National Association of People with AIDS
1413 K Street NW, Suite 700
Washington, DC 20005
(202) 898-0414

National AIDS Hotline
(800) 342-2437

National AIDS Information Clearinghouse
(800) 458-5231

National Gay and Lesbian Task Force
2320 17th Street NW
Washington, DC 20009
(202) 332-6483

People with AIDS Hotline
(800) 828-3280

Gay and Lesbian Services

Lambda Legal Defense and Education Fund, Inc.
666 Broadway
New York, NY 10012
(212) 995-8585

National Gay and Lesbian Task Force
and Policy Institute
2320 17th Street NW
Washington, DC 20009
(202) 332-6483

National Lesbian and Gay Health Association
1407 S Street NW
Washington, DC 20009
(202) 939-7880

Self-Help Services

Resolve, Inc.
5 Water Street, Arlington, MA 02174
(617) 643-2424
(for couples experiencing infertility problems)

Sex Addicts Anonymous
P.O. Box 70949
Houston, TX 77270
(713) 869-4902

Rape and Sexual Assault

National Directory: Rape Prevention and Treatment
U.S. Department of Health and Human Services
National Center for the Prevention and Control of Rape
(301) 443-3728

Rape Crisis Centers
Check the local listings in your phone book

Violence and Traumatic Stress Research
National Institute of Mental Health

5600 Fishers Lane, Room 10C-24
Rockville, MD 20857
(301) 443-3728

Incest and Sexual Abuse

Adults Molested as Children United
232 East Gish Road
San Jose, CA 95112-4703

Child Help USA Information Center
6463 Independence Avenue
Woodland Hills, CA 91367
(800) 422-4453

Incest Resources, Inc.
Cambridge Women's Center
46 Pleasant Street
Cambridge, MA 02139
(617) 354-8807

Incest Recovery Association
4300 MacArthur
Dallas, TX 75209
(214) 559-2170

Incest Survivors Anonymous
P.O. Box 17245
Long Beach, CA 90807-7245
(310) 428-5599

National Center on Child Abuse and Neglect
P.O. Box 1182
Washington, DC 20013
(202) 205-8813

National Resource Center on Child
Abuse and Neglect
63 Inverness Drive East
Englewood, CO 80112-5117
(800) 227-5242

National Resource Center on Child
Sexual Abuse Information Service
106 Lincoln Street
Huntsville, AL 35801
(800) 543-7006

National Committee for Prevention of Child Abuse
332 South Michigan Avenue, Suite 1600
Chicago, IL 60604-4357

National Center for Missing
and Exploited Children
2101 Wilson Blvd., Suite 550
Arlington, VA 22201
(800) 843-5678

VOICES (Victims of Incest Can Emerge
Survivors) in Action, Inc.
P.O. Box 148309
Chicago, IL 60614
(314) 327-1500

Sexuality and Gender in Society

Sexuality and Gender in Society

Janell L. Carroll
Baker University

Paul Root Wolpe
University of Pennsylvania

HarperCollins*CollegePublishers*

Acquisitions Editor: Jill Lectka
Developmental Editor: Maxine Effenson Chuck
Project Coordination and Text Design: Electronic Publishing Services Inc.
Cover Designer: Mary McDonnell
Cover Photographs: Three nudes by Keith Tishken. Flower by Digital Stock Professional.
Art Studio: Precision Graphics
Photo Researcher: Julie Tesser
Electronic Production Manager: Mike Kemper
Manufacturing Manager: Helene G. Landers
Electronic Page Makeup: Electronic Publishing Services Inc.
Printer and Binder: R. R. Donnelley & Sons Company
Cover Printer: New England Book Components, Inc.

For permission to use copyrighted material, grateful acknowledgment is made to the copyright holders on pp. 813–816, which are hereby made part of this copyright page.

Sexuality and Gender in Society

Library of Congress Cataloging-in-Publication Data

Carroll, Janell L.
    Sexuality and gender in society / Janell L. Carroll, Paul Root
  Wolpe.
       p.   cm.
    Includes bibliographical references and index.
    ISBN 0-06-500872-3
    1. Sex. 2. Sex (Psychology) 3. Sex (Biology) I. Wolpe, Paul
  Root. II. Title.
    HQ21.C42 1996   95-35191
    306.7-dc20   CIP

95 96 97 98 9 8 7 6 5 7 3 2 1

Brief Contents

For Greg and Valerie, to whom this book is dedicated;
and to Ariel, Kendra, and Reagan, for whom it is intended.

Detailed Contents

Preface

The decision to spend years researching and writing an introductory textbook is not an easy one. Yet we decided to write **Sexuality and Gender in Society** because we felt that none of the available sexuality textbooks had the combination of features we were looking for: a focus on the social aspects of sexuality, an inclusion of the voices of those whose sexuality is usually hidden, and, most importantly, a text that is accessible and answers the questions *students* want to know about sexuality. In that sense, this is truly a student-centered text.

By addressing these concerns, we believe we have created the most innovative sexuality textbook available on the market. Some of our unique features include:

- *SexTalk Questions:* Over the last five years, we have collected thousands of students' questions about sexuality. Questionnaires have been distributed to students across the country and in a number of foreign countries, asking: What questions would you *really* like to ask a member of the other sex about sexuality? A member of you own sex? An expert? These questions both informed the writing of the text itself and appear explicitly in a special Q&A feature called *SexTalk. SexTalk* questions appear in each chapter, allowing us to pose and answer the most interesting and provocative questions students have on the topic under discussion.

- *A Social Focus:* In addition to a comprehensive discussion of the biological and psychological levels of human sexuality, we provide a unique sociological view, including a strong cross-cultural perspective on sexual behavior, a recognition of the role of politics and law, a studiously non-heterosexist orientation, and an emphasis on exploring the changing nature of gender roles. Almost every chapter incorporates cross-cultural elements. The opening chapter itself offers the most sweeping and comprehensive historical and global overview of sexuality of any available textbook, and the text goes on to discuss such things as homosexuality in China, female circumcision in Africa, contraception in Sweden, and the erotic sculptures in India.

- *Enriching Personal Sexuality:* We do not shy away from a frank discussion of the "how-tos" of sexual behavior. *Enriching Personal Sexuality,* a special focus chapter written in response to student requests, instructs students on how to be more sensitive and skillful lovers, how to communicate with their partners, and how to get the most out of their sexual lives.

- *Core Curriculum Feature:* The typical human sexuality textbook on the market has twenty-one to twenty-five chapters, an impossible number to assign in an average semester. For that reason, we have organized our book in a unique manner. The book begins with fifteen *Core Curriculum Chapters,* which alone comprise a comprehensive Human Sexuality Curriculum. The *Core Curriculum* includes full treatments of sexual biology, pregnancy, birth, contraception, and sexually transmitted diseases; chapters describing adult sexual behavior, adult sexual relationships, sexual orientation, sexual variations, sexual dysfunctions; and full chapters on gender roles, love and intimacy, and power and coercion, among others. These are supplemented by six shorter *Special Focuses,* which provide in-depth treatment of special topics that can be used by those who desire a longer or more specialized curriculum. The *Special Focuses* include discussions of the media and pornography; prostitution; morality, religion, and law; sex education; sexual humor; and enriching personal sexuality.

- *Student Accessibility:* The text is well-written, interesting, and thought-provoking. We have tried to strike a balance between making this text more accessible to students and making it more comprehensive, scientifically rigorous, and up-to-date than comparable texts in the field. The writing style is informal and entertaining, and the special features emphasize the interpersonal aspects of sexuality and bring ideas to life for students. At the same time, however, we have included many studies, findings, and cross-cultural behaviors that are simply absent from other human sexuality texts.

- *Personal Voices Boxes:* Anecdotal accounts from students and published, first-person narrative accounts are sprinkled liberally throughout the text to translate the text's theoretical information into personal experiences that the student can appreciate. We have chosen these accounts very carefully, and they provide a singular glimpse into the world of sexual behaviors and beliefs.

- *Other Boxed Features:* In addition to the *Personal Voices* and *SexTalk* boxes described above, *Sexuality and Gender in Society* includes other special boxes to supplement the text. Up to date information on all aspects of sexual behavior, attitudes, and current events are highlighted in a feature called *Sexuality Today*. To emphasize the scientific nature of sexology, *Sex Facts* boxes summarize important and interesting scientific research in sexuality, including many lesser known findings that provide unique insights into gender and sexuality. *Focus on Diversity* presents research on sexuality in other countries and historical eras in almost every chapter. Finally, *Where Do I Stand?* boxes provide self-tests to allow students to explore their own assumptions and knowledge about the chapter's subject matter.

- *Other Features:* A number of other pedagogical features are designed into the text. All relevant terms are defined in margin definitions, and a comprehensive glossary is included in the back of the text. Every chapter ends with: 1) a summary of important points; 2) *Reflections on Sexuality,* a series of study and thought questions; and 3) a list of suggested readings. The text includes names and addresses of agencies and information resources, such as rape crisis hotlines and special interest agencies for students who need help or want further information. *Sexuality and Gender in Society* also features an exceptional art program, with original, four-color art by Precision Graphics. Photos have been carefully chosen to illustrate textual material, and occasional cartoons provide a glimpse into the lighter side of sexuality.

Special Content Areas

Sexuality and Gender in Society also includes the following unique contributions:

- A **comprehensive introduction chapter** that reviews the history of sexual behaviors from the emergence of *Homo sapiens* to the present day, covering Western and Eastern civilizations, the contributions of the major religions, and historical eras such as the Renaissance, and concludes with a history of sexuality in the United States.

- A focus on **gender issues,** ranging from discussions of fertility symbols and witchcraft, to modern biological theories of brain differentiation, to the influence of sexism and media portrayals of gender roles.

- A special chapter on **sexual dysfunction and disability,** with full sections on sexuality and cancer, chronic disease, and substance abuse.

- A strong focus on **making ethical decisions** in sexual relationships, including important sections on religious values in sexual relationships.

- Discussions of the **political and policy implications** of sexuality issues.

- Up-to-date information on **childhood and adolescent sexuality,** including discussions of the role of the teenage father and racial factors in teenage pregnancy.

- **Discussions of STDs are integrated** into chapters on contraception, sexual orientation, and challenges to sexual functioning, in addition to the full chapter on STDs and AIDS.

- Up-to-the-minute statistics on sexual behavior in the United States, including the findings of the 1994 *Social Organization of Sexuality* study by Laumann, Gagnon, Michael and Michaels.

- A unique chapter on **sexual humor**.

- Important coverage of the **gay rights** and **feminist movements**.

- The latest updates in **contraceptive research,** including Norplant, Depo Provera, RU-486, and methotrexate.

- Descriptions of the most current techniques in **infertility**.

- Discussion of the **effects of rape on special populations,** such as lesbians, the elderly, and prostitutes, as well as rape of males.

- And much more!

Supplemental Materials

To supplement the text, we have created an unparalleled set of materials. The *Instructor's Manual* offers scores of helpful suggestions for the teachers of sexuality courses, including teaching tips, chapter summaries, lecture and discussion modules, class activities, and supplemental resources. The *Student Manual* does more than reiterate the material. It is almost a complementary text, with strategies for getting the most out of a course on human sexuality. We also offer a wonderful video tape, with original film clips that cannot be found anywhere else, as well as carefully chosen commercially produced clips. The test bank offers hundreds of questions that can be used directly or can serve as reference points for your own exams. It is also available in *Testmaster,* the computerized version, which comes in both IBM- and Macintosh-compatible formats. To selected adopters, HarperCollins will make available a classroom contraception sample kit, which is available on a limited basis. It contains a variety of real contraceptive devices, so that students can become familiar with them.

Acknowledgments

Somehow one knows, when beginning a textbook such as this one, that it will be longer and harder than he or she imagines. Each chapter of an introductory textbook is, in effect, a new book, and, in the rapidly changing field of human sexuality, new findings and studies appear almost daily that need to be incorporated into the text. And coordinating such a complex project is made that much more difficult when the two authors live a thousand miles away from each other.

Yet this collaboration has been joyful, mutually reinforcing, and, even during the most frustrating moments, fun. The text is in every sense fully collaborative and equal, with faxes, fedexes, and phone calls flying between us almost daily. This book has truly been a labor of love and it has been shared by a number of others who have made contributions to its completion.

Thanks go to those who reviewed chapters, including Lisa Henderson of the University of Massachusetts, Amherst; Frank Furstenberg of the University of Pennsylvania; Andrea Braverman of Pennsylvania Hospital; and Stephen Wolpe of Pro Neuron, Inc. Thanks also for the helpful comments of the HarperCollins reviewers: Christine Ahmed of the University of Oregon, Sylvester W. Allred of Northern Arizona University; Myles Jon Anderson of Walla Walla Community College; Wayne Anderson of the University of Missouri, Columbia; Ann Auleb of San Francisco State University; Sue Balinsky of the College of Charleston; Kenneth Becker of the University of Wisconsin, La Crosse; Betsy Bergen of Kansas State University; Irv Binik of McGill University; Peter Chroman of the College of San Mateo; Shae Coleman of Northeastern State University; Donald Craft of Wytheville Community College; Beverly A. Drinnin of Des Moines Area Community College; Philip J. Elias Duryea of the University of New Mexico; Eugenio Galiandro of El Paso Community College; Grace Galliano of Kennesaw State College; Dawn Graff-Haight of Portland State University; Robert Hackman of the University of Oregon; Fred A. Johnson of the University of Washington, D.C.; Robin Kowalski of Western Carolina University; Tom Langley of the College of Charleston; Mark R. Leary of Wake Forest University; Phil Marty of the University of South Florida; Susan McFadden of the University of Wisconsin; Angela P. McGlynn of Mercer County Community College; Kay R. Murphy of Oklahoma State University; Elaine Osborne of Humboldt State University; Beverly Palmer of California State University; Ryda Rose of the University of Pennsylvania; Robert Slechta of Boston University; Norman Smith of San Joaquin Delta College; Fran Thomas of Lane Community College; Thomas Tighe of Moraine Valley Community College; Lou Ann Wieand of Humboldt State University; and Michael Young of the University of Arkansas. Special thanks to Denise Hawkins Walinsky, who helped considerably with the chapter on biology, and William Stayton, who came through in a pinch. Thanks also to Joel Braverman, Laudan Aron, Victoria Jensh, Howard Wills, Susan Sergent, Erin Ragan, Jaime Thiessen, Ann Bobek, and Gina Macconi, for their help. Thanks also to our agent, Sydelle Kramer.

Finally, as all authors (and their families) know, books cannot be written without the care, tolerance, and support of spouses and children. To Greg and Reagan, and to Valerie, Ariel, and Kendra—our love and thanks are immeasurable.

JANELL L. CARROLL

PAUL ROOT WOLPE

Note to Students

"Why are you taking that course?" is one of the first questions often asked of students who enroll in a human sexuality course. Many students feel that by the time they reach college, they should know everything there is to know about sex. However, learning about sexuality is a lifelong process, not one that ends when we reach a certain age.

While there are many reliable sources that address issues in sexuality, it is hard to find which is the most reliable and current resource. That's why taking a course is so useful. As we grow and mature, our questions about sex don't go away, rather, they change. Are your questions the same as they were five years ago? Do you think they will be the same five years from now?

Students have many different motivations for taking a course in human sexuality. Some of the reasons we have heard include:

- to help me learn more about the opposite sex
- to learn more about my own sexuality
- to be able to study sex in a socially acceptable format
- to help me communicate better with my partner
- to get answers to questions I'm unable, unwilling, or too embarrassed to ask
- to see if I am normal
- to understand why people are different from me sexually
- to understand the influences of society on sexuality
- to explore my personal values about sex
- to meet members of the opposite sex
- to become a better lover

As you read this list, which reasons are closest to your own for taking the course? All of these are sound and legitimate reasons to take a course in human sexuality.

You may have some fears and trepidations as you begin this class. Consider for a moment your fondest hope and worst nightmare about taking this course. Students have often reported to us that some of their hopes included:

- having the opportunity to discuss difficult issues
- learning more about sex in general
- becoming more confident as a person and a sexual being
- becoming more open-minded when confronted with issues to which they previously were not exposed
- meeting a potential partner
- and, of course, getting an A in the course

Some of their fears included:

- finding oneself in disagreement with other students and feeling in the minority
- saying something "stupid"
- becoming embarrassed
- learning about things that may make one uneasy
- having the "secrecy" or "mystery" taken out of sex

After a sexuality course ends, many students realize that these are unfounded fears.

We can sum up our feelings about this course by sharing a comment from one of our students: *"Taking a course in human sexuality has taught me a lot about myself. It made me realize how much I have changed. I am no longer afraid of sex and know that sex is not a dirty act but one of great love. I wish this course was required of all students."* By the way, we are continuing to collect questions from students on human sexuality. If you have questions, please send them to us in care of the publisher.

We hope this textbook offers you an opportunity to learn more about yourself and the society in which you live. We also hope that it will serve as a resource to help you make informed and responsible decisions regarding your own sexuality.

JANELL L. CARROLL

PAUL ROOT WOLPE

About the Authors

Janell L. Carroll received her B.A. from Denison University where she studied Psychology, and then went on to receive a Ph.D. from the University of Pennsylvania in Human Sexuality Education. Janell has been an associate professor of psychology at Baker University, where she also served as Director of the Counseling Center. Her research interests include gender differences in sexual behavior and attitudes and the psychology of relationships. She has also conducted cross-cultural sexuality research in both Australia and New Zealand. Janell has published articles in several journals, including *The Journal of Sex and Marital Therapy, Archives of Sexual Behavior, AIDS Care,* and *Urology.*

Janell L. Carroll

An AASECT-Certified Sexuality Educator, Janell has been teaching human sexuality for more than ten years and was named "Sexuality Educator of the Year" by Planned Parenthood of Greater Kansas City for her extensive work in the field of sexuality. In addition, she has been honored with a variety of teaching awards for students. Janell has brought sexuality education into the mainstream by hosting one of the first nightly radio call-in programs on sexuality in Kansas City. She presents workshops and guest lectures to a wide variety of groups and organizations and is the author of a popular syndicated sexuality newspaper column. Janell lives in Avon, Connecticut, with her husband, Greg Henke, and their daughter, Reagan.

Paul Root Wolpe received his B.A. in the Sociology and Psychology of Religion from the University of Pennsylvania, and then went on the receive a Ph.D. from Yale University under a National Institute of Mental Health Training Grant in the Sociology of Medicine. Paul has taught in the Department of Sociology at Penn since 1986, and for five years was the Director of Research for the Department of Psychiatry at Jefferson Medical College. He is now a Faculty Associate of the Center for Bioethics at Penn. Paul has published a wide range of articles in both the medical and the social science literature.

Paul Root Wolpe

Paul lectures widely on issues of bioethics, medicine, and sexuality. He was chosen as a "Superstar Teacher of America," and his courses on the Sociology of Sexuality and Theories of Deviance are distributed nationally. His courses at the University of Pennsylvania are extremely popular, winning him a regular place in the Undergraduate Course Guide's "Hall of Fame." He is also the recipient of numerous writing awards. Paul lives in Narberth, Pennsylvania, with his wife, Valerie, and his daughters, Ariel and Kendra.

Sex in Other Times and Places

> Sex lies at the root of life, and we can never learn to reverence life until we know how to understand sex.
>
> —*Havelock Ellis*

> It requires far more genius to make love than to command armies.
>
> —*Ninon de Lenclose*

WHAT IS SEXUALITY?

Human beings are unique in the animal kingdom. While most other animals engage in some kind of sexual behavior in order to reproduce, only human beings have gone beyond instinctual mating to create ideas, laws, customs, fantasies, and art around the sexual act. In other words, while sexual intercourse is common in the animal kingdom, **sexuality** is a uniquely human trait.

sexuality: A general term for the feelings and behaviors of human beings concerning sex.

Human sexuality is grounded in biological functioning, emerges in each of us as we develop, and is expressed by cultures through rules about sexual contact, attitudes about moral and immoral sexuality, habits of sexual behavior, patterns of sexual relations between the sexes, and so on. Sexuality is studied by biologists, psychologists, physicians, anthropologists, historians, sociologists, political scientists, those concerned with public health, and almost every other scholarly discipline. For example, political scientists may study how sexuality reflects social power; powerful groups may have more access to sexual partners or use their control over laws to try to restrict the sexual behaviors of less powerful groups.

There are few areas of human life as contradictory and confusing as sexuality. We come from a society that is often called sexually "repressed," yet sexuality is all around us, in advertising, movies, and television. We all think that everyone else is "doing it"; still, most of us are uncomfortable talking about it. Some feel that we should all be free to explore our sexuality; others believe that there should be strong moral restrictions around sexual behavior. To some, only sex between a man and a woman is natural and acceptable; others believe that other kinds of sexual expression are equally "natural" and valid. Most of us find it puzzling that some people want to have sex with children, animals, in public, while being choked, or while dressed in diapers. While parents teach their children about safe driving, safe use of fire, and safe hygiene, many are profoundly uncomfortable instructing their children on safe sexual practices.

We begin our exploration of such questions in this chapter by taking a sweeping look at the history of human sexuality from prehistoric time to the present. Of course, in the space of one chapter, we cannot begin to cover the variety and richness of human sexual experience. We hope this overview gives you an idea of how varied human cultures are, while at the same time showing that human beings throughout history have had to grapple with the same sexual issues that confront us in American society today.

OUR APE ANCESTORS

Walking Erect

Our ape ancestors began walking upright over three million years ago, according to recent fossil records. Before that, our ancestors were mostly **quadrupeds** who stood only for brief moments—as baboons do now—to survey the terrain. The evolution of an upright posture changed forever the way the human species engaged in sexual intercourse.

In our closest primate relatives, such as chimpanzees, when the female is in **estrus** her vulva, visible from behind, becomes swollen and brightly colored. This signals her sexual availability and attracts the male, who mounts the female from behind. Most primate females allow males to mount them only during estrus. In an upright female, however, swollen genitalia would be uncomfortable and less visible to the male. Over time, therefore, human females lost their indications of estrus and instead developed the menstrual cycle. Since the menstrual cycle provides no outward indications of when a woman is ovulating and therefore fertile, sexual intercourse was no longer restricted to certain times each month.

The development of menstruation may even have been a factor in the development of **monogamous** relationships. If when the fertile stage of the cycle is hidden, the female can be sexually available at all times, the male need not go searching for other females. Also, since he can never be certain when his partner is is fertile, the male is encouraged the to stay with one female and guard against her having sex with other males. (Gibbons are one of the few monogamous primates, and female gibbons are one of the few primates that menstruate.) Whatever the reasons, the loss of estrus seems to correspond to the development of human monogamy.

There are other important sexual implications in humans learning to walk upright (Rancour-Laferriere, 1985). For example, eyesight became more important than the sense of smell. When the male genitals and female breasts became more visible, sexual attraction began shifting from the sense of smell to visual stimuli. In an upright posture, the male genitals are rotated to the front of the body, so merely approaching someone involves displaying the genitals. Since male confrontation often involved acts of aggression, the **phallus**—the male symbol of sex and potency—became associated with displays of aggression. In other words, upright posture may have also contributed to a new tie between sexuality and aggression (Rancour-Laferriere, 1985). (See the in-text photo on page 4.)

The upright posture of the female also emphasized her breasts (and hips), which became larger and more prominent in humans than in any other primate species. The rotation of the female pelvis forward (the vagina faces the rear in most quadrupeds) also resulted in the possibility of face-to-face intercourse. Since more body area is in contact in face-to-face intercourse than in rear entry, the entire sensual aspect of intercourse was enhanced, manipulation of the breasts became possible (the breasts are sexual organs only in humans), and the female clitoris was much more easily stimulated. Only in human females does orgasm seem to be a common part of sexual contact.

quadruped: Any animal that walks on four legs.

estrus: The (usually monthly) state of female mammals in sexual excitement; in higher primates, it is accompanied by a swelling and coloration of the hindquarters. (In males, the corresponding word is *rut*.)

monogamous: Being married to one mate; often used to mean not having sexual relations outside the marital unit.

phallus: The penis; often used to refer to the penis as a symbol of power and aggression.

Note the brightly colored hindquarters of the baboon, intended to attract males while the female is in estrus. Some sociobiologists suggest that the practice of using makeup, jewelry, and bright clothing, universally found in human women, may be an evolutionary attempt to mimic the lost coloration of estrus.

SEX TALK

QUESTION 1.1 Do female primates experience orgasm?

Yes, some do, though it is relatively rare compared to human females. Female primates rarely masturbate, though occasionally they stimulate themselves manually during intercourse. Though some chimpanzees, such as the bonobos, do have face-to-face intercourse on occasion and may reach orgasm, the primate clitoris seems not to be significantly stimulated by the rear-entry intercourse most use (Margulis & Sagan, 1991).

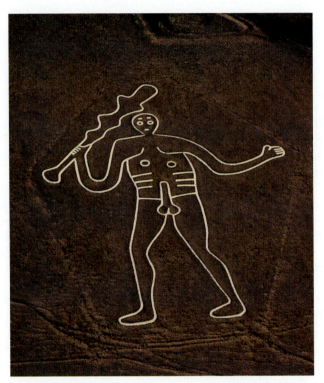

Many ancient drawings associate power, aggression, and erections, as the Cerne Abbas Giant above, carved into an English countryside.

Humans Beings Before the Great Civilizations

Homo sapiens: The technical name for the species that all human beings belong to.

About two hundred thousand years ago, **Homo sapiens** appeared on the scene. We do not know much about how these early ancestors behaved or what they believed. However, we do know that they were generally monogamous, living in fairly stable sexual pairings.

Since early *Homo sapiens* probably did not know that childbirth was related to intercourse, only the female's contribution to the perpetuation of the species was known. The value of the female must have therefore been very high (Tannahill, 1980). This may be why the majority of carved images and fetishes that have survived from this period depict females (See Focus on Diversity 1.1).

Focus
on Diversity
——————— *1.1*

The "Venuses": Fertility Goddesses or Ancient Pin-ups?

Look at the picture of the "venus" (right), as the form has come to be known. Note the exaggerated breasts and thighs; note also that the figures lack facial features. Many archaeologists have suggested that these figures were magical fertility figures—in part because the (male) archaeologists believed that these figures were too fat and exaggerated to be representations of "sexy" females.

Indeed, they may have been fertility figures, but we must remember that in climates and times when food is scarce and the weather cold, fat becomes a sign of health and desirability. Ever since the Neolithic age (the "stone age"), carvings of women have shown ample breasts, hips, thighs, and buttocks—all the places where estrogen promotes fat storage (Frisch, 1988). When a woman's body fat declines below a certain level, she stops ovulating and eventually stops menstruating,

becoming temporarily infertile. In the harsh and demanding conditions of neolithic life, a well-proportioned figure may well have been the ideal of health—*and* sexual desirability.

Women with ample body fat have also been considered very sexy in other times and places—many cultures (such as Middle Eastern cultures) and many Western artists (such as Renoir or Rubens) celebrated women with full figures. In fact, extremely thin women did not even become a symbol of desirability in the United States until recently. The sex symbols of the 1940s and 1950s—Marilyn Monroe, Jane Russsel—had ample bosoms and hips, not the emaciatingly thin waists we see on many of today's models.

Venus of Willendorf

Model Anna Nicole Smith

Life among early humans tended to be exceedingly difficult, with high infant mortality, disease, malnutrition, and a harsh environment. Living conditions began to improve about 11,000 years ago, when human beings discovered agriculture and began to settle down into permanent communities. Since women typically did the gathering, they understood plant life better than men. Women therefore probably first discovered how to cultivate plants, generally considered one of the two greatest discoveries—with harnessing fire—in the history of humankind.

SEXUALITY IN THE ANCIENT WORLD*

As the first civilizations were established, cities began to grow and people began living together in larger and larger groups. Cities require a more formal way of structuring social life, and so the first codes of law began to develop. Codes of law and other legal sources, however, tend to tell us only about what was forbidden. We can also learn about ancient people's behavior from carved or painted pictures (which are scarce) or from the occasional written account (few of which go into explicit detail). So determining how ancient people engaged in their daily sexual lives is not really possible. Yet we are able to reconstruct some ideas based on the clues left to us.

—————————————
* Large portions of the following sections are based on the books *Sex in History* by Tannahill (1980) and *The Subordinate Sex* by Bullough (1973).

From writings and art we know a bit about ancient accounts of venereal disease (some ancient medical texts discuss cures), menstruation (there were a variety of laws surrounding menstruation), circumcision (which was first performed in Egypt and possibly other parts of Africa), and contraception (Egyptian women inserted sponges or other objects in the vagina). Since having as many children as possible was crucial—especially sons for inheritance—abortion was usually forbidden; for example, Assyrian women who had abortions were "to be impaled and not given burial" (Tannahill, 1980). Prostitution was common, and **temple prostitutes** often greeted worshippers. Even in Egypt, the first civilization to eliminate sexual intercourse and prostitution as part of temple worship, some Egyptian women did make their livings through prostitution. In fact, Herodotus writes that King Cheops, the ruler who built the three great pyramids, was said to have prostituted his own daughter in order to get the money and bricks to build his tomb (Manniche, 1987).

Monogamy as practiced in the ancient world had a double standard. Complete fidelity was required for women, while men could visit prostitutes and have **concubines**; wealthy men often had more than one wife. Women could not inherit property, which made them economically subservient to men. Early wedding ceremonies involved the groom or the groom's family paying money for the bride—they literally bought her from her father (Bullough, 1973). The Egyptian home, for example, was ruled by men, and women were primarily wives, slaves, or prostitutes. The high number of arm fractures found in the skeletons of lower class women have led anthropologists to suggest that the limbs were broken as the women put up their arms to ward off the blows of their husbands (Tannahill, 1980). Female adultery was a **transgression** against a husband's property, while sleeping with an unmarried woman was a transgression against her father's property. As Tannahill (1980) puts it, a woman was the property of her father until marriage, when she became the property of her husband.

Men's dominance over women in public life throughout most of human history has effectively silenced women's voices; we know far more about what men thought, how they lived, and even how they loved than we know about the lives of women. In fact, it was only relatively recently in human history that women's voices have begun to be heard on a par with men's in literature, politics, art, and other parts of public life.

Some ancient civilizations had surprisingly modern attitudes about sex. Though the ancient Egyptians condemned adultery, especially among women, there is ample evidence that it was still fairly common and was the subject of much sexual joking. A woman in Egypt had the right to divorce her husband, a privilege, as we will see, that was not allowed to Hebrew women. Egyptians seem to have invented male circumcision, and Egyptian workers left behind thousands of pictures, carvings, and even cartoons of erotic scenes. All told, the Egyptians had sexual lives that do not seem all that different from the way humans engage in sex throughout the world today.

temple prostitutes: Women in many ancient cultures who would have sex with worshippers at pagan temples to provide money for the temple or as a form of worshipping the gods.

concubine: Primarily in older societies, a woman who served as a secondary wife, whose social and legal status was inferior to that of the primary wife but whose children were considered legitimate.

transgression: Sin

The Egyptians left many erotic drawings and carvings that were hidden by embarrassed archaeologists for many years.

SEX TALK

QUESTION **1.2** **If women were so valued and important among prehistorical human beings, why did their status slip once civilization started?**

There are many theories that try to explain why women have occupied a subordinate status in so many human societies. A sociobiological explanation suggests that a woman always passes on her genes when she gets pregnant, while a man must be certain he impregnates a woman to pass his on; therefore, men tried to dominate women (and to forbid adultery among women) to ensure that their individual genes were passed on. A more social explanation suggests that in hunter-gatherer societies it was the men, as hunters, who controlled the rarer resource (meat), which gave them more power. Or it may be that women's childbearing functions kept them too busy to devote time to political issues. A psychological theory suggests that both boy and girl infants identify with the mother, but boys must separate from the mother and identify with a male role model, which is a very painful separation; in order to release their emotional hold on the mother, they denigrate all that is female. All these theories have weaknesses and are discussed in greater depth in Chapter 5.

Of all the ancient civilizations, modern Western society owes the most to the interaction of three ancient cultures: the Hebraic, Hellenistic (Greek), and Roman. From the Greeks we trace our views of art and architecture, secular philosophy, and folklore; from the Romans our legal, military, and institutional structures; and from the Hebrews our views of religion, morality, and family structure. Each made a contribution to our views of sexuality, so it is worthwhile to examine each culture briefly.

The Hebrews

The Hebrews rejected the common religious thinking of their day, which included worshipping idols and having local gods that ruled only over a particular group of people. The Hebrews believed a single deity had a supreme place in the universe and ruled over all tribes and peoples. With a single, universal God came the idea of a single, absolute set of truths, given by God, that instructed people how they must live.

The Hebrew Bible, which was put into written form some time between 800 and 200 B.C., contains very explicit rules about sexual behavior, such as forbidding adultery, homosexual contact, and sex with a variety of family members and their spouses. The Bible tells tales of sexual misconduct, from incest, to sexual betrayal, to sex outside of marriage, to sexual jealousy, even by its most admired figures. It even contains a book of erotic poetry, the Song of Solomon. Yet, the Bible also tells tales of marital love and the importance of sexuality in marital relations (see Special Focus 1).

The attitude of the Hebrews toward women, sex, and procreation is complex. This is illustrated by the two different accounts of the creation of man and woman in Genesis (Bullough, 1973). Chapter One of Genesis reads: "God created mankind in His own image, in the image of God He created them; male and female He created them." Note that here there is no indication that man is created before woman or that woman is created from his side; both man and women are created "in [God's] own image." In Chapter Two of Genesis, however, the story is retold. This time Adam is created first, and then God decides that Adam could use a "helpmeet," and so God creates Eve from Adam's side, giving woman a secondary place in the story. The rest of the Bible reflects this ambivalence about women; while Eve leads Adam astray and Delilah betrays Samson, Deborah is portrayed as a great judge and Ruth is held up as the Bible's premier example of loyalty and integrity.

"Be fruitful and multiply" are the very first words God addresses to Adam, and so marriage and procreation were taken very seriously by the Hebrews. Deuteronomy (24:5) states that "when a man hath taken a new wife, he shall not go out to war, neither shall he be charged with any business; but he shall be free at home for one year, and shall cheer up his wife which he hath taken." To strengthen marriage and promote reproduction, the Bible has a generally positive attitude toward sexuality. The Bible often uses the intimate phrase "to know" to mean that two people have had sex ("And Abraham knew his wife Sarah"), showing that the Bible views sex as a means to deepen one's understanding of one's spouse. Intercourse creates a sense of union: "A man leaves his father and his mother and cleaves to his wife, and they become one flesh" (Genesis 2:24). Though marital sexuality was important in and of itself, procreation was the ultimate goal, and so the Bible forbids many sexual acts that are not aimed at procreation, such as homosexuality, adultery, incest, sex during menstruation, and sex with animals.

In biblical times, property was usually inherited through the male line, so having sons was very important. Men could divorce their wives, marry second wives, or take concubines in the attempt to have a son. In fact, if a man died childless, it was the obligation of his brother to impregnate his wife in order to provide a male heir. Onan, the son of Judah, refused to do this and spilled his seed on the ground instead of ejaculating into his brother's wife. For this transgression, God slew Onan. Not only does this show the importance the Bible places on procreation but also on semen, the fluid of procreation, which should not be wasted. A man who had a **nocturnal emission** was considered unclean and must bathe himself and all the clothes his semen touched.

nocturnal emission: Also called a "wet dream," an ejaculation by a man while asleep.

The legacy of the Hebrew attitude toward sexuality has been profound. The focus on marital sexuality and procreation and the prohibition against such things as homosexuality were taken up by Christianity and formed the basis of sexual attitudes in the West for centuries thereafter. On the other hand, as opposed to the Greeks, the Hebrew Bible sees the marital union and its sexual nature as an expression of love and affection, as a man "cleaves to his wife, and they become one flesh."

Greece (1000–200 B.C.)

The Greeks were more sexually permissive than the Hebrews. Their stories and myths were full of sexual exploits, incest, rape, and even **bestiality** (as when Zeus, the chief god, takes the form of a swan to rape Leda). Yet there were also tragic stories of love and loss; Achilles wept bitter tears when he looked into the eyes of the woman he had just impaled with his sword, Penthesilea, and realized that she was his equal and that he could have loved her. The Greeks clearly distinguished between love and sex in their tales, even giving each a separate god; Aphrodite was the goddess of sexual intercourse, while Eros (her son) was the god of love.

bestiality: The act of having intercourse with an animal.

Greece was one of the few major civilizations in Western history to institutionalize homosexuality successfully, though the practice was widespread only among the upper class. In Greek **pederasty**, an older man would befriend a post-pubescent boy who had finished his orthodox education and aid in the boy's continuing intellectual, physical, and sexual development. In return, the boy would have sex with his mentor. The mentor was always the active partner, the penetrator, while the student was the passive partner.

pederasty: Sexual contact between adult men and (usually) post-pubescent boys.

Personal

VOICES

Voices of Love and Sexuality in the Hebrew Bible

The Hebrew Bible talks openly about love, even sexual love. Though love between people is mentioned often, there are few personal declarations of love in the Bible. One exception is the love between Jacob and Rachel:

Jacob loved Rachel; and said [to Rachel's father] "I will serve thee seven years for Rachel thy younger daughter....And Jacob served seven years for Rachel; and this seemed to him but a few days for the love he had to her. (Genesis 29:118–20)

Love also seems to get Biblical characters into trouble. King David is punished for sleeping with Bathsheba and sending her husband off into battle to be killed. Jacob's excessive love for his son, Joseph, results in Joseph being sold into slavery; once in Egypt, his master's wife tries to seduce Joseph, and his refusal lands him in jail. Samson reveals the secrets of his strength to prove his love for Delilah, and she betrays him, leading to his death.

Love of God is the only love that is portrayed as pure in the Bible. The Hebrew Bible often portrays the relationship between God and Israel in terms of two people in love. Sometimes God refers to Israel as a beloved child:

When Israel was a child, then I loved him, and called my son out of Egypt (Hosea 11:1)

At other times God speaks of Israel as His betrothed, and even implies that the depth of the relationship rivals the knowledge of sexual relations (remember: the Bible often uses the word "know" to mean that a couple had sexual intercourse):

I will even betroth thee unto me in faithfulness and thou shalt know the Lord.

The Song of Solomon (or Song of Songs) is an explicit, sexual love poem and was only included in the Bible (after much controversy) because it was taken to be an allegory of the love between Israel and God. It speaks of the ecstasy of love and of the passion of sex, alternating the voice of the female and the male:

The voice of my beloved! Behold he cometh leaping upon the mountains, skipping upon the hills. My beloved is like a roe or a young hart... behold he spake, and said unto me, Rise up, my love, my fair one, and come away (Song of Solomon 2:8–10)

Thou hast ravished my heart, my sister, my spouse; thou hast ravished my heart with one of thine eyes, with one chain of thy neck. How fair is thy love, my sister, my spouse! How much better is thy love than wine! And the smell of thine ointments than all spices! Thy lips, O my spouse, drop as the honeycomb; honey and milk are on thy tongue. (Song of Solomon 4:9–11)

Adapted from Bergmann (1987)

Socrates, for example, was supposed to have enjoyed the sexual attentions of his (all male) students, and his students expressed jealousy when he paid too much physical attention to one or another. Many Greek leaders had young boys as lovers, and, in fact, more than a few were assassinated by boys they had seduced. This pederasty was considered a natural form of sexuality; when Plato has a character in his writings think about a society where pederasty is outlawed, he concludes that the idea is inconceivable (Winkler, 1990).

In Greece, men and the male form were idealized. When the ancient Greek philosophers spoke of love, they did so almost exclusively in **homoerotic** terms. Man's nonsexual love for another man was seen as the ideal love, superior to the sexual love of women. Plato discussed such an ideal love, and so we have come to call friendships without a sexual element **platonic**.

homoerotic: Artistic or literary works that focus on the sexual or love relations between members of the same sex.

platonic friendship: Named after Plato's description, a deep, loving friendship between men (and now also between men and women) that is devoid of sexual contact or desire.

Greeks did not think about sexual behavior as being "homosexual" and "heterosexual," as Americans do today, but as dominant/masculine and submissive/female. Masculine power was symbolized by the act of male penetration, while the woman was submissive and an inferior complement to man. The Greek male saw the act of penetration as a powerful, masculine act, and, as a famous Greek philosopher commented, it "hardly matters what you are penetrating." That is why adult Greek males rarely had homosexual contact with each other; one of them would have to be penetrated, and adult men willing to adopt such a "feminine" role were viewed with contempt (Winkler, 1990).

SEX TALK

QUESTION **1.3** **How could the Greeks think that men having sex with boys was a "natural" form of human sexuality? Couldn't they see that it was perverted?**

One society's perversion is another society's normal sexual practice. Every culture sees its own forms of sexuality as natural and obvious—including ours. Not too long ago in our own society, it was "obvious" to most people that things like oral sex and anal sex were perversions (they are still technically illegal in many states) and that masturbation was a serious disease that could lead to mental illness. Now most people see these acts as part of healthy sexual life. Sexual beliefs and practices change over time and are different in different cultures.

Pederasty was only a small part of Greek sexual life. In the great stories of Homer, such as the *Iliad* and the *Odyssey,* we find descriptions of deep heterosexual love, of caring marriages, of tenderness for children, and of conjugal and maternal affections

Greek cups, plates, and other pottery often depicted erotic scenes, such as this pederastic scene from the fifth century, depicted on a cup.

(Flacelière, 1962). Coupled with the obvious admiration Greeks had of the feminine form—such as the Venus de Milo—it is a mistake to take Greek pederasty as the basic form of Greek sexuality.

Women in Greece had few rights and lived cloistered lives, and (male) Greek philosophers did not speak highly of women in general. Aristotle, for example, was clearly contemptuous of women. Women were seen as driven by their need to reproduce, and their sexual nature lay primarily in the desires of the womb, while men were seen to have a higher, mental sexual desire (Halperin, 1990).

On the other hand, a Greek woman is the first in history to offer us female views of love and sex. Sappho (who lived in the sixth century B.C.) wrote poetry that extolled feminine traits, setting them up against the masculine love of war (Bergmann, 1987). Sappho wrote love poetry to women and thus is reputed to have been a lesbian (Sappho was from the island of Lesbos, which is why we call female homosexuals "lesbians"). However, she also wrote poems about heterosexual relationships, such as this poem about the orgasmic bliss awaiting a bride on her wedding night:

Song of the Wedding Bed

Bride, warm with rose-
colored love, brightest
ornament of the Paphian,
come to the bedroom now,
enter the bed and play
tenderly with your man.
May the Evening Star
lead you eagerly
to that instant when you
will gaze in wonder
before the silver throne
of Hera, queen of marriage.

Contemporary historians of sexuality, following the work of philosopher Michel Foucault (1978, 1987, 1988), have been writing about sexuality in society as a reflection of social power. In the ancient Greek city of Athens, for example, only a small group of men were consider "citizens," and they held all the political and social power. Sex became a symbol of that power, and it was therefore acceptable for citizens to have sex with any of the other, less powerful groups in society—women, slaves, foreigners, or children. In other words, a powerful male, wielding the symbol of masculine power (the penis), could penetrate those who were his social inferiors, reinforcing their place in the social order.

Rome (Fifth Century B.C. to Seventh Century A.D.)

In Rome, marriage was viewed as a means to improve one's economic and social standing; passionate love almost never appears in the accounts handed down to us. Bride and groom need not love each other, for that kind of relationship was to grow over the life of the marriage; more important was fair treatment, respect, and mutual consideration. Wives even encouraged their husbands to have slaves (of either gender) for the purposes of sexual release (Boswell, 1980). Rome had few restrictions about sexuality until late in the history of the empire, and so early Romans had very permissive attitudes toward homosexual and bisexual behaviors, which were entirely legal until the sixth century A.D. (Boswell, 1980).

In Rome, as in Greece, adult males who took the passive sexual position in homosexual encounters were viewed with scorn, while the same behavior by youth, foreigners, slaves, or women was seen as an acceptable means to try to please a person who could improve one's place in society (Boswell, 1980). Still, long-term homosexual unions were not unknown. The emperor Elagabalus married a male athlete and demanded that all other athletes at court who wished to advance should do the same; and the Emperor Nero publicly married two men, one of whom was accorded all the honors of an empress, accompanied Nero to public functions, and stayed with him until he died (Boswell, 1980).

Women in Rome had slightly more freedom than their Greek counterparts, but they were still primarily seen as wives and mothers whose job was to produce children. Legally, they were not individuals but part of the man's familial possessions—women even lacked individual names, being named after their families, and only male children were listed on their parents' tombstones (Bullough, 1973). After Rome became wealthy, and some women began to accumulate their own wealth and freedom, many writers began to suggest that women had gone too far, not like the glorious women of the past who knew their place. Cato, the Roman politician and scholar, argued for laws returning women to their place as subordinate to men and wrote:

> *If each of us citizens, had determined to assert his rights and dignity as a husband with respect to his own spouse, we should have less trouble with the sex as a whole . . . The moment they begin to be your equals they will be your superiors.*

> *Quoted in Bullough (1973:88)*

Roman women and men knew about contraception, and a number of techniques they used have survived in the literature (Tannahill, 1980). Pliny suggested "mouse dung . . . applied in the form of a liniment," while Soranus suggested the undoubtedly more effective technique of wool plugs, inserted in the vagina and doused with gummy substances. There is also evidence that goat bladders may have been used for a kind of condom.

The Ancient Civilizations
China

Chinese civilization never developed a Western-style concept of God, a conscious being who determines correct behavior. Instead, Chinese philosophy emphasizes the interdependence of all things, unified in the Tao, which represents the basic unity of the universe. The Tao is usually translated as "The Way" or "The Path" but is itself unknowable; people can only try to live in harmony with the Tao, but they can never actually get to know it (much as the Western view of God considers God to be unknowable). The Tao itself is made up of two principles, **yin** and **yang**, which represent the opposites of the world: yin is feminine and yang masculine, yin is passive and receptive, while yang is active and assertive, and so on. Sexuality in Chinese thought is not a matter of moral or allowable behavior but, rather, is a natural procreative process, a joining of the yin and yang, the masculine and feminine principles. The goal of Taoist life is harmony, the effortless blending of yin and yang.

yin and **yang:** The Chinese belief that the universe is run by the interaction of two fundamental principles—one (yin) negative, passive, weak, yielding, and female, and the other (yang) positive, assertive, active, strong, and male.

Since sex itself was part of the basic process of knowing the Tao, sexual instruction and sex manuals were common and open in early Chinese society. These texts were very explicit, with pictures of sexual positions and instruction on how to stimulate partners, and were often given to brides before their weddings. Yet the interplay between the sexes still involved male initiation and female shyness, as this quote, which accompanies pictures showing how to make love, illustrates:

When the red flower [the vagina] shows its beauty
And exhales its heady perfume,
While she stays with you in the night
and you play and take your pleasure with her,
Pointing at the pictures, you follow their sequence,
While she blushes and looks abashed
And coyly protests. . . .

Chang Hêng, Ch'i-pien: quoted in Tannahill (1980:169)

Since women's essence, yin, was inexhaustible, while man's essence, yang (embodied in semen) was limited, man should feed his yang through prolonged contact with yin. In other words, intercourse should be prolonged as long as possible, without the man ejaculating, which releases all the yin energy that has been saved up. (The man may orgasm without ejaculation, however, and techniques were developed to teach men how to do that.) Men should try to have sex with many different women to prevent the yin energy of any single women from getting depleted. It is also important for the man to experience the woman's orgasm, when yin is at its peak, in order to maximize his contact with yin energy. The Chinese were unique in stressing the importance of female orgasm.

Chinese sexual philosophy discussed the kinds and numbers of partners a person should sleep with, the sexual positions one should engage in, the ways to prepare the partner for the sex act, the means to avoid pregnancy, the best times to conceive, and techniques for producing boys or girls. The great philosophers of sexuality also instructed on how to make sex tender, caring, pleasurable for both partners, and mutually respectful.

Homosexuality and lesbianism were not discouraged, though male homosexuality was viewed as a wasteful use of sperm, for semen was seen as precious and primarily for impregnation (see Chapter 7 for more on Chinese views of homosexuality). Aphrodisiacs were developed, as were drugs for all kinds of sexual problems. So were sexual devices such as penis rings to maintain erection, balls and bells that were grafted under the skin of the head of the penis to increase its size and therefore the women's pleasure, and balls (usually two or three) containing mercury and other substances that were to be inserted in the vagina, where their motion against each other brought sexual pleasure ("Ben-wa" balls).

Taoists believed that yin and yang were equally necessary complements of all existence, so one might guess that men and women were treated more equally in China than in the West. Yet since yin is the passive, inferior principle, women were seen as subservient to men throughout their lives: first to their fathers, then their husbands, and finally their sons when their husbands died. **Polygamy** was practiced until very late in Chinese history, and the average middle class male had between three and a dozen wives and concubines, with the nobility having thirty or more. A husband's adultery was tolerated, and only men could initiate divorce. Women were often denied the right to be seen

polygamy: The practice of men or women marrying more than one partner.

in public, and those who worked in the home or, occasionally, outside the home, did so for the husband's benefit. In fact, some men set up businesses where all the female workers were also their concubines (Bullough, 1973).

India

karma: The idea that there is a cycle of birth, death, and rebirth and that deeds in one's life affect one's status in a future life.

Hinduism, the religion of India for most of its history, concentrates on an individual's cycle of birth and rebirth, or **karma**. *Karma* involves a belief that a person's unjust deeds in this life are punished by suffering in a future life, and suffering in this life is undoubtedly punishment for wrongs committed in previous incarnations. The goal, then, is to live a just life to avoid suffering in the future, and one of the responsibilities in this life is marriage and procreation. Sex is an important part of those responsibilities, so sex was generally viewed as a positive pursuit.

patriarchal: A society ruled by the male as the figure of authority, symbolized by the father's absolute authority in the home.

There are legends about great women rulers early in India's history, and women had important roles in ceremonies and sacrifices. Still, India's social system, like others we have mentioned, was basically **patriarchal**, and Indian writers (again, mostly male) shared many of the negative views of women that were characteristic of other civilizations. Being born a woman was seen as itself a punishment for sins committed in previous incarnations. In fact, murdering a woman was not seen as a particularly serious crime, and female infanticide was not uncommon (Bullough, 1973). Still, Indian women did have power within their families, and when the fathers of the house grew into late middle age, many followed a religious prescription to leave the family and become a hermit or beggar. This left the mother with most of the authority in the household (Tannahill, 1980).

By about the third or fourth century B.C., the first and most famous of India's sex manuals appeared, the *Kamasutra*. India is justifiably famous for this amazing book. The *Kamasutra* talks not just of sex but also of the nature of love, how to make a good home and family, and moral guidance in sex and love. The *Kamasutra* is obsessive about naming and classifying things. It describes eight kinds of love-biting, eight stages of oral sex, and nine ways to move the lingham (penis) in the yoni (vagina). Men fell into one of three categories of lingham size: there was a hare man, a bull man, or a horse man, while a woman might be a deer, mare, or cow-elephant depending on the capacity of her yoni. A good match in size was preferred, but barring that, a tight fit was better than a loose one (Tannahill, 1980).

The *Kamasutra* recommends that women learn how to please their husbands, and so it gives instruction on sexual techniques and portrays many sexual positions, some of which are virtually impossible for anyone who cannot twist his or her body like a pretzel. Intercourse should be a passionate activity and includes scratching, biting, and blows to the back, accompanied by a variety of animal noises (there were eight kinds of nail marks, eight different animal sounds to be made . . .). On the other hand, the *Kamasutra* gives no advice about contraception or abortion because it believed that sex and procreation were part of the cycle of birth and rebirth (which does not mean that Indian women did not know about contraception—clearly, courtesans practiced a variety of contraceptive techniques) (Tannahill, 1980).

SEX TALK

QUESTION **1.4** **When I read about other cultures, I have trouble deciding if they are just like us or completely different from us. Which is it?**

Both, most likely. All human beings share certain traits and behaviors, from eating, to wearing clothes, to adorning the body, to disciplining children, to making love. Yet the ways these behaviors are thought about in a society, and the rituals and restrictions put around them, differ greatly.

Marriage was an economic and religious obligation, and families tried to arrange good marriages by betrothing their children at younger and younger ages, though they did not live or have sex with their husbands until after puberty. Since childbearing began so young, these women were still in the prime of their lives when their children were grown, and they were able to assert themselves in the household over elderly husbands. When a husband died, his wife was forbidden to remarry, and she had to live simply, wear plain clothes, and sleep on the ground. She was to devote her days to prayer and rituals that ensured her remarriage to the same husband in a future life. Many women chose to (or were forced to) end their lives as widows by the ritual act of *satî* where they threw themselves on their husband's burning funeral pyre.

A depiction of one of the more difficult positions in the *Kamasutra* and the erotic carvings on the facade of the Kandarya-Mahadeva Temple in India.

SEXUALITY FROM ROME TO THE MIDDLE AGES

Christianity

Perhaps no single system of thought had as much impact on the Western world as Christianity and nowhere more so than in its views on sexuality.

Christianity Until the Fall of the Roman Empire (476 C.E.)

Christianity began as a small sect following the teachings of Jesus. It was formalized into a religious philosophy by Paul (who was a Hellenized Jew—that is, a Jew who was heavily influenced by Greek culture) and by other early leaders who were influenced by Roman legal structure. Within a few hundred years, this little sect would become the predominant religion of the Western world and would influence the attitudes of people towards sexuality until the present day.

Jesus himself was mostly silent on sexual issues such as homosexuality or pre-marital sex. Jesus was born a Jew and was knowledgeable in Jewish tradition, and his attitudes were probably compatible with mainstream Jewish thought of the time. He preached that men should be held to the same standards of adultery, divorce, and remarriage as women were held to, leading some disciples to complain that it would be better not to marry at all if Jesus' teaching was enforced (Bullough, 1973). The Gospels also show that Jesus was liberal in his recommendations for punishing sexual misadventures. When confronted with a woman who had committed adultery, a sin for which the Hebrew Bible had mandated stoning, Jesus replied with his famous comment, "Let he who is without sin cast the first stone." It was not Jesus, but Paul and later followers such as St. Jerome and St. Augustine, who established the Christian view of sexuality that was to dominate Western thought for the next 2,000 years. St. Paul condemned sexuality in a way not found in either Hebrew or Greek thought and also not found anywhere in the teachings of Jesus. Paul suggested that the highest love was love of God and that the ideal was not to allow sexual or human love to compete with love for God. Therefore, though sexuality itself was not sinful when performed as part of the marital union, the ideal situation was **celibacy**. **Chastity**, for the first time in history, became a virtue; abstaining from sexual intercourse became a sign of holiness (Bergmann, 1987). Paul felt that those unable to make a commitment to chastity should engage in marital sex, though occasionally abstaining for periods of prayer and devotion. (Paul never suggested that the clergy should be celibate, by the way; the First Epistle of Timothy clearly shows that Bishops and Deacons were to be "the husband of one wife.")

As Christianity developed, Greek, Roman, and other philosophies influenced the Church's developing views on sexuality. St. Jerome (347–420 C.E.) and St. Augustine (died 604 C.E.), were both powerful influences on the early church's views of sexuality. Both had been sexually active before converting to a life of chastity, and both felt ongoing sexual temptation; perhaps that is why they were so strong in condemning sexual activity, as they themselves were struggling with their erotic feelings. St. Augustine prayed to God: "Give me chastity—but not yet!" (Tannahill, 1980). St. Jerome declared sexuality itself unclean and even taught that one who feels ardent (erotic) love for his *own wife* is committing adultery! (Bergmann, 1987).

Women were seen as the source of temptation and evil for men (perhaps since it was women who St. Jerome and St. Augustine had such a hard time putting out of their minds). St. John Chrysostom (347–407 C.E.) declared that "The beauty of women is the

celibacy: The state of remaining unmarried; often used today to refer to abstaining from sex.

chastity: The quality of being sexually pure, either through abstaining from intercourse or by adhering to strict rules of sexuality.

greatest snare." Jesus never suggested that women were "temptresses" and even confided in many women; nevertheless, after St. Paul, women were forbidden to teach in the church and were ordered to keep silent. Women were to obey their husbands, submit meekly to their husbands' instruction, and be ruled by their husbands as the church was ruled by God.

The legacy of early Christianity was a general association of sexuality with sin. All nonprocreative sex was strictly forbidden, as was contraception, masturbation, and sex for pleasure's sake. The result was that the average Christian associated the pleasure of sexuality with guilt. Christianity's view of sex has been one of the harshest of any major religious or cultural tradition.

The Middle Ages (476 C.E. to about 1500 C.E.—the Renaissance)

In the early Middle Ages, the influence of the church slowly began to increase. Christianity had become the state religion of Rome, and though the church did not have much formal power, its teachings had an influence on law. For example, homosexual relations (even marriage) had been legal for the first two hundred years that Christianity was the state religion of Rome, and the church was very tolerant of homosexuality. Eventually, however, church teachings changed and became much more strict. For example, the emperor Justinian outlawed homosexuality by invoking scripture and the teachings of the church and mandated castration as a punishment, saying that "because of such crimes there are famines, earthquakes, and pestilences" (quoted in Boswell, 1980:171).

Between the years of about 1050 and 1150 (the "High" Middle Ages) sexuality once again became liberalized. For example, a gay subculture was established in Europe that produced a body of gay literature that had not been seen since the Roman Empire and would not happen again until the nineteenth century (Boswell, 1980). Mabod, the Bishop of Rennes, France, had a male lover, and the style of his erotic poetry to boys was copied throughout Europe. Male brothels appeared, defenses of homosexual relations began to appear in print, and homosexuality was a fairly accepted part of the general culture.

However, the homosexual subculture disappeared in the thirteenth century when the church cracked down on a variety of groups—including Jews, Muslims, and homosexuals (Boswell, 1980). In the year 1215, the Church instituted **confession**, and soon guides appeared to teach priests about the various sins **penitents** might have committed. The guides seem preoccupied with sexual transgressions and used sexual sins more than any other kind to illustrate their points (Payer, 1991). All sex outside of marriage was considered sinful, and even certain marital acts were forbidden. But penance also had to be done for such things as nocturnal emissions and violations of modesty (looks, desires, touches, kisses). One set of statutes, for example, mandated that for the sin of masturbation the penitent was to flagellate (whip) himself every week for *seven years!* (Payer, 1991).

confession: A Catholic practice of revealing one's sins to a priest.

penitents: Those who come to confess sins (from the word *penance*, meaning "to repent").

Women and Love in the Later Middle Ages. European women in the early Middle Ages were little better off than they had been under the ancient Greeks or Romans. By the late Middle Ages, however, new ideas of women were being brought back by the Crusaders from Islamic lands (see *Islam,* below). Women were elevated to a place of purity and were considered almost perfect. Eve, who caused Adam's downfall, was replaced as the symbol of ideal womanhood by Mary, the mother of God (Tannahill, 1980). Woman was no longer a temptress but a model of virtue. Treatises began to

The artists of the Middle Ages did not shy away from erotic depictions. To the right is the central panel and below a detail of Bosch's famous *Garden of Earthly Delights* showing people engaging in explicitly sexual behaviors; note the man caressing the woman in the detail.

appear praising women, such as Christine de Pizan's defense of her sex, in which she extolled women's abilities in a way not seen again until the Renaissance (Bornstein, 1979). The idea of romantic love was first created at this time, and it spread through popular culture as balladeers and troubadours traveled from place to place singing songs of pure, spiritual love, untroubled by sex.

At the same time that women were seen to be virtuous, however, they were also said to be the holder of the secrets of sexuality (Thomasset, 1992). Before marriage, men would employ the services of an **entremetteuse** to teach them the ways of love. These old women procured young women (prostitutes) for the men and were said to know the secrets of restoring potency, restoring virginity, and concocting potions. It was a small step from the scary accounts of these old women's powers to the belief in witches. By the late fifteenth century, the church began a campaign against witchcraft, which they said was inspired by women's insatiable "carnal lust" (Covey, 1989). Thousands of women were killed, and the image of the evil witch became the symbol of man's fear of women for centuries to come.

entremetteuse: A woman who procures sexual partners for men; in older days, one who also taught men about lovemaking.

Thomas Aquinas. Perhaps no person from the Middle Ages had a stronger impact on subsequent attitudes toward sexuality than the theologian (and later St.) Thomas Aquinas (1225–1274). Aquinas established the views of morality and correct sexual behavior that form the basis of the Catholic Church's attitudes toward sexuality even today. In his *Summa theologiae,* intended to answer Christians' questions on all moral issues, Aquinas drew from the idea of "natural law" to suggest that there were "natural" and "unnatural" sex acts. Aquinas argued that the sex organs were "naturally" intended for procreation, and other use of them was unnatural and immoral; in fact, he argued that semen and ejaculation were intended only to impregnate, and any other use of them was immoral. But Aquinas recognized a problem: if the reason that, for example, homosexual intercourse was wrong was because it was an unnatural use of the sex organs, then was it not wrong to use other parts of the body for other uses? Is it immoral, for example, to walk on one's hands, which were not naturally designed for that (Boswell, 1980)? Aquinas solved that problem by arguing that the sin was that misuse of sexuality got in the way of procreation. But he himself had argued that individuals are *not* obligated to reproduce, for the Christian church thought celibacy and voluntary virginity was the highest virtue. Aquinas' own logic led him to admit that certain sex acts are immoral simply because of popular sentiment. Yet Aquinas' strong condemnation of sexuality, and especially homosexuality, which he called the worst of all sexual sins, set the tone for Christian attitudes towards sexuality for many centuries.

Islam

In the sixth century, a man named Muhammad began to preach a religion that drew from Jewish and Christian roots and added Arab tribal beliefs. Islam became a powerful force that conquered the entire Middle East and Persian lands; swept across Asia, and so touched China in the East; spread through Northern Africa and, from there, north into Christian Europe, particularly Spain. Between about the eighth and twelfth centuries, Islamic society was the most advanced in the world, developing a new system of mathematics (Arabic numbers) to replace the clumsy Roman system and having the world's most sophisticated medicine, warfare, and science.

Muslim societies often have strong rules of *satr al-'awra,* or modesty, which involve covering the private parts of the body (which in women means almost the entire body). Muhammad had tried to preserve the rights of women; he made sure that women were treated fairly in marriage, had the right to inherit (though in lesser amounts than males), and could keep the rights to their dowries (Bullough, 1973). There are examples in the **Koran**, the Muslim Bible, of female saints and intellectuals, and powerful women often held strong informal powers over their husbands and male children. Still, women in many Islamic lands were subjugated to men, were segregated and not permitted to

Koran: The holy book of Islam.

venture out of their homes, and were forbidden to interact with men who were not members of their family.

In Islamic law, as in Christian law, sexuality between a man and a woman was only legal when the couple was married or when the woman was a female concubine (Coulson, 1979). Sexual intercourse in marriage was a good religious deed for the Muslim male, and the Koran likens the wife to a field that men should cultivate as frequently as they want. The man with a strong sex drive is advised to marry many wives, even more than the normal limit of four (Bürgel, 1979). **Fornication** is punishable by one hundred lashes and adultery is punished by stoning to death, so Islam takes restricting sex to the marital union very seriously.

Women who were married to wealthy men usually lived in secluded areas in their husbands' homes, called **harems**. Harems were not the dens of sex and sensuality that are sometimes portrayed but, rather, were self-contained communities where women learned to become self-sufficient in the absence of men. Among the middle and lower classes, men had less wealth to offer potential wives, which gave women more power. In a letter from medieval Egypt, for example, a man pleading with his estranged wife promises that she will be the queen of the house and he will be her slave (Goitein, 1979).

Islamic society has a much freer, more open attitude to sexuality than Christian society. Erotic and love writings from medieval Islam are very common, and some of the books are quite explicit. There are many Arab love poems that are clearly sexually charged poems of the love of boys (Roth, 1991), for, like Greeks, Arabs celebrated young boys as the epitome of beauty. But even these homoerotic writings were religious in nature, often starting with the formula "in the Name of God, the Merciful, the Compassionate" (Bürgel, 1979).

The Sultans of the **Ottoman Empire**, which ruled most of the Islamic world from the fifteenth to the twentieth century, had between 300 and 1,200 concubines, mostly captured or bought slaves. The Sultan's mother ruled the harem and even sometimes ruled the empire itself if she was strong and her son was weak-willed (Tannahill, 1980). Since each woman might sleep with the Sultan at best once or twice a year, **eunuchs** were employed to guard against the women finding sexual satisfaction elsewhere. Some eunuchs had their testicles removed, some their penises, and some both; young eunuchs might have their testicles crushed. Many died under the surgeon's knife.

THE RENAISSANCE TO THE TWENTIETH CENTURY

The Reformation (1517–1558)

In the sixteenth century, Martin Luther challenged papal power and founded a movement known as Protestantism. Instead of valuing celibacy, Luther saw in the Bible the obligation to reproduce, saw marital love as blessed, and considered sexuality a natural function. Calvin, the other great Protestant reformer, suggested that women were not just reproductive vessels but men's partners in all things.

To Luther, marriage was a state that was blessed by God, and sexual contact was sinful primarily when it was done out of wedlock, just as any indulgence was sinful. Marriage was inherent in the nature of man, had been instituted in paradise, and was confirmed in the fifth commandment and safeguarded by the seventh (Bullough,

fornication: Engaging in sexual intercourse while unmarried.

harem: Abbreviation of the Turkish word *harêmlik* (*harâm* in Arabic) meaning "women's quarters" or "sanctuary."

Ottoman Empire: An empire based in Turkey that lasted over 600 years and ruled over large parts of Asia, Europe, and Africa until its collapse after World War I.

eunuchs: From the Greek word for "bed-watcher," castrated males (or less often, with their penises removed) who guarded harems. At times, children were also made eunuchs in childhood in order to sing soprano in church choirs. Jesus even mentions eunuchs who castrated themselves for religious reasons.

1973).* (Luther himself married an ex-nun, and had few illusions about the difficulties of marriage. He wondered how often Eve must have said to Adam, "You ate the apple!" and Adam had replied, "But you gave it to me!") If marriage was so important, then a bad marriage should not continue. So Luther broke with the Catholic church and allowed divorce.

Sexuality was permissible only in the marital union, but it had other justifications besides reproduction, such as "to avoid fornication, or to lighten and ease the cares and sadnesses of household affairs, or to endear to each other"—a very different perspective on sex than was preached by the Catholic church. Calvin, in fact, saw the marital union as primarily a social and sexual relationship. Though procreation was important, companionship was the main goal of marriage.

Luther did accept the general subjugation of women to men in household affairs and felt that, of men and women, women were weaker and should humble themselves before their fathers and husbands. Despite his preaching that men and women were equal, he also excluded women from the clergy because of standards of "decency" and of women's inferior aptitudes for ministry. Though Calvin and Luther tried to remove from Protestantism the overt disdain of women they found in some older Christian theologians, they did not firmly establish women's equal place with men. "In effect," Tannahill (1980:328) puts it, "they upgraded the position of 'wife' without upgrading the women who held it."

The Renaissance (The Fourteenth Through Sixteenth Centuries in Europe)

The Renaissance may be summed up as a time when intellectual and artistic thought turned from a focus on God to a focus on human beings and their place in the world; from the sober and serious theology of the Middle Ages to a renewed sense of joy in life; from asceticism to sensuality; from religious symbolism to a focus on naturalness; and from a belief in tradition to experimentation in the pursuit of knowledge (New, 1969). Part of the cultural shift of the Renaissance was new views of sexuality and, to some degree, the roles of women in society. (See Focus on Diversity 1.2 for a discussion of sexuality in Central and South America during this period of history.)

Note the unashamed nudity of Botticelli's Venus.

---

* The fifth commandment is to honor one's mother and father, which (Luther believed) assumes a marital unit, and the seventh is the prohibition against adultery.

Focus
on Diversity
1.2

Sexuality in Pre-European Central and South America

When the Spaniards began to conquer the New World, they found natives there whose cultures and sexual practices were fundamentally different than theirs. An argument emerged among them: were these "irrational savages" little more than beasts who could therefore be killed and robbed of their lands with impunity; or, as the Spanish Pope Alexander VI Borgia declared, were they simply "misguided" human beings who had the capacity to understand Christianity and should therefore be missionized and treated with common decency? As the riches of the new land favored those who would conquer by the sword, their version of Native Americans—savages who engaged in cannibalism, sodomy, adultery, rape, and murder and were therefore little more than animals—won the day. The Spanish massacred the Aztecs, Incas, Mayans, and other groups, burned all their writings and books of knowledge, and sold many into slavery.

The Mayans accepted adult homosexuality (which was not accepted by the Aztecs or Incas), which deeply shocked the Spanish. All three American civilizations accepted teenage homosexuality as natural, but the Mayans also believed that some portion of adult males were predisposed to homosexuality, and to the Spanish, that was enough to brand them all as sinners and sodomites (in Spain, homosexuality was not uncommon, but it was performed in private while being censured publicly). The Mayans had carvings and amulets of men together in sexual positions, and so the Spanish assumed all of the New World was populated with "sodomites." Actually, adult homosexuality was severely punished by the Aztecs, using brutal torture and executions.

The Incas had a system of laws that was aimed at increasing the population. No man could remain a bachelor, and the Inca himself (the leader of the civilization) would perform mass weddings. Inca men had concubines or harems, and the Inca had a large harem replenished by selecting the most beautiful girls of the land and putting them in a special convent until they were ready to be chosen for his harem. Inca law mandated death for any man who raped a virgin (unless she agreed to marry him), though there is evidence that consensual premarital sex was allowed. Incest was forbidden except for the Inca himself, who, since he was believed to be descended from the sun, could not marry a mortal and so married his sister. Adultery and abortion were also forbidden.

The Aztecs had the problem of replenishing a population that was depleted by war and by their practice of human sacrifice. Some anthropologists suggest they may have sacrificed up to a quarter of a million people a year! It is not surprising that they penalized all non-procreative practices, such as homosexuality and abortion, and practiced polygamy.

Prostitutes were common in the civilizations of the Americas. Among some groups, prostitution was not legal, while in others, new prostitutes were consecrated with great festivals. Spaniards took advantage of these prostitutes, but they also raped native women with impunity. The Spanish also introduced a variety of diseases—venereal and otherwise—which killed millions upon millions of natives and effectively emptied the land of its population so that the Spanish could settle.

Adapted from Tannahill (1980)

In Renaissance art, sexuality and nudity are treated as positive, even glorious, while in the Middle Ages, nudity had been used to indicate shame or sinfulness (Lucie-Smith, 1991). For example, Renaissance art showed the humanness of the child Jesus by showing his legs splayed wide open, his penis exposed, often erect, and even being fondled by St. Ann (Steinberg, 1983). In fact, that Jesus lived on after his crucifixion is often symbolized by his being shown draped in his death shroud with an erection, a symbol of life and potency. Showing Jesus' nudity was seen as a positive portrayal, even though many such Renaissance pictures were later painted over by offended Christians.

During the Renaissance, women made great strides in education and began to become more prominent in political affairs (Bornstein, 1979). Anti-female tracts still had wide circulation, but they gave rise to pro-female tracts, and a lively debate arose on the worth and value of women. Henricus Cornelius Agrippa published a tract in 1532 arguing that each of God's creations in Genesis is superior to the one before, and since the human female is the last thing God creates, she must be his most perfect creation. In the Bible, Agrippa continues, a male is the first sinner; men introduce polygamy, drunkenness, and murder into the world; and men are aggressive and tyrannical. Women, on the other hand, are more peaceful, chaste, refined, and faithful. Agrippa concludes that what holds women back is the tyranny of men and that women should be liberated and educated (Bornstein, 1979).

But as seems to happen so often in history when women make some modest gains, there was a backlash. By the seventeenth century, witchcraft trials appeared once again in Europe and in the New World, symbols of the fears that men still held of women's sexuality (see Focus on Diversity 1.3).

Focus on Diversity — *1.3*

Witchcraft

Many images of women have been created by men throughout history, some of which have expressed male fears of female sexuality and have helped to keep women subjugated. The woman as whore, as temptress, as shrew, as simple-minded, as virtuous, as perfect—all have prevented men from seeing women as simply the other half of the human species. But perhaps none has been so dangerous to women's lives as the image of the witch.

Though the idea of the witch has been around at least since the Bible (which mandates killing witches), the Catholic church did not take witches seriously until the thirteenth century, when Aquinas suggested they still existed. Witch hunting became an obsession in Europe when Pope Innocent VIII decreed that witches should be wiped out in 1486. A pamphlet released in that year (which went through thirteen editions) claimed witches were more likely to be female because women were the source of all evil, had defective intelligence, tried to dominate men, and "know no moderation whether in goodness or vice" (Bullough, 1973).

In Germany, over 100,000 people (mostly women) were executed for witchcraft. Cardinal Albizzi wrote of his trip to Cologne: "A horrible spectacle met our eyes. Outside of the walls of many towns and villages, we saw numerous stakes to which poor, wretched women were bound and burned as witches" (quoted in Bullough, 1973: 224). In England, where most of the women accused were married, executions for witchcraft continued until 1712.

Witchcraft trials seem to happen at times of social disruption, religious change, or economic troubles. At such times, it is easier to blame evil forces, and women, than to look to causes in the greater society. Such was the case in Salem, Massachusetts, in 1692, where three young girls began acting strange, running around, falling to the ground in convulsions, and barking like dogs. Soon the other girls of Salem began to follow suit, and the doctors decided that they had been bewitched. Forced to identify the witches that had put spells on them, the girls began with the adults they did not particularly like and went on to name names from every corner of the village. Not one suspect dragged before the courts was acquitted, and twenty-two were executed or died in prison. When the tide finally turned, 150 people were in prison awaiting trial and another 200 stood accused. All were finally released (Erikson, 1986).

The accusations of witchcraft were often used as a way to punish women who did not conform to the social expectation of women's behavior. It was also a means to reaffirm men's dominance over women. Even in many contemporary tribal cultures where witchcraft is very much a part of the cultural beliefs, women are seen as potentially more malevolent and evil creatures than men Janeway (1971).

The Enlightenment and the Victorian Era (the Eighteenth and Nineteenth Centuries)

The Enlightenment

The Enlightenment, an intellectual movement of the eighteenth century, prized rational thought over traditional authority and suggested that human nature was to be understood through a study of human psychology. Enlightenment writers argued that human drives and instincts are part of nature's design, so one must realize the basic wisdom of human urges and not fight them (Porter, 1982). Sexual pleasure is therefore also natural and desirable. In fact, of all the earthly pleasures, enlightenment thinkers praised sexuality as supreme. Darwin had demonstrated that asexual reproduction had given way, in evolution, to sexual reproduction, and so sex was seen as a great evolutionary achievement. Travelers began to write of the sexual habits of far away civilizations, "free love" was often discussed, and sex manuals and erotic literature became very popular (Porter, 1982). Sexuality had become so free that there was an unprecedented rise in premarital pregnancy and illegitimate births; up to one-fifth of all brides in the late seventeenth century were pregnant when they got married (Trumbach, 1990).

As liberal as the Enlightenment was, many sexual activities, such as homosexuality, were condemned and persecuted. For example, starting in 1730, there was a two-year "sodomite panic" in the Netherlands, and hundreds of men were executed and hundreds more fled the country. France burned homosexuals long after it stopped burning witches. Yet there were also times of relative tolerance. Napoleon so eased laws against homosexuality that by 1860 homosexuality and lesbianism were tolerated and male prostitutes were very common in France (Tannahill, 1980).

The Victorian Era (1837–1901—the Reign of Queen Victoria of England)

The Victorian Era, which lasted into the twentieth century, was a time of great prosperity in England. Propriety and public behavior became more important, especially to the upper class, and sexual attitudes became more conservative. Sex was not to be spoken of in polite company and was to be restricted to the marital bed, in the belief that preoccupation with sex interfered with higher achievements. At least that was the *public* attitude. Privately, Victorian England was not as conservative as it has been portrayed, and pornography, extramarital affairs, and prostitution were common. Still, the most important aspect of Victorian society was public propriety, and conservative values were often preached if not always practiced.

During this period, the idea of male chivalry returned, and women were considered as virtuous, refined, delicate, fragile, vulnerable, and remote; certainly, no respectable Victorian woman would ever admit to a sexual urge. The prudery of the Victorian Era sometimes went to extremes. Victorian women were too embarrassed to talk to a doctor about their "female problems" and so would point out areas of discomfort on dolls. Women were supposed to be interested in music but could not play the flute because pursing the lips was unladylike; the cello was unacceptable because it had to be held between the legs; the brass instruments were too difficult for the delicate wind of the female; the violin forced the woman's neck into an uncomfortable position. Therefore only keyboard instruments were considered "ladylike" (Bullough, 1973).

At the same time, men were seen as the gallant knights of their homes. One woman, expressing a common sentiment, wrote in 1842 that it was essential for women to recog-

In the late nineteenth and early twentieth centuries, many doctors taught that masturbation was harmful, and so devices were created to keep children (especially boys) from achieving unwanted erections, such as the two barbed rings and the shock-box above.

nize "the superiority of your husband simply as man . . . In the character of a noble, enlightened, and truly good man, there is a power and a sublimity so nearly approaching what we believe to be the nature and capacity of angels" (quoted in Tannahill, 1980:349).

Sexuality was repressed in many ways. Physicians and writers of the time often argued that semen was precious and should be conserved; Sylvester Graham recommended sex only twelve times a year. In fact, Graham invented a cracker (now called the Graham Cracker) that was supposed to be bland and boring and therefore reduce sexual desire. He argued that sexual indulgence led to all sorts of ailments and infirmities, such as depression, faintness, headaches, blindness—the list is almost endless (Money, 1985).

The Victorian Era had great influence on the sexuality of England and the United States. Many of the conservative attitudes that Western countries have held until the modern day are holdovers from Victorian standards.

SEX IN AMERICAN HISTORY*

Early American Life

American society has been influenced most strongly by Europe and particularly by England. Yet, it also developed its own unique mix of ideas and attitudes, tempered by the contributions of the many cultures its immigrants brought with them. Let us look at some of these influences.

The Puritans

The **Puritans** were a religious group who fled England and tried to set up a biblically based society in the New World. They had severe sanctions for sexual transgressions; in New England, for example, the death penalty was applied for sodomy, bestiality, adultery, and rape. In Puritan ideology, the entire community was responsible for upholding morality (D'Emilio and Freedman, 1988). Yet the Puritans were not as closed-minded about sex as their reputation suggests and believed that sexuality was good and proper within marriage. In fact, men were obligated to have intercourse with their wives. The Puritans also tolerated most mild sexual transgressions as long as people accepted their punishments and repented.

Puritan: A sixteenth- and seventeenth-century religious movement from England that wanted to purge the church of elaborate ceremonies and simplify worship; has come to mean any person or group which is excessively strict in regard to sexual matters.

The Colonies

As the New World began to grow, it suffered from a lack of women, and the reputation in Europe was that any woman seeking a man should come to America. America offered women greater independence than Europe. On the island of Nantucket, for example, whaling kept the men at sea for months. The women took over the island's business, and prestige was granted to those who managed to make the money grow while their husbands were away (Bullough, 1973). Still, women were generally expected to tend to their domain of the home and children.

---

* Much of this section is drawn from D'Emilio and Freedman's (1988) history of sexuality in the United States, entitled *Intimate Matters*.

Sexuality was also a bit freer, and courting youth would wander into barns or look for high crops in the field to obscure their necking and groping. There was also a custom called **bundling**, where young couples were allowed to share a bed as long as they were clothed, wrapped in sheets or bags, or had a wooden "bundling board" between them. The high number of premarital pregnancies suggest that couples found ways to get around their bundling impediments, but in most such cases, the couple would quickly marry (D'Emilio and Freedman, 1988).

bundling: An American practice of putting a wooden board, hanging sheets in the middle of the bed, or wrapping the body in tight clothes, in order to allow an unmarried couple to spend the night together without sex.

Post-Revolutionary America

The Liberalization of Sex.
After the Revolutionary War, the church's power began to diminish in the United States. Communities began abolishing church courts, which had previously heard cases of divorce and other sexual crimes. The United States entered a period of practical, utilitarian philosophy (such as Benjamin Franklin's maxims: "Early to bed and early to rise . . . ", etc.), which stressed the individual's right to pursue personal happiness. People began to speak more openly about sexuality and romantic love, and women began to pay more attention to appearance and sexual appeal. Children stopped consulting parents about marriage or would simply become pregnant if they wanted to marry. By the late eighteenth century, as many as one-third of all brides in some parts of New England were pregnant (D'Emilio and Freedman, 1988).

The liberalization of sexual conduct had many results. In 1720, prostitution was relatively rare, and, for example, William Byrd could not find a single prostitute in Williamsburg, Virginia; by the late eighteenth century, angry mobs were attacking brothels in cities all over the Eastern seaboard (D'Emilio and Freedman, 1988). Contraception, such as early condoms, were readily available (Gamson, 1990), and newspapers and almanacs often advertised contraceptive devices and concoctions to induce abortion. The birth rate dropped and abortion rates rose through the use of patent medicines, folk remedies, self-induced abortion by inserting objects into the uterus, or medical abortions. Within marriage, sexuality was much celebrated, and many diaries and letters survive where couples speak of passion and longing for each other. "I anticipate unspeakable delight in your embrace," one husband wrote to his wife, imagining her "caressing hands" and "voluptuous touch." She responded "How I long to see you . . . I'll drain your coffers dry next Saturday I assure you" (quoted in D'Emilio and Freedman, 1988:79). Extramarital affairs were not uncommon, and some of the diaries that survive quite explicitly record extramarital sexual passion.

Slavery.
Before the influx of slaves from Africa, the southern colonies had made use of **indentured servants**. Sexual contact and even rape of female indentured servants was fairly common. After 1670, African slaves became common in the South. The sex lives of slaves was different than that of colonists, due to the relative lack of females among the slaves, the restrictions put on contact with members of the opposite sex, and the different cultural traditions of Africa. Early on, interracial sex was legal, and southern white men often took black slaves as wives. As slavery became more established, many states passed **anti-miscegenation laws**, but they were often not obeyed. The relations between whites and blacks continued, ranging from brutal rape to genuinely affectionate, long-term relationships; mixed race children accounted for one-fifth of the children born out of wedlock in Virginia by the end of the eighteenth century (D'Emilio & Freedman, 1988).

African slaves were accused by whites of having loose morals, for females tended to have children by different fathers and children slept in the same rooms as their copulating parents. These sexual habits of slaves were used as an excuse to rape them, break

indentured servants: People who became servants to pay off a debt and were often treated as little more than slaves.

anti-miscegenation laws: Laws forbidding sexuality, marriage, or breeding between members of different races.

up families, and even, at times, kill them. Of course, slave owners did not consider that it was they themselves who forced the slaves to live that way. The fear that freed black men would rape white women (or accusations that they had) was often used as a justification to keep blacks segregated or to lynch them, even though it was far more common for white men to rape black slaves and servants. White women, on the other hand, had their movements and freedoms restricted for fear that they would "lose their virtue" to black males. The paradox was that the sexual availability of female black slaves severely damaged the sexual relations of white men and women.

The slaves themselves developed a social system to protect the few freedoms they had. Adults formed and tried to maintain stable unions when possible (marriage was officially illegal between slaves). Despite their harsh conditions, there was a strong sense of morality within the slave community, and slaves tried to regulate sexual behavior as much as possible, forcing men to take care of the women they impregnated and sanctioning girls who were too promiscuous. The myth of slave sexual looseness is disproved by the lack of prostitution and very low venereal disease rates among slaves (D'Emilio and Freedman, 1988). It is difficult, however, to maintain sexual unions when the woman's body is legally owned by the white master or when sexual favors might free one from harsh labor in the cotton fields. Still, despite the fact that plantation owners often condemned the promiscuity of the blacks (and therefore excused their own sexual exploitation of them), the premarital sexual activity of slaves was probably not much different than that of poor whites.

Settlers throughout early American history used the sexuality of minorities as an excuse to disdain or oppress them. Native Americans had their own cultural system of sexual morality; nonetheless, they were branded as savages for their acceptance of premarital sex and their practice of polygamy, which they needed because of the large number of males killed in war. White men freely raped female Native Americans, for

Indians, blacks, and other minorities were often killed for allegedly raping white women. Colonial settlers produced fanciful drawings of Indians raping white women, such as the one to the left, and many Indians were killed on those grounds; later, blacks were lynched for the same reason. In fact, such rapes were extremely rare.

whites could not be convicted of rape, or any crime, solely on the testimony of a "savage Indian." Similarly, Americans used sexual imagery to criticize the Mexicans they encountered in the West and Southwest; one writer claimed that all "darker colored" races were "inferior and syphilitic" (D'Emilio and Freedman, 1988). Mexicans, who were religious Catholics with strict sexual rules, were considered promiscuous by the Protestants because they did not consider it wrong to dance or show affection in public. The settlers often criticized others of sexual behaviors, such as homosexuality and pre-marital sex, that were not uncommon in their own communities.

The Nineteenth Century

Free Love Movement: A movement of the early nineteenth century that preached that love should be the factor that determines whether one should have sex (not to be confused with the free love movement of the 1960s). They were against promiscuity, which does not include true love of partner.

The nineteenth century saw the rise of a number of controversial social movements focusing on sexuality. **The Free Love Movement**, which began in the 1820s, preached that love, not marriage, should be the prerequisite to sexual relations. Free love advocates criticized the sexual "slavery" of women in marriage, often condemned the sexual exploitation of slaves, and condemned uncontrolled sexuality not connected to love (though their critics often claimed that they preached promiscuity). Another controversial group was the Church of Jesus Christ of Latter Day Saints, or Mormons, whose announcement in 1852 that many of its members practiced polygamy almost cost Utah its statehood. As with the free love movement, Americans accused the Mormons of loose morals, even though, despite their acceptance of polygamy, they were very sexually conservative (Iverson, 1991). A number of small communities that practiced alternative forms of sexual relations were also begun during this time, such as the Oneida community, which preached group marriage, and the Shakers who, frustrated with the all the arguments over sexuality, practiced strict celibacy.

By the close of the nineteenth century, the medical model of sexuality began to emerge. Americans became obsessed with sexual health, and physicians and reformers began to advocate self-restraint, abstention from masturbation, and eating "non-stimulating" foods.* Doctors also argued that women were ruled by their wombs, and many had their ovaries surgically removed to "correct" masturbation or sexual passion. An influential group of physicians even argued that women were biologically designed for procreation and should stay in the marital union, for they were too delicate to work or undergo the rigors of higher education. These theories completely ignored the fact that lower class women often worked twelve and fifteen hours a day at very difficult labor.

In the nineteenth century, homosexuality was underground, though there were some open same-sex relationships that may or may not have been sexual. For example, there are a number of cases of women who dressed and passed as men and even married other women. There were also men who wrote of intimate and loving relationships with other men, without an explicit admission of sexual contact. The great poet Walt Whitman, now recognized as having been homosexual, at times confirmed his erotic attraction to men, while at other times he denied it. In accordance with the developing medical model of sexuality, physicians began to argue that homosexuality was an illness rather than a sin, a view that lasted until the 1970s (Hansen, 1989) (see Chapter 7).

---

* A man named John Kellogg opened a sanitarium in Battle Creek, Michigan, where he created and served bland cereals so as not to excite the patients; a century later, his company, Kellogg's Foods, advertises its cereals as exciting and energizing!

The pressures for a more open sexuality were countered by strong voices to return the country to a more religious and chaste morality, a struggle that still goes on today. In the 1870s, Anthony Comstock, a dry-goods salesman, singlehandedly lobbied the legislature to outlaw obscenity. The resulting Comstock Act of 1873 prohibited the mailing of obscene, lewd, lascivious, and indecent writing or advertisements, including articles that aided contraception or abortion. Comstock himself was the act's most vigorous enforcer, and he reported hundreds of people to the authorities, even for such things as selling reprints of famous artwork containing nudity or famous books that mentioned prostitution. Literally thousands of books, sexual objects, and contraceptive devices were destroyed, denying many people sophisticated contraceptive devices or information for almost sixty years (D'Emilio and Freedman, 1988).

The Twentieth Century and Sexual Reform Movements

In a study of one thousand women born shortly before the turn of the century, 74% used some form of contraception (despite Comstock), most made love at least once a week, and 40% acknowledged masturbating during childhood or adolescence (while others began after marrying). These statistics reflect the freedom women found as they moved to the cities, lived on their own, and began working more outside the home (Irvine, 1990). Yet less than half the women polled considered sex crucial to their mental or physical health, and an overwhelming majority still considered reproduction the primary goal of sex. In part, this may be because information about sex was generally unavailable; there was a high correlation between lack of sexual instruction, distaste for sex, and unhappiness in marriage (D'Emilio and Freedman, 1988).

By the turn of the century, moral crusaders and those trying to liberalize sexuality were fighting to try to guide the rapid changes taking place in American sexual behaviors. Moral crusaders pointed to the spread of prostitution, high rates of venereal disease, and youth who rejected traditional morality for nightclubs, dances, and long-delayed marriages. Liberalizers argued that modern industrial society could not sustain the coercive sexual standards of past centuries. These battles are still being fought today, as the twentieth century comes to a close.

The Social Hygiene Movement

In response to high venereal disease rates, a New York physician, Prince Morrow, started a movement in 1905 that was a curious mixture of both liberal and traditional attitudes. The social hygiene movement convinced legislators that scores of "virtuous" women were catching venereal diseases from husbands who frequented prostitutes, and so laws were passed mandating blood tests before marriage. They argued that sex in marriage was for pleasure, not just reproduction, though they were against premarital sex and felt that masturbation harmed one's future sex life. Most important, they were early (if unsuccessful) advocates for sex education in the schools for all students, male and female (D'Emilio and Freedman, 1988).

Sexology

Beginning in the early part of the century and increasingly by midcentury, the pioneers of sexual research were beginning scientific research into sexuality. Rejecting the reli-

Posters appeared in the 1920s from the American Social Hygiene Association trying to curb rising venereal disease rates through sex education. The motto of the movement was "Keep Thyself Pure."

gious and moral teachings about how people "should" behave, they brought sex out into the open as a subject worthy of medical, scientific, and philosophical debate. We discuss these researchers at length in the following chapter, but here we should note that they had a profound impact on the way people began to talk and think about sexuality. For example, by midcentury Kinsey's large-scale surveys of American sexual behavior were promising to settle some of the debates and confusion about sexuality by promising a scientific solution to questions of how people behaved, and Masters and Johnson were trying to do the same for the physiology of the sexual response. The work of these sexologists helped to demystify sex and to make it more respectable to discuss publicly the sexual behaviors and problems of real people. Much of this work was condemned by moral crusaders, who criticized its lack of connection to traditional standards of morality (Irvine, 1990).

Feminism

There have always been women who protested against the patriarchy of their day, argued that women were as capable as men in the realms of work and politics, and defied their culture's stereotypes about women. Yet, the twentieth century has seen the most successful feminist movement in history. The **women's suffrage** movement of the early twentieth century first put women's agendas on the national scene, but it was Margaret Sanger who most profoundly influenced women's sexuality in the first half of the twentieth century.

 Sanger, a thirty-year-old housewife, attended a lecture on socialism that transformed her into an advocate for the rights of workers and their children. Sanger defied the Comstock laws by arguing that poor workers, who were having child after child,

women's suffrage: The movement to get women the right to vote.

needed birth control. Her statement: "It is none of society's business what a woman shall do with her body" has remained the centerpiece of feminist views on the relation between the state and sexuality ever since. Because she published information about birth control, she was forced to flee to England to avoid arrest for violating the Comstock laws. She finally returned when a groundswell of support in the United States convinced her to come back and face trial. Intellectuals from across Europe wrote to President Woodrow Wilson on her behalf, and the public was so outraged by her arrest that the prosecutors dropped the case. She then opened a birth control clinic in Brooklyn (which eventually evolved into the Planned Parenthood organization), which led to her being arrested again and again, evoking much protest from her supporters.

After Sanger, organized feminism did not reemerge until the 1960s. The middle of the twentieth century saw women increasingly enter institutions of higher education and also enter the labor force in great numbers while men were off fighting World War II. However, it also saw the rise of divorce rates and single motherhood and the post-war baby boom in which middle class women married and stayed at home. Social conditions had given women more power just as their roles were being restricted again to wife and mother. A backlash was soon to come.

The modern feminist movement can best be summarized by the work of three women authors (Ferree & Hess, 1985). In her 1957 book, *The Second Sex,* Simone de Beauvoir showed that women were not granted an identity of their own but were described instead as the objects of men's wishes and anxieties. Betty Friedan followed in 1963 with *The Feminine Mystique,* a ten-year follow-up of the lives of her graduating class from Smith College, in which she found that these educated, bright women felt trapped in the role of housewife and wanted careers to have happier, more fulfilled lives. Finally, at the height of the Vietnam War in 1969–1970, Kate Millet's *Sexual Politics* argued that patriarchy breeds violence and forces men to renounce all that is feminine in them. According to Millet, rape is an act of aggression aimed at keeping women docile and controlling them, and men see homosexuality as a "failure" of patriarchy and so it is violently repressed.

Feminists of the 1960s argued that they were entitled to sexual satisfaction, that the relations of the sexes as they existed were exploitative, and that women had a right to control their lives and their bodies. Some of the more radical feminists advocated lesbianism as the only relationship not based on male power, but most feminists fought for a transformation of the interpersonal relationship of men and women and of the male-dominated political structure. Part of the freedom women needed was the freedom to choose when to be mothers, and the right to choose abortion became a firm part of the feminist platform.

Feminism has made great cultural and political strides and has changed the nature of American society and sexual behavior. The pursuit of sexual pleasure is now seen as a woman's legitimate right, and men are no longer expected to be the sexual experts relied upon by docile, virginal mates. Feminists were at the forefront of the abortion debate and hailed the legalization of abortion as a great step in achieving women's rights over their own bodies. More recently, women have begun entering politics in record numbers, and the senate, congress, and governorships are increasingly counting women among their members. Women still have many struggles. Men are paid more than women for the same work, poverty is increasingly a problem of single mothers, and rape and spousal abuse are still major social problems in America. In addition, some have argued that the pursuit of equal rights for women has created a backlash against women in American society (Faludi, 1991). Still, feminism as a movement has had a major impact on the way America views sexuality.

Gay Liberation

The period after World War II was a period of challenge to homosexuals (Adam, 1987). Senator Joseph McCarthy, who became famous for trying to purge America of communists, also relentlessly hunted homosexuals. Homosexuals were portrayed as perverts, lurking in schools and on corners ready to pounce on unsuspecting youth, and many were thrown out of work or imprisoned in jails and mental hospitals. The news media participated in this view, as in a 1949 *Newsweek* article that identified all homosexuals as "sex murderers." Medical men tinkered with a variety of "cures," including lobotomies and castration. Churches were silent or encouraged the witch-hunts, Hollywood purged itself of positive references to homosexuality, and many laws initiated during this period, such as immigration restrictions for homosexuals and banning gay men from the military, have lasted in some form until today (Adam, 1987).

In 1951, an organization for homosexual rights, the Mattachine Society, was founded in the United States by Henry Hay. The Daughters of Bilitis, the first postwar lesbian organization, was founded by four lesbian couples in San Francisco in 1955. Though these groups began with radical intentions, the vehement anti-homosexuality of American authorities forced the groups to lay low throughout the late 1950s (Adam, 1987).

Though gay activism had been increasing in America with protests and sit-ins throughout the 1960s, modern gay liberation is usually traced to the night in 1969 when New York police raided a Greenwich Village gay bar called Stonewall. For the first time, the gay community erupted in active resistance, and the police were greeted by a hail of debris thrown by the gay patrons of the bar. Though there had been previous acts of resistance, the Stonewall riot became a symbol to the gay community and put the police on notice that homosexuals would no longer passively accept arrest and police brutality (Adam, 1987).

Following Stonewall, gay activism began a strong campaign against prejudice and discrimination all over the country. Groups and businesses hostile to gays were picketed, legislators were lobbied, committees and self-help groups were founded, legal agencies were begun, and educational groups tried to change the image of homosexuality in America. For example, in 1973 strong gay lobbying caused the American Psychiatric Association to remove homosexuality from the Diagnostic and Statistical Manual (DSM), the list of official psychiatric disorders. Almost overnight, people who had been considered "sick" were suddenly "normal." The deletion of homosexuality from the DSM removed the last scientific justification for treating homosexuals any differently than other citizens and demonstrated the new national power of the movement for homosexual rights. Soon gay liberation was a powerful presence in the United States, Canada, Australia, and Western Europe (Adam, 1987).

The decade of the 1970s was, in many ways, the Golden Age of gay life in America. In cities like San Francisco and New York, gay bathhouses and bars became open centers of gay social life, and gay theater groups, newspapers, and magazines appeared. The gradual discovery of the AIDS epidemic in the United States and Europe in the beginning of the 1980s ended the excitement of the 1970s as thousands of gay men began to die from the disease (see Chapter 13). Historically, when such fearsome epidemics arise, people have been quick to find a minority group to blame for the disease, and homosexuals were quickly blamed by a large segment of the public (Perrow and Guillén, 1990; Shilts, 1987). The AIDS tragedy has mobilized the gay community, and they have successfully established health clinics, information services, sex education programs, and political lobbies to fight AIDS.

The gay liberation movement has been at the forefront of trying to change sexual attitudes in the country, not only by pressing for recognition of homosexuality as a legitimate sexual choice, but also by arguing that all sexual minorities have a right to sexual happiness. In some states, gay couples can register as "domestic partners," and in Hawaii homosexual couples may soon be allowed to marry. Still, gays and lesbians are subject to prejudices in America, and some states are passing laws making it illegal for homosexuals to be considered a minority group worthy of special protections.

OUR SEXUAL LEGACY

We are the sum total of our history. Our attitudes and beliefs reflect all our historical influences, from the ancient Hebrews and Greeks to the Christianity of the Middle Ages to the modern feminist and gay liberation movements. The great difficulty most of us have is in recognizing that our own constellation of beliefs, feelings, and moral positions about sex are a product of our particular time and place and are in a constant state of evolution. It is important to keep this in mind as we explore the sexual behaviors of other people and other cultures throughout this book.

Summary

- Sexuality in our primate ancestors began to change when they adopted an upright posture, which resulted in the loss of estrus in women and in face-to-face intercourse. It may have also encouraged monogamy.
- The Hebrews, through the laws recorded in the Bible, established both the sanctity of marital sexuality and proscriptions against nonprocreative sex acts, such as adultery, prostitution, homosexuality, bestiality, and incest.
- The Greeks were sexually permissive, and upper class men often engaged in pederasty, guiding a young teen through the lessons of adulthood in exchange for sexual activity. Greek culture idealized the male and female forms, and it divided the world into masculine (penetrator) and feminine (penetrated).
- Rome had a very permissive attitude towards things such as homosexuality and saw marriage and marital sexuality in a practical way. Roman emperors sometimes had male lovers or even male "wives."
- Chinese civilization's belief in yin-yang led to a philosophy of sexual balance and even sexual disciplines that teach people how to maximize their sexuality.
- India also has a long history of sexual freedom, including great temples adorned with sexual carvings. Women in India, on the other hand, have often been dominated by men.
- Christianity, through St. Paul and subsequent thinkers such as Sts. Augustine, Jerome, and Aquinas, condemned sexuality, saw abstinence as the most exalted state, and outlawed

almost everything but face-to-face marital intercourse for the purpose of procreation. By the time the church reached dominance in the Middle Ages, there was a general association of sexuality and sin.
- Islam is a more sex-positive religion than Christianity, even though there are strict laws of marital fidelity and modesty.
- Three great movements that influenced modern sexuality were the Reformation, where Martin Luther introduced Protestantism and its belief in the use of sexuality to build the marital union; the Renaissance, in which sexuality was portrayed as beautiful; and the Enlightenment, which praised sexuality as one of the highest forms of earthly pleasure. These tendencies declined during the Victorian Era in England.
- Though Puritans came to America with strict Christian views of sexuality, those attitudes were challenged as America grew. The struggle between conservative and liberal attitudes towards sexuality still persists to this day in the United States.
- In the twentieth century, three major trends have profoundly influenced sexuality: Sexology, pioneered by Kinsey, Masters and Johnson, and others, seriously began to explore sex scientifically; feminism argued that women have been dominated by men and male power; and gay liberation brought homosexuality into the public eye and opened the way for many other people whose sexuality was underground and hidden.

R *eflections on Sexuality*

1. How much of human sexuality do you think can be understood by appealing to explanations like prehistoric changes in our posture or the development of the menstrual cycle?

2. The Bible has had a profound impact on our attitudes towards sexuality. Do you think that it is still influential? In what way?

3. Is it acceptable to judge the morality of a civilization's sexuality by modern standards? Was Greece's pederasty "immoral"?

4. How "foreign" do China's and India's sexual histories seem to you? How different are they from Western views of sexuality?

5. After the Middle Ages, what were the biggest influences on the modern development of ideas of sexuality? What did the Reformation contribute? The Renaissance? The Enlightenment?

6. What are the two most important movements to change sexuality in the latter part of the twentieth century? What did each contribute?

S *uggested Readings*

BULLOUGH, VERN L. (1973) *The Subordinate Sex: A History of Attitudes toward Women.* Urbana, IL: University of Illinois Press.

D'EMILIO, JOHN, AND ESTELLE FREEDMAN. (1988) *Intimate Matters: A History of Sexuality in America.* New York: Harper and Row.

HALPERIN, DAVID M. (1990) *One Hundred Years of Homosexuality: and Other Essays on Greek Love.* New York: Routledge.

KLAPISCH-ZUBER, CHRISTIANE (Editor). (1992) *A History of Women in the West, Volume II: Silences of the Middle Ages.* Cambridge, England: Belknap Press.

LUCIE-SMITH, EDWARD. (1991) *Sexuality in Western Art.* London: Thames and Hudson.

MANNICHE, LISE. (1987) *Sexual Life in Ancient Egypt.* London: KPI Ltd.

MARGULIS, LYNN, AND DORION SAGAN. (1991) *Mystery Dance: On the Evolution of Human Sexuality.* New York: Summit Books.

MONEY, JOHN. (1985) *The Destroying Angel.* Buffalo: Prometheus Books.

SALISBURY, JOYCE E. (Editor). (1991) *Sex in the Middle Ages.* New York: Garland Publishing, Inc.

TANNAHILL, REAY. (1980) *Sex in History.* New York: Stein and Day.

2

Theory and Research

"How does early sexual abuse affect adult sexuality?"
"What factors motivate an adolescent to engage in sex?"
"What contributes to the development of an exhibitionist?"
"How does alcohol affect sexual desire?"
"What causes someone to be gay or lesbian?"
"Does early termination of a pregnancy cause future miscarriages?"
"How do our thoughts influence our sexual attractions?"
"Do societal attitudes influence sexuality?"

You might wonder why reviewing theory and research in a sexuality textbook is important. Since theories guide our understanding of sexuality and research helps answer our many questions, understanding how theories are formulated and research is pursued will give you insight into the information that is provided in the chapters to come. Recently, we asked our students to imagine that they were sexuality researchers who were designing a new study. What topic would most interest them? We found that students have a wide range of interests: some wanted to examine gender differences; others were interested in how we acquire our attitudes about sexuality. A few of their research questions are presented at the beginning of this chapter. If you were to do a study in some area of sexuality, what would you be most interested in studying? Once you have decided your area of interest, what comes next? How is a research study done? What are some of the obstacles to doing sexuality research? How can these difficulties be avoided? Why are theories important?

The results of sexuality studies seem to appear everywhere today—in magazines, in the newspaper, on television. But how do you know if this research has been carried out properly? In this chapter, we explore both the theories and the research methods that underlie the study of sexuality. We also present information on the major sexuality studies that have been done. This material provides a foundation on which to build further understanding of sexuality.

Sigmund Freud, the father of psychoanalysis, set the stage for all other psychological theories.

theory: A formal statement about the relationship between constructs or events.

THEORIES ABOUT SEXUALITY

The study of sexuality is multidisciplinary. Biologists, psychologists, theologians, physicians, sociologists, anthropologists, and philosophers all perform sexuality research. The questions each discipline asks and how they transform those questions into research projects differ greatly. However, the insights of these disciplines complement each other, and no single approach to the study of sexuality is better than another.

A **theory** is a set of assumptions, principles, or methods that help a researcher understand the nature of the phenomenon being studied. A theory provides information on how to conceptualize, implement, and interpret a topic, such as human sexuality. The majority of researchers will begin with theories about human behavior that guide the kind of questions they ask about sexuality. For example, suppose a researcher subscribes to the theory that sexuality is innate and biologically determined; he or she would probably design studies to examine such things as how the hypothalamus in the brain influences our sexual behavior, or the monthly cycle of hormones. It is unlikely he or she would be interested in studying how society influences sexuality. A person who believes sexuality is determined by environmental influences, on the other hand, would be more likely to study how the media influences sexuality rather than genetic patterns of sexuality.

SEX TALK

QUESTION **2.1** **When scientists come up with new theories, how do they know they are true?**

They don't. Theories begin as ideas that must undergo testing and evaluation. Many early theories of sexuality were simply developed out of work with patients, such as the work by Sigmund Freud. However, the researchers never really know whether their theory is true or not. Some scientists become so biased by their own theory that they have trouble seeing explanations other than their own for certain behaviors. That is why scientific findings should always be tested and confirmed by other scientists.

Thomas Kuhn (1962), a noted philosopher, used the word **paradigm** to explain how theories guide our questioning. A paradigm is a shared view in a particular area of science. Usually people with similar paradigms see things in similar ways; for example, people with environmental paradigms would not see much value in a biological study of homosexuality. This is often easier to conceptualize if you think about a paradigm as a camera lens. Once it is in place, the world is seen in a certain way and only when the lens is changed does the view of the world also change.

There are several paradigms that guide much of our thinking about sexuality. These include psychological, biological, sociological, and sociobiological ways of viewing human sexuality. In addition, over the last few years, feminist theory has also become an important paradigm. We will first explore each of these and look at how they influence sexuality research.

paradigm: A plan of research based on specific concepts.

Psychological Theories

Of all the psychological theories of sexuality, the most influential was the psychoanalytic theory of Sigmund Freud. Freud felt that the sex drive was one of the most important forces in life and he spent a considerable amount of time studying sexuality.

Psychoanalytic Theory

Sigmund Freud (1856–1939) spent most of his life in Vienna, Austria. He was a neurologist by training, and later in his life he became interested in **neurosis** and **hysteria**. Through the use of **free association**, he discovered that patients could recall information that had previously been in their **unconscious**. Often these memories involved traumatic experiences, such as a past history of sexual abuse (which Freud also thought could be hysterical fantasies). Freud believed that all infants had sexual desires and energy, and he published many books about his ideas. In 1909, he was invited to the U.S. to lecture on the sexual roots of behavior and conflicts between sex and society.

Sigmund Freud gathered a group of psychologists together to further his ideas, and he became the founder of the psychoanalytic school. He is also indirectly responsible for the foundation of a host of other theories that followed psychoanalytic theory, maintaining some of its concepts, and modifying or rejecting others. Some of these theories will be presented in the following sections.

Personality Formation. According to Freud, human behavior is motivated by instincts and drives. Two of the most powerful instincts are the **libido**, which is the life

neurosis: A category of psychological disorders in which an individual experiences emotionally distressing symptoms.

hysteria: A psychological disorder characterized by excessive or uncontrollable fear or other strong emotion.

free association: A technique used in psychoanalytic therapy in which a client flows with any feelings or thoughts by reporting them immediately without censorship.

unconscious: In Freud's theory, all the ideas, thoughts, and feelings of which we are not and cannot normally become aware.

libido: According to Freud, the energy generated by the sexual instinct; also known as the "life" instinct.

thanatos: According to Freud, the self-destructive instinct, often turned outward in the form of aggression; also known as the "death" instinct.

conscious: In Freud's theory, the part of the personality that contains the material of which we are currently aware.

preconscious: In Freud's theory, the part of the personality that contains thoughts that can be brought into awareness with little difficulty.

id: In Freud's theory, the collection of unconscious urges and desires that continually seek expression.

ego: According to Freud, the part of the personality that mediates between environmental demands (reality), conscience (superego), and instinctual needs (id).

superego: According to Freud, the social and parental standards an individual has internalized; the conscience.

or sexual instinct, and **thanatos**, which is the death or aggressiveness instinct. Of these two, the libido is the more powerful.

Freud believed that there were two divisions to the personality. In the first division, he identified three levels in which the personality operates. These levels included the **conscious**, **preconscious**, and unconscious. The conscious level contains information that we are aware of—for instance, right now as you are reading this page, you are aware of the fact that you are doing so, and you might also be aware of other things going on around you. You are *consciously* aware of all of this information. However, there are some things that you might not be aware of, but you could recall them if you wanted to or someone asked you to. For instance, what did you have for dinner two nights ago? This information is stored in your *preconscious* level. The third level of the personality, the *unconscious,* Freud believed, was the most important part. The unconscious level contains information that we have no access to, such as conflicts or anxiety-producing memories. However, even though we have no access to the unconscious, it is responsible for much of our behavior. For example, perhaps there are unconscious reasons why we choose the partners we do. Freud explored ways to bring unconscious material into consciousness.

The second division of the personality contains the id, ego, and superego. At birth, a child only has the **id** portion of the personality, which functions as the pleasure center. A child is only interested in things that bring immediate satisfaction. Children want their needs met immediately; for example when they cry, they want food. The id operates totally within the unconscious part of the mind. If the id were the only part of the personality that developed, we would always be seeking pleasure and fulfillment with little concern for others; in other words, most animals operate only through the id. As humans get older, however, the id balances its desires with other parts of the personality.

By the second year of life, the **ego** develops as the child begins to interact with his or her environment. The ego constitutes the reality part of the personality and it keeps the id in check by being realistic about what the child can and cannot have. Because the majority of the id's desires may be socially unacceptable, the ego works to keep it in check. The ego can move between the conscious, preconscious, and unconscious.

By five years of age, the last portion of the personality, the **superego**, develops. It contains both societal and parental values and puts more restrictions on what we can and cannot do. It acts as our conscience and its most effective weapon is guilt. For example, let's say that a woman was raised in a very religious family and learned that premarital sexual activity was wrong. One night she becomes overly passionate with her long-term boyfriend (an id action). This activity feels pleasurable and the id is being fulfilled. Suddenly, reality kicks in (the ego) and she realizes that she is engaging in sexual activity with her boyfriend in the back seat of a car, which is parked at a busy convenience store—she could be discovered at any moment! This causes her to become aware of the reality of the situation, and she will probably feel guilty (a superego action) because she has been taught that premarital sexual activity is wrong. Throughout our lives, the id, ego, and superego are in a constant struggle with each other, but it is the ego, or the realistic portion of our personality, that keeps the other two parts balanced.

If the ego doesn't balance the other two parts of the personality, two things can occur. First, the superego could take over, and a person could be paralyzed by guilt. Freud believed that a guilty person has a superego that dominates his or her personality. If, on the other hand, the id takes over, the person constantly searches for pleasure with little concern for others. Freud believed that the only way to change these conditions was for the person to undergo **psychoanalysis**.

Psychosexual Development. Probably one of Freud's most controversial ideas was his theory of **psychosexual development**. He believed that our basic personality is formed by events that happen to us in the first six years of life. During each stage of development, Freud identified a different **erogenous zone** where libido energy was directed. If the stage was not successfully completed, the libido energy would be tied up and the child could experience a fixation. We will explain this more in a moment.

The first stage of psychosexual development is known as the **oral stage**, and it lasts throughout the first eighteen months of life. The erogenous zone is the mouth, and most babies who are this age put everything in their mouths. Enjoyment comes from eating, sucking, and biting. However, if a traumatic event happens during this time (for instance, if a child is not allowed to eat when he or she needs to), the child may develop an oral fixation later in life. According to Freud's theory, this would lead the individual to desire oral satisfaction such as cigarette smoking, overeating, fingernail chewing, or alcohol abuse. Freud believed that people with these problems had oral personalities and exhibited this through personality traits such as dependency or aggression.

After eighteen months, children enter into the second stage, the **anal stage**. During this stage most children are being toilet trained, and the erogenous zone is the anus. Children realize that their parents are pleased when they learn to use the toilet. Many parents will cheer and clap when their child takes his or her first bowel movement in the potty. Usually, this happiness is due to the fact that the parents won't have to clean diapers anymore, but the child believes that the feces must be valuable. For what other reason would his or her parents become so excited? One of our students informed us that when he was a child, he thought that his feces were so valuable that every time he had a bowel movement, he collected them from the toilet bowl and stored them in boxes underneath his bed. Imagine his mother's surprise when she finally found them!

If there are any traumatic experiences with toilet training (such as taking an excessive period of time to learn) the child could develop an **anal fixation**. Traits of an anal personality include stubbornness, orderliness, or cleanliness.

According to Freud, the most important stage is the next one, the **phallic stage**, which occurs between the ages of three and six. During this stage, the genitals (the penis in boys and the clitoris in girls) become the erogenous zone, and masturbation increases. Freud believed that during the phallic stage, boys go through the Oedipus complex (which derives its name from the Greek story of Oedipus, who unknowingly killed his father and married his mother), which causes them to fall in love with their mother. Although they want her all to themselves, to do so would mean having to kill their father, which causes castration anxiety, a fear that the father might retaliate by cutting off their penis, and they may lose it (like girls obviously did). The Oedipus complex is resolved when the child realizes he cannot have his mother, and he renounces his desire for her.

Freud was less clear about what happened to girls. He believed that girls go through an Electra complex, in which they love their father and want to be impregnated by him. However, they realize they cannot have this, and they eventually come to identify with the mother. During this time, Freud believed that women develop penis envy. When a girl sees a boy's penis, she realizes that she is lacking one and feels inferior. Freud believed that the Electra stage for girls is never fully resolved and that women were less psychologically mature than men.

psychoanalysis: The system of psychotherapy developed by Freud that focuses on uncovering the unconscious material responsible for a patient's disorder.

psychosexual development: The childhood stages of development (oral, anal, phallic, latency, genital) during which, according to Freud, the id's pleasure-seeking energies focus on distinct erogenous zones.

erogenous zones: According to Freud (in psychoanalytic theory), the mouth, anus, and genital regions are particularly sensitive to touch, and the various pleasures associated with these regions are sexual.

oral stage: The psychosexual stage of development in which the mouth, lips, and tongue together are the primary erogenous zone.

anal stage: The psychosexual stage of development in which the anal region is the primary erogenous zone.

anal fixation: If the conflict of the anal stage is not successfully resolved, anal character traits such as excessive stubbornness, orderliness, or cleanliness might result.

phallic stage: The psychosexual stage of development in which the genital region is the primary erogenous zone and in which the Oedipus complex develops.

SEX TALK

QUESTION **2.2** **Why did Freud call it "penis envy" when guys are always trying to get into our pants? Shouldn't we call it "pussy envy"?**

Karen Horney, a follower of Freud, believed that it could be argued that men had "womb envy" rather than women having "penis envy." Many modern feminists—some who are psychoanalysts—have reframed psychoanalytic theory to be less biased against women and women's experience. Freud chose the penis because it fit with his theory—and perhaps because he had one.

The resolution of the phallic stage is important for boys and girls because when they identify with the same-sex parent, they adopt appropriate masculine or feminine characteristics. The superego begins to develop during this time as well, and most children adopt their parents' values. Keep in mind, however, that the conflicts associated with the Oedipus and Electra complexes are **repressed**, and how they are resolved affects future behavior.

Prior to puberty, the child passes through the **latency stage** in which all libido and sexual interest go underground. The fear and strength of the previous stage makes all sexual urges and interests disappear. In fact, during this stage, little boys often think little girls have "cooties" (and visa versa) and childhood play primarily exists in same sex groups. At puberty, the **genital stage** begins and is the final stage of psychosexual development. The erogenous zone once again becomes the genitals. During this stage, sexuality becomes less internally directed and more directed at others as erotic objects. Freud believed that if there was no trauma or fixation in any of the above mentioned stages, a child would be heterosexual. To Freud, homosexuality and bisexuality were a result of problematic psychosexual development (we'll discuss this more in Chapter 7).

Freud's ideas were controversial in the Victorian time period in which he lived. His claims that children were sexual from birth and that children lusted for the opposite-sex parent caused tremendous shock in the conservative community of Vienna. However, Freud's theories set the foundation for the rest of the psychological theories which followed his. He was also the first to uncover the importance of the unconscious. Yet even so, Freud and the psychoanalytic theory have received a considerable amount of criticism. The most predominant criticism was that his theory was unscientific and did not lend itself to testing. How could a researcher study the existence of the phallic stage? If it is indeed unconscious, then it would be impossible to hand out surveys to see when a child was in each stage. His work was also based primarily on work with individuals he was working with, which may have been biased. Because Freud based his theories on the patients he saw, he has been accused of creating his theories around people who were sick; consequently they may not apply to healthy people (we will discuss this more in research methodology). Finally, Freud has also been heavily criticized because of his unflattering psychological portrait of women (see Sexuality Today 2.1).

repression: A coping strategy by which unwanted thoughts or prohibited desires are forced out of consciousness and into the unconscious mind.

latency stage: The psychosexual stage of development that follows resolution of the Oedipus complex and in which sexual desires are weak.

genital stage: The final psychosexual stage in which the ability to engage in adult sexual behavior is developed.

B.F. Skinner, a radical behaviorist, believed that rewards and punishments control all of our behavior.

behaviorists: Theorists who believe that behavior is learned through rewards and punishments and can be altered using the same technique.

Behavioral Theory

Behaviorists believe that it is necessary to observe and measure behavior in order to understand it. Psychological states, emotions, the unconscious, and feelings are not measurable and therefore are not valid for study. Only overt behavior can be measured, observed, and controlled by scientists. Radical behaviorists, such as B.F. Skinner (1953), claim that environmental rewards and punishments determine the types of

SEXUALITY*Today*   2.1

Clitoral Versus Vaginal Orgasms

Most of Freud's theory of sexuality did not view female sexuality in a positive light. Perhaps this had to do with the conservative time period in which Freud lived. His ideas about the nature of the female orgasm are still very controversial today. He proposed that women are capable of two kinds of orgasms—clitoral and vaginal. Clitoral orgasms result from clitoral stimulation (such as masturbation), while vaginal orgasms result from vaginal stimulation (such as sexual intercourse). Freud felt clitoral orgasms were immature, and in order for a woman to experience mature orgasms, she needed to transfer the site of arousal from the clitoris to the vagina. Only vaginal orgasms were mature or "authentic." Freud felt that if a

woman was unable to have orgasms during sexual intercourse, it was due to problems during psychosexual development.

Because of Freud's views on female orgasm, many women were considered neurotic or deficient for not being able to reach vaginal orgasms. However, as you will see, Masters and Johnson's work in the laboratory showed that all female orgasms are physiologically similar, no matter what type of stimulation causes them. However, the emotional reactions to different types of orgasms may differ. A woman may *prefer* orgasms that occur during sexual intercourse, or she may *prefer* those during masturbation.

---

behaviors in which we engage; thus, they believe that we do not actually *choose* how we behave. This process is referred to as **operant conditioning**.

We learn certain behaviors through reinforcement and punishment, including most sexual behaviors. Reinforcements encourage a person to engage in a behavior by associating it with pleasurable stimuli, while punishments make it less likely that a behavior will be repeated by associating it with unpleasant stimuli. For instance, if a man decided to engage in extramarital sex with a colleague at work, it may be because of the positive reinforcements he receives, such as the good feelings or the excitement of going to work. If, on the other hand, a man experiences a problem with his erection the first time he has sexual intercourse outside of his marriage, it may make it less likely he will try the behavior anytime soon. The negative experience reduces the likelihood that he will engage in the behavior again.

To help change unwanted behavior, behaviorists use **behavior modification**. For example, if a man only engages in sex with adolescent boys, a behavioral therapist might use **aversion therapy**. To do so, the therapist might show the man slides of young boys and when he responds with an erection, an electrical shock is administered to his penis. If this is repeated several times, behaviorists believe his body may soon learn not to have this reaction. The punishment has changed the behavior. Contrast this form of therapy to a psychoanalytic therapist, who would probably want to study what happened to this man in the first six years of his life. A behavior therapist would primarily be concerned with changing the behavior and is less concerned with its origins.

Social Learning Theory

Social learning theory actually grew out of behaviorism. Scientists began to question whether or not behaviorism was too limited in its explanation of human behavior. Many believed that thoughts and feelings had more influence on behaviors than the behaviorists claimed. A noted social learning theorist, Albert Bandura (1969), argued that both internal and external events influence our behavior. By this, he meant that external events, such as rewards and punishments, influence behavior, but so do internal events,

operant conditioning:
Learning resulting from the reinforcing response a subject receives following a certain behavior.

behavior modification:
Therapy based on operant conditioning and classical conditioning principles, used to change behaviors.

aversion therapy: (In behavior therapy) a technique that reduces the frequency of maladaptive behavior by associating it with real or imagined aversive stimuli during a conditioning procedure.

such as feelings, thoughts, and beliefs. Bandura began to bridge the gap between behaviorism and cognitive theory, which we will talk about next.

Social learning theorists believe that imitation and identification are also important in the development of sexuality. For example, we identify with our same sex parent, and begin to imitate him or her, which helps us develop our own gender identity. In turn, we are praised and reinforced for these behaviors. Think for a moment about a young boy who identifies with his mother and begins to dress and act like her. He will probably be ridiculed or even punished, which may lead him to turn his attention to a socially acceptable figure, most likely his father. Peer pressure also influences our sexuality. We want to be liked and therefore we may engage in certain behaviors because our peers encourage it. We also learn what is expected of us on television, from our families, even from music.

Cognitive Theory

cognitive theory: A theory that proposes that our thoughts are responsible for our behaviors.

So far, the theories we have looked at believe that either internal conflicts or external events control the development of personality. Unlike these, **cognitive theory** holds that people differ in how they process information, and this creates personality differences. We *feel* what we *think* we feel, and our thoughts also affect our behavior (Walen and Roth, 1987). Our behavior does not come from early experiences in childhood or from rewards or punishments; rather it is a result of how we perceive and conceptualize what is happening around us.

As far as sexuality is concerned, cognitive theorists believe that the biggest sexual organ is between the ears (Walen and Roth, 1987). What sexually arouses us is what we *think* sexually arouses us. We pay attention to our physical sensations and label these reactions. For example, if a woman does not have an orgasm during intercourse, she could perceive this in one of two ways. She might think that having an orgasm when her partner does is not really all that important, and maybe next time she will have one, or she could think that she is a failure since she did not have an orgasm when her partner did and as a result feel depressed. What has caused the depression, however, is not the lack of an orgasm but her perception of it.

Humanistic Theory

self-actualized: Fulfillment of an individual's potentialities; the actualization of aptitudes, talents, etc.

unconditional positive regard: Accepting others unconditionally, without restrictions on their behaviors or thoughts.

conditional love: Accepting others conditionally, making restrictions on their behaviors or thoughts.

Humanists believe that we all strive to develop ourselves to the best of our abilities and to become **self-actualized**. This is easier to do if we are raised with **unconditional positive regard**. Unconditional positive regard involves accepting and caring about another person without any stipulations or conditions. There are no rules a person must follow in order to be loved. An example of unconditional positive regard would be a child being caught playing sexual games with her friends and the parents explaining that they loved her but disapproved of the behavior. If, on the other hand, the parents responded by yelling at the child and sending her to her room, she learns her that when she does something wrong, her parents will withdraw their love. This is referred to as **conditional love**. The parents make it clear that they will love their child only when she acts properly. Children who grow up with unconditional positive regard learn to accept the parts of themselves that may be negative, while children who have experienced conditional love may try to ignore these negative aspects since they knows others would not approve. Accepting our faults and weaknesses leads us toward self-actualization.

Self-actualization occurs as we learn our own potential in life. We want to do things that make us feel good about ourselves. For the majority of us, casual sex with an uncaring partner would not make us feel good; therefore, it does not contribute to our own growth. Sexual intimacy in a loving and committed relationship does feel good and helps contribute to our own self-actualization.

Biological Theory

The biological theory of human sexuality claims that sexual behavior is primarily a biological process. The acts of sexual intercourse, hormonal release, ovulation, ejaculation, conception, pregnancy, and birth are controlled physiologically (DeLamater, 1987). These theories also point out that human sexual behavior, including gender roles and sexual orientation, are primarily due to inborn, genetic patterns and are not functions of social or psychological forces. Sexual problems are believed to be due to physiological causes, and intervention often includes medications or surgery.

SEX TALK

QUESTION **2.3** **How might researchers study whether homosexuality is biological or not?**

A person who believes in the biological theory would look for physical or genetic differences to explain homosexuality. This would include differences in the anatomy of the brain, hormones, or neurochemicals. To do research on the anatomy of the brain, researchers usually use cadavers (dead bodies) to look for brain differences.

Sociological Theories*

Sociologists are interested in how the society we live in influences sexual behavior. Even though the capacity to be sexual is biologically programmed, *how* it is expressed varies greatly across societies, as we saw in the last chapter. For instance, there are differences in what societies tolerate, what the roles of men and women are, and how sexuality is viewed. A behavior that may be seen as normal in one society may be considered abnormal in another. For instance, on the island of Mangaia in the South Pacific, women are very sexually assertive and often initiate sexual activity. From an early age, they are taught by elders how to have multiple orgasms. However, in Inis Beag in Ireland, sexuality is repressed and is considered appropriate only for procreation. Couples engage in sexual intercourse fully clothed, with only the genitals exposed. Each society has regulated sexual behaviors.

Sociologists believe that institutions influence the rules a society holds about sexual expression (DeLamater, 1987). These institutions include the family, religion, economy, medicine, law, and the media. Each dictates certain beliefs about the place of sexuality in one's life, and these beliefs can determine what is seen as normal within the society.

The family is the first institution that influences our values about what is sexually right and wrong. Our parents and family provide strong messages about what is acceptable and unacceptable. Religion also influences how a society views sexuality. As we discussed in Chapter 1, Christian doctrine stated that sex before marriage was wrong

---

* Much of this section is drawn from DeLamater's (1987) work.

because sex was primarily for procreation. Some religions provide strong opinions on issues such as premarital and extramarital sex, homosexuality, sexual variations, abortion, masturbation, contraception, and sex education. Many people within society look to religious institutions and leaders for answers to their questions about sexuality. We will discuss this more in Special Focus 1.

The economy is another institution that affects the societal view of sexuality. The U.S. economy is based on capitalism, which involves an exchange of services for money. This influences the availability of services such as prostitution, pornography, sex shops, and certain birth control methods. They exist because they generate money. If people did not purchase these services, they probably would not exist in our society.

The medical community also affects the societal views of sexuality. For example, many years ago physicians taught that masturbation was a disease that could lead to permanent mental illness. The medical community's attitude influenced societal opinions of masturbation. Other behaviors that physicians urged people not to engage in included anal intercourse, extramarital sex, homosexuality, and bisexuality. In turn, society's values about these behaviors were guided by the medical community's attitudes and beliefs.

A fifth institution that regulates sexual behavior in the United States is the law. The law establishes what sexual behaviors are "officially" right and wrong. For instance, laws regulate things like the practice of sodomy (or anal intercourse), the availability of certain contraceptive methods, and abortion. In turn, this affects how society feels about these practices. Laws help establish societal norms. We will discuss this more in Special Focus 1.

The media is another institution that influences societal attitudes about sexuality. Television, magazines, and popular music portray what is acceptable sexual behavior. There is, for example, a strong heterosexual bias in the media that tells us that heterosexuality is the only acceptable form of sexual behavior. To be homosexual or even **abstinent** is unacceptable. All of these influence social views of sexuality and what practices we believe are right and wrong. We discuss the powerful influence of the media more in Special Focus 4.

abstinence: The state of not engaging in sexual activity.

Sociobiological Theories

sociobiology: A theory that incorporates both evolution and sociology and looks for trends in behaviors.

Sociobiology incorporates both evolution and sociology to understand sexual behavior. In order to understand sexual behavior in humans, sociobiologists study animal sexual patterns and look for evolutionary trends. Sexuality exists, according to sociobiologists, for the purpose of reproducing the species, and individual sexuality is designed to maximize the chances of passing on one's genes. According to sociobiologists, the winners in the game of life are those who are most successful at transmitting their genes to the next generation.

Think about the qualities you look for in a partner. Students often tell us that they are looking for someone who is physically attractive, monogamous, has a sense of humor, is intelligent, honest, extroverted, fun, and sensitive. A sociobiologist would argue that these qualities have evolved because they ensure that a person would be able to provide healthy offspring. A physically attractive person is more likely to be physically fit and healthy. Could this be important to us because of their reproductive capabilities? Sociobiologists would say so. They would also argue that qualities such as monogamy, honesty, and sensitivity would help ensure that a partner will be reliable and help raise the offspring.

Some sexual activities have evolved to ensure a survival of the species. Sociobiologists believe that premarital sex is resisted because pregnancy in a single woman would be much less desirable for the species. They also believe that orgasms have evolved to make sexual intercourse pleasurable; this, in turn, increases the frequency that people engage in it and therefore the possibility of reproduction is increased. Discrepancies between the sexes in sexual desire and behavior are also thought to have evolved. The double standard, which states that men are free to have casual sex while women are not, exists because of the fact that men produce millions of sperm per day while women produce only one ovum per month. Men need to "spread their seed" in order to ensure the reproduction of their family line. Women, on the other hand, need to protect the one ovum they produce each month. When they become pregnant, they have a nine-month commitment ahead of them (and some would argue a lifelong commitment as well).

Sociobiological theory has received a considerable amount of criticism. This has been directed primarily at the fact that sociobiologists tend to ignore the influence of both prior learning and societal influences on sexuality.

Feminist Theory

Many feminist researchers believe that **sexology** in the United States is still dominated by white, middle class, heterosexist attitudes, which permeate sexuality research (Irvine, 1990). Others add that sexuality research has been based on a model of male sexuality, which also promotes heterosexuality as the norm (Jackson, 1984).

sexology: The scientific study of sexuality.

Feminist scholars believe that the social construction of sexuality is based on power, which has been primarily in the hands of men for centuries. They believe there is sexual gender inequality which, for the most part, sees women as submissive and subordinate. This power over women is maintained through acts of sexual aggression such as rape, sexual abuse, sexual harassment, pornography, and prostitution (Jackson, 1984; MacKinnon, 1986). In addition, feminists argue that male sexuality consistently views sex as an act that involves only a penis in a vagina. For "sex" to occur, the erect penis must penetrate the vagina and thrust until the male ejaculates. MacKinnon (1986:75) suggests that society believes that "what is sexual gives a man an erection." All of this has led to the repression of female sexuality and, as a result, a lack of attention to the female orgasm. Even in sexuality education the female orgasm is neglected. Michelle Fine (1988) refers to this as the "hegemonic floating phallus." Students are often taught about erections, ejaculation, and the male orgasm but very rarely are given information on the female orgasm. Andrea Dworkin (1987), one of the more radical feminists, takes this one step further; she believes that sexual intercourse itself is a punishment of women by men. Thrusting during sexual intercourse is painful for women, Dworkin claims, and this pain is to prove to the woman who is in charge and possesses the power.

Feminist researchers also believe that there is much to be gained from collaborative or group research which uses interviews to gain information since they can provide rich, qualitative data. Strict control of research, such as the use of controlled experiments, has been viewed as more "masculine" in structure (due to the rigid nature of experiments). Such experiments, within the laboratory, remove the study from the social context, which affects the outcome of the study (Peplau and Conrad, 1989). With respect to quantitative versus qualitative research, feminists believe that "qualitative data permit an in-depth understanding of individuals" (Peplau and Conrad, 1989:388). We will discuss this more later in this chapter.

In Sexuality Today 2.2, we present examples of studies that researchers with different theoretical backgrounds might be interested in doing. Now let us turn our attention to some of the important sexuality studies that have been done.

SEXUALITY RESEARCH

Even though it seems as though just about everybody is interested in sex these days, the topic has not always been a legitimate area for scientific research. Research into sexuality began in the nineteenth and early twentieth centuries. During the Victorian Era, the majority of sex research was thwarted in many subtle, and not so subtle, ways. Some researchers found that they suddenly lost their professional status, were accused of having the very sexual disorders they studied, or were viewed as motivated solely by lust, greed, or fame. However, as the interest in medicine grew, researchers began to explore how to improve health and peoples' lives. This included researching various aspects of sexuality.

The majority of the early sexuality studies were done in Europe, primarily in Germany. In the early twentieth century, Iwan Bloch was the first to coin the term "sexual science" or "sexology" (Reiss, 1982). He hoped that one day sexual science would have the same structure and objectivity as other sciences. At the time, sex research was

SEXUALITY *To d a y*   **2.2**

What Questions Would They Ask?

Different theorists are interested in different types of studies, for a theory helps determine what questions a researcher might want to ask. Below are a few examples of studies that different theorists might propose.

Psychoanalytic—How do children become fixated at certain psychosexual stages? How does this cause problems to develop later in their lives? How do children resolve the Oedipal and Electra complexes?

Behavioral—What reinforces a person's attraction to partners of the same sex? What reinforces a college student to use contraception? Why would a person want to lose his or her virginity?

Social Learning—How does peer group pressure influence our sexuality? What effects does the media have? Are children influenced by sexual advertising they see on television?

Cognitive—What is the decision-making process related to contraceptive choice? Do children cognitively understand sexuality? How do men view erectile dysfunction?

Humanist—How do negative parental reactions to first sexual experience affect teenagers? How does self-actualization affect sexuality?

Biological—How do genetics influence sexuality? What are the effects of hormone levels on sexual desire? Does menstruation affect sexual desire in women?

Sociological—How does religion influence sexuality? How does the threat of AIDS affect society? Do laws affect sexual behavior?

Sociobiological—Why are women the ones who usually control the level of sexual activity? How has monogamy developed?

protected by being considered part of medical research, even though holding a medical degree did not always offer complete protection. Some researchers used pseudonyms to publish their work, some were attacked, and others had their data destroyed. In 1921, several prominent European doctors attempted to set up an organization called the Committee for Research in Problems of Sex. After much hard work, the organization established itself but experienced problems in low membership rates and a lack of research and publishing support. However, because of strong beliefs and persistence by the founders, the group continued.

As a result of all the negative reactions and problems with sexuality research, it gradually moved from Germany to the United States, which has led the way in sexuality research ever since (see Table 2.1). During the 1940s and 1950s, sex research began to flourish in the United States. Perhaps this was because young people began to leave home and pursue their own futures and therefore gained more sexual freedom. Increasing autonomy may have led to a favorable climate for sexual science and sexual research. Even so, today, there are many people who are opposed to sexuality research and some believe that the mystery surrounding sexuality should not be taken away by science.

Researchers, educators, and clinicians who specialize in sexuality are called **sexologists**. Sexologists often are involved in research projects and may publish their work. Unfortunately, they may also be ridiculed, not viewed as "real" scientists, and accused of studying sexuality because of their own sexual hang-ups or because they are voyeurs. Geer and O'Donohue (1987) claim that unlike other areas of science, sex research is often evaluated as either moral or immoral. The majority of sexual practices tend to be viewed as immoral by society, such as masturbation, homosexuality, premarital, and extramarital sex. Only marital sex for procreation is viewed as completely acceptable and moral. Money (1986) takes this one step further and adds that the sexuality *researcher* is evaluated on moral grounds. Researchers are encouraged not to invade the privacy of intimate relationships or to study the sexuality of certain age groups (either young or old). Methodological problems also have made it difficult for the field of sexuality research. We will discuss these more later in this chapter.

sexologist: A professional who studies sexuality.

Academic programs that specialize in human sexuality appeared in the 1970s, and many still flourish today. There are many programs offering advanced degrees in sexology across the United States. In addition, several groups exist today to promote sexuality research and education, including: *The Kinsey Institute for Research in Sex, Gender, and Reproduction; The Society for the Scientific Study of Sexuality; American Association for Sexuality Counselors, Educators, and Therapists; Society for Sex Therapy and Research;* and *The Sexuality Information and Education Council of the U.S.,* to name just a few. Many medical schools and universities now teach sexuality courses as a part of the curriculum. In addition, today there are various funds available for support of sexuality research. The AIDS crisis, and our desire to understand it better, has also helped establish the importance of sexuality research.

The Society for the Scientific Study of Sexuality holds regional and national meetings in the United States.

Although sexuality research is still in its early stages, it has done much to help remove the mystery surrounding sexuality. This mystery was fueled by ignorance and fear, which contributed to irresponsible behavior. Sexuality research has helped sex become a topic of discussion rather than a subject that is taboo. Today, sexuality has become increasingly important to psychologists, physicians, educators, theologians, and scientists. In this section we will outline some of the most important sexuality researchers and studies.

T a b l e **2.1**

SEX RESEARCH: CHRONOLOGY AND PATTERNS OF INFLUENCE

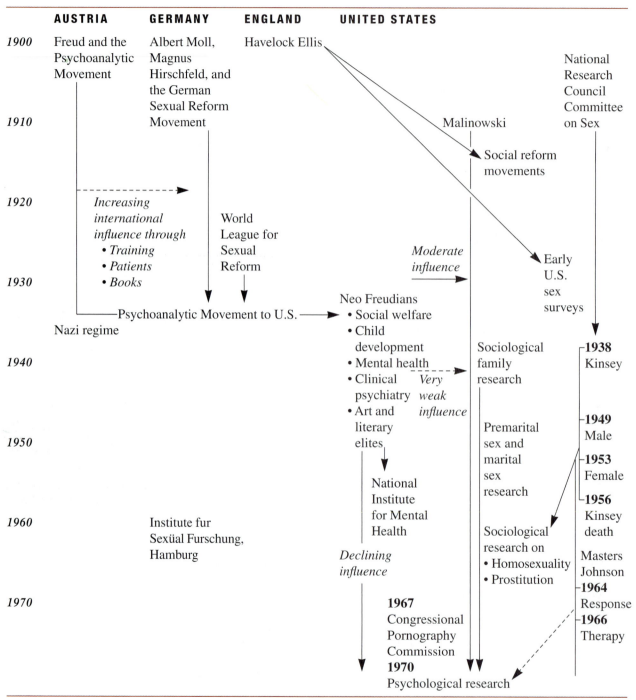

	AUSTRIA	GERMANY	ENGLAND	UNITED STATES		

Reprinted with permission from Gagnon (1977:35)

Richard von Krafft-Ebing

Society was conservative about sexuality in the late 1800s, and this repression was furthered by a German named Richard von Krafft-Ebing (1840–1902). He believed that deviant sexual behavior was the result of engaging in nonreproductive sexual practices, including masturbation. In 1886, he published a book entitled *Psychopathia Sexualis,* which explored approximately 200 case histories of individuals who had experienced **sexual pathology**, including people who had sex with children (pedophiles) and homosexuals. These behaviors were seen as abnormal and deviant. His work was the first detailed classification of sexual disorders. Although Krafft-Ebing supported sympathetic concern for victims of these so-called "deviations" and worked to help change existing laws that discriminated against them, he also increased suspicion about differences in sexuality by lumping all forms of sexual variation together with what is now judged to be normal sexual behavior.

sexual pathology: Sexual disorders.

Havelock Ellis

Havelock Ellis (1859–1939), an English citizen, also grew up in Victorian society but began to rebel against the secrecy surrounding sexuality. In 1875, when he was sixteen years old, he decided to make sexuality his life's work but at the time was unaware of what a big task he had taken on (Grosskurth, 1980).

Upon publication of his famous six-volume *Studies in the Psychology of Sex* (1897–1910), Ellis established himself as an objective and nonjudgmental researcher. He claimed that homosexuality and masturbation were not abnormal and should not be labeled as such (Reiss, 1982). In 1901, the *Lancet,* a prestigious English medical journal, reviewed his early volumes and wrote:

> [Studies in the Psychology of Sex] *must not be sold to the public, for the reading and discussion of such topics are dangerous. The young and the weak would not be fortified in their purity by the knowledge that they would gain from these studies, while they certainly might be more open to temptation after the perusal of more than one of the chapters.*
>
> ***Quoted in Grosskurth (1980:222)***

Unfortunately, Ellis's book is also fairly dry and boring, and as a result, and much to his dismay, Ellis never found the fame and fortune that Freud did.

Havelock Ellis, a sex researcher, was a key figure in the early study of sexuality.

Magnus Hirschfeld

Magnus Hirschfeld (1868–1935) was born in Kolberg, Germany. After completing his medical degree, he went on to specialize in public hygiene and was known as a kind, compassionate, and caring physician. His work with patients convinced him that negative attitudes toward homosexuals were inhumane and without reason. This inspired his dedication to the field of sexual problems.

Using a pseudonym, Hirschfeld wrote his first paper on sexology in 1896. In this paper, he argued that sexuality was the result of certain genetic patterns that could result in a homosexual, bisexual, or heterosexual. He fought for a repeal of the laws that made homosexuality and bisexuality punishable by prison terms and heavy fines. In 1899, he began the *Journal of Intermediate Sex Stages,* which was published for the purpose of

Magnus Hirschfeld worked hard to establish sexuality as a legitimate field of study.

educating the public about homosexuality and other sexual "deviations." Thousands of people came to Hirschfeld for his help and advice about sexual problems, and in 1900, Hirschfeld began distributing questionnaires on sexuality. By this time, he had also become an expert in the field of homosexuality and sexual variations and testified as an expert witness in court cases of sexual offenders. Probably his most controversial finding was that homosexuality was a biological phenomenon. Hirschfeld brought strict control of methodology and science to all of his work.

In 1913, he founded the Medical Society for Sexual Science, and in 1918 he opened the Institute for Sexual Science in Berlin, which was the first of its kind in the world. Soon afterward, it became known as the Magnus Hirschfeld Foundation, and many similar centers rapidly appeared for the treatment of sex problems. Even though many books had been published by Krafft-Ebing, Havelock Ellis, and others, Hirschfeld was the first to develop an actual center, which was an important step in the history of sexology. In 1919, Hirschfeld presented his institute, which contained his libraries, laboratory, and lecture halls, to the German people. Over the next few years the institute continued to grow in size and influence.

All of this took a turn for the worse during World War II when the Nazi government condemned him for his pacifist ideology and his interest and work in the field of sexuality. In 1933, as the climate grew more tense, Hirschfeld left Germany and soon learned that the Magnus Hirschfeld Foundation in Berlin had been destroyed, its contents publicly burned, and those who were working there sent to concentration camps. Hirschfeld decided to stay in France, where he began another institute. He continued this work until his death in 1935.

All of the above researchers and their publications helped give credibility to the area of sexual research. While some of the researchers adopted Freud's psychoanalytic theory, others developed their research without adopting specific theories of sexuality. Though they had introduced scientific principles into the study of sexual behavior, their influence was mostly limited to the field of medicine.

The rise of behaviorism in the 1920s added a new dimension to this research. The idea of studying specific sexual behaviors became more acceptable. The formulation of more sophisticated scientific research techniques provided researchers with more precise methods for sexual research. Many researchers attempted to compile data on sexual behavior, but the results were inconsistent and the data was poorly organized. This led Alfred Kinsey, an American researcher, to undertake a large scale study of human sexuality.

Alfred Kinsey

Alfred Kinsey implemented the first large-scale survey of adult sexual behavior in the United States.

In 1938, Alfred Kinsey (1894–1956), a Professor of Zoology at Indiana University, was asked by the University President to teach a sexuality course for married students. Soon after the course began, students came to Kinsey with sexuality questions that he could not answer, and the existing literature was little help. This encouraged him to begin collecting data on the sex lives of his students. His study grew and soon included students who were not in his classes, faculty members, friends, and nonfaculty employees. In 1941 he obtained a grant which enabled him to hire people to help with data collection.

Conflict arose with other colleagues and persons within the University who felt that the marriage course and the sexuality research were immoral. Fortunately for Kinsey, the President of Indiana University still believed in and was committed to Kinsey's work.

The growing negativity toward the marriage course eventually did force Kinsey to give it up, even though he continued to collect the sexual histories. After he stopped teaching the course, students waited in line to make appointments to talk with Kinsey.

In his early work, Kinsey claimed to be **atheoretical**. He felt that since sexuality research was so new, it was impossible to construct theories and hypotheses without first having a large body of information. The original questionnaire that Kinsey had designed for his students soon proved to be inappropriate for certain other groups. For instance, it did not contain questions about extramarital sex or the sexuality of divorced or widowed partners. However, Kinsey refused to change the original structure of the questionnaire because this would have made it impossible to compare responses to earlier questionnaires. He decided to amend the questionnaire by adding more questions.

atheoretical: Research that is not structured by a particular theory.

Kinsey's procedure involved collecting information on each subject's sexual life history, with an emphasis on specific behaviors and orgasms (Gebhard and Johnson, 1979). A total of thirteen areas were covered in the interview, including demographics, physical data, early sexual knowledge, adolescent sexual behaviors, masturbation, orgasms in sleep, heterosexual petting, sexual intercourse, reproductive information, homosexual activity, sexual contact with animals, and sexual responsiveness. In order to build rapport with their subjects, each of the interviewers working with Kinsey were required to memorize all questions and not to use an actual questionnaire during the interview. They were also to use appropriate terminology that subjects would understand. Finally, subjects were assured that the information they provided would remain confidential.

The sampling procedures Kinsey used were also a strength of his research. He believed that he would have a high refusal rate if he used **probability sampling**. Because of this, he used "quota sampling accompanied by opportunistic collection" (Gebhard and Johnson, 1979:26). This meant that if he saw that a particular group such as young married women was not well represented in his sample, he would find organizations with a high percentage of these subjects and include them in his sample. Overall, his subjects were obtained from twenty-three colleges and universities, twenty-one hospitals, eight prisons, two mental hospitals, two institutions for young delinquents, four churches and synagogues, five groups of people with sexual problems, nine settlement houses; homosexual groups in Chicago, Los Angeles, New York, Philadelphia, and San Francisco; and members of various groups including the YMCA and YWCA (Gebhard and Johnson, 1979:29). In these groups, every member was strongly encouraged to participate in the project to minimize volunteer bias. Kinsey referred to this procedure as **100% sampling**.

probability sampling: A research strategy that involves acquiring a random sample for inclusion in a study.

100% sampling: A research strategy in which all members of a particular group are included in the sample.

Institute for Sex Research

In 1947, the Institute for Sex Research was established by Kinsey with the help of Clyde Martin, Wardell Pomeroy, and Paul Gebhard. This center was established primarily to maintain the confidential data that had been collected and to claim royalties from any published work (Gebhard and Johnson, 1979). Not coincidentally, two of Kinsey's most popular and lucrative works were published soon afterward—in 1948, *The Sexual Behavior of the Human Male* appeared, and in 1953, *The Sexual Behavior of the Human Female*. These books were overnight best-sellers and provided the institute with the financial ability to continue its work. Both books helped to break down the myths and confusion surrounding sexuality, while providing scientifically derived information about the sexual lives of men and women. Many practices that had previously been seen as perverse or unacceptable in society (such as homosexuality, masturbation, and oral sex) were found to be widely practiced (as you could guess, these findings were very controversial and created strong reactions from religious organizations). However, as a result of his work, feelings of guilt and negativity that people had about their sexuality were reduced, and people were allowed to express their sexuality without worrying, "Am I normal?" However, continued controversy toward Kinsey's work resulted in the termination of several research grants. This lack of funds was very frustrating for Kinsey, who did not like to ask people for money because he felt that to do so would be self-serving (Pomeroy, 1982). Obtaining private funds was difficult, too, since the public would view those who donated as "supporting sex research!"

By the time of Kinsey's death in 1956, his collection of interviews totaled 18,000, which was considerably less than his original dream of 100,000. Many people believe that his early death at the young age of sixty-two was because of the constant criticism and struggle he lived under as he tried to legitimize the field of sexuality research. In fact, colleagues of Kinsey believed he literally worked himself to death trying to do all he could with the money and time he had (Pomeroy, 1982). Kinsey was also frustrated by the lack of respect many had for his controversial findings in this taboo area. However, after his death *The New York Times* wrote:

> *The untimely death of Dr. Alfred C. Kinsey takes from the American scene an important and valuable, as well as controversial, figure. Whatever may have been the reaction to his findings—and to the unscrupulous use of some of them—the fact remains that he was first, last and always a scientist. In the long run it is probable that the values of his contribution to contemporary thought will lie much less in what he found out than in the method he used and his way of applying it. Any sort of scientific approach to the problems of sex is difficult because the field is so deeply overlaid with such things as moral precept, taboo, individual and group training and long established behavior patterns. Some of these may be good in themselves, but they are no help to the scientific and empirical method of getting at the truth. Dr. Kinsey cut through this overlay with detachment and precision. His work was conscientious and comprehensive. Naturally it will receive a serious setback with this death. Let us earnestly hope that the scientific spirit that inspired it will not be similarly impaired.*
>
> *Quoted in Pomeroy (1982:441)*

Sex & Morality in the U.S.

In 1989, the Kinsey Institute published *Sex & Morality in the U.S.* The report contained data that had been collected in the United States in the 1970s, but political disputes within the institute had delayed its publication. This study, designed to examine Americans' moral attitudes toward sexuality, was meant to complement Kinsey's work, which had concentrated on sexual behaviors but not the thoughts, feelings, and attitudes behind these behaviors. In this new study, the researchers explored public opinions about premarital and extramarital sex, prostitution, homosexuality, masturbation, incest, and sex with children.

The Kinsey Institute New Report on Sex

The Kinsey Institute receives thousands of letters and phone calls each year about sexuality. Researchers at the institute have wondered whether these questions were universal and how much people knew about sex. In an attempt to understand knowledge levels about sex, the Institute gave 1,974 American adults a sexuality quiz in 1989. People who took the test did not score very high. The Kinsey Institute found that the majority of Americans did not know much about issues such as AIDS, homosexuality, birth control, or sexual problems.

There were some interesting findings revealed in this study. Older persons generally scored the lowest, which may have to do with the lack of sexuality education when they were young. However, it was also found that when older people did not know the answer to a question, they admitted it, while younger people tended to be "confident in their ignorance" (Reinisch, 1990:19). Other findings included higher scores for those who had some college education, lived in the Midwest, and were politically liberal. We will discuss more of these findings in the following chapters.

Morton Hunt

In the early 1970s, the Playboy Foundation commissioned a study to update Kinsey's earlier work on sexual behavior. Morton Hunt (1974) eventually published these findings in his book *Sexual Behavior in the 1970's*. In addition, he reviewed his findings in a series of articles in *Playboy* magazine.

Hunt gathered his sample through random selection from telephone books in twenty-four U.S. cities. This sampling technique was thought to be an improvement over Kinsey's techniques, although there were also drawbacks. People without telephones, such as college students or institutionalized persons, were left out of the study. Each person in Hunt's sample was called and asked to participate in a group discussion about sexuality. Approximately 20% agreed to participate. Subjects participated in small group discussions about sexuality in America and, after doing so, were asked to complete questionnaires about their own sexual behavior and attitudes. A total of 982 males and 1,044 females participated in his study. However, since his sample was such a small percentage of those he contacted and volunteer bias may interfere with his results, they are probably not similar to the population as a whole, so this study may not be **generalizable** and must be interpreted with caution. We will discuss some of his findings in some of the following chapters.

generalizable: Able to be applied to the general population.

Masters and Johnson

Although Alfred Kinsey first envisioned physiological studies on sexual arousal and orgasm, it was Masters and Johnson who were actually the first modern scientists to observe and measure the act of sexual intercourse in the laboratory. William Masters, a gynecologist, and Virginia Johnson, a psychologist, began their sex research in 1954. They were primarily interested in the anatomy and physiology of the sexual response and later also explored sexual dysfunction. One of the aspects of Masters and Johnson's work that was different than prior research was that they offered a dual sex-therapy team. This way both male and female opinions were represented, and there was less chance for gender bias. Much of the work done by Masters and Johnson was supported by grants, the income from their books, and individual/couple therapy.

Masters and Johnson's first study, published in 1966, was entitled *Human Sexual Response*. In an attempt to understand the physiological process that occurs during sexual activity, the researchers actually brought 700 people into the laboratory to have their physiological reactions studied during sexual intercourse. In the beginning, Masters and

Virginia Johnson and William Masters are experts on the physiology of sexual behavior.

chronic pelvic congestion:
A vasocongestive buildup in the uterus that can occur when arousal does not lead to orgasm.

random sample: A number of cases taken from the entire population of persons, values, scores, etc. in such a way as to ensure that any one selection has as much chance of being picked as any other and that the sample will be a valid representation of the entire population.

penile strain gauge: A device that was used by Masters and Johnson to measure penile engorgement during arousal.

photoplethysmograph: A device used to measure physiological sexual arousal in females.

Johnson had difficulty recruiting volunteers, so they used prostitutes. They soon realized that prostitutes often suffered from a condition known as **chronic pelvic congestion**, which interfered with normative physiological functioning. Soon, several middle-class volunteers were included in the study. These volunteers participated for financial reasons (financial incentives were given for participation), personal reasons, and even for the release of sexual tension (Masters and Johnson both stated that they felt some volunteers were looking for legitimate and safe sexual outlets). Since Masters and Johnson were studying behaviors they felt were normative (i.e., they happened to most people) they did not feel they needed to recruit a **random sample**.

When a volunteer was accepted as a subject in the study, he or she was first encouraged to engage in sexual activity in the lab without the investigators present. It was hoped that this would make him or her feel more comfortable with the new surroundings. Our students often ask us how sex could be "natural" in the sterile conditions of a lab. Many of the volunteers reported that after a while they did not notice the fact that they were being monitored. During the study they would be monitored for physiological changes with an electrocardiograph to measure changes in the heart and an electromyograph to measure muscular changes. Changes were also noted in penile erection and vaginal lubrication with **penile strain gauges** and **photoplethysmographs**.

Through this research, Master and Johnson discovered several interesting aspects of sexual response, including the potential of multiple orgasms in women and the fact that sexuality does not fade away in old age. They also proposed a four stage model for sexual response. We will discuss each of these in more detail in Chapter 9.

In 1970, Masters and Johnson published another important book entitled *Human Sexual Inadequacy,* which explored sexual dysfunction. Again they brought couples into the laboratory but this time only those who were experiencing sexual problems. They evaluated these couples physiologically and psychologically and taught them exercises to regain sexual functioning. Frequent follow-ups were done to measure the therapeutic results—some subjects were even contacted five years after the study was completed. One of the most interesting findings from Masters and Johnson's work on sexual dysfunction is that there is often a dual sexual dysfunction in couples (i.e., males who are experiencing erectile problems often have partners that are also experiencing sexual problems). The study also refuted Freud's theory that women are capable of vaginal (mature) and clitoral (immature) orgasms and that only vaginal orgasms resulted from intercourse, finding instead that women need clitoral stimulation in order to have orgasms (see Sexuality Today 2.1). They also noted the impact of fear of failure and performance anxiety on sexual behavior.

Both of Masters and Johnson's books were written from a medical, rather than a psychological, perspective. Many professionals have speculated that this was a tactic to avoid censorship of the book. As a result, the books were not geared towards the general public. For instance, consider this quote from *Human Sexual Response:*

> [Subjects were observed performing] *manual and mechanical manipulation, natural coition with the female partner in supine, superior, or knee-chest positions and, for many female study subjects, artificial coition in supine and knee-chest positions.*

Even with this scientific and medical base, their work did not proceed without controversy. Many people viewed Masters and Johnson's work as both unethical and immoral.

Age-Specific Studies

A few sexuality studies have been done on specific populations. Most notably, studies have focused on adolescents and the elderly. Below we will review a few of these studies.

Adolescent Studies

In 1973, a study was done by Robert Sorenson entitled *Adolescent Sexuality in Contemporary America.* This study provided baselines of sexual activity in 411 adolescents aged thirteen to nineteen. With a nearly 50% response rate, Sorenson was able to collect information on frequency of masturbation, sexual activity, and homosexuality. However, we must keep in mind that many parents did not allow their teenagers to participate in the study. Therefore, we must use caution in generalizing the results of this study.

Sorenson used questionnaires to gather information and should be credited with the first comprehensive study of adolescent sexuality. We will discuss specific findings from this study more in Chapter 4.

Melvin Zelnik and John Kantner also did research on adolescent sexuality. In 1971, 1976, and 1979, they studied the sexual and contraceptive behavior of fifteen to nineteen-year-old females. In 1979, they included males in their sample. A total of 7,995 females and 917 males were included in their studies. Although this is an impressive sample of females, the work of Zelnik et al. (1981) was criticized as for the small number of males, as well as for the limited focus of their study (very little information was collected on sexual behaviors other than sexual intercourse).

Elderly Studies

In Kinsey's studies, the elderly were underrepresented. Recognizing this, in 1981, Bernard Starr and Marcella Weiner decided to explore the sexuality of 800 adults who were between the ages of sixty and ninety-one years old. Sixty-five percent were female and thirty-five percent were male (Starr and Weiner, 1981). The questionnaires were given to the subjects after a lecture about sexuality in later years. Each participant was given a fifty-item questionnaire and a self-addressed, stamped envelope in which to return it. The response rate was 14%, which is very low; therefore, the statistics may not be accurate for all seniors. The questionnaire was composed of fifty open-ended questions about sexual experience, changes in sexuality that have occurred with age, sexual satisfaction, sex and widows, sexual interest, masturbation, orgasm, sexual likes and dislikes, and intimacy.

This study revealed that an interest in sexuality continues into the later years and that many older people feel that sex is important for physical and emotional health. Although Kinsey had found that those over sixty had sexual intercourse once every two weeks, participants in Starr and Weiner's group reported their frequency was 1.4 times a week. Many reported that they wished this number was higher. Many respondents thought that sexuality was better in the later years, that masturbation was acceptable, that oral sex was very pleasurable, and that their sex lives were similar to, or better than, their younger years.

In 1983, another study was done by Edward Brecher and the editors of Consumer Reports Books and was published in a book entitled *Love, Sex, and Aging* (Brecher et al., 1984). This study also explored sexuality in the later years. A total of 4,246 men and women who were over the age of fifty were included in this study. The survey included questions on attitudes about sex, behaviors, and sexual concerns. Again it was found that older adults were indeed sexual, even though society still thought of them in nonsexual terms. We will discuss these findings more in Chapter 9.

Studies on Homosexuality

Although many research studies have been done on homosexuality, there have been very few actual wide-scale studies. Here we will review two of these studies.

Evelyn Hooker

In the early 1950s, a researcher named Evelyn Hooker (1957) undertook a study on male homosexuality. Hooker compared two groups of men, one gay and the other straight, who were matched for age, education, and IQ levels. She collected information about their life histories, personality profiles, and psychological evaluations and asked professionals to try to distinguish between the two groups on the basis of their profiles and evaluations. They could not, demonstrating that there was little fundamental psychological difference between gay and straight men. Hooker's study was the first to provide evidence that homosexuality was not a psychological disorder. Today, many studies have shown that there is no psychological difference between heterosexual and homosexual men and women. We will discuss this more in Chapter 7.

Bell and Weinberg

Alfred Kinsey's death prevented him from publishing a book on homosexuality as he had hoped. He had collected a large number of case histories from homosexuals and had learned that a large number of people had experienced homosexual behavior in childhood and adulthood. Homosexuality, to Kinsey, was not as "abnormal" as society had thought. In 1967, a task force was established within the National Institute of Mental Health to examine homosexuality. A total of 5,000 homosexual men and women were interviewed and 5,000 heterosexual men and women were used for comparison. The interviews contained 528 questions and took two to five hours to complete. In 1978, Alan Bell and Martin Weinberg published *Homosexualities,* which explored the results of this study (see Sex Facts 2.1).

Prior to this research, many people believed that homosexuals were sexually irresponsible and had psychological problems which needed to be cured (Bell & Weinberg, 1978). However, this study revealed that the majority of homosexuals do not conform to stereotypes. They do not push unwanted sexual advances onto people, nor do they seduce children. In fact, heterosexual men were found to be more likely to seduce children than were homosexual men. The homosexual community was also found to be similar to the heterosexual community in its types of intimate relationships. We will discuss these studies more in Chapter 7.

SEX *Facts*

A Study on Homosexuality

Bell and Weinberg (1978) did a study to examine a variety of dimensions of the homosexual experience. They wanted to explore levels of sexual desire, frequency of sexual behavior, and number of sexual partners. The sample of homosexual men and women was collected from the San Francisco Bay area, and subjects were recruited from public advertising, bars, personal contacts, gay baths, organizations, mailing lists, and public places. A heterosexual comparison group was recruited from the general population in San Francisco. All subjects were interviewed, primarily by graduate students who attended local universities. They found:

- The majority of homosexual men and women were relatively covert ("in the closet"), as opposed to overt.
- For the majority of homosexuals, sex was not a predominant concern.
- Public cruising was infrequent among lesbians. Among homosexual men who cruised in public places, most conducted their sexual activity in the privacy of their homes.
- Gay bars were the most popular cruising locales.
- Homosexual men tended to have more partners than did lesbians and were more apt to engage in sexual activities with persons who were virtual strangers to them.

Other Sexuality Studies

Shere Hite conducted studies to explore sexuality from a feminist perspective. Below we examine her trilogy of books.

The Hite Reports

In 1976, Shere Hite published the *Hite Report,* which examined female sexuality (Hite, 1987). It included responses from 3,019 American women. Hite distributed her questionnaires (which contained between fifty and sixty questions about orgasm, sexual activities, relationships, and life stages) to several women's groups, including chapters of the National Organization of Women, university centers, and abortion rights groups. Notices were also put in several magazines, including the *Village Voice, Mademoiselle, Brides,* and *Ms.* Over 100,000 questionnaires were distributed and 3,000 received, which resulted in an extremely small response rate of 3%. Small response rates mean that we cannot be sure the study is generalizable.

The *Hite Report on Male Sexuality* was published in 1981 (Hite, 1981). Both of Hite's books received a great deal of criticism because neither study used a random sample and the return rates were so small. Critics of these studies point out that those who felt more comfortable with their sexuality may have responded to the questionnaire, while those who were uncomfortable did not. Therefore, the studies cannot be generalized to the general population. However, both of these studies revealed rich, qualitative material on male and female sexuality.

Shere Hite, a feminist scholar, worked to establish baselines for female sexuality. She later did a study on male sexuality.

Women and Love: The 1987 Hite Report on Women

In 1987, Shere Hite published the third book of her trilogy, entitled *Women and Love: A Cultural Revolution in Progress* (Hite, 1987). Included in this volume were responses from 4,500 women. Overall it found that women were experiencing unsatisfying emotional relationships with men (see Sex Facts 2.2). Again, critics argued that primarily women who were unhappy would take the time to complete the questionnaire. Hite made it clear that she was following a feminist theory, which, as discussed earlier, values qualitative over quantitative research. The voices of the individual women were important to Hite. However, without the structure of scientific experimentation, we cannot generalize any of Hite's information from this study. Nonetheless, the report presents some interesting findings about how a group of women was feeling about its relationships with men.

The Janus Report

In 1993, Drs. Samuel and Cynthia Janus published the *Janus Report on Sexual Behavior* (Janus and Janus, 1993). It was touted as the most comprehensive study of sex in America since Kinsey's work in the 1950s. The Janus Report was based on data obtained from nearly 3,000 questionnaires. Overall, the authors claimed that there had been a redistribution of values in American society with regard to sex. They found that people were more willing to engage in a variety of sexual behaviors and that there had been an increase in sexual interest and behavior in elderly Americans. In addition, the report examined the sexual behavior of people according to where they lived—the South, Northeast, West, and the Midwest. Although one study cannot fill in the all the gaps in knowledge about sexual attitudes and behaviors in the United States, this study did yield valuable information on sexuality, such as:

SEX *Facts*   *2.2*

Women and Love

In 1987, Shere Hite published the findings from her third study in a book entitled *Women and Love: A Cultural Revolution in Progress,* (1987). In this book, 4,500 women of all backgrounds and ages filled out questionnaires about their relationships with men. Overall, Hite found that many women were dissatisfied with their relationships with men. Some of the findings from her study includes the following:

- 98% of the women said they would like more verbal closeness with their male partners.
- 83% said they initiated most deep talks and tried to get their partners to open up.
- 17% said the communication in their relationships was good and made them happy.

- In 47% of relationships, the only way to get real verbal communication was to have a fight eventually.
- 67% of the women said that men do much more complaining than women.
- 89% of the women said that men do not really hear what they are saying during fights.
- 57% of the single women said most men do not end relationships gracefully.

Do you think that women who took the time to answer Hite's questionnaire are representative of the majority of women? Hite's study was criticized because of very low response rates, therefore, her findings must be interpreted with caution.

- Americans in their sixties and seventies are experiencing greatly heightened levels of sexual activity.
- Married couples reported the highest level of sexual activity and satisfaction.
- Three out of five married people said their sex lives improved after marriage.
- Areas in which people live influence overall sexual attitudes and behaviors. Midwesterners were found to have the least sexual activity, while those in the South reported the earliest ages of sexual initiation and the highest rates of premarital sex.
- People who are ultra-conservative are more likely to be involved in frequent or ongoing extramarital affairs than are those who are ultra-liberal.
- Men and women are both initiating sexual activity.

National Health and Social Life Study

In late 1994 a national survey on sexual behavior was completed by researchers at the University of Chicago and was entitled the National Health and Social Life Study (Laumann et al., 1994). This $1.6 million survey was also touted as the most comprehensive, scientifically accurate study of its kind in the United States. Originally, the study was designed to examine Americans' sexual practices with respect to the AIDS crisis. The federal funding for this project was initially received in the late 1980s, but the project was postponed because of political opposition. It was finally completed with private funds. Ninety-minute interviews were done with 3,432 adults, ages eighteen to fifty-nine, in randomly selected households across the United States. Preliminary data reveals that Americans may be more sexually conservative than previously thought. The majority of people were found to have sex a few times a month or less and have three sex partners over a lifetime. The results also indicated that sexual choices that people make are restricted by their social networks (i.e., friends and family).

This was the first study to explore sexuality in its social context, rather than from a psychological or biological perspective. Among the findings:

- The median number of sexual partners since the age of eighteen was six for men and two for women.
- 75% of married men and 80% of married women do not engage in extramarital sexuality.
- 2.8% of men and 1.4% of women describe themselves as homosexual or bisexual.
- 75% of men claimed to have consistent orgasms with their partners, while 29% of women did.
- More than one in five women said they had been forced by a man to do something sexual.

In the following chapters, we will explore more of the results of this study.

SEX RESEARCH METHODS

Now that we have explored some studies in sexuality, let us look at the specifics of how these studies are conducted. Each study that we have presented in this chapter was scientific, yet researchers used different experimental methods depending on the kind of information they were trying to gather. For example, Freud relied on a **case study**

case study: A research methodology that involves an in-depth examination of one subject or a small number of subjects.

participant-observation: A research methodology that involves actual participation in the event that is being researched.

correlations: Numbers that indicate a degree of a relationship between two variables.

validity: The property that a measuring device measures what it is intended to measure.

reliability: The dependability of a test as reflected in the consistency of its scores upon repeated measurements of the same group.

generalizability: Pertaining to objects, symbols, principles, etc. formulated in such a manner that they have wide applicability.

representative sample: A sample that resembles the breakdown of the general population. Certain factors (such as ethnicity, gender, or age) are appropriately proportioned.

methodology, while Kinsey used questionnaires to gather data. There are other ways that researchers collect information, such as interviews, laboratory experiments, direct observation, **participant-observation**, and **correlations**.

Whatever techniques they use, researchers must be certain that their experiment passes standards of **validity**, **reliability**, and **generalizability**. Tests of validity determine whether or not a question or other method is measuring what it is designed to measure. For example, the people who read the question need to interpret it the same way as the researcher who wrote it. Reliability refers to the consistency of the measure. If we ask a question today, we would hope to get a similar answer if we ask it again in two months. Finally, if a study is generalizable, the answers of a few subjects can be applicable to the general population. A study can be generalized only if a random sample is used. **Representative samples** can also be used. All of the methods we review below must fit these three criteria.

Case Study

When a researcher does a case study, he or she explores individual cases to formulate general hypotheses. Freud was famous for his use of this methodology. Using this method, however, does not allow researchers to generalize to the general public since the sample is so small. Even so, it may generate hypotheses that can lead to larger, generalizable studies.

Questionnaire Versus Interview

Questionnaire or survey research is generally used to identify the attitudes, knowledge, or behavior of large samples. For instance, Kinsey used this method to obtain information about his many subjects, and questions have since been raised about Kinsey's validity and reliability. Kinsey recognized these problems and tried to increase the validity by using interviews to supplement the questionnaires. Some researchers prefer to use interviews instead of questionnaires; there are advantages and disadvantages to each method. An interview allows the researcher to establish a rapport with each subject and emphasize the importance of honesty in his or her study. In addition, the researcher can vary the order of questions and skip questions that are irrelevant. However, there are also some limitations to interviews. First, they are more time-consuming and expensive than questionnaires. Also, it has been argued that questionnaires provide more honesty since the subject may be embarrassed to admit things to another person that they would be more likely to share with the anonymity of a questionnaire. Research has revealed that when people answer sexuality questionnaires they are likely to leave out the questions that cause the most anxiety, especially questions about masturbation (Catania et al., 1986).

Direct Observation

Masters and Johnson used direct observation for their research on sexual response and physiology. This method is the least frequently used since it is difficult to find subjects who are willing to come into the laboratory to have sex while researchers monitor their bodily functions. However, if it can be done, it does provide information that cannot be obtained elsewhere. The researchers can actually monitor behavior as it happens, which gives the results more credibility. A man may exaggerate in a self-report and claim that he experiences three erections per sexual episode, but he cannot exaggerate in a laboratory. Direct observation is much more expensive than any of the other methods and may not be as generalizable since it would be impossible to gather a random sample. In addition, direct observation focuses on behaviors and, as a result, ignores feelings, attitudes, or personal history.

Participant-Observation

Participant-observation research involves researchers going into an environment and monitoring what is happening naturally. For instance, a researcher who wants to explore male and female flirting patterns and alcohol might watch interactions between men and women in bars. This would entail several visits and specific note taking on all that occurs. However, it is difficult to generalize from this type of research since the researcher could subtly, or not so subtly, influence the research findings. Also, much of sexual behavior occurs in private, where researchers have no access.

Experimental Methods

Experiments are the only research method that allow us to isolate cause and effect. This is because in an experiment, strict control is maintained over all variables so that one variable can be isolated and examined. For example, suppose you want to teach high school students about AIDS, but you don't know which teaching methodology would be most beneficial. You could design an experiment to examine this more closely. First, you choose a high school and **randomly assign** all the students to one of three groups. You might start by giving them a questionnaire about AIDS to establish baseline data about what they know or believe. Group one then listens to a lecture about AIDS, group two is shown a video, and group three listens to a person with AIDS talk about his or her experience. Strict care is taken to make sure that all of the information that is presented in these classes is identical. The only thing that differs is the teaching method. In scientific terms, the type of teaching method is the **independent variable**. It is manipulated by the researcher. After each class, the students are given a test to determine what knowledge they have gained about AIDS. This measurement is to determine the effect of the independent variable on the **dependent variable**, which in this case is knowledge about AIDS. If one group shows more learning after one particular method was used, we might be able to attribute the learning to the type of methodology that was used.

Experiments are much more costly than any of the other methods discussed, both in terms of finances and time commitment. It is also possible that in an attempt to control the experiments, a researcher may cause the study to become too sterile or artificial (not anything like it would be outside of the laboratory) and the results may be faulty or may not apply to the real world. Finally, experiments are not always possible in certain areas of research, especially in the field of sexuality. For instance, what if we wanted to examine whether or not early sexual abuse contributed to adult difficulties with intimate relationships? It would be entirely unethical to abuse children sexually in order to examine whether or not they develop these problems later in life.

randomly assign: Assigning subjects to groups in an experiment such that each subject has an equal chance of being assigned to each group.

independent variable: The variable controlled by the experimenter and applied to the subject in order to determine its effect on the subject's reaction.

dependent variable: A variable in which changes are contingent upon changes in the independent variable.

Correlations

Correlations are often used when it is not possible to do an experiment. For example, in a sexual abuse study we would study a given population and see if there is any correlation

correlational: Research that examines the relationship between two or more variables.

between past sexual abuse and later difficulties with intimate relationships since it is unethical to do a controlled experiment. The limitation of a **correlational** study is that it does not provide any information about cause. We would not learn if past sexual abuse causes difficulties with intimacy, even though we may learn that these factors are related. The intimacy difficulties could occur for several other reasons including factors such as low self-esteem or a personality disorder.

PROBLEMS AND ISSUES IN SEX RESEARCH

There are many problems that are more difficult to contend with in sexuality research than other types of research. These include ethical issues, volunteer bias, sampling problems, and reliability.

Ethical Issues

informed consent: Informing subjects about what will be expected of them before they participate in a research study.

There are many ethical issues that apply to all psychological research and to sexuality research in particular. Prior to a person's participation in a study of sexuality, it is necessary to obtain his or her **informed consent**. This is especially important in an area such as sexuality since it is such a personal area to research. Informed consent means that the person knows what to expect from the questions and procedures, how the information will be used, how his or her confidentiality will be assured, and to whom he or she can address questions. Once he or she has decided to participate, subjects need to be assured that **confidentiality** will be maintained. Another ethical question that has generated controversy is whether or not children should be asked questions about sexuality.

confidentiality: Keeping all materials collected in a research study private and confidential.

Volunteer Bias

If we wanted to administer a questionnaire about college students' attitudes towards sexuality and we recruited volunteers from your class, do you think those who volunteer would be different from those who do not? Research indicates that they may indeed differ. As early as 1969, Rosenthal and Rosnow (1975) claimed that those who volunteer for psychological studies often have a special interest in the studies in which they participate. Volunteers have also been found to be brighter, less authoritarian, higher in occupational status and in their need for approval, and better adjusted than nonvolunteers (Rosenthal and Rosnow, 1975; Barker and Perlman, 1975). In sexuality studies, volunteers have been found to be more liberal, more sexually active, have higher rates of masturbation, experience more unusual sexual behaviors, view erotic materials more, experience less guilt, have higher educational levels, value sex research more, and are often older (Morokoff, 1986; Wolchik et al., 1985). Although women are more likely to volunteer for conventional research (such as psychological research), men are more likely to volunteer for unconventional research including sexuality studies (Wolchik et al., 1985; Rosenthal and Rosnow, 1975).

You might be wondering how a researcher would know whether his or her volunteer sample is different from the nonvolunteer sample. After all, how can the researcher know anything about nonvolunteers who are not in the study? Researchers have designed ways of overcoming this problem. Prior to asking for volunteers to take part in a sexuality study, researchers ask all subjects to fill out a questionnaire, which contains personality measures and sexuality questions. Subjects are then asked whether or not they would volunteer for a sexuality study. Since the researchers already have information from both volunteers and nonvolunteers, they simply compare this data.

Since volunteers appear to differ from nonvolunteers, it is impossible to generalize the findings of a study that used a volunteer sample. The Kinsey studies attempted to decrease volunteer bias by obtaining full participation from each member of the groups they studied.

Sampling Problems

Sexuality studies routinely involve the use of college age populations. Brecher and Brecher (1986) refer to these populations as **samples of convenience** because the subjects used are convenient for researchers who tend to work at universities. Kinsey used such samples in his initial research at Indiana University. The question is, can these studies be generalized to the rest of the population? Are college students similar to noncollege students of the same age or people who are older or younger? Probably not. These samples also miss certain groups, such as those who do not go to college, and may also underrepresent minorities and the disabled.

samples of convenience: A research methodology that involves using samples that are easy to collect and acquire.

Reliability

How reliable are studies on sex? Some studies have found that couples who are sexually satisfied tend to overestimate their frequency of sexual behavior, while those who are unsatisfied underreport them (James, 1971). In 1967, a study was done to evaluate the reliability of the reporting of sexual activity. Men were required to keep daily logs of when they engaged in sexual activity and also to provide daily urine samples. These samples were microscopically evaluated for semen to substantiate their logs of sexual activity. Reports were found to be consistent with their written logs.

SEX TALK

QUESTION **2.4** **How do you know that what people tell you is true?**

> **The fact is that we just don't know, and we hope that people are being honest. Researchers also anticipate that subjects will understand the questions asked and have the ability to tell us the answers. In actuality, researchers may take many things for granted.**

Some critics claim that changes in frequency of sexual behavior over time may be due more to changes in the *reporting* of behavior than to actual changes in frequency (Kaats and Davis, 1971). For instance, if we had done a study in 1995 of the number of college students who engage in premarital sex and compare this to data collected in 1963, we would undoubtedly find more people having premarital sex in 1995. However, it could be that these higher numbers are due to the fact that more people feel comfortable talking about premarital sex than they did in 1963. To ensure that we know that the increase in numbers is actually due to an increase in behavior, it is necessary to take the time and location of the study into account while evaluating the results.

Another problem affecting reliability involves the subject's memory. Since many sexuality researchers ask questions about behaviors that might have happened in one's adolescence, people may not always have the capacity to remember this information.

For instance, if we were to ask a fifty-two-year-old man the age at which he first masturbated, chances are good that he would not remember how old he was. He would probably *estimate* the age at which he first masturbated. Estimates are not adequate for scientific study.

SEXUALITY RESEARCH IN OTHER COUNTRIES

Many studies have been done to examine sexuality in cultures outside the United States. Some have been general studies that examine knowledge levels and attitudes in different populations; others have evaluated specific areas such as pregnancy, rape, homosexuality, or sex education. Many times these studies are done by researchers in other countries, but some have also been done by American researchers.

The largest comprehensive study of sexual behavior was recently completed in France. It was funded by a $2.5 million grant from France's Health Ministry and the National AIDS Research Agency, and it examined the sexual practices of 20,000 people between the ages of eighteen and sixty-nine (*The New York Times,* 1992a) Interviews were done primarily by telephone, and the majority of those people contacted agreed to participate. Findings revealed that many teenagers do not use condoms during sexual intercourse because they are too expensive; that rates of extramarital sexual behavior are decreasing; and that the average French heterosexual engages in sex approximately two times per week. This was the largest study done in France in over twenty years.

Of all the topics that have been studied cross-culturally, we have probably learned the most about how societies influence sexuality. Every culture develops its own rules and regulations about what sexual behaviors are encouraged and which will not be tolerated. As we discussed earlier, on the South Pacific Island of Mangaia, men and women are taught to be very open-minded about sexuality. On another small island named Inis Beagin in Ireland, sexuality is very repressed. The United States falls somewhere in between these two. In 1971, Donald Marshall and Robert Suggs published *Human Sexual Behavior*, which was an anthropological study to examine how sexuality was expressed in several different cultures (Marshall and Suggs, 1971). There were some interesting findings, including:

- Masturbation is rare in preliterate groups.
- In the majority of societies, foreplay is engaged in prior to sexual intercourse.
- Foreplay is usually initiated by males.
- Sexual intercourse is most commonly engaged in at night prior to falling asleep.
- Female orgasmic frequency varies greatly from culture to culture.

Societal influences affect all aspects of sexuality. Throughout this book we explore cross-cultural studies on sexuality and examine how cultures vary from each other.

SEX RESEARCH IN THE FUTURE

In September of 1991, the National Institutes of Health canceled a nationwide sexuality study entitled the *Survey of Health and AIDS Risk Prevalence*, which was to examine the sexual behavior of Americans. A sexuality study on such a wide scale had not been done since the Kinsey studies. Pressure from conservative politicians was instrumental in causing the study to be canceled. Also canceled was a sexuality study entitled the *American Teen Study* (ATS), which was aimed at understanding teenagers and high risk sexual behavior. The ATS was to shed some light on what types of sexual activities teenagers engage in and how they comprehend the risks of their behavior. Some claim that funding for these studies was cut because the questions asked were too "invasive" and "explicit" and because the studies were seen as unnecessary and a waste of taxpayers' money (Youngstrom, 1991). Supporters felt the study would aid in our understanding of teenage sexual behavior.

Many people argue that politics should not interfere with wide-scale studies of sexuality. Although funding for these projects might be difficult to come by, it is very important in the long run. Without knowledge about what types of sexual behaviors people are engaging in, it is difficult to plan educational interventions. In turn, without education, we may not be able to combat the rising numbers of sexually transmitted disease and infection with the AIDS virus.

In order to be federally funded, all sexuality studies must be **peer-reviewed**, must be approved by the investigator's **Institutional Review Board**, and must also be seen as necessary to promote public health. Once a study passes these requirements, it can then be considered for funding by federal agencies. Since the federal funding has been cut for the ATS study, which involved the interviews of 24,000 adolescents (with parental permission), researchers are hoping to secure $18 million from a private foundation. Due to the high cost of the study, however, private funding seems unlikely.

In the future, perhaps federal funds will again be available to researchers who are interested in studying sexuality. As of 1994, many researchers and scientists were avoiding extensive sexuality research because of the expense involved and the decreasing possibility of being funded even after maneuvering through the appropriate channels—which is time-consuming in itself.

peer-reviewed: A process of research study approval, prior to the study being carried out. Usually universities have a committee that approves proposals.

Institutional Review Board: A committee at universities that works to approve research proposals.

Summary

- The major psychological theories about human sexuality include psychoanalytic, behavioral, social learning, cognitive, and humanistic. Other theories include biological, sociological, sociobiological, and feminist. Theorists in different disciplines differ in the questions they raise about sexuality and also the methods they use to obtain data.

- Krafft-Ebing, Hirschfeld, Ellis, and Freud were the first to discuss sexuality in a modern scientific way. Alfred Kinsey designed the first large-scale study of sexuality in the United States; Morton Hunt tried to update Kinsey's data in the 1970s. The first studies of the physiology of human sexuality were done by Masters and Johnson.

- Many special studies have been done on specific populations including adolescents, the elderly, homosexuals, and females.

- Researchers use several different methods to obtain information about sexuality. These include case study, questionnaire, interview, direct observation, experiments, and correlations. Each has advantages and disadvantages.

- Several difficult issues affect sexuality research including ethical and sampling problems. Sexuality researchers need to be aware of these issues and the impact they have on research.

- Volunteer bias can also affect sexuality researchers. Many issues affect reliability, including reporting variations and problems with memory and estimates of sexual behavior.

- Cross-culturally we have learned that every society regulates the sexual behaviors it will encourage and those it will not tolerate.

- The future of sexuality research in the United States is shaky; however, some researchers have found private funding for their studies. In the future, it is hoped that federal funds will be available for sexuality research.

*Reflections on Sexuality*___

1. Is sexuality research as valid and reliable as other areas of research? Explain.
2. Do you think that people would be more honest about their sex lives if they were filling out an anonymous questionnaire or if they were being interviewed by a researcher? Which method of research yields the highest degree of honesty? With which method would you feel the most comfortable?
3. Why do you think couples volunteered to be in Masters and Johnson's study? Would you have volunteered for this study? Why or why not?
4. Although there have been a limited number of studies on adolescent sexuality, none have been done on pre-adolescent sexuality. Why do think this might be? What are the advantages and disadvantages of such a study? Is it ethical to do such a study?
5. If you could do a study on sexuality, what area would you choose? What methods of collecting data would you use? Why? How would you avoid the problems that many sex researchers face?
6. Describe two major sexuality studies that have been done over the years. What have they found?

*Suggested Readings*___

GILLIGAN, CAROL. (1982) *In a Different Voice: Psychological Theory and Women's Development.* Cambridge, MA: Harvard University Press.

IRVINE, JANICE. (1990) *Disorders of Desire: Sex and Gender in Modern American Society.* Philadelphia: Temple University Press.

JANUS, SAMUEL, AND CYNTHIA JANUS. (1993) *The Janus Report on Sexual Behavior.* New York: John Wiley and Sons.

LAUMANN, EDWARD O., JOHN H. GAGNON, ROBERT T. MICHAEL, AND S. MICHAELS. (1994) *The Social Organization of Sexuality.* Chicago: University of Chicago Press.

MICHAEL, ROBERT T., JOHN H. GAGNON, EDWARD O. LAUMANN, AND GINA KOLATA. (1994) *Sex in America: A Definitive Survey.* Boston: Little, Brown and Co.

3

Human Sexual Biology

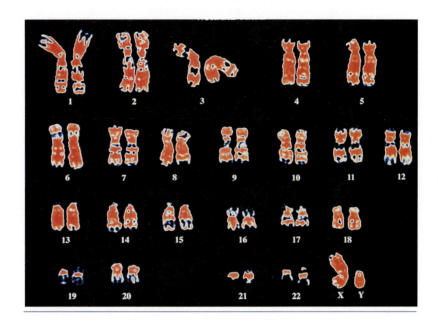

Are there really such things as hermaphrodites, born with the sex organs of both men and women?

Can you tell if a woman is a virgin by examining her hymen?

Why does a man need millions of sperm in one ejaculation to impregnate a woman?

Does the G-spot actually exist?

How do I check my breast for signs of breast cancer?

Do men go through menopause?

Is circumcision necessary?

Is my (breast size, penis size, frequency of erection, menstrual pains, etc.) normal?

Considering the number of sex manuals and guides that line the bookshelves of American bookstores, it may seem surprising that the majority of questions that students ask about sex are fundamental, biological questions. Yet it becomes less surprising when we realize that parents are still uncomfortable about discussing sexual biology with their children, and younger people often do not know who to approach or are embarrassed about the questions they have. But questions about sexual biology are natural, for the reproductive system is complex and there are probably more myths and misinformation about sexual biology than any other single part of human functioning. The purpose of this chapter is to tell the complex yet intriguing story of our biological development as sexual beings.

PRENATAL DEVELOPMENT

Biologists sometimes joke that a chicken is just an egg's way of making another egg. In other words, reproduction is the evolutionary goal of all species, and biological organisms have therefore evolved to maximize their ability to create more biological organisms. Human beings share this biological urge to reproduce and so are in some sense "designed" to be sexual beings; any species that does not have good reproductive equipment and a strong desire to use it will not last very long.

sexual reproduction: The creation of offspring through the combination of the genes of two parents.

Simpler organisms, such as amoeba, simply split in two, creating a pair genetically identical to the parent amoeba. More complex organisms, however, reproduce through **sexual reproduction**, where two parents each donate a **gamete**, or **germ cell**, which combine to create a new organism. The advantage of sexual reproduction is that mixing genetic material from both parents increases genetic diversity and avoids inbreeding bad traits into the species.

gamete or **germ cell:** A male or female reproductive cell; the spermatozoon or ovum.

The tiny germ cells from the male (sperm) and the much larger but also microscopic cell from the female (egg, or ovum) each contains half of the new person's **genes** and determine his or her sex, hair and eye color, general body shape, chances of having twins or triplets when they mature, the likely age at which they will reach puberty, and literally millions of other aspects of their physiology, development, and emotional nature. The genes direct the development of the genitals and the reproductive organs and set the biological clock running to trigger puberty and, for the female, menopause.

gene: A basic unit of genetic material that is carried in a particular point on a chromosome. A gene is made up of DNA.

chromosome: A threadlike structure in the nucleus (central body) of a cell that carries the genetic information of the cell.

Most cells in the human body contain forty-six **chromosomes** (twenty-three inherited from the mother and twenty-three from the father), arranged in twenty three pairs. Twenty-two of the pairs look almost identical and are referred to as autosomes; the

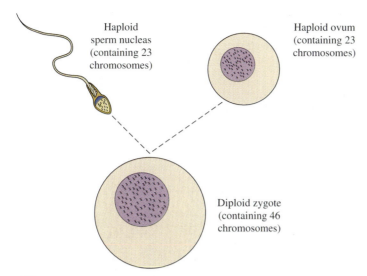

Figure **3.1**

The haploid cells from the father and the mother (the sperm and ovum) combine to create a cell with all forty-six chromosomes.

exception is the twenty-third pair, the **sex chromosomes**. The two sex chromosomes (which determine whether a person is male or female) are made up of an X chromosome donated by the mother through the ovum and either an X or Y chromosome donated by the father's sperm. In normal development, if the male contributes an X chromosome, the offspring will be female (XX), and if it is Y, the offspring will be male (XY). Therefore, it is the father's contribution that determines whether the child is a boy or girl.

sex chromosomes: The twenty-third pair of chromosomes, designated X and Y, that determines the genetic sex of an individual; in males the pair is XY and in females it is XX.

SEX TALK

QUESTION **3.1**   **Does the father's sperm really determine the sex of the child?**

Yes, but it is not that simple. The woman does have a role to play; there are differences between X and Y sperm (X are heavier and slower, but live longer; Y are faster but die more quickly), and a woman's vaginal environment or ovulation cycle may favor one or the other. But the sex of the child does depend on whether an X chromosome sperm or a Y chromosome sperm, donated by the father, joins with the ovum (which is always an X). The irony is that for many years, in many cultures, men routinely blamed and even divorced women who did not produce a child of a certain sex (usually a boy), when in fact the man's sperm had much more to do with it.

All the cells of the body (somatic cells), except gametes, contain all twenty-three pairs of chromosomes and are called diploid. But if a merging sperm and egg also had twenty-three pairs each, they would create an offspring with forty-six pairs, or ninety-two chromosomes in all! So gametes are haploid, meaning they contain half the number of chromosomes (twenty-three) as a somatic cell. During **fertilization**, a haploid sperm and haploid egg join to produce a diploid **zygote**, containing forty-six chromosomes, half from each parent (see Figure 3.1). The zygote can now undergo **mitosis**, reproducing its forty-six chromosomes as it grows.

fertilization: Penetration of the ovum by a spermatozoon and the subsequent union of the nuclei of the two cells.

zygote: The single cell resulting from the union of a male and female gamete; the fertilized ovum.

mitosis: The division of the nucleus of a cell into two new cells such that each new daughter cell has the same number and kind of chromosomes as the original parent.

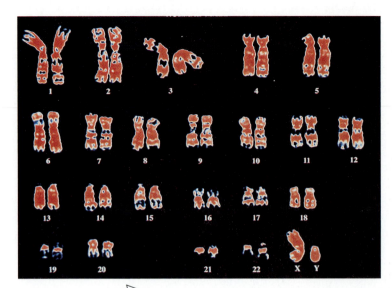

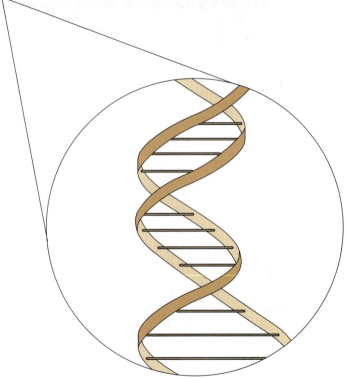

F i g u r e **3.2**

The twenty-three pairs of chromosomes in the normal male. Chromosomes contain DNA, the genetic blueprint for the developing human being. Note that in the last pair, one chromosome is smaller than the other; this shows that these are XY, and that these chromosomes come from a male.

The forty-six chromosomes are threadlike bodies made up of over 100,000 genes, each of which contains deoxyribonucleic acid (DNA) (see Figure 3.2). DNA acts as a blueprint for how every cell in the organism will develop. At first, the zygote reproduces exact copies of itself. Soon, however, the cells begin a process of differentiation. Differentiation is one of the great mysteries of human biology—all of a sudden, identical cells begin splitting into liver cells, brain cells, skin cells, and all the thousands of different kinds of cells in the body. Though the DNA determines the order in which cells differentiate and a cell's position may determine to some degree what type of cells it will become, still no one has yet been able to figure out how the cells "know" when to begin differentiating or how a particular cell is directed to become a nerve cell or a liver cell.

Whether the zygote will develop into a male or female is determined at the moment of conception, and part of the process of differentiation includes the development of our sexual characteristics. If sexual differentiation goes well, the zygote will develop into a fetus with typically male or typically female sexual characteristics. However, things can go wrong at any time during development, which can later influence the person's biological sex or the person's own sense of whether they are male or female.

Sexual Differentiation

A human embryo normally undergoes about nine months of **gestation**. At about four to six weeks, the first tissues that become the embryo's **gonads** develop. Sexual differentiation begins a week or two later, and is initiated by the sex chromosomes, which control at least four important aspects of sexual development: 1) the internal sexual organs (for example, whether the fetus develops ovaries or testicles); 2) the external sex organs (such as the penis or clitoris); 3) the hormonal environment of the embryo; and 4) the sexual differentiation of the brain (Money and Norman, 1987).

Internal Sex Organs

In the first few weeks of development, XX (female) and XY (male) embryos are identical. Around the fifth to sixth week the primitive gonads form, and at this point they can potentially develop into either **testes** or **ovaries**. The "default" development is female; without the specific masculinizing signals sent by the Y chromosome, the gonads will develop as female.*

In most males, the testes begin to evolve from the gonads by the seventh to eighth week following conception. In most females, the gonads begin to evolve into ovaries by the tenth or eleventh week. The primitive duct system, the **Müllerian** (female) **duct** or the **Wolffian** (male) **duct,** also appear at this time. Once the gonads have developed, they then hormonally control the development of the ducts into either the female or male reproductive system.

In female embryos, the lack of male hormones results in the regression and disappearance of the Wolffian ducts, and the Müllerian duct fuses to form the uterus and inner

gestation: The period of intrauterine fetal development.

gonads: The glands that produce gametes and hormones; the ovary in the female and the testis in the male.

testicles or **testes:** The male gonads, or sex glands, that rest in the scrotum and are responsible for the production of sperm and certain male sex hormones. The word "testes" comes from the Latin word "to testify," for Roman soldiers would put their hand over their genitals (presumably their most valued possessions) when they took an oath.

ovary: The female gonad, responsible for the production of ova and female sex hormones.

Müllerian duct: One of a pair of tubes in the embryo that will develop, in female embryos, into the Fallopian tubes, uterus, and part of the vagina.

Wolffian duct: One of a pair of structures in the embryo that, when exposed to testosterone, will develop into the male reproductive system.

---

* As this chapter is being written, new findings suggest that becoming female may not be the passive, "default" process it had been believed; a new gene has been discovered that can feminize a male even in the presence of testosterone. This indicates that certain genes may be able to override testosterone and actively stimulate female development.

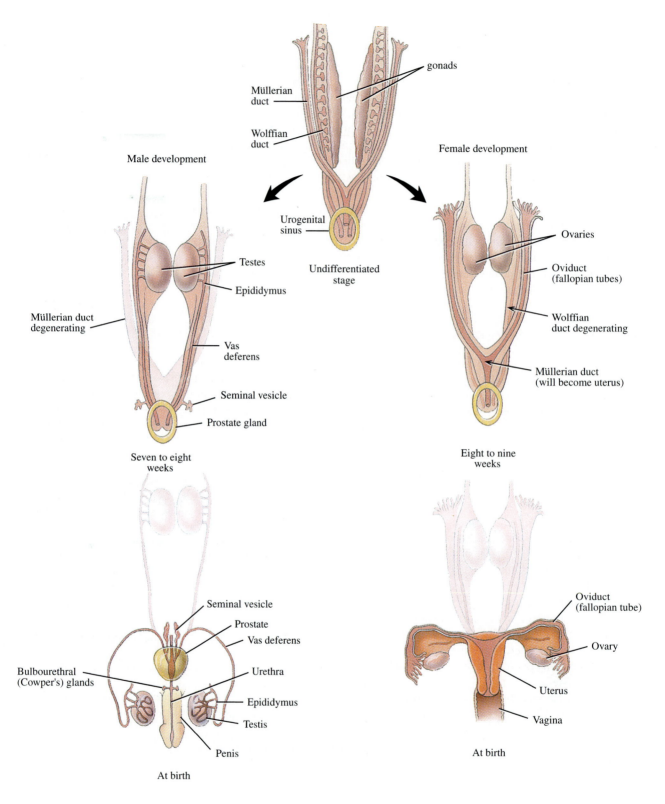

Figure **3.3**
Development of the male and female internal reproductive systems from the undifferentiated stage.

third of the vagina (see Figure 3.3). The unfused portion of the duct remains and develops into the two oviducts or Fallopian tubes (see The Female Sexual and Reproductive System below).

In the presence of a Y chromosome, the gonads develop into testes, which soon begin producing **Müllerian inhibiting factor** (MIF) and **testosterone**. MIF causes the Müllerian ducts to disappear during the third month, and testosterone stimulates the Wolffian duct to develop into the structures surrounding the testicles (see Male Sexual and Reproductive Organs below) (Picard et al., 1989). The body converts some testosterone into another androgen, called dihydrotestosterone (DHT), to stimulate the development of the male external sex organs.

External Sex Organs

External genitals follow a pattern similar to internal organs, except that male and female genitalia all develop from the same tissue. Male and female organs that began from the same prenatal tissue are called homologous.

Until the eighth week, the undifferentiated tissue from which the genitalia will develop exists as a mound of skin, or tubercle, beneath the umbilical cord (see Figure 3.4). In females, the external genitalia develop under the influence of female hormones produced by the placenta and by the mother. The genital tubercle develops into the clitoris, the labia minora, the vestibule, and the labia majora.

In males, the testes begin **androgen** secretion by the eighth or ninth week, which begins to stimulate the development of male genitalia. The genital tubercle elongates to form the penis, in which lies the **urethra**, culminating in an external opening called the urethral meatus. Part of the tubercle also fuses together to form the scrotum, where the testicles will ultimately rest when they descend (see Sex Facts 3.1).

Hormonal Development and Influences

Hormones play an important role in human development. Table 3.1 lists the various sex hormones and the roles they play. **Endocrine glands**, such as the gonads, secrete hormones directly into the bloodstream to be carried to the target organs. The ovaries, for example, produce the two major female hormones, **estrogen** and **progesterone**. Estrogen is an important influence in the development of female sexual characteristics

Müllerian inhibition factor: A hormone secreted in male embryos that prevents the Müllerian duct from developing into female reproductive organs.

testosterone: A male sex hormone (androgen) secreted by the Leydig cells of mature testes; controls the growth and development of male sex organs, secondary sex characteristics, spermatozoa, and body growth.

androgen: The general name for male hormones such as testosterone and androsterone.

urethra: The tube from the urinary bladder to the exterior of the body that conveys urine in females and urine and semen in males.

endocrine glands: Glands that secrete hormones into the blood.

estrogen: A general term for female sex hormones produced by the ovaries (and elsewhere) and concerned with development and maintenance of female reproductive structures and secondary sex characteristics, such as estradiol and estriol.

SEX *Facts*   3.1

Testicular Descent and Cryptorchidism

The testicles begin high in the abdomen near the kidneys, and, during the eighth and ninth months, are supposed to descend into the scrotum through the inguinal canal. Sometimes the testes fail to descend into the scrotum, a condition called cryptorchidism. (A similar condition can occur in males with an inguinal hernia, where the intestine enters the scrotum through the inguinal canal and may fill it completely, leaving no room for the testicles.)

The temperature of the abdomen is too high to support sperm production, so if the testes remain in the abdomen much past the age of five, the male will likely be infertile. Cryptorchid testes also carry a thirty to fifty times increased risk of testicular cancer. In most infants, cryptorchidism can be corrected by surgically relocating the testes in the scrotum.

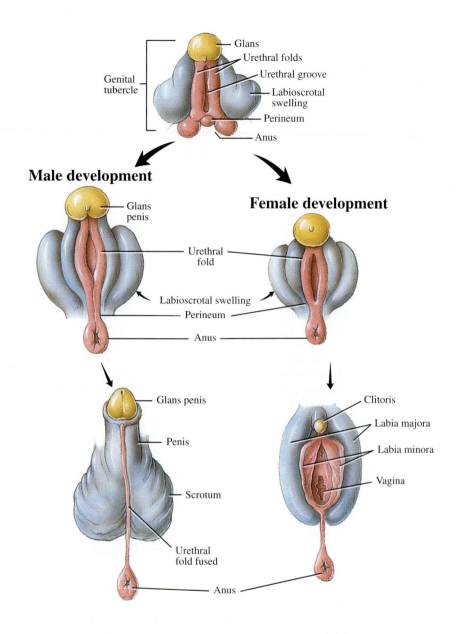

Figure **3.4**

Development of the male and female external genitalia from the undifferentiated genital tubercle.

progesterone: A female sex hormone produced by the ovaries that helps prepare the endometrium for implantation of a fertilized ovum and the mammary glands for milk secretion.

throughout fetal development and later life, while progesterone regulates the menstrual cycle and prepares the uterus for pregnancy. The testicles produce androgens, which are quite important to the male, since even a genetically male embryo will develop female characteristics if androgens are not secreted at the right time or if the fetus is insensitive to androgens (see Atypical Sexual Development on page 76).

Table **3.1**

THE SEX HORMONES

HORMONE	PURPOSES
Androgens	A group of hormones that control male sexual development and includes *testosterone* and *androsterone*. Androgens stimulate the development of male sex organs and secondary sex characteristics such as beard growth and a deepening voice. Testosterone also has an important role to play (in both sexes) in stimulating sexual desire. The testes produce androgens in men (stimulated by luteinizing hormone), though a little is also produced by the adrenal glands. Women's ovaries also produce a small amount of androgens, which helps stimulate sexual desire; too much production by the ovaries causes masculinization in women.
Estrogen	A group of hormones that control female sexual development and include estriol, estrone, and estradiol. Estrogen controls development of the female sex organs, the menstrual cycle, parts of pregnancy, and secondary sex characteristics such as breast development. The ovaries produce most of the estrogen in women, although the adrenal glands and the placenta also produce small amounts. Testes also produce a small amount of estrogen in men; if they produce too much, feminization may occur.
Progesterone	A female hormone secreted by the ovaries. Progesterone helps to prepare the lining of the uterus for the implantation of the fertilized ovum, to stimulate milk production in the breasts, and to maintain the placenta. Progesterone works in conjunction with estrogen to prepare the female reproductive system for pregnancy.
Gonadotropin-Releasing Hormone (GnRH)	GnRH is a hormone that affects the nervous system. It is produced in the hypothalamus of the brain and transported through the bloodstream to the pituitary gland. Gonadotropin means "gonad stimulating" and GnRH stimulates the pituitary to release hormones, such as follicle stimulating hormone (FSH) and luteinizing hormone (LH), which themselves induce the ovaries and testes (as well as other glands) to secrete their hormones.
Follicle-Stimulating Hormone (FSH)	A hormone released by the pituitary gland when stimulated by GnRH, which stimulates the ripening of the follicles in females and the formation of sperm in the male.
Luteinizing Hormone (LH)	A hormone released by the pituitary gland when stimulated by GnRH that stimulates ovulation, helps the formation of the corpus luteum in the ovary, and stimulates the release of other hormones, notably progesterone in the female and testosterone in the male. It is also called interstitial-cell-stimulating hormone (ICSH) because it stimulates the interstitial (Leydig) cells in the testes to produce testosterone.
Prolactin	A pituitary hormone that stimulates milk production after childbirth and also stimulates production of progesterone in the corpus luteum.
Oxytocin	A pituitary hormone that stimulates the ejection of milk from the breasts and causes increased contractions of the uterus during labor (it is often given to mothers to induce labor artificially).
Inhibin	A hormone produced by the sertoli cells of the testes that signals the anterior pituitary to decrease FSH production if the sperm count is getting too high.

Brain Differentiation

Most hormonal secretions are regulated by the brain, in particular by the hypothalamus, which is the body's single most important control center. Yet hormones also affect the development of the brain itself, both in the uterus and after birth. Male and female brains have different tasks to do and so undergo different development. For example, female brains control menstruation and therefore must signal the release of hormones in a monthly cycle, whereas male brains signal release continuously. With the brain, as with sexual organs, the presence of androgens during the appropriate critical stage of development may be the factor that programs the central nervous system to develop male sexual behaviors (Imperato-McGinley, 1979).

Atypical Sexual Differentiation

Prenatal development depends on carefully orchestrated developmental stages. At any stage, sex hormone irregularities, genetic abnormalities, or exposure of the fetus to inappropriate maternal hormones can result in atypical sexual differentiation. The result can be a child born with ambiguous genitals or with the external genitals of one sex while being genetically of the other sex.

Sex Chromosome Disorders

Sometimes, a person's sex chromosomes will include an extra X or Y chromosome or will be missing one. Though medical researchers have identified over seventy such abnormalities of the sex chromosomes, we will discuss the three most common. Table 3.2 lists these three sex chromosome abnormalities as well as some hormonal irregularities.

Klinefelter's syndrome, which occurs in about one in 700 live male births, occurs when an ovum containing an extra X chromosome is fertilized by a Y sperm (designated XXY), giving the offspring forty-seven chromosomes altogether. The Y chromosome triggers the development of male genitalia, but the extra X prevents them from developing fully. Men with Klinefelter's syndrome are infertile, have small testicles, low levels of testosterone, can have **gynecomastia**, and are tall with feminized body contours. These men often show low levels of sexual desire, probably due to the lack of testosterone. **Testosterone therapy**, especially if it is begun during adolescence, can enhance the development of **secondary sexual characteristics**.

Turner's syndrome is very uncommon, occuring in about one in 2,500 live female births. Turner's syndrome results from an ovum without any sex chromosome being fertilized by an X sperm (designated X0), which gives the offspring only forty-five chromosomes altogether (if an ovum without a chromosome is fertilized by a Y sperm and so contains no X sex chromosome, it will not survive). Though the external genitalia develop to look like a normal female's, the woman's ovaries do not develop fully, causing **amenhorrea** and infertility. In addition, Turner's syndrome causes short stature, immature breast development, and abnormalities of certain internal organs, as well as mental retardation. Therapeutic administration of estrogen and progesterone, especially during puberty, can help enhance some sexual characteristics and slightly increase height.

Klinefelter's syndrome: A genetic disorder in which there are three sex chromosomes, XXY, instead of two; characterized by small testes, low sperm production, breast enlargement, and absence of facial and body hair.

gynecomastia: Abnormal breast development in the male.

testosterone therapy: The use of testosterone to replace missing hormones in males with hormone disorders.

secondary sexual characteristics: The physical characteristics, other than the genitalia, that distinguish male from female; for example, breasts, sex-based distribution of body hair, voice pitch, body shape, and muscle development.

Turner's syndrome: A genetic disorder in females where there is only one X sex chromosome instead of two; characterized by lack of internal female sex organs, infertility, short stature, and mental retardation.

amenhorrea: The absence of menstruation.

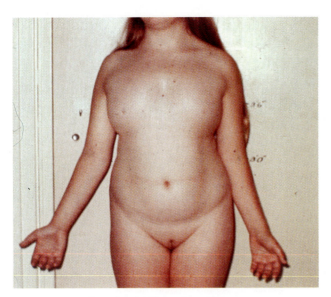

Female with Turner's syndrome.

XYY syndrome and **triple-X syndrome** are very rare disorders. As the names imply, these syndromes occur when a normal ovum is fertilized by a sperm that has two Y chromosomes or two X chromosomes or when an ovum with two X chromosomes is fertilized by a normal X sperm. The XYY individual may grow up as a normal male and the XXX as a normal female, and so often their unusual genetic status is not detected. However, many do suffer from slight mental retardation and some genital abnormalities, and often fertility is either decreased or they are infertile. There is no effective treatment for XYY or XXX syndrome.

Hormonal Irregularities

A **hermaphrodite** is born with fully formed ovaries *and* fully formed testes, which is very, very rare. Most people called hermaphrodites are actually **pseudohermaphrodites**, whose external genitals resemble to some degree the genitals of both sexes. Let us look at a few examples of pseudohermaphroditism.

Adrenogenital syndrome (AGS) occurs when a genetically normal female (XX) is exposed to large amounts of androgens during crucial stages of prenatal development. All women produce some androgens in their adrenal glands, and AGS may develop if the adrenal glands produce too much. A similar syndrome can also develop if the mother takes male hormones or drugs whose effects mimic male hormones (a number of pregnant women were prescribed such drugs in the 1950s, resulting in a whole group of AGS babies). Depending on the amount of male hormone, different degrees of masculinization can occur. Though the internal organs remain female and are not affected, the clitoris enlarges, even sometimes developing into a true penis containing a urethra. Underneath the penis, the two labia may fuse to resemble a scrotum, but it contains no testicles.

If the adrenal glands continue to produce excessive androgens, masculinization can continue throughout the AGS female's development. When a child is born with the genital traits of AGS today, a chromosomal analysis is usually performed, so AGS females

Table 3.2
SOME PRENATAL SEX DIFFERENTIATION SYNDROMES

SYNDROME	CHROMOSOMAL PATTERN	EXTERNAL GENITALS	INTERNAL STRUCTURES	DESCRIPTION	TREATMENT
Klinefelter's syndrome	47, XXY	Male	Male	Testes small, breasts may develop (gynecomastia), low testosterone levels, impotence and mental retardation are common, unusual body proportions, usually infertile.	Testosterone during adolescence may help with body shape and sex drive.
Turner's syndrome	45, X0	Female	Uterus and Oviducts	No menstruation or breast development, broad chest with widely spaced nipples, loose skin around the neck, nonfunctioning ovaries, infertility.	Androgens during puberty can help increase height, and estrogen and progesterone can help breast development and menstruation.
XYY syndrome	47, XYY	Male	Male	Likelihood of slight mental retardation, some genital irregularities, decreased fertility or infertility.	None.
Triple-X syndrome	47, XXX	Female	Female	Likelihood of slight mental retardation, decreased fertility or infertility.	None.
Androgenital syndrome (pseudohermaphroditism)	46, XX	Some male and some female traits	Female	Internal organs normal, external organs may be fused together. Fertility is unaffected.	Surgery to correct external genitals.
Androgen-insensitivity syndrome (AIS)	46, XY	Female (with a shortened vagina)	Male gonads in the abdomen	Usually raised female, breasts develop at puberty, but menstruation does not begin. Has shortened vagina. Has no internal sexual organs, and so remains sterile.	Surgery can lengthen vagina to accommodate penis for intercourse.

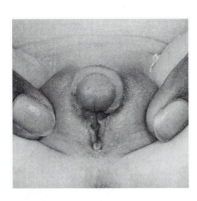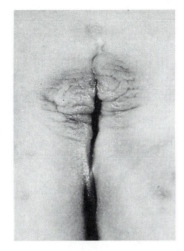

Genitalia of fetally androgenized female on the left and androgen-insensitivity male with feminized body on the right.

are typically diagnosed at birth. Corrective surgery can be done to form female genitalia and drugs can be prescribed to control adrenal output. Since the internal organs are unaffected, even pregnancy is possible in many AGS females.

Androgen-insensitivity syndrome (AIS) is, in some ways, the opposite of AGS. It is often first detected when a seemingly normal teenage girl fails to menstruate, and chromosomal analysis discovers that she is XY, a genetic male. In this syndrome, the gonads develop into testes and produce testosterone normally, but, for some reason, the AIS individual's cells cannot absorb it; in other words, the testosterone is there but has no effect on the body. Since the Wolffian ducts did not respond to testosterone during the sexual differentiation phase, no male genitalia developed, but since the gonads, which are male, did produce Müllerian inhibiting factor, the Müllerian ducts did not develop into normal female internal organs either. The AIS individual ends up with no internal reproductive organs except two testes, which remain in the abdomen producing testosterone that the body cannot use.

The AIS infant has the "default" female genitals, but since the Müllerian ducts also form the last third of the vagina, the infant has only a very shallow vagina. Usually the syndrome is undetected at birth, and the baby is brought up female. Since males do produce a small amount of estrogen, the breasts do develop, so it is only when the teen fails to menstruate that AIS is usually diagnosed. Surgery can then be initiated to lengthen the vagina to accommodate a penis for intercourse, though, without any female internal organs, the woman remains infertile. Even though they are genetically male, most AIS individuals seem fully feminized and live as women.

androgen-insensitivity syndrome (AIS): A condition where a genetic male's cells are insensitive to androgens, resulting in the development of female external genitalia (but no internal reproductive organs). People with AIS are raised as females.

THE FEMALE SEXUAL AND REPRODUCTIVE SYSTEM

Children are naturally curious about their genitals and spend a good deal of time touching and exploring them. However, they are often taught that this exploration is something to be ashamed of, that their genitals are dirty and forbidden. While boys genitals protrude, girls' are more hidden and recessed, and since girls are often discouraged from making a thorough self-examination, they tend to be less familiar with their genitals than boys are. This may be reinforced as females mature and are taught that menstruation is "dirty." These attitudes are even reflected in ads for "feminine hygiene" products, which suggest that the vagina is unsanitary and unpleasant to smell.

gynecologist: A physician who specializes in gynecology, the branch of medicine dealing with the study and treatment of disorders of the female reproductive system.

It is important for women (and men) to understand the structure of the female reproductive system, which is really a marvel of biological engineering. Women who have not done a thorough genital self-examination should do so, not only because it is an important part of the body to learn to appreciate, but also because any changes in genital appearance should be brought to the attention of a **gynecologist** or other

SEXUALITY *Today*   *3.1*

Female Genital Self-Examination

A genital self-examination can teach you about your body and make you more comfortable with your genitals. It is also important because many female health problems can be identified when changes are detected in the internal or external sexual organs; therefore, self-examination has an important health function as well.

Begin by examining the outside of your genitals; using a hand mirror can help. Using your fingers to spread open the labia majora, try to identify the other external structures—the labia minora, the prepuce, the introitus (opening) of the vagina, and the urethral opening. Look at the way your genitals look while sitting, lying down, standing up, squatting. Feel the different textures of each part of the vagina, and look carefully at the coloration and size of the tissues you can see. Both coloration and size can change with sexual arousal, but such changes are temporary and the genitals should return to normal within a couple of hours after sexual activity. Any changes over time in color, firmness, or shape of the genitals should be brought to the attention of a health professional.

If it is not uncomfortable, you may want to move

back the prepuce, or hood, over the clitoris and try to see the clitoral glans. Though the clitoris is easier to see when erect, note how it fits beneath the prepuce. Note also if there is any whitish material beneath the prepuce; fluids can accumulate and solidify there, and so you should gently clean beneath the prepuce regularly.

Don't be afraid to put your fingers inside your vagina and feel around. You should be able to feel the pubic bone in the front inside part of your vagina. It is slightly behind the pubic bone that the G-Spot is supposed to be, but it is hard for most women to stimulate the G-Spot with their own fingers. Squat and press down with your stomach muscles as you push your fingers deeply in the vagina, and you may be able to feel your cervix at the top of the vagina, which feels a little like the tip of your nose. Note how it feels to touch the cervix (some women have a slightly uncomfortable feeling when their cervix is touched). Feeling comfortable inserting your fingers into your vagina will also help you if you choose a diaphragm, contraceptive sponge, or cervical cap as your form of contraception, all of which must be inserted deep within the vagina at the cervix (see Chapter 11).

health care provider. See Sexuality Today 3.1 for instructions on performing a genital self-exam.

External Sex Organs

Though many people refer to the female's external sex organs collectively as the "vagina," that is technically incorrect; a more accurate term for the whole region is **vulva,** or **pudendum**. The vulva, as we will see, is made up of the mons veneris, the labia majora and labia minora, the vestibule, the perineum, and the clitoris (Figure 3.5). Though the vagina does open into the vulva, it is mainly an internal sex organ and will be discussed in the next section.

Mons Veneris

The fatty cushion resting over the front surface of the pubic bone is called the **mons veneris** or **mons pubis**. The mons veneris becomes covered with pubic hair after puberty, and though it is considered a stimulating place to caress during lovemaking, it serves largely as a protective cushion for the genitals, especially during sexual intercourse.

vulva: Literally meaning "covering," the collective designation for the external genitalia of the female; also called the pudendum.

pudendum: Derived from a Latin word meaning "that about which one should have modesty," a name for the female genitalia.

mons veneris or **mons pubis:** Literally Latin for "mountain of Venus" (Venus was the Roman goddess of love and beauty), the mound of fatty tissue over the female pubic bone, also called mons pubis, meaning "pubic mound."

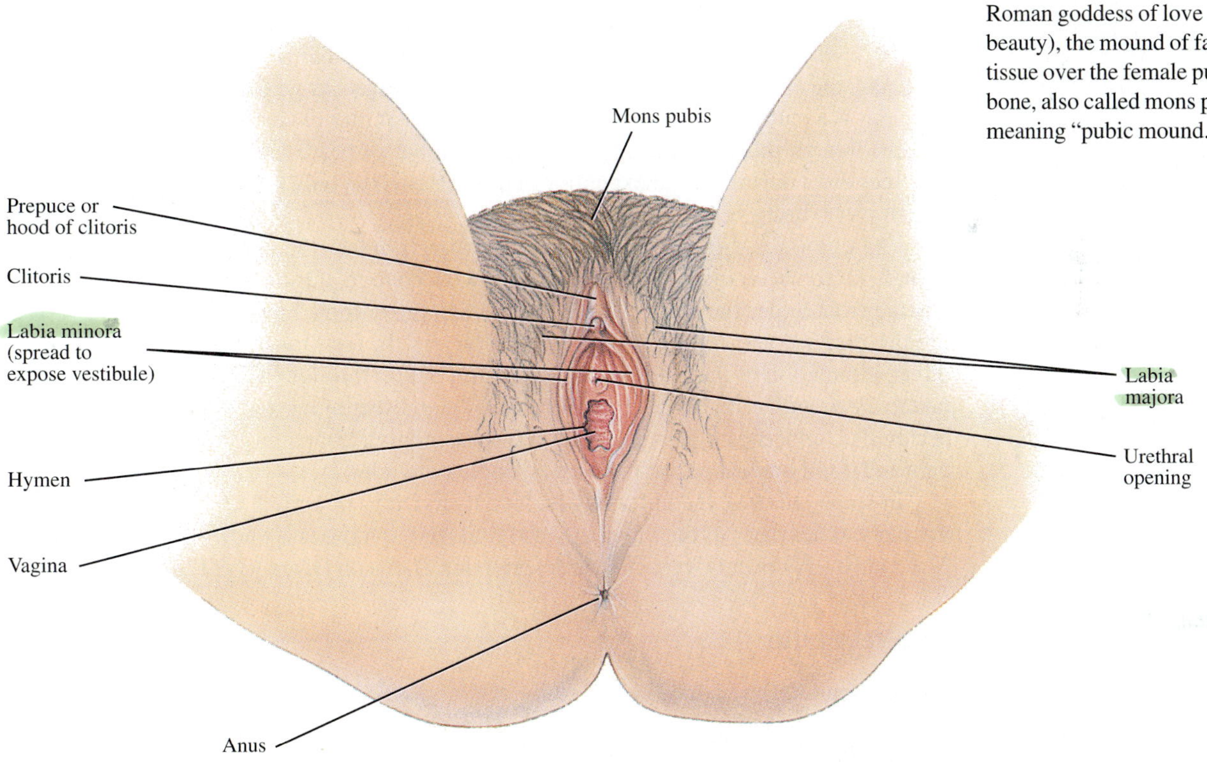

Prepuce or hood of clitoris

Clitoris

Labia minora (spread to expose vestibule)

Hymen

Vagina

Anus

Mons pubis

Labia majora

Urethral opening

Figure 3.5

The external genital structures of the mature female.

Labia Majora

The labia majora ("outer lips") are two longitudinal folds of fatty tissue that extend from the mons, frame the rest of the female genitalia, and meet at the perineum. The skin of the outer labia majora is pigmented and covered with hair, while the inner surface is hairless and contains sebaceous (oil) glands. During sexual excitement, the labia majora fill with blood and engorge, which makes the entire pubic region seem to swell. Since the labia majora is homologous to the male scrotum, the sensation of caressing it may be similar to that of caressing the scrotum for a male.

Labia Minora

The labia minora ("inner lips") are two smaller red skin folds situated between the labia majora and the vestibule (see below). They are generally more delicate, shorter, and thinner than the labia majora and join at the clitoris to form the prepuce, the "hood" over the clitoris. The labia minora contain no hair follicles, although they are rich in sebaceous glands. They also contain some erectile tissue and serve to protect the vagina and urethra. The labia minora can differ considerably in appearance in different women.

The Clitoris

clitoris: An erectile organ of the female located under the prepuce; it is an organ of sexual pleasure and is homologous to the male penis.

smegma: The collected products of sweat and oil glands that can accumulate under the clitoral hood or penile foreskin in cases of insufficient cleanliness.

circumcision: Surgical removal of the foreskin (prepuce), the fold of skin over the glans penis, or, in some societies, the removal of the clitoris in women.

infibulation: The ritual removal of the clitoris, prepuce, and labia and the sewing together of the vestibule. Practiced in many African societies, there are now movements to try to eliminate the practice.

The **clitoris** is a small cylindrical erectile tissue located under the prepuce, made up of the glans, which is the exposed portion, the shaft, and the internal crura. Homologous to the penis, the clitoris is richly supplied with blood vessels as well as nerve endings, and the glans is a particularly sensitive receptor and transmitter of sexual stimuli. In fact, the clitoris, though much smaller, has the same number of nerve endings as the penis and becomes erect during sexual excitation. The clitoris is the only human organ whose sole function is to bring sexual pleasure.

The clitoris is difficult to see in many women unless the prepuce is pulled back, though in some women the clitoris may swell enough during sexual excitement to emerge from under the prepuce. It is easy to feel the clitoris, however, by gently grasping the prepuce and rolling it between the fingers. In fact, most women do not enjoy direct stimulation of the clitoris and prefer stimulation through the prepuce. It is important to clean under the prepuce, for sebaceous gland secretions and other secretions can accumulate underneath in a material known as **smegma**. Smegma can harden and cause pain and if left uncleaned can produce an unpleasant odor.

In some cultures, the clitoris is removed surgically in a ritual **circumcision**, while in others, other parts of the vulva are also removed in a process known as **infibulation**. The controversy over this practice is described in Focus on Diversity 3.1.

The Vestibule

The vestibule is the name for the entire region between the labia minora and can be clearly seen when the labia are held apart. The vestibule contains the opening of the urethra and the vagina and the ducts of Bartholin's glands.

The Urethral Meatus. The opening, or meatus, to the urethra lies between the vagina and the clitoris. The urethra, which brings urine from the bladder to be excreted, is much shorter in women than in men, where it goes through the penis.

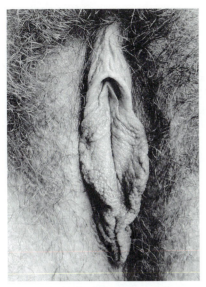 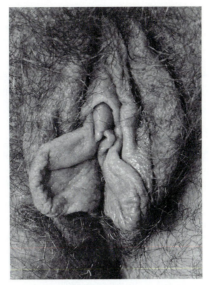 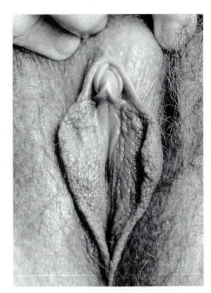

The female genitalia come in a variety of shapes and pigmentations, and pubic hair can be thick or thin, dark or light.

The Introitus and the Hymen.   The entrance, or **introitus**, of the vagina also lies in the vestibule. The introitus is usually covered at birth by a fold of tissue known as the **hymen** (see Figure 3.6). The hymen varies in thickness and extent and is sometimes absent. The center of the hymen is usually perforated, and it is through this perforation that the menstrual flow leaves the vagina and that a tampon is inserted. If the hymen is intact it will usually rupture easily and tear at several points during the first coitus, often accompanied by a small amount of blood. If the woman is sexually excited and well lubricated, the rupture of the hymen usually does not cause more than a brief moment's discomfort. In rare cases a woman has an **imperforate hymen**, which is usually detected because her menstrual flow is blocked. A simple surgical procedure can open the imperforate hymen.

An intact hymen has been a symbol of "purity" throughout history, a sign that a woman has not had sexual intercourse. In reality, many activities can shred the hymen, including vigorous exercise, horseback or bike riding, masturbation, or the insertion of tampons or other objects into the vagina. Still, in many cultures during many periods in history, the absence of blood-stained sheets on the wedding night was enough to condemn a woman as "wanton" (promiscuous), and some knowing mothers encouraged their newlywed daughters to have a little vial of blood from a chicken or other animal to pour on the sheet of their bridal bed, just in case.

Bartholin's Glands.   The "greater vestibular glands," or **Bartholin's glands**, are bean-shaped glands whose ducts empty into the vestibule in the middle of the labia minora (see Figure 3.5). Historically, Bartholin's glands have been presumed to provide lubrication for penile penetration of the vagina; however they do not actually secrete enough lubrication for intercourse. It is also thought that they might be responsible for creating a genital scent.

introitus: Any entrance to a body cavity, such as the vagina.

hymen: A thin fold of vascularized mucous membrane at the vaginal orifice.

imperforate hymen: An abnormally closed hymen that usually does not allow exit to menstrual fluid.

Bartholin's glands: A pair of glands on either side of the vaginal orifice that open by a duct into the space between the hymen and the labia minora; also called greater vestibular glands.

Focus on Diversity

3.1

Female Circumcision and Infibulation

In many parts of Africa and in a few other countries around the world, female circumcision and infibulation are practiced. These practices have been performed throughout history to distinguish "respectable" women from prostitutes or slaves. Many cultures believe that without removing the source of female pleasure, women will become promiscuous or cheat on their husbands.

The procedure is usually done between the ages of four and eight years old, though in some cultures it is later. The procedure is done without anesthesia or antiseptic. In circumcision, the prepuce and clitoris are cut off with a knife, while in infibulation the labia minora and majora are also removed, and the remaining tissue is sewn together:

> *The remaining outer edges of the labia majora are then brought together so that when the wound has healed they are fused so as to leave only a pinhole-sized opening. The resultant infibulation is, in effect, an artificially created chastity belt of thick, fibrous scar tissue. Urination and menstruation must thereafter be accomplished through this remaining pinhole-sized aperture.*
>
> *Lightfoot-Klein (1989:378)*

The tighter the girl's infibulation, the higher the bride price will be for her. Estimates are that 85–114 million women, mostly Muslim, have undergone the procedure (Kaplan 1993).

The day that a woman is circumcised is thought to be the most important day in a woman's life, and it is accompanied in most cultures by rituals. Since menstruation is often very difficult through the pinhole opening, marriage usually takes place soon after menstruation begins. Marital penetration of the infibulation can take anywhere from three to four days to several months, and, in 15% of cases, men are unable to penetrate their wives at all. Often penetration results in severe pain, possible hemorrhaging or infection, which may lead to death. Anal intercourse is common in some of these cultures, since the vagina may not be penetrable.

Recently, there has been controversy over what Americans and others should do to try and discourage this practice. Some African American women's groups, the National Organization of Women, and some African groups are trying to end the practice through education and legislation (Ragab, 1993). Female circumcision is actually illegal in many of the countries where it is practiced. But it is hard to end a deeply ingrained social practice, especially among the rural and tribal peoples who have been performing the ritual for many centuries. Some argue that those outside of Africa have no right to comment on a religious ritual, just as Africans have no right to oppose the circumcision of American men. However, African governments and other groups are beginning to make some headway in decreasing the prevalence of this practice.

The Perineum

The perineum is the tissue between the vagina and the anus. During childbirth, the baby can stretch the perineum and even tear it, so an incision is often made, called an **episiotomy**, to allow more room for the baby's head to emerge (See Chapter 11).

episiotomy: A cut made with surgical scissors to avoid tearing of the perineum at the end of the second stage of labor.

Internal Sex Organs

The female's internal sex organs include the vagina, the uterus, the Fallopian tubes, and the ovaries.

Variations in the Hymen

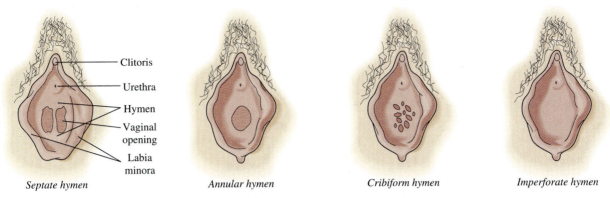

Septate hymen   Annular hymen   Cribiform hymen   Imperforate hymen

F i g u r e 3.6
Hymens can have different types of perforations, including being imperforate.

The Vagina

The **vagina** is a thin-walled tube extending from the cervix of the uterus to the external genitalia and serves as the female organ of intercourse, a passageway for the arriving sperm, and a canal through which menstrual fluid and babies can pass from the uterus. It is tilted toward the back in most women and so forms a ninety-degree angle with the uterus, which is commonly tilted forward (see Figure 3.7). The vagina is approximately four inches in length when relaxed but contains numerous folds that help it expand somewhat like an accordion. The vagina can expand to accommodate a penis during intercourse and can stretch four to five times its normal size during childbirth.

vagina: A muscular tubular organ, situated between the urinary bladder and the rectum in the female, that leads from the uterus to the vestibule and is used for sexual intercourse and the passage of the newborn from the uterus.

SEX TALK

QUESTION **3.2**   **My girlfriend told my that my penis is too large for her vagina and that it causes her pain during intercourse. How far can the vagina expand?**

Although it is true that the vagina expands and lengthens during sexual arousal, not every vagina expands to the same degree. If a man's penis is very large, it can bump against the woman's cervix during thrusting which can cause discomfort. In such cases it is particularly important to make sure the woman is fully aroused before attempting penetration and to try a variety of positions to find which is most comfortable for her. The female superior position or the rear entry positions (see Chapter 10) may help her control the depth of penetration. Either partner's hand around the base of the penis (depending on the position) may also prevent full penetration, as will some devices such as "cock rings," which are sold through adult catalogues or in adult stores. If the woman's pain continues, she should consult with her gynecologist to rule out a physiological problem and to get more advice and information. And remember—there are other sexual behaviors that bring pleasure besides intercourse.

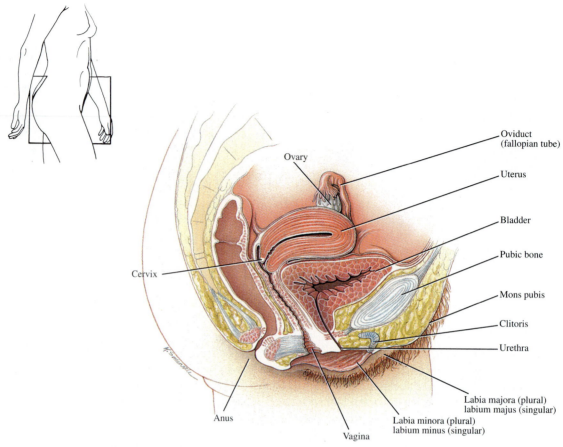

F i g u r e 3.7
Above, opposite: the female internal reproductive system.

The vagina does not itself contain glands but lubricates through small openings on the vaginal walls during engorgement, almost as if the vagina is sweating, and by mucus produced from glands on the cervix. While the first third of the vaginal tube is well endowed with nerve endings, the inner two-thirds are practically without tactile sensation; in fact, minor surgery can be done on the inner part of the vagina without anesthesia.

Grafenberg Spot (G-Spot): A controversial structure that is said to lie on the anterior (front) wall of the vagina and that is reputed to be a seat of sexual pleasure when stimulated.

The Grafenberg Spot and Female Ejaculation. The **Grafenberg spot (G-spot)** and female ejaculation are two controversial issues in the field of human sexuality. The G-Spot, first described by Grafenberg in 1950, is a spot about the size of a dime or quarter in the lower third of the front part of the vagina and is particularly sensitive to stimulation. The G-Spot is found about two or three inches up the anterior (front, or stomach) side of the vagina, just past the pubic bone. There is some controversy over whether this spot is a separate physiological entity, with some arguing that the entire anterior wall (and even parts of the posterior wall) of the vagina is generally sensitive (Alzate and Moch, 1986). Others argue that the G-spot is homologous to the male prostate.

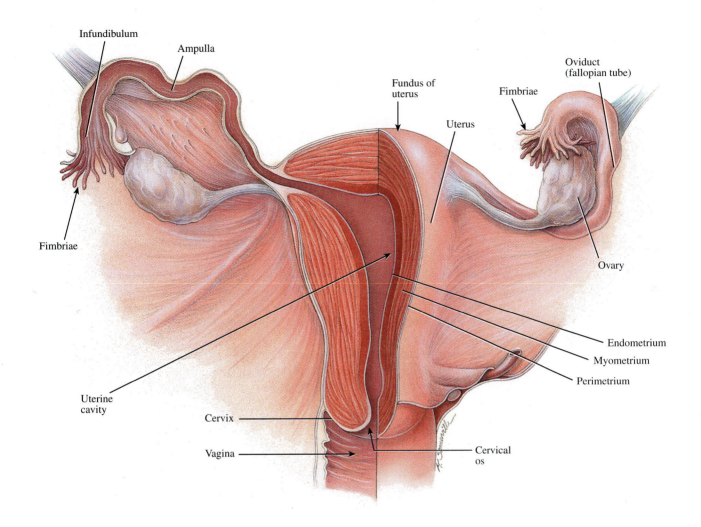

Stimulating the G-Spot causes pleasant vaginal sensation in some women and can result in powerful orgasms accompanied by the forceful expulsion of fluid (female ejaculation). Some suggest that all women have the capacity to ejaculate and that female ejaculation and orgasm are separate processes (Sevely and Bennett, 1978). Women may ejaculate up to four ounces of fluid, which may come from the Skenes glands on either side of the urethra (Heath, 1984); however, some researchers argue that female ejaculate is chemically indistinguishable from urine (Alzate, 1985). (See Special Focus 6 for an explanation of how to find the G-Spot on yourself or your partner.)

The Uterus

The **uterus** is a thick walled, hollow, muscular organ in the pelvis sandwiched between the bladder in front and the rectum behind. It is approximately the shape of an inverted

uterus: The hollow muscular organ in females that is the site of menstruation, implantation of the fertilized ovum, and labor; also called the womb.

cervix: The donut-shaped bottom part of the uterus that protrudes into the top of the vagina and contains an opening (os) through which sperm enter and menstrual fluid and babies exit the uterus.

perimetrium: The outer wall of the uterus.

myometrium: The smooth muscle layer of the uterus.

endometrium: The mucous membrane lining the uterus.

os: The opening of the cervix that allows passage between the vagina and the uterus.

pear, with a dome-shaped top (fundus), a hollow body, and the donut-shaped **cervix** at the bottom. The uterus provides a path for sperm to reach the ovum, undergoes a cycle of change every month that leads to menstruation, nourishes and protects the fetus during gestation, and provides the contractions for expulsion of the mature fetus during labor. The uterus is about three inches long and flares to about two inches wide, but it increases greatly in size and weight during and after a pregnancy and atrophies after menopause.

The uterine wall is about one inch thick and is made up of three layers. The outer layer, or **perimetrium**, is part of the tissue that covers most abdominal organs. The muscular layer of the uterus, the **myometrium**, contracts to expel menstrual fluid and to push the fetus out of the womb during delivery. The inner layer of the uterus, the **endometrium**, responds to fluctuating hormonal levels, and its outer portion is shed with each menstrual cycle (Tortora and Grabowski, 1993).

Cervix. The cervix is the lower portion of the uterus that contains the opening, or **os**, leading into the body of the uterus. It is through the os that menstrual fluid flows out of the uterus and that sperm gain entrance. Glands of the cervix secrete mucus with varying properties during the monthly cycle: during ovulation, the mucus helps sperm transport through the os, and during infertile periods, it can block the sperm from entering. During childbirth, the cevix softens and the os dilates to allow the baby to pass through.

The cervix can be seen with a mirror during a pelvic exam, and women should not hesitate to ask their gynecologist or other medical professional to show it to them. The cervix can also be felt at the top end of the vagina (see Sexuality Today 3.1, above).

The Fallopian Tubes

Fallopian tubes: The ducts that transport ova from the ovary to the uterus; also called oviducts.

oviducts: See **Fallopian tubes.**

infundibulum: The funnel- or trumpet-shaped, open end of the Fallopian tube.

fimbria: The branched, fingerlike border at the end of each Fallopian tube.

Fallopian tubes, also called **oviducts**, are four-inch long trumpet-shaped tubes that extend laterally from the sides of the uterus. From the side of the uterus, the tube expands into an ampulla, or widening, which curves around to a trumpet-shaped end, the **infundibulum**. The infundibulum has fingerlike projections that curl around the ovary, poised to accept ova when they are released.

Once a month an ovary releases an ovum that is swept into the Fallopian tube by the waving action of the **fimbriae**. The fimbriae sense the chemical messages released from the ovary that signal the release of the ovum and begin a series of muscular contractions to help move the ovum down the tube. If the Fallopian tube is long and flexible, it may even be able to catch the released ovum from the opposite ovary; some women with a single active ovary on one side and a single functioning Fallopian tube on the other have been known to get pregnant (Nilsson, 1990).

The inner surface of the Fallopian tubes are covered by hairlike projections whose constant beating action creates a current along which the ovum is conducted toward the uterus. The entire transit time from ovulation until arrival inside the uterus is normally about three days. Fertilization of ova usually takes place in the ampulla because, after the first twelve to twenty-four hours, post-ovulation fertilization is no longer possible. Occasionally, the fertilized ovum implants in the Fallopian tube instead of the uterus, causing a potentially dangerous *ectopic pregnancy* (see Chapter 10).

The Ovaries

The mature ovary is a light gray structure most commonly described as the size and shape of a large almond shell. With age, the ovaries become smaller and firmer, and after menopause they become difficult for gynecologists to feel. The ovaries have a dual responsibility—to produce ova and to secrete hormones.

The ovary is the repository of oocytes, also known as ova, or eggs, in the female. A women is born with 200,000 ova in each ovary, each sitting in its own primary follicle. The primary follicle contains an immature ovum surrounded by a thin layer of follicular cells. Follicle stimulating hormone (FSH) and luteinizing hormone (LH) are released in sequence by the pituitary gland during each menstrual cycle, causing about twenty primary follicles at a time to begin maturing. Usually only one follicle finishes maturing each month, which is then termed a **secondary follicle**, containing a secondary oocyte. At ovulation, the secondary follicle bursts, and the ovum begins its journey down the Fallopian tube. The surface of a mature ovary is thus usually pitted and scarred at sites of previous ovulations. An average woman will produce about 450 mature ova in her lifetime.

Ovulation can occur each month from either the right or left ovary. No one knows why one or the other ovary releases an ovum any given month; sometimes they take turns, while at other times they do not. It seems to be mostly a matter of chance. If one ovary is removed, however, the other ovary will often ovulate every month (Nilsson, 1990).

The ovaries are also the female's most important producer of female sex hormones, such as estrogen, which we will discuss below.

Other Sexual Organs

The organs involved with reproduction are not the only organs involved in a woman's sex life. The secondary sex characteristics of a woman also contribute to sexual pleasure. While most people consider the breast a sexual part of the body, other erogenous zones may not be as obvious.

The Breasts

Breasts, or mammary glands, are modified sweat glands that produce milk to nourish a newborn child. The breasts contain fatty tissue and milk-producing glands and are capped by a **nipple** surrounded by a round, pigmented area called the areola. The breast contains between fifteen and twenty lobes, made up of a number of compartments that contain alveoli, the milk-secreting glands. Alveoli empty into **secondary tubules**, which in turn pass the milk into the **mammary ducts** and then into the **lactiferous sinuses** where the milk is stored until the **lactiferous ducts** release it from the nipple (Figure 3.8). When **lactation** begins, infant suckling stimulates the posterior pituitary gland to release **prolactin**,which signals milk synthesis, and **oxytocin**, which allows the milk to be ejected.

SEX TALK

QUESTION **3.3** **Does a woman's breast size have anything to do with how much milk she can produce?**

secondary follicle: The name of the site in the ovary where the matured ovum sits before being released.

nipple: A pigmented, wrinkled protuberance on the surface of the breast that contains ducts for the release of milk.

secondary tubules: The tubes that transport milk from the alveoli of the breast to the mammary ducts.

mammary ducts: The tube that deposits the milk into the lactiferous sinuses.

lactiferous sinuses: The area of the breast where milk is stored for eventual secretion from the nipple.

lactiferous ducts: The openings in the nipple through which milk is secreted.

lactation: The collective name for milk creation, secretion, and ejection from the nipple by the mammary glands.

prolactin: A hormone secreted by the pituitary gland that initiates and maintains milk secretion by the mammary glands.

oxytocin: A hormone secreted by the hypothalamus that stimulates contraction of both the uterus for delivery of the newborn and the ducts of mammary glands for the secretion of milk from the nipple.

No. The breast is made up mostly of fatty tissue, which does not produce milk. A small-breasted woman usually just has less fat and can have as many or more milk-producing glands as a large-breasted woman.

Most people see the breasts as an erogenous zone and include stimulation of the breasts in sexual arousal and masturbation. Some women can even experience orgasm from breast and nipple stimulation alone.

Many women in American society are uncomfortable about the size and shape of their breasts. Since breasts are a constant source of attention in our society and are considered an important part of a woman's attractiveness, women may worry that their breasts are unattractive, too small, or too large. Yet the ideal breast differs in other cultures. For example, large breasts are valued in the United States, and so over 80% of breast surgeries are to increase the size of the bust. In France, however, breast attractiveness is not related to size, and the majority of surgical alterations of the breasts in France are to *decrease* their size!

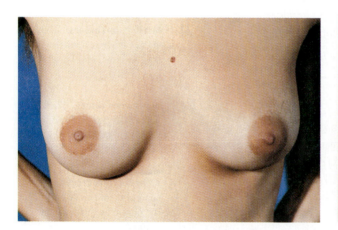
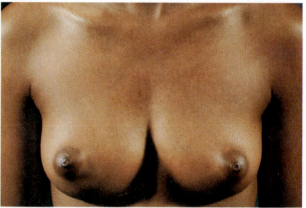
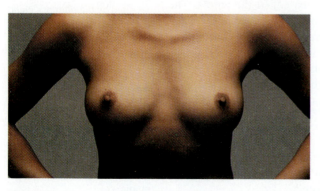
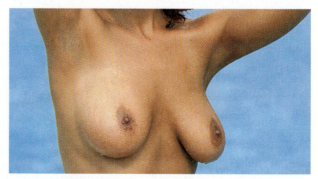

The female breast is mostly fatty tissue and can take various shapes and come in different sizes.

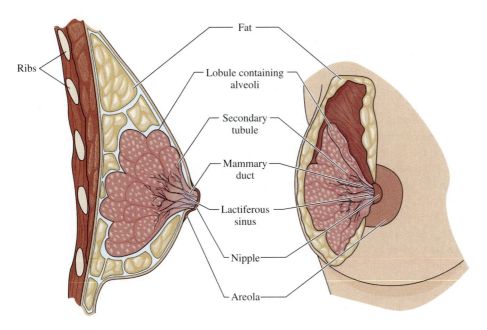

Fat

Ribs

Lobule containing
alveoli

Secondary
tubule

Mammary
duct

Lactiferous
sinus

Nipple

Areola

Figure **3.8**
The female breast.

Other Erogenous Zones

There are many other erogenous zones on the body that can be considered part of a woman (or man's) sexual organ system. In fact, the largest sexual organ of all is the skin, and there is no part of it that cannot be arousing if caressed in the right way at the right time during lovemaking. Some areas, such as the lips or the ears, are commonly used to increase sexual pleasure, while others, such as the back of the knee, the armpit, or the base of the neck, for example, may be arousing to certain people. Some people find stimulation of the anus, or anal intercourse, extremely erotic, while others may not. Of course, the most important sexual organ is one that you can only stimulate indirectly—the brain.

The Female Maturation Cycle

Female Puberty*

After birth, the female's sexual development progresses slowly until puberty. Puberty lasts from three to five years on average, and the first stirrings begin at about the age

---

* See Chapter 4, Childhood and Adolescence, for a discussion of the psychological and physiological changes of female puberty.

pituitary gland: A small endocrine gland lying beneath the hypothalamus, nicknamed the "master gland" because of its importance in hormonal secretion.

of eight in girls but can begin as late as fourteen or fifteen. No one really knows how the body knows its own age or that it is time for puberty to begin. Somehow the girl's internal clock signals the **pituitary gland** to begin secreting the hormones FSH and LH, which stimulate the ovaries to produce estrogen while the girl sleeps. Between the ages of eleven and fourteen, FSH and LH levels begin to increase during the day as well.

As puberty continues, the ovaries, in response to stimulation by the pituitary gland, begin to release more and more estrogen into the circulatory system. Estrogen is responsible for the development and maturation of female primary and secondary sexual characteristics. Under its influence, the Fallopian tubes, the uterus, and the vagina all mature and increase in size. The breasts also begin to develop as fat deposits increase and the elaborate duct system develops. The pelvis broadens and changes from a narrow funnellike outlet to a broad oval outlet, flaring the hips. The skin remains soft and smooth under estrogen's influence, fat cells increase in number in the buttocks and thighs, and pubic hair develops. The growing end of certain longer bones in the body, which are responsible for height, fuse with the bone shaft and growth stops. (In the absence of estrogen, females usually grow several inches taller than average.)

The changes that accompany puberty prepare the woman for mature sexuality, pregnancy, and childbirth. At some point during puberty, usually at about the age of eleven or twelve, the woman will begin to ovulate. Most women are unable to feel any internal signs during ovulation. In a few women, however, a slight pain or sensation accompanies ovulation, referred to as **mittelschmerz**. The pain may result from a transitory irritation caused by the small amount of blood and fluid released at the site of the ruptured follicle.

mittelschmerz: German for "middle pain," a pain in the abdomen or pelvis that some women feel that indicates ovulation has occurred.

menarche: The start of menstrual cycling, usually during early puberty.

The beginning of ovulation closely corresponds to **menarche** in most girls, though some may begin menstruating a few months before their first ovulation, while others may ovulate a few times before their first full menstrual cycle. In some cultures in the past, as soon as a girl reached menarche she was considered ready to marry and begin bearing children. In our culture the age of menarche has been steadily falling, and most people believe that there is a difference between being physiologically capable of bearing children and being psychologically ready for sexual intercourse and childbearing (see Sex Facts 3.2)

S E X *F a c t s*   *3.2*

Age of Menarche

The average age of menarche in the United States is about 12.8 years old, but the age has been steadily decreasing each decade. One hundred years ago, the average age of first menstruation was about sixteen years old. It has been estimated that the average age of menarche has decreased by four months every decade since 1830 (Welch, 1992). In other, less developed countries, the age of menarche is later.

It is hard to say exactly why this is true, but better nutrition and environmental changes may be partially responsible. Even as menarche has been getting earlier, menopause has been getting later, which means that the fertile range of modern women is many years greater than in the last century. Menopause used to occur, on average, in a woman's middle forties, but now most women do not experience menopause until their late forties or early fifties.

Menstruation

The menstrual cycle lasts from twenty-four to thirty-five days, but the average is twenty-eight. The cycle can be divided into four general phases: the follicular phase, ovulation, the luteal phase, and the menstrual phase.

SEX TALK

QUESTION **3.4** **When I started college, I began having very severe menstrual cramps—often to the point of nausea, fatigue, and backache. What causes bad cramps and how can I reduce them?**

Menstrual cramps are usually caused by prostaglandins, which stimulate the uterus to contract and expel the endometrial lining during menstruation. The uterine muscles are powerful (they must push the infant out at birth), and the menstrual contractions can be strong and are sometimes quite painful. However, there are many things that can make the cramps worse. Poor eating habits, an increase in stress, alcohol use, insufficient sleep, and a lack of exercise can aggravate the problem. Reducing salt, sugar, and caffeine intake, moderate exercise, warm baths, and gentle massage of the lower back sometimes help. Orgasm, either through masturbation or with a partner, also helps relieve menstrual cramps in many women.

The *follicular phase* begins after the last menstruation has been completed and lasts anywhere from six to thirteen days. Only a thin layer of endometrial cells remains from the last menstruation. As the follicles in the ovaries begin to ripen with the next cycle's ova, estrogen released by the ovaries stimulates regrowth of the endometrium's outer layer to about two to five millimeters thick.

During the *ovulation phase,* an ovum is released, usually about the fourteenth day of the cycle. The particulars of ovulation are described in the section on the ovaries and Fallopian tubes, above.

The third phase is the *luteal phase.* Immediately following ovulation, a small, pouchlike gland, the **corpus luteum**, forms on the ovary. The corpus luteum secretes additional progesterone and estrogen for ten to twelve days, which cause further growth of the cells in the endometrium and increases the blood supply to the lining of the uterus. The endometrium reaches a thickness of four to six millimeters during this stage (about a quarter of an inch), in readiness to receive and nourish a fertilized egg. If fertilization does not occur, however, the high levels of progesterone and estrogen signal the hypothalamus to decrease LH and other hormone production. The corpus luteum begins to degenerate as LH levels decline. Approximately two days before the end of the normal cycle, the secretion of estrogen and progesterone decreases sharply as the corpus luteum becomes inactive, and the menstrual stage begins.

In the *menstrual stage,* the endometrial cells shrink and slough off. The uterus begins to contract in an effort to expel the dead tissue along with a small quantity of blood (it is these contractions that cause menstrual cramps, which can be painful in some women). During menstruation, approximately thirty-five milliliters of blood, thirty-five milliliters of fluid, some mucus, and the lining of the uterus (about four tablespoons of fluid in all) are expelled from the uterine cavity through the cervical os and ultimately the vagina. (If a woman is using oral contraceptives, the amount may be significantly smaller; see Chapter 11.) This menstrual flow is called **menses**. Menses usually stops about three to seven days after the onset of menstruation.

corpus luteum: Meaning "yellow body," a yellowish endocrine gland in the ovary formed when a follicle has discharged its secondary oocyte; it secretes estrogen and progesterone to help prepare the uterus for implantation.

menses: The blood and tissues discharged from the uterus during menstruation.

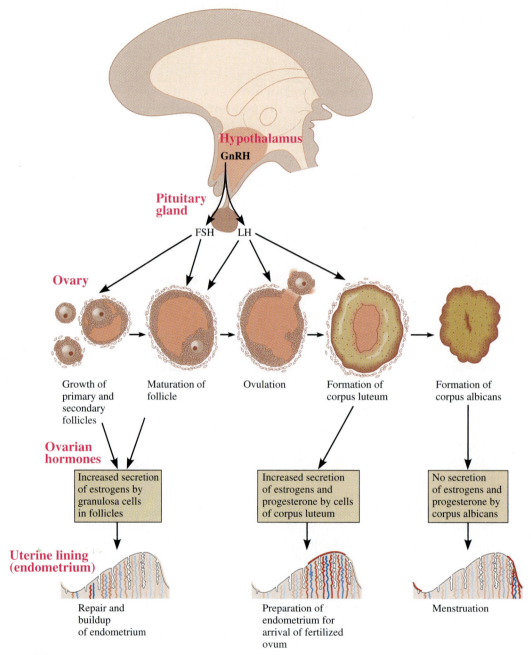

F i g u r e **3.9**

The female menstrual cycle and the monthly hormonal cycle.

This monthly cyclical process involves a negative feedback loop, where one set of hormones controls the production of another set, which in turn controls the first. It works like this: estrogen and progesterone are produced by the ovaries at different levels during different parts of the menstrual cycle. As these levels increase, the hypothalamus is stimulated to decrease its production of GnRH, which sends a message to the pituitary to decrease levels of FSH and LH. The decrease in FSH and LH signals the ovaries to decrease their production of estrogen and progesterone, so the hypothalamus increases its level of GnRH and it all begins again. It is similar to a thermostat; when temperatures go down, the thermostat kicks on and raises the temperature, until the rising heat turns off the thermostat and the heat begins slowly to fall (see Figure 3.9).

SEX TALK

QUESTION **3.5** **Someone once told me that women who live together often experience menstruation at the same time. Why does this happen?**

> **Menstrual synchronicity, as this phenomenon is called, is common, and women who live in the same apartment or house often notice that they begin to cycle together. This happens because of pheromones, chemicals that are produced by females (more powerfully in animals) during their fertile periods that signal their reproductive readiness. Women who live together detect each other's pheromones (unconsciously), and slowly their fertile periods begin to converge. Men also have sexual odors that are commonly referred to as pheromones.**

Variations in Menstruation

Amenorrhea, the absence of menstruation, can take two forms. In primary amenorrhea a woman never even begins menstruation, while in secondary amenorrhea, previously normal menses stops before the woman has gone through menopause. Primary amenorrhea may result from malformed or underdeveloped female reproductive organs, glandular disorders, general poor health, emotional factors, or excessive exercise. The most common cause of secondary amenorrhea is pregnancy, although it can also occur with excessive exercise, eating disorders, emotional factors, certain diseases, surgical removal of the ovaries or uterus, or hormonal imbalance caused naturally or through the ingestion of steroids. If amenorrhea persists, a physician should be consulted.

Some women suffer from **menorrhagia**, or irregular periods. Often oral contraceptives are prescribed to make menses lighter and more regular.

menorrhagia: Excessive menstrual flow.

SEX TALK

QUESTION **3.6** **My roommate has been on a strict diet (she might be anorexic), and recently she stopped having her periods. Could this be due to her eating disorder?**

> **Absolutely. Once the female body drops below a certain percentage of body fat, a woman will cease to menstruate. This is common in women with eating disorders or women who are malnourished because of starvation or disease. It also occurs in female athletes who train hard and reduce their body fat to below the critical level for menstruation. It is probably an evolutionary mechanism that prevents women from getting pregnant when there is too little food available to**

support the pregnancy. Over long periods of time, this kind of cessation of menstruation and ovulation can lead to infertility.

dysmenorrhea: Painful menstruation.

Dysmenorrhea, or painful menstruation, may be caused by a variety of inflammations, by constipation, or by psychological stress. In the past there was a tendency to believe that cramps were always due to some organic cause, and some women even had operations in an attempt to stop the pain, but such strategies usually failed. Today, doctors recommend medication, relaxation, relief from stress, yoga, and massage, all of which can bring some relief from dysmenorrhea.

Premenstrual Syndrome

premenstrual syndrome (PMS): Symptoms of physical and emotional stress occurring late in the postovulation phase of the menstrual cycle.

Premenstrual syndrome (PMS) refers to physical or emotional symptoms that appear in some women during the latter half of the menstrual cycle, which can affect their relationships and/or ability to function. Estimates of the incidence of PMS vary widely depending on how it is defined, but only a small number of women find it debilitating. The most frequent symptoms associated with PMS are abdominal bloating, breast tenderness, backache, headache, constipation, low abdominal pain, fatigue, irritability, and symptoms related to depression. PMS symptoms seem to have both biological and lifestyle components (Huerta-Franco and Malacara, 1993), and so both medication and lifestyle changes can help.

PMS has been controversial. The term became well known in the early 1980s when two separate British courts reduced the sentences of women who had killed their husbands on the grounds that severe PMS reduced their capacity to control their behavior (Rittenhouse, 1991). Though no successful trials using that defense occurred in the U.S., publicity over the trials led to much discussion about PMS. Some women objected to the idea of PMS, suggesting that it would reinforce the idea that women were "out of control" once a month and were slaves to their biology, while others supported it as an important biological justification of the symptoms they were experiencing each month. The extreme views of PMS have calmed down somewhat, and women who suffer from it can now find sympathetic physicians and a number of suggestions for coping strategies; in fact, "premenstrual dysphoria disorder," the technical name for PMS, is listed in the DSM IV (1994), the latest guide to the accepted disorders of the American Psychiatric Association.

Female Menopause

menopause: The cessation of menstrual cycling in women.

climacteric: The combination of physiological and psychological changes that develop at the end of a female's reproductive life; usually includes menopause.

Female **menopause** refers to a woman's final menstrual period but is often (incorrectly) used a synonym for the **climacteric**. These terms refer to the period in which the woman's estrogen production begins to wane, culminating in the cessation of menstruation, usually, between the ages of forty-seven and fifty-nine. In smokers, for reasons that are unclear, menopause often occurs earlier (Baron et al., 1990). As they age, women's ovaries become less responsive to hormonal stimulation from the anterior pituitary, resulting in decreased hormone production. The first sign is often a menstrual cycle that does not include ovulation, followed by irregular cycles. Amenorrhea may occur for two or three months, followed by a menstrual flow. In most cases, menstruation does not stop suddenly.

Diminishing estrogen production also results in atrophy of the primary sexual glands. The clitoris becomes smaller, the labia are reduced in size, and degenerative changes occur in the vaginal wall. At the same time, the ovaries and uterus also begin to shrink. Changes in the secondary sex characteristics because of estrogen reduction can include loss of pubic hair, increasing sparseness of head hair, growth of hair on the upper lip and chin, drooping of the breasts and wrinkling of skin due to loss of elasticity, and **osteoporosis**, resulting in brittle bones. However, these changes are usually mild rather than dramatic.

Many women go through menopause with few problems and find menopause to be a liberating time, signaling the end of their childbearing years and a newfound freedom from contraception. In some women, however, the hormonal fluctuations can cause **hot flashes**, headaches, and insomnia. Common sexual complaints include loss of desire (or a sudden increase in desire), decreased frequency of sexual activity, painful intercourse, and diminished sexual responsiveness; sometimes this is associated with dysfunction in the male partner as well (Sarrel, 1990). Hormonal therapy can help lessen or reverse many of these symptoms.

Certain surgeries, such as removal of the ovaries, can result in a surgically induced menopause because of estrogen deprivation. For this reason, surgeons try to leave at least one ovary in premenopausal women to allow the patient to enter menopause naturally.

osteoporosis: An age-related disorder characterized by decreased bone mass and increased susceptibility to fractures as a result of decreased levels of estrogens.

hot flashes: A symptom of menopause consisting of the feeling of sudden heat often accompanied by a flush.

FEMALE REPRODUCTIVE AND SEXUAL HEALTH

In order to maintain reproductive health, all women should undergo routine gynecological examinations once they begin menstruating and certainly before they begin having sexual intercourse. Routine gynecological exams include a general medical history and a general check-up, a pelvic examination, and a breast examination (see below). During the pelvic examination, the health care provider inspects the genitals both internally and externally and manually examines the internal organs.

In a pelvic exam, the health professional will often use a **speculum** to hold open the vagina to examine the cervix (though there is a sense of stretching, it is not generally painful). A **Papanicolaou (Pap) smear** will be taken from the cervix (see Cervical Cancer, below). The practitioner will then insert two fingers in the vagina and press down on the lower abdomen to feel the ovaries and uterus for abnormal lumps or pain. A recto-vaginal exam may also be performed, where the practitioner inserts one finger into the rectum and one into the vagina to feel the membranes in between.

It is important to choose a gynecologist or nurse practitioner with care, for they should be a resource for sexual and birth control information as well. Referrals from friends or family members, college health services, women's health centers, and Planned Parenthood Centers can direct you to competent professionals. Do not be afraid to change practitioners if you are not completely comfortable.

speculum: An instrument for dilating the vagina to examine the cervix and other internal structures.

Papanicolaou (Pap) smear or **test:** Named for its inventor, a test that scrapes some cells from the cervix to detect cervical cancer.

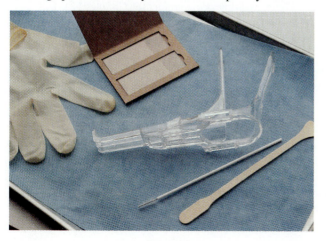

During a pelvic examination, the health professional may use a speculum to see the internal parts of the vagina and should perform a Pap smear.

*Cancer of the Female Reproductive Organs**

Breast Cancer

Breast cancer is the most common cancer in women and is the second most common cause of death from cancer in American women (lung cancer is the first). One in nine American women (about 11%) will develop carcinoma of the breast in her lifetime (Harris et al., 1992). About 180,000 new cases are diagnosed each year, up from 130,000 in the late 1980s. With early detection, about 90% of women survive for at least five years; still, over 50% die within ten years after detection.

Unfortunately, there is no known method of preventing breast cancer, so it is extremely important to detect it as early as possible. Every woman should regularly perform breast self-examinations (see Sexuality Today 3.2), especially after the age of thirty-five. Women should also have their breasts examined during routine gynecological check-ups, which is a good time to ask for instruction on self-examination if you have any questions about the technique. Another important preventive measure is **mammography**, which can detect tumors too small to be felt during self-examination. There is some controversy about when a woman should begin receiving regular mammography examinations, with some claiming that the research shows that it does not have a significant benefit in women under fifty; others suggest mammograms every two years from age forty; still others recommend regular mammograms for all women. Whether mammography is appropriate for you, and if so, how often, should be discussed with your health care provider.

Breast cancer is most commonly discovered by a postmenopausal woman who discovers a breast lump with no other symptoms. However, breast cancer can also cause breast pain, nipple discharge, changes in nipple shape, and skin dimpling. It should be noted here that the discovery of a lump or mass in your breast does not mean you have cancer; most masses are **benign**, and many do not even need treatment. If it is **malignant** and left untreated, however, breast cancer usually spreads throughout the body, which is why it is very important that any lump be immediately brought to the attention of your physician or other medical practitioner.

Treatment. In the past, women with breast cancer usually had a **radical mastectomy**. Today, few women need such drastic surgery. More often, a partial or modified mastectomy is performed, which leaves many of the underlying muscles and lymph nodes in place. If the breast must be removed, many women choose to undergo breast reconstruction, where a new breast is formed from existing skin and fat (see Chapter 12).

If the tumor is contained to its site and has not spread, a **lumpectomy** may be considered. A lumpectomy involves the removal of the tumor itself, along with some surrounding tissue, but the breast is left intact. A lumpectomy does not usually severely alter the appearance of the breast and is followed by radiation therapy and/or chemotherapy to try to kill any remaining cancer cells.

Risk Factors. A number of risk factors have been identified for breast cancer. Early menarche or late menopause increases chances of developing breast cancer, probably due to prolonged estrogen exposure. Family history is also an important risk factor in

mammography: A procedure for internal imaging of the breasts to evaluate for breast disease or screen for breast cancer.

benign: Not malignant; favorable for recovery; a mild disease.

malignant: Technically, a cancerous condition that will spread; often used to mean any life-threatening condition.

radical mastectomy: A surgical procedure where the breast, its surrounding tissue, the muscles supporting the breast, and axillary (underarm) lymph nodes are removed.

lumpectomy: A modern surgical procedure for breast cancer where the tumorous lump and a small amount of surrounding tissue are removed.

---

* In this section, we review preventive measures for detecting or avoiding common female health problems. See Chapter 13 for information on sexually transmitted diseases and Chapter 12 for more information on how illnesses affect women's lives and sexuality.

SEXUALITY *Today* 3.2

Breast Self-Examination

A breast self-examination (BSE) is an important part of any woman's health and personal hygiene program. As you make BSE a monthly routine, you will become familiar enough with your breasts that any irregularity will be easily detectable. If you do detect a lump, however, do not panic; 80–90% of all lumps are non-cancerous and can be easily treated.

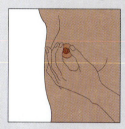

Since the shape and feel of the breasts change during ovulation and menstruation, it is best to perform a BSE about one week after menstruation. BSE should be done at a regular time during each cycle. Postmenopausal women should also perform a BSE at a regular time, such as on the first day of each month.

In the Mirror

The first step of a BSE is inspection. Look at your breasts in a mirror to learn their natural contours. With arms relaxed, note any elevation of the level of the nipple, dimpling, bulging, and peau d'orange ("orange peel skin," which results from edema, or swelling). Compare the size and shape of the breasts, remembering that either (though usually the left) is normally slightly larger. Next, press the hands down firmly on the hips to tense the pectoral muscles, and then raise the arms over the head looking for a shift in relative position of the two nipples. These maneuvers also bring out any dimpling, bulging, or peau d'orange. After doing BSEs over time, any changes will become obvious, which is why it is best to begin BSEs early rather than later in life.

In the Shower

The shower is a good place to do a breast palpation

(pressing)—fingers glide well over wet or soapy skin. Press the breast against the chest wall with the flat of the hand, testing the surface for warmth, and moving the hand to test mobility. Pay close attention to increased heat or redness of the overlying skin, tenderness, dilated superficial veins, peau d'orange, and retraction (dimpling, asymmetry, decreased mobility). Feel the tissue carefully in all four quadrants of the breast being sure to include the tissue that extends up towards the armpit, and examine the armpit itself for any lymph node enlargement. Finally, gently squeeze the nipple inward and upward to see if there is any discharge.

Lying Down

Finally, lie down and put a folded towel or a pillow under your left shoulder. Placing your left hand behind your head, use your right hand to press firmly in small, circular motions all around the left breast, much like you did in the shower. Imagine a clock: starting at the top of the breast, Twelve o'clock, move to one o'clock, two o'clock, etc., on the outside rim of the breast, and then move in one inch towards the nipple and repeat. Make at least three circles, and end up on the nipple itself. You will feel the normal structures of the breast beneath your fingers, but look for a distinct lump or hardness. Repeat entire procedure for your other breast.

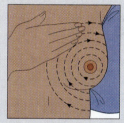

Finally, squeeze each nipple again gently, looking for any discharge, whether clear or bloody. Any discharge or any other irregularities or lumps should be reported to your doctor without delay.

Adapted from the American Cancer Society

breast cancer. If a first-degree relative (mother, sister, daughter) has had bilateral (both breasts) premenopausal breast cancer, the odds of a woman getting breast cancer are increased nine times. Recently, medical researchers have discovered a gene called BRCA1, whose presence seems to indicate a greatly increased risk of developing breast cancer. The gene is only present in about 5% of women, some of whom are choosing to have prophylactic (preventive) mastectomies before breast cancer can develop (Cowley, 1993).

Early pregnancy (having a first child before the age of thirty) seems to have a protective effect against getting breast cancer, though no one understands exactly why. There has also been some controversy over the effect of oral contraceptives on breast cancer rates, with many contradictory studies, some finding an increased risk and others finding none (Johnson, 1989). A comprehensive study conducted by the FDA concluded that there is no concrete evidence that the pill causes or influences the development of breast cancer; however, the long-term effects of using oral contraception are not yet certain, and those with a family history of breast cancer might want to use other forms of contraception.

Uterine Cancer

Cancer can attack almost any part of the uterus, though the most common forms are cervical and endometrial cancer.

Cervical Cancer. Carcinoma of the cervix is the second most common cancer of the female's reproductive tract. The Pap smear, taken during routine pelvic exams, tests for cervical cancer. A few cells are painlessly scraped from the cervix and are examined under a microscope for abnormalities. Cervical cancer has high cure rates because it starts as an easily identifiable lesion, called a **cervical intraepithelial neoplasia (CIN)**, which usually progresses slowly into cervical cancer. Better early detection of cervical cancer has led to a sharp decrease in the numbers of serious cervical cancer cases (Chu and White, 1987).

CIN occurs more frequently in women who have had sexual intercourse early in their lives as well as women with multiple sexual partners (Herrero et al., 1990). Women who begin to have children at an early age, such as teenage mothers, are also at increased risk. Chronic inflammation of the cervix (cervicitis) has also been found to be frequently associated with cervical cancer (Grunebaum et al., 1983; Schneider et al., 1987). Since a number of viral infections of the genitals can lead to lowgrade cervicitis, it is particularly important for those with a diagnosis of genital warts or herpes to have annual Pap smears. Oral contraceptive users have two to four times the risk for developing cervical cancer, particularly if they have used oral contraceptives for more than five to ten years, and so there, too, annual Pap smears are important (Beral et al., 1988). Of course, good gynecological health care requires that *all* women have annual Pap smears.

There are simple and effective treatments for CIN, which have resulted in cure rates up to 90% in early stage disease and a dramatic decline in mortality rate for cervical cancer. If the disease has progressed, a **hysterectomy*** followed by radiation and chemotherapy is common.

Endometrial Cancer. Cancer of the lining of the uterus is the most frequent gynecological cancer. Though it can also be detected with a Pap smear, a D&C (**dilation and curettage**) is more reliable. Endometrial cancer generally affects women over fifty and

cervical intraepithelial neoplasia (CIN): The lesion that signals the possible beginning of cervical cancer.

hysterectomy: The surgical removal of the uterus.

dilation and curettage: The surgical scraping of the uterine wall with a curette (spoon-shaped instrument).

---

* See Chapter 12 for a discussion of hysterectomies.

is a major cause of hysterectomies in that age group. If detected at an early stage, the five-year survival rate is over 90%. Use of birth control pills decreases the incidence of endometrial cancer.

Ovarian Cancer

Ovarian cancer strikes over 22,000 American women each year. Though it is not as common as uterine or breast cancer, it is the most deadly of all gynecologic cancers; 61% of women die within five years of developing it. Ovarian cancer invades the body silently, with few warning signs or symptoms until it reaches an advanced stage. A woman who detects an ovarian lump need not panic, however, for most lumps turn out to be relatively harmless **ovarian cysts**; about 70% of all ovarian tumors are benign.

The cause of ovarian cancer is unknown. An increased incidence is associated with being childless, undergoing early menopause, eating a high fat diet, and being of a higher socioeconomic status; a decreased incidence is associated with having children, using oral contraceptives, or undergoing late menopause. Women who were pregnant at an early age or who had several pregnancies have particularly low rates. Recently, a study demonstrated that women who undergo tubal ligation (having their tubes tied to prevent pregnancy) also have significantly lower rates of ovarian cancer (Stolberg, 1993).

Ovarian cancer is often detected when a health care provider examines the ovary and feels a lump. Early symptoms may include vague abdominal discomfort, loss of appetite, indigestion, and anorexic symptoms, and later a patient may become aware of an abdominal mass or of diffuse abdominal swelling. At this stage, nausea and vomiting may also be prominent due to intestinal obstruction. The only treatment is removal of the ovaries (with or without accompanying hysterectomy) and radiation and chemotherapy. Early detection is crucial to maximizing the chance of a cure.

ovarian cysts: Small, fluid-filled sacs that can form on the ovary, which do not pose a health threat under most conditions.

Other Problems

Endometriosis

Endometriosis occurs when endometrial cells begin to migrate to places other than the uterus. They may implant on any of the reproductive organs or other abdominal organs and then engorge and atrophy every month with the menstrual cycle, just like the endometrium in the uterus. Endometriosis is most common in women between twenty-five and forty years of age who have never had children and has been called the "career woman's disease" because it is more common in professional women.

The cause of endometriosis is still unknown, though some have suggested that it is due to menstrual flow regurgitating back into the Fallopian tubes (Tortora and Grabowski, 1993). The symptoms of endometriosis depend on where the endometrial tissue has invaded but commonly include painful menstrual periods, lower back pain, and pain during intercourse. Symptoms often wax and wane with the menstrual cycle, starting a day or two before menstruation, becoming worse during the period, and gradually decreasing for a day or two afterwards. The pain is often sharp and can be mistaken for menstrual cramping.

Many women discover their endometriosis when they have trouble becoming pregnant. The endometrial cells can affect fertility by infiltrating the ovaries or Fallopian tubes and interfering with ovulation or ovum transport through the Fallopian tube.

endometriosis: The growth of endometrial tissue outside the uterus.

laparoscope: Instrument inserted through a small abdominal incision to view organs, remove fluids and tissues, drain ovarian cysts, stop bleeding, or perform other procedures.

toxic shock syndrome: An infection of Staphylococci bacteria usually caused by tampons that includes high fever, vomiting and diarrhea, and sore throat, and that, if left untreated, may lead to shock, loss of limbs, or death.

Endometriosis is diagnosed through biopsy, or the use of a **laparoscope**. Treatment consists of hormone therapy, surgery, or laser therapy to try to remove endometrial patches from the organs. Endometriosis declines during pregnancy and disappears after menopause.

Toxic Shock Syndrome

Toxic shock syndrome (TSS) first hit the news in the early 1980s, when a number of women died or lost limbs to the disease. Many of the infected women used a brand of tampons called *Rely,* which was designed to be inserted and kept in the vagina over long periods of time. Using a single tampon for a long period of time allows bacteria to build up and can result in infection, and the TSS cases of the 1980s were believed to be due to a buildup of toxins produced by an infection of vaginal staphylococcus aureus bacteria (Reingold, 1991).

TSS is an acute, fast-developing disease that can result in multisystem failure. Symptoms of TSS usually include fever, sore throat, diarrhea, vomiting, muscle ache, and a scarlet-colored rash. It may progress rapidly from dizziness or fainting to respiratory distress, kidney failure, shock, and heart failure and can be fatal if medical attention is not received immediately.

TSS can occur in persons of any age, gender, or race, but most reported cases have occurred in younger menstruating women using tampons. There has been a substantial reduction in the incidence of TSS in the last ten years, which is primarily attributed to the changes in absorbancy and composition of tampons available to the consumer (Schuchat and Broome, 1991). Today, TSS is most common in women who forget to remove a tampon, which becomes a breeding ground for bacteria over a few days. TSS can be avoided by using less absorbent tampons, changing tampons regularly, or using sanitary pads instead of tampons.

Infections

A number of different kinds of infections can afflict the female genital system, and those that are sexually transmitted are discussed in Chapter 13. However, some infections of the female reproductive tract are not necessarily transmitted sexually. For example, on occasion one or both of the Bartholin's glands can become infected, just as any gland of the body can become infected if bacteria get inside and multiply. It may happen because of poor hygiene practices and is more frequent in those who engage in sexual intercourse frequently. When infected, the glands can swell and cause pressure and discomfort and can interfere with walking, sitting, or sexual intercourse. Usually a physician will need to drain the infected glands with a catheter and will prescribe a course of antibiotics.

THE MALE SEXUAL AND REPRODUCTIVE SYSTEM

Most men are fairly familiar with their penis and scrotum. Boys learn to hold their penises while urinating, certainly notice them when they become erect, and generally talk more freely about their genitals among themselves than girls do. Yet the male reproductive system is a complex series of glands and ducts, and few men have a full understanding of how the system operates physiologically.

External Sex Organs

The Penis

The **penis** is the male sexual organ. It contains the urethra, which carries urine and semen to the outside of the body. The penis has the ability to engorge with blood and stiffen, which allows easier penetration of the vagina in order to deposit sperm near the cervical os for its journey toward the ovum. Though there is no bone and little muscle in the human penis (there are both in some animals' penises), the root of the penis is attached to a number of muscles that help eject semen and that allow men to move the penis slightly when erect. (See Sexuality Today 3.3 for a look at the anxiety over penis size experienced by some men.)

The penis is composed of three cylinders, each containing erectile tissue—sponge-like tissue that fills with blood to cause **erection**. Two lateral **corpora cavernosa** lie on the upper sides of the penis, while the central **corpus spongiosum** lies on the bottom and contains the urethra. The three are bound together with connective tissue to give the outward appearance of a single cylinder and are permeated by blood vessels and spongy tissues that fill with blood when the penis is erect.

penis: The male copulatory and urinary organ, used both to urinate and introduce spermatozoa into the female vagina; it is the major organ of male sexual pleasure and is homologous to the female clitoris.

erection: The hardening of the penis (or clitoris) caused by blood engorging the erectile tissue.

corpora cavernosa: Plural of corpus cavernosum (cavernous body), areas in the penis and clitoris that fill with blood during erection.

corpus spongiosum: Meaning "spongy body," the erectile tissue in the penis that contains the urethra.

SEX TALK

QUESTION **3.7** **I heard that some women can capture a penis in their vagina, using their muscles, so that the man cannot get it out. Is that true?**

You are referring to a phenomenon known as "captive penis." Captive penis is found in some animals, where the penis really is trapped in the vagina once intercourse is initiated. For example, there is a bone in the penis of the male dog that allows the penis to be inserted into the vagina before erection occurs. Once inside, the erection occurs and the head of the penis enlarges inside the female's vagina. The vagina swells and prevents the male dog from withdrawing until ejaculation occurs and erection of the penis subsides. Although some people and some cultures believe that captive penis can happen in human beings too, there is not one authentic case on record—not even in the seven scientifically documented cases of men born with bones in their penises!

The Glans Penis. The corpus spongiosum ends in a conelike expansion called the **glans penis**. The glans penis is made up of the **corona**, the **frenulum**, and the meatus (see Figure 3.10). The glans is very sensitive to stimulation, and some males find direct or continuous stimulation of the glans irritating.

The prepuce of the glans penis is a circular fold of skin usually called the **foreskin**. The foreskin is a continuation of the loose skin that covers the penis as a whole to allow it to grow in size during erection. The foreskin can cover part or all of the glans and retracts back over the corona when erect.

In many cultures, the foreskin is removed surgically through a procedure called a circumcision. Circumcision is practiced by many groups, such as Jews and Muslims, as a religious or cultural ritual; however, there are hygienic reasons why other cultures routinely circumcise their infants. If good hygiene is not practiced, smegma, secretions from small glands in the foreskin, can accumulate, causing a foul odor and sometimes infections. It has also been observed that women married to circumcised men tend to have a lower incidence of cancer of the cervix, while circumcised men have a lower

glans penis: The flaring, enlarged region at the end of the penis.

corona: The ridge of the glans penis.

frenulum: Any small fold of mucous membrane that connects two parts of an organ and limits movement.

foreskin: The fold of skin that covers the glans penis, often removed by circumcision; also called the prepuce.

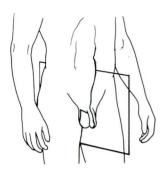

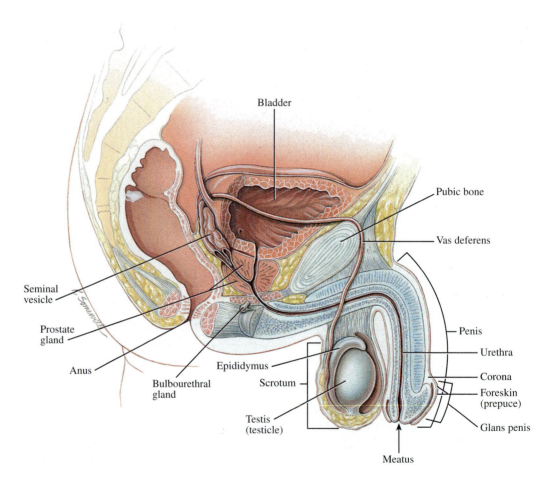

F i g u r e **3.10**

Above, opposite: the male reproductive organs and the internal structures of the penis.

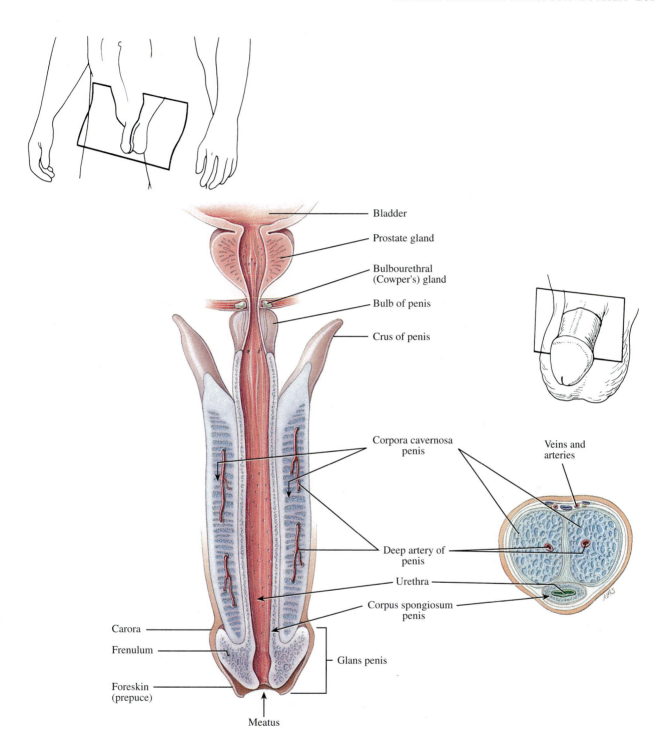

Bladder

Prostate gland

Bulbourethral
(Cowper's) gland

Bulb of penis

Crus of penis

Corpora cavernosa
penis

Veins and
arteries

Deep artery of
penis

Urethra

Corpus spongiosum
penis

Carora

Frenulum

Glans penis

Foreskin
(prepuce)

Meatus

SEXUALITY *Today*   *3.3*

Penis Size and Male Anxiety

The penis has been defined as the symbol of male sexuality throughout history. Concerns about the function and dimensions of the penis have often plagued men, especially when it comes to anxiety about penis size.

Many men assume that there is a correlation between penis size and masculinity, or sexual prowess. Other men may have concerns that they are not "normal." Most assume that women prefer large penises. While there may be a psychological preference for large penises among some women (just as some men desire women with large breasts), penis size has no correlation with the ability to excite a woman sexually during intercourse or to bring her to orgasm.

The *average* flaccid penis is between three and four inches long, and the *average* erect penis is six inches in length. Men often express doubt at this fact, thinking it is stated just to reassure them. In fact, the exaggerated opinion most men have of average penis size comes from pornographic films (which tend to use the largest men

they can find); from men's perspective on their own penises (which, from the top, look smaller than from the sides); and from overestimates of actual penis size (researchers consistently find that people's estimation of the size of penises they have just seen is exaggerated).

Still, men continue to be anxious about their penis size. Some succumb to the advertisements for devices promising to enlarge their penises. Men who purchase these devices are bound to be disappointed, for there is no nonsurgical way to enlarge the penis, and many of these techniques (most of which use suction) can do significant damage to the delicate penile tissue. Other men refrain from sex altogether, fearing they cannot please a woman or will be laughed at when a woman sees them naked. Yet, the vast majority of women report that penis size is not a significant factor in the quality of a sex partner. Besides, women are often so worried that their breasts are too small or too large or that they are too fat that they do not have time to pay that much attention to men's penis sizes.

incidence of cancer of the penis, though know one knows exactly why. Recently, some medical professionals have begun to question the health value of circumcision, which is the single most common surgical procedure performed on male patients in the United States.

The Root. The root of the penis enters the body just below the pubic bone and is attached to internal pelvic muscles. The corpus spongiosum on either side ends in a crus (singular of crura; see The Clitoris). The root of the penis goes further into the body then most men realize; it can be felt in the perineum (between the scrotum and anus), particularly when the penis is erect.

Erection. Erection can occur with any form of stimulation the individual perceives as sexual—visual, tactile, auditory, olfactory, or cognitive. Excitement causes nerve fibers to swell the arteries of the penis, allowing blood to rush into the corpora cavernosa and corpus spongiosum, while veins are compressed to prevent the blood from escaping. The erectile tissues thus fill with blood and the penis becomes erect. The penis returns to its flaccid state when the arteries constrict, the pressure closing off the veins is released, and the sequestered blood is allowed to drain.

Erection is basically a spinal reflex, and men who have spinal injuries can sometimes achieve reflex erections, where their penises become erect even though they can feel no sensation there. These erections generally occur without cognitive or emotional excitement (see Chapter 12). Most men also have regular erections during their sleeping cycle and often wake up with erections, which shows that conscious sexual excitement is not necessary for erection.

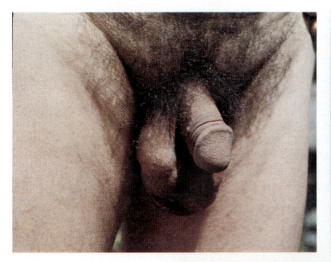
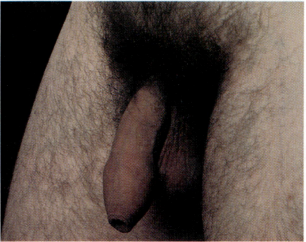
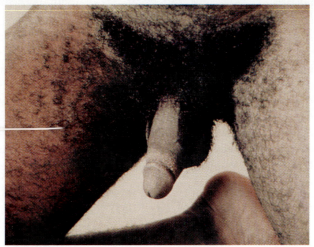

The human penis can be of various sizes and shapes and may be circumcised or uncircumcised.

SEX TALK

QUESTION **3.8** **Why do men so often wake up with erections?**

Men's penises (and women's clitorises) become erect during a part of sleep known as the REM (rapid eye movement) cycle. Some physiologists have suggested that nighttime erections help keep the cells of the penis supplied with blood. Both men and women cycle into REM sleep many times each night, and often we are in a REM cycle right before we wake up. That is why men often awaken with an erection. Some men believe that having a full bladder makes the morning erection firmer and makes it last longer, though there is little medical evidence for this. Since men have no control over nighttime erections, physicians often check to see if impotent men (men who cannot achieve erection) are having erections when they sleep, which can indicate whether their problem is physiological or psychological (see Chapter 12).

The Scrotum

The scrotum is a loose, wrinkled pouch beneath the penis, covered with sparse pubic hair. The scrotum contains the testicles, each in a sac, separated by a thin layer of tissue.

Why do the man's gonads sit outside the body in the scrotum while the woman's are in her abdomen? The production and survival of sperm require a temperature that is about three degrees centigrade lower than the body's temperature, so the scrotum is actually a kind of cooling tank for the testicles. If the testicles become too hot, sperm production is halted; in fact, soaking the testicles in hot water has been used as a form of birth control. (Of course, such a technique is highly unreliable, and it only takes a few hardy sperm to undo an hour of uncomfortable soaking. We do not recommend that you try it!) Likewise, after a prolonged fever, sperm production may be reduced for as long as two months. It has also been suggested that men who are trying to father a child wear loose-fitting underwear, for tight jockstraps or jockey shorts have been shown to reduce sperm counts somewhat, though the effects are reversible (Shafik, 1991). Semen quality has even been shown to undergo seasonal changes, with decreasing quality of semen in the summer in warm climates (Levine et al., 1990).

The scrotum is designed to regulate testicular temperature using two different mechanisms. First, the skin overlying the scrotum contains many sweat glands and sweats freely, which cools the testicles when they are becoming too warm. Second, the **cremaster muscle** of the scrotum contracts and expands: when the testicles become too cool, they are drawn closer to the body to increase their temperature; when warm, they are lowered away from the body to reduce their temperature. Men often experience the phenomenon of having the scrotum relax and hang low when taking a warm shower, only to tighten up when cold air hits it after exiting the shower. The scrotum also contracts and elevates the testicles in response to sexual arousal, which may be to protect the testicles from injury during intercourse.

Internal Sexual Organs

The Testes or Testicles

The testes or testicles are egg-shaped glands that rest in the scrotum, each about two inches in length and one inch in diameter. One testicle hangs lower than the other (usually the left hangs lower than the right, though that can be reversed in left-handed men), which helps one slide over the other instead of crushing together when compressed. The testicles serve two main functions: **spermatogenesis** and testosterone production.

Spermatogenesis. Sperm is produced and stored in some 300 microscopic tubes located in the testes and known as **seminiferous tubules**. Uncoiled, this network of tubes would extend over a mile! Figure 3.11b shows the development of the **spermatozoon** in the seminiferous tubules. First, a **spermatogonium** develops in the cells lining the outer wall of the seminiferous tubules and progressively moves toward the center of the tubules. Sertoli cells located in the seminiferous tubules secrete nutritional substances for the developing sperm. As the spermatogonium grows, it becomes a primary **spermatocyte** and then divides to form two secondary spermatocytes. As the developing sperm approach the center of the seminiferous tubules, the secondary spermatocytes divide into two **spermatids**. The spermatid then reorganizes its nucleus to form a compact head, topped by an acrosome, which contains enzymes to help the

cremaster muscle: The "suspender" muscle that raises and lowers the scrotum to control scrotal temperature.

spermatogenesis: The production of sperm in the testes.

seminiferous tubules: The tightly coiled ducts located in the testes where spermatozoa are produced.

spermatozoon: A mature sperm cell.

spermatogonium: The immature sperm cells that will develop into spermocytes.

spermatocyte: The intermediate stage in the growth of a spermatozoon.

spermatids: The cells that make up the final intermediate stage in the production of sperm.

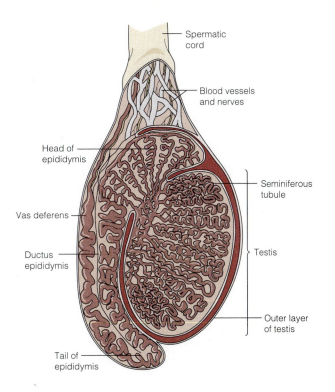

Spermatic
cord

Blood vessels
and nerves

Head of
epididymis

Seminiferous
tubule

Vas deferens

Testis

Ductus
epididymis

Outer layer
of testis

Tail of
epididymis

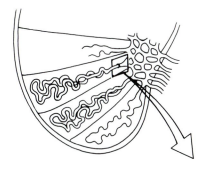

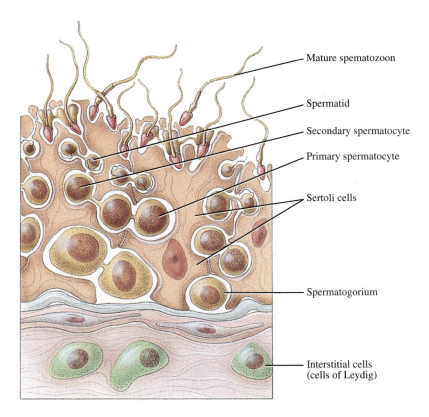

Mature spematozoon

Spermatid

Secondary spermatocyte

Primary spermatocyte

Sertoli cells

Spermatogorium

Interstitial cells
(cells of Leydig)

Figure **3.11**
The testis is the site of spermatogenesis.

flagellum: The taillike end of a spermatozoon that propels it forward.

sperm penetrate the ovum. The sperm also develops a midpiece, which generates energy, and a **flagellum**, which propels the mature spermatozoon. Human sperm formation requires approximately seventy-two days, yet the human male produces about 300 million sperm per day.

SEX TALK

QUESTION **3.9** **If a man's testicles produce so much sperm every day, is it harmful if the sperm do not regularly exit the body? Can sperm build up and cause a problem?**

More than one male has used this argument to try to persuade a partner of the necessity of sexual release, but it has no basis in fact. Sperm are so tiny that even 300 million of them would form a mere drop or two of fluid; the vast majority of male ejaculate is fluid from other glands, not sperm. Also, sperm is regularly reabsorbed by the body as it sits in the epididymis and vas deferens, and sertoli cells secrete a hormone to signal the pituitary to decrease FSH production if the sperm count is getting too high. Many men go days, weeks, months, perhaps even years without ejaculating at all without any physiological damage, and if the body really "needs" to ejaculate, wet dreams relieve that pressure.

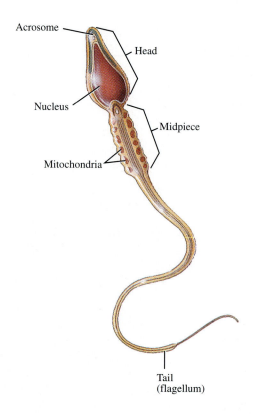

Figure **3.12**
The mature spermatozoon.

Testosterone Production. Testosterone is produced in the testicles in interstitial or **Leydig cells** and is synthesized from cholesterol. Testosterone is the most important male hormone; we will discuss its role when we examine male puberty, below.

Leydig cells: The cells in the testes that produce hormones.

The Epididymis. Once formed, immature sperm enter the seminiferous tubule and migrate to the ductus epididymis, where they mature for about ten to fourteen days and where some faulty or old sperm are reabsorbed. The ductus epididymis sits within the epididymus itself, a comma-shaped organ that sits atop the testicle and can be easily felt if the testicle is gently rolled between the fingers. If uncoiled, the ductus epididymus would be about twenty feet in length. After maturation, the epididymus pushes the sperm into the vas deferens, where they can be stored for several months.

The Ejaculatory Pathway

The **vas deferens**, or ductus deferens, is an eighteen-inch tube that carries the sperm from the testicles, mixes it with fluids from other glands, and propels the sperm towards the urethra during ejaculation. **Ejaculation** is the physiological process whereby the seminal fluid is forcefully ejected from the penis (see Ejaculation). During ejaculation, sperm pass successively through the epididymis, the vas deferens, the ejaculatory duct, and the urethra, picking up fluid along the way from three glands—the seminal vesicles, the prostate gland, and the bulbourethral gland.

vas deferens: One of two long tubes that convey the sperm from the testes and in which other fluids are mixed to create semen.

ejaculation: The reflex ejection or expulsion of semen from the penis.

The Seminal Vesicles. The vas deferens hooks up over the ureter of the bladder and ends in an ampulla. Adjacent to the ampulla are the **seminal vesicles**. The seminal vesicles contribute rich secretions, which provide nutrition for the traveling sperm and make up about 60–70% of the volume of the ejaculate. The vas deferens and the duct from the seminal vesicles merge into a common **ejaculatory duct**, a short straight tube that passes into the prostate gland and opens into the urethra.

seminal vesicles: The pairs of pouchlike structures lying next to the urinary bladder that secrete a component of semen into the ejaculatory ducts.

The Prostate Gland. The **prostate gland**, a walnut-size gland sitting at the base of the bladder, produces several substances that are thought to aid sperm in their attempt to fertilize an ovum. The vagina maintains an acidic pH to protect against bacteria, yet an acidic environment slows down and eventually kills sperm. Prostatic secretions, which comprise about 25–30% of the ejaculate, effectively neutralize vaginal acidity almost immediately following ejaculation.

ejaculatory duct: A tube that transports spermatozoa from the vas deferens to the urethra.

The prostate is close to the rectum, so a doctor can feel the prostate during a rectal examination. The prostate gland can cause a number of physical problems in men, especially older men, including enlargement and the development of prostate cancer (see below, under Male Reproductive and Sexual Health). Annual prostate exams are recommended in men over thirty-five years of age.

prostate gland: A doughnut shaped gland that wraps around the urethra as it comes out of the bladder which contributes fluid to the semen.

Cowper's Glands. The **bulbourethral** or **Cowper's glands** are two pea-size glands that flank the urethra just beneath the prostate gland. The glands have ducts that open right into the urethra and produce a fluid that cleans and lubricates the urethra for the passage of sperm, neutralizing any acidic urine that may remain in the urethra. The drop of pre-ejaculatory fluid that many men experience during arousal is the fluid from the Cowper's glands. Be aware, however, that the fluid may contain some live sperm, especially in a second act of intercourse if the male has not urinated in between; the Cowper's gland fluid often accounts for the failure of withdrawal as a means of birth control.

bulbourethral gland: One of a pair of glands located under the prostate gland on either side of the urethra that secretes a fluid into the urethra; also called a **Cowper's gland**.

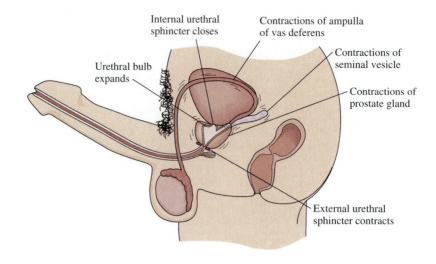

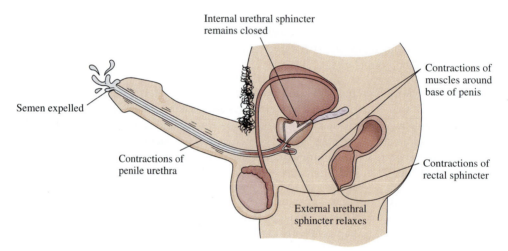

F i g u r e **3.13**
The ejaculatory pathway.

Ejaculation. Ejaculation, like erection, begins in the spinal column. Unlike erection, there is seldom a "partial" ejaculation; once the stimulation builds to the threshold, ejaculation usually continues until its conclusion (see Figure 3.13).

When the threshold is reached, the first stage of ejaculation begins: the epididymis, seminal vesicles, and prostate all empty their contents into the urethral bulb, which swells up to accommodate the semen. The bladder is closed off by an internal sphincter so that no urine is expelled with the semen. Once these stages begin to happen, some men report feeling that ejaculation is imminent, that they are going to ejaculate and nothing can stop it; however, others report that this feeling of inevitability can be stopped by immediately ceasing all sensation.

If stimulation continues, strong, rhythmic contractions of the muscles at the base of the penis squeeze the urethral bulb and the ejaculate is propelled from the body, usually accompanied by the pleasurable sensation of orgasm. Most men have between five and fifteen contractions during orgasm, and many report enjoying strong pressure at the base of the penis during orgasm. This may be an evolutionary way of encouraging deep thrusting at the moment of ejaculation to deposit semen as deeply as possible within the woman's vagina.

Once orgasm subsides, the arteries supplying the blood to the penis narrow, the veins taking the blood out enlarge, and the penis usually becomes limp. Depending on the level of excitement, the person's age, the length of time since the previous ejaculation, and his individual physiology, a new erection can be achieved almost immediately or not for over an hour, though the average is about ten to twenty minutes.

SEX TALK

QUESTION **3.10 Can a male have an orgasm without an ejaculation?**

> **Yes. Before puberty, boys often orgasm without ejaculation. Some men report feeling several small orgasms before a larger one that includes ejaculation, while other men report that if they have sex a second or third time, there is orgasm without ejaculatory fluid. There are also some Far East sexual disciplines, like Tantra, that try to teach men to achieve orgasm without ejaculation because they believe that retaining semen is important for men.**

Ejaculate. The male ejaculate, or semen, averages about two to five milliliters—about one or two teaspoons—in quantity. Semen normally contains secretions from the seminal vesicles and the prostate gland and about 50–150 million sperm per milliliter. If there are less than twenty million sperm per milliliter, the male is likely to be infertile—even though the ejaculate can have almost 100 million sperm altogether! Sperm is required in such large numbers because only a small fraction ever reach the ovum. Also, the sperm work together to achieve fertilization; for example, many die to plug up the os of the cervix for the other sperm, and the combined enzyme production of all sperm are necessary for a single spermatozoon to fertilize the ovum.

Once ejaculated, semen initially coagulates into a thick mucuslike liquid, probably to keep it from leaking back out of the vagina. After five to twenty minutes, the prostatic enzymes contained in the semen cause it to thin out and liquify. If it does not liquify normally, coagulated semen may be unable to complete its movement through the cervix and into the uterus.

Other Sexual Organs

The Breasts

Men's breasts are mostly muscle, and though they do have nipples and areolas, they seem to serve no functional purpose. Transsexual males, who want to change their sex (see Chapter 5), can enlarge their breasts to mimic the female breast by taking estrogen. Some men experience sexual pleasure from having their nipples stimulated, especially during periods of high excitement, while others do not.

Other Erogenous Zones

Besides the penis, many men experience pleasure from stimulation of the scrotum, testicles (usually through gentle squeezing), and anus. As with women's **erogenous zones,**

erogenous zone: Any part of the body which, when stimulated, induces a sense of sexual excitement or desire.

there is no part of the male body that is not erogenous if caressed in the right way and at the right time during lovemaking. When the body is sexually stimulated, almost all moderate sensation can enhance excitement—which is why gentle pinching, scratching, and slapping can be exciting for some lovers.

The Male Maturation Cycle

Male Puberty*

During a boy's early life, the two major functions of the testes (to produce male sex hormones and to produce sperm) remain dormant. No one knows exactly what triggers the onset of puberty or how a boy's internal clock knows that he is reaching the age where

---

* See Chapter 4, Childhood and Adolescence, for a discussion of the psychological and physiological changes of male puberty.

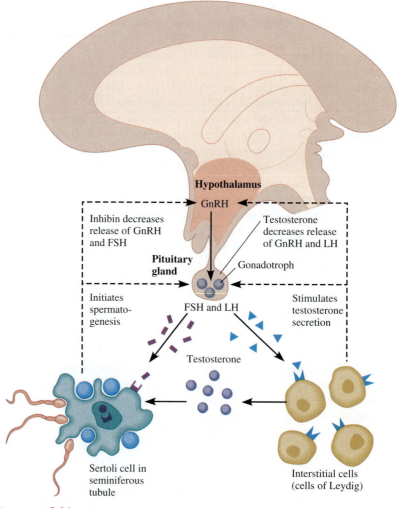

F i g u r e **3.14**
The cycle of male hormones.

SEX*Facts*

Anabolic-Androgenic Steroids

Male sex hormones, or androgens, are also referred to as anabolic steroids. During puberty, the release of androgens increases weight and muscle size, and they can also increase endurance and aggressiveness. Some athletes have therefore used these drugs in an attempt to enhance performance. The level of anabolic-androgenic steroid (AAS) use in sport and exercise appears to have increased notably during the past three decades, and use is no longer restricted to elite athletes or adult males (Yesalis, 1993). Estimates based on data from the National Household Survey on Drug Abuse indicated that there were more than one million current or former anabolic-androgenic steroid users in the United States, with more than half of the lifetime user population being twenty-six years of age or older (Yesalis et al., 1993).

However, AAS use comes at a high price. AAS use has been associated with many damaging changes in the physiologic characteristics of organs and body systems.

The best documented effects are to the liver, serum lipids, and the reproductive system, including shrinkage of the testicles (Wilson, 1988; Yesalis et al., 1989). Other areas of concern include cerebrovascular accidents (stroke), prostate gland changes, and impaired immune function (Friedl, 1993). In younger athletes, steroids can cause early fusion of bone-growth plates, resulting in permanently shortened stature. Use of AAS has also been associated with changes in mood and behavior. Schizophrenia, increases in irritability, hostility, anger, aggression, depression, hypomania, psychotic episodes, and guilt have all been reported among AAS users (Strauss et al., 1983; Dimeff and Malone, 1991).

The bottom line is this: steroids can cause impotence, overly aggressive behavior, mental problems, increased chances of various diseases, shrinkage of the testicles in men, and masculinization in women. It is simply not worth the risk.

---

these functions of the testes will be needed. Still, at an average of ten years of age, the hypothalamus begins releasing gonadotropin releasing hormone (GnRH), which stimulates the anterior pituitary gland to send out follicle-stimulating hormone (FSH) and luteinizing hormone (LH). These flow through the circulatory system to the testes where LH stimulates the production of the male sex hormone, testosterone, which, together with LH, stimulates sperm production. As in females, a negative feedback system regulates hormone production; when the concentration of testosterone in blood increases to a certain level, GnRH release from the hypothalamus is inhibited, causing inhibition of LH production and resulting in decreased testosterone production. Alternately, when testosterone levels decrease below a certain level, it stimulates GnRH production by the hypothalamus, which increases the pituitary's LH production and testosterone production goes up. Figure 3.14 illustrates the cycle of male hormones, while Sex Facts 3.3 examines the abuse of anabolic steroids.

As puberty progresses, the testicles increase in size, and penis size begins increasing about a year later. The epididymis, prostate, seminal vesicles, and bulbourethral glands also increase in size over the next several years. Increased testosterone stimulates an overall growth spurt in puberty, as bones and muscles rapidly develop. This spurt can be dramatic; teenage boys can grow three or four inches over the space of a few months. The elevation of testosterone and DHT affects a number of male traits: the boy develops longer and heavier bones, larger muscles, thicker and tougher skin, a deepening voice due to growth of the voice box, pubic hair, facial and chest hair, increased sex drive, and increased metabolism.

Spermatogenesis begins at about twelve years of age, but ejaculation of mature sperm usually does not occur for about another year or year-and-a-half. At puberty, the hormone FSH begins to stimulate sperm production in the seminiferous tubules, and the increased testosterone induces the testes to fully mature. The development of spermatogenesis and the sexual fluid glands allows the boy to begin to experience his first wet orgasms, though, at the beginning, they tend to contain a very low live sperm count.

Male Menopause

andropause: The hormonal changes accompanying old age in men that correspond to menopause in women.

As men age, their blood testosterone concentrations decrease. Men do not go through an obvious set of stages as menopausal women do but experience a less well-defined symptom complex termed **andropause** in their seventies or eighties. Though men's ability to ejaculate viable sperm is often retained past the age of eighty or ninety, spermatogenesis does decrease, the ejaculate becomes thinner, and ejaculatory pressure decreases. FSH and LH levels also significantly decrease in andropause (Janczewski et al., 1992). The reduction in testosterone production results in decreased muscle strength, fewer viable sperm, and decreased libido; however, this can be a very gradual process in men.

MALE REPRODUCTIVE AND SEXUAL HEALTH

Cancer and Other Diseases of the Male Reproductive Organs

Testicular Cancer

Testicular cancer is the most common malignancy in men aged twenty to forty-four years (Raghavan, 1990). There are few symptoms until the cancer is advanced, which is why early detection is so important. Most men first develop testicular cancer as a pain-

SEXUALITY *Today*   3.4

Testicular Self-Examination

When detected early, testicular cancer is easily treatable. Yet testicular cancer has no obvious symptoms. That is why testicular self-examination (TSE) is a good idea; it is the only early detection system for testicular cancer that we have. Yet most men do not do regular TSEs.

Just like breast self-examinations in women, men should examine their testicles at least monthly.

To examine the testicles, compare both simultaneously by grasping one with each hand, using thumb and forefinger. This may be best done while

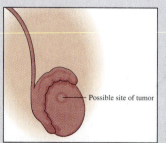

Possible site of tumor

taking a warm shower, which causes the scrotum to relax and the testicles to hang lower. Determine their size, shape, and sensitivity to pressure.

Above the testicles you will feel a softer section. That is the epididymis. As you get to know the exact shape and feel of the testicles, you will be able to notice any swelling or lump or any unusual pain as you do a TSE. Report any such occurrence to your physician without delay, but do not panic; most lumps are benign and nothing to worry about.

less testicular mass or a harder consistency of the testes. If there is pain or a sudden increase in testicular size, it is usually due to bleeding into the tumor. Sometimes lower back pain, gynecomastia, shortness of breath, or urethral obstruction may also be found.

Though the incidence of testicular cancer has doubled in the last twenty years (Iammarino and Scardino, 1991), the survival rate has increased dramatically from 10% in the 1970s to 90% in the 1990s (Richie, 1993). This increase is due to improvements in clinical practice that have now made testicular cancer one of the most curable solid tumors. Treatment may involve the removal of the testicle, which does not affect a man's fertility or virility. Many men opt to get a prosthetic testicle implanted, which gives the appearance of having two normal testicles. Early diagnosis is very important, as the treatment is less severe early on, and one's chance of being cured is greater. All men should do testicular self-examinations monthly (see Sexuality Today 3.4).

Penile Cancer

A wide variety of cancers involving the skin and soft tissues of the penis can occur, though cancer of the penis is not common. Any lesion on the penis must be examined by a physician, for benign and malignant conditions can be very similar in appearance, and venereal diseases also often appear as lesions. Even though most men handle and observe their penis daily, there is often significant delay between a person's recognition of a lesion and seeking medical attention. Fear and embarrassment may contribute most to this problem, yet almost all of these lesions are treatable if caught quickly.

Prostatic Disease

As men age, their prostate glands enlarge. In most cases, this natural occurrence, **benign prostatic hypertrophy (BPH)**, causes few problems. Because of its anatomical position surrounding the urethra, BPH may block urination, and surgeons may need to remove the prostate if the condition becomes bad enough.

Of far more concern than BPH is prostatic cancer, the most common cause of cancer deaths among men over sixty in the United States. About 35,000 men died of prostate cancer in 1993, and over 100,000 new cases are diagnosed each year. Autopsies find cancerous cells in the prostates of 30–40% of men over fifty and half of men in their eighties. Cancer of the prostate is 25% more common in African American men than in white men.

Signs of possible prostatic cancer (or BPH) include loss in force of the urinary stream, urinary dribbling, blood in the urine, and frequent nighttime urination. Many deaths from prostate cancer are preventable since a simple five or ten second rectal examination by a physician, to examine for hard lumps on the prostate, detects over 50% of cases at a curable stage. A recently developed test called the PSA (for prostate-specific antigen) tests the blood for a protein found only in the prostate. Though not all tumors will show up on a PSA test, a high reading does indicate that something (such as a tumor) is releasing prostatic material into the blood, and a biopsy or further examination is warranted.

There are many treatments for prostatic disease, and almost all are controversial. Some argue that, in older men especially, the best thing is to leave it alone, since most men will die of other causes before the prostate cancer spreads. Some argue for a **radical prostatectomy**, while others argue for radiation treatment, each of which leave some men impotent or incontinent. A new technique called **cryosurgery** uses a probe to

benign prostatic hypertrophy: The common enlargement of the prostate that occurs in most men after about age fifty.

radical prostatectomy: The surgical removal of the prostate.

cryosurgery: Surgery using freezing techniques to destroy part of an organ.

freeze parts of the prostate and has had good success in reducing the occurrence of post-surgical impotence and incontinence. Carefully controlled clinical studies are necessary to discover the best treatment for different stages of prostate cancer.

Summary

- Human beings use sexual reproduction to combine the twenty-three chromosomes in the mother's gamete with the twenty-three in the father's. The zygote then begins to undergo cell differentiation, which leads to sexual differentiation into a girl (if the twenty-third chromosome pair is XX) or a boy (if the twenty-third chromosome pair is XY).
- Male internal genitalia develop from the Wolffian ducts, while female genitalia develop from the Müllerian duct. Both male and female external genitalia develop from the same tubercle so that many male and female genital structures are homologous.
- Endocrine glands produce hormones. Female reproductive hormones include estrogen and progesterone, while the primary male reproductive hormone is testosterone.
- A number of prenatal problems can develop, usually due to the fetus's inability to produce or respond to hormones or due to the mother ingesting hormones.
- The woman's external sex organs, collectively called the vulva, include a number of separate structures, including the mons veneris, labia majora, and labia minora. The clitoris is a cylindrical erectile tissue located under the prepuce, which becomes erect during sexual excitement and is the seat of female sexual pleasure. In the vestibule, the space between the labia minora, lie the urethra, the opening or introitus of the vagina, and the Bartholin's glands.
- The female's internal sexual organs include the vagina, the uterus, the Fallopian tubes, and the ovaries. The vagina serves as the female organ of intercourse and the passageway to and from the uterus.
- The uterus is a thick-walled, hollow, muscular organ that provides a path for sperm to reach the ovum and provides a home for the developing fetus. Fallopian tubes extend laterally from the sides of the uterus and bring the ovum from the ovary into the uterus. The mature ovaries contain a woman's oocytes (ova or eggs) and are the major producers of female reproductive hormones.

- The breasts are modified sweat glands that contain fatty tissue and milk-producing glands. Milk creation, secretion, and ejection from the nipple are collectively called lactation.
- Female puberty occurs when the ovaries begin to release estrogen, which stimulates growth of the woman's sexual organs and menstruation. A number of menstrual problems are possible, including amenhorrhea, dysmenorrhea, and premenstrual syndrome.
- As women age, hormone production wanes, leading to menopause and the cessation of menstruation.
- Regular gynecological examination is recommended for all women to help detect uterine, cervical, and ovarian cancer. Breast self-examination is also an important part of women's health behavior.
- Men's external sexual organs include the penis and scrotum. The penis consists of the glans (covered at birth with a foreskin), the shaft, and the root, which anchors the penis within the body. The scrotum is a sack below the penis that contains the testicles.
- The testicles are egg-shaped glands that sit in the scrotum and produce sperm and androgens, such as testosterone. About 300 million sperm per day are produced and stored in over a mile of seminiferous tubules.
- Ejaculation is the physiological process whereby the seminal fluid is forcefully ejected from the penis. An average, fertile male ejaculates between 100 and 750 million sperm.
- At puberty, testosterone stimulates the development of males' secondary sexual characteristics, such as pubic hair and enlarged genitalia. Spermatogenesis begins at about twelve years of age, and ejaculation about a year later. Older men go through andropause where their libido and strength decrease.
- Men can suffer from three types of reproductive cancers—testicular cancer, penile cancer, and prostate cancer. Self-examination of the testicles and regular prostate check-ups are an important part of male preventive health.

R eflections on Sexuality

1. We don't seem to need to know how the digestive system works to eat. Why is a detailed knowledge of the sexual functioning of men and women important in human sexuality?

2. What are some common misconceptions about human sexual biology? Why do you think they are so widespread?

3. Describe the process whereby the gonads influence the duct system to become either male or female. What would happen in the absence of hormones?

4. Men and women start as embryos with the exact same structures, until sexual differentiation begins. Does that make you feel that you have more in common with the opposite sex than you thought?

5. Do you practice good sexual hygiene? Why or why not? What do you think stands in the way of women and men performing regular self-exams or talking to their health professionals about sexual questions?

6. What is the physiological process by which a man gets an erection? Can a man with a spinal-cord injury, who has no sensation in his penis, get an erection?

7. Can you trace the path of an egg through the various female internal reproductive organs until it is expelled in menstrual fluid?

8. Describe the path taken by a sperm from the moment it is a spermatogonium until it is ejaculated. What other internal male organs donate fluids to the semen along the way?

S uggested Readings

BECK, WILLIAM S., KAREL F. LIEM, AND GEORGE GAYLORD SIMPSON. (1991) *Life: An Introduction to Biology*. New York: HarperCollins.

MASTERS, WILLIAM H., VIRGINIA E. JOHNSON, AND ROBERT C. KOLODNY. (1993) *Biological Foundations of Human Sexuality*. New York: HarperCollins.

TORTORA, GERALD J., AND SANDRA GRABOWSKI. (1993) *Principles of Anatomy and Physiology, 7th Edition*. New York: HarperCollins.

Childhood and Adolescent Sexuality

My first and only experience with sexual intercourse, I thought, was going to be great. I couldn't wait. It happened over just this past summer. It was awful; it wasn't anything like I expected it to be. Sure, I know that the first time is painful, but it really didn't hurt that much. My feelings towards sex now are that I'm really not curious about it any more and don't really care to do it again in the near future unless I find someone who is exceptionally wonderful and that I care a lot for. Right now I would much rather just be with someone than have intercourse again. (Author's files)

I started my period in April of my 8th grade year. All my friends had already started, and my Mom had talked to me about it so I wasn't really scared. I thought it was really gross and painful because of the cramps. I was scared to use a tampon because I thought it would hurt. I wore a pad for my first period, and I was really embarrassed because I had to go church and I thought people could see my pad. (Author's files)

Some names preschoolers used, in one study, to refer to a girl's vulva: cat, cookie, coochie, dingle, feefee, fluzzy, heinie, lapoopoo, muffin, peepee, pie, pooch, pussy, teetee, weewee, winkie, winnie. Names they used to refer to a boy's penis: boner, dingaling, dick, dingdong, dink, dodo, dollywacker, hose, monkey, nuts, pee-dee, pee-pee, pee-wee, peter, petereater, piddlewiddle, shinyinie, teetee, tinker, tweeter, weenie, weewee, wiener. (Wurtele et al., 1992)

GENDER AND SEXUALITY IN CHILDHOOD

The idea of "childhood" is a recent invention. Throughout most of history, children were treated simply as miniature adults, and concepts such as "childhood"—and certainly "adolescence"—did not exist (Aries, 1962). Though accommodations were made for age, most children worked, dressed, and were expected to behave (as much as they were capable) like adults. Life was not segmented into stages; today we have many: first you are an infant, then a baby, a toddler, a preschooler, a kindergartner, etc.; then, once you reach adulthood, you become a young adult, reach early middle age, and so on. Thinking of life in these types of stages became popular only in the latter half of the nineteenth century, when the single-room schoolhouse and mixed classes gave way to age-grading in education (Vinovskis, 1986). Sexuality Today 4.1 looks at gender identity in children.

One aspect of childhood that *was* considered different than adulthood in Western history, particularly during the nineteenth century, was sexuality. Children were considered pre-sexual and referred to as "innocents," meaning that they had no knowledge of, nor desire for, sexual contact. Some people still view children as sexual innocents who can be "corrupted" if exposed to sexual information or images. Others see children as naturally curious about sexuality, with culture determining how the child's view of sexuality will be constructed (Plummer, 1991).

Children's sexuality is not adult sexuality, and it is a common mistake to project adult feelings and attitudes toward sexuality onto children. Sexuality is socially constructed; that is, though the desire for sex may be an innate drive, the ways in which we think about sex and even perform sexual acts are not innate but learned. When a five-year-old boy and a five-year-old-girl sharing a bath reach out to touch each others'

These children from a village in Kenya live a very different life from American children, but they still play, learn about growing up, and dress up on special occasions, and they are curious about adult sexuality.

genitals, the meaning that they ascribe to that action cannot be considered "sexual" in any adult sense. As Plummer (1991) notes, a child having an erection shows simply that his physiology functions normally; seeing the erection as "sexual" is to overlay a social meaning onto the physiology. The child is probably not even aware of the "sexual" nature of his erection and, indeed, may not even be aware that he *is* erect. On the other hand, children do have urges for touching and caressing, and that can include genital contact. Perhaps it is best to suggest that children are sexual, but not as adults are sexual; childhood sexuality is a different kind of sexuality.

Age grading in the social structure is the most universal feature of human societies (Constantine and Martinson, 1981). In other words, every society distinguishes between young and old; every society also creates rules around the sexuality of the young. In this chapter, we will explore the development of sexuality as the child matures. Sexual growth involves a host of factors—physical maturation of the sexual organs, psychological dynamics, familial relations, and peer relations, all within the social and cultural beliefs about gender roles and sexuality.

age grading: The tendency of cultures to determine people's social positions and allowable behaviors in terms of their chronological age.

Research on Childhood Sexuality

It is very difficult to carry out research on children's sexuality in American society. Many parents are opposed to questioning their younger children about sexuality, often believing that child sexuality research will somehow encourage promiscuity. Others seem to believe that if we do not talk about children's sexuality, it will just go away. Teenagers are becoming increasingly sexually active, yet national survey data on teens was not even collected until 1971, and a nationwide survey of American sexuality proposed in the early 1990s was cancelled by Congress in part because of concern about questioning children about their sexual habits.

In response to increasing teenage pregnancy rates, the growing awareness of child abuse and incest, and concern over teenage rates of sexually transmitted diseases, some researchers have been forging ahead in their study of children's sexual behavior, despite opposition. Certain types of research, such as studying fertility control in children, have increased in recent years. Yet there is very little research on frequency of sexual behav-

SEXUALITY*Today* 4.1

Aspects of Gender Identity

This list of terms differentiates the different ways a child can be thought of as having a gender identity. The first six are biologically oriented, and the last two are psychologically oriented. Note how many there are and the ways they differ; though all six are consistent in most individuals, there are a number of problems that can develop prenatally or postnatally that can make one or more of these variables conflict with the others. For example, one can be born with a female chromosomal gender and yet have male traits in all other categories. The transsexual may have female traits in categories one through five but have a male gender identity.

1. **Chromosomal gender:** This refers to whether one is genetically male or female, that is, whether one has XX or XY chromosomes.
2. **Gonadal gender:** Whether one has testes or ovaries.
3. **Prenatal hormonal gender:** The presence of the correct amounts of estrogen and progesterone in the female and testosterone in the male.
4. **Internal accessory organs:** The presence of a uterus and vagina in females or of the prostate gland and seminal vesicles in males.

5. **External genital appearance:** Having a clitoris and vaginal openings in females and a penis and scrotum in males; some children are born with genitals that seem to be a cross between male and female genitals (see pseudohermaphrodites, page 77).
6. **Pubertal hormonal gender:** At puberty, whether the body releases estrogen and progesterone, as it usually does in the female, or testosterone, as in the male.
7. **Assigned gender:** The gender the child is considered to be at birth; the gender in which the child is raised.
8. **Gender identity:** People's inner sense of gender; the way they conceive of themselves and integrate the idea of "being male" or "being female" into their sense of identity.

Do not confuse these eight categories with *sexual orientation,* that is, the gender of the sexual partners one chooses (being homosexual, bisexual, or heterosexual; see Chapter 7). The gender of those we choose as sexual partners is not necessarily related to the other aspects of gender identity listed above.

Adapted from *Money* **(1987)**

iors other than intercourse, differences in gender, ethnicity, race, religion, and social class, same-sex preferences and behavior, cross-cultural research, and the meaning of eroticism and sexuality in the lives of the young (Brooks-Gunn and Furstenberg, 1989). Still, the data that does exist shows some things about childhood sexuality that you might find surprising. Before you read the rest of the chapter, take the self-test in Where Do I Stand? 4.1 to see how much you know about childhood and adolescent sexuality.

INFANCY (BIRTH TO AGE TWO)

Physical Sexual Development

Our sexual equipment becomes functional even before we are born; ultrasound has shown male fetuses with erections in the uterus, and some babies develop erections shortly after birth—even before the umbilical cord is cut (Masters et al., 1982). Female babies are capable of vaginal lubrication from birth (Martinson, 1981a). Young children are even capable of orgasm! Kinsey (1948, 1953) established that one-half of boys between the ages of three and four could achieve the urogenital muscle spasms of orgasm (though no fluid is ejaculated), and almost all boys could do it by three to five years before puberty. Kinsey did not collect systematic data on the abilities of young

WHERE DO I *Stand?*   *4.1*

girls to reach orgasm, though he did include some anecdotal stories on the subject (Kinsey, 1953). Still, there is no reason to think that girls should be any less able than boys to orgasm.

Babies are born with immature sexual organs that develop very slowly until puberty. Infant girls do produce some estrogen from the adrenal glands before puberty, while infant boys have small testes that produce very small amounts of testosterone.

Psychosexual Development

There are few sights more touching than a newborn child with its parents. The sense of love is there almost instantaneously for many couples; they hold, caress, and coo over the newborn baby, despite the fact that the baby is oblivious to their presence and will

Parental attention and touch is important in the normal development of the infant.

not recognize them for months. The bond between the mother and child is more than psychological; a baby's crying actually helps stimulate the secretion of the hormone oxytocin in the mother, which releases her milk for nursing (Rossi, 1978).

The single most important aspect of infant development is the child's relationship to its parents or caregivers. The infant is as helpless a creature as one can imagine; it is incapable of obtaining nourishment or warmth, or relieving its own pain or distress. Equally as important, almost all infants have a deep need for holding, cuddling, and close contact with their caregivers. The need for warmth and contact in infancy was demonstrated in Harlow's (1959) famous experiment, where rhesus monkeys were separated at birth from their mothers. When offered two surrogate mothers, one a wire figure of a monkey equipped with milk bottles, and one a terrycloth-covered figure, the monkeys clung to the terrycloth figure for warmth and security and ventured over to the wire

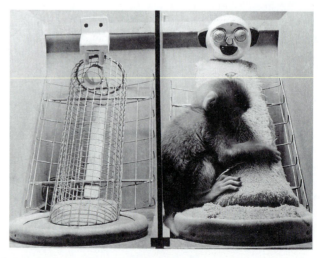

Though the wire figure offered the infant monkeys food, Harlow's famous experiment showed that the monkeys spent much more time with the figure that could offer them warmth and comfort.

figure only when desperate for nourishment. The need for a sense of warmth and security in infancy overwhelms even the desire to eat.

Infants between one and two years of age begin to develop their **gender identity** (Lewis, 1987). After about the age of twenty-four months, it becomes increasingly difficult to change the child's gender identity (which is occasionally done when, for example, a female with an enlarged clitoris is mistakenly identified at birth as a boy). It takes a little longer to achieve **gender constancy**, and young children often believe they will become a member of the other sex sometime in the future. By the second year, there is usually strong identification with one gender, which becomes a fundamental part of a child's self-concept. Along with this identification begins knowledge of **gender role behavior**, the behaviors that society teaches are appropriate for a person of that gender. Though gender role behavior undoubtedly has some biological component, it is primarily a product of modeling and direct teaching by the parents and others. We will discuss the development of gender roles in depth in the next chapter.

gender identity: The inner sense of one's maleness or femaleness.

gender constancy: The realization in the young child that one's gender does not normally change over the life span.

gender role behavior: The learned set of behaviors that are expected of a person of one's gender.

Sexual Behavior

In infancy, the child is busy making sure all of the bodily organs work and learning to control them. The sexual system is no exception. For example, male babies will often have erections while nursing (which can be very disconcerting to the mother). Girls, too, will have clitoral erections, but this is less likely to be noticed. The baby's body (and mind) have not yet differentiated sexual from other functions, and the pleasure of nursing, as well as the stimulation from the lips, mouth, and tongue, create a generalized neurological response that stimulates the genital response.

Masturbation

Many infants start touching their genitals as soon as their hands are coordinated enough to do so, after about three or four months (Gundersen et al., 1981). Some babies only occasionally or rarely touch themselves, while others masturbate frequently. Infants and babies do not masturbate to achieve orgasm, though they clearly derive pleasure from the activity and do not appreciate being interrupted when caressing themselves. Masturbation is soothing to the baby. In fact, in some cultures it is a common practice for mothers to calm a baby down by stroking the baby's genitals. Masturbation at this age is normal and natural, and parents should be more concerned if babies show absolutely no curiosity about exploring their world and their bodies than if they touch themselves.

EARLY CHILDHOOD (AGES TWO TO FIVE)

Physical Sexual Development

Early childhood is a crucial period for physical development, though not particularly of the sexual organs. Children of this age must learn to master the basic physical actions, such as eye-hand coordination, walking, talking, and generally learning to control their bodies. Think of all the new things a child must learn: all the rules of speaking and communicating; extremely complex physical skills such as self-feeding, walking, and running; how to interact with other adults and children; control of bodily wastes through toilet-training; and handling all the frustrations of not being able to do most of the things they want to do when they want to do them. Though this period of childhood is not a particularly active one in terms of physical sexual development, children may learn more in the first few years of childhood about the nature of their bodies than they learn in the entire remainder of their lives. It is truly a time of profound change and growth.

Psychosexual Development

In early childhood, children begin serious exploration of their bodies. It is during this period that children are usually toilet trained, and they go through a period of intense interest in their genitals and bodily wastes. They begin to ask the first, basic questions about sex, usually about why boys and girls have different genitals and what they are for. This is also the period that Freud believed the child goes through his or her first sexual stage and first sexual crisis, the Oedipal or Electra Complex (see Chapter 2).

Children at this age are beginning to explore what it means to be "boys" or "girls," and they turn to their parents, siblings, or television for models of gender behavior. Sometimes children at this age will appear flirtatious or engage in sexual behaviors such as kissing in an attempt to understand gender roles. However, it is almost certainly wrong to suggest that these behaviors are motivated by sexual desire at this young age.

Sexual Behavior

Early childhood sexuality is more about a general sense of being cared for, soothed, and nurtured than about stimulating the genitals for pleasure. Still, young children do masturbate and engage in some sexual behaviors.

Masturbation

It is natural for young children to have curiosity about their genitals and to enjoy caressing them.

Both girls and boys masturbate. There is some controversy over whether boys actually masturbate more than girls, but that may be because girls can do it more subtly, by rubbing their legs together (Langfeldt, 1981b). Masturbation is actually more common in early childhood than later childhood, though it picks up again after puberty (Friedrich et al., 1991). Masturbation may be deliberate and obvious and may even become a preoccupation; some children insist on keeping their pants and underwear off to have easy access to their genitals. Boys at this age are capable of erection, and some proudly show it off to visitors. Parental reaction at this stage is very important; strong disapproval may teach their children to hide the behavior and to be secretive and even ashamed of their bodies, while parents who are tolerant of their children's emerging sexuality can teach them to respect and take pride in their bodies. It is perfectly appropriate to make rules about the times and places that such behavior is acceptable, just as one makes rules about other childhood actions such as the correct time and place to eat or to urinate.

Sexual Contact

Even when young children fondle their genitals and express pleasure, their behaviors are only "sexual" within the limited cognitive abilities of the child's age. Child sex play often begins with games exposing the genitals ("I'll show you mine if you show me yours . . . ") and, by the age of four, may move on to undressing and touching followed by asking about sex around the age of five (Friedrich et al., 1991). Sometimes young children will rub their bodies against each other, and in the case of boys, penile erections may occur (girls, too, may get clitoral erections during such play, though it has not been documented) (Langfeldt 1981a). Such rubbing commonly happens between members of the same sex at this age and probably stimulates a general sense of tactile pleasure. Since the amount of sexual behavior actually declines as the **prepubescent** child ages, the ages of two to five include the most sex-play of any age before adolescence (Friedrich et al., 1991).

prepubescent: The period just before puberty.

SEX TALK

QUESTION **4.1** **Is it damaging to a child to see his or her parents naked? What about accidentally seeing them making love?**

For many years in Western society, it has been thought that children would be somehow traumatized by seeing their parents naked. In fact, nudity is natural and common in many cultures, such as Scandinavian countries, which have a reputation for physical health and beauty. Parents' casual nudity, openness to sexual questions, and willingness to let their children sleep in their beds has been found to be correlated with positive overall effects on the well-being of children (Friedrich et al., 1991; Lewis and Janda, 1988). If parents are caught making love, their best tactic is not to be upset but to tell the child calmly that the parents are showing each other how much they love each other and would prefer to do it in private. Then they should teach the child to knock on their bedroom door in the future. More trauma can come from the parents' overreaction than from the sight of lovemaking.

Sexual Knowledge and Attitudes

During the period of early childhood, the child learns that the genitals are different than the rest of the body. They remain covered up, at least in public, and touching or playing with them is either discouraged or to be done only in private. This is the beginning of the sense of secrecy surrounding sexuality.

Words for the sexual organs are among the first words children learn. However, they rarely learn the anatomically correct names for their genitals. In one study, children knew the correct anatomical terms for body parts like eyes, arms, and legs, but only 6.3% knew the term "penis" and only 3% "vagina" (Wurtele et al., 1992) (see Table 4.1). However, these children were easily capable of learning the correct terminology when taught at home by their parents. Why is it that we teach our children the correct names for all the body parts except their genitalia? Do you think it sends children a subtle message when we use cute play words like "dinkle" or "piddlewiddle" for their genital organs?

In our culture, boys are taught very early a name for their focus of sexual pleasure, the penis, but girls rarely are taught about the focus of their sexual pleasure, the clitoris. Children are usually taught about their genitals in order to teach them about elimination, not sexuality, and young children often confuse eliminative and sexual functions (Chilman, 1983). Therefore, most parents see little need to teach girls about the different parts of their genitals. Boys' sexual organs are more obvious and the erection is more

T a b l e **4.1**

PRESCHOOLERS' KNOWLEDGE OF GENITAL TERMS

Researchers in this study examined preschoolers' knowledge and use of words for their genitals. They recorded how many gave incorrect, slang, or correct terms for each body part, and how many said "private part." Note how few knew the correct terms for their genitals, while all seemed to know the correct terms for other parts of their body.

PERCENTAGES (AND NUMBER) OF CHILDREN WHO USED VARIOUS LABELS FOR BODY PARTS (N=271)

BODY PART	INCORRECT		SLANG		"PRIVATE PART"		CORRECT	
	%	N	%	N	%	N	%	N
Genital								
Breasts	33.9	(92)	52.4	(142)	5.5	(15)	8.1	(22)
Vagina	51.7	(140)	27.7	(75)	17.7	(48)	3.0	(8)
Penis	41.3	(112)	34.7	(94)	17.7	(48)	6.3	(17)
Buttocks	20.7	(56)	10.0	(27)	10.7	(29)	58.7	(159)
Nongenital								
Eyes	2.2	(6)	—	—	—	—	97.8	(265)
Arms	1.1	(3)	—	—	—	—	98.9	(268)
Legs	1.5	(4)	—	—	—	—	98.5	(267)

From Wurtele et al. (1992:118). Reprinted with permission from Guilford Publications, Inc.

prominent, which focuses attention on the penis. Boys, therefore, tend to discuss their penises more often than girls do their sexual organs (Langfeldt, 1981). Boys also tend to know more sexual words than girls, even though girls, in general, have larger vocabularies than boys (Bem, 1989; Gundersen et al., 1981). In addition, the appearance of the penis seems to fascinate both girls and boys—while boys tend to be relatively uninterested in girls' genitals, girls are quite interested in boys' penises (Gundersen et al., 1981). An extra effort has to be made by parents to introduce girls to their genital anatomy.

CHILDHOOD THROUGH PREADOLESCENCE (AGES SIX TO TWELVE)

Physical Sexual Development

Until a child's body starts the enormous changes involved in puberty, the sexual organs grow in size only to keep up with general body growth and change very little in their physiological activity. At about the age of nine or ten, the first signs of puberty begin; in girls, breast buds appear and pubic hair growth may begin. In boys, pubic hair growth generally starts a couple of years later than in girls, and, on average, girls experience menarche before boys experience their first ejaculation. Preadolescent boys experience frequent erections, even to nonerotic stimuli (Martinson, 1981). These changes can be frightening if the child is not prepared for them, and, even if prepared, the onset of puberty can be emotionally, psychologically, and physically difficult for many children.

Psychosexual Development

Freud believed that children enter a sexual "latency" period during their childhood in which sexual issues remain fairly unimportant until they reemerge with the coming of puberty (see Chapter 2). Though the issue of latency is still controversial, most researchers disagree with Freud and believe that psychosexual development issues remain important throughout childhood (Janus and Bess, 1981; Martinson, 1981). In fact, research seems to show that sexual interest and activity in societies across the world steadily increases during childhood (Goldman and Goldman, 1982).

The latency thesis may have been formulated because, as the child matures, overt sexual behavior lessens. However, such behavior may lessen because it becomes less tolerated by parents and adults as the child grows older. For example, it is common to see a three-year-old happily holding or stroking her genitals in public; such behavior would be shocking in a nine-year-old. Children are quickly socialized into correct sexual behaviors and learn to restrict them to moments of privacy (Friedrich et al., 1991). Personal Voices 4.1 examines what children from kindergarten to grade 6 think about the opposite sex and sexuality.

Sexual Behavior

Children through the middle and late childhood years masturbate, engage in heterosexual and homosexual contact, enjoy displaying their genitals and seeing those of other children, and sometimes even attempt intercourse. This is the age of sexual discovery; it is likely during this time that children will first learn about adult sexual behaviors such as intercourse and will assimilate cultural taboos and prejudices concerning unconventional sexual behavior. For example, it is at this age that children (especially boys) first begin to use sexual insults with each other, questioning their friends' desirability or sexual orientation. As the child enters the later years of preadolescence, frequency and sophistication of sexual activity often increases.

Sexual Fantasies

Children as young as four or five have fantasies with erotic content, and children between the ages of six and ten can become sexually aroused by thinking about sexual events (Langfeldt, 1981a). Children are sometimes fearful of their fantasies, worrying that thinking about certain acts would lead them to actually perform them (Langfeldt, 1981b). As children grow older, their fantasies have more and more erotic content and are more often used during masturbation.

Masturbation

By the later childhood years, most children have the ability to stimulate themselves to orgasm. A consistent finding about childhood and adolescent masturbation is that boys

Children's Discussion of Sexual Issues by Grade

Janus and Bess (1981) interviewed children of different grade levels about their views of the opposite sex. Note the progression of ideas about sexuality as the children mature.

Kindergarten and Grade One

If a boy kissed me, I would kiss him more. And I would say I like you. I like Carlos because he is very nice with me. And he took me on a date. I like Carlos more than anybody in my class. I want him to want me. And do you know what? He came to my house and gave me a big, big, big kiss. The first time he saw me I was wearing a beautiful dress and it popped his eyes out.—*Migdalia*

Whoever kisses me I will slap his face. He was a strong boy, but he was a nice boy. I asked his name, and he didn't answer me. I got so angry that I wanted to throw him out the window. But I couldn't believe that I was going to have a baby. I had the baby and I was glad because that was what I wanted. That was what he told me.—*Noreen*

If I was sleeping in the morning and my husband came and kissed me in the neck, I'd kiss him in his mouth and I'd wink my eye at him.—*Louisa*

Grades Two and Three

I don't like boys because they are nasty. They look under your dress and try to kiss you. Boys are very dirty. I don't like sissies. When you go up the bus they look under your dress. They kiss the girls. They give me the creeps. They are silly. That is what I don't like about boys. They come from Mars. They asked me for a date. I said no and closed the door. Don't come back, I said. If you come back, I will scream.—*Rhonda*

I like about the girls. I like when a girl is not very smart but has good manners. I like when their breasts are not flat, and their legs are not fat, and they are not conceited. I don't like when they think they could have any boy. I like when they wear short dresses.—*Anonymous*

A boy is someone who looks handsome. A boy can be someone with pimples. Some boys grow up to be men. Boys are fellows. Fellows are boys that grow to be men. Boys can be husbands and actors and singers. Boys can get married. Boys can be fathers. Boys are good. Boys can be polite if they know how to handle a girl. But one thing he has to know how to act with girls. You must say you like them, take them out every night, propose to them. Say you want to marry me.—*Carlotta*

Grades Four and Five

I like girls. They are beautiful. I am going to marry one. I really like girls. They look beautiful. They dress up beautiful. They dance good. Their legs are lovely. Some girls have long hair and short but I like their hair every way they fix it. They wear beautiful clothing. When girls grow up they are ladies and have children.—*Wilfus*

Most boys are very strong with their muscles. The boys I like are tall, dark, and handsome. If you go on a date, boys are well mannered. Some boys when they come over to your house, they compliment you. This makes a girl feel real good on the inside, a burning sensation. Without boys, girls or women would be helpless. You couldn't share your love, or if you got mugged, then a policeman would come to the rescue and save you. Some boys are dream bosses.—*Linda*

I would like to take my girl out someday when I grow up tall. I would get marry, and sure I will have twin babies. I will stick my dick in her pussy. I will suck her lips.—*Willis*

I like the shape in general. Legs, waist, face, and breasts. I think I want to be a photographer of nude women. I like what they do with men. I do not like fat women. P.S. I wish I was twelve years older.—*Bill*

Grade Six

I think that a girl can get pregnant at any age above thirteen because she should know what she is doing if her mother tells her about sex. My father thinks that I should not have a boyfriend. I think that if a girl wants a boy to feel her, it is her business not her parents. I think that a girl can kiss a boy at any time, my father thinks I shouldn't.—*Delilah*

Somedays I see pretty girls walking along the street. They have good ass and a good waist and a good nouck and I will find another sweet ho that suck dick.—*Harold*

I think that miniskirts should be worn, but my parents think that miniskirts are temptations for boys. They say that they might rape you if you walk with a miniskirt. They put down the hems of your dresses without telling you. I think that sex education should be taught, because if something happens to you, you want to know what's wrong with you. About making the baby, they think, if you learn about it you would immediately go out and get pregnant. They don't let you with boys because you'll go to lover's lane and get pregnant. If you ask questions about sex, they tell you to mind your business and you'll learn someday.—*Female Anonymous*

Reprinted with permission from Constantine (1981).

masturbate more than girls (boys about twice a week, girls about once a month) and that boys reach orgasm more frequently (Sorenson, 1973). Boys often learn masturbation from each other, though this is not common for girls (Langfeldt, 1981b). It is not uncommon for boys to masturbate together in group situations, which is also less frequent for girls.

Boys and girls masturbate a variety of different ways. Boys masturbate manually or by rubbing their penis against soft objects like their bedsheets or stuffed animals. Girls also masturbate manually and by pelvic rubbing and thrusting and also may put objects such as pillows between their legs. Many girls experience pleasure and even orgasm by rhythmically rubbing their legs together. Some children find creative ways to masturbate; one child loved to take "rides" on the washing machine during the wash and rinse cycles because the vibrations were sexually pleasurable to her (Authors' files).

Sexual Contact

Children from the age of five to puberty engage in a variety of heterosexual and homosexual play. It is common during this period to engage in sex games, such as spin the bottle or post office, that structure sexual looking and contact under the guise of a "game." Play, in a sense, is the "work" of childhood, teaching interpersonal and physical skills that will be developed as we mature. Sex play helps the child discover the differences and similarities between the sexes and is tolerated to a greater or lesser degree in different cultures (see Focus on Diversity 4.1).

Rates of sexual contact among school-age children are difficult to come by, and most experts still cite Kinsey's data of 1948 and 1953. Kinsey found that 57% of men and 46% of women remembered engaging in some kind of sex play in the preadolescent years. By the age of twelve, about one boy in four reported having at least attempted heterosexual intercourse, and about 10% had their first ejaculation in sex play with a girl. Girls' activity tended to taper off as they approached preadolescence, and they reported the majority of their experiences before the age of eight. Only about 3% reported having sex play just before puberty. Boys who did not finish high school retained a high level of sexual activity into adolescence, while boys who went on to college reported a drop-off in activity. The drop-off of girls' activity that Kinsey found may have been due in part to parents' increased vigilance and restrictions on behavior as girls reached puberty and entered adolescence (Martinson, 1981).

There is much dispute about the numbers of boys who have homosexual contact before puberty, and most research is done by asking adults to recall childhood sexual contacts that, as we have noted before, can be very inaccurate. Research seems to suggest that between 9% and 14% of teenage boys engage in sexual contact with other teenage boys (Haas 1979; Michael, 1994). In contrast to the way girls' heterosexual activity declines as they reach puberty, girls report a steadily increasing rate of homosexual activity as they approach adolescence, with between 11% and 33% of girls reporting at least some homosexual contact (Haas 1979; Reevy, 1967).

Sexual Knowledge and Attitudes

Children's knowledge of sexuality slowly increases as they age. Children under seven really understand very little about adult sexual behavior, though knowledge does increase even among younger children each year (Gordon et al., 1990). Children get information from many different sources, much of it contradictory, from which they must construct a **sexual script** (Plummer, 1991). The sexual script can have different

sexual script: The sum total of a person's internalized knowledge about sexuality.

Focus
on Diversity
4.1

Childhood Sexuality Among the Muria

The Muria are a non-Hindu tribal people in the State of Basar in the central hill country of India. They have a very different view of childhood sexuality than we do in the West.

Beautiful Jalaro, twelve years old, slips out of her parents' thatched-roof hut, heading for the *ghotul* compound at the edge of the village . . . . Tonight Jalaro hopes to sleep with Lakmu, her favorite of all the *ghotul* boys. Only last week, she had her first menstrual period, and now all the village boys are eager to sleep with her. She has made love to many of them during her years in the *ghotul*, but now beautiful Jalaro is a real woman at last . . . .

With a rush of noise and laughter, the girls swarm through the gate, assembling first in front of their own fire and then dispersing to mingle with the boys. One group of boys and girls pairs off and begins singing sexual, taunting songs. Another group settles down by the fire, talking and joking. From a third group, in a different part of the compound, there is the sudden beat of a drum, and half-naked bodies begin to bob and weave in the darkness.

Later on, when the singing and dancing have died down and the smaller children have begun to fall asleep, the Belosa (the girls' headmistress) tells each one whom she will massage and with whom she will sleep. These assignments are made arbitrarily by the headmistress, but Jalaro smiles and lowers her eyes when the Belosa, wise and fair for her seventeen years, orders her to massage Lakmu and then share his sleeping mat.

Before long, Jalaro is kneeling on the ground a short distance from the fire; Lakmu sits on the ground between her thighs. She takes one of the beautiful hand-carved combs from her head and begins to comb out his long, black tangles, talking softly as she works.

When this is done, she massages his back, chest, arms, and legs—slowly at first, but building up to a violent intensity. Then she runs the teeth of her comb all over his body to stimulate his skin. Finally, she finishes by taking each of his arms in turn and cracking every joint from shoulder to fingertip.

This same scene is repeated in a great many other places throughout the compound. Soon the sleeping mats will be unrolled, and the unmarried young of the Muria will be well engrossed in the lovemaking and sexual play. The adults like this arrangement because it gives them privacy in their small, crowded huts at night. And to the Muria, the enjoyment of sex—in private and without interference from children—is one of the supreme pleasures of married life.

In this technologically simple society, where privacy is all but impossible to find and where sex—like work, play, food, and sleep—is openly accepted as a normal and natural part of life, children of three or four are already familiar with the basic facts of sexual behavior. And by the time a Muria child is twice that age, sexual innocence is a thing of the past. The traditional cultures of the West generally take the attitude that children are not naturally sexual creatures, should not *be* sexual creatures, and should at all costs be kept away from sexual knowledge and ideas lest they somehow *become* sexual creatures before their appointed hour arrives. Yet the members of relatively few cultures studied by anthropologists would have anything but derision for such notions. Indeed, the overwhelming majority of preindustrial cultures consider sex to be an inevitable and harmless aspect of childhood.

Reprinted with permission from Currier (1981:9–12)

themes, depending on the sexual ideas and values communicated to the child by the culture and his or her specific environment.

Plummer (1991) offers some examples of sexual scripts. One theme is the scripting of *absence.* That is, because of the reluctance parents have about talking frankly about sex, children may have gaps of knowledge and gaps of vocabulary and may have to create these words or ideas for themselves. Another is the scripting of *values;* the child comes to realize that sexuality is "heavily embedded in judgments and emotion" (Plummer, 1991:239), and these judgments and emotions are, in many cases, presented to the child as negative ("touching yourself is bad"). These two scripts can lead to a third—*secrecy.* Sexuality is segregated from the rest of life, and children come to realize that integrating sexuality into the rest of their lives is not allowed, that performing sexual acts at their age is unacceptable to adults, and that even asking questions makes adults uncomfortable. A final example is the script of *utility,* or the social uses to which sexuality can be put. For example, children learn that sexuality can be used to intimidate other children, to defy authority with adults, as a form of play, or, in the cases of abuse, as a means to gain love.

Sexuality and Relationships

All of our intimate relationships influence our sexuality in one way or another. We learn different aspects of sexuality from different sources; for example, we may learn taboos from our parents, information from our siblings, or techniques from our peers.

Relationship with Parents and Caretakers

Parents and caretakers are the main sources of information and attitudes on sexuality for most children until well into preadolescence. Parents who do not talk about sex can still transmit powerful messages to their children—that sex is unacceptable or dirty, for example. Children often receive mixed messages even from parents who think they are open to their children's sexuality.

In a study of parental attitudes towards masturbation, for example, Gagnon (1985) found that a large majority of parents accepted the fact that their children did masturbate, and about 60% said that it was all right for their children to masturbate (Table 4.2). Yet, less than half wanted their children to have a positive attitude toward masturbation, and that attitude was transmitted to their children. In Table 4.3, parents who report knowing about their children's masturbation (who were already a select group) report how they reacted. A small minority approved, and another minority resorted to punishment; the rest of the parental responses were generally negative or disapproving. Telling their children to stop, distracting them, or telling them that it is harmful all send a message that the behavior is not acceptable. Note that mothers are more likely to approve of their sons' masturbating than their daughters' and are much more likely to discuss morality with their daughters. This may reflect the double standard that boys' sexuality is normal and uncontrollable, while girls' sexuality is subject to moral codes of behavior. Notice also the large percentage who simply ignored the behavior.

Parents can be extremely upset and confused when they discover that their children are engaged in sexual play. One therapist noted that though parents often come to see him because they are worried that their children are showing sexual interests they think are too precocious, no parents ever come because their children show a *lack* of any sexual interest, which may be a much greater cause for concern (Harry, 1977). There also tends to be a double standard when parents discover the sex play of their children. Boys' sex play may be tolerated or even encouraged, while girls are more likely to be sanctioned, to be told that "nice" girls don't act like that. Double messages and mixed messages are common. We will explore this double standard in the next chapter's discussion of gender roles.

Relationship with Peers

Same-sex Peers. As children age and try to determine how they will fare in the world outside the family, their peer groups increase in importance. Learning acceptable peer-

Tables 4.2 and 4.3 describe how a sample of parents responded to their children's masturbatory activities. In the first table, parents answer questions about the frequency of their own, and their children's, masturbation and their attitudes towards it. In the second table, they describe how they actually handled discovering a son's or daughter's masturbation.

Table **4.2**

PARENTS' REACTIONS TO THEIR CHILDREN'S MASTURBATION: ATTITUDES

PARENTS' RESPONSES TO SURVEY QUESTIONS ABOUT MASTURBATION BY GENDER OF PARENT AND CHILD (NUMBERS ARE PERCENT ANSWERING YES, FOLLOWED BY THE ACTUAL NUMBER IN PARENTHESES)

| | MOTHERS OF | | FATHERS OF | |
	SONS	DAUGHTERS	SONS	DAUGHTERS
Have you (parent) discussed the topic with your child?	19.6 (440)	14.0 (412)	13.5 (318)	6.6 (271)
Do most preteen children masturbate?	91.6 (385)	87.3 (391)	82.5 (280)	81.2 (252)
Is preteen masturbation all right?	67.1 (399)	57.4 (360)	61.9 (293)	63.0 (348)
Did [your child] masturbate?	47.0 (389)	27.1 (372)	29.8 (279)	19.9 (231)
Do you want child to have positive view of masturbation as an adolescent?	46.2 (424)	34.5 (385)	42.5 (306)	36.0 (270)
Did you (parent) masturbate as a preteen?	25.7 (417)	23.9 (380)	46.7 (301)	49.8 (260)

Reprinted with permission from Gagnon (1985:455, 463)

Table **4.3**

PARENT'S REACTIONS TO THEIR CHILDREN'S MASTURBATION: REACTIONS

| | MOTHERS OF | | FATHERS OF | |
RESPONSE	SONS (%)	DAUGHTERS (%)	SONS (%)	DAUGHTERS (%)
Punished child	5.9	3.9	5.9	0.0
Said "Stop!"	8.8	5.6	15.7	18.7
Told child it was harmful	9.4	24.6	4.6	12.4
Discussed morality	4.7	14.2	8.8	11.0
Distracted the child	13.7	10.7	10.8	8.7
Ignored the behavior	30.3	22.8	31.2	27.8
Explained partly	3.6	1.8	1.4	5.6
Said "Do it in private"	17.6	10.6	14.3	7.0
Discussed feelings about the behavior	2.9	4.6	3.2	6.0
Approved of the behavior	4.1	1.1	3.4	2.8

Reprinted with permission from Gagnon (1985:455, 463)

group sexual standards is as important as learning all the other attitudes and behaviors that are expected by peers, such as how to play common games and sports or knowing about the latest media trends.

Peers are the main sources of voluntary sexual experimentation with others. Sexual communication and contact are carefully negotiated, as both partners are usually a little frightened and nervous about the initiation of sexuality. Often initial sexual experimentation takes place among preadolescents of the same sex. As one boy relates:

> *It was at summer camp, about eleven or twelve years old, and I went for a walk with a friend. We were in the woods, and we began to dare each other to do things. My friend was always considered a bit effeminate, and I dared him to take off his clothes, which he did. I ended up daring him to put my penis in his mouth, which he resisted initially but finally did for a few seconds. We then got dressed and left and remained friends and never spoke of that experience again.*

> *Authors' files*

Homosexual experimentation is quite common in childhood, even among people who grow up to be predominantly heterosexual (see Chapter 7). The majority of most children's time between the ages of about ten and late adolescence is spent in same-sex groupings, and the opportunities for sexual experimentation and contact is often restricted to members of the same sex.

Other-sex Peers. Dating behaviors usually begin some time in preadolescence, though a great deal of it involves pairing off within larger groups or at parties. Individual dates also begin at this time, and couples may involve themselves in sexual exploration, especially kissing and petting. Preadolescents seem to be dating at younger ages, and desire for contact with members of the other sex at younger ages has increased markedly (Miller et al., 1986). This may be due to the general level of sexual information and sexual content of television shows geared even to the young; sex itself is increasingly seen as glamorous and accessible to all.

Sibling Sex. Another fairly common childhood experience is sexual contact with siblings or close relatives such as cousins. Sometimes this occurs as abuse, with an older relative coercing a younger one into unwanted sexual activity. However, more often it involves mutual sexual curiosity, for siblings are, after all, the most accessible sexual partners to most children. Greenwald and Leitenberg (1989) found that 17% of a sample of college students reported having sibling sexual contact before the age of thirteen. Only a small percentage involved force or threat, and intercourse was rare.

There are a number of myths about sibling sex, including that it only happens in dysfunctional families, that it only happens to younger children, that it is as devastating as parental abuse, or that it is perfectly harmless. Sibling sex is common in a great diversity of family types, and children can have sibling contact at all ages from three through adolescence. Sibling sexual contact can be either heterosexual or homosexual. Finklehor (1980; 1981) found that about one quarter of sibling experiences involved force or verbal threat, especially when one sibling was significantly older than the other. Finklehor also found that females reporting such contact had higher current levels of sexual activity. Sexual contact with much older siblings before the age of nine resulted in lower levels of self-esteem.

Is sibling sex "normal" and acceptable? Finklehor and others' research seems to suggest that sibling sex can be as destructive as other forms of incest when there is a large difference between the ages of siblings or when coercive force is used. It is probably not a good idea, therefore, to encourage boys going through puberty to bathe with their younger sisters or to share a bedroom with a brother four or five years younger. Yet the normal sexual experiences of minor touching or looking at siblings of approximately the same age is usually innocent and harmless.

ADOLESCENCE (AGES TWELVE TO EIGHTEEN)

puberty: The period of life at which both males and females develop the capacity to reproduce.

Adolescence begins a couple of years after the onset of **puberty** and is, in part, our emotional and cognitive reactions to puberty. Adolescence ends when the person achieves "adulthood," signified by a sense of individual identity and an ability to cope independently with internal and external problems (Lovejoy and Estridge, 1987). Adolescence can be fairly quick, ending around the age of eighteen, or it can drag out into the person's twenties; people reach adulthood at different times. It is recognized the world over as a time of transition, as the entrance into the responsibilities and privileges of adulthood. Most societies throughout history have developed rites of passage around puberty; the Jewish Bar or Bat Mitzvah and Christian Confirmation come to mind, and other cultures have other rites.

Adolescence is a time of physical, emotional, and cognitive change. There is no other time in the life cycle that so many things happen at once: the body undergoes rapid change; the individual begins a psychological separation from the parents to enter adulthood; peer relationships, dating, and sexuality increase in importance; and attention turns to career or college choices. It is during this period that many people have their first experience with sexual intercourse and that some confirm their homosexuality (especially males; women tend to discover their homosexuality later than men). It is no wonder that many adults look back on their adolescence as both a time of confusion and difficulty and a time of fond memories. However, though some researchers portray adolescence as a time of great stress, others argue that really only a small proportion of adolescents find it to be a particularly difficult period (Chilman, 1983).

Physical Sexual Development

Puberty is one of the three major stages of sexual development in the human body, along with prenatal sexual differentiation and menopause. Puberty marks the transition from sexual immaturity to maturity and ushers in the reproductive years. In Chapter 3, we discussed the physiological and hormonal changes that accompany puberty, so here we will only review those physical changes that have an effect on the nature of adolescent sexuality.

Puberty begins anywhere between the age of eight and thirteen in most girls and nine and fourteen in most boys. Actually, the age of puberty has been steadily declining, especially among girls, probably due to better nutrition during childhood. American girls reach menarche at the mean age of 12.5, and a study in Israel found that boys' mean age of first conscious ejaculation was 14.3 (Reiter, 1986). Parents are often shocked at

Many cultures have rituals of passage that signify the entry of the child into adulthood; Apache society marks a female's entrance into puberty through a pollen ceremony; the Jewish Bar Mitzvah, performed at age thirteen, serves the same purpose for a Jewish boy.

the extreme changes that puberty can bring; a boy can grow up to five or six inches in less than a year, develop pubic hair, his voice can drop, and his body begins to take on a decidedly adult physique. Girls begin to develop breasts, pubic hair, and an enlargement of the genitals. Though we tend to concentrate on the development of the sexual organs, biological changes take place in virtually every system of the body and include changes in cardiovascular status, energy levels, sexual desire, mood, and personality characteristics (Hamburg, 1986). If those changes are difficult for a parent to cope with, imagine how much more difficult it is for the person going through it!

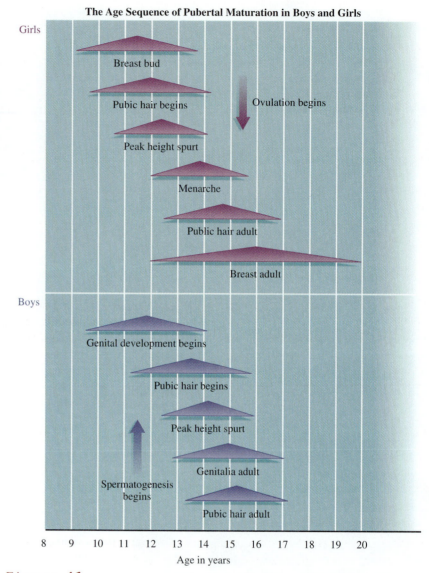

The Age Sequence of Pubertal Maturation in Boys and Girls

Girls

Breast bud

Pubic hair begins

Ovulation begins

Peak height spurt

Menarche

Public hair adult

Breast adult

Boys

Genital development begins

Pubic hair begins

Peak height spurt

Genitalia adult

Spermatogenesis begins

Pubic hair adult

8 9 10 11 12 13 14 15 16 17 18 19 20

Age in years

F i g u r e **4.1**

This graph illustrates the average ages when boys and girls go through the major bodily changes of puberty. **Reprinted with permission from Lancaster (1986:20).**

The physiological changes of puberty almost seem cruel. At just the time when attractiveness to potential sexual partners begins to become important, the body starts growing in disproportionate ways; fat can accumulate before muscles mature, feet can grow before the legs catch up, the nose may be the first part of the face to begin its growth spurt, and one side of the body may even grow faster than the other (Diamond and Diamond, 1986). Add acne, a voice that squeaks at unexpected moments, and unfamiliarity with limbs that have suddenly grown much longer than one is accustomed to, and it is no wonder that adolescence is often a time of awkwardness and discomfort.

Fortunately, the rest of the body soon catches up, so the awkward phase does not last too long.

Maturing early or late can also be awkward for boys or girls. Since girls' growth spurts happens earlier than boys', there is a period of time where girls will be at least equal in height and often taller than boys; this reversal of the cultural expectation of male height often causes both sexes to be embarrassed at dances. Being the last boy (or the first) in the locker room to develop pubic hair and have the penis develop can be a humiliating experience that many remember well into adulthood. Similarly, girls who are the first or last to have their breasts develop often suffer the cruel taunts of class-mates. It may be this combination of nascent sexual exploration, changing bodies, and peer pressure that results in the average adolescent having a negative **body image** (Peterson and Crockett, 1986).

body image: A person's feelings and mental picture of his or her own body's beauty.

Females

For most girls, the first signs of puberty are the beginnings of **breast buds**, the appear-ance of pubic hair, the widening of the hips, and the general rounding of the physique. Increased estrogen levels stimulate the growth of the breasts, labia, and clitoris, the enlargement of the uterus and widening of the vaginal canal, and increased activities of the sweat glands. In other words, the adolescent's body is adding oily skin, fat, sweat, and odor—is it any wonder that girls become self-conscious during this period, when the entire advertising industry advises us that these are the most undesirable traits of the human body?

breast buds: The first swelling of the area around the nipple that indicates the beginning of breast develop-ment.

Menarche is the hallmark of female puberty. It usually begins fairly late in the sequence of pubertal change after the peak of the growth spurt and generally (but not always) before regular ovulation. However, ovulation does sometimes occur early in puberty, so unprotected intercourse can result in pregnancy. Menarche can be a scary time for a girl who is uninformed about what to expect and an embarrassing time if she is not taught how to correctly use tampons or pads.

SEX TALK

QUESTION **4.2** **I keep reading about how terrible people's adolescence was, and mine was fine—I mean I had the normal problems, but it was no big deal. Am I weird?**

Adolescence is a time of great change and development, and how people handle it depends on a host of factors, including their biology (such as fluctuat-ing hormone levels), their family, their personality, and their social relations. Adolescence in general may not be as upsetting or disturbing to most people as theorists tend to portray it (Brooks-Gunn and Furstenburg, 1990). If you had (or are having) a wonderful adolescence, that makes you fortunate, not "weird." Be sympathetic to others who may not have had your resources—whether biologi-cal, psychological, or social—as they went through adolescence.

Girls often worry that their maturation is too fast or too slow, that their breasts will not grow or that they will be extremely large-chested, that one breast will be much dif-ferent than the other, or that their menstrual period is too soon or too late. Girls who consider themselves to be "on time" feel more attractive and positive about their bodies than those who consider themselves "early" or "late" (Hamburg, 1986). While boys' first sign of sexual maturity—the ejaculation—is generally a pleasurable experience which is overtly associated with sexuality, girls' sign of maturity is not associated with sexual pleasure and may be accompanied by cramps and discomfort, as well as embarrassment if the onset is at the wrong moment. Unfortunately, some girls begin menstruation with little idea of what is happening or with myths like it being bad to bathe, swim, exercise, or engage in sexual activities (see Personal Voices 4.2). Many are unfamiliar with their genital anatomy, making tasks such as inserting tampons difficult and frustrating (Diamond and Diamond, 1986).

Males

Male puberty is different from female puberty in many ways. Unlike ovulation, which occurs late in female puberty, spermatogenesis and ejaculation occur early in male puberty—ejaculation may even precede secondary sexual characteristics such as body hair and voice changes. Some boys become capable of impregnating a female even while appearing sexually immature (Lancaster, 1986). Boys' voices change more drastically than girls', and their growth spurts tend to be more extreme and dramatic, usually accompanied by an increase in appetite. Since boys' pubertal growth tends to be more uneven and sporadic than girls', the adolescent boy will often appear gangly or awkward. As a boy's testicles begin to increase their production of testosterone, his scrotum darkens and the testes and penis enlarge. As puberty progresses, pubic hair appears, the larynx enlarges, bones grow, and the frame takes on a more adult appearance.

Early development in boys is usually not as embarrassing as it is in girls; a larger penis may be a symbol of status, and beginning to shave may be seen as a sign of maturity and adulthood. Unfortunately, penis comparisons begin even at this young age, as those who develop early seem to have dramatically larger penises than those who have not begun puberty. Adolescent boys also experience frequent spontaneous erections, which may have no association with sexuality and which can be quite embarrassing. Their increased sexual desire may also be released through **nocturnal emissions** and increased masturbation.

nocturnal emissions: Male orgasm and ejaculation while sleeping, often during erotic dreams; also known as wet dreams.

Psychosexual Development

Though puberty is only one of three major physical changes in the body over the life cycle, it is the most psychologically and socially difficult. There are a number of tasks that adolescents struggle with: achieving comfort with their bodies, developing an identity separate from their parents', trying to prove their capacity to establish meaningful intimate and sexual relationships, and beginning to think abstractly and futuristically (Grant and Demetriou, 1988). It may help to examine these stages by splitting adolescence into three general stages: early adolescence, middle adolescence (or "adolescence proper"), and late adolescence (Lawlis & Lewis, 1987).

Early Adolescence (About Ages Ten to Thirteen)

In early adolescence, pre-teens begin to shift their role from child to adolescent, trying to forge an identity separate from their family's by establishing stronger relationships

Personal
V O I C E S
4.2

Reflections on Menstruation

Below, college students recall how they first learned about menstruation, had their first periods, and what their periods are like now. Note how important having reliable information was to girls' first experiences of menstruation.

Female: I was prepared for menstruation because my Mom had talked with me since I was about eleven years old. It was still a little bit embarrassing when I had to tell my Mom because to her it marked an important stage in my life (so I told my sister first).

Male: I think that I learned about menstruation from those old Massengil commercials (the one where Mom and daughter are walking on a secluded beach and the daughter asks in a very uneasy voice, "Mom, do you douche?")

Female: I noticed it in the locker room of gym class, but it wasn't until I got home later that evening that I caught on to what it was. My Mom was at a meeting that evening. So I just took care of it myself (and didn't tell my Dad). The next morning my Mom came into my room and I told her and started to cry. When I went out into the kitchen, Dad said "Oh. So that's why you were talking in your sleep so much last night." I was so embarrassed that my Dad knew. I guess I thought he wouldn't understand what was going on.

Male: I had always wondered what those diaperlike things I saw in my parents' bathroom trashcan were all about. So I asked my Dad, and he told me all about it. I understood then why my Mom was such a grouch every once in a while.

Female: I think men also get PMS. I do not know exactly why or how, but they seem to go through phases like women do. Men are just difficult to figure out in general.

Male: I think I might have PMS right now.

Author's files

with peers. Perhaps you remember developing a close friendship at this age—another adolescent with whom you became extremely close (and from whom you may have moved apart later on). Such same-sex friendships are common by the eighth grade and serve as role models that help us determine appropriate behaviors as we move into adolescence proper (Buhrmester and Furman, 1987). First homosexual contacts are sometimes experienced in these relationships (Lawlis and Lewis, 1987). "Crushes" on adults who have idealized characteristics (teachers or celebrities) are also very common at this age.

This is also the age at which groups or "cliques" are formed, usually of the same sex. Early adolescence is marked by entry into junior high school, which, as you probably remember, is filled with in-group and out-group behavior. Peers are increasingly relied upon to establish correct standards of behavior, and self-esteem and self-image generally worsens for a while as we judge ourselves in relation to others (Peterson and Crockett, 1986).

Dating also often begins at this age. In one study of junior high school girls in San Francisco, 47% reported that they were involved in heterosexual dating and social behaviors. The average age of initiating dating was between twelve and thirteen years; but many (31%) went out once a week or less (Gibbs, 1986). As dating increases and the changes of puberty begin, many adolescents become preoccupied with their bodily appearance and may experiment with different "looks." Perhaps surprisingly, girls' body

The body changes rapidly in both girls and boys during adolescence, often causing the gangliness characteristic of many teens.

images tend to improve as they progress through adolescence, while boys' tend to worsen (Peterson and Crockett, 1986), perhaps because of the positive image of the youthful female in our culture. On the other hand, girls' general self-images tend to worsen as they grow older, while boys' increase (see Chapter 5).

Middle Adolescence (About Ages Fourteen to Sixteen)

During middle adolescence, heterosexuals increase the frequency of dating as they try to integrate sexuality into their growing capacity for adult-to-adult intimacy. This does not mean the adolescent will achieve the goal; rather, in various ways, the adolescent will "try on" different roles and different ways of being intimate with others (Johnson and Alford, 1987).

Dating for the average middle adolescent consists of going to movies or eating lunch together at the school cafeteria or spending time together after school or on weekends. (The experiences of the very poor, those who drop out of school, those who are sexually abused, runaways, or those who go to work early may be very different.) During this period, couples develop longer-term and more exclusive relationships, and early sexual experimentation (deep kissing, fondling) may also begin. Many couples exchange rings, bracelets, necklaces, or some other token to signify exclusivity. These relationships are typically short-lived, although the memories may be long-lived. Do you remember your first date? You might remember just sitting together, going to a restaurant or a movie, shopping, or just hanging out. Early dating is often quite informal, and double-dating is popular. Even so, dating in the adolescent years is serious business!

Younger adolescents tend to value superficial characteristics of their partners (such as appearance and popularity) and peer approval more than older adolescents, who tend to be more concerned with their partners' goals and future career plans (Roscoe et al., 1987). Differences in attitudes toward sex have also been found between adolescents who begin dating early and those who delay dating. Those with early dating patterns often have more permissive attitudes and engage in more premarital sexual behavior (Miller et al., 1986).

The pattern for young adolescents who have identified their homosexual feelings may be quite different than that of their heterosexual counterparts. Often, gay adolescents feel that they don't really fit into the dating scene and may try to hide their disinterest in the discussions of the other sex that so fascinate their friends. Though life can still be difficult for the gay adolescent today, there is evidence that young people are becoming more accepting of their gay peers.

Since the development of the adolescent sense of self is a delicate process, adolescents may be very sensitive to perceived slights and threats to their emerging ideas of "manhood" or "womanhood." There is an unfortunate tendency among adolescents to portray certain partners as "desirable" (football captain, cheerleader) and others as undesirable or outcast, which as you can imagine (or remember) can be extremely painful if you are on the wrong side of that judgment. Also, for homosexual youth, family reactions or self-expectations may result in depression or confusion. The development of a gay identity may challenge long-held or socially taught images of the correct way to be a man or a woman.

Late Adolescence (About Ages Seventeen to Adulthood)

There is no clear line between adolescence and adulthood. Almost all cultures allow marriage and other adult privileges in late adolescence, though there still may be certain restrictions (such as needing parental permission to marry). Late adolescence was, until recently, the stage that people in Western cultures were expected to begin their search for marital partners through serious dating. With the increased sexual freedoms of the last thirty years, however, young adults have been pushing marriage further back and spending more time in temporary sexual relationships.

Sexual Behavior

Almost every survey shows that sexual activity has increased among teens over the past few decades. The reasons are complex (White and DeBlassie, 1992). Teenagers have become more independent and autonomous, as, for example, most colleges and universities no longer set curfews or rules about when members of the other sex can be in dormitories. Society itself has become eroticized, with sexual images being commonly used in advertising, movies, music, and other media—much of which is directed at teens. Teens can also see sexuality as a "quick fix" for the perceived problems of adolescence, such as loneliness, feelings of awkwardness, or estrangement from the family.

Adolescence is a time for exploring sexual intimacy.

Sexual Fantasies

Sexual fantasies are used as a means to test out sexual situations for their potential erotic content and to help determine emotional reactions to sexual situations. Most research shows that boys use more visual imagery in their sexual fantasies, and that their fantasies include explicit sexual behavior and interchangeable partners. Girls' fantasies focus more on emotional involvement, romance, committed partners, and physical touch, and girls tend to be more complex and vivid (Chick and Gold, 1987–88; Ellis & Symons, 1990). One retrospective study asking adults to remember their first fantasies found that men reported more explicit and shorter fantasies, had more positive emotional responses to having indulged in fantasy, and responded more to visual cues, while women's first fantasies tended to come in response to relationships (Gold and Gold, 1991). Both men and women tended to fantasize about adults they knew, such as teachers, and famous people, such as celebrities.

Masturbation

Masturbation sharply increases as boys and girls enter adolescence, and the activity is more directed toward achieving orgasm than simply producing pleasurable sensations. Kinsey et al. (1953) found a sharp increase between the ages of thirteen and fifteen in boys, with 82% of boys having masturbated by age fifteen. The girls' pattern was more gradual, with 20% having masturbated by age fifteen and no sharp increase at any point. More recently, a study by Leitenberg et al. (1993) found that twice as many college-age males as females had ever masturbated, and men who masturbated during adolescence did so three times more frequently than women who masturbated. The authors also note that no relationship was found between the frequency of masturbation as an adolescent and later experience with sexual intercourse, sexual satisfaction, sexual arousal, or sexual difficulties in relationships. They conclude that early masturbatory experience is neither beneficial nor harmful to later sexual adjustment (Leitenberg et al., 1993).

Almost all studies find that at every age from adolescence into adulthood, more males masturbate, and masturbate more frequently, than females. Many boys worry that they masturbate more than other boys, but a 1985 study of one group of male adolescents found that the *average* male teen masturbated about five times a week (Lopresto et al., 1985). Boys' masturbatory activities decrease when they are having regular sexual intercourse, while girls' increase; this may be because boys masturbate significantly more than girls in general (see SexTalk Question 4.3). Also, nonvirgins, male or female, are more likely to masturbate than virgins (Chilman, 1983).

SEX TALK

QUESTION **4.3** **I am 19 years old and I masturbate at least twice a week, even if I am having good sex with my girlfriend. But she tells me that she rarely masturbates. Why do teenage men masturbate so much more than teenage women?**

There are interesting differences in masturbation patterns between the sexes. Though women masturbate more now than they did in years past

(Kolodny, 1980), girls are less likely than boys to report reaching orgasm while masturbating and less likely to report enjoying masturbation. Also, boys tend to reinforce the social acceptability of masturbation by talking about it more freely among themselves and even engaging occasionally in group masturbation. This is important because both girls and boys report feeling guilty about their masturbatory activities. There may also be biophysiological reasons for more frequent male masturbation, such as the obvious nature of the male erection, levels of testosterone, and so forth.

Sexual Contact

Kissing and Petting. Kissing and touching are the first sexual contacts most people have with potential sexual partners. Coles and Stokes (1985) reported that 73% of thirteen-year-old girls and 60% of thirteen-year-old boys had kissed at least once. Since younger girls tend to date older boys, they have higher rates of these kinds of activities at earlier ages than boys do, but the differences diminish over time. For example, 20% of thirteen-year-old boys reported touching a girl's breast, while 35% of thirteen-year-old girls reported having their breasts touched, a difference that disappears within a year or two. By the age of eighteen, about 60% of boys and girls report vaginal touching, and about 77% of boys and girls report penile touching.

Oral Sex. Oral sex has increased in acceptance among young people. Kinsey et al. (1948, 1953) reported that 17% of adolescents reported engaging in **fellatio** and 11% in **cunnilingus**. By 1979, about one-third of fifteen- and sixteen-year-olds and about half of seventeen- and eighteen-year-olds reported engaging in oral sex at least once (Haas, 1979a). In a more recent survey, Newcomer and Udry (1985) found that 50% of all adolescent males and 41% of females reported having engaged in cunnilingus (males giving, females receiving), while 44% of males and 32% of females reported having engaged in fellatio. In a survey of college students (many of whom are presumably postadolescent), fully 86% of males and 80% of females reported at least one experience with oral sex in the previous twelve months (Gladue, 1990). Whether due to fear of sexually transmitted diseases* or increased acceptability of oral sex in American society, adolescents have become more likely to include oral sex in their sexual repertoire.

fellatio: The act of sexually stimulating the penis with the mouth.

cunnilingus: The act of sexually stimulating the female genitals with the mouth.

Sexual Intercourse. Intercourse rates among adolescents have increased steadily over the last thirty to forty years, especially among females (see Table 4.4); another way of putting that is that average age of first intercourse has decreased. In 1970, 28.6% of women reported being nonvirgins by their late teens; by 1979, just nine years later, the rate had risen to 49% for females (and 53% for males) (Zelnick and Kantner, 1980). In a 1994 poll, men and women born in the decade between 1933 and 1942 reported first having sex at an average age of about eighteen, while those born twenty to thirty years later had sex, on average, six months earlier; (Laumann et al., 1994). By 1994, 59% of teenagers had lost their virginity by the age of 17 and 82% by

---

* It is important to remember that many sexually transmitted diseases *can* be transmitted orally; see Chapter 13.

the age of 19 (Ingrassio 1994). Compare that steady rise over the last fifteen years or so to the fact that in the forty years between 1925 and 1965, the rates changed very little, remaining at about 10% for high school females and 25% for high school males (Chilman, 1986).

Almost all studies of adolescent intercourse show that boys have intercourse earlier than girls, although recently the gap has been closing. Sexual performance is an important factor for male adolescent identity but less so for females (Bolton and MacEachron, 1988). In 1988, 81% of both white and black women aged nineteen were sexually active, while 85% of white, 96% of black, and 82% of Hispanic nineteen-year-old males were sexually active (Voydanoff and Donnelly, 1990). Though most studies report that African Americans rates of teenage intercourse, in general, are higher than white rates of intercourse, black rates leveled off in the early 1980s while white rates continue to rise (Voydanoff and Donnelly, 1990). A 1994 study reported that half of all black men had intercourse by the time they were fifteen; half of all Hispanic men had intercourse by the time they were about sixteen-and-a-half; half of all black women had intercourse by the time they were nearly seventeen; and half the white women and Hispanic women had intercourse by the time they were nearly eighteen (Michael et al., 1994). Table 4.5 compares the age of first intercourse for black, Hispanic, and white females; the most significant differences are between blacks and the other two groups. However, these differences may be more related to poverty than race since adolescents from poorer classes tend to have higher levels of sexual activity than in the wealthier classes and blacks tend to be poorer than whites and Hispanics.

Researchers are very interested in teenage *pregnancy,* so there are many studies of rates of first intercourse, choice of first partners, and contraception; yet we know very little about how youth feel about their first experiences, with whom they share sexual information, or how they decide to have intercourse for the first time (Brooks-Gunn and Furstenberg, 1990). Teenagers tend to report that they did not plan to have intercourse the first time they did it; in a Philadelphia survey of adolescents, almost two-thirds of girls said that their first intercourse "just happened," one-fifth said that sex was "unplanned but not entirely unexpected," and only 15% said that they had planned to have intercourse (Brooks-Gunn and Furstenberg, 1990).

The decision to have intercourse for the first time is difficult for many teens. Many do not plan their first time at all; they say it "just happened." Others do think about their decision and may worry about pregnancy, about whether it will change their relationship with their partner, about their skills and techniques, or about moral and ethical questions of sexuality. (Personal Voices 4.3 takes a look at some people's recollections of first intercourse.) There is often a difference in the reactions of boys and girls to first intercourse; as a report by the Children's Defense Fund (1988) puts it, "Although they have equal levels of anxiety about first intercourse, girls are more likely to be worried about whether they are doing the right thing, while boys are worried about whether they are doing the thing right." Boys tend to report more positive feelings about losing their virginity and less guilt (Haas, 1979a).

Michael et al. (1994) found that more than 90% of men said they wanted to have intercourse the first time they did it; more than half were motivated by curiosity, while only a quarter said they had intercourse out of affection for their partner. About 70% of women, too, reported wanting to have intercourse, though 24% said they just went along with it (fewer than 8% of men said that). Nearly half of women said they had sex the first time out of affection for their partner (the vast majority said they were in love with their first partner), while a quarter cited curiosity as their primary motivation. Four percent of

Table **4.4**

SUMMARY OF STUDIES OF AGE OF FIRST INTERCOURSE AMONG WOMEN
(PERCENT OF FEMALES HAVING HAD INTERCOURSE AT EACH AGE)

AGE	KINSEY ET AL. (1953)	LAKE (1967)	SORENSON (1972)	ZELNICK AND KANTER (1976)	ZELNICK AND KANTER (1979)	OSTROV ET AL. (1985)	GLADUE (1990)
13	1%	—	9%	—	—	1%	2%
14	2%	—	15%	—	—	2%	6%
15	3%	6%	26%	19%	23%	8%	13%
16	5%	*	35%	29%	38%	16%	29%
17	9%	13%	37%	43%	49%	37%	50%
18	14%	*	—	52%	57%	—	68%
19	17%	18%	45%	60%	69%	—	73%

*Lake combined 16–17 and 18–19 age groups.

Table **4.5**

1994 STUDY OF AGE OF FIRST INTERCOURSE AMONG WOMEN OF VARIOUS RACIAL GROUPS
(APPROXIMATE PERCENT OF FEMALES HAVING HAD INTERCOURSE AT EACH AGE)

AGE	BLACK WOMEN	HISPANIC WOMEN	WHITE WOMEN
13	5%	4%	2%
14	11	8	5
15	21	14	10
16	39	22	22
17	59	35	40
18	78	54	58
19	83	68	69
20	89	78	77
21	93	83	83

Adapted from Michael et al. (1994)

Personal

V O I C E S

<u>4.3</u>

Experiences of First Intercourse

Below, college students recall their first experience with sexual intercourse. Note how varied the memories are; to some it was scary, to others wonderful, to others no big deal.

Male: I thought it was great, it was a big relief to finally get it over with.

Female: I felt as if I was an entirely different person after I lost my virginity. I often hear horror stories that people were drunk or regret who they had sex with for the first time. I am glad to say I didn't then and don't regret who I was with. I had this plastered grin on my face for at least two days straight. I wasn't so sure I did the right thing but the good feelings I had seemed to overwhelm the wondering.

Female: I always wished that someone would have told me beforehand what sexual intercourse was like for the girl. No one would tell me. They said I'd have to find out for myself. I was scared to death. I had no idea what to expect (how much pain, etc.). I'm sure that the not knowing made it even worse. (All of the nervousness and anxiety probably didn't relax my muscles much!) I couldn't believe how much it hurt. I had tears streaming down my face. All I could think of was how much it hurt but if I stopped, it'd be just

as bad the next time so I continued on and took it with a grain of salt.

Male: My first sexual contact was in the form of sexual intercourse. I was seventeen and terribly inexperienced. My girlfriend at the time was the same age but far more experienced. Because of her experience, she took a leadership role which I'd like to think does not bother me, but I think it does. As far as outside reactions, my friends were all pretty happy about it since I was the last of my clique to have intercourse.

Female: I really hated it. It was painful and certainly not enjoyable. I felt ashamed and regretted the entire experience. Now that I think back to that time, I recall that I really didn't know any facts or biological information concerning sex. I think that was a bigger mistake than having sex itself.

Female: My first experience with intercourse was hilarious. It was unplanned and very spontaneous. It wasn't romantic, like it is viewed to be on TV. The man involved was very gentle and caring, but because of my inexperience it didn't go very well. However, it was not traumatic in any way. It didn't matter that it was not perfect sex. We both had fun and lots of laughs and will probably remember that night for the rest of our lives.

Author's files

---

women reported being forced to have sex the first time, while about three men in a thousand (0.3%) reported being forced.

One misconception that people have (even some sexuality researchers) is that a woman who reports having had intercourse at least once is "sexually active." Rubin (1991) found that fully two-thirds of teenage women surveyed said they had tried it once and then "put the issue on hold." So having lost one's virginity is not necessarily an indication that the person is now actively engaging in intercourse.

SEX TALK

QUESTION **4.4** **Sometimes I feel I should have intercourse just to get it over with—being a virgin is embarrassing! Its pretty hard to resist when everybody else seems to be doing it.**

The issue of abstinence has become muddled in the whole adolescent pregnancy discussion. It used to be that it was shameful (especially for women) to admit to having had sexual intercourse; now it often seems shameful to admit to being a virgin. Some sexuality teachers are even embarrassed to discuss abstinence because it is "old-fashioned," or it may sound like they are in agreement with religious fundamentalists, or they fear insulting those in the class who have had sex (Peterson, 1988). Yet the decision to have sex is a serious one and is too often taken without consideration of its consequences—for example, whether we feel psychologically or emotionally ready and whether our partner does. Sex should never be the result of pressure (by our partner, our friends, or ourselves), and there may be many reasons that we want to delay sexual experimentation—including moral or religious reasons. Teens also usually overestimate the numbers of their friends who are engaging in intercourse. Due to AIDS and other sexually transmitted diseases and in response to the high rates of teen pregnancy, virginity is becoming fashionable again (Ingrassia, 1994).

Anal Intercourse. Rates of anal intercourse are hard to determine because there are very few adolescent (or adult) studies on the topic, especially among heterosexuals (the AIDS epidemic did result in studies of rates of anal intercourse among gay men—see Chapter 7). Gladue (1990) found that 17% of female and 15% of male college students (many of whom were presumably postadolescent) reported at least one experience with anal intercourse over the previous twelve months. It is not known, however, how many of the male students were reporting heterosexual and how many were reporting homosexual anal intercourse or how many males were reporting penetrating another and how many were being penetrated.

Homosexuality. Homosexual contact is not uncommon in adolescence, both for those who will go on to have sexual partners predominantly of the other sex and those who will have partners predominantly of the same sex. There is a difference between homosexual activity and a predominantly homosexual orientation. Until recently, adolescent homosexuality was not treated seriously and was considered simply a "phase"; it was not until 1983 that the American Academy of Pediatrics formally acknowledged the existence of adolescent homosexuality and called upon pediatricians to recognize and to address the needs of homosexual youths (Bidwell and Deisher, 1991).

It is difficult to determine actual figures for adolescent homosexual contact. In 1973, Sorenson found that about 6% of adolescent males between thirteen and fifteen and 17% between sixteen and nineteen had homosexual experiences, while 6% of adolescent females as a whole report having homosexual experiences. But the research is over twenty years old, and it relies on self-reports; people may define homosexual differently, deny experiences, or lie due to the stigma on homosexuality that continues to prevail in our society. Many people also do not consider homosexual contact—even repeated contact—indications of homosexuality, seeing it as a "passing phase," and thus they do not report it (Bolton and MacEachron, 1988).

Discovering one's homosexuality during adolescence can be a painful and difficult process. Even those who report having felt "different" from their peers from as early as four or five years old may not label that difference as homosexual attraction until adolescence (Martin, 1991). Many hide their orientation due to fears of being taunted by classmates or rejected by family members. Others, however, come to terms with their identity and find ways to establish a positive self-image (see Chapter 7).

Other Sexual Situations. There are many other types of sexual situations that adolescents can experience. Teenage prostitution—both male and female—is not uncommon, especially among runaways. These young people can also make money by becoming involved in child pornography, posing for pictures while nude or performing sexual acts. While there are few comprehensive studies of the results of engaging in prostitution and pornography while an adolescent (or younger), there is every clinical indication that it results in many sexual and psychological difficulties later on.

Many of the sexual variations seen in adults, such as transvestism, exhibitionism, voyeurism, etc., may begin in adolescence, though it is more common for these desires to be expressed in early adulthood. We discuss sexual variations in depth in Chapter 14.

abstinence: In sexuality, the refraining from intercourse and often other forms of sexual contact.

Abstinence. The focus on teenage sexual activity may draw attention away from the fact that many heterosexual teens delay sexual activity, or at least intercourse, until marriage. After all, if about half of women report being nonvirgins at seventeen (see Table 4.4), then about half are still virgins. When asked why they should delay intercourse, teens cite the dangers of disease (65%) and of pregnancy (62%), followed by what their parents would do (50%) and what their peers would think (29%) (Peterson, 1988). There are many reasons to delay sexual activity, including the feeling that one is simply not ready.

After a period where virginity seemed to become out of fashion, it is becoming more acceptable again to wait until marriage. Groups advocating abstaining from sex until marriage are cropping up throughout the country, with mottos like "Save Sex, not Safe Sex" and "Trust Me, I'm a Virgin." A number of celebrities have started campaigns supporting virginity, such as A.C. Green's "athletes-for-abstinence," and television shows such as *Beverly Hills 90210* have prominent characters who defend their virginity (Ingrassia, 1994). Historical trends tend to go in cycles, and there is evidence that we are returning to a more conservative attitude towards premarital sex.

Influences on Adolescent Sexuality

Why do teens engage in sex? Perhaps the better question is, Why *don't* teens engage in sex? After all, sexuality is a basic human drive, a drive that first emerges in its adult form in adolescence. Many authors portray the emergence of adult sexual feelings in adolescence as a "runaway train" or as practically irresistible desires. On the other hand, many teens do not take sex lightly and understand that exploring the intimacy of sexual activity is a major life step. What are the influences on teenage sexual activity?

Peer Influences

Many people believe that the single most important influence on adolescent sexual behavior is peer pressure, and adolescence is certainly a time that the influence of one's friends and peers is at a peak. However, there are two sides to the peer-influence story. On the one hand, there is evidence that a person's *perceptions* of what their peers are doing have a greater influence over sexual behavior than peers' actual behavior (Brooks-Gunn and Furstenberg, 1989), and adolescents with strong family relationships tend to be less influenced by peers (Chilman, 1983). On the other hand, peer pressure among adolescent males may exert pressure to "prove" one's masculinity, leading to early sexual activity. Also, as Figure 4.2 indicates, many adolescents cite peer pressure as the

Table **4.6**

REASONS FOR HAVING FIRST INTERCOURSE

ATTRIBUTED REASON	FIRST INTERCOURSE WANTED		FIRST INTERCOURSE NOT WANTED, BUT NOT FORCED	
	MEN	WOMEN	MEN	WOMEN
Affection for partner	25%	48%	10%	38%
Peer pressure	4	3	29	25
Curiosity/readiness for sex	51	24	50	25
Wanted to have a baby	0	1	0	1
Physical pleasure	12	3	7	2
Under influence of alcohol/drugs	1	0	3	7
Wedding night	7	21	1	3

From Michael et al. (1994)

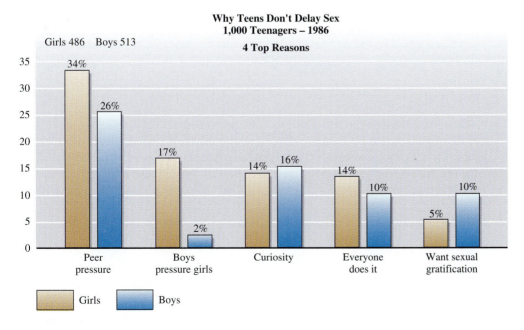

Figure 4.2

This graph represents the percentage of teens who cite each reason for not delaying intercourse (peer pressure and boys pressuring girls are part of the same question). **Peterson (1988:2). Reprinted with permission from SIECUS.**

number one reason they do not wait to engage in intercourse. The relationship between peer influences and sexual activity in teens is complex.

As might be expected, sexual activity is correlated with dating; those who do not date have lower levels of sexual activity. Male adolescents who date more than one partner are more likely to be sexually active than other males, but females who date more than one partner are no more likely to be active sexually than females with a steady partner (Melchert and Burnett, 1990). Adolescents who are sexually active may be more likely to seek out friends and dating partners who share their perspective on sexuality, so it is unclear in which direction such influences go.

It should also be mentioned that siblings have an important influence over sexual activity, especially older siblings. Younger children with sexually active older siblings are more likely to become sexually active themselves (Rodgers and Rowe, 1988).

Relationship with Parents

Communication, family harmony, coming from a two-parent home, and having a sense of closeness with parents are all associated with later onset of first intercourse and likelihood to use contraception (Brooks-Gunn and Furstenberg, 1989; Chilman, 1986). Close families are more likely to transmit their sexual values and integrate their children into their religious and moral views. Ostrov et al. (1985) found that among adolescents reporting that their parents get along very well, 56% of boys and 38% of girls had sexual intercourse, while among those reporting that their parents did not get along, 77% of boys and 60% of girls had intercourse. Children from single parents and divorced homes are also more likely to initiate early intercourse. Both overly strict and overly permissive parents have children who engage in earlier and more frequent sexual intercourse than parents who are moderately strict but those from overly permissive families seem to be the most active and have the greatest risk of pregnancy (Miller et al., 1986).

Religion

Although the relationship between religiosity and sexual activity is complex, in general, more religious youth tend to have lower levels of premarital sexual activity and tend to have sex with fewer partners (Chilman, 1986). Young people who attend church frequently and who value religion in their lives have less permissive attitudes and are less sexually experienced (White and DeBlassie, 1992). Not only do major Western religions discourage premarital sex, but religious adolescents also tend to develop friendships and relationships within their religious institutions and thus have strong ties to people who are more likely to disapprove of early sexual activity.

School

Sexual activity is influenced by the environments the adolescent frequents—the family, the church, peer groups, and school. Teens who are not doing well in school and have lower educational aspirations are more likely to have sex in adolescence than those who do well in school (Brooks-Gunn and Furstenberg, 1989). There is also controversy about whether sex education significantly influences teen rates of intercourse and contraceptive use; we discuss this further in Special Focus 2.

Adolescent Contraception and Pregnancy

Contraceptive Use

Sexually active American adolescents tend to be erratic users of contraception, which is not surprising since American adults are also erratic users of contraception (see Chapter 11). This may be in part because Americans are exposed to mixed messages about contraceptive use. Until recently, words like "condom" have been taboo on television, and contraception is not generally advertised in magazines or other media. Access to contraceptive devices (except condoms) is difficult for teens, and many forms of birth control are expensive. Most other industrialized countries provide free or low-cost birth control to adolescents.

A 1985 poll of high school students found that only 10% claimed to always use some form of birth control, and 20% said that they never used it during intercourse (Ostrov et al., 1985). Another poll found only 33% of females claimed to always use contraception during intercourse (Chilman, 1986). It has also been found that the most ineffective users of contraception are also the most sexually active (Morrison, 1980). Since one-half of teen pregnancy occurs during the first six months following first intercourse, consistent use from the start is important to prevent unwanted pregnancy.

Studies of low-income African American teens show that they have more negative attitudes towards birth control, value fertility more highly, and are less effective contraceptors than white teens; yet black teens exposed to good contraceptive education were *more* likely than similarly exposed white teens to adopt good contraceptive methods (Gibbs, 1986). While sex education does not necessarily affect the age or frequency of intercourse among teens, those who receive sex education are more likely to use contraception and less likely to become pregnant.

Birth control responsibilities among teens, as among adults, often fall on the females. Females become pregnant, and females must either carry the baby for nine months or undergo abortion. Thus, it is difficult to impress on teenage boys the need for shared contraceptive responsibility. One study found that inner-city black adolescent boys felt that they had little or no responsibility for birth control (Reis and Herz, 1989). Perhaps the fear of AIDS and the growing public discussion of condom use may finally convince boys that contraception, like sexuality itself, is best when shared between people who care for each other's well-being.

Misinformation about contraception is widespread among teens. A 1985 poll of high school seniors found that many students erroneously believed that a girl can become pregnant only if she "wants to be" and that a girl cannot become pregnant the first time she has intercourse (Ostrov et al., 1985). That is why parental guidance and information about contraception is so important. Baker et al. (1988) found that although parents did not have that much influence on whether or not adolescents engaged in sexual activity, they did have significant influence on whether or not adolescents used contraception when they did have sex.

Chilman (1986) lists a number of factors that are correlated with patterns of contraception use. For example, adolescents who are younger than eighteen, unmarried, poor, belong to racial minorities, and belong to fundamentalist Protestant groups tend to use contraception less often during intercourse. On the other hand, those who are in steady relationships, who have been pregnant before, who have easy access to contraception, who plan for intercourse, and who have good communication about sexuality with their parents tend to use contraception more consistently. Finally, failure to use contraception is also correlated with attitudes of fatalism, powerlessness, alienation, incompetence, anxiety, passivity, dependency, and adopting traditional female roles. Low self-image and feelings of lack of control are reflected in the care with which people treat their bodies. Positive self-image leads to good contraceptive care.

Teenage Pregnancy

The United States has the highest rates of teenage pregnancy, abortion, and childbirth of any Western country. The likelihood of a child of fourteen or younger becoming pregnant in the United States is much higher than that of any other Western country; for example, it's seven times higher than in the Netherlands, and seventeen times higher than in Japan (Hardy, 1988; Society for Adolescent Medicine, 1991). Teen pregnancy is probably the most studied aspect of adolescent sexual behavior because of its many impacts on the life of the teenager, the teenager's family, and society as a whole.

There are many examples of teenagers who become pregnant and raise healthy babies while living fulfilling lives. However, the problems a teenage mother faces are many, especially if there is no partner participating in the child's care. Baker et al. (1988) discuss four major problems identified in the literature. First, babies born to teenage mothers are more likely to be of lower birth weight and to die than are babies of women over twenty. Second, the mother's mortality rates are higher for adolescent mothers. Third are the social costs on the parents: teenage mothers and fathers are less likely to finish high school and have lower mean incomes and lifetime earnings than their peers, which starts some families on cycles of poverty that are difficult to overcome. Finally, the children of teenage parents in general tend to have increased educational and cognitive deficits. There are many other problems as well. Adolescent fathers are more likely to divorce, abandon their families, end their education, and have lower paying jobs (Bolton and MacEachron, 1988). These types of problems do not even address the impact of teen parenting on others, such as the parents of the teens (who may end up having to take care of their children's children), and on society in general since these parents are more likely to need governmental assistance. Again, these are general trends, and individual cases differ, but, clearly, delaying pregnancy past the teenage years has many advantages.

Pregnancy Rates. Between 1971 and 1979, the percentage of teenage women who became pregnant increased from 8.5% to 16% (Alan Guttmacher Institute, 1981). It is estimated that about 40% of white women and 64% of black women had experienced a pregnancy before their twentieth birthdays in 1990 (Society for Adolescent Medicine, 1991). On the other hand, pregnancy rates have been declining since 1980 (Society for Adolescent Medicine, 1991). In 1985, the majority of teens who become pregnant report that they did not intend nor desire to become pregnant. Determining exactly how many teenagers become pregnant, how many give birth, and how many have abortions is not an easy task. The Society for Adolescent Medicine estimates 1,014,620 teens became pregnant in 1987, with 50% ending in birth, 36% in abortion, and 14% in miscarriage (Society for Adolescent Medicine, 1991).

Birth Rates. Most people think that teenage birth rates have been climbing over the last twenty years. In fact, birth rates have been declining since about 1957, even as pregnancy rates have risen, because a high percentage of teen pregnancies end in abortion. Teen birth rates actually reached close to an all-time low in 1978! Then why all the

Though many teens make loving and caring parents, the pressures on teenagers who have children are great.

concern over teen pregnancy? The problem is that, due to the post-World War II baby boom, there are many more teenagers than before. In 1970, there were 43% more teenagers in the United States than in the previous decade, so even though *rates* fell, the *numbers* of babies born to teenagers rose (Williams, 1991). Also, birth rates were falling among older women, so there was a rise in the *proportion* of all births to teens; between 1955 and 1970 the adolescent share of births rose from 12 to 18% of all births (Hudson and Ineichen, 1991). Recently, however, the numbers of births to teenagers has been declining, from a high of 656,460 in 1970 to 472,081 in 1986.

One of the more alarming trends in teenage pregnancy and birth rates, however, is the increasing birth rate in younger teens, fifteen and under. This was the only group that has experienced a steady increase in births, rising from about 7,500 in 1960 to 10,000 in 1981 to 10,200 in 1985 (Williams, 1991). And for every birth to a girl under fifteen, about three pregnancies end in abortion. A high percentage of these pregnancies are to black teenagers.

Sixty percent of teenagers who have a child before the age of seventeen will be pregnant again before the age of nineteen. While the number of births to teens has decreased, the percentage of those births that are to unmarried teens has been rising; in 1984, 56% of all births to women under twenty years old were to unmarried women, compared with 30% in 1970 (Hardy, 1988).

In studies of teen pregnancy, most of the focus has been on the mothers, who often bear the brunt of the emotional, personal, and financial costs of childbearing. Adolescent fathers are more difficult to study. Many teenage fathers ignore the women they impregnate and run as soon as they learn of the pregnancy, and thus the problem of single women raising children can be traced in part to the lack of responsibility of teen fathers. Society asks little of the teenage male, and there are few social pressures on him to take responsibility for his offspring.

Yet many of these fathers also feel isolated, rejected, or are treated punitively (Bolton and MacEachron, 1988). Recent research has found that many adolescent fathers do accept their role in both pregnancy and parenthood and realistically assess their responsibilities toward the mother and child. Many feel both stress over the birth and guilt. Fathers should be reintegrated into the lives of their children and should be expected to take equal responsibility for the results of their sexual activities; if teen fathers neglect their partners and children, it is at least in part due to the fact that society does not demand or even encourage that they do otherwise.

Abortion. The legalization of abortion in 1973 had the greatest impact on the ratio of teen pregnancies to births. Teenagers accounted for more than a quarter of all abortions in the United States in 1985 (Hudson and Ineichen, 1991). In Britain, the age group sixteen to nineteen has a higher abortion rate than any other age group, and one in four pregnancies to teens under fifteen ends in abortion (Hudson and Ineichen, 1991).

Race, Poverty, and Teen Pregnancy. Many Americans believe that the majority of teen pregnancies and births happen to poor, black, inner-city youth. In fact, that is a myth; adolescent parenthood affects every race, every income group, and every part of American society. Two-thirds of adolescent births are to white teens, two-thirds are to teens who do not live in big cities, and two-thirds are to teens from nonpoor families (Adams et al., 1989).

The reason that many more white teens get pregnant than blacks and Latinos is because there are so many more whites than minorities in this country; a higher *proportion* of blacks and Hispanic youths get pregnant than whites. In 1986, the birth rate for white women fifteen to nineteen years old was 4.2%, while to black women of the same age it was 9.8% (Voydanoff and Donnelly, 1990). Eighty-nine percent of those black mothers were unmarried, which is more than twice the white rate. Still, the 1986 rates represent a decrease among white teens of 26% since 1970 and a 30% decrease among black teens. White teens are more likely than black teens to terminate a pregnancy with an abortion and are also more likely to marry once they discover they are pregnant (Adams et al., 1989).

Unmarried mothers and their children are more likely to live in poverty than any other segment of the population. Even though only about a third of teen pregnancies happen to people officially listed as "poor," many others are to people just above the official poverty line, and for these mothers pregnancy may carry with it the end of a person's educational history and decreased job opportunities. Society has become less willing to grant benefits to teenage and single mothers, believing (against most of the data) that such aid simply perpetuates dependency on welfare and leads to the children of teenage mothers becoming teenage mothers themselves (Williams, 1991). Hardy (1988) found that 9% of the adolescent mothers in his sample were refused medical care because they could not pay; 16% had no family planning services available to them; and 16% reported having trouble feeding themselves and their children. Only 4% received subsidized day care for their children, making it extremely difficult for the others to work. In many other countries, teenage mothers can find social services and support that allow them to finish their schooling or attend vocational training; in the United States, we are far less supportive of teenage mothers.

What Should be Done About Teen Pregnancy? Teen pregnancy is a complex problem that is too often discussed as if teenagers are divorced from the rest of the culture and as if the only influences on teen sexuality were peers and individual sexual desire. Yet the United States has significantly higher rates of teenage pregnancy than other Western countries, which shows that it is more than teenagers' hormones at work here but important social factors.

What is it about American society that seems to foster such high rates of teenage pregnancy? It is a complex series of factors. American society is extremely conflicted about the issue of sexuality in general; our teens are exposed to sexual scenes in movies and television, yet we hesitate to discuss sex frankly with them; we allow advertising to use blatantly sexual messages and scantily clothed models yet will not permit advertising for birth control; and there is significant resistance to sex education in the schools.

Today, when teenagers do become pregnant, opportunities may be limited; it is difficult to have a baby and attend high school all day or work at a job. The United States is far behind most other Western countries in providing day care services that would help single or young parents care for their children. Better counseling, birth control, day care services, and hope for the future can help assure that the teenagers who are at risk for unwanted pregnancies and the children of those unwanted pregnancies are cared for by our society.

S ummary

- Children's sexuality develops through the life cycle according to biological, psychological, and social influences.
- Infants are born with functional sexual organs and can achieve erections, vaginal lubrication, and perhaps orgasm.
- The most important influence on sexual development, the child's relationship to the caregiver, should be warm and caring for the child to develop normally. Children first develop gender identity, a recognition that they are male or female, then gender constancy, the realization that one cannot change one's gender. Eventually they begin to learn gender role behavior, the socially prescribed ways people of their gender are supposed to behave.
- Children under seven or eight years of age usually mimic the same-sex parent in an attempt to master their gender roles. They also begin to learn the names for genitals, the differences between the sexes, and the secrecy surrounding sexuality. Most children of this age freely masturbate unless severely reprimanded by parents, and they may engage in child sex play with same or opposite sex peers.
- In preadolescence the body begins gearing up for puberty. Preadolescents begin to solidify their "sexual scripts" that define their understanding of sexuality, learning from caretakers, peers, and the media. Preadolescents may begin dating, and they engage in sexual behaviors, such as masturbation and the beginnings of sexual fantasizing.
- Puberty prepares the body for adult sexuality and reproduction. Girls' breasts begin to develop, their figures take on an adult appearance, and they begin menstruation, while boys' voices deepen, their muscles and frames grow and mature, and they experience their first ejaculations. Adolescence is the time when individuals learn to achieve comfort with their bodies and their sexuality, where primary sexual orientation often emerges (homosexuality or heterosexuality), and where people experiment with establishing long-term relationships with sexual partners.
- In early adolescence (about ten to thirteen years old), identity is forged separate from the family, strong same-sex friendships are developed, and dating may begin. In middle adolescence sexual identity is established, and different ways of being intimate are explored. Late adolescence capacity for independent judgment improves and impulses come under greater control.
- Adolescents tend to fantasize about sex and masturbation sharply increases, especially for boys. Mature sexual experimentation begins, often with kissing and petting, though a fairly large number of adolescents remain abstinent throughout their teen years. Homosexual contact is not uncommon in adolescence.
- Intercourse rates among adolescents have increased dramatically over the last half-century, with boys tending to have intercourse earlier than girls, blacks and Latinos earlier than whites and Asians, and the lower classes earlier than the upper classes.
- Adolescents are poor users of contraception, which, coupled with increasing sexual activity, results in high pregnancy rates. The United States has the highest rates of pregnancy, abortion, and childbirth of any Western country.

R eflections on Sexuality

1. How is the sexuality of the young child different from that of the adolescent? Is the young child, in your opinion, "sexual"?

2. Should masturbation in young children be encouraged, ignored, or discouraged? What message do you think it sends to children when parents encourage their children to discover and play with their toes, ears, and fingers but pull the child's hands away when the child discovers his or her genitals?

3. Young children often play sex games, like "doctor," with each other. Is this acceptable? How should a parent respond?

4. Why do you think same-sex experimentation among preadolescents is so common?

5. Where should children get their sexual knowledge? Should children learn everything from their parents, school, or the church? Are some things actually better coming from peers?

6. Why is adolescence a difficult time for many people? What can be done to make the transition through adolescence easier?

7. People today are having sex relatively early in life, often in their middle or early teens. Is that a good time to experiment with intercourse, or is it too early? What do you think is the "ideal" age to lose your virginity? Why?

8. Why has teen pregnancy been increasing so dramatically? What are the drawbacks of such early pregnancy?

S uggested Readings

ARIES, PHILIPPE. (1962) *Centuries of Childhood: A Social History of Family Life.* New York: Vintage Books.

LANCASTER, JANE B., AND BEATRIX A. HAMBURG, EDS. (1986) *School-age Pregnancy and Parenthood: Biosocial Dimensions.* New York: Aldine DeGruyter.

ALLEN-MEARES, PAULA, AND DAVID A. SHORE, EDS. (1986) *Adolescent Sexualities: Overviews and Principles of Intervention.* New York: The Haworth Press.

SKOLNICK, ARLENE. (1992) *The Intimate Environment.* New York: HarperCollins Publishers.

VOYDANOFF, PATRICIA, AND BRENDA DONNELLY. (1990) *Adolescent Sexuality and Pregnancy.* Newbury Park, CA: Sage Publications.

5

Gender Roles

Picture These Scenes:

A little league batter leaves the on-deck circle and enters the batter's box. The kid looks kind of scrawny, so you don't expect much, until you notice the gaze of determination and concentration in the batter's eyes and the coach's confident stance. The pitcher winds up, throws—and the kid swings, the bat cracks, and the ball sails sharply over the left-fielder's head. The kid rounds second to third, stares down the third baseman, and executes a perfect slide. Then the batter turns, takes off her cap and lets her long hair fall free, and flashes her winning smile at her third-base coach.

The nurse wipes the sweat from the surgeon's brow. The hip replacement surgery is going well, and the saw buzzes in the hand of the skillful surgeon as it is carefully moved through the pelvic bone. The work is demanding and physical. The nurse is adept at handing the surgeon each instrument at exactly the right moment; they have worked together before and make a good team. Now it is time to close, and as the nurse prepares the sutures for the surgeon, a brief smile breaks out. "I am good at what I do," the nurse thinks to himself as he once again reaches over to wipe the surgeon's brow. The surgeon smiles in gratitude, grateful that she has such dedicated and able professionals working with her.

Robin undresses, feeling nervous and apprehensive, and then feels silly. After all, the photographer is a professional and has probably seen a thousand naked bodies, so what is one more? All that work in the weight room, the aerobics—why not show off, after all the work it took to get a such a tight body? "I should be proud," Robin thinks, slipping into the robe thoughtfully provided by the photographer. Once exposed to the lights of the studio, Robin gets another pang of doubt but dismisses it and drops the robe. The photographer suggests a seated pose, and Robin strikes it, but he drops his hands to cover his genitals. "Move your hands to your knees, please," the photographer says gently. After all, she is a professional and knows how to put her models at ease.

The purpose of the stories above, as you undoubtedly have guessed, is to show how quickly our minds fall into stereotypes of gender and how unsettling it is to readjust the mind when gender stereotypes are violated. Gender stereotypes are fundamental to our ways of thinking, which makes it difficult to realize how thoroughly our conceptions of the world are shaped by gender issues. For example, when a baby is born, the very first question we ask is "Is it a boy or a girl?" The parents proudly display a sign in their yard or send a card to friends, proclaiming "It's a girl!" or "It's a boy!" as the sole identifying trait of the child. The card does not state "It's a redhead!" or "It's over eight pounds!" From the moment of birth onward, the child is thought of first as male or female, and all other characteristics—whether the child is tall, bright, an artist, Irish, disabled, gay—are seen in light of the person's gender. Gender is what sociologists call a **master status** (Risman and Schwartz, 1988), meaning a fundamental concept that we use to categorize each other, as well as ourselves.

Most people become confused and uncomfortable when they are denied knowledge of a person's gender. In one study, adults were asked to interact with a baby but were not told its gender. Every single adult in the study attributed a gender to the child, deciding that it was "soft" and so must be a girl or "strong" and so must be a boy, even though they all played with the same child (Seavey et al., 1975). It is very difficult to know how

master status: A primary characteristic or role that determines the way one is regarded; for example, being African American, gay, a movie star, or female.

to interact with someone whose gender we do not know because we are so programmed to react to people first according to their gender. You may be familiar with the character "Pat," who was on the television program *Saturday Night Live*. It was impossible to tell whether Pat was a male or female, and the skits were built around the ploys people used to try to discover Pat's gender. No one seemed to ask why it was so important for people to figure out Pat's gender in the first place; the need to categorize people by gender was taken for granted. But why is it so important?

Even our language is constructed around gender. English has no neutral pronoun, meaning that every time you refer to a person, you must write either "he" or "she." Therefore, every sentence you write about a person reveals his or her gender, even if it reveals nothing else about that person. Writing the vignettes that opened this chapter without using "he" or "she" until the last few sentences was a very difficult task.

Many of our basic assumptions about gender, however, are open to dispute. Gender research has been growing explosively over the past thirty years, and many of the results challenge long-held beliefs about gender differences. Still, research into gender runs into some serious problems. For example, even gender researchers are socialized into accepted gender roles from birth, which may make it very difficult for them to avoid projecting their own gender biases onto the research (Shaklee, 1983). Despite these types of problems, the data do seem to report certain findings consistently. Before you read the rest of this chapter, take the self-test in Where Do I Stand? 5.1 on the following page to see how much you know about the current research on gender. The results might surprise you.

GENDER ROLES

Gender roles are culturally defined behaviors that are seen as appropriate for males and females, including the attitudes, personality traits, emotions, and even postures and body language that are considered fundamental to being male or female in a culture. Gender roles also extend into social behaviors, such as the occupations we choose, how we dress and wear our hair, how we walk (men traditionally walk on the street side, open doors, etc.), how we talk (men often interrupt more, women defer more), and the ways in which we interact with others.

gender roles: A set of culturally prescribed behaviors that determines how members of each gender are expected to behave in a particular society.

Note that by saying that gender roles are *culturally* defined, we are suggesting that such differences are not primarily due to biological, physiological, or even psychological differences between men and women but, rather, are due to the ways in which we are taught to behave. Yet many people believe that many gender differences in behavior are biologically programmed. Who is correct? Another way to ask the question is: Which of our gender-specific behaviors are gender *roles* (that is, culturally determined) and which are **gender *traits*** (that is, innate or biologically determined)? If gender-specific behaviors are biologically determined, then they should remain constant in different societies; if they are social, then we should see very different gender roles in different societies. In fact, there are some gender-specific behaviors that seem to be universal and therefore are probably gender traits related to differences in biology; still others *may* have biological bases. The majority of gender-specific behaviors, however, differ widely throughout the world and are determined primarily by culture.

gender traits: Biologically determined characteristics that differentiate men from women.

Masculinity and Femininity

What is masculine? What is feminine? Not too long ago, the answers would have seemed quite obvious: Men naturally have masculine traits, meaning they are strong,

WHERE DO I $Stand$? 5.1

How Much Do You Know About Gender?

Decide whether each of these statements is true or false:

1. "Gender" is a biological category.   T   F
2. Most behavioral differences between men and women are due to hormonal and biological factors.   T   F
3. Men are innately more aggressive than women.   T   F
4. In all societies, men are responsible for the aggressive needs of society while women stay at home.   T   F
5. Some societies recognize more than two genders.   T   F
6. Every individual has one, unified gender.   T   F
7. Masculine and feminine traits appear in both men and women.   T   F

Answers:

1. *False.* The term "gender" is generally used to refer to the social aspects of one's biological sex.
2. *False.* A few behavioral characteristics in men and women may be different due to biological factors. Still, the overwhelming majority of gender behaviors are socially determined.
3. *True.* Practically the only biologically determined behavioral difference between men and women for which there is overwhelming evidence is that males tend to be more aggressive than women, a trait that is evident even in small children.
4. *False.* Even though male aggression may have biological roots, culture can overcome it. In the Tchambuli tribe, described by Margaret Mead, the women take a more aggressive social role than the men.
5. *True.* Though all societies recognize at least two sexes, some societies treat certain individuals as members of a third gender category.
6. *False.* Transsexuals are people who believe that they are really members of the gender opposite their biological ones; for example, a male transsexual may feel he is a woman "trapped" in a man's body and may undergo sex reassignment surgery to bring his body into conformity with his mind. Another rare case is the biologically asexual person who is born with a total absence of internal or external sexual organs, therefore having no sexual hormones—and no gender.
7. *True.* Research tools, such as Bem's Sex Role Inventory, which measure masculine and feminine traits, find that most people have a combination of traits. Some people measure high in both masculine and feminine traits, and these people are considered androgynous.

stable, aggressive, competitive, self-reliant, and emotionally undemonstrative; women are naturally feminine, meaning they are intuitive, loving, nurturing, emotionally expressive, and gentle. Even today, many would agree that such traits describe the differences between the sexes. These gender stereotypes, however, are becoming less acceptable as our culture changes.

masculinity: The set of behavioral expectations of men in a particular culture.

femininity: The set of behavioral expectations of women in a particular culture.

Masculinity and **femininity** refer to the ideal cluster of traits that society attributes to each gender. Most societies have cultural heroes and heroines who are supposed to embody the traits of masculinity and femininity and serve as models for socializing youths into their gender roles. In some societies, these models are provided by gods and goddesses, religious leaders, warriors, or mythical figures. In modern American society, entertainers and sports figures serve the purpose of providing gender models of behavior. In fact, a good way to understand the changing nature of masculinity and femininity in American society over the last fifty years is to watch movies from each time period. You can see how clearly the relationship between the sexes has changed and evolved; but you might also be surprised to find that movies from the 1940s and 1950s featured strong women and that gender roles were often intentionally violated for comic or dramatic effect.

Eleanor Maccoby (1987) suggests that the terms "masculinity" and "femininity" are used in three distinct ways in society. First, a masculine or feminine person is one who exemplifies those characteristics that have been shown to differentiate the sexes. For example, as we go through the life cycle, different behaviors are considered appropriate for boys and girls: masculine four-year-old boys are supposed to play with trucks and avoid dolls; feminine ten-year-old girls have one or two close girl friends, pay attention in class, and like romantic television shows. Second, we use the terms to refer to the extent to which adults adhere to socially prescribed gender roles; so, as one example, masculine men do not become secretaries and feminine women do not become construction workers. Finally, masculinity and femininity refer to sexual characteristics: Feminine women are those who are attractive to men, and masculine men are those sought after by women. That is why homosexual men are so often labeled "feminine" and lesbians considered "masculine," even if they display no other traits associated with the terms. These models of masculinity and femininity change over time and differ from culture to culture.

SEX TALK

QUESTION **5.1**   **Why are men so into macho sexual behavior? Why do women seem to go after the macho guys instead of the nice guys? Why are women so preoccupied with how they look? Why do guys seem to go for appearances instead of looking for the nice, intelligent girls?**

Men and women always seem to wonder why people of the other sex behave the way they do. Yet society itself supports those kinds of behaviors. Is it really any surprise that men often seem to pursue appearance over substance in women when advertising, television, and women's and men's magazines all emphasize appearance of women? Also, don't women themselves encourage the behavior when they buy millions of dollars worth of beauty products? Is it surprising, conversely, that some women pursue "macho" men when society teaches them to admire male power? Society determines the way we view gender relationships, and each of us is responsible to some degree for continuing those attitudes (see Wolf, 1991; Mosher and Tomkins, 1988).

Models of masculinity and femininity are changing rapidly in modern American society. Women are taking jobs traditionally reserved for men, such as construction, policing, race-car driving, and politics. Men are taking jobs traditionally reserved for women, such as child care, nursing, and switchboard operation. Women dress in slacks and cut their hair short; men sport earrings and wear their hair in pony tails. Female executives have male secretaries. Women explore new domains by traveling into space, and men explore new domains by changing their children's diapers.

Changing gender roles can also result in confusion, fear, and even hostility in society. Gender roles exist, in part, because they allow comfortable interaction between the sexes. If you know exactly how you are supposed to behave and what personality traits you are supposed to assume in relation to the other sex, interactions between the sexes go more smoothly. When things are changing, determining correct behaviors becomes more difficult. For example, when construction sites were the exclusive domain of men, a very "male"-oriented culture arose that included sexual joking, whistling at passing

Movies have captured the changing sexual roles over time. Although strong women have been shown in the cinema since the days of silent movies, they usually occupied stereotypical roles of mother and lover. In *Casablanca,* Bergmann tells Bogart that he must do the thinking for them both. Katharine Hepburn often played women who entered the workforce or violated stereotypes; Linda Hamilton in *Terminator II* shows the modern trend toward androgyny, where women can be warriors.

Women are commonly found today in occupations traditionally reserved for men.

women, etc. Now that women have become part of the construction team, men complain that they do not know how to behave anymore: Are sexual jokes and profanity still okay or are they sexual harassment? Some people yearn for the old days when male and female behaviors were clearly defined, and they advocate a return to traditional gender roles. Other people still see inequality in American society and argue that women need to have more freedom and equality.

Are Gender Roles Innate?

As gender stereotypes evolve, a trait may no longer be seen as the exclusive domain of a single gender. For example, many people have been trying to change our current stereotypes of men as "unemotional" and women as "emotional." The constellation of traits that has been traditionally seen as masculine and feminine may be changing, becoming less rigid. For many centuries, these types of gender traits were seen as innate, immutable, part of the biological makeup of the sexes. Few scientists suggested that the differences between men and women were primarily social; most believed that women were fundamentally different than men. For example, E.D. Cope wrote in 1887 (quoted in Gould, 1981:117–118):

> *The gentler sex is characterized by a greater impressibility;. . . warmth of emotion, submission to its influence rather than that of logic; timidity and irregularity of action in the outer world. All these qualities [also] belong to the male sex, as a general rule, at some period of life . . . probably most men can recollect some early period of their lives when the emotional nature predominated—a time when emotion at the sight of suffering was more easily stirred than in maturer years. . . . Perhaps all men can recall a period of youth when they were hero-worshippers—when they felt the need of a stronger arm, and loved to look up to the powerful friend who could sympathize with and aid them. This is the "woman stage" of character.*

In other words, not only was the difference in the sexes innate, but men were seen as superior, having developed past the "emotional" nature of women. In fact, scientists and philosophers throughout history (most of whom were, of course, male) often wrote of the natural superiority of men. There is even common reference in the nineteenth century to "women, children, and savages" when scientists were discussing the "inferior" or less-developed groups of human beings when compared to white males (Gould, 1981). Unfortunately, these attitudes still exist, both subtly in cultures like our own and overtly in cultures where women are allowed few of the rights granted to men.

How many of our gender behaviors are biological and how many are socially transmitted? The truth is that the world may not split that cleanly into biological versus social causes of behavior. Behaviors are complex and are almost always interactions between one's innate biological capacities and the environment in which one lives and acts. Behaviors that are considered innately "male" in one culture may be assumed to be innately "female" in another. Even when modern science suggests certain gender traits that seem to be based on innate differences between the sexes, culture can contradict that trait or even deny it.

For example, most researchers accept the principle that males display more aggression than females; adult males certainly demonstrate this tendency, which is probably the result, in part, of higher levels of testosterone. When female bodybuilders, for example, take steroids, they often find themselves acquiring male traits, including losing breast tissue, growing more body hair—and becoming more aggressive. However, the difference is also demonstrated in early childhood, where boys are more aggressive in play while girls tend to be more compliant and docile. Yet Margaret Mead's (1963) famous discussion of the Tchambuli tribe of New Guinea shows that such traits need not determine gender roles. Among the Tchambulis, the women performed the "aggressive" occupations such as fishing, commerce, and politics, while the men were more sedentary and artistic and took more care of domestic life. The women assumed the dress appropriate for their activities—plain clothes and short hair—while the men dressed in bright colors. So even if we accept biological gender differences, societies like the Tchambuli show that human culture can transcend biology.

Are any gender traits commonly considered biological? Physically, males tend to be larger and stronger, with more of their body weight in muscles and less in body fat than females. Females, however, are born more neurologically advanced than males, and they mature faster. Females are also biologically heartier than males; more male fetuses miscarry, more males are stillborn, the male infant mortality rate is higher, males acquire more hereditary diseases and remain more susceptible to disease throughout life, and men die at younger ages than women. Males are also more likely to have developmental problems such as learning disabilities. It has long been believed that males are better at mathematics and spatial problems, while females are better at verbal tasks; for example, female children learn language skills earlier than males. Yet many of these traits may be the result of socialization rather than biology. The research on the gender gap in intellectual abilities is contradictory and controversial, with researchers on both sides arguing for their interpretations of the data (Holden 1991).

Another aspect of gender that is said to be in some sense innate in females is "mothering" or the "maternal instinct." Do women really have a maternal instinct that men lack? For example, is there a psychological bonding mechanism that happens to women who carry babies in their wombs, one that fathers are unable to experience? Historians have pointed out examples (such as France and England in the seventeenth and eighteenth centuries) where maternal feelings seem almost nonexistent; children were considered a nuisance, and nursing was seen as a waste of time. Poor children were often abandoned (birth control for the poor was almost nonexistent), while the children of the wealthy were sent to the countryside for care by a **wet nurse**. Infant mortality was high, and the records of the time often show little concern for the dead child, who was replaced later by another (Gergen, 1991). So the question of an innate female desire for childrearing is far from settled.

wet nurse: A woman brought in to breast feed an infant for another woman.

Boys and girls do show some differences in behavior that appear to be universal. For example, in a study of six different cultures, Whiting and her colleagues (Whiting and Whiting, 1975; Whiting and Edwards, 1988) discovered that certain traits seemed to characterize masculine and feminine behavior in three-to six-year-olds. In almost all countries, boys engaged in more-insulting behavior and rough-and-tumble play, and boys "dominated egoistically" (tried to control the situation through commands), while girls more often sought or offered physical contact, sought help, and "suggested responsibly" (dominated socially by invoking rules or appealing to greater good). Interestingly, though their strategies were different, both boys and girls often pursued the same ends; for example, rough-and-tumble play among boys and initiation of physical contact among girls are both strategies for touching and being touched. However, Whiting suggests that even these behaviors might be the result of different kinds of pressures put on boys and girls; for example, in their sample, older girls were expected to take care of young children more often than boys, and younger girls were given more responsibility than younger boys. These different expectations from each gender may explain later differences in their behaviors. So even behaviors that are spread across cultures may not prove to be innate differences.

There has always been evidence that men's and women's brains were different; autopsies showed that men's brains were more assymetrical than women's, and women seemed to recover better from damage to the left hemisphere of the brain (as in strokes), where language is situated. Yet it has always been unclear what facts such as these mean. Recently, newer techniques in brain imagining have provided evidence that women and men actually use their brains differently while thinking (Kolata 1995a; 1995b). While it is too early to know what these differences mean, future studies may be able to provide clearer pictures of the different ways men and women think.

Aside from the above traits, almost no differences between the sexes are universally accepted by researchers. This does not mean that there are not other biological gender traits; we simply do not know for sure. We must be careful not to move too far in the other direction and suggest that there are no innate differences between the sexes. Many gender traits remain controversial, such as relative levels of activity and curiosity and facial recognition skills. But these are relatively minor differences. Even if it turns out, for example, that female infants recognize faces earlier than males, as has been postulated, or that male children are more active than females, would that really account for the enormous gender role differences that have developed over time? Though biologists still study innate differences between the sexes, many researchers have been turning their attention recently to gender similarities.

CATEGORIES OF GENDER

sex typing: The development of stereotypical ideas about men and women that are then applied to particular individuals and provide expectations of how that individual will behave.

Culture and social structure interact to create **sex typing**, a way of thinking that splits the world into two basic categories—male and female—and suggests that most behaviors, thoughts, actions, professions, emotions, and so on fit one gender more than the other (Epstein, 1988). In fact, when given a set of adjectives, most people can easily begin to separate those adjectives into male and female groups. This is true even of objects. For example, think of these two animals—a bear and a gazelle. Which of the two is more masculine, and which is more feminine? Of course, there are male and female bears and male and female gazelles, but the *idea* of masculinity encompasses traits like strength, size, aggression, and so on that leads us to consider bears more "masculine," while we consider the graceful, slim, delicate gazelle "feminine."

These stereotypes become so basic to our way of thinking that we do not even realize the powerful hold they have over our ways of conceiving of the world. Many cultures build their entire views of the world around masculinity and femininity. Some cultures have taken these ideas and created models of the universe based upon masculine and feminine traits; the Chinese concept of yin and yang refer to the feminine and masculine side of all things and are accompanied by a series of traits that are considered associated with each. Yang represents the masculine, firm, strong, sides of life, and yin represents the feminine, weak, yielding side; there are also thousands of other yin-yang polarities, and the goal of Chinese life is to keep these forces in balance (see Chapter 1).

Gender is socially constructed; that is, societies decide how gender will be defined and what it will mean. For example, in American society, conceptions of "masculinity" and "femininity" have been seen as mutually exclusive; that is, a person who is feminine cannot also be masculine and vice versa (Spence, 1984). But research has shown that masculinity and femininity are independent traits that can exist in people separately

(Spence, 1984; Bem, 1978). Bem (1978) suggests that this can lead to four types of personalities: those high in masculinity and low in femininity; those high in femininity and low in masculinity; those low in both ("undifferentiated"); and those high in both ("androgynous"). Such categories may challenge traditional thinking about gender. So may examples of ambiguous gender categories, such as transsexualism or asexuality. In fact, the more one examines the categories of gender that really exist in the social world, the clearer it becomes that gender is more complicated than just splitting the world into male and female.

Masculinity

From the moment of birth, almost every society has different expectations of its males and females. In many societies, men must go through trials or rights of passage in which they earn their right to be men; few societies have such trials for women. For example, the !Kung bushmen have a "Rite of the First Kill" that is performed twice for each boy—once after he kills his first large male animal and once after he kills his first large female animal (Collier and Rosaldo, 1981). During the ceremony, a gash is cut in the boy's chest and filled with a magical substance that is supposed to keep the boy from being lazy. Hunting prowess is ritually connected with marriage, and men acquire wives by demonstrating their ability at the hunt. For example, a boy may not marry until he goes through the Rite of First Kill, and, at the wedding, he must present a large animal he has killed to his bride's parents. Even the language between killing and marrying is linked; !Kung myths and games equate marriage with hunting and talk of men "chasing," "killing," and "eating" women just as they do animals (Collier and Rosaldo, 1981).

Figure **5.1**
In the Chinese symbol of yin-yang, the yin (black) represents the feminine and the yang (white) the masculine, each wrapped up in the other and necessary to make a whole. Note that there is a seed of the masculine in the feminine and vice versa, showing that men and women each have aspects of the other as part of their fundamental nature.

SEX TALK

QUESTION **5.2** **Why is there such peer pressure on men to be sexually active and to "conquer" women?**

Many explanations have been suggested. One is sociobiological; women always know their genes will be passed along no matter who impregnates them, while men can never be 100% sure their genes will be passed along. Therefore, the best genetic strategy for males, some argue, is to try to impregnate as many women as possible. However, in some cultures men are not expected to engage in sexual "conquests." Another approach would be to try to understand the nature of male and female power in society. Men tend to gain prestige by competing successfully for society's resources, and women have often been considered simply another resource over which men compete. These attitudes are a primary target of those who criticize modern gender relationships.

Williams and Best (1982) collected data about masculinity and femininity in thirty different countries and found that all had a general view of men as stronger, more active, and higher in achievement, autonomy, and aggression. Differences also exist; for example, they found that women are viewed more positively in Catholic countries than in Protestant countries. In a study of thirty-seven countries, Buss (1989) found that women and men value different qualities in each other; women, more than men, tended to value the qualities of being "good financial prospects" and "ambitious and industrious" in the other sex. This finding was true in all thirty-seven countries, showing that throughout the world masculinity is judged, at least in part, in terms of a man's ability to succeed as a provider and as an aggressive worker.

American society has similar stereotypes. Men are often judged by their "prowess" in business, with successful men receiving society's admiration. Despite the fact that men tend to have privileges women do not have in many societies, and despite the fact that male traits in many societies are valued more than female traits (which we discuss in further detail below), it is not easy for men to live up to the strong social demands of being male. Great contradictions are inherent in the masculine role: The man is supposed to be the provider and yet is not supposed to live entirely for his work; he is often judged by his sexual successes and yet is not supposed to see women as sexual objects to be conquered; he is supposed to be a strong, stable force, yet must not cut his emotions off from his loved ones; and he is never supposed to be scared, inadequate, impotent, inexperienced in sexuality, or financially dependent upon women. Also interesting is another set of stereotypes about men, expressed by Epstein (1988:237):

> *There has always been a theme in women's folklore, at least in the Western world, that women know best what men need, that men are often childlike and incompetent, that their egos need bolstering because they are unsure of themselves and easily threatened at work, that they are vulnerable weak reeds depending on a woman's strength in matters of emotion, and that they cannot cope with children, the home, and other aspects of life in the female domain.*

Men in all societies live with these types of contradictions. In some cases, men simplify their lives by exaggerating the "macho" side of society's expectations, becoming hypermasculine males who play out the script of the warrior in their relations to the world (Mosher and Tomkins, 1988). To these macho men, violence is manly, danger is exciting, and sexuality must be pursued callously. Men who rape often express this type of hypermasculinity (Scully and Marolla, 1985).

Another side of the masculine way of being must also be addressed, however. David Gilmore (1990) notes that men often must go through trials to prove their masculinity, except in those few societies where people are totally free of predators and enemies and where food is plentiful. In those societies, there is no stress on proving "manhood" and little pressure to emphasize differences between men and women. Gilmore concludes that in most societies masculine socialization prepares men to adopt the role of safeguarding the group's survival, to be willing to give their own lives in the hunt or in war to assure the group's future by protecting the women's ability to reproduce. Gilmore's point is that men are not concerned with being macho as an end in itself but are concerned with the ultimate welfare of society. In fact Gilmore argues, men are as much nurturers as women, concerned with society's weaker and more helpless members, willing to give their energy and even their lives for the greater social good.

Though masculinity has its privileges, it has its down side too. Men do not live as long as women, in part because of the demands of the male role. For example, men are more likely to die of stress-related illnesses, including lung cancer (men smoke more than women), motor vehicle accidents (men drive more than women, often because of work-related need), suicide (women attempt suicide more often, but men are more successful at actually killing themselves), other accidents (men do more dangerous work activities than women), cirrhosis of the liver (there are more male alcoholics and drug addicts), and heart disease (Gilmore, 1990; Harrison, 1978). Men also die more often in wars.

In fact, with all the attention on the ways stereotypes of gender harm women, men are equally the victims of society's expectations. Male stereotypes tend to be narrower than female stereotypes, and men who want to conform to society's ideas of masculinity have *less* flexibility in their behavior than women who want to live up to feminine stereotypes (Hort et al., 1990). For example, it is still unacceptable for men to cry in public except in the most extreme of circumstances. Crying is the body's natural response to being upset. Boys are taught not to cry, but that is difficult when they are emotionally moved; so they stop allowing themselves to be moved emotionally—and then are criticized for shutting themselves off (Resnick, 1992).

Recently, many authors in American society have been trying to redefine the male role. Part of the feminist project was to redefine men's roles and the ways men looked at gender differences. More recently, the "Men's Liberation" movement has argued that men can escape from stereotypical men's roles by cultivating their nurturing, caring side without losing those qualities that make them men. Two books, *Iron John* by Robert Bly (1990) and *The Fire in the Belly* by Sam Keen (1991), argue that men have lost their traditional roles as warriors, which were less about killing than about group solidarity and the ritual of male contact. What is needed, they suggest, is a new definition of masculinity that does not destroy what is unique about being male.

Femininity

When someone says, "she is a very feminine woman," what image comes to mind? Is the first image that comes to mind a woman in a business suit, or the president of a corporation? Usually we associate femininity with qualities such as beauty, softness, empathy, concern, and modesty. A feminine women knows how to flatter a male's ego and how to flirt gracefully, without being too obvious (Maccoby, 1987). In fact, in almost every culture, femininity is defined by being the opposite of masculinity (Ortner and Whitehead, 1981).

On the other hand, ideas of femininity are not static. Sheila Rothman (1978) has argued that modern American society has gone through a number of basic conceptions of what "womanhood" (and, by extension, femininity) should be. For example, the late nineteenth century emphasized the value of "virtuous womanhood," whereby women brought "morality" to society by starting women's clubs that brought women together and eventually led to the battling of perceived social ills. The Women's Christian Temperance Union, for example, started a movement to ban alcohol, which eventually succeeded. By the early part of the twentieth century, the concept of the ideal woman shifted to what Rothman calls "educated motherhood," whereby the woman was supposed to learn all the new, sophisticated theories of childrearing and was to shift her attention to the needs of children and family. Over the next few decades, the woman's role was redefined as a "wife-companion," and she was supposed to redirect her energy away from her children and toward being a sexual companion for her husband. Finally, Rothman argues, the 1960s began the era of "woman as person," where a woman began to be seen as autonomous and competent and able to decide the nature of her own role in life independent of gender expectations.

Among feminist scholars, ideological battles rage about the meaning of being a woman in today's society; for example, many have faulted feminism for its attitude, at least until recently, that women who choose to stay in the home and raise children are not fulfilling their potential. Yet women with young children who do work often report feelings of guilt about not being with their children (*The New York Times,* 1992). Many argue that the idea of femininity itself is an attempt to mold women in ways determined by men. In fact, such feminist theorists as Catherine MacKinnon (1987) argue that men have always set the definitions of what gender, sexual difference, and masculinity and femininity are, and so gender itself is really a system of dominance rather than a social or biological fact.

For example, the pressure on women to stay thin, to try to appear younger than they are, and to try to appear as beautiful as possible can be seen as reflections of male power (Wolf, 1991). Businesswomen must still try to appeal to men, while men in business need not dress or act in ways that are designed to appeal to women. Sexually, as well, women are supposed to conform to feminine stereotypes and be passive, naïve, and inexperienced. The media reinforce the ideals of feminine beauty, and the pressures on women to conform to these ideals are what lead to eating disorders and the surge in cosmetic surgery (Wolf, 1991).

The messages a woman receives from the culture are contradictory; she needs a job for fulfillment but should be home with her children; she is more than her looks, but she had better wear makeup and stay thin; she has every opportunity men have but only on men's terms. Though femininity has moved away from classic portrayals of women as docile and subservient to men, the pressures are still strong to appeal to those outdated stereotypes.

Androgyny

androgyny: The strong presence of both masculine and feminine gender role characteristics in a single individual.

The breakdown of traditional stereotypes about gender has refocused attention on the idea of **androgyny**. Bem (1978), as we mentioned earlier, suggested that people have different combinations of masculine and feminine traits. She considers those who have a high score on both masculinity and femininity to be androgynous. Androgyny, according to Bem, allows greater flexibility in behavior because people have a greater repertoire of possible reactions to a situation. For example, Hemmer and Kleiber (1981) have suggested that female and, to a lesser extent, male children who are labeled with cross-sex behavior (girls who are "tomboys," boys who are "sissies") may, in fact, demonstrate more flexibility and creativity in their behavior than peers who conform to gender-specific roles. Bem (1974; 1975; 1977) has tried to show that androgynous individuals can display "masculine" traits (such as independence) and "feminine" traits (such as playfulness with a kitten) when situations call for them.

Due to Bem's early research on masculinity, femininity, and androgyny, people suggested that androgynous attitudes were a solution to the tension between the sexes. Even though there was very little research on what androgyny actually meant and how an androgynous personality compared to other types of personalities, people who were working on gender roles saw androgyny as a potential way to overcome gender stereotypes. Bem also portrayed androgyny as a desirable state. Writing about the androgynous male, she claimed: "Clearly, he is a liberated companion for the most feminist among us" (Bem, 1976:58). Androgynous individuals were found to be generally more loving than sex-typed individuals (Coleman and Ganong, 1985). Androgynous males were more likely to be warmly complementary than sex-typed males, and androgynous females were better at saying "no" to unreasonable requests (Kelly et al., 1981). Androgynous men and women seemed to have more positive attitudes toward sexuality than sex-typed individuals (Walfish and Myerson, 1980), and androgynous women reported more orgasms than feminine women (Radlove, 1983). Still, androgyny may not be the answer to all of the world's gender problems, for suggesting that people should combine aspects of masculinity and femininity may simply reinforce and retain outdated ideas of gender. Bem later reassessed her evaluation of androgyny, which

> . . . *continues to presuppose that there is a feminine and masculine within us all, that is, that the concepts of "femininity" and "masculinity" have an independent and palpable reality rather than themselves being cognitive*

constructs derived from gender schematic processes. A focus on androgyny thus fails to prompt serious examination of the extent to which gender organizes both our perceptions and our social world.

Bem (1984: 221–22)

Transsexualism

Transsexualism has profound implications for the ways in which we conceive of gender categories. In the Western world, we tend to think of gender in terms of biology; if you have XX chromosomes and female genitalia, you are female, and if you have XY chromosomes and male genitalia, you are male. This is not universally true, however. A male transsexual is convinced that he is really a female "trapped" in a man's body, even though he has a fully male biological and anatomical gender. Another way to put it is that a transsexual's gender identity is inconsistent with his or her biological sex. This is called **gender dysphoria**.

transsexualism: Extreme gender dysphoria that has persisted without fluctuation for at least one or two years.

SEX TALK

QUESTION **5.3** **I don't understand transsexualism. Is a transsexual a homosexual who has taken things to an extreme?**

gender dysphoria: The state of feeling and believing that one is not really a member of one's anatomical gender (see **transsexualism**).

Transsexualism is difficult to understand because even the experts are not sure what the phenomenon means about human sexuality. One thing is certain: These are not just people with homosexual desires taken to an extreme. In fact, a significant percentage of transsexuals change sex, let's say from male to female, and then have sex exclusively with females! That is, they are heterosexual before the surgery and become "homosexual" afterwards. Our difficulty in understanding transsexualism comes from the natural assumption that everyone's biological sex and psychological gender are unified. Transsexualism shows clearly that the way we feel about our gender may be unrelated to the biological equipment we were given.

Some cases of transsexualism have received great publicity. In 1952, George Jorgenson, an ex-marine, went to Denmark to have his genitals surgically altered to resemble those of a female. George changed his name to Christine, went public, and became the first highly publicized case of a transsexual who underwent **gender (or sex) reassignment surgery**. Christine recalled having desired to be a girl from an early age, avoided rough sports, and was a small, frail child with underdeveloped genitals (Jorgenson, 1967). Jorgenson's story is typical of other transsexuals, who knew from an early age that they were somehow different.

gender reassignment surgery: Surgery for transsexuals, designed to re-form male genitals into female genitals or female genitals into male.

Another famous case was that of Richard Raskind, an eye doctor and tennis player, who had sex reassignment surgery and then tried to play in a professional women's tennis tournament as Renee Richards. More recently, in the early 1990s, the case of Barry Cossey received much publicity. Cossey was passing as a female showgirl by the age of 17, eventually underwent sex reassignment surgery, and became known as "Tula."*

For a long time, Tula kept her sex change a secret and went on to become a well-known model, even appearing in bathing suit and brassiere advertisements. After

---

* It should be noted that in Tula's case, she was born with a chromsomal abnormality: she has XXXY chromosomes, compared to XX for a normal female and XY for a normal male. In most cases of transsexualism, however, no abnormal chromosomes are found.

receiving a role in the James Bond spy thriller *For Your Eyes Only* (where she appeared primarily in a skimpy bathing suit), a British tabloid uncovered her past and announced: "James Bond Girl Was a Boy!" Tula then wrote an autobiography and began appearing on the talk-show circuit as a crusader for the rights of transsexuals. She even appeared fully nude in *Playboy* (1991)!

More males than females experience gender dysphoria, though the exact degree of difference is in dispute. Transsexuals may have either homosexual desires or heterosexual desires. For example, depending upon the study, somewhere between 25% and 53% of male-to-female transsexuals report a preference for male partners, and an equal number report preferring a female partner; about 20% report being bisexual; and, in one study, 27% denied any sexual activity (Blanchard et al., 1987). In other words, some male transsexuals become female and limit their sexual contact to other females. Among female-to-male transsexuals, almost all desired female partners after surgery. Transsexuals need not make the change when they are young; one study of older female-to-male transsexuals found women who were requesting sex reassignment surgery for the first time while in their fifties.

Most transsexuals report a life-long desire to be a member of the other sex. The desire is often temporarily satisfied by cross-dressing, but, unlike transvestites, transsexuals do not find cross-dressing satisfying in itself. The personal accounts of transsexuals are usually tales of suffering and confusion over who they are and what gender they belong to, and therapy is useful only in establishing for them that they do, in fact, deeply believe themselves to be emotionally and psychologically of the other sex. Gender reassignment surgery was developed to help bring transsexuals' biology into line with their inner lives. See Sexuality Today 5.1 for a description of the process of gender reassignment.

Transsexuals want to live as members of their *psychological* gender, not their biological sex. This desire suggests a difference between the two: Biology alone cannot determine how gender is defined. In fact, to the transsexual, psychological gender is *more* important than biological gender. However, the issue of gender is even more complicated than that, for even the transsexual often accepts the idea that there are two fundamental genders. Yet that is not true in every culture.

Third Genders

Transsexuals stretch our usual concepts of gender by suggesting that there can be a fundamental and irreconcilable break between our psychological and biological genders. However, some cultures challenge our notions and even having a gender category that is neither male nor female—a third gender.

Many traditional Native American societies had a category of not-men/not-women known as **berdaches**. The berdache was usually (but not always) a biological male who was effeminate or androgynous in behavior and who took on the social role of females (Williams, 1986; Blackwood, 1984). The berdache often married a male Native American (and adopted children), though not all married or engaged in sexual behavior with males. Berdachism was considered a vocation, like being a hunter or warrior, which was communicated to certain boys in their first adult vision. In all social functions, the berdache was treated as a female. The berdache held a respected, sacred position in society and was believed to have special powers.

Biologically female berdaches also lived in Native American tribes. Female berdaches began showing interest in boys' activities and games during childhood

berdache: A social role among some Native American tribes in which people of one biological gender lived their lives as members of the other biological gender.

SEXUALITY*Today*   *5.1*

Sex Reassignment Surgery

The process of seeking gender reassignment is long and complicated. The first step is psychological counseling to confirm that the individual is truly gender dysphoric; one cannot just see a doctor and demand a sex change. The next step is to live as a member of the other sex, and if a person does so successfully for a designated period of time, hormones are then administered to masculinize or feminize his or her appearance. Finally, sex reassignment surgery (SRS) is performed. It may take three or more surgeries to complete the transition.

For male-to-female transsexuals, the scrotum and testicles are removed. The penis is removed, but the penile skin, with all its sexually sensitive nerve endings, remains attached. This skin is then used to form the inside of the vagina, which is constructed along with a set of labial lips to simulate female genitalia as closely as possible. Finally, silicone implants create breasts. Male-to-female transsexuals have normal intercourse as females and achieve orgasm. Many also report that their male lovers cannot tell they have had SRS.

Female-to-male transsexuals have a number of choices to make. First, the female internal sex organs are usually removed. Since the testosterone they take enlarges their clitoris, many do not have artificial penises constructed but make do with an enlarged clitoris (which can be anywhere from one to three inches long). Others have an artificial penis constructed from the skin of their abdomen, and a scrotum is made from the labia, into which are placed prosthetic testicles. These penises look fairly real, but of course they cannot achieve a natural erection, so penile implants of some kind are usually used (see Chapter 12 for more on

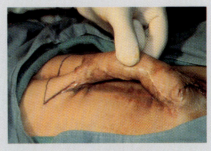

Doctors shape a penis from abdominal skin.

A completed female-to-male transsexual.

penile implants). The results of female-to-male SRS are rarely as good as that of male-to-female.

In fact, SRS in general is controversial, and some transsexuals end up worse off after the surgery, unable to have sex as a man or as a woman. Some clinics have stopped performing transsexual surgery altogether. But for others, who have longed for years to bring their bodies into line with their sense of gender identity, SRS is the ultimate goal. As surgical techniques improve, some of the problems of SRS may be resolved.

(Blackwood, 1984). Adults, recognizing this desire, would teach the girls the same skills the boys were learning. (In one tribe, a family with all girl children might select one daughter to be their "son," tying dried bear ovaries to her belt to prevent conception!) These females were initiated into puberty as men, and thereafter they were, for all purposes, considered men. They hunted and trapped, fought in battle, and performed male ceremonial tasks. Among the Alaskan Ingalik, for example, these biological women would even participate in nude, men-only sweat baths, and the men would ignore the female genitalia and treat the berdache as a man. The female berdache could marry a woman, though the unions remained childless, and the berdache would perform the appropriate rituals when her partner menstruated but would ignore her own menses.

Female berdaches became prominent members of some Native American societies, and in at least one case, a female berdache became chief of the tribe (Whitehead, 1981).

Other cultures have similar roles. The Persian Gulf country of Oman has a class of biological males called the *xanīth* (Wikan, 1977). The *xanīth* are exempt from the strict Islamic rules that restrict men's interaction with women, because *they are not considered men*. They sit with females at weddings and may see the bride's face; they may not sit with men in public nor do tasks reserved for men. Yet the *xanīth* are not considered females either; for example, they retain men's names.

Another important example are the *hijra* of India (Nanda, 1986). The *hijra* are men who undergo ritual castration in which all or part of their genitals are removed, and they spend their lives in communes worshiping the Mother Goddess Bahuchara Mata. They are believed to have special powers to curse or bless male children, and supposedly they make their livings selling their blessings to new parents, though many actually engage in prostitution. *Hijra* dress as women, though they do not really try to "pass" as women; their mannerisms are exaggerated, and some even sport facial hair. In India, the *hijra* are considered neither men nor women but inhabit a unique third social gender (Nanda, 1986).

Other cultures have similar roles. In Thailand, there is a group of people called the *kathoey,* who are very similar to Oman's *xanīth.* Two other examples are the *aikane* of native Hawaii, who were attached to the court of the chiefs and served sexual, social, and political functions (Morris, 1990), and the *mahu* of Tahiti (Herdt, 1990). The belief in these societies that it is neither obvious nor natural that there are only two genders should make us carefully reconsider our own assumptions about gender.

Asexualism

A final type of gender category is asexuality. On occasion, usually due to the mother taking hormones, a child is born without sexual organs of any kind. This means that the child has no ovaries, uterus, or vagina, has no penis or testicles, and usually has only a bladder and a urethra ending in an aperture for the elimination of urine. Though such a child has a genetic gender (that is, has XX or XY chromosomes) the child has no *biological* gender. Most are assigned a gender in childhood, are given hormones, and live as male or female. Personal Voices 5.1 tells the story of an asexual named Toby, who chose to live without any social gender at all.

GENDER ROLE THEORIES

When a baby is born, it possesses no knowledge and few instinctual behaviors. But by the time the child is about three or four, he or she can talk, feed himself or herself, interact with adults, describe objects, and use correct facial expressions and body language. The child also exhibits a wide range of behaviors that are appropriate to his or her gender. The process whereby this infant who knows nothing becomes a toddler who has the basic skills for functioning in society is called **socialization**. Some would argue that almost everything we know, think, and do is a product of our socialization to one degree or another; for example, the fact that we get hungry is biological; what we eat, when we eat, how we eat, and with whom we eat are all determined by our socialization.

As we saw in the last chapter, different types of sexual socialization occur at different ages and levels of development. The same is true of socialization into gender roles, which is closely related to socialization about sexuality. It is interesting to note that over

socialization: The process whereby social values and knowledge are taught to and assimilated by individuals throughout the life cycle.

Personal

V O I C E S

<u>**5.1**</u>

Toby: An Asexual Person

Toby was born without any internal or external reproductive organs; Toby has no penis, scrotum, or testicles, and Toby has no vagina, ovaries, or uterus. Therefore, Toby also has no male or female sex hormones, except the small amount secreted by the adrenal glands on the kidneys. Though at a molecular level Toby is either XX or XY, it has no impact on Toby's life; therefore, Toby has no real gender and has adopted the term "neuter" rather than male or female. Since Toby has no gender, terms like "he" or "she" are also inappropriate to refer to Toby. Toby therefore uses the word "xe," instead, to use for those who have neither a male or female gender.

Toby was assigned a female gender at birth because the doctor saw no penis. Toby was raised as a girl until the age of about twelve, when Toby began refusing female hormones because xe did not "feel" like the girl everyone thought xe was. Of course, without hormones, Toby could not begin puberty at all. During Toby's early teens, xe also spent some time taking male hormones. But that did not feel right either. Between the ages of thirteen and eighteen, the doctors began to experiment with Toby's gender. Finally, at eighteen, when Toby was no longer a minor, she refused to take any more hormones and has been living as a neuter ever since.

When official or school forms ask for the person's sex, Toby writes in "neuter"; Toby has the first driver's license in the state of Kansas with the designation "O" under sex. Toby uses whichever restroom is less crowded, dresses in jeans and other unisex, casual clothes, and has close friends of both sexes. Toby also taught Sunday school, where, after a period of intense interest, the children decided the fact that their teacher was neither a male nor female was no big deal. Here Toby talks about what it means to be a neuter and to be asexual.

I conclude that I'm neuter because I don't see anything in being male or being female that I can relate to. It's partly a matter of anatomy; the basic medical definitions of maleness and femaleness involve the presence of body parts which I don't have. Most people who don't have those body parts still somehow relate to the idea that there are these things called maleness and femaleness, and everybody has to be one or the other, and therefore I must be one or the other because everyone is. Therefore there has to be something wrong with me that has to be "fixed." I have to be "repaired"—I have to have hormones, I have to have surgery, I have to pretend, or acquire somehow these characteristics that I didn't start out with. I didn't do that. I started out saying, "I don't know what being male or female means; I read the definitions, I looked at myself, they didn't match, and my conclusion was, therefore: I must not be either male or female, therefore it must not be true that everyone has to be one or the other." And that is what I mean when I say that I am neuter.

Being "asexual" means that when I read about feelings and behaviors that are described as sexual, and when I hear people talking about feelings and behaviors that are sexual, I can't relate that to any of my own experience. It doesn't mean anything to me. I do have ways of relating to people that do mean something to me, and to define my ways of relating in terms of sexuality seems to deny, overlook, trivialize everything that matters to me. So I say, OK, we're going to leave all of this behind, sexuality is irrelevant, what I am doing [in relationships] is not sexual. I don't have words for it, but I know it's not sex.

Author's files

the past twenty years or so, many parents have tried to raise their children in "gender-neutral" homes, where traditional stereotypes of gender are not used as extensively in defining children's behavior. Though some positive results are achieved, in general, these children go through stages where their behavior and self-definition follow closely the traditional stereotypes—boys want to dress and act like other boys and play with traditionally male toys (guns, trucks); girls insist on wearing dresses and express a strong desire to do traditionally "female" things, such as playing with dolls and cooking toys. Is this behavior innate, or are gender stereotypes still getting through to these children through television and in playing with their peers? The answer depends on which theory of gender role development you accept.

Theories of Gender Role Development

In Chapter 2 we reviewed general theories of sexuality, and the debates there centered on how much of human sexuality is programmed through our genes and physiology and how much is influenced by culture and environment. Gender role theory struggles with the same issues, and different theorists take different positions. Social learning theorists believe that we learn gender roles almost entirely from our environment, while cognitive development theorists believe that children go through a set series of stages that correspond to certain beliefs and attitudes about gender. Recently, theorists are beginning to try to synthesize these two sides to formulate a theory that includes both biology and culture.

Social Learning Theory*

Social learning theory suggests that we learn our gender roles from our environment, from the same system of rewards and punishments that we learn our other social roles. For example, research shows that parents commonly reward gender-appropriate behavior and disapprove of (or even punish) gender-inappropriate behavior. Telling a boy sternly not to cry "like a girl," approving a girl's use of makeup, taking a Barbie® doll away from a boy and handing him a Power Ranger®, making girls help with cooking and cleaning and boys take out the trash—these little, everyday actions build into powerful messages about gender. Children learn to model their behavior after the same-gender parent to win parental approval. They may learn about gender-appropriate behavior from parents even if they are too young to perform the actions themselves; for example, they see that mommy does the sewing while daddy fixes the car. Children also see models of the "appropriate" ways for their genders to behave in their books, on television, and when interacting with others. Even the structure of our language conveys gender attitudes about things such as the dominant position of the male; for example, the use of male words to include men and women (using "actor" or "waiter" to refer to both men and women).

Cognitive Development Theory

Cognitive development theory assumes that all children go through a universal pattern of development, and there really is not much parents can do to alter it. As the child's brain matures and grows, the child develops new abilities and new concerns, and at each stage, his or her understanding of gender changes in predictable ways. This theory follows the ideas of Piaget (1951), the child development theorist who suggested that social attitudes in children are mediated through their processes of cognitive development. In other words, children can only process a certain kind and certain amount of information at each developmental stage.

As children begin to be able to recognize the physical differences between girls and boys and then to categorize themselves as one or the other, they look for information about their genders. Around the ages of two to five, they form strict stereotypes of gender based on their observed differences—men are bigger and stronger and tend to do

---

* The following discussion is taken largely from Albert and Porter (1988).

aggressive jobs like being policemen or superheroes; women tend to be associated with motherhood through their physicality (e.g., the child asks what the mother's breasts are and are told they are used to feed children) and through women's social roles of nurturing and emotional expressiveness. These "physicalistic" thought patterns are universal in young children and are organized around ideas of gender.

As the child matures, he or she becomes more aware that gender roles are, to some degree, social and arbitrary, and cognitive development theory predicts therefore that rigid gender role behavior should decrease after about the age of seven or eight. So cognitive development theory predicts what set of gender attitudes should appear at different ages; however, the research is still contradictory on whether its predictions are correct (see Albert and Porter, 1988).

New Gender Role Theory

Newer theories of gender role development try to combine social learning theory and cognitive development theory, seeing weaknesses in both. Cognitive development theory neglects social factors and differences in the ways different groups raise children. On the other hand, social learning theory neglects a child's age-related ability to understand and assimilate gender models and portrays the child as too passive; in social learning theory, the child seems to accept whatever models of behavior are offered without passing them through his or her own thought processes.

Gender Schema Theory. Sandra Bem's (1981; 1983; 1987) theory is a good example of a theory that tries to overcome the difficulties posed by the other theories. According to Bem, children (and, for that matter, all of us) think according to **schemas**, which are cognitive mechanisms that organize our world. These schemas develop over time and are universal, like the stages in cognitive development theory; the difference lies in Bem's assertion that the *content* of schemas are determined by the culture. Schemas are like maps in our heads that direct our thought processes.

schema: A network of associations that organizes and guides an individual's perceptions.

Bem suggests that one schema we all have is a **gender schema**, which organizes our thinking about gender. From the moment we are born, information about gender is continuously presented to us by our parents, relatives, teachers, peers, television, movies, advertising, etc. We absorb the more obvious information about sexual anatomy, "male" and "female" types of work and activities, and gender-linked personality traits. But society also attributes gender to things as abstract as shapes (rounded, soft shapes are often described as "feminine" and sharp, angular shapes as "masculine").

gender schema: The network of ideas and associations that guides the way we think about gender and gender roles.

Gender schemas are very powerful in our culture. When we first meet a man, we immediately use our masculine gender schema and begin our relationship with an already-established series of beliefs about him. Meeting a man evokes our particular sets of ideas about men; perhaps, for example, we believe that men are funny, or assertive or tend to hit on women. We even turn to our developing gender schema to make sense of things that are not related to gender; for example, Bem suggests, we might categorize "nightingale" as feminine and "eagle" as masculine, even though we have other schemas (such as an "animal" schema) that fits them better. Our gender schema is more powerful than other schemas and is used more often, Bem argues, because our *culture* puts so much emphasis on gender and gender differences. This is where she parts company with cognitive development theorists, who argue that gender is important to children because of their naturally physicalistic ways of thinking.

The gender schema becomes so ingrained that we do not even realize its power. For example, some people so stereotype gender concepts that it would never occur to them

SEX *Facts*   *5.1*

Martin and Halverston's Study

Carol Lynn Martin and Charles Halverson, Jr. (1983) showed five- and six-year-old children a set of sixteen drawings, eight showing activities consistent with gender stereotypes (such as a boy playing with a train) and eight showing activities inconsistent with gender stereotypes (such as a girl sawing wood). The experimenters had the children identify the gender of the person in each picture, and they corrected the children if they misidentified the gender in the picture.

One week later, the children were asked if they could recall the gender of the people portrayed in various pictures, with questions such as "Do you remember seeing a picture of someone sawing wood in the pictures I showed you last week? Was it a boy, a girl, a man, or a woman?"

Two interesting findings came out of this study. First, when the activity shown in the picture was gender consistent, children were more likely to remember it if it was a female doing it (that is, they were more likely to remember a female washing clothes than a male fixing a car). However, if the activity was gender inconsistent, they were more likely to remember a male doing it (that is, they were more likely to remember a male sewing than a female carrying a heavy object).

The second finding is even more interesting. When the gender behavior was inconsistent, children tended to change the gender of the figure in the picture! In other words, if the picture showed a female sawing wood, they were likely to say that they remembered a man sawing wood. The children tended to switch the gender of the actors in order to turn gender-inconsistent information into gender-consistent information. The children's gender schemas were so firmly set that they had a very hard time assimilating any information that violated those structures.

---

to say "My, how strong you are becoming!" to a little girl, while they say it easily to a little boy. We do not see girls on one end and boys on the other of a weak-to-strong continuum; rather, Bem argues, "strong" as a feminine trait *does not exist* in the female schema for many people, so they rarely invoke the term "strong" to refer to women. This was shown in the interesting study by Martin and Halverson (1983) that we describe in Sex Facts 5.1, where children could not even remember the gender of figures who violated stereotypes.

Gender Hierarchy Theories

gender hierarchy: The ranking of the genders, with one gender (usually male) being dominant and considered superior.

Men tend to be more frequently assigned to formal positions of power and authority in society, creating what we might call a **gender hierarchy**. Though women have held formal positions of power across cultures and tend to wield power in more subtle ways than men, it is still indisputable that, viewed as a whole, women have been restricted from roles of formal power in most societies.

Why are women's roles considered subordinate to, and often inferior to, that of men in many societies? In those societies (and for many theorists, such as Freud) men seem to be the standard against which women are judged. In other words, masculinity is held up as the basic model from which femininity is a deviation. Why is this so? Why are masculine traits in our society more valued than feminine traits? Why is being a female "tomboy" considered admirable, while a male "sissy" is subject to taunting and cruelty? Of course, finding a satisfactory answer to such a complex question, one that will explain every society throughout all of history, is unlikely. Nevertheless, let us briefly examine a few of the many theories that try to get at the basic reasons societies might value traits they see as male over traits they see as female.

Chodorow's Developmental Theory

One example of a psychological theory of gender hierarchy is found in the work of Nancy Chodorow (1978). Chodorow draws from psychoanalytic theory to argue that girls and boys undergo fundamentally different psychological developmental processes. Since females have always been the primary childrearers, Chodorow suggests, we must explore what it means to boys and girls to be brought up by women. Both boys and girls create a powerful bond with their mothers; the mother becomes the source of personal identification for both. But, argues Chodorow, boys have a dilemma: They must separate themselves from their mothers and re-identify themselves as males. This is a very difficult process, and boys do it by devaluing the female role. Since their attachment to the mother is so profound, the only way they can overcome it and adopt a male role, is by deciding that being female is inferior to being male.

On the other hand, girls have a different problem: They can continue to identify with their mothers, but they cannot continue to love their mothers as they mature into heterosexual adults. Boys can carry over their original love for their mothers into adulthood, but heterosexuality in adult girls to some extent involves the loss of the mother. Girls cope with that separation by idealizing the qualities of the father (and therefore all men).

This brief description of Chodorow's rich and complex theory shows how the psychological needs of boys and girls both result in a devaluation of the female and an overvaluation of the male. Perhaps, Chodorow suggests, the overall social gender hierarchy can be traced back to these important psychological processes.

Ortner's Culture/Nature Theory

While Chodorow draws from the experiences of individuals, Ortner's (1974) theory looks at society as a whole. Ortner argues that a universal tendency in cultural thought is to align things male and masculine with "culture" and things female and feminine as closer to "nature." Men are outwardly oriented, going out from the tribe or group to hunt, make war, etc., while women's concerns with childbirth, breast feeding, etc. are more biological and inward. Since culture, in the broad sense, sets human beings apart from animals, while childbirth and child-rearing are traits of all animals, men's cultural role's are valued over women's more biological roles.

Other theorists have taken that idea and developed it (Ortner and Whitehead, 1981). For example, both Strathern (1981), who studied the Mt. Hegeners of New Guinea, and Llewelyn-Davies (1981), who studied the Massai in Africa, differentiate between women's involvement in "self-interest" and men's in the "public good." Women are seen in these two cultures as more involved with local, parochial, and private concerns of the family and children, while men are more concerned with the welfare of society as a whole; another way to put it is that women are concerned with the "domestic domain" and men with the "public domain." The public domain *includes* the domestic domain, which means that women's sphere of influence—the family—is subordinate to man's. Ortner and Whitehead (1981:7-8) conclude their discussion of these kinds of oppositions by suggesting:

> It seems clear to us that all of the suggested oppositions—nature/culture, domestic/public, self-interest/social good—are derived from the same central sociological insight: that the sphere of social activity predominantly associated with males encompasses the sphere predominantly associated with females and is, for that reason, culturally accorded higher value.

MacKinnon's Dominance Theory

Catharine MacKinnon (1987), a feminist scholar, believes that the gender hierarchy is the result of men's attempt to dominate social life. MacKinnon dismisses biological arguments about gender and argues that gender itself is fundamentally a system of dominance rather than a system of biological or social differences. Sometime back in ancient times, she suggests, men assumed the power to define "difference" in society and especially the "difference gender makes." Though she is not clear on how men achieved that first act of dominance ("probably by force," she writes), understandings of sexual differences have since been masculine constructions that are presented as if they are objectively neutral. In other words, men define what is male, what is female, and what difference that makes, but they try to present these ideas as though they were scientifically or objectively true rather than a result of male dominance. "Male" and "female" are therefore not biological categories, MacKinnon suggests, but social and political categories, "a status socially conferred upon a person because of a condition of birth."

MacKinnon argues that these basic gender definitions mean that men and women are never socially equal—they never even start at the same place in society—and therefore, all the attempts to pass laws or otherwise help women are doomed to fail. MacKinnon can see no end to this fundamental inequality except through wholesale social change.

GENDER ROLE SOCIALIZATION THROUGH THE LIFE CYCLE

Socialization into gender roles begins at birth and, nowadays, may begin even before birth! Since we now have accurate ways to determine the gender of a fetus, parents can know months before birth whether it is a boy or a girl and can begin to prepare accordingly. They may set up the nursery in pink or blue and buy dresses or pants. Parents even speak to the unborn child—a mother simply by talking and the father by putting his mouth close to the mother's belly—and communicate ideas about their "little boy" or "little girl." In a real sense, then, these parents may begin trying to communicate gender-specific messages before the child is even born (whether the child actually is influenced by these sounds diffusing into the womb is, of course, another question). In some cultures, it is believed that what a mother eats during pregnancy may effect the gender of the child, so nutrition may differ depending on which gender the mother believes she is carrying or which gender she desires. In any case, parents awaiting the birth of a child are filled with gender expectations, stereotypes, and desires.

Childhood

From the moment the doctor declares, "It's a boy!" or "It's a girl!" a child's life is largely defined by its gender. From the baby's name to how it is dressed to how its room is decorated, gender suffuses the newborn's life. Not only do parents construct different environments for boys and girls from birth, they tend to treat them differently as well. Girls are treated more delicately, as if they are more fragile (they are not), while boys are subject to rougher play (Doyle, 1985), and parents tend to be more restrictive of girl babies and allow boys more freedom and less intervention (Block, 1983; Skolnick, 1992).

Parents tend to dress their children according to gender standards. Imagine the reaction of friends and family if a parent kept a newborn boy in a bedroom decorated in lace, put him in a crib full of Barbie® dolls, and dressed him in pink!

SEX TALK

QUESTION 5.4 **Is there anything really wrong with letting boys and girls act like boys and girls? Why try to discourage boys from playing with guns and girls with dolls? Everyone I know grew up that way and they are okay.**

The same people who believe that they "grew up okay" are often the first to complain about the nature of gender relations in the United States. Perhaps we should not forbid boys from ever playing with toy guns (anyway, they would probably just make their fingers or sticks into guns) or forbid girls to play with dolls, but trying to encourage children to appreciate the activities of the opposite sex can only help matters. Emphasizing differences between the sexes and suppressing a child's desire to explore the activities of the other sex (like stopping a boy from playing with dolls) only further alienates the sexes from each other.

As early as age two, **modeling behavior** begins to emerge, and children begin to realize that objects and activities are appropriate to specific genders. The rules that a child develops at this point are not flexible but universal; to the child, *only* women can wear skirts, and *only* men can use an electric razor. In fact, cross-gender humor is very

modeling behavior: The act of young children mimicking the behavior of adults, usually their parents, in an attempt to learn adult behaviors.

SEXUALITY *Today* 5.2

Play Like a Boy! Play Like a Girl!

For a child, playing is not a game, it is serious business. Play is what teaches the child physical coordination, eye-hand coordination, the rules of gravity and cause and effect, and other physical and motor skills. As the child matures, playing with peers also teaches the child lessons of social interaction, sharing, letting go of things he or she wants, winning and losing, and compromise. Yet strong gender messages are also typically communicated to children during play, even in infancy.

Boys and girls are provided different toys and different play environments from birth. One study, comparing the physical environment of 120 infant girls and boys, found that boys were provided with more sports equipment, tools, and large and small vehicles, while girls had more dolls, fictional characters, and children's furniture (Pomerleau et al., 1990). Parents send a powerful message by the way they decorate nurseries and stock them with playthings, and the message is "There are boy toys and girl toys. You are a boy; therefore you will play with boy toys." In fact, children as young as twenty-four months old can label the gender appropriateness of many toys (Shaklee, 1983). In a study of the toys children request for Christmas, Etaugh and Liss (1992) found that children requested, wanted, received, and best liked sex-appropriate toys. However, when a child *did* request a gender-inappropriate toy, the parent was likely to give them something else. So even when a child wants to escape from toy stereotypes, parents generally do not cooperate.

Walk through a toy store one day. Even though the aisles may not be marked "for boys" and "for girls," it is very clear for which gender an aisle is intended. Boys' toys are often geared toward aggression and destruction, while girls' toys are geared toward domestic life and appearance. Yet many of these preferences are learned. Children in one study were shown a movie in which Muppets assigned masculine, feminine, or sex-neutral attributes to various toys (Cobb et al., 1982). Then the children were put in a playroom where those toys appeared along with other comparison toys. Children of both sexes tended to play more with the test toys when they had been identified by the Muppets as appropriate for their sex; when the videotape identified the toys as appropriate for the other sex, however, children tended to play with the comparison toys. In other words, it was not the toys *themselves* that were desirable but whether the children believed they were "for boys" or "for girls" (Cobb et al., 1982).

The same patterns tend to hold true in other countries too. In a study of play differences between Canada and Poland, Richer (1990) found that boys tended to draw pictures of competitive activities and situations, while girls did not; even when showing the same picture, such as children shooting basketballs, boys would set up a competitive situation (such as someone trying to block the shot) while girls would show more noncompetitive situations. Almost every culture has its own gender-appropriate toys. In Russia, the dolls available to the average child are bulky and have simple, bland clothes. But they also have pink or blue hair to indicate whether they are girl or boy dolls. In fact, when Barbie® came to Russia, complete with sequined outfits and blond hair and toy Ferrari cars, the Russians would often spend over a month's salary to have the doll. When some mothers who were staring longingly at the Barbie® in the store window were asked by a reporter whether Barbie® might not teach their daughters bad lessons, such as the idea that blond hair and Ferraris bring happiness, they looked blank and confused (Kansas City Star, 1992). It seems that Americans are not the only ones who overlook the gender messages of their toys.

funny to young children; a television program that shows a man dressed up in a woman's clothes or a woman who appears on TV sporting a mustache will elicit gales of laughter.

As the child begins to show more complex behaviors, he or she is usually rewarded for displaying gender-stereotyped behavior and discouraged or punished for nonstereotyped behaviors. A boy picks up a bat and hits a ball and hears his parents call, "Good

Children learn much of their gender role behavior by modeling.

boy!" while no such encouragement is forthcoming when he mimics his mother sewing. A daughter watches her father fix the car and receives no instruction about what the parent is doing, while a son is taught the parts of the car. Similarly, when a daughter wanders into the kitchen, the mother who is cooking may begin instructing her on how to mix ingredients, while a son gets no such guidance (see Sexuality Today 5.2).

Early in childhood, gender segregation in play begins, also known as **homosocial play**. Children tend to gravitate to same-sex partners and, as early as the age of two-and-a-half or three, children play more actively and more interactively with same-sex playmates (Maccoby, 1987). This tendency is universal. Researchers have tried rewarding children for playing with the other sex, but as soon as the reward is discontinued, play reverts back to same-gender groupings. Gender segregation may be due to the different playing styles of boys and girls, the attraction of children to others like themselves, or to learned social roles; most probably, it involves a combination of all these factors.

During the school years, gender roles become the measure by which children are judged by their peers. (See Personal Voices 5.2 for a look at how children are bombarded by gender stereotypes in the media.) As early as the preschool years, male gender-stereotyped behavior is linked with perceived competence and peer acceptance and, to a lesser extent, female stereotyped behavior to competence (Cramer and Skidd, 1992). Children who violate sex-typed play are usually rejected (and not kindly) by their peers (Moller et al., 1992). This is especially true of boys, who experience more rejection from their peers when they violate gender stereotypes than girls do. The classroom itself can also strongly reinforce gender stereotypes. Even though teachers believe they show equal attention to boys and girls, research shows that teachers spend more time with boys, give them more attention, both praise and criticize boys more, use more follow-up questions to boys, and tolerate more bad behavior among boys than girls (AAUW, 1992; Sadker and Sadker, 1985). Girls are also steered away from math and science courses and use biased textbooks that reinforce gender stereotypes (AAUW, 1992). Boys who question the teacher are considered curious, while girls who question are considered aggressive. Also, teachers stereotype the tasks they ask boys and girls to do; boys may be asked to help move desks, while girls are asked to erase the blackboard.

homosocial play: The tendency for children to play with others of their own gender.

Gender Roles in the Media*

An enormous amount of research looks at the ways the media help to form gender stereotypes and perpetuate them. Research has shown that stereotypical portrayals of gender roles exist in commercials (Bretl and Cantor, 1988; Mamay and Simpson, 1981; Lovdal, 1989), on television (Kalisch and Kalisch, 1984), in the Sunday comics (Barbant and Mooney), in advertising (Soley and Kurzbard, 1986), in rock videos (Hansen and Hansen, 1988), and even in children's books such as Dr. Seuss (Lurie, 1990)! Not only do these stereotypes exist, but research shows that people react to them. Though the television industry is rapidly becoming more conscious of the gender biases in its programming, the following account, written by a concerned mother in 1992, shows the absence of positive female-gender images for children.

Take a look at the kids' section of your local video store. You'll find that features starring boys, and usually aimed at them, account for nine out of ten offerings. Clicking the television dial one recent week—admittedly not an encyclopedic study—I came across not a single network cartoon or puppet show starring a female.

Contemporary shows are either essentially all-male or are organized on what I call the Smurfette principle: a group of male buddies will be accented by a lone female, stereotypically defined. In the worst cartoons—the ones that blend seamlessly into the animated cereal commercials—the female is usually a little-sister type, a bunny in a pink dress and hair ribbons who tags along with the adventurous bears and badgers. But the Smurfette principle rules the more carefully made shows, too. Thus, Kanga, the only female in "Winnie-the-Pooh," is the mother. Piggy, of "Muppet Babies," is a pint-size version of Miss Piggy, the camp glamour queen of the Muppet movies. April, of the wildly popular "Teen-Age Mutant Ninja Turtles," functions as a girl Friday to a quartet of male superheroes. The message is clear. Boys are the norm, girls the variation; boys are central, girls peripheral; boys are individuals, girls types. Boys define the group, its story and its code of values. Girls exist only in relation to boys.

Well, commercial television—what did I expect? The surprise is that public television, for all its superior intelligence, charm, and commitment to worthy values, short-changes preschool girls, too. Mister Rogers lives in a neighborhood populated mostly by middle-aged men like himself. "Shining Time Station" features a cartoon in which the male characters are train engines and the female

characters are passenger cars. And then there's "Sesame Street." True, the human characters are neatly divided between the genders (and among the races, too, which is another rarity). The film clips, moreover, are just about the only place on television in which you regularly see girls having fun together: practicing double Dutch, having a sleep-over. But the Muppets are the real stars of "Sesame Street," and the important ones—the ones with real personalities, who sing on the musical videos, whom kids identify with and cherish in dozens of licensed products—are all male. I know one little girl who was so outraged and heartbroken when she realized that even Big Bird—her last hope—was a boy that she hasn't watched the show since.

Well, there's always the library. Books about girls are a subset in a field that includes a much larger subset of books about boys (12 of the 14 storybooks singled out for praise in last year's Christmas roundup in Newsweek, for instance) and books in which the sex of the child is theoretically unimportant—in which case it usually "happens to be" male. Dr. Seuss's books are less about individual characters than about language and imaginative freedom—but, somehow or other, only boys get to go on beyond Zebra or see marvels on Mulberry Street. Frog and Toad, Lowly Worm, Lyle the Crocodile, all could have been female. But they're not.

Do kids pick up on the sexism in children's culture? You bet.

The sexism in preschool culture deforms both boys and girls. Little girls learn to split their consciousness, filtering their dreams and ambitions through boy characters while admiring the clothes of the princess.

Boys, who are rarely confronted with stories in which males play only minor roles, learn a simpler lesson: girls just don't matter much.

"We're working on it," Dulcy Singer, the executive producer of "Sesame Street," told me when I raised the sensitive question of those all-male Muppets. After all, the show has only been on the air for a quarter of a century; these things take time. The trouble is, our preschoolers don't have time. My funny, clever, bold, adventurous daughter is forming her gender ideas right now. I do what I can to counteract the messages she gets from her entertainment, and so does her father—Sophie watches very little television. But I can see we have our work cut out for us. It sure would help if the bunnies took off their hair ribbons, and if half of the monsters were fuzzy, blue—and female.

Pollitt (1991)

*See also Special Focus 6, Sexual Images.

Classrooms are places where gender stereotypes are often reinforced. Studies show that teachers pay more attention to boys than to girls.

Adolescence

By adolescence, gender roles are firmly established, and they guide adolescents through their exploration of peer relationships and different "love styles" with potential partners. Part of the task of adolescence is to figure out what it means to be a "man" or a "woman" and to try to adopt that role. Boys quickly learn that to be popular they should be interested in and good at sports, should express interest in sex and in women, should not be overly emotional, and should not display interests that are seen as feminine or girlish. (See Personal Voices 5.2 to see how these learned roles affect career choices.) Girls, on the other hand, seem to have more latitude in their behavior but are supposed to express interest in boys and men, show concern with their appearance, and exercise a certain amount of sexual restraint. When boys deviate from gender role behavior the consequences of being seen as unmasculine or suspected of being homosexual are more severe than when girls deviate. Girls have, traditionally, been sanctioned more than boys when they violate gender stereotypes of *sexuality* (such as being promiscuous). We discuss some reasons that masculine roles are narrower than feminine roles in a later section.

Adolescence can be a particularly difficult time for those with a homosexual orientation. There tends to be little tolerance for homosexuality in adolescence, because homosexuality is seen as the *opposite* of what the teenage male is supposed to be striving for—genuine "masculinity." Though female homosexuality is also seen as deviant and lesbians can be the subject of taunts, females tend to discover their sexual orientation later than males, so fewer "come out" in adolescence. The life of an emerging gay or lesbian adolescent may be fraught with tension and gender role confusion, which contributes to the high suicide rate among gay and lesbian teens.

As teenaged girls move from elementary to junior high and high school, they seem to lose a good deal of the confidence and self-esteem they had before, while boys' confidence and self-esteem increases. Young girls are very self-confident, and they resist norms of female behavior that they find objectionable or harmful until they are eleven or twelve years old. As they enter adolescence, their strong voice tends to become more muted, more tentative and conflicted (Rogers and Gilligan, 1988). They are beginning to recognize that they have a unique understanding of the human social world, but they are not expected to be assertive in their knowledge, while boys are being increasingly rewarded for asserting their opinions.

*P*ersonal

V O I C E S

5.3

How High School Boys and Girls Think About Careers

In her book on gender matters in school and in the work-place, Jane Gaskell (1992) quotes Canadian high school students about their future plans. When asked about who should work, who should stay home, and who should do the housework and child care, high school students of both sexes expressed a lot of ambivalence about the appropriate roles of men and women today.

Females

[A woman's] main job is doing things that, you know, [the man] likes. And making the house their own. Making it a nice and comfortable place to come home to. Supporting him and his problems, sort of thing.

You get bored staying at home. Women should get into things more. My mum is at home. She doesn't know what is going on in the world.

If I had a job that was really important, I probably wouldn't be able to raise my children the way I want to.

I considered engineering pretty seriously [but] . . . if I'm going to get married that's the most important thing I'm looking forward to.

I'd rather be home. I don't want to work the rest of my life. I'd rather do the housework.

I think women should be able to work. My mum did. She didn't do it because we were starving or anything. She did it because we she was really bored. She needed to come out of her shell.

I don't think men are very good at raising children. From what I have seen of fathers, I don't think they could

hack it. I guess that it is just the way they were brought up when they were young. Women have a better knack for it than men do.

Women with small children shouldn't work. It's hard on the kids.

Males

I wouldn't let her work if I could support the family.

I don't think it should be equal. I think the wife should stay home and clean the house and cook while the male goes out and works.

Women should be able to work outside the home. We shouldn't expect them to get married, have babies, and stay home. They do have their own freedom, their own life. They can enjoy it.

When the kids get to be about sixteen and they're in school all day and she's got five hours to kill, she should go out and get a job not far from home so she can get home and make supper.

I can't picture myself staying at home and looking after the kids for five years while she works. I'd just feel sheer lazy.

[Child care] is sort of an equal responsibility too. If a man's home, why not be involved. He sort of groans changing those diapers. I'd probably end up doing it. Changing the kid at two o'clock in the morning . . . yuck.

I could stay home with the kids if her job was more [money] than mine . . . times change. I haven't heard of any men staying home, but it could be all right.

It may be that these teenage gender roles are changing. For example, girls are much more willing to assert themselves and call boys on the phone or ask them out than they were twenty-five years ago, when they would have been considered either "desperate" or "sluts." Yet such changing roles are also confusing; adolescent girls and boys still receive contradictory messages about their roles. Traditional male attitudes value sexual achievement, control of the sexual relationship, and suppression of emotionalism. However, today, teenaged boys are being approached by girls, they are not necessarily more sexually experienced than the girls they date, and they are expected to be sensitive to issues of female equality. Women, on the other hand, have often been taught to be dependent upon males but now are expected to assert their independence. In addition, the tables have turned on achievement to the point that girls who express a wish to become mothers and stay at home may be denigrated for lacking ambition. So, even with all the changes that have lessened the differences between the sexes, it is still not easy for adolescents to negotiate their way into sexual adulthood.

Adulthood

As men and women grow into adulthood, they tend to derive their gender identity primarily in two realms—their careers and their family lives. While many believe that ideas about gender are firmly established by the time we reach adulthood, recent social changes in sex roles show that adults do have the capacity to revise their thoughts about gender roles.

Careers

For many years in Western society, men have been encouraged to develop "careers" while women (insofar as they have been encouraged to work at all) have been taught to get a job that will occupy their time until marriage and children remove them from the workforce. The tendency still exists, especially in the lower classes, for women to choose low-prestige occupations and to subordinate their careers to their husbands'. Socialization pressures shape our career choices and can lead to the devaluation of female work in a number of ways (Eisenhart and Holland, 1992). First, parental and media influences often portray female work as unimportant. The jobs that are visible and exciting to children, such as firefighters, police officers, cowboys, doctors, and even superheroes and cartoon characters, are portrayed as predominantly male. Girls soon learn that "people working" almost always means "men working" while "bringing up children" means "women bringing up children" and that even those jobs traditionally held by women often involve answering to men: nurses answer to male doctors, secretaries to businessmen, teachers to male principals, etc.

As they grow, girls are taught to derive satisfaction from courtship, marriage, the family, and home life. A job is seen as a potential disruption to their "true" fulfillment through relationships and reproduction. Girls learn from early in childhood that women's work is not valued by society; even in college, women often find that their peers encourage them to assess themselves in terms of their romantic successes and not in terms of their career or academic achievements (Eisenhart and Holland, 1992).

Men are also socialized into career choices. Society teaches men that career achievement is, in large part, the measure of their worth. Being the "bread winner" is a crucial part of male identity, and a man's success is often measured in dollars earned.

Women's roles in the workplace are changing, and more women are pursuing careers and are holding positions of responsibility and leadership. In politics, for instance, the election of 1992 was supposed to have ushered in the "Year of the Woman;" even though the Congress is still predominantly male, more women are running than ever before. More and more women are pursuing professions and looking toward careers for at least part of their personal fulfillment. Yet powerful pressures still exist for women to retain primary responsibility for home life, which means that women in high-pressure jobs may have more responsibility than men in similar jobs.

Sandra Day O'Connor, Supreme Court Justice, exemplifies how women have been assuming positions of greater power in American society.

Women and Family Life

We tend to idealize the family in the United States. We like to believe in a time in the not-too-distant past when families were "stable," when most families consisted of a mother at home and a father working; we think of these as happier, simpler times. For example, the 1950s are often portrayed as a time of stable families, the "decade of the suburb," where women were supposed to be content living in beautiful homes with all the modern conveniences (Rothman, 1978). Yet in 1957, Betty Friedan began interviewing her fellow Smith College graduates who were presumably happily married housewives. Her results, published as *The Feminine Mystique* in 1963 (Friedan, 1963), showed that these women were actually lonely, isolated, unhappy, and felt like prisoners trapped in their homes. As one woman put it, "The problem is always being the children's mommy, the minister's wife, and never being myself" (Friedan, 1963:13). Searching for a sense of identity, Friedan said, many women began to focus on sex and their marriages as their sole source of fulfillment. To the husbands, who found meaning in their work, sex was a pleasurable diversion; to these woman, the focus on sex and the marital union itself (rather than what it could accomplish) grew disproportionately in importance, until they literally drove their husbands away; male-initiated divorce grew significantly in the 1950s.

So our stereotypes of the family roles of women in the past may be wrong, yet we often use them to continue encouraging women into the same old patterns. For example, throughout most of history, women worked outside the home, and even today, in most countries, women (especially the poor) are a major part of the workforce. Yet, most women in the United States and elsewhere are still taught that their primary sense of satisfaction and identity should be derived from their roles as wives and mothers. Classic Freudians have claimed that women are best defined by the mothering role and that withdrawal from that role tends to make women neurotic. Many modern writers, even those who consider themselves feminists, still portray women as biologically (Rossi, 1977) or psychologically (Chodorow, 1978) "programmed" to have a special, central mothering role that fathers are unable to assume. Yet, studies show that women whose sole identities are as wives and mothers have higher rates of mental illness and suicide than single or married women who work (Epstein, 1988).

Women receive two conflicting messages from American society: the first is the conservative message that a woman must be married and have children to be fulfilled; the second, a feminist message, is that to be fulfilled, women must have a career outside the home. Women who try to do both find themselves with two full-time jobs. Researchers of domestic life point out that "housework" involves far more than its stereotype of dusting and ironing and includes creating an atmosphere of good family relations, planning the budget and educating oneself in consumer skills, evaluating educational options, being the liaison between the family and outside services (such as appliance repair, etc.), and so on (Epstein, 1988). Single working women with children must assume both roles; but even when a working woman has a working (male) partner, research shows that the woman tends to do a significantly larger percentage of household tasks, though the man does assume some of the burden (Douhitt, 1989).

Many women therefore live with a double sense of guilt. If they work, they feel they are not spending the time they should with their children and are leaving the important task of child-rearing to a nanny, day care center, or other relatives. If they decide to stay at home and raise their children, they may feel, as one highly educated graduate from Stanford University put it, "like I'm a disappointment for the women who have worked so hard to broaden opportunities for other women" (*The New York Times,* 1992b). Many women do not even have that choice because economic circumstances require that they work, and most would not be able to stay at home full-time without public assistance. This dispute has been called the "mommy wars," as working mothers and stay-at-home mothers each try to defend their decisions. Nearly half the stay-at-home mothers in one survey said employed mothers did not spend enough time with their children; among employed mothers, half said they would keep their jobs even if they could get the same salary without working. The debates over working mothers will not end soon, for women are continuing to enter the workforce in great numbers. Over 60% of all women in the United States now work, 75% of women with children younger than eighteen work, and 55% of women with at least one child under three years old work (*The New York Times,* 1992b). As long as society portrays a woman's "real" job as that of mother, women will feel guilty when they choose to be productive outside the family.

Men and Family Life

Because of the traditional view that the family is the primary domain of women and the workplace is the primary domain of men, we have relatively few studies of men's roles in the home. For example, enormous amounts of literature have been dedicated to discussing the "unmarried mother," but it is only recently that the fathers of children born outside of marriage have begun to get any attention (Furstenberg and Harris, 1992). A growing field of men's studies looks at the role of being a "man" in modern society, including the changing domestic demands on men as more women enter the workforce.

Studies do show that men with working wives have begun to share more responsibility for home life (Douhitt, 1989). When men become fathers, they begin to carry out many tasks that are stereotypically female, such as feeding and dressing the baby. Research has found that when men become fathers, their masculine sex-role stereotyping decreases (Archer and Lloyd, 1985). Women still tend to retain primary responsibility for organizing the daily household and for physical chores like preparing meals and doing laundry. Men tend to take on other types of chores, such as heavy-lifting chores and specific projects in the home. Still, even working women spend more hours on household chores than men do.

Because of the changing workforce, the numbers of unemployed men, whose wives are the primary wage earners, are increasing. These "house husbands" assume domestic chores and become the primary caretakers for the children. It is interesting, however, that we consider men who choose to keep house "unemployed" while women who do the same tasks are usually considered outside the wage-earning workforce. There is still an assumption that a man "should" be working, while women may choose to stay home.

The Senior Years

Heterosexual couples can experience either a great sense of loneliness or a newfound freedom as their children grow and leave the home. A few women, especially those with traditional roles as wife and mother, experience the "empty nest syndrome," becoming depressed about losing their primary roles as caretakers and mothers. On the other hand, men (and, more and more, women also) may have trouble adjusting to retirement if they

Many men are assuming traditionally female social roles without feeling a threat to their masculinity.

derived a large sense of their identity from their work. In other words, whether a career or family life is the source of a person's gender identity, significant changes are common in the senior years that may involve difficult adjustments.

As people age, gender roles relax and become less restrictive. For example, older men tend to do more housework than younger men. Many are retired and spend more time at home, or some find that their spouses are becoming less able to handle the household by themselves. Similarly, women who are widowed or whose husbands become disabled must learn to care for their finances or learn other skills that their husbands may have previously handled.

TOWARD GENDER EQUALITY

Can we create a society that avoids gender stereotypes, a society of total gender equality? Would you want to live in such a society? Does a gender-equal society mean that women must be drafted into the army and that we must have unisex bathrooms, or is it something subtler, referring to a sense of equal opportunity and respect?

SEX TALK

QUESTION **5.5** **It seems to me that men and women are just different. Why then are people trying so hard to make them the same?**

> **A common criticism of feminists and other theorists and activists is that they are trying to erase the differences between the sexes. Some theorists may advocate that, but they are in the minority. The agenda for most is not to erase all differences but to erase *inequality.* Inequality comes from differences that are imposed from the environment, not biology. For example, it is a "difference" that women can get pregnant and men cannot, but no one has seriously advocated that we try to get men pregnant. On the other hand, men and women often earn different wages for the same work—and that we can correct (see Epstein, 1988).**

Epstein (1986; 1988) believes that gender distinctions begin with basic, human, dichotomous thinking—the splitting of the world into opposites like good-bad, dark-light, soft-hard, and male-female. This very basic human process tends to exaggerate differences between things, including the sexes, and society invests a lot of energy in maintaining those distinctions.

Many religious and cultural systems clearly define gender roles. Advocates of such systems deny that differentiating gender roles means that one gender is subordinate to the other. For example, Rogers (1978) has argued that we cannot apply Western notions of gender equality to countries with fundamentally different systems. She argues that inequality can only exist in society if women and men are seen in that society as fundamentally similar. In Oman, for example, women are subject to strict social rules that we in the West would clearly see as subordination. Yet Rogers argues that women in Oman see themselves as quite different from men and are uninterested in the male role and male definitions of power. Is it appropriate for us to impose our categories on their society and suggest that women in Oman are exploited and subordinate even though they themselves do not think so? Such questions go to the heart of the discussion of power in society.

The goal for many is not a society without gender distinctions; a world without differences is boring. Yet, a world that restricts people's ability to express difference because of the color of their skin, their religious beliefs, or the type of genitalia they happen to have is unjust. It is the *content* of gender roles, not their existence, that societies can alter to provide each person an opportunity to live without being judged by stereotypes of gender.

Summary

- Gender roles are the culturally determined pattern of behaviors that societies prescribe to the sexes. Gender traits are the biologically determined characteristics of gender. Little agreement exists on which gender characteristics are innate and which are learned in society. Most people agree that males are larger, stronger, and more aggressive, while females are neurologically more advanced than males, mature faster, and are biologically heartier. Some also cite evidence that males may have more spatial abilities and females more verbal abilities.

- Three types of theories about gender role development have been offered: social learning theories, which postulate that almost all gender knowledge is dependent on what children are taught; cognitive development theories, which suggest that children go through a universal set of stages during which they can only learn certain types of information about gender; and newer theories, such as Bem's gender schema theory, which suggest that children do go through developmental stages and that the kinds of things they learn at each stage are largely culturally determined.

- Gender hierarchy theories try to explain why masculine traits tend to be valued in society over feminine traits. Nancy Chodorow's developmental theory suggests that boys must make the switch from identifying with their mothers to identifying with their fathers, which is a very difficult process, and so devalue feminine traits in order to reject them; girls, on the other hand, must learn to love males romantically and so idealize masculine traits. Ortner suggests that women's domain is "nature" since women perform the biological functions of reproduction (domestic duties), while men's domain is "culture" (the public domain), and that the domestic domain is subordinate to the public domain, while culture is valued over nature. Finally, Catharine MacKinnon argues that men get to define what is fundamentally "male" and "female" in society and what the implications of those differences are; therefore, men control gender definitions in society.

- Androgyny is a combination of masculine and feminine characteristics, and some advocate androgyny as a way to transcend gender stereotypes. Transsexuals, people who believe their biological and psychological genders are incompatible, show us that gender is more complex than simply determining *biological* gender. Some societies identify gender categories that are neither male nor female; in other words, some societies identify a third gender. Finally, some people are born without internal or external sex organs and therefore have no real gender at all.

- Infants are socialized into gender roles early through the way they are dressed and treated and through the environments in which they are brought up. As they enter school, children strongly reinforce appropriate gender activity through ridiculing children who violate gender boundaries. Adolescents "try on" adult gender roles and attitudes.

- Careers have been seen as the domain of men, and women have tended to gravitate toward lower-paying jobs and to subordinate their careers to their husbands'. Family life has traditionally been the domain of women, but as women enter the workforce in greater numbers, more men are assuming a larger portion of childrearing and household duties.

- As people age, gender roles become more flexible, and the elderly may have to make adjustments to their stereotypes once they retire or once the children leave the home.

R eflections on Sexuality

1. What are the differences between gender roles and gender traits? Which types of behaviors do you think are gender roles and which are gender traits?

2. How are definitions of masculinity and femininity changing in society? Are many of the old stereotypes still powerful?

3. In what ways are stereotypes of women's abilities and roles limiting to them? In what ways are men's stereotypes limiting to them?

4. Can one truly be androgynous? Is that a desirable or undesirable trait?

5. What questions does transsexualism raise about the nature of gender? Does it support the idea that gender is innate or that it is socially learned?

6. We have suggested that third genders are more than just men or women pretending to be members of the opposite sex. In what sense are third genders really third genders?

7. Why is gender so important to children's development?

8. Is it "natural" for parents to reinforce strong gender models in their children? Is it desirable?

9. Which theory of gender hierarchy do you favor? What are its strengths and weaknesses?

S uggested Readings

BLY, ROBERT. (1990) *Iron John: A Book About Men.* Reading, MA: Addison-Wesley.

EPSTEIN, CYNTHIA FUCHS. (1988) *Deceptive Distinctions: Sex, Gender, and the Social Order.* New Haven: Yale University Press.

GILMORE, DAVID D. (1990) *Manhood in the Making: Cultural Concepts of Masculinity.* New Haven: Yale University Press.

MACKINNON, CATHERINE. (1987) *Feminism Unmodified: Discourses on Life and Law.* Cambridge: Harvard University Press.

ORTNER, SHERRY B., AND HARRIET WHITEHEAD, EDS. (1981) *Sexual Meanings: The Cultural Construction of Gender and Sexuality.* Cambridge: Cambridge University Press.

REINISCH, JUNE M., LEONARD A. ROSENBLUM, AND STEPHANIE A. SANDERS, EDS. (1987) *Masculinity/ Femininity: Basic Perspectives.* New York: Oxford University Press.

WOLF, NAOMI. (1991) *The Beauty Myth: How Images of Beauty Are Used Against Women.* New York: William Morris.

Love, Intimacy, and Communication

One word frees us of all the weight and pain of life: That word is love.

(Sophocles, Oedipus at Colonus*)*

Love is a kind of warfare.

(Ovid, Ars amatoria*)*

They do not love that do not show their love.

(Shakespeare, Two Gentlemen of Verona, *I, ii)*

You mustn't force sex to do the work of love or love to do the work of sex.

(Mary McCarthy, The Group*)*

Love is a grave mental disease.

(Plato)

WHAT IS LOVE?

Love. One of the great mysteries of humankind is the capacity to love, to make attachments with others that involve deep feeling, selflessness, and commitment. Throughout history, literature and art have portrayed the saving powers of love; how many songs sing of its passion, and how many films depict its power to change people's lives? Yet after centuries of writers discussing love, philosophers musing over its hold on men and women, and religious leaders teaching of the necessity to love one another, how much do we really know about love? Are there different, separate kinds of love—friendship, passion, love of parents—or are they all simply variations on one fundamental emotion? Does love really "grow"? Is love different at fifteen than at fifty? What is the relationship between love and sexuality? See Where Do I Stand? 6.1 to explore your own feelings about these questions.

Senator William Proxmire once suggested that research on love was foolish, that "right at the top of things we don't want to know is why a man falls in love with a woman." Yet though we understand his point that the mystery of love is part of its attrac-

No matter which culture or which time in history, the language of love is universal, as between this couple in New Guinea.

tion, we go through life trying to come to terms with loving, trying to figure out why we are attracted to certain types or why we fall in love with all the wrong people. We are surrounded with images of love in the media and are taught from the time we first listen to fairy tales that love is the answer to most of life's problems. Why then should we not try to understand what love is?

Love in Different Times and Places

The desire for love is as old as humankind. Each new generation somehow imagines that it was the first, the inventor of "true love," but look at this poem from the Late Egyptian empire, more than 3,000 years ago:

I found my lover on his bed,
and my heart was sweet to excess.
I shall never be far away (from) you
while my hand is in your hand,
and I shall stroll with you
in every favorite place.
How pleasant is this hour,
may it extend for me to eternity;
since I have lain with you
you have lifted high my heart.
In mourning or in rejoicing
be not far from me.

Quoted in Bergmann (1987:5)

Or this more recent poem from a small group of aborigine tribesmen in the Polynesian islands (Quoted in Bergmann, 1987:9):

As the rapid flow of the current at Onoiau,
And as the swollen torrent from the valley,
So flows my yearning heart after thee,
O Aitofa, have compassion on thy lover, lest he die!
As a great cloud obscuring the sky is his grief,
The grief of the husband mourning for his estranged wife,
And like the sky darkened by its rising is my distress for her.

Love has a place in the hearts and minds of people in every culture and every period in history. According to Greek mythology, the Greek goddess of love, Aphrodite, had as her lover the god of war, Ares. Peace reigned on earth whenever Ares lay in Aphrodite's arms, showing the Greek belief in the power of love over conflict (Bergmann, 1987). The Hebrew Bible speaks of God's love of Israel, and the metaphorical imagery in the Song of Solomon, usually interpreted as depicting God and Israel as lovers, is highly erotic and sexual. Jacob had to work for seven years to win Rachel's hand, but these seven years "seemed to him to be but a few days, for the love he had for her" (Genesis 29:20). The Middle Ages glorified the modern idea of **romantic love**, including loving from afar or loving those one could not have (**unrequited love** as in Sir Lancelot's love for Queen Guinevere in the tale of King Arthur) (see Chapter 1).

Not until the nineteenth century did people begin to believe that romantic love was the most desirable form of loving relations. Through most of Western history, marriage

romantic love: The type of love that is focused on physical attraction, feelings of ecstasy, and passion, romance, and exclusivity. Only recently in history has romantic love become the preferred love leading to long-term relationships.

unrequited love: Love for another that is not returned by the person loved.

W H E R E   D O   I *S t a n d ?*   6.1

How Do You Feel About Love?

Number a paper 1 to 11 and write down whether you agree or disagree with the statements below:

1. Loving someone is different from being "in love" with them.
2. Self-love is necessary before we can love someone else.
3. Loving *adds* to your freedom and your partner's freedom.
4. You always like someone you love.
5. Jealousy shows that a loving relationship has depth.
6. Secrets are okay to have even in a loving relationship.
7. Loving someone involves accepting risk.
8. Some relationships should end even when there is still love.
9. Fulfilling love relationships are possible even without sex.
10. Fulfilling sexual relationships are possible even without love.
11. If you are unfaithful in a love relationship, you have an obligation to tell your partner.

After you have read this chapter, go back and do this test again. Have your feelings about any of these statements changed? Discuss your answers with your friends—you will find that people have very different views of love.

was an economic union, arranged by the parents. Once wed, husbands and wives were encouraged to learn love for one another, to *develop* love; how different that is from the modern romantic ideal of love preceding marriage or from the unrequited romantic love of Lancelot and Guinevere.

THE FORMS AND ORIGIN OF LOVE

We must admire those intrepid researchers who are willing to tackle a difficult subject such as the origins of love or the different forms of love. We all love, and one of the characteristics of love is that we often believe that the intensity of the emotion is unique to us, that no one else has ever loved as we have loved. We also feel many different kinds of love, such as love of a friend, love of a parent, love of a celebrity, or love of a cat. Philosophers, historians, social scientists, and other scholars have made attempts to untangle these types of love.

Romantic Versus Companionate Love

Romantic love is the all-encompassing, passionate love of romantic songs and poetry, of tearjerker movies and romance novels, and has become the prevailing model of sexual relationships and marriage in the Western world. Romantic love is also sometimes called passionate love, infatuation, obsessive love, and even love sickness. With it comes a sense of ecstasy and anxiety, physical attraction, and sexual desire. We tend to idealize the partner, ignoring faults in the newfound joy of the attachment. Dorothy

Set me as a seal upon thine heart, as a seal upon thine arm; for love is strong as death; jealousy is cruel as the grave; the coals thereof are coals of fire, which hath a most vehement flame. Many waters cannot quench love, neither can the floods drown it.

(Solomon's Song)

Tennov (1979) coined the term **limerence** to capture many of the aspects we associate with romantic or passionate love, such as intrusive cognitive activity (you cannot think about anything else) and acute longing for, and dependency upon, another person. Passionate love blooms in the initial euphoria of a new attachment to a sexual partner, and it often seems as if it happens *to* us; that is why we say we "fall" in love or even fall "head over heels" in love.

limerence: A term coined by Dorothy Tennov, referring to a sense of passionate obsession with the object of desire, a preoccupation with love feelings, and a sense of dependency on the other person, similar to infatuation.

SEX TALK
QUESTION **6.1** Why is love so confusing?

Love is confusing because it evokes a host of other emotions and personal issues, such as self-worth and self-esteem, fears of rejection, passion and sexuality, jealousy and possessiveness, great joy and great sadness. Dealing with those emotions is confusing enough, but in love, we try to communicate and share intimacies with another human being who is going through the same kinds of confused feelings that we are. When so many emotions are fighting for attention, it comes as no surprise that the mind does not seem to work that well!

There are few feelings as joyous or exciting as romantic love. The explosion of emotion is often so intense that people talk about being unable to contain it; it feels as if it spills out of us onto everything we see, making the flowers a bit more beautiful and birds' songs a little sweeter. Some people joke that there is nothing quite so intolerable as a person in love; they are just so annoyingly *happy* all the time! It is not surprising that such a powerful emotion is celebrated in poetry, story, and song. It is also not surprising that such a powerful emotion seems as if it will last forever. After all, isn't that what we learn when the couples in fairy tales "live happily ever after" and when the couples in movies ride off into the sunset?

Unfortunately, perhaps, passion of that intensity fades after a time. If the relationship is to continue, romantic love must develop into **companionate** or **conjugal love**. Companionate love involves feelings of deep affection, attachment, intimacy, and ease

companionate or **conjugal love:** A love that develops over time in committed couples, involving a sense of intimacy, trust, mutual respect, comfort and ease, and deep affection. Companionate love can also be quite sexual and sensual but usually without the sense of urgency found in romantic love.

Conjugal or companionate love often develops over time, as a couple becomes comfortable and at ease with each other.

The magic of first love is our ignorance that it can ever end.

(Benjamin Disraeli)

Personal

VOICES

<u>6.1</u>

"Do You Love Me?"
A Song of Conjugal Love

This song is from the long-running Broadway musical and, later, motion picture, *Fiddler on the Roof.* Tevye, Golde, and their five daughters live a hard life in Eastern Europe in the early twentieth century. Tevye and Golde's marriage had been arranged by their parents, and they met each other for the first time on their wedding day. Now, twenty-five years later, Tevye is puzzled by new concepts of love and by his daughters' insistence that they marry the men they love rather than the men he chooses for them. It occurs to Tevye that he and his wife have never spoken of love. So, for the first time, he asks Golde the question:

Tevye: Golde. Do you love me?

Golde: Do I *what*?!

Tevye: Do you love me?

Golde: Do I love you?
With our daughter getting married,
and there's trouble in the town—
you're upset, you're worn out,
go inside, go lie down.
Maybe its indigestion!

Tevye: Golde, I'm asking you a question!
Do you love me?

Golde: You're a fool!

Tevye: I know. But do you love me?

Golde: Do I love you?
For twenty-five years I've washed your clothes,
cooked your meals,
cleaned your house,
given you children,
milked the cow
After twenty-five years, why talk about love
right now?

Tevye: Golde. The first time I met you was on our
wedding day.
I was scared.

Golde: I was shy.

Tevye: I was nervous.

Golde: So was I.

Tevye: But my father and my mother
said we'd learn to love each other.
And so I'm asking, Golde.
Do you love me?

Golde: I'm your wife!

Tevye: I know. But, do you love me?

Golde: Do I love him?
For twenty five years I've lived with him,
fought with him,
starved with him,
twenty-five years my bed is his—
if that's not love, what is?

Tevye: Then you love me!

Golde: I suppose I do.

Tevye: And I suppose I love you, too.

Golde & Tevye: It doesn't change a thing,
But even so—
After twenty-five years,
Its nice to know.

Golde and Tevye

with the partner, and it includes the development of trust, loyalty, a lack of undue criticalness, and a willingness to sacrifice for the partner (Critelli et al., 1986; Shaver et al., 1987). Though it does not have the passionate high and low swings of romantic love, passion is certainly present for many companionate lovers. Companionate love may even be a deeper, more intimate love than romantic love.

No, there's nothing half so sweet in life
As love's young dream.

(Thomas Moore, Love's Young Dream)

It can be difficult for couples to switch from passionate love to the deeper, more mature companionate love (Peck, 1978). Because the model of love we see in television and movies is the highly sexual, swept-off-your-feet passion of romantic love, some may see the mellowing of that passion as a loss of love rather than a development of a different kind of love. Yet the mutual commitment to develop a new, more mature kind of love is, in fact, what we *should* mean by "true love" (see Personal Voices 6.1).

John Alan Lee and the Colors of Love

"How do I love thee? Let me count the ways . . . " wrote Elizabeth Barrett Browning, who seemed to agree that there is more than one way to love, that even within one person love can take many forms. Psychologist John Alan Lee (1974, 1976, 1977) suggests that more forms of love exist than merely romantic and companionate love. Lee collected statements about love from hundreds of works of fiction and nonfiction, starting with the Bible and including both ancient and modern authors. He then gathered a panel of professionals in literature, philosophy, and the social sciences and had them sort the thousands of statements he found into categories. Lee's research identified six basic ways to love, which he calls "colors" of love, to which he gave Greek and Latin names. Lee's categories are described in Sexuality Today 6.1.

SEXUALITY *Today* 6.1

Lee's Colors of Love

John Alan Lee has described the six "colors" of love, six different styles of loving.

1. *Eros:* Eros is like romantic love. Erotic loves speak of their immediate attraction to their lover, to his or her eyes, skin, fragrance, or shape. Most have the picture of an ideal partner in their minds, which a real partner cannot fulfill; that is why purely erotic love does not last.

2. *Ludus:* Ludic lovers play the "game" of love, enjoying the act of seduction. Commitment, dependency, and intimacy are not valued, and ludic lovers will juggle several relationships at the same time. Don Juan and Casanova were examples of ludic lovers.

3. *Storge:* Storgic love is a quiet, calm love that builds over time, similar to companionate love. Storgic lovers do not suddenly "fall in love" and do not dream of some idealized, romantic lover; marriage, stability, and comfort within love is the goal. Should the relationship break up, the storgic partners would probably remain friends, a status unthinkable to erotic lovers who have split.

4. *Mania:* Manic lovers are consumed by thoughts of the beloved. Each encouraging sign from the lover brings joy; each little slight brings heartache, which makes their lives dramatic and painful. Manic lovers fear separation; they may sit by the phone waiting for the beloved to call, or they may call their beloved incessantly. They tend to wonder why all their relationships ultimately fail.

5. *Pragma:* Pragmatic lovers look at their love relationships realistically. Pragmatic lovers want a deep, lasting love, but they believe the best way to get it is to assess their own qualities and make the best "deal" in the romantic marketplace. They tend to be planners—planning the best time to get married, have children, and even a divorce ("Well, in two years the house will be paid for and Junior will be in high school, so that would be a good time to get divorced...").

6. *Agape:* Altruistic, selfless, never demanding, patient, and true is agape love. Never jealous, not needing reciprocity, agapic love tends to happen in brief episodes; Lee found very few long-term agapic lovers. Lee gives the example of a man whose lover was faced with a distressing choice between him and another man, and so he gracefully bowed out.

Reprinted with permission from Lee (1974)

Lee's colors of love have generated a substantial body of research, much of which shows that his lovestyles are independent of each other and that each can be measured to some degree (Hendrick and Hendrick, 1989). Lee points out that two lovers with compatible styles are probably going to be happier and more contented with each other than two without compatible styles. Couples who approach loving differently often cannot understand why their partners react the way they do or can hurt their partners unintentionally. Imagine how bored an *erotic* lover would be with a *pragmatic* lover or how much a *ludic* lover would hurt the feelings of a *manic* lover. Each would consider the other callous or even cruel, suggests Lee, when in fact people simply tend to love differently.

SEX TALK

QUESTION **6.2** **How do I know the difference between love and infatuation? How do I know if I am in "true love" or whether it is just sexual attraction?**

Each individual must struggle with these questions as he or she matures, particularly in the teenage and early adulthood years when they have less experience with romantic love. There is no easy answer, but there are some indications that a relationship may be infatuation rather than love, such as a compulsion (rather than a desire) to be with the person, a feeling of lack of trust (such as a need to check up on the partner), extremes of emotions (ecstatic highs followed by depressing lows), and a willingness to take abuse or behave in destructive ways that one would not have before the relationship. Some questions to ask yourself about your love relationship are these: Would I want this person as a friend if he or she were not my partner? Do my friends and family dislike this person or think they the person is not right for me (friends and family are often more level-headed judges of character than the infatuated individual)? Do I really know this person, or is my fantasy replacing a realistic assessment of his or her actual behavior?

Robert Sternberg and Love Triangles

Robert Sternberg (1986; 1987; 1988) suggests that different strategies of loving are really different ways of combining the basic building blocks of love. He has proposed that love is made up of three elements that can be combined in different ways. The three elements are passion, intimacy, and commitment.

Passion is sparked by physical attraction and sexual desire and drives a person to pursue a romantic relationship. Passion instills a deep desire for union, and although it is often expressed sexually, self-esteem, nurturing, domination, submission, and self-actualization may also contribute to the experience of passion. Passion is the element that identifies romantic forms of love; it is absent, for example, in love of a parent or child. Passion fires up quickly in a romantic relationship, but it also quickly fades.

Intimacy involves feelings of closeness, connectedness, and bondedness in a loving relationship. It is the emotional investment one has in the relationship and includes such things as the desire to help the other, happiness, mutual understanding, emotional sup-

How do I love thee? Let me count the ways.
I love thee to the depth and breadth of height
My soul can reach, when feeling out of sight
For the ends of being and ideal grace.

(Elizabeth Barrett Browning, Sonnets from the Portuguese, 43)

port, and communication. The intimacy component of love is experienced in many loving relationships, such as parent–child, sibling, and friendship.

Commitment is the third element. In the short term, this element is the *decision* to love someone; in the long term, it is the commitment to maintain that love. This element can sustain a relationship that is temporarily (or even permanently) going through a period without passion or intimacy. The marriage ceremony, for example, is a public display of a couple's commitment to each other.

Sternberg combines these elements into eight forms of love, which are described in Sex Facts 6.1. A person may experience different forms of love at different times; romantic love may give way to companionate love, or the infatuated lover may find a person to whom he or she is willing to commit and settle down. In the emotionally healthy person, as we shall see, love evolves and changes as we mature.

MEASURING LOVE

Based on these types of theories, theorists have tried to come up with scales that *measure* love. But theorists cannot simply ask people, "How deeply do you love _____?" Each

SEX *Facts* 6.1

Sternberg's Eight Forms of Love

Sternberg believes that love is made up of three traits: passion (P), intimacy (I), and decision/commitment (D/C), each of which may be present or absent in a relationship. Below are the eight forms of love Sternberg derives by combining the three traits in different ways.

 Nonlove: In most of our casual daily relationships there is no sense of intimacy, passion, or commitment.

 Liking: When there is intimacy without (sexual) passion and without strong personal commitment, we are friends. Friends can separate for long periods of time and then pick the relationship up as if it had never ended.

 Infatuation: Passion alone leads to infatuation. Like Tennov's idea of limerence, infatuation refers to physiological arousal and a sexual desire for another person. Infatuation quickly fades, often to be replaced with infatuation for someone else!

 Empty love: Empty love involves commitment alone, as in a couple who stays together even though their relationship long ago lost its passion and intimacy. However, relationships can *begin* with commitment alone and develop intimacy and passion, as in Tevye and Golde's arranged marriage.

 Romantic love: Passion and intimacy lead to romantic love, which is often the first phase of a relationship. Romantic love is often an intense, joyful experience.

 Companionate love: Companionate love ranges from long-term, deeply committed friendships to married or long-term couples who have experienced a decrease in the passionate aspect of their love.

 Fatuous love: Love is fatuous (which means silly or foolish) when one does not really *know* the person to whom one is making a commitment. Hollywood often portrays two people who meet, become infatuated, and make a commitment by the end of the movie. However, a committed relationship continues even after passion fades, and so it makes sense to know one's partner *before* making a commitment.

 Consummate love: Consummate, or complete, love has all three elements in balance. Even after achieving consummate love, we can lose it; passion can fade, intimacy can stagnate, commitment can be undermined by attraction to another. But it is consummate love we all strive for.

Reprinted with permission from Sternberg (1986)

subject will interpret love in his or her own way. One strategy is to create a scale that measures love by measuring something strongly associated with love. Zick Rubin (1970; 1973) was one of the first to try to scientifically measure love. Rubin thought of love as a form of attachment to another person, and he created a "Love Scale" that measured what he believed to be the three components of attachment: Degrees of *Needing* (If I could never be with _____, I would feel miserable); *Caring* (I would do almost anything for ____); and *Trusting* (I feel very possessive about ____). Rubin's scale proved to be extraordinarily powerful as a tool to measure love; for example, how couples score on the "Love Scale" is not only correlated with their rating of the probability that they will get married; their score even predicts how often they will gaze at each other!

Others have since tried to create their own scales. Keith Davis and his colleagues (Davis and Todd, 1982; Davis and Latty-Mann, 1987) created the Relationship Rating Scale (RRS), which measures six aspects of relationships, such as intimacy, passion, and conflict. Hatfield and Sprecher (1986) created the Passionate Love Scale (PLS), which tries to measure the degree of intense passion or "longing for union." Look over the questions that are used in the PLS in Sexuality Today 6.2.

Will measures of love eventually tell us what love is made of? Well, as you can imagine, many problems are inherent in trying to measure love. Most scales of love really focus on romantic love and are not as good at trying to measure the degree of companionate love (Sternberg, 1987). Also, measuring degrees of love, or types of love, is different from saying what love actually consists of. Finally, when people are asked questions about love, they can only answer with their conscious attitudes toward love. Many theorists suggest that people do not consciously know why they love, how they love, or even how much they love. Other theorists argue that people do not realize to what degree love is physiological (see Physiological Arousal Theories, below). So we may only be measuring how people *think* they love.

WHERE DOES LOVE COME FROM?

Why do we love in the first place? What purpose does love serve? After all, most animals mate successfully without experiencing "love." The theories of researchers who try to understand why we form emotional bonds in the first place can be grouped into four general categories: behavioral reinforcement theories, cognitive theories, physiological arousal theories, and sociobiological theories.

Behavioral Reinforcement Theories

One group of theories suggests that we love because another person reinforces positive feelings in ourselves. Lott and Lott (1961) suggested that a rewarding or positive feeling in the presence of another person makes us like them, even if the reward has nothing to do with the other person. For example, they found that children who were rewarded continually by their teachers came to like their classmates more than children who were not equally rewarded (Lott and Lott, 1968). The opposite is also true. Griffitt and Veitch (1971) found that people tend to dislike people they meet in a hot, crowded room, no matter what the new person's personality is like. Behavioral reinforcement theory suggests that we like people we associate with feeling good, and love people if the association is very good. Love develops through a series of mutually reinforcing activities.

Love begins with love; friendship, however warm, cannot change to love, however mild.

(La Bruyere)

SEXUALITY *Today*   6.2

Hatfield and Sprecher's (1986) Passionate Love Scale (PLS)

The purpose of Hatfield and Sprecher's PLS is to create a scale that measures passionate rather than companionate love. Hatfield and Sprecher tested a number of questions and drew from other love scales to come up with questions that measure what they believe to be three basic components of passionate love: (1) cognitive aspects such as intrusive thoughts, idealization, and desire to know and be known (questions 5, 10, 19, and 21); (2) emotional aspects such as attraction, desire for union, and arousal (questions 12, 16, 18, and 23); and (3) behavioral aspects such as studying the other, serving the other, and physical closeness (questions 4, 6, 25, and 27). Each question is supposed to be ranked from one to nine, as indicated below. Do you think such a scale is a reasonable measure of passionate love?

1	2	3	4	5	6	7	8	9
Not at all true				Moderately true			Definitely true	

Score

_5_ 1. Since I've been involved with _____, my emotions have been on a roller coaster.

_9_ 2. I would feel despair if _____ left me.

_9_ 3. Sometimes my body trembles with excitement at the sight of _____.

_9_ 4. I take delight in studying the movements and angles of _____'s body.

_9_ 5. Sometimes I feel I can't control my thoughts; they are obsessively on _____.

_9_ 6. I feel happy when I am doing something that makes _____ happy.

_9_ 7. I would rather be with _____ than with anyone else.

_9_ 8. I'd be jealous if I thought _____ were falling in love with someone else.

_7_ 9. No one else could love _____ the way that I do.

_8_ 10. I yearn to know all about _____.

_9_ 11. I want _____—physically, emotionally, mentally.

_9_ 12. I will love _____ forever.

_8_ 13. I melt when looking deeply into _____'s eyes.

_8_ 14. I have an endless appetite for affection from _____.

_8_ 15. For me, _____ is the perfect romantic partner.

_9_ 16. _____ is the person who can make me feel the happiest.

_7_ 17. I sense my body responding when _____ touches me.

_8_ 18. I feel tender toward _____.

_9_ 19. _____ always seems to be on my mind.

_9_ 20. If I were separated from _____ for a long time, I would feel terribly lonely.

_9_ 21. I sometimes find it difficult to concentrate on work because thoughts of _____ occupy my mind.

_8_ 22. I want _____ to know me—my thoughts, my fears, my hopes.

_9_ 23. Knowing that _____ cares about me makes me feel complete.

_7_ 24. I eagerly look for signs indicating _____'s desire for me.

_8_ 25. If _____ were going through a difficult time, I would put away my concerns to help him/her out.

_7_ 26. _____ can make me feel effervescent and bubbly.

_8_ 27. In the presence of _____, I yearn to touch and be touched.

_9_ 28. An existence without _____ would be dark and dismal.

_9_ 29. I possess a powerful attraction for _____.

_9_ 30. I am extremely depressed when things don't go right in my relationship with _____.

Cognitive Theories

Cognitive theories of liking and loving are based on an interesting paradox: the less people are paid for a task, the more they tend to like it. In other words, a person tends to think: "Here I am painting this fence, and I'm not even getting paid for it. Why am I doing this? I must *like* to paint!" The same things happen in relationships. If we are with a person often and find ourselves doing things for them, we ask: "Why am I with her so often? Why am I doing her laundry? I must like her—I must even *love* her!" This theory suggests the action comes first, and the interpretation comes later.

Physiological Arousal Theories

How does love feel? Most people describe physiological sensations: "I felt so excited I couldn't breathe"; "My throat choked up"; "I felt tingling all over." But if you look at those descriptions, couldn't they also be descriptions of fear? Anger? Excitement? Is there a difference between being in love and being on a roller coaster?

Perhaps not. In a famous experiment, Schachter and Singer (1962) gave students a shot of epinephrine (adrenaline), which causes general arousal, including sweaty palms, increased heart rate, increased breathing, etc. They split the students into four groups: one was told exactly what was happening and what to expect; another was told the wrong set of symptoms to expect (itching, numbness, a slight headache); a third group was told nothing; and a fourth group did not get epinephrine but an injection of salt water.

Each group was put into a waiting room with another student, a confederate, who was actually part of the study. In half the cases, the confederate acted happy and in half angry. The interesting result was that the students in the informed group, when they felt aroused, assumed they were feeling the effects of the epinephrine; but the other groups *tended to believe they were experiencing the same emotion as the other person in the room.* They thought they were happy, or they thought they were angry. Schachter and Singer concluded that an emotion happens when there is general physiological arousal for whatever reason and then a label is attached to it—and that label might be *any* emotion.

In other words, people should be vulnerable to experiencing love (or another emotion) when they are physiologically aroused for whatever reason (Walster and Berscheid, 1974). A famous example of this was a clever experiment done by Dutton and Aron (1974). They had men between the ages of nineteen and thirty-five walk across one of two bridges. The first was high over a gorge, narrow, had low handrails, and swayed in the wind. The second was close to the ground and stable. As the men crossed the bridge, they were met by an attractive male or female research assistant, who asked them to answer a few questions and tell a story based on a picture. The assistant also mentioned that the men could call him or her at home for more information. Those men who met the female on the high bridge, where they were more physiologically aroused by the sense of danger, told stories with more erotic content and were most likely to call the female assistant at home and try to arrange a more personal rendezvous. The men were aroused by the danger and interpreted that arousal as a response to the attractive research assistant.

So, is love just a label we give to sweaty palms? The idea may explain why we tend to associate love and sex so closely; sexual excitement is a state of intense physiological arousal, and certainly, arousal of some sort is a necessary component of love—would you want to be in love with someone who was not the least bit excited when you entered the room? Love, however, is almost certainly more than arousal alone. Perhaps arousal has a stronger connection to initial attraction than to love. Maybe that is why lust is so often confused with love.

Love is the triumph of imagination over intelligence.

(H.L. Mencken)

Sociobiological Perspectives

Sociobiologists try to understand the evolutionary advantages of human behaviors. Love, they believe, developed as the human form of three basic instincts: the need to be protected from outside threats, the instinct of the parent to protect the child, and the sexual drive (Wilson, 1981). Love is an evolutionary strategy that helps us form the bonds we need to reproduce and pass our genes on to the next generation. We love in order to propagate the species.

To sociobiologists, that would explain why we tend to fall in love with people who we think have positive traits; we want to pass those traits along to our children. In fact, sociobiologists argue that their perspective can explain why men look for attractive women, and women look for successful men, the world over (see Attraction in Different Cultures, on page 215). Men want a fit, healthy woman to carry their offspring, and women want a man with the resources to protect them and help care for the infant in the long period they devote to reproduction (for most of history, that included nine months of pregnancy and over a year of nursing). Love creates the union that maximizes each partner's chance of passing his or her genes on to the next generation.

LOVE THROUGH THE LIFE CYCLE

Throughout our lives, we love others. First we love our parents or caretakers and then siblings, friends, and lovers. Love is different at each stage of development, and it becomes more complex as we grow older. Let us walk through the different stages of individual development and look at the different ways love manifests itself as we grow.

Childhood

At each stage of life we learn lessons about love that help us mature into the next stage. In infancy, the nature and quality of the bond with the caregiver can have profound effects on the ability of the person to form attachments throughout life (see Chapter 4). Loving, attentive caregivers tend to produce secure, happy children. Those who do not experience intimacy growing up may have a harder time establishing intimate relationships as adults. For example, three-quarters of the subjects in one study who had experienced or observed abusive behavior in their homes reported using the same forms of abuse on their own partners in their intimate relationships (Bernard and Bernard, 1983). Of course, it is also true that many people who had difficult upbringings are successful at developing deep and intimate relationships.

Adolescence

There is something attractive about young love, which is why it is celebrated so prominently in novels and movies. The love relationship seems so important, so earnest, and so passionate at the time and yet so innocent and bittersweet in retrospect. Why are the dips and

Love is an egotism of two.

(Antoine de la Sale)

Reprinted from *Binky's Guide to Love* ©1994 by Matt Groening. All rights reserved. Reprinted by permission of Harper Perennial, a division of HarperCollins Publishers, New York

rises of our loves so important to us in adolescence? Because adolescent love is to adult love what a child's play is to adult work: it teaches us how to react to love, to manage our emotions, and to handle the pain of love; it lays the groundwork for adult intimacy. Adolescents must learn to establish a strong personal identity separate from their family. Experimentation with different approaches to others is very natural, and during adolescence

Love is a hole in the heart.

(Ben Hecht)

we develop our **role repertoire** that follows us into adulthood. Similarly, we experiment with different intimacy styles (Johnson and Alford, 1987) and develop an **intimacy repertoire**, a set of behaviors that we use to forge close relationships throughout our lives.

The importance of this experimentation to our lives explains why adolescent relationships can be so intense and fraught with jealousy and why adolescents often are unable to see beyond the relationship (Johnson and Alford, 1987). Our first relationships often take the form of a "crush" or infatuation or are directed toward unattainable partners such as teachers or movie stars. Sometimes the first lessons of love are painful, as we learn that love may not be returned, that feelings of passion fade, and that love itself does not preclude conflict. Yet managing such feelings helps us develop a mature love style. The emotions are so powerful that adolescents may feel that they are the only ones to have gone through such joy, pain, and confusion; they may gain some comfort in knowing that almost everyone goes through the same process to some degree. Confusion about love certainly does not end with adolescence.

SEX TALK

QUESTION **6.3** **Why is love often so painful?**

Human beings are both blessed and cursed with the ability to form strong attachments. When those attachments are reciprocated, we feel joy; when they are not, or even when we fear they are not, we feel pain. What is mourning, for example, except the pain of losing a person with whom one felt strong attachment? When we are young, and those attachments are made quickly and are used to reinforce our sense of identity and self-worth, the ups and down of love seem more drastic and frequent. Though love still has its pain as we get older, we usually experience fewer hills and valleys.

Attachment Styles

Perhaps you have trouble getting close to people. You *want* intimacy, but it is not as easy for you as it seems to be for others. Maybe you do not feel you need intimacy as much as some other people, that you are happy with just one or two special people or are happy being a loner. On the other hand, you may be a person who seems to make close friends easily.

The type of intimate relationships you form may be due primarily to the type of attachment you formed as a child. Hazan and Shaver (1987; Shaver et al., 1988), building on the work of Ainsworth and her colleagues (1978), suggest that infants form one of three types of attachment behaviors that follow them throughout life. *Secure* infants tolerate caregivers being out of their sight because they believe the caregiver will respond if they cry out or need them. Similarly, the secure adult easily gets close to others and is not threatened when a lover goes away. *Anxious/Ambivalent* babies cry more than secure babies and panic when the caregiver leaves them. Anxious/ambivalent lovers worry that their partners do not not really love them or will leave them and that their need for others will scare people away. *Avoidant* babies often have caregivers who are uncomfortable with hugging and holding them and tend to force separation on the child at an early age. In the adult, the avoidant lover is uncomfortable with intimacy and finds trusting others difficult.

Hazan and Shafer found that adults report the same rates of each type of behavior as Ainsworth found in infants. People with secure attachment styles also reported more

role repertoire: A set of roles we learn in adolescence (for example, our role as "friend," "lover," "student," "car driver," etc.), each of which has certain behaviors and attitudes associated with it. We carry these roles throughout life.

intimacy repertoire: The set of attitudes and behaviors we learn in adolescence about how to form close friendships and love relations. For example, we might learn that a different set of behaviors is appropriate for a love interest than for a person with whom we plan to have a casual sexual relationship.

A book of verses underneath the bough
A jug of wine, a loaf of bread—and thou
Beside me singing in the wilderness.

(Edward Fitzgerald, The Rubaiyat of Omar Khayyam)

positive childhood experiences and had higher self-esteem than others (Feeney and Noller, 1990). We may develop an attachment style as a child that reemerges as we begin to form romantic attachments in adolescence.

Adult Love and Intimacy

Love relationships can last many years. As time goes by, relationships grow and change, and love grows and changes. Trying to maintain a sense of stability and continuity while still allowing for change and growth is probably the single greatest challenge of long-term love relationships.

The attainment of intimacy is different than loving. We can love from afar, and we can love anonymously; we can love our cat, our favorite movie star, or a great leader. But intimacy requires reciprocity; it takes two. Intimacy is a dance of two souls, each of whom must reveal a little, risk a little, and try a lot. In some ways, therefore, true intimacy is more difficult to achieve than true love because the emotion of love may be effortless, while the establishment of intimacy always requires effort.

Attraction

Imagine that you are in a public place, such as a bar, a museum, or a sports event. Suddenly you see someone and feel an immediate attraction. As you approach him or her with your favorite opening line, you muse to yourself: Why I am so attracted to this person and not to someone else?

"Haven't I seen you here before?" One of the most reliable predictors of who a person will marry is proximity: people are most likely to find lovers among the people they know or see around them. The vast majority of people have sex with, love, and marry people who are very much like them in ethnic, racial, and religious background (Michael et al., 1994). This is in part because we tend to meet many more such people as we go through our normal lives. We have a cultural myth about seeing a stranger across a crowded room, falling in love, and finding out that the stranger is from an exotic place and has lived a much different life. In fact, such a scenario is rare; we are much more likely to meet our mates at a party, school, religious institution, or friend's house, where the other guests are likely to come from backgrounds very similar to our own.

"You know, we really have a lot in common." Folklore tells us both that "birds of a feather flock together" and that "opposites attract." Only the first saying is supported

Young love tends to be passionate, volatile, and short-lived.

Love is like an hourglass, with the heart filling up as the brain empties.

(Jules Renard)

by the evidence; people tend to be attracted to those who think like they do (Byrne and Murnen, 1988). The majority of people who fall in love share similar educational levels, social class, religion and degree of religiousness, desired family size, attitudes toward gender roles, physique and physical attractiveness, family histories, and political opinions (Byrne and Murnen, 1988; Rubin, 1973). In other words, most people marry people from their general communities who are very much like them.

"You have such beautiful eyes." Physical attractiveness is so important to most people that physically attractive people are assumed by others to have more socially desirable personalities and to be happier and more successful; also, physical attractiveness is commonly cited by men as the single most important feature in potential mates (it is high on women's lists also) (Buss, 1989). Physical appearance is usually the first thing we perceive about a potential lover, although it tends to fade in importance over the life of the relationship. The media put such a premium on physical appearance that the majority of people in the United States report they are unhappy with their appearance and would change it if they could. However, the more that people report that appearance is important to them, the less likely they are to form close romantic relationships, and many people find other traits much more important than physical attractivenes in their choice of mates.

"You seem so warm and understanding." On the other hand, it should be some relief to those of us not blessed with cover-model looks that a large percentage of people cite personality as the most important factor in how they choose their partners. Although people tend to be attracted to others with personalities like theirs, the general traits cited as most important are openness, sociability, emotional stability, a sense of humor, and receptivity (Snyder et al., 1985).

Different cultures and times have very different standards of beauty.

Many a man has fallen in love with a girl in a light so dim he would not have chosen a suit by it.

(Maurice Chevalier)

"By the way, have I shown you my Porsche?" What do women find sexy in men? Very often, their occupation and earning potential. Research has shown that, in almost every culture, a woman's most important asset on the marriage market is her physical attractiveness, while a man's is his occupational status (Buss, 1989; see next section). Rubin (1973) reports that all women found high-status occupations to be desirable in their marriage partners, while most said they were not interested in men with low-status occupations such as bartending and custodial work. Perhaps not surprisingly, the less attractive a woman was, the more likely she was to accept men in the middle-status occupations, such as electricians. Attractive women often understand that they have the asset most men desire, and so they seek a higher-status partner.

"So, can I see you again?" What is it, finally, that we really look for in a mate? Despite all the other factors, people are in surprising agreement on what they want in an ideal partner. A study of homosexual, heterosexual, and bisexual men and women showed that, no matter what their sexual orientation or gender, all really wanted the same thing: partners who had similar interests, shared their religious beliefs, had similar values, and were intelligent, honest, affectionate, financially independent, dependable, and physically attractive (Engel and Saracino, 1986). Now that doesn't seem too much to ask, does it?

SEX *Facts*   6.2

Buss's Cross-Cultural Research

The table below shows how males and females from different countries rate the importance of a mate's looks and financial prospects and what their ideal age difference is. In the "Good Looks" and "Good Financial Prospect" categories, the subjects rated importance from 0 (unimportant) to 3 (indispensable); in other words, the higher the number, the more males or females thouught good looks or good financial prospects were important. (The standard deviation (S.D.) tells how much people disagreed within the category; the higher the score, the more disagreement there was.) In the "Age Difference" category, the number refers to how much younger (a negative number) or older (positive number) subject want their mate to be.

The results show that, almost universally, men value good looks higher in a mate, and women value good financial prospects. Also, almost universally, men want their mates to be a few years younger than they are, and women want their mates to be a few years older.

SUBJECTS:	GOOD LOOKS		GOOD FINANCIAL PROSPECT		AGE DIFFERENCE	
	MALE MEAN (S.D.)	FEMALE MEAN (S.D.)	MALE MEAN (S.D.)	FEMALE MEAN (S.D.)	MALE MEAN (S.D.)	FEMALE MEAN (S.D.)
Nigeria	2.24 (.67)	1.82 (.72)	1.37 (.82)	2.30 (.76)	−6.45 (5.04)	4.90 (2.17)
China	2.06 (.62)	1.59 (.68)	1.10 (.98)	1.56 (.94)	−2.05 (2.47)	3.45 (1.73)
Japan	1.50 (.75)	1.09 (.74)	0.92 (.75)	2.29 (.58)	−2.37 (2.29)	3.05 (1.62)
Poland	1.93 (.83)	1.77 (.76)	1.09 (.82)	1.74 (.80)	−2.85 (2.94)	3.38 (3.02)
Australia	1.65 (.74)	1.24 (.73)	0.69 (.73)	1.54 (.80)	−1.77 (2.34)	2.86 (2.72)
France	2.08 (.81)	1.76 (.77)	1.22 (.97)	1.68 (.92)	−1.94 (2.47)	4.00 (3.17)
Italy	2.00 (.70)	1.64 (.83)	0.87 (.69)	1.33 (.80)	−2.76 (2.77)	3.24 (2.41)
Norway	1.87 (.83)	1.32 (.83)	1.10 (.84)	1.42 (.97)	−1.91 (4.14)	3.12 (2.36)
Brazil	1.89 (.75)	1.68 (.86)	1.24 (.89)	1.91 (.78)	−2.94 (3.35)	3.94 (3.23)
Canada (English)	1.96 (.50)	1.64 (.71)	1.02 (.82)	1.91 (.76)	−1.53 (1.93)	2.72 (2.01)
Canada (French)	1.68 (.64)	1.41 (.65)	1.47 (.83)	1.94 (.63)	−1.22 (1.69)	1.82 (1.83)
USA	2.11 (.69)	1.67 (.69)	1.08 (.88)	1.96 (.82)	−1.65 (2.62)	2.54 (1.90)

Derived from Buss (1989)

Attraction in Different Cultures

Do men and women look for the same traits in every culture? For example, are more males than females looking for physically attractive mates in Nigeria? Is earning potential more important in males than females in China? David Buss (1989) has done an ambitious study comparing the importance of, among other things, physical attractiveness, earning potential, and age difference to men and women in thirty-seven different cultures. His results confirm what we have been claiming about the nature of mate attraction (although Buss assumed all his respondents were heterosexual and, therefore, assumed they were all talking about the opposite sex). He found that across all thirty-seven cultures, men valued "good looks" in a partner more than women did, and in all thirty-seven cultures, women valued "good financial prospect" in a partner more than men did. Also interesting is that in all thirty-seven cultures, men preferred mates who were younger than they were while women preferred mates who were older. Selected results of Buss's study appear in Sex Facts 6.2.

Intimate Relationships

What exactly *is* intimacy? Think about the word; what does it imply to you? The word is derived from the Latin *intimus,* meaning "inner" or "innermost" (Hatfield, 1988). Keeping our innermost selves hidden is easy; revealing our deepest desires, our longings, and our insecurities can be scary. Intimates reveal beliefs and ideas to each other, disclose personal facts, share opinions, and admit to their fears and hopes. In fact, **self-disclosure** is so important to intimacy that early researchers thought that willingness to self-disclose was itself the definition of intimacy (Clark and Reis, 1988). True self-disclosure, however, involves sharing feelings, fears, and dreams, not just facts and opinions. People respond more positively to those who display emotional openness than to people who are only willing to self-disclose thoughts and experiences (Berg and Archer, 1980).

self-disclosure: The act of telling or showing another person intimate aspects of one's cognitive or emotional life. One can self-disclose facts, opinions, vulnerabilities, fears, hopes, insecurities, etc.

Intimacy involves a sense of "closeness, bondedness, and connectedness" (Sternberg, 1986). The Bible describes the intimate friendship of David and Jonathan by saying that their lives were "bound up one to the other." People who value intimacy tend to express greater trust in their friends; are more concerned for them; tend to disclose more emotional, personal, and relational content; and have more positive thoughts about others. They also tend to be seen as more likable and noncompetitive by peers; smile, laugh, and make eye contact more often; and report better marital enjoyment (Clark and Ries, 1988).

But all types of disclosure are risky; the other person may not understand or accept the information offered or may not reciprocate (Beach and Tesser, 1988). Thus, risk-taking and trust are crucial to the development of intimacy. Because intimacy makes us vulnerable and because we invest so much in the other person, intimacy can also lead to betrayal and disappointment, anger and jealousy. We explore the dark side of intimacy later in this chapter.

Male and Female Styles of Intimacy

Do men and women love differently? If any area of research in love and intimacy has yielded conflicting findings, it is the question of gender differences. Clark and Ries (1988) suggest that the subject remains murky because many other variables are at work. Perhaps the most important factor is culturally transmitted gender roles. Men and women

The word love has by no means the same sense for both sexes, and this is one cause of the serious misunderstandings that divide them.

(Simone de Beauvoir)

Personal

V O I C E S

6.2

In the Men's Locker Room

I played organized sports for 15 years and they were as much a part of my "growing up" as Cheerios, television, and homework. My sexuality unfolded within this all-male social world of sport where sex was always a major focus. I remember, for example, when we as prepubertal boys used the old "buying baseball cards" routine as a cover to sneak peeks at Playboy and Swank magazines at the newsstand. We would talk endlessly after practices about "boobs" and what it must feel like to kiss and neck. Later, in junior high, we teased one another in the locker room about "jerking off" or being virgins, and there were endless interrogations about "how far" everybody was getting with their girlfriends.

Eventually, boyish anticipation spilled into real sexual relationships with girls which, to my delight and confusion, turned out to be a lot more complex than I ever imagined. While sex (kissing, necking, and petting) got more exciting, it also got more difficult to figure out and talk about. Inside, most of the boys, like myself, needed to love and be loved. We were awkwardly reaching out for intimacy. Yet publicly, the message that got imparted was to "catch feels," be cool, connect with girls but don't allow yourself to depend on them. Once when I was a high school junior, the gang in the weight room accused me of being wrapped around my girlfriend's finger. Nothing could be further from the truth, I assured them, and in order to prove it, I broke up with her. I felt miserable about this at the time and I still feel bad about it.

Within the college jock subculture, men's public protests against intimacy sometimes became exaggerated and ugly. I remember two teammates, drunk and rowdy, ripping girls' blouses off at a mixer and crawling on their bellies across the dance floor to look up skirts. Then there were the Sunday morning late breakfasts in the dorm. We jocks would usually all sit at one table and be forced to listen to one braggart or another describe his sexual exploits of the night before. Though a lot of us were turned off by such kiss-and-tell, ego-boosting tactics, we never openly criticized them. Real or fabricated, displays of raunchy sex were also assumed to "win points." A junior fullback claimed to have defecated on a girl's chest after she passed out during intercourse. There were also some laughing reports of "gang-bangs."

When sexual relationships were "serious," that is, tempered by love and commitment, the unspoken rule was silence. It was rare when we young men shared our feelings about women, misgivings about sexual performance, or disdain for the crudeness and insensitivity of some of our teammates. I now see the tragic irony in this: we could talk about superficial sex and anything that used, trivialized, or debased women, but frank discussions about sexuality that unfolded within a loving relationship were taboo. Within the locker room subculture, sex and love were seldom allowed to mix. There was a terrible split between inner needs and outer appearances, between our desire for the love of women and our feigned indifference toward them.

Reprinted with permission from Sabo (1990:1617)

report equally *desiring* and *valuing* intimacy, some suggest, but men grow up with behavioral inhibitions to *expressing* intimacy. We are taught how to be male and female in society, and from a very young age, boys are discouraged from displaying vulnerability or doubt about intimacy. Read one man's experience in Personal Voices 6.2: The message the author received from his peers was loud and clear: talk of sex was acceptable, but talk of intimacy was taboo. While the author's experience may have been extreme, exaggerated by the all-male atmosphere of the athletic team, such attitudes are communicated in subtle ways to most men. Men may therefore remain unexpressive about intimacy, however strongly they may desire it. However, others have suggested that men are just as intimate as women. They argue that men simply express intimacy differently; either they express intimacy more through actions than words (Gilmore, 1990), or they use a language of intimacy that women do not always recognize (Tannen, 1990).

That's the nature of women, not to love when we love them, and to love when we love them not.

(Cervantes, Don Quixote)

One study compared men and women who scored high on a scale of masculinity or femininity to those who scored high on both (androgyny—see Chapter 5) (Coleman and Ganong, 1985). Androgynous people were more aware of their love feelings, more expressive, and tolerated their partner's faults more than those who scored high only on the masculinity scale; they were also more cognitively aware, willing to express faults, and tolerant than those who scored high only on the femininity scale. The importance of accepting traditional gender roles is also reflected in comparisons of homosexual and heterosexual men; although homosexual and heterosexual men agree on the ideal characteristics of love partners and express the same amounts and kinds of love, homosexuals are more likely to believe that "you should share your most intimate thoughts and feelings with the person you love" (Engel and Saracino, 1986:242). Physical intimacy was also more important to homosexual men. Since homosexual men tend to adopt fewer stereotyped beliefs about gender roles than heterosexual men, this may be more evidence that sex role belief is more important than biological sex.

However, some evidence indicates that the differences in attitudes between the genders may be changing. Research showing strong differences between the sexes tends to be older. The women's movement and, more recently, the men's movement have tried to challenge old stereotypes of gender and intimacy. Hatfield and Rapson (1987) suggest that while in the past women were more comfortable with intimate encounters while men were more comfortable taking independent action, now a new, more androgynous breed of men and women may be emerging who are more comfortable in both roles. If so, maybe we can expect greater ease in intimacy between the genders in the upcoming generations of men and women.

Intimacy in Different Cultures

Love and intimacy seem to be basic human emotions. Aren't "basic human emotions" the same everywhere? Isn't anger the same in Chicago and Timbuktu, and sadness the same in Paris and Bombay? In fact, the ways people think about and express emotion are very different in different cultures. For example, passionate love as we conceive of it is unknown in Tahiti (Peele, 1988). In the United States, dependency is considered to be a sign of a problem in a relationship; in Japan, dependency on another is seen as a key aspect of love, a positive trait that should be nurtured. In China, people's sense of self is entirely translated through their relationships with others. "A male Chinese would consider himself a son, a brother, a husband, a father, but hardly himself. It seems as if . . . there was very little independent self left for the Chinese" (Chu, 1985, quoted in Dion and Dion, 1988:276). In China, love is thought of in terms of how a mate would be received by family and community, not in terms of one's own sense of romance.

Culture has a large part in determining how we view love. In a study of France, Japan, and the United States, intimacy style was directly related to whether the culture was individualistic (United States), collectivistic (Japan), or mixed (France) and also to how much the culture had adopted stereotypical views of gender roles (how much it tended to see men as assertive and women as nurturing) (Ting-Toomey, 1991). The Japanese, with a collectivistic culture and highly stereotypical gender roles, had lower scores in measures of attachment and commitment and were less likely to value self-disclosure than the French or Americans. Americans also have stereotypical gender roles, but because of the highly individualistic culture in the United States, Americans tend to

Love makes itself felt not in the desire for copulation (a desire that extends to an infinite number of women) but in the desire for a shared sleep (a desire limited to one woman).

(Milan Kundera)

Personal
V O I C E S
<u>6.3</u>

Murray and Frances:
A Tale of Committed Love

Frances has multiple sclerosis and is institutionalized in a home for the severely disabled called Inglis House. Her husband, Murray, works.

Murray:

When I married Frances, I swore that I would stay with her till death do us part, see, and I'm keeping my word—that's all. This is what I wanted; now, I wouldn't want any other woman. Even if she'd give me a divorce today, I wouldn't want any other woman. I've had a marvelous—a *beautiful*—life with her, even with her handicaps. She's humorous, she's smart—and we talk the same language: we don't even have to come out with the exact words. I can say *one word* and she knows what I am thinking about . . . because [of] living with me that length of time [fifty years of marriage, the last thirty-five with multiple sclerosis— the last fifteen of these at Inglis House]. I come here four or five times a week. Her love *draws* me out here. When I come here I feel *good*; I look for the moment when I have to get in the car to come out here.

So it must be *in me* to want to do that. And we can have a difference of opinion. And I can leave her in a huff here, but the next time I come—its just like nothing happened. And I daren't walk in that room without kissing her!...So, we're still on our honeymoon, even though she's incapacitated to the point where she's not really a *wife* to me. But as far as a companion? She's all I want. So, that's the way it is. . . . Yep.

Frances:

I know there are a lot of things to be thankful for . . . after all there are women in here whose husbands just put them in here and *forgot* about them. And I think that's sad. In fact, when I told my husband how worried I was about him once when he wasn't feeling well, he said "Don't worry"—not to "worry about me"—and I said to him: "Don't you *dare* deprive me of that! That's one of my *privileges*." The people for whom I feel sorry are the people that have nobody to worry about. . . . It's a reciprocal thing.

From Stehl (1985:127)

have high levels of confusion and ambivalence about relationships. Interestingly, the French, who have a culture with high individual motivation yet with a strong group orientation, and who also have a more balanced view of masculine and feminine gender roles, had the lowest degree of conflict in intimate relationships. Thus, culture plays a role in how we experience and express both love and intimacy.

Long-Term Love and Commitment

The ability to maintain love over time is the hallmark of maturity. Many people regard love as something that happens *to* them, almost like catching the flu. This attitude hides an important truth about love: it takes effort and commitment to maintain love—not only commitment to the other person, but commitment to build on and improve the quality of the relationship continually. Most long-term relationships that end do so not because the couple "fell out of love" but because somewhere down the line they stopped

Love is not love until love is vulnerable.

(Theodore Roethke)

working together on their relationship. In this sense, the old saying is true: the opposite of love is not hate but indifference.

Sternberg (1986), you may recall, claimed that passion, intimacy, and commitment are the three elements of love; in consummate love, he says, all three are present. Yet, one hears little talk of commitment in our culture, with its great emphasis on passionate love. Read the account of the man and wife in Personal Voices 6.3. It is this sense of commitment that is the test of love. Couples going through hard times can persevere and even build stronger and more intimate relationships when their commitment reflects such a deep sense of trust.

Try to observe an elderly couple who have been together for many years. There is often an ease together, a comfort born of many years of trust. Long-term relationships without intimacy or commitment can be very lonely. Men report feeling lonelier in marriages where there is less intimacy, less liking, and less communication. Women report more loneliness in marriages where there is less liking, less marital satisfaction, less self-disclosure, and less love (Sadava and Matejcic, 1987). Love itself does not necessarily fade over time; passionate love may, but the decreased importance of passion allows other kinds of love to move to the forefront of the relationship, if the couple makes the commitment to do so.

SEX TALK

QUESTION **6.4** **How can you stay with only one person your whole life and not become bored?**

Love grows and changes when two people commit themselves to work on a relationship. Are you the person you were ten years ago? What makes you think you will be the same ten years from now? When two people allow each other to grow and develop, they find new experiences and new forms of love all the time. People grow bored primarily when they lose interest, not because the other person has no mysteries left.

Loss of Love

Popular songs are often about the loss of love; "the blues" is a whole genre of music built on the experience of losing love, and country-western music is well known for its songs of lost love. People experience loss of love in many ways. The couple may realize that their relationship was based on passion and cannot develop into long-term love. One partner may decide, for his or her own reasons, to end a relationship that is still valued by the other partner. Also, a partner may be lost to disease or may die.

The loss of love is a time of mourning and going through a period of sadness and depression, as well as anger at the partner, is natural. Most people are also very vulnerable after the loss of a love relationship—vulnerable to rushing into an ill-advised relationship to replace the lost partner, and vulnerable to self-blame, loss of self-esteem, and distrust of others (Timmreck, 1990).

No easy solutions exist to decreasing the pain of a breakup. Often being good to yourself can help, taking some time to do the things that make you happy. Readjusting your schedule can be difficult if your day was built around the other person; you may feel the most sense of loss at just those times that you used to be together (dinner time, bedtime). Try to find new activities and new patterns in your day. Call on your family and

I want to do with you
What spring does
With the cherry trees.

(Pablo Neruda)

friends for support. As you go through the grieving process, remember: almost everyone has experienced what you are feeling at one time or another, and you will pull through.

LOVE, SEX, AND BUILDING INTIMATE RELATIONSHIPS

One way to express deep love and intimacy is through sexuality, but sexuality itself is not necessarily an expression of love or intimacy. How are love and sex related?

Love and Sex

The decision to engage in a sexual relationship may or may not be related to feelings of love. Casual sex has become much more common and accepted than it was thirty-five or forty years ago when young people (especially women) were strongly advised to save their "greatest asset," their virginity, for marriage. However, one can also enter a sexual relationship too casually without a close examination of how both partners will feel afterward. Sex can be used as a substitute for intimacy or as a substitute for love. Also, casual sex has become more physically risky with the spread of sexually transmitted diseases (see Chapter 13).

When we begin to feel attracted to others, we begin to act intimate; we gaze longer at each other, lean on each other, and touch more (Hatfield, 1988). People meeting each other for the first time tend to reveal their levels of attraction by their body language. Perper (1985) observed couples approaching each other in bars. The first stage is the initial contact and conversation (which, by the way, Perper found to be commonly initiated by the female). If the couple is mutually attracted, they will begin to turn their bodies more and more toward each other until they are facing one another. Then the first tentative touches begin, a hand briefly on a hand or a forearm, for example, and increase in duration and sexual intimacy over time (also often initiated by the female). Finally, the couple shows "full body synchronization"; their facial expressions, posture, and even breathing begin to mirror their partner's.

SEX TALK

QUESTION **6.5** **How can I tell the difference between being in love and just deeply liking someone?**

> Unfortunately, no one has come up with a foolproof way of making that distinction. Being "in love" can feel a lot like being in "deep like." One would hope we deeply like those whom we love; and, in fact, we probably love those we deeply like. The element that may be missing from those we deeply like is sexual passion; but sometimes we do not realize that we are not in *love* with them until after we develop a sexual relationship. The discovery can be painful to both parties, which is why it is advisable to be very careful before initiating a sexual relationship with a friend.

How do we make the decision to have sex? There are many levels of relationships that can lead to sex. Casual sex can happen between people who barely know each other,

Love, such as it is in society, is only the exchange of two fantasies, and the contact of two bodies.

(Sebastian R. N. Chamfort, Maximes et penses)

"one-night stands" whose pleasure is generated by excitement, novelty, and pure physical pleasure. Sex can be an expression of affection and intimacy without considering it an expression of passionate love. Sex can also be engaged in purely for procreation, or sex can be an extension of a loving relationship, an expression of love. Problems can develop when one partner has one view of the developing sexual relationship, while the other partner takes a different perspective. For example, research shows that men in the United States have considerably more permissive attitudes toward casual sex than females do (Oliver and Hyde, 1993). If the decision to engage in a sexual relationship is not discussed beforehand, the man might assume, for example, that the sex is casual, while the women might assume it is an expression of deeper feelings.

Since the decision to engage in sexual contact involves the feelings and desires of another person, as well as your own needs, examining your own motivations as well as your partner's is important. When making the decision to initiate a sexual relationship with another person, consider the following:

1. *Clarify your values.* At some point, each of us needs to make value decisions regarding intimacy, sex, and love. How do I feel about casual sexual contact? What role does love play in my sexual decisions? How will I reconcile these values with those I have learned from my family, my friends, and my religion?

2. *Be honest with yourself.* Honesty with oneself is often more difficult than honesty with others. Entering a relationship with another person takes close self-examination. What do I really want out of this encounter, out of this person? Am I hoping the sexual contact will lead to something deeper, or am I in it simply for the sex? What will I do if I (or my partner) gets pregnant? If I find that I (or my partner) has a sexually transmitted disease? Will I feel better or worse about myself tomorrow? Am I in this because I want to be or because I feel some kind of pressure to be sexual—from myself or from my partner? Could I say "no" comfortably? Am I ready for a sexual relationship with this person?

3. *Be honest with your partner.* Another person's feelings and needs are always at issue in any relationship, and part of our responsibility as caring human beings is not to hurt or exploit others. Why is my partner interested in sex with me? Do his or her expectations differ from mine? Will he or she be hurt if our relationship does not develop further? Have we discussed our feelings? Does he or she really want to do this, or is he or she afraid of losing my love or friendship?

Developing Intimacy Skills

Self-Love

Developing intimacy begins with understanding ourselves and *liking* ourselves. Many people look to others for indications of their own self-worth. But making others the guardians of our self-worth is not fair to them. We must first take responsibility to know ourselves (self-intimacy) and then to accept ourselves as we are (self-love). Self-love is different from conceit or **narcissism**; it is not a process of promoting ourselves but of being at ease with our positive qualities and forgiving ourselves for our faults. If you are not willing to get to know yourself and to accept your own faults, why would others think you are any more interested in them or that you would judge them any less harshly?

Once we like ourselves, we can reach out to others. What attracts people to others? What skills can we develop to enhance our ability to form intimate relationships?

Let there be spaces in your togetherness.

(Kahill Gibran, The Prophet)

narcissism: Obsession with the self, conceit, and selfishness, named for the Greek mythical character Narcissus, who gazed at his own reflection in a pool and fell in love with himself. Unlike healthy self-love, narcissism involves total self-absorption.

Receptivity

Many of us think we are receptive to others when actually we are sending subtle signals that we do not want to be bothered. Receptivity can be communicated through smiling, eye contact, and a warm, relaxed posture. This allows the other person to feel comfortable and makes us approachable.

Listening

As we will see below, true communication begins with listening, and nothing shows you care about another person quite as much as your full attention. Who is more of a bore than a person who talks only of him or herself, who sees any comment made by another person primarily in terms of how it relates to them? Remember the experiment we mentioned above where people were liked better by others when they responded to self-disclosure with emotional support rather than with their own self-disclosure (Berg and Archer, 1980). Learning to listen truly enhances intimacy.

Affection

Do you want to learn to display affection? Watch a loving parent with his or her child. Parents *attend* to their children, smile at them, touch them in affectionate ways, look in their eyes, and hug and kiss them. Most people want the same things from their intimate friends and lovers. Affection shows that you feel a sense of warmth and security with your partner.

Trust

To trust another is an act of courage because it grants that person the power to hurt or disappoint you. However, intimacy requires trust. Those who totally trust their partners show an ease in their relationship, a contentment not found in those who do not trust.

Respect

We enter relationships with our own needs and desires, and sometimes these cloud the fact that the other person is different from us and has his or her own special needs. Respect is the process of acknowledging and understanding that person's needs, even if you do not share them.

The Dark Side of Love

Love evokes powerful emotions; this is both its strength and its weakness. Many of the emotions that can come from strong feelings about another person are destructive to a relationship, and these emotions require great maturity or a strong act of will to overcome. Let us examine three of the dark sides of love.

Jealousy: The Green-Eyed Monster

Imagine that you are at a party with a person with whom you are in an exclusive, sexual relationship. You notice the person standing close to another person, talking and laugh-

It is easier to live through someone else than to become complete yourself.

(Betty Friedan)

ing, and occasionally putting a hand on the other person's arm. At one point, you notice your partner whispering in the other person's ear, and they both laugh. Then they walk out to the dance floor, where they dance together, still talking and laughing.

How does that make you feel? Are you jealous? But wait, we forgot to tell you: the person your partner was talking to and dancing with was of the same sex as your partner (if you are heterosexual) or the opposite sex (if you are homosexual). Are you still jealous? Oh yes, one more thing. The other person was your partner's younger sibling. *Now* are you jealous?

Jealousy is "the thoughts and feelings that arise when an actual or desired relationship is threatened" (Salovey and Rodin, 1985). But a threat is a matter of interpretation; people who deeply trust their partners may not be able to imagine a situation where the relationship is really threatened. According to a survey in *Psychology Today* done by Salovey and Rodin (1985), we are most jealous in the situation above when the person flirting with our partner has traits we ourselves want (or we fantasize that they do). Maybe we imagine that our partner will find them more desirable than us, sexier, or funnier. The survey found a correlation between jealousy and self-esteem; the more often a person is jealous, the lower is his or her self-esteem. We imagine that the partner sees in the other person all those traits we believe that we lack.

Jealousy exists in all cultures, but what *evokes* jealousy may be very different. In the former Yugoslavia, for example, having your partner flirt with another evokes a strong jealousy response, while having your partner kiss another or hearing your partner's sexual fantasies about another person had the lowest jealousy response of all nations studied. The Dutch, on the other hand, seem to have a hard time with sexual fantasies about other people (Buunk and Hupka, 1987).

Although many people think that their jealousy shows that they really care for a person, in fact it shows a lack of trust in the partner. Jealousy is not a compliment; it is a demonstration of lack of trust and low self-esteem. Jealousy is also a self-fulfilling prophecy; jealous individuals can drive their mate away, even into the arms of another lover, which convinces them that they were right to be jealous in the first place. Jealousy can be contained by trying to improve one's own self-image; by turning it around into a compliment (not "she is flirting with other men" but "look at how lucky I am—other men also find her attractive"); and by trust of one's partner.

Compulsiveness: Addicted to Love

Being in love can produce a sense of ecstasy, euphoria, and a feeling of well-being, much like a powerful drug. In fact, Liebowitz (1983) argues that love causes the body to release the drug phenylethylamine, which produces these feelings. (Phenylethylamine is also present in chocolate, which may be why we love it so much, especially during a breakup!) Some people do, in fact, move from relationship to relationship as if they were love-addicted, trying to recreate that feeling continually, or else obsessively hang on to a love partner long after his or her interest has waned. (See Lee's description of mania in the Colors of Love, page 205.)

Love addiction is reinforced by the popular media's portrayals (even as far back as Shakespeare's *Romeo and Juliet*) of passionate love as all-consuming, fostering the belief that only one person is fated to be your "true love," that love is always mutual, and that you will live "happily ever after." Some people feel the need to be in love because

Perhaps that is what love is—the momentary or prolonged refusal to think of another person in terms of power.

(Phyllis Rose)

society teaches that only then are you really whole, only then are you happy, and only then have you fulfilled your role as a woman or a man. Yet love based solely on need can never be truly fulfilling. In Peele and Brodsky's (1976) book *Love and Addiction,* they argue that love addiction is more common than most believe and that it is based on a continuation of an adolescent view of love that is never replaced as the person matures. Counseling or psychotherapy may help the person come to terms with their need to constantly be in love relationships.

Possessiveness: Every Move You Make, I'll Be Watching You

Since love also entails risk, dependency to some degree, and a strong connection between people, there is always the danger that the strength of the bond can be used to manipulate the other. Abusive love relationships exist when one partner tries to increase his or her own sense of self-worth or to control the other's behavior through withdrawing or manipulating love.

For intimacy to grow, partners must nurture each other. Controlling behavior may have short-term benefits (you might get the person to do what you want for a while), but in the long term, it smothers the relationship. No one likes the feeling of being manipulated, whether it is subtle, through the use of guilt, or overt through physical force. Part of love is the joy of seeing the partner free to pursue their desires and to appreciate the differences between partners. Although every relationship has its boundaries (being free to pursue your desires does not mean being free to engage in sex with others while in an exclusive relationship), freedom within those agreed-upon constraints is what encourages the growth and maturation of both partners.

stalking: Obsessively following and spying on another person, usually to see if they are involved romantically with someone else. Stalking is now against the law in most states.

Possessiveness indicates a problem of self-esteem and personal boundaries, and it can eventually lead to **stalking**. Most states have passed stalking laws, which allow a person (usually, but not always, a woman) to have someone arrested who constantly shadows them or makes threatening gestures or claims (see Chapter 15). Thinking about another person with that level of obsession is a sign of a serious psychological problem, one that should be brought to the attention of a mental health professional.

COMMUNICATION

For love and intimacy to grow, each partner must know how the other feels. Good communication is the hallmark of a healthy, developing relationship; however, it is never quite as easy as it seems. Couples who rate their communication skills high while dating tend to have greater satisfaction later in the relationship (Markham, 1979; 1981). Good communication skills can be applied to all aspects of life, from developing a love relationship, to discussing sexuality with a partner, to improving family relationships, to being more effective in relationships at school or work. Note that having good communication skills and using them are two different things; partners who have no trouble talking about their feelings in general, for example, may still have trouble telling each other how they want to change their sex life.

Communication about sexuality is extremely difficult for many people. We grow up in society instilled with a sense of shame about our sexuality and are taught at an early

It requires far more genius to make love than to command armies.

(Ninon de Lenclose, ascribed)

age that talking about sex is "dirty." Approaching the subject of sex for the first time in a relationship implies moving on to a new level of intimacy, which can be scary. (It also opens the way for rejection, which can be painful.) We often expect that in love, our partner will somehow know exactly what we want without our having to say so.

Sexuality is also an area in which many people feel insecure. People may wonder if they are good lovers and worry that their partners do not think they are. At the same time, however, they may be hesitant to make suggestions to improve their partner's techniques or to request new sexual positions or experiences, worrying that they might hurt their partner's ego. Anxieties like these do not foster a sense of open and mutual communication.

Sexuality seems to magnify all the communication problems that exist in any close relationship. Let us explore the nature of communication between the sexes, and perhaps we can uncover guidelines to good communication.

Gender and Communication

Do men and women communicate differently? Is part of the communication problem in heterosexual couples incompatibility between how men and women communicate so that the content of the communication gets lost in the form it takes? Researchers have looked at this question, and many suggest that there is, in fact, a "male" and "female" mode of communication.

Communication Styles

Research has shown that men use more nonstandard forms of speech (slang), talk more about money and business, refer more to time, space, quantity, destructive actions, physical movements, and objects, and use more hostile verbs than women. Women are more supportive in speech, are more polite and expressive, talk more about home and family, and use more words implying feeling, evaluation, interpretation, and psychological states (Haas, 1979b; Tannen, 1990). Research has also shown that men know and use more synonyms for sexual intercourse, and that the sexes differ in word preference (e.g., when speaking informally, men prefer "fuck" where women prefer "screw"; women also use the phrase "make love" more often) (Simkins and Rinck, 1982).

Men and women have different communication styles, especially when in sex-segregated groups. Note that the men above space themselves more widely than the women do.

The best part of married life is the fights—the rest is merely so-so.

(Thornton Wilder)

genderlects: Deborah Tannen's word for the fundamentally different strategies males and females use to communicate.

Women tend to use more nonverbal behaviors in flirting than men do.

Deborah Tannen (1990) suggests that there are fundamental differences between the way men and women communicate, which she calls **genderlects**. Men tend to see the world as a place of hierarchical order where they must struggle to maintain their position. They therefore interpret comments more often as challenges to their position and attempt to defend their independence. Women, on the other hand, see the world more as a network of interactions, and their goal is to form connections and avoid isolation. Tannen suggests that men more often engage in *report-talk,* imparting knowledge, while women more often engage in *rapport-talk,* establishing relationships and connections.

Men and women also differ in the flow of language, Tannen suggests. Men believe that women constantly interrupt them; but women claim that men interrupt them more than other women do. Tannen responds that, in keeping with a *report-talk* style, men tend to speak one at a time, and so another comment is seen as an interruption. Women use more overlapping talk, where it is alright for a second person to speak over the first as long as they do not change the subject or try to take over being the primary speaker. When men interrupt women, they expect to become the primary speaker; when women overlap, they "interrupt" without expecting that the conversation will turn to them.

Men and women also differ in how they respond to problems. Men tend to give advice and try to fix others' problems; women tend to try and confirm the other person's feelings and sympathize. Many misunderstandings can arise between the sexes because of this, says Tannen. Women resent men's tendencies always to try to fix their emotional problems, and men complain that women refuse to take action to solve their problems.

Tannen suggests these genderlects develop because young boys and girls tend to play in same-sex groups, which are often organized very differently. Boys jockey for status by telling jokes or showing off or claiming they are the best at things, and individual leaders tend to emerge. Boys spend more time than girls in sports organized with captains and a hierarchy of better and worse players. Girls, on the other hand, tend to play in smaller groups or pairs or to have a best friend. Levels of intimacy are the goal, and the games they play when young (playing house, for example) less often have winners and losers. They usually do not solve problems by jockeying for power or by trying to become the group leader but by negotiating.

The different ways boys and girls communicate and solve problems follow them through life. In one experiment, young boys, told to sit and discuss something serious, fidgeted in their chairs, made dirty jokes, teased each other, and made fun of the researcher. Young girls sat quietly, faces almost touching, and told stories they thought were serious. Interestingly, when adult men and women watched the tapes of these children, they had very different reactions. Women found the girls cute and wondered why the boys could not sit still and had to make fun of everything; men, though, thought the girls were trying to kiss up to the experimenters and admired the boys' impulse to poke fun at the situation and defy the experimenter. Tannen notes that two-year-old girls have more in common with twenty-five-year-old women than with two-year-old boys; we grow up in different worlds, but we judge each other's world by our own.

Nonverbal Communication

In addition to having different styles of communication, men and women may also have different abilities. Judith Hall (1978) reviewed seventy-five studies of the ability of males and females to understand nonverbal communication and found that, overall, females were significantly better than men at decoding nonverbal cues. Perhaps that is why women try

A good marriage is that in which each appoints the other guardian of his solitude.

(Alexander Pope, The Rape of the Lock)

to use nonverbal cues more. For example, women engage in more nonverbal flirting behaviors; they are more likely to gaze toward their partners, use positive facial expressions, engage in brief touching, and exhibit more self-grooming behaviors, and they are, perhaps surprisingly, more likely to initiate flirtation (McCormick and Jones, 1989).

With all these differences, are men and women destined to try to communicate over a giant chasm of misunderstanding? Not necessarily. First of all, these ways of communicating are only trends, and plenty of men and women are good at different techniques of communication. Second, understanding and patience play a key role. Those willing to work at improving their communication skills can significantly enhance their intimate relationships both with members of the other sex and with members of their own gender.

Being a More Effective Communicator

How can we communicate more effectively? A number of techniques can help us.

1. **Talk about good communication.** When you need a good icebreaker to move into a conversation about love, intimacy, and sex, a safe place to start is to talk about talking. It is an intimate topic that is not threatening, and it can easily move into more personal and sexual areas.
2. **Learn to accommodate the style of the other sex.** Tannen (1990) notes that when groups of men meet or when groups of men and women are together, the conversation tends to adopt men's conversational and body-language styles. Only when women are alone do they feel able to relax their posture and assume their natural style. Understanding the style of the opposite sex and accepting it (that is, not seeing it as selfish, stupid, or a threat) will go a long way to improving communication.
3. **Give helpful, supportive feedback.** A good listener tries to understand what the person who is speaking is really trying to say and what he or she really wants in return. Knowing your partner means knowing when your partner wants advice and when he or she just wants a sympathetic ear.

WHERE DO I *Stand?* 6.1

How Do You Feel About Love?

Remember at the beginning of the chapter we asked you to repeat Where Do I Stand? 6.1 after completing this chapter? Here it is. Number a paper 1 to 11 and write down whether you agree or disagree with the statements below:

1. Loving someone is different from being "in love" with them.
2. Self-love is necessary before we can love someone else.
3. Loving *adds* to your freedom and your partner's freedom.
4. You always like someone you love.
5. Jealousy shows that a loving relationship has depth.
6. Secrets are okay to have even in a loving relationship.
7. Loving someone involves accepting risk.
8. Some relationships should end even when there is still love.
9. Fulfilling love relationships are possible even without sex.
10. Fulfilling sexual relationships are possible even without love.
11. If you are unfaithful in a love relationship, you have an obligation to tell your partner.

Have your views of love changed at all because of what you've learned in this chapter?

4. **Do not wait until you are angry before discussing something.** According to an ancient Chinese book of wisdom, the truly wise person handles things when they are small, before they grow too big. Therefore, they never seem like great men or women because they never have to solve really big problems. Let this guide you in your relationships. Discuss problems when you first realize them, while they are still small, and avoid the big, blow-out fights.

5. **Let go of the need to be right.** In relationships, establishing who is "right" and "wrong" is never fruitful. What is fruitful is establishing how to improve communication and how to increase intimacy.

6. **Ask questions.** How are you really going to know your partner's needs, desires, and thoughts unless you ask?

7. **Be responsible.** Most people cannot read their partners' minds. What is obvious to you may not be obvious to your partner. If you want something, ask for it, and do not be vague; be direct. For example, suppose you want your partner to be more romantic. "You never do anything romantic" is a challenge; "Let's plan a romantic evening together" is a more direct and less threatening way to request the same thing.

8. **Be supportive.** Mix praise with your criticisms; say things in positive rather than negative ways. In the example above, an even better way to put it would be: "I love being alone with you, together, just talking. Let's go out for a candlelight dinner tonight, just the two of us."

9. **Learn to say no, gently.** People sometimes get into relationship trouble because they do not know how to say "no" to their partners and then end up resenting that they are doing things they do not want to do. Every person has a right to say no; in fact, it is a sign of trust and respect for your partner to believe that you can say no and still retain his or her love and affection. But saying no to a request is different from rejecting the person making it; no must be said in a way that reassures the partner that it is only the requested action you are refusing.

10. **Be forgiving.** In all love relationships, we make mistakes. We hurt our partners, we are sometimes thoughtless, and we do a thousand little things we wish we could change. We are all human. Bringing up slights from the past is never helpful. When communication is done in a spirit of unconditional positive regard (which, we realize, is a very difficult state to achieve), all the other qualities of good communication will fall into place.

S u m m a r y

- *Romantic love* is the passionate, highly sexual part of loving. *Companionate love* involves feelings of affection, intimacy, and attachment to another person. In many cultures, marriages are based on companionate love, assuming that passion will grow as the couple does.

- John Alan Lee suggests there are six basic types of love, enumerated in Sexuality Today 6.1. Robert Sternberg suggests that love is made up of three elements, passion, intimacy, and commitment, which can combine in different ways in relationships, creating eight basic ways to love.

- Where does love come from? Behavioral reinforcement theorists argue that we love those who make us feel good, who reinforce positive traits in ourselves. Cognitive theorists sug-

gest love is our interpretation of being with someone a lot or thinking about them a lot; the action comes first, the interpretation later. Physiological arousal theorists argue that love happens when we enter a general state of arousal in the presence of a potential love object. Sociobiologists suggest that love is a combination of our sexual drive and our instincts to protect and to procreate.

- Love develops over the life cycle. In infancy, we develop attachments to our caregivers; receiving love in return has an influence on our capacity to love later in life.

- In adolescence, we deal with issues of separation from our parents and begin to explore adult ways of loving. Adolescents tend to experience romantic love. Attachment styles we learn in infancy, such as secure, avoidant, and ambivalent styles, may last through life and influence how we begin to form adult attachment in adolescence.

- As we mature and enter adulthood, forming intimate relations becomes important. We tend to become attracted to people like us, and men tend to look more for beauty and women for security in almost every culture. Developing intimacy is risky, and men and women have different styles of intimacy, but intimacy is seen as an important component of mature love in our culture. As we grow older, commitment in love becomes important, and passion decreases in importance.
- Relationships take effort, and when a couple stops working on the relationship they can become very lonely, love can fade, and intimacy can evaporate. When love is lost, for whatever reason, it is a time of pain and mourning. The support of family and friends can help us let go of the lost love and try to form new attachments.
- Men and women may have different intimacy styles. For example, men may learn to suppress communication about intimacy as they grow, or they may learn to express it in different ways.
- The decision to be sexual is often confused with the decision

to love. Values need to be clarified before a sexual relationship is begun.

- Love also has its negative side. Jealousy plagues many people in their love relationships, while others seem addicted to love, going in and out of love relationships. Some people also use love as a means to manipulate and control others.
- Honest, open communication is a key part of a loving relationship. However, men and women communicate differently. Men see the world hierarchically and interpret communication in terms of power and pecking order; men also tend to use advice to solve problems. Women see the world as a web of interconnections and see communication as a means of forging intimacy; women tend to use support to help those with problems.
- We can become more effective communicators. We need to open channels by giving helpful feedback to our partners, discussing things early, before they get out of hand, and letting go of the need to be right all the time. Each partner must be responsible for asking questions and telling the other partner what is on his or her mind in a direct, honest, and supportive way. Finally, generosity and forgiveness, although often difficult, are the greatest gifts we can give our partners.

R eflections on Sexuality

1. Is love the same in all ages and times? Can we speak of an "evolution" of the idea of love?
2. What is the difference between romantic and companionate, or conjugal, love? What kind of love relationship do you hope to have with your mate?
3. What do you think of the attempts of John Alan Lee or Robert Sternberg to enumerate all the types of love? Do you think that can be done?
4. Where does the feeling of love come from? Is it no more than a general state of arousal to which we add a label, as Schachter and Singer claim?
5. What makes love relationships so difficult and changeable

for many adolescents? Why do you think those highs and lows even out as we get older?
6. How does research on attraction and mate selection debunk the idea of "one true love"?
7. Which of the three attachment styles described by Ainsworth et al. and Hazan and Shaver is most like yours?
8. Do you accept the idea that men and women communicate differently? Why or why not?
9. What can we learn from the fact that, although sexual jealousy is found in almost all cultures, the things that make people jealous can be quite different in different societies?
10. Why is communication about sex and love so difficult?

S uggested Readings

ABBOTT, F., ED. (1990) *Men and Intimacy.* Freedom, CA: The Crossing Press.

FROMM, ERICH (1956) *The Art of Loving.* New York: Harper.

LEE, JOHN A. (1977) "A typology of styles of loving." *Personality and Social Psychology Bulletin* 3: 173–182.

LIEBOWITZ, M.R. (1983) *The Chemistry of Love.* Boston: Little, Brown.

STERNBERG, ROBERT J. (1988) *The Triangle of Love. Intimacy, Passion, Commitment.* New York: Basic Books.

STERNBERG, ROBERT J., AND M.L. BARNES, EDS. (1988) *The Psychology of Love.* New Haven: Yale University Press.

TANNEN, DEBORAH (1990) *You Just Don't Understand: Women and Men in Conversation.* New York: Ballantine Books.

7

Sexual Orientation

Bill is a twenty-one-year-old male. When he was in his teens, he and a male friend stroked each other to orgasm on three occasions. Although he now dates only women, every so often while masturbating he fantasizes about those experiences, which enhances his orgasm. He considers himself heterosexual and is a bit uneasy about his fantasies.

Anthony is a thirty-one-year-old married man with two children. He enjoys a healthy sexual life with his wife, whom he loves, and has not had sex with another woman since his marriage. However, about once every two or three months, Anthony drives to a town about two hours away from where he lives and picks up a man for quick, anonymous sex. He finds these encounters to be the most exciting part of his sex life.

Peter is a twenty-six-year-old male who has been incarcerated for five years for dealing drugs. While in prison, he engaged in anal and oral sex with other men, usually fantasizing that they were women. He longs for his scheduled release a few months from now when he plans to resume having sex exclusively with women, as he did before being sent to prison.

Susan is a forty-five-year-old female who has lived for twenty-one years in an exclusive, monogamous lesbian relationship with Michele. After eight years with Michele, Susan decided she wanted a child and had sex a few times with a friend of hers named Jonathan. When asked, she says that sex with a man was better than she remembered it, but she has little desire to repeat the experience. She now has a thirteen-year-old son. Seeing how much Susan enjoyed having a child, Michele decided she wanted one, too, but had herself artificially inseminated because she had no desire to have intercourse with a man.

Don and Kiko are swingers who enjoy engaging in group sex with other couples. In these group sex sessions, sexual contact is very free, and often Don will find himself fellating a man, or Kiko will engage in sexual contact with women. Both are very comfortable with such contact, feeling that sexual pleasure is sexual pleasure no matter who is administering it.

DEFINING SEXUAL ORIENTATION

Read through the five examples of sexual lifestyles listed above. How would you categorize these people? Who is heterosexual? Who is homosexual? Who is bisexual? Are any of them difficult to characterize? What about Bill, who is now exclusively heterosexual in his behavior but has fantasies of past homosexual behavior? Anthony has occasional sex with other men, while Peter and Susan both have had sex outside their usual lifestyles for purely practical reasons—Peter because he is in prison and women are not available to him, and Susan because she wanted to get pregnant. Don and Kiko seem to move fluidly between heterosexuality and homosexuality without worrying about their "orientation."

sexual orientation: A term used to denote the gender(s) one is sexually attracted to.

heterosexual: A person who is predominantly sexually attracted to the opposite sex.

Sexual orientation refers to the gender(s) that a person is attracted to sexually and romantically. **Heterosexuals** are predominantly attracted to members of the other sex;

WHERE DO I *Stand?*   7.1

How Much Do You Know About Homosexuality?

Test your knowledge about homosexuality by deciding whether the statements below are true or false.

1. Most homosexuals are cross-dressers.   T (F)
2. You can tell gay persons by the way they look, act, or talk.   T (F)
3. People could stop being homosexual if they wanted to.   T (F)
4. Most homosexuals adopt a sexual role— they are usually either the passive partner or the active partner in sex.   T F
5. Most male homosexuals are incapable of having sex with women.   T F
6. Male homosexuals are gay because they have a psychological fear of women.   T F
7. Lesbians are more masculine in build—bigger, more muscular—than straight women.   T F

8. Homosexuals often try to recruit others to their sexual preference.   T F
9. Homosexuals can stop desiring members of the same sex if they get therapy.   T F
10. Homosexual behavior is found only among humans.   T F
11. Homosexuals are more likely than heterosexuals to abuse children.   T F
12. Being brought up by gay parents increases your chance of being gay yourself.   T F
13. Most countries in the world today have outlawed homosexuality.   T F
14. The Christian church has always been strongly opposed to homosexuality.   T F

Answers:

All of the above statements are false!

---

homosexuals to members of the same sex; and **bisexuals** are attracted to both men and women. (The word *gay* is often used to refer to homosexuals as well, particularly male homosexuals.) Although such distinctions may seem simple, the examples above illustrate that human sexual behavior does not always fit easily into such neat boxes (see also Where Do I Stand? 7.1).

How should we categorize a person's sexual orientation? The simplest way seems to be through their behavior: with whom do they have sex? However, if that

homosexual: A person who is predominantly sexually attracted to the same sex.

bisexual: A person who is sexually attracted to both sexes.

Homosexual attraction has appeared in almost every society throughout human history.

straight: A commonly used colloquial word for heterosexual.

were our sole criterion, we would have to call Peter (third entry on page 234) homosexual—after all, he has sex exclusively with other men. Since Peter fantasizes only of sex with women, can we really call him homosexual? Maybe, then, the secret life of sexual fantasies determines sexual orientation. Bill, however, sometimes fantasizes about sex with men, even though he considers himself **straight** and has sex only with women.

Perhaps we should consider romantic love instead of sex to determine a person's sexual orientation. Who do you love, or who *could* you love? Anthony loves his wife romantically and would never consider an emotional attachment to the men he picks up. Would you consider Anthony 100% heterosexual just because he loves only his wife? Maybe we should just let people decide for themselves; if people believe they are heterosexual, they are, no matter how they behave. Yet when people's behavior and beliefs about themselves are in conflict, social scientists usually define them by their behavior.

SEX TALK

QUESTION **7.1** **If I played sex games with a friend of the same sex when I was fifteen, am I homosexual?**

Sexual experimentation and sexual orientation are two different things. It is very common, especially in the teenage years and before, to experiment with same-sex contact (and for people who are predominantly homosexual to experiment with the other sex). Yet, only a fairly small percentage of people will become predominantly homosexual (Fay et al., 1989).

The problem may be that we tend to think of sexual orientation in discrete categories: you are either homosexual or heterosexual (or, occasionally, bisexual). The full variety and richness of human sexual experience, however, cannot be easily captured in such restrictive categories. People can show enormous variety in their sexual behavior, sexual fantasies, emotional attachments, and sexual self-concept; yet, each contributes to a person's sexual orientation.

In this chapter, we explore the nature of sexual orientation and the ways researchers and scholars think about it. Heterosexuality is a sexual orientation, and the question: why is he or she heterosexual? is no less valid than asking: why is he or she homosexual? Here, however, we focus our attention primarily on the research and writing about homosexuality and bisexuality.

Models of Sexual Orientation

Kinsey and his colleagues (Kinsey et al., 1948) believed that relying on the categories "homosexual" and "heterosexual" to describe sexual orientation was inadequate. They also suggested that using a category such as "homosexual" was not as helpful as talking about homosexual *behavior*. Trying to decide "who is a homosexual" is difficult; trying to compare amounts or types of homosexual behavior (including fantasies and emotions) is easier. Based on both people's sexual behaviors and their erotic feelings, Kinsey introduced a seven-point scale, ranging from exclusively heterosexual behavior (0) to exclusively homosexual behavior (6). The Kinsey Continuum was the first scale to suggest that people engaged in complex sexual behaviors, which were not reducible simply to "homosexual" and "heterosexual." Many modern theorists agree that sexual

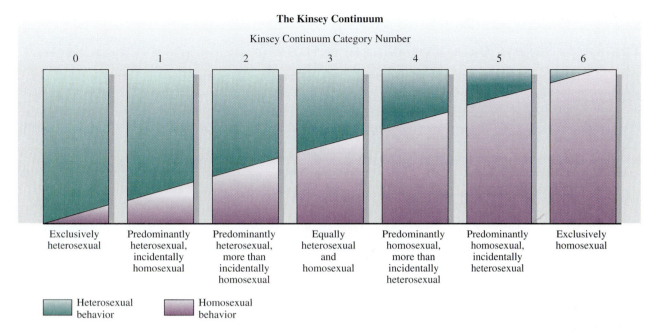

Figure 7.1

The Kinsey Continuum. Reprinted with permission from Kinsey (1948).

orientation is a *continuous variable* rather than a *categorical variable*—that is, there are no natural cut-off points that would easily separate people into categories such as "heterosexual" or "homosexual" (Berkey et al., 1990; Ellis et al., 1987).

The Kinsey scale is not without its problems, however. First of all, Kinsey emphasized people's behavior (although he did consider other factors such as fantasies and emotions). But some researchers suggest that people's emotions and fantasies are the most important determinants of sexual orientation (Storms, 1980, 1981; Bell et al., 1981). A second problem is that the scale is static in time; how recently must one have had homosexual contact to qualify for "incidents" of homosexual behavior? Or consider Anthony from the vignettes that opened this chapter. If Anthony slept with twelve men over the last year and had sex with his wife once a week, is he in category five (since he had sex with twelve men and only one woman) or category two (because he had fifty-two experiences with a female, but only twelve with males) (Klein, 1990)?

Other models, such as the Klein Sexual Orientation Grid (KSOG) (see Table 7.1), try to take the Kinsey Continuum further by including the missing elements of time, fantasy, social and lifestyle behavior, and self-identification (Klein et al., 1985). Try taking the KSOG to create a profile of your sexual orientation.

Prevalence of Different Sexual Orientations

How prevalent are homosexuality, heterosexuality, and bisexuality in society? Kinsey et al. (1948) found that 37% of men and 13% of women reported that they had had at least one adult sexual experience with another member of the same sex that resulted in orgasm and that about 4% of men and 3% of women were lifelong homosexuals. He also reported that 10% of white men had been mostly homosexual for at least three years

Table **7.1**

THE KLEIN SEXUAL ORIENTATION GRID (KSOG)

The KSOG is designed to examine seven dimensions of an individual's sexual orientation to determine if any of these dimensions have changed over time and to look at a person's fantasy of their "ideal" sexual orientation. There are no right or wrong answers; the KSOG gives a set of numbers that can be compared to determine rates of different sexual orientations.

Using the Kinsey Continuum's categories of 0–6, rate yourself as follows:

A through E: 0=same sex only; 1=mostly same sex, incidental other sex; 2=mostly same sex, more than incidental other sex; 3=both sexes equally; 4=mostly other sex, more than incidental same sex; 5=mostly other sex, incidental same sex; 6=other sex only.

F and G: Use Kinsey's regular scale; for example, if your self-identification is 100% heterosexual, put a "0" in the space; if it is mostly homosexual with incidental heterosexual attraction, put a "5," and so on.

	PAST	PRESENT	IDEAL
A. Sexual Attraction			
B. Sexual Behavior			
C. Sexual Fantasies			
D. Emotional Preference			
E. Social Preference			
F. Self-Identification			
G. Heterosexual/ Homosexual Lifestyle			

Derived from Klein (1990)

between the ages of sixteen and fifty-five, and this statistic became the one most people cited when estimating the prevalence of homosexuality in the United States. However, due to the problems with Kinsey's sampling (see Chapter 2), these figures may be unreliable.

Modern studies have found numbers lower than Kinsey's. Fay et al. (1989) found that about 20% of adult men had indicated some same-gender sexual experience, but only 1.4% reported they had same-gender sex "fairly often" after the age of twenty. Another 1.9% reported "occasional" same gender sex after twenty, meaning that 3.3% had adult same-sex experiences after their teenage years. Harry (1990) did a phone sample that keyed in on those groups of American men usually underrepresented in such studies (such as older, minority, less educated, and small-town men) and found that 3.7% of subjects reported that they were homosexual or bisexual. Laumann et al. (1994) found that while 5.5% of women said they found the thought of having sex with another woman appealing, only about 4% said they had sex with another woman after the age of eighteen, and less than 2% had sex with another woman in the past year. Similarly, while

9% of men said they had sex with another male since puberty, a little over 5% had sex with a man since turning 18, and only 2% had sex with a man in the past year. National studies in France, Britain, Norway, Denmark, and Canada all found homosexual behavior in 1% to 3% of men and a slightly lesser percentage of women (Muir, 1993).

Another problem is distinguishing between homosexuals and bisexuals for these purposes. For example, Janus and Janus (1993) found that about 9% of men and 5% of women reported having homosexual experiences "frequently" or on an "ongoing" basis; yet 5% of men considered themselves bisexual while only 4% considered themselves homosexual, and 3% of the women considered themselves bisexual while only 2% considered themselves homosexual.

Although there are problems with each of the studies cited above—for example, they concentrate on homosexual behavior, not fantasies or desires—scholars generally agree that the percentage of males who are predominantly homosexual is between 2% and 5%, with another 2–5% who are bisexual. The number of lesbians is slightly lower.

SEX TALK

QUESTION **7.2** **Isn't it easy to tell a homosexual from a heterosexual just by the way they talk and act?**

No. Berger et al. (1987) used videotapes of homosexual and straight men and women to see if subjects, including other homosexual and straight men and women, could tell who was gay or lesbian and who was straight by watching them. No group did better than chance at determining who was homosexual, although women, gays, and lesbians did a bit better than men. Although some homosexuals enjoy dressing or acting like members of the other sex (as do many heterosexuals) and some adopt a style of speech or gait to identify themselves as gay, most are indistinguishable from heterosexuals.

WHY ARE THERE DIFFERENT SEXUAL ORIENTATIONS?

It seems that everybody who has ever written about homosexuality has a theory on why some people are attracted to the opposite sex and some to the same sex. K.M. Benkert, the nineteenth-century coiner of the word *homosexuality,* had a theory that people are born homosexual:

> *In addition to the normal sex urge in men and women, nature in her sovereign mood has endowed at birth certain male and female individuals with the homosexual urge, thus placing them in a sexual bondage which renders them physically and psychically incapable—even with the best intention—of normal erection. This urge creates in advance a direct horror of the opposite sex, and the victim of this passion finds it impossible to suppress the feeling which individuals of his own sex exercise upon him.*
>
> *Benkert (1869), quoted in Bullough (1976)*

In the 1930s and 1940s, a group of scientists tried to explain homosexuality by looking for "masculine" traits in lesbians and "feminine" traits in homosexual men. They claimed that homosexuals had broad shoulders and narrow hips (indicating "immature skeletal development") and lesbians had abnormal genitalia, including larger than average vulvas, longer labia minora, a larger glans on the clitoris, a smaller uterus, and higher eroticism, shown by their tendency to become sexually aroused when being examined (Terry, 1990)! Modern research has failed to find any significant nonneurological physical differences between homosexuals and heterosexuals, although some attempts to examine physical differences still exist (e.g., Perkins, 1981).

Today's theories can be divided into two basic types: **essentialist** and **constructionist**. Essentialism suggests that homosexuals are innately different from heterosexuals, a result of either biological or developmental processes. Early essentialist theories implied that homosexuality was an abnormality in development, which contributed to the argument that homosexuality is a sickness. More recently, gay and lesbian scholars, in an attempt to prove that homosexuality is not a "lifestyle choice" as antihomosexual forces have argued, have themselves been arguing that homosexuality is a biologically based sexual variation. Constructionists, on the other hand, suggest that homosexuality is a social role that has developed differently in different cultures and times, and therefore nothing is *innately* different between homosexuals and heterosexuals.

Scholars in different fields tend to take different approaches to why some people are homosexual. Note, however, that almost all the researchers we discuss below assume there are two, exclusive, nonoverlapping categories: homosexual and heterosexual. Few of these theories have anything significant to say about bisexuals.

essentialism: The scientific theory that sexual orientation is innate, part of a person's biological makeup.

constructionism: The scientific theory that sexual orientation is a product of social forces rather than an innate part of a person's biological makeup.

Biological Theories

Biological theories are essentialist; that is, they claim that differing sexual orientations are due to differences in physiology. This difference can be due to genetics, hormones, or simple physical traits.

SEX TALK

QUESTION **7.3** **Why are men often turned on by watching two females having sex but are turned off by watching two males?**

> Heterosexual men's magazines often feature women together in sexual positions but almost never two men. This may be because heterosexual men see being penetrated as feminine and thus unacceptable (Forstein, 1988). Two women are not threatening because neither has the masculine symbol of penetration—the penis. (Even heterosexual women's magazines rarely show two men together sexually.) These pictorials always imply that the women are still attracted to men, waiting for them, just biding their time until a man arrives. That is why many men feel uneasy with genuine lesbian erotica, which often involves a very masculine, "butch" female and a feminine counterpart. Those pictures clearly communicate that men are neither desired nor required, and thus they provide no space for heterosexual male fantasies.

Genetics

Beginning with Franz Kallman in 1952, a number of researchers have tried to show that there is a genetic component to homosexuality. Kallman used identical twins (who come from one zygote and have the same genes) compared with fraternal twins (who come from two zygotes and have about 50% of the same genes). Though Kallman found a strong genetic component to homosexuality, his study had a number of problems and is unreliable. More recently, J. Michael Bailey and his colleagues have done a number of studies of twins to try to determine the genetic basis of homosexuality. They report that, in homosexual males, 52% of identical twins, 22% of fraternal twins, and 11% of adoptive brothers were also homosexuals, showing that the more closely genetically related two siblings were, the more likely they were to share a sexual orientation (Bailey and Pillard, 1993). Among females, 48% of identical twins, 16% of fraternal twins, and 6% of adoptive siblings of lesbians were also lesbians (Bailey et al., 1993). They also found that homosexual males were more likely to have lesbian sisters and lesbians more likely to have homosexual brothers (Bailey and Benishay, 1993; Bailey and Bell, 1993).

However, identical twins share much more than genetics. They also share many more experiences than do other kinds of siblings (Adler, 1992). So the studies cannot tell how much of the concordance is due to genetic factors and how much is due to the identical twins having grown up under similar environmental influences. A more interesting finding is the one by Dean Hamer (1993) of the National Cancer Institute. Hamer found that homosexual males tended to have more homosexual relatives on their mother's side, and he traced that to the existence of a gene, passed through the mother, that he found on thirty-three of forty gay brothers. It is unclear whether Hamer has found a "gay gene," a subtype of people who may be more likely to become homosexual because of genetics or a coincidence; more research is needed.

If homosexuality were solely a genetic trait, it should have disappeared long ago. Since homosexuals have been less likely than heterosexuals to have children, each successive generation of homosexuals should have become smaller, until genes for homosexuality disappeared from the gene pool. Yet, rates of homosexuality seem to have remained constant. Although there probably is a genetic component to homosexuality, even Bailey and his colleagues agree that environmental factors are also very important.

Hormones

Hormonal theories can concentrate either on hormonal imbalances before birth or on hormone levels in adults.

Prenatal Factors. If certain hormones are injected into pregnant animals such as rats or guinea pigs at critical periods of fetal development, the offspring can be made to exhibit homosexual behavior (Dorner, 1976). However, it is unclear whether the same is true in human beings. Some researchers have found evidence that homosexual men had lower levels of androgens than heterosexuals during sexual brain differentiation (Dorner, 1988), but others found no differences (Hendricks et al., 1989). In a retrospective study, Ellis et al. (1988) suggested that stress during pregnancy (which can influence hormonal levels) made homosexual offspring more likely. Evidence also exists that boys who show early effeminate behavior may have had a higher incidence of prenatal difficulties than other boys (Zuger, 1989). Other researchers, however, have concluded that the evidence for the effect of prenatal hormones on both male and female homosexuality is weak (Meyer-Bahlburg, 1977, 1979; Whalen et al., 1990). A study of female rhesus monkeys who were given masculine hormones before birth revealed that their environment after birth was as important to their sexual behavior as the hormones (Money, 1987). In other words, even if prenatal hormones are a factor in sexual orientation, environmental factors may be equally important.

Adult Hormone Levels. Many studies have compared blood androgen levels in adult male homosexuals with those in adult male heterosexuals, and most have found no significant differences (Green, 1988). Of five studies comparing hormone levels in lesbians and straight women, three found no differences between the two groups in either testosterone, estrogen, or other hormones, and the other two found higher levels of testosterone in lesbians (and one found lower levels of estrogen) (Dancey, 1990). Thus, studies so far do not support the idea of adult hormone involvement. Another discomfirming factor is that injecting hormones into adults in no way influences their sexual orientation.

Physiology

Two articles in the early 1990s reported finding differences between the brains of homosexual and heterosexual men (Swaab and Hofman, 1990; LeVay, 1991). Both studies looked at the hypothalamus, known to play a strong role in sexual urges, and found that certain areas of the hypothalamus were either larger or smaller in homosexual men than in heterosexual men. The studies are very preliminary, cannot determine if the differences were there from birth or developed later in life, and cannot prove that the differences were due primarily to the men's sexual orientation. However, brain physiology is an area of research that will certainly grow in the future.

Homosexual behaviors are common in the animal kingdom. Here two male giraffes engage in sexual mounting behaviors.

SEX TALK

QUESTION **7.4** **Is homosexuality found only in humans, or do some animals also exhibit homosexual behavior?**

> Many mammal species, from rats to lions to cows to monkeys, exhibit same-sex mounting behavior. Males mount other males, and females mount other females (though they rarely do it when a male is present) (Money, 1987). Female rhesus monkeys probably mount each other to establish dominance hierarchies, and cows may mount to coordinate their reproductive cycles. On the other hand, no one has reliably reported on cases where individual animals display *exclusively* homosexual behavior; that seems to be restricted to human beings. However, we should be very careful in extending animal analogies to humans. The fact that animals exhibit such mounting behavior teaches us little or nothing about homosexuality in human beings.

Developmental Theories

Developmental theories focus on a person's upbringing and personal history to find the origins of homosexuality. Developmental theories tend to be constructionist; that is, they see the development of homosexual behavior as a product of social forces rather than being innate in a particular individual. First we discuss the most influential development theory, psychoanalytic theory, and then gender-role noncomformity, peer-interaction theories, and behavioristic theories of homosexuality.

Freud and the Psychoanalytic School

Sigmund Freud seemed to be of two minds about homosexuality. On the one hand, he believed that the infant was "polymorphous perverse," that is, the infant sees all kinds of things as potentially sexual. Since both males and females are potentially attractive to the infant, thought Freud, all of us are inherently bisexual. He therefore did not see homosexuals as being sick; he wrote, in a famous letter to a concerned American mother, that homosexuality "is nothing to be ashamed of, no vice, no degradation, it cannot be classified as an illness" (Freud, 1951, quoted in Friedman, 1986). He even found homosexuals to be "distinguished by specially high intellectual development and ethical culture" (Freud, 1905, quoted in Friedman, 1986).

On the other hand, Freud saw male heterosexuality as the result of normal maturation and male homosexuality as the result of an unresolved Oedipal complex (see Chapter 2 for a more complete discussion). An intense attachment to the mother coupled with a distant father could lead the boy to fear revenge by the father through castration. Female genitalia, lacking a penis, could then represent this castration and evoke fear throughout his life. After puberty, the child shifts from desire for the mother to identification with her, and he begins to look for the love objects she would look for—men. Fixation on the penis allows the man to calm his castration fears, and by renouncing women he avoids rivalry with the father.

Freud's view of female homosexuality was less coherent, but he basically argued that the young girl becomes angry when she discovers she lacks a penis, and blames her mother. Unable to have her father, she defensively rejects him and all men and minimizes her anger at her mother by eliminating the competition between them for male affection.

Freud saw homosexuality as partly **autoerotic** and narcissistic; by making love to a body like one's own, one is really making love to a mirror of oneself. Freud's generally tolerant attitude toward homosexuality was repudiated by some later psychoanalysts, especially Sandor Rado (1949). Rado claimed that humans were not innately bisexual and that homosexuality was a psychopathological condition—a mental illness. This view (not Freud's) became standard for the psychiatric profession until at least the 1970s.

autoerotic: Characterized by sexual desire for or sexual behavior with oneself.

Another influential researcher who followed Rado's perspective was Irving Bieber. Bieber et al. (1962) studied 106 homosexual men and 100 heterosexual men who were in psychoanalysis. He claimed that all boys had a normal, erotic attraction to women. However, some had overly close and possessive mothers who were also overintimate and sexually seductive. Their fathers, on the other hand, were hostile or absent, and this **triangulation** drove the boy to the arms of his mother, who inhibited his normal masculine development. Bieber thus blamed homosexuality on a seductive mother who puts the fear of heterosexuality in her son. But Bieber's subjects were all in psychoanalysis and thus may have been particularly troubled. Also, less than two-thirds of the homosexuals fit his model, and almost a third of heterosexuals came from the same type of family and yet did not engage in homosexual behavior.

triangulation: The psychological dynamic of three family members where two ally themselves against the third.

Rado and Bieber both portrayed male homosexuals as running away from the love of women. Wolff (1971) studied the families of more than 100 lesbians and claimed that a majority had a rejecting or cold mother and a distant father. For lesbians also, therefore, some theorists have claimed that inadequate love from the mother leads to the girl searching for that love in other women.

A pioneer in gay studies who tried to combat the psychoanalytic view that homosexuality was an illness was Evelyn Hooker (1957) (see Chapter 2). Hooker used psychological tests, personal histories, and psychological evaluations to show that homosexuals were as well adjusted as heterosexuals and that no real *evidence* existed that homosexuality was psychopathology. Although it took many years for her ideas to take hold, many modern psychoanalysts have shifted away from the pathological view of homosexuality. Lewes (1988) demonstrated that psychoanalytic theory itself could easily portray homosexuality as a result of healthy development and that previous psychoanalytic interpretations of homosexuality were based more on prejudice than on science. Some psychoanalysts still maintain that homosexuality is the result of early developmental disturbance (Socarides, 1981), but recent books have tried to create a more positive psychoanalytic view of homosexuality (Isay, 1989).

SEX TALK

QUESTION **7.5** **Is there any therapy that can change a person's sexual orientation?**

A number of therapists have tried to "cure" homosexuality. Although the psychoanalyst Irving Bieber (Bieber et al., 1962) reported changing the sexual orientation of 27% of his sample of gay men, more recent psychoanalytic studies have had far less impressive success, and how long such "conversions" last is questionable. Behavior therapists have tried to alter male homosexual orientation through administering electroshocks or inducing nausea while showing nude pictures of men, or substituting pictures of nude men with nude women while the subjects were aroused, without much result or success (Green, 1988). Therapists who claim to have changed the sexual orientation of their patients usually turn out only to have convinced them not to act on their desires, and that decision may not last over time. No good evidence exists that a person's fundamental sexual orientation can be changed by therapy.

Gender-Role Nonconformity

gender-role nonconformity: The act of not behaving as society expects of one's gender.

One group of studies that has begun to fuel debate about the role of early childhood in the development of homosexuality is **gender-role nonconformity** studies. The studies are based on the observation that boys who exhibit cross-gender traits, that is, who behave in ways more characteristic of girls of that age, are more likely to grow up to be homosexual. One therapist who works with homosexual men reports that they saw themselves as

> *more sensitive than other boys; they cried more easily, had their feelings more readily hurt, had more aesthetic interests, enjoyed nature, art, and music, and were drawn to other "sensitive" boys, girls and adults. Most of these men also felt they were less aggressive as children than others of their age, and most did not enjoy participating in competitive activities. They report that they experienced themselves as being outsiders since these early childhood years.*
>
> *Isay (1989:23)*

Green (1987) did a prospective study by comparing sixty-six pervasively feminine boys with fifty-six conventionally masculine boys as they matured. Green calls the feminine boys "sissy-boys," an unfortunate term for him to use. However, he found that these boys cross-dressed, were interested in female fashions, played with dolls, avoided rough play, wished to be girls, and did not desire to be like their fathers from a young age. Three-fourths of them grew up to be homosexual or bisexual, while only one of the masculine boys became bisexual. The "sissy-boys," however, also tended to be harassed, rejected, and ignored more by their peers, were more sickly than other boys, and had more psychopathology (Zucker, 1990).

One cannot tell from these types of studies whether these boys are physiologically or developmentally different (an essentialist view of homosexuality) or whether society's reaction to their unconventional play encouraged them to develop a particular sexual orientation (a constructionist view of homosexuality). A constructionist might point out that girls are permitted to exhibit masculine play without being ridiculed, and gender nonconformity in girls, being a "tomboy," does not correlate with later tendency to become a lesbian. Whether right or wrong, gender-role nonconformity theory cannot be the sole explanation of homosexuality, for many, if not most, gay men were not effeminate as children, and not all effeminate boys grow up to be gay.

Peer Group Interaction

Storms (1981) suggests a purely constructionist theory of development. Noting that a person's sex drive begins to develop in adolescence, Storms suggests that those who develop early begin to become sexually aroused before they have significant contact with the other sex. Since dating usually begins around the age of fifteen, boys who mature at the age of twelve still play and interact in predominantly same-sex groupings, and so their emerging erotic feelings are more likely to focus on boys. Storm's theory is supported by the fact that homosexuals do tend to report earlier sexual contacts than heterosexuals. Also, men's sex drive may emerge at a younger age than women's, if such things as frequency of masturbation are any measure, which may explain why there are fewer lesbians than gay men. Yet, Storm's theory also has its problems. On page 251, we discuss the example of Sambian boys who live communally and have sex with other boys from an early age until they are ready to marry. If Storms is right and one becomes a male homosexual because only males are available at the time of sexual awakening, then all male Sambians should be homosexuals. However, almost all go on to live heterosexual lives.

Behaviorist Theories

Behavioral theories of homosexuality consider it a learned behavior, brought about by the rewarding or pleasant reinforcement of homosexual behaviors or the punishing or negative reinforcement of heterosexual behavior (Masters and Johnson, 1979) (see Chapter 2). For example, a person may have a same-sex encounter that is pleasurable, coupled with an encounter with the other sex that is frightening; in their fantasies, they may focus on the same-sex encounter, reinforcing its pleasure with masturbation. Even in adulthood, some may move more and more toward homosexual behaviors if they have bad heterosexual ecounters and pleasant homosexual ones (Masters and Johnson, 1979).

Sociological Theories

Sociological theories are constructionist and try to explain how social forces produce homosexuality in a society. They suggest that concepts like homosexuality, bisexuality, and heterosexuality are products of our social imagination and are dependent upon how we as a society decide to define things. In other words, we learn our culture's way of thinking about sexuality, and then we apply it to ourselves.

The idea of "homosexuality" is a product of a particular culture at a particular historical moment; the idea did not even exist before the nineteenth century. Some have argued that the use of the term "homosexuality" as a way to think about same-sex behavior only arose after the Industrial Revolution freed people economically from the family unit and urbanization allowed them to choose new lifestyles in the cities (Adam, 1987). Thus, the idea that people are either "heterosexual" or "homosexual" is not a biological fact but simply a way of thinking that evolves as social conditions change. In other countries, as we note below, the terms are not used, and a person's sexuality is not defined by who his or her partners are. Scientists often assume that homosexuality and heterosexuality are unproblematic categories, without considering whether they might not be products of their particular culture.

Sociologists are interested in the models of sexuality that society offers its members and how individuals come to identify with one model or another. For example, maybe effeminate young boys begin to behave as homosexuals because they are *labeled* homosexual, are called "faggot" by their peers, are ridiculed by their siblings, and even witness the worry and fear on the faces of their parents. They begin to doubt themselves, search for homosexuality in their own behavior, and eventually find it. If American society did not split the sexual world into "homosexual" and "heterosexual," perhaps these boys would move fluidly through same-sex and opposite-sex contacts, without having to choose between the "gay community" and the "straight community."

HOMOSEXUALITY AND HETEROSEXUALITY IN OTHER TIMES AND PLACES

Homosexuality remains controversial in the United States. Some people see homosexuality as a mortal sin; others argue that homosexuals are a "bad influence" on society and children and, for example, believe they should not be teachers. Others defend homosexual rights and attack America's whole view of sexuality. Many other countries are much more tolerant of homosexuality than the United States, even other Western, predominantly Christian countries. Western history has included many periods when homosexuality was generally accepted. In fact, Gilbert Herdt, a prominent scholar of homosexuality, states that the modern American attitude is much harsher toward homosexuality than most other countries throughout most of history (Herdt, 1988). The history of social attitudes toward homosexuality can teach us something about our own attitudes today.

Homosexuality in History

The Ancient World

sodomy: A vague legal category for "unnatural" sex acts that can include oral sex, anal sex, and/or sex with animals.

buggery: A term used in some legal documents and in popular circles for anal sex.

The way we define, think about, and evaluate homosexuality in twentieth century America is uniquely American, a product of our own history and cultural background. Seeing a person as "a homosexual"—that is, using their sexual orientation as the primary way you think of them—is very recent (Risman and Schwartz, 1988). Before the nineteenth century, men who engaged in homosexual acts were accused of **sodomy** or **buggery**, which were simply seen as sex crimes and not considered part of a person's fundamental nature.

Ancient societies left many artifacts that showed that same-sex behavior was not uncommon.

John Boswell (1980) has written a comprehensive history of early views of male homosexuality in his book, *Christianity, Social Tolerance, and Homosexuality.* Boswell begins with ancient Rome and shows how the idea of homosexuality and the idea of it being immoral and illegal developed over time. In early Rome, homosexual acts were not punished. In fact, of the first fifteen Roman emperors, only Claudius seems to have been exclusively heterosexual. Homosexual activity was common, homosexual prostitution was taxed by the state, and the writers of the time seemed to consider men loving men as natural as men loving women. Even after Rome became Christian, there was no antihomosexual legislation for more than two hundred years.

Lesbian love seems to have puzzled ancient writers (who were almost all men). The Greek writer Ovid, for example, had one of his characters discourse on the oddness of lesbian love while seeming to find male homosexuality perfectly normal (Boswell, 1980). The word *lesbian* itself comes from the island of Lesbos, in Greece, where the poet Sappho lived about 600 B.C. (lesbians used to be called "Sapphists"). Sappho was married and had a daughter, but she wrote erotic love poetry to other women. Lesbianism was rarely explicitly against the law in most ancient societies (in fact, two or more unmarried women living together has usually been seen as proper, while a woman living alone was viewed with suspicion) (Bullough, 1979).

Contrary to popular belief, homosexuality was not treated with concern or much interest by either early Jews or early Christians. The only place where homosexual acts are expressly mentioned in the Bible is in the book of Leviticus, which twice states that

lesbian: A woman who is attracted to and/or has sex with other women; comes from the Greek island of Lesbos, where Sappho, who wrote love poetry to women, lived.

it is forbidden to "lie with mankind as with womankind." In the first century A.D., the Council of Jerusalem, which was charged with deciding which Jewish laws must be kept by gentile converts to Christianity, did not even include homosexual relations as a forbidden act (Boswell, 1980). In fact, many pagans objected to Christianity because of sexual looseness among its adherents, including rampant homosexuality. Neither ancient Greek nor Hebrew had a word for homosexual; in the entire Bible, same-gender sexual behavior is only explicitly mentioned in the prohibition in Leviticus; Saint Paul never explicitly condemned homosexuality, and Jesus made few pronouncements on proper or improper sexuality (except fidelity) and never mentioned homosexuality. Why, then, did Christianity become so antihomosexual?

The Middle Ages

By the ninth century, almost every part of Europe had some sort of local law code based on Church teachings, and although these codes included strong sanctions for sexual transgressions, including rape, adultery, incest, and fornication, homosexual relations were not forbidden in any of them (Boswell, 1980). Church indifference to homosexuality lasted well through the thirteenth century; in other words, for the first 1300 years of Christianity, the Church showed very little interest in homosexuality and did not generally condemn the behavior. In fact, Saint Peter, who was vehemently antihomosexual, could not convince Pope Saint Leo IX to do anything about homosexuality, even among priests! In England, the people were not even informed that homosexuality was considered sinful, and as we mentioned in Chapter 1, in the High Middle Ages a gay subculture was established in Europe, which produced a large body of gay literature (Boswell, 1980). Mabod, the Bishop of Rennes, France, had a male lover and wrote erotic poetry to boys. Ganymede, a beautiful Greek god, became a symbol for gay people in the Middle Ages, and the term "Ganymede" became slang for homosexuals. Male brothels appeared, defenses of homosexual relations began to appear in print, and homosexuality became a fairly accepted part of the general culture until the late Middle Ages.

In the late Middle Ages, especially in the second half of the thirteenth century, both the state and the Church began to demand conformity of thought and of action. By the fifteenth century, the worst possible crime was heresy, which meant believing something in conflict with Church teachings. This led to persecution of anyone seen as different, including women, Jews, the poor, Muslims, lepers, and others; homosexuals were often persecuted and were accused of being heretics.

Homosexuality was completely legal in most countries in Europe in the year 1250. By 1300, however, the new intolerance of differences resulted in homosexuality being punishable by death almost everywhere. This view, from the late Middle Ages, has influenced the Western world's view of homosexuality for the last 700 years.

The Modern Era

From the sixteenth century on, homosexuals were subject to periods of tolerance and periods of severe repression. In the American colonies, for example, homosexuality was a serious offense. The first recorded case of homosexual acts in American legal annals was in Plymouth in 1637, where John Alexander and Thomas Roberts were found "guilty of lewd behavior and uncleane carriage one with another, by often spendinge their seed one upon another" (Bullough, 1979:43). In 1656, the New Haven Colony prescribed death for both male and female homosexual acts. The severe attitude toward homosexuality in America reflects its Puritan origins, and America remains, even today, more disapproving of homosexuality than Europe.

Even in times when homosexual acts were condemned, however, homoerotic poems, writings, and art were created. Openly homosexual communities also appeared now and then. For example, in England in the seventeenth century, homosexual men called "fops" or "mollies" organized themselves into "mollies clubs" (Trumbach, 1990). Other cultures also had periods of relative tolerance of homosexuality. In Japan, for example, the Edo period (1600–1868) saw a flourishing homosexual subculture, with openly gay clubs, geisha houses, and a substantial gay literature (Hirayama and Hirayama, 1986).

During the nineteenth and early twentieth centuries in the United States, it was not uncommon for single, upper-middle-class women to live together in committed, lifelong relationships, although they may not all have engaged in genital sexuality (Nichols, 1990). At the same time, **passing women** disguised themselves as men, entered the work-force, and even married women—who sometimes never knew their husbands were female! In most cases, of course, the wife knew, and the couple probably lived as lesbians in a disguised heterosexual marriage. Some of these passing women held offices of great power, and their biological sex was not discovered until their death (Nichols, 1990).

In the nineteenth and early twentieth centuries, physicians and scientists began to suggest that homosexuality was not a sin but an illness, which, if left "untreated," would spread like a contagious disease (Hansen, 1989). In 1935, the "Committee for the Study of Sex Variants" in New York City published a book to help clinicians treat "sexual mal-adjustment" so that it would not spread into the general population (Terry, 1990). The dangers of this perspective were realized in Nazi Germany, where homosexuals were imprisoned and murdered along with Jews, Gypsies, epileptics, and others as part of the program to purify the "Aryan race" (Adam, 1987). In America, psychiatry continued to view homosexuality as a mental disorder well into the 1970s—and some psychiatrists still do today.

Ironically, the medical model's view of homosexuality, which influenced modern ideas of sexual orientation, changed the politics of homosexuality. Since physicians saw homosexuality not as just a behavior but as a built-in trait, it became a primary part of the way people looked at each other—"a master status" (Risman and Schwartz, 1988). Homosexuals began to argue: "If homosexuality is something I *am,* not just something I *do,* then I should have a right to be 'who I am' just as blacks, women, and other groups have a right to be who they are." The new view of homosexuality as a master status encouraged homosexuals to band together and press for recognition of their civil rights as a minority group, which led to the modern gay and lesbian liberation movement we described in Chapter 1.

The history of homosexuality in the Western world has been strongly influenced both by the hostility of the Judeo-Christian tradition to homosexuality and by the diffi-culty the Western world has incorporating minorities into its political structures. The study of history is instructive, for it shows that Western, predominantly Christian soci-eties have often existed without the hostility to homosexuality that characterizes modern America and that Christianity itself has had periods of tolerance. Equally important to realize is that different attitudes toward homosexuality exist throughout the world today, and other cultural traditions do not view homosexuality with the suspicion and disap-proval that characterizes Europe and North America.

passing women: Women, predominantly in the early twentieth century, who dressed, acted, and lived as men—even marrying other women—without revealing their true gender to the public.

Homosexuality in Other Cultures

We all have a natural tendency to believe that others see the world the way we do. Yet, that which we call "homosexuality" is viewed so differently in other cultures that the word itself does not apply. In many societies, men and/or women have same-gender sexual relations as a normal part of their life cycles. This can be mild as in Cairo, Egypt, where heterosexual men casually kiss and hold hands, or it can be fully sexual as in the sequential homosexuality of Papua New Guinea, where young males have sexual contact exclusively with other males until getting married at the age of eighteen, after which they have sexual contact only with women (see page 251). Applying American conceptions of "homosexuality" and "heterosexuality" to cultures for whom such ideas are meaningless can be extremely misleading. Theories of sexual orientation often neglect the experiences of other countries and just assume that there are "homosexuals" and "heterosexuals" everywhere.

Same-sex sexual behavior is found in every culture, and its prevalence remains about the same no matter how permissive or repressive that culture's attitude is toward it (Mihalik, 1988). Broude and Greene (1976) examined forty-two societies for which there were good data on attitudes toward homosexuality. Nine (21.4%) either accepted or ignored homosexuality; five (11.9%) mildly disapproved of homosexuality; six (14.3%) ridiculed or scorned homosexuality but did not punish it; seventeen (40.9%) strongly disapproved of and punished homosexuality; and five (11.9%) had no conception of homosexuality at all in the culture. Note that a substantial number of the cultures in the sample have an accepting or only mildly disapproving view of homosexual behavior, and less than half punish homosexuals for their sexual activities.

Latin American Countries

machismo: A Spanish term for standards of masculinity.

In Central and South America, people do not tend to think in terms of homosexuality and heterosexuality but masculinity and femininity. Male gender roles, for example, are defined through what makes one a man, or **machismo**, and that is defined by being the penetrator, the active partner in sex. Therefore, one is *not* considered homosexual for taking the active, penetrating role in intercourse, *even if he is penetrating other men.* As long as one is penetrating, one is a man.

In Nicaragua, for example, penetrating another man does not make you homosexual; a man who is the active partner in same-sex anal intercourse is called *machista* or *hombre-hombre* ("manly man"), a term used for any masculine male (Lancaster, 1988). In fact, penetrating other men is seen as a sign of manliness and prestige. The same is true in Brazil, where only the passive partner, the *viado* ("deer") or *bicha* ("bitch"), is stigmatized, for he violates cultural norms of manliness (Parker, 1989). In the Mexican state of Jalisco, where the *charro* (Mexican cowboy) originated and defending one's honor with a gun is common, being the active partner in anal sex with other men is seen as a sign of healthy sexuality (Carrier, 1989). In other words, these Latin American countries look at sexuality in a fundamentally different way than we do; the basic categories of manhood are not homosexual or heterosexual but masculine and feminine. Masculine men sometimes penetrate other men and are admired, while feminine men allow themselves to be penetrated and are generally scorned.

Note that the implicit message of such cultures is that to mimic female behavior is disgraceful and shameful in a male. This attitude reflects the general nature of these societies, which tend to be patriarchal, with women lacking political and social power. Since women are, in general, considered inferior to men, men who mimic women are to be ridiculed.

Arab Cultures

Homosexuality has never been treated as harshly in the Muslim world as in the Christian world. Classic works of Arab poetry use homoerotic imagery, and young boys were often used as the standard of beauty and sexuality in Arab writing (Boswell, 1980). Homosexuality, especially during adolescence, is not generally punished or stigmatized in Arab lands as it is in the West. Estimates in some communities are that up to 90% of the male population has had some same-sex experience (El-Islam, 1982). In Chapter 5, we discussed the *xanīth* in the Arab country of Oman, who dress like women, wear perfume, and walk a swishy, feminine walk. The Omani see being a *xanīth* as part of a person's inevitable nature and none of anyone else's business (Wikan, 1977).

Asian Countries

In China, homosexuality was generally accepted and even honored in many periods of history. Chinese emperors often had court lovers, at least until the reign of Kangxi (1622–1722), who initiated sanctions against even consensual sodomy (100 heavy blows and a month's imprisonment) (Hinsch, 1990). Under communism, however, homosexuality has been considered a "revolting behavior," punishable by prison or labor camps (Ruan and Tsai, 1988).

On the other hand, China traditionally considered male homosexuality and lesbianism unrelated (Ruan and Bullough, 1992). Although lesbianism was hidden, stories and paintings that depict lesbian scenes in various periods of Chinese history do exist, and organized lesbian groups were occasionally established. One, started by a Buddhist nun, lasted several hundred years and included marriage ceremonies for lesbian couples. Under communism, however, lesbianism is against the law, and so lesbians tend to remain secretive.

Other Asian societies have different views of homosexuality. Buddhism does not condemn homosexuality, and so Buddhist countries generally accept it. In Thailand, for example, men may live sexually with boys over thirteen, who are considered old enough to make their own decisions (Williams, 1990). In fact, General Prem, Thailand's popular Prime Minister, and Dr. Seri Wongmontha, one of the most famous and prominent people in the country, both live openly and freely as homosexuals (Williams, 1990).

India has historically had no prejudice against homosexuality, although homosexuality is technically illegal as a holdover from British rule. Hinduism is the majority religion of India, and its main gods—Krishna, Vishnu, and Shiva—all had homosexual relations at some point. The religious shrines of Ayyappa, a homosexual god of the state of Kerala, attract millions of visitors every year (*The New York Times*, 1991a).

Sambia

A famous and much discussed example of a very different cultural form of sexual relations, called **sequential homosexuality**, is found in a number of cultures in the Pacific islands. The Sambia tribe of Papua New Guinea has been described in depth by Gilbert Herdt (1981; Stoller and Herdt, 1985). Life in Sambia is difficult because food is scarce and war is common; warriors, hunters, and many children are needed to survive. Sambians believe that mother's milk must be replaced by man's milk (semen) for a boy to reach puberty, and so, at the age of seven, all Sambian boys move to a central hut where they must fellate the postpubescent Sambian boys and drink their semen. After a

sequential homosexuality:
In some cultures, homosexuality is structured into a particular part of a person's life, to be followed by periods of heterosexuality; age-structured homosexuality is one example (see Focus on Diversity 7.1).

boy reaches puberty, he no longer fellates others but is himself sucked by the prepubescent boys until he reaches the age of marriage at about nineteen. Despite his long period of same-sex activity, he will live as a heterosexual for the rest of his life.

The Lesson of Cross-Cultural Studies of Homosexuality

With all these very different cultural forms of sexuality, trying to pigeonhole people or ways of life into our restrictive, Western "homosexuality–heterosexuality–bisexuality" model seems inadequate. This is a good time to think about your personal theory about homosexuality and to ask yourself: can my theory account for the *xanīth*? For the idea of the *hombre-hombre*? For the lives of the men of Sambia?

LIVING AS A HOMOSEXUAL

Homosexuals in America face particular problems that are not faced by most heterosexuals (see Where Do I Stand? 7.2). Homosexuals must struggle with discrimination, prejudice, laws that do not recognize same-sex unions, the lack of spousal benefits for their partners, and families who may reject them. On the other hand, many gay and lesbian couples live together in stable, happy unions, living lives not really that much different than the heterosexual couple next door. Gay and lesbian lifestyles are as varied and different as those of the rest of society; yet, examining the special challenges and circumstances that gay and lesbian people face can be instructive.

Homosexuality Through the Life Cycle

Growing Up Gay or Lesbian

Imagine what it must be like to be an adolescent and to either believe or know that you are gay or lesbian. (A number of you reading this book do not have to *imagine* it.) All your life, from the time you were a toddler, you were presented with a single model of sexual life: you were expected to be attracted to the other sex, to go on dates, and eventually to marry. No other scenario was seriously considered; if you are heterosexual, you probably have never even reflected on how powerfully this "presumption of heterosexuality" (Herdt, 1989) was transmitted by your parents, your friends, television and movies, newspapers and magazines, even the government. Advertisements on TV and in magazines always show heterosexual couples; your friends probably played house, played doctor, or played spin the bottle assuming everyone was attracted to the other sex; your grade school, parties, and social activities were organized around this presumption of heterosexuality. There were open questions about many things in your life: what career you would pursue, where you might live, what college you would attend. But one thing was considered certain: you were going to marry (or at least date) someone of the other sex.

But imagine that while all your friends were talking about the other sex, dating, and sex, you were experiencing a completely different set of emotions. Why, you wondered, can't I join in on these conversations? Why can't I feel the attractions that all my friends feel? Then, at some point in your early teens, you began to realize *why* you felt differently from your friends. All of a sudden you understood that all the models you had taken for granted your whole life did not apply to you. You began to look for other models that

WHERE DO I *Stand?*   7.2

A "Presumption of Heterosexuality" Questionnaire

The questionnaire below challenges the "presumption of heterosexuality" by taking questions that are usually asked of gay and lesbian people and asking the same of heterosexuals. When asked of heterosexuals, some of the questions seem rather silly; why, then, do we ask them of homosexuals?

1. What do you think caused your heterosexuality?
2. When and how did you first decide you were heterosexual?
3. Isn't it possible your heterosexuality is just a phase you may grow out of?
4. If you have never slept with someone of the same sex, how do you know you wouldn't prefer it?
5. If heterosexuality is normal, why are a disproportionate number of mental patients heterosexual?
6. To whom have you disclosed your heterosexual tendencies? How did they react?
7. Your heterosexuality doesn't offend me as long as your don't try to force it on me. Why do you people feel compelled to tell others about your sexual orientation?
8. If you should choose to have children, would you want them to be heterosexual knowing all the problems they would face?
9. The great majority of child molesters are heterosexual. Do you really consider it safe to expose your children to a heterosexual teacher?
10. Heterosexuals are known for assigning themselves and each other narrowly restricted stereotyped sex roles. Why do you adopt such unhealthy role playing?
11. With all the support marriage receives, the divorce rate is spiraling. Why are there so few stable relationships among heterosexuals?
12. How could the human race survive if everyone were heterosexual, considering the menace of overpopulation?
13. Does heterosexual acting-out necessarily make one a heterosexual? Can't a person have loving friends of the opposite sex without being labeled a heterosexual?
14. Why do you make a point of attributing heterosexuality to famous people? Is it to justify your own heterosexuality?

Adapted from the Gay and Lesbian Services of Kansas

described your life and your feelings—and they simply were not there. In fact, in hundreds of subtle and not-so-subtle ways, society taught you that what you are is perverted, sinful, illegal, or disgusting. *Now* what are you supposed to do? Who do you turn to? How can you possibly tell anyone your deep, painful secret?

The experiences of many gays and lesbians, at least until recently, followed this scenario, although the timing and intensity vary with individual cases (see Personal Voices 7.1). For example, many male homosexuals grew up with close male friends, enjoyed sports, and differed only in their secret attraction to other boys, while others remember feeling and acting differently from their friends as early as four or five years old (Martin, 1991). In those boys, atypical gender behavior often provoked anxiety from parents, teachers, and friends: "Why don't you act like other boys?" This kind of pressure can lead to strong psychosocial problems (Plummer, 1989). Because group sports and heterosexual dating are focal to male adolescents forming peer group bonds, homosexual youth can feel unattached and alienated (Herdt, 1989). The same is true of young lesbians, although the pressure and alienation may be slightly less early in life because same-sex affection and touching is more accepted for girls and because lesbians tend to determine their sexual orientation later than gay men.

Personal

VOICES

<u>7.1</u>

Being Young and Gay in Different Cultures

English *(male):* Between the ages of 13 and 15 I closed myself off from the outside world. I would rarely go out and would never dare to go places where other people of my own age would be. The only thing I knew was that homosexuality was bad (Plummer, 1989:204).

East Indian living in Canada *(female):* My family holds Western culture somehow responsible for off-beat youth. They think my being a lesbian is my being young, and confused, and rebellious. They feel it has something to do with trying to fit into white culture. . . . They're waiting for me to stop rebelling and go heterosexual, go out on dates, and come home early (Tremble et al., 1989:260).

Mexican *(male):* I thought myself very bad, and many times I was at the point of suicide. I don't know if I really might have killed myself, but many times I thought about it and believed it was the only alternative. That caused me many problems with my friends. I felt they thought me to be different, homosexual, and really sick. It made me separate from them. I felt myself inferior and thought I was the only one these things happened to (Carrier, 1989: 238).

Chinese *(male):* I am longing to love others and to be loved. I have met some other homosexuals, but I have doubt about this type of love. With all the pressure I was afraid to reveal myself and ruined everything. As a result, we departed without showing each other homosexual love. As I am growing older my homosexual desire increases. This is too troubling and depressing for anyone. I thought about death many times. When you are young you cannot fall in love and when you are old you will be alone. Thinking of this makes the future absolutely hopeless (Ruan and Tsai, 1988:194).

Canadian *(female):* I feel like I am the terrific person I am today because I'm a lesbian. I decided I was gay when I was very young. After making that decision, which was the hardest thing I could ever face, I feel like I can do anything (Schneider, 1989:123).

Scottish *(Male):* I don't like being gay. I wouldn't choose to be gay, and I don't like the gay scene. It's too superficial. I've got high moral standards. Lust is a sin but love isn't. In the gay scene people use other people and throw them away again (Burbidge and Walters, 1981:41).

Asian-American *(gender not identified):* I wish I could tell my parents—they are the only ones who do not know about my gay identity, but I am sure they would reject me. There is no frame of reference to understand homosexuality in Asian-American culture. (Chan, 1989:19)

SEX TALK

QUESTION **7.6** **Aren't homosexuals more creative than heterosexuals and more likely to be in the arts? Aren't more male body-builders gay and more female professional athletes lesbian?**

The stereotype that gays and lesbians choose certain types of professions over others has never been supported by research (Dressler, 1978). If, indeed, homosexuals are overrepresented in certain professions, it may be because those professions were more accepting of gays and lesbians rather than because they have some "natural talents" in those areas. Jews entered the entertainment industry in the twentieth century because the industry was accepting of Jews while other professions were closed to them; the same may be true for homosexuals, although it has not yet been proven, and some theorists have even suggested that Hollywood was more hostile to homosexuals than to most other groups (Russo, 1987).

Coming Out

Special challenges confront the person who believes he or she is gay or lesbian. One is the need to establish a homosexual self-identity and communicate it to others; this is known as **coming out** (see Sexuality Today 7.1). A number of models have been offered as to how this process proceeds (see, for example, Cass, 1979, 1984; Coleman, 1982; Martin, 1991; Schneider, 1989; Troiden, 1989). Coming out refers, first of all, to acknowledging one's sexual identity to oneself; many homosexuals have their own negative feelings about homosexuality to overcome. The difficult and anxiety-ridden process of disclosing the truth to family, friends, and eventually the public at large comes later.

coming out: The process of a person recognizing his or her own homosexuality, coming to personal terms with it, and then informing his or her family and the public.

The average age of coming out for men has dropped in America, from a reported 19.3 years in 1971 to 14 in 1987; lesbians tend to come out later, although the differences have been decreasing (Herdt, 1989). Women are more likely to discover their homosexuality through a close relationship with another woman, while men are more likely to do it through casual social/sexual contacts (Troiden, 1989). Once people have begun accepting their own homosexuality, they usually enter a period of exploration, trying to determine what that means both socially and sexually. One woman tells of the frightening moment in her early twenties when she realized the implications of her new-found homosexuality:

> *I went to a disco with some [heterosexual] friends, and they paired off and began dancing. And I looked out over the dance floor, men and women dancing together, and it suddenly struck me: this is not my life! I was standing next to a giant, six foot speaker, blaring music, but I couldn't even hear it; I just put my head against it and cried.*
>
> *Author's files*

Coming out does not just happen overnight; being homosexual may mean for some a lifetime of "information management," disclosing different amounts of information to family, friends, and strangers in different contexts (Cain, 1991). Deciding whether and how to tell friends and family is a difficult decision. One study (Wells and Kline, 1987) found that gay males and lesbians tended to come out first to people they trusted most. Men were more likely than women to tell strangers and acquaintances, while women were more likely to tell only other lesbians.

Discovering one's own homosexual identity can be painful and confusing. One woman commented:

> *Here I was, with a good job, close friends who I knew would not abandon me when they learned I was gay. I had many gay friends, so I had a support network. My family is open, so I wasn't worried about them rejecting me. And still, I cried myself to sleep every night and woke up each morning feeling like I had been kicked in the solar plexus.*
>
> *Author's files*

SEXUALITY *Today*   7.1

A Model of Coming Out

A number of authors have created models of the process of coming out. For example, Vivienne Cass (1979, 1984) has proposed the following six-stage model of homosexual identity formation. Not all homosexuals reach the sixth stage; it depends, at each stage, how comfortable one is with one's homosexuality.

Stage 1: Identity Confusion. The individual begins to believe that his or her behavior may be defined as homosexual. There may be a need to redefine one's own concept of homosexuality, with all the biases and misinformation that most people have. The person may accept that role and seek information, may repress it and inhibit all homosexual behaviors (and even perhaps become an antihomosexual crusader), or may deny its relevance at all to his or her identity (like the man who has same-sex behavior in prison but doesn't believe he is "really" homosexual).

Stage 2: Identity Comparison. Accepts *potential* homosexual identity; rejects heterosexual model but has no substitute. May feel different, lost. If willing to even consider a homosexual self-definition, may begin to look for appropriate models.

Stage 3: Identity Tolerance. Here the person shifts to the belief that he or she is probably homosexual, and begins to seek out a homosexual community for social, sexual, and emotional needs. Confusion declines, but self-identity is still more tolerated than truly accepted. Usually, the person still does not reveal new identity to heterosexual world but maintains double lifestyle.

Stage 4: Identity Acceptance. A positive view of self-identity is forged, and a network of homosexual friends is developed. Selective disclosure to friends and family is made, and the person often immerses himself or herself in homosexual culture.

Stage 5: Identity Pride. Pride in homosexuality is developed and anger over treatment may lead to rejecting heterosexuality as bad. One feels validated in one's new lifestyle.

Stage 6: Identity Synthesis. As one truly becomes comfortable with one's lifestyle and as nonhomosexual contacts increase, one realizes the inaccuracy of dividing the world into "good homosexuals" and "bad heterosexuals." No longer is sexual orientation seen as the sole identity by which an individual can be characterized. One lives an open, gay lifestyle so that disclosure is no longer an issue, and one realizes that there are many sides and aspects to personality of which sexual orientation is only one. The process of identity formation is complete.

From Cass (1979, 1984)

If a woman with all the support and advantages possible experienced such difficulties, imagine how much more difficult it is for youths who thinks their family and friends will reject them. One sixteen-year-old wrote in her diary:

> *Please help me. Oh shit, I have to talk to someone. Help me please. My feelings are turning into gnawing monsters trying to clamber out. Oh please, I want to just jump out that window and try to kill myself. Maybe I'll get some sympathy then. Maybe they'll try to understand. I have to tell someone, ask someone. Who?!! Dammit all, would someone please help me? Someone, anyone. Help me. I'm going to kill myself if they don't.*

> *Heron (1983:10)*

The plea of this young woman that she might try to kill herself is not an idle threat. Between 20% and 35% of gay and lesbian youth have attempted suicide, a much higher rate than among straight youths (Herdt, 1989).

Other homosexual youth have more positive experiences. A seventeen-year-old male reports:

> *I like who I am. I have come to accept myself on psychological as well as physical terms. I not only like myself, I like everyone around me. Today, for women, gays and especially our youth, that is really hard to say.*
>
> *Heron (1983:15)*

Parents of a homosexual also often have a difficult time learning to accept their child's homosexuality. Because we tend to think of homosexuality as something one "is," parents may suddenly feel they do not know the child, that he or she is a stranger, and they may even go through a kind of mourning for the child they knew (Strommen, 1989). The family must go through its own "coming out," as parents and siblings slowly try to accept the idea and then tell their own friends. The importance of positive resolution in the family has prompted the formation of a national organization, the *Federation of Parents and Friends of Lesbians and Gays* (PFLAG), who help parents learn to accept their children's sexual lifestyle.

People may come out at different periods in their life, even after they are married. Between 14% and 25% of gay men and about a third of lesbians marry the other sex at some point, either before they recognize that they are gay or lesbian or because they want to try to fit into heterosexual society. Many remain married, either with or without their spouses knowing that they are homosexual (Strommen, 1989). Coming out to your family is very difficult on the spouse and the children, and divorce is common. In some couples, though, the partners develop a platonic relationship and pursue sexual gratification outside the marriage (Hays and Samuels, 1989).

Living a Gay or Lesbian Life

Looking for Partners. Meeting other homosexuals in the heterosexual world is difficult, and so the gay community has developed its own social institutions to allow people to meet each other and socialize. Teenage homosexuals under the drinking age have trouble finding places where they are comfortable and open with their homosexuality (Schneider, 1989), but adults often frequent **gay bars** or discos that cater primarily to same-sex couples. In one study of ninety-two gay male couples, 40% had initially met in a gay bar (Berger, 1990). **Gay baths**, which were popular in the 1970s, have largely been closed since the start of the AIDS epidemic. Gay magazines like the *Advocate* carry personal ads, and ads for dating services, travel clubs, resorts, bed and breakfasts, theaters, businesses, pay phone lines, sexual products, and other services to help homosexuals find partners.

gay bar: A bar that serves a predominantly homosexual clientele.

gay baths: Public baths that served a predominantly homosexual clientele and were often used for sexual pick-ups; many were closed, voluntarily or involuntarily, as the AIDS epidemic became known.

SEX TALK

QUESTION **7.7** **Is homosexuality natural?**

The question itself is biased: Is heterosexuality "natural"? Also, the question seems to assume that if it is "natural," then it is okay; yet much that is natural, such as killing, is reprehensible. Some people suggest that a human behavior is "natural" if it is found in animals; other animals do display homosexual behavior, and so perhaps it is natural in that sense. Still, many human qualities—humor, language, religion—are not shared by animals and yet are considered "natural." Humans are so immersed in culture and so lacking in instincts that it is impossi-

ble to say what is natural. Perhaps the only measure we can use is to ask whether a behavior is found universally, that is, in all or almost all human cultures. By that measure, homosexuality is quite natural.

Gay and Lesbian Couples. When most straight people imagine how gay or lesbian people live, they do not picture a committed, monogamous couple living together in a household. Yet, in one sample of thirty-six- to forty-five-year-old homosexuals, 71% of men and 82% of women were living with a partner (Cabaj, 1988). Contrary to the image of gay and lesbian couples having a dominant and a submissive partner, such relationships are actually characterized by greater role flexibility and partner equality than are heterosexual relationships (Risman and Schwartz, 1988) and lower levels of sexual jealousy (Hawkins, 1990). Gay and lesbian couples often live together as happily as straight couples; their main challenge tends to be society's intolerance for their lifestyle.

While gay and lesbian marriages are legal in Denmark, Norway, and Sweden and while other countries, such as Canada, are considering it, no state in the United States allows gay or lesbian couples to become legally married. Although many gay and lesbian couples do go through religious or other ceremonies to affirm their mutual commitment, these do not have any legal standing. However, the supreme court of the state of Hawaii recently invalidated the law preventing homosexual marriage, and now the Hawaiian legislature must decide whether or not to permit homosexual marriage. Since all states recognize the marriages performed in other states, this may open the way for homosexual couples to get married in Hawaii and then live as legally recognized married couples in other U.S. states (see Chapter 8). In response, some states, such as Utah, South Dakota, and Alaska, have introduced or passed legislation so that gay marriages, if they do become legal in Hawaii, will not be recognized in those states (Dunlap, 1995).

Gay and Lesbian Sexuality. Homosexuals, like heterosexuals, make love for a variety of reasons and use a variety of positions. Sexuality, for all people, heterosexual or homosexual, can be an expression of deep love, affection, or lust. Homosexuals tend to have earlier first sexual experiences; of 312 homosexuals interviewed by McWhirter and Mattison (1984), three-quarters had their first homosexual experience before the age of sixteen, and only 20 had not had a homosexual experience by the time they were twenty-one. Since most people identify the gay and lesbian community primarily by its sexuality (gay men and lesbians themselves tend to see their community as broader, with sexuality as only one component), there is an increased awareness of and attention to what can only be called sexual *style;* in gay social, political, and cultural life, sexuality is always close to the surface.

Masters and Johnson (1979) found that arousal and orgasm in homosexuals was physiologically no different than in heterosexuals. They also found, however, that homosexuals tend be slower, more relaxed, and less demanding with each other during sex. Male and female homosexual couples spend more time sexually "teasing" and caressing each other, bringing their partners to the brink of orgasm and then withdrawing, before beginning direct genital stimulation. Heterosexuals tend to be more goal oriented, to spend less time at each phase of arousal, and to be less involved in their partner's subjective states than homosexuals. Perhaps, Masters and Johnson suggest, this is because men and women know what pleases them, and so they have an immediate, intuitive understanding of what would please another member of their own sex. (For more details on gay and lesbian sexuality, see Chapter 9.)

Gay and Lesbian Parents. Research suggests that about 10% of gay men and 16% of lesbians have children, although the actual numbers may be much higher (Strommen, 1989). Gay and lesbian parents cite most of the same reasons for wanting to be parents that straight parents do (Bigner and Jacobson, 1989b). Courts have often granted straight parents custody over gay or lesbian parents, fearing that gay parents might "make their children homosexual" or at least promote sex role confusion. The research shows differently. No significant differences have been found between the offspring of lesbian and straight mothers, including the sexual orientation of their children (Golombok et al., 1983; Green et al., 1986; Kirkpatrick et al., 1981). In fact, lesbian mothers are not even significantly different in their sex role guidance of their children (Hoeffler, 1981). Yet, courts often assume that lesbian mothers are emotionally unstable or unable to assume a maternal role (Falk, 1989). Research on gay fathers found that children tended to take the news that their father was homosexual better than most gay fathers feared (Bozett, 1989), and gay fathers are no different than straight fathers in their degree of involvement with their children (Bigner and Jacobson, 1989a). All the scientific evidence suggests that gay men and lesbians make good parents who raise the same mix of heterosexual and homosexual children as straight parents.

When lesbian couples want to become parents, they may become pregnant through intercourse or artificial insemination. It is not uncommon, in fact, for lesbians to ask gay friends to donate sperm for that purpose. However, gay male couples who want children do not have that option. Some gay men have tried to adopt children (as have some lesbians), but many are refused adoption because of their homosexuality. Two states, Florida and New Hampshire, specifically bar homosexuals from adopting. Other gay men have tried paying surrogate mothers to have their children who they then adopt, but that can be very expensive, and such women are difficult to find. New organizations, such as the PFLAG, are trying to support gay and lesbian parents and make it easier for homosexuals to adopt (Griffin, 1992).

Gay and lesbian couples encounter many problems that heterosexual parents do not face. Since homosexual marriages are not yet legally recognized in the United States, gay couples may have trouble gaining joint custody of a child, and the nonbiological parent may not be granted parental leave and may not be able to get benefits for the child through their workplace. The couple may also experience discrimination and disapproval from family, friends, and the community. Most official forms ask about mothers and fathers (not mothers and mothers, or fathers and fathers). Yet, gay and lesbian couples today are creating new kinds of families, and the social system is going to have to learn how to deal with them. Many states are beginning to allow adoptions and registration of children of gay and lesbian couples (Weston, 1991).

Gay and Lesbian Seniors. Some experts used to believe that homosexuals often died alone and isolated; yet research disputes that stereotype. The older male couples that McWhirter and Mattison (1984) interviewed tended to be in solid relationships that stood the test of time, and studies reveal few differences between aging homosexual and heterosexual men (Lee, 1989; Lipman, 1986). Older lesbians tend to be in excellent mental health and have positive views of aging (Deevey, 1990). However, older homosexuals may find themselves isolated from the rest of the homosexual community, which has been slow to provide a place for the elderly in their community (Lee, 1989).

Gay and Lesbian Problems. One study found that homosexuals are substantially more likely to use alcohol, marijuana, or cocaine than heterosexuals and to have higher rates of alcoholism (McKirnan and Peterson, 1989). Homosexuals are also significantly more likely to have been in therapy (Pillard, 1988). For many years, psychiatrists and other therapists argued that this showed that homosexuals had greater psychopathology than heterosexuals. In fact, the problems of gay and lesbian life may not be due to psychopathology but to the enormous pressures of living in a society that discriminates against them. Most other minorities also have higher rates of these types of behaviors.

Gay and Lesbian Organizational Life

Gay and lesbian newspapers and magazines are now published in almost all major cities in the United States.

Because many organizations misunderstand the needs of homosexuals, gay and lesbian social services, medical, political, entertainment, and even religious organizations have been formed. For example, the *National Gay and Lesbian Task Force* (NGLTF) and its associated *Policy Institute* advocate for gay civil rights, lobbying Congress for such things as a Federal Gay and Lesbian Civil Rights Act, health care reform, AIDS policy reform, and hate-crime laws. In 1978 they successfully lobbied the Public Health Service to stop certifying all gay immigrants as "psychopathic personalities," and they helped establish the Hate Crimes Statistics Act in 1987, which identifies and records hate crimes (NGLTF, 1991b). Also well known are the *Lambda Legal Defense and Education Fund,* which pursues test-case litigation of concern to the gay and lesbian community, and the *Human Rights Campaign Fund,* which lobbies Capital Hill on gay and lesbian rights, AIDS, and privacy issues. Since the advent of the AIDS epidemic, many organizations have been formed to help homosexuals obtain medical, social, and legal services (see Chapter 13). Local gay and lesbian organizations have been established in almost every reasonably sized city in the United States, including counseling centers, hotlines, legal aid, and AIDS information. New York City even has a full-time, accredited high school exclusively for homosexual students (Green, 1991). Students from across the country come there to study in an environment where their sexual orientation is accepted and where they will not be ridiculed, ostracized, or assaulted, as many were in the schools they came from.

A large gay and lesbian media has also developed over the last thirty years, which includes countless magazines and newspapers across the country. The largest and best-known gay magazine is the the *Advocate,* a national publication that covers news of interest, entertainment reviews, commentaries, gay-oriented products and services, and hundreds of personal ads. The Daughters of Bilitis publish their own newspaper, called the *Ladder;* there are national publications for lesbians, such as *On Our Backs,* and Los Angeles also has the *Lesbian News.* Most major cities have their own gay newspaper, some of which get national exposure; some noteworthy examples are New York's *New York Native,* Philadelphia's *Au Courant* and the *Philadelphia Gay News*, Boston's *Gay Community News,* and the *Seattle Gay News.* These papers are often the best first sources for the young gay man or lesbian who is looking for the resources available in his or her community. Although they are far less numerous, there now are also some organizations and magazines directed toward the bisexual community.

HETEROSEXISM AND HOMOPHOBIA

In 1989, students at Southwest Missouri State University put on a play called
The Normal Heart, *by Larry Kramer, which is about a gay man's effort to bring*

attention to the AIDS epidemic. A Missouri lawmaker denounced the college, said the play "promoted a homosexual lifestyle," and proclaimed that hetero-sexual students who acted in the play would become homosexuals.

Mayhook (1990)

In 1991, a fraternity at Syracuse University distributed T-shirts which read, "Club Faggots, Not Seals" on the back, with a picture of the fraternity mascot, a crow, holding a spiked club over the prone body of a faceless man. The front of the shirt read "Homophobic and Proud of It!"

The New York Times (1991b)

A song released in 1990 by the rap group Audio Two included the lyrics, "I can't understand why you lookin' this way/Whats the matta witcha boy, are ya gay?/Yo I hope that ain't the case, 'cause gay mothers get punched in the face/I hate faggots. They're living in the Village like meat on some maggots."

NGLTF (1991a)

For years the gay community of Houston complained of continual harassment. Finally, after the beating and stabbing death of a 27-year-old gay banker, the police department set up an undercover operation where officers posing as gay couples walked the streets. The police were shocked to find that in the very first week of the program, officers were spat upon, attacked with mace, and beaten with baseball bats, and thirteen people were arrested.

The New York Times (1991c)

What Is Homophobia?

Many terms have been proposed to describe the negative, often violent reactions of many straight people toward homosexuality—antihomosexualism, homoerotophobia, homo-sexism, homonegativism, and **homophobia**. The popularity of the term *homophobia* is unfortunate, for *phobia* is a medical term describing an extreme, anxiety-provoking, uncontrollable fear accompanied by obsessive avoidance. The word is also used to describe very different negative views of homosexuality, including cultural, attitudinal, and personal biases (Fyfe, 1983). Still, the term is generally accepted, and so we will use it here to refer to strongly negative attitudes toward homosexuals and homosexuality.

homophobia: A deep antipa-thy, disgust, or dislike of homosexuals.

Are people really homophobic? Survey results show that anywhere from two-thirds to three-quarters of the public believe that sexual relations between members of the same sex are always wrong, a statistic that has been used to claim that homophobia is rampant (*Newsweek*, 1983). However, different types of reactions to homosexuality exist: individuals might accept homosexuality intellectually and yet still dislike being in the presence of homosexuals, or people might object to homosexuality as a practice and yet have acceptable personal relationships with individual homosexuals (Forstein, 1988). When compared with those with favorable views of gays and lesbians, people who hold negative views are less likely to have had contact with lesbians or gay men, are likely to be older and less well educated, are more likely to be religious and to subscribe to a conservative religious ideology, have more traditional attitudes toward sex roles and less support for equality of the sexes, are less permissive sexually, and are more likely to be authoritarian (Herek, 1984).

heterosexism: An attitude where heterosexuality is assumed to be the norm and where social power is used to promote the validity of one heterosexual model of loving over other forms.

Even bigger than the problem of homophobia for most gay men and lesbians is **heterosexism**. Heterosexism has a sociological, rather than a medical implication: it describes the "presumption of heterosexuality" discussed earlier and the social power used to promote it (Neisen, 1990). Since only heterosexual relationships are seen as "normal," the heterosexist feels justified in suppressing or ignoring those who do not follow their model. Even those with no ill feelings toward homosexuality are often unaware that businesses will not provide health care and other benefits to the partners of homosexuals, for example. Heterosexism, in other words, can be passive rather than active, a lack of awareness rather than active discrimination.

Heterosexism is reflected in the lack of positive portrayals of homosexuals on television, in movies, in newspapers, or from our government. It is also revealed in how homosexuality had been largely ignored in academic circles. For example, the enormous literature on the interesting youth movements of England (such as punks, skinheads, rockers, teddy boys, etc.) has virtually ignored the significant gay elements of these groups (Plummer, 1989). Newspaper obituaries of homosexuals often state that the deceased has "no survivors," even if they have left behind a lifelong partner (Herek, 1986). The gay liberation movement has been successful at changing some of these assumptions, especially in larger cities, but heterosexism still dictates a large part of the way the average American considers his or her world.

Polls show that many Americans still think homosexuality is immoral. In three national polls in 1993, more than 50% of the respondents thought that homosexuality was immoral (NGLTF, 1994a). Most people also believed that homosexuals are discriminated against and that such discrimination is wrong, although a majority do not favor protective legislation. These kinds of conflicting feelings reflect America's general ambivalence about homosexuality.

Hate Crimes

Throughout history, persecution of minorities has been based on philosophies that portrayed those minorities as illegitimate, subhuman, or evil. Homophobia, likewise, is not just a set of attitudes; it creates an atmosphere where it is seen as permissible to harass, assault, and even kill homosexuals. Homosexuals are victimized four times more often than the average American, and a 1987 National Institute of Justice report suggested that homosexuals are probably the most victimized minority in the United States (NGLTF, 1994b). Hate crimes against gays and lesbians are extremely violent; one hospital spokesman remarked:

> *Attacks against gay men were the most heinous and brutal I encountered. They frequently involved torture, cutting, mutilation, and beating, and showed the absolute intent to rub out the human being because of his [sexual] preference.*
>
> ***Quoted in Hentoff (1991:96)***

After an assault, a homosexual may suffer from what is called "secondary victimization"—losing one's job, being denied public services, or being harassed by the police in response to being the victim of an antigay attack (Berrill and Herek, 1990). For that reason, a large percentage of hate crimes against homosexuals go unreported.

A 1990 study of hate crimes in six major U.S. cities found 1,588 reported incidents, ranging from harassment to murder (NGLTF, 1991a). Compared with 1989, antigay hate crimes rose, for example, 20% in Los Angeles, 65% in New York City, and 113% in Minneapolis/St. Paul. From 1992 to 1993, hate crimes against homosexuals fell about 14%, the first fall after years of a dramatic rise; from 1987 to 1993, the incidence of violence against homosexuals rose 127% (NGLTF, 1994b). These numbers, remember, do not reflect the large percentage of antigay crimes that are never reported or that are reported but not classified as antigay.

Hate crimes on college campuses are also common and troublesome. In one study of college students, half said they found homosexuality disgusting and 30% would have preferred a college environment with only heterosexuals (D'Augelli and Rose, 1990). Almost three-quarters of lesbians and gay men on college campuses report having been verbally abused, over one-quarter having been threatened with physical violence, and over half fearing for their physical safety (D'Augelli, 1989; NGLTF, 1991a). Yet 90% of homosexual students at one Ivy League university and 94% at a large state university experienced at least one incident they did not report (NGLTF, 1991a). Most of the harassment was from male students, who tend to show greater hostility toward homosexuality than females (Dressler, 1979; D'Augelli and Rose, 1990).

Why Are People Homophobic?

What motivates people to be homophobic? A number of theories have been suggested. Since rigid, authoritarian personalities are more likely to be homophobic, it may be a function of personality type; for such people, anything that deviates from their view of "correct" behavior elicits disdain (Smith, 1971). Another common suggestion is that straight people fear their own suppressed homosexual desires or are insecure in their own masculinity or femininity (Herek, 1986). Perhaps people are simply ignorant about homosexuality and would change their attitudes with education. Most likely, all of these are true to some degree in different people (Herek 1986).

SEX TALK

QUESTION **7.8** **Are people really homophobic because they fear that they themselves are homosexuals?**

> **The question is difficult to answer, but many psychologists believe that fear of one's own sexual desires is a factor in homophobia. The best evidence is the level of brutality of gay hate crimes; the degree of violence suggests that there is a deep fear and hatred at work. Why such hatred of somebody you don't even know? The answer must lie within oneself.**

People also tend to confuse sexual orientation with gender identity. Sexual orientation refers to who your sexual partners are; gender identity has to do with definitions of masculinity and femininity. People react negatively when they see males or, to a lesser extent, females violating gender roles; for example, they dislike men portrayed either as effeminate or as hypermasculine (Laner and Laner, 1979). In almost every culture, violating "correct" masculine or feminine behavior is unacceptable, although what is thought to be "correct" masculine or feminine behavior varies from society to society. That is why there is no stigma in being the penetrator in anal sex in cultures where masculinity is defined by being the active partner in intercourse.

What Can Be Done About Homophobia and Heterosexism?

Heterosexism is widespread and subtle and therefore is very difficult to combat. Adrienne Rich (1983), a prominent scholar of lesbian studies, uses the term *heterocentrism* to describe the neglect of homosexual existence, even among feminists. Perhaps we can learn from the history of a similar term: *ethnocentrism.* Ethnocentrism refers to the belief that all standards of correct behavior are determined by one's own cultural background, leading to racism, ethnic bigotry, and even sexism and heterosexism. Although ethnocentrism is still rampant in American society, progress has been made through passing new laws, using the media to highlight abuses, and improving education. Perhaps a similar strategy can be used to combat heterosexism.

Laws. Although more than twenty states have passed laws to monitor "hate crimes," only twelve of those statutes originally include antigay crimes (NGLTF, 1991a). In fact, five states specifically blocked or amended antihate legislation to remove sexual orientation from the statute (Berrill and Herek, 1990). Note, however, that "monitoring" or "recording" hate crimes does not necessarily mean putting any resources into improving enforcement or prevention. Only eight states and the District of Columbia have laws explicitly prohibiting discrimination based on sexual orientation. But even laws protecting homosexuals from abuse can be thwarted by homophobia. A Texas judge named Jack Hampton gave a man convicted of murdering two homosexual men a lenient sentence, remarking: "I put prostitutes and queers at the same level. . . . And I'd be hard put to give somebody life for killing a prostitute" (quoted in Berrill and Herek, 1990:404).

In 1990, President Bush signed into law the *Hate Crime Statistics Act,* the first *federal* law ever to include a "sexual orientation" provision (NGLTF, 1991a). Other, newer laws are beginning to be introduced as well. In 1994, for example, Governor William Weld of Massachusetts signed a bill that effectively added homosexuals to the list of groups protected against discrimination in public schools. Twenty-two states, the District of Columbia, and several counties and cities have now enacted hate crime legislation that includes sexual orientation (NGLTF, 1994b).

The Media. Homosexuals have begun to demand more positive portrayals of homosexuality on television and in films (*The New York Times,* 1991d). Homosexual activists protested the portrayals of gays and lesbians in popular movies such as *Basic Instinct* and *Silence of the Lambs,* where they are shown as sex perverts and murderers. More recently, however, the portrayals of gays and lesbians in feature films have taken a positive turn, and a number of films about gay and lesbian life, made by homosexual filmmakers, have begun to appear in movie theaters.

On television, gay or lesbian characters or episodes involving homosexuals do appear. However, many have been blocked by conservatives who protest to networks or who threaten advertising sponsors with boycotts if they do not withdraw their commercials. With all the pressure, television executives find it easier to just avoid the topic. Homosexual characters in television, as in films, therefore more often show up only as murderers or perverts, or as comic relief (*The New York Times,* 1991d). Recently, the taboo against homosexual characters on television had begun to erode. The situation comedy *Roseanne,* for example, had Martin Mull playing Roseanne's gay boss and Sandra Bernhard playing a lesbian friend of Roseanne's. In 1994, *Roseanne* featured an episode where a lesbian makes a pass at Roseanne, kissing her on the lips; although there were predictions of public outrage, the network got few calls of protest even though the show was seen by almost 32 million viewers. So perhaps the public is becoming more comfortable with portrayals of gay and lesbian sexuality.

Another important development is the explosion of gay fiction, nonfiction, plays, and movies that portray gay and lesbian life in America more realistically. Where once these types of media were shocking and hidden, now they appear in mainstream bookstores and movie theaters.

Education. Finally, an important step to stopping heterosexism is education. Homosexuality is still a taboo subject in schools, and most proposals to teach about sexuality in general, never mind homosexuality in particular, encounter strong opposition by certain parent groups (see Special Focus Chapter 2). No school would teach about George Washington Carver, Malcolm X, or Martin Luther King without mentioning that they were black; why then teach about Leonardo Da Vinci, Walt Whitman, Oscar Wilde, James Baldwin, Bessie Smith, or Gertrude Stein without exploring the fact that they were homosexual?

Where Do The States Stand On Hate Crime?
National Gay & Lesbian Task Force Policy Institute
February 1991

States with hate crime laws that *include* crimes based on sexual orientation (12 states and the District of Columbia)

States with hate crime laws *that do not include* crimes based on sexual orientation (14 states)

Figure **7.2**
A map of the United States indicating which states have hate crime laws.

SOME HOMOSEXUAL SUBPOPULATIONS

Since homosexuality exists in almost every ethnic, racial, and religious group, many homosexuals also belong to other minority groups. Below, we discuss the unique situation of some of these groups.

Lesbians

Younger lesbians today are willing to adopt traditionally feminine appearances that older lesbians had rejected in order to make a political statement about gender roles.

Research focusing on lesbian life and the lesbian community in particular lags far behind research on gay men. This is ironic because many of the gains homosexuals made in the 1960s and 1970s were due to the close relationship between lesbians and the overall feminist movement. The lack of interest in lesbian studies may itself be a result of the lower value society puts on women and women's issues.

Most of the writing and research about lesbian life in the United States is by lesbians themselves. Scholarship by lesbians tends to be strongly political, in part because lesbians have to deal with both sexism and heterosexism. Friction has arisen between the more radical lesbians and heterosexual feminists, with many lesbians seeing themselves as the vanguard of feminism and seeing heterosexist life as practically synonymous with male domination (Rich, 1983; Risman and Schwartz, 1988).

Yet the lesbian community is a vibrant one. Bars, coffeehouses, bookstores, sports teams, political organizations, living cooperatives, media, and lesbian-run and -owned businesses often represent a political statement about the ways in which women can live and work together. A number of lesbian musicians, such as K.D. Lang, Holly Near, Chris Williamson, and Meg Christian, sing of issues important to the lesbian community and yet have strong crossover appeal to the straight community. Many lesbian magazines are published that are dedicated to lesbian fiction, erotica, current events, and photography. Lesbian and feminist journals provide a forum for the lively and argumentative debates between lesbian scholars. For example, pornography has been the subject of an ongoing dispute among lesbian (and feminist) writers. Some are "anti-porn," seeing most sexually explicit materials as debasing portrayals of women. On the other side, the "*anti*-anti-porn" group argues that suppressing expressions of sexuality—even ones we disagree with—is a dangerous practice and limits female and lesbian sexual expression just as new forms of that expression are beginning to appear (Henderson, 1991) (see Special Focus Chapter 4).

In younger lesbian circles, a revolution in attitudes seems to be occurring. The new generation of lesbians, who do not have to fight as many battles as the older generation did, are rejecting the political ideologies of the previous generation (Gallagher, 1992). As one young lesbian put it:

> It was unheard of ten years ago for a lesbian to dress provocatively in a women's bar. I remember the first time I walked into Sneakers [a lesbian bar in Philadelphia], and it was every straight person's stereotype of us. You know, short hair, flannel shirts, a very masculine persona, and I was very, very confused as I stood there in my makeup and long hair. . . . Now I see girls wearing whatever they want and being more assertive about who they want."
>
> *Gallagher (1992:D20)*

Bisexuals

We began this chapter by discussing the variety and fluidity of people's sexual behavior and by examining the premises of those who split the world into only homosexuality and heterosexuality. Yet barely a mention has been made of bisexuality. The reasons are mainly historical. Homosexuals have tended to see bisexuals either as on their way to becoming homosexual or as people who want to be able to "play both sides of the fence," being homosexual in the gay community and heterosexual in straight society. Heterosexuals tend to lump bisexuals in with homosexuals. Even some sexuality scholars have claimed that bisexuality is a myth, or an attempt to deny one's homosexuality, or identity confusion, or an attempt just to be "chic" or "trendy" (Berkey et al., 1990). Bisexuals themselves have begun to speak of **biphobia**, which they suggest exists in both the straight and gay and lesbian communities.

biphobia: A suspicion, antipathy, or dislike of bisexuals whether coming from heterosexuals or homosexuals.

SEX TALK

QUESTION **7.9** **Are bisexuals really equally attracted to both sexes?**

It depends on the bisexual. Some are more attracted to one sex than the other, while others say that they have no preference at all (Klein, 1978). Masters and Johnson (1979) found that both heterosexuals and homosexuals have at least some "cross-preference" fantasies; so perhaps if social pressures were not as strong as they are, many more people would be bisexual to some degree.

Recently, however, bisexuals have begun their own "coming out," declaring that their sexual identity is different from both homosexuals and heterosexuals (Paul, 1984; Hutchins and Kaahumanu, 1990); a cover article in *Newsweek* in 1995 trumpeted that "a new sexual identity" has emerged (*Newsweek*, 1995). Bisexuals see themselves as having the best of both worlds. As one bisexual put it, "the more I talk and think about it, and listen to people, I realize that there are no fences, no walls, no heterosexuality or homosexuality. There are just people and the electricity between them" (quoted in Spolan, 1991). In our society, fear of intimacy is expressed through either homophobia if you are straight, or **heterophobia** if you are gay or lesbian; no matter what your sexual preference is, one gender or another is always taboo—your sexually intimacy is always restricted (Klein, 1978). From that perspective, bisexuality is simply lack of prejudice and full acceptance of both sexes.

heterophobia: The antipathy or dislike that homosexuals feel toward heterosexuals.

More people in American society exhibit bisexual behavior than exclusively homosexual behavior (Klein, 1990). In **sequential bisexuality**, the person has sex exclusively with one gender followed by sex exclusively with the other; **contemporaneous bisexuality** refers to having sexual partners of both sexes during the same time period (Paul, 1984). Numbers are very hard to come by because bisexuality itself is so hard to define. How many encounters with both sexes are needed for a person to be considered bisexual? One? Fifty? And what of fantasies? Masters and Johnson (1979) found that fantasies that crossed the sexual orientation line—straight fantasies among gays or gay fantasies among straights—were quite common for all their subjects, homosexual and heterosexual. Only half the lesbians in Bell and Weinberg's (1978) sample considered themselves exclusively homosexual. In McWhirter and Mattison's (1984) study, almost all the gay subjects had, at some point, had sexual relations with women, many had been married, and a large number expressed sexual attraction to women.

sequential bisexuality: When bisexuals have sex exclusively with one sex in any given period; the opposite of **contemporaneous bisexuality.**

contemporaneous bisexuality: When bisexuals have sex with members of both sexes in the same time period.

Some people come to bisexuality through intimate involvement with a close friend of the same sex, even if they have not had same-sex attractions before. Others have come to it through group sex or swinging, where, in the heat of passion, a body is a body and distinctions between men and women easily blur. For some, bisexuality is a philosophy of sexuality that advocates the freedom to love both sexes (Blumstein and Schwartz, 1976). The new bisexual movement may succeed in breaking through the artificial split of the sexual world into homosexuals and heterosexuals. Perhaps we fear the fluid model of sexuality offered by bisexuals because we fear our own cross-preference encounter fantasies and do not want to admit that most of us, even if hidden deep in our fantasies, are to some degree attracted to both sexes.

Minority Homosexuals

Many homosexuals who belong to other minority groups must deal with the prejudices of society toward both groups, as well as both groups' prejudices toward each other.

Special problems confront homosexuals who are members of racial or ethnic minorities in the United States. Homosexuality is not accepted by many ethnic groups, and yet the gay community does not easily accommodate expressions of ethnic identity. Many end up feeling torn between the two communities. As one gay Asian-American put it:

> *While the Asian-American community supports my Asian identity, the gay community only supports my being a gay man; as a result I find it difficult to identify with either.*
>
> *Chan (1989)*

Gay African-Americans can find their situation particularly troubling, as they often have to deal with the heterosexism of the African-American community and the racism of the homosexual and straight communities. In 1981, for example, a group of interracial gay couples filed suit against a gay disco that they said discriminated against nonwhites (Altman, 1982). In the African-American community, the strong disapproval of homosexuality has prevented black politicians and church leaders from taking a firm stand in combatting AIDS, even though black Americans are at higher risk than whites for contracting the disease (Quimby and Friedman, 1989). Some progress is being made, however. Books such as *In the Life, a Black Gay Anthology* (Beam, 1986) and its sequel, *Brother to Brother: New Writings by Black Gay Men* (Hemphill, 1991), have raised the issue in public, and journals such as *Other Countries: Gay Black Voices* and *BLK* have provided a forum for discussion of black gay life. Many feminist and lesbian anthologies, such as *Home Girls: Black Feminist Anthology* (Smith 1983), and most lesbian and feminist journals include writings explicitly by minority lesbians.

Same-Sex Behavior in Prison

situational homosexuality: When people have sex with members of the same sex because of a situation that does not allow them access to the opposite sex; same-sex activity in prison and on naval vessels are examples.

Homosexual behavior is fairly common in prisons, where members of the other sex are not available. Yet those who engage in such behavior usually claim that they are not homosexuals and plan to return to heterosexual relationships exclusively once they are released. This **situational homosexuality** is also found in other places where men must spend long periods of time together, such as on naval ships.

Many people think that the majority of homosexual contacts in prisons are due to rape. In fact, less than 3% of men report being raped in prison (Nacci and Kane, 1983). Still, these kinds of numbers depend on what we mean by "rape"; a man who is scared for his life and provides sexual services to a more powerful man for protection may feel coerced by his circumstances (see Chapter 15). On the other hand, homosexual attachments in prison can be strong and jealously guarded; for example, homosexual activity has been found to be the leading cause of inmate homicide in U.S. prisons (Nacci and Kane, 1983). Inmates speak of loving their inmate partners, and relations can become extremely intimate, even among those who return to a heterosexual life upon release.

Because of the hostility of much of Western organized religion toward homosexuals, some have started their own congregations where they can worship without feeling condemned.

HOMOSEXUALITY IN RELIGION AND THE LAW

Homosexuality and Religion

Religion has generally been considered a bastion of antihomosexual teachings and beliefs. In reality, though, only traditional Judaism and Christianity have strongly opposed homosexual behavior. The changes in social attitudes toward homosexuality over the last thirty years have provoked conflict over homosexual policies in many religious denominations. In 1991, Presbyterians overwhelmingly rejected a report written by a church panel that recommended relaxing prohibitions against sexual relations among homosexuals (*The New York Times,* 1991e). After the Episcopal Bishop of Washington ordained a confirmed lesbian (*The New York Times,* 1991f), Episcopal leader called for a moratorium on gay ordinations even as they advocated greater outreach to homosexuals (Briggs, 1994). In response, the Greek Orthodox Church broke off its relations with both the Episcopal Church and the larger National Council of Churches (*The New York Times,* 1991g). The Lutheran Church recently ordained three gay men, although the church's official policy is that homosexuals should not be ordained.

Only the United Church of Christ, the Unitarian Universalists, and Reconstructionist Judaism have *openly* accepted homosexual clergy (Clark et al., 1989). A number of organizations lobby particular religious denominations to change their policies, such as Dignity, which is a gay Catholic organization, or Lutherans Concerned for Gay People. Recently religious scholars, both homosexual and heterosexual, have begun to promote arguments based on religious law and even scripture that argue for a more liberal attitude toward homosexuality. For example, some Jewish scholars have argued that since homosexual orientation is not a free choice but an unalterable feature of the personality, it is immoral to punish someone for it (Kahn, 1989–90).

Homosexuality and the Law

Throughout history, laws have existed in the Western world that prohibited homosexual behavior, even on pain of death. In the United States, sodomy has been illegal since colonial days, and it was punishable by death until the late eighteenth century. Fellatio was technically legal until the early twentieth century, although it was considered to be "loathsome and revolting" (Murphy, 1990). All fifty states outlawed homosexual acts until 1961. Twenty-four states and the District of Columbia still regard some form of consensual sex between adults as illegal, and seven states prohibit sodomy only between people of the same gender (*Harvard Law Review,* 1990). In sixteen states, sodomy is a felony; in Michigan, sodomy is theoretically punishable by life in prison, and in Washington, D.C., sodomites are officially considered "sexual psychopaths" (Knopp, 1990).*

SEX TALK
QUESTION **7.10** **I have heard of a new gay group called "Queer Nation." Why would gay people want to use a word like *queer,* which is used against them as a slur?**

Radical homosexuals use the word *queer* for its shock value. The motto of Queer Nation, a group loosely organized to combat gay bashing, is: "We're Here/We're Queer/Get Used to It." By reclaiming the words used to intimidate them and using them with pride, homosexuals are making a statement. Similarly, the symbol used for homosexuality is a pink triangle, which homosexuals were compelled to wear in Nazi Germany but now wear with pride. Yet, some older homosexuals are very uncomfortable with the word, and it may also be a sign of divisions between gay radicals and moderates (*The New York Times,* 1991h).

Little legal recourse exists for homosexuals discriminated against on the job. Homosexuals are often denied equal housing rights through exclusionary zoning, rent control, and rent stabilization laws. Even in long-term, committed, same-sex couples, partners are routinely denied the worker's compensation and health care benefits normally extended to a spouse or dependents (*Philadelphia Inquirer,* 1991). Some homosexuals have even resorted to adopting their partners officially in order to extend benefits they would otherwise be denied (*Harvard Law Review,* 1990). In addition, gay couples are denied tax breaks, Social Security benefits, rights of inheritance, and even cheaper hunting licenses, all of which are available to married couples.

Why Do Laws Discriminate Against Homosexuals?

Canada, our neighbor to the north, has been much more active than the United States in passing gay rights laws (Walsh, 1993). Canada is well on its way to allowing homosexual marriage, with all the benefits of heterosexual marriage, including adoption. Seven of Canada's twelve provinces explicitly prohibit discrimination on the basis of sexual orientation, and Canada has passed federal legislation proscribing such discrimination. Canada has granted political asylum to at least one homosexual fearing persecution in his home country, Argentina (Farnsworth, 1992), and Canada has ended its ban on homosexuals in the armed forces (see Sexuality Today 7.2).

In contrast, a number of American states have been proposing laws over the last few years to try and limit homosexual rights. Oregon proposed a measure that would have lumped homosexuality with sadomasochism and pedophilia as "abnormal, wrong, unnatural, and perverse" and would have mandated that school systems and local governments actively discourage homosexuality; however, the law was defeated (Woestendiek, 1992). Colorado, on the other hand, passed a constitutional amendment in 1993 that bars state agencies from enacting or enforcing any law that protects gay men or lesbians from discrimination (PFLAG, 1993), although the courts have blocked its implementation (*The New York Times,* 1994a) and the Supreme Court is considering its legality (Greenhouse, 1995).

---

* See Special Focus 1 for a discussion of the famous *Bowers* v. *Hardwick* case of 1986, where the Supreme Court upheld the constitutionality of the State of Georgia's antisodomy laws.

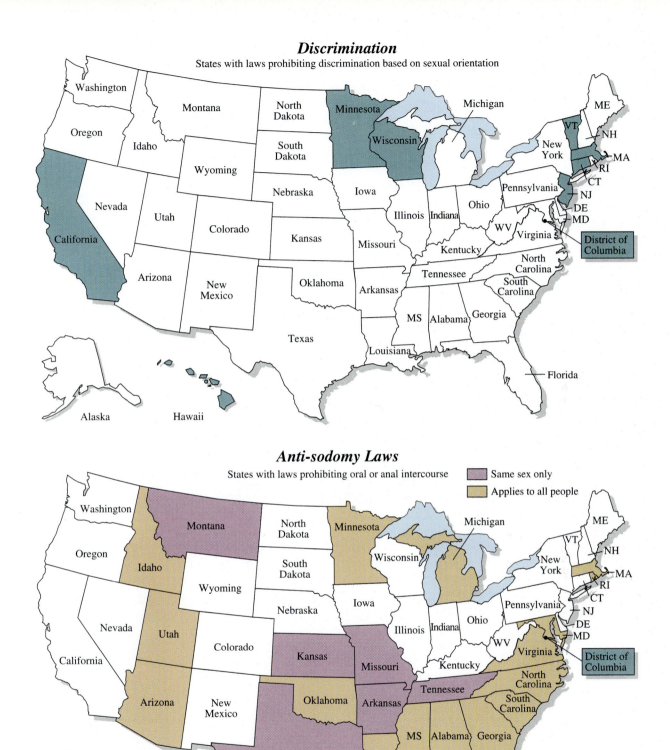

Discrimination

States with laws prohibiting discrimination based on sexual orientation

Anti-sodomy Laws

States with laws prohibiting oral or anal intercourse

Same sex only

Applies to all people

Figure 7.3

Maps of the United States indicating which states have anti-discrimination (top, green) and anti-sodomy laws (bottom, see key).

Why are homosexuals in the United States so routinely denied the rights that the rest of the country takes for granted? What is the justification for denying homosexuals protection against housing discrimination, job discrimination, and invasions of their sexual privacy? Those who are appointed to guard our rights in this country—judges and the legal community—still hold predominantly negative views of those with minority sexual orientations (Berrill and Herek, 1990; *Harvard Law Review,* 1990). The efforts of local, grassroots gay organizations, as well as the national efforts of groups like the *Lambda Legal Defense and Education Fund,* may yet break through the wall of legal inaction that makes homosexuals unable to fight the discrimination and victimization they experience in the United States.

A FINAL COMMENT

When the American Psychiatric Association (APA) decided in 1973 to remove homosexuality from its list of official mental diseases, many psychiatrists were outraged. They demanded a vote of the full APA membership. Think about that. Is that how ques-

---

SEXUALITY*Today*   7.2

Homosexuals in the Military

When Bill Clinton was running for President, he promised to end the existing ban on homosexuals serving in the armed forces. Once he was elected, however, he found that ending the ban was not as easy as he thought; strong opposition was voiced by the religious right, conservative Republicans, many high-ranking members of the armed forces, rank-and-file soldiers, and even his own political allies. Defenders of the ban argued that heterosexual soldiers will not tolerate homosexual soldiers. Opponents retorted that the same arguments were made against allowing blacks and whites to serve together in the military, that homosexuals have always been in the armed forces, and that other nations allow homosexuals to serve without problems.

In fact, of the sixteen nations in the North Atlantic Treaty Organization (NATO), only four (Greece, Turkey, Britain, and the United States) ban homosexuals in the military, and of these four the United States and Britain are slowly reevaluating their policies (Baldwin, 1993). To the nations that allow homosexuals to serve, the American policy is baffling, for almost no problems have been reported, except for an occasional disciplinary action against someone caught having sex on base (just as those caught having heterosexual sex on base are also punished).

Because of the controversy, President Clinton settled for a "don't ask, don't tell" policy; recruits are no longer asked about their sexual orientation, and (if they are homosexual) they are not to mention it or discuss it. Of course, heterosexuals in the armed forces are free to discuss their sexual orientation as often and as loudly as they wish. However, all such rules may be eliminated even without presidential or congressional action. In 1995, a federal judge struck down the policy, saying it violated the Constitution and catered to the fear and prejudices of heterosexual troops. The ruling will be appealed; however, a judicial consensus may be building that the ban is unconstitutional. Australia ended its ban on gays in the military in November 1992. For about a month, controversy reigned, and then the ruckus died down and the military got back to business (Baldwin, 1993). The same process will likely happen eventually in the U.S. armed forces as well.

Keith Meinhold was discharged from the Navy for admitting his homosexuality in November 1992 and sued in federal court. He was reinstated three days later.

tions of science should be decided—by a *vote?* Can you imagine a vote on whether cancer or pneumonia should be considered a disease? But the whole question of homosexuality had become so politicized, so emotional, that the psychiatrists could not even see the implications of what they were doing (Bayer, 1981).

For 100 years or so, homosexuality was considered a sickness. Yet, only when scientists dropped that assumption did they make real progress in understanding homosexuality. The enormous complexity of the human brain allows highly flexible human behavior patterns in almost every aspect of life, and human sexuality is not an exception to that rule. Why do we accept and even rejoice in human differences in so many other areas of life and call it pathological only in sexual orientations (Mihalik, 1988)?

Theories of sexual orientation change as society changes. Our society is grappling with its acceptance of new forms of sexual relationships. Only time will tell whether that yields increased tolerance or intolerance for people of all sexual orientations.

S ummary

- Sexual orientation includes homosexuality, bisexuality, and heterosexuality. While sometimes thought of as three distinct ways of being, in fact, they are fluid categories that often are hard to define.
- There are different theories of sexual orientation. Biological theories tend to be essentialist, meaning that they believe sexual orientation is innate. Developmental theories look at individual development to discover when sexual orientation is established. Sociological theories tend to be constructionist, meaning that they believe that orientation is a social category that changes in meaning over time.
- Same-sex behavior has existed in almost every recorded society, although few have had a concept of "homosexuality" as such. Each society has its own attitudes toward homosexual behavior, such as ancient Greece's acceptance of sex between men and postpubescent boys. In other cultures, especially Christian cultures, homosexuality has been condemned.
- Because of the "presumption of heterosexuality" in American society, many gay men and lesbians grow up con-

fused and fearful about their sexuality and may delay their "coming out." Gays and lesbians form sexual relationships—some stable and long-lasting, others fleeting—just as heterosexuals do. Some choose to become parents, and their children are little different from those of heterosexual couples.
- Homophobia is a problem for gays and lesbians. Some people are quite vocal, even violent, in their opposition to homosexuality. Others are heterosexist and fail to realize the ways that society discriminates against homosexuals.
- Although research on lesbians is less common than that on gay men, new researchers have been focusing on lesbian communities. These communities are changing as younger lesbians begin to develop their own views of politics and lesbian life.
- Bisexuality is another understudied part of sexuality. Bisexuals have been rejected by both the homosexual and heterosexual communities in the past, but they have recently become more vocal.
- The law in the United States has been used both to press for homosexual rights and as a weapon against homosexuals.

R eflections on Sexuality

1. Did you start this chapter with a strong view of homosexuality one way or another? Have the facts you have read so far altered your view of homosexuality in any way?
2. How many different sexual orientations are there?
3. Do you think people are born heterosexual or homosexual, or does orientation develop as they grow? Does it matter to you how sexual orientation arises?
4. Do you think it contradictory that a culture, such as Latin American culture, can value masculinity so highly and still accept certain types of same-sex contact as being mascu-

line and natural?
5. Where do you think the negative view of homosexuals as parents come from? Do you think there is a reason that gay people should not have children? How would you react if you discovered that a parent of yours was gay or lesbian?
6. Why do you think someone's sexual orientation is of more concern to people than his or her height, race, hobbies, or any other aspect of their personality?
7. Look inside yourself. Do you have negative feelings about people with different sexual orientations from you? Why?

8. Suppose you found a way to make it so that all people were born and grew up heterosexual. Would you do it? Why or why not?

9. Why do you think crimes against homosexuals are so much more violent than crimes against other minorities?

10. Do you support the passage of a law that would make it illegal to discriminate against homosexuals in housing, jobs, benefits, marriage, and so on?

S u g g e s t e d   R e a d i n g s

ANDREWS, N. (1994) *Family: A Portrait of Gay and Lesbian America.* San Francisco: HarperSan Francisco.

BOSWELL, J. (1980) *Christianity, Social Tolerance, and Homosexuality: Gay people in Western Europe from the Beginning of the Christian Era to the Fourteenth Century.* Chicago: The University of Chicago Press.

HAMER, D.H. (1994) *The Science of Desire: The Search for the Gay Gene and the Biology of Behavior.* New York: Simon and Schuster.

MARCUS, E. (1992) *Making History: The Struggle for Gay and Lesbian Civil Rights.* New York: HarperCollins.

MARCUS, E. (1993) *Is it a Choice? Answers to 300 of the Most Frequently Asked Questions About Gays and Lesbians.* San Francisco: HarperSan Francisco.

WESTON, K. (1991) *Families We Choose.* New York: Columbia University Press.

8

Adult Sexual Relationships

A lot of people ask me why I want to get married right when I graduate from college. I guess it's a good question, but I never thought of being single then. I have always wanted a husband, kids, a family life. These are the most important things to me. I don't care about a job or money. I guess I'm just not a materialistic person.

—a nineteen-year-old female college student, engaged to be married

I have had a number of partners over the last four years, and a few of them were really close. But I am really worried about finding a partner that I could love and live with for the long term. With all the pressures of life these days, even straight couples have a hard time making relationships work, so imagine how hard it is if you are gay. I just hope I can find somebody.

—a twenty-year-old male college student

My wife of three-and-a-half years is divorcing me, and I want reconciliation more than anything in the world. I feel that I have been/was a good provider and husband to my wife in almost every way. She is the only woman with whom I have ever had sex, as I saved myself for marriage. I still love my wife with all my heart, and I am still very much committed to the marriage in my heart and mind, but she will not consider coming back to me. I get the "I want my freedom" story, but I NEVER kept her from socializing, seeing friends, or anything else while we were married. I just don't understand what makes a person do something like this and in turn hurt another human being so badly. I am not a bleeding-hearted liberal, but I do try to treat human beings with respect and the same courtesies that I like to be treated with. Divorce is so hard.

—a twenty-seven-year-old male

In the last five years, I have had sex with my spouse maybe four times. However, I do have a special friend who I meet maybe three times a year in St. Louis and we have seven hours of total love making and total sex. She is also married. She loves sex, is very responsive, takes the initiative on occasion, and is accepting of doing and trying new things and *all* things. When we are together we totally satisfy each other and there is nothing in sex that a man and woman could possibly do together that we don't do.

—a married fifty-year-old male

Author's files

Every society has rules to control the ways that people develop sexual bonds with other people. Until recently, in many parts of the world, parents or other family members arranged for their children to meet members of the opposite sex, marry them, and begin their sexual lives together. The expectation was that couples would remain sexually faithful and that marital unions would end only in death. In such societies, adult sexual relationships were clearly defined, and deviating from the norm was frowned upon.

In our society today, people openly engage in a variety of adult sexual relationships, including premarital, marital, extramarital, and homosexual relationships. (Note that a term like "premarital sex" assumes eventual marriage; for people who never marry, their entire lives' sexualities are considered "premarital!") These relationships can change and evolve over the course of a lifetime, and at different times a person might live alone and date, cohabitate with a partner or partners, marry, divorce, or remarry. In this chapter, we will look at how people live as adults in sexual relationships with others.

DATING

The freedom to choose among a variety of partners or to develop exclusive relationships with many potential mates before choosing one for marriage is a relatively modern development. Much can be understood about a society just by examining the customs and rules it sets up for choosing a mate. The level of patriarchy in society, its ideals about masculinity and femininity, the roles of women and men, the value placed on conformity, the importance of childbearing, the authority of the family, attitudes toward childhood, pleasure, responsibility, and a host of other traits can be learned just from looking at dating patterns.

SEX TALK
QUESTION **8.1** **How do you know if a person is interested in dating you?**

People show their interest in various ways. Some may feel comfortable telling you of their interest, while others may be more subtle. Constant eye contact, touching, and other nonverbal signs often indicate interest. Some people try to use "pick-up" lines to show their interest (see Personal Voices 8.1), although the majority of people do not like pick-up lines being used on them. The important thing is to be outgoing and friendly, and if you are unsure about a person, try asking him or her first to join you for lunch or a walk or another low-pressure situation where you can get to know him or her better.

The process of dating—meeting people socially for possible mate selection—may seem like a casual and fun process, but it is, in fact, serious business. (Personal Voices 8.1 takes a humorous look at terrible pick-up lines.) Sociologists describe dating as a "marriage market," in which prospective spouses compare the assets and liabilities of eligible partners to choose the best available mates (Benokraitis, 1993). It is true that dating serves an important recreational function in that many teens spend a good deal of their free time having fun on dates. For most people, however, this leads to progressively more serious dating and eventually to final mate selection.

Today, it is not uncommon for men and women to date many people prior to settling down into their first serious relationship. This is not to say that a relationship cannot work if the partners have not dated others, but dating helps us clarify what we look for in a partner. In fact, many people feel that it is risky to marry without having spent some time dating first. If a couple meets each other, and two weeks later they decide to get married, do you feel they have dated long enough? Today, probably not. But consider that not too long ago, parents arranged marriages between people who had known each other for only a few hours, days, or weeks.

People date with many goals in mind. In one study of college students, both men and women felt that "to have a good time with someone" and "to have a friend of the opposite sex" were the most important goals for their current relationships (Peplau and Gordon, 1985). Studies show that those who date are in better physical and emotional health than those who do not. For example, college-age women who are involved in intimate relationships have better physical health than women not involved in intimate relationships (Riessman et al., 1987). College women who are involved in intimate relationships have

Personal

V O I C E S

The Worst Pick-up Lines Ever Heard

- If I told you you have a beautiful body, would you hold it against me?
- I'm majoring in human sexuality. Would you like to help me with my homework?
- Wanna see my room?
- Your pants are so clean I can see myself in them!
- Were you ever a dancer? You sure have the body of one.
- Wanna go back to my place and do the things I'm gonna tell my friends we did anyway?
- I think I love you. What was your name again?
- Are you really Polish? Could I see your sausage?
- If I swore you were an angel, would you treat me like the devil tonight?
- Please, I only have a week to live.
- Beauty is only a light switch away.
- I'm not trying anything. I always put my hand there.
- Do you want to have pizza and get laid? What—you don't like pizza?
- Your jeans look great—but they'd look even better on my bedroom floor.

Author's files

been found to be more independent from their families and engage in more social interactions. Steady dating in adolescence is associated with higher self-esteem and sex-role identity (Samet and Kelly, 1987). Relationships provide companionship, emotional support, and even, at times, economic support. Of course, the key may be the kind of dating relationships people have. Both the pressure to have sex and engaging in sex before the person is ready may turn a healthy dating experience into a detrimental one.

Dating and courtship behaviors vary in different social classes and racial groups (Zinn and Eitzen, 1993). Upper-class parents tend to have more control over the dating activities and partners of their children because dating is more likely to take place in private schools, country clubs, parties, and other places that conform to adult rules. Middle-class youth have more freedom than the upper classes, but many of their interactions are also structured by school or church-sponsored activities. Lower-class youth are more likely to just "hang out" in places where their interactions are less structured, such as bowling alleys, skating rinks, or street corners.

Young gay and lesbian people have a much harder time finding dates and developing sexually than their straight counterparts because of the stigma of homosexuality and the difficulty in determining who are potential sexual partners. Some communities are tolerant of gay and lesbian teen dating, while others still severely stigmatize gay youth and make it difficult for them to admit their sexual orientation.

As we discussed in Chapter 6, many social factors influence who we date.

Types of Dating

The problem with discussing courtship behavior is that there are no agreed-upon words for different levels of commitment. "Dating," "going out," "going steady," "boyfriend and girlfriend," "seeing each other"—these terms mean different things to different couples. Even a term like "engaged" can mean different things—to some it means the wedding date is set; to others it simply means that they have decided that someday they will marry each other, although they are in no rush to say when. Researchers often have a hard time understanding what their subjects mean by such terms (especially when doing courtship studies of other cultures).

The "dating years" in American society begin in earnest in high school, and how they develop depends on whether the person goes to college or directly to work. People with more free time tend to date more, and so college students pursue dating behaviors longer than those who begin working. Of course, now that people are getting married later and later, they can continue to date for many more years, even into their thirties and forties—and dating may even begin again after a divorce. But the late teens and early twenties are a special time for dating, for then dating patterns become more firmly established and sexual maturity is reached.

In "traditional" dating, which occurred before the 1970s (and is portrayed on old sitcoms like *My Three Sons*), the boy would pick up the girl at her house, giving the father and mother time to meet with or chat with the boy (jokes were always made about the girl being late in those shows!), then they would go to a well-defined event (a "mixer"—a chaperoned, school-sponsored dance—or a movie), and she would be brought home by the curfew her parents imposed (Benokraitis, 1993). Today, however, formal dating has given way to more casual dating, in part because of the almost universal access of teenagers to cars and the more permissive attitudes toward the early mixing of the sexes. Teenagers still go to movies and dances, but just as often they will get together at someone's house or go for a drive. In casual dating, there are more opportunities for couples to find time alone away from parents or chaperones, which is one reason why the age of first intercourse has steadily decreased over the last thirty years.

The most difficult part of dating is the initial invitation; it is difficult to ask someone out and risk rejection. Whether a person is straight or gay, asking someone out can be risky. The ego can be bruised if the desired person is not interested. In college, men are more active at initiating dates, although in one study, 72% of women reported having initiated dates with men within the previous six months (McNamara and Grossman, 1991).

The problems of dating change as one gets older, as there are fewer organized ways to meet other single people. Socializing and going out to bars and clubs may work for some, but others are uncomfortable with the "meat market," as it is often called. Perhaps the best way to meet others as one gets older is to get involved in community, religious, and singles groups and to find community events and programs where other single people go. Evening classes at local universities are also a good way to meet people. Often partners are introduced to each other by friends or family (see Figure 8.1).

The gay community has been ahead of the straight community in providing opportunities for meeting partners, but recently many businesses and organizations have begun to realize that there is a lucrative market in arranging for straight singles to meet each other. For example, a movie theater in Kansas City started a singles' night giving people an opportunity to socialize before the film and then sit together for the show. Many other theaters and clubs are now offering similar opportunities. The Philadelphia Museum of Art began a singles' night, which has become one of the most popular events for singles in the city, and it is now being copied by other cultural institutions. Dating services, computer bulletin boards, and classified ads are also becoming more popular with older singles (see Sexuality Today 8.1).

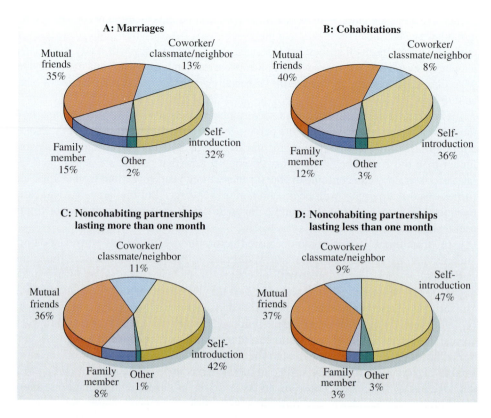

Figure **8.1**
Who introduced partners to each other. **Michael et al. (1994)**

Sexuality in Dating Relationships

Dating is, to a great extent, about love and sex, and the endless struggle seems to be how much of each occurs in any one relationship. Many men rate sex as being more important than love in dating relationships, while many women rate love as being more important than sex. We have to keep in mind, however, that this may be what men and women report rather than what they believe—or how they may act. (See Sexuality Today 8.2 for a look at the kind of additional twist long distances can put on a dating relationship.)

In relationships, some couples wait for months, years, or until marriage before they engage in sexual intercourse, while others feel this is less important and may begin having a sexual relationship right away. Their individual sexual scripts (see Chapter 4), that is, their full sets of beliefs about appropriate sexual behavior, also affect how quickly the relationship becomes sexual. Men and women tend to have different sexual scripts, which is why men tend to be the ones who encourage sexual contact while women often limit the level of sexual intimacy (Benokraitis, 1993). Male homosexual couples also tend to have different sexual scripts than heterosexual couples and, therefore, tend to engage in sex more quickly than heterosexual couples.

SEX TALK

QUESTION   **8.2   I have heard that if a couple has sexual intercourse on their first date, there is little chance that the relationship can grow into a long-term one. Is this true?**

Some researchers claim that it is necessary to have a friendship prior to engaging in a sexual relationship, while others claim that relationships can grow out of sexual intimacy. The decision to become sexual in a relationship and how long to wait may have to do with how a couple views sexuality. Some couples believe sexual intimacy should be reserved for marriage, while others feel it is acceptable in strong, emotionally committed relationships, and still others feel it is acceptable if the couple is attracted to one another. Those who believe that sex is primarily or only for procreation will wait until after marriage, and those who feel emotional closeness is necessary will wait until they fall in love (usually within six months to a year); still, those who do decide to have sex more quickly have not eliminated the possibility that their relationship will grow into a long-lasting one. Many long-time married couples (although you might not be able to get them to admit it!) had sexual relations soon after they began dating.

SEXUALITY *Today*   8.1

Personals

WOMEN SEEKING MEN

LONELY REDHEAD
SWF, 42 looks 32, likes blues, good food and conversation. Like men who pay attention to me, not themselves. Want considerate, sensitive man. ☎1207.

LET'S CREATE FANTASIES TOGETHER
Hey! Are you ready to have some fun and excitement? I'm full of adventures to share with you. Me: SWF 23, 5'5", brunette. You: SWM with good personality, and a great sense of humor. Let's see how creative we can be. ☎1083.

SWF, FORMER PLAYBOY BUNNY/MODEL
Wish to meet a successful professional businessman over 50 for equally rewarding relationship. Likes travel, jewelry, mink coats, beautiful clothes, and looks good in them. ☎1081.

5'4", INTELLIGENT, ATTRACTIVE, DBF
Tall, attractive, fun loving man over 55, who likes books, movies, sports, classical concerts, eating out, and other clean fun, for companion and possible further relationship. Race unimportant. Smoker, LD ok. ☎1107.

ARE YOU TALL?
Attractive, professional, in your 40s or 50s, with a quest for living, and friends- not creditors at your door? Slim, attractive, energetic, shorthaired blond, with a sense of humor, and diverse interests, is looking for someone to share her love of travel and adventure. If people say you're goofy, don't apply. If you live on a golf course, I look forward to hearing from you! ☎1155.

MEN SEEKING WOMEN

TIRED OF SEARCHING
Bored, not desperate SPM seeks F 24- 40 for friendship, romance, maybe more. Me: Tall, dark, handsome (?), mid-30s, intelligent, music, movies, dancing, discussions, intense, witty, non- conformist. You: Literate, open-minded, good looking, humorous, shapely, adventurous, fashion forward. ☎1203.

LAST OF THE GOOD GUYS
SBM, 49, affectionate, 5'8", 165. In search of attractive SF or DF who wants a one-on-one passionate, meaningful relationship. ☎1209.

TRAGICALLY COOL
SWM, 36, fun-loving, easy-going, open- minded, seeking full-figures S/DF, 22-40, for friendship, maybe more. I enjoy concerts, movies, CD shopping, late night outings. All responses will be answered. ☎1206.

LOOKING FOR A LOVER
SBM, 50, 5'8", 162, like a great number of things but don't have to do but what you want. In search of attractive, 35-45, queen size ok, romantic, passionate SF for possible committed relationship. ☎1213.

WHEN IT FLOWS-IT GOES
DWPM, homeowner, 38, 5'5", 135. In search of loyal, fun, happy, SW/HF, 30-40. She enjoys travel, camping, Harley's, dancing, sexy outfits, boating, and mutual spoilage. Long term relationship possible, kids ok, friend and lover. ☎1212.

MEN SEEKING MEN

UNPREDICTABLE, HANDSOME GBM
30, 5'6", a cut above the rest. Seeks M (any race) who is handsome, discreet, versatile, and confident. Not into bars. Take a chance, I won't be a disappointment to you. ☎1205.

GWM, 28
I like music, outdoors, hockey, soccer, tennis, and the arts. With good health and personality. In search of a GM, open minded, sincere, romantic, spontaneous, but down to earth. Looking for a 22-34 year old, for friendship/relationship, but no games. ☎1204.

SON WANTED
GWM, 6'5", 195, late 40s, seeks compatible son over 28. Are you physically, emotionally, and mentally able to maintain my pace? Give a call and let's find out. Athletic and muscular a plus. ☎1142.

DIVERSITY WANTED
GWM, 35, 6'0", 225, discreet, healthy, wanting to meet Native American, Hispanic, Asian, (21-49) interested in friendship, quiet times, and watching movies/videos. No smokers, drugs, femmes or fats. ☎1173.

SWM, 32
Likes fishing, bicycle riding, movies, like to meet SWM, good personality, and hobbies, for friendship maybe relationship. ☎1171.

WOMEN SEEKING WOMEN

TIRED OF LIVING IN DENIAL
SGWF, 26, athletic, academic. In search of SGWF, 30-40, who is career oriented, and preferential to good conversation, movies, and working out. Have just found the courage to take a chance. ☎1211.

I'M A LF, 29
Interested in meeting other LF for friendship. If you are 25-35, enjoy clubs, movies, sports, etc. Maybe we should meet. Persons responding should be drug-free and open to having fun. Friendship begins with hello. ☎1183.

LET'S TAKE A RISK!
You: attractive SGF, N/S, no drugs, little or N/D, sincere, likes the outdoors, movies, dining, and quiet evenings. Me: same as above but ND, low-keyed, SGBF, 43, 5'7", 145 lbs., I may be the person you're looking for. ☎1165.

Key for Personal Ads
A=Asian
B=Black
C=Christian
D=Divorced
DP=Disabled Person
F=Female
G=Gay
H=Hispanic
J=Jewish
LD=Light Drinker
M=Male
ND=No Drinking or Drugs
NS=Nonsmoker
S=Single
W=White
WW=Widowed

SEXUALITY*Today*   8.2

Long-Distance Relationships

With a shrinking job market and limited opportunities in any one place for employment, more and more people find themselves in relationships with partners residing in different states. One thirty-year-old male who was involved in a long-distance relationship said:

We met about four years ago and I really liked her. However, at the time I had no intentions of becoming serious with her. My career was going very well and there were many things I wanted to do professionally before I settled down. After about a year into our relationship she was offered a job 1000 miles away. We talked about our relationship but neither of us felt ready for a more serious commitment. We dated "long distance" for two years. During that time of flying back and forth to see each other, we grew closer and closer. Soon I was willing to move to be with her.

I would never have guessed that I would move, or switch jobs, for a woman. At this point, we have discussed marriage, and both of us feel established enough in our careers to start the next aspect of our lives. Some people haven't understood our strong desire for our respective careers, but it's the way we wanted it to be.

Author's files

Can long-distance relationships work? It has been found that they can indeed work, but survival chances are better if the couple has good communication skills and if there are frequent visits. The biggest problem couples encounter is the pressure of feeling that they must always get along while they are together. They may hesitate to disagree or challenge each other, which can lead to a lack of communication.

Couples who abstain from sexual intercourse tend to hold more conservative attitudes about sex, and have less prior sexual experience. If both partners are virgins in a long-term relationship, there is a 50% chance that they will have sexual intercourse with their partner (Peplau et al., 1977). When both partners have been sexually active in the past, they are very likely to continue to be sexually active in their present relationship. In couples where one partner has been sexually active in the past and the other is a virgin, the woman's past experience is a stronger predictor of the sexual behavior of the couple. Virginal men often do not resist the opportunity to have sexual intercourse with an experienced woman. Peplau et al. (1977) found in a study of college students that every male virgin who dated a sexually experienced female engaged in sexual intercourse. However, when a virginal female dated a sexually experienced man, only one-third of couples had sexual intercourse. Virgins are more likely to have at least one close friend who is a virgin, whereas nonvirgins are unlikely to have either of their two closest friends be virgins. This relationship is usually stronger among women than men.

Today we are finding that more and more adults are standing up for their virginity instead of being embarrassed by it. Even some famous athletes have spoken out about their virginity (see Personal Voices 8.2).

Although we discussed adolescents' first sexual intercourse in Chapter 4, we will explore the research that has been done on first sexual intercourse in adult relationships here. For many couples, first intercourse takes place within a month of dating. Both men and women often experience first sexual intercourse with older partners, but women are more likely to be in a committed relationship when they first have intercourse, and women also often have intercourse again with the same partner (Darling et al., 1992).

Because women have been taught that they should be in love before engaging in sexual intercourse, many feel this is the only socially acceptable justification for sexual intimacy. Men, on the other hand, have typically been afforded more leeway in deciding

*P*ersonal
V O I C E S

8.2

Sports and Virginity

Recently, some professional athletes have spoken about their desire to remain virgins until their wedding day. A. C. Green, a thirty-one-year-old professional basketball player for the Phoenix Suns, is one man who chooses to speak out about his desire to maintain his virginity.

I just finished my tenth season in the NBA, and it's nice to take a break. Not only does my body take a physical toll, but it isn't easy dealing with the constant travel and the media requests for interviews. It's also hard to escape the public eye. I'm 6-foot-9 and, like most basketball players, pretty easy to spot in a crowd.

As a professional athlete, I have to deal with groupies in many cities. It seems as though my teammates and I are often confronted by young women wanting to meet us from the time we arrive to the time we depart. They hang out everywhere—airports, hotel lobbies, restaurants and sports arenas— always trying to catch our eyes.

Not many resist their advances. I don't know how many virgins there are in the NBA, but you can probably count them on one hand. Pro basketball players have this larger-than-life image, and it doesn't help when a former player such as Wilt Chamberlain boasts about bedding 20,000 women in his lifetime.

While I've remained sexually pure, I still hear the locker-room talk about the latest sexual conquests. But I don't let that weaken my resolve because I have chosen to follow God's standard. I've communicated my stand to my teammates. Some—in a humorous vein—have threatened to set me up with women who would make themselves available to me; "Let's see how strong you really are," they joke.

Don't get me wrong. Sex itself isn't bad. It's just a matter of when *to experience it. God created it for enjoyment, but He also reserved it for marriage. So I'm waiting. The Bible tells me in Philippians 4:13 that "I can do all things through Christ, who strengthens me," and I've taken that verse to heart. I also know God's Word tells me that He will not give me any temptation too great.*

I want young people to hear this message: It is possible to wait. Not everybody is doing it. Five years ago, I started the A. C. Green Youth Foundation *in Los Angeles. We put together basketball camps, help kids find summer jobs, and try to give inner-city youth some direction. As part of that outreach, last summer several pro athletes—including Daryl Green and David Robinson—along with a Christian rap group called Idol King joined me to make a video called "It Ain't Worth It." It's a rap song dealing with teenage love, broken hearts, the dilemma of abortion, and the fallacy of the "safe sex" message.*

Of course, some young kids listening to me have been sexually active for years. That's when I tell them about the concept of secondary virginity. "You may have had sex in the past and think you don't have a reason to wait now," I say. "But there's a better way, and that's following God's way. Perhaps you feel guilty or not worthy, but the Lord can forgive you. After that, you can commit yourselves to remaining pure until your wedding day."

Sometimes I'm asked if I have a girlfriend. Yes, I do. She really respects herself, and she has high morals and values. We share the same vision and goals, particularly when telling teens about the values of abstinence. That's what I really like telling kids: You have to learn to respect yourself before you can start respecting other people.

Reprinted with permission:
Focus on the Family Magazine
(June 1993: pp. 2–3)

when and with whom to have sexual intercourse. In casual sexual encounters where a couple does not have an established relationship, women are more likely than men to not enjoy the encounter and to feel guilt (Herold and Mcwhinney, 1993).

There is a stereotype that men have an easier time engaging in sex without love and women need to have love in order to feel good about engaging in sexual behavior, and there seems to be some validity to this stereotype. Carroll et al. (1985) found that when college students were asked about their motives for engaging in sexual intercourse, males' motives were often more physical, while females' were more emotional. Typical reasons that males gave for engaging in sexual intercourse included:

> *To satisfy my needs.*
> *To gratify myself.*
> *Need it.*

Typical female answers included:

> *Love, to feel loved, to express love to someone.*
> *Wanting to share myself with someone I love, needing to be needed.*
> *My motives for sexual intercourse would all be due to the love and commitment I feel for my partner.* (Carroll et al., 1985:137)

Once again, we need to be careful in evaluating these responses. It may be easier for males to *report* that physical pleasure is more important, while females may have an easier time reporting emotional motives.

Men often initiate sexual behavior, even though men and women often report similar interest levels (see Figure 8.2). In fact, both females who initiate sexual activity and males who avoid sexual activity are often viewed negatively (Muehlenhard, 1988). However, in relationships that are rated as the happiest, both partners initiate sex equally, and both feel free to say no if they do not feel like having sex (Heiman and LoPiccolo, 1992).

When a partner in a long-term relationship initiates sex, he or she is successful in approximately 75% of attempts, according to one study (Byers and Heinlein, 1989). In fact, some people feel obligated to have sex with their partners when asked. If they say no to sex, it is usually because they are too tired or do not have enough time. There are also differences in how interest and noninterest are shown. If a partner wants to have sex, usually he or she shows this interest nonverbally, through touch or body movements. If a partner is not interested, he or she often expresses this verbally (Byer and Heinlein, 1989).

Sorenson (1973) found that young men often experience a decrease in their masturbatory activity when they are having sexual intercourse, while masturbation in young women increases. Perhaps this is due to the fact that women are less likely to be orgasmic during sexual intercourse and it is easier to reach orgasm through masturbation.

Finally, in the majority of couples, there is very little communication during the transition from thinking about having sexual intercourse to actually having sexual intercourse (Wight, 1992). It is almost as if talking about it will reduce the possibility of it happening and increase the vulnerability of one or both of the partners if they do not want to engage in sexual intercourse. We often hear people claim that "it just happened." Although there may be very little communication, there are often signals or clues that indicate the partner's willingness to have sex. For instance, if a couple is lying on the floor kissing and fondling each other and they move to the bed, there is an understanding

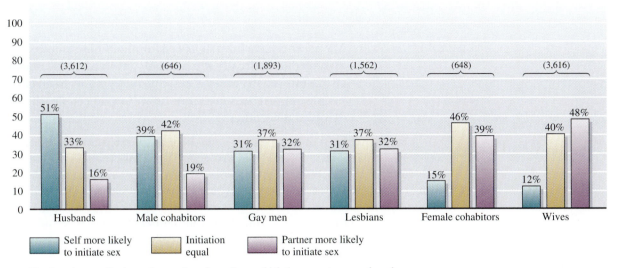

Sexual Initiation

Numbers in parenthesis are the number of people on which the percentages are based.

Figure **8.2**

The graph above shows which partner is more likely to initiate sexual behavior in homosexual and heterosexual couples. Reprinted with permission from **Blumstein and Schwartz (1983: 207).**

about what is to follow (Wight, 1992). Although all couples should discuss their sexual history (partners and use of condoms) prior to their first sexual intercourse, the majority of couples do not (Ingham et al., 1991).

Dating After Divorce or Widowhood

After a divorce or the death of a spouse, it can be very difficult to get back into the "dating scene." Many of these people have been involved in committed relationships for many years; consequently, they find that the dating environment has changed drastically since they were younger. For example, consider a sixty-two-year-old man and woman who have been married since 1950. In 1994 they decide to divorce. Dating in 1994 was considerably different from dating in 1950. The relationship between the sexes has changed, women initiate dates and sexual activity, casual dating is more common, sexual activity may be more frequent, and one has to be more worried about sexually transmitted diseases. It is not uncommon for newly divorced people to feel frustrated or confused about this unfamiliar environment. Widowed men and women often experience similar difficulties. One widowed, forty-nine-year-old man said:

> It was very hard for me to get into the dating scene again. I had married very young. Honestly, there is no one to match my late wife. I don't know if I am still responding to the wonderful life I had in my marriage or have just lost all interest in romance. I meet quite a few young women and can see that they are attractive, and to someone else may be desirable, but I hardly give it a blink.
>
> **Janus and Janus (1993:8)**

Today, more and more groups and organizations are being created to help divorced and widowed people ease back into the dating scene.

SEX TALK

QUESTION **8.3** **My parents have been divorced for about nine months, and my dad is already romantically involved with someone else. However, my mom is not. She really wants to meet people but just does not know how. How do people who are divorced meet others?**

It is often difficult to begin dating again after a divorce. However, there are several organizations that have been designed to help divorced people restart their dating activities. Parents Without Partners (PWP) is one such group offering support and social opportunities. PWP has dances and parties, and members attend sporting and social events together. You might help your mom get in touch with this group. Another way that divorced people often meet others is through mutual friends, social events, and other daily activities (such as grocery shopping).

As married people age, one spouse eventually dies, and the partner may find himself or herself single again for the first time in many years. Even though many of these people are not interested in marrying again, they may still be interested in dating (Bulcroft and Bulcroft, 1991). The likelihood that an older man will choose to date is predicted by his age and social involvement, while older women are influenced more by their health and mobility. Some older women do decide to take on younger lovers, even though society may consider it less acceptable than older men with younger women. Older adults, on the other hand, overwhelmingly approve of older women dating younger men. One seventy-six-year-old female said: "Let them enjoy themselves. I wish I had one for myself" (Starr and Weiner, 1981:174). We discuss dating after the death of a spouse among the elderly in more detail below (see Marriages in Later Life).

Interracial Dating

In 1967, the Supreme Court struck down state antimiscegenation laws, which outlawed interracial relationships (see Chapter 1). Since the early 1980s, the number of interracial couples has nearly doubled, although the overall proportion of interracial marriages is still low (about 1.8% of all marriages). In 1992, there were approximately 1.2 million marriages between Hispanic and non-Hispanics, 883,000 between whites and other races (such as Asian, Pacific Islander, or American Indian), including 246,000 between African-Americans and whites; and 32,000 between African-Americans and other races. Despite these trends, there are still very strong social forces that keep the races separate and make it difficult for people of different races to meet or maintain relationships. Although the number of people who approved of interracial marriages exceeded the number who disapproved for the first time in 1990 (48% approved, 42% disapproved, 10% had no opinion), a large minority does not accept such marriages (Benokraitis, 1993).

It should also be noted that race is not the only factor that influences whether people think dating is acceptable; some disapprove of dating people of different religions, ethnic groups, ages, or social classes, or who are disabled. Such couples may also face some of the same challenges that interracial couples do.

SEX TALK

QUESTION **8.4** **Why is it that people stare at couples who are different races? I just don't understand what the big deal is if they really love each other.**

Americans have a history of disapproving of relationships that take place between blacks and whites. After all, we must remember that such relationships were actually illegal in many states until the Supreme Court overturned these laws in 1967. In many other countries, interracial couples are not unusual. Latino–white relationships, as well as Asian–white, Native American-white, Latino–black, and other combinations—while still often looked upon negatively— are more acceptable in the United States than black–white. Unfortunately, these negative feelings can lead to discrimination against such couples and their children.

COHABITATION

Gay and lesbian partners who decide to join in a committed relationship still cannot be officially married in the United States; their only choice is **cohabitation**, or living together. Heterosexual partners, on the other hand, do have a choice, and they have been choosing cohabitation in increasing numbers. Today, cohabitation has become so common that many sociologists regard it as a stage of courtship (Thomson and Colella, 1992). Modern surveys and questionnaires started using the category of POSSLQ— "People of Opposite Sex Sharing Living Quarters." Since this category assumes that sexual relationships are heterosexual, surveys now often ask about "partners." Still, there is no accepted term for heterosexual and homosexual sexual partners that is widely used in surveys or by the government.

Between 1960 and 1990, the number of unmarried couple households rose from 430,000 to 2,851,000 (Benokraitis, 1993) (see Figure 8.3). But the United States still does not compare with Sweden, where 90% of married couples lived together before marriage, or Denmark, where 80% cohabit.

Cohabiting heterosexual couples tend to share some characteristics, including being under the age of thirty (if never before married), living in a metropolitan area, being well educated, and both being employed but having relatively low incomes (Glick and Spanier, 1981). But there are many exceptions; for example, many elderly people who do not want to get married (often because it would increase their taxes) also decide to live together.

There are advantages and disadvantages to cohabitation. Cohabitation allows couples to move into marriage more slowly, learn more about each other, and not be legally or economically tied together. It allows a couple who loves each other to be older, more mature, and more financially stable when they finally marry. It is more realistic than dating because it gives couples the opportunity to learn of their partners' bad habits and idiosyncrasies. Yet there are also problems. Parents and relatives may not support the

cohabitation: Living together in a sexual relationship when not legally married.

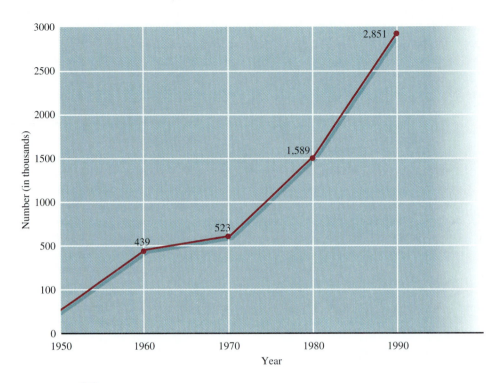

Number of unmarried-couple households from 1960 to 1990. **Benokraitis (1993)**

union, and society as a whole tends not to recognize people who live together for purposes of health care, taxes, etc. Also, partners may want different things out of living together, such as when one sees it as a trial marriage and the other as a way for a more accessible sexual partner. People can feel cut off from their friends, and the couple can become too enmeshed and interdependent (Benokraitis, 1993).

common law marriage: A marriage existing by mutual agreement over a period of years, rather than through legal means, between a man and a woman.

Thirteen states do recognize **common-law marriage**, which means that if a couple lives together for a certain number of years, they are considered married. There are also cases of individuals who have successfully sued partners they lived with for alimony or shared property (called **palimony**), claiming that their partner promised them marriage or lived together with them as if married. If the couple has a baby, of course, both partners are responsible for its upbringing, even if they separate afterward. So living together may entangle a couple in legal issues they did not anticipate.

palimony: Payments awarded by a court to a woman (usually), from a man with whom she has cohabitated.

Some people believe that when couples live together, they can smooth out the rough spots in their relationships and see if they would be able to be happily married to each other. Research indicates, however, that the reverse may be true. Cohabiting couples tend to either marry or separate after just a few years. Those who marry are at increased risk of divorce, and longer cohabitation has been found to be associated with higher likelihood of divorce (Thomson and Colella, 1992). Even in Sweden, women who cohabited before marriage had almost an 80% higher rate of marital dissolution than those who did not (Benokraitis, 1993).

Why might couples who live together be less successful as marriage partners? Bennett et al. (1988) believes that higher rates of divorce in couples who cohabit for a long period of time may be due to the fact that these couples develop as separate individuals during that time (since they are not married, they maintain their own "life" outside of the relationship), and this may lead to a higher risk for divorce. Without the legal commitment of marriage, couples may just be "playing house," unprepared for the real problems of married couples. Also, most cohabiting couples do not get joint checkbooks, have expensive mortgages, etc., and may not be prepared for the financial pressures of marriage (money fights are a major reason for divorce).

However, there are several possible shortcomings of the above findings. It may not be that cohabitation itself increases the chance of divorce, but that the type of people who are willing to cohabit are the type who are also more likely to divorce when marriage gets difficult. Cohabiting couples may feel that they would not be happy in a marriage; they may be more accepting of divorce; they may be less religious and less traditional in the first place; or they may be less committed in the beginning of the relationship. Since we do not know about the samples in the studies on cohabiting couples, it is difficult to generalize their findings.

SEX TALK

QUESTION **8.5** **Do couples who are dating, living together, or married have more conflict and arguments?**

Studies have shown that the things that anger men about women and women about men are just about the same regardless of the type of relationship they are in. Men tend to complain that women sexually reject them; are unresponsive to sex; are moody; and are too self-absorbed (i.e., spend too much time on their appearance, face, hair, clothes, etc.). Women complain that men make too many sexual demands on them; are condescending, or treat them like their opinion is not valid because they are female; hide emotions to act macho or tough; are unreliable; fail to say "I love you"; and are thoughtless (belching, leaving the toilet seat up, etc.). These issues seem to affect couples who are dating, living together, or married (Buss, 1989).

The *reasons* a couple decides to live together may have a lot to do with whether or not the relationship survives marriage. If a couple lives together for economic reasons, or because of timing (say they are planning to marry in the near future), this will generally result in a healthy marital relationship. However, complications arise when couples live together because they are nervous about making a commitment of marriage or they want to "test" their relationship. Obviously, if they need to test a relationship to see if it will work, they are not ready for marriage.

MARRIAGE

Throughout history, there has been a long-standing love–hate relationship with the institution of marriage. Writers have often cursed it and have often praised it, but no matter what their attitude toward it, almost all have done it. Even today, 95% of the population marry at least once, and if they divorce (especially if they are younger), the majority will remarry. See how much you know about marriage by taking the quiz in Where Do I Stand? 8.1.

In almost all societies on earth, women are more likely to marry partners older than themselves, while men are more likely to marry younger women (Buss, 1989). In adolescence, these age preferences are less strong, but they increase as one ages.

WHERE DO I *Stand*? 8.1

Critical Issues / The Marriage Quiz

1. A husband's marital satisfaction is usually lower if his wife is employed full time than if she is a full-time homemaker. T F
2. Today most young, single, never-married people will eventually get married. T F
3. In most marriages, having a child improves marital satisfaction for both spouses. T F
4. The best single predictor of overall marital satisfaction is the quality of the couple's sex life. T F
5. The divorce rate in the United States increased between 1960 and 1980. T F
6. A greater precentage of wives are in the work force today than in 1970. T F
7. Marital satisfaction for a wife is usually lower if she is employed full time than if she is a full-time homemaker. T F
8. "If my spouse loves me, he/she should instinctively know what I want and need to be happy." T F
9. In a marriage in which the wife is employed full time, the husband usually assumes an equal share of the housekeeping. T F
10. For most couples, marital satisfaction gradually increases from the first year of marriage through the childbearing years, the teenage years, the empty-nest period, and retirement. T F
11. "No matter how I behave, my spouse should love me because he/she is my spouse." T F
12. One of the most frequent marital problems is poor communication. T F
13. Husbands usually make more lifestyle adjustments in marriage than do wives. T F
14. Couples who cohabited before marriage usually report greater marital satisfaction than do couples who do not. T F
15. "I can change my spouse by pointing out his/her inadequacies, errors, and so forth." T F
16. Couples who marry when one or both partners are under the age of 18 are more likely to divorce than are those who marry when they are older. T F
17. "Either my spouse loves me or does not love me; nothing I can do will affect the way my spouse feels about me." T F
18. The more a spouse discloses positive and negative information to his/her partner, the greater the marital satisfaction of both partners. T F
19. "I must feel better about my partner before I can change my behavior toward him/her." T F
20. Maintaining romantic love is the key to marital happiness over the life span, for most couples. T F

Scoring the Marriage Quiz

Cross out items 2, 5, 6, 12, and 16 (filler items to disguise the pattern of responses), which are true. The rest are false. The greater the number of true responses, the greater the belief in marital myths. Larson found that college students answer about 50 percent of the items incorrectly, and women miss about 10 percent fewer items than do men. For a more in-depth explanation of the items, see Larson, 1988:8–9.

Jeffry Larson, *"The Marriage Quiz: College Students' Beliefs in Selected Myths about Marriage,"* Family Relations 37, no. 1 (January): 3–11. Copyright © 1988 by the National Council on Family Relations, 3989 Central Ave. N.E., Suite #550, Minneapolis, MN 55421. Reprinted by permission.

Evolutionary explanations suggest that men want to ensure conception and pregnancy (more likely with a younger, healthy wife), while women want to be sure they will be taken care of (more likely with an older, more established husband). Sociological models say instead that social gender roles value wealth and power in men (more likely in older men) and physical beauty in women (more likely in younger women).

SEX TALK

QUESTION **8.6** In a good marital relationship, do couples pursue mutual interests or self-interests more?

It is important for a couple to pursue both mutual and self-interests in any relationship. In a good marriage, couples support each other's individual development as well as their development as a couple. Balancing these two is harder than many people realize, however, because too much attention to oneself threatens a marriage, while too much focus on being a "couple" can end up feeling stifling.

What do married couples think is important for a good marriage? Studies have shown that women tend to feel that emotional closeness and verbal self-disclosure are the most important ingredients, while men report that spending time with their spouse and putting their spouse's needs first are crucial (Parelman, 1983). Both men and women report that they would like a partner whom they get along with well, who is also affectionate and understanding. For husbands, sexual satisfaction was more strongly related to overall marital satisfaction than for wives, while communication was more important to wives (Peplau and Gordon, 1985). Marital satisfaction for men was also found to be related to the frequency of pleasurable instrumental activities (doing things together) in the relationship, while for women it was related to the frequency of pleasurable activities that focus on emotional closeness.

Most married couples believe that they achieve these goals, because the majority of husbands and wives report that their marriages are happy and satisfying. More than 60% of couples in a study by Greeley (1991) reported that their marriages were happy. In general, slightly more women than men report being happy in their marriages, although the difference has been declining since the early 1970s. African-American women, on the other hand, typically report lower marital happiness than African-American men perhaps because they report feeling overwhelmed by employment and household work (Benokraitis, 1993).

Why do some marriages last, while others end in divorce? Lauer and Lauer (1990) asked 351 married couples why their marriages have lasted. They found that marriages seem to last most when both partners have a positive attitude toward the marriage, view their partner as a best friend, and like their partner as a person. Another important aspect of marriage is the belief that marriage is a long-term commitment. To make it work, couples need to be willing to work through the difficulties that are part of any relationship.

Researchers have found that marriage seems to be good for a person's health. People who are married tend to be happier, healthier, and have longer lives than either widowed or divorced persons of the same age (Gore et al., 1983). Marriage has also been found to reduce the impact of several potentially traumatic events including job loss, retirement, and illness. Overall, however, marriage seems to provide more health benefits to men than women. For instance, while married men have better physical and mental health, more self-reported happiness, and experience fewer psychological problems than either divorced, single, or widowed men (Gore, 1972), married women tend to be less healthy than married men (Benokraitis, 1993). Perlman et al. (1978) found that widowed men were significantly more lonely than married men, while no differences were found in loneliness between married and widowed women. Suicide rates for single men are twice as high as those of married men, and single men have been found to experience more psychological problems such as depression and even nightmares (Faludi, 1991). This may be because women have had multiple role responsibilities; for example, working women still tend to do the bulk of the housework and disproportionately take care of the children. As Collins (1988:289) puts it, for men "[marriage] largely means receiving household services, whereas for women it means giving services."

Marital Sexual Relationships

Sexuality is an essential part of most marriages. Many young people see marriage as an unproblematic feast of sexual pleasure; after all, you have your partner there all the time, and you just make love anytime you want to. (Figure 8.4 illustrates frequency of sex in marriage as compared to other types of relationships.) But others wonder if sex with the same person might not become boring after a while. The number of books promising to teach couples how to put zing back into the marital bedroom indicates that marriage is not always an unending string of sexual encounters.

Greenblat (1989) interviewed eighty people, married five years or less, about their sexual habits. Respondents had sex as often as forty-five times a month or as rarely as once a month (see Table 8.1). Laumann et al. (1994) found that 40% of married people have sexual intercourse two or more times a week, while 50% engage in it a few times each month. No matter how often couples had sex, most reported a decline over time— only 6% reported an increase in sexual frequency over time. More than a third reported that they made love less than 60% as often as they did in the first year of marriage. The reasons had less to do with getting bored with their partners than it had to do with the pressures of children, jobs, commuting, housework, and finances. However, even with these life changes, after ten years or more of marriage only 15% of married couples have sex less than once a month, and 63% report having sex once a week or more (Heiman and LoPiccolo, 1992). The frequency of sexual activity and satisfaction with a couple's sex life have been found to be positively correlated (Blumstein and Schwartz, 1983); that is, the higher the frequency of sexual behavior, the higher the sexual satisfaction. However, it is not known if increased sexual frequency causes more satisfaction, or if increased satisfaction with the marriage is responsible for the increase in frequency of sexual behavior.

Some couples feel that decreasing frequency of sexual behavior is a positive change. One woman said:

> *Maybe it's not a necessity anymore. We have other ways of expressing our feelings, and intercourse is one of the ways. When we first got married we thought it was the only way, and now we realize it is not. And the quality of our sex life has improved. Now it gives us so much satisfaction, it's not really necessary that we have it every single night.*

> *Greenblat (1989:187)*

Frank and Anderson (1989) studied 100 couples and found that sexuality changes as one moves through different stages of marriage. During the early years, about the first five years, sexuality is more frequent and generally satisfying, with both partners feeling that they can satisfy the other. During the next fifteen or so years, the middle stage, other aspects of life take precedence over sex, and the couple may experience difficulty in maintaining sexual interest in each other. In this stage, the couple begins to report more sexual dissatisfaction, with husbands troubled by an increasing interest in other women and wives troubled by a decreasing interest in sex itself. In the later years, twenty or more, sex gets more difficult as frequency and potency decline; still, men report being generally satisfied with their sex lives. Women, on the other hand, report being much less satisfied, saying they feel a sense of resignation that their sex lives are not exciting to them anymore.

Frequency and type of marital sex has been found to differ by social class (Collins, 1988). Contrary to the stereotype of the uninhibited lower class, the upper

Sexual Frequency

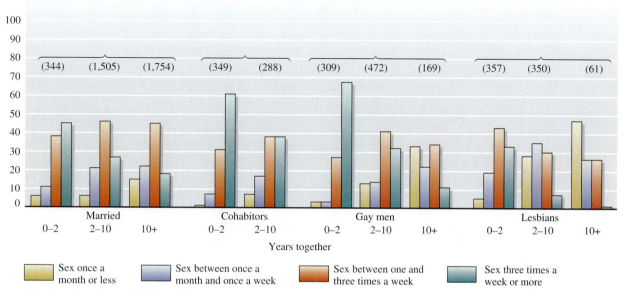

Note: Very few of our cohabitors had been together more than 10 years.
Numbers in parentheses are the number of couples on which the percentages are based.

Figure **8.4**

The figure above shows the frequency of sexual behavior in various types of relationships by years together. **Blumstein and Schwartz (1983:196)**

Table **8.1**

FREQUENCY OF INTERCOURSE PER MONTH, BY YEARS MARRIED

YEARS MARRIED	NUMBER OF COUPLES	MEAN FREQUENCY	RANGE
1	12	14.8	4–45
2	10	12.2	3–20
3	19	11.9	2–18
4	7	9.0	4–23
5	18	9.7	5–18
6	8	6.3	2–15

Greenblat (1989:182)

classes actually tend to have marital sex more frequently, use more sexual positions, and practice more oral sex and other varieties of sexual contact. This may be because of more leisure time, because of more space and privacy, or perhaps because lower classes tend to have more traditional gender roles. Still, class differences in marital sexuality have been decreasing in recent years.

asexual: Relationships that do not involve sexual behavior.

Some marriages are **asexual**, which means the partners do not engage in sexual intercourse. This is usually a mutual decision, and it may be because the partners do not have sexual desire for each other anymore. One man who claimed he had been happily married for thirty-six years said:

> *After about a month or two into the marriage, I could have gone without any marital sex. I just kept having sex because I felt I had to. We haven't had sex in years and years. She doesn't seem to mind, either.*
>
> **Kansas City Star (1993a)**

Finally, masturbation is often taboo in marital relationships. The myth is that if a married man masturbates, his wife cannot be satisfying him sexually. However, this is not true. Forty-four percent of American husbands masturbate weekly or more, while only 16% of wives do (Janus and Janus, 1993). Michael et al. (1994:165) found that masturbation is often stimulated by other sexual behavior—"[T]he more sex you have of any kind, the more you may think about sex and the more you may masturbate." (We will discuss masturbation more in Chapter 9.)

Having Children or Remaining Childless

Children can be born at any period before or during a marriage or outside of marriage, and the timing of having children has effects on the quality of marital life. Some people get married in order to have children, others get married because they are pregnant and want to make their child "legitimate," and other couples decide to get married even though neither partner wants children. In any case, the decision to have or raise children is one that most people face at one time or another.

Many single women who wish to remain childless report that they do not expect to marry (Callan, 1986), and approximately 6% of married women between the ages of eighteen and thirty-four plan to remain childless (Baber and Monaghan, 1988).

Some research suggests that having children may actually adversely affect overall marital quality. Marital happiness is higher before the children come, declines steadily until it hits a low when the children are in their teens, and then begins to increase once the children leave the house (Collins, 1988). Why is this? First, unhappily married people may stay together "for the sake of the children." Also, many couples have not agreed on roles after childbearing, and the female may find, for example, that her husband just assumes that she will take primary care of the children (Benokraitis, 1993). Many couples do not realize how time consuming children are, and they find themselves with little time to work on their marriage.

Marriages in Later Life

Over half of Americans over the age of sixty-five are married and living with their spouse and family. By the age of seventy-five, however, 70% of men are still married versus only 22% of women. This is because women often outlive their spouses and older men tend to marry younger women.

Most older couples report that their marriages improved over time and that the later years are some of the happiest. Elderly men often report more satisfaction with marriage than do women, who complain of increased responsibilities in caring for infirm husbands or planning activities if he is retired. This is further complicated by the fact that older persons usually have very few places to turn to for emotional assistance. They have fewer relatives and friends, no coworkers, and often feel uncomfortable sharing problems with their children. In addition, counseling services are limited.

Many older people who experience the death of a spouse will remarry. Older men are twice as likely to remarry, however, because women outnumber men in older age and also because older men often marry younger women (Atchley, 1985). White males remarry more often than other groups; the remarriage rates for African-Americans are lower, and they have longer intervals between marriages (Brubaker, 1985). Marriages that follow the death of a spouse tend to be more successful if the couple knew each other for a period of time prior to the marriage, if their children and peers approve of the marriage, and if they are in good health, financially stable, and have adequate living conditions. One seventy-three-year-old man said:

> *I can't begin to tell you how happy I am. I am married to a wonderful woman who loves me as much as I love her. My children gave me a hard time of it at first, especially because she is a bit younger than me, but they finally accepted the relationship and came to our wedding. In fact, they gave me away at the ceremony. That's a switch, isn't it? I put some humor into this situation when my oldest son, who is in the business with me, objected. He was telling me that marrying again and trying to have a lot of sex—imagine that, saying to me trying to have sex—could be dangerous to the marriage. So, I said to him with a straight face, "Do you think she'll survive it?" He was so shocked, he laughed.*
>
> *Janus and Janus (1993:8)*

Extramarital Sexual Relationships

All societies regulate sexual behavior and use marriage as a means to control the behavior of its members to some degree. Our society is one of the few that have traditionally forbidden sexual contact outside of marriage; research estimates that less than 5% of all societies are as strict about forbidding extramarital intercourse as ours has been (Leslie and Korman, 1989). Our opposition to sex outside of marriage stems from our Judeo-Christian background, and although today it is not as shocking as it used to be, there is still a strong feeling among Americans that extramarital sex is wrong. In the United States, adults are more tolerant of premarital sexuality than of extramarital sexuality (Cochran and Beeghley, 1991; Rubinson and deRubertis, 1991). Overall, college students are more accepting of extra-premarital sexual relations (cheating on a boyfriend or girlfriend) than of extramarital ones (Lieberman, 1988).

Even for those couples who never consider sex outside of marriage, the possibility looms, and people wonder about it—what it would be like, or if their partners are indulging in it. Even if their marriage is secure, they may have friends or relatives who are engaged in it and so must decide how to judge it (Blumstein and Schwartz, 1983). A study done by the National Opinion Research Center in 1993 found that the majority of Americans do not engage in extramarital sex (*Kansas City Star,* 1993b). Laumann et al. (1994) found that more than 80% of women and 65% to 85% of men of all ages reported that they had no extramarital affairs while they were married.

Extra-premarital sex also occurs. Although these are not called extra*marital* affairs, they can have a similar effect on the relationship. Blumstein and Schwartz (1983) found that these types of affairs were very common in gay couples. Overall, married couples are the most deceptive about sexual affairs outside of their relationship. Both nonmarried heterosexual couples and lesbians who live together have been found to be less deceptive and secretive than married couples.

There appear to be some gender and racial differences in acceptance of extramarital affairs. Males tend to be more accepting of extramarital sex than females (Wilson and Medora, 1990), while black men are more likely than white men to engage in extramarital sex and to have more partners outside of marriage (Weinberg and Williams, 1988). In Figure 8.5 we present statistics on when extramarital affairs tend to occur.

Thompson (1984) claims that there are three types of extramarital affairs: sexual but not emotional; sexual and emotional; and emotional but not sexual. Twenty-one percent of respondents having extramarital sex were involved in predominantly sexual affairs; 19% in both sexual and emotional affairs; and 18% in affairs that were emotional but not sexual (the remaining affairs did not fit clearly into any of these categories). Affairs that are both emotional and sexual appear to affect the marital relationship the most, while affairs that are primarily sexual affect it the least.

Gender differences play a role in the type of extramarital sexual relationships that occur. Women are more likely than men to have emotional but not sexual affairs, and twice as many men have sexual affairs. Research has also found that the more positive a woman's attitude is toward sexuality, the longer she will stay in a primarily sexual extramarital affair. However, attitudes about sex are often unrelated to the length of the emotional type of extramarital affair. Age differences have also been found—men are more likely to have extramarital affairs when they are younger, while women are more likely to do so when they are older. In addition, women who have extramarital affairs are less sex-typed and are more independent and assertive than women who do not (Hurlbert, 1992).

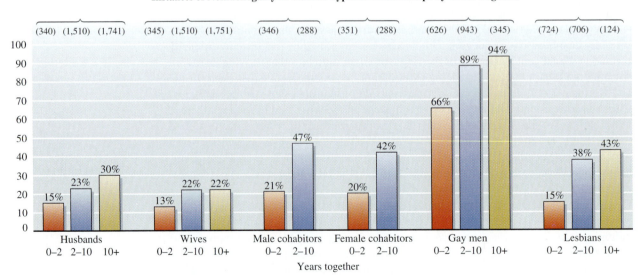

Instances of Nonmonogamy in Various Types of Relationships by Years Together

Note: Very few of our cohabitors had been together more than 10 years.
Number in parentheses are the number of people on which the percentages are based.

Figure **8.5**
The figure above shows what percentage of partners "cheat," organized by type of partner and numbers of years together. Reprinted with permission from **Blumstein and Schwartz (1983:274)**

Although people often report that they believe that affairs "just happen," and that a casual meeting or a relationship with someone who was a friend just blossoms into an affair (See Table 8.2), most researchers and clinicians believe that marital problems are a primary factor behind many extramarital affairs (Macklin, 1980). In fact, when asked, the majority of people claim that marital dissatisfaction is a justifiable reason for engaging in an extramarital affair (Taylor, 1986). Laumann et al. (1994) found that, overall, couples are faithful to each other as long as the marriage is intact and satisfying.

Can a marital relationship continue after an extramarital affair? Yes, but it can be difficult. Often the male partner who has an extramarital affair adds further distress to his wife by mislabeling her reactions and emotions (Gass and Nichols, 1988). For example, he may try to distort reality so that his wife thinks she is imagining things. Overall, however, men are more disapproving of extramarital relationships and less optimistic about the continuation of a marriage after an affair than women (Buunk, 1987).

Open Marriages

Some married couples open up their relationships and encourage their partners to have extramarital affairs or to bring other partners into their marital beds, believing that sexual variety and experience enhance their own sexual life. In 1972, George and Nena O'Neill published a book entitled *Open Marriages* (O'Neill and O'Neill, 1972). In this book, they explained that "sexual adventuring" was fine, as long as both spouses knew about it. In open marriages, each partner is free to seek out sexual partners outside of the marriage. Although open marriages became slightly more popular in the 1970s, they have decreased in popularity today. Janus and Janus (1993) found that 6% of men and women had participated in an open marriage lifestyle. A fear of STDs may have contributed to the decrease.

Most couples who allow this, however, have strict rules meant to protect the marriage; sexuality in those cases is seen as separate from the loving relations of marriage. However, many couples also find that maintaining that kind of openness is more difficult than they anticipated.

GAY AND LESBIAN RELATIONSHIPS

In many ways, gay and lesbian relationships have changed more than heterosexual relationships over the last few decades. First, gay and lesbian relationships came out of the closet in the 1960s and 1970s, where there was almost a euphoria of multiple partners (primarily in gay men) and a blossoming of a gay subculture. Then, the advent of AIDS resulted in fewer sexual partners and more long-term, monogamous relationships in the gay community. Although we discussed many aspects of gay and lesbian relationships in Chapter 7, here we will explore sexuality in gay and lesbian relationships, the advent of gay and lesbian marriages, and some of the controversies over gay and lesbian childrearing.

Sexuality in Gay and Lesbian Relationships

Earlier in this chapter, we discussed gender differences in initiating sexual activity in heterosexual relationships. In heterosexual couples, men often initiate sex. Does this mean that lesbians may be uncomfortable initiating sex or that gay men never have

T a b l e **8.2**

ADULTERY: HOW IT HAPPENS AND WITH WHOM

ADULTERY: HOW IT HAPPENS

HOW	PERCENTAGE OF RESPONDENTS
Casual meeting/met at a bar	28%
Just happened/accident	12
Growing friendship	10
Introduced by friend	7
Sexual attraction	7
Pursued by eventual lover	7
Old flame	3
Midlife crisis	2

...AND WITH WHOM

WHOM	PERCENTAGE OF RESPONDENTS
Friend	24%
Co-worker	23
Old flame	21
Stranger	20
Friend of spouse	15
Prostitute	9
Boss	7

Reprinted with permission from Patterson and Kim (1991)

problems doing so? According to Blumstein and Schwartz (1983), this may be the case. They found that some lesbians do have difficulty initiating or balancing sex in their relationships. As with heterosexual relationships, often one partner initiates more than the other. One woman explains:

The problem is that I want more than she does. And she feels guilty about wanting less. Recently, we've been to a counselor to talk about it. I think we've come to a point of deciding that we probably are not going to be able to solve it . . . that we've gone around in circles long enough.

Blumstein and Schwartz (1983:214)

Problems with initiating sex in lesbian relationships may be due to the social pressures women have while growing up. One thirty-three-year-old woman said:

> *Women have a hesitancy to initiate. My forthrightness makes sex happen. [Lesbians] don't ask; they wait. All that "boy asking them to dance" stuff. It's not alright for women to ask for things for themselves. . . . Sometimes I have gotten these messages from my partner. It's very subtle. Subtly to imply I am too intense. If you're the only person asking, you get to feel pretty weird. I ask, "What do you want," and they say "Whatever you want." So I start to pull back on asking for what I want.*
>
> *Blumstein and Schwartz (1983:215)*

In lesbian couples, it is often the more emotionally expressive partner who is responsible for maintaining the couple's sex life.

Like those involving lesbian women, in relationships between gay men the more emotionally expressive partner is usually the one who initiates sexual activity (see Figure 8.2). However, gay men are much less bothered by their role of initiator. Again, this may lead to other problems, with one partner feeling he is always the initiator. One gay man said:

> *I don't want sex enough, according to him. He would like me to be more aggressive. But sometimes I'm just beat and I don't feel like having sex. . . . I used to be more dominant, but he would turn me off because he felt so uncomfortable about [receiving anal intercourse], and although we never articulated it, it embedded itself as a memory that he felt he wouldn't be able to satisfy me, so we'd better not start. So in a sense he trained me not to be as dominant or as insistent as I might have been. So now, in a sense, the seesaw has changed direction and I have to remind him occasionally that I've gotten used to his not wanting it and now I don't want it so much.*
>
> *Blumstein and Schwartz (1983:216)*

Gay men engage in sexual behavior more often than lesbian women do. Lower rates of sexual behavior in lesbian couples have been explained in three ways. First, the biological nature of the sex drive may be higher in male couples. Second, it may have to do with the fact that, traditionally, males initiate sexual activity, while females feel less comfortable doing so. Finally, as we discussed earlier, women may be less likely than men to express their feelings through sex.

Same-Sex Marriage

As we discussed in Chapter 7, in 1993 the supreme court of the state of Hawaii invalidated the law preventing homosexual marriage. The highest court ruled that a ban on gay and lesbian marriages would violate the state constitution's prohibition against sex discrimination. Now the state must decide whether or not homosexual couples can legally be married (the case will probably be heard sometime in 1995). Although no other state allows marriages between gays and lesbians, each state recognizes marriages performed in other U.S. states, and so homosexual couples who marry in Hawaii would have to have their marriages recognized in other states. This would entitle these couples to marital benefits such as tax breaks, health benefits, and also survivor benefits in the case of death.

Many gay and lesbian couples in other places "marry" their partners in ceremonies that are not recognized by the states in which they live. Gay marriages, whether legally

A gay couple kisses after exchanging vows along with eight other homosexual couples at a mass gay wedding in Trafalgar Square in England in June 1991. A crowd of 500 watched the symbolic ceremonies, held to publicize gay couples' demands for equal recognition with heterosexual couples.

recognized or not, often suffer from the same jealousies, power struggles, and "divorces" as heterosexual marriages; they may even be more unstable because of the added pressures of social disapproval (Collins, 1988). Gay and lesbian couples interviewed by Blumstein and Schwartz (1983) complained about their partners' lack of attention, sexual incompatibility, and the same mundane, day-to-day struggles that straight couples deal with. In addition, these couples often have to cope with the disapproval of their families and, sometimes, the stress of hiding their relationship.

Homosexual activists have begun to try to get states to set up "domestic partner" acts, where same-sex couples who live together in committed relationships can have some of the benefits granted to married couples. Many cities have been considering passing some type of domestic partnership ordinances. Seattle, for example, grants sick leave and bereavement leave to city employees who have domestic partners. Also, Berkeley and a few other California cities extend family leaves to unmarried employees and health insurance to their partners. San Francisco voters defeated a 1989 ballot proposition that would have granted health insurance to partners of city employees, but they passed a law to allow citizens to register domestic partnerships. Insurance companies often will not agree to cover domestic partners, so that in Seattle, for example, the city had to become partially self-insured (Zinn and Eitzen, 1993).

DIVORCE

What causes a couple to end their marriage? The question is complicated because not all unstable or unhappy marriages end in divorce. Couples stay together for many reasons—for the children, because of lack of initiative, because of religious prohibitions against divorce—even though they have severe problems in their marriages. Similarly, couples with seemingly happy marriages separate and divorce, sometimes to the surprise of one of the partners who did not even know the marriage was in trouble.

There has been a lot of concern over the rising divorce rates in the United States, but it is important to realize that rates have been on a steady rise for the last 130 years (see Figure 8.6). If current levels persist, 60% of the current marriages in the United States will end in divorce. However, since about 1981, the U.S. divorce rate has been declining, which may signal the beginning of a downward trend (Zinn and Eitzen, 1993).

Divorce rates vary among age groups. They are at their highest in women in their teens and decline with increasing age (see Figure 8.7). Perhaps the most consistent finding about divorce is that those who marry early are more likely to divorce eventually. Still, since most people marry later, the majority of divorces take place in couples who were married between the ages of twenty and twenty-four. Generally, divorce occurs early in the marriage; the median duration of marriage at divorce in 1988 was 7.1 years (see Figure 8.8). First marriages have been found to last approximately two years longer before divorce than do second marriages, which last two years longer than third or higher marriages (Centers for Disease Control, 1991).

African-Americans, Native Americans, and Puerto Ricans show the highest separation and divorce rates in the United States; Korean, Asian-Indian, and Chinese Americans have the lowest rates; and Mexican Americans, Cubans, and whites lie somewhere in between (Skolnick, 1992). Interracial marriages also have higher divorce rates than marriages within racial groups (Zinn and Eitzen, 1993). The marital instability of African-Americans has received considerable attention, in part because it has increased dramatically over the last thirty years. In 1960, 65% of African-American women aged

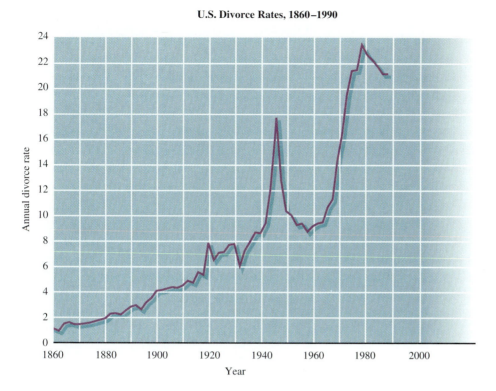

U.S. Divorce Rates, 1860–1990

Figure 8.6
Annual divorce rates in the United States from 1860 to 1990. National Center for Health
Statistics, births, marriages, divorces, and deaths for September 1994. Monthly vital statistics
report; 43 (9). Hyattsville, MD: Public Health Service, 1995. **Reprinted with permission from
Zinn and Eitzen (1993).**

thirty to thirty-four were in intact marriages, while in 1990, the percentage dropped to
39% (Zinn and Eitzen, 1993). While many cultural factors contribute to the high rates of
divorce, such as the legacy of slavery or the unwillingness of black women to put up
with male-dominated marriages, the main reasons for the increased divorce rates are
probably the unemployment, economic dislocation, and increasing poverty within the
African-American community.

A mutually shared decision to divorce is actually uncommon. Usually, one partner
wants to terminate a relationship more than the other partner, who is still strongly
attached to the marriage and who is more distraught at its termination. In fact, the declaration that a partner wants a divorce often comes as a shock to his or her spouse. When
one partner is the initiator, it is usually the female. One study found that women initiated
75% of nonmutual divorces (Kelly, 1989).

Why Do People Get Divorced?

It is very difficult to determine why some marriages fail; every couple has its own story.
Sometimes the spouses themselves are at a loss to understand why their marriage failed.
Below we explore some of the social, predisposing, and relationship factors that may
contribute to divorce.

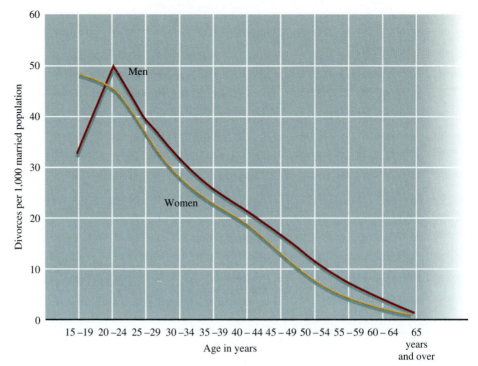

Age-specific Divorce Rates for Men and Women in 1988

Figure **8.7**
This graph shows the percentage of men and women who divorced in each age group in 1988.
Clarke (1995)

Social Factors Affecting Divorce

no-fault divorce: The legal dissolution of a marriage without having to establish one partner's guilt.

Divorce rates are influenced by changes in the legal, political, religious, and familial patterns in the United States. For example, most states have instituted **no-fault divorce**, where neither partner needs to be found guilty of a transgression (such as having sex outside marriage) in order to dissolve the marriage. The growth of low-cost legal clinics and the overabundance of lawyers have made divorce cheaper and thus more accessible (Benokraitis, 1993). Additionally, the more equitable distribution of marital assets has made some people less apprehensive about losing everything to their spouses.

In recent years, divorce has become generally more acceptable in American society. While thirty or forty years ago it was very difficult for a divorced person to attain high political office, the fact that Ronald Reagan was divorced was not even an issue in his presidential campaign. Also, many religious groups are less opposed to divorce than they used to be; many Catholic parishes, for example, no longer ostracize parishioners who divorce (Benokraitis, 1993).

Predisposing Factors for Divorce

Certain situations may predispose a couple to have more marital problems. Couples who marry at a young age often suffer more marital disruption than older couples (Morgan and Rindfuss, 1985), due in part to emotional immaturity. Also, couples who marry because of an unplanned pregnancy are more likely to divorce (Becker et al., 1977).

Percent Distribution of Divorces by Duration of Marriage in 1988

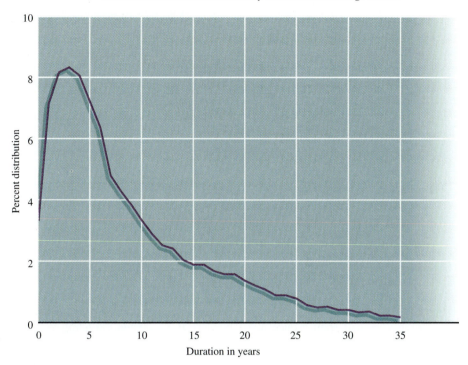

Figure **8.8**

This graph shows how long couples are married before they are divorced. Note that the highest number of divorces occur in the first few years of marriage. **Clarke (1995)**

Marital stability increases as couples have children but then decreases if the couple has more than five (Zinn and Eitzen, 1993). The interval between marriage and the arrival of children is also an important factor; waiting longer promotes marital stability by giving couples time to get to know each other prior to the arrival of children and may also allow them to become more financially secure (Morgan and Rindfuss, 1985). Catholics and Jews are less likely to divorce than Protestants, and divorce rates tend to be high for marriages of mixed religions. Marriages between people having no religious affiliation at all have particularly high divorce rates (Skolnick, 1992).

People who have been divorced before or whose parents have divorced have more accepting attitudes toward divorce than those who grew up in happy, intact families (Amato and Booth, 1991). In addition, people who have divorced parents are significantly more likely to report marital problems in their own relationships than people from intact families, and they also tend to be more skeptical about marriage in general (Kinnaird and Gerrard, 1986).

Although for years divorce was seldom discussed, today many lawyers actually advertise in magazines, on television, on billboards, or on store fronts.

Relationship Factors in Divorce

In general, couples who divorce have known for a long time that there were difficulties in their marriage, although they may not have contemplated divorce. These problems are made worse, in most cases, by communication problems. Some warning signs are communication avoidance (not talking about problems in the relationship); demand and withdrawal patterns of communication, where one partner demands that they address the problem and the other partner pulls away; and little mutually constructive communication (Christensen and Shenk, 1991).

A California divorce study demonstrated that women and men tend to complain about different things about their mates (Kelly, 1989). Women's most frequent complaint was that they were feeling unloved by their partner. That was followed by a feeling that their competence and intelligence were belittled by their husbands and that their husbands were hypercritical of them. Men, on the other hand, complained most that their wives were inattentive or neglectful of their needs and that they and their wives had incompatible interests, value, or goals. Both sexes mentioned sexual incompatibility or loss of sexual interest as a problem.

Many of the problems of people's marriages are there before they decide to get married. As one woman put it:

> *I had a queasy feeling before the marriage. There were signs. When we were studying for the Bar [both are lawyers], he became critical of me in ways he hadn't been before. "Whoa! Where did this come from? I don't need this!" We had discussions about it before the marriage. He'd say, "That's the way I am." It didn't get settled.*
>
> *Blumstein and Schwartz (1983:357)*

Many couples make the mistake of believing that the little annoyances or character traits that they dislike in their potential spouses will disappear after marriage or that they will be able to change their spouse once married. Marrying a person intending to change their personality or bad habits is a recipe for disaster.

Divorce and Sexual Behavior

Few studies have focused on sexual behavior among people who are divorced. Common sense tells us that a person who is depressed or angry about a divorce may have a decrease in both levels of sexual activity and sexual satisfaction. Stack and Gundlach (1992) found that age was inversely related to sex among the divorced: the older a person was at divorce, the less sexual activity occurred afterwards. Another relationship was found between religiosity and sex: the more religious a divorced person was, the less likely he or she was to have another sex partner. Whether or not a person has sexual partners after a divorce also depends on whether their attitudes are liberal toward sex and the presence or absence of children. Divorced persons without children are more likely to have sexual partners than those with children. After a divorce, men are more likely to have one or more partners, while women are less likely to find new partners, especially if they are middle-aged or older (Laumann et al., 1994).

Adjusting to Divorce

One year after a divorce, 50% of men and 60% of women reported being happier than they were during the marriage (Faludi, 1991). Even ten years later, 80% of the women and 50% of the men said that their divorce was the right decision. However, for some, divorce can be very painful, both emotionally and physically. One recently divorced twenty-seven-year-old man said:

> *My mind is unclear, my body aches, my dreams run rampant, and I feel a loss like I've never felt before. Maybe I'm old-fashioned, but I have always dreamed*

of a wife, a home, and a decent job. I spent time with her, I sent her flowers for no reason, a movie, dinner, and our sex life was very satisfying on both accounts. The bottom line is that I miss her and the only emotion I can feel is love for her and a desire to overcome our problems and go on with life. We were married for three-and-a-half years. I can honestly say that I would rather she had died in an accident than to be facing and feeling this type of hurt for the rest of my life.

Author's files

After a divorce, economic adjustment is often harder for women because women's income tends to decline more than men's. A woman's income declines about 30% after a divorce, while a man's only decreases about 19%; but accounting for the fact that the woman usually has to take care of the children as well, her standard of living decreases about 30% while the average man's actually rises about 175% (Collins, 1988). Many women who, before divorce, lived in a middle-class family find themselves slipping below the poverty line after divorce. The situation is made worse if the ex-husband refuses to pay his alimony or child support; about 20% of divorced fathers never provide any form of assistance for their children, including nonfinancial burdens like meeting with teachers, helping with homework, taking the children on trips, etc. (Benokraitis, 1993). Many states are trying to find ways to deal with "deadbeat dads," fathers who do not pay child support. For example, in Iowa the names of delinquent fathers are published in a statewide paper and the public is asked to help locate them.

On the other hand, some women's careers improve after a divorce, even more than men's do (*Working Woman,* 1991). Some career women who divorce find they have improved performance evaluations and feel more motivated and satisfied with their jobs because they put the time and energy they had invested in their relationship into their work instead. Men tend to be more work focused, and so divorce may not give them as much free time—instead, some men may have to learn how to cook, clean, do their own laundry, etc. Women may also get more emotional support from their friends and coworkers than men do. Over time, the majority of people seem to adjust to divorce. Often, social support from friends and family can be very helpful.

ADULT SEXUAL RELATIONSHIPS IN OTHER PLACES

Courtship

In most industrialized countries, mate selection through dating is the norm. There are still a few industrialized cultures where arranged marriages take place, although those are often in the upper classes. In Japan's business class, for example, arranged marriages are common (Hamabata, 1990). But there are also some cultures where all the classes' marriages are arranged by families.

In some cultures, courtship is a highly ritualized process in which every step is defined by one's kin group or tribe (Hutter, 1981). For example, the marriages of the Yaruros of Venezuela are arranged and highly specified; a man must marry his "cross-cousin," that is, the daughter of either his father's sister or his mother's brother. The marriages are arranged by the shaman or religious leader in consultation with one of the boy's uncles. The Hottentots of South Africa also marry their cross-cousins, but here the boy can choose which cousin he wants to marry; once he does, he informs his parents, who send someone to seek permission from the girl's parents. Tradition dictates that they must refuse. The youth then approaches the girl, going to her house late at night once everyone is asleep and lying down next to her. She then gets up and moves to the other side of the house. The next night he returns, and if he finds her back on the side where he first lay next to her, he lies down again with her and the marriage is consummated (Hutter, 1981).

For 2,000 years, marriages in China were arranged by parents and elders, and emotional involvement between prospective marriage partners was frowned upon; if a couple appeared to like having their marriage arranged, the marriage was called off! In China, the primary responsibility of each person was supposed to be to his or her extended family. If there was a marriage bond that was very strong outside of that extended family, it could jeopardize the cohesiveness of the group. This all began to change with the communist revolution of 1949. Through contact with the West, these customs began to erode. Only eight months after coming to power, the Communist leaders established the *Marriage Law of the People's Republic of China,* in which, among other things, they tried to end arranged marriages and establish people's right to choose their spouse freely. Today in China, although arranged marriages still take place in the rural areas, people date and meet each other in public places—a condition that was virtually unknown a few generations before. Focus on Diversity 8.1 lists what women in China, now free to choose their own partners, desire in a mate.

*Focus
on Diversity
8.1*

**Criteria in
Mate Selection in
Chinese Women**

In 1982, a Chinese sociologist asked 158 unmarried women working in a silk mill in Hiangsu Province their attitudes toward marriage. Most accepted the Chinese government's standard of having few children and getting married late (around twenty-four years of age was the modal response), and many agreed that it was good to have parents involved in mate selection. Below are listed, in order, the traits that these women most valued in a potential mate.

RANK	CRITERIA	PERCENT AGREEING
1	Male is in good health	89.2
2	Male is honest and sincere	82.9
3	Male's parents are genial	62.0
4	The two can get along	61.4
5	Male clever and deft	49.4
6	Male is from same village	24.1
7	Male is good looking	17.7
8	Male's family is well-off	6.3
9	Male is a worker	4.4
10	Nature of male's parent(s) occupation	2.5
11	Male has much housing	1.9

Xian (1983–84)

In many parts of Africa, too, parents used to be involved in mate selection (Kayongo-Male and Onyango, 1984). Marriages were made between families, not really individuals, and each family had a set of expectations about the other's role. Courtship was highly ritualized, with the groom's family paying a "bridewealth" to the bride's family. The rituals that preceded marriage were intended to teach the couple what their particular tribe or culture believed married couples needed to know in order to keep their marriage successful. However, young people did have some say in who they were to marry; in many cases, young people would reject their parents' choices or meet someone they liked and ask their parents to arrange a marriage. One Egyptian boy commented:

We all know the girls of our village. After all, we played together as kids, and we see them going back and forth on errands as they get older. One favorite place for us to get a glimpse of girls is at the village water source. The girls know that and like to linger there. If we see one we like and think she might be suitable, we ask our parents to try to arrange a marriage, but usually not before we have some sign from the girl that she might be interested.

Rugh (1984:137)

Today, however, mate selection in most places is a much more individual affair. However much we in the West believe in the right of individuals to choose their own mates, there were some advantages to parental participation in mate selection, and the transition to individual mate selection in traditional societies is often difficult.

Cohabitation

Cohabitation is rarer in more traditional societies where, even if a couple has sex before or instead of marriage, social customs would never tolerate an unmarried heterosexual couple living together openly. Asian societies still frown upon it, although it is sometimes allowed, and it is severely discouraged in Islamic societies. Most Western countries, on the other hand, now have substantial numbers of couples who live together. In France, for example, the number of cohabiting couples rose from 67,000 in 1968 to 589,000 in 1985. By 1990, one out of five couples was living together outside of marriage (Forsé et al., 1993).

In some countries, cohabitation is often a step toward marriage or is seen as a "lower form" of marriage. As one female student in the former Yugoslavia put it: "I have nothing against living together out of wedlock, but marriage is something more elevated" (Blagojevic, 1989:226).

Marriage

Marriage ceremonies take place in every society on earth, but marriage customs vary widely from culture to culture. In some cultures, girls can be married as young as nine years old (although they do not have sex with their husbands until puberty). Other cultures mandate marriages between certain relatives, while still other cultures allow multiple spouses. Most cultures celebrate marriage as a time of rejoicing and have rituals or ceremonies that accompany the wedding process. Among different Berber tribes in Morocco, for example, wedding rituals can include performing a sacrifice, painting the heels of the couple's feet with goat's blood, having a feast, having fish cast at the feet of the bride, and feeding bread to the family dog (Westermack, 1972).

Marriage ceremonies outside the United States may vary greatly. Above is a traditional wedding in northern India.

In many preliterate cultures (and in some literate ones, too) there is a tendency to believe that the main purpose of being female is to get married and have babies. Among the Tiwi, a group of Australian aborigines, this was taken to its logical conclusion; a woman was to get married, and there was no word in their language for a single woman, for there was, in fact, no female—of any age—without at least a nominal husband. The Tiwi believed that pregnancy happens because a spirit entered the body of a female, but one could never be sure exactly when that happened; so the best thing to do was to make sure that the woman was married at all times. Therefore, all Tiwi babies were betrothed before or as soon as they were born, and widows were required to remarry at the gravesides of their husbands, no matter how old they were (Hart and Pilling, 1960).

Some countries allow the practice of polygamy. Usually, this takes the form of **polygyny**, or having more than one wife, which is a common practice in many areas of Africa and the Middle East, among other places. Although it is rarely practiced in the United States, there are some small Mormon fundamentalist groups in the Middle West that do practice polygyny. Most commonly, a polygynous marriage involves two or three wives, though in Islam a man is allowed up to four.

polygyny: The practice of having more than one wife at a time.

Some have suggested that polygyny began as a strategy to increase fertility, but the suggestion is controversial. In fact, a number of studies have found that polygyny is associated with lower fertility among wives (Anderton and Emigh, 1989), although other studies have found no differences (Ahmed, 1986), and a few have even found higher rates of fertility (Arowolo, 1981). However, the majority of the research supports the conclusion that wives in polygynous marriages have lower fertility rates. This is because husbands in polygynous marriages must divide their time between each of their wives, which decreases the chance of impregnation for each individual wife. Therefore, it may be more likely that polygyny developed as a strategy for men to gain prestige and power by having many wives, while women could gain the protection of a wealthy man.

In Islam, a woman may have sex with only one man, but a man may marry up to four wives. Al-Ghazali, the great Islamic thinker and writer of the eleventh century, believed that polygyny was permitted due to the desires of men. What determines whether a Muslim man has multiple wives in most Islamic countries today is his wealth more than anything else, for he usually sets up a different household for each wife. Another reason for polygyny in many Muslim countries is the desire for a male child; if one wife does not deliver a male heir, the man may choose to try a second and third wife to try for a boy (Donnan, 1988).

polyandry: The practice of having more than one husband at a time.

consanguineous marriage: A marriage that takes place between persons who are related by blood or family lineage.

Polyandry is much less common than polygyny, and when it happens, it is usually for reasons of keeping together inheritance. For example, in Tibet, a woman may marry several brothers in order to avoid cutting up the inherited property. The same rationale is used in many **consanguineous marriages**, in which a woman marries her own relative to maintain the integrity of a family property. In the majority of U.S. states, consanguineous marriage is illegal and has been since the late nineteenth century. However, in many Muslim countries in northern Africa, western and southern Asia, North, East, and Central India, and the middle Asian republics of the former Soviet Union, marriages take place between relatives between 20% and 55% of the time (Bittles et al., 1991). In Islamic societies marriages between first cousins are most common, while in Hindu states of South India uncle–niece and first cousin marriages are equally common. Incidentally, marriages between certain cousins are legal in many U.S. states.

Attitudes toward marriage vary in different cultures in different times. For example, in Germany in 1963, 89% of people believed that the institution of marriage was necessary and only 3% believed it was obsolete; by 1985, only 64% of people believed it was necessary and 14% said it was obsolete (Glatzer et al., 1993). In a study done a few years ago in the former Yugoslavia, approximately half of all young men and women held a positive view of marriage, while 19% of men and 8% of women held negative views (Blagojevic, 1989). Many of the women in this study gave idealistic views of what they thought marriage should be like. For instance, several women wrote:

> *Marriage is what true, great love should strive for. A person affirms himself through marriage, he or she gains a fuller understanding of the value of life. He or she is ready to make sacrifices, feels stronger and safer.*

> *If two people love each other, then marriage is the best solution for their life.*

> *Marriage is the most optimum form for two people to live together.*

> *Blagojevic (1989:219–220)*

Some responses from men include:

> *Marriage is a port where a person can always find a refuge.*

> *Life becomes more beautiful and interesting, and life's problems are far easier to bear and resolve.*

> *Marriage is a happy obligation.*

> *Blagojevic (1989:220–221)*

Research on marital roles in the People's Republic of China has found that compared with American students, Chinese students hold a more male-dominated attitude about marriage (Chia et al., 1985). However, recently more Chinese women are adopting more egalitarian ideas of marriage, which may be a sign that Chinese culture is gradually becoming less repressive and oppressive to women.

Finally, same-sex marriages are legal in some countries outside of the United States. In 1989, Denmark became the first country to allow same-sex marriages. Norway soon followed and then Sweden. In these countries, gay couples are given the same benefits as heterosexual married couples (such as inheritance and tax breaks). However, these countries do not allow gay couples to adopt children or become impregnated through artificial insemination.

Polygyny, or having more than one wife, is a common practice in many areas of Africa and the Middle East, among other places. This man has forty-nine wives, aged fourteen to thirty-five years old. He has a total of thirty-two children—so far.

Extramarital Sex

Extramarital sex is forbidden in many cultures, but often it is tolerated even in cultures where it is technically not allowed. For example, infidelity is considered a grave transgression in Islam and is punishable according to the Koran by 100 lashes for both partners (Farah, 1984). However, there are a number of Muslim societies, such as many in Africa (Kayongo-Male and Onyango, 1984) or Pakistan (Donnan, 1988) where adultery is tacitly accepted as a fact of life.

Those countries that tolerate extramarital sex often find it more acceptable for men than for women. In Zimbabwe, for example, women were asked what they would do if they found out their partners were engaging in extramarital sex: 80% reported they would confront their partners, 15% said they would caution their husbands, and 5% were indifferent. But when men were asked the same question, 60% replied they would divorce their wives, 20% would severely beat their wives, 18% would severely caution her, and 2% would express disappointment and ask their partner to change (Mhloyi, 1990).

In some cultures, extramarital relations are replacing polygamy. In some African societies where having multiple wives is becoming less accepted, men may set up a secret second household where a woman is kept as his wife without a ceremony—and without any of the legal rights that accrue to a wife (Kayongo-Male and Onyango, 1984).

Divorce

Divorce is common in almost all societies, but it is changing its nature as societies develop. In societies such as the United States, Japan, Sweden, Russia, and most European countries divorce is relatively simple and has little stigma. The exceptions are countries that are largely Roman Catholic; because Catholicism does not allow divorce, it can be difficult to obtain in Catholic countries. In Latin America, for example, many countries have restrictive divorce legislation, which means that only the wealthy find it easy to divorce because they can fly to Mexico or other countries where divorce is easier (Hutter, 1981).

Many traditional societies had ways to assure that divorces did not disrupt the community. In Africa, for example, traditional societies had rituals for peacefully dissolving marriages, but today divorces can be disruptive and messy as couples fight in court over marital assets and custody (Kayongo-Male and Onyango, 1984). Traditional laws about divorce can still be enforced, especially in more patriarchal cultures. In Egypt, for example, it is far easier for men to divorce than for women; Islamic law, like traditional Jewish law, allows a man to divorce his wife simply by repudiating her publicly three times. A wife, on the other hand, must go to court to dissolve a marriage (Rugh, 1984). Therefore, only about 33% of divorces in Egypt are initiated by females. In Israel, women need their husband's permission for a divorce, and councils have been set up to try to convince men to let their wives have a divorce.

The reasons that people get divorced are numerous, although different patterns emerge in different societies. In Egypt, the most common reason given for divorce is infidelity by the husband, while among the Hindus of India, the most common reason for divorce is cruelty (either physical or mental) from their partner (Pothen, 1989). In Focus on Diversity 8.2, the most important reasons for divorce in four different cultures are listed.

Some countries have interesting ways of decreasing divorce rates. For example, one insurance company in China began offering a marriage insurance policy in 1993 (*Philadelphia Inquirer*, 1994). If a couple stays together for the duration of the policy (25, 40, or 50 years), they will receive *at least* seven times their initial premium. In the first year the policy was available, more than 40,000 policies were sold to Beijing couples.

Overall, divorce rates seem to be going up in most countries in the world as they modernize and as traditional forms of control over the family lose their power. Only time will tell, however, whether a backlash will stabilize marriage rates as they seem to be doing in the United States.

Summary

- Dating provides an opportunity to get to know another person. For the most part, early dating is practice for progressively more serious dating, which leads to mate selection.
- After college it can be more difficult to find dates since social interactions are fewer. Today, more and more college graduates are being forced to date long-distance because of the necessity of relocating for employment.
- How soon a dating relationship becomes sexual depends on the couple's sexual scripts. There are often gender differences in sexual scripts.
- After a death or divorce, it may be difficult for individuals to begin dating again. There are different organizations that can help ease the transition to the dating "scene."
- Although interracial relationships are legal, there are still very strong social forces that keep the races separate and make it difficult for individuals to meet or maintain relationships.

Reasons for Divorce in Four Cultures

Below are the reasons given for divorce in four cultures: among the men of the Muria, a tribal group in India; among couples in the African country of Cameroon; among Chinese couples registering for divorce in Shanghai, China; and among couples in the United States.

Rank of Reasons for Divorce Among Men of the Muria Tribe (Stephens, 1963)

1. She ran away. (No other reasons given)
2. I could not satisfy her. (sexually)
3. My older wife could not stand it when I married a second wife.
4. My elder wife drove out the second.
5. We quarreled over work.
6. She was a bitch.
7. We did not like each other.
8. Impotence.
9. She did not like me.
10. I was ill and she didn't like to stay with me.
11. She was a thief.
12. She was of bad character.

Reasons for Divorce in Couples in Cameroon, Africa (Kayongo-Male and Onyango, 1984)

1. Ill treatment of wife by husband.
2. Marriage forced by parents against daughter's wishes.
3. Extensive neglect of wife by husband.
4. Marriage of husband to a second wife.
5. The husband was a Muslim and the parents did not like him.
6. The wife delivered the child in a hospital and had it baptized.
7. The wife's parents hated the husband.
8. The mother-in-law quarreled with the wife a lot.
9. The husband wanted sexual relations with his wife when the baby was only three months old.
10. One of the children died suddenly and people blamed the wife.
11. The husband threatened to kill his wife.
12. The husband sold the cassava farm without his wife's permission.

Rank of Reasons Given in Shanghai, China, for Divorce (Class of 1978, 1983–84)

1. Insufficient premarital foundation.
2. Don't get along in style, personality, or moral values.
3. Inadequate or no sex life.
4. Economic problems.
5. Other.

The Top Ten Reasons Behind Divorces in America (Patterson and Kim, 1991)

1. Communication problems.
2. Spouse's infidelity.
3. Constant fighting.
4. Emotional abuse.
5. Falling out of love.
6. Unsatisfactory sex.
7. Spouse didn't make enough money.
8. Physical abuse.
9. Falling in love with somebody else.
10. Boredom.

- Over the last few years, cohabitation has become more popular. Findings on whether or not cohabiting leads to happier marriages are contradictory.
- The majority of people marry at least once in their lives. Married people have been found to be happier, healthier, and live longer than either widowed or divorced persons of the same age. Marriage has been found to provide more health benefits to men than women.
- Some qualities that help ensure a happy marriage include emotional closeness, verbal self-disclosure, sexual satisfaction, long-term commitment, viewing partner as a best friend, and liking your partner as a person.
- Over the course of most marriages and long-term relationships, frequency of sexual behavior decreases. Some marriages become asexual.
- Several factors influence whether or not a couple decides to have children. These include both educational level and career aspirations.
- Since women often outlive their spouses, many elderly women will end up widowed later in life. Older men are twice as likely as women to remarry after the death of a spouse.
- Overall, attitudes about extramarital sex are mostly negative. Men are more likely to have sexual affairs, while women are more likely to have emotional affairs.
- In homosexual couples, lower rates of sexual behavior have been found in lesbians. This may be due to several factors such as a claimed greater sex drive in men, lack of initiating activity in women, or because women are less likely to use sex as a way to express emotions.
- In 1993, the supreme court of the state of Hawaii invalidated the law preventing homosexual marriage, and the Hawaiian legislature is deciding whether or not homosexual couples can be legally married there.
- Couples who divorce have been found to be likely to have communication difficulties. In addition, couples who marry at a young age or marry because of a pregnancy divorce more often than other couples. Divorce is less frequent in older couples.
- Although polygyny is rarely practiced in the United States, it is a common practice in many areas of Africa and the Middle East. Polyandry is also practiced in some countries, where a woman marries several brothers in order to avoid cutting up property.
- Attitudes toward extramarital sex and divorce vary cross-culturally, and they have to do with the overall societal atmosphere.

Reflections on Sexuality

1. Compare the societal traditions for dating in the states and in some of the countries mentioned, and explain why the rituals occur the way they do.
2. How does past sexual history help determine whether or not a couple who is dating will engage in sexual intercourse?
3. What are some factors that make it difficult for divorced or widowed partners to begin dating again? What can be done to ease their transition back into the dating scene?
4. Why do you think marriages between two people of a young age often end in divorce?
5. Would you live with your partner? Why or why not? What does the research conclude on the stability of marriages between couples who cohabitate prior to marriage?
6. What does the research show about frequency of sexual activity in long-term relationships?
7. What are some reasons that people engage in extramarital sexual relationships? Do you feel extramarital relationships are wrong in all cases? Explain.
8. Explain why lesbians engage in less sexual behavior then gay men.
9. What do we know about gay and lesbian marriages and childrearing? What do you think of these practices?
10. What are the most common reasons couples give for getting divorced?

Suggested Readings

BLUMSTEIN, P. AND R. SCHWARTZ. (1983) *American Couples: Money, Work, Sex.* New York: William Morrow and Co.

BUTLER, R. AND M. LEWIS. (1988) *Love and Sex After Sixty.* New York: Harper and Row.

RISMAN, B.J., AND P. SCHWARTZ. (1989) *Gender in Intimate Relationships.* Belmont, CA: Wadsworth Publishing Company.

WESTON, K. (1991) *Families We Choose: Lesbians, Gays, and Kinship.* New York: Columbia University Press.

CHAPTER

9

Adult Sexual Behavior

Sue considers herself happily married. She enjoys sexual intercourse with her husband and usually reaches orgasm. However, just as she approaches the peak, she imagines that she is tied to a table while several men caress her, touch her genitals, and have intercourse with her. It is a fleeting image; as she passes into orgasm it disappears.

Hariton (1973:39)

When I was about 13, our preacher gave me a book to read. It said boys who masturbate would become bald, diseased and insane, lead a life of crime, and end up in hell. When my sexual urges became overpowering, I did indeed indulge in what they called in those days "self-abuse" and suffered tremendous anxiety and wretched feelings of guilt. Every morning I woke up wondering if I had gone insane during the night or developed some outward sign that would let the world know of my "unpardonable sin." That terrifying misinformation carried over to my adult life, and it took a long time before I could be a loving husband.

Landers (1992:C2)

I feel that sex is great, it's important, but you got to think of the other person too, and you've gotta live within the rules that God instructed man to live with. I listen to my friends, guys like to brag, and some of them sound like they don't care about anyone, just their own pleasure. . . . [My girlfriend and I] feel that it is a beautiful thing for a girl to be a virgin until she is married, and to give this as a gift to her husband. But what about nature; sex is a drive, and at my age it really demands attention, so we worked out a way to handle sex without guilt.

—24 year old male; in Janus & Janus (1993:234).

Human sexuality is a complex part of life, with cultural, psychological, and biological influences; people, therefore, express their sexuality in a variety of ways. In this chapter, we will discuss adult sexual behaviors from early adulthood through the senior years. We will explore the frequency and techniques of sexual behaviors as well as the physiology of sexual behavior. Before reading any further, answer the questions in Where Do I Stand? 9.1 on p. 316.

FREQUENCY OF SEXUAL BEHAVIOR

Heterosexual behavior includes a range of different sexual activities, beginning with abstinence, which has increased in popularity in the United States. A study in 1994 found that 14% of men and 10% of women reported that they had had no sexual partners in the past year (Laumann et al., 1994). People may choose abstinence because they want to wait for marriage or the right partner, because they fear sexually transmitted diseases or intimacy, or for religious reasons. Some people who are abstinent still masturbate, while others do not. Overall, abstinence is more prevalent among widowed men and women.

Some people remain abstinent their whole lives and have no partners, others may go through life with just one partner, and still others have multiple partners. Janus and

Janus (1993) found that 28% of men and 42% of women had ten or fewer sexual partners; 32% of men and 39% of women had between eleven and thirty partners; and 21% of men and 9% of women had between thirty-one and sixty partners. However, they also found that 10% of men and 4% of women had over one hundred partners.

In contrast, Laumann et al. (1994) found that 26% of Americans had only one sexual partner; 30% had between two to four; 22% had between five to ten; 11% had between ten to twenty; and 9% had twenty-one or more. Overall, they found that the more educated people are, the more partners they have over their lifetimes. Men are more likely than women to have a large number of sexual partners, and the majority of partners for both men and women are accumulated during their twenty's.

Gender differences in numbers of sexual partners may not be entirely accurate. Men may overreport the number of partners they have, while women may underreport the number of partners. So, in reality, each may report what they feel "should" be the case rather than what is true. In addition to age and gender, marital status also affects the number of partners a person has in his or her lifetime. Widowed adults have been found to have the fewest sexual partners, followed by those who are married, those who are divorced, and those who have never married.

MODELS OF SEXUAL RESPONSE

There is a series of physiological and psychological changes that occur in the body during sexual behavior; this is referred to as our "sexual response." Over the years, several models have been proposed to explain the exact progression and nature of the human sexual response. These models are beneficial in helping therapists identify how dysfunction, disease, illness, and disability affect sexual functioning. The most popular model has been Masters and Johnson's sexual response cycle.

The Sexual Response Cycle

Based on their laboratory work (see Chapter 2), William Masters and Virginia Johnson proposed a four-phase model of physiological arousal known as the **sexual response cycle**. This cycle occurs during all sexual behavior in which a person progresses from excitement to orgasm, whether it is through oral or anal sex, masturbation, or sexual intercourse (see Figure 9.1). In addition, these physiological processes are similar for heterosexual, homosexual, and bisexual persons.

The four phases of the sexual response cycle are **excitement**, **plateau**, **orgasm**, and **resolution**. The two primary physical changes that occur during the sexual response cycle are **vasocongestion** and **myotonia**, which we will discuss in greater detail below.

Sexual Response Cycle in Women

Sexual response patterns vary among women (and in the same woman) at different times. These variations can be attributed to the amount of time spent in each phase (for example, the orgasmic response may be greater if more time is spent during arousal in foreplay). The intensity of the response may also be affected by such things as whether or not a woman has had children and where she is in her menstrual cycle. However, even with these differences, the basic physical response is always the same (see Figure 9.2).

sexual response cycle: The four-stage model proposed by Masters and Johnson that indicates the physiological changes during sexual activity.

excitement: The first stage of the sexual response cycle, in which an erection occurs in males and vaginal lubrication occurs in females.

plateau: The second stage of the sexual response cycle, occurring prior to orgasm, in which vasocongestion builds up.

orgasm: The third stage of the sexual response cycle, which involves an intense sensation during the peak of sexual arousal and results in a release of sexual tension.

resolution: The fourth stage of the sexual response cycle, in which the body returns to the pre-aroused state.

vasocongestion: An increase in the blood concentrated in the male and female genitals, as well as in the female breasts, during sexual activity.

myotonia: Involuntary contractions of the muscles.

WHERE DO I *Stand?* 9.1

Myth or Reality?

Below are some statements about sexual behavior. Take a few minutes to see which you think are true or false.

Female Sexuality

1. Sex is only for those under fifty. T F
2. Women have an orgasm every time they have sex. T F
3. All women can have multiple orgasms. T F
4. Pregnancy and delivery reduce women's sexual responsiveness. T F
5. A woman's sex life ends with menopause. T F
6. There are different kinds of orgasms that are related to a woman's personality. T F
7. Vaginal orgasms are more feminine and mature than clitoral orgasms. T F
8. A sexually responsive woman can always be "turned on" by her partner. T F
9. Nice women aren't aroused by erotica (books, films, and so on). T F
10. A woman is frigid if she doesn't like the more exotic forms of sex. T F
11. If a woman can't have an orgasm quickly and easily, there is something wrong with her. T F
12. Feminine women don't initiate sex or become wild and unrestrained during sex. T F
13. A woman is frigid if she doesn't have sexual fantasies. T F
14. All women have a rape fantasy. T F
15. When women say "no" they really mean "yes." T F

Male Sexuality

1. Men should not have, or at least not express, certain feelings. T F
2. For men, in sex, as elsewhere, it's performance that counts. T F
3. The man must take charge of and orchestrate sex. T F
4. A man always wants and is always ready to have sex. T F
5. For men, all physical contact must lead to sex. T F
6. Sex equals intercourse for men. T F
7. Sex requires an erection. T F
8. Good sex for men is a linear progression of increasing excitement terminated only by orgasm. T F
9. Sex should be natural and spontaneous. T F
10. In this enlightened age, the preceding myths no longer have any influence on us. T F

All of the above statements are myths about female and male sexuality and are false. Notice how these myths often imply what is "normal" and "abnormal" as far as sexual functioning is concerned. You may not have heard or believed every one of these myths; however, significant numbers of people do believe each myth.

Adapted from Heiman and LoPiccolo (1992) and Zilbergeld (1978)

---

transudation: The passing of a fluid through a membrane, especially the lubrication in the vagina during sexual arousal.

tenting effect: During sexual arousal in females, the cervix and uterus pull up, making a larger opening in the cervix—presumably for the sperm to pass through. In addition, the upper third of the vagina balloons open.

Excitement Phase. The first phase, *excitement,* begins with vasocongestion. Many different things can induce excitement, including visual or auditory stimulation, fantasy, or touch. Within thirty seconds, vasocongestion causes the vaginal walls to begin lubricating, a process called **transudation**. If a woman is lying down, the process of lubricating the vaginal walls may take a little longer than if she is standing up, which may be one reason it takes most women longer than men to get ready to have sexual intercourse. During the excitement phase, the walls of the vagina, which usually lie flat together, expand. This has also been called the **tenting effect** (see Figure 9.2).

The breasts also experience changes during sexual excitement. Nipple erections may occur in one or both breasts and the areolas enlarge (see Figure 9.3). The breasts

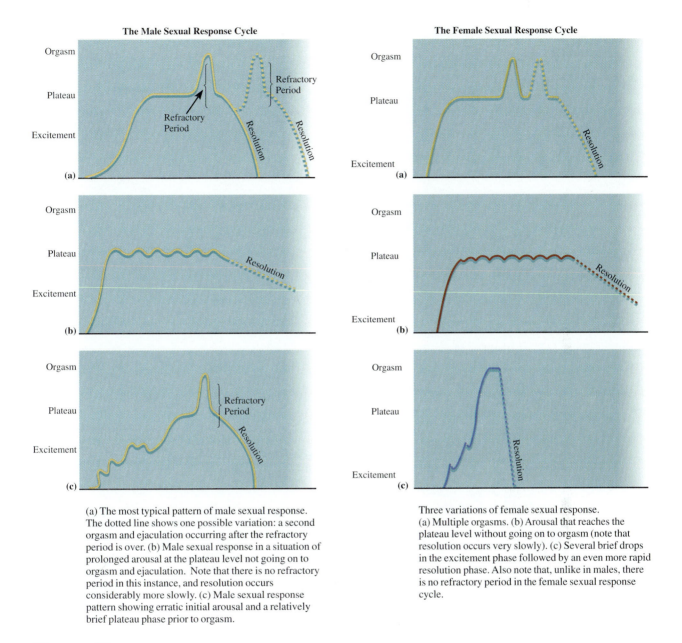

(a) The most typical pattern of male sexual response. The dotted line shows one possible variation: a second orgasm and ejaculation occurring after the refractory period is over. (b) Male sexual response in a situation of prolonged arousal at the plateau level not going on to orgasm and ejaculation. Note that there is no refractory period in this instance, and resolution occurs considerably more slowly. (c) Male sexual response pattern showing erratic initial arousal and a relatively brief plateau phase prior to orgasm.

Three variations of female sexual response. (a) Multiple orgasms. (b) Arousal that reaches the plateau level without going on to orgasm (note that resolution occurs very slowly). (c) Several brief drops in the excitement phase followed by an even more rapid resolution phase. Also note that, unlike in males, there is no refractory period in the female sexual response cycle.

Figure **9.1**

Male and female sexual response cycles. **Reprinted with permission from Masters et al (1994).**

enlarge, which may cause an increased definition of the veins in the breasts, especially if they are large and the woman is fair skinned.

In women who have not had children, the labia majora thin out and become flattened and may pull slightly away from the introitus. The labia minora often turn bright pink and begin to increase in size. The increase in size of the vaginal lips adds an average of one-half to one inch of length to the vaginal canal. It is believed that these changes create a type of funnel into the vagina, which directs the penis (Sherfey, 1972).

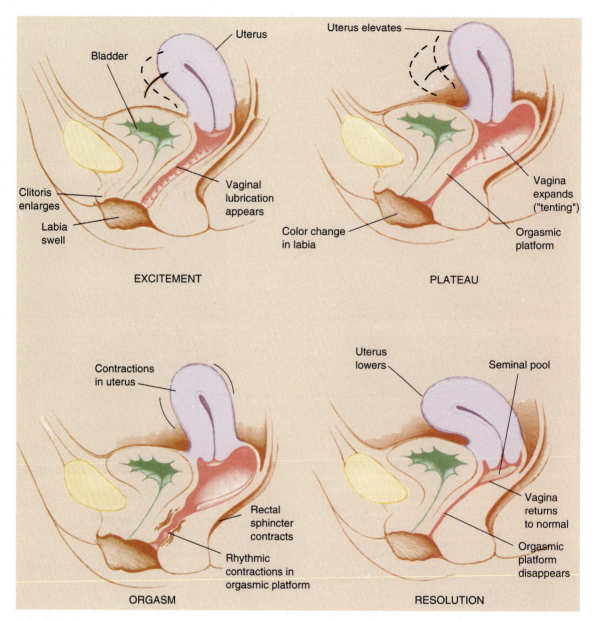

F i g u r e **9.2**
Internal changes in the female sexual response cycle. **Reprinted with permission from Masters et al (1994).**

sex flush: A temporary reddish or rashlike color change that sometimes develops during sexual excitement; mostly occurs on the chest and abdomen but can spread to other parts of the body.

Women who have had children have a more rapid increase in vasocongestion and enlargement of both the labia majora and minora, which may become two to three times larger by the end of the excitement phase. Vasocongestion may also cause the clitoris to erect, depending upon the type and intensity of stimulation. The more direct the stimulation, generally, the more erect the clitoris will become.

The excitement phase can last anywhere from a few minutes to hours. Toward the end of the excitement phase, a woman may experience a **sex flush**, which resembles a rash. This usually begins on the chest and, during the plateau stage, spreads from the

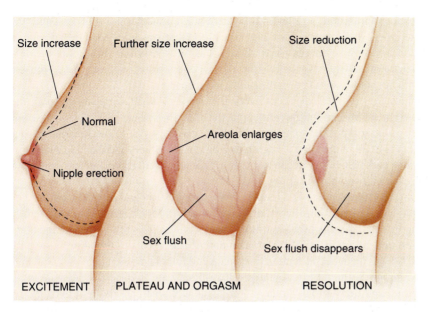

F i g u r e **9.3**
Breast changes during the female sexual response cycle. **Reprinted with permission from Masters et al (1994).**

breasts to the neck and face, shoulders, arms, abdomen, thighs, buttocks, and back. Women report varied sensations during the excitement phase, which are often felt all over the body, rather than being concentrated in one area.

Plateau Phase. Breast size continues to increase during the *plateau* phase and the nipples may remain erect. The clitoris retracts behind the clitoral hood anywhere from one to three minutes before orgasm, and, just prior to orgasm, the clitoris may not be visible at all. Masters and Johnson (1966) believe that hood rubbing and pulling the clitoris is responsible for the orgasm during sexual intercourse.

During sexual arousal in women who have not had children, the labia majora are difficult to detect, due to the flattened-out appearance. The labia minora, on the other hand, often turn a brilliant red. In women who have had children, the labia majora become very engorged with blood and turn a darker red, almost burgundy. At this point, if sexual stimulation were to stop, the swelling of the clitoris and labia, which can continue for anywhere from a few minutes to hours, can be very uncomfortable. Hite (1976:75–76) found that some women felt strongly about this:

> *When orgasm is in doubt, I have conflicting feelings about arousal. It is pleasurable for itself, but after a certain point I am left tense and angry and disappointed, and . . . depressed. Ultimately I have to come and know I will enjoy it.*

Orgasm helps to relieve this pressure, whether it occurs during masturbation or during sexual behaviors with another person. Overall, the plateau stage may last anywhere from thirty seconds to three minutes.

Orgasm Phase. At the end of the plateau phase, vasocongestion in the pelvis creates an **orgasmic platform** in the lower third of the vagina, labia minora (and labia majora in women who have had children), and the uterus (see Figure 9.2). When this pressure

orgasmic platform: The thickening of the walls of the outer third of the vagina, which occurs during the plateau stage of the sexual response cycle.

reaches a certain point, a reflex in the surrounding muscles is set off, causing vigorous contractions. These contractions expel the blood that was trapped in the surrounding tissues and in doing so causes pleasurable orgasmic sensations. Myotonia of the uterine muscles is primarily responsible for these contractions; without these muscles, the orgasmic response would be significantly reduced.

Muscular contractions occur every 0.8 seconds during orgasm. In total, there are about eight to fifteen contractions, and the first five or six are felt most strongly. In women, contractions last longer than in men, possibly due to the fact that vasocongestion occurs in the entire pelvic region in women and is very localized in men (mainly in the penis and testicles). Because of this, women need more muscle contractions to remove the built-up blood supply.

During orgasm, there is a release of vasocongestion and muscle tension. The body may shudder, jerk uncontrollably, or spasm. In addition, orgasms may involve facial grimacing, groans, spasms in the hands and feet, contractions of the gluteal and abdominal muscles, and contractions of the orgasmic platform. Peaks in blood pressure and respiration patterns have been found in both male and female orgasms.

Although Sigmund Freud claimed that there were two types of female orgasms—the clitoral and the vaginal—today all orgasms in women are thought to be the result of direct or indirect clitoral stimulation (see Chapter 2, Sex Facts 2.1). Michael et al. (1994) found that while 75% of men report always reaching orgasms during sexual activity, only 29% of women do.

Some women begin sneezing during arousal and orgasm. This may be because the mucous membranes in the vagina and in the nose are similar and both have the capability of swelling and becoming moist during excitement. Other women report feeling nausea after orgasm, which may be caused by the intensity of the uterine contractions (Sherfey, 1972).

SEX TALK

QUESTION **9.1** **Why would a person fake orgasm?**

Many women have faked orgasms at some point in their lives. Some women who never have orgasms rely on faking them. It could be that either she or her partner are unaware of what would help her to reach orgasm, and so faking becomes habitual. Other women claim that they fake orgasm in order to end a sexual encounter or to make their partners feel good. Men are also able to fake orgasm—if a man is losing his erection during sexual intercourse, he may fake orgasm in order to avoid a confrontation with his partner. Although you might think his partner would be aware of his lack of orgasm because of the lack of ejaculation, this is often not the case.

Resolution Phase. During the last phase, *resolution,* the body returns to preexcitement conditions. The blood leaves the genitals and erections disappear, muscles relax, and heart and breathing rates return to normal. During resolution, women are able to be restimulated to orgasm, and some women can experience **multiple orgasms** (see Figure 9.1). Masters and Johnson believe that multiple orgasms are more likely to occur from manual stimulation of the clitoris, rather than from penile thrusting during sexual intercourse. There has also been some research into the female G-Spot (see Chapter 3) that indicates that some women may have an area inside the vagina that, when stimulated, causes intense orgasms and possibly female ejaculation of fluid.

multiple orgasms: More than one orgasm experienced within a short period of time.

After orgasm, the skin is often sweaty and the sex flush slowly disappears. The breasts begin to decrease in size, which usually takes between five and ten minutes. Many women appear to have nipple erections after an orgasm because the breast as a whole quickly decreases in size while the areola are still engorged. The clitoris returns to its original size but remains extremely sensitive for several minutes. Most women do not like the clitoris to be touched during this time.

The menstrual cycle in women may influence sexual responsiveness. For example, sexual excitement has been found to occur more frequently during the last fourteen days of the menstrual cycle (Sherfey, 1972). During this time, more lubrication is produced during the excitement phase, which may be due to the increased vasocongestion. As we discussed in Chapter 3, orgasms can be very helpful in reducing cramps during menstruation, presumably because they help to relieve pelvic congestion and vasocongestion.

Sexual Response Cycle in Men

The sexual response cycle in males is similar to that of females, with vasocongestion and myotonia leading to physiological changes in the body (see Figure 9.4). However, in men, the four phases, are less well defined. During the excitement phase, the penis, like the clitoris in women, begins to fill with blood and erect. Erection begins very quickly during excitement, generally within three to five seconds (although the speed of this response lengthens with age).

Excitement Phase. The excitement phase of the sexual response cycle in men is often very short, unless a man uses deliberate attempts to lengthen it (some men, in an attempt to prolong the excitement stage, replay parts of an NFL game or some other event in their minds). Often this causes a gradual loss of **tumescence**, which is referred to as **detumescence**. Distractions in sexual activity during the excitement phase may also cause detumescence. However, once the plateau stage is reached, an erection is often more stable and less sensitive to outside influences. Women take longer to reach the plateau phase due to their more intense pelvic congestion, which takes longer to develop.

During the excitement phase, the testicles also increase in size, becoming up to 50% larger. This is both a vasocongestive and myotonic response. The **dartos** and cremastic muscles pull the testicles closer to the body to avoid injury during thrusting. If sexual stimulation were to stop at this point, the swelling in the testicles could be uncomfortable (see Sex Talk Question 9.2).

tumescence: The swelling of the penis due to vasocongestion, causing an erection.

detumescence: The return of an erect penis to the flaccid state.

dartos muscles: Muscles in the scrotum that are responsible for raising and lowering the testes.

SEX TALK

QUESTION **9.2** **Does the condition "blue balls" really exist?**

The concept of blue balls refers to a pain in the testicles that is experienced by men if sexual arousal begins and is not followed by an orgasm. It is true that the pressure felt in the genitals, which is caused by vasocongestion, can be uncomfortable. However, this discomfort can easily be relieved through masturbation. The excuse that a man must have sexual intercourse once he is sexually aroused "or else he'll have blue balls" is one that should be greeted with the reply "go masturbate, then." By the way, women also experience a similar condition if they are sexually aroused and do not reach orgasm. There can be pressure, pain, or a bloating feeling in the pelvic region, which can also be relieved through masturbation.

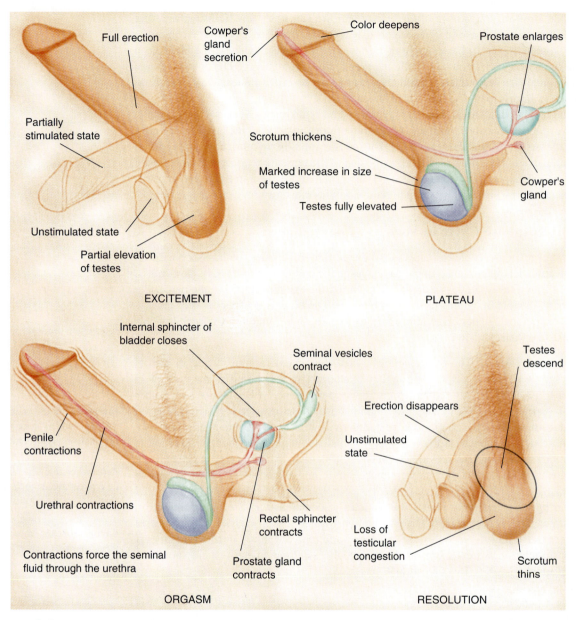

F i g u r e 9.4
External and internal changes in the male sexual response cycle. **Reprinted with permission from Masters et al (1994).**

Plateau Phase. All of these physical changes continue during the plateau phase. Some men may experience a sex flush, which is identical to the sex flush women experience. In addition, it is not uncommon for men to have nipple erections. Just prior to orgasm, the glans penis becomes engorged (this is comparable to the color changes in the labia in women).

Orgasm Phase. During orgasm, ejaculation occurs in two stages. During the first stage, which lasts only a few seconds, there are contractions in the vas deferens, seminal vesicles, and prostate gland. These contractions lead to **ejaculatory inevitability**. Next, the semen is forced out of the urethra by muscle contractions (in the same set of muscles that contract in female orgasms). The first three or four contractions are the most forceful and pleasurable and are responsible for depositing the majority of the semen deep into the vagina. The force of the ejaculation can propel semen up to twenty-four inches, and generally this distance is longer in younger men (Welch, 1992). After these major contractions, minor ones usually follow, even if stimulation stops. As with women, the muscular contractions during orgasm occur about every 0.8 seconds.

ejaculatory inevitability: A feeling , just prior to orgasm, that ejaculation can no longer be controlled; the vas deferens, seminal vesicles, and prostate have already started to contract.

Resolution Phase. Directly following ejaculation, the glans of the penis decreases in size, even before general penile detumescence. During the resolution phase of sexual response, when the body is returning to its prearousal state, men go into a **refractory stage** in which they cannot be restimulated to orgasm for a certain time period. The refractory period gets longer as a man gets older (we discuss this more later in this chapter). Younger men, on the other hand, may experience an erection soon after an ejaculation.

refractory stage: The period of time after an ejaculation in which men cannot be stimulated to further orgasm.

The refractory period prevents multiple orgasms in most males. However, one study found that men are capable of anywhere from two to sixteen orgasms prior to ejaculation, though the ability to have them decreases with age (Dunn and Trost, 1989).

Kaplan's Model of Sexual Response

Another model of the sexual response cycle has been proposed by Helen Singer Kaplan (1974). Kaplan believes that a sexual response occurs in three, rather than four, distinct phases—sexual desire, excitement, and orgasm.

Kaplan's model has often been referred to as a **triphasic model** of sexual response and includes sexual desire, vasocongestion of the genitals, and muscular contractions during orgasm. Notice that two of these phases are physiological (vasocongestion and muscular contractions), while the other is psychological. Sexual desire is of paramount importance to Kaplan because, without sexual desire, the other two physiological functions would not occur. We discuss the importance of the desire phase and disorders associated with it in Chapter 12.

triphasic model: A model of sexual response proposed by Kaplan in which there are three phases—sexual desire, vasocongestion, and muscular contractions.

All three phases of the triphasic model are controlled by separate systems. For example, vasocongestion is a vascular response, while myotonia is a muscular response. An advantage to Kaplan's model is that, in some ways, the triphasic model is easier to conceptualize than Masters and Johnson's model. For example, most of us can recognize and differentiate desire, excitement, and orgasm but may have a difficult time recognizing when we are in Masters and Johnson's plateau phase.

ADULT SEXUAL BEHAVIOR

Our culture, our religion, and social, economic, psychological, and biological factors all contribute to the way we behave sexually. As we grow, we learn strong messages about acceptable and unacceptable behaviors from the culture at large, our ethnic groups, our social classes, and even our language (see Sexuality Today 9.1). Religiosity and strength of religious beliefs also influence sexual behavior (Sneddon and Kremer, 1992). Generally, the more religious people are, the more conservative their sexual behavior tends to be (see Special Focus 1). Cultural factors, such as sex-role stereotypes, may also influence sexual behavior, as can biological factors, such as physical health. All of these influences help us define what is considered acceptable and unacceptable sexual behavior. Some people experiment with different techniques, while others accept a smaller set of sexual behaviors. In the following section, we examine the range of common sexual behaviors.

Sexual Fantasy

Over the last few decades, views about sexual fantasy have been changing. Sigmund Freud believed that only unsatisfied people fantasized about sex. Today, many researchers not only believe that sexual fantasies are normal and healthy but that sexual fantasies may be a driving force behind human sexuality. Fantasies are most often used to increase sexual interest and arousal. Liberal attitudes and more sexual experience have been found to be associated with longer and more explicit sexual fantasies (Gold and Chick, 1988: Person et al., 1992), and those who do not have sexual fantasies have been found to experience a greater likelihood of sexual dysfunction (Nutter and Condron, 1985) and sexual dissatisfaction (Cado and Leitenberg, 1990).

College Students and Sexual Fantasy

In one study, 84% of college students were found to use fantasy at least some of the time during sexual activity (Cado and Leitenberg, 1990). The majority of college students who use sexual fantasies feel little guilt about it and feel it is normal, moral, common, socially acceptable, and more beneficial than harmful. However, some college students feel a considerable amount of **sex guilt** about using sexual fantasies, and those students often have fewer, shorter, and less explicit sexual fantasies than those with low sex guilt. Sex guilt has been found to cause a person to be less likely to engage in more intimate types of sexual behavior (DiVasto et al., 1981).

sex guilt: A generalized expectancy for self-mediated punishment for violating or anticipating violating internalized standards of proper sexual conduct.

Women's Sexual Fantasies

Women's sexual fantasies emphasize more touching, feeling, and partner response, their own physical and emotional responses, and more ambiance than men's (Ellis and Symons, 1990). Women's fantasies are often about a current or past partner. One study found that 97% of females use sexual fantasy, with the most common fantasy being sexual intercourse with one's boyfriend or future husband (Pelletier and Herold, 1988). Females have also been found to have more passive sexual fantasies than males, involving something being done to *them* rather than doing something to someone else (Gold and Chick, 1988). Many women report that they use sexual fantasy to increase their arousal if necessary.

Overall, female sexual fantasies tend to be more romantic than male fantasies, as seen by this fantasy from a twenty-one-year-old female:

SEXUALITY *Today* 9.1

Sexual Terminology

In Western history, there have always been both "proper" and popular (slang) terms to refer to sexual behaviors. In his book *The Dictionary of Sexual Slang*, Alan Richter (1993) explores the origins and meanings of different modern terms for sexual behavior.

Analingus: Oral stimulation of the anus. Word derives from the Latin *anus*, meaning "ring," and *lingere*, meaning "lick."

Blowjob: An act of oral sex on a man or woman. Blow is probably a euphemism for suck, since suck is simply the converse of blow—both being oral actions.

Cunnilingus: Oral stimulation of the female genitals. Derived from the Latin *cunnus*, meaning "vulva," and *lingere*, meaning "lick." First used in the late nineteenth century.

Fellatio: Oral stimulation of the penis. Derives from the Latin *fellare* meaning "suck." Term has been used since the nineteenth century.

Fuck: Sexual intercourse. Earliest recorded use of the term was in 1503 in northern England. It probably derives from either Middle English *fuken* or German *ficken*, meaning "strike."

Greek sex: Anal intercourse. Derived from the homosexual practices of ancient Greece.

Jack off: Male masturbation. Derived from either the common male name or from the lifting device. May also derive from the Latin *jacere*, meaning "throw."

Jill off: Female masturbation. Often used by lesbians in the twentieth century.

Masturbate: To stimulate the genitals manually. This term dates back to the seventeenth century. It may derive from the Latin *manustupare*, meaning "defile with the hand."

Missionary position: Sexual intercourse with the couple facing each other and the man on top of the woman. This term dates back to the nineteenth century and derives from the position allegedly favored by European missionaries in newly explored lands, as opposed to the indigenous peoples they encountered, who performed sexual intercourse in other ways.

Orgasm: Peak of sexual excitement. Term dates back to the eighteenth century. The word derives from the Greek *orgasmos*, meaning "grow and swell," and is related to the Greek *ergon*, meaning "work."

Screw: Sexual intercourse. The sexual meaning stems from the standard sense of rotating into something. Has been used since the eighteenth century.

Sixty-nine: Mutual oral sex. Based on the number 69, representing two clinched and inverted bodies facing each other.

Thirty-nine: Analingus. Based on the number 3, which resembles buttocks.

Tribadism: Lesbianism. Term derives from the Greek *tribein*, meaning "rub."

Richter (1993)

My ultimate fantasy would be with a tall, strong man. We would spend a whole day together—going to a beach on a motorcycle, riding horses in the sand, and making love on the beach. Then we'd ride the motorcycle back to town, get dressed up and go out to dinner. After dinner we'd come home and make love by the fire. Or we could make love in a big field of tall grass while it is raining softly.

Author's files

F i g u r e **9.5**
These cartoons depict activities stereotypically desired by each sex, both of which culminate in a sexual encounter.

Lesbians also use sexual fantasy. One twenty-year-old lesbian shared her sexual fantasy with us:

> *A woman in a suit and tie waits in the rain. She has black hair and a crew cut. I stop the car and motion her to get in. She walks quickly, with a slight attitude. She gets in with silence—her hands and eyes speak for her. I take her home and she pulls me in. I undress her and she is ready for me. Down on the bed she goes, and down on her I go. With legs spread, her clitoris is swollen and erect, hungry for my touch. I give her what she wants. She moans as orgasm courses through her body. She is my lover of thirteen years.*

> *Author's files*

Sexual fantasies are commonly used by elderly women as well. In fact, using fantasies may be a prerequisite for reaching orgasm in older women (Brecher et al., 1984). One sixty-four-year-old woman, who always uses fantasy during masturbation, described one sexual fantasy:

THE PERFECT DAY *Continued*

I see myself (younger than I am) with a man who is strong and sure and tender.
I see us dancing, driving, parking on the cliff to watch and hear the sea crash-
ing on the rocks—always aware of each other, always reaching toward the
ultimate, wondrous culmination, yet prolonging the anticipation. I feel his
hands gently removing my dress, my underclothes, lingering on my body,
caressing me as I caress him. I feel his body against mine and desire rises,
rises, filling me, filling me, and I want that moment to last forever and ever.
And I dream that this time, THIS time, there will be that perfect, earth-shaking
realization of sexual love. An overwhelming joy in each other, then quiet and
peace and sleep in each other's arms.

Brecher et al. (1984:385)

In Denmark, Lunde et al. (1991) found that sexual fantasies were used during masturbation by 50% of seventy-year-old women, 48% of forty-year-old women, and 68%
of twenty-two-year-old women. Although the content of the fantasies of older and
younger women may vary, both groups use sexual fantasy to enrich their sexual lives.

Over the years, there has been some exploration of forceful sexual fantasies in
women (rape fantasies). It is true that some women do fantasize about being forced to
engage in certain sexual behaviors. However, being forced in a sexual fantasy and being

forced in real life are two very different things. In a fantasy, the woman is in control. One study found that the development of rape fantasies was related to an early exposure to pornography (Corne et al., 1992). In addition, women who have a history of sexual abuse often have more force in their sexual fantasies and begin fantasizing earlier in life than women who have not been sexually abused.

Men's Sexual Fantasies

Men's fantasies differ from women's. They are more frequent, involve imagined sexual partners, are more impersonal, are dominated by visual images, move more quickly to explicit sexual acts, and often focus on the imagined partner as a sex object. These fantasies generally include visualizing more body parts, specific sexual acts, group sex, a great deal of partner variety, and less romance. Unlike female fantasies, male sexual fantasies often involve doing something *to* someone else. Below are some examples of some young males' fantasies:

> *My sexual fantasy is to be stranded on an island with beautiful women from different countries (all of them horny, of course). I'm the only male. I would make all of them have multiple orgasms and I would like to have an everlasting erection so I could please them all nonstop.—twenty-year-old male*

> *I walk into my room and see Madonna totally naked on my waterbed. She is singing "Justify My Love," only she is adding different words to it. Basically, she is telling me to make love to her. Without hesitation, I begin and we do it for twelve straight hours, twenty-seven positions, and every known act of foreplay. After finishing she says to me, "you were the best I've ever had. Thank you!"—twenty-one-year-old male.*

> *Author's files*

Like older women, older men also use sexual fantasy. For some older men, fantasy is necessary to reach orgasm. One sixty-year-old man says he fantasizes about:

> *. . . the person I met at a party, the hitchhiker picked up on a long trip, the teenager wanting an adult to take her to an R-rated movie. . . . Such things don't happen to me except in fantasies. . . . Yet the excitement about it all has enough power to suggest yes, I'd like to try it—and know I never will!*

> *Brecher et al. (1984:387)*

Men who have been forced into sexual behavior tend to have more sexually explicit and less emotional sexual fantasies, more sexual experience, and common themes of either much older or younger partners (Gold and Clegg, 1990).

Once again, we have to be careful in interpreting these findings. It could be that men have an easier time discussing their sexual fantasies than women. One study from Canada found no significant differences in male and female sexual fantasies (Rokach, 1990).

Both heterosexual and homosexual men have been found to use sexual fantasy (Keating and Over, 1990). Overall, the most sexually arousing fantasies for heterosexual men were oral sex with a woman, sexual intercourse, manual stimulation of the penis by a woman, and either undressing a woman or being undressed by her. For gay men, the most common sexual fantasies were oral sex by a man, manual stimulation of the penis by a man, anal intercourse, and kissing a man's lips. When asked about his favorite sexual fantasy, one twenty-one-year-old gay man reported:

My favorite sexual fantasy consists of a purely coincidental meeting between myself and an old friend from high school, Jason. I remember never being sure whether or not he was gay, but I was pretty sure that he was not. We would eventually end up at my house and talk for hours about what each of us had been up to for the last few years. Eventually, the conversation would become one of his talking about trouble with a girlfriend or something of that nature. Jason tells me that he was always aware that I was gay and that he had been thinking about that a lot lately. He tells me that he has always wondered what it would be like to have sex with another man. I offer to have sex with him. He agrees and we engage in passionate, loving sex.

Author's files

It is important to point out that a gay man fantasizing about sex with a straight man does not mean that he would want this to happen in real life. It is similar to a heterosexual fantasy of an unavailable partner or sexual encounter. The unavailability makes it even more taboo.

Sexual fantasies are a normal part of sexual activity. They can help increase sexual arousal and desire. Try thinking for a moment about your own sexual fantasies. Where do they take place? With whom? What activities do you engage in? (Remember that having a fantasy does not necessarily mean we want to engage in that particular activity or be with that particular person.) If you feel comfortable, you might try sharing your fantasies with your partner.

Masturbation

For a period in the nineteenth and early twentieth centuries in the United States and Europe, there was a fear that masturbation caused terrible things to happen. Myth had it that masturbation resulted in insanity, death, or even sterility. Parents would go to extremes to protect their children from the sins of masturbation. In fact, aluminum gloves were sold to parents for the purpose of covering children's hands at bedtime so that masturbation was impossible. A variety of other devices were used to discourage adolescent masturbation (see Chapter 1). Many of these beliefs have lasted, even to the present day (see the opening quote from an Ann Landers column).

The reality is, however, that masturbation decreases sexual tension and anxiety, provides an outlet for sexual fantasy, and fulfills a variety of different needs for different people at different ages (Janus and Janus, 1993). In addition, it allows people the opportunity to experiment with their bodies to see what feels good (see Sexuality Today 9.2). Masturbation is an important part of our sexuality; for the majority of American boys, their first ejaculation result from masturbation, and it is the main sexual outlet during adolescence (see Chapter 4). Janus and Janus (1993) found that 48% of single men masturbate weekly or more, while 28% of women do so.

Mutual masturbation can also be very pleasurable, although it may make reaching orgasm difficult. It can be frustrating to concentrate both on feeling aroused and pleasuring your partner.

mutual masturbation:
Simultaneous masturbation of both sexual partners by each other.

College Students and Masturbation

Twice as many male college students as female college students masturbate (Leitenberg et al., 1993). Men who masturbate do so three times more frequently than women do during the same periods. The reported percentages of masturbation in college women

SEXUALITY *Today*   9.2

Learning to Masturbate

Below is a series of exercises on learning to masturbate, which can be very pleasurable. After you learn to masturbate, it may be helpful to share this information with your partner so he or she can also learn how to best stimulate you. Masturbation can also be exciting for couples to use during sexual activity. They may masturbate themselves or each other, either simultaneously or one at a time.

Women

Unlike men, the female genitals don't hang outside of the body. For this reason, it helps to use a small, self-standing mirror while you are exploring your own genitals. This will help you to see better and also allow your hands to be free. In a well-lit area, get into a comfortable sitting position and spread your legs. This will give you access to your vulva. Slowly explore your genitals, pulling the labia apart, and taking a good look inside. The size of the labia differ in all women—they can be long or short, textured and/or smooth (see Chapter 3). Notice what yours look like. Play with them. Next, examine the clitoris and the clitoral hood. Pull the hood back over the clitoris and expose the tip of the clitoris. How does this feel? What does the clitoris look like? Is it red? Pink? Soft? Hard? Lightly touch your clitoris and notice the sensations you experience. You might try lubricating your fingers with some KY jelly, which will add to these sensations. Notice how the clitoris erects when it is stimulated. It may even turn a deeper shade of pink when stimulated.

Next, use your lubricated finger and penetrate the opening of the vagina. What does the inside feel like? Are the muscles tight? If you flex these muscles, can you feel it in your vagina? If you push your finger up higher into the vagina, you will feel the tip of your cervix. What does it feel like? While your fingers are still inside of your vagina, relax your entire body, becoming more aware of the sensations in your vagina. Press your finger around inside your vagina, noting where touch feels the best. You will notice that as you become more and more aroused, the vagina will begin to lubricate.

Withdraw your finger and notice the vaginal lubrication on them. What does it look like? What does it feel like? What does it smell like? These vaginal secretions often change day to day.

Take your time to explore your own body. Go back to any areas that felt especially pleasurable and continue the stimulation. You may feel an orgasm beginning and that is okay. Pay attention to the sensations of your own body.

Men

Like female genitalia, male genitals come in all different shapes and sizes. Notice the size and shape of your own penis. What does it look like? Feel like? Does it begin to get hard as your explore it? What do the testicles look like? Gently explore both of them.

Examine the head of your penis. What does it look like? If you are not circumcised, you will notice a flap of skin lying over the glans of the penis. Pull the foreskin back and expose the glans. If you are circumcised, your glans will be totally exposed. Explore different areas of the head by rubbing your lubricated fingers around, noticing the different sensations. Move underneath the penis and lightly trace the penis along the shaft to the base. How does it feel? Where does touch feel the best?

Touch your scrotum and feel the two testicles inside. How does it feel to touch and massage the testicles? How much pressure feels the best? How much pressure is too much?

Take your time and explore your own body. Go back to any areas that felt especially pleasurable and continue the stimulation. You may feel an orgasm beginning and that is okay. Pay attention to the sensations of your own body.

Adapted from Dodson (1987:136–139)

ranges from 45% to 78% (Davidson and Moore, 1994). However, only 50% of college women believe that masturbation is "healthy" (Weis et al., 1992).

People masturbate in a variety of different ways. In Personal Voices 9.1 we list some responses to the question, How do you masturbate?

Many men and women feel guilty and inadequate about their masturbating because of the lasting cultural taboos against this behavior. In relationships, masturbation is the most commonly kept sexual secret between the partners (Klein, 1988). Outside of the United States, attitudes towards masturbation differ. In some cultures, masturbation is acceptable and may be practiced openly and casually in public (as in certain areas of Melanesia),

Figure **9.6**
Mutual masturbation.

while in others, it is prohibited. Prohibition often simply relegates masturbation to private locations. These cultural views towards masturbation have much to do with how "normal" masturbation is perceived to be in a particular culture.

Female Masturbation

Women have been found to masturbate much less than men (Leitenberg et al., 1993). However, it is also true that many women are embarrassed to admit that they masturbate. This is because the masturbation taboo is stronger for women than it is for men. Again, this goes back to the double standard and the stereotype that women are not supposed to enjoy and take pleasure in sexual activities. In general, women are more likely to report guilt about their masturbatory activity than men (Davidson and Darling, 1986). This guilt may interfere with physiological and psychological sexual satisfaction in general (Davidson & Darling, 1993).

Kinsey et al. (1953) reported that the average woman could reach orgasm in 95% or more of her masturbatory attempts. In addition, masturbation can produce the most intense orgasms in women (Masters and Johnson, 1970). In Chapter 12 we'll discuss how masturbation is being used in therapy for women who are unable to have orgasms.

When women are asked about their masturbatory activity, some feel very comfortable about it:

F i g u r e **9.7**
Female masturbation.

> *I never masturbated when I was young, and when I found out about it, I was*
> *filled with a sense of power and liberation. Masturbating helped me learn a*
> *great deal about the changes my body goes through in achieving orgasm.*
>
> *Hite (1976:11)*

However, even with all of the benefits of masturbation, many women feel guilty about their own masturbation. One woman said:

> *I only started to masturbate recently, after a long abstinence since childhood.*
> *It was hard to begin—I felt self-conscious and a little silly. Physically I enjoy it,*
> *but psychologically I still have difficulties—a fantasy is necessary.*
>
> *Hite (1976:7)*

Male Masturbation

Many men are also embarrassed to admit that they masturbate. There are many advantages to masturbation including sexual release, relaxation, and the fact that it doesn't require a partner:

> *It's good to get unemployment when you can't find work, right?*

> *I'm beginning to realize that masturbation is necessary for everyone's own*
> *sexual independence and that I shouldn't always have to rely on my mate to*
> *satisfy or arouse me. I used to never masturbate because she always did such a*
> *good job on me. Also, I guess all the things drilled in your head before you can*
> *think made me think that it was degrading, selfish, a waste of time, and why do*
> *it yourself when a woman is much better. Lately I've been doing it more, mainly*
> *for arousal purposes. It feels so-o-o good.*
>
> *Hite (1981:488,491)*

Personal
V O I C E S
9.1

How Do You Masturbate?

Men and women use a variety of different techniques to masturbate, some of which are described for us below.

In Women:

During masturbation, some women like to use vibrators, fingers, rubbing, or vaginal insertion. Some women lie on their backs, while others prefer their sides, or stomachs. Some women also stimulate their breasts during clitoral stimulation. Overall, the majority of women use some type of manual clitoral stimulation during masturbation. However, the methods for stimulating the clitoris may differ:

I usually use my fingers and rub in a circular motion. Sometimes for variety I use objects to rub my clitoris, such as the rounded handle of my hairbrush, any object I have on hand at the moment, but I don't usually do that. I like my legs to be very far apart.

I prefer to be wearing tight blue jeans and pulling so that the seam is pressed against the tip of the clitoris. Otherwise I use my fingers to provide genital press-release pressure to the top of the clitoris. My legs are usually together, and I move very little. I can even do it in public without being observed, I think, with the tight blue jean method.

I masturbate with an electric toothbrush. I put a dampened washcloth over the toothbrush and lubricate my clitoris with lotion. I lie on my back with my legs spread. With my left hand, I spread the labia to expose the clitoris, and I hold the vibrator with my right hand and gently press it on my clitoris. Sometimes I move it up and down; sometimes I leave it in one spot, depending on what feels good.

I usually suspend myself against a piece of furniture and rub myself against it in an up and down, *slow, circular motion. I never heard of it being done like this before, and I don't know where I picked it up, but at an early age it gave me a quick orgasm, or several. It's a good way, only it gives you calluses on the palms of your hands.*

Hite (1976:29, 33, 48, 49)

In Men:

For men, the most frequent method of masturbation involves direct stimulation of the penis with the hand. Many men also use other types of stimulation, such as breast, anal, testicular, or other body stimulation. It appears that the up and down movement of the hand or movement around the penis during masturbation is what is necessary for an orgasm:

I masturbate with my right hand, with my thumb on top and fingertips on the bottom—pumping up and down, taking care not to touch the glans with my thumb until ready to trigger ejaculation. Occasionally I masturbate with a condom on because of the sexy, slinky feeling of the rubber on my flesh.

Masturbating is easy for me. I am not circumcised and have a full foreskin that easily goes over the whole of the head of my penis even when erect. My hand does not have to move against the skin then, but rather I move the whole skin back and forth.

Sometimes I fill a condom with lotion and lying on the bed face down make as though I was in a vagina. It's more work, but a better orgasm.

I almost always do it lying on my back, holding the penis in my hand, and rubbing my hand up and down. Sometimes I may run my other hand over my stomach or thigh, as it is very sensual, but the narcissism of that frightens me.

Hite (1981:504, 506, 508, 523)

However, some men feel that masturbation is not acceptable for them:

I'm still hung up on the idea that though there is nothing wrong with masturbation, a sexually successful person shouldn't need it.

Hite (1981:487)

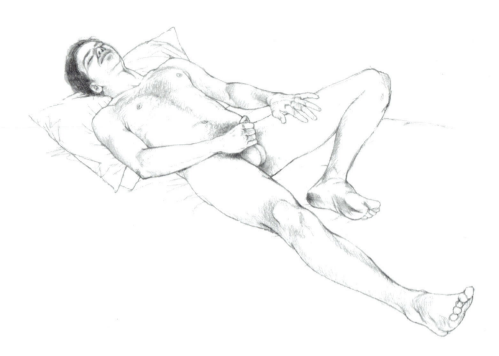

F i g u r e **9.8**
Male masturbation.

One final word about masturbation: Some may choose not to do it for personal or religious reasons. That is fine. Your sexual behavior should include only that which is comfortable for you.

Manual Sex

Manual sex (also referred to as a "hand jobs") refers to the physical caressing of the genitals during solo or partner masturbation. Generally, people think of manual sex as something that happens *before* sexual intercourse, but it has become more popular over the years as a form of safer sex. This is because during manual sex, there is no exchange of body fluids (we will talk about safe sex later in this chapter). In order to learn how best to stimulate your partner manually, it may help to watch how he or she masturbates. After all, most people know best how to stimulate their bodies. However, this can be very anxiety-producing for some couples. If your partner is hesitant, try again another time, or volunteer to go first.

Manual Sex on Women

Many men do not know exactly what to do with the female genitals. Do I rub? If so, where and how much? Could I rub too hard? Too light? Will it hurt? Can I break something? When does she like to have it touched? Where does she like it to be touched? Men who worry about these questions may become overly cautious or eager in touching a woman's clitoris and vulva. Figure 9.9 illustrates a variety of ways to manually stimulate the clitoris.

Since each woman differs on how she likes her clitoris stroked or rubbed, it is important to talk to your partner. Only she can tell you precisely how she likes to have her clitoris stimulated. The majority of women enjoy a light caressing of the shaft of the clitoris, along with an occasional circling of the clitoris, and maybe digital penetration of the vagina. Other women dislike direct stimulation and prefer to have the clitoris rolled between the lips of the labia.

Clitoral stimulation feels best when the fingers are well lubricated. Use some KY jelly, or some of your partner's own lubrication to help with this. Some women like to have the entire area of the vulva caressed, while others like the caressing to be focused on the clitoris.

Begin by lightly caressing the thighs, stomach, and entire mons area. Some women like to have their partners gently part the labia and softly explore the inner vulva. Don't immediately head for the clitoris though; take your time and explore her body. She will begin to breathe more deeply, her muscles will become tense, and she may moan. This usually means she is close to orgasm. You might ask, "Does this feel OK?" It can be very frustrating if you change your techniques when a woman is close to orgasm. Again, it is best to ask what your partner enjoys the most.

Manual Sex on Men

Many women do not know how to hold or caress the male penis. Can I rub too hard? Too lightly? Will it hurt? Can I break something? When does he like to have it touched? Where does he like to be touched? Therefore, they become overly cautious in touching the penis. To reach orgasm, however, many men like to have the penis stimulated with strong and consistent strokes. Again, it helps if he can communicate this to his partner. Figure 9.10 illustrates a variety of ways in which the penis can be manually stimulated.

At the beginning of sexual stimulation, most men like soft, light stroking of the penis and testicles. Often, women fail to understand how pleasurable it is to have the testicles fondled, tickled, and stroked. Most women are afraid they will hurt the testicles. It is true that the testicles can be badly hurt by rough handling, but a light, feathery stroking can feel wonderful. This is an individual preference; some men enjoy having

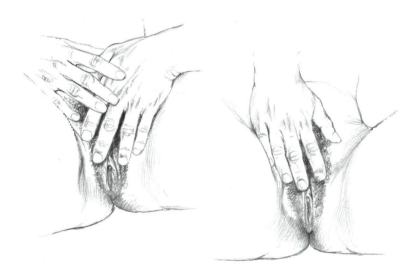

Figure **9.9**
There are many different ways to stimulate the vagina.

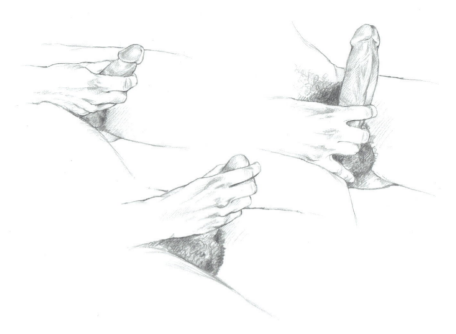

F i g u r e **9.10**
There are a variety of ways to stimulate the penis.

the testicles firmly but carefully squeezed right before orgasm, while others do not enjoy it. A good rule to follow is that most men do not like to have their testicles squeezed any harder than a woman would like to have her breasts squeezed. Remember, also, that the friction of a dry hand can cause irritation, so you might try using hand lotion, baby oil, or KY jelly while manually stimulating the penis. However, if you proceed to have vaginal or anal intercourse, make sure to wash off any lotion or oil (although it is fine to leave KY jelly on for lubrication).

Since many women do not know how best to stimulate a man's penis, they often switch positions, pressures, and techniques fairly often. Mainly, this is due to the fact that they are unaware of what feels the best for their partners. Unfortunately, this can be very frustrating for a man who feels almost at the brink of an orgasm when his partner changes the stimulation. Most women want help with this; ask him what feels best or have him show you by placing his hand over yours as a guide.

Another common mistake that many women make when fondling the male genitals is to grasp the penis far down near its base. Although this can feel pleasurable, there are fewer nerve endings in the base of the penis than there are in the tip. The most sensitive part of the male penis is the glans and tip, which are very responsive to touch. In fact, some men can masturbate by rubbing only the glans of the penis. For others, stimulation at the base may help bring on orgasm because it mimics deep thrusting.

All men have their own individual techniques for masturbating. However, the most common techniques involve a quick up-and-down motion that is applied without a great deal of pressure. Try varying the pressure every once in awhile (harder and then softer). These motions are what will lead to orgasm. When he begins to breathe deeper, his muscles become tense, his heart rate increases, and maybe he begins to moan, you will know he is close to orgasm. At this point, use a stronger and deeper stroke, which focuses on the glans of the penis. Like women, men can be very frustrated if stimulation is suddenly

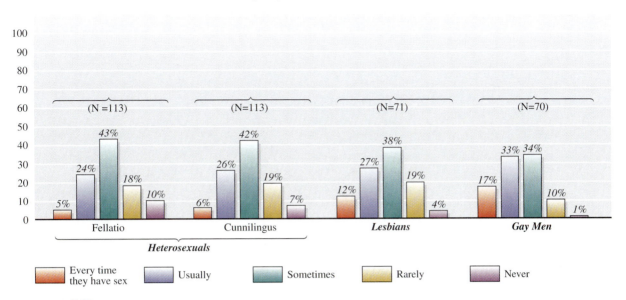

Figure 9.11

This graph demonstrates how often couples of various kinds engage in oral sex. Note the similarity in rate of heterosexual fellatio and cunnilingus. **Reprinted with permission from Blumstein and Schwartz (1983:236)**

stopped when they are close to orgasm. At the point of orgasm, it is important to continue firm stroking on the top and sides of the penis but not on the underside. Firm pressure on the underside of the penis during orgasm can restrict the urethra, which can be very uncomfortable during ejaculation.

Oral Sex

Oral sex (also called **cunnilingus** and **fellatio**) has been practiced throughout history. Ancient Greek vases, tenth-century temples in India, and even nineteenth-century playing cards, all portrayed couples engaging in different types of oral sex (see Special Focus Chapter 4). Over the years, there have been many taboos associated with oral sex. For some, oral sex is not an option. They consider it against their religions or beliefs or even find it disgusting, sickening, or even like "licking a toilet seat" (Author's files). However, for many people, oral sex is an important part of sexual behavior. The majority of Americans report that they engage in oral sex at least occasionally. Between 68% and 72% of college women have experienced cunnilingus, and between 73% and 86% of college men have experienced fellatio (Davidson and Moore, 1994). Janus and Janus (1993) found that 88% of men and 87% of women approved of oral sex. In Figure 9.11, we present the frequency of oral sex in relationships. Overall, oral sex is less common among the less educated and among African-Americans (Laumann et al., 1994). It is most popular among young, better-educated whites.

Some people like to perform oral sex as a form of foreplay. Others like to have oral sex instead of other sexual behaviors, and some may engage in **sixty-nine** (see Figure 9.12). This position, however, can be very challenging for some couples and may not provide the best stimulation for either of them. **Analingus**, another form of oral sex,

cunnilingus: Oral stimulation of the clitoris or vulva.

fellatio: Oral stimulation of the penis.

sixty-nine position: Oral sex that is performed simultaneously.

analingus: Oral stimulation of the anus.

F i g u r e **9.12**
The sixty-nine position.

involves oral stimulation of the anus. However, it is important to keep in mind that without meticulous hygiene, oral-anal activity on an infected partner can spread intestinal infections, hepatitis, and various sexually transmitted diseases.

One note of caution here: If your partner does not like oral sex, do not force it. There is nothing worse than being forced to engage in a sexual activity that you do not want to do. One man said:

I really want my girlfriend to go down on me. I keep trying to put myself in a position in bed where my cock is close to her lips, but she doesn't seem to take the hint. Once I actually took hold of her hair and tried to push her down there, but she got upset and after that I didn't know what else to do.

Masterson (1987:9)

Some people feel that engaging in oral sex is less intimate than sexual intercourse and may not like it for this reason. Since there is little face-to-face contact during cunnilingus or fellatio, it may make partners feel emotionally distant. Other people report that engaging in oral sex is one of the most intimate behaviors that a couple can engage in because it requires total trust and vulnerability. In general, the majority of men and women are more interested in receiving oral sex rather than giving it (Laumann et al., 1994).

If there is a conflict in your relationship concerning oral sex, try talking about it and seeing if you can come up with some compromises. Maybe you could agree to engage in oral sex once or twice a month in exchange for back rubs or some other agreed-upon trade-off.

Cunnilingus

Many women express concern about the cleanliness of their vaginas during oral sex. In the United States, women have historically been inundated with negative messages about their vaginas—though never more so than today. Shelves full of products, including powders, douches, creams, jellies, and other scented items, all designed to help make the vagina "better," are marketed to women. These products and the advertisements that sell them have convinced women that they need *something* to improve their vaginas. When their partners try to have oral sex with them, fears and anxieties often prevent women from enjoying the sexual experience. When coupled with many women's lack of familiarity with their own genitals, women often feel extremely strong discomfort with oral sex.

One woman remarked:

If I were a man I would never do it!
I am always self-conscious that I might smell or look disgusting.

Hite (1976:250;258)

Some men report that the taste of the vaginal secretions is arousing to them and they feel that cunnilingus is extremely erotic. They find the female vulva beautiful and sexy, including its smell and taste. Overall, when we are highly aroused, we are less alert to sensory impressions than if we were not stimulated. This means that when we are aroused, the flavor of the vagina or of semen may be more appealing than it would be if we were not aroused. However, if the odor and taste of the vagina is offensive to you or your partner, you might try taking a bath or shower together before you engage in oral sex. You might also try using whipped cream or grape jelly to improve its flavor!

SEX TALK

QUESTION **9.3** **Do women like their partners to kiss them right after they have performed cunnilingus on them?**

Some women do; some do not. For some women, sharing a kissing after cunnilingus can be very erotic and sensual. However, other women feel uncomfortable with the taste of their own genitals. It would be best to ask your partner to see what her individual pleasure is. Do not assume it is okay with her and go ahead and do it—this can be a big turn-off for her.

Often the best way to approach oral sex with a woman is to be slow and gradual in your actions. Do not immediately head for her vulva during oral sex; take your time. Start at her lips and then slowly move to her neck and shoulders. From there, move down to her breasts. Do this slowly, concentrating on each part of the body and gradually move down to the vulva. Kiss the outer lips and caress the mons. Explore the area with your mouth and lips prior to stimulating the clitoris directly. Use your hands and caress the breasts or other body parts while you are exploring the vulva. Many women like to have the lips of their vaginas parted gently during this exploration. You might try using your tongue to explore the inner areas of the vulva and run it up and down from the clitoris to the vaginal opening. Try using your hands to open up the lips of the vagina, and explore the inside with your tongue. A persistent rhythmic caressing of the tongue on the clitoris will cause many women to reach orgasm. During cunnilingus, some women enjoy a finger being inserted into their vagina or anus for extra stimulation.

Cunnilingus is the most popular sexual behavior for lesbians. In fact, the more oral sex a lesbian couple has, the happier the relationship and the less they fight (Blumstein and Schwartz, 1983) (see Figure 9.11). Although women in heterosexual relationships often worry that their partners may find the vagina unappealing, this is not so in lesbian relationships. Perhaps this is due to the fact that each is more accepting of the other's genitals since they are both women. One woman said:

Gay women are very much into each other's genitals. They're very comfortable with and attracted to women's genitals. Not only accepting, but truly apprecia-

Figure **9.13**
Cunnilingus.

tive of women's genitals and bodies. My feeling about my body and my genitals has significantly been enhanced by my experience with women. Lesbians are really into women's bodies, all parts.

Blumstein and Schwartz (1983:238)

In performing cunnilingus with a pregnant woman, never be blow air into her vagina. This can force air into her uterine veins, which can cause an air embolism that could result in death.

Fellatio

The majority of men also enjoy having their genitals orally stimulated. Many men are displeased if their partners do not like to perform fellatio (Blumstein and Schwartz, 1983). However, some men do not even desire such stimulation:

This is by far my favorite sexual activity. I always orgasm and it is more intense for me than an intercourse orgasm.

I have never had fellatio. I have no desire to have it done, it is repulsive to me.

Hite (1981:527;532)

In gay male couples, the more oral sex occurs, the more sexually satisfied the couple is (Blumstein and Schwartz, 1983). Fellatio is the most popular sexual behavior for gay men.

Prior to fellatio, many men enjoy having their partners stroke and kiss various parts of their bodies, gradually getting closer to their penises and testicles. Some men like to have their partners take one testicle gently into their mouth and slowly circle it with their tongues. The head of the penis can be gently sucked while you slowly move your hand up and down the shaft. Be sure to keep your teeth covered with your lips; exposed teeth

Figure **9.14**
Fellatio.

can cause pain. Some men like the sensation of being gently scratched with teeth during oral sex, but you must be very careful.

Pornographic movies tend to show women who take the entire penis into their mouths, but this is not necessary. In fact, it may be uncomfortable due to the gagging response. Some men make the mistake, during fellatio, of holding their partners' heads during orgasm. This makes it impossible for the partner to remove the penis and to control the ejaculate. In fact, a bad experience in which a man forces his partner to swallow can negatively affect the partner for a long time.

To avoid a gagging response, it is often very helpful to place a hand around the base of the penis while you are performing fellatio. By placing a hand there, the penis will be kept from entering the back of the mouth, thus reducing the urge to gag. In addition, the hand can be used to provide more stimulation to the penis during fellatio.

SEX TALK

QUESTION **9.4** **Do men want their partners to swallow the ejaculate after their orgasms?**

Some men do; some do not. Again, there is not only one way to perform fellatio. Swallowing the ejaculate can be a very intimate experience for both partners. There is nothing in the ejaculate that could harm a person. However, some people find it uncomfortable to swallow and prefer to remove the penis prior to ejaculation.

Some partners are concerned about having their partners' ejaculate in their mouths after fellatio. Performing fellatio and swallowing the ejaculate is not considered a form of safe sex. So many clinicians advise using a condom so that a partner is not exposed to the ejaculate. However, if your partner is HIV negative and free from all sexually transmitted diseases, swallowing the ejaculate is fine. Some women enjoy the taste, feel, and idea of tasting and swallowing ejaculate, while others do not. Some women allow their partners to ejaculate in their mouths, but spit it out instead of swallowing it. Some men see this as a "rejection," but, in fact, just allowing a man to ejaculate in your mouth is an intimate, accepting act.

How much semen a man ejaculates during fellatio often depends on how long it has been since his last ejaculation. If a long period of time has gone by, generally the ejaculate will be larger. An average ejaculation is approximately one to two teaspoons and consists mainly of fructose, enzymes, and different vitamins. It contains approximately five calories. The taste of the ejaculate can also vary, depending on a man's use of drugs and/or alcohol, stress level, and diet. Coffee and alcohol can cause the semen to have a bitter taste, while fruits (pineapple in particular) can result in sweet-tasting semen. Men who eat lots of red meat often have very acid-tasting semen. The taste of semen also varies from day to day.

If you really dislike performing oral sex on your partner, try talking about it. Find out if there are things that you can do differently (using your hands more) or that your partner can vary (ejaculating outside of your mouth). Barbara DeAngelis (1990), a relationship expert, notes that disgust over fellatio often comes from the *thought* of having oral sex. Thinking *"I can't believe his penis is in my mouth!"* can destroy any possible pleasure you might feel. DeAngelis (1990:193-4) suggests to trying the following exercise: Hold out the palm of your hand and imagine holding a miniature version of your partner. If your partner was only six inches tall, how could you show him your feelings? You would probably want to stroke and kiss him. Now, think of the smaller version of your partner as his penis. When you are kissing his penis or caressing it, you are really caressing his whole being. It shows your feelings for the whole person, not only his penis.

SEX TALK

QUESTION **9.5** **I have heard that you can get genital herpes if your partner performs oral sex on you and has a cold sore on his or her lip. Is this true?**

From what we understand about the herpes virus, this is true. It appears that, even though oral herpes (cold sores) are caused by another strain of the virus, when oral sex is performed, this virus can infect the genitals and lead to genital herpes. It is best to avoid oral sex when either partner has a cold sore.

Heterosexual Sexual Intercourse

People have always been curious about how frequently other couples engage in sexual intercourse. A 1994 study found that one-third of Americans between the ages of eighteen and fifty-nine engage in sexual intercourse as often as twice a week (Laumann et al., 1994). Overall, Americans fall into three groups: those who have sexual intercourse at least twice a week (one-third); those who engage in sexual intercourse a few times a month (one-third); and those who engage in sexual intercourse a few times a year or have no sexual partners (one-third).

Sexual intercourse involves inserting the penis into the vagina. However, there are a variety of ways in which couples perform this action. Below we will discuss various positions for sexual intercourse. Most heterosexual couples engage in sexual intercourse almost every time they have sex (Blumstein and Schwartz, 1983), and, when most people think of "sex," they think of vaginal intercourse (Michael et al., 1994). In fact, the majority of men and women report that their preferred way to reach orgasm is through sexual intercourse (Janus and Janus, 1993), even though many women need additional clitoral stimulation to reach orgasm.

It is important for couples to delay vaginal penetration until after lubrication has begun. During arousal, the vagina becomes lubricated, which makes penetration easier and feels better for both partners. Penetrating a dry vagina, forcefully or not, can be very uncomfortable for both partners. If the woman is aroused but there is little vaginal lubrication, extra lubrication (such as KY jelly) should be used.

Many men believe that women want hard and fast thrusting during sexual intercourse, but faster is *not* always better. One man said:

> I believe women want huge, hard ramming. Part of me thinks that if I do it real slow, she'll be totally mine. But when I'm having sex, I listen to my primal self, and my primal self says I must do it hard, and not just at the climax either— because there's some guy out there who can do it even harder, all night long. I never fantasize that I can do it more "feathery" than the next guy.
>
> *Jake (1993)*

Pornography helps reinforce the idea that women like thrusting to be fast and rough during sexual intercourse. Tape after tape shows men engaged in hard and fast thrusting—and women asking for more. In reality, many women like a slower pace for intercourse. It can be very intimate and erotic to make love very slowly, circling the hips, varying pressure and sensations, while maintaining eye contact. Men, too, enjoy a woman who can move her hips, squeeze the penis with her vaginal muscles, and vary the pace and strength of intercourse.

If thrusting during sexual intercourse is not comfortable for you, try slowing each other down. When one partner works up to a quicker pace, stop him or her by holding his or her hips or buttocks. This nonverbal communication can be very helpful, but also remember to communicate verbally to make sure you are both happy with the pace of intercourse.

Traditionally, the end of sexual intercourse is signified when a man ejaculates. Although many men may wish to time their orgasm with their partners, this can be difficult to do. Many times, men will try to delay ejaculation until their partners are satisfied with the length of thrusting; however, longer thrusting does not always mean that women will be closer to orgasm. If intercourse lasts for too long, the vagina may become dry, and this can be very uncomfortable. Couples should communicate what is best for them.

Each time a couple engages in sexual intercourse, there are a variety of needs, feelings, and desires the partners bring together. They may want to stretch out the time and make it last longer, or they may desire a "quickie." Ointments have long been sold to men to allow them to lengthen their thrusting time. However, these are often counterproductive in that they tend to psychologically separate the man and his penis and may desensitize the woman's genitals as well. In Chapter 12 we will discuss treatment for erectile difficulties.

Schnarch (1993) analyzed the sexual practices of average couples and found that the majority of couples do not have eye contact during sexual intercourse, regardless of their positions. He believes this may be due to the fact that eye contact intensifies intimacy and most couples cannot handle that. In addition, over time, we have learned to close our eyes during intimate interactions (such as kissing, making love, or oral sex). To increase the intensity of sexual behavior, try keeping your eyes open!

Positions for Sexual Intercourse

According to the *Complete Manual of Sexual Positions,* there are 116 vaginal entry positions, and, in *The New Joy of Sex* (Comfort, 1991), 112 positions are illustrated. Of course, we cannot describe all of these positions, so we will limit ourselves to the four main positions for sexual intercourse: male-on-top, female-on-top, rear entry, and side-by-side. There are advantages and disadvantages to each of these positions, and each couple must choose the sexual positions that are best for them.

Male-on-Top

The male-on-top (also called the "missionary" or "male superior") position is one of the most common positions for sexual intercourse. In the male-on-top position, the woman lies on her back and spreads her legs, often bending her knees to make penetration easier. The man positions himself on top of the woman, between her legs (see Figure 9.15). Since his full weight is usually uncomfortable and perhaps even painful for the woman, he should support himself on his elbows and knees. Either partner may guide the penis into the vagina. This position allows deep penetration during intercourse and enables the partners to look at each other, kiss, and hug during sexual intercourse. The woman can move her legs up around her partner or even put them on his shoulders. She can also use a pillow under her hips to increase clitoral stimulation. For some couples, this position is the most comfortable since the male is more active than the female. In fact, couples with traditional sexual values limit their sexual positions to this one (Blumstein and

F i g u r e **9.15**
The male-on-top position for sexual intercourse.

Schwartz, 1983). Another advantage to this position is that it may be the most effective for procreation. In the male on top position, the penis can be thrust deep into the vagina, which allows the semen to be deposited as deeply as possible, and since the woman is lying on her back, the semen does not leak out as easily.

However, there are also some disadvantages to this position. If either partner is obese, or if the female is in the advanced stages of pregnancy, this position can be very uncomfortable. Also, the deep penetration that is possible in this position may be uncomfortable for the woman, especially if her partner has a large penis, which can bump the cervix. This position also makes it difficult to provide clitoral stimulation for the female, though recently there has been some talk of the "coital alignment technique," in which the partners try to align their bodies so that the man "rides high" on his partner so that his pelvic bone stimulates her clitoris. However, there has been very little research done to see if this technique actually works for most couples. Another disadvantage to this position is that the woman may be prevented from moving her hips or controlling the strength and/or frequency of thrusting. Finally, in the male-on-top position, it may be difficult for the man to support his weight, and his arms and knees may get too tired. He may also experience difficulties controlling his erection and ejaculation. For this reason, sex therapists often advise couples with erectile difficulties to use different positions.

Female-on-Top

The female-on-top position (also called "female superior") has become more popular in the last decade. In this position, the man lies on his back, while his partner positions herself above him (see Figure 9.16). She can either put her knees on either side of him or lie between his legs. By leaning forward, she can increase clitoral stimulation, or she can sit

Figure **9.16**
The female-on-top position for sexual intercourse.

Figure **9.17**
A variation of the female-on-top position for sexual intercourse, which allows for clitoral stimulation by either partner.

intromission: Insertion of the penis into the vagina or anus.

upright and manually stimulate herself (see Figure 9.17). Other variations of this position include the woman sitting astride the man facing his feet or the woman sitting on top of her partner while he sits in a chair (see Figure 9.18). Since **intromission** can be difficult in this position, many couples prefer to begin in the male-on-top position and roll over.

In the female-on-top position, the female can control clitoral stimulation either by manual stimulation or through friction on her partner's body. She can also control the depth and rhythm of thrusting. Her partner's hands are also free so that he can caress her body during sexual intercourse. Since this position is face-to-face, the partners are able to see each other, kiss, and have eye contact.

Sex therapists often recommend this position for couples who are experiencing difficulties with premature ejaculation or a lack of orgasms since the female-on-top position can extend the length of erection for men and facilitates female orgasm. For women who are in the advanced stages of pregnancy, the female-on-top position may be a very good position (see Figure 9.19). Finally, if a man is not able to support his weight or is tired or infirm, this position is often helpful.

However, there are also some drawbacks to the female-on-top position. Some women may feel shy or uncomfortable about taking an active role in sexual intercourse.

Figure 9.18
A variation of the female-on-top position for sexual intercourse.

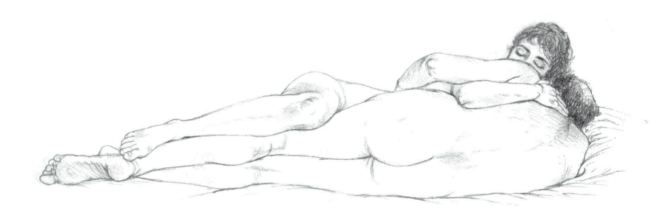

Figure 9.19
The side-by-side position for sexual intercourse.

Likewise, some men feel uncomfortable letting their partners be on top. This position also puts the primary work responsibility on the female. Also, some men do not receive enough penile stimulation in this position to maintain an erection.

Side-by-Side

The side-by-side position takes the primary responsibility off both partners and allows them to relax during sexual intercourse. In this position, the partners lie on their sides and the woman lifts one leg to facilitate penile penetration (see Figure 9.19). This is a good position for playful couples who want to take it slow and extend sexual intercourse. Both partners have their hands free and can caress each other's bodies. In addition, they can see each other, kiss, and talk during sexual intercourse.

Disadvantages of the side-by-side position include the fact that sometimes couples in this position have difficulties with intromission. It can also be difficult to get a momentum going, and even more difficult to achieve deep penetration. Women may also have a difficult time maintaining contact with the male's pubic bone during sexual intercourse.

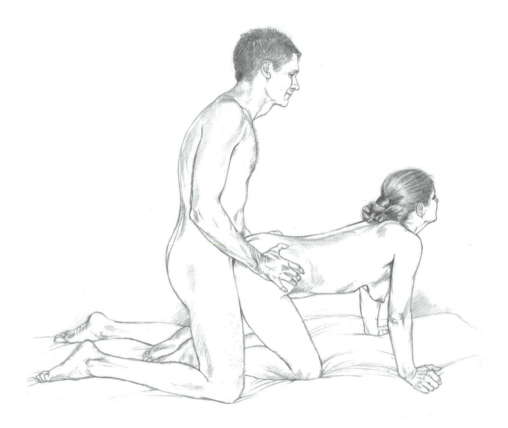

F i g u r e **9.20**
The rear-entry ("doggie-style") position for sexual intercourse.

Rear-Entry

There are many variations to the rear-entry position of sexual intercourse. Intercourse can be fast or slow depending on the variation chosen. One variation involves a woman on her hands and knees (often referred to as "doggie style"), while her partner is on his knees behind her (see Figure 9.20). The female can also be lying on her stomach with a pillow under her hips while the male enters her from behind. Another variation is to use the side-by-side position where the male lies behind his partner and his penis is introduced from behind (see Figure 9.21).

The rear-entry positions provide the best opportunity for direct clitoral stimulation, either by the male or the female. It may also provide direct stimulation of the G-Spot. The rear-entry position also can be a good position for women who are in the later stages of pregnancy or who are obese.

However, there are some drawbacks to this position. Many couples do not like the fact that there is no face-to-face contact during rear-entry. Some couples view this position as "kinky" or degrading. It's also important to make sure that the penis does not inadvertently rub against the anus during intromission or thrusting because this can cause bacteria to enter the vagina. Some couples notice that the penis often falls out of the vagina in this position and that thrusting is difficult to maintain. Finally, many couples notice that during rear-entry the vagina may make strange noises due to the displacement of air during thrusting. For some couples, this is a turn off.

Anal Intercourse

During anal intercourse (also called "Greek" sex), the man's penis enters his partner's anus. Although many people think of anal sex as a homosexual activity (with the anus being used as a substitute for the vagina), anal stimulation is very pleasurable for many

Figure **9.21**
The side-by-side (rear-entry) position for sexual intercourse.

people and so is practiced by both heterosexual and homosexual men and women. There are many nerve endings in the anus and it is frequently involved in sexual response, even if it is not directly stimulated (the anus spasms during orgasm).

In one study, one-third of college students reported engaging in anal intercourse (Rubin, 1991). Others have found that between 18% and 20% of female college students have engaged in anal intercourse (Trocki, 1992; Weis et al., 1992), and approximately 15% of college men have done so (Gladue, 1990). One quarter of American men and women have engaged in anal sex in their lifetimes, 10% within the last year. Even with these percentages of people who engage in anal intercourse in the United States, 69% of men and 74% of women believe that anal sex is unusual or kinky (Janus and Janus, 1993). Some heterosexuals may find the idea of anal sex very unappealing, and heterosexual men may have a difficult time viewing the penetration of the anus as pleasurable (Blumstein and Schwartz, 1983). However, men and women can experience orgasms during anal intercourse, especially with simultaneous penile or clitoral stimulation.

Since the anus is not capable of producing lubrication and the tissue is so fragile, it is important that additional water-soluble lubrication (such as KY Jelly®) be used. Oil-based lubricants (such as Vaseline®) may cause problems later since the body cannot easily get rid of it. Without lubrication there may be pain, discomfort, and possibly tearing of the tissue in the anus. During anal intercourse, the **anal sphincter** muscle must be relaxed, which can be facilitated by gentle stroking and digital penetration of the anus. If it is not, intercourse can be very painful. It is very important to take it very slowly if you and your partner decide to engage in anal sex. Also, a condom is a must (unless you are in a long-term, exclusive, monogamous relationship). Couples who engage in anal intercourse should know that it is one of the riskiest of all sexual behaviors and has been implicated in the transmission of AIDS (we will discuss this more in Chapter 13). In addition, a heterosexual couple who decides to engage in anal sex should *never* transfer the penis from the anus to the vagina without changing the condom or washing the penis. The bacteria in the anus can cause severe vaginal infections in women.

Before engaging in anal sex, make sure that you and your partner have discussed and agreed upon it. Forcing anal sex can be very painful and even dangerous. The anal sphincter is delicate tissue that can tear if not treated gently. One man said:

> *One night I got kind of carried away and tried penetrate my girlfriend up the backside. That was virtually the end of our relationship. I hurt her quite badly and she said I was brutal and clumsy and an animal. It's not only broken up our relationship, it's also destroyed my confidence in myself as a lover.*
>
> *Masterson (1987:9)*

Again, communication is key. If you would like to engage in anal sex but you are afraid your partner would not, discuss it openly. Perhaps you can try digital penetration of the anus first, during foreplay or intercourse, to see if that feels pleasurable; you might be surprised to learn that your partner is interested in exploring some of the same areas as you are.

anal sphincter: A ring-like muscle that surrounds the anus; it usually relaxes during normal physiological functioning.

HOMOSEXUAL SEXUAL TECHNIQUES

Though the similarities between heterosexual and homosexual sexual behavior are many, there are some differences. The differences tend to be in the frequency and, sometimes, the types of sexual behaviors engaged in.

Gay Men

Gay men use a variety of sexual techniques, which refutes the stereotype that most gay men assume only one role (either passive or active) in their relationships. The most frequent techniques used by white homosexual males are fellatio, followed by mutual masturbation, anal intercourse, and body rubbing. Gay men engage in oral sex more often than heterosexual or lesbian couples (see Figure 9.11).

Gay men fall into three categories in relation to anal sex: those who rarely engage in it (30%); those who regularly engage in it, reciprocally (27%); and those who regularly engage in it, with one partner as the dominant one (43%) (Blumstein and Schwartz, 1983). However, it is important to note that this study was done prior to the AIDS crisis. Today among gay males, anal sex is less common than oral sex. Another sexual technique is **fisting** (also called "handballing"), which involves the insertion of the fist and even part of the forearm into the anus. A survey of gay males in San Francisco found that about half had tried fisting at least once, and many described the

fisting: Sexual technique that involves inserting the fist and even part of the forearm into the anus.

Figure **9.22**
Gay men use a variety of sexual techniques in their lovemaking.

practice as producing sexual ecstasy and feelings of intimacy with their partners (Lowry and Williams, 1983).

Gay male sexual behavior has changed significantly in the era of AIDS. Undoubtedly due to the massive education efforts initiated in the gay community, studies indicate that safe sex practices have increased (at least in the major cities) among male homosexuals (Catania et al., 1989).

Lesbians

Overall, lesbians have been found to be more sexually responsive and more satisfied with their sexual relationships than heterosexual women and to have lower rates of sexual problems. On the other hand, research also suggests that the frequency of sexual contact among lesbians declines dramatically in their long-term, committed relationships (Nichols, 1990).

Lesbians in committed relationships tend to enjoy body contact, kissing, and caressing before beginning stimulation of the breasts or genitals (Masters and Johnson, 1979). Manual stimulation of the genitals is the most common sexual practice among lesbians, though lesbians tend to use a variety of techniques in their lovemaking. Two-woman

F i g u r e **9.23**
Lesbians have been found to be more sexually responsive and more satisfied with their sexual relationships than heterosexual women.

couples kiss more than couples with one man and one woman, while two-man couples kiss least of all. After manual stimulation, the next most common practice is cunnilingus, which most lesbians report is their favorite sexual activity (Bell and Weinberg, 1978) (see Figure 9.11). Another common practice is **tribadism**, also called the genital apposition technique, where the women rub their genitals together. Some lesbians also use dildos or vibrators, which are inserted into the vagina, often accompanied by manual or oral stimulation.

A nonscientific survey was done of over 100 members of a lesbian social organization in Colorado (Munson, 1987). When asked what sexual techniques they had used in their last ten lovemaking sessions, 100% reported kissing, sucking on breasts, and manual stimulation of the clitoris; over 90% reported French kissing, oral sex, and fingers inserted into the vagina; and 80% reported tribadism. Though only 9% of women in their twenties reported using a dildo, 27% of women over forty used them. Lesbians in their thirties were twice as likely as other age groups to engage in anal intercourse (presumably with a dildo) (41%) and fisting (14%). About one-third of women used vibrators, and there was a small number who reported using a variety of other sex toys, such as dildo harnesses, leather restraints, and handcuffs (see Sexuality Today 9.3).

Lesbians (as well as gay men) also engage in role-playing, sometimes (though by no means always) assuming the roles of **"butch"** and **"femme."** Ponse (1980) reports little such role-playing in her observations of lesbians; however, the Colorado survey reported that 25% engaged in fantasy or role-playing (Munson, 1987).

tribadism: Body rubbing.

butch: Lesbian role-playing of a masculine-type female.

SEXUALITY *Today* 9.3

Sex Toys

There are a variety of toys that can be purchased to increase pleasure during sexual activity. These include vibrators, dildos, creams, oil, and other products. There is a myth that lesbians are predominant users of vibrators or dildos, but many heterosexual, homosexual, and bisexual individuals and couples also use these products.

Vibrators and dildos (penis-shaped objects) are used to increase genital stimulation. They are used more frequently by women, although men use them as well. There are many types of vibrators and dildos on the market today, which are often used to either stimulate or penetrate the vagina or anus. Vibrators that come with the ability to vary speed are usually the most popular. In the past few years, vibrators have been used as a treatment for women who cannot reach orgasm (see Chapter 12).

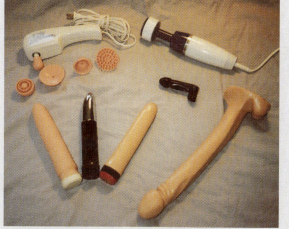

Creams, oils, and lotions can be very erotic in sexual play. They can be sensuously rubbed on your partner's body or used during mutual masturbation. Some are even flavored or contain spermicides. Other toys, such as blow-up dolls and artificial vaginas, are also available.

Sex toys can be purchased in many stores today but are probably most often sold through mail-order companies. Good Vibrations and Eve's Garden* carry a variety of vibrators, oils, lubricants, dildos, and much more.

*Good Vibrations, 1210 Valencia Street, San Francisco, CA 94110 (415) 550–7399. Eve's Garden, 119 West 57th Street, New York, N.Y. 10019 (212) 757–8641.

SEXUAL BEHAVIOR LATER IN LIFE

When we picture people making love, we rarely think of two people over the age of sixty. This is because we live in a society that equates sexuality with youth (see Sex Facts 9.1). However, the majority of elderly persons maintain an interest in sex and sexual activity, and many engage in sexual activity (Bergstrom and Nielsen, 1990), including those who are institutionalized (White, 1982).

Many older Americans change their preferences for certain types of sexual behaviors as they age (Turner and Adams, 1988). They may engage in sexual intercourse less and oral sex more, for example. These changes happen because many women do not discover their own sexual desires or try new sexual behaviors until later in life. Also, normal physiological changes that occur when one ages may make sexual intercourse less pleasurable or not possible (see Chapter 3). However, we also find that age positively correlates with sex guilt; the older the generation, the more sex guilt it has (DiVasto et al., 1981). This sex guilt can interfere with sexual activity.

Four out of five elderly (over the age of seventy) men who remain in good health report continued interest in sex, although with advancing age, the number of men who continue to engage in sexual intercourse decreases (Pfeiffer et al., 1972). The majority of healthy elderly males (64%) have no difficulties either obtaining or maintaining erections and have regular sexual intercourse (White, 1982). Kinsey et al. (1948) found that by the age of sixty, 20% of men could not engage in sexual intercourse and this percentage grew to 75% by the age of eighty. Whether or not a man remains sexually interested and active has to do with a variety of factors, including his age, what medications he is taking, his overall health, his present life satisfaction, and the availability of a partner.

One-third of women in their sixties report continuing sexual interest, with one-fifth reporting ongoing sexual activity. Personal Voices 9.2 offers a poetic of sexual desire among the elderly. For women, the most important factor in whether or not they continue sexual activity is an available and interested partner. When sexual intercourse stops in a marital relationship, it is usually because of the *male's* refusal or inability to continue,

SEX *Facts*   9.1

Sexuality and the Elderly

Because of the misconception that the elderly are not interested in sex, most people know little about geriatric sexuality. Below are some general findings about the sexual behavior of senior citizens.

1. The majority of the elderly are still interested in maintaining an active sex life.
2. The sexual attitudes and behaviors that one has in old age are a result of continuous lifelong patterns that have existed since youth.
3. When sexual interest and/or behavior end in an elderly female, it is most likely due to the declining interest

of or illness in the male partner or lack of a partner.

4. The majority of males and females experience a decline in sexual activity with advancing age.
5. Decreases in sexual activity occur because of physiological changes, but this does not account for all decreases. It may also be due to a person's interpretation of these physical changes.
6. We know more about sexual behavior in elderly males than we do about elderly females since more research is done on males.
7. Many studies of sexual behavior in older populations suffer from sample bias and research problems.

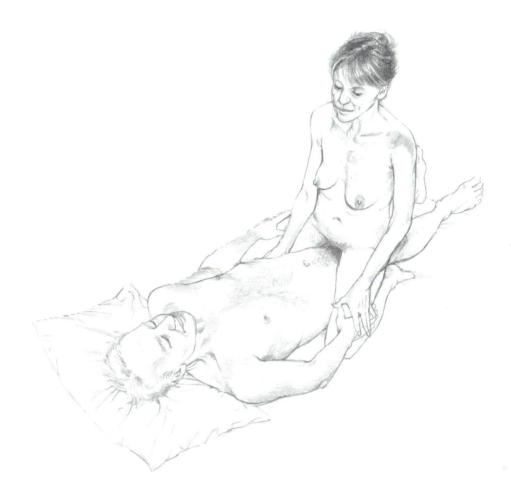

Figure **9.24**
The majority of elderly persons maintain an interest in sex and sexual activity.

rather than the wife's disinterest. This is often due to the existence of an erectile problem, which may be caused by physiological aging, illness, medication, or psychological issues (we will discuss this more extensively in Chapter 12). The most common sexual behaviors for men and women over the age of eighty are touching and caressing without sexual intercourse, masturbation, and sexual intercourse (Bretschneider and McCoy, 1988).

Despite the myth that menopause and hysterectomies may further decrease a woman's sexual desire, Kaplan (1974:111) found that these factors may actually *increase* sexual desire:

> *Again, the fate of libido seems to depend on a constellation of factors which occur during this period, including physiologic changes, sexual opportunity and diminution of inhibition. From a purely physiologic standpoint, libido should theoretically increase at menopause because the action of the woman's androgens, which is not materially affected by menopause, is now*

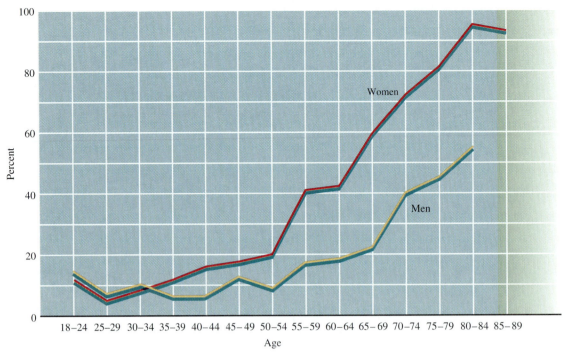

U.S. Adults with No Sexual Partner in the Past Twelve Months

9.2

V O I C E S

**Elderly Sexuality:
Finding the Fountain**

*The slim young man I married
Has slowly gone to pot;
With wrinkled face and graying pate,
Slender he is not!
And when I meet a mirror,
I find a haggard crone;
I can't believe the face I see
Can really be my own!
But when we seek our bed each night,
The wrinkles melt away:
Our flesh is firm, our kisses warm,
Our ardent hearts are gay!
The Fountain of Eternal Youth
Is not so far to find;
Two things you need—a double bed,
A spouse who's true and kind!*

Brecher et al. (1984:379)

unopposed by estrogen. Indeed, some women do seem to behave in this manner, especially if they are not depressed and can find interested and interesting partners.

Many older couples who experience problems in sexual functioning may lack adequate knowledge about sexuality. In fact, some may give up on sex at the first signs of any sexual difficulties, believing that "sex is over." After raising a family, one or both of the partners may also feel that recreational sex is inappropriate and therefore will stop having sex. It is for these reasons that it is important to increase sexual knowledge among the elderly and help them understand the implications of any physiological changes they may be experiencing. Many people, young and old, are not aware of the physical changes that can affect sexual functioning. One seventy-nine-year-old man said:

> *These days, my erections tend to come and go a bit unpredictably, but it doesn't particularly matter. It usually comes back again pretty soon if stimulation is continued. And in any case, it only affects vaginal intercourse, and sex can be very good by other techniques.*
>
> *Hite (1981:883–4)*

As people age, their bodies go through many changes. In Chapter 3, we discussed the effects of menopause and andropause on sexual functioning. There are also changes in the sexual organs, which in turn affects sexual functioning (see Sex Facts 9.2). These changes do not mean that elderly people cannot engage in sex but only that their sexual functions may slow down or change.

In elderly men, decreases in sexual desire and also in the ability to perform are two of the most frequent complaints (Kaplan, 1974). Because of these changes, masturbation increases, while rates of sexual intercourse decrease (White, 1982). Masturbation

SEX *Facts*   9.2

Physical Changes in Older Men and Women

As men and women age, there are changes in the sexual response cycle. Although the stages and physiological processes remain the same, the time and length of these stages may vary. Better knowledge of these changes would help the elderly anticipate changes in their lovemaking.

IN MEN:

1. Delayed and less firm erection.
2. More direct stimulation is needed for erection.
3. Extended refractory period (twelve to twenty-four hours before arousal can occur).
4. The elevation of the testicles is reduced.
5. The vasocongestive response in the testicles and scrotum is reduced.
6. Fewer expulsive contractions during orgasm.
7. Less forceful expulsion of seminal fluid and a reduced volume of ejaculate.
8. Rapid loss of erection after ejaculation.
9. Ability to maintain an erection for a longer period.
10. Less ejaculatory urgency.
11. Decrease in size and firmness of the testes, changes in testicle elevation, less sex flush, and decreased swelling and erection of the nipples.

IN WOMEN:

1. Sexual interest may be reduced.
2. Menopausal changes may lead to painful intercourse.
3. Decreased volume of vaginal lubrication.
4. Decreased expansive ability of the vagina.
5. Pain may occur during orgasm due to less flexibility.
6. Thinning of the vaginal walls.
7. Shortening of vaginal width and length.
8. Decreased sex flush, reduced increase in breast volume, and longer postorgasmic nipple erection.

may continue among the elderly so that they can reassure themselves that they are not the asexual persons that society labels them (Catania and White, 1982). Also, when an older adult finds that his or her partner is no longer interested in sexual activity, masturbation often becomes an important outlet. This can also be an important activity for elderly persons who have lost their sexual partners because it offers a sexual release that may help decrease depression, hostility, or frustration. Other physical problems, such as arthritis, diabetes, and osteoporosis can also interfere with sexual functioning. We will discuss many other physical problems, such as illness, surgery, and injuries that can affect sexual functioning in Chapter 12.

Following the death of a spouse, a widow or widower may become abstinent for a period of time or perhaps for the rest of his or her life. Masters and Johnson referred to this as this **widow/widower syndrome**, and it occurs because of the grief he or she feels over their partner's loss or perhaps because the person has never had other sexual partners and feels it is too late to start. If he or she does decide to resume sexual activity, sexual problems often occur. Men may experience erectile difficulties, and women may have less flexibility and lubrication in the walls of the vagina as a result of sexual inactivity. These problems may be reduced if the man or woman continues to masturbate.

The stereotype that sex worsens with age is not inevitably true. A key to sexual enjoyment later in life is for partners to learn more about each other and to be patient and understanding with each other. As one man in Hite's (1981:900) study said:

> *The age of one's mind and spirit is the determiner that affects all relationships and sex at any age. Age is irrelevant, our culture has made too much of this. We must ignore the public relations commercials in regard to age and sex (always young male and female couples) and begin to see each other as loving persons who need, desire, and can give love—whatever our ages.*

Physical fitness, good nutrition, adequate rest and sleep, a reduction in alcohol intake, and positive self-esteem can all enhance sexuality later in life.

widow/widower syndrome: A range of symptoms, including sexual dysfunction, that many widows and widowers experience after losing their sexual partners.

SAFE-SEX BEHAVIORS

safe sex: Sexual behaviors that do not pose a risk for the transmission of sexually transmitted diseases.

safer sex: Sexual behaviors that reduce the risk of transmission of a sexually transmitted disease.

What exactly is **safe sex**? It refers to specific sexual behaviors that are "safe" to engage in because they protect against the risk of acquiring sexually transmitted diseases. However, there are no sexual behaviors that protect a person 100% of the time (with the exception of abstinence, solo masturbation, and sexual fantasy). Therefore, maybe the real question is "Is there really any such thing as *safe* sex?" In response to that question, it may be more appropriate to refer to **safer sex** behaviors since we do know there are some sexual behaviors that are safer than others. In Sexuality Today 9.4, we present some safer sex behavior guidelines.

Most people believe that safer sex involves wearing a condom and reducing the number of sexual partners (Wight, 1992). However, this is not necessarily true. All sexually active people should be aware of the risks associated with various sexual behaviors. Not only should people decrease the number of sexual partners, they must learn more about the backgrounds of their partners, avoid unprotected anal intercourse and other risky activities, and use latex condoms with spermicide (DeBuono et al., 1990). Since the advent of AIDS, there have been very few changes in the heterosexual behavior of male and female college students; in fact, no significant changes in sexual behavior have been noted. Overall, sexual activity has increased in the past several years, and even

SEXUALITY*Today*   9.4

Safer Sex Behavior Guidelines

Below are some sexual activities that are regarded as either no-risk, or minimal-risk, low-risk, moderate-risk, or high-risk. However, you should know that recommendations for safer sex are frequently changing. You should contact your local health clinic or AIDS organization for more information.

No-Risk Sexual Behaviors

Hugging
Using one's own sex toys such as vibrators
Sexual fantasy
Self masturbation

Minimal-Risk Sexual Behaviors

Dry social kissing
Body massage
Body-to-body rubbing
Mutual masturbation

Low-Risk Sexual Behaviors

(depends on using barrier or special precautions)

Anal or vaginal intercourse with a latex condom (not lambskin)
Fellatio without ejaculation

Fellatio with a condom
Mouth-to-mouth kissing (deep kissing)
Oral-vaginal or oral-anal contact with a protective barrier (such as a dental dam)
Manual-anal contact with a latex glove
Manual-vaginal contact (internal) with a latex glove

Moderate-Risk Sexual Behaviors

(transmission of STDs possible but not proven)

Fellatio to orgasm
Oral-anal contact
Cunnilingus
Manual-rectal contact
Sharing sex toys
Ingestion of urine

High-Risk Sexual Behaviors *(transmission proven)*

Receptive anal intercourse without a condom
Insertive anal intercourse without a condom (risk less than in receptive partner)
Vaginal intercourse without a condom (both partners)

Adapted from Heiman and LoPiccolo (1992)

---

though most people feel anxious about the possibility of acquiring an STD, there have been very few increases in heterosexual safer sex behaviors (Janus and Janus, 1993; Davidson and Moore, 1994). An increase in condom use is the only behavior that has slowly been changing but still not as much as it needs to. Even with college students who are knowledgeable about AIDS, there is little change in sexual behavior (Carroll, 1991). However, an increase in condom use has been found in gay populations. In fact, more gay men than heterosexual men use condoms (Treffke et al., 1992).

Outside of college, few adults use condoms. One study found that only one-third of the population uses condoms consistently (Geringer et al., 1993). Another study found that of those people with multiple partners, less than 50% use condoms (Pepe et al., 1993). Women are more likely than men to demand a condom be worn or to use a power strategy, such as "no condom, no sex" (Edgar and Hammond, 1992). As a form of safer sex, Kaplan (1991) recommends **dry sex** as an alternative sexual activity, which involves no mixing of bodily fluids such as semen, blood, or saliva.

Drinking alcohol increases unsafe sexual activities, which may increase AIDS risk (Siegel et al., 1989). In addition, women who drink alcohol often appear "more sexual" to men than women who have not been drinking (George et al., 1988). In fact, women who drink are rated as being more aggressive, sexually available, and more likely to

dry sex: Sexual activity that does not involve the transfer of any bodily fluids.

Frequency of Condom Use in Past Twelve Months with Primary and Secondary Sex Partners

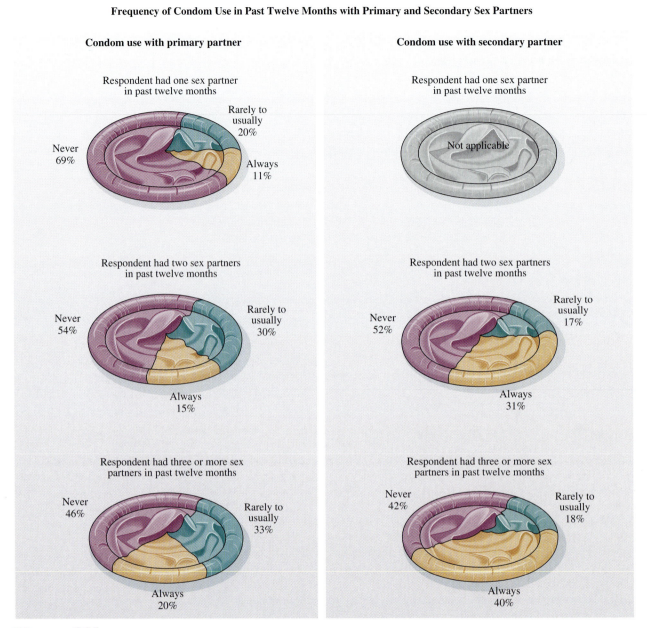

Condom use with primary partner   Condom use with secondary partner

Respondent had one sex partner in past twelve months

Never 69% — Rarely to usually 20% — Always 11%

Not applicable

Respondent had two sex partners in past twelve months

Never 54% — Rarely to usually 30% — Always 15%

Never 52% — Rarely to usually 17% — Always 31%

Respondent had three or more sex partners in past twelve months

Never 46% — Rarely to usually 33% — Always 20%

Never 42% — Rarely to usually 18% — Always 40%

F i g u r e **9.26**
The above figure illustrates the percentage of people who use condoms, both with primary and secondary partners. **Reprinted with permission from Michael et al. (1994:197).**

engage in foreplay and sexual intercourse. This was increasingly likely if a man bought the drinks for her. Among sexually active college women, 57% have engaged in sexual intercourse while intoxicated, while 47% of the men did so. (Butcher et al., 1991).

To learn more about your partner's sexual history, it is important to talk about each other's past sexual relationships prior to engaging in sexual intercourse or sexual activity.

However, this may cause embarrassment or uncomfortable feelings for many people and may even lead them to misrepresent their pasts. People worry that asking about the possibility of a partner being HIV positive may imply that the partner is promiscuous, bisexual, a drug user, or a carrier of a sexually transmitted disease (Wight, 1992). However, to ensure safer sex practices, communication is key. Talk to your partner honestly and ask that same honesty from them in return. Communication was discussed in Chapter 6.

How do we encourage people to engage in safer sex? We do not know a great deal about what causes a person to change his or her sexual behaviors (Wight, 1992). We do know that homosexual men have dramatically changed their sexual behavior since the advent of AIDS, which has reduced the transmission of the virus in the gay community. One reason is undoubtedly the strong threat that gay men have to confront each time they learn that a gay friend or acquaintance has AIDS. It may also be due to the strong gay community's AIDS educational campaign (Wight, 1992). Among heterosexuals, since the AIDS threat is less prevalent at this time, sexual behaviors are changing more slowly. (Smith, 1991).

S u m m a r y

- The majority of Americans have between one and thirty sexual partners, with men having more sexual partners than women.
- The sexual response cycle involves four physiological phases including excitement, plateau, orgasm, and resolution. During these phases, vasocongestion and myotonic changes occur.
- Kaplan's model of sexual response has three stages—desire, excitement, and orgasm.
- Many people use fantasy to help increase their sexual excitement, and people use them both during periods of sexual activity and inactivity. Female sexual fantasies often reflect personal sexual experiences, whereas male fantasies are more dependent on erotica and images.
- Homosexual couples engage in many of the same sexual activities as heterosexual couples do. Lesbians tend to be more sexually satisfied than heterosexual women and have lower rates of sexual problems.
- Although fear of masturbation has existed for many years, many people engage in it. Generally, females feel more guilty about their masturbatory activity than do males.
- In manual sex, no exchange of bodily fluids occurs. Men and women both have concerns about how best to manually stimulate their partners.
- Fellatio and cunnilingus are becoming more popular as forms of sexual behavior. Both heterosexual and homosexual couples engage in oral sex.

- Couples engage in sexual intercourse in a variety of ways. They may use a variety of positions and techniques. Each position has advantages and disadvantages.
- Both heterosexual and homosexual couples engage in anal sex and can experience orgasm from this technique. Water-soluble lubricants should be used to decrease discomfort and possible tearing of the tissue. After anal intercourse, the penis should never be transferred from the anus to the vagina because of the risk of infection.
- In comparing the sexual behavior of homosexuals and heterosexuals, more similarities than differences have been found.
- The majority of elderly persons maintain an interest in sex and sexual activity, even though society often views them as asexual. A lack of education about the physiological effects of aging on sexual functioning may cause an elderly person to think his or her sex life is over when a sexual dysfunction is experienced. It is not uncommon for widows and widowers to experience sexual dysfunction after the loss of their partners.
- There may be no such thing as "safe" sex; instead, we refer to "safer" sex. Besides abstinence, solo masturbation, and sexual fantasy, there are no 100% safe sexual behaviors.
- Very few changes in the heterosexual behavior of male and female college students has occurred as a result of the AIDS crisis. Men and women should learn the sexual histories of all their sexual partners and use latex condoms consistently.

*R*eflections on Sexuality

1. Explain the sexual response cycle proposed by Masters and Johnson. What physiological changes occur?
2. What are the differences between the Masters and Johnson model of sexual response, and the Kaplan model?
3. What factors influence the sexual behaviors that an individual engages in?
4. What gender differences have been found in men's and women's sexual fantasies?
5. What is the most commonly kept sexual secret between partners? Explain why this might be so.
6. Explain the advantages and disadvantages of various positions for sexual intercourse.
7. Are sexual relations within a lesbian or gay relationship more similar to or different from the sexual relations within a heterosexual relationship? Explain.
8. Explain the physiological changes during the sexual response cycle in later life.
9. What might you do now to maintain a healthy sex life later in your own life?
10. What are the differences between "safer sex" and "safe sex"?
11. Has your own sexual behavior been affected by the current AIDS crisis? Explain.

*S*uggested Readings

BARBACH, LONNIE (1984) *For Each Other: Sharing Sexual Intimacy.* New York: Penguin Books.

DODSON, BETTY (1987) *Sex For One: The Joy of Self Loving.* New York: Crown Trade Paperbacks.

MICHAEL, R.T., J.H. GAGNON, E.O. LAUMANN, G. KOLATA. (1994) *Sex in America: A Definitive Survey.* Boston: Little Brown & Co.

OGDEN, GINA (1994) *Women Who Love Sex.* New York: Pocket Books, A Division of Simon & Schuster Inc.

Pregnancy and Birth

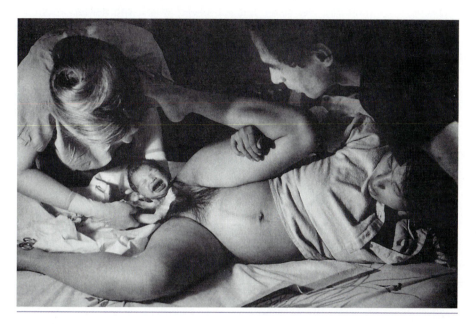

The record-holder for most children born to one mother is a Russian woman who produced 69 children between 1725 and 1765: 16 pairs of twins, 7 sets of triplets, and 4 sets of quadruplets. The modern record-holder is Leontina Albina of Chile, who by 1980 had produced 44 children. Dunham et al. (1992:18)

On Mother's Day, 1992, Margie Walsh received an unusual card that read "thanks for baby-sitting us for 8½ months." Walsh had carried her sister's biological children in her own womb, and had given birth to her sisters' triplets that day. Her sister, Michele Lewis, was in the delivery room when her girls were born. Michele had tried to have children through artificial insemination and surgery with no success. *Kansas City Star* (1992b:A6)

In Holland, women educate themselves about pregnancy and make their own choices about how they will give birth; this gives them greater control over the childbirth experience. It is interesting that Holland boasts one of the lowest statistical rates in the world for childbirth-related problems, such as episiotomy, the use of forceps, vacuum extraction, and Cesarean section. Dunham et al. (1992:68)

There are more than five billion people in the world, and approximately 238,000 more are born each day (Hatcher et al., 1988). In 1990, 4,179,000 babies were born in the United States—the largest number of births since 1961 (National Center for Health Statistics, 1991). Although the average woman in the United States will bear fewer than two children in her seventy-nine-year lifetime, an average woman in Rwanda will bear eight children in her fifty-one-year lifetime (Hatcher et al., 1994). In this chapter we will begin to explore issues related to fertility, infertility, options for infertile couples, pregnancy, and childbearing.

PART ONE—CONCEPTION

Most parents, sooner or later, must confront the moment when their child asks: "*Where did I come from?*" The answer depends on the parent, the child, the situation, and the culture. Every culture has its own myths of where babies come from. The Australian aborigines, for instance, believe that babies are created by the mother earth and, therefore, are products of the land. The spirit of children rests in certain areas of the land, and these spirits enter a young woman as she passes by (Dunham et al., 1992). Women who do not want to become pregnant either avoid these areas or dress up like old women to fool the spirits.

In western Africa, a tribe of people believe babies are the result of using certain words:

To impregnate a woman, a man must gently whisper the ancient stories of the ancestors into her ear before making love. His words will enter her ear, pass through her throat and liver, and spiral around her womb, where they form the celestial germ of water that can receive a man's seed.

Dunham et al. (1992:12)

In Malaysia, the Malay people believe that since man is the more rational of the two sexes, babies come from men. Babies are formulated in the man's brain for forty days before moving down to his penis for eventual ejaculation into a woman's womb.

For our own culture, we take a more scientific view of where babies come from, and so it is important to understand the biological processes involved in conceiving a child, being pregnant, and giving birth.

FERTILITY

The biological answer to the question *"Where did I come from?"* is that we are created from the union of an ovum and a spermatozoon. You may recall from Chapter 3 that fertilization and conception are dynamic processes that result in the creation of new life, a process so complex it is often referred to as "The Incredible Journey."

Our bodies are biologically programmed to help pregnancy occur. For instance, at ovulation, a woman's sexual desire is usually at its peak. Female orgasm helps push the semen into the uterus; once there, the orgasmic, muscular contractions of the vagina and uterus help pull sperm up toward the Fallopian tubes (pregnancy can certainly still occur, however, without the woman having an orgasm). Almost immediately after ejaculation, semen thickens to help it stay in the vagina. Twenty minutes later, when the sperm has had a chance to move up into the uterus, it becomes thin again.

For most of a woman's menstrual cycle, there is a **mucus plug** in the cervix, which makes it difficult for sperm to enter. During ovulation, this plug disappears and the mucus changes in consistency (becoming thinner and stretchy), making it easier for sperm to move through the cervix. The consistency of this mucus also creates wide gaps, which vibrate in rhythm with the tail motion of normal sperm, helping to quickly move the healthy sperm and detain abnormal sperm. The cervical mucus also helps filter out any bacteria in the semen.

With all the help our bodies are programmed to give, the process of getting pregnant may appear rather easy; however, this is not always the case. The process of becoming pregnant is complex, and things can and do go wrong. Also, the female's immune system itself begins to attack the semen immediately after ejaculation, thinking it is unwanted bacteria. Although many sperm are killed by the woman's immune system, this process is usually not a threat to conception.

Because the ovum can live for up to twenty-four hours and sperm can live up to seventy-two hours in the female reproductive tract, pregnancy may occur if intercourse takes place either a few days before or after ovulation. Although it is not clear how the sperm locates the ovum, preliminary research indicates that the ovum releases chemical signals that indicate its location (Palca, 1991). Throughout their trip into the Fallopian tube, the sperm haphazardly swim around, bumping into things. When (and if) they reach the jellylike substance that surrounds the ovum, they begin wriggling violently. Several sperm may reach the ovum, but usually only one will fertilize it. The sperm secretes a fluid called **acrosin**, a chemical that bores a hole through the outer layer of the ovum and allows the sperm to penetrate for fertilization. The outer layer of the ovum undergoes a **zona reaction**, which makes it impossible for any other sperm to enter. This entire process takes about twenty-four hours. Fertilization usually occurs in the ampulla (the funnel-shaped open end of the Fallopian tube—see Chapter 3); after fertilization, the fertilized ovum is referred to as a **zygote**.

mucus plug: A collection of thick mucus in the cervix that prevents bacteria from entering the uterus.

acrosin: The chemical in the head of the spermatozoon that breaks down the outer membrane of the ovum to allow penetration.

zona reaction: The reaction of ovum to the penetration by a spermatozoon that makes the ovum impenetrable by any other sperm.

zygote: The fertilized single cell created by the penetration of an ovum by a spermatozoon.

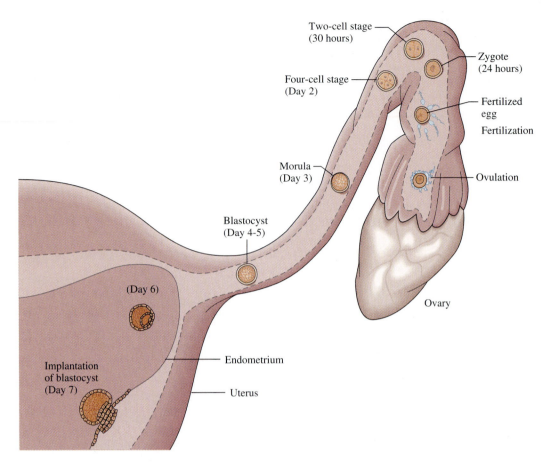

Two-cell stage
(30 hours)

Zygote
(24 hours)

Four-cell stage
(Day 2)

Fertilized
egg

Fertilization

Morula
(Day 3)

Ovulation

Blastocyst
(Day 4-5)

(Day 6)

Ovary

Implantation
of blastocyst
(Day 7)

Endometrium

Uterus

Figure **10.1**

After ovulation, the follicle moves through the Fallopian tube until it meets the spermatozoon. Fertilization takes place in the wide outer part of the tube. Approximately twenty-four hours later, the first cell division begins. For some three or four days the fertilized ovum remains in the Fallopian tube, dividing again and again. When the fertilized ovum enters the uterus, it sheds its outer wall in order to be able to implant in the wall of the uterus.

As discussed in Chapter 3, the sperm carry the genetic material from the male. Each sperm contains twenty-three chromosomes, including the X or Y sex chromosome, which will determine the gender of the fetus. Other information is determined by both the male and female genes, including eye and hair color, skin color, and weight. Approximately twelve hours after the genetic material from the sperm and ovum join together, the first cell division begins. At this point, it is referred to as a **blastocyst**. The blastocyst will divide into two every twelve to fifteen hours, doubling in size. As this goes on, the cilia in the Fallopian tube gently push the blastocyst toward the uterus. Fallopian tube muscles also help to move the blastocyst by occasionally contracting. Once the blastocyst enters the uterus, it implants in the uterine wall.

blastocyst: The hollow ball of embryonic cells that enters the uterus from the Fallopian tube and eventually implants. Once implantation has been achieved, pregnancy has begun.

INFERTILITY

A great deal of importance is placed on the ability to have children in almost every culture. Rice was originally thrown at couples after marriage, in fact, because onlookers

Many sperm arrive at the ovum and try to penetrate the hard outer covering.

As the head of the spermatozoon enters the ovum, the ovum prevents penetration by another spermatozoon.

hoped that the great fertility of the rice plant would be transferred to the married couple (Dunham et al., 1992). The same is true of the baby's breath plant, which is traditionally used in the bride's bouquet.

Being fertile is something most of us take for granted. Being able to conceive, however, is not always easy for couples. About one out of every five couples in the United States, or 3.5 million couples, are **infertile** (Burns, 1990). Infertility is defined as the inability to conceive (or impregnate) after one year of regular sexual intercourse without the use of any form of birth control (Benson, 1983). Approximately 15% of couples who try to get pregnant are not able to conceive within one year (Hatcher et al., 1988). In 1990, more than one million people sought medical help for their infertility problems. The problem can be traced to one of the partners 70% of the time (40% of the time the female, and 30% of the time the male). In 20% of cases there is a combined problem, and in 10% the reason is unknown (Afek, 1990). Historically, women have been blamed

infertile: The inability to conceive (or impregnate) after one year of regular sexual intercourse without the use of birth control.

for infertility problems, and until recently, men were not even considered a possible part of the problem. In Sex Facts 10.1, we provide some of the causes of infertility.

Being the partner responsible for infertility can be emotionally devastating. In Personal Voices 10.1, we present reflections on infertility from both a male and a female. Researchers have found that many people, upon discovering their infertility, tell their partners that they would understand if they wanted a divorce (Andrews et al., 1991). Although many studies report that infertility is a great stress on most couples, some couples are actually brought closer by the trials of infertility (Greil et al., 1988).

Emotional reactions to infertility can include depression, anxiety, anger, self-blame, guilt, frustration, and fear. Since the majority of people have no experience dealing with infertility, many of those who find out they are infertile isolate themselves and try not to think about it. Infertile couples often feel ashamed and keep it a secret. Although both men and women are emotionally affected by infertility, women tend to experience more emotional difficulties. As one woman reported:

> *I can't emphasize how devastating infertility is to one who has spent a lifetime basing her self-esteem on "what I can do." When you can't have children—the most natural and important aspect of life—none of your previous accomplishments seem important. They are overshadowed by this supreme failure.*
>
> *Mahlstedt (1987:131)*

Support groups for persons experiencing infertility are often very helpful. One of these groups, RESOLVE,* offers resources for couples struggling with infertility. RESOLVE helps couples see that they are not alone and provides a safe and healthy environment in which to discuss relevant issues.

---

* RESOLVE, Inc., P.O. Box 494, Belmont, Massachusetts 02178; (617) 643-2424.

SEX *Facts*   10.1

Possible Causes of Infertility

Possible Causes of Female Infertility Include:

- Vaginal or cervical mucus that does not allow for sperm transport
- Lack of ovulation or Fallopian tube blockage
- A uterus incapable of maintaining pregnancy
- A malfunctioning hormonal system
- Development of antibodies to sperm or to the fetus
- Exposure to multiple sexual partners, which may increase exposure to sexually transmitted diseases
- Endometriosis or excessive radiation
- Excessive stress

Possible Causes of Male Infertility Include:

(For males to be considered fertile, their sperm count must be at least 20 million sperm per ml of semen. Forty percent of these must swim, and 60% must be of normal shape and size.)

- Abnormal spermatogenesis, or ejaculatory or erectile difficulties
- Exposure to multiple sexual partners, which may increase exposure to sexually transmitted diseases
- Exposure to excessive radiation (i.e., work conditions)
- Undescended testes, infected prostrate gland, varicocele
- Adult mumps
- Excessive stress
- Increased temperature, which may be caused by hot baths and saunas, frequent use of athletic supporters, or workplaces with excessive heat
- Genital injury
- Autoimmunity to sperm
- Excessive alcohol, drug, or cigarette use

Adapted from Hotchner (1984:47–55)

Infertile couples usually seek professional help, although research indicates that women are often more committed than their partners to finding a solution to the infertility. However, if there is a disagreement about a potential solution, the male partner's wishes usually prevail (Ulbrich et al., 1990). Childbearing in the United States is part of what defines being female, and so women who are infertile often feel less valued than fertile women. The **motherhood mandate** refers to the idea that something is wrong with a woman if she has not had children by a certain age (usually thirty to thirty-five in the United States). As one woman put it:

> *[Infertility] is a wound that never heals . . . or maybe it heals but it has a thin scab that can be penetrated very easily. I still feel less than other people—not as valuable—different.*
>
> *Mahlstedt (1987:132)*

Between 10% and 90% of all infertility is due to gonorrhea, chlamydia, or pelvic inflammatory disease (Hatcher et al., 1994), which is one of the reasons college

motherhood mandate: The belief that there is something psychologically wrong with a woman if she is childless at a certain age.

Personal

VOICES
10.1

Personal Reflections on Infertility

Woman

The thing I remember most about our involvement with infertility is our sense of isolation. I felt separated from the "normal" world because my calendar was geared to temperature charts, ovulation predictor kits, and legs up in stirrups for inseminations and hospital personnel who were always too busy. It was too painful to share with friends who were either still practicing birth control or had just begun their families.

There was absolutely nothing "extra" I could do to make this pregnancy happen. The loss of control was profound and the dependency on doctors, nurses, and kits for something so personal and, seemingly, so effortless for everyone else, was difficult. There was no psychological support from the medical team, particularly on a professional level (e.g., psychologist, psychiatrist, etc.).

Infertility was like a stain that marked my thoughts and feelings. To this day, after having two magical and beautiful daughters, I still react with a twinge of jealousy when I hear of someone who got pregnant. I suppose, no matter how many children I may have, that I will always feel infertile. The feelings surrounding my infertility were almost primal in the amount of pain they brought; these

feelings are equally as powerful and wonderful about my daughters and bring into focus why the desire to have children is so basic.

Man

Although my infertility did not come as a surprise to me (I knew of it years before I was married), my reaction to needing help in starting a family was nevertheless unexpected. The need to seek the help of strangers (albeit "professionals" in the medical field) in this most personal of matters was galling. I had predicted that I would react in the mature and modern way, that is, very nonchalant about the whole infertility treatment. But instead, as matters progressed, I became more and more resentful of my lack of privacy and antagonistic toward all those involved.

Compounding this situation was the shocking absence of any professional guidance to aid in explaining and aiding my feelings and reactions. My wife and I were surrounded with technology and technicians to treat our bodies but had nowhere to turn to seek help in understanding our feelings and easing our pain.

Fortunately, we worked things through together, my wife and I, and are the stronger for it, and today I know there are therapists who specialize in infertility counseling. It's a lesson we learned the hard way—infertility is as much a state of mind as of body.

Author's files

students are encouraged to have regular medical checkups and women are encouraged to have regular Pap smears. If an STD is treated early, there is less chance that it will interfere with fertility (see Sex Facts 10.1, page 368). For some men and women who experience reproductive problems, changing lifestyle patterns, reducing stress, avoiding rigorous exercise, and maintaining a recommended weight may restore fertility. (Laversen and Bouchez, 1991). For other couples, professional intervention offers new possibilities.

Options for Infertile Couples

Problems with infertility have given rise to artificial means of conception. Reproductive technologies that have been developed in the last few years enable some couples to have children even if one of them is infertile. These technologies, although exciting, may also contribute to the further anguish and stress for the infertile couple, particularly if they fail. Many of these options are very time consuming, expensive, and do not guarantee success. One woman said:

> *The waiting and uncertainty was the most stressful aspect of the infertility treatment—not knowing if any of the time, the money, or the pain would pay off. It's bad enough if you can never achieve a pregnancy, but having no end to the quest is the worst. You just want someone to tell you to forget it because it's hopeless or to hang in there because you will finally be successful.*
>
> *Mahlstedt (1987:143).*

There are a large number of technologies available to the infertile couple, although many are expensive (see Sexuality Today 10.1). In addition, many ethical and legal issues have emerged as these procedures have become more common (see Sexuality Today 10.2). Below we explore these options in more detail.

Fertility Drugs

human chorionic gonadotropin (hCG): The hormone that stimulates production of estrogen and progesterone to maintain pregnancy.

As discussed in Chapter 3, ovulation and sperm production are a result of a well-balanced endocrine system (pituitary, hypothalamus, and gonads). Some women and men have hormonal irregularities that may interfere with the process of ovulation or sperm production. Although we do not always know why these hormonal problems develop, many problems can be treated with fertility drugs. Fertility drugs such as Clomiphene, Pergonal, Pregnyl [or **human chorionic gonadotropin (hCG)**], and Gonadatropin-Releasing Hormone (GnRH) are most commonly used. Clomiphene, Pergonal, and GnRH are used to help a woman ovulate and produce healthier ova. Pregnyl is used to trigger the release of the ovum and help maintain the levels of progesterone in the luteal phase of the menstrual cycle. Since these drugs work to increase ova production in women, there is an increased possibility of multiple births. All of these drugs are also used by males who are experiencing fertility problems.

Surgery

laparoscopy: A procedure that allows a physician to have a direct view of all the pelvic organs, including the uterus, Fallopian tubes, and ovaries; also allows a physician to perform a number of important surgical procedures.

varicocele: An unnatural swelling of the veins in the scrotum that may lead to sterility in males.

Cervical or vaginal abnormalities that prevent conception may be corrected surgically. Scar tissue, cysts, tumors, or adhesions, as well as blockages inside the Fallopian tubes, may be surgically removed. The use of diagnostic techniques such as **laparoscopy** are also common.

In men, surgery may be required to reverse a prior sterilization procedure, remove any blockage in the vas deferens or epididymis, or repair a **varicocele**.

The Costs of Infertility Tests, Treatments, and Adoption

Procedure	Charge
Initial Visit, Interview, Physical Exam—Female	$250 plus any lab work ordered
Initial Visit, Interview, Physical Exam—Male	$100–$150 plus any lab work ordered
Semen Analysis	$75–$100
Postcoital Test (PCT)	$75
Sperm Antibody Test	$75–$150
Hysterosalpingogram	$400–$500 for radiologist and hospital charges
Various Hormonal Blood Tests for Women and Men	$50 per test
Testicular Biopsy	$800–$2000 depending on whether performed in physician's office or hospital
Endometrial Biopsy	$250 for physician's and laboratory charges
Sperm Penetration Assay (SPA)	$250–$400
"Fertility Drug" Treatment with hMG (Pergonal)	$1500–$2500 per cycle for drug and monitoring
Donor Insemination (DI)	$225 per insemination
Laparoscopy plus Laparoscoptic Surgery	$8000–$8500 for surgeon, anesthesiologist and outpatient hospital charges
Zygote intrafallopian transfer (ZIFT) Gamete intrafallopian transfer (GIFT)	About $8000–$10,000 per attempt
In Vitro Fertilization (IVF)	$8,000–$10,000 per attempt, depending on procedures and individual program
Frozen Embryo Transfer (FET)	$1000
Major Surgery for Removal of Tubal Blockages, Adhesions, or Severe Endometriosis	$5000 or more for surgeon, assistant surgeon, and anesthesiologist charges, plus hospital charges of $7000 or more, depending on length of stay, time in operating room, medications, etc.
Vasectomy Reversal	$2500–$6000 $1500–$4000
Variocele Surgery	$4000–$7000
Duct Obstruction Surgery	Male surgery charges for surgeon, assistant surgeon, and anesthesiologist and hospital, depending on length of surgery and type of anesthesia
Independent Adoption	$2000–$10,000, depending on birthmother's and newborn's needs for living, counseling, and medical costs plus $3000–$4000 for attorney's fees and other legal costs
Agency Adoption	Varies from several hundred dollars for some types of public agency adoptions to thousands of dollars for some private agency and international adoptions
Surrogate Arrangements	From about $12,000 for an arrangement based on the independent adoption model to $35,000 or more when fees for surrogate and agency services are added.

Harness (1992)

Artificial Insemination

artificial insemination:
Inserting semen into a
woman's vagina or uterus for
the purpose of inducing pregnancy by means other than
sexual intercourse.

Artificial insemination is the process of introducing sperm into a woman's reproductive tract without sexual intercourse. Sperm, collected through masturbation, can come
from a partner or from a sperm donor. Although seldom used a few decades ago, in the
United States today approximately 250,000 babies are conceived each year using artificial insemination (Holbrook, 1990). Men who decide to undergo sterilization or who
may become sterile because of surgery or chemotherapy may collect sperm prior to the
procedure. It can be frozen for up to ten years in a **sperm bank**. Recently, both heterosexual and homosexual single women who want children have been using artificial
insemination.

sperm bank: A place that
stores frozen sperm for later
use.

Prior to using these artificial insemination procedures, doctors often prescribe fertility drugs to increase the chances that there will be healthy ova present when the
sperm is introduced. This practice has become so successful that the majority of clinics
today use fertility drugs with all artificial insemination procedures (Lauersen and
Bouchez, 1991).

After collecting the semen sample, the sperm is specially treated and washed, and
healthy sperm are allowed to swim up to the top of the wash. In men with a low sperm
count, several samples may be combined to increase the number of healthy sperm. Once
washed, sperm are deposited inside the vagina. Sperm can also be deposited just above
the cervix, which is helpful when hostile cervical mucus exists. Intrauterine (in the
uterus) and intratubal (in the Fallopian tubes) inseminations have also been used.

In Vitro Fertilization

in vitro fertilization: A procedure in which a woman's
ova are removed from her
body, fertilized with sperm in
a laboratory, and then surgically implanted into her
uterus.

Another reproductive technology is **in vitro fertilization (IVF)**, or **test-tube babies**
(see Figure 10.2). In 1978, Louise Brown, the first test-tube baby, was born in
England. Since that time, several babies have been conceived in this fashion. The
name is a bit deceiving, however, because these babies are not *born* in a test tube,
rather they are *conceived* in a petri dish. Most of the women who use this method have
Fallopian tube blockage, which does not allow for fertilization in the tube. Women
who undergo this process are first given fertility drugs to help the ovaries release multiple ova, and between four and six ova are retrieved (with the use of microscopic
needles inserted into the abdominal cavity). However, not all of them will be able to
implant.

test-tube baby: A slang term
for any zygote created by
mixing sperm and egg outside
a woman's body.

The ova are collected and mixed with washed sperm from the father. Once fertilization has occurred, the zygotes are transferred to the woman's uterus, where they
develop normally. Implantation problems with IVF are the biggest hurdle to overcome;
for some unknown reason, many of the zygotes refuse to implant. It is estimated that
after implantation 20% to 25% of these fertilized embryos are spontaneously aborted
(Cohen, 1991).

Gamete Intra-Fallopian Tube Transfer

**gamete intra-Fallopian tube
transfer:** A reproductive
technique in which the sperm
and ova are collected and
injected into the Fallopian
tube prior to fertilization.

Although **gamete intra-fallopian tube transfer (GIFT)** is similar to IVF in that ova
and sperm are mixed in an artificial environment, the main difference is that both the
ova and sperm are placed in the Fallopian tube *prior* to fertilization. Fertilization is
allowed to occur naturally in the Fallopian tube, rather than in an artificial environment. This has resulted in a much higher implantation rate. Fertility drugs and sperm
washing are also used.

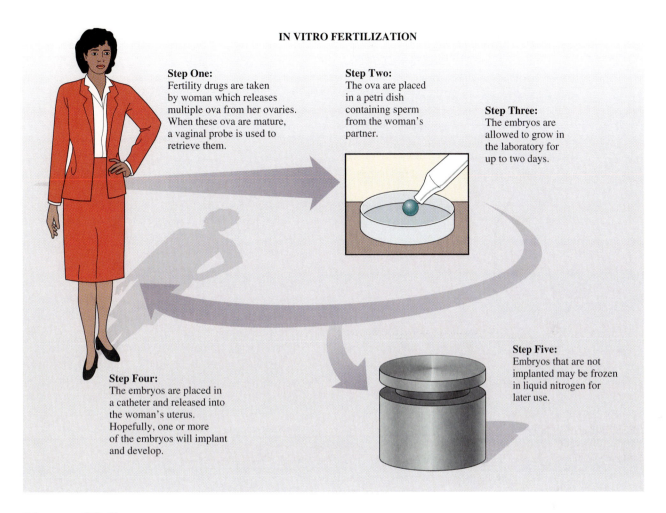

IN VITRO FERTILIZATION

Step One:
Fertility drugs are taken by woman which releases multiple ova from her ovaries. When these ova are mature, a vaginal probe is used to retrieve them.

Step Two:
The ova are placed in a petri dish containing sperm from the woman's partner.

Step Three:
The embryos are allowed to grow in the laboratory for up to two days.

Step Four:
The embryos are placed in a catheter and released into the woman's uterus. Hopefully, one or more of the embryos will implant and develop.

Step Five:
Embryos that are not implanted may be frozen in liquid nitrogen for later use.

F i g u r e **10.2**
In vitro fertilization.

Zygote Intra-Fallopian Transfer

Similar to both IVF and GIFT, the **zygote intra-fallopian transfer (ZIFT)** procedure allows ova and sperm to meet outside the body, where fertilization occurs. Directly following fertilization, the embryo is placed in the woman's Fallopian tube, allowing it to travel to the uterus and implant naturally. Fertility drugs and sperm washing are also used. This procedure has been found to yield higher implantation rates than IVF but not higher than GIFT.

zygote intra-Fallopian transfer: A reproductive technique in which the sperm and ova are collected and fertilized outside the body, and the fertilized zygote is then placed into the Fallopian tube.

Intravaginal Cultures

Intravaginal cultures are used in conjunction with IVF and ZIFT; they use a woman's uterus as an incubator. The ova and washed sperm are placed in a small container that is sealed and placed in a woman's vagina. The container is held in place by a vaginal diaphragm. Fertilization is allowed to occur in the proper temperature and atmosphere. Forty-eight hours later the vial is removed; if fertilization has occurred, it will be transferred to the woman's uterus.

SEXUALITY*Today* 10.2

Ethical, Legal, and Moral Issues Involved in Reproductive Technology

Many of the reproductive technologies raise ethical, legal, and moral questions with which many scientists and researchers are grappling. Should we be allowed to artificially join the ovum and sperm outside of the uterus? Will this one day give rise to the manipulation of certain traits or genes in the creation of a "perfect" baby? In addition, all of these procedures are very expensive. One women reported:

I want to take out a second mortgage for another shot at GIFT, but my husband thinks that would be foolish. We've already spent the money we'd saved for college, so our only other option now is earmarking next year's tax return

Hopkins (1991).

Expensive technologies produce very expensive children. Does expensive mean "better"? Does this set up higher expectations for these children? Will people be disappointed if their expensive children are difficult in the future? Why are people willing to risk their life savings on having biologically related children when there are children waiting to be adopted?

In addition to these ethical and moral questions, several legal questions have also arisen. What should be done with embryos that are fertilized and frozen for later use if a couple divorces? Whose property are they? Should they be equitably distributed to both partners? Should they simply be disposed of? Also, since this field is so lucrative, some physicians have been known to perform expensive infertility procedures when they may not be necessary.

In 1992, infertility specialist Dr. Cecil Johnson was found guilty of artificially inseminating 52 women with his own sperm. After DNA testing, it was found that he had fathered 15 of the children, though some claim this number was as high as 75.

What do you think about these reproductive techniques? Should a woman be able to "rent" her uterus for the development of someone else's child? Should fertilization be allowed to occur in a petri dish? Many feminists argue that these reproductive techniques make money at the expense of emotionally distraught women.

Zonal Dissection

Sometimes ova are resistant to fertilization due to problems with the enzyme in the head of the sperm, which is supposed to break down the hard outer covering of the ovum and allow fertilization. Zonal dissection involves drilling a hole in the ovum with a very small needle, making a small slit in the side of the jellylike coating, or using a chemical to dissolve the outer shell. Unfortunately, one drawback to this procedure is that several sperm may enter the ovum and cause developmental problems in the resulting embryo.

Sperm Injections

A new procedure, sperm injection, involves injecting one sperm into the center of an ovum under a microscope. This procedure can be beneficial for men who produce insufficient or weak sperm. So far, the results have been promising, but there are some difficulties. The ovum can be damaged during the procedure, and there also may be an increased risk of chromosomal defects. In addition, scientists do not know how nature chooses one sperm for fertilization, and choosing one randomly may not be appropriate. It is still too early to know whether this procedure will be successful.

Embryo Transplants

Women who are not able to produce their own ova may use a donor ovum. An embryo transplant involves artificial insemination of a donor's ovum with the male partner's (washed) sperm. After fertilization has occurred, the embryo is transferred from the donor's to the woman's uterus. To be successful, it is imperative that fertility drugs be used to synchronize both women's menstrual cycles.

Surrogate Parenting

In women who cannot carry a pregnancy to term, **surrogate parenting** is an option. If a woman cannot carry a pregnancy but has healthy ova, she may "rent" another woman's uterus to carry the pregnancy to term. The couple's sperm and ovum are combined and the zygote is implanted in a second woman, called a **gestational carrier**. One gestational carrier said:

> *It's wonderful being a carrier. It's not easy, but it's wonderful. You feel all the emotions, it's like a rollercoaster. You try and help the parents cope, but at the same time, you're trying to deal with your own emotions. I feel very proud when I see the little one I carried—I love watching him with his parents; it's so overwhelming sometimes. They gave him life; I sustained that life and gave birth to him. It's wonderful. A very good high; I could burst with pride sometimes just watching him.*
>
> *Author's files*

If a woman is neither capable of carrying a pregnancy nor producing her own ova, she may "rent" another woman's uterus and have one of the surrogate's ovum fertilized by her partner's sperm. The woman who carries the fetus is called a **surrogate mother**. At birth, the child is given to the woman and her partner. But as the case in Sexuality Today 10.3 demonstrates, surrogate parenting is fraught with emotional and ethical dilemmas. It is estimated that, in 1989, there were 198 attempts at this type of surrogate parenting, and in 33 of these cases a baby was born (*The New York Times,* 1991i). In 1992, surrogacy was illegal in seventeen states.

Other Options

Other options for infertility involve the freezing of embryos and sperm for later fertilization. This can be beneficial for men and women who are diagnosed with illnesses (such as cancer) that interfere with their ability to manufacture healthy sperm or ova. Recently, researchers in South Korea have been experimenting with freezing unfertilized ova. Although it is uncertain whether this will work, if it does, women who choose to delay childbearing until later in their lives could store ova while they are young. At this time, only sperm and embryos can be frozen for use later on.

GENDER SELECTION

Throughout history, there have been techniques that were recommended for parents to try to select the gender of their children. Aristotle believed that if a couple had sexual intercourse in the north wind, they would have a male, and if intercourse took place in

surrogate parenting: Use of a woman who, through artificial insemination or in vitro fertilization, gestates a fetus for another woman or man.

gestational carrier: A woman who carries another couple's zygote to term for them.

surrogate mother: A woman who donates her ovum (which is fertilized by the father's sperm) and then carries the zygote to term.

SEXUALITY *T o d a y* 10.3

The Baby M Case

Probably the most famous case of surrogate parenting gone wrong is the 1986 "Baby M" case. In this case, William Stern contracted with Mary Beth Whitehead to bear him a child through artificial insemination. Stern's wife, Elizabeth, was infertile. Stern agreed to pay Whitehead $10,000 upon Whitehead's terminating her parental rights and giving the child to him and his wife.

Ms. Whitehead, a married mother of two, agreed to be artificially inseminated with Stern's sperm. On March 27, 1986, she gave birth to a girl (named Sara by Whitehead, Melissa by the Sterns). Ms. Whitehead had requested that no one at the hospital know about the surrogacy arrangement. Three days after Sara's birth, the Whiteheads took her home from the hospital. Ms. Whitehead turned the baby over to the Sterns shortly thereafter.

However, Ms. Whitehead quickly changed her mind and wanted the baby back. She begged the Sterns to let her have the baby back temporarily, or she threatened to kill herself. The Sterns allowed her to have the baby back temporarily.

Soon afterward, the Whiteheads and Sara disappeared. For more than three months they ran, avoiding police. However, they were eventually apprehended. In 1987, a lower court ruled that the surrogacy contract was valid and that it was in the child's best interest to remain with the Sterns. The judge allowed Mr. Stern's wife to legally adopt Melissa. Later, however, the New Jersey Supreme Court ruled that surrogacy contracts were invalid and also voided Mrs. Stern's adoption of the child. The court also ruled that paying a woman to give birth may constitute "baby selling," which is a criminal act. The court decided that even though Whitehead was child's legal mother, the child's best interests would be served by giving custody to Mr. Stern. Ms. Whitehead was awarded visitation rights.

Many feminists and others were up in arms about this decision, claiming that there was a bias toward favoring the rich over the poor because the Sterns were wealthy and Ms. Whitehead was not. Other states began to question the legality of surrogacy contracts, and today many states have outlawed the practice.

Other ethical questions soon arose. In surrogacy arrangements, will the parent who has a genetic link with the child have a stronger bond with him or her? What happens if the child is born with a defect? What if the couple decides they do not want the baby anymore?

Who do you think should have had custody of Baby M? For what reason? The legal battle that ensued over this case set a legal agenda for the future of surrogate motherhood.

Adapted from Annas (1988)

the south wind, they would have a female. Hippocrates believed that males formed on the right side of the uterus and females on the left, and so to conceive a daughter, a woman was advised to lie on her left side directly after intercourse. The ancient Greeks thought that if a man cut or tied his left testicle, a couple would not have girls because male sperm were thought to be produced in the right testicle (Dunham et al., 1992). Although some of these suggestions sound absurd today, many people in many cultures—even in the United States—still hold myths of how to choose and how to know the gender of their child (see Focus on Diversity 10.1).

Although some couples simply prefer a male or female child, others desire to choose the gender of their children for medical reasons. For example, certain inherited diseases are more likely to affect one gender (such as hemophilia, which affects more males). Modern-day methods of gender selection were popularized by Shettles and Rorvik (1960) in their groundbreaking book *Your Baby's Sex—Now You Can Choose.* By using microscopic observation, they claimed that they could distinguish between X (female) and Y (male) sperm. They found that each of these types of sperm live better in different types of vaginal environments (either acidic or alkaline). By douching prior to

Focus
on Diversity
──────── *10.1*   **Is it a Boy
or a Girl?**
────────────────

It's a Girl		It's a Boy
Baby sits on the left side of the womb	**Nyinba, Napal**	Baby sits on the right side of the womb
Mother puts her left foot first crossing the threshold	**Bihar, India**	Mother puts her right foot first crossing the threshold
Mother's left eye is brighter and her left breast is bigger	**Hippocrates**	Mother's right eye is brighter and her right breast bigger
Baby sits low in the belly	**Lepchas, Himalayas and Bedouin Tribes**	Baby sits high in the belly
Baby sits high in the belly	**Ancient Egypt**	Baby sits low in the belly
If you're grumpy with women	**Dinka, Africa**	If you're grumpy with men
Fetus moves slow and gentle	**Dustin, North Borneo and Egypt**	Fetus moves fast and rough
If you first feel baby move when you're outside	**Serbs, Yugoslavia**	If you first feel baby move when you're at home
Dreams of human skulls	**Maori, New Zealand**	Dreams of *huisa* feathers
Dreams of prayer beads, necklaces, round parsnips	**Nyinba, Nepal**	Dreams of long radishes, aubergine, cutting tool
Dream of a headkerchief	**Egypt**	Dream of a handkerchief
Cravings for spicy foods	**Nyinba, Nepal**	Cravings for bland foods
Mother has red, fat cheeks	**Nyinba, Nepal**	Mother has thin, white face
Mother's face has yellow spots	**Poland**	Mother looks well
Belly is long	**India**	Nipples are black
Baby "play in stomach" before sixth month	**Nyinba, Nepal**	Baby "plays in stomach" after sixth month

Dunham et al. (1991)

intercourse, a woman can change the acidity or alkalinity of her vagina. In addition, since there are ways to favor an X or Y sperm getting to the ovum first, Shettles and Rorvik made other recommendations. To have a boy, a couple should have intercourse close to ovulation (to allow the faster-swimming Y sperm to get there first) and douche with a mixture of baking soda and water (which creates an alkaline vagina and favors male sperm). For a girl, a couple should time intercourse two to three days prior to ovulation (since X sperm tend to live longer) and douche with a mixture of vinegar and water (which creates an acidic vagina and favors female sperm).

amniocentesis: A diagnostic procedure in which amniotic fluid is extracted from a pregnant woman's uterus to examine fetal cells for chromosomal defects that can cause genetic disorders or other abnormalities in the unborn child.

amniotic fluid: The fluid in the amniotic cavity; initially produced by the mother's blood and later from fetal urine.

female infanticide: The killing of female infants; practiced in some countries that value males more than females.

Other formulas for gender selection include various dieting routines, spinning the semen in a centrifuge (which separates the X and Y sperm) followed by artificial insemination, and separation of the sperm with an electrical charge. However, at present there are no 100% reliable methods of gender selection.

During the sixteenth or seventeenth week of pregnancy, a procedure called **amniocentesis** can determine, among other things, the gender of the fetus. Some **amniotic fluid** is extracted from the womb using a needle and is evaluated for chromosomal abnormalities. An amniocentesis is strongly advised for women over the age of thirty-five because they are at a higher risk for chromosomal abnormalities. This test is also important in the early discovery of sex-linked abnormalities. However, amniocentesis also raises many moral, sociological, and ethical issues about gender selection. For example, controversy surrounds whether or not parents should be able to choose the gender of a child through selective abortion. Some believe that in these cases, if a couple is carrying a boy and want a girl, they should not be allowed to terminate the pregnancy.

The government of the Peoples Republic of China (PRC) has instituted a series of laws trying to combat overpopulation by restricting every family to one child. Yet there is a strong preference for male children because they can continue the family name. Because of this, many people believe that **female infanticide** has been used to allow couples to have a male child. A recent article in *Health Magazine* reported that a total of sixty million female babies are unaccounted for in populations of China, India, Pakistan, Bangladesh, Nepal, Egypt, and western Asia (Health, 1992). It is believed that this is a result of female infanticide and a lack of care for female babies from birth onward. Female babies are given less food and medical treatment in these countries.

SEX TALK

QUESTION **10.1 I have missed my period now for two months in a row. Does this mean that I am pregnant? What should I do?**

If you have been engaging in sexual intercourse, there is certainly a chance that you are pregnant. However, if you are not pregnant, missing your period may happen for several reasons. Stress, losing weight, active participation in sports, or changes in eating patterns can affect menstrual patterns. In any case, it is a good idea to see a gynecologist or your school nurse for an evaluation.

PART TWO—PREGNANCY

Approximately three to four days after conception, the blastocyst enters the uterus. For two or three days it remains in the uterus and absorbs nutrients secreted by the endometrial glands. On about the sixth day after fertilization, the uterus secretes a chemical that dissolves the hard covering around the blastocyst, allowing it to implant in the uterine wall (Jones, 1984). Implantation usually occurs five to eight days after fertilization. To facilitate implantation, the endometrium must have been exposed to the appropriate levels of estrogen and progesterone. Most of the time, implantation takes place in the upper portion of the uterus, and once this occurs the woman's body and the developing embryo begin to exchange chemical information. Hormones are released into the woman's bloodstream, which can be detected through pregnancy tests. If implantation does not occur, the blastocyst will degenerate and the potential pregnancy will be terminated.

Some women report that they knew conception had occurred, even prior to a pregnancy test:

> *As I laid there right after we finished having intercourse, I felt a very strange feeling inside of me. At that moment, I knew for sure that I was pregnant. For the next couple of days I felt the same sensations again. When the pregnancy test confirmed this, I was not surprised.*
>
> *A 25-year-old first-time mother; Author's files*

It is fascinating that a woman's body allows the blastocyst to implant when so many of our body's defenses are designed to eliminate foreign substances. Apparently there is some weakening of the immune system that allows for an acceptance of the fertilized ovum (Nilsson, 1990). Some women do continually reject the fertilized ovum and experience repeated miscarriages. We will discuss this in greater detail later in this chapter. Here, Sexuality Today 10.4 discusses ways to increase the chances of pregnancy.

After implantation, the blastocyst divides into two layers of cells, the ectoderm and endoderm. A middle layer, the mesoderm, soon follows. These three layers will develop into the adult tissues. From the second through the eighth weeks, the developing human is referred to as an **embryo**.

Soon the **amnion** begins to grow over the developing embryo, and the amniotic cavity begins to fill with amniotic fluid. This fluid supports the fetus and protects it from shock. The **placenta** supplies nutrients to the developing fetus. It also aids in respiratory and excretory functions, and it secretes hormones necessary for the continuation of the pregnancy. The **umbilical cord** connects the fetus to the placenta. By the fourth week of pregnancy the placenta covers 20% of the wall of the uterus, and at five months the placenta covers half of the uterus (Jones, 1984). Toward the end of pregnancy, approximately seventy-five gallons of blood will pass through the placenta daily.

The majority of women deliver a single fetus. However, in 2 out of every 100 couples there is a multiple birth (Eisenberg et al., 1991). This can happen in two ways. Sometimes two ova are released by the ovaries, and if both are fertilized by sperm, **fraternal twins** (nonidentical) will be born. These twins are **dizygotic**, and they can be either the same or different genders. Dizygotic twins are no more closely genetically related than any two siblings. Two-thirds of all twins are fraternal. The tendency to have fraternal twins may be inherited from the mother, and older women (over the age of thirty) seem to have fraternal twins more often than younger women (due to erratic ovulation and an increased possibility of releasing more than one ova). **Identical twins** occur when a single zygote divides into two separate zygotes. This process produces twins who are genetically identical and are referred to as **monozygotic** twins. They often look very much alike and are always of the same gender. In rare cases, the zygote fails to divide completely and two babies may be joined together at some point in their bodies; these are known as **Siamese twins**. In some instances, many ova are released and fertilized, and **triplets** or **quadruplets** may result. While the odds of having twins are about 1 in 80, triplets and quadruplets are even rarer, with chances at 1 in 6400 and 1 in 512,000 respectively (Jones, 1984). Recently, the number of multiple births has been increasing as more older women become pregnant and fertility drug usage increases.

embryo: The unborn organism during the first eight weeks after fertilization.

amnion: The innermost fetal membrane that holds the fetus suspended in amniotic fluid.

placenta: The structure through which the exchange of materials between fetal and maternal circulations occurs.

umbilical cord: The long, ropelike structure containing the umbilical arteries and vein that connect the fetus to the placenta.

fraternal twins: Two offspring developed from two separate ova fertilized by different spermatozoon.

dizygotic: Pertaining to or derived from two separate zygotes.

identical twins: Two offspring developed from one single ovum fertilized by one spermatozoon.

monozygotic: Pertaining to or derived from a single zygote.

Siamese twins: Twins who are born physically joined together in any manner.

triplets: Three offspring having coextensive gestation periods and delivered at the same birth.

quadruplets: Four offspring having coextensive gestation periods and delivered at the same birth.

SEXUALITY *Today* 10.4

Increasing the Chances of Pregnancy

Although many college-aged students try to avoid pregnancy, many couples wish to increase their odds of conception. With infertility affecting 3.5 million couples in the United States, there have been many recommendations for couples who are trying to become pregnant. A few of these are listed here.

1. Maintain a healthy and satisfying sex life. This can bolster endorphins, which help increase fertility.

2. Avoid lubricants that contain oil-based products because these can change the natural pH level of the vagina.

3. Avoid hot tubs, which can interfere with ova production and sperm development.

4. Women should maintain a healthy weight for their body. Hormonal shutdown can occur if a woman's body fat falls too high or low. Women with eating disorders (including obesity) often experience difficulties conceiving.

5. Reduce participation in endurance sports, such as marathon running, excessive jogging, frequent high-energy aerobics, or triathlon training. All of these influence the hypothalamus of the brain, which regulates hormone production.

6. Increase participation in low aerobic activities, such as swimming, walking, moderate aerobics, stretching, and moderate tennis workouts.

7. Reduce stress. Stress has also been found to affect the hypothalamus and hormone production.

8. Smile a lot. Smiling has been found to cause a biochemical reaction that causes the brain to produce endorphins.

9. Avoid artificial sweeteners, soda pop, high-sugar fruit drinks, and candy. High sugar levels have been found to cause lower blood sugar, which can affect hormonal levels.

10. Avoid caffeine. Caffeine has been found to affect the hypothalamus and may lead to ovulation problems. Although caffeine is found in coffee, tea, cola, and chocolate, it is also present in many over-the-counter drugs, such as extra-strength Excedrin, maximum-strength Midol, No-Doz, and Dexatrim diet pills.

11. Use the male-on-top position, with a pillow under the woman's hips. This causes her uterus to tilt backward. Reduce movement directly following intercourse. Avoid the woman-on-top, bending over, or standing positions for sexual intercourse.

12. Spend some time in the sun. Exposure to sunshine may increase levels of vitamin D (Soltriol), which affects hormone production.

13. Males should wear boxer shorts instead of briefs. Boxer shorts allow the testicles to hang freely, which may increase sperm production.

14. Both males and females should reduce exposure to computers. Prolonged exposure to the video display terminal may damage various areas of the reproductive system.

15. Reduce frequency of air travel. Frequent air travel exposes men and women to high levels of atmospheric radiation, which may reduce fertility.

Adapted from Lauersen and Bouchez (1991)

EARLY SIGNS OF PREGNANCY

morning sickness: One of the signs of pregnancy that most women experience; it can occur at any time of day.

If the zygote does implant, most women experience physical signs very early in pregnancy that alert them their pregnancy. These include missing a period, breast tenderness, frequent urination, and **morning sickness**. Morning sickness is due to the increase in estrogen during pregnancy, which may irritate the stomach lining. It is often worse in the morning because there is no food in the stomach to counter its effects, although it can happen at any point during the day. Although the majority of women stop menstruating during pregnancy, there are some who continue to menstruate in the first two months of pregnancy; it is not clear why this happens.

QUESTION **10.2** **Why do some women have really bad morning sickness?**

> **Since every woman is unique, each one will respond differently to the increase in hormones during pregnancy. Only one-third to one-half of women experience morning sickness. Some may notice very few symptoms, while others have many symptoms. A woman's expectations may influence the severity of her morning sickness. Research has found that women who are unhappy about the pregnancy tend to experience severe morning sickness, while those who are excited about their pregnancy experience none (Eisenberg et al., 1991). Also, genetics and biology seem to play some role; however, the research is still unclear.**

Identical twins develop when a single zygote divides into two separate zygotes. These twins are genetically identical.

In rare cases, **pseudocyesis**, or false pregnancy, occurs. This is a condition in which a woman believes she is pregnant when she is not. Her belief is so strong that she begins to experience several of the signs of pregnancy. She may miss her period, have morning sickness, and gain weight. Although the majority of cases of pseudocyesis have a psychological basis, there are some that have physical causes. For instance, a tumor on the pituitary gland may cause an oversecretion of prolactin, which in turn can cause symptoms such as breast fullness and morning sickness. Pseudocyesis has been found to be more common in women who believe childbearing is central to their identity, have a history of infertility and/or depression, or have had a miscarriage (Whelan and Stewart, 1990). Although expectant fathers have also been found to experience pseudocyesis, it is more typical for them to experience a related condition called **couvade**. These men experience the symptoms of their pregnant wives. They may begin to gain weight and even experience morning sickness. While not extremely common, approximately 11% of men experience some psychogenic symptoms that are related to their partner's pregnancy (Whelan and Stewart, 1990; Shapiro and Nass, 1986).

pseudocyesis: A condition in which a woman believes she is pregnant and experiences signs of pregnancy, even though she is not.

couvade: The experiencing of the symptoms of pregnancy and/or childbirth.

PREGNANCY TESTS

If you have had sexual intercourse without using birth control or have experienced any of the signs of pregnancy, it is a good idea to have a pregnancy test. Over-the-counter pregnancy tests can be purchased in drug stores, but it can be less expensive to go to a clinic. Pregnancy tests measure for a hormone in the blood called human chorionic gonadatropin (hCG), which is produced during pregnancy (this is the same hormone used in the treatment of infertility). The hormone hCG is manufactured by the cells in the developing placenta and can be identified in the blood or urine eight to nine days after ovulation. The presence of hCG helps build and maintain a thick endometrial layer and prevents the menstrual period. Peak levels of hCG are reached in the second and third month of pregnancy and then drop off.

Home pregnancy tests are inaccurate if taken too soon after conception, and some women who postpone pregnancy tests until after the twelfth week may have a **false negative** pregnancy test because the hCG levels are too low to be detected by the test. **False positive** test results may occur in the presence of a kidney disease or infection; an over-

false negative: An incorrect result of a medical test or procedure that wrongly shows the lack of a finding, condition, or disease.

false positive: An incorrect result of a medical test or procedure that wrongly shows the presence of a finding, condition, or disease.

radioimmunoassay (RIA): A procedure in which a radioactive substance known to react with a certain protein is injected into the bloodstream to detect the amount of that protein in the body.

spontaneous abortion: A natural process whereby the body expels a developing embryo.

ectopic pregnancy: The implantation of the fertilized egg outside the uterus, for example, in the Fallopian tubes or the abdomen.

active thyroid gland; or large doses of aspirin, tranquilizers, antidepressants, or anticonvulsant medications (Hatcher et al. 1994).

Of all pregnancy tests, **radioimmunoassay (RIA)** tests are the most accurate. These are blood tests that can detect hCG within a few days after conception. RIA tests are also useful for monitoring the progress of pregnancies that may be in jeopardy. Because hCG levels rise so sharply early on, doubling in concentration every two days, if a woman's hormones do not increase following this pattern, it may indicate a possible **spontaneous abortion** or **ectopic pregnancy**. We will discuss both of these later in this chapter.

Reactions to positive pregnancy tests differ depending on the woman's life situation. If she feels prepared and ready for a child, her reaction may be elation and trepidation. One woman reported:

I was horrified when I found out my test was positive. I did not want to be pregnant. I had thought that even though I was married, I would wait until I was at least thirty-three to have my first child. My career wasn't set and this just wasn't a part of my plan. I was crying hysterically when my husband found out. He was so excited that he started to cry, which made me cry harder. We held each other and it felt so good. I think I was terrified because I thought he wasn't ready either. When I saw his enthusiasm, I was relieved and excited.

A twenty-nine-year-old first time mother; Author's files.

due date: The projected birth date of a baby; it gives a general idea of the day of birth but is not meant to be exact.

Naegeles Rule: A means of figuring the due date by subtracting three months from the first day of the last menstrual period and adding seven days.

After a woman's pregnancy is confirmed, her physician helps her to calculate a **due date**. Most physicians date the pregnancy from the first day of the last menstrual period rather then the day of ovulation or fertilization. The standard for due date calculation is called the **Naegeles Rule**—subtract three months from the first day of the last period and add seven days (for example, if the last period was on August 1st, subtract three months and add seven days, which means that the due date would be May 8th) This rule works most effectively with women who have standard twenty-eight-day menstrual cycles.

PRENATAL DEVELOPMENT

trimester: A period of three months; pregnancies usually consist of three trimesters.

sonography: Another name for ultrasound; a way of seeing the developing fetus by bouncing sound waves off it.

Pregnancy can vary from thirty-six to thirty-eight weeks in length, and it is divided into three three-month periods called **trimesters**. Throughout the pregnancy, physicians use electronic monitoring and **sonography** to check on the status of the fetus. Below we will explore physical development in each of these trimesters.

First Trimester

The first trimester includes the first three months of pregnancy (one to twelve weeks). It is the trimester where the most important embryonic development takes place. By the end of the first month of pregnancy, the fetal heart is formed and begins to pump blood. In fact, the circulatory system is the first organ system to function in the embryo (Rischer and Easton, 1992). In addition, many of the other major systems develop, including the digestive system, beginnings of the brain, spinal cord, nervous system, muscles, arms, legs, eyes, fingers, and toes. By the end of the third month, the liver, kidneys, intestines, and lungs have begun to develop. In addition, the circulatory and urinary systems are operating and the reproductive organs have developed. By the end of the first trimester, the fetus weighs one-half ounce and is between two-and-a-half and three inches long.

Second Trimester

The second trimester includes the second three months of pregnancy (thirteen to twenty weeks). The fetus becomes noticeably more human-looking (see Photo 10.4c). By the end of the fourth month, the fetus is four inches long. He or she has developed tooth buds and reflexes, such as sucking and swallowing. Though the gender of the fetus is determined at birth, it is not immediately apparent during development. Finger- and toeprints develop, and by the end of the fifth month the fetus is between eight and ten inches in length. During the second trimester, the mother will often feel the fetus moving around inside of her uterus. Soft hair, called **lanugo,** and a waxy substance, known as **vernix caseosa,** both cover the body of the fetus. These may develop to protect the fetus from the constant exposure to the amniotic fluid (see Photo 10.4d). By the end of the second trimester, the fetus is approximately thirteen inches long and weighs about one-and-three-quarters pounds. If birth takes place at the end of the second trimester, the baby may be able to survive with intensive medical care. We discuss early birth later in this chapter.

Third Trimester

The third trimester includes the third three months of pregnancy (twenty-one to thirty-six weeks). By the end of the seventh month, the fetus begins to develop fat deposits. She or he can react to pain, light, and sounds. Some fetuses develop the hiccups or begin to suck their thumb. If a baby is born at the end of the seventh month, there is a good chance of survival. In the eighth month, the majority of the organ systems are well developed, although the brain continues to increase in size. By the end of the eighth month, the fetus is eighteen inches long and weighs about five pounds. In the ninth month, the fetus moves very little because there is very little room to move. At birth, an infant on average weighs approximately seven-and-a-half pounds and is twenty inches in length.

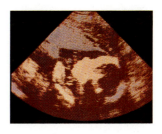

Ultrasound or sonography uses ultrasonic sound waves to photograph the fetus in utero. This is an ultrasound of the fetus at twelve weeks.

lanugo: The downy covering of hair over the fetus.

vernix caseosa: Cheesy substance that coats the fetus in the uterus.

SEX TALK

QUESTION **10.3** **What is the advisable amount of time to wait before announcing a planned pregnancy to family and friends?**

How long a couple waits to share their news really depends on the couple. For some couples, it is hard not to share the news as soon as they know. Others choose to wait. If a couple has experienced a pregnancy loss or problems getting pregnant, they may wait longer than couples who have not had these experiences. Because the risk of miscarriage is highest during the first trimester and drops significantly after then, some couples wait until the thirteenth week of pregnancy to share their news. However, there are other factors that need to be taken into consideration. For example, some women feel that it may put their jobs in jeopardy if they tell their employers they are pregnant too soon.

CHANGES IN THE PREGNANT MOTHER

When a woman becomes pregnant, her entire system readjusts. Her heart pumps more blood, her weight increases, her lungs and digestive system work harder, and her thyroid gland grows. All of these changes occur to encourage the growth of the developing fetus. Most women experience specific signs during each trimester of pregnancy.

In the first trimester, common symptoms include nausea, excessive salivation, fatigue, breast changes, constipation, and increased urination. Certain food cravings or aversions often develop, along with a sensitivity to smells and odors. While some women feel physically uncomfortable because of all these changes, they may also feel excited and happy about the life growing within them. The final, definite sign of pregnancy—a fetal heartbeat—can be a joyous moment that offsets all the discomforts of pregnancy. This is usually heard by the end of the first trimester.

During the second trimester, nausea begins to subside as the body adjusts to the increased hormonal levels. Breast sensitivity also tends to decrease during the second trimester. However, fatigue often sets in, as well as an increase in appetite, heartburn, **edema** (ankle or leg swelling), and a noticeable vaginal discharge. Skin pigmentation changes can occur on the face. As the uterus grows larger and the blood circulation slows down, constipation and muscle cramps bother some women. Internally, the cervix turns a deep red, almost violet color, due to an increased blood supply. As the pregnancy

edema: An excessive accumulation of fluid in a part of the body, causing swelling.

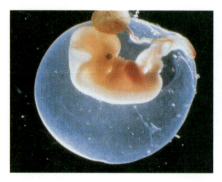

A four-week embryo.

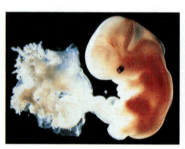

A six- or seven-week embryo.

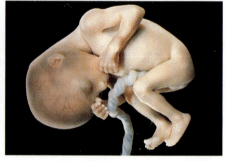

At four months, the fetus is becoming more and more lively. It can turn its head, move its face, and make breathing movements.

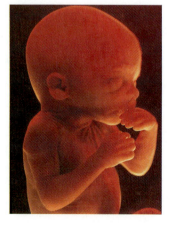

At five months, the fetus is covered by lanugo and vernix caseosa. By the time of birth, most of this lanugo will have disappeared.

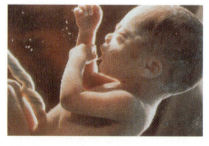

The fetus at nine months.

progresses, the increasing size of the uterus and the restriction of the pelvic veins can cause more swelling of the ankles. Increased problems with **varicose veins** and **hemorrhoids** also occur. Fetal movement is often felt in the second trimester, sometimes as early as the sixteenth week. Usually women feel movement earlier in their second or subsequent pregnancies because they know what to feel for.

The second trimester of pregnancy is usually the most positive time for the mother. The physiological signs of pregnancy such as morning sickness and fatigue lessen, and the mother-to-be finally feels better physically. This improvement in physical health also leads to positive psychological feelings including excitement, happiness, and a sense of well-being. Many women report an increased sex drive during the second trimester, and for many couples, it is a period of high sexual satisfaction. As the developing fetus begins to move around, many women feel reassured after anxiously wondering whether the fetus was developing at all. In fact, many women report that the kicking and moving about of the developing fetus is very comforting (unless, of course, it routinely happens at three in the morning!).

Some women keep their pregnancy a secret during their first trimester because they want to make sure the pregnancy will be viable. By the second trimester, however, since there are more positive psychological feelings and fewer physical problems, many women report feeling more comfortable with the pregnancy. The transition to maternity clothes often results in more positive feelings, probably because it is now obvious and public knowledge that the woman is pregnant.

During the third trimester, there is often stronger and more frequent fetal movement, which will slow down toward the ninth month (since the fetus will have less room to move around). Many of the symptoms from the second trimester continue, with constipation and heartburn increasing in frequency. Backaches, leg cramps, increases in varicose veins, hemorrhoids, sleep problems, shortness of breath, and **Braxton–Hicks contractions** also occur. At first these contractions are scattered and relatively painless (the uterus hardens for a moment and then returns to normal). In the eighth and ninth months, the Braxton–Hicks contractions become stronger. A clear liquid called **colostrum** is secreted from the nipples as the breasts prepare to produce milk for breast-feeding. It is also important to mention that many women are not bothered by these physical changes in their bodies, and they enjoy being pregnant. One woman said:

> I'm now in the middle of my third trimester and I can't tell you how happy I am to be pregnant. Each symptom I experience reminds me that I am indeed pregnant and I just smile. All of these changes are so exciting!
>
> *A thirty-four-year-old first-time mother; Author's files*

In the third trimester, many women feel an increase in apprehension about labor and delivery and their role as a mother. Dreams about the baby are frequent. Toward the end of the third trimester, it is not uncommon to wish that the pregnancy were over. Impatience and restlessness are common.

varicose veins: Unnaturally swollen veins.

hemorrhoids: Dilated or varicosed blood vessels in the anal region.

Braxton–Hicks contractions: Intermittent contractions of the uterus after the third month of pregnancy that do not indicate that labor has begun.

colostrum: A thin, yellowish fluid, high in proteins and antibodies, that is secreted from the nipples at the end of pregnancy and during the first few days after delivery.

FATHER'S ROLE DURING PREGNANCY

For men, pregnancy can be a time of joy and anticipation. One man reported:

> I was so excited the day that I found out she was pregnant. At first, she had told me that she was one week late and then we got a home pregnancy test. I didn't

There are a variety of devices that simulate pregnancy. Here a partner tries on one of these devices.

really believe it was true until we went to the doctor's office. The nurse came out and told me and I thought "Wow, this is it!"

A twenty-nine-year-old first-time father; Author's files

However, there can also be stress and anxiety. Feelings about parenting in combination with the many changes their partners are undergoing can all add to men's feelings of vulnerability. Some men report that they wish they could know how it feels to be pregnant so that they could understand what their partner is going through. For such people, there is a product called the *Empathy Belly*. It weighs thirty-three pounds (which is approximately how much weight is usually gained in a pregnancy) and, when strapped on, it simulates twenty of the most common signs of the pregnancy including lower back pain, an increase in urination, shortness of breath, and blood pressure elevation. This device also has two seven-pound lead weights, which put pressure on the ribs of the wearer just as a developing fetus's knees and feet would.

Some men report that it is very difficult for them to think about the impending birth. As one man stated:

I think that the most dreaded and scariest moment that I can possibly think about is the birth process. I don't want to see my wife in that much pain. There are also so many things that can go wrong. As she gets closer and closer to this day she has begun to have difficulties getting around, and she has more frequent doctor's visits. It's really scary. I don't know what to expect. Sometimes I just wish we could jump ahead to having a kid without the birth process.

A twenty-nine-year-old first-time father; Author's files

Many men report a decrease in sexual interest during the pregnancy. A common reason for this is their fear of causing injury to the fetus during sexual activity. Other men report increases in sexual desire and find the pregnant woman particularly sexy and attractive. As we will discuss later in this section, sexual intercourse during pregnancy is safe up until the last month.

In the United States today, fathers are allowed and encouraged to be in the delivery room. However, this was not always the case. At one time, fathers were told to go to the waiting room and sit until the baby was born. In some other cultures, such as in Bang Chan, Thailand, the father aids in the actual birth of his child (Dunham et al., 1992). The role of the father in pregnancy varies in other cultures. Some fathers are required to remain on strict diets during the course of the pregnancy or to cater to their partners' food cravings at all times.

SEX TALK

QUESTION **10.4** Do men ever feel left out because the woman gets all the attention while she is pregnant?

Some do. However, it is important to keep in mind that both mothers- and fathers-to-be share the pregnancy experience, both the excitement and the fears. Many years ago, male involvement in pregnancy and birth ended once a sperm fertilized the ovum. Today, many physicians recommend that fathers be included in many aspects of the pregnancy experience. They can go to the monthly obstetrician appointments with their partners, help out with their partner's special diet needs by going on a diet themselves, read as many books as

possible on pregnancy, talk to friends who have children about their experiences, talk to the baby while it is still in the womb, help shop for necessary baby items, take childbirth classes with their partners, and coach the mother through the birth itself. Overall, probably the most important thing that parents-to-be can do is to be open and honest about their feelings and communicate with each other.

SEX DURING PREGNANCY

In some cultures, sex during pregnancy is strongly recommended because it is believed that the father's semen is necessary for proper development of the fetus (Dunham et al., 1992). In the United States, many women continue to have satisfying sexual relations during pregnancy. Sexual intercourse during pregnancy is safe for most mothers and the developing child up until the last several weeks of pregnancy. During a woman's first pregnancy, sexual interest is often decreased because of physical changes, including nausea and fatigue. One woman reported:

> *I felt terrible during the first trimester. I was nauseous all the time and very, very tired. At three in the afternoon I would have to take a nap just to get through the rest of the day. I had no energy whatsoever. Sex wasn't on my mind at all!*
>
> *A twenty-nine-year-old first-time mother; Author's files*

Sexual interest usually begins to subside as the woman and fetus grow during the third trimester. The increasing size of the stomach puts pressure on many of the internal organs and also makes certain sexual positions difficult. During the first and part of the second trimester, the male-on-top position is used most often during sexual intercourse (see Chapter 9). However, later in pregnancy, the side-by-side, rear-entry, and female-on-top positions are used more frequently because they take the weight and pressure off the uterus. During the last two to eight weeks of pregnancy, many physicians advise their patients to avoid sexual intercourse. The main reasons that the frequency of sexual activity declines are physical discomfort, fear of fetal injury, awkwardness, or physician recommendation.

Orgasm during pregnancy is safe, but occasionally it may cause painful uterine contractions. Cunnilingus can also be safely engaged in during pregnancy, although changes in vaginal aroma and discharge may make couples uncomfortable. As we discussed in Chapter 9, air should never be blown into the vagina of a pregnant woman because it may be fatal.

Although there may be a decrease in a woman's desire for sexual activity during the last trimester, this does not mean that there is a decrease in her need for affection. Many women report an increase in their desire for touching, hugging, and caressing. This need especially increases during the last ten weeks of the pregnancy, when she may be feeling most frightened and vulnerable.

EXERCISE AND NUTRITION DURING PREGNANCY

How much exercise should a woman get during pregnancy? A woman's exercise routine should not exceed her pre-pregnancy exercise levels. If a woman exercised vigorously prior to her pregnancy, keeping up with a moderate amount of exercise during the pregnancy is

Apgar: A numerical expression of the condition of a newborn infant based on the combined assessment of heart rate, respiratory effort, muscle tone, reflex irritability, and color evaluated one minute after birth.

fine. In fact, many physicians strongly advise light exercise during pregnancy; it has been found to result in heavier birthweight, fewer surgical births, higher **Apgar** scores (standard scale used to evaluate a newborn's condition at birth), and shorter hospital stays (Hamilton, 1991).

It is a myth that too much exercise may cause a miscarriage or harm the developing fetus. Hundreds of pregnant women learned this prior to the legalization of abortion when they tried to exercise excessively or punch their abdomens in an unsuccessful attempt to dislodge the fertilized ovum. The implanted embryo is difficult to dislodge. However, there are certain sports that should be avoided during pregnancy, such as water skiing, scuba diving, and horseback riding since these may cause injuries in both the mother and her fetus.

During pregnancy, a woman must increase her caloric intake. Nutritional requirements call for extra protein, iron, calcium, folic acid, and vitamin B6 (found in foods such as milk, yogurt, beef, legumes, and dried fruits). Failure to follow these nutritional requirements may result in low-birthweight children or even spontaneous abortion. Both under- and overweight women are at greater risk of impaired pregnancy outcome, and they are advised to gain or lose weight prior to pregnancy. An underweight woman may give birth to a low-birthweight baby, which may be more susceptible to disease and premature death. In fact, nutritional deficiencies in the mother and low birthweight of the infant cause more than half of deaths reported for children five years and younger (Hamilton, 1991). Obese women are also at risk because of the possibilities of developing diabetes, hypertension, and infection. Food cravings can occur, and some women report a craving for specific foods, such as ice cream, pickles, and/or pizza. Sometimes these food cravings can indicate a deficit in nutritional requirements.

SEX TALK

QUESTION **10.5** **I've heard women say that if the average baby weighs about seven pounds, then they will gain no more than ten pounds while pregnant. Is that safe to do? How small of a weight gain is considered healthy? What about anorexics and bulimics?**

The average weight gain for a pregnancy is twenty-five pounds. This includes the fetus, amniotic fluid, placenta, breasts, and muscle and fat increases. Gaining less than this is not healthy for either the developing baby or the mother. Anyone who has an eating disorder should consult with a physician before getting pregnant to determine an appropriate weight gain. If the nutritional requirements cannot be met, she should postpone a pregnancy.

It is estimated that the average pregnant woman will gain twenty-two to twenty-eight pounds during her pregnancy. Ideally, three to four pounds should be gained in the first trimester, and one pound per week from there on (Hamilton, 1991). To see how the weight gain is distributed, see Table 10.1.

During the second trimester, a woman is advised to increase her caloric intake by 300 calories per day, and protein requirements increase from forty-five grams to sixty grams. For vegetarians, it is necessary to increase consumption of vegetables, whole grains, nuts, seeds, and also a possible soy-based protein supplement to help ensure adequate protein intake. An increase in calcium is also needed to help with bone

Table **10.1**

WEIGHT GAIN DURING PREGNANCY

Fetus	7½ lbs.
Amniotic Fluid	1¾ lbs.
Placenta	1½ lbs.
Maternal Blood Volume	2¾ lbs.
Uterine Enlargement	2 lbs.
Maternal Breast Tissue	1 lb.
Fat Deposits	7 lbs.
Fluids in Maternal Tissue	3 lbs.

Total: 26½ pound overall weight gain

Adapted from Eisenberg et al. (1991:148)

calcification of the growing fetus. Since a woman's blood volume increases as much as 50% during pregnancy, iron may be diluted in the blood; thus many pregnant women are advised to take prenatal vitamins, which include iron supplements.

On occasion the expectant father may also gain weight along with his pregnant wife. This happens for several reasons. One new father shared that he felt compelled to cook healthy meals for his wife to ensure her nutritional health. He also added, however, that he was purposely gaining weight "so that she wouldn't feel guilty or bad about her own weight gain" (Author's files).

DRUGS AND ALCOHOL DURING PREGNANCY

There are several substances that physicians recommend to avoid during pregnancy, such as caffeine, nicotine, alcohol, marijuana, and other drugs. (Focus on Diversity 10.2 describes activities women in other cultures are told to avoid.) All of these substances can cross the placenta, enter into the developing fetus's bloodstream, and cause physical or mental deficiencies. Alcohol intake has also been linked with **fetal alcohol syndrome (FAS)**. FAS occurs when a woman drinks heavily during pregnancy, producing an infant who is undersized and mentally deficient. These abnormalities are irreversible. Even women who drink very little put their developing babies at risk. Presently, there is no safe level of alcohol use during pregnancy.

Research indicates that approximately 20% to 25% of pregnant American women smoke cigarettes throughout their pregnancies, which has been associated with spontaneous abortion, low birthweight, and prematurity (Benowitz, 1991). In other countries, even more pregnant women smoke; when the United States, United Kingdom, Canada, Australia, New Zealand, and Norway are counted together, the percentage of women who

fetal alcohol syndrome (FAS): A disorder involving growth deficiencies, nervous system damage, and facial abnormalities found in the offspring of mothers who consumed large quantities of alcohol during pregnancy.

Focus on Diversity 10.2

Avoid the Sun?

In the United States, most physicians recommend avoiding substances such as alcohol, tobacco, and drugs and certain dangerous activities such as scuba diving and horseback riding during pregnancy. However, in other cultures, there are several additional activities that are avoided. These include:

• Lying too long in the sun, which may cause the baby to melt (*Ibo, Nigeria*).

• Eating hot food or drinking hot liquid, which may scald the fetus (*East Africa*).
• Sitting in front of a door for an extended period, which may cause the baby to have a big mouth and to cry too much (*Java, Indonesia*).
• Sleeping on one's back, which may cause the umbilical cord to wrap around the baby's neck (*Bariba, People's Republic of Benin*).
• Hanging the washing out, which may cause the umbilical cord to become knotted (*Navajho Indians, United States*).
• Gazing at the eclipse of the moon, which may cause a baby to be born with a cleft palate (*Aztecs, Mexico*).

Adapted from Dunham et al. (1992:41)

smoke during pregnancy may be closer to 30% (Dunham et al., 1992). Fathers who smoke around their pregnant partners are also jeopardizing the future health of their baby.

PREGNANCY IN WOMEN OVER THIRTY

Until the late 1980s, the majority of women had their first child in their early or mid-twenties. Today, more and more women are delaying childbearing because of educational or career goals. In the United States, since 1980, pregnancy among thirty to thirty-four-year-old women has increased 33%, and among thirty-five to thirty-nine-year-old women, 39% (U.S. Bureau of Census, 1991).

Delayed pregnancy does carry some risks, which include an increase in spontaneous abortion, first-trimester bleeding, low birthweights, labor time, **cesarean sections** (c-section), and chromosomal abnormalities (Berkowitz et al., 1990). The likelihood of a chromosomal abnormality increases each year in women over thirty and in men over fifty-five. Remember that women are born with a set number of follicles that will develop into ova. As she ages, so do these follicles. However, the good news is that recent research reveals that although an older women may have higher rates of conception and delivery complications, if they are healthy and have regular prenatal health checks, they will have little risk of problems during pregnancy or delivery (Berkowitz et al., 1990).

cesarean section: A surgical procedure in which the woman's abdomen and uterus are cut open and the child is removed; used when vaginal birth may endanger a mother and/or child.

PROBLEMS IN THE PREGNANCY

The majority of women go through their pregnancy without any problems. However, understanding how complex the process of pregnancy is, it should not come as a surprise that occasionally something goes wrong. Below we will discuss some of these problems.

Ectopic Pregnancies

Most zygotes travel through the Fallopian tubes and into the uterus. In an ectopic pregnancy, the zygote implants outside of the uterus. Ninety-six percent of ectopic pregnancies occur when the fertilized ovum implants in the Fallopian tube. These are called tubal pregnancies. The remaining 4% occur in the abdomen, cervix, or ovaries. About 1 in 100 pregnancies are ectopic (Eisenberg et al., 1991), and this number has been steadily increasing in the past two decades in the United States. Ectopic pregnancy is very dangerous and is the primary cause of maternal mortality in the first trimester of pregnancy (Handler et al., 1989). Recent research also indicates that smokers may be at increased risk for ectopic pregnancies. Nicotine has been found to change the tubal contractions and muscular tone of the Fallopian tubes, which may lead to tubal inactivity, delayed ovum entry into the uterus, and changes in the tube's ability to transport the ovum (Handler et al., 1989). Another possible cause of ectopic pregnancy is past infection with sexually transmitted diseases.

The Fallopian tubes, cervix, and abdomen are not designed to support a growing fetus. If a growing fetus implants in one of these places, it can cause a rupture, causing internal hemorrhaging and possibly death. Symptoms of ectopic pregnancy include abdominal pain (usually on the side of the body that has the tubal pregnancy), cramping, pelvic pain, vaginal bleeding, nausea, dizziness, and fainting. Immediate abdominal surgery is needed to remove the embryo and control the internal bleeding. This often includes the removal of the affected Fallopian tube. It is possible that in the next few years, there will be a test to detect an ectopic pregnancy prior to rupture.

Spontaneous Abortions

A spontaneous abortion, or **miscarriage**, refers to a natural termination of a pregnancy before the time that the fetus can live on its own. Approximately 10% of all diagnosed

miscarriage: A spontaneous abortion or pregnancy that terminates on its own.

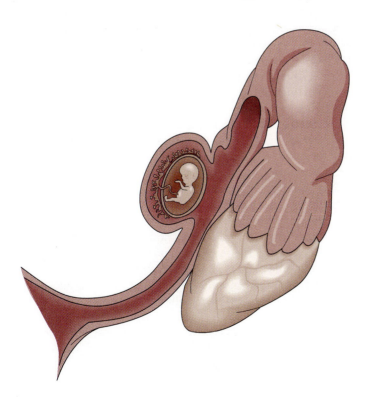

Figure **10.3**
In an ectopic pregnancy, the fertilized ovum implants outside of the uterus. In most cases, it remains in the Fallopian tube.

pregnancies end in miscarriage, and 20% to 40% of pregnancies end before a pregnancy diagnosis is made (Eisenberg et al., 1991). Miscarriages can also occur during the second and third trimesters of pregnancy, although the percentage drops dramatically after the first trimester. A miscarriage is very difficult emotionally for both the woman and her partner.

In 40% to 60% of miscarriages, there is some chromosomal abnormality (Jones, 1984). The body somehow knows that there is a problem in the developing fetus and rejects it. In other cases, where there are no chromosomal problems, the uterus may be too small, too weak, or abnormally shaped, or the miscarriage may be caused by maternal stress, nutritional deficiencies, excessive vitamin A, drug exposure, or pelvic infection. Symptoms may include vaginal bleeding, cramps, and lower back pain.

A normal menstrual period usually returns within three months after a miscarriage, and future pregnancies may be perfectly normal. However, some women experience continual spontaneous abortions, often due to an **incompetent cervix**. Tests are being developed to try to predict when a spontaneous abortion will occur.

Chromosomal Abnormalities

We have already discussed the process of an amniocentesis, which identifies chromosomal abnormalities in the sixteenth to seventeenth week of pregnancy. Once an abnormality is detected by amniocentesis, a woman must decide whether to continue or terminate the pregnancy; yet the woman is already four months into the pregnancy. Because of this, a procedure known as **chorionic villus sampling (CVS)** has been used, where a sliver of tissue from the chorion is removed (the tissue that gradually develops into the placenta) and is checked for chromosomal abnormalities. Unlike amniocentesis, CVS can be done between the eighth and twelfth week of pregnancy. However, some CVS tests will result in a false positive, since the sample may have a different chromosomal composition than the fetus. In addition, there is an increased risk of miscarriage and limb deformities associated with this test. However, these risks must be carefully weighed in women who's fetuses are at risk for genetic deformities. Another test, the **maternal-serum alpha-fetoprotein screening (MSAFP)**, is used to detect defects such as **spina bifida** or **anencephaly**. MSAFP is a simple blood test done between the sixteenth and eighteenth week of pregnancy. However, there has been a high frequency of false positive test results with this test, and so second screenings are recommended.

Chromosomal abnormalities can result in many different problems. Sometimes physicians are certain of where the chromosomal problem lies and how it will manifest itself; at other times they are not. The most common chromosomal abnormality occurs on the twenty-first chromosome and is known as **Down's syndrome**. In Down's syndrome, an extra chromosome has been added to the twenty-first chromosome; although most of us have forty-six chromosomes (twenty-three from each parent), a Down's syndrome child has forty-seven.

The risk of having a child with Down's syndrome increases as a woman ages. The risk is 1 in 10,000 for twenty-year-old mothers, 3 in 1000 for thirty-five-year-old mothers, and 1 in 100 for forty-year-old mothers (Eisenberg et al., 1991). Although Down's syndrome is often blamed on ova that have aged, it can also be due to deficient sperm. In fact, 25% of Down's syndrome cases are due to defective sperm. A child with Down's syndrome often exhibits mental retardation, slanted eyes, and a flat face (see photo on the facing page).

---

incompetent cervix: A condition in which the cervix begins to open prematurely without labor or contractions and may result in premature delivery or miscarriage.

chorionic villus sampling (CVS): The sampling and testing of the chorion for fetal abnormalities.

maternal-serum alpha-feto-protein-screening (MSAFP): A blood test used during early pregnancy to determine neural tube defects such as spina bifida or anencephaly.

spina bifida: A congenital defect of the vertebral column in which the halves of the neural arch of a vertebra fail to fuse in the midline.

anencephaly: The absence of all or part of the brain.

Down's syndrome: A problem that occurs on the twenty-first chromosome of the developing fetus that can cause mental retardation.

Rh Incompatibility

The Rh factor naturally exists on the red blood cells of some people. You may know what blood type you are, followed by a "+" or "−". If your blood type is "+", you are "Rh positive," and if not, "Rh negative." This is important when you are having a blood transfusion or if you are pregnant. If the father is Rh positive, the baby often inherits his blood type. If the mother's blood is Rh negative in this case, any of the fetal blood that comes into contact with hers (which happens during delivery, not pregnancy) will cause her to begin to manufacture antibodies against the fetal blood. This may be very danger-ous for any future pregnancies. Since the mother has made antibodies to Rh positive blood, she will reject the fetal Rh positive blood, which can lead to fetal death. After a Rh negative woman has delivered, she is given **Rhogam**, which prevents antibodies from forming and ensures that her future pregnancies will be healthy. An Rh negative woman who has a miscarriage or an abortion must also have a Rhogam injection within seventy-two hours.

Toxemia

In the last two to three months of pregnancy, 6% to 7% of women experience **toxemia**, a form of blood poisoning caused by kidney disturbances. Symptoms include rapid weight gain, fluid retention, an increase in blood pressure, and/or protein in the urine. If toxemia is allowed to progress, it can result in **eclampsia**, which involves convulsions, coma, and, in approximately 15% of cases, death. Toxemia and eclampsia occur primar-ily in women who neglect good prenatal care, and they are relatively rare in women with good medical care. A recent study found that the longer a woman has a monogamous relationship before she conceives, the less likely she is to develop pre-eclampsia and eclampsia (Clark, 1994). It has been suggested that longer relationships will produce an immune response in the female to certain chemicals in the sperm that may lead to com-plications with pre-eclampsia.

PART THREE—BIRTH

The average length of a pregnancy is nine months, but a normal birth can occur more than two weeks before or after the due date. It is estimated that only 4% of American babies are born exactly on the due date predicted (Dunham et al., 1992). Early delivery may occur in cases where the mother has exercised throughout the pregnancy, the fetus is female, or the mother has shorter menstrual cycles (Jones, 1984). No one really knows why, but there is also a seasonal variation in human birth. More babies are born between July and October (more conceptions occur during the late fall and early winter). It has been hypothesized that this evolved because of the increased food supply available dur-ing the late summer and early fall months (although perhaps more couples engage in sexual intercourse to keep warm in the cold winter months!). There are also more babies born between the hours of 1 and 7 A.M., and again this is thought to have evolved because of the increased protection and decreased chances of predator attacks (Jones, 1984).

In the United States, if the birth process is taking too long, physicians may adminis-ter the drug **pitocin** to speed up labor. In Bolivia, however, certain groups of people

Rhogam: A drug given to mothers whose Rh is incom-patible with the fetus's; it prevents the formation of antibodies that can imperil future pregnancies.

toxemia: A condition of a mother involving high blood pressure, edema, protein in the urine, and convulsions during the later half of preg-nancy; may result in coma or death of a mother.

eclampsia: A progression of toxemia with similar, but worsening, symptoms.

Down's syndrome, a chromo-somal defect, can cause mental retardation, slanted eyes, and a flat face.

pitocin: A drug used during delivery to induce uterine contractions.

believe that nipple stimulation helps the birth move quicker. So if a birth is moving too slowly, a woman's nipples may be massaged (Dunham et al., 1992). Biologically, nipple stimulation leads to a release of oxytocin, which is a natural form of pitocin. In some Guatemalan societies, long and difficult labors are believed to be due to a woman's sins, and so she is asked to confess. If this does not help speed up labor, her husband is asked to confess his sins. If neither of these confessions helps, the father's loincloth is wrapped around the woman's stomach to assure her that he will not leave her once the baby is born (Dunham et al., 1992).

We do not know exactly what starts the birth process. It appears that in fetal sheep there is a chemical in the brain that signals it is time for birth (Palca, 1991). Perhaps this may also be true in humans, but the research is still incomplete.

SEX TALK

QUESTION **10.6** **What determines how long a woman is in labor? Why do they say a woman's first baby is hardest? A friend of mine was in labor for thirty-six hours!**

Usually, first labors are the most difficult. Second and subsequent labors are usually easier and shorter than the first one because there is less resistance from the birth canal and the surrounding muscles. Overall, the biggest differences are in the amount of time it takes for the cervix to fully dilate and the amount of pushing necessary to move the baby out of the birth canal. The first labor can take anywhere between eight and fourteen hours, while second and subsequent labors can take anywhere between four and nine hours. However, labor can, and often does, last up to twenty-four hours. We do not really know why some women have easier labors than others. Perhaps it could be due to other factors such as diet and/or exercise during the pregnancy.

PREPARATION FOR BIRTH

Lamaze method: A prepared childbirth method in which couples are provided information about the birth process and are taught breathing and relaxation exercises to use during labor.

engagement: When the fetus moves down toward the birth canal prior to delivery.

breech birth: An abnormal and often dangerous birth during which the baby's feet, knees, or buttocks emerge before the head.

As the birth day comes closer, many women (and men too!) become anxious, nervous, and excited about what is to come. This is probably why baby showers became traditional (Dunham et al., 1992). Showers enable women (and more recently, men) to gather and discuss the impending birth. Personal experiences and helpful hints are often shared. This ritual may help couples to prepare themselves emotionally and to feel more comfortable.

Increasing knowledge and alleviating anxiety about the birth process are the main concepts behind the **Lamaze method** of childbirth. In Lamaze, women and their partners are taught what to expect during labor and delivery and how to control the pain through breathing and massage. Tension and anxiety during labor have been found to increase pain, discomfort, and fatigue. Many couples feel more prepared and focused after taking these courses.

A few weeks before delivery, the fetus usually moves into a "head down" position in the uterus. This is referred to as **engagement**. Ninety-seven percent of fetuses are in this position at birth (Nilsson, 1990). If their feet or buttocks are first (**breech birth**), the physician may either try to rotate them prior to birth or recommend a cesarean section. We will discuss this later in this chapter.

HOSPITAL AND HOME BIRTH

Approximately 80% of the world's babies are born at home (Dunham et al., 1992). In nonindustrialized countries, nearly all babies are born at home. Some people believe that babies can be safely delivered at home with the help of a **midwife**. These people argue that it has been the medical establishment that has moved delivery into hospitals as a way of making money and controlling women's bodies. If women can safely deliver at home, should they be encouraged to do so with the help of a midwife, or should they be encouraged to have children in the hospital?

midwife: A person who assists women during childbirth.

In the United States, the majority of babies are born in hospitals. A relatively recent development are birthing centers within hospital settings. These center provide very comfortable rooms, often complete with soothing music, televisions, cheery colors, and showers. A bed may also be available for the father-to-be.

POSITIONS FOR BIRTH

Although women can assume a variety of positions during childbirth, in the United States, the majority of hospitals have a woman in the semi–lying-down position with her feet up in stirrups. Some feminist health professionals claim that this position is easier for the doctor rather than the woman, and that it is the most ineffective and dangerous position for labor (Boston Women's Health Book Collective, 1992). Recently, women have been given more freedom in deciding how to position themselves for childbirth. A woman on her hands and knees or in the squatting position allows her pelvis and cervix to be at its widest. In addition, the force of gravity can be used to help in the birth process. A woman may also give birth on her side (see photo on next page).

In different areas of the world, positions for birth vary. "Rope midwives" in rural areas of the Sudan hang a rope from the ceiling and have the mother grasp the rope and bear down in a squatting position. In Bang Chan, Thailand, a husband cradles his pregnant wife between his legs and digs his toes into her thighs. This toe pressure is thought to provide relief from her pain (Dunham et al., 1992).

A recent development in birthing is the underwater birth, which originated in Russia. A woman is seated in a warm bath or Jacuzzi and is allowed to give birth underwater. It is thought that the warmth of the water makes labor less painful for the woman. In addition, proponents of underwater birth claim it is less traumatic for infants. Because the baby gets its oxygen from the mother until the umbilical cord is cut, there is very little danger to the baby.

cervical effacement: The stretching of the cervix in preparation for birth.

dilation: The expansion of the opening of the cervix in preparation for birth.

STAGES OF BIRTH

Birth itself takes place in three stages: **cervical effacement** and **dilation**, expulsion of the fetus, and expulsion of the placenta. The beginning of birth is usually marked by an expulsion of the mucus plug from the cervix. This plug protects the fetus from any harmful bacteria that enters the vagina during pregnancy. The mucus plug is often combined with blood, giving it the name **bloody show**.

bloody show: The combination of the mucus plug and some blood that are expelled from the vagina before labor begins.

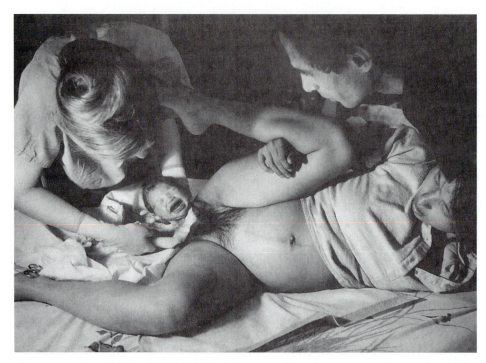

There are a variety of different positions for birth. In the United States, the most common position is the semi-lying-down position. This photo shows a woman giving birth on her side.

Stage One

The first stage of labor can last anywhere from twenty minutes to twenty-four hours and is longer in first births. When true labor begins, the Braxton–Hicks contractions increase. The cervix begins dilation (opening up) and effacement (thinning out) to allow for fetal passage (this phase is called Early Labor). Toward the end of this stage, the amniotic sac usually ruptures (however, this may happen earlier in some women). Contractions may last for about thirty to sixty seconds with intervals of between five and twenty minutes. Couples are advised to time the contractions and the interval between contractions and report these to their physician. When they are about five minutes apart, the physician will advise the couple to come to the hospital.

When the contractions begin to last longer (one minute or more), are more intense, and increase in frequency (every one to three minutes), dilation of the cervix is becoming complete (this phase is called Active Labor). The entrance to the cervix (the os) increases from zero to ten centimeters to allow for the passage of the fetus (see Figure 10.4). The contractions that open the os can be very painful, and nurses will usually monitor the progress of cervical dilation.

The last phase in Stage One is called **transition**, which for most women is the most difficult part of the birth process. Contractions are very intense, long, and have shorter periods in between. The fetus moves into the base of the pelvis, creating an urge to push; however, the woman is advised not to push until her cervix is fully dilated. By this time, the woman is beginning to feel exhausted.

The woman's body produces pain-reducing hormones called **endorphins**, which dull the intensity of the contractions (see SexTalk Question 10.7). Should a woman feel

transition: The last period in labor, in which contractions are strongest and the periods in between contractions are the shortest.

endorphins: Neurotransmitters, concentrated in the pituitary gland and parts of the brain, that inhibit physical pain.

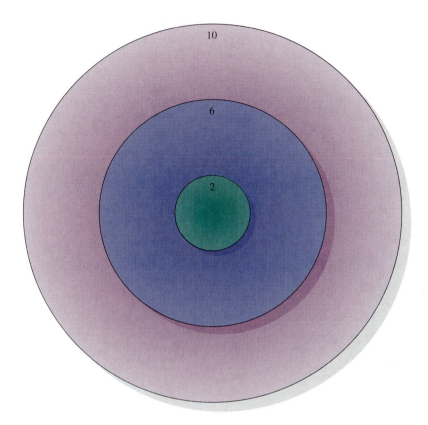

Figure **10.4**
For birth to occur vaginally, the cervix must dilate a full ten centimeters. The drawing is the actual size of the dilated cervix.

the need for more pain relief, she can also be given various pain medications. However, the risks are that she may become drowsy, nauseated, and/or the drugs may affect the fetus. In the past several years, there has been a movement away from the use of drugs during delivery. Methods of relaxation, breathing, hypnosis, and acupuncture have been encouraged (Nilsson, 1990).

SEX TALK
QUESTION **10.7** **Is it safe to use drugs to lessen the pain of labor and birth?**

While some women believe in a "natural" childbirth (one without pain medications), other women want to use them. The search for a perfect drug to relieve pain, one that is safe for both the mother and her child, has been a long one. Every year, more and more progress is made. Medication is often recommended when labor is long and complicated, the pain is more than the mother can tolerate or interferes with her ability to push, forceps are required during the delivery, or when a mother is so restless and agitated that it inhibits labor progress. In all cases, the risks of drug use must be weighed against the benefits. The most commonly used pain medications include analgesics (pain relievers), anesthetics (produce a loss of sensation), and tranquilizers. Which drug is used depends on the mother's preference, past health history, present condition, and the baby's condition. The epidural block, which is a tranquilizer, is increasingly popular for the relief of severe labor pain. However, how well a pain medication works depends on the mother, the dosage, and other factors (Eisenberg et al., 1991).

epidural block: A nerve block used during delivery that is administered through a needle in the back into the space between the spinal cord and the outer membrane.

fetal distress: When a fetus has an abnormal heart rate or rhythm.

Fetal monitoring is done to check for signs of **fetal distress**. This can be monitored either through the woman's abdomen or the fetus's scalp through the cervix. It is done to determine whether or not the fetus is in any danger to allow a quicker delivery or a cesarean section.

Stage Two

After the cervix has fully dilated, the second stage of birth begins, which is the expulsion of the fetus. Contractions are somewhat less intense, lasting about sixty seconds with one to three minute intervals. An **episiotomy** may be performed to reduce the risk of a tearing of the tissue between the vaginal opening and anus as the fetus emerges.

episiotomy: An incision sometimes made from the bottom of the entrance to a mother's vagina down toward the anus to give a baby's head more room to emerge and to prevent the tearing of vaginal and anal tissues during childbirth.

crowning: The emergence of a baby's head at the opening of the vagina at birth.

As the woman pushes during contractions, the top of the head of the baby soon appears at the vagina, which is known as **crowning**. Once the face emerges, the mucus and fluid in the mouth and nostrils are removed by suction. The baby emerges and, after the first breath, usually lets out a cry. The umbilical cord, which is necessary for oxygen, is cut after the baby's first breath; this is painless for the mother and child. Eye drops are put into the baby's eyes to prevent bacterial infection. Directly following birth, many physicians and midwives place the newborn directly on the mother's chest to begin the bonding process. However, sometimes the father may be the first to hold the child, or the nurses will perform an Apgar test. A newborn with a low Apgar may require intensive care after delivery.

SEX TALK

QUESTION **10.8** Carol Burnett once said that giving birth is like taking your bottom lip and pulling it over your head. Is it really that painful?

Women report a variety of experiences, some ranging from relatively painless to extremely painful. Research is beginning to reveal that perhaps exercise during the pregnancy can help ensure a less painful delivery. After delivery, some women block out the pain they experienced during the birth, not recalling it later on. Other women state that the pain they experienced was worth it for their new baby.

Stage Three

During the third stage of labor, the placenta is expelled from the uterus (sometimes referred to as the afterbirth). Strong contractions continue after the baby is born in order to push the placenta out of the uterus and vagina. Most women are not aware of this

squatting   standing   kneeling

Figure **10.5**
There are a variety of birthing positions.

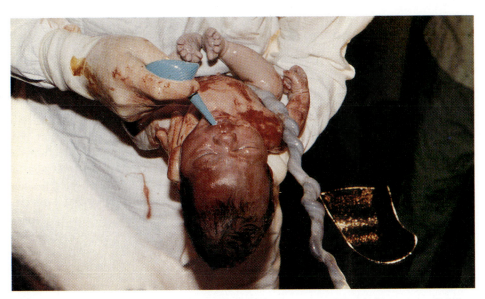

At birth, the mouth and nostrils are suctioned to remove any mucus. Many babies appear slightly bluish in color. As they begin to breathe on their own, their coloring changes.

process because of the excitement of giving birth. The placenta must be checked to make sure all of it has been expelled. If an episiotomy was performed, the cut will be sewn up after the placenta is removed. Usually this stage lasts about thirty minutes or so.

In parts of Kenya, the placenta of a female baby is buried under the fireplace and the placenta of a male baby is buried by the stalls of baby camels. This practice is thought to forever connect the children's future and these locations (Dunham et al., 1992). Other cultures hang the placentas outside the home to show that a baby indeed arrived!

PROBLEMS DURING THE BIRTH PROCESS

For most women, the birth of a newborn baby proceeds without problems. However, a number of problems can arise, as described below and in Personal Voices 10.2.

Prematurity

premature: A baby born early, weighing less than 5.5 pounds.

The majority of babies are born late rather than early. If birth takes place before the thirty-sixth week of pregnancy, it is considered **premature**. About 8% of births in the United States are premature. Prematurity increases the risk of birth-related defects and infant mortality (Palca, 1991). Close to 100% of the fetuses born at forty weeks can survive, 50% at thirty-one weeks of development, 10% at twenty-seven weeks, and less than 1% survive at less than twenty-three weeks of development (Jones, 1984). Those that do survive have higher risks for developmental difficulties.

Premature birth may occur early for several reasons, including early labor, early rupture of the amniotic membranes, or because of a maternal or fetal problem. It is common for women who have had one premature birth to have subsequent premature births. Approximately 50% of all twin births are premature, and delivery of multiple fetuses occurs about three weeks earlier, on average, than single births. There are several risk factors that may cause a premature birth, such as smoking during pregnancy, alcohol or drug use, inadequate weight gain or nutrition, heavy physical labor during the pregnancy, infections, and teenage pregnancy.

Breech Birth

In 97% of all births, the fetus emerges in the head-down position. However, in 3% to 4% of cases, the fetus is in the breech position, with the feet and buttocks against the cervix. Interestingly, about half of all fetuses are in this position before the seventh month of pregnancy, but most rotate before birth (Jones, 1984). Sometimes doctors are aware of the position of the fetus prior to delivery and can try to change the fetus's position for normal vaginal delivery. However, if this is not possible, or if it is discovered too late into delivery, labor may take an unusually long time. A cesarean section may be necessary for the health and well being of both the mother and her child.

Stillbirth

stillbirth: An infant who is born dead.

The most common cause of **stillbirth** is a failure in the baby's oxygen supply, heart, or lungs. For example, some babies are born dead because the umbilical cord is tightly wrapped around their neck during delivery. The majority of the time, a woman's body continues to produce milk, not knowing that the baby has died. Over the years, many women have blamed themselves for a stillbirth delivery, although medical experts agree that it often has little to do with what a woman has done (unless she has been using drugs during her pregnancy).

Cesarean Section Delivery

A cesarean section (c-section) involves the delivery of the fetus through an incision in the abdominal wall. In 1990, the number of women having c-sections fell, which was

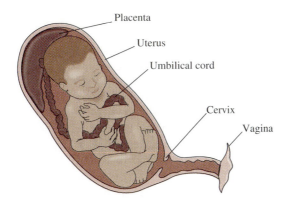

F i g u r e 10.6
In 3% to 4% of cases, the fetus is in the breech position,
with feet and buttocks against the cervix.

the first time it has done so in twenty years (*Kansas City Star*, 1992c). C-sections are needed when the baby is too large for a woman to deliver vaginally, the woman is unable to push the baby out the birth canal, the placenta either blocks the cervix (**placenta previa**) or separates from the baby prior to birth, or if the baby is in fetal distress. If a doctor decides that a cesarean is necessary, the woman is moved to an operating room and is given either a general anesthestic or an epidural. The operation usually lasts between twenty to ninety minutes and these women tend to stay in the hospital longer than women who deliver vaginally. Although a woman may be able to deliver her next baby vaginally after a c-section, many choose to have another c-section to avoid the pain of vaginal labor. Prior to 1990, the number of cesarean sections increased for several reasons: women were waiting longer to have children, which increased labor complications; the procedure became easier and safer to perform than it was several years before; and doctors performed cesarean sections to reduce the risks associated with vaginal delivery due to their fear of malpractice suits.

placenta previa: A condition in which the placenta is abnormally positioned in the uterus so that it partially or completely covers the opening of the cervix.

PART FOUR—POSTPARTUM

The majority of women and men are excited about being parents. However, many couples may not be prepared for the many physical and emotional changes that occur after the child is born. They may also find changes in their sex lives because of the responsibility and exhaustion that often accompanies parenthood.

PHYSICAL CHANGES

Following delivery, the uterus returns to its original shape in about six weeks. Many women report painful contractions for a few days after birth. These contractions are caused by the secretion of oxytocin, which is produced when a woman nurses and is

Great Expectations

There are numerous books, classes, and, of course, all the unsolicited advice that educate you when you are pregnant. It starts at the moment of conception and continues through delivery. The Lamaze instructors, the gynecologist, and the written material encourage you to write a birth plan so that you are prepared and can anticipate this experience. The Lamaze class itself teaches about the phases of birth, what the contractions will feel like, the duration of the contractions, the role of the coach in helping understand when the contraction is starting and how much longer it is likely to last. It prepares you for a "typical" birth experience. What the classes and the books don't prepare you for is anything else.

My water broke on Saturday night (around 10 P.M.) prior to feeling any kind of labor symptoms or contractions. I called my doctor, and he told me to try to get some sleep because it was likely to be a long thirty-six hours ahead (to prevent infection, most doctors want the baby out within thirty-six hours after your water breaks). He told me to call when the contractions were three to five minutes apart or at 8 A.M. the next morning, which ever came first.

I was quite surprised when I slept through the night and woke up without any signs of labor. I called the doctor; he had me go to the hospital for an exam. Once he confirmed that my water had been broken, he sent me home hoping labor would start on its own but advised that he would induce me at 8 P.M. if nothing had happened.

We left the hospital and did what any other parents-to-be would do . . . we went to the movies. That night I was induced. They warned me that it could take until noon or so the following day. Once at the hospital, after trying to get an I.V. in my arm for about an hour and a half (and three different nurses), they started the pitocin drip. It took about forty-five minutes to start feeling the effects, and then it kicked in.

The contractions were coming so fast that my husband couldn't tell when they were staring and when they were over. There was also some sort of time delay on the monitor, so he couldn't tell me when I reached the peak of the contractions and when they would start to taper off. Then they started to double upon each other, so I was not getting a break in between, as we had learned in Lamaze.

After about two hours of this nonsense, I asked for the epidural. Pain medication had not been in my birth plan, but it was necessary. The pain shifted from my uterus to the top of my thigh as the epidural started to take effect. I was experiencing a "window" where the epidural does not take effect. At that point, I was four centimeters dilated.

After about twenty minutes, I received another dose of the epidural. Then they checked my progress, and I was eight centimeters dilated. Ten minutes later I was fully dilated, and I began to push. The doctors were concerned that the cord might be around the baby's neck, so they asked me to push and they watched his heart rate on another monitor. For awhile it looked like we were going to be able to go ahead with the vaginal delivery. Then the baby's heart rate dropped and stayed there. An emergency cesarean section was required within minutes.

I had a general anesthesia and woke up two hours later to an eight-pound, nine-ounce baby boy. He was born at 2:53 A.M. Tommy was in intensive care for a day, which is standard for all babies if the water breaks in advance. Two days later he came down with a fever, and a nurse and doctor came into my room, woke me up, and told me that my baby was sick. They advised me that tests were being done to find out if the cause was viral or bacterial and that they were going to put him on antibiotics and monitor his heartbeat and of course move him back to intensive care.

At that point my husband had come down with the flu, so he was not allowed to come back to the hospital. I was given a room so that I could breast-feed the baby and stay on in the hospital as long as he had to stay. I breast fed him in ICU and left for two hours in between feedings. While all this was going on, I experienced postpartum depression. I was very worried about the baby, and my hormones were in a tailspin. It was not very easy to take control of the situation, and I had to handle everything alone since my husband was home sick in bed.

The bottom line in all this is that today Tommy is fine, in perfect health. After all that, I looked back at the previous week and realized that nothing went according to my expectations. My "birthplan" was irrelevant. I missed the romantic image that I learned in the movies. I missed the doctor saying, "It's a Boy!" I missed the look on my husband's face when he got to hold the baby for the first time, and I missed the first scream. I've since learned—and hopefully I will apply the lesson next time—not to have Great Expectations.

Author's files

responsible for the shrinking of the uterus. In breast-feeding women, the uterus returns to its original size quicker than in non-breast-feeding women. A bloody discharge persists for a week or so postdelivery. It soon turns yellow-white and lasts for ten days in mothers who nurse their child and up to a month or so in women who do not. An increase in frequency of urination occurs, which can be painful if an episiotomy was performed. Women who did undergo an episiotomy may be advised to take warm baths to reduce the pain of the incision and to quicken the healing process.

PSYCHOLOGICAL CHANGES

The majority of women feel both excitement and exhaustion after the birth of a child. However, for some, it is a very difficult time of depression, crying spells, and anxiety. Minor depression occurs in 25% to 67% of women (Jones, 1984). In severe cases, this is referred to as **postpartum depression**. Physical exhaustion, physiological changes, and an increased responsibility of childrearing all contribute to these feelings. Hormonal changes (including a sudden drop in progesterone) also trigger postpartum depression. Men have also been found to experience some degree of postpartum depression. In the most severe cases, mental disturbances, called **postpartum psychosis**, occur and in rare cases women have killed or neglected their babies after delivery.

In many mammals, it is quite common for the mothers to eat the placenta after delivery, a process known as **placentophagia**. Although this does not sound very appetizing to us, it does serve two very important purposes. The placenta is rich in progesterone and, once digested, the progesterone is quickly released into the bloodstream, causing the levels of progesterone to temporarily stabilize. This stabilization of progesterone has been hypothesized as a way to decrease the incidence of postpartum depression (Jones, 1984). In addition, in animals, eating the placenta also avoids attracting predators.

postpartum depression: The feelings of sadness found in some women after childbirth, usually mild, but that can, in rare cases, result in deep, clinical depression; also called baby blues.

postpartum psychosis: The rare occurrence of severe, debilitating depression or psychotic symptoms in the mother after childbirth.

placentophagia: The act of eating the placenta directly following childbirth.

POSTPARTUM SEXUALITY

Although most physicians advise waiting six weeks postpartum before resuming intercourse, in an uncomplicated vaginal delivery (with no tears or episiotomy), intercourse can safely be engaged in two weeks after delivery. This period is usually needed to ensure that no infection occurs and that the cervix has returned to its original position. If an episiotomy was performed, it may take up to three weeks for the stitches to dissolve. Intercourse can take place at this time if there is no pain during penetration. Cesarean section incisions usually take approximately two weeks to heal, and sexual intercourse is safe after this time. To reduce the risk of infection, it is best to avoid cunnilingus until a woman is certain she has no cuts or lacerations as a result of the delivery.

Directly after delivery, many women report slower and less intense excitement stages of the sexual response cycle and a decrease in vaginal lubrication (Masters and Johnson, 1966). However, at three months postpartum, most women return to their original levels of desire and excitement. Research has also shown that women who breast-feed often report higher levels of sexual interest. It is important to remember that women who have just given birth experience an increase in tension, fatigue, and physical

SEXUALITY*Today*   10.5

To Breast-Feed or Not to Breast-Feed?

In the early 1900s virtually every baby was breast-fed. However, as women began to fight for equality in the home and the workplace, bottle-feeding increased in popularity. Formulas and mixes were used instead of breast milk. Today, each woman must make her own decision about whether or not to breast-feed her baby. Below we will explore some of the advantages and disadvantages to breast-feeding.

Advantages to Breast-feeding:

- Breast milk is uniquely suited to an infant's needs. Unlike other milk, breast milk contains exactly the right balance of vitamins and nutrients for human beings. As the baby grows, the composition of breast milk changes to accommodate these needs.
- Breast milk is easier to digest than cow's milk. Even infants who cannot tolerate any other food can easily digest breast milk.
- Breast milk helps to strengthen the infant's immune system. Colostrum, which is secreted before milk production, is high in antibodies and protects a child from infection. Breast-fed babies are less likely to become ill in the first year of life.
- Breast-fed babies have fewer health problems, such as constipation, diarrhea, allergies, indigestion, future tooth decay, and skin disorders, than infants who have been bottle-fed. In addition, breast-fed babies are less likely to be overweight as infants or adults.
- Bowel movements of breast-fed babies are better smelling than bottle-fed babies, and they cause less diaper rash.
- Breast milk is always fresh and never spoils.
- Breast milk is convenient. It is always available and kept at the right temperature.

- Breast-feeding is inexpensive. The only necessity is that the mother needs to be on a healthy and nutritious diet.
- Breast-feeding helps to shrink the uterus back to its original size.
- Breast-feeding *may* suppress ovulation and menstruation for as long as a woman breast-feeds.

Disadvantages to Breast-feeding:

- Breast-feeding may be very time consuming, especially with multiple births.
- Breast-feeding may make it difficult for a mother to work outside the home.
- Breast-feeding does not allow the father the opportunity to bond with the infant during feeding, unless the breast milk is expressed and given by bottle.
- Breast-feeding may interfere with a couple's sex life. Lactation hormones may cause the vagina to become dry. In addition, the breasts often leak breast milk during lovemaking.
- Breast-feeding mothers must monitor their diets very closely. They must avoid hot or spicy foods and increase their intake of nutritious foods.
- Breast-feeding may be uncomfortable for a woman who feels uneasy about the intimacy of this type of feeding.
- A woman who breast-feeds may experience sore nipples or breasts and painful engorgement of the breasts.
- Breast-feeding may be uncomfortable after a cesarean section.

Adapted from Eisenberg et al. (1991:251–253) and *Boston Women's Health Book Collective* (1992:478–480)

discomfort, and many do not feel like having sexual intercourse. However, this does not mean women do not want affection. Men also experience similar feelings and may lose their erections during the first few sexual attempts after a baby is born. This may occur out of fear of hurting their partner, general anxiety, or conflicts involved in viewing the birth process.

BREAST-FEEDING

Breast-feeding became very popular again in the United States in the late 1980s and early 1990s. Within an hour after birth, the newborn baby usually begins a **rooting reflex**, which signals hunger. The baby's sucking triggers the flow of milk from the breast. This is done through receptors in the nipples, which signal the pituitary to produce prolactin, a chemical necessary for milk production. Another chemical called oxytoxin is also produced, which helps increase contractions in the uterus.

In the first few days of breast-feeding, the breasts release a fluid called colostrum. Colostrum is very important in strengthening the baby's immune system. This is one of the reasons that breast-feeding is recommended to new mothers. However, for some women, breast-feeding is not possible. Time constraints and work pressures may also not allow for breast-feeding. In poor countries, a child who is bottle-fed is more likely to die than a breast-fed one (Dunham et al., 1992). This is probably due to unsterilized bottles, water, and equipment often being used. For the most part, however, under sanitary conditions bottle feeding is perfectly safe.

Some women who want to breast-feed but who also wish to return to work use a breast pump (see photo). This allows a woman to express milk from her breasts that can be given to her child while she is away. Breast milk can be kept in the refrigerator or freezer, but it must be heated prior to feeding.

Some women use electric breast pumps to express milk from the breast for later use.

rooting reflex: When a hungry infant keeps its head in contact with an object that touches its mouth or cheek.

Summary

- Every culture has its own myths about where babies come from. These myths are passed down from generation to generation. Because the sperm can live for up to seventy-two hours, pregnancy can occur if sexual intercourse occurs a few days before or after ovulation. The ovum can live for up to twenty-four hours.
- One out of every five couples in the United States are infertile. Today, there are many options for infertile couples, including fertility drugs, surgery, artificial insemination, IVF, GIFT, ZIFT, intravaginal cultures, zonal dissection, sperm injections, embryo transplants, and surrogate parenting.
- Some couples wish to select the gender of a child. There have been a variety of formulas proposed for gender selection, although at the present time there is no known 100% reliable method for gender selection.
- Early signs of pregnancy include missing a period, breast tenderness, frequent urination, and nausea. Pregnancy tests measure for a hormone in the urine called human chorionic gonadatropin. It is secreted by the developing placenta.
- A nine-month pregnancy is divided into three trimesters. During each trimester, there are various physical developments in the fetus. Developmentally, the first trimester is the most important.

- During each trimester, the mother experiences various physical signs of the pregnancy. During the second and third trimester, she may have decreased nausea and breast sensitivity and increased heartburn and leg and ankle swelling. The breasts may begin to leak fluid.
- Many men also feel apprehensive as the birth date approaches. Today, many fathers are in the delivery room during labor.
- Sexual intercourse during pregnancy is safe for most mothers and the developing child up until the last several weeks of pregnancy.
- Exercise levels during pregnancy should never exceed pre-pregnancy levels. Caloric intake must be increased during pregnancy.
- If a woman drinks during her pregnancy, Fetal Alcohol Syndrome (FAS) can occur. FAS infants are undersized and mentally deficient. These deficits are lifelong.
- More women are delaying childbearing, although older women may run into problems with pregnancy such as an increase in spontaneous abortions, first-trimester bleeding, low birthweights, labor time, cesarean sections, and chromosomal abnormalities. However, if she is healthy and has regular prenatal checkups, there is little increased risk of problems.

- Possible problems in pregnancy include chromosomal abnormalities, toxemia, ectopic pregnancies, spontaneous abortions, and Rh incompatibility.
- In the United States, the majority of women give birth in the semi–lying-down position, which is not the easiest position. The easiest positions are either on hands and knees or squatting. In other cultures, a variety of birthing positions are used.
- Problems in the birth process include prematurity, breech birth, stillbirth, and cesarean section. Most women have no problems in the birth process.

- After the birth of a child, most men and women feel excited and relieved. However, a few experience postpartum depression. Sexual activity can resume within two weeks after delivery, if there was an uncomplicated vaginal delivery. This wait reduces the possibility of infection.
- Breast-feeding is an option available to most women. They must weigh advantages and disadvantages to determine what works best for them.

R e f l e c t i o n s   o n   S e x u a l i t y

1. Explain how culture affects our views of fertility.
2. Trace the development of the ovum and spermatozoon from maturation to fertilization and implantation.
3. What are the options for infertile couples today? Explain each of these options.
4. What ethical issues arise as a result of the advanced technological standing of gender selection research?
5. What are the signs of pregnancy? Why do they occur?
6. Differentiate between a false positive and false negative pregnancy test.
7. When is sexual intercourse safest during pregnancy? Explain.
8. How do nutritional requirements change during pregnancy? How can smoking or drug use affect a developing fetus?
9. Is pregnancy safe after the age of thirty? Explain.
10. Explain the potential problems that may develop during a pregnancy.
11. Explain the stages of the birth process. What is occurring at each stage?
12. What potential problems may arise during the birth process?
13. What are the physical and psychological changes associated with the postpartum?
14. Discuss the advantages and disadvantages to breast-feeding. Do you favor one method over the other? Why or why not?

S u g g e s t e d   R e a d i n g s

DUNHAM, C., and the Body Shop Team (1992) *Mamatoto: A Celebration of Life.* New York: Viking Penguin Books.

EISENBERG, A., H. E. MURKOFF, and S. E. HATHAWAY. (1991) *What To Expect When You're Expecting.* New York: Workman Publishing.

LAUERSON, N., and C. BOUCHEZ. (1991) *Getting Pregnant: What Couples Need To Know Right Now.* New York:

Ballatine Books.

MAYLE, P., and L. STUART. (1977) *Where Did I Come From?* New York: Coral Publishing Group.

NILSSON, L. (1990) *A Child is Born.* New York: Bantam Doubleday Dell Publishing Group.

SALZER, L. (1991) *Surviving Infertility.* New York: HarperCollins.

Contraception and Abortion

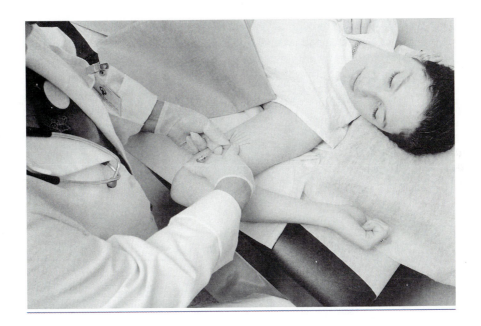

I've always felt that the birth control pill is the best option for me. After all, I'm not very good at remembering birth control in the heat of the moment. This way, I'm always prepared.

nineteen-year-old female

I hate to admit it, but I feel like birth control is a woman's job. Men don't get pregnant. Condoms just make sex feel terrible.

twenty-year-old male

Going through an abortion was one of the toughest things I had ever done. My parents had adopted me when I was a baby, and I've always had such respect for my mom for allowing me to be born. Unfortunately, I didn't feel adoption was an option for me at this time in my life.

eighteen-year-old female

Abortion is wrong. We should do everything in our power to make abortion illegal. The murder of innocent children must stop.

twenty-year-old male
Author's files

PART ONE—CONTRACEPTION

contraception: Prevention of pregnancy by abstinence or the use of certain devices or surgical procedures to prevent ovulation, fertilization, or implantation.

The typical American woman spends over one-half of her life from menarche to menopause trying not to get pregnant (Forrest, 1993). In fact, only 10% of an average woman's life is spent either pregnant or attempting to become pregnant (Gold, 1990). Although approximately 90% of women who are at risk for pregnancy use **contraception** (Hatcher et al., 1994), studies have found that only 47% of couples between the ages of fifteen and forty-four use contraception the first time they have sexual intercourse (Mosher and Bachrach, 1987).

In the early 1950s, a tremendous increase in reproductive and contraceptive research occurred in the United States, resulting in a new selection of modern birth control methods. These choices are made even more complex by disputes about the effectiveness of different methods, their side effects, and the increased use of some methods, such as condoms, in the prevention of AIDS and other sexually transmitted diseases. These factors make knowledge about contraception even more important.

Overall, women who know more about contraception tend to take fewer risks than women who do not know about contraception (Miller, 1986). In addition, motivation to use contraception increases when couples are able to communicate with their partners. Other factors that have been found to affect whether or not a couple uses contraception include the cost of the method, effectiveness rates, their frequency of sexual intercourse, their motivation to avoid pregnancy, the method's side effects, and their openness about sexuality. Couples are also less likely to use contraception while under the influence of alcohol.

In this chapter, we explore the array of contraceptive methods available today, investigate their strengths and weaknesses, and discuss abortion.

THE HISTORY OF CONTRACEPTION

Although many people believe that contraception is a modern invention, its origins actually go far back in history. The ancient Greeks used magic, superstition, and possibly herbs and drugs to try and control their fertility. The ancient Egyptians used several techniques to help prevent pregnancy, including fumigating the female genitalia with certain mixtures; inserting a tampon into the vagina that had been soaked in herbal liquid and honey; and inserting a mixture of crocodile feces, sour milk, and honey (Dunham et al., 1992). Another strategy was to insert objects into the vagina that could entrap or block the sperm. Objects such as vegetable seed pods (South Africa), a cervical plug of grass (Africa), sponges soaked with alcohol (Persia), and empty pomegranate halves (Greece) have also been used. These methods may sound far-fetched to us today, but they worked on many of the same principles as modern methods.

In the early 1800s, several groups in the United States were interested in controlling fertility in order to reduce poverty. However, contraception was considered a private affair, to be discussed only between partners in a relationship. As we learned in Chapter 1, Anthony Comstock worked with Congress in 1873 to pass the Comstock Laws, which prohibited the distribution of all obscene material; this included contraceptive information and devices. Even medical doctors were not allowed to provide information about contraception (although a few still did). Margaret Sanger, the founder of Planned Parenthood, was one of the first people to publicly advocate the importance of contraception in the U.S. (see Special Focus Chapter 2).

METHODS OF CONTRACEPTION

Several methods of contraception, or **birth control**, are currently available. There are also several methods currently being evaluated for possible approval by the **Food and Drug Administration (FDA)**. No single method of birth control is best for everyone. The best method of birth control for you is one that you and your partner will use correctly *every time* you have sexual intercourse.

Before choosing a method of birth control, you must consider your particular lifestyle. Issues that are important in choosing a method include your own personal health and health risks; the number of sexual partners you have; how often you have sexual intercourse; your risk of acquiring a sexually transmitted disease (STD); how responsible you are; the cost of the method; and the advantages and disadvantages of the method. In the United States, oral contraceptives are the most popular form of birth control (10.7 million users), followed by female sterilization (9.6 million), condoms (5.1 million), and male sterilization (4.1 million) (Mosher and Pratt, 1990).

Before deciding on a method of contraception, there are a number of questions you should ask yourself. In Where Do I Stand? 11.1, we present a short questionnaire that will help you weigh your options.

In the following sections, we discuss hormonal, barrier, chemical, intrauterine, natural, postcoital, and permanent methods of contraception. For each of these methods, we present how they work, **effectiveness** and **failure rates**, cost, advantages and disadvantages, and cross-cultural patterns of usage.

Effectiveness rates refer to how effectively the contraceptive method can protect a woman from pregnancy. Failure rates, on the other hand, refer to how often a woman

birth control: Another term for *contraception*.

Food and Drug Administration: An agency in the U.S. federal government, which has the power to approve and disapprove new drugs.

effectiveness rates: Estimated rates of the number of women who do not become pregnant each year using each method of contraception.

failure rates: Measurable rates of the number of women who become pregnant each year using each method of contraception.

WHERE DO I *Stand?* 11.1

Am I Going to Be Comfortable and Succeed with This Method?

It is important to choose a method of birth control that works well for you. Below are some questions that will help you clarify whether a particular type of birth control method will work well for you.

What type of birth control are you considering? _____
_____

Circle answer

Are you afraid of using this method?	yes	no	don't know
Would you rather not use this method?	yes	no	don't know
Will you have trouble remembering to use this method?	yes	no	don't know
Have you ever become pregnant while using this method?	yes	no	don't know
Will you have trouble using this method carefully?	yes	no	don't know
Do you have unanswered questions about this method?	yes	no	don't know
Does this method make menstrual periods longer or more painful?	yes	no	don't know
Does this method cost more than you can afford?	yes	no	don't know

Does this method ever cause serious health problems?	yes	no	don't know
Do you object to this method because of religious beliefs?	yes	no	don't know
Have you already had problems using this method?	yes	no	don't know
Is your partner opposed to this method?	yes	no	don't know
Are you using this method without your partner's knowledge?	yes	no	don't know
Will using this method embarrass you?	yes	no	don't know
Will using this method embarrass your partner?	yes	no	don't know
Will you enjoy intercourse less because of this method?	yes	no	don't know
Will this method interrupt lovemaking?	yes	no	don't know
Has a nurse or doctor ever told you not to use this method?	yes	no	don't know

"Yes" answers mean that potential problems may arise. In general, the more "yes" answers you have, the less likely you are to use this method consistently and correctly every time you have sexual intercourse.

**Reprinted with permission from
Hatcher et al (1994:130)**

---

typical use: Refers to the probability of contraceptive failure for a typical user of each method.

perfect use: Refers to the probability of contraceptive failure for a perfect user of each method.

becomes pregnant using a particular method. Since failure rates are directly measurable and effectiveness rates are not, failure rates are more reliable. Failure rates take into consideration both **typical** and **perfect use** of each method. Table 11.1 shows failure rates for different contraceptive methods.

Barrier Methods

Barrier methods of contraception work by preventing the sperm from entering the uterus. These methods include the condom, diaphragm, cervical cap, and sponge.

Table **11.1**

CONTRACEPTIVE EFFECTIVENESS

Below are both typical and perfect use failure rates for several contraceptive methods.

PERCENT OF WOMEN EXPERIENCING AN ACCIDENTAL PREGNANCY WITHIN THE FIRST YEAR OF USE

METHOD	TYPICAL USE	PERFECT USE
cervical cap		
women who have had children	36	26
women without children	18	9
condom		
male	12	3
female	21	5
combination birth control pills	3	0.1
Depo Provera	0.3	0.3
diaphragm	18	6
female sterilization	0.4	0.4
intrauterine device	2	1.5
male sterilization	0.15	0.10
Natural Family Planning	20	4
Norplant	0.09	0.09
spermicides	21	6
sponge		
women who have had children	36	20
women without children	18	9
withdrawal	19	4
no method	85	85

Hatcher et al. (1994:113)

Condom

Penile coverings have been used as a method of contraception since the beginnings of recorded history. In 1350 B.C., Egyptian men wore decorative sheaths over their penises. Eventually, sheaths of linen and animal intestines were developed. In 1844 the Goodyear company improved the strength and resiliency of rubber, and by 1850 rubber **condoms** were available in the United States (McLaren, 1990).

The past decade in the United States has seen a tremendous increase in condom use. With the advent of AIDS in the 1980s, condoms have become popular not only for their contraceptive abilities, but also for the protection they provide from STDs. In fact, while

condom: A latex or animal membrane sheath that fits over the penis and is used for protection against pregnancy and sexually transmitted diseases; latex female condoms, that protect the vaginal walls, are also available.

just a few years ago in the United States the majority of condoms were purchased by men, today women purchase almost half of all condoms.

In 1993, female condoms became available, marketed under the brand name *Reality*. The female condom is about seven inches long and has two flexible polyurethane rings. The female condom is inserted fully into the vagina, with the exception of the outer ring, which lies on the outside of the vagina. The inner ring serves as an insertion device and helps to hold the condom in place.

Costs for male condoms range from $5 to $10 per dozen, depending on what they are made of. Lambskin intestine condoms (also called "skins," because they are very thin) are considerably more expensive than latex, costing approximately $7 for three condoms. Female condoms cost approximately $2.50 each.

How It Works. The male condom ("rubber" or "prophylactic") is placed on an erect penis prior to vaginal penetration. Condoms must be put on before there is any vaginal contact by the penis because sperm may be present in the pre-ejaculatory fluid. After being rolled onto the penis, a one-half-inch empty space is left at the tip of the condom to allow room for the ejaculatory fluid (see Figure 11.1). To prevent tearing the condom, the vagina should be well lubricated. Although some condoms come prelubricated, if extra lubrication is needed, water, contraceptive jelly or cream, or KY jelly should be used. Hand or body lotion, petroleum jelly, baby oil, massage oil, or vegetable oil should never be used, as they may damage the latex and cause the condom to break. To avoid the possibility of semen leaking out of the condom, withdrawal must take place immedi-

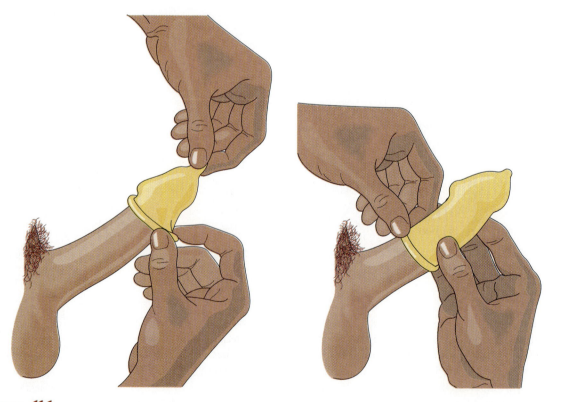

F i g u r e **11.1**
As the condom is rolled onto an erect penis, space should be left in the top of the condom so that the force of the ejaculate does not break the condom.

ately after ejaculation, while the penis is still erect, and the condom should be grasped firmly at the base to prevent its slipping off into the vagina during withdrawal.

SEX TALK

QUESTION **11.1** Do some men have problems maintaining an erection when they use a condom?

Some men do report that they have more difficulties maintaining an erection when they use a condom. Lubricated condoms may help maintain erections by increasing sensitivity. Condoms must be on hand when you need one. Nothing ruins the moment more than having to search the room hurriedly for a condom. On the other hand, men who experience problems with premature ejaculation report that condoms can help maintain erections.

Some couples complain that wearing a condom is like "taking a shower with a raincoat on," or that it decreases sensitivity during sexual intercourse. For men, adding two or three drops of a lubricant, such as KY jelly, into the condom before rolling it on to the penis can improve penile sensitivity. Many women also report that putting a small amount of a lubricant into their vagina prior to intercourse helps increase their pleasure and sensitivity while using a condom. Lambskin condoms offer more sensitivity than latex condoms, but they do not offer the same protection.

There are many different types of male condoms on the market, including lubricated, colored, spermicidal, reservoir tip, or ribbed texture condoms. For protection from STDs, the best condoms are rubber (latex) and contain a spermicide called **nonoxynol-9**. Nonlatex artificial condoms were approved for manufacturing by the FDA in late 1993. They are made of polyurethane, which is twice as strong as latex and half as thick. These condoms are not damaged by oil-based products, such as Vaseline or baby oil. However, they will probably be considerably more expensive than latex condoms.

Effectiveness. If male condoms are used correctly, every time you engage in sexual intercourse, their perfect-use effectiveness is 98%. However, if used properly, in conjunction with spermicidal jelly, this method approaches 100% effectiveness. Typical-use effectiveness rates for condoms are 88%. Preliminary tests reveal 74% typical-use effectiveness rate for female condoms.

Condoms that contain nonoxynol-9 have been found to be very effective in deactivating sperm, killing the HIV virus, and preventing other STDs. In addition, latex condoms have been found to be effective barriers against the transmission of herpes, chlamydia, gonorrhea, and HIV (Cates and Stone, 1992). While lambskin condoms block sperm, they may have microscopic holes big enough for the transmission of certain viruses. Therefore, they are not recommended for the prevention of STDs or the HIV virus.

Some couples worry that condoms will break. All condoms made in the United States are tested and must meet very stringent quality control requirements. Studies have demonstrated that the overall risk of condom breakage, if used correctly, is 1.9% (Grady and Tanfer, 1994). Using a condom after the expiration date is the leading cause of breakage. However, if a condom does break while you are using it, the best thing to do is to insert a spermicidal jelly or cream into the vagina immediately.

As we stated earlier, using certain products with condoms may cause them to tear. These include petroleum products, oils, and creams for vaginal infections (such as Monistat and Vagisil). Exposure to heat can also cause a condom to break when used. Since carrying a condom in your pocket exposes it to heat, these condoms may be more

A variety of condoms are available, including latex, polyurethane, skins, and female condoms. Male condoms come in many colors and shapes.

Nonoxynol-9: A spermicide that has been found to be highly effective for the prevention of pregnancy and protection from sexually transmitted diseases.

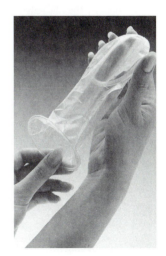

Female condoms have been available since 1994.

likely to break. Therefore, instead of carrying a condom in your wallet, it might be better to have it in a purse or backpack.

postcoital drip: A vaginal discharge (dripping) that occurs after sexual intercourse.

Advantages. Latex condoms offer the most protection from sexually transmitted diseases, including the virus that causes AIDS. In addition, latex condoms encourage male participation in contraception, are inexpensive (depending on how sexually active the couple is), do not require a prescription, may reduce the incidence of premature ejaculation, reduce **postcoital drip**, and have no medical side effects. Lubricated condoms may also make intercourse more pleasurable by reducing friction.

Disadvantages. The use of condoms reduces spontaneity since they require a couple to interrupt foreplay to put one on. In addition, condoms may reduce sensation and cause a slight allergic reaction to a specific type of condom or lubricant. Some condoms only come in a single size, while others come in a variety of sizes and shapes. Female condoms are also quite expensive.

Cross-Cultural Use. Condoms are popular outside of the United States. In Australia, pizza parlors will deliver condoms after 10 P.M., and in Japan, 40% of condoms are sold door-to-door (Hatcher et al., 1988; Coleman, 1983). Studies reveal that 78% of Japanese couples use condoms, 40% of couples in Denmark and Sweden, 30% in Singapore, and 5% in western European countries (Bulatao et al., 1990). In fact, Japan has the highest rate of condom usage in the world. Condom use has also significantly increased in France, where there are the highest number of AIDS cases in Europe (Moatti et al., 1991). Finally, after the fall of the U.S.S.R., condoms have been readily available, and Russian companies have begun to develop and market their own condoms (*New Republic,* 1992). In Brazil, on the other hand, condoms are six times more expensive than they are in the United States, which drastically reduces their use.

Diaphragm

diaphragm: A birth-control device consisting of a latex dome on a flexible spring rim; used with spermicidal cream or jelly.

Rubber **diaphragms** became popular in the 1880s, and since then many new developments have taken place. In 1983, a new model with a soft flexible rim was introduced. Today, diaphragms come in several different sizes and shapes. In the United States, diaphragms range in cost from $10 to $20, and the accompanying spermicidal cream or jelly costs approximately $10 per tube. Again, these are less expensive at family planning clinics. In the United States, approximately 15% of single women use a diaphragm (Janus and Janus, 1993).

How It Works. The diaphragm is a barrier method of contraception, and it must be used with a spermicidal jelly to ensure that sperm do not live if they should get past the barrier. Since diaphragms come in several different sizes and shapes, they also must be prescribed by a physician or other health-care provider to ensure a proper fit over the cervix. Prior to insertion, the diaphragm rim is covered with spermicidal jelly and one tablespoon of the jelly is put into the dome of the diaphragm. More spermicidal jelly must be inserted into the vagina if intercourse takes place again. After applying the spermicidal jelly, the diaphragm is folded in half and inserted into the vagina. For insertion, a woman can be standing with one leg propped up, squatting, or lying on her back (see Figure 11.2). The diaphragm is pushed downward toward the back of the vagina, while the front rim is tucked under the pubic bone. The diaphragm can be inserted by the woman or her partner, and insertion may take place immediately prior to sexual intercourse or up to six hours before. Once a diaphragm is in place, a woman should not be able to feel it; if she does, it is improperly inserted. After insertion, the diaphragm must

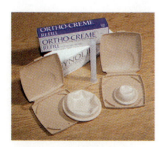

Diaphragms come in a variety of different sizes and must be fitted by a health-care provider.

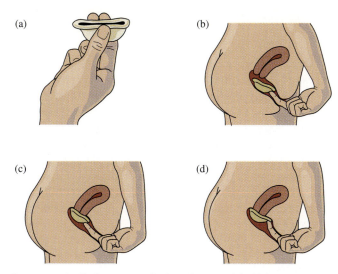

Proper use of a diaphragm: (a) After inserting spermicidal jelly or cream, the rim of the diaphragm is pinched between the fingers and thumb. (b) The folded diaphragm is gently inserted into the vagina and pushed downward as far as it will go. (c) To check for proper positioning, feel the cervix to be certain it is completely covered by the soft rubber dome of the diaphragm. (d) A finger is hooked under the forward rim to remove the diaphragm.

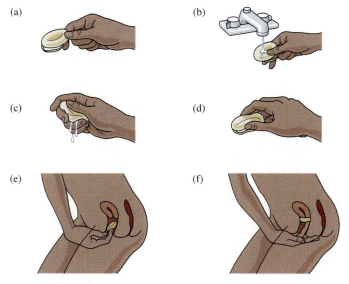

Proper insertion of the sponge: (a) Remove the sponge from the inner pack and hold with dimple side up. The loop should dangle under the sponge. (b) The sponge will feel slightly moist. Wet it further with a small amount of clean water (about two tablespoons). (c) Squeeze the sponge gently to remove excess water. It should feel moist and soapy, but not dripping wet. (d) Fold the sides of the sponge upward with a finger along each side to support it. The sponge should look long and narrow. Be sure the string loop dangles underneath the sponge from one end of the fold to the other. (e) From a standing position, squat down slightly and spread your legs apart. Use your free hand to spread apart the lips of the vagina. You may also stand with one foot on a stool or chair, sit cross-legged, or lie down. The semisquatting position seems to work best for women. Slide the sponge into the opening of the vagina as far as your fingers will go. Be careful not to push a fingernail through the sponge. Check the position of the sponge by sliding your finger around the edge of the sponge to make sure your cervix is not exposed. You should be able to feel the string loop.

Figure **11.2**
Instructions for proper use of a diaphragm and sponge.

be checked to ensure it is properly placed on the cervix. This is done by inserting two fingers into the vagina and feeling for the diaphragm covering the cervix.

After intercourse, the diaphragm must be left in place for at least six to eight hours. To remove the diaphragm, a finger is hooked over the front of the diaphragm rim, and then it is pulled down and out of the vagina. The diaphragm must be washed with soap and water and replaced in its container. As with condoms, petroleum-based products should never be used with a diaphragm, as they may damage the rubber. If properly cared for, diaphragms can last for several years. However, if a woman loses or gains more than ten pounds or experiences a pregnancy (regardless of how the pregnancy was resolved—through birth, miscarriage, or **abortion**), she must have her diaphragm refitted by her health-care provider.

abortion: Induced termination of a pregnancy before fetal viability.

SEX TALK

QUESTION **11.2** Is it okay to borrow someone else's diaphragm if I can't find mine?

> **Absolutely not. The diaphragm works by creating a suction on the cervix, which prevents sperm from entering the uterus. To get this suction, a health-care provider must measure the cervix and prescribe the right size diaphragm for each individual woman. If you use someone else's diaphragm, it may be the wrong size and, thus, ineffective. Also, because of the risk of acquiring a sexually transmitted disease, it is not a good idea to share diaphragms.**

Effectiveness. In order to be effective, a diaphragm must be used every time a woman has sexual intercourse. Perfect-use effectiveness rates are 94%, but since many people forget to put them in or do not use spermicidal jelly every time, typical-use effectiveness is 82%. Research has found that users who are less than thirty years old or who have intercourse more than four times a week have a double risk of failure (Hatcher et al., 1988). This is probably because younger women and women who have sexual intercourse several times per week are less likely to use the diaphragm consistently and effectively.

Advantages. The diaphragm can be inserted prior to beginning sexual activity, which increases spontaneity. In addition, the spermicidal cream or jelly provides some protection from sexually transmitted diseases and **pelvic inflammatory disease (PID)**, and it also reduces the risk of cervical dysplasia and/or cancer. The diaphragm can be used during the menstrual cycle, does not affect hormonal levels, and is relatively inexpensive. Finally, men can be active in the insertion of the diaphragm.

pelvic inflammatory disease (PID): Widespread infection of the female pelvic organs.

Disadvantages. A physician fitting and prescription is necessary to use the diaphragm. In addition, a woman must be taught insertion and removal techniques. The diaphragm has also been found to increase the risk of toxic shock syndrome (Schwartz et al., 1989), the risk of urinary tract infection, and postcoital drip. It may also move during different sexual positions and become less effective and develop a foul odor if left in place too long. An allergic reaction to the spermicide may also develop. Finally, a woman who uses the diaphragm must be comfortable touching her genitals and checking the diaphragm for proper placement.

Cross-Cultural Use. The diaphragm has low usage rates in other cultures. This may be due to the lack of promotion of this method of contraception (Coleman, 1983). Other factors that may contribute to low usage rates include the necessity of physician fitting; availability of spermicidal cream or jelly; cost; and the necessity of touching the genitals. Many women in other cultures are not comfortable touching the vagina or inserting anything into it (in fact, tampon use is also much lower in countries outside the United States). A shortage of physicians to fit diaphragms may also inhibit its use.

Contraceptive Sponge

In the early 1800s, sponges were recommended as birth control. In fact, in France, a damp sponge tied to a ribbon, used in conjunction with a douche or bidet, was seen as a "*woman's best protection*" (McLaren, 1990:184). More than 100 years later, in 1983, the *Today* sponge, another barrier method of contraception, was approved by the FDA. It is a round, concave sponge that fits over the cervix and contains nonoxynol-9 spermicide. In the United States, **contraceptive sponges** cost approximately $8 to $10 for six sponges.

In early 1995, however, the makers of *Today* contraceptive sponges decided to discontinue manufacturing the sponge because of stringent new government safety rules. As a result, the future of the contraceptive sponge is very uncertain at best.

contraceptive sponges: Polyurethane sponges impregnated with spermicide, inserted into the vagina for contraception.

How It Works. Contraceptive sponges work in three ways: as a barrier, which blocks the entrance to the uterus; through the absorption of sperm; and by deactivating sperm. Sponges can be purchased in a drug store, and they come in one size. Prior to vaginal insertion, the sponge is moistened with water, which activates the spermicide. It is then folded in half and inserted deep into the vagina (see Figure 11.2). Like the diaphragm, the sponge must be checked to make sure it is covering the cervix. Intercourse can take place immediately after insertion or at any time during the next twenty-four hours. Intercourse can occur as many times as desired without adding additional spermicidal jelly or cream. However, the sponge must be left in place for six hours after intercourse. For removal, a cloth loop on the outside of the sponge is grasped to gently pull the sponge out of the vagina. Like the diaphragm, the sponge can be inserted and removed by either the woman or her partner.

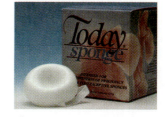

Effectiveness. Perfect-use effectiveness rates of the sponge are 83%, but typical-use effectiveness rates are lower, at 75.5%. These rates depend upon the user, and like the diaphragm, failure rates are higher in women under the age of thirty or those who have frequent sexual intercourse.

The *Today* contraceptive sponge.

Advantages. Contraceptive sponges can be purchased without a prescription. Once inserted, sexual intercourse can take place as many times as desired during a twenty-four-hour period. The sponge can be also be put in prior to sexual intercourse, which may increase sexual spontaneity. Sponges do not affect hormonal levels, are disposable, and do not require routine cleaning. In addition, men can be involved in the insertion of the contraceptive sponge.

Disadvantages. The contraceptive sponge may increase the risk of toxic shock syndrome and urinary tract infections. Unlike the diaphragm, the sponge cannot be left in place during a woman's menstrual period. Other disadvantages include required touching of the genitals, which may be uncomfortable for some women; a foul odor if left in place too long; a spermicide-caused allergic reaction in the woman or her partner; high expense if used frequently; and difficulty for some couples to insert. In addition, some men can feel the sponge inside and may find it uncomfortable.

Cross-Cultural Use. There is little research on the cross-cultural use of the contraceptive sponge. However, we do know that for years women in France have been using vaginal sponges, which have been dipped in various chemicals to avoid pregnancy. These sponges are washed and used over and over. This practice is not recommended, however, because of the risk of infection and toxic shock syndrome. As with diaphragms, sponges tend to have low usage rates in other cultures, which may be due to such factors as the lack of availability of spermicidal cream or jelly or the necessity of touching the genitals.

Cervical Cap

cervical cap: A plastic or rubber cover for the cervix that provides a contraceptive barrier to sperm.

The **cervical cap** was approved by the FDA in 1988. There are several different types of cervical caps, but only the Prentif cap has FDA approval. The cervical cap is a thimble-shaped rubber dome that is placed in the vagina over the cervix. It is similar to the diaphragm, but it is smaller and can remain in place for up to forty-eight hours. In the United States, the cost is approximately $30, and spermicidal cream or jelly is also necessary.

How It Works. The cervical cap works by blocking the entrance to the uterus and deactivating sperm through the use of spermicidal cream or jelly. After insertion, a woman must check to see that the cap is covering her cervix. Like a diaphragm, it can be inserted prior to intercourse and must be left in place for six to eight hours after intercourse. Additional spermicide must be inserted into the vagina for each act of sexual intercourse. The cervical cap comes in four sizes and must be properly fit by a physician.

Effectiveness. Since the cap fits the cervix more snugly than the diaphragm, effectiveness rates are generally better. Perfect-use effectiveness rates are 98%, but typical-use effectiveness rates are much lower, at 82%. The primary reason for failure is inconsistent or incorrect use.

The *Prentif* cervical cap.

Advantages. The cervical cap can be left in place for up to forty-eight hours (Klitsch, 1988), and it can be inserted earlier and left in longer than either a diaphragm or contraceptive sponge. Effectiveness rates are also higher than the diaphragm or sponge. The cervical cap does not affect hormonal levels.

Disadvantages. The use of a cervical cap may increase a woman's risk of toxic shock syndrome, cause abnormal Pap smears (Masters et al., 1994), increase the risk of urinary tract infections, cause possible allergic reactions to the rubber (Hatcher et al., 1994), increase vaginal odors, cause cervical damage, and increase postcoital drip. In addition, it must be fit by a physician, may be felt by the male partner during sexual intercourse, may dislodge during penile thrusting, and may cause discomfort.

Cross-Cultural Use. The cervical cap, designed in London, is widely used in England. However, in less-developed countries it is used infrequently, probably due to insertion problems and the necessity of checking cervical placement. Also, it is unclear whether or not this method has been actively promoted.

Hormonal Methods

By changing hormonal levels, production of ova can be interrupted and fertilization and implantation can be also be prevented. Hormonal methods of contraception include oral contraceptives, Norplant, and Depo Provera.

Oral Contraceptives

oral contraceptives: The "pill"; a preparation of synthetic female sex hormones that blocks ovulation.

Margaret Sanger was the first to envision **oral contraceptives** (the birth control pill, or simply "the pill"). Many researchers had been working with chemical methods to inhibit pregnancy in animals, but they were reluctant to try these methods on humans because they feared that increasing hormones could cause cancer. The complexity of a woman's body chemistry and the expense involved in developing the pill inhibited its progress. Finally, in 1960, the birth control pill was federally approved as a contraceptive method.

At first, the pill was much stronger than it needed to be. In the search for the most effective contraception, *more* estrogen was seen as *more* effective. However, within three to four years physicians realized that many women were experiencing negative side effects due to the high dosage of estrogen, and it was reduced. Today's birth control pills have less than half the dose of estrogen than the first pills did. In the United States, birth control pills are used by approximately 10.7 million women (Mosher and Pratt, 1990).

Combination birth control pills, which contain synthetic estrogen and a type of progesterone, are the most commonly used contraceptive method in the United States (Forrest and Fordyce, 1993). They range between $12 and $25 per month, and they are less expensive in family planning clinics than in drug stores. A physician prescription is necessary.

How It Works. The hormones estrogen, progesterone, LH, and FSH fluctuate during a woman's menstrual cycle. These fluctuations control the maturation of an ovum, ovulation, the development of the endometrium, and menstruation (see Chapter 3). The synthetic hormones replace a woman's own natural hormones but in different amounts. The increase in estrogen and progesterone prevent the pituitary gland from sending hormones to cause the ovaries to begin maturation of an ovum. The woman's body is actually tricked into believing that it is pregnant, and so ovulation does not occur. Birth control pills also work by thickening the cervical mucus (which inhibits the mobility of sperm) and by reducing the buildup of the endometrium.

Combination birth control pills can either be **monophasic** or **multiphasic**. Monophasic pills contain the same amount of hormones in each pill, while multiphasic pills vary the hormonal amount. Birth control pills can be taken on either a twenty-one-day or twenty-eight-day regimen. Seventy percent of pill users are on a twenty-eight-day regimen. If a woman takes a twenty-eight-day regimen, she will take one pill every day for twenty-eight days. However, the last seven pills in the pack are **placebo pills**. These pills are taken, but since they contain no hormones, a woman begins menstruation. In a twenty-one-day regimen, one pill is taken every day for twenty-one days, and then no pills are taken for one week (seven days). During this week, the woman will

combination birth control pills: An oral contraceptive containing synthetic estrogen and progesterone.

monophasic: Oral contraceptives containing stable levels of hormones during the entire month; the doses and types of hormones do not vary.

multiphasic: Oral contraceptives that contain varying levels of hormones during the month; each week the hormonal dosage is changed.

placebo pills: Seven pills that are at the end of a 28-day cycle of oral contraception; these pills are sugar pills and do not contain any hormones; used to help a woman remember to take a pill every day.

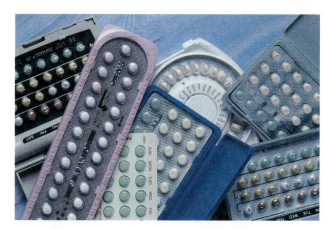

A variety of birth control pills are available, and a health-care provider can prescribe the one that will work best for you.

begin menstruation. Since the twenty-eight-day regimen requires a woman to continue taking a pill every day (although seven of them are placebos), it is often easier to use. Women on twenty-one-day regimens must remember to start the pills again after the one-week period. Birth control pills can be started on the first or fifth day of menstruation or on the first Sunday after menstruation. **Start days** vary depending on the pill manufacturer. The majority of manufacturers recommend a Sunday start day, which enables a woman to avoid menstruating during a weekend.

Each pill must be taken every day, at approximately the same time. This is important because they work by maintaining a certain hormonal level in the bloodstream. If this level drops, ovulation may occur. If one pill is forgotten, it should be taken as soon as it is remembered, even if this means taking two pills at one time. If two pills are forgotten, many physicians recommend taking two pills for the next two days and using a backup method of contraception for the remainder of the cycle. If any pills are missed, check with your health care provider and the birth control pills package insert for information on what to do.

Women who take birth control pills usually have lighter menstrual periods because the pills decrease the buildup of the endometrium. Menstrual discomfort, such as cramping, is also reduced. Since oral contraception also increases menstrual regularity, some women with irregular periods are advised to take birth control pills to regulate their periods even if they do not need contraception.

Since different pills contain different dosages of hormones, a health-care provider needs to determine the sensitivity of a woman's endocrine system to prescribe the appropriate level of hormones. There are approximately fifty-six different brands of pills, containing different amounts of estrogen and progesterone. There is no one type of pill that is "better" for everyone, based on side effects or effectiveness rates.

When a woman wants to use birth control pills, she must first have a full medical examination. Women with a history of circulatory problems, strokes, heart disease, breast or uterine cancer, migraine headaches, hypertension, diabetes, and undiagnosed vaginal bleeding are generally advised not to take oral contraceptives. If a woman can use birth control pills, physicians usually begin by prescribing a low-dose estrogen pill, and they increase the dosage if **break-through bleeding** or other symptoms occur.

Triphasil pills were introduced in the 1990s and have been growing in popularity (see Photo 11.5). They contain three different sets of pills for the month. Each week, the hormonal dosage is increased, rather than keeping the level at the consistently high levels like monophasic pills. When first introduced, many physicians liked this pill because it seemed to follow the natural cycle. However, many women who use triphasil pills report an increase in break-through bleeding due to the fluctuating hormone levels.

start day: The actual day that the first pill is taken in a pack of oral contraceptives.

break-through bleeding: Slight blood loss which occurs from the uterus when a woman is taking oral contraceptives.

triphasil pills: A type of multiphasic oral contraceptive that contains three different types of pills, each of which contains a different hormonal dosage.

SEX TALK

QUESTION **11.3** Last week I lost my pack of birth control pills and did not have time to go to the student health center. My roommate let me take a few of her pills. Is this okay?

This is not a good idea. Since there are many different types of pills, with different levels of hormones in them, your roommate may not be taking the same kind of pill. Also, with the new triphasil pills, if you took someone else's pills and they were not the same, you could be at risk of getting pregnant. The best idea would be to make time to get to the student health center to refill your own prescription and use another method of contraception until you start a new pack of pills.

Since birth control pills trick the body into believing that it is pregnant, it is not surprising that many women experience signs of pregnancy. These signs may include nausea, increase in breast size, breast tenderness, water retention, headaches, increased appetite and weight gain, fatigue, depression, decreased sexual drive, and high blood pressure (Hatcher et al., 1988) (see Chapter 10). Symptoms usually disappear within a couple of months, once a woman's body becomes used to the hormonal levels. Physicians should reevaluate a woman on birth control pills after three months to see if she is experiencing any problems, in which case a different dosage may be indicated. Although birth control pills can be used for an extended period, some physicians recommend taking a break from the pill after four years, although it is not clear how long of a break would be beneficial (Knowlden, 1990). It is a good idea to check with your physician about how long to stay on the pill. When a woman wants to discontinue oral contraceptives, she should wait until the end of the month and then stop taking it, rather than quitting midcycle.

Another type of birth control pill, the **minipill**, contains only progesterone. Because there is no estrogen, there are lower rates of side effects. However, minipills are also less effective than combination pills.

minipill: A type of birth-control pill that contains only synthetic progesterone and no estrogen.

If a woman using the pill experiences abdominal pain, chest pain, severe headaches, vision or eye problems, and severe leg or calf pain, she should contact her physician immediately (Hatcher et al., 1988). In addition, a woman who takes birth control pills should always inform her physician of her oral contraceptive use, especially if she is prescribed other medications. Certain drugs may have negative interactions with oral contraceptives (see Sexuality Today 11.1).

Effectiveness. Perfect-use effectiveness rates for combination birth control pills are 99.5%, while typical-use effectiveness rates are 97%. Typical-use effectiveness rates for minipills are between 90% and 95% (Masters et al., 1994). To be effective, the pill must be taken every day, at the same time of day.

Advantages. If used correctly, oral contraceptives have one of the highest effectiveness rates, do not interfere with spontaneity, reduce the flow of menstruation, menstrual cramps, and premenstrual syndrome, and increase menstrual regularity. Oral contraceptives also decrease incidence of pelvic inflammatory disease, offer protection from ovarian and endometrial cancer, lower the risk of ovarian cysts and fibroid tumors of the uterus (Masters et al., 1994), reduce noncancerous breast tumors by 75%, may help in preventing osteoporosis (Kleerekoper, 1991), and reduce the risk of rheumatoid arthritis (Spector et al., 1990). In addition, use of oral contraceptives may increase sexual enjoyment because fear of pregnancy is reduced and they are convenient and easy to use.

Disadvantages. Oral contraceptives offer no protection from sexually transmitted diseases and may increase a woman's susceptibility to STD infection and other vaginal infections. In addition, physical and psychological side effects are common, there are increased risks for women who smoke, they can be expensive, a pill must be taken every day, there is decreased effectiveness when certain other medications are used, and oral contraceptives place all of the responsibility for contraception on the female. Finally, some women with certain medical conditions cannot use oral contraceptives.

Cross-Cultural Use. Birth control pills have been used by more than 150 million women throughout the world, and by 50 million women in the United States (Hatcher et al., 1988). In the United Kingdom, the pill is used more than any other method of contraception (Bromwich and Parsons, 1990). Bracher and Santow (1992) found that birth control pills were the most successfully used contraceptive method in Australia, although recently many women have been opting for more "natural" or "healthy" alter-

SEXUALITY*Today*   *11.1*

Drugs That Interact with Oral Contraceptives

Many drugs and prescription medications may lower the effectiveness of the pill, and the pill may interfere with another drug's effectiveness. When you take medications, you should *always* let your physician know that you are on birth control pills. Drugs that interact with oral contraceptives include the following:

Drug	Birth Control Pills
acetaminophen	decreases effect of pain relief
alcohol	increases alcohol's effects
anticoagulants	decreases anticoagulant effect
antidepressants	increases antidepressant effect
barbiturates	decreases birth control pill effectiveness
penicillin	decreases birth control pill effectiveness
tetracycline	decreases birth control pill effectiveness
vitamin C	increases estrogen concentration with possible negative effects with 1 gram or more a day

Hatcher et al. (1988:222–223)

natives, such as the contraceptive sponge. In Denmark, more than 80% of reproductive-age women are taking birth control pills (David, 1994). Japan has had a longtime ban on birth control pills, perhaps due to the fact that birth control pills may increase a woman's susceptibility to STDs.

Norplant

Norplant: A hormonal method of birth control using doses that are implanted in a woman's arm and that can remain in place for up to five years.

Another hormonal method of contraception is **Norplant**, which was approved by the FDA in 1980. Norplant consists of silicone cylinders, which are implanted in a woman's forearm through a small incision. The procedure takes about ten minutes and is usually performed in a physician's office. Norplant can be left in place for five years, after which the cylinders must be surgically removed. They also must be removed if the woman wants to become pregnant. The most important advantage of these implants is their long-term ability to protect against pregnancy. However, removal can be difficult, taking three to four times as long as insertion, because the body grows protective scar tissue around the implants. In mid-1994, a group of women filed a lawsuit against the makers of Norplant, claiming that they suffered permanent injury during removal of the implants. In the future, scientists are hoping to find a way to have the cylinders dissolve so that removal is unnecessary.

How It Works. The matchstick-sized cylinders contain time-released chemicals (synthetic progestin) that suppress ovulation, thicken cervical mucus, and render the endometrium inhospitable to the zygote. Since there is no estrogen in Norplant, the side effects typically associated with oral contraceptives are reduced. Norplant is effective immediately after implantation. In the United States, insertion and the cylinders costs from $500 or more, depending on the physician's fees. Women using Norplant may experience irregular bleeding or other menstrual problems, arm pain, bleeding from injection site, headaches or vision problems, dizziness, cramping, nausea, weight gain or loss, hair growth or loss, and general weakness (Hatcher et al., 1990). Some women experience no menstrual bleeding for months at a time.

Effectiveness. The perfect-use effectiveness rate for Norplant is approximately 99% in the first year of use (Sivan, 1988). Since this method is relatively new, there are no typical-use rates for usage. The effectiveness rate decreases consistently in the second, third, and fourth year of use. Also, women who weigh more than 154 pounds have a greater chance of becoming pregnant than do thinner women because of lower hormonal concentration in the blood.

Advantages. Norplant is a highly effective and long-lasting contraceptive method. It involves a simple implantation procedure, is reversible, has no estrogen side effects, decreases menstrual flow and cramping, decreases risk of endometrial cancer, and increases spontaneity. In addition, women who are not able to use oral contraceptives may be able to safely use Norplant.

Disadvantages. Disadvantages to Norplant include expensive implantation and physician fees ($500 to $700), lengthy and painful removal procedures, no protection from STDs, menstruation problems and other potential side effects, visible injection site and cylinders, and possible scars after removal. As for oral contraceptives, other drugs have been found to interfere with Norplant's contraceptive effects. Finally, since Norplant has been only recently approved, its long-term effects are unknown.

Cross-Cultural Use. Prior to FDA approval in the United States, Norplant had been used throughout Europe, Latin America, and Asia (Masters et al., 1994). In addition, injectable contraceptive devices, which are similar to Norplant, have been available in several countries over the past few years. *Noristerat,* a long-acting drug, provides circulating levels of hormones to suppress ovulation and to make the endometrium inhospitable to the ovum. In the future, injectable contraceptives may become more popular because of their long-term effectiveness, reversibility, lack of day-to-day responsibility on the part of the user, and lack of long-term physician involvement.

Norplant is implanted into a woman's arm during a physician's office visit.

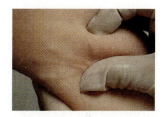

When implanted, the cylinders may be slightly visible.

Depo Provera

In late 1992, the FDA approved the use of another hormonal method of contraception, **Depo Provera**. Prior to 1992, Depo Provera had been approved for medical treatment, but not for contraceptive use. It had been scheduled for FDA approval for contraceptive use back in 1973, and then again in 1978. Because of its links with cervical, liver, and breast cancer, Depo Provera was never approved for contraceptive use. In the early 1990s, studies revealed that the cancer link was not as strong as previously thought. However, the use of Depo Provera has remained controversial, in part because it has been used as "chemical castration" for male sex offenders (see Chapter 14). When men take Depo Provera, it reduces their sexual drive.

For contraception, Depo Provera must be injected into the muscle of a woman's arm or buttock once every three months, and each injection costs approximately $40. Depo Provera begins working within twenty-four hours after the injection.

How It Works. Depo Provera is an injectable form of contraception that contains synthetic progesterone, and it works chiefly by preventing ovulation and thickening cervical mucus. Supporters of Depo Provera cite the fact that it does not contain estrogen (like birth control pills), which has been found to cause other serious side effects.

Depo Provera: Medroxyprogesterone, an injectable contraception available in the United States and in many other countries.

Opponents claim that the risk of breast cancer from use of Depo Provera is too high, and this risk increases after two years of use.

Effectiveness. Similarly to oral contraceptives, Depo Provera has a 99% perfect-use effectiveness rate (Hatcher et al., 1990).

Advantages. Depo Provera is a highly effective method of birth control, and one injection lasts for three months. It is only moderately expensive, reversible, does not contain estrogen, and does not restrict spontaneity. Menstrual periods may stop altogether after several injections of Depo Provera.

Disadvantages. Potential side effects include weight gain, menstrual irregularity, fatigue, dizzy spells, weakness, and an increase in headaches. In addition, use may increase risk of cervical, liver, and/or breast cancer, and it cannot be used by women with a history of liver disease, breast cancer, or unexplained vaginal bleeding or blood clots. It may take up to one year to become fertile again after discontinuing Depo Provera. Finally, Depo Provera has not been approved long enough to know all the long-term effects of use.

Cross-Cultural Use. Depo Provera has been available in more than eighty countries, including Britain, France, Sweden, Norway, Germany, New Zealand, and Belgium (Hatcher et al., 1990).

Chemical Methods

Chemical methods of contraception include spermicides such as creams, jellies, foams, suppositories, and films. Spermicides work by reducing the survival of sperm in the vagina.

Spermicides

vaginal contraceptive film (VCF): Spermicidal contraceptive film that is placed in the vagina.

As the incidence of STDs and AIDS continues to climb, the use of spermicides will become increasingly important. Spermicides can be found in some condoms, suppositories, creams, foams, and jellies. **Vaginal contraceptive film (VCF)**, produced in England, is now available over the counter in the United States. The film is two inches square, contains nonoxynol-9, and comes in packages of twelve. The film is wrapped around the index finger and inserted up into the vagina. In the United States, the cost for most spermicides ranges from $5 to $10, depending on the brand and where they were purchased. They are generally less expensive in clinics.

How It Works. Spermicides contain two components: one is an inert base such as jelly, cream, foam, or film, which holds the spermicide close to the cervix, and the second is the spermicide itself. In the United States, nonoxynol-9 is the most commonly used spermicidal product (Hatcher et al., 1994). Foams, jellies, creams, and film can all be purchased in drugstores and are usually inserted into the vagina with an applicator. Suppositories must be given ten to thirty minutes to melt after insertion in the vagina, and VCFs must be given approximately five minutes to melt; it is important to read manufacturer's directions carefully. Douching and tampons should be avoided for six to eight hours following the use of spermicides, as they interfere with effectiveness rates.

Effectiveness. Perfect-use effectiveness rates are 97%, while typical-use effectiveness rates are much lower, at 79%. Foam is generally considered more effective than either jelly, cream, film, or suppositories. However, the most successful type of spermicide is one that a couple feels comfortable with and uses consistently. It is not clear if it is the spermicides alone or in their use conjunction with barrier methods that prevents STD infection. Spermicides are considerably more effective when used in conjunction with a diaphragm or condom.

Spermicides are chemical methods of contraception.

Advantages. Spermicides can be purchased without a physician's prescription, and they are simple to use. In addition, spermicides provide lubrication during intercourse, a partner can participate in inserting them, and there are no serious medical side effects. Finally, spermicides are effective in killing most STDs, including gonorrhea, trichomoniasis, herpes, chlamydia, and HIV (Cates and Stone, 1992).

Disadvantages. Spermicides must be used each time sexual intercourse occurs, which may be expensive depending on frequency of intercourse. In addition, there is an increase in postcoital drip, some couples may be allergic or have reactions to certain types of spermicides, spermicides often have an unpleasant taste, and they are less effective if used alone. Finally, preliminary research has shown that consistent use of nonoxynol-9 may cause a woman to become more susceptible to HIV infection, because it may weaken vaginal tissue (Niruthisard et al., 1991).

Cross-Cultural Use. Spermicides are not widely used in other countries, probably due to the relatively high cost. Often sterilization and IUDs are free, but diaphragms, condoms, and spermicides must be purchased for a fee (Bulatao et al., 1990). An unwillingness to touch the vagina may also restrict the use of spermicides.

Intrauterine Methods

Intrauterine Device (IUD)

In the 1970s, approximately 10% of women using contraceptives in the United States used an **intrauterine device** or IUD (Hatcher et al., 1988). However, after that time, an increase in the number of problems associated with IUDs led to fewer types on the market, negative attitudes toward them, and a decrease in the number of IUD users. As of 1990, there were only two IUDs available, Progestasert and the Paraguard, and only 1% of women in the United States were using them (Hatcher et al., 1990).

intrauterine device: A small, plastic device that is inserted into the uterus for contraception.

The Dalkon Shield was a popular type of IUD up until the mid-1980s when the A. H. Robins company recommended that they be removed from all women who were using them. At that time, women who had IUDs experienced many problems including severe pain, bleeding, and pelvic inflammatory disease (PID), which even led to sterility in some cases. Many of the women who had been using an IUD felt that A. H. Robins knew of the problems associated with the Dalkon Shield and did not adequately warn them of the dangers. As a result, lawsuits and litigation totaling $480,000,000 were filed against A. H. Robins (Hatcher et al., 1988). Because of the problems with the Dalkon Shield, several other companies stopped production of their IUDs as well, although some are still available today outside the United States. In the United States, the cost for an IUD can range from $150 to $300.

The *Progestasert* and *Paraguard* IUDs.

How It Works. How IUDs work is not clearly understood. Since an IUD is placed inside of the uterus, it has long been thought that it interferes with the implantation of the fertilized ovum. IUDs have been found to create a low-grade infection in the uterus, which may either break apart the fertilized ovum, inhibit implantation, and/or increase prostaglandins (Hatcher et al., 1988). The IUD may also interfere with sperm mobility and block sperm from passing into the Fallopian tubes.

IUDs must be inserted by a physician, usually during a woman's menstrual period to make certain she is not already pregnant. A string hangs down from the cervix, and a woman must check for the string once a month, to make certain the IUD is still in place. Some men have reported that they can feel this string during intercourse. Because of the risk of pelvic inflammatory disease and sterility, IUDs are not recommended for college-aged students who have not had children.

Effectiveness. Perfect-use effectiveness rates for the IUD are 98%, and the typical-use effectiveness rate is approximately 97%. Effectiveness also depends upon the age of the woman and her past pregnancy history. A woman who has never been pregnant is more likely to expel the IUD through her cervix. Some IUDs can be left in place for up to eight years, while others need to be changed yearly.

Advantages. IUDs are the least expensive method of contraception over time, and they do not interfere with spontaneity. In addition, they have long-lasting contraceptive effects.

Disadvantages. Women with several sexual partners who use the IUD are at increased risk of pelvic inflammatory disease (Masters et al., 1994). In addition, there is no protection from STD infection (and may be an increase in STD and HIV transmission), an increase in amount of menstrual flow and severity of cramping, risk of uterine perforation, and painful insertion and removal procedures. The IUD may also be expelled from the uterus and may create partner discomfort.

Cross-Cultural Use. As of 1988, IUDs were used by eighty-five million women all over the world, 70% of whom were in China (Hatcher et al., 1990). In Korea, the IUD

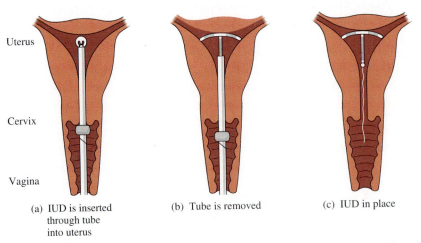

Uterus		
Cervix		
Vagina		
(a) IUD is inserted through tube into uterus	(b) Tube is removed	(c) IUD in place

Figure **11.3**
Insertion of an IUD: (a) tube containing the IUD is inserted into the uterus; (b) IUD positioned up to the top wall of the uterus; (c) tube is removed.

was the most popular method of contraception in 1966 because it was promoted by the government and was easy to administer to less-educated women (Larson, 1981). However, because of the unpleasant side effects, many women requested IUD removal. In India, 910,000 IUDs were inserted in 1966, and although this number has currently dropped to 500,000 per year, the number of IUD users is increasing (Bulatao et al., 1990). In Europe, the increase in IUD use may be due to adverse publicity about the side effects of birth control pills.

Natural Methods

Natural methods of contraception do not alter any physiological function. They include natural family planning and fertility awareness, withdrawal, and abstinence.

Natural Family Planning and Fertility Awareness

With **natural family planning** (or the **sympto-thermal method**), a woman charts her menstrual periods by taking a daily **basal body temperature (BBT)** and checking cervical mucus in order to determine when she ovulates. During ovulation, she abstains from sexual intercourse. While this may also be referred to as the **rhythm method**, generally the rhythm method does not involve monitoring the signs of ovulation. When charting is used in conjunction with another form of birth control, it is referred to as **fertility awareness**.

How It Works. With natural family planning, a woman takes her BBT every morning before she gets out of bed and records it on a basal body temperature chart (see Figure 11.4). Changes in hormonal levels cause body temperature to rise 0.4–0.8°F (0.2–0.4°C) immediately before ovulation, and it remains elevated until menstruation begins. A woman using this method monitors her cervical mucus, which becomes thin and stretchy during ovulation to help transport sperm. At other times of the month, cervical mucus is thicker. After six months of consistent charting, a woman will be able to estimate the approximate time of ovulation, and she can then either abstain from sexual intercourse or use contraception during her high risk times (usually this period is between one and two weeks). Most women who use this method are spacing their pregnancies and are not as concerned about preventing pregnancies. The rhythm method involves abstaining from intercourse midcycle, when ovulation is probable, but usually this does not include BBT or cervical mucus charting. Recently, ovulation kits have appeared to help women who desire pregnancy to determine their fertile days. It is possible tests like these may also be used in natural family planning, but at this time they are too expensive to be used this way.

Effectiveness. Perfect-use effectiveness rates for natural family planning are 90%, while typical-use effectiveness rates are approximately 80%. The majority of failures with this method are due to couples engaging in intercourse too close to ovulation. In addition, a woman may ovulate earlier or later than usual because of diet, stress, or alcohol use.

Advantages. Natural family planning is an acceptable form of birth control for those who cannot use another method for religious reasons. It is also inexpensive, teaches couples about the menstrual cycle, may encourage couples to communicate more about contraception, can involve the male, and has no medical side effects. It also helps women if they eventually want to get pregnant, because they know when they ovulate.

natural family planning: A contraceptive method that involves calculating ovulation and avoiding sexual intercourse during ovulation and at unsafe times.

sympto-thermal method: A contraceptive method that involves monitoring both cervical mucus (sympto) and basal body temperature (thermal) to determine ovulation.

basal body temperature (BBT): The body's resting temperature, which is taken first thing in the morning prior to arising and used to calculate ovulation in the sympto-thermal method of contraception.

rhythm method: A contraceptive method that involves calculating the date of ovulation and avoiding sexual intercourse around this time.

fertility awareness: Basal body temperature charting used in conjunction with another method of contraception.

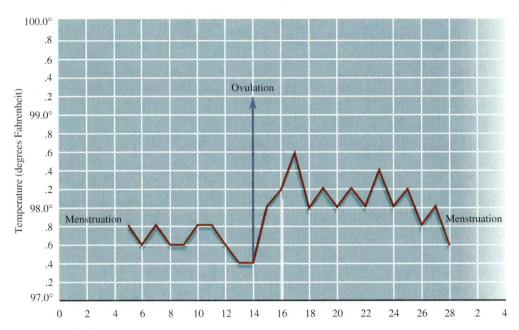

F i g u r e **11.4**
A basal body temperature chart.

Disadvantages. Natural family planning provides no protection from STD infection and restricts spontaneity. In addition, this method has low effectiveness rates, takes time and commitment to learn, and requires several cycles of records before method can be used reliably. In addition, women who have irregular cycles may have difficulty in interpreting their charts.

Cross-Cultural Use. In Peru, Sri Lanka, the Philippines, and Ireland, natural family planning and the rhythm method are the most popular methods of contraception (Bulatao et al., 1990). This is primarily because they are inexpensive and involve little assistance from physicians. In addition, in Catholic countries such as Ireland, this may be the only form of contraception available or acceptable. Many women's groups from the United States have gone to undeveloped countries to teach natural family planning.

Withdrawal

coitus interruptus: A contraceptive method involving withdrawal of the penis from the vagina prior to ejaculation.

coitus reservatus: A contraceptive method that involves stopping sexual intercourse prior to ejaculation and allowing the penis to detumesce.

In the Bible, Onan is described as "spilling his seed" to prevent impregnating his brother's wife. This is referred to as **coitus interruptus**, or withdrawal. In the mid-1800s, withdrawal was the most popular method of birth control. At that time, some physicians recommended partial withdrawal, in which a man pulled his penis away from the cervix but not out of the vagina while he ejaculated, which (they thought) kept the sperm out of the uterus. However, this method proved ineffective. Another method, called **coitus reservatus**, in which a man refrains from ejaculating, was also ineffective (McLaren, 1990). Today in the United States, approximately 2% of couples use withdrawal as a method of birth control (Hatcher et al., 1994).

How It Works. Withdrawal does not require any advance preparation. A couple engages in sexual intercourse, and prior to ejaculation, the male withdraws his penis from the vagina. The ejaculate does not enter the uterus.

Effectiveness. Perfect-use effectiveness rates are approximately 80%, while typical-use effectiveness rates are 75%. Failures often occur because the preejaculatory fluid contains sperm. If a couple engages in sexual intercourse, the preejaculatory fluid (present on the tip of the penis) contains enough sperm for pregnancy to occur.

Advantages. Withdrawal is another acceptable method of birth control for those who cannot use another method for religious reasons. In addition, it may be a good method for couples who do not mind if they become pregnant, and it is better than not using any method at all.

Disadvantages. Withdrawal provides no protection from STD infection and has low effectiveness rates. In addition, withdrawal may contribute to premature ejaculation in some men and may be extremely stressful for both men and their partners. It also requires an act of will from the male and trust from the female partner.

Cross-Cultural Use. Although some research indicates that there are fewer couples using withdrawal than other traditional methods of contraception, other studies suggest that it is used by more than 50% of couples practicing contraception in Czechoslovakia, Ireland, Poland, Romania, Spain, and the former Yugoslavia (Bromwich and Parsons, 1990). In other countries, such as Turkey, withdrawal has been found to be the number one contraceptive method. In Africa, there is a reluctance to use modern methods of contraception; therefore, many women rely on withdrawal. For couples with limited contraceptive choices, withdrawal is a popular method.

Abstinence

Historically, abstinence (or not engaging in sexual intercourse at all) has probably been the most important factor in controlling fertility. It is the only 100% effective method of contraception. Couples may choose abstinence to prevent pregnancy, to protect against STDs, or for other reasons such as illness or disease. Couples who practice abstinence may or may not engage in other sexual behaviors. Periodic abstinence can be used in combination with natural family planning.

Postcoital Methods

Throughout the world, many women have tried to design their own **postcoital methods** of contraception, which include jumping up and down, douching with certain liquids, taking certain vitamins, and inserting various objects into the vagina. Many of these methods, however, have only been successful in hurting the woman. Effective postcoital methods of contraception do exist, but they are used only in emergency situations and must be given within seventy-two hours of the act of intercourse. Although the FDA has not approved any postcoital methods (Hatcher et al., 1994), physicians have been using them, primarily to treat rape victims, for close to twenty years. Although certain areas of Germany and Great Britain have approved postcoital methods, the United States and Canada have not because postcoital methods have been seen as **abortifacients**.

postcoital methods: Methods of birth control that are used after a pregnancy is confirmed or suspected.

abortifacients: Any substance or device that causes an abortion.

"morning after" pill: A contraceptive method that involves taking a high dose of hormones to interrupt a pregnancy within forty-eight hours of conception.

DES: Diethstilbestrol, a potent synthetic estrogen.

menstrual extraction: Removal of the contents of the uterus prior to a positive pregnancy test.

Postcoital techniques include the **"morning after" pill**, **DES**, and **menstrual extraction**. The "morning after" pill is a combination pill, which contains various types of estrogen. Several pills are taken directly following intercourse (preferably within twelve to twenty-four hours) and then again twelve hours later (Hatcher et al., 1988). The pills work by changing the endometrial layer of the uterus, effectively blocking implantation. These pills can cause severe nausea, abdominal pain, headaches, breast tenderness, and/or depression. A menstrual period usually begins within two to three weeks of taking the pill. At one time, DES, a synthetic form of estrogen, was a popular method of postcoital contraception. It was taken for five days, and it worked by changing the endometrial layer of the uterus and by decreasing the production of certain hormones necessary to continue pregnancy (Hatcher et al., 1988). However, since DES was found to contribute to cancer in the offspring of women who used it, it is seldom used today.

Menstrual extraction, or the removal of uterine contents after missing a menstrual period, has also been used as a postcoital method. This procedure, although often viewed as a form of abortion, is used prior to a positive pregnancy test. A thin tube is placed in the uterus and suction removes the uterine contents. Since it is performed before a pregnancy test is done, it has been performed on many women who were not pregnant.

Permanent Methods

sterilization techniques: Surgical contraceptive methods that cause permanent sterility.

vasectomy: A surgical procedure in which the vas deferens are cut, tied, or cauterized for permanent contraception.

tubal sterilization: A surgical procedure in which the Fallopian tubes are cut, tied, or cauterized, for permanent contraception.

cauterization: A sterilization procedure that involves burning or searing the Fallopian tubes or vas deferens for permanent sterilization.

ligation: A sterilization procedure that involves the tying or binding of the Fallopian tubes or vas deferens.

The first **sterilization techniques** in the United States were performed on psychiatric patients to regulate the reproduction of the "unfit" (McLaren, 1990:253). In the 1970s, sterilizations were also forced on poor minority women who sought abortions. In the United States, sterilization may be the most popular form of contraception today (Bulatao et al., 1990). Married couples are more likely to use sterilization methods than any other form of birth control (48% use female sterilization, while 11% use **vasectomy**) (Forrest and Fordyce, 1993).

The primary difference between sterilization and other methods of contraception is that sterilization is usually irreversible and requires surgery. Although some people have been able to have their sterilizations reversed, this can be very expensive, time consuming, and in some instances, dangerous (in males, their bodies may have developed antibodies against sperm, which can damage new, developing sperm). The majority of people who request sterilization reversals do so because they have remarried and desire children with their new partners.

Female Sterilization

Female sterilization, or **tubal sterilization**, is the most widely used method of birth control in the world (Church and Geller, 1990). In a tubal sterilization, a physician may sever or block both Fallopian tubes so that the ovum and sperm can not meet. Blocking the tubes can be done with **cauterization**, a ring, band, or clamp (which pinches the tube together), or **ligation**. The procedure takes between twenty and thirty minutes, and can be done under local or general anesthesia. Recently, some of these procedures have been done using clips or silicone plugs instead of severing the tubes, which may enable physicians to reverse the operation in the future. However, at the present time, female sterilization is considered irreversible.

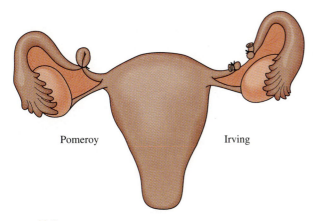

Figure **11.5**

Two types of tubal ligation.

Sterilization procedures can be done during **outpatient surgery** or directly following childbirth in a hospital. The sterilization procedure is generally done with the use of a **laparoscope** through a small incision either under the naval or lower in the abdomen. After this is done, a woman continues to ovulate, but the ovum does not enter the uterus. Female sterilization costs approximately $1000 to $2500.

As with any other surgery, potential risks exist. A woman may feel side effects from the anesthesia or experience bleeding, infection, and possible injury to other organs during the procedure. In a few cases, the surgery is unsuccessful and must be repeated. On the positive side, however, tubal sterilization has been found to substantially reduce the risk of ovarian cancer (Hankinson et al., 1993).

outpatient surgery: Surgery performed in the hospital or doctor's office, after which a patient is allowed to return home; inpatient surgery requires hospitalization.

laparoscope: A tiny scope that can be inserted through the skin and allows for the viewing of internal organs.

Male Sterilization

Male sterilization, or vasectomy, blocks the flow of sperm through the vas deferens (see Chapter 3). After a vasectomy, the testes continue to produce viable sperm cells, but with nowhere to go, they die and are absorbed by the body. Semen normally contains approximately 98% fluid and 2% sperm, and after a vasectomy, the man still ejaculates semen, but the semen contains no sperm. All other functions, such as the manufacturing of testosterone, erections, and urination, are unaffected by a vasectomy procedure. In the United States, between 400,000 and 500,000 vasectomies are performed each year.

The surgery for a vasectomy is done on an outpatient basis in a physician's office. The physician makes two small incisions about one-quarter to one-half inch long in the scrotum. The vas deferens is then clipped or cauterized under local anesthesia, which usually takes approximately twenty minutes. Immediately following a vasectomy, enough sperm remains for twenty more ejaculations, and so sperm counts are taken two to three months later to check sterility (Bromwich and Parsons, 1990). The procedure costs between $250 and $500.

Vasectomy does have some risk involved, including internal bleeding, infection, pelvic congestion, and **recanalization**. In 1993, men who underwent a vasectomy were reported to be at an increased risk of developing prostate cancer (*Wall Street Journal,* 1993). However, more studies need to be done to document these findings. With the availability of newer, long-term contraceptive options for women, fewer men are choosing vasectomy.

recanalization: The rejoining of the vas deferens or Fallopian tubes after a sterilization procedure.

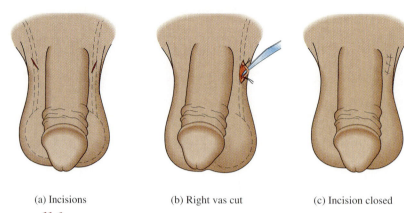

(a) Incisions   (b) Right vas cut   (c) Incision closed

F i g u r e **11.6**

The vasectomy. In an actual procedure, both sides must be completed.

Effectiveness. Tubal sterilizations are effective immediately, while vasectomies require semen analysis for two months after the procedure to ensure no viable sperm remains. Effectiveness for both procedures is between 99% and 100%.

Advantages. Sterilization is a highly effective permanent method of contraception. It does not interfere with spontaneity, has no ongoing medical risks, and may increase sexual desire and frequency of sexual intercourse (Shain, 1991).

Disadvantages. Sterilization provides no protection from STD infection. Surgery is required, and this procedure is considered irreversible.

Cross-Cultural Use. Worldwide, by 1984, approximately thirty-three million couples were protected by vasectomy and ninety-five million by tubal sterilization (Shain, 1991). In Korea by 1979, female sterilization was used by the majority of contracepting women (Bromwich and Parsons, 1990). In Malaysia, sterilization was used primarily by educated women with higher incomes (Bulatao et al., 1990). In Thailand, Fiji, Hong Kong, Panama, El Salvador, and Singapore, female sterilization is also quite common. In countries where family planning clinics are sparse, many women travel long distances to be sterilized. As we have discussed before, access to and promotion of a certain method also contribute to its popularity. In many countries, sterilization is the only method of contraception available. Financial incentives also regulate the use of sterilization; for instance, in Bangladesh men and women who undergo sterilization are paid the equivalent of $5.50 U.S. dollars (which is to them a considerable amount of money).

Ineffective Methods

Douching involves using a syringe-type instrument to inject a stream of water (which may be mixed with other chemicals) into the vagina. In the mid-1800s, douching was actually advised by physicians as a contraceptive. As a method of contraception, douching is ineffective. In fact, by the time a woman gets up to douche after intercourse, most of the sperm are already up in her uterus, and those that are not are helped in by the force of the douche. Many physicians recommend that women not douche at all because it has been found to lead to a higher degree of pelvic infections and STDs. Douching often removes the healthy infection-fighting bacteria.

MALE CONTRACEPTION

Historically, birth control has been considered a female's responsibility, and that may be why the condom and vasectomy are the only birth control methods available to men. Many feminists claim that the lack of research into male methods of birth control has to do with the fact that birth control research is done primarily by men. As a result, women are responsible for using birth control and must suffer through the potential side effects. Others claim that there are few male methods because of the fact that men produce one billion sperm for each ovum a woman produces. It is easier to interfere with one ovum, once a month, than billions of sperm at each ejaculation. They also argue that since men are constantly producing sperm from puberty to old age, chemical means of stopping sperm production may in some way harm future sperm production (Bromwich and Parsons, 1990). Chemical contraception may also interfere with testosterone production, which is responsible for the male sexual drive.

There is hope, however, that men will have more options to choose from in the future. Some possibilities include implants (similar to Norplant for women), hormonal and drug treatments, and **gossypol injections**. Gossypol is an ingredient in cottonseed oil that reduces the quantity of sperm produced. However, sperm production has not been found to increase to original levels after discontinuation. **Inhibin**, another hormone, has also been studied. Another alternative involves weekly injections of testosterone, which causes sperm production to decrease. Side effects may include increased aggression, acne, weight gain, depression, and fatigue. Researchers are also experimenting with longer-acting formulas that can be injected every three or four months instead of weekly.

In some countries, such as Sweden, even though there are a limited number of contraceptive options for men, men are still encouraged to be involved in contraceptive decision making. They are also routinely involved in counseling and physician appointments with their partners.

gossypol injections: An ingredient in cottonseed oil that, when injected or implanted, may inhibit sperm production.

inhibin: A hormone that, when injected or implanted, inhibits sperm production.

CONTRACEPTION IN THE FUTURE

Societal attitudes about contraception have been changing slowly. In the United States today, more and more people feel comfortable asking physicians about contraception or purchasing condoms. Condoms are also being handed out freely in clinics, many universities, and even in some high schools. Many restaurants and gas stations have condom-vending machines in the bathrooms.

While there is not a lot of contraceptive research being done in the United States today, some developments are under way. Condoms are becoming ecologically sound and able to dissolve in water. Spermicides are now being developed in a range of flavors to offset the disadvantage of their current unpleasant taste (Bromwich and Parsons, 1990). Disposable diaphragms, coated with spermicide, and vaginal rings containing hormones, which can be left in the vagina for up to six months, may also be available soon. The time-released hormones in the vaginal rings will prevent ovulation and change cervical mucus (Bromwich and Parsons, 1990). Even contraceptive nasal sprays are being studied. However, because of the side effects of vaginal dryness and thinning of the bones, more research is needed before nasal sprays will be approved for contraceptive purposes.

Scientists are also beginning to look for vaccines that would cause infertility until pregnancy is desired. In 1992, scientists in India claimed to have developed the first birth control vaccine for women (*Kansas City Star,* 1992d). This vaccine may prevent the fertilized ovum from implanting in the endometrium. However, it may be several years before we know whether this vaccine will be a valid contraceptive option.

Many natural methods of contraception are also being studied. Saliva and urine tests may help natural planning by allowing a woman to determine whether she is ovulating. Temporary sterilization techniques are also being evaluated. While we still have a long way to go in making better methods available for controlling whether pregnancy occurs, many improvements are in the works and may be available in the near future.

PART TWO—ABORTION

The abortion debate in the United States has been very emotional and even violent. One thing is clear and consistent: everyone has a strongly held opinion about abortion. **Pro-life supporters** believe that human life, and therefore personhood, begins at conception, and so an embryo, at *any* stage of development, is a person. Therefore, they believe that aborting a fetus is murder, and that the government should make all abortions illegal. One pro-life supporter said:

pro-life supporters: People who believe that abortion should be illegal or strictly regulated by the government.

> [a woman] has the right to control her body by using birth control, but once a baby is created it's out of her hands; she has no right to kill what God has created: it's in her body, but it is separate, put there by an act of will.
>
> *Parsons et al. (1990:110)*

pro-choice supporters: People who believe that the abortion decision should be left up to the woman and not regulated by the government.

On the other side of the issue, **pro-choice supporters** believe that the embryo has the *capacity* to become a full-fledged human life. Pro-choice supporters differ on when they believe personhood begins. For some, it may be in the second trimester of pregnancy, and for others, the third trimester. However, since not everyone agrees that personhood begins at conception, it is a woman's choice whether or not to have an abortion, and they strongly believe that the government should not interfere with her decision. One pro-choice supporter said:

> Everybody should be able to control their own lives, to choose what happens to them, and every woman has the right to decide what's best for her; she must be able to choose abortion because having a child changes your life completely, and she has to decide if she wants her life to change.
>
> *Parsons et al. (1990:110)*

The abortion debate often polarizes people into pro-life and pro-choice camps, with each side claiming moral superiority over the other. Approximately 10% of the population in the United States believes that abortion is wrong in almost all circumstances, while 30% believes that abortion is a right that must be left up to the woman (Podell, 1990). The remaining 60% of people may be firm in their beliefs but fall somewhere between the two extremes, such as believing abortion is acceptable in some situations but not others.

WHERE DO I *Stand ?* 11.2

Abortion Attitude Scale

Please answer the following questions on the scale given below. Please think about each statement and then choose your answer by writing the number of the answer below in the space provided. Be as honest as you can.

    (1) SA = strongly agree
    (2) A = agree
    (3) SLA = slightly agree
    (4) SLD = slightly disagree
    (5) D = disagree
    (6) SD = strongly disagree

_____ 1. The Supreme Court should strike down legal abortions in the United States.

_____ 2. Abortion is a good way of solving an unwanted pregnancy.

_____ 3. A mother should feel obligated to bear a child she has conceived.

_____ 4. Abortion is wrong no matter what the circumstances are.

_____ 5. A fetus is not a person until it can live outside its mother's body.

_____ 6. The decision to have an abortion should be the pregnant mother's.

_____ 7. Every conceived child has the right to be born.

_____ 8. A pregnant female not wanting to have a child should be encouraged to have an abortion.

_____ 9. Abortion should be considered killing a person.

_____ 10. People should not look down on those who choose to have abortions.

_____ 11. Abortion should be an available alternative for unmarried, pregnant teenagers.

_____ 12. Persons should not have the power over the life or death of a fetus.

_____ 13. Unwanted children should not be brought into the world.

_____ 14. A fetus should be considered a person at the moment of conception.

To tabulate your score, first reverse score items 1, 3, 4, 7, 9, 12, and 14. (This means if it is a 1 make it a 6, a 2 = 5, a 3 = 4, a 4 = 3, a 5 = 2, and a 6 = 1). Then add up your total score. Use the following scale to interpret your results.

    84–56 strong pro-life
    55–44 moderate pro-life
    43–27 unsure
    26–16 moderate pro-choice
    15–0   strong pro-choice

Reprinted by permission from Berne (1988)

ATTITUDES TOWARD ABORTION

How do you feel about abortion? Abortion is an powerful, emotional issue, and because of this, we all must decide for ourselves what we believe. Where Do I Stand? 11.2 provides a short quiz, which can help you clarify your thoughts and feelings about abortion.

INCIDENCE

More than half of the six million American pregnancies each year are unintended (Gold, 1990). Of the unintended pregnancies, approximately 1.4 million will be carried to term, 400,000 will be miscarried, and 1.6 million will be aborted (Gold, 1990). In the United States, approximately one out of five women of reproductive age (21%) have had a legal abortion, the majority of whom were under the age of twenty-five, unmarried, and had not been pregnant before (Gold, 1990). In 1992, 1,529,000 abortions were performed in the United States, the lowest number of abortions performed since 1979 (Henshaw and VanVort, 1994). Overall, the largest number of abortions are performed in California, New York, and Texas. Along with Florida and Illinois, these states account for nearly half of all abortions in the United States. Worldwide, it was estimated that in 1987, 26,000,000–31,000,000 legal abortions and 10,000,000–22,000,000 illegal abortions were performed (Henshaw, 1990).

HISTORICAL PERSPECTIVES

Abortion has been practiced in many societies throughout history; in fact, there are few large-scale societies where it has not been practiced (see Chapter 1). Before the common era, pagans, Jews, and Christians alike used abortion, usually to hide sexual activity. Aristotle argued that abortion was necessary as a backup to contraception. He believed that a fetus was not alive until certain organs had been formed; for males, at

Table **11.2**

WHO HAS AN ABORTION IN THE U.S.?

PERCENT	AGE
1%	<15 years
11%	15–17 years
13%	18–19 years
33%	20–24 years
22%	25–29 years
12%	30–34 years
6%	35–39 years
2%	≥40 years

PERCENT	RELATIONSHIP STATUS
63%	never married
19%	married
11%	divorced
6%	separated
1%	widowed

PERCENT	SCHOOL ENROLLMENT
69%	not in school
31%	in school

Gold (1990:14)

forty days after conception, and for females, ninety days. In early Roman society, abortions were also allowed, but husbands had the power to determine whether or not their wives would undergo abortion.

For most of Western history, religion determined general attitudes toward abortion, and both Judaism and Christianity have generally condemned abortion and punished those who used it. Still, throughout recorded history, abortions were performed. By the nineteenth century, more than twenty-five different chemical abortifacients were being advertised in or sold by the patent-medicine industry, said to help "interrupted menstruation" (D'Emilio and Freedman, 1988). Many died or were severely injured by illegal surgical abortions performed by semiskilled practitioners. Although it was little discussed publicly, abortion was apparently quite common; the Michigan Board of Health estimated in 1878 that one-third of all pregnancies in that state ended in abortion (D'Emilio and Freedman, 1988).

Still, abortion remained illegal until New York became the first state to permit physicians to perform abortion on request until twenty-four weeks into the pregnancy. In all other states, abortion was still illegal, and so women flocked to New York to obtain abortions. However, only wealthy women could afford to travel and pay for an abortion, and those who could not either had the baby or had to acquire an illegal abortion. Illegal abortions, known as **back-alley abortions**, were very dangerous because they were often performed under unsanitary conditions and resulted in multiple complications, sometimes ending in death. See Personal Voices 11.1 for one woman's account of an illegal abortion.

back-alley abortions:
Illegal abortions, which were all that were available prior to the legalization of abortion.

At the head of the movement to legalize abortion was a woman named Norma McCorvey. In 1969, Norma McCorvey was a twenty-one-year old divorced woman living in Texas with a five-year-old daughter. In September 1969, while traveling and working with a carnival, Norma became pregnant again. Unable to afford an illegal abortion or to travel to states that could provide a legal abortion, she contracted a lawyer to help her put her child up for adoption. The lawyer introduced her to two female lawyers, Linda Coffee and Sarah Weddington. Coffee and Weddington had been working together to try to find ways to overturn the Texas abortion laws, which had stood for more than 100 years. In order to do this, they needed to file a lawsuit against the state of Texas. However, to do so required the help of a pregnant woman who was willing to sue the state of Texas.

When Coffee and Weddington met Norma McCorvey, they felt she was a good plaintiff and decided to use her to build their case. Both lawyers realized that since the court process was so slow, by the time the case was over Norma would already have had the child and put it up for adoption. After informing Norma of this, she decided to go along with their plan under one condition—she did not want any publicity. This led to the adoption of her pseudonym, Jane Roe. This secret identity remained for more than ten years, until she finally broke her silence.

Norma McCorvey's case was served to the District Attorney Henry Wade on March 16, 1970. Jane Roe was suing Wade to prevent the state from interfering with a woman's right to an abortion. This case became known as *Roe* v. *Wade*. A three-judge court ruled that the Texas abortion laws violated the Constitutional right to privacy, and the case was appealed to the U.S. Supreme Court, where it was heard in December 1971. It was a slow process because it was also heard in October 1972 and for the final time, on January 22, 1973. The Supreme Court finally agreed that the Texas abortion laws were unconstitutional.

The Supreme Court's decision resulted in the affirmation of abortion as a right that was guaranteed under the constitutional right to privacy. Another decision, *Doe* v.

Personal

Illegal Abortion

What follows is a personal account from a woman who underwent an illegal abortion.

In the mid–1950s I was very brutally raped, and this act resulted in pregnancy. At first suspecting that this might be the case, I went immediately to my doctor, told him what had happened, and pleaded for help. But, of course, he couldn't give it. To have performed an abortion would have meant chancing up to 20 years in prison, both for him and for me. Knowing nowhere else to turn, and completely terrified by all I had heard about the local abortionist, I went home and proceeded to try all the sundry "home remedy" things I had heard of—things like deliberately throwing myself down a flight of stairs, scalding the lower half of my anatomy in hot tubs, pounding on my abdomen with a meat mallet, and even drinking a full pint of castor oil. The single notable effect of all these efforts and more was that I became very black and blue and about a month more pregnant than I had been when I started. And so, as a final desperate measure, I took the only option left. I went to see the local back-alley abortionist . . . .

I think the thing I will always remember most vividly was walking up those three flights of darkened stairs and down that corridor and knocking at the door at the end of it, not knowing what lay behind it and not knowing whether I would ever walk back down those stairs again. More than the incredible filth of the place . . . more than the fact that the man was an alcoholic and was drinking throughout the procedure . . . more than the indescribable pain, the most intense pain I have ever been subjected to; more than the humiliation of being told, "You can take your pants down now, but you shoulda'—ha! ha!—kept 'em on before"; more than the degradation of being asked to perform a deviant sex act after he had aborted me (he offered me $20 of my $1000 bucks back for a "quick blowjob"); more than the hemorrahaging and the peritonitis and the hospitalization that followed; more even than the gut-twisting fear of being "found out" and locked away for perhaps 20 years; more than all of these things, those stairs and that dank, dark hallway, and the door at the end of it, stay with me and chill my blood still.

**National Abortion Rights Action League
(1989:5–6)**

Bolton, challenged a Georgia statute that abortions could only be done in hospitals. This decision, along with *Roe* v. *Wade,* resulted in the following Supreme Court decisions:

- In the first twelve weeks of pregnancy, the decision to have an abortion is up to the woman and her physician;
- In the second and third twelve weeks, the state can regulate the availability of abortion; and
- The state may regulate or proscribe abortion for the life or health of the pregnant woman.

These decisions supported a woman's right to privacy in the first trimester of pregnancy but also supported the "potential life" in the second and third trimesters. Immediately following these decisions, an organized national movement against abortion began.

Today, states vary on the abortion cutoff date. For instance, in California abortion is legal until the twentieth week (five months), while in New York and South Dakota, abortion is legal up until the twenty-fourth week (six months), and later if it is necessary to save a woman's life (NARAL, 1992).

Federal funding for abortion has also been controversial. In 1977, the *Hyde Amendment* was enacted by Congress; this restricted the use of Medicaid money for abortion unless the woman's life was at risk. Poor women who could not afford an abortion were forced to either continue the pregnancy or find a way to come up with enough money to have an abortion. Studies indicate that approximately 20% of women who would have chosen a Medicaid-funded abortion were forced to have children when this funding was cut (Family Planning Perspectives, 1991). Federal funding restrictions make it more likely that poor women will bear unwanted children, continue a potentially health-threatening pregnancy to term, and undergo abortion procedures that would endanger their health.

In 1979, the Supreme Court ruled that minors need parental consent or approval from a judge prior to obtaining an abortion. In 1989, abortion rights were further restricted by *Webster* v. *Reproductive Health Services,* another case heard by the Supreme Court. The *Webster* decision allowed states to

- Restrict public employees from performing, or assisting in abortion procedures, unless a woman's life was in danger;
- Prohibit public facilities (such as clinics) from performing abortions;
- Require physicians to test all fetuses over twenty weeks for **viability**; and
- Discard the trimester system from *Roe* v. *Wade* (allowing the state to interfere at any point in the pregnancy).

viability: When a fetus is capable of living and reaching a stage of development that will permit survival under normal conditions.

Since this ruling, many bills that include restrictions on abortion have been proposed. These bills involve parental and spousal/partner notification, a reduction in financial assistance for those who cannot pay, clinic licensing, insurance coverage, informed consent, waiting periods, and/or restrictions on fetal tissue research. In *Rust* v. *Sullivan* in 1991, the Supreme Court allowed the implementation of the "gag rule," which prohibited federally funded family-planning clinics from promoting, advocating, or encouraging abortion or even giving out any information about it. Some clinics decided to forego federal funds rather than comply with these regulations.

Two states, Louisiana and Utah, and the territory of Guam have enacted laws prohibiting virtually all abortions, although the laws are not enforceable. North Dakota technically bans all abortion, except to save the woman's life or in cases of rape or incest that are reported within thirty days (AGI, 1991). In fact, there is only one abortion provider in both North and South Dakota (Henshaw and VanVort, 1994).

In June 1992, the Supreme Court heard *Planned Parenthood of Southeastern Pennsylvania* v. *Casey,* which challenged a law requiring spousal notification, a twenty-four-hour waiting period, and a requirement that women be given materials on alternatives to abortion (NARAL, 1992). Although *Roe* v. *Wade* was upheld in a five-to-four decision, the states were given power to impose restrictions on abortion. For example, the Supreme Court's decision allowed Pennsylvania to pass a law requiring that women go through counseling sessions, be given materials on fetal development and abortion alternatives, and then wait at least twenty-four hours before undergoing an abortion. A requirement to notify husbands was found to be unconstitutional.

Both sides of the abortion debate are becoming more bitter, vocal, and determined to continue their struggle. The *Freedom of Choice Act* (FOCA) was presented to Congress shortly after the *Pennsylvania* case was heard in 1992. It attempted to limit the state's power to restrict the right to choose abortion. FOCA was not approved prior to the end of the 103rd Congress in 1994, and it may be reintroduced in 1995. However, approval of FOCA is uncertain at this time because of a strong conservative voice in Congress in 1995.

In early 1993, President Bill Clinton overturned several restrictions on abortion, including:

- Removing the "gag rule";
- Ending restrictions that had prevented federally funded U.S. programs from providing information or counseling on abortion;
- Giving overseas U.S. military hospitals the right to perform abortions as long as they are paid with private funds; and
- Initiating trials of chemical methods of abortion in the United States.

In late 1993, President Clinton continued his struggle for abortion rights by issuing a directive that said that poor women who are survivors of rape or incest are eligible for Medicaid-funded abortions.

In the United States today, strong pressure exists to reverse the Supreme Court's decision in *Roe* v. *Wade* and make abortion illegal. The bitter battle between the pro-choice and pro-life factions has also resulted in picketing and demonstrations outside abortion clinics. In July 1994, the Supreme Court upheld a decision barring antiabortion demonstrators from getting within thirty-six feet of an abortion clinic. This ruling was sparked by the fatal shooting of Dr. David Gunn outside of his abortion clinic in Pensacola, Florida. In August 1993, Dr. George Tiller was shot in both arms during an antiabortion protest in Wichita, Kansas. In 1994, another abortion provider, Dr. John Britton, and his escort were shot and killed by Paul Hill. In late 1994, Paul Hill was convicted of murder and was sentenced to die in the electric chair.

LEGAL VERSUS ILLEGAL

Since the legalization of abortion in the United States in 1973, the number of deaths of pregnant women from abortion have declined dramatically. It is hard to say by how many, because the numbers of deaths from illegal abortions are difficult to determine because many abortion-related deaths were not noted on death certificates (Gold, 1990). The legalization of abortion ensured that sanitary conditions were strictly followed, and if infections developed the patients were treated immediately. As of 1992, there were 2380 abortion providers in the United States (Henshaw and VanVort, 1994).

Pro-life supporters believe that prior to *Roe* v. *Wade,* women were more careful about becoming pregnant. Since abortion was not a legal choice, many women used birth control consistently, and if necessary they gave birth. The legalization of abortion, according to the pro-life camp, has caused women and men to become irresponsible about sexuality and contraceptive use. By making abortion illegal, pro-life supporters believe that people will become more responsible about contraception and may delay sexual activity.

SEX TALK

QUESTION **11.4 In the future, is abortion going to be illegal?**

The Supreme Court may eventually overturn the *Roe* v. *Wade* decision, passed in 1973. Should this happen, each state will be able to determine its own abortion policies. Researchers claim that if this happens, the states most likely to ban abortion include Alabama, Louisiana, Michigan, Mississippi, Missouri, Nebraska, Ohio, and Pennsylvania, while some of the least likely states to ban abortion include Arizona, California, Colorado, Florida, Hawaii, Washington, and the District of Columbia (NARAL, 1992).

TYPES OF ABORTIONS

Abortion Procedures

In ancient Greece and Rome, abortions were performed by either inserting certain substances into the vagina and cervix or by orally ingesting chemicals that killed the fetus. Certain plant potions were devised to cause fetal death. Some women even wrapped themselves tightly around the abdomen to cause fetal expulsion (Gorman, 1982).

SEX TALK

QUESTION **11.5** **Does the fetus feel pain during an abortion?**

The American College of Obstetricians and Gynecologists (ACOG) claims that there is no scientific information that supports the claim that a fetus experiences pain early in pregnancy. Since the brain and nervous system are not completely developed, ACOG believes there is probably no experience of pain.

Today, the majority of abortion procedures are performed in specialized abortion clinics (Henshaw et al., 1987). However, this has not always been the case. After *Roe* v. *Wade* in 1973, most abortions were performed in hospitals. The move away from hospitals and into clinics has reduced the cost of an abortion. Like all surgical procedures, there are risks involved with pregnancy termination. The most serious risks include **uterine perforation**, **cervical laceration**, severe hemorrhaging, infection, and anesthesia-related complications. These risks are greater when general anesthesia is used. In fact, the risk of death during a general anesthesia abortion is two to four times greater than during one with local anesthesia (Tietze, 1983).

Abortions can be performed as either first- or second-trimester procedures. **First-trimester abortions** are done before thirteen weeks gestation, and they are simpler and safer than those done after thirteen weeks. In the United States, approximately 90% of abortions are done in the first trimester of pregnancy, with half of them being performed in the first eight weeks (Santee and Henshaw, 1992). **Second-trimester abortions**, or late abortions, are those done between fourteen and twenty-one weeks.

First-Trimester Abortion

A first-trimester abortion (**vacuum aspiration** or suction abortion) is usually performed on an outpatient basis, using local anesthesia. Ninety-seven percent of abortions are performed by instrumental evacuation, usually vacuum aspiration (Henshaw et al., 1991). In this procedure, a woman lies on an examining table with her feet in stirrups, and a speculum is placed in her vagina to view the cervix. Local anesthesia is injected into the cervix, which numbs it slightly. **Dilation rods** are used to open the cervix and usually cause mild cramping of the uterus. The amount of dilation depends on how far along the pregnancy is. Once dilated, a **cannula** is inserted into the cervix and is attached to a **vacuum aspirator**, which empties the content of the uterus.

A first-trimester abortion usually takes between five and ten minutes. After it is completed, most clinics require a woman to stay in a recovery room for a certain amount of time before she can go home to make sure no complications arise. Once home, she is advised to rest, not to lift heavy objects, to avoid sexual intercourse, not to douche or use tampons for at least two weeks, and not to take baths; all of these activities increase the

---

uterine perforation: Tearing a hole in the uterus.

cervical laceration: Cuts or tears on the cervix of the uterus.

first-trimester abortions: Termination of pregnancy within the first twelve weeks of pregnancy.

second-trimester abortions: Termination of pregnancy between twelve and twenty-four weeks of pregnancy.

vacuum aspiration (suction): The termination of a pregnancy by using suction to empty the contents of the uterus.

dilation rods: A series of graduated metal rods that are used to dilate the cervical opening during an abortion procedure.

cannula: A tube, used in an abortion procedure, through which the uterine contents are emptied.

vacuum aspirator: A vacuum pump that is used during abortion procedures.

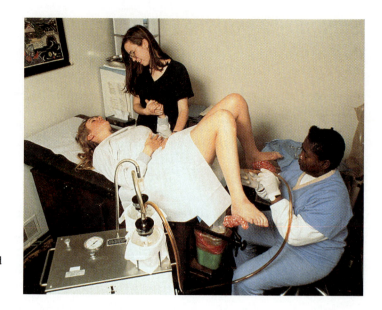

First-trimester abortion procedures are usually performed in clinics on an outpatient basis.

risk of hemorrhaging and infection. She will also experience bleeding and perhaps cramping, as she would during a normal period. Her menstrual period will return within four to six weeks.

There are several potential risks associated with a first-trimester abortion, including excessive bleeding, possible infection, and uterine perforation. However, because these risks are much lower than for a second-trimester procedure, most physicians advise women who are considering abortions to have a first-trimester procedure.

A **dilation and curettage (D&C)** is another first-trimester abortion procedure, which involves general anesthesia and use of sharp **curettes** to scrape the lining of the uterus. D&C procedures are also performed on nonpregnant women for medical reasons. This procedure is similar to a vacuum aspiration abortion, except that curettes are used instead of a vacuum pump. The risks include excessive blood loss, increased pain, and a higher incidence of an incomplete abortion. General anesthesia contributes to higher procedural risks.

dilation and curettage (D&C): A first-trimester abortion procedure that involves cervical dilation and then scraping out the contents of the uterus; may also be used for certain nonpregnancy medical problems.

curette: A surgical instrument, which is shaped like a spoon or scoop, used to empty the uterus during an abortion procedure.

Second-Trimester Abortion

Sometimes women who seek abortions do not do so until the second trimester of their pregnancy. There may be several reasons for this, including medical complications, fetal deformities that were not revealed earlier, divorce or marital problems, miscalculation of date of last menstrual period, financial or geographic problems, or a denial of the pregnancy until the second-trimester. Second-trimester abortions are riskier than first trimester procedures and involve more potential problems.

SEX TALK

QUESTION **11.6** I've heard that the majority of abortions occur in the second trimester—is this true? How many second-trimester abortions occur?

In the United States, 90% of all abortions are done in the first trimester of pregnancy. However, 10% of the time women do choose to undergo a second-trimester procedure. Of these, less than 1% occur after twenty weeks of pregnancy.

Between thirteen and twenty weeks of pregnancy, a **dilation and evacuation (D&E)** is the most commonly used procedure (Castadot, 1986). The procedure is similar to a D&C, although it combines both the vacuum aspiration and D&C methods. General anesthesia is administered, and the cervix is dilated more than in a first-trimester abortion. Dilators, such as **laminaria**, may be used to help begin the dilation process and may be inserted into the cervix twelve to twenty-four hours prior to the procedure. When a woman returns to the hospital, she may first be given intravenous pain medication and local anesthesia, which is injected into the cervix. The dilators are removed and the uterus is then emptied with suction and various instruments. If fetal development has progressed far enough, the fetal skull may need to be crushed to allow passage through the cervix. This procedure generally takes between fifteen and thirty minutes. The risks associated with this type of abortion include increased pain, blood loss, and cervical trauma.

Some physicians may use either a **saline** or **prostaglandin procedure** instead of a D&E in the second trimester. In these cases, a needle is injected into the amniotic sac and amniotic fluid is removed. Then saline or prostaglandin can be injected into the amniotic sac. If saline is used, it will cause fetal death. If prostaglandins are used, uterine contractions force the fetus out of the uterus. Usually, after a saline or prostaglandin injection, the fetus is delivered within nineteen to twenty-two hours. Women who have undergone saline or prostaglandin procedures experience more depression, anger, and guilt than those who undergo a D&E (Kaltreider et al., 1979). Since a D&E takes place under general anesthesia, most women are not aware of the procedure. During a saline or prostaglandin procedure, she is not only awake and aware, but she also experiences labor, which ends with the delivery of a dead fetus. Overall, D&E procedures are safer, less painful, quicker, and less expensive than either saline or prostaglandin procedures. Both of these procedures are very painful emotionally and physically. Complications may include nausea, diarrhea, and cervical problems, and the risk of death from a second trimester abortion procedure is twenty-five times greater than from an abortion in the first trimester (Tyler, 1981).

A **hysterotomy** is a rare type of abortion procedure that may be used if either of the above methods is contraindicated or if the woman's life is in immediate danger. In this procedure, the abdominal cavity is opened up to remove the fetus, similar to a cesarean section. This is done under general anesthesia and requires a hospital stay of between five and seven days. Since it is a major operation, the possible risks are much greater and include problems with general anesthesia, prolonged recovery, and possible death. These risks have significantly reduced the use of this procedure. Another procedure that is rarely used today is a hysterectomy, which is a removal of the fetus and uterus.

dilation & evacuation (D&E): A second-trimester abortion procedure that involves cervical dilation and vacuum aspiration of the uterus.

laminaria: Seaweed that grows in cold ocean waters and can swell three to five times its original diameter; when dried, laminaria may be used in second-trimester abortion procedures to dilate the cervix.

saline abortion: A second-trimester abortion procedure in which amniotic fluid is removed and replaced with a saline solution, which causes premature delivery of the fetus.

prostaglandin procedure: A second-trimester abortion procedure that involves injecting the uterus with prostaglandins, which cause uterine contractions and fetal expulsion.

hysterotomy: A second-trimester abortion procedure that involves a surgical removal of the fetus through the abdomen.

SEX TALK
QUESTION **11.7** How much does an abortion cost?

A first-trimester abortion costs approximately $200 to $400 in an abortion clinic. These fees usually include an examination, laboratory tests, anesthesia, the procedure, and a follow-up examination. In a private physician's office, this procedure can run as high as $2000. A second-trimester abortion can run anywhere from $500 to $2000, and even higher for later procedures. Women who need Rhogam (see Chapter 10) must pay an additional fee (approximately $35 to $50).

REACTIONS TO ABORTION

In the late 1980s, President Ronald Reagan asked Surgeon General Dr. C. Everett Koop to prepare a report on the physical after-effects of women who have undergone elective abortions. The Surgeon General reported that scientific studies had documented that physiological health consequences, including infertility, incompetent cervix, miscarriage, premature birth, and low birth weight are no more frequent among women who experience abortion than they are among the general population of women. The Surgeon General's findings do not support claims by pro-life advocates who state that there are severe psychological and physiological symptoms associated with abortion.

The decision to have an abortion is a difficult one. Terminating an unintended pregnancy or an intended pregnancy with a deformed fetus can be very painful. The physiological and psychological effects vary from person to person, and they depend on many factors.

Physiological Symptoms

Physiological reactions to abortion depend on the type of procedure used. After an early abortion, many women report increased cramping, heavy bleeding with possible clots, and nausea. These symptoms may persist for several days, but if any of these are severe, a physician should be seen for an evaluation. Severe complications are much more frequent in late abortion procedures and, as we discussed, include hemorrhaging, cervical laceration, uterine perforation, and infection (Tieze and Henshaw, 1986). Of these complications, uterine perforation is the most serious, although the risk of occurrence is small. While some people believe that early abortion is a risky procedure, studies have shown that the death rate from an abortion before nine weeks is 1 in 260,000.

SEX TALK

QUESTION **11.8** If you had an abortion, could that make you infertile later on?

Women who undergo an abortion can become pregnant and give birth later on in their life without complications (Frank, 1991). However, repeated abortions may create an incompetent cervix and could cause future miscarriages. Also, there are rare cases of unexpected complications of abortion that can lead to infertility or even hysterectomy, such as uterine perforation or severe infection.

Psychological Symptoms

How a woman feels after an abortion has a lot to do with how the society in which she lives views abortion. For example, a woman who underwent an illegal abortion in the 1960s might have felt an incredible sense of guilt and shame because abortion was illegal and therefore viewed as "bad." Psychological reactions also vary among women, as the stories in Personal Voices 11.2 indicate.

11.2

Having an Abortion

Stacy

My boyfriend, Jeff, and I had been sexually active for about two years and were using condoms for protection. However, one night after a party, we had been drinking and forgot to use a rubber. About three weeks later, my period was late. I was worried, and I also knew that my period had been late before, so I tried to convince myself that that was all I was—late. I went to the store and bought a home pregnancy test. It turned out positive. I could not stop crying. I felt so scared and nervous. I told Jeff about the pregnancy (he had known that I was late). We talked about our options, but deep down I knew what would happen. I would not be able to keep this baby.

The next day, I went to a women's health clinic, but they told me I couldn't have an abortion for about a month because it was too early. I remember finding that out and feeling "Oh my God, I have to wait another month." That was awful. I felt pretty bad.

The procedure was scheduled and Jeff drove me there. When we arrived at the clinic, there were several protesters outside, which made me feel terrible. I wished that I didn't have to do what I was doing. When we got inside, they asked me to fill out a questionnaire. I felt like I was in a dream and nothing was real. I did my best to be brave, but honestly I didn't feel brave that day. I was in a group of about five other girls, and we were all taken to a room together. Here they talked to us about exactly what would happen in the procedure and what instruments they would be using. I started to cry. We had to talk about ourselves and how we felt about our decision. There was one girl who was fifteen years old in my group and another who had been in this same situation a couple of times before. The nurse asked me if I was sure about my decision to have an abortion. I wasn't, but I just really felt there wasn't any other choice. Neither Jeff or I felt that we could handle a baby at that point in our life. But I didn't know if I could handle an abortion at that point either. I just cried and felt very afraid and alone.

Soon afterwards, we went into the preparation room. There were probably thirty-five to forty girls in there. We were given some medicine to make us kind of drowsy, but I still was aware of what was going on. I talked to another girl in there, who was very nice and supportive. After about an hour, a nurse came and took me into the exam room. There they put me on a table and helped put my feet in stirrups. I felt very sick. The doctor stuck something in me to open me up, like a Pap smear, and then started this vacuum thing. I remember screaming and crying. The nurse was telling me to be still, but it was hurting. I didn't want them to do this, but it was too late. It was done.

I don't remember going to the recovery room. I just remember lying there, feeling like I was in shock. I had a big pad on and remember laying there for awhile, crying the whole time. Finally, a nurse came to me with a list of people I could call for counseling. She told me that she really felt I should talk with someone about the abortion. After awhile, I got up and left. They gave me a list of instructions of things I could and could not do. I remember feeling extremely faint when I started to walk. Jeff was there, and I just started crying again when I saw him.

When we got home, I immediately went to bed. Jeff was great. He didn't leave my side—taking care of me and getting me whatever I needed. I think he was really feeling bad because he just had no idea of what was going on. The next morning I was still in a daze. I felt like I was in a dream (or more like a nightmare). Jeff was really concerned because I wouldn't talk to him. All I could do was lie there.

From this time until now, it has all seemed like a very, very bad dream. I made a huge mistake and had to deal with it basically alone. Jeff was there, but I kind of shut him out of my feelings. He wanted me to see a counselor right away, but most of the counselors cost money—money that I didn't have if I wanted to return to school. Plus, I didn't want to talk about it. I really wanted to forget it.

Today when I see babies, I wonder what mine would have looked like. Would it have been a girl or a boy? What would he or she be like? These are the things that I constantly wonder. I guess now I just wish I could make peace with myself. It seems so long ago that all of this happened, but I still feel the guilt. I don't know how I finally decided to talk to someone, but it was really good for me. It was painful at first but I'm still working on it. It may take me a long time, but someday I hope to feel at peace with myself.

Author's files

The majority of evidence from scientific studies indicates that most women who undergo abortion have very few psychological side effects later on (Zolese and Blacker, 1992; Adler et al., 1992). In fact, relief is the more prominent response for the majority of women (Janus and Janus, 1993; Turell et al., 1990). However, although relief may be a prominent immediate feeling, some researchers point out that there are actually three categories of psychological reactions to abortion. *Positive emotions* include relief and happiness; *socially based emotions* include shame, guilt, and fear of disapproval; and *internally based emotions* include regret, anxiety, depression, doubt, and anger, which are based on the woman's feelings about the pregnancy (Adler et al., 1990). A woman may cycle through each of these reactions—feeling relief one minute, depression and/or guilt the next.

SEX TALK

QUESTION **11.9** **My friend had an abortion two months ago but she still seems very depressed. How long does this last?**

It is hard to say how long the psychological reactions to abortion will last; it depends on the person. It might be helpful for your friend to talk things over with either a school counselor or health-care provider.

In contrast to the Surgeon General's Report, some research that claims that some women do experience intense, negative psychological consequences that include guilt, anxiety, depression, and regret. In 10% of these cases, these feelings are severe (Zolese and Blacker, 1992). Other possible psychological symptoms include self-reproach, increased sadness, and a sense of loss.

Certain conditions may put a woman more at risk for developing severe psychological symptoms. These include being young; not having family or partner support; being persuaded to have an abortion when a woman does not want one; having a difficult time making the decision to have an abortion; blaming the pregnancy on another person or on oneself; having a strong religious and moral background; having an abortion for medical or genetic reasons; having a history of psychiatric problems before the abortion; and having a late abortion procedure (Zolese and Blacker, 1992; Dagg, 1991; Mueller and Major, 1989). Women who blame the unplanned pregnancy on some aspect of their character (i.e., "*I am a bad person*") often experience more psychological symptoms than do those who do not blame their character (Major et al., 1985). Women who decide to tell no one about their decision to abort, because they encounter a lack of support, were found to have more negative psychological symptoms following the procedure (Major et al., 1990).

Being denied an abortion when a woman wants one has also been found to cause negative effects. A review of 225 studies on the psychological effects of abortion found that many women who were denied abortions showed ongoing resentment that lasted for several years. The children that were born to these women had many social, interpersonal, and occupational difficulties that lasted into adulthood (Dagg, 1991). They also were found to have an increase in various medical illnesses, fewer friends, and a poorer school performance, and in their adult years, many experienced difficulties with jobs, friends, crime, and drug use (David, 1994).

Thus, although discovering an unplanned pregnancy and deciding to abort are very stressful decisions, in the majority of cases the emotional aftermath does not appear to be severe (Mueller and Major, 1989; Burnell and Norfleet, 1987; Major et al., 1985).

Still, it is very beneficial for a woman (and her partner) who is contemplating an abortion to discuss this with a counselor or nurse. When looking for a reliable abortion clinic, check with someone you trust. In the last five years, many "fake" abortion clinics have been set up; while these appear to provide full health care for women, they only provide a pregnancy test and strong anti-abortion information (Mertus, 1990).

A few studies have examined the psychological reactions of abortion clinic workers (Kaltreider et al., 1979). In Personal Voices 11.3, we present one clinic worker's thoughts.

WHY DO WOMEN HAVE ABORTIONS?

Many people claim that women have abortions because they do not use contraception. However, studies indicate that 70% of women who undergo an abortion had either been using a method or had discontinued use within three months of conception (Henshaw and Silverman, 1988). Some of these women were using methods incorrectly or inconsistently. Approximately 9% of women who have abortions never have used any contraception.

Women who have abortions do so for a variety of reasons. The majority of women report that a baby would interfere with other responsibilities, such as educational or career goals. Other reasons include

- An inability to financially provide for a child;
- Difficulties in the relationship with the father;
- Not wanting people to know they are sexually active;
- Pressure from their partners or families;
- Fetal deformity;
- Risks to mother's health;
- Having several children already; and
- Rape or incest.

The reasons given for abortion may differ depending on the woman's age (Torres and Forrest, 1988). For example, younger women were more likely to cite the fact that a baby would change their lives, they were not mature enough, or they did not want others to know they were sexually active; women over thirty years old were less likely to cite these reasons. Women who were undergoing late abortion procedures were more likely to cite reasons that were out of their own control, such as a health problem or a result of rape or incest (Torres and Forrest, 1988). From this research, the only thing that is clear is that there is no simple answer to the question of why a woman decides to have an abortion. The decision-making process is difficult and has no easy answers.

How do you feel about these reasons? Do any of these circumstances seem more justified than others? Do you feel that there are legitimate reasons for aborting a fetus?

NEW DEVELOPMENTS

The last few years have seen many new developments in the abortion arena. Below we will explore **RU-486** and **Methotrexate**.

RU-486: A drug that, when taken early in pregnancy with prostaglandin, causes a nonsurgical termination of the pregnancy.

Methotrexate: An experimental drug being tested as a postcoital method of contraception or abortion; when taken, it causes a fertilized ovum to be expelled.

Personal

V O I C E S

11.3

Reactions of an Abortion Counselor

When we think about psychological reactions to abortion, we do not often think about the emotional reactions of the clinic workers. What follows is an account of a woman who worked in an abortion clinic.

"How can you stand it?" Even the clients ask. They see the machine, the strange instruments, the blood, the final stroke that wipes away the promise of pregnancy. Sometimes I see that too: I watch a woman's swollen abdomen sink to softness in a few stuttering moments and my own belly flip-flops with sorrow. But all it takes for me to catch my breath is another interview, one more story that sounds so much like the last one. There is a numbing sameness lurking in this job: the same questions, the same answers, even the same trembling tone in the voices. The worst is the sameness of human failure, of inadequacy in the face of each day's dull demands.

In describing this work, I find it difficult to explain how much I enjoy it most of the time. We laugh a lot here, as friends and as professional peers. It's nice to be with women all day.

I grew up on the promise of birth control. Like many women my age, I took the pill as soon as I was sexually active. To risk pregnancy when it was so easy to avoid seemed stupid, and my contraceptive success, as it were, was part of the promise of social enlightenment. But birth control fails far more frequently than trials predict. Many of our clients take the pill; its failure to protect them is a shocking realization. We have patients who have been sterilized, whose husbands have had vasectomies; each one is a statistical misfit, fine print come to life. The anger and shame of the women I hold in one hand, and the basin in the other. The distance between the two, the length I pace and try to measure, is the size of an abortion.

It is when I am holding a plastic uterus in one hand, a suction tube in the other, moving them together in imitation of the scrubbing to come, that women ask the most secret question. I am speaking in a matter-of-fact voice about "the tissue" and "the contents" when the woman

suddenly catches my eye and asks, "How big is the baby now?" These words suggest a quiet need for a definition of the boundaries being drawn. It isn't so odd, after all, that she feels relief when I describe the growing bud's bulbous shape, its miniature nature. Again I gauge and sometimes lie a little, weaseling about its infantile features until its clinging power slackens.

But when I look in the basin, among the curdlike blood clots, I've seen an elfin thorax, attenuated, its pencilline ribs all in parallel rows with tiny knobs of spine rounding upwards. A translucent arm and hand swim beside.

If the human bond to a child were as primitive and unflinchingly narrow as that of other animals, there would be no abortion. There would be no abortion because there would be nothing more important than caring for the young and perpetuating the species. No reasons for sex but to make babies.

I have fetus dreams, we all do here: dreams of abortions one after the other; of buckets of blood splashed on the walls; trees full of crawling fetuses. I dreamed that two men grabbed me and began to drag me away. "Let's do an abortion," they said with a sickening leer, and I began to scream, plunged into a vision of sucking, scraping pain, of being spread and torn by impartial instruments that do only what they are bidden. I woke from this dream barely able to breathe and thought of kitchen tables and coat hangers, knitting needles striped with blood, and women all alone clutching a pillow in their teeth to keep the screams from piercing the apartment-house walls. Abortion is the narrowest edge between kindness and cruelty. Done as well as it can be, it is still violence—merciful violence, like putting a suffering animal to death.

Abortions require of me an entirely new set of assumptions. It requires a willingness to live with conflict, fearlessness, and grief. I imagine a world where [abortion] won't be necessary, and then return to the world where it is.

Podell (1990).
Reprinted with permission
from Sally Tisdale

RU-486

Mifepristone (RU-486), a drug manufactured by Roussel-UClaf, is approved for nonsurgical termination of pregnancies in France, the United Kingdom, and Sweden. RU-486 blocks the development of progesterone, which is an essential hormone for maintaining a pregnancy. Three RU-486 pills are taken, and two days later a woman takes an oral dose of prostaglandin. This causes uterine contractions that expel the fertilized ovum. In higher dosages, the mean time for expulsion is approximately four-and-a-half hours, and in smaller doses it was between thirteen and nineteen hours (Silvestre et al., 1990). Effectiveness rates are between 95% and 97%. In a few cases, women have changed their mind about terminating their pregnancy after taking RU-486 and did not take the prostaglandins. These pregnancies were found to progress normally, and a healthy fetus was delivered. In France, RU-486 can only be taken up to the seventh week of pregnancy, and in Britain up until the ninth week. Approximately 25% of abortions in France are done with RU-486 (Henshaw, 1990).

There are some serious potential side effects, however, which include prolonged uterine bleeding, hemorrhaging, gastrointestinal difficulties, and cramping. The prolonged bleeding and the length of time to expulsion (days compared with minutes) make RU-486 less appealing than a vacuum aspiration abortion. However, with RU-486, surgery is unnecessary, and there is no possibility of uterine perforation. The cost of RU-486, approximately $48 (not including the cost of the prostaglandin), is also much lower than a vacuum aspiration abortion.

RU-486 also has other medical purposes including treatment for breast cancer, brain tumors, and Cushing's Syndrome (a disorder of the endocrine system). However, since it is also an abortifacient, most drug companies will not market it. In 1994, Roussel UClaf donated its RU-486 patents to The Population Council, a U.S. not-for-profit organization. In the fall of 1994, testing of RU-486 began on 2000 U.S. women. Along with clinical trials of RU-486, a manufacturer must be identified and a new drug application must be submitted to the FDA. This could potentially lead to the availability of RU-486 in the United States by 1996.

Methotrexate

Another experimental abortion drug, called Methotrexate, has been touted as America's answer to the French RU-486 pill (Creinin and Darney, 1993). Similar to RU-486, Methotrexate is used in combination with a vaginal prostaglandin-type drug. Both drugs are already approved by the FDA for treatment of breast cancer, leukemia, rheumatoid arthritis, and psoriasis, and they are inexpensive. Trials on methotrexate began in the United States in the fall of 1994.

TEENAGERS AND ABORTION

In the United States, 84% of teenage pregnancies are unintended, and 40% of teenagers who become pregnant choose to have an abortion (National Abortion Federation, 1988) (See Chapter 6). In a study of options in teenage pregnancy, it was found that among white adolescents, abortion was the most popular choice, while among black adolescents, single parenthood was most popular. The majority of Hispanic adolescents had the baby and either married or lived with their partners (Buchanan and Robbins, 1990).

parental notification:
Abortion legislation that requires the notification of the parents of a minor prior to an abortion procedure.

parental consent: Abortion legislation that requires the consent of the parents of a minor prior to an abortion procedure.

judicial bypass option:
Abortion legislation that allows for a judge to bypass parental consent or notification for a minor to acquire an abortion.

Many states have passed laws that control teenagers' access to abortion. For instance, some states require **parental notification**, **parental consent**, or offer a **judicial bypass option**. As of April 1994, sixteen states required parental notification, while twenty-one required parental consent (NARAL, 1992). However, studies have shown that in states without mandatory parental consent or notice requirements, 75% of minors involve one or both parents (Henshaw and Kost, 1992). Those who do not usually have strong reasons for not doing so, and these laws make it difficult for many of them to obtain an abortion.

PARTNERS AND ABORTION

When a woman chooses to have an abortion, it forces a couple to reevaluate their relationship and ask themselves some difficult questions. Do we both feel the same about each other? Is this relationship serious? Where is this relationship going? Keeping the lines of communication open during this time is very important. Some studies claim that abortion causes couples to break up, but there is also evidence that if couples can communicate about their thoughts, feelings, and fears while facing an unplanned pregnancy, an abortion may actually bring them closer. When the male partner is involved, it makes the abortion experience less traumatic for the woman; in fact, women whose partners support them and help them through the abortion show more positive responses after abortion (Adler et al., 1990; Moseley et al., 1981). Women who have no support from their partners or who make the decision themselves often experience greater emotional distress.

Some people believe that abortion is a difficult decision only for the woman because she is the one who carries the pregnancy. However, men also have a difficult time with the decision to abort, and they often experience sadness, a sense of loss, and fear for their partner's well being. Many men feel isolated and angry at both themselves and their partners. What makes it even more difficult for most men is that they often do not discuss the pregnancy with anyone other than their partner. Their own feelings are buried under the desire to help their partner get through it. Oftentimes they will become very rational, intellectual, and claim "*the best thing to do is. . . .*" These are emotional defenses used to cover their underlying anxiety. Since counseling services for men are often not available at abortion facilities, this is further evidence to the men that they should be able to deal with their feelings on their own. Attending counseling, either with their partners or alone, can be very helpful for these men. Personal Voices 11.4 includes a poem that was given to one of the authors by a male student whose girlfriend was undergoing an abortion, written while he was in the waiting room.

CROSS-CULTURAL ASPECTS OF ABORTION

In some countries, abortion is strictly prohibited or allowed *only* to save the life of the mother (Henshaw, 1990). This includes most of the Muslim nations in Asia, two-thirds of Latin America, the majority of African countries, and four European countries (Ireland, Spain, Portugal, and Belgium) (Podell, 1990). In countries such as India, Japan, some of the Eastern and Central European states, abortion is legal under certain circumstances. It is legal upon request (with some restrictions) in the United States, Austria, China, Denmark, Italy, the Netherlands, and the former Soviet Republics (see

VOICES
11.4

Men and Abortion

The following poem was written by a male whose girl-friend was undergoing an abortion procedure. The pain and suffering he was experiencing is something that professionals often do not help men with.

Here the poor boy lays in wait,
Knowledge uncertain, only fear,
Demons torment through the silence,
Pain his beloved shall endure.

Searching for comfort in a sea of fire,
Finding only shame and sorrow.
Darkness captures another soul,
Leaving hatred in its wake.

Relief found only in departure,
Quickly subsiding to misconceptions,
Desire to prolong this union,
We have left only ourselves to heal.

Author's files

Table 11.3). However, rules vary with respect to parental consent, waiting periods, and cost. For example, spousal notification requirements exist in Kuwait, Taiwan, and Turkey (Henshaw, 1990).

In 1992, two years after the reunification of Germany, East Germany allowed abortion on demand, while West Germany prohibited abortion. As of 1994, the abortion debate continues to divide the country. It has been estimated that there are 200,000 abortion-related deaths each year, 99% of which occur in undeveloped countries (Magai, 1992).

In England and Wales, the incidence of abortion has been increasing, and researchers suggest that this may be due to a decrease in the age at which people first have sexual intercourse. In China, nearly half of all women were found to have had at least one abortion; 18% had had two or more (Li et al., 1990). In Japan, abortion is also heavily relied upon, but it is used more by married, rather than unmarried, women. This may be due to an underreporting of statistics for unmarried women or because of the low rates of premarital sexual activity for both males and females in Japan (Coleman, 1983). In the United States, approximately 70% of abortions are performed on unmarried women. However, in India, China, and Japan, more than 90% of abortions are performed on married women (Podell, 1990).

In Brazil, abortion is illegal, yet studies indicate that Brazilian women have an equal or greater number of abortions than do American women (*The New York Times,* 1991j). The majority of these procedures are illegal, and they cause more than 400,000 cases of abortion complications each year. Many police are trying to locate illegal abortion centers and shut them down.

The least restrictive abortion laws may be in Sweden. In 1975, the Abortion Act was enacted, which gave women the right to choose an abortion and provided abortion and

Table **11.3**

COUNTRIES, BY RESTRICTIVENESS OF ABORTION LAW, ACCORDING TO REGION, JANUARY 1, 1990

LAW	AFRICA	ASIA & OCEANIA	EUROPE	NORTH AMERICA	SOUTH AMERICA
To save a woman's life	Angola Benin Botswana Burkina Faso Central Afr. Rep. Chad Côte d'Ivoire Gabon Libya Madagascar Malawi Mali Mauritania Mauritius Mozambique Niger Nigeria Senegal Somalia Sudan Zaire	Afghanistan Bangladesh Burma Indonesia Iran Iraq Laos Lebanon Oman Pakistan Philippines Sri Lanka Syria United Arab Emirates Yemen Arab Rep. Yemen, Peoples' Democratic Rep.	Belgium Ireland	Dominican Rep. El Salvador*,[†] Guatamala Haiti Honduras Mexico* Nicaragua Panama	Brazil* Chile Columbia Ecuador* Paraguay Venezuela
Other maternal health reasons	Algeria Cameroon* Congo Egypt[†] Ethiopia Ghana*,[†] Guinea Kenya Lesotho Liberia*,[†] Morocco Namibia*,[†] Rwanda Sierra Leone South Africa*,[†] Tanzania Uganda Zimbabwe*,[†]	Hong Kong*,[†] Israel*,[†] Jordan* Korea, Rep. of*,[†] Kuwait[†] Malaysia*,[†] Mongolia Nepal New Zealand*,[†] Papua New Guinea Saudi Arabia Thailand*	Albania Northern Ireland Portugal*,[†] Spain*,[†] Switzerland	Costa Rica Jamaica Trinidad & Tobago	Argentina* Bolivia* Guyana Peru
Social and social-medical reasons	Burundi Zambia[†]	Australia[†] India*,[†],[**] Japan*,[†],[§§] Korea. Dem. Rep.*,[†] Taiwan*,[†]	Bulgaria*,[†],[‡],[††] Finland*,[†],[‡],[‡‡] German Fed. Rep.*,[†],[‡‡],*[†] Great Britain[†] Hungary*,[†],[‡],[‡‡] Poland*,[§§],[‡‡]		Uruguay*,[§]
On request	Togo Tunisia[‡‡]	China Singapore Turkey[††] Vietnam	Austria[‡‡],*[†] Czechoslovakia[‡‡] Denmark[‡‡] France[‡‡] German Dem. Rep.[‡‡] Greece[‡‡] Italy[‡‡] Netherlands Norway[‡‡] Romania[‡‡] Soviet Union[‡‡] Sweden*[‡] Yugoslavia[††]	Canada Cuba[††] Puerto Rico United States	

*Includes judicial grounds, such as rape and incest.

[†]Includes abortion for genetic defects.

[‡]Approval is automatic for women who meet certain age, marital and/or parity requirements.

[§]Not permitted for health reasons but may be permitted for serious economic difficulty.

[**]During the first 20 weeks.   [††]During the first 10 weeks.   [‡‡]During the first three months or 12 weeks.

[§§]No formal authorization is required, and abortion is permitted in doctor's office; thus, abortion is de facto available on request.

*[†]Gestational limit is for interval since implantation.   *[‡]During the first 18 weeks.

Notes: Table does not include countries with fewer than one million inhabitants or those for which information on the legal status of abortion could not be located (e.g., Bhutan and Kampuchia). All abortions are permitted only prior to fetal viability unless otherwise indicated in footnotes.

Henshaw (1990:4)

counseling free of charge. The most restrictive abortion laws in Europe are in Ireland. In early 1992, there was a case involving a pregnant fourteen-year-old girl who had been raped by her girlfriend's father. Since abortion is illegal in this predominantly Catholic country, this girl and her parents went to England. They decided to call the police in Ireland to ask whether or not they should keep some of the abortion products to prove that she was raped. The police and the courts of Ireland forced her to come back to her country without having the abortion. The case was then heard by Ireland's Supreme Court, which voted to allow her to go to have the abortion done in England. This case sharply divided the people of Ireland and no doubt will force them to reevaluate their abortions laws.

Abortion remains a controversial procedure in the United States as well as in the rest of the world. Both sides of the issue battle from what they believe are basic principles; one side from a fetus's right to be born, the other from a woman's right to control her own body. In the early 1970s, the right-to-choose group won an important victory with *Roe* v. *Wade;* in the early 1990s, the right to life group scored a victory with the decision that a state can limit access to abortion. Although new developments like RU-486 may take the fight out of the abortion clinics and into women's homes, the only real certainty about the future of abortion is that it will remain one of the most controversial areas of American public life.

S u m m a r y

- In the United States, people are more likely to use contraception if they are knowledgeable about it and can communicate with their partner.

- Several contraceptive methods are available. These include barrier, hormonal, chemical, intrauterine, natural, postcoital, and permanent methods of contraception. Barrier methods include the condom, diaphragm, cervical cap, and sponge. Hormonal methods include oral contraceptives, Norplant, and Depo Provera. Chemical methods include spermicides. Natural methods include natural family planning and fertility awareness, withdrawal, and abstinence. In addition, IUDs, postcoital methods, and permanent methods of contraception, such as tubal ligation and vasectomy, are available.

- In the United States, birth control pills are the most popular form of contraception. Methods that have recently been approved by the FDA include Norplant, Depo Provera, female condoms, and cervical caps. Female sterilization is the most widely used method of birth control in the world.

- With the advent of HIV and the increases in STDs, many more people are seeking effective methods of birth control that offer both contraception and protection from STDs.

- The abortion debate often polarizes people into pro-life and pro-choice groups. Pro-life groups believe that human life begins at conception, while pro-choice groups believe that

women should have the right to decide whether or not they want to have an abortion.

- Since 1973, abortion has been legal up until the second trimester. After the second trimester, each individual state can regulate the availability of abortion.

- Abortion procedures are divided into first- and second-trimester procedures. First-trimester procedures include vacuum aspiration and D&C. Second trimester procedures include D&E, and saline and prostaglandin abortions. Rare, late second-trimester procedures, a hysterotomy or hysterectomy, may also be performed.

- Physiological reactions to abortion may include cramping, heavy bleeding, and nausea. These symptoms may be more severe in later abortion procedures and include hemorrhaging, cervical laceration, uterine perforation, and infection. Psychological symptoms may include relief, guilt, anxiety, depression, and anger. Studies have found that men also experience many different emotional reactions to abortion, including anger, isolation, and sadness.

- Women choose abortion for many reasons, including inability to provide financially for a child, difficulties in the relationship with the father, not wanting people to know they are sexually active, pressure from their partners or families, fetal deformity, risks to mother's health, having several children already, and rape or incest.

- Over the last few years, there have been many new developments in the abortion arena. Two of these are the drugs RU-486 and Methotrexate. Although not available at this time in the United States, both interrupt a pregnancy and cause a spontaneous abortion.

- Cross-culturally, restrictions on abortions vary depending on the country. In the next few years the abortion debate will probably become more vocal and bitter. There are no simple answers to this complex problem.

R *eflections on Sexuality*

1. Differentiate between hormonal, barrier, chemical, intrauterine, natural, postcoital, and permanent methods of contraception. Give one example of each and explain how this method works.
2. What factors should a person consider when deciding what type of contraception to use? What method do you feel would be best for you?
3. What are the advantages and disadvantages of the various methods of contraception?
4. Do you feel postcoital contraception or menstrual extraction should be available to women? Why or why not?
5. Do you feel that teenagers should be given information on abortion? Should teenagers be required to acquire parental consent for an abortion? In all cases? In some cases? Where do you draw the line? Why?
6. Explain why there are more female than male methods of contraception. What new developments are taking place?
7. Differentiate between pro-life and pro-choice ideologies. Make an argument for each side of this debate, and defend your argument.
8. Explain the political developments in the abortion debate since *Roe* v. *Wade*. What does the future look like for abortion?
9. Differentiate between the different types of abortions. What side effects and risks are associated with each?
10. Explain the physiological and psychological reactions to abortion. What conditions may put a woman more at risk for developing severe psychological symptoms?
11. What are some of the reasons women choose to have abortions? Explain.
12. What is RU-486, and how does it work?
13. Should there be more support services available to men whose partners are going through an abortion? Why or why not?
14. Explain how abortion is viewed outside of the United States.

S *uggested Readings*

CHESLER, E. (1992) *Woman of Valor.* New York: Simon & Schuster.

FAUX, M. (1988) *Roe* v. *Wade: The Untold Story of the Landmark Supreme Court Decision that Made Abortion Legal.* New York: Macmillan Publishing Co.

GORMAN, M. J. (1982) *Abortion and the Early Church.* Mahwah, NJ: Paulist Press.

HATCHER, R., et al. (1994) *Contraceptive Technology,* Sixteenth Revised Edition. New York: Irvington Publishers.

LUKER, K. (1984) *Abortion and the Politics of Motherhood.* Berkeley, CA: University of California Press.

SHOSTAK, A. B., et al. (1984) *Men and Abortion: Lessons, Losses, and Love.* New York: Praeger Publishers.

Challenges to Sexual Functioning

[Mrs. Reynolds] was a 55-year-old married woman who [had] a lifelong history of sexual disinterest. For the past year, she had absolutely refused to engage in any sexual activity with her spouse of 20 years. The history revealed that [she] had been sexually coerced into engaging in genital contact with her maternal uncle for a 2-year period, between the ages of 8 and 10. Although she had confided in her parents, they failed to protect her from further contact with her uncle, leading her to feel betrayed and abandoned by her parents and abused by her uncle. (Rosen and Leiblum, 1987)

[Tom] is a 54-year-old recovering alcoholic who had received a surgical penile implant following a diagnosis of organic impotence due to alcoholic neuropathy. Despite [his] new found ability to perform intercourse at will, in the two years following surgery he made infrequent use of the prosthesis. His wife became increasingly distressed by his disinclination to either initiate or respond with any enthusiasm to her overtures for sexual contact. In reviewing [his] history, it became apparent that his loss of sexual desire had preceded the erectile failure and that the absence of desire appeared to be the primary problem. Unfortunately, both the urologist and Tom's wife had assumed that once the capacity for intercourse was restored, sexual interest would re-emerge unassisted. (Rosen and Leiblum, 1987:153)

The general public does not think of handicapped people as sexual beings because handicapped people seem to be so radically different from them that it is very difficult to realize that they have feelings just like their own. When they meet handicapped people they are so busy worrying about whether they can communicate with them, how intelligent they are, how much help they want or resent, and perhaps even being repulsed by drooling, an external urine bag, or lack of eye contact, that the last thing that occurs to them is whether they'd like to go to bed.

Prudy Sutherland, cerebral palsy sufferer; Sutherland (1987:27)

Healthy sexuality depends on good mental and physical functioning. Challenges to sexual functioning include anxiety, sexual dysfunctions, illness, disease, and disability. However, learning to adapt to these challenges is very important in maintaining a positive view of sexuality. In this chapter, we will discuss the various sexual dysfunctions, treatments, disabilities, diseases, and illnesses, and how these may challenge one's sexual functioning.

SEXUAL DYSFUNCTION

What constitutes a sexual dysfunction? Not being able to get an erection one night? Experiencing difficulties having an orgasm during sexual intercourse? Having no sexual desire for your partner? Do sexual dysfunctions have to happen for extended periods of time, or do they happen only once in awhile? There are many types of sexual dysfunctions, and they can happen at any point during sexual activity. In fact, problems with sexual functioning happen periodically to even "normal" couples. Frank et al. (1978) evaluated the incidence of sexual dysfunction in 100 couples who had never sought help for sexual problems and found that although 80% of the couples reported a happy and satisfying marital and sexual life, 40% of the men reported that they had experienced erectile or ejaculatory dysfunction, and 63% of the women reported arousal or orgasmic dysfunction at some point in their marriage.

In addition to sexual dysfunctions, many men and women reported sexual *problems,* the most common of which are insufficient foreplay, lack of enthusiasm for sex, and the inability to relax. However, even though couples with more sexual dysfunctions and problems had lower frequencies of sexual intercourse, they still feel very positive about their sexual relationships. This is an important finding because people often assume that having a sexual dysfunction decreases both satisfaction and happiness in a relationship.

Anxiety plays an important role in developing and maintaining sexual dysfunctions. Both **performance fears** and an excessive need to please a partner interfere with sexual functioning (Masters and Johnson, 1970; Kaplan, 1974). When anxiety levels are very high, physiological arousal may be impossible. Therefore, sex therapy usually begins by overcoming performance fears, feelings of sexual inadequacy, and other anxieties.

performance fears: The fear of not being able to perform during sexual behavior.

Sexually dysfunctional men and women also tend to underreport their own levels of sexual arousal (Barlow, 1986). A man who has trouble maintaining an erection may begin thinking "I'm a failure," or "I can't have an erection," and his anxiety leads him to avoid sex and dampens his sexual desire. Distractions, shifts in attention, or preoccupation during sexual arousal may interfere with the ability to become aroused, as can **spectatoring**.

spectatoring: Acting as an observer or judge of one's own sexual performance.

Sex roles and gender roles may also influence sexual functioning. One study found that a "hypermasculine role definition" was associated with psychological causes of erectile failure (Derogatis et al., 1976). Some have also claimed that modern, sexually assertive women have intimidated many men, leading to increased male sexual dysfunction (Spencer and Zeiss, 1987). There is no scientific evidence for this. In fact, although more androgynous men and women tend to have more positive feelings about their sexuality, they do not seem to have lower incidences of sexual dysfunction (Spencer and Zeiss, 1987). So the relationship of gender and sex roles to sexual dysfunction awaits more research.

primary sexual dysfunction: A sexual dysfunction that has always existed.

TYPES AND CAUSES OF DYSFUNCTIONS

Sexual dysfunctions are categorized as either primary or secondary, and situational or global. A **primary sexual dysfunction** is one that has always existed, while a **secondary sexual dysfunction** is one in which a problem developed after a period of adequate functioning. A **situational sexual dysfunction** is a difficulty that occurs during certain sexual activities or with certain partners (for instance, a man who can get an erection with his girlfriend but not his wife; or a woman who can have orgasms during masturbation but not during oral sex). A **global sexual dysfunction** is a problem that occurs in every situation, during every type of sexual activity, and with every sexual partner. It is important to clarify these differences, for they may affect treatment strategies. For instance, primary problems tend to have more biological or physiological causes, while secondary problems tend to have more psychological causes.

secondary sexual dysfunction: A sexual dysfunction in a person who has functioned well in the past.

situational sexual dysfunction: A sexual dysfunction that occurs only in specific situations.

global sexual dysfunction: A sexual dysfunction that occurs in every sexual situation.

Helen Singer Kaplan (1929–1995), a sex therapist and researcher, described inhibited sexual desire as a lack of "sexual appetite."

A therapist's first task is to ascertain whether a problem is psychological, physiological, or mixed. Psychological and physiological problems can overlap. Some psychological causes include unconscious fears, ongoing stress, anxiety, depression, guilt, anger, fear of infidelity, partner conflict, fear of intimacy, dependency, abandonment, or loss of control, all of which may impair the ability to respond sexually. As we discussed in Chapter 8, the various pressures and time commitments of two-career families may often lead to an absence of sexual intimacy. Problems may also arise from the desire to have children, commitment demands, the children leaving home, or guilt about past sexual relationships.

Physical causes such as disease, disability, illness, and many commonly used drugs can interfere at any point in the sexual response cycle in both men and women. They may cause a loss of sexual desire, erectile or ejaculatory problems, or orgasm problems in women. Nonprescription drugs such as tobacco, alcohol, marijuana, LSD, and cocaine can also cause erectile dysfunction (Morales, 1993). Since many medications cause sexual dysfunction, lowering the drug dosage or changing medications may result in a reversal of these difficulties. We will discuss illness and physical causes later in this chapter, but now let us turn to the symptoms that can be the result of various sexual dysfunctions.

Arousal Disorders

arousal disorders: Sexual dysfunctions that occur during the excitement stage of sexual response.

Arousal disorders interfere with an individual's level of sexual excitement. A person with an arousal disorder can still function sexually; however, he or she often does not feel interested in sex. Women are more likely than men to view an absence of sexual desire as problematic in a relationship (Rosen and Leiblum, 1987).

discrepancy in desire: Differences in levels of sexual desire in a couple.

Sometimes it is not one partner's level of desire that is the problem but the **discrepancy in desire** between the partners. Many couples experience differences in their levels of desire—one partner may desire sex more often than the other. Some couples may have sex only once a month, while others may desire sex once a day. Often, the partner with a lower level of desire will show up at a therapist's office and not the partner with higher desire (Rosen and Leiblum, 1987). If the partner with the lower level of desire was paired with someone with an equal level of sexual desire, there would be no problem. Often, people experiencing low levels of sexual desire turn to **aphrodisiacs** for help (see Sexuality Today 12.1).

aphrodisiac: A substance that increases, or is believed to increase, a person's sexual desire.

Inhibited Sexual Desire

inhibited sexual desire (ISD): A sexual dysfunction in which a person experiences very low sexual desire.

When someone has **inhibited sexual desire** (ISD), the person is uninterested in sex. The number of cases of ISD has increased significantly in the last few years (Rosen, 1994). ISD may be manifested in several different ways. There may be a lack of sexual fantasies, a reduction of or absence in initiating sexual activity, a lack of physiological response when sexually stimulated, or a decrease in self-stimulation. Sexually stimulating someone with ISD often evokes anger, anxiety, tension, or disgust. These reactions begin early in the sexual response cycle, when the first thought of sex is greeted with a focus on the negative (Rosen and Leiblum, 1987).

Primary ISD, the least common type, is diagnosed when a person has a lifelong pattern of complete disinterest in sex. Secondary ISD, which is the most common, refers to a problem in which desire was normal for a certain period of time but is no longer occurring.

SEXUALITY *Today* 12.1

What Is an Aphrodisiac?

Aphrodisiacs have been used for centuries by primitive—and not so primitive—cultures to enhance sexual interest and performance. Throughout history, people have always searched for the "ultimate" aphrodisiac. Oysters, for example, have been reported to increase sexual desire, although this has never been proven. The idea that oysters are an aphrodisiac may have originated from their resemblance to male testicles. Ancient people believe that food with the shape or qualities of the genitals possessed aphrodisiac abilities. In various cultures, carrots, cucumbers, caviar, chili peppers, rhino horns, eggs, and various seafoods were thought to increase sexual desire.

There are no incontrovertible aphrodisiacs. However, if people think something will increase their sexual desire, it just might do so. Just believing may cause it to work. Below are some of the most popular substances that have been thought to increase sexual desire.

Alcohol: Although some people believe that alcohol increases their sexual desire, in actuality in low doses it only decreases anxiety and inhibitions. In large amounts, alcohol can impair sexual functioning.

Amyl Nitrate: Used by both homosexuals and heterosexuals, amyl nitrate (also called "snappers" or "poppers") is thought to increase orgasmic sensations. It is inhaled from capsules that are "popped" open for quick use. Amyl nitrate causes a rapid dilation of arteries that supply the heart and other organs with blood, which may cause warmth in the genitals. Amyl nitrate may dilate arteries in the brain, causing euphoria or giddiness, and relax sphincter muscle to ease penetration during anal sex. Side effects include severe dizziness, migraine headaches, and fainting. In addition, amyl nitrate is used by cardiac patients to reduce heart pain.

Cocaine: Thought to increase frequency of sexual behavior, sexual desire, and orgasmic sensations. In actuality, cocaine may reduce inhibitions. possibly leading to risky sexual behaviors. Long-term use can result in depression, addiction, and increased anxiety.

Ginseng: An herb that has been thought to increase sexual desire. It has not been found to have any specific effects on sexuality.

Marijuana: Reduces inhibitions and may increase mood. No proven effect on sexual desire.

Spanish Fly: Consists of ground-up beetle wings (cantharides) from Europe, which when taken, cause inflammation of the urinary tract and dilation of the blood vessels. Although some people find the burning sensation arousing, Spanish fly may cause death from its toxic side effects.

Yohimbine: From the Yohimbe tree that grows in West Africa. Injections may increase sexual arousal and performance in lab animals. Has been prescribed by physicians to increase the frequency of erections.

Although some people use street drugs to increase sexual desire, the majority of these drugs can result in decreased sexual functioning. Overall, the best things to use to increase sexual desire include regular exercise, a healthy diet, candlelight, the use of scents, romantic music, special garments, and intimacy.

Psychological causes for ISD include a lack of attraction to one's partner, fear of intimacy and/or pregnancy, marital or relationship conflicts, religious concerns, depression, and other psychological disorders. ISD can also result from negative messages about female sexuality while growing up, treating sex as a chore, a concern over a loss of control, or a negative body image (Heiman and LoPiccolo, 1992). Sexual coercion or abuse can also result in decreases in sexual desire. In one study of 181 survivors of sexual assault, more than half had long-lasting problems with sexual desire (Becker et al., 1986).

Although there appear to be fewer cases of male inhibited sexual desire than female, these lower reports may be because men feel less comfortable discussing the problem. ISD in both men and women may also be due to biological factors such as hormonal problems, medication side effects, and illness. Chronic use of alcohol, marijuana, and/or cocaine have also been implicated in ISD (Abel, 1985).

Sexual Aversion

sexual aversion disorder: A phobia or irrational fear of sexual activity or the thought of sexual activity that leads to an avoidance of sexual situations.

Sexual aversion disorder involves an actual fear or disgust associated with sexual activity. Unlike ISD, in which a person might be able to engage in sexual activity even though he or she has little or no desire to do so, a person with a sexual aversion reacts with strong disgust or fear to a sexual interaction. These feelings block the ability to become sexually aroused.

Overall, sexual aversion affects more women than men, and it is not uncommon for survivors of sexual abuse to experience sexual aversion (Rosen, 1994). This is especially true if the sexual abuse was forced, abusive, guilt-producing, or pressured.

Pain Disorders

Pain disorders can occur at any stage of the sexual response cycle. Although pain disorders are more frequent in women, they also occur in men. We will discuss vaginismus, a female disorder, and dyspareunia, which can affect both males and females.

Vaginismus

pubbococcygeus muscle: A muscle that surrounds and supports the vagina.

vaginismus: Involuntary spasms of the muscles around the vagina in response to attempts at penetration.

The **pubbococcygeus muscle** surrounds the entrance to the vagina and controls the vaginal opening. **Vaginismus** involves involuntary contractions of this muscle, which can make penetration during sexual intercourse virtually impossible. Forced penetration can be very difficult and may cause a woman severe pain. Vaginismus may be situation-specific, meaning that a woman may be able to allow penetration under certain circumstances but not in others (say during a pelvic exam, but not during sexual intercourse) (LoPiccolo and Stock, 1986).

Vaginismus is very common in women who have been sexually abused or raped, and it is often present along with other sexual difficulties such as sexual aversion and/or difficulties becoming aroused. The muscle contractions that occur during vaginismus are in reaction to anticipated vaginal penetration. One woman had been in a relationship with her partner for more than three years, but they had never been able to engage in penile–vaginal intercourse because she felt as if her vagina "was closed up" (Author's files). Penetration of her vagina with her partner's fingers was possible and enjoyable, but once penile penetration was attempted, the vagina closed off. She also shared that she had been forced to engage in sex with her stepfather for several years of her early life.

Dyspareunia

dyspareunia: Painful intercourse.

Women who experience vaginismus often experience **dyspareunia**, or painful intercourse, as well. In addition, women who have dyspareunia may also develop vaginismus. Dyspareunia may occur prior to, during, or after sexual intercourse and may involve only slight pain, which does not interfere much with sexual activity. However, in its extreme, it may make sexual intercourse difficult, if not impossible.

A number of things may cause such pain, from physical problems to allergies or infections. Psychological problems can also cause dyspareunia, and so a full diagnosis from a health professional is imperative.

QUESTION **12.1** Every time I have sexual intercourse, the pain in my vagina is so intense, I almost feel like I should stop having sex altogether. Could this have anything to do with the fact that I was forced to have sex with my brother for several years while I was growing up?

The pain you experience during sexual intercourse may be due to the sexual abuse you experienced as an adolescent, as well as stress, fear, and anxiety. You should consider talking to a counselor to help clarify what is contributing to this pain and also have a full medical evaluation. In the meantime, try engaging in other sexual activities besides intercourse to relieve the anxiety that is associated with penetration through the anticipation of pain.

Contrary to popular belief, men can also experience dyspareunia, which may cause pain in the testes or penis, both during or after sexual intercourse. Dyspareunia in men is caused by the same physiological and psychological factors as in females.

Orgasm Disorders

Every individual reaches orgasm differently and has different wants and needs to build sexual excitement. Some people need very little stimulation, others need a great deal of stimulation, and some never reach orgasm. The most common sexual problems that women experience involve arousal and orgasm, especially anorgasmia, which we discuss first. Afterward we cover premature ejaculation, retarded ejaculation, and erectile dysfunction.

Anorgasmia

Anorgasmia refers to a condition in which a man or a woman cannot reach orgasm during sexual stimulation. Although male anorgasmia can occur, anorgasmia is much more common in women; therefore, we primarily focus on female anorgasmia here. Historically, this female sexual dysfunction was referred to as "frigidity," which had negative implications about the woman. Primary anorgasmia describes a condition in which a woman has never had an orgasm. Secondary anorgasmia refers to a condition in which a woman was able to have orgasms previously but becomes nearly anorgasmic. Situational anorgasmia is used to refer to women who can only have orgasms with one type of stimulation.

anorgasmia: An inability to reach orgasm.

QUESTION **12.2** I seem to have problems achieving orgasm with my partner, yet I am able to with the help of a vibrator. Are there different levels of orgasms? Sometimes it is so deep and complete and emotional; other times

it is very satisfying but not to the tips of my toes! Is this normal? I would love to be able to achieve the same satisfaction with my partner as I can by myself or with a vibrator.

There are different levels of sexual satisfaction that result from orgasms. Orgasms differ based on stress, emotions, thoughts, physical health, menstrual cycles, sexual position, and method of stimulation. However, Masters and Johnson did find that masturbation usually evoked more powerful orgasms than intercourse. In order to experience these orgasms with your partner, you might try masturbating together or using a vibrator with your partner.

Anorgasmic women, compared with orgasmic women, have more negative attitudes about masturbation, believe more myths about sexuality, and possess greater degrees of sex guilt (Kelly et al., 1990). They also have more difficulties in asking their partners for direct clitoral stimulation, discussing how slow or fast they want to go, or how hard or soft stimulation should be. Some women worry about what their partners might think if they made sexual suggestions or feel uncomfortable receiving stimulation (such as cunnilingus or manual stimulation) without stimulating their partners at the same time. Distracting thoughts, such as "his hand must be falling asleep" or "he can't be enjoying this" can interfere with orgasm (Kelly et al., 1990). After repeated failures to reach orgasm, a person may grow to expect failure.

If the woman displays no physical problems, most cases of orgasmic difficulties are presumed to be **psychogenic** in nature (Andersen, 1981). Several psychological issues have been found to interfere with orgasmic response, including a lack of sex education and fear or anxiety related to sexuality (Kelly et al., 1990). In addition, anorgasmia has been found to be associated with other psychological problems such as personality disorders. In Where Do I Stand? 12.1, we present some questions about your own personal life history that may help clarify issues that may affect your own orgasmic functioning.

Physical factors can also cause anorgasmia. Severe chronic illness and disorders such as diabetes, neurological problems, hormonal deficiencies, and alcoholism can all interfere with orgasmic response. Certain prescription drugs can also impair this response.

psychogenic: Relating to psychological causes.

Premature Ejaculation

Defining **premature ejaculation** has always been difficult for professionals. Does it depend on how many penile thrusts take place before orgasm, how many minutes elapse between actual penetration and orgasm, or whether a man reaches orgasm prior to his partner? All of these definitions are problematic since they involve individual differences in sexual functioning and also make the assumption that females always reach orgasm during sexual intercourse. Although the time it takes to ejaculate may vary based on a man's age, sexual experience, health, and stress level, premature ejaculation usually refers to a man reaching orgasm just prior to, or directly following, penetration. If the couple believes there is a problem, then it is often treated like one (Rosen, 1994). However, in some cultures premature ejaculation is not seen as a problem because only male pleasure is considered important in sexual encounters.

We do not know exactly what causes premature ejaculation. Some sociobiologists claim that premature ejaculation may actually have offered a biological advantage in that a male will be able to impregnate more women over a shorter time period. Both

premature ejaculation: Unintentional ejaculation either during foreplay, during penetration, or soon after intercourse begins.

WHERE DO I *Stand?* 12.1

A Personal Sex History

We know that a variety of personal issues (such as religious influences, early childhood experiences, past sexual experience, and current attitudes and beliefs) may interfere with sexual functioning (Heiman and LoPiccolo, 1992). Below we present a list of questions that may help you to clarify the impact of certain life circumstances on your sexuality. Take a few moments to answer each question. Try to search for your own feelings and attitudes about each. You might want to write your answers down on a piece of paper.

1. Was religion an active force in your early life? How important was it to you and your family?
2. In what ways did your religious upbringing influence your attitudes toward sex?
3. How do your religious beliefs *currently* influence your attitudes about sex?
4. As you were growing up, were you allowed to ask questions about or to discuss sexual topics?
5. Did your parents show physical affection?
6. What was the attitude toward nudity (or modesty) in your home?
7. How did your siblings or friends influence your sexuality or what you thought about sex? Did you ever discuss sex with friends or siblings? Was sex the subject of jokes and embarrassment? Was sex considered "dirty"?
8. Do you recall playing any games with sexual content as a child (such as "doctor")?
9. At what age did you first experiment with masturbation (or any other solitary activity that produced genital feelings of pleasure)? How and where did you do this? How often? How did you feel about doing this? In what ways did you explore your own sexuality?
10. In terms of closeness and respect, how did you feel toward your mother? Your father?
11. At what age did you start to date? In groups? On single dates?
12. What kinds of petting did you engage in?
13. Did you ever engage in nonmarital intercourse? If so, what was it like the first time?
14. When and where do you usually engage in sexual behavior?
15. Have you ever had any problems with sexually transmitted diseases such as chlamydia, gonorrhea, or syphilis?
16. Have you ever experienced pain during sexual behavior?
17. Did you ever have any sexual fantasies accompanying masturbation, petting, or intercourse? If so, are there common themes or images?
18. What is your attitude toward sex in general? What specific activities do you find enjoyable? Do you ever feel inhibited, embarrassed, or guilty about any aspects of sex?
19. As you think back over your personal sex history, what would you change if you could? Why would you or wouldn't you?

Adapted from Heiman and LoPiccolo (1992)

Kinsey et al. (1948) and Kedia (1983) proposed that premature ejaculation occurred in men who had low levels of sexual activity; however, it remains unclear which comes first, the low sexual activity because of the premature ejaculation or the premature ejaculation because of the low sexual activity. Kaplan (1974) believed that premature ejaculation occurs in men who are unable to accurately judge their own levels of sexual arousal, which would enable them to use self-control to avoid rapid ejaculation. We also know that erectile problems, including premature and retarded ejaculation, have been found to be associated with depression, drug and alcohol abuse, and personality disorders (Grinspoon, 1990).

Retarded Ejaculation

retarded ejaculation:
Condition in which ejaculation is impossible or occurs only after strenuous efforts.

Retarded (or inhibited) **ejaculation** refers to a situation in which a man may be unable to reach orgasm during certain sexual activities. Therapists distinguish between primary and secondary retarded ejaculation in diagnosing and treating this sexual dysfunction. A man with primary retarded ejaculation has never been able to have an orgasm during certain sexual activities, but he may be able to reach orgasm through masturbation. Secondary retarded ejaculation involves problems that have not always been present. Retarded ejaculation may be due to both physical and psychological factors. It may also be situational (e.g., he may be able to have an orgasm during masturbation but not during sexual intercourse). Retarded ejaculation may also be caused by diseases, injuries, or medications. Recent research suggests that men with retarded ejaculation get erections quickly, but arousal is slow to catch up (Rosen, 1994).

Erectile Dysfunction

erectile dysfunction: The inability to obtain or maintain an erection firm enough for penetration.

Erectile dysfunction (or impotence) is the inability to either obtain or maintain an erection. Kinsey found that approximately 42% of men reported that they had had difficulties either getting or keeping an erection at some point in their lives (Gebhard and Johnson, 1979). This was often due to factors such as having too much to drink, fatigue, or interruption.

SEX TALK

QUESTION **12.3** Is erectile dysfunction hereditary?

> No, erectile dysfunction itself is not hereditary. However, certain diseases such as diabetes mellitus may be inherited and can lead to erectile dysfunction or other sexual dysfunctions. It is important to catch these diseases early so that medical intervention can decrease any possible sexual side effects.

More recent research shows that neurologic, vascular, and hormonal problems can play an important role in erectile dysfunction, and in many cases both psychological and physical factors contribute (LoPiccolo and Stock, 1986). Hormonal abnormalities are, in fact, rare in cases of erectile dysfunction (Morales, 1993). On the other hand, diabetes mellitus is the leading cause of organic erectile dysfunction (Bernstein, 1989). Unfortunately, when a physician locates a physical problem (say, hypertension), he or she might not continue to explore the psychological factors; or if a psychological problem is found first (such as a recent divorce), the physician might not perform a medical evaluation. Overall, erectile problems in younger men (twenty to thirty-five years old) are more likely to be psychological in nature, while erectile problems in older men (sixty or more years old) are more likely to be due to physical factors (Rosen, 1994).

nocturnal penile tumescence (NPT) test: A study that is done to evaluate erections during sleep; tumescence of the penis is noted during certain stages of sleep, and this helps clarify the erectile dysfunction etiology.

Masters and Johnson (1970) once reported that 95% of cases of erectile dysfunction were due to psychological factors. For example, an intact sense of masculinity is necessary for satisfying sexual functioning in men (Dormont, 1989). This sense of masculinity can be shaken by feelings of inadequacy, a life-threatening illness or injury (car accident or physical illness), and even athletic injuries, which can interfere with a man's erectile response.

To diagnose the causes of erectile dysfunction, physicians use tests such as the **nocturnal penile tumescence test (NPT)**. Men normally experience two or three erections while sleeping during stages of rapid eye movement (REM) sleep. If these erections do not occur, it is a good indication that there is a physiological problem, while if they do, erectile problems are more likely to come from psychological causes. While an NPT requires a man to spend at least three nights in a sleep laboratory hooked up to several machines, newer devices allow a man to monitor his sleep erections in the privacy of his own home. Rigiscan, a portable diagnostic monitor, measures both rigidity and tumescence at the base and tip of the penis. In addition, stamp tests and other at home devices are used. A stamp test uses perforated bands, resembling postage stamps, which are placed on the base of the penis prior to retiring for the night. In the morning the stamps are checked to see if they have ripped. If so, this indicates that the man had an erection while sleeping.

Other Sexual Problems

In addition to the above dysfunctions, there are other sexual problems that may lead to relationship difficulties. Although faking orgasms is not generally considered a sexual dysfunction, we discuss it here because it often stems from an inability to reach orgasm.

Faking Orgasms

Faking orgasms often occurs as a result of a dysfunction. To a man or woman who experiences anorgasmia or retarded ejaculation, faking an orgasm may seem the best way to end the sexual activity or to please the partner. However, such deceptions are not healthy in a committed relationship, and partners are generally advised to discuss any sexual problems they have instead of covering them up.

SEX TALK

QUESTION **12.4** Why do women fake orgasms rather than honestly telling their partners what they are doing wrong?

Women fake orgasms for many reasons: to end sexual intercourse, to make a partner feel better, or to avoid having to think about what might really turn her on. A woman (or a man) may have a difficult time communicating sexual needs and desires. So, instead of talking to her partner about what sexually excites her, she hopes that he knows how to do it. She may feel too embarrassed or vulnerable to tell him what to do. In this society, we expect men to know exactly what turns a woman on. However, what feels best to one woman may not feel good to another, and what feels good may change over time. Many variables can also interfere with sexual pleasure, such as stress, fatigue, anxiety, or depression. It is important that couples communicate so that they can make their sex lives satisfying for both partners.

Peyronie's Disease

Although **Peyronie's Disease** is not a sexual dysfunction in and of itself, it can cause sexual dysfunction. Peyronie's is a disorder that occurs in the connective tissue of the penis, and although some cases are asymptomatic, others develop penile nodules, which can cause severe erectile pain (Gelbard, 1988). Severe cases can cause curvature in the penis, which can make sexual intercourse impossible.

Peyronie's Disease: Abnormal calcifications in the penis, which may cause painful curvature, often making sexual intercourse impossible.

No one knows what causes Peyronie's Disease. It is possible that crystal deposits in the connective tissue, trauma, excessive calcium levels, or calcification may contribute to this disorder (Gelbard, 1988). Usually this disease lasts approximately two years and may go away just as suddenly as it appears. It is often treated with medication or surgery.

TREATMENT OF SEXUAL DYSFUNCTION

The success rate of treatment for sexual dysfunctions ranges from about 60% in those with primary erectile dysfunction to 97% in premature ejaculation; rates of about 80% have been reported in anorgasmia in women. Different types of therapies also tend to report different success rates. In addition, gender differences exist in the treatment of sexual dysfunctions. Women tend to have lower levels of self-acceptance when experiencing a sexual dysfunction and higher levels of mate acceptance if their partner is experiencing a problem. However, men are more self-accepting and less accepting of their partners with sexual dysfunctions. This may be due to the fact that men typically deny problems or put the blame on someone or something else, while women tend to assume responsibility for problems and, as a result, may experience a decrease in self-esteem (DeAmicis et al., 1985).

Sex Therapy

Sex therapy, which was originally developed by Masters and Johnson (1970), is often recommended for the treatment of sexual dysfunctions. Originally, Masters and Johnson's program consisted of a two-week intensive treatment program that required couples to go to their clinic in St. Louis. Two therapists, a man and woman, would meet with individual couples daily and help establish better communication patterns, provide information about sex, and teach specific sexual techniques.

sexual surrogate: A professional who may work with a sex therapy team and serves as a sexual partner for the client while the client is in therapy.

Since many of the therapies for sexual dysfunction required the presence of a willing and cooperative partner, Master and Johnson originally provided a **sexual surrogate** for a person without a sexual partner. A surrogate was a trained professional who would work with the patient and teach him/her sexual skills to use with future sexual partners. However, this practice has stopped because of questions raised about its ethics, value, psychological effects, and use in normal sexual relations. Many critics of this practice claimed that surrogates were merely acting as prostitutes and that this was not beneficial for patients. It has been found to be more beneficial to treat other issues in single men with sexual dysfunctions, such as their assertiveness, knowledge, and attitudes about sex. If a partner refuses to cooperate in therapy, a dysfunctional partner can still be treated with education, self-exploration, body awareness, fantasy, and masturbation training. Also today, books on sexual dysfunction allow partners to improve sexual functioning at home.

Masters and Johnson's work still influences the treatment of sexual dysfunction today. This is rather surprising, given that the treatments for other psychological disorders have changed dramatically over the years. Minor changes have occurred in the length of sex therapy (weekly instead of daily) and the number of therapists (one therapist instead of a male–female team). In addition, partners need not travel away from home.

Sex therapists prescribe a number of exercises to clients. Homework and **sensate focus** exercises are used to increase sensory awareness and to improve communication. Sexual intercourse as a part of therapy is usually reserved for the end of treatment in order to remove any demands for sexual performance.

Sex therapy in America has been criticized for its adherence to Western sexual attitudes and values, with an almost total ignorance of cultural differences in sexual dysfunction and therapy. Above we have presented the aspects of therapy that generally include the Masters and Johnson techniques involving sensate focus, **nondemand pleasuring**, male–female therapy teams, exercises and homework, increased knowledge, and better communication skills. All of these work under the assumption that sexual activity is pleasurable, both partners are equally involved, couples need and want to be educated about sex, and communication is important to have good sexual relationships (Lavee, 1991). However, these ideas might not be shared outside the United States or in different ethnic groups.

Cross-Cultural Aspects of Treating Sexual Dysfunctions

In the United States, as well as in other countries, there is often the expectation that a man's sexual pleasure is more important than the woman's. In cultures where low female sexual desire is not viewed as a problem, anorgasmia would not be viewed as a sexual dysfunction; it would be an acceptable part of sexuality. In some Muslim groups, for example, the only problems that exist are those that interfere with the man's sexual activity (Lavee, 1991). Other cultures believe in supernatural causes of sexual dysfunction (such as the man being cursed by a powerful woman or being given the evil eye).

One Asian approach to sexuality is a Tantric ceremonial sex ritual, which involves five exercises (Voigt, 1991). First, a couple develops a private ritual in which they decide what would prepare them to share sexual expression. This may involve the lighting of candles, using perfume, lotions, music, a special bed or room, certain lighting patterns, massage, reciting poetry together, or meditating. Then they synchronize their breathing by lying together and "getting in touch" with each other. Eye contact is sustained throughout the ritual. Many couples report that they initially felt uncomfortable using eye contact. However, it became very powerful with practice. Next, "motionless intercourse" begins, where the couple remains motionless at the peak of the sensual experience. For many couples, this may be during the time of initial penetration. At first, this may last only a few minutes, building up to increasingly longer periods. Finally, the fifth aspect of the Tantric process is to expand the sexual exchange without orgasm. This is similar to Masters and Johnson's idea of delaying orgasm to enjoy the physical sensations of touching and caressing. In the Asian ritual, this results in an intensification of the sexual-spiritual energy (Voigt, 1991).

The Western view of sex tends to emphasize values such as sex is good (or at least natural), there is an interactional basis of sexual activity, and there is equality between the partners in the relationship (Lavee, 1991). However, Reiss (1986) points out that sexual goals are different among cultural groups that believe in an egalitarian ideology than among those that do not. While an egalitarian ideology views mutual sexual pleasure and communication as important, nonegalitarian ideologies view heterosexual intercourse as the goal, and men's sexual pleasure is more important than women's. Double standards in sexual pleasure are common, for example, in many Portuguese, Mexican, Puerto Rican, and Latino groups. Some Asian groups also often have strong

sensate focus: A series of touching experiences (nonsexual and sexual) that are assigned to couples in sex therapy to teach nonverbal communication and reduce anxiety.

nondemand pleasuring: Non-goal-oriented sexual activity.

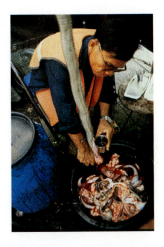

In Bangkok, Thailand, a vendor is pushing cobra blood to increase sexual drive. Customers get to choose their own snake, and then the snake is split open with a razor blade. An incision is made in the major artery of the snake and all blood is drained into a wine glass. The blood is then mixed with bile from the snake's gall bladder, warm whiskey, and a dash of honey. Users believe it helps their sex drive. Prices for the cobras vary: a three- or four-year-old cobra goes for $10; a king cobra is $150; a twelve-year-old king cobra is $350; and an albino cobra with red eyes is $1200.

cultural prohibitions about discussing sexuality. So American values such as open communication, mutual satisfaction, and accommodation to a partner's sexuality may not be appropriate to many other cultures.

Specific Treatments

Arousal Disorders

multimodal: Using a variety of techniques.

Arousal disorders are considered by many therapists to be the most complicated sexual dysfunction to treat. Often, treatment must be **multimodal.** Treatment first involves a medical workup to identify any physiological causes. As we discussed previously, it is also important to evaluate any past sexual trauma or abuse that may interfere with sexual arousal. Intensive psychotherapy can be done to identify and resolve these causes and can also explore the motivations for avoiding intimacy. Homework exercises can be given to help identify these motivations.

Since testosterone is largely responsible for male sexual desire, low male sexual desire has historically been treated with testosterone injections. However, the majority of men who experience low sexual desire have normal levels of testosterone (Schiavi and White, 1976). Given the causes we outlined earlier in this chapter, the treatment for inhibited sexual desire in men is often accomplished through medical evaluation and sex therapy to help explore all possible contributing factors. Research is currently being done on drug treatment for ISD.

Pain Disorders

People who experience any of the pain disorders often believe that they have to live with the problem. As a result, they do not seek help. However, medical evaluations and counseling can help isolate possible causes and solutions.

dilators: A graduated series of metal rods used in the treatment of vaginismus.

Vaginismus. Women who are experiencing vaginismus should consult with a physician and bring their partner as well. After the diagnosis is confirmed, many therapists recommend a series of **dilators**, which are used at home by the couple. At the woman's direction, her partner slowly inserts the dilators, gradually increasing the size, even leaving them in overnight if necessary. If these procedures are successful, penile penetration can be attempted. In some cases, however, it may be necessary to use a dilator just prior to penetration.

Couples should also be receiving information and education about vaginismus and sexuality to reduce their anxiety or tension. If a history of sexual abuse or rape exists, it is very important to work through the trauma prior to beginning work with the dilators, or treatment for vaginismus may be unsuccessful.

Dyspareunia. Like vaginismus, dyspareunia should be evaluated medically prior to treatment. Several physical and psychological issues can contribute to painful intercourse. If there is a physical problem, such as an infection, medical treatment will usually result in a lessening or total elimination of the pain. Psychological causes of dyspareunia, such as performance anxieties or a fear of intimacy, must be treated through counseling or psychotherapy.

Orgasm Disorders

Today, the majority of treatment programs for anorgasmia are multimodal. This means they involve a combination of different treatment approaches such as homework assignments, sex education, communication skills training, cognitive restructuring, desensitization, and other techniques (Kelly et al., 1990).

Anorgasmia. The most effective treatment for primary orgasmic dysfunction in women was developed by LoPiccolo and Lobitz (1972) and involves teaching a woman to masturbate to orgasm. On a psychological level, masturbation also helps increase the pleasurable anticipation of sex. Kegel (1952) also found that women who strengthen their pubococcygeus muscle through exercise also experience an increase in orgasm frequency.

Another treatment, **systematic desensitization** has resulted in 75% of subjects experiencing orgasm either during treatment or shortly after treatment (Andersen, 1981). Systematic desensitization and directed masturbation have been found to be equally effective at increasing the orgasmic response. Systematic desensitization is often helpful in cases where there is a great deal of sexual anxiety.

LoPiccolo and Lobitz (1972) also include education, self-exploration, and body awareness in their masturbation training for orgasmic problems. In addition, information is provided about sexual technique, and communication skills are often taught. Masturbation exercises begin with a woman examining her body and vagina with mirrors. Then she is instructed to find which areas of her body feel the most pleasurable when touched and to stroke them. If this does not result in orgasm, a vibrator is used. As a woman progresses through these stages, she may involve her sexual partner so that the partner is able to learn which areas are more sensitive than others. Although masturbation training is the most effective treatment for anorgasmia, it is somewhat controversial, and so some therapists do not incorporate it into their treatment. Interestingly, improving orgasmic responsivity does not always increase sexual satisfaction. Women often prefer and engage in sexual intercourse over masturbation because it provides more intimacy and closeness, even though masturbation may be a better means of reaching orgasm (Jayne, 1981).

Premature Ejaculation. In order to successfully treat premature ejaculation, a couple has to believe that treatment is possible. Without this belief, treatment may be unsuccessful.

Two techniques used to treat premature ejaculation are the **squeeze** and the **stop–start techniques**. Both involve stimulating the penis to the point just prior to ejaculation. With the squeeze technique, sexual intercourse or masturbation is engaged in just short of orgasm and then stimulation is stopped. The man or his partner puts a thumb on the frenulum and the first and second fingers on the dorsal side of the penis (see Figure 12.1). Pressure is applied for three to four seconds, until the urge to ejaculate subsides. This technique can also be used during female-superior intercourse. The woman must remain fairly motionless and, prior to ejaculation, either the man or the woman uses the squeeze technique. With the stop–start technique, stimulation is simply stopped until the ejaculatory urge subsides. Stimulation is then repeated up until that point, and this process is repeated over and over. These techniques must be used for six to twelve months or whenever necessary to control premature ejaculation. For a man to gain some control over his erection often takes two to ten weeks, and within several months, he can have excellent control.

It is believed that these techniques may help a man get in touch with his arousal levels and sensations. Suggested effectiveness rates have been as high as 98%, although it is unclear how this effectiveness is being measured. In addition, many studies fail to mention whether or not the treatment permanently solves the problem or if periodic repetition of the techniques is necessary. Directly following treatment for premature ejaculation, men showed significant gains in length of foreplay, satisfaction with sexual relationships, and increased mate acceptance (DeAmicis et al., 1985). However, these

systematic desensitization: A treatment method for sexual dysfunction that involves neutralizing the anxiety-producing aspects of sexual situations and behavior by a process of gradual exposure.

squeeze technique: A technique used for the treatment of premature ejaculation in which the ejaculatory reflex is reconditioned using a firm grasp on the penis.

stop–start technique: A technique used for the treatment of premature ejaculation in which the ejaculatory reflex is reconditioned using intermittent pressure on the glans of the penis.

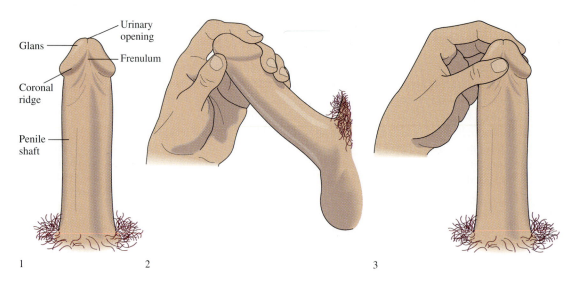

Urinary opening

Glans

Frenulum

Coronal ridge

Penile shaft

1   2   3

Figure 12.1
The squeeze technique used in the treatment of premature ejaculation.

improvements were not maintained three years later, and the frequency and desire for sexual contact, duration of sexual intercourse, and marital satisfaction all decreased. As of 1994, research is being initiated on the effectiveness of medications for the treatment of premature ejaculation (Rosen, 1994).

Retarded Ejaculation. Although psychological factors have been primarily implicated in retarded ejaculation, we still do not really understand what causes this problem, which makes treatment difficult. To treat retarded ejaculation, the man uses those situations where he is able to achieve ejaculation to help him during those where he is not. For example, if a man can ejaculate during masturbation while fantasizing about being watched during sexual activity, he is told to use this fantasy while he is with his partner.

Gradually, the man is asked to incorporate his partner into the sexual fantasy and to masturbate while with the partner. Finally, he is to allow the partner to masturbate him to orgasm. Retarded ejaculation can be very difficult to treat; in many cases, psychotherapy is used to help work through some of these issues as a part of treatment. One forty-three-year-old man reported that he had been experiencing a lifelong problem in reaching orgasm with his partner. He had been sexually abused as a child for many years by an uncle who was a few years older than he, and during this abuse the uncle tried to make him reach orgasm. However, the boy learned to withhold the orgasmic response, much to the dismay of the uncle. Later on in life, this pattern continued even though he was not consciously trying to do so (Author's files).

Erectile Dysfunction. The success rate for treating erectile dysfunction ranges from 50% to 80% (Kerfoot and Carson, 1991). For some unknown reason, erectile dysfunction has been found to improve without treatment in at least 15% to 30% of cases if the cause is not organic (Grinspoon, 1990). In some cases, placebo medications have been found to work as well as sex therapy. Three years after treatment, men show significant improvement in the ability to maintain erections during intercourse, in mate acceptance, and in duration of foreplay (DeAmicis et al., 1985). Depending on the cause, treatment for erectile dysfunction includes psychological treatment, hormonal and intracavernous injections, vascular surgery, vacuum constriction devices, and prosthesis implantation.

Psychological issues that may affect erectile functioning include fear of failure and performance anxiety. Anxiety has been found to have a cyclical effect on erectile functioning. In other words, if a man experiences a problem getting an erection one night, the next time he tries to have intercourse he remembers the failure and becomes anxious. This anxiety, in turn, interferes with his ability to have an erection. Psychotherapy can help reduce these feelings of anxiety and can evaluate issues that are interfering with erectile response.

Hormonal injections may be used to help improve erections in men with hormonal problems such as hyperprolactinemia (too much prolactin) or hypogonadism (too little gonadal hormones) (Morales, 1993). Excessive prolactin can interfere with adequate secretion of testosterone and can cause impotence. Hypogonadism can be treated by intramuscular injections of testosterone every three to four weeks. Although hormonal injections have been popular in the last few years, there are many possible side effects, including liver damage and tumor development (LoPiccolo and Stock, 1986).

Intracavernous injections are a relatively new development in the treatment of erectile dysfunctions. Men and their partners are taught to self-inject these preparations directly into the corpora cavernosa while the penis is gently stretched out (see Figure 12.2). The majority of patients report very minor pain from these injections. Each time a man desires an erection, he must use this injection. The higher the dosage of medication, the longer the erection will last. However, **priapism**, a possible side effect of treatment, occurs in 4% to 8% of cases. Other side effects may include pain during injections, hematoma, and bruising, which may occur from inappropriate injection sites.

Vacuum constriction devices, which use suction to induce erections, have become more popular in the last several years, in part because they are less invasive and safer than injections. One such device, the *ErecAid System,* involves putting the flaccid penis into a vacuum cylinder and pumping it to draw blood into the corpora cavernosa. To keep the blood in the penis, a constriction ring is rolled onto the base of the penis after it is removed from the vacuum device. This ring is left on the penis until the erection is no longer desired. When it is removed, the man will lose his erection.

Side effects include possible bruising, hematomas, and, in rare cases, testicular entrapment in the vacuum chamber (Morales, 1993). Overall, these devices can be expensive, bulky, noisy, and require use before having an erection, which some patients find unappealing.

In the last few years, surgical intervention has increased as a treatment for erectile dysfunction (Barlow, 1986). In some cases, physicians perform **revascularization** to improve erectile functioning.

For organic problems that cause permanent erectile dysfunction, however, **prosthesis implantation** may be recommended. Acrylic implants for erectile dysfunction were first used in 1952, but they were replaced by silicone rubber in the 1960s, and then by a variety of synthetic materials in the 1970s. Today there are two main types of implants: **semirigid rods**, which provide a permanent state of erection, and inflatable devices that become firm when the patient pumps them up (McCarthy and McMillan, 1990). Sexual intercourse may safely be engaged in four to eight weeks after surgery. Although some believe that a man cannot ejaculate with a prosthesis, it is not true. Orgasms, the ability to ejaculate, and the ability to impregnate are unaffected (McCarthy and McMillan, 1990).

Between 10% and 20% of patients remain dissatisfied, dysfunctional, or sexually inactive even after prosthetic surgery (McCarthy and McMillan, 1990). In some cases, if a man has psychological factors that contribute to his erectile difficulties, these issues

intracavernous injections: A treatment method for erectile dysfunction in which vasodilating drugs are injected into the penis for the purpose of creating an erection.

priapism: A condition in which erections are long lasting and often painful.

vacuum constriction devices: Treatment devices for erectile dysfunction used to pull blood into the penis.

revascularization: A procedure used in the treatment of vascular erectile dysfunction in which the vascular system is rerouted to ensure better blood flow to the penis.

prosthesis implantation: A treatment method for erectile dysfunction in which a prosthesis is surgically implanted into the penis.

semirigid rods: Flexible rods that are implanted into the penis during prosthetic surgery.

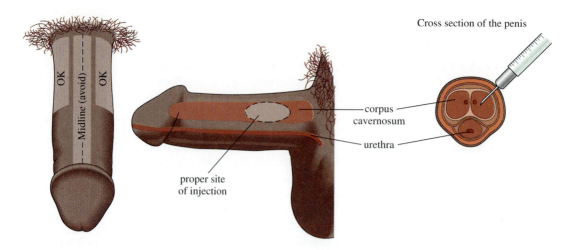

Cross section of the penis

corpus cavernosum

urethra

proper site of injection

Figure 12.2
To use self-injections, a man must gently stretch the penis out and inject the medication directly into the corpora cavernosa.

are likely to resurface once a prosthesis is implanted. However, it was found that after prosthesis implantation, men tend to engage in more kissing and to increase the frequency of meaningful conversation.

Research is being done on several other possible treatments. For example, some substances, such as **yohimbine**, have been tested as an oral treatment for erectile dysfunction (Morales, 1993). Preliminary trials suggest it may bring significant improvement in erectile functioning to both organic and psychogenic erectile dysfunction.

yohimbine: This substance is derived from the bark of a tree and has been used as an aphrodisiac.

OTHER TREATMENTS FOR SEXUAL DYSFUNCTION

Bibliotherapy

bibliotherapy: Using books and educational materials for the treatment of sexual dysfunction.

Bibliotherapy has been found to be particularly helpful in cases of orgasmic difficulties. One study found that women who participated in a treatment method that involved reading a self-help manual at home improved their orgasmic functioning and maintained these gains at six-week follow-up appointments (Dodge-Tripet et al., 1982). Over the past few years, several good books have been written on sexual dysfunction, many of which are available through your local bookstore. Several of them are listed at the end of this chapter.

A variety of penile prostheses are available.

Hypnosis

Hypnotherapists use relaxation and direct suggestion to help improve sexual functioning. One patient who was experiencing sexual apathy and anorgasmia was told during a hypnotic session to "please herself in bed" (Andersen, 1981). The next week she reported having her first orgasm, and two months later she reported an orgasmic frequency of 75%. At this time, little clinical evidence exists on the success of hypnosis in the treatment of sexual dysfunction.

Drugs

Medications that act like aphrodisiacs are also being evaluated to help in the treatment of low sexual desire. *Wellbutrin,* which was originally developed as an antidepressant, has been found in preliminary trials to increase sexual desire. Wellbutrin is a nonhormonal prescription drug, which can be taken by those who have been advised to avoid hormones. More research needs to be done on this drug.

SEXUALITY IN ILLNESS AND DISABILITY

[When a child looks at me on the street] the mother will pull her away and perhaps slap her. Much the same thing happens when the child begins to explore her own sexuality. Handicapped people are forbidden and sex is forbidden, so it's no wonder that the sexuality of handicapped people is doubly forbidden.

Prudy Sutherland, cerebral palsy sufferer; Sutherland (1987:27)

We all need love, and we all need touching and contact with others. Yet somehow we have grown to think that sexuality is the privilege of the healthy. We tend to exclude ill or disabled people from our visions of the sexual, and so we deny them a basic human right (see Personal Voices 12.1). If you were suddenly disabled or developed a chronic illness, would *you* lose your desire to love and be loved, to touch and be touched, to be regarded by another as sexy and desirable?

Physical illness and its treatment can interfere with a person's sexual desire, physiological functioning, or both. Sexual functioning involves a complex physiological process, which can be impaired by pain, immobility, changes in bodily functions, or medications (Levay et al., 1981). More often, though, the problems are psychological. Sudden illness causes shock, anger, resentment, anxiety, and depression, all of which can adversely affect sexual desire and functioning. Many illnesses cause disfiguration and force a person to deal with radical changes in body image; after removal of a limb or a breast or the need to wear an external bag to collect bodily waste, many people wonder: How could anyone possibly find me sexually attractive?

Serious illness often puts strains on loving relationships. A partner may be forced to become nurse, cook, maid, and caretaker as well as lover. The caretaker of an ill person may worry that the sick partner is too weak or fragile for sex or be too concerned with his or her illness to want sexual contact. Still, many couples do enjoy loving, full relationships (see Personal Voices 12.2 on page 481).

A majority of the research on the sexuality of the disabled has been done on men, and physicians are more likely to talk to their male patients about sexual issues than their female ones. Health-care workers often assume that female patients do not want to have sex or that they are only interested in whether or not they can still do it; yet the little research that exists on gender differences in the sexuality of the disabled has found that disabled women have a harder time than disabled men (Fine and Asch, 1988). Another common assumption is that all patients are heterosexual, and so, for example, disabled lesbians may be given contraceptive advice without being asked if they need it (O'Toole and Bregante, 1992). Heterosexual women looking for information about sexuality and their particular disability may find little, and lesbians may find none at all.

The *real* questions that sick people and their partners have about their sexuality are too often ignored by medical professionals. They may be questions of mechanics—"What

"I Want Sex—Just Like You"

For years, because of my cerebral palsy and certain other physical difficulties, I doubted my ability to give and receive pleasure in sexual intercourse. For a long time I did not want to ask my doctors about sex because I felt that a negative answer would make me regard myself as nonhuman—such is the value our society places on sexuality.... I asked the doctor, in what I thought was a simple, forthright manner, if I could give and receive sexual pleasure. Extremely nervous laughter ensued—but no answer.... Several times I asked my question, with similarly depressing nonanswers.

Finally, since I was extremely hazy about what physical movements were involved in coitus, I decided to go to a movie. I reasoned that a movie would provide an uninhibited, graphic illustration. But none of my friends took me seriously.

One dark night, with a young man with whom I was just getting acquainted, I took off and pulled up at a sleazy, red carpeted theater complete with groaning old men in raincoats. They let me in for nothing, and I am still not sure whether that was because I was a woman or because I was a cripple. After the first two minutes I got the idea down pat and saw that I was perfectly capable of performing. My self-image skyrocketed. I, just like other women, had something sexual to offer a man!

Perhaps the most amazing thing about this educational adventure was the reaction of my friends.... Strangely enough, many of my friends were anxious to tell me that what I had seen on the screen was not love, as if I did not know what love was. I knew that men jumping in and out of women and women sucking men was not love, that the movies had contained little foreplay and no tenderness. I had not needed to go to a movie to find out what love was. I had needed to go to a movie to find out the physical manipulations involved in coitus, because "legitimate" society was too insecure to provide me with the information....

There are various reasons why sexuality of the handicapped was avoided for so long and why it makes many professionals intolerably uncomfortable. First, most physical disabilities alter the looks of the person—deformities, bizarre head and arm motions, drooling, and poor eye-contact. The majority of the handicapped do not meet the popular standard of physical attractiveness. When was the last time you saw a woman in a wheelchair advertising Ultra-Brite? Few professionals are able to see their patients as sexually desirable, and there is even the subtly expressed attitude that there is something a bit wrong with anyone who is sexually attracted to a disabled person. You can image what such an attitude does to the self-esteem of the handicapped person—"Anyone who wants me must be nuts!"

The couple too disabled to have sex by themselves must decide whether they want to forego sex because of the invasion of privacy or whether they want to make love in spite of needing help to do so. Theirs is a completely amoral decision. There are many reasons for making love —recreation, bribery, consolation, procreation, the desire for one-on-one attention, religious experience. Some of the reasons are more amenable than others to third-party participation. But I feel strongly that no couple who wants to have sex should be denied the necessary help to do so, and that, if they live in a health-care facility, it is the duty of the health-care professional to provide such help. After all, many able-bodied people enjoy a ménage à trois!

Initial access to potential partners is extremely limited, in large part due to the barrier thrown up by my distorted speech. Opportunities to meet are few, and when they do exist, men who are not trained to work with handicapped people tend to shy away from me. Somehow I hardly think the father of young children who held me in his arms as he helped me into the YWCA swimming pool was making plans to have me as a future bed partner.

Even if I did get to know a guy well enough so that the moment for sex drew near, there would be the problem of birth control. An able-bodied woman can have herself fitted with a diaphragm with very little failure, and furthermore she can insert the device herself at the opportune time....

Yet an even more basic problem for me, at least, is my mistrust of my own body. Intellectually I know that sexually I can perform—the movie proved it. Yet at what might be called the subintellectual level I doubt my body's ability to give another pleasure. Rarely does my body give me pleasure. When I tell it to do something as often as not it does exactly the opposite, or else it flares out in wild, tantrum-like motions. How could my body possibly conform to the wishes of an expectantly excited lover? This is the question I still ask myself.

Sutherland (1987:25,27)

positions can I get into now that I have lost a leg?" Questions of function—"Will my genitals still work now that I have a spinal-cord injury?" Questions of attractiveness—"Will my husband still want me now that I have lost a breast?" Even questions of appropriateness—"Should I allow my retarded teenage daughter to pursue a sex life when she may not understand the consequences?" Below, we review a sample of physical and mental challenges that confront people and also some of the sexual questions and problems that can arise.

Cardiovascular Problems

Heart Disease

Heart disease, including **hypertension**, **angina**, and **myocardial infarctions (MIs)**, is the number one cause of death in the United States. A person with heart disease—even a person who has had a heart transplant—can return to a normal sex life shortly after recovery. Most cardiologists allow intercourse as soon as the patient feels up to it, although they usually recommend waiting from four to eight weeks to give the incision time to heal. However, researchers have found that the frequency of sexual intercourse after MIs, for example, can decrease from 40% to 70% (Schover and Jensen, 1988). Why does sexual activity decrease so much after cardiac incidents?

One reason is fear. Many patients (or their partners) fear that their damaged (or new) heart is not up to the strain of intercourse or orgasm. This fear can be triggered by the fact that when a person becomes sexually excited, his or her heartbeat and respiration increase, and he or she may break out into a sweat (these are also signs of a heart attack). Some people with heart disease actually do experience some angina during sexual activity. Although not usually serious, these incidents may be frightening. Most of the anxiety, however, is based on misconceptions. Except for the patients with very serious heart conditions, sex puts no more strain on the heart than walking up a flight or two of stairs.

Not all problems are psychological, however. Since achieving an erection is basically a vascular process, involving the flow of blood into the penis, some forms of heart disease can result in erectile difficulties (in fact, many men who have had an MI report having had erectile difficulties before their heart attack). Some heart medications also can dampen desire or cause erectile problems, or less often, women may experience a decrease in lubrication (see Sexuality Today 12.2). Sometimes, adjusting medications can help couples who are experiencing such problems.

After a heart attack or other heart problems, it is not uncommon to have feelings of depression, inadequacy (especially among men), or loss of attractiveness (especially among women) (Schover and Jensen, 1988). As one man observed:

> *Some people I know who have suffered heart attacks move into massive states of depression. Why? Because anytime you become sick, if you're a man, somehow you're less a man. One of the first questions that's asked in the therapy groups is, "Can my wife and I have sex?" Now they may not even have had it with any regularity before, but it just seems to be the question.*
>
> *Register (1987:38)*

In addition, after a heart attack, the patient's partner often assumes the responsibility of enforcing the doctor's orders: "Don't smoke!" "Don't eat fatty foods!" "Don't drink alcohol!" "Don't get so excited!" "Don't put so much salt on that!" "Get some

hypertension: Abnormally high blood pressure.

angina: Though the term technically refers to any spasmodic or choking pain, it is usually used by the lay public to refer to the chest pains that accompany heart disease.

myocardial infarction (MI): A cutoff of blood to the heart muscle, causing damage to the heart; also called a heart attack.

SEXUALITY*Today*   *12.2*

Specific Drugs and Symptoms of Sexual Problems

Listed below are different drugs that have been found to interfere with the sexual response cycle by interfering with sexual desire, erections, ejaculation, or orgasm and also by contributing to conditions such as Peyronie's Disease, Priapism, or Gynecomastia (breast enlargement).

Type of Drug	Possible Problems
ANTIHYPERTENSIVES (blood pressure medications)	
Aldomet	reduced sexual desire, erectile and ejaculatory problems, impaired orgasm
Inderal	reduced sexual desire, erectile problems
Catapres	reduced sexual desire, erectile problems
Lopressor	reduced sexual desire, Peyronie's Disease
Minipress	reduced sexual desire, erectile problems
TRANQUILIZERS	
barbiturates	reduced sexual desire, erectile problems
Valium and Xanax	reduced sexual desire, ejaculatory problems, impaired orgasm
ANTIDEPRESSANTS	
Clomipramine	reduced sexual desire, erectile and ejaculatory problems, impaired orgasms
Desyrel	erectile problems, priapism
Elavil	reduced sexual desire, erectile and ejaculatory problems, testicular swelling
ANTIPSYCHOTICS	
Mellaril	reduced sexual desire, erectile and ejaculatory problems, priapism, gynecomastia, menstrual problems
Stelazine	erectile and ejaculatory problems, priapism, gynecomastia, menstrual problems
Thorazine	erectile and ejaculatory problems, priapism, menstrual problems
ULCER MEDICATION	
Tagamet	reduced sexual desire, erectile problems, gynecomastia
Xantac	reduced sexual desire, erectile problems
OTHER DRUGS	
Antabuse (alcoholism)	erectile problems
Naproxen (antiinflammatory)	erectile and ejaculatory problems
Alkeran (cancer)	reduced sexual desire, erectile problems, gynecomastia, menstrual problems

Reinisch et al. (1990)

---

exercise!" This is hardly a role that leads to good feelings and sexual desire. Any combination of these factors may lead one or both partners to avoid sex. Consequently, distance in the relationship may grow, and the couple may drift apart just when they need each other most (Sandowski, 1989). Physicians should address potential sexual problems with patients directly and calm their anxieties and concerns. It is equally important for the couples to discuss their sexual issues directly with each other.

Stroke

strokes: Occur when blood is cut off from part of the brain, usually because a small blood vessel bursts.

hemiplegia: Paralysis of one side of the body.

aphasia: Defects in the ability to express and/or understand speech, signs, or written communication, due to damage to the speech centers of the brain.

Strokes, also called cerebral vascular accidents (CVAs), happen when blood is cut off from part of the brain, usually because a small blood vessel bursts. Although every stroke is different depending on what areas of the brain are damaged, some common results are **hemiplegia**, **aphasia**, and other cognitive, perceptual, and memory problems. As with other types of brain injury (such as those caused by automobile accidents), damage to the brain can affect sexuality in a number of ways.

In most cases of stroke, sexual functioning itself is not damaged, and many stroke victims do go on to resume sexual activity. The problems that confront a couple with normal functioning are similar to those with cardiovascular disease: fear of causing another stroke, worries about sexual attractiveness, and the stresses and anxieties of having to cope with a major illness.

However, a stroke can also cause physiological changes that affect sexuality. Some men find that after a stroke their erections are crooked because the nerves controlling the erectile tissue on one side of the penis are affected. Hemiplegia can result in spasticity (jerking motions) and reduced sensation on one side of the body. Paralysis can also contribute to a feeling of awkwardness or unattractiveness. In addition, aphasia can affect a person's ability to communicate or understand sexual cues.

Some stroke victims also go through periods of **disinhibition,** where they exhibit behavior that, before the stroke, they would have been able to suppress. Often this includes **hypersexuality**, where the patient may make lewd comments, masturbate in public, disrobe publicly, or make inappropriate sexual advances (Larkin, 1992). Others may experience **hyposexuality** and show decreased sexual desire or impotence. Sexual intervention programs have been designed for use in rehabilitation hospitals, and they can be of great help in teaching couples how to deal with the difficulties of adjusting to life after a stroke.

Cancer

Cancer is one of the most dreaded diseases, can involve almost any organ of the body, and has a reputation of being invariably fatal. In fact, cure rates have increased dramatically, and some cancers are now more than 90% curable. Still, cancer *can* kill, and a diagnosis of cancer is usually accompanied by shock, numbness, and gripping fear. Also, as in other illness, partners may need to become nursemaids, and roles can change. For these reasons, cancer can lead to a decrease in sexual desire and activity, even when it attacks nonsexual organs.

For example, surgery is required for a number of cancers of the digestive system, and it can lead to **ostomies**. People with cancer of the colon often need to have part or all of the large intestine removed; the rectum may be removed as well. A surgical opening, called a **stoma**, is made in the abdomen to allow waste products to exit the body. This is collected in a bag which, for many patients, must be worn at all times (others can take it off periodically). Ostomy bags are visually unpleasant and may emit an odor, and the adjustment to their presence can be very difficult for some couples. Having a new opening on the body to eliminate bodily wastes is itself a hard thing to accept for many people, but most people eventually adjust to it and, barring other problems related to their disease, go on to live healthy and sexually active lives. One woman wondered how an ostomy would change her self-image:

> I had to go through a total reevaluation of my physical appearance. I couldn't ever imagine myself attracting somebody in a bikini or in any of those normal, stereotypical ways. I would eventually have to confront the reality that I was having this ostomy, and if I was to develop any kind of an intimate relationship with anybody, that was going to have to be dealt with. So I had to look deeper down beyond the flesh. It was like having someone say, "OK, all your usual ways of relating to people have to be completely changed." I had always used my body and my appearance. . . . You wonder, if something happened to my husband or if our relationship broke down completely, how would I tell somebody? What would I do? Would they want me? Would I be afraid to be sexually involved?

> *Register (1987:38–39)*

disinhibition: The loss of normal control over behaviors such as expressing sexuality or taking one's clothes off in public.

hypersexuality: Abnormally expressive or aggressive sexual behavior, often in public; the term usually refers to behavior due to some disturbance of the brain.

hyposexuality: Abnormal suppression of sexual desire and behavior; the term usually refers to behavior due to some disturbance of the brain.

ostomies: Operations to remove part of the small or large intestine or the bladder, resulting in the need to create an artificial opening in the body for the elimination of bodily wastes.

stoma: Surgical opening made in the abdomen to allow waste products to exit the body.

Cancer can affect sexual functioning in other ways as well. Physical scars, the loss of limbs or body parts, changes in skin texture when radiation therapy is used, the loss of hair, nausea, bloatedness, weight gain or loss, and acne are just some of the ways that cancer and its treatment can affect the body and one's body image. In addition, the psychological trauma and the fear of death can lead to depression, which can inhibit sexual relations. Perhaps the most drastic situations, however, occur when cancer affects the sexual organs themselves.

Cancer in Women's Reproductive Organs

Breast Cancer.* Breast cancer is the most common female cancer, affecting about one out of every nine women in America. It is also the leading cause of cancer-related deaths in women. In the late 1980s and early 1990s, many women who were involved in writing about health issues began to feel that researchers were not spending enough time and effort on women's diseases. They subsequently began pressing federal funding agencies to focus more attention on breast cancer. Newspapers began to expand their coverage of women's health, and breast cancer became a major focus of national funding agencies such as the National Institute of Health.

mastectomy: The surgical removal of a breast.

simple mastectomy: The surgical removal of the breast tissue.

In American society, breasts are a focal part of female sexual attractiveness, and women often invest much of their feminine self-image in their breasts. For many years, a diagnosis of breast cancer usually meant that you lost that breast; **mastectomy** was the preferred treatment. **Simple mastectomies** meant that the breast tissue alone was removed, while radical mastectomies involved the removal of the breast, along with other tissues and lymph nodes. Today, the numbers of mastectomies have decreased, and many women are opting for lumpectomies. These are often coupled with chemotherapy, radiation therapy, or both. Still, some women must undergo radical mastectomies and must contend not only with having cancer, but also with an altered image of their sexual identity.

There might be very little time to prepare oneself psychologically for the loss of a breast. One woman who had a mastectomy years ago reported: "It all happened so fast. I was told on Friday, and on Monday it [the breast] was off" (Sandowski, 1989:166). A woman who loses a breast may worry that her partner will no longer find her attractive or desirable. Some go so far as to wear their bras when making love or to avoid looking in mirrors when nude. In order to wear the clothes they are used to wearing, many woman missing a breast (or both breasts) will wear a prosthesis. Other women choose to undergo breast reconstruction, where tissue and fat from other parts of the body are molded into the shape of a breast and implanted under a fold of skin. Years ago, reconstructed breasts were not very satisfactory in appearance, but recent advances in reconstructive techniques can create a much more natural-looking breast. Surgery can also create a realistic looking nipple, although some women are satisfied with just the form of a breast (Sandowski, 1989).

There is no reason that a mastectomy should interfere with normal sexual functioning. The most important factor in resuming a normal sexual life is the encouragement and acceptance from the woman's sexual partner, assuring her that she is still sexually attractive and desirable.

---

* We discuss breast cancer, including warning signs and how to do a breast self-examination, in Chapter 3.

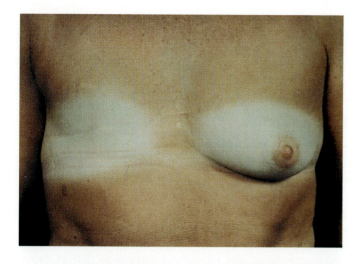

During a mastectomy, one or both of the breasts are completely removed.

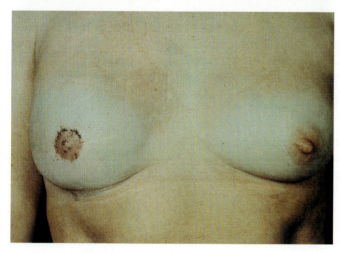

Breast reconstruction surgery can be done to make the breast look more realistic after surgery.

Pelvic Cancer and Hysterectomies. Cancer can also strike a woman's vagina, uterus, or ovaries. Often, cancer of these organs will result in a hysterectomy. In a total hysterectomy, the uterus and cervix (which is part of the uterus) are removed, and in a radical hysterectomy, the ovaries are also removed (**oophorectomy**), along with the Fallopian tubes and surrounding tissue. Hysterectomies are also performed for conditions other than cancer. In fact, they were done so often that by the early 1980s, they were one of the most common surgeries in the United States. Many critics began to claim that American surgeons were much too quick to remove a woman's uterus; in France, for example, doctors performed less than one-fifth the number of hysterectomies as in the United States. Because of this criticism, the number of hysterectomies performed in the United States has been dropping.

Physicians may neglect to discuss the sexual implications of losing a uterus with their patients because they know that the uterus does not directly influence sexuality and they assume that the woman feels the same way. Yet many women believe that their uterus is needed for normal sexual functioning and worry that removal will affect their

oophorectomy: The surgical removal of the ovaries.

sexual desire or their ability to have normal relations. In one study, close to 40% of women who had undergone hysterectomies reported a deterioration in their sexual relationships, which they associated with the operation (Levay et al., 1981).

There are a number of ways hysterectomy can affect sexual functioning and pleasure. The ovaries produce most of a woman's estrogen and progesterone, and so when they are removed, hormonal imbalances follow. Even with hormone replacement therapy, reduced vaginal lubrication, mood swings, and other bodily changes can occur. Also, many women find the uterine contractions of orgasm very pleasurable, and when the uterus is removed, they lose that aspect of orgasm. In some cases, part of the woman's upper vagina may be removed, and the vagina may then be shorter, making intercourse uncomfortable or painful.

Depression and the disruption of marital relationships are common after a hysterectomy. In part, how a woman feels about her hysterectomy reflects other needs in her life. Older women who are through with childbearing may find it less disturbing, and in fact, some women are happy to be free of menstrual periods and the need for contraception (especially if the hysterectomy was for reasons other than cancer). Other women may feel a profound sense of loss because they may have wanted to bear children or because they are mourning the loss of a cherished part of their body and female identity. Sexual partners must be sensitive to how the woman tries to work out her new relationship to her sexuality. If intercourse is painful, trying different positions and using artificial lubrication may help. Perhaps the most important element in adjusting to hysterectomy is time (Sandowski, 1989).

Cancer in Men's Reproductive Organs

Prostate Cancer. Almost all men will experience a normal enlargement of the prostate gland if they live long enough (see Chapter 3). Prostate cancer is one of the most common cancers in men over fifty. When prostate cancer is diagnosed or if the normal enlargement of the prostate progresses to the point where it affects urination, a **prostatectomy** (sometimes along with a **cystectomy**) must be performed. In the past, a prostatectomy involved cutting the nerves necessary for erection, resulting in erectile dysfunction. Newer techniques, however, allow more careful surgery, and fewer men suffer impotence as a result.

One result of prostatectomy may be **incontinence**, sometimes necessitating an **indwelling catheter**. Many couples fear that this means the end of their sex life, because removing and reinserting the catheter can lead to infection. However, the catheter can be folded alongside the penis during intercourse or held in place with a condom (Sandowski, 1989). For men who are rendered impotent from the surgery, penile prostheses or intracavenous injections are possible. As in all surgeries of this kind, the man must also cope with the fear of disease, concern about his masculinity and body image, concern about the reactions of his sexual partner, and the new sensations or sexual functioning that can accompany prostate surgery.

Testicular Cancer. Cancer of the penis or scrotum is rare, and cancer of the testes is only slightly more common. Still, the sexual problems that result from these diseases are similar to those with prostate cancer. The surgical removal of a testicle (orchiectomy) due to cancer usually does not affect the ability to reproduce, as the remaining testicle produces enough sperm and, usually, adequate testosterone. However, some men experience psychological difficulties, due to feelings that they have lost part of

prostatectomy: The surgical removal of the prostate gland.

cystectomy: The surgical removal of the bladder.

incontinence: The inability to withhold defecation or urination.

indwelling catheter: A permanent catheter, inserted in the bladder, to allow the removal of urine in those who are unable to urinate or are incontinent

their manhood or fears about the appearance of their scrotum. However, the appearance of the scrotum can be helped by inserting a testicular prosthesis that takes the place of the missing testicle. In some rare cases, cancer of the penis may necessitate a partial or total **penectomy**. In a total penectomy, the man's urethra is redirected downward to a new opening that is created between the scrotum and anus. Even with a penectomy, some men can have orgasms by stimulating whatever tissue is left

penectomy: The surgical removal of the penis.

Personal

V O I C E S

12.2

Stories of Love Among the Disabled

ANDY: For a while, sure I felt bad [about breaking up with previous partner], but I went on and picked myself up, and I feel this [relationship with Carol] will be better for me.... It's doing me a lot of good so far, and I hope she feels that way.... For me, I don't want to lose her....

CAROL: I'm looking for the same thing he's looking for —security. I thought I had it in the past, but I didn't. [Security is] being with each other and having the ability to talk to one another....

AL: She means everything to me.... As soon as I get my divorce—put this in the book!—I'll marry her.

BEV: No matter how good or bad the situation is, he's there for me, loving me—letting me know he loves me.... Like everything else, you have to find your own way of intimacy. There's nothing that I can give to Al that he can't give back to me. It's mutual.

Earl and Gina

EARL: Some people don't look at it [an older person's sex life] as [important and healthy]. "Oh, that dirty, dirty old man!" [He's sixty-five, she's thirty-three.] I'm sick and tired of listening to that "dirty old man" talk! I think it's wrong when they say that. What the man needs is *love*, just like I'm giving Gina. Love makes me feel happier. But a lot of people don't understand it because not only am I older—I'm handicapped. I say to hell with that! Handicap or no handicap, we're all *human*. We're *all* human....

GINA: Above all, he has an inner strength in him that has reflected on me and gotten through to me so that I'm more able to cope with life. He has a much better inner strength than I have seen in any other person.... I can talk with him about anything and everything under the sun, and he can make me feel *so* much better and so much more at ease.

Stehle (1985)

Al and Bev

*Photographs reprinted with permission, © Bernard F. Stehle, 1985. *INCURABLY ROMANTIC* by Bernard F. Stehle, Philadelphia: Temple Univ. Press, 1985.

where the penis was, and the ejaculate leaves the body through the urethra (Schover and Jensen, 1988).

Chronic Illness

Many people born with chronic diseases, or who develop them later in life, suffer for many years with their condition. They must learn to make adjustments in many parts of their lives, including their sexual behaviors.

Chronic pain from illnesses such as arthritis, migraine headaches, and lower back pain can make intercourse difficult or impossible at times. A study of lower back pain patients found that all 100 subjects had reduced sexual activity after the onset of their symptoms, with the majority showing a 50% reduction or more (Kolk et al., 1992). A female describes the results of her painful condition:

> *It is difficult to express sensual pleasures—intercourse, touching, holding, hand-holding, hugging—when my body hurts. I often feel pain when trying new positions, which is also affected by my limited range of motion. Sexual expression was limited. My husband was afraid to try new things and positions sometimes because of the fear he might physically hurt me. I was afraid of trying new things because I might hurt myself or cry out in pain and spoil the mood or feel embarrassed.*

> *Kohler et al. (1990:95)*

Still, with gentle, caring lovemaking and an avoidance of those positions that are too painful or stressful, many people report that sexual activity actually provides them some respite from their pain.

Another group of conditions that affects sexual functioning is the **chronic obstructive pulmonary diseases (COPD)**, which include asthma, emphysema, tuberculosis, and chronic bronchitis. These diseases affect sexual functioning not only because they may make physical exertion difficult, but because perceptual and motor skills can also be impaired. The twenty million people who have COPD learn to take medicine before sexual activity, slow down their pace of lovemaking, and use positions that allow the partner with COPD to breathe comfortably.

Many other chronic illnesses call for special types of sexual counseling and understanding. In order to understand the challenges that chronic illness poses to sexual functioning, we will review a sample of such conditions and examine the types of sexual challenges they present below.

> **chronic obstructive pulmonary diseases (COPD):** Diseases of the lung and breathing.

Diabetes

Diabetes is caused by the inability of the pancreas to produce insulin, which is used to process blood sugar into energy. Diabetes may affect children (*type I diabetes*), who must then depend on insulin injections for the rest of their lives, or it may appear later (*type II diabetes*) and may then be controlled through diet or oral medication. Diabetes is a serious condition that can ultimately lead to blindness, renal failure, and other problems.

Diabetes is often used to demonstrate the effects of disease on sexuality because diabetics tend to exhibit multiple and complex sexual difficulties. In fact, sexual problems (especially difficulty in getting an erection for men and vaginitis or yeast infections in women) may be one of the first signs of diabetes. Both type I and II diabetic men tend to have a significantly higher rate of erectile dysfunction and may have lower sexual desire than unaffected men, although it is not clear if this is a separate effect or secondary to the erectile difficulty (Levay et al., 1981). A large number of men in the later stages of diabetes have penile prostheses implanted. Type I diabetic women, aside from some problems with vaginal lubrication, do not seem to have significantly more problems than unaffected women. Type II diabetic women, however, show loss of desire, difficulties in lubrication, less satisfaction in sex, and difficulty reaching orgasm (Schover and Jensen, 1988).

Differentiating between how much of a person's sexual difficulty is due to underlying physiological problems and how much is due to psychological issues is often difficult. For example, although diabetics do experience physiological changes that directly affect sexual functioning (such as neurological problems), men with sexual difficulties sometimes find that they lessen or disappear when they form a new relationship or when conflicts are resolved in their present relationship (Schover and Jensen, 1988). Depression, fear of impotence or lack of sexual response, anxiety about the future, and the life changes that diabetes can bring all can dampen sexual desire. Sexual counseling is an important part of diabetes treatment.

Multiple Sclerosis

Multiple sclerosis (MS) involves a breakdown of the myelin sheath that protects all nerve fibers, and it can be manifested in a variety of symptoms, such as dizziness, weakness, blurred or double vision, muscle spasms, spasticity, and loss of control of limbs and muscles. Symptoms can come and go without warning, but MS is progressive and worsens over time. MS often strikes people between the ages of eighteen and forty, at a time when they are establishing sexual relationships and families.

MS can affect sexual functioning in many ways. Men can experience erectile difficulties or premature, delayed, or lack of ejaculation. Women may have lack of vaginal lubrication, altered feelings during orgasm, or difficulty experiencing orgasm. Both men and women may become hypersensitive to touch, experiencing even light caresses as painful or unpleasant. Such things as fatigue, spasms of the muscles, and loss of bladder and bowel function can also inhibit sexual contact. Sexual counseling, penile prostheses in men, and artificial lubrication in women can help overcome some of these difficulties.

MS is a debilitating disease, and marriages often do not survive it. One woman seems amazed that her husband stays with her through it all:

> I think, "How come he doesn't leave?" You hear of so many people getting divorced. I said, "Why do you stay? Are you going to leave me?" He said, "No, I don't think so." That's the way he always is. He isn't one to say, "Oh, how could you think that?" Then you'd question. . . . My husband never, ever lies. He says yes, I get on his nerves after he has to watch me struggle. It would be easier on him if he didn't have to see that.
>
> *Register (1987:136)*

With MS, as with many other similar diseases, a loving partner (and, at times, a sense of humor) can overcome many of the physical limitations of the disease.

Muscular Dystrophy

Muscular dystrophy (MD) affects more males than females and is characterized by progressive loss of muscle strength. MD causes a decreased range of motion, lowered endurance, atrophy of certain muscles, and loss of coordination as it progresses. The genitals' ability to function sexually is not usually impaired, except at the end stages of the disease. Pillows to support the body, certain positions that lessen strain or avoid atrophied muscles, slowing down sexual motion, and increasing nonintercourse sexuality (such as oral sex) can help partners maintain their sexual contact. Changing expectations so that coitus is not the goal of every sexual encounter can also help (Sandowski, 1989). Even so, the realization that one's life will undergo profound changes, including eventually losing normal functions, having to stop working, losing independence and self-reliance, and depending on the partner or caretaker more and more for daily life, takes its toll on sexual relationships.

Alcoholism

Alcohol is the most common type of chemical dependency in the United States and Western Europe; about one-third of American families have at least one problem drinker in their midst, and alcohol is the third leading cause of death in the United States. Ethyl alcohol is a general nervous system depressant that has both long- and short-term effects on sexual functioning. It can impair spinal reflexes and decrease serum testosterone levels, which can lead to erectile dysfunction. Paradoxically, even as serum testosterone levels drop, luteinizing hormone (LH) levels can increase, leading to increased libido (Buffum et al., 1981).

hyperestrogenemia: Having an excessive amount of estrogens in the blood.

Long-term alcohol abuse can have drastic consequences. **Hyperestrogenemia** can result from the liver damage due to alcoholism, which, combined with lower testosterone levels, may cause feminization, gynecomastia, testicular atrophy, sterility, impotence, and the decreased libido seen in long-term alcoholic males. In women, liver disease can lead to decreased or absent menstrual flow, ovarian atrophy, loss of vaginal membranes, infertility, and miscarriages. Alcohol can affect almost every bodily system, and after a while the damage it causes, including the damage to sexual functioning, can be irreversible, even if the person never drinks alcohol again.

Alcohol has a reputation of being an aphrodisiac. After surveying many people who believe that alcohol increases sexual pleasure, however, these same people were not able to cite a single instance when it actually functioned that way for them (Schover and Jensen, 1988). Advertising reinforces this stereotype, portraying sexual relationships enhanced by a beer or a mixed drink. It is true that one drink or two at the most may help a person relax; any more, though, and alcohol works as a general nervous system depressant that can cause erectile problems, lack of arousal in females, or the inability to reach orgasm. It may surprise those who accept the image of alcohol as a sexual enhancer that up to 80% of alcoholic men are impotent!

Alcoholism also has a dramatic impact on families. It often coexists with anger, resentment, depression, and other familial and marital problems. Some people become abusive when drunk, while others may withdraw and become noncommunicative. Neither of these behavior patterns is conducive to a healthy sex life. People react to alcohol-induced behavior in a number of ways. For example, sex may be withheld by a partner as punishment for intoxicated behavior, leading to further withdrawal and estrangement. If the couple or the individual realize the problem and seek help and if the alcoholism has not progressed too far, medical treatment or programs such as Alcoholics Anonymous can address the basic problem and eventually reverse the sexual dysfunction.

Female alcoholics often report histories of sexual promiscuity, sexual abuse, extramarital affairs, rape, incest, or prostitution. Some women become more sexually active while drinking or find it necessary to drink in order to have sex. For both sexes, problem drinking may lead them in a spiral of guilt, lowered self-esteem, and even to thoughts of suicide. Recovery is a long, often difficult process, and one's body and sexuality need time to recover from periods of abuse. The most important thing for recovering alcoholics to remember is to give themselves time to adjust, even time to learn to enjoy sexuality in the absence of artificial substances.

Spinal Cord Injuries

The spinal cord brings impulses from the brain to the various parts of the body; damage to the cord can cut off those impulses in any areas served by nerves below the damaged section. Therefore, to assess the dysfunctions that result from a spinal cord injury (SCI) (or a spinal tumor), a physician must know exactly where on the spine the injury occurred and how extensively the cord has been damaged. Though some return of sensation and movement can be achieved in many injuries, most people are left with permanent disabilities.

Men are four times more likely than women to experience SCI. If the injury is above the T12 vertebra (see Figure 12.3) and the cord is not completely severed, a man may still be able to have an erection through the body's reflex mechanism, although it may be difficult to maintain as he will not be able to feel skin sensations in the penis. Injuries to the lower part of the spine are more likely to result in erectile difficulties in men, but they are also more likely to preserve some sensation in the genitals. Men without disabilities maintain erections in part through psychic arousal, such as thoughts and feelings and fantasies about the sex act, but with SCI, psychic arousal cannot provide continuing stimulation. Most men with SCI who are capable of having erections are not able to climax or ejaculate, which involves a more complex mechanism than an erection.

Women with SCI remain fertile and can bear children, and so they must continue to use contraception. Although they remain fertile, women with SCI can also lose sensation in the genitals and with it the ability to lubricate during sexual activity. In one survey, 52% were able to achieve an orgasm after SCI, but half said that the orgasm felt different than before (Kettl et al., 1991). Some women (and men) report experiencing "phantom orgasm," a psychic sensation of having an orgasm without the corresponding physical reactions. Also, skin sensation in the areas unaffected by the injury can become greater, and new erogenous zones can appear.* The breasts, for example, may become even more sexually sensitive in women who retain sensation there.

In more extreme cases, SCI can result in total or partial **paraplegia** or total or partial **quadriplegia**. In these cases, the person is rendered extremely dependent on his or her partner or caretaker. Sexual problems develop over time as the full impact of their situation takes effect. While only 9% of SCI patients in one study rated their sexual adjustment as poor upon release from the hospital, two years later the number had risen to 38% (Cole and Cole, 1981). Women in one study rated their bodies as only half as attractive as they were before the injury (Kettl et al., 1991). In addition, the life changes brought on by SCI can be devastating. In a study of twenty-six women with spinal cord

paraplegia: Paralysis of the legs and lower part of the body, affecting both sensation and motor response.

quadriplegia: Paralysis of all four limbs.

---

* Sandowski (1989) tells of a doctor who was embarrassed when a female paraplegic asked him to remove a hand he had casually placed on her shoulder because her shoulders had become sexually sensitive!

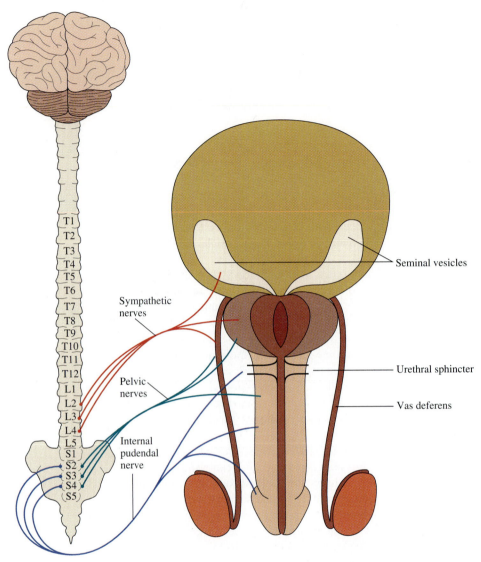

Figure **12.3**
Injury to any of the above areas of the spinal cord can result in impaired sexual functioning.

injuries, fifteen lost their husbands or lovers after the injury, five lost custody of their children, and eight more gave up plans to have children (Bonwich, 1985).

Rehabilitation from SCI is a long, difficult process. Still, with a caring partner, meaningful sexual contact can be achieved. Men incapable of having an erection can still use their mouths and sometimes their hands. If penetration is desired, couples can consider a penile prosthesis or use the technique of "stuffing," where the flaccid penis is pushed into the vagina. Couples must learn to shift the focus of their lovemaking from erections and penetration to other pleasurable and loving contact.

Sexual life after SCI can also be affected by a person's beliefs and fears. In a study of ten paraplegic men in Hong Kong, one had no sex because he believed that semen was manufactured in his spinal cord and that sex would weaken his spine and kill him faster; another believed that his condition could be inherited by his children, and so he would not have sex with his wife in case she accidentally got pregnant and had a paraplegic child (Pearson and Klook, 1989). Most of the men felt that if they could not achieve erection, sex was pointless and incomplete. As one man put it:

> *Without penetration, it seems incomplete and not natural. . . . Sometimes when I fail to have an erection even with manual stimulation from my wife, I would like to masturbate my wife. But usually she would reject me in a laughing manner, saying that it would be useless and lead to nowhere. I think she is right.*
>
> **Quoted in Pearson and Klook (1989:289)**

None of these men received sexual counseling. The situation is slightly better in the United States. In a survey returned by 251 people with SCI, 45% reported receiving sexual education and counseling in their rehabilitation programs. Men were twice as likely to receive the counseling as women. Still, only 48% of those who received the services felt that the services met their needs (Tepper, 1992). There is still a long way to go to insure that SCI patients have the sexual information they need.

SEXUALITY *Today* 12.3

Sexual Implications of Other Disabilities

Disability	Sexual Issues	Contraceptive Issues
Amputation	Masturbation for those with amputations of arms or hands is difficult; some positions may be uncomfortable.	Help with diaphragm insertion or condom wearing necessary if arms or hands are amputated.
Cerebral Palsy	Stimulation and arousal may increase spasms, and spasms or muscle tightness may make certain positions difficult.	Diaphragm or condom may be difficult to use; oral contraceptives unusable if circulation is poor.
Polio	Intercourse in certain positions may be difficult, paralysis and hand limitations may make masturbation difficult, fatigue and lack of energy a problem; respirator can interfere with sexual contact.	Oral contraceptives may be unusable, IUD may lead to increased anemia in women with respiratory difficulties.
Renal Disease (End-Stage)	Intercourse should be planned in high-energy times between dialysis treatments. To lessen feelings of being disabled, sex should take place in a room other than the room with home dialysis equipment. Techniques that minimize problems with male's erectile difficulties or female's problems with lubrication should be used.	Oral contraceptives may be unusable.
Scoliosis (Curvature of the Spine)	Intercourse in certain positions may be difficult.	Pelvic deformity may make diaphragm difficult to insert or fit.

Adapted from Bogle et al. (1980); Schover and Jensen (1988)

AIDS and HIV

In other chapters we discussed the influence that AIDS has had on the sexual behaviors and attitudes of people in the United States. Because the HIV virus is communicable and can be passed to others through sexual activity, millions of Americans have changed their sexual lifestyles to include safer sex practices. But what of those who discover that they are HIV positive or have developed AIDS? How does this knowledge and the disease itself affect their sexual functioning?

As the disease progresses, people who are HIV+ may feel tired, lose their appetite, lose weight, have a fever, diarrhea, night sweats, and swollen glands.* Once opportunistic diseases set in, other symptoms appear, both those specific to the opportunistic disease and others such as pain and dementia. Depression is also common in AIDS sufferers (Noh et al., 1990). As the disease enters its final stages, men often experience erectile difficulties or impotence, and men and women may lose all desire for sexual (although not emotional) contact.

Caught up in the tragedy of their situation, their fear of infecting others, and often their shame, some people cease all sexual activity. Others limit their sexual contact to hugging, kissing, and caressing. However, the existence of the HIV virus in the bloodstream need not mean the end of one's sexual life. HIV+ people need to be careful and considerate with their partners, avoiding exchange of body fluids and keeping clean to avoid accidental infection. However, there is ample opportunity for loving, sexual relations while maintaining safety. Wearing a condom reduces (although it does not eliminate) the risk of sexually transmitting the disease during oral, vaginal, or anal sex (Schover and Jensen, 1988). Mutual massage, mutual masturbation, the use of vibrators or other sex toys, and kissing without the exchange of saliva are all safe practices if care is taken (for example, the ejaculate of an infected partner should not come into contact with skin if the skin has cuts or abrasions) (Sandowski, 1989). Sexuality can be very important to those infected with HIV, for in the midst of the world's fear and rejection, sexuality reaffirms that they are loved, cared for, and accepted by their partners.

Mental Illness and Retardation

People with psychiatric disorders have sexual fantasies, needs, and feelings, and they have the same right to a fulfilling sexual expression as do others. However, historically they have been treated either as asexual, or their sexuality has been viewed as illegitimate, warped, or needing external control (Apfel and Handel, 1993). Yet a sudden or drastic change in sexual habits may be a sign of mental illness or a sign that a mentally ill person is getting worse (or better, depending on the change). Therefore, understanding the sexual problems of the psychiatric patient can be quite complex (Schover and Jensen, 1988).

People with **schizophrenia**, for example, can be among the most impaired and difficult psychiatric patients. **Neuroleptics**, the class of medicines that schizophrenics take, can cause increased or decreased desire for sex; painful enlargement of the breasts, reproductive organs, or testicles; difficulty in achieving or maintaining an erection; delayed or retrograde ejaculation; and changes, including pain, with orgasm. In one study, schizophrenic men on neuroleptics had trouble ejaculating, which may be why

schizophrenia: Any of a group of mental disorders that affects the individual's ability to think, behave, or perceive things normally.

neuroleptics: A class of antipsychotic drugs.

* See Chapter 13.

34% of schizophrenic men in another study reported no sexual activity or feelings at all; 42% had erections only rarely; 32% could not reach orgasm; and only 2% had had sex with a partner in the last year (Schover and Jensen, 1988).

Yet, outside of the effects of neuroleptics, people with schizophrenia have been found to grapple with the same sexual questions and dysfunctions as other people. The same is true of people with **major depression** and other **affective disorders**. They may experience hyposexuality when depressed or hypersexuality in periods of **mania**. Both can also occur as a result of antidepressive medications. Otherwise, their sexual problems do not differ significantly from those of people without major psychiatric problems (Schover and Jensen, 1988).

On the other hand, mental illness is very difficult to live with and can be very trying on a marriage. One man with major depression appreciated how hard it was on his wife:

> *I guess the thing I'm worried about the most is the marriage. Look at it from Sandy's point of view: Here I was, pretty non-functional for four and a half years. She was trying to run the household. She had a baby in the midst of all this. Her mother died in the midst of all this. She had to admit me to the hospital five times. We have a very large house. There's a lot of space that needs to be taken care of. We had financial problems during the whole time. It was just a mess.*

> *Register (1987:134)*

Sexual issues among the mentally ill are neglected in psychiatric training, and physicians who treat the mentally ill have often been more interested in controlling and limiting patients' sexual behaviors than they have been in treating sexual dysfunction. For years, the mentally retarded population has been kept from having sexual relationships, and those who are institutionalized are often discouraged from masturbating. It is as if an otherwise healthy adult is supposed to display no sexual interest or activity at all. Recently, some therapists have begun to design special sexuality education programs for the mentally retarded and developmentally disabled to make sure that they express their sexuality in a socially approved manner (Monat-Haller, 1992). But to deny people with psychiatric problems or retardation the pleasure of a sexual life is cruel and unnecessary.

Many people with mental disabilities (and physical disabilities) must spend long periods of their lives—sometimes their entire lives—in institutions. That makes developing a sex life difficult. Whether people with severe mental illness can consent to mutual sex in an institutional setting is a difficult question (Kaeser, 1992). However, institutions differ greatly in the amount of sexual contact they allow; some allow none whatsoever, while others allow mutually consenting sexual contact, with the staff carefully overseeing the patients' contraceptive and hygienic needs (Trudel and Desjardins, 1992).

One aspect of institutional life involves the sexual exploitation of mentally ill and retarded patients. This is well known by those who work in such institutions, although it is seldom discussed. About half of all women in psychiatric hospitals report having been abused as children or adolescents, and many are then abused in a hospital or other institutional setting. Even outside the hospital system such people are more likely to be victimized, either because the abuser convinces them that it is not abuse or because they are not believed due to their illness or disability. Children who grow up with developmental disabilities are between four and ten times more likely to be abused than children without those difficulties (Baladerian, 1991). Therefore, it is difficult to

major depression: A persistent, chronic state in which the person feels he or she has no worth, cannot function normally, and entertains thoughts of or attempts suicide.

affective disorders: A class of mental disorders that affect mood.

mania: A symptom of mental disorder characterized by excessive activity, feelings of elation, overtalkativeness, and irritability.

separate the sexual problems of retardation, developmental disability, and psychiatric illness from histories of sexual abuse (Apfel and Handel, 1993; Monat-Haller, 1992).

Conclusion

People who are ill or disabled have the same sexual needs and desires as everyone else (see Sexuality Today 12.3 on page 487 for effects of diseases not discussed in the preceding paragraphs). In the past, these needs have too often been neglected, not because the disabled themselves were not interested in sexuality but because physicians and other health care professionals were themselves uncomfortable learning about the sexual needs of the disabled and discussing these needs with their patients. Fortunately, that is beginning to change, and now sexuality counseling is a normal part of the recuperation from many diseases and injuries in many hospitals. It is important for all of us, not just health professionals, to learn that the disabled are just like everybody else and simply desire to be treated like anyone else.

GETTING THE HELP YOU NEED

If you are experiencing problems with sexual functioning, illness, or disability, it is important to seek help as soon as possible. Often, when the problems are ignored, they lead to bigger problems down the road. If you are in college and have a student counseling center available to you, this may be a good place to start looking for help. Request a counselor who has received training in sexuality or ask to be referred to one who has.

Today, many sex therapists are receiving specific training in sexuality. One of the best training organizations in the United States is the *American Association of Sexuality Educators, Counselors, and Therapists* (AASECT) in Chicago, Illinois. This organization offers certification programs in human sexuality for counselors, educators, and therapists and can also provide information on those who are certified as therapists or counselors. To receive information on professionals in your area who are trained in the field of sexuality, call or write AASECT, 435 N. Michigan Avenue, Suite 1717, Chicago, Illinois 60611; (312) 644-0828.

S u m m a r y

- Some studies have found that many happily married couples also experience sexual dysfunction that does not interfere with their marital satisfaction. The most common complaints are insufficient foreplay, lack of enthusiasm for sex, and the inability to relax during sex.
- Sexual dysfunctions are classified as either primary or secondary, and global or situational. These differences may affect treatment strategies. Often therapists first attempt to evaluate what is contributing to the sexual dysfunction and determine whether it is primarily psychogenic or physical.
- Psychological factors can include such things as unconscious fears, ongoing stress, anxiety, depression, guilt, anger, or fear of intimacy, while physical causes include disease, disability, illness, certain medications, and alcohol or drug use.

- Sexual dysfunctions can occur at any stage of the sexual response cycle. Most commonly, they occur during arousal or interfere with orgasm. Pain disorders can also interfere with sexual functioning.
- Arousal disorders include inhibited sexual desire and sexual aversion. A therapist must take into consideration the person's age, years married, socioeconomic class, degree of religiosity, and life circumstances in making these diagnoses. Unlike inhibited sexual desire, a person with sexual aversion may be able to engage in sexual activity even though they may not enjoy it.
- Pain disorders include vaginismus and dyspareunia, which both can interfere with sexual intercourse. Both of these are more common in men and women who have been sexually abused.

- Orgasm disorders include anorgasmia, which is an inability to reach orgasm during sexual stimulation. Anorgasmia can be due to physical and/or psychological factors. Other orgasm disorders include premature ejaculation, retarded ejaculation, and erectile dysfunction.
- Sex therapy is often recommended for the treatment of sexual dysfunctions. Masters and Johnson developed an intensive two-week program involving a male–female sex therapy team. Minor changes to their original program include shorter length of time in therapy, one therapist rather than two, and no travel away from home. Sensate focus exercises are often used in sex therapy to increase sensory awareness and improve communication.
- Sex therapy in the United States has been criticized for its adherence to Western sexual attitudes and values with an almost total ignorance of cultural differences in sexual dysfunction and therapy. It is important to consider the clients' values and to fit the therapy to their values, rather than attempting to teach the client a new set of values.
- Treatment methods vary for the sexual dysfunctions. First, it is important to clarify what is contributing to the sexual difficulties. Often, therapists recommend a complete medical evaluation to ascertain whether or not there are any physical factors that might be contributing.
- Psychological problems are generally treated with psychotherapy, while physical problems may be treated medically. Often, psychological and physical problems overlap, and these problems must each be dealt with.
- Newer treatment options include bibliotherapy, or using books and educational materials, and hypnosis to help reduce sexual problems. Both of these have been found to improve sexual functioning.
- Sexual functioning can also be affected by surgery, illness, or disease. This is why a complete medical screening is necessary before treatment of sexual dysfunction.
- Cardiovascular problems (such as heart disease and strokes), cancer, chronic illness (such as diabetes, multiple sclerosis, muscular dystrophy, alcoholism), spinal cord injuries, mental illness and retardation, and infection with HIV and AIDS all present specific challenges to sexual functioning. People who are ill or disabled have the same sexual needs and desires that healthy people do.
- People who are experiencing sexual dysfunction, illness, disease, or disability should seek treatment as soon as possible in order to avoid the development of further problems.

R eflections on Sexuality

1. What is a sexual dysfunction?
2. Differentiate between arousal, pain, and orgasm disorders. Give an example of each.
3. Differentiate between psychogenic and physiological causes for sexual dysfunction.
4. What is sex therapy? Why has it been criticized for ignoring cultural differences?
5. Give some examples of how sexual dysfunctions are treated outside the United States.
6. Explain the various types of treatment for sexual dysfunctions in the United States.
7. How can psychological factors cause sexual dysfunction in a person with an illness or disease?
8. Explain how cardiovascular problems, cancer, chronic illness, spinal cord injuries, AIDS, and mental illness and retardation can affect sexual functioning.
9. How have the needs and desires of people who are ill or disabled been neglected in the past? What do you think could improve this situation? Why?
10. What are some of the concerns of handicapped individuals in regard to their sexual lives? What problems might they encounter, and what can be done to aid in their enjoyment of a healthy sexual relationship?
11. What are some of the possible solutions to erectile dysfunction in men? What are some of the drawbacks to each of these treatments? How does this dysfunction affect the man's relationship with his partner?

S uggested Readings

BARBACH, L. (1975) *For Yourself: The Fulfillment of Female Sexuality.* New York: Doubleday and Co.

BARBACH, L. (1984) *For Each Other: Sharing Sexual Intimacy.* New York: Signet Publishers.

HEIMAN, J., and J. LO PICCOLO. (1992) *Becoming Orgasmic: A Sexual and Personal Growth Program for Women.* New York: Simon and Schuster.

KAPLAN, H. S. (1987) *The Illustrated Manual of Sex Therapy,* Second Edition. New York: Brunner/Mazel.

KAPLAN, H. S. (1989) *How to Overcome Premature Ejaculation.* New York: Brunner/Mazel.

ZILBERGELD, B. (1992) *The New Male Sexuality.* New York: Bantam Books.

13

Sexually Transmitted Diseases and Acquired Immune Deficiency Syndrome

It had been a fun night. I felt great and knew that I looked good. I went to a party that night, which was something that I don't often do. We were drinking and partying, just having a lot of fun. Soon I was in a deep conversation with Cindy, who I had never been on campus before. We talked and laughed a lot. Finally, we decided to go back to my room. I knew about sexually transmitted diseases, so when things heated up I said "no." I just didn't feel safe having sexual intercourse. However, when she offered to give me a blow job, I agreed. That was the only night I was ever with Cindy. A few weeks later I noticed an open sore on my penis. Several months later, herpes was diagnosed.

Author's files

I had been seeing Brad for about a year; we had been sexually active for half of that time. When it was time for my yearly pelvic exam I went to see my gyne-cologist. She informed me that I had venereal warts. I had not had any symptoms and neither had Brad. We learned that, unfortunately, warts do not always have symptoms. By the time I had discovered them I had probably been infected for a few months.

Author's files

Having AIDS is of course a unique experience for every person who has it. A big part of having AIDS is "change.". . . One of the biggest changes has been the loss of my career goals. My original career goal was to study the develop-ment of sexual orientation and teach at the university level. . . . These career goals (seemed) difficult enough to achieve, since I would have to overcome the discriminatory barriers that a gay man normally faces as a university employee. But at least I saw my goals as possible, however unlikely. Now, since my AIDS diagnosis, those goals seem farther away than ever.

Berg (1988:3)

Years ago, the general public believed that gonorrhea and syphilis were the only sexual-ly transmitted diseases (STDs) in existence, but today there are many "new" STDs such as chlamydia, crabs, herpes, genital warts, and the human immunodeficiency virus (HIV). In the past, people thought that only prostitutes and people who were very sexu-ally active got STDs, while today we know that *all* sexually active people are at risk for contracting a STD, regardless of their level of sexual activity. In fact, one study has esti-mated that the risk of getting a STD each time a person has sexual intercourse is higher than the risk of getting pregnant (Platt et al., 1983).

All states require that syphilis, gonorrhea, and chancroid be reported to public health centers (Hatcher et al., 1994). In addition, many states require reporting cases of chlamydia, genital herpes, genital warts, the human immunodeficiency virus (HIV), and the acquired immune deficiency syndrome (AIDS). Reporting these diseases helps to identify disease trends and communities that may be at high risk. In this chapter we will discuss attitudes, incidence, diagnosis, symptoms, treatment, and prevention of STDs, including AIDS.

SEX TALK

QUESTION **13.1** **How can you know if your partners have any STDs before becoming sexual with them?**

You should ask your partner, prior to any sexual involvement, whether or not he or she has had or currently has a STD. You can also check his or her genitals prior to engaging in sex. Look for open sores on the penis, lips, vulva, or anus. You can also get tested for STDs to determine whether or not you have been exposed. But keep in mind that many STDs do not have any symptoms and that there is no way to know for sure whether or not your partner has a STD; therefore, it is very important to engage only in safer sex behaviors.

ATTITUDES AND SEXUALLY TRANSMITTED DISEASES

The sudden appearance of a new disease has always elicited fear about the nature of its **contagion**. Cultural fears about disease and sexuality in the early twentieth century gave way to many different theories about casual transmission (Brandt, 1985). At the turn of the twentieth century, physicians believed that STDs could be transmitted on pens, pencils, toothbrushes, towels, and bedding. In fact, during World War I, the United States Navy removed doorknobs from its battleships, claiming that they were responsible for spreading infection.

contagion: Disease transmission by direct or indirect contact.

STDs have historically been viewed as symbols of corrupt sexuality (Brandt, 1985). When compared with other diseases such as cancer, attitudes about STDs have been considerably more negative, and many people believe that a person so afflicted "got what they deserved." This has been referred to as the **punishment concept** of disease. In order to acquire a STD, it was generally believed, one must break the silent moral code of sexual responsibility. Those who become ill therefore have done something bad, for which they are being punished.

punishment concept: The idea that people who had become infected with certain diseases, especially STDs, had done something wrong and were being punished.

Kopelman (1988) suggests that this conceptualization has endured because it serves as a defense mechanism. By believing that a person's behavior is responsible for acquiring a STD, we believe ourselves to be safe by not engaging in whatever that behavior is. For example, if we believe that herpes only happens to people who have more than ten sexual partners, we may limit our partners to two or three to feel safe. Whether we *are* safe, of course, depends on whether our beliefs about the causes of transmission are true or not.

SEX TALK

QUESTION **13.2** How did STDs start? I have heard it was from having sex with animals. Is this true?

Everyone has different theories on how STDs started. Some claim that it was a punishment for being sexually active; others thought that it was a result of promiscuity. STDs are caused by bacteria and viruses. When a person comes into contact with these bacteria and viruses, they are at risk of developing a STD. We do not know where these different infectious agents came from, just as we do not know where the common cold virus or the flu originated.

College students often act as if they are invincible; they may believe that although others may get STDs, it will not happen to them. In one study, students were asked if they would refuse to have sex with someone because of the fear of acquiring a STD. Neither males nor females said that the fear of acquiring a STD would be an important

prevalence: The state of widely or commonly occurring or existing.

factor in the decision to be sexually active (Jedlicka and Robinson, 1987). Even the advent of AIDS has had little effect on the incidence of premarital sexual intercourse (Davidson and Moore, 1994). Yet the increasing **prevalence** of STDs *should* be considered when deciding whether to become sexually active.

What are your attitudes about sexually transmitted diseases? In Where Do I Stand? 13.1, we present a test to measure your own beliefs, feelings, and behaviors with respect to STDs.

SEXUALLY TRANSMITTED DISEASES

Approximately 50% of Americans will acquire a STD by the age of thirty-five (Handsfield, 1992). Although the spread of syphilis and genital warts is usually equal between the sexes, women tend to be more susceptible to gonorrhea, chlamydia, and HIV (although the prevalence of HIV was higher in men in the late 1980s, women are still more susceptible if they have sexual intercourse with an infected partner). STDs also tend to strike more young people than old; in fact, approximately two-thirds of all STDs occur in individuals under twenty-five years old (Hatcher et al., 1994).

asymptomatic: Describes diseases that occur without recognizable symptoms.

Studies also indicate that women are at greater risk for long-term complications from STDs because of the fragility of the female reproductive tract. In addition, many more women are **asymptomatic**; therefore, they do not know that they are infected. There are also some racial differences in the incidence of STDs. Syphilis, gonorrhea, chancroid, herpes, hepatitis B, and HIV infections are increasing in young black and Hispanic inner-city populations at a faster rate than in white populations (Kassler and Cates, 1992), in part because minority populations tend to engage in sexual intercourse earlier and engage in more high-risk behaviors, including drug use and unsafe sexual practices.

latency: A period in which a person is infected with a STD but does not test positive for it; the length of latency varies for different diseases.

Some diseases, such as herpes and HIV, also have properties of **latency**. A person can have the virus that causes the disease but be asymptomatic, and sometimes even tests will show up negative. As a result, the person may be unaware that he or she is infecting others.

Contraceptive methods offer varying levels of protection from STDs. In 1993, the Food and Drug Administration approved labeling contraceptives for STD protection. Barrier methods (such as condoms, diaphragms, or contraceptive sponges) and the use of nonoxynol-9 spermicide may also decrease the risk of acquiring a STD. The most effective contraceptive method for reducing the risk of acquiring a STD, however, is the condom used in conjunction with nonoxynol-9 spermicide (see Chapter 11). Even a condom has it limitations; it cannot always protect the vulva or parts of the penis or scrotum that are not covered. Nonoxynol-9 spermicide can kill the organisms that cause gonorrhea, herpes, trichomonasis, syphilis, and AIDS (Hatcher et al., 1994). The IUD offers no protection against STDs; in fact, it increases both the risk of pelvic inflammatory disease (PID) and the transmission of several STDs, including HIV.

The role of oral contraceptives in preventing STDs is complicated. The increased hormones change the cervical mucus and the lining of the uterus, which can help prevent any infectious substance from moving up into the genital tract. In addition, the reduced buildup of the endometrium decreases the possibility of an infectious substance growing (since there is less nutritive material for bacteria to survive). On the other hand, oral contraceptives may also cause the cervix to be more susceptible to infections because of changes in the vaginal environment.

STD Attitude Scale

This scale measures your beliefs, feelings, and behaviors about sexually transmitted diseases. Using the key to the right of each question, mark an X through the letter that best describes how much you agree or disagree with each idea.

SA – strongly agree
A – agree
U – undecided
D – disagree
SD – strongly disagree

1. How one uses his/her sexuality has nothing to do with STDs. SA A U D SD
2. It is easy to use the prevention methods that reduce one's chances of getting STDs. SA A U D SD
3. Responsible sex is one of the best ways of reducing the risk of STDs. SA A U D SD
4. Getting early medical care is the main key to preventing harmful effects of STDs. SA A U D SD
5. Choosing the right sex partner is important in reducing the risk of getting STDs. SA A U D SD
6. A high rate of STDs should be a concern for all people. SA A U D SD
7. People with STDs have a duty to get their sex partners to medical care. SA A U D SD
8. The best way to get a sex partner to STD treatment is to take him/her to the doctor with you. SA A U D SD
9. Changing one's sex habits is necessary once the presence of a STD is known. SA A U D SD
10. I would dislike having to follow the medical steps for treating STDs. SA A U D SD
11. If I were sexually active, I would feel uneasy doing things before and after sex to prevent getting STDs. SA A U D SD
12. If I were sexually active, it would be insulting if a sex partner suggested we use a condom to avoid STDs. SA A U D SD
13. I dislike talking about STDs with my peers. SA A U D SD
14. I would be uncertain about going to the doctor unless I was sure I really had a STD. SA A U D SD
15. I would feel that I should take my sex partner with me to a clinic if I thought I had a STD. SA A U D SD

16. It would be embarrassing to discuss STDs with one's partner if one were sexually active. SA A U D SD
17. If I were to have sex, the chances of getting a STD make me uneasy abouthaving sex with more than one person. SA A U D SD
18. I like the idea of sexual abstinence (not having sex) as the best way of avoiding STDs. SA A U D SD
19. If I had an STD, I would cooperate with public health persons to find the sources of the STD. SA A U D SD
20. If I had a STD, I would avoid exposing others while I was being treated. SA A U D SD
21. I would have regular STD checkups if I were having sex with more than one partner. SA A U D SD
22. I intend to look for STD signs before deciding to have sex with anyone. SA A U D SD
23. I will limit my sex activity to just one partner because of the chances I might get a STD. SA A U D SD
24. I will avoid sex contact anytime I think there is even a slight chance of getting a STD. SA A U D SD
25. The chance of getting a STD would not stop me from having sex. SA A U D SD
26. If I had a chance, I would support community efforts toward controlling STDs. SA A U D SD
27. I would be willing to work with others to make people aware of STD problems in my town. SA A U D SD

SCORING: Items are divided into three different scales. **Belief subscale**: items 1–9; **Feeling subscale**: items 10–18; and **Intention to Act subscale**: items 19–27. Calculate the total points for each subscale and total scale using the following point values. For items 1, 10–14, 16, and 25: strongly agree = 5, agree = 4, undecided = 3, disagree = 2, and strongly disagree = 1. For items 2–9, 15, 17–24, 26, and 27: strongly agree = 1, agree = 2, undecided = 3, disagree = 4, and strongly disagree = 5. High subscale or total scale scores are interpreted as reflecting an attitude that predisposes one to engage in high-risk STD behavior; a lower score predisposes the person toward low-risk STD behavior.

Yarber et al. (1988)

SEX TALK

QUESTION **13.3 Can STDs be transmitted through oral sex?**

If there are open sores on the penis or vulva, it is possible that a STD may be transmitted to the mouth through oral sex. If there are active cold sores on the mouth or lips and a person performs oral sex, it is possible to transmit the virus to the genitals. Oral sex with a partner infected with gonorrhea or chlamydia may cause an infection in the throat, which can also be transmitted (Schwebke, 1991). As for the AIDS virus, some researchers have found that oral sex is an unlikely method of transmission for the virus (Mayer and DeGruttola, 1987); however, other studies indicate that there is a slight risk of infection during oral sex (Kassler and Cates, 1992).

STDs can be caused by several different agents. Some are caused by bacterial infection, while others are caused by viral infection. The causal agents are important in treating STDs. Overall, persons with multiple sexual partners over a short period of time are at higher risk for bacterial STDs, while those with multiple sexual partners during their lifetime are at greater risk for viral STDs (see Figure 13.1). We will discuss bacterial STDs first and then move on to viral STDs.

Lifetime Rates of Sexually Transmitted Infections by Number of Partners and Gender

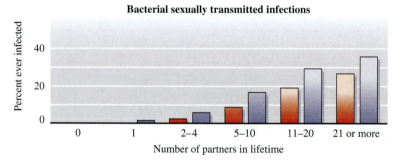

Note: Bacterial STIs include gonorrhea, chlamydia, syphilis, NGU, and PID.

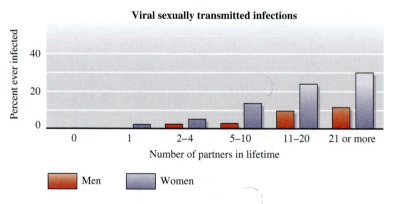

Note: Viral STIs include genital warts, genital herpes, hepatitis B, and HIV/AIDS

F i g u r e **13.1**
Above are the lifetime rates of STD infection, by the number of partners and gender. Notice how STD infection increases as the number of partners increases. **From Michaels et al. (1994:193)**

Gonorrhea

Gonorrhea (the "clap" or "drip") is caused by the bacterium *Neisseria gonorrhoeae,* which can survive only in the mucus membranes of the body. These areas, such as the vagina, penis, mouth, throat, rectum, urethra, and even the eyes, provide moisture and warmth that help the bacterium survive. *Neisseria gonorrhoeae* is actually very fragile and can be destroyed by exposure to light, air, soap, water, or a change in temperature, and so it is nearly impossible to transmit gonorrhea nonsexually. The only exception to this is the baby who is born to an infected mother.

Transmission of gonorrhea occurs when mucus membranes come into contact with each other. One study estimates that if an infected man has sexual intercourse with an uninfected woman, he will transmit the disease to her two-thirds of the time (Platt et al., 1983), while an infected woman transmits the disease to her uninfected partner only one-third of the time (Hooper et al., 1978).

gonorrhea: A STD that is caused by an infection with *Neisseria gonorrhoeae;* symptoms in men include a puslike discharge and frequent urination; many women are asymptomatic; if left untreated, gonorrhea can lead to serious complications.

Incidence

In 1992, approximately 700,000 cases of gonorrhea were reported in the United States (Hatcher et al., 1994). This made gonorrhea the most commonly reported **communicable disease**. Rates of gonorrhea had declined in the 1970s and early 1980s but began to rise again in the mid-1980s in certain sections of the population (Schwebke, 1991). Overall, gonorrhea rates have been declining in the United States but have increased in minority and lower socioeconomic groups. One study indicates that young African-American women are at highest risk of acquiring gonorrhea (Handsfield et al., 1989). Sexually active persons under the age of twenty-five account for two-thirds of the reported cases of gonorrhea (Cates, 1990; Adler, 1990). The incidence of gonorrhea in some studies has been found to be associated with prostitution and drug use.

communicable diseases: Diseases that can be transmitted from one person to another.

Symptoms

The majority of women who are infected with gonorrhea are asymptomatic and do not know that they are carrying the disease; however, they are still able to infect their partners. The bacteria enters the small tears and cracks in the skin. In women, the cervix is the most common site of infection, and a pus-filled cervical discharge may develop. If there are any symptoms, they develop within three to five days and include an increase in urinary frequency, abnormal uterine bleeding, and bleeding after sexual intercourse, which results from an irritation of the cervix. The cervical discharge also irritates the vaginal lining, causing pain and discomfort and eventually causing the vagina to fuse together. Urination is difficult and painful. If left untreated, gonorrhea can move up into the cervix, uterus, and Fallopian tubes, and it can cause PID. In fact, gonorrhea has been found to cause approximately 40% of the cases of PID (Hatcher et al., 1994). We will discuss PID later in this chapter.

Seventy-five percent of men who are infected with gonorrhea are symptomatic and experience urethral discharge, painful urination, and an increase in the frequency and urgency of urination (Hatcher et al., 1994). Symptoms usually appear between two and six days after infection. However, 25% of men with gonorrhea are asymptomatic, although they are able to transmit the disease.

If a person has engaged in anal sexual intercourse, rectal gonorrhea (in both men and women) may cause bloody stools and a puslike discharge. Another potentially serious complication of infection with gonorrhea is blood poisoning. Gonorrhea can move

Seventy-five percent of men infected with gonorrhea are symptomatic and experience urethral discharge and painful urination.

throughout the body and settle in various areas, including the joints, causing swelling, pain, and pus-filled infections. A person who is infected with gonorrhea should also be checked for other STDs because it is not unusual for a person infected with gonorrhea to be infected with other STDs such as chlamydia, syphilis, and/or HIV.

SEX TALK

QUESTION **13.4** What STDs do gynecologists check for during a regular exam?

> During a yearly visit, health-care providers perform a Pap smear. It is possible that some of the STDs, such as cervical warts and herpes, may show up on the Pap smear. However, if you think that you may have been exposed to any STDs, it is important for you to ask your health-care provider to perform specific tests to screen for these. Specific tests can be run for syphilis, gonorrhea, chlamydia, herpes, genital warts, or HIV.

Diagnosis

gonococcus bacterium: The bacterium that causes gonorrhea (*Neisseria gonorrhoeae*).

Testing for gonorrhea involves collecting a sample of the discharge from the cervix, urethra, or another infected area with a cotton swab. The discharge is incubated to allow the bacteria to multiply. It is then put on a slide and examined under a microscope for the presence of the **gonococcus bacterium**.

Treatment

Gonorrhea can be treated effectively with antibiotics. Antibiotics are usually administered orally, but in severe cases intramuscular injections may be necessary. However, some strains have become resistant to certain antibiotics (Schwebke, 1991), and so it is important that a person be reexamined one week after treatment to make sure that the antibiotic is effective and that the patient takes the whole course of the prescribed antibiotic. If the antibiotic works, the person will become free from the infection.

Syphilis

syphilis: A STD that is caused by an infection with *Treponema pallidum;* syphilis is divided into primary, secondary, and tertiary stages.

Syphilis is caused by an infection with the bacterium *Treponema pallidum*. Like *Neisseria gonorrhoeae,* these bacteria can only live in the mucus membranes of the body. The bacteria enter the body through small tears in the skin and are able to replicate themselves. Syphilis is transmitted during sexual contact, and it usually first infects the cervix, penis, anus, lips, or nipples. It has been estimated that there is a 30% chance of acquiring syphilis from an infected partner during one sexual interaction (Wendel, 1989). Syphilis may also be transmitted from an infected mother to her baby during delivery.

Incidence

Each year, there are 40,000 cases of syphilis in the United States (Hatcher et al., 1994). In the United States, the incidence of syphilis rose in late 1970s and early 1980s and was highest among homosexual and bisexual men. From 1982 to 1985, the incidence began to decrease, probably as a result of safer sex practices in homosexuals as a result of the

AIDS crisis. The incidence of syphilis began to rise again in the heterosexual community in 1985; in fact, from 1985 to 1990, the incidence of the disease increased 75% (Hook and Marra, 1992).

Syphilis rates differ geographically, with lower rates in the Midwest and higher rates in the South, although this may be due to differing racial compositions; rates are highest in minority groups. In Philadelphia alone, the incidence of syphilis from 1985 to 1989 increased 551% (Schwebke, 1991). Syphilis rates may be increasing because of its association with HIV; many of those infected with HIV are also infected with syphilis. There has also been an increase in the incidence of syphilis in populations of crack cocaine users, especially in groups that trade crack for sex.

chancre: A small, red-brown sore that results from syphilis infection; the sore is actually the site in which the bacteria entered the body.

Symptoms

Infection with syphilis is divided into three stages. The first stage of infection, primary or early syphilis, occurs approximately ten to ninety days after infection. During this stage there may be one or more small, red-brown sores, called chancres that appear on the vulva, penis, vagina, cervix, anus, mouth, or lips. The chancre, which is a round sore with a hard raised edge and a sunken center, is usually painless and does not itch. If left untreated, the chancre will heal in three to eight weeks. However, during this time the person can still transmit the disease to other sexual partners.

Once the chancre disappears, the infected person enters into the second stage, secondary syphilis, which begins anywhere from one week to six months after infection, with the average being approximately six weeks (Wendel, 1989). During this stage, the syphilis invades the central nervous system. The infected person develops reddish patches on the skin that looks like a rash or hives (see photo on page 502). Generally these patches do not itch. The patches or sores sometimes ooze a clear liquid, which is highly infectious. If the rash develops on the scalp, hair loss can also occur. The lymph glands in the groin, armpit, neck, or other areas enlarge and become tender. Additional symptoms at this stage include headaches, fevers, anorexia, flulike symptoms, and fatigue.

In the third and final stage of the disease, tertiary or late syphilis, the disease goes into remission. The rash, fever, and other symptoms go away and the person usually feels fine. They are still able to transmit the disease for about one year, but after this time they are no longer infectious. Left untreated, however, tertiary or late syphilis can cause neurological, sensory, muscular, and psychological difficulties and is eventually fatal. Syphilis causes more severe symptoms and progresses much more quickly in patients who have been diagnosed with the HIV virus (Gregory et al., 1990). A pregnant woman who is infected with syphilis can transmit the disease to her developing child, and this is called congenital syphilis.

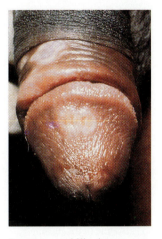

In men, a syphilis chancre can appear on the penis, anus, mouth, or lips.

Diagnosis

Anyone who develops a chancre should immediately go to a health-care provider to be tested for the presence of the syphilis-causing bacteria. This diagnosis can be made in several ways. A culture can be taken from one of the lesions and microscopically examined. When magnified, it is possible to detect spirochetes. Blood tests can also be used to diagnose syphilis. These tests check for the presence of antibodies, which develop once a person is infected with the bacteria. Test results usually indicate syphilis within one to three weeks after infection (Lowhagen, 1990). However, it has been estimated that up to 30% of patients with primary syphilis test negative, although it is unclear why

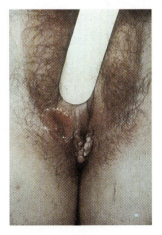

In women, a syphilis chancre can appear on the vulva, vagina, cervix, anus, mouth, or lips.

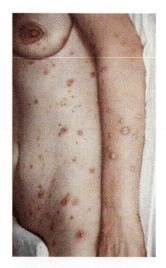

During secondary syphilis, a rash may develop on the body. In addition, headaches, fevers, and other flulike symptoms may develop.

chlamydia: A STD that is caused by an infection with *Chlamydia trachomatis;* although often asymptomatic, it is also one of the most damaging of all the STDs.

nongonococcal urethritis (NGU): Urethral infections in men that are usually caused by an infection with chlamydia.

(Handsfield, 1992). During late syphilis, blood tests may be negative or weakly positive even if the infection exists (Lowhagen, 1990). If a person thinks that he or she may have been exposed to syphilis but tests negative, he or she should engage only in safer sex activity and consult with his or her health-care provider immediately.

Treatment

Although there have been several different treatments for syphilis over the years, antibiotics are the treatment of choice today. They may cause a temporary increase in fever or symptoms, which subside in a few hours. Follow-up examinations are necessary to make sure that the disease has been successfully treated. Many physicians today recommend HIV tests and counseling for patients who have syphilis.

Chlamydia and Nongonococcal Urethritis

Chlamydia is the common name for infections caused by a bacterium called *Chlamydia trachomatis*. Risk factors for chlamydia are similar to those for other STDs and include multiple sexual partners, a partner who has had multiple sexual partners, being below the age of twenty-five years, the lack of consistent use of barrier contraceptives (such as condoms), and a history of STDs.

The bacterium that causes chlamydia can also cause **nongonococcal urethritis (NGU)** in men. In fact, chlamydia has been found to cause 50% of all cases of NGU (Kassler and Cates, 1992). NGU may also be caused by the trichomonas or herpes organism; however, 40% of the cases of NGU seem to have no direct cause (Baldassare, 1991).

Incidence

Chlamydia infection is the most common bacterially induced STD in the United States, and the leading cause of infertility (Hatcher et al., 1994). Chlamydia infects approximately one in seven adolescent females and one in ten adolescent males (Hersch, 1991), resulting in approximately four million cases per year in the United States. However, it is impossible to know the exact number since reporting is not mandatory. Chlamydia is most common in heterosexual populations, but it also occurs in lesbian women (Freund, 1992). On college campuses, rates of chlamydia infection range from 5% to 20% (Estrin and Do, 1988).

Symptoms

In approximately 75% of women and 25% of men, chlamydia is asymptomatic (Kassler and Cates, 1992). If there are symptoms, they will usually begin within seven to twenty-one days and can include an unusual vaginal discharge, burning during urination, pain during sexual intercourse, and pain in the lower abdomen. Chlamydia increases a woman's chance of developing PID, which can cause sterility or even death. Although chlamydia does not often produce symptoms, it is very contagious, which is why its incidence is increasing. Chlamydia can affect the cervix, urethra, rectum, or throat, and it often occurs with other STDs. In fact, coinfection with gonorrhea has been found in 30% to 50% of all cases of chlamydia (Freund, 1992).

In most women, the cervix is the site of infection with chlamydia, and so cervical bleeding or spotting may occur. Vaginal discharge, however, is rare and is more likely an indication of another STD (Freund, 1992). Men who are infected with chlamydia can experience **epididymitis** (infection of the epididymis), which can be treated with antibiotics (Baldassarre, 1991).

epididymitis: An inflammation of the epididymis in men, usually resulting from STDs.

In approximately 40% of cervical cases of chlamydia, the bacteria moves into the uterus, even if the infected woman has no symptoms (Krogh, 1990). From the uterus, the bacteria can spread to the Fallopian tubes and ovaries, leading to PID. In fact, infection with chlamydia is thought to be one of the agents most responsible for the development of PID (Krogh, 1990). Women who are infected with cervical chlamydia, and who undergo an elective (or possibly spontaneous) abortion or vaginal birth, are also at increased risk of developing PID (McGregor, 1989). All women who undergo childbirth or an abortion should be screened for chlamydia prior to these operations. During childbirth, an infected woman can infect her child, although the risk is lower if a woman has a cesarean section delivery.

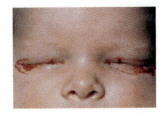

This newborn baby has neonatal chlamydial conjunctivitis, which was transmitted during pregnancy. A blood-stained discharge oozes from the swollen eyes.

Diagnosis

Since chlamydia testing is not routine, women who have had unprotected sexual intercourse with several partners should ask their health-care provider to perform chlamydia tests during their yearly physical examinations, even if they are asymptomatic. A health-care provider will culture the cervical discharge and examine the cells microscopically, or use a blood test. Blood tests are easier, more reliable, less expensive, and offer quicker results (Freund, 1992). Urine tests are available to screen for chlamydia in men. Over the past few years, there has been a call for a nationwide screening program for chlamydia to help curb the growing prevalence. In 1994, the Rockefeller Foundation announced a $1 million prize for the development of an easy, low-cost, diagnostic test for chlamydia and gonorrhea (*Los Angeles Times,* 1994).

Treatment

Antibiotics have been used to treat chlamydia, but like gonorrhea, chlamydia has become highly resistant. Antibiotics are usually taken for at least seven to ten days, depending on the severity of the infection. An infected person's sexual partners over the three months prior to the diagnosis should be referred to a health-care provider for treatment, whether or not they are experiencing symptoms. This is necessary to avoid reinfection, further complications, and the spread of chlamydia to others (McGregor, 1989). Follow-up examinations should be performed to ensure that the bacteria is no longer present.

Pubic Lice

Pubic lice (or "crabs") are very small, wingless insects that can attach themselves to pubic hair with their claws. They feed off the tiny blood vessels just beneath the skin and are often difficult to detect on light-skinned people. Under closer observation, it is possible to see the movement of their legs. They may also attach themselves to other hairy parts of the body, although they tend to prefer pubic hair. When not attached to the human body, pubic lice cannot survive more than twenty-four hours. However, they reproduce rapidly and the female cements her eggs to the sides of pubic hair. The eggs hatch in seven to nine days, and the newly hatched nits (baby pubic lice) reproduce within seventeen days.

pubic lice: Parasites that primarily infest the pubic hair and can be transmitted through sexual contact; also called crabs.

Pubic lice attach to pubic hair and feed off the tiny blood vessels beneath the skin.

SEX TALK

QUESTION **13.5** **Can crabs be spread through casual contact, such as sleeping on the same sheets or sharing clothes? What if someone with crabs sat on my couch and I sat down right after them?**

If a person who was infected with crabs sat down on your couch without clothes on and you sat down directly after them without clothes on yourself, there is a chance that you could get crabs. Although crabs are usually spread through sexual contact, it is possible to acquire them if you share towels, linens, articles of clothing, combs and brushes, or toilet seats with a person who is infected. They can also be transferred while sharing a bed even if there is no sexual contact.

Symptoms

The most common symptom is a mild to unbearable itching, which often increases during the evening hours. This itching is thought to be a result of an allergic reaction to the saliva that the lice secrete during their feeding. People who are not allergic to this saliva may not experience any itching.

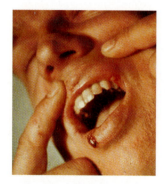

HSV-1 infection often causes blisters on the lips or mouth.

herpes: A highly contagious viral infection that causes eruptions of the skin or mucous membranes.

herpes simplex virus (HSV): The virus that causes herpes.

herpes simplex I (HSV-1): A viral infection that causes cold sores on the face and lips.

herpes simplex II (HSV-2): A viral infection that is sexually transmitted and causes genital ulcerations.

Diagnosis

The itching usually forces a person to seek treatment, though some people detect the lice visually first. Diagnosis is usually made fairly quickly since the pubic lice and eggs can be seen with the naked eye.

Treatment

To treat pubic lice, it is necessary to kill both the insects and their eggs. In addition, the eggs must be destroyed on sheets and clothing. Health care providers can prescribe *Kwell* ointment, which comes in a shampoo or cream. The cream must be applied directly to the pubic hair and left on for approximately twelve hours, while the shampoo can be applied and directly rinsed off. There are also some fairly effective over-the-counter products that can be purchased in drugstores; however, these products are usually not as effective as *Kwell*. Some people attempt more extreme treatment such as dousing the pubic hair in alcohol or shaving the genital area. These practices should be avoided because they may cause further irritation of the area and could possibly cause infection. Sheets and all articles of clothing should either be dry cleaned, boiled, or machine washed in very hot water. As with the other STDs, it is important to tell all sexual partners to be checked for lice since they are highly contagious.

Herpes

Herpes (herpes simplex, herpes genitalis) is caused by an infection with the **herpes simplex virus (HSV)**. Once people acquire the virus, they have it for the rest of their lives. The virus can infect the mouth and face (**herpes simplex I** or **HSV-1**), or the genitals (**herpes simplex II** or **HSV-2**), where they cause sores to appear.

HSV-2 can be transmitted during sexual intercourse or to the genitals during oral sex if either partner has HSV-1, although genital herpes is usually caused by HSV-2. After a certain length of time, the virus will seem to disappear, although this does not mean that it is gone. HSV can lie dormant in the body so that even if an infected person does not have symptoms, he or she may be able to transmit the virus to another person.

It is possible for people who are infected with HSV to reinfect themselves on another part of their body. For instance, if someone with HSV-1 touches an open lesion, and then rubs another part of his or her body, he or she may **autoinoculate** themselves. He or she could also transmit HSV to his or her partner's genitals in this manner.

autoinoculate: To cause a secondary infection in the body from an already existing infection.

Incidence

The U.S. Centers for Disease Control estimate that there are between 200,000 and 500,000 new cases of herpes each year (Adler, 1990). It is estimated that anywhere from twenty to thirty million people in the United States are infected with HSV (Kassler and Cates, 1992).

prodromal phase: The tingling or burning feeling in the genitals that precedes the development of herpes blisters.

Symptoms

The first symptoms of herpes usually appear within six days of infection, but they can appear anywhere from one to twenty-six days later. The first occurrence of HSV sores is generally the most painful, and women tend to have more severe symptoms with HSV-2 than men. At the onset, there is usually a tingling or burning feeling in the affected area, which can grow into an itching and a red, swollen appearance of the genitals (this period is often referred to as the **prodromal phase**). The sores usually last anywhere from three to six weeks, and the amount of pain they cause can range from mild to severe. Depending on the amount of pain, urination may be difficult. Small blisters may appear externally on the vagina or penis. The blisters, which are usually red and sometimes have a grayish center, will eventually burst and ooze a yellowish discharge. As they begin to heal, a scab will form over them. Other symptoms of HSV include a fever, headaches, pain, itching, vaginal or urethral discharge, and general fatigue. These symptoms peak within four days of the appearance of the blisters. A few patients with severe symptoms require hospitalization.

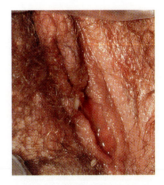

In women, HSV-2 infection can cause blisters on the vulva, vagina, or any place where the virus entered the body.

SEX TALK

QUESTION **13.6** Because herpes is not curable, when people are in their "down time" between flare-ups, can they still transmit it?

Although many people believe that the herpes virus cannot be transmitted if there are no active lesions, there is now evidence that it can be transmitted even in the absence of active lesions. In one study, couples with one partner having herpes were told to abstain from sexual intercourse while the herpes lesions were active; yet at the end of the study period, 10% had transmitted the virus during nonactive lesion times (*Health Magazine,* 1992a). People infected with the HSV-2 should always use condoms so that they do not infect their partners. Transmission from men to women is easier because the lining of the vagina is less durable than the skin covering the penis.

The frequency and severity of recurrent episodes of herpes depends on several things, including the amount of infectious agent, the severity of the infection, the type of

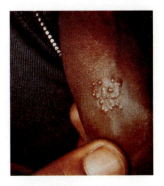

In men, HSV-2 infection can cause blisters on the penis or any place where the virus entered the body.

herpes, and the timing of treatment (Kroon, 1990). If treatment is begun within four days of initial symptoms, recurrence rates may decrease. Fifty-five percent of HSV-1 patients and 88% of HSV-2 patients experience a recurrent episode, usually less than a month later, with HSV-2 recurrence being more frequent. In recurrent episodes, women experience more and longer lasting pain than men (Corey et al., 1983).

Psychological reactions to herpes outbreaks can include anxiety, guilt, anger, frustration, helplessness, a decrease in self-esteem, and depression (Aral et al., 1988). Persons with supportive partners and social relationships tend to do better psychologically. In addition, those who receive psychological support services experience a greater reduction in recurrent episodes of herpes and an improvement in their emotional health (Longo et al., 1988). Physical and emotional stress may increase the likelihood of recurrent episodes. People who have been infected with the herpes virus are advised to get plenty of sleep, to eat and exercise properly, to reduce alcohol intake and cigarette smoking, and to reduce stress.

Recent research reveals that people who are infected with HSV-2 are at greater risk for acquiring HIV if they engage in unprotected sexual intercourse because the herpes blisters facilitate the transmission of HIV. Women who are infected with the herpes virus have also been found to be more likely to develop cervical cancer and pregnancy complications later on. If a woman is experiencing active lesions at the time of delivery, a health-care provider will usually perform a cesarean delivery, for it is possible to infect a child during childbirth (Kroon, 1990). The herpes virus can also cause fetal death.

Diagnosis

The presence of blisters caused by the herpes virus is often enough to diagnose the disease. Like gonorrhea, herpes is often accompanied by other STDs, and tests must be performed to rule out other infections. Pap smears from routine gynecological visits can show changes in the cell structure, which indicate infection with the herpes virus. No tests for the detection of HSV-1 or HSV-2 are 100% accurate (Kroon, 1990) because tests depend on the amount of infectious agent and the stage of the disease. Even blood tests are unreliable for distinguishing between different strains of the virus (Handsfield, 1992). Newer, more reliable tests have been developed that offer some promise, but as of 1995, these are still in the research stage.

Treatment

There is no cure for infection with the herpes virus. Once infected, a person will always carry the virus in his or her body. Medications may only help to reduce the severity and frequency of the herpes outbreaks. Some patients can benefit from applying topical **acyclovir** cream, while those with more severe symptoms can be treated with daily doses of oral acyclovir (Kroon, 1990). In mid-1994, the manufacturers of acyclovir sought FDA approval to sell the drug over the counter as a nonprescription drug; however, this had not been approved by early 1995.

acyclovir: A topical ointment used to reduce the pain and swelling of the herpes blisters.

Natural remedies for herpes outbreaks include applying an ice pack to the affected area during the prodromal phase and applying cooling or drying agents such as witch hazel. Increasing intake of foods rich in certain amino acids, such as L-lysine, which includes fish or yogurt, and decreasing the intake of sugar and nuts (which are high in arginine) may also help reduce recurrences (Vukovic, 1992). Lysine can also be purchased from the vitamin section of any drugstore.

Genital Warts

Genital warts (condyloma acuminata, venereal warts), which are similar to warts that appear on other parts of the body, are caused by the human papilloma virus (HPV). HPV can be transmitted through sexual intercourse, oral sex, or anal sex. It is more common in people with other STDs and also in women who use birth control pills.

genital warts: Wartlike growths on the genitals; also called venereal warts, condylomata, or papilloma.

Incidence

In the United States, HPV is the most common symptomatic viral STD (Koutsky et al., 1988). It is estimated that three million HPV cases are diagnosed each year in the United States (Hatcher et al., 1994). The incidence of HPV in sexually active populations probably ranges between 5% and 30% and is higher in adolescents and young adults (Krilov, 1991). Genital warts may be the most common STD in college-age populations (Sawyer and Moss, 1993). In one study, 46% of college women examined were found to be infected with HPV (Bauer et al., 1991). Seventy percent of women who attended one STD clinic and 20% of women who attended a family planning clinic were found to be infected with HPV (Handsfield, 1992).

Symptoms

Many people who are infected with HPV are asymptomatic, while others develop genital warts as late as six weeks to nine months after infection (Lilley and Schaffer, 1990). Warts are usually flesh-colored and may have a bumpy type surface (see the photos on this page). Warts develop in women on the vagina, vulva, or cervix, and in men on the penile shaft, head, scrotum, and rarely, the urethra (Krilov, 1991). Warts can also appear on the anus. In some areas, warts may grow together and have a cauliflowerlike appearance. These lesions are generally asymptomatic, and so people do not notice them and thus unknowingly infect other sexual partners. There can also be a foul-smelling discharge, which may cause some itching and pain. Children who are infected with HPV at birth are at risk of developing viral growths in the respiratory tract, which can cause respiratory distress and hoarseness (Fletcher, 1991). Because of the contagious nature of genital warts, approximately 65% of sexual partners of people with cervical warts develop warts within three to four months of contact (Krilov, 1991).

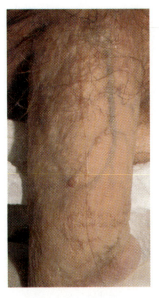

Genital warts on the penis.

Diagnosis

In some instances health-care providers can identify genital warts during a woman's routine pelvic exam. Ten to twenty percent of the time, Pap smears reveal the presence of HPV (Kassler and Cates, 1992). Other times, a *ViraPap* test must be performed to identify presence of the virus. To magnify the cervical cells, a health-care provider may use magnified examination known as colposcopy, and he or she may also soak the infected area with acetic acid (white vinegar) to aid in detection. Since warts can grow and multiply, it is important to seek treatment immediately. Using condoms and avoiding multiple sexual partners can reduce the chances of acquiring genital warts.

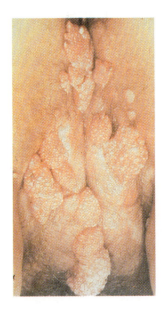

Genital warts on the labia.

Treatment

Genital warts can be treated in several ways. Treatment alternatives include using podophyllin (an acidic solution), freezing the warts with liquid nitrogen, using a burning needle to burn the warts, using high-intensity lasers to destroy the warts, and/or using a topical solution to burn the skin and destroy the warts. Podophyllin is a popular treatment if the warts are on either the penis or vagina. It may be necessary to try several treatment methods, and repeat applications are common. Genital warts frequently reoccur after treatment due to the residual virus in the body (Krilov, 1991).

To decrease transmission of HPV to a sexual partner, an infected person should use condoms and nonoxynol-9 spermicide during sexual intercourse for at least six months following treatment (Lilley and Schaffer, 1990); it may be prudent to use condoms long-term because it is possible to transmit the virus even when no lesions are present.

Research indicates that there may be a link between genital warts and cervical and vaginal cancer (Bauer et al., 1991). Women who have been diagnosed with genital warts are encouraged to have pelvic exams and Pap smears at least once a year. Some studies indicate that folic acid (vitamin B) may help to keep HPV in check in women who have been diagnosed with genital warts (*Health Magazine*, 1992b). It is not known exactly how folic acid may help reduce the effects of HPV, but it is thought that it helps to strengthen the cervical cells. Folic acid can be found in green leafy vegetables, yeast breads, and liver.

Vaginal Infections

trichomoniasis: A vaginal infection caused by the protozoan called *Trichomonas vaginalis,* which may result in discomfort, discharge, and inflammation.

There are several common vaginal infections that may also be associated with sexual intercourse, including **trichomoniasis**, **hemophilus**, **nonspecific vaginitis**, and **yeast infections**. All of these may cause a vaginal discharge.

Trichomoniasis (also called trich or TV) is a form of vaginitis that is caused by *Trichomonas vaginalis*. The organism is acquired through sexual intercourse, and symptoms usually appear anywhere from three to twenty-eight days after infection. The most common symptom for women is an increase in vaginal discharge, which may be yellowish or green-yellow in color, frothy, and foul-smelling; it may cause a burning or itching sensation in the vagina. In men, trichomoniasis infection is often asymptomatic, although there may be a slight increase in burning on the tip of the penis. The most common treatment for trichomoniasis is metronidazole *(Flagyl),* which can cause side effects such as nausea, headaches, loss of appetite, diarrhea, cramping, and a metallic taste in the mouth. Anyone taking this medication should not drink alcohol until twenty-four hours after treatment.

hemophilus: A vaginal infection caused by the organism *Hemophilus vaginalis;* often this infection is asymptomatic.

Hemophilus is caused by the organism *Hemophilus vaginalis,* which lives in moist places like the vagina. Although the majority of women are asymptomatic, some may experience a vaginal discharge, which is thin and gray in color and tends to have a foul smell. It is common for hemophilus to occur along with trichomoniasis and other vaginal infections. Treatment includes oral antibiotics or vaginal suppositories. Nonspecific vaginitis is another vaginal infection that is caused by the *Hemophilus* bacteria. The symptoms are similar to other infections and include an increase in vaginal discharge, soreness, itching, and burning; the treatment also consists of antibiotics.

nonspecific vaginitis: A vaginal infection caused by the bacteria hemophilus; symptoms may include an increase in vaginal discharge, soreness, and itching.

yeast infections: Vaginal infections caused by the fungus *Candida albicans,* which is often sexually transmitted.

Yeast infections (also called moniliasis or candidiasis) can be very troubling to women, especially those who are prone to them. Yeast infections are difficult to get rid of, and it is common to have several recurrences. The infections are caused by a fungus called *Candida albicans*. This fungus is normally present in the vagina, but it multiplies when the pH balance of the vagina is disturbed because of antibiotics, regular douching, pregnancy, oral contraceptive use, diabetes, or careless wiping after defecation (yeast is present in fecal material, and so it is important to make sure it does not come into contact with the vagina). Yeast infections can also be transmitted from a man to a woman (or vice versa) during sexual intercourse.

A yeast infection often causes heavy discharge that is white, thin, watery, can include thick white chunks, and has a foul-smelling odor. Additional symptoms include burning, itching, increased urination, and some pain. Treatment includes either an anti-fungal prescription or over-the-counter drugs (such as Monistat, Gyne-Lotrim, or Mycelex), which are applied topically on the vulva and are inserted into the vagina. Plain yogurt can provide relief to women suffering from a yeast infection. The yogurt can be applied to the outside of the vulva, and a tampon can be dipped into the yogurt and inserted into the vagina. Eating one cup of yogurt daily can also sometimes reduce recurrences. *Lactobacillus,* a type of bacteria found in the vagina of healthy women, is also present in yogurt and can help the vagina to produce more of it.

Lactobacillus: Bacteria in the vagina that help maintain appropriate pH levels.

Men are less likely to have problems with yeast infections because the penis does not provide the warm and moist environment that the vagina does. However, if a woman has recurrent yeast infections, her health-care provider may recommend that her partner come in to be checked for candidae.

Other STDs

Hepatitis

Hepatitis is caused by an infection with the hepatitis B virus (HBV). There are 150,000 new cases of HBV each year in the United States (Hatcher et al., 1994). Between 5% and 20% of the general public has been infected with the hepatitis B virus, although heterosexual intercourse has become the predominant mode of HBV transmission (Alter et al., 1990). Most of the time, infection with HBV is asymptomatic. If there are symptoms, they may include nausea, vomiting, jaundice, headaches, fever, a darkening of the urine, moderate liver enlargement, and fatigue. Long-term risks of hepatitis infection include chronic hepatitis, liver disease, kidney failure, and possible death. Blood tests are used to identify HBV infection. HBV is the only STD for which a vaccine is available (Hatcher et al., 1994).

Chancroid

Although a **chancroid** may look similar to a syphilis chancre, the difference lies in its soft edges compared with the hard edges of a syphilis sore. Chancroids are transmitted sexually through the *Hemophilus ducreyi* bacteria. The incidence of chancroid is on the rise in the United States. Diagnosis is often difficult, and a result of ruling out other STDs. Women are often asymptomatic. In men, a small lesion or several lesions appear on the penis that develop into painful ulcers. The infection may spread to the lymph nodes of the groin, which can cause swelling and pain.

chancroid: A bacterial STD that is characterized by small bumps that eventually rupture and form painful ulcers.

Chancroids are treated with antibiotics. Counseling about HIV and testing are often recommended because chancroids tend to increase the risk of acquiring HIV. Regular follow-ups are advisable until the ulcer is completely healed. All recent sexual contacts should be contacted for testing and treatment.

PELVIC INFLAMMATORY DISEASE

Pelvic inflammatory disease is an infection of the endometrium, Fallopian tubes, and the lining of the pelvic area. It can be caused by many different agents, but the two that have been most often implicated are *Chlamydia trachomatis* and *Neisseria gonorrhoeae.*

Approximately 40% of cases of PID have been found to be caused by infection with chlamydia. Long-term complications include ectopic and tubal pregnancies, chronic pelvic pain, and infertility. Between 100,000 and 150,000 women who have PID become infertile each year (Kassler and Cates, 1992), which means that approximately 10% to 20% of initial episodes of PID result in infertility (Handsfield, 1992).

In the United States, it has been estimated that there are one million cases of PID each year, and one out of every seven women of reproductive age are found to have at least one episode of PID by the age of thirty-five (Handsfield, 1992). Women who are diagnosed with PID tend to be young, be unmarried, have multiple sexual partners, have had a STD in the past, have first engaged in sexual intercourse at a young age, be members of a minority group (Cates et al., 1990), and use douches (Aral et al., 1991).

One of the major symptoms of PID is acute pelvic pain. Antibiotics are used in the treatment of PID, and depending on severity, hospitalization may be necessary. In the United States, approximately 180,000 hospitalizations for PID occur each year (Hatcher et al., 1994).

ACQUIRED IMMUNE DEFICIENCY SYNDROME (AIDS)

acquired immune deficiency syndrome (AIDS): A condition of increased susceptibility to opportunistic diseases; results from an infection with the HIV, which destroys the body's immune system.

There are several factors that set **acquired immune deficiency syndrome (AIDS)** apart from other STDs and also shed some light on why the AIDS debate has become so politically charged. AIDS appeared at a time when modern medicine was believed to be well on its way to reducing epidemic disease (Altman, 1986). In addition, AIDS was first identified among homosexual males, and as of 1995, the largest number of cases in this country were gay and bisexual men and intravenous drug users. Because of this early identification, the disease was linked with "socially marginal" groups in the population (Altman, 1986; Kain, 1987). The media gave particular attention to the lifestyle of "victims" and implied that social deviance has a price. Social, cultural, and historical issues have a profound influence on the patterning of AIDS, as well as on other sexually transmitted diseases (Brandt, 1985). For example, in Africa, AIDS is not predominantly a disease of homosexuals and intravenous drug users, and so there is less stigma in contracting AIDS than there is in the United States (see Focus on Diversity 13.1).

human immunodeficiency virus (HIV): The retrovirus responsible for the development of AIDS; can be sexually transmitted.

AIDS is caused by the **human immunodeficiency virus (HIV)**, which is primarily transmitted through body fluids, including semen, vaginal fluid, and blood. During sexual or anal intercourse, this virus can enter the body through the rectum, vagina, penis, or mouth. It is also possible to transmit the virus during intravenous drug use by sharing needles. Through December 1990, 63% of AIDS cases were sexually transmitted; 58% between homosexual or bisexual couples, and 5% between heterosexual couples in which one person engaged in a high risk behavior (Kassler and Cates, 1992). Behaviors that seem to transmit the virus include receptive anal sex and unprotected vaginal sex. Having a partner who has another STD can also increase the chances of transmitting the virus. Babies are also able to acquire the AIDS virus from their infected mothers through breast-feeding.

While some researchers have found that oral sex is an unlikely method of transmission (Mayer and DeGruttola, 1987), other studies indicate that there is a slight risk of acquiring HIV through receptive oral sex (Lane et al., 1991). Although transmission between females is unlikely, there are a few cases where this has occurred (Greenhouse, 1987). As of 1992, there were an increasing number of cases in which no identifiable

Focus
on Diversity
————— *13.1*
Cross-Cultural Aspects of STDs

STDs are on the rise all over the world. The global increase in STDs may be due to earlier ages of first intercourse, an increase in premarital sex, a decrease in the age at menarche, and a change in contraception away from barrier methods (Adler, 1990). Countries are using different strategies to deal with the increasing numbers of STDs, as we illustrate below.

United Kingdom

As in the United States, STDs are increasing in the United Kingdom. As of 1990, the most common STD in the United Kingdom was chlamydia (Adler, 1990). However, other STDs including trichomoniasis, genital herpes and warts, hepatitis B, and HIV have also been rapidly increasing. It naturally follows that since the incidence of these STDs is increasing, so too is PID.

Africa

Sexually transmitted diseases are a major health problem in Africa (Latif, 1990). The most common STD in Africa is gonorrhea, which presents the biggest health problem because of the complications associated with PID. Interestingly, in Nigeria infection with gonorrhea is thought to be a sign that a person has reached adolescence and sexual potency (Ogunbanjo, 1989).

Chlamydial infections are also increasing, which is resulting in increased infertility problems. In Ethiopia, congenital syphilis is the fourth leading cause of infant death (Latif, 1990). Prostitution also contributes to the high incidence of certain STDs. For instance, in Somalia, prostitutes were found to have a 58% prevalence rate for syphilis, while the general population had a 3% rate (Goeman and Piot, 1990).

Southeast Asia

The bacterial STDs continue to be the biggest problems in this region, with gonorrhea and chlamydia being the two most common STDs (Thirumoorthy, 1990). Many Asian countries have high rates of prostitution, and numerous international tourists visit these prostitutes. Many of these prostitutes also travel across international borders. In Southeast Asia, bacterial STDs have become resistant to antibiotic treatment, in part because nonprescription antibiotics are available to prostitutes, who often medicate themselves and their partners. Overuse of antibiotics increases the resistance of various strains of the diseases (Thirumoorthy, 1990).

In Singapore and Thailand, gonorrhea is the most common STD, although rates of genital warts, chlamydia, herpes, and HIV are also increasing (Thirumoorthy, 1990). It was not until the mid–1980s that HIV and AIDS were considered to be problems, and not surprisingly, they first began to appear in the prostitute and intravenous drug using populations. Recently the HIV rates in Southeast Asia have been increasing rapidly.

Sweden

In Sweden, chlamydia infections dominate the STD scene. Gonorrhea, syphilis, and herpes are also present. Diagnosis and treatment of STDs are free of charge and easily accessible in Sweden; in fact, every county has a physician who specifically treats STDs.

---

high risk behaviors had been engaged in, and so it was thought that transmission was from heterosexual intercourse (Kassler and Cates, 1992). From 1978 to 1985, people who received blood transfusions were at high risk for HIV because the blood supply was poorly screened for HIV (Catania et al., 1989). Many hemophiliacs, who require frequent transfusions, were infected during this period. Today in the United States, the blood used in transfusions is carefully tested for HIV.

Like the herpes virus, HIV never goes away; it remains in the body for the rest of a person's life. Unlike the herpes virus, however, the HIV infection is often fatal. After a person is infected, the virus may remain dormant for a period of time and cause no symptoms. This is why some people who are infected may not realize that they are. However, a blood test can be taken to reveal whether or not someone is HIV positive.

T-lymphocytes (T-helper cells): Type of white blood cell that helps to destroy harmful bacteria in the body.

Even though a person may not know he or she has been infected, he or she can transmit the virus to other people immediately after infection.

HIV attacks the **T-lymphocytes (T-helper cells)** in the blood. Usually, when there is a foreign invader in our bloodstream, antibodies develop that are able to recognize the invader and destroy it. However, if the antibodies cannot do this or if there are too many viruses, a person will become ill. These antibodies can be detected in the bloodstream anywhere from two weeks to six months after infection, which is how the screening test for HIV works. The immune system also releases many white blood cells to help destroy invaders.

reverse transcriptase: A chemical that is contained in the RNA of HIV; it helps to change the virus to DNA.

The HIV virus attaches itself to the T-helper cells and injects its infectious RNA into the fluid of the helper cell. The RNA contains an enzyme known as **reverse transcriptase**, which is capable of changing the RNA into DNA. The new DNA takes over the T-helper cell and begins to manufacture more HIV (see Figure 13.2).

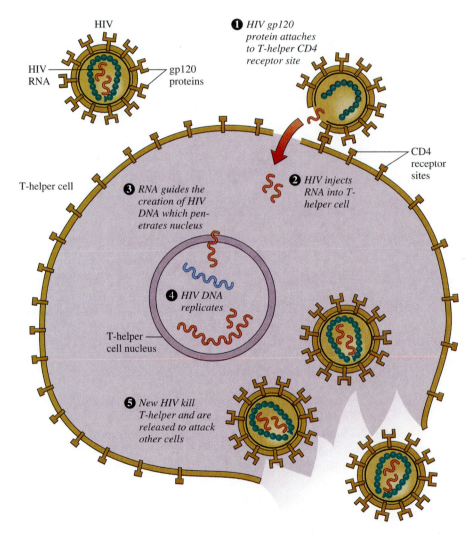

F i g u r e **13.2**

HIV attacking a T-helper cell. (1) The gp120 protein on the surface of HIV fits the CD4 receptor on the surface of the T-helper cell. (2) HIV RNA enters the T-helper cell and uses the cell's machinery to create HIV DNA. (3) HIV DNA enters the nucleus, where it (4) replicates and (5) forms new HIV molecules that destroy the cell and go looking for new T-helper cells.

The attack on the T-helper cells causes the immune system to be less effective in its ability to fight disease, and so many diseases infect people with AIDS that a healthy person could easily fight off. We will discuss these diseases later in this chapter. No one knows exactly why some people acquire the virus from one sexual encounter while others may not be infected even after repeated exposure. It appears that a person is more at risk for acquiring HIV if they already have another STD (Kassler and Cates, 1992). Research indicates that infections with syphilis, chancroid, herpes, gonorrhea, chlamydia, and trichomoniasis can increase the risk of acquiring and transmitting HIV (Wasserheit, 1992; Cates and Hinman, 1991). Having HIV also decreases the immune system's ability to fight the other STDs.

SEX TALK

QUESTION **13.7 Can you get AIDS from drinking from the same cup after someone who is infected with AIDS? How about from someone with AIDS that I am around a lot?**

Many people have unfounded fears about casual contact with someone with AIDS. Scientific evidence, however, shows that it is not spread through casual, everyday contact. It cannot be acquired from talking to someone with AIDS, shaking hands, hugging, toilet seats, gyms, or swimming pools. AIDS is transmit-

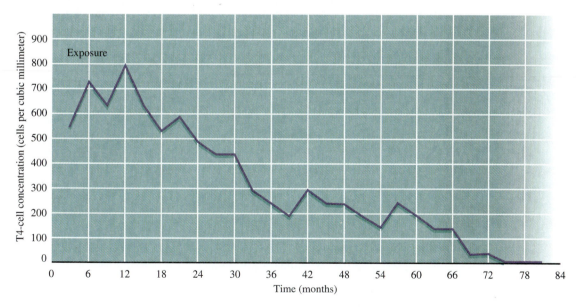

DECLINE in T4-cell count (rounded to the nearest 50) was tracked in the blood of a young man whose disease followed a typical course. About three months after sexual exposure to HIV the patient tested positive for the virus; his immune system temporarily controlled the infection. He developed chronic lymphadenopathey at nine months and at 51 months, after a long, slow decline in his T4-cell count (by 36 months it was chronically below 400), exhibited chronic, subtle abnormalities of delayed hypersensitivity. He displayed persistent anergy (the complete absence of delayed hypersensitivity) at 63 months, when he developed thrush and oral hairy leukoplakia, a tongue infection. Less than a year later he was besieged by opportunistic infections, including cytomegalovirus infection, which made him blind. He died at 83 months.

Figure **13.3**

T-4 cell count of an HIV-infected person. **Reprinted with permission from *Scientific American*.**

ted through the exchange of bodily fluids. The AIDS virus is very fragile, and it quickly dies outside of the body. That is why people who live with and care for a friend or relative with AIDS almost never become infected.

It is unknown where the HIV virus came from, although some believe that the infectious agent came from Africa. The disease came to light in mid-1981 when a number of gay men, mostly in Los Angeles and New York City, began coming down with rare forms of pneumonia and skin cancer. Physicians began calling the disease GRID for "gay-related immunodeficiency syndrome." It was hypothesized that there was a new infectious agent causing the disease, that the immune system was being suppressed by a drug that the infected persons were using, or that perhaps a sexual lubricant was involved. In 1984, Dr. Robert Gallo from the National Institute of Health identified a virus that seemed to cause AIDS. At precisely the same time, Dr. Luc Montagnier, a physician at the Pasteur Institute in Paris, announced that he had also identified the virus. There was some controversy as to who discovered the virus first. However, in 1993, these two researchers agreed to combine their efforts to search for more AIDS treatments (*Washington Post,* 1993).

Many physicians felt that this infectious agent would quickly be isolated and wiped out. However, HIV is difficult to detect and kill. Today, it is anticipated that the AIDS virus will continue to infect people for the next several decades without a cure. However, there is some hope that a vaccine will be available sooner than a cure.

In 1995 UCLA researchers documented for the first time a case in which an infant infected with HIV at birth cleared the virus from his body by his first birthday (Bryson et al., 1995). This case indicates that it is possible for the immune system to fend off HIV infection. Researchers are hopeful that this case will help provide some insight into the development of an AIDS vaccine.

Incidence

By 1988, AIDS was the third leading cause of death among American males who were between twenty-five and forty-four years old, and by 1989, it had moved up to second place (Centers for Disease Control, 1991). As of 1991, AIDS was the fifth leading cause of death for American women between the ages of twenty-five and forty-four (*Kansas City Star,* 1992d).

It is estimated that one million people have been infected with HIV in the United States, many of whom do not know their infection status (Centers for Disease Control, 1994). As of June 1994, the total estimated number of people with AIDS in the United States is 401,749. The incidence of AIDS differs from state to state (see Table 13.1).

Although in the beginning of this epidemic the largest at risk group in the United States were homosexual men, soon IV drug users, hemophiliacs, blood transfusion recipients, heterosexuals, and children also became infected. In 1993, the largest proportionate increase in AIDS cases was within the heterosexual population. The World Health Organization estimates that by the year 2000 heterosexual transmission will account for 70% of infections in the United States, homosexual transmission will account for 10%, and IV drug use will be 10%.

In the past few years, women's risk for infection with HIV has increased. In a study done at the University of California in San Francisco, only 1% of HIV-infected heterosexual women transmitted the virus to their partners, while 20% of the HIV-infected men passed it on to their partners (AIDS Update, 1991). In fact, women have been found to be seventeen times more likely to be infected by their partners than they are to give

Table 13.1

AIDS CASES BY STATE

AIDS cases and annual rates per 100,000 population, by state, reported April 1990 through March 1991, April 1991 through March 1992; and cumulative totals, by state and age group, through March 1992

STATE OF RESIDENCE	CUMULATIVE TOTALS		
	ADULTS/ ADOLESCENTS	CHILDREN <13 YEARS OLD	TOTAL
Alabama	1,353	35	1,388
Alaska	122	3	125
Arizona	1,642	11	1,653
Arkansas	682	14	696
California	40,763	279	41,042
Colorado	2,142	13	2,155
Connecticut	2,477	76	2,553
Delaware	422	5	427
District of Columbia	3,538	52	3,590
Florida	20,258	552	20,810
Georgia	5,987	59	6,046
Hawaii	863	7	870
Idaho	116	2	118
Illinois	6,590	99	6,689
Indiana	1,485	11	1,496
Iowa	336	3	339
Kansas	630	4	634
Kentucky	709	9	718
Louisiana	3,254	55	3,309
Maine	285	2	287
Maryland	4,280	90	4,370
Massachusetts	4,454	95	4,549
Michigan	2,892	51	2,943
Minnesota	1,057	9	1,066
Mississippi	924	18	942
Missouri	2,650	27	2,677
Montana	85	1	86
Nebraska	260	2	262
Nevada	932	11	943
New Hampshire	247	5	252
New Jersey	12,902	372	13,274
New Mexico	482	2	484
New York	43,179	997	44,176
North Carolina	2,341	38	2,379
North Dakota	25	—	25
Ohio	3,092	51	3,143
Oklahoma	985	12	997
Oregon	1,352	7	1,359
Pennsylvania	5,876	99	5,975
Rhode Island	490	9	499
South Carolina	1,473	29	1,502
South Dakota	30	1	31
Tennessee	1,552	18	1,570
Texas	15,070	166	15,236
Utah	492	12	504
Vermont	96	2	98
Virginia	2,837	57	2,894
Washington	2,927	16	2,943
West Virginia	254	4	258
Wisconsin	892	9	901
Wyoming	54	—	54
U.S. Total	**207,836**	**3,501**	**211,337**
Guam	11	—	11
Pacific Islands U.S.	2	—	2
Puerto Rico	6,662	187	6,849
Virgin Islands U.S.	98	4	102
Total	**214,609**	**3,692**	**218,301**

the infection (Padian et al., 1991). Fifty-one percent of women have been infected through IV drug use and 29% through heterosexual behavior (Ellerbrock et al., 1991). In 1991, it was estimated that at least three million women were infected with HIV world-wide (Williams, 1991).

A study of university students found that 2 out of every 1000 are HIV positive (Gayle et al., 1991), while adolescents represent only 1.2% of all AIDS cases (Hersch, 1991). In 1990, the incidence of AIDS in adolescent women increased by 67% (which was twice the rate for males). Runaway youths are the most at risk for contracting HIV because of their use of IV drugs, lack of consistent condom use, and the practice of trading sex for money or drugs (Rotheram-Borus et al., 1991). Although 65% of runaways are sexually active, only 18% report consistent condom use.

A report by the Harvard University Global AIDS Policy Coalition claims that by the year 2000, there will be more than 110 million adults in the world infected with AIDS (*Kansas City Star,* 1992e). Other groups are more conservative in their estimates, such as the World Health Organization, which predicts that 40 million will be infected by the year 2000. The great variety in the estimates of future AIDS cases (the above two studies have a 70 million case difference) shows how difficult it is to predict the course of the AIDS epidemic.

In prison populations, AIDS is becoming the leading cause of death (Brewer and Derrickson, 1992). The major risk factor for the development of AIDS in prison is IV drug use.

Knowledge and Attitudes About AIDS

College students are at risk for HIV because of high rates of sexual activity, multiple sexual partners, lack of protection during sexual activity, and sexual activity that takes place after a couple has been drinking. Knowledge levels among college students is generally high (Gamba,1990); on the other hand, students also tend to overestimate how knowledgeable they actually are about AIDS. Many college students report that they are "highly knowledgeable" about AIDS, but then score low on knowledge tests. Unfortunately, higher knowledge levels about AIDS has not been found to be consistently correlated with behavior changes or the practice of safer sex (Caron et al., 1992).

Studies indicate that individuals of all ages are more knowledgeable about HIV/AIDS than any other STD (Benton et al., 1993). However, sexually active teenagers tend to be less knowledgeable about HIV and less fearful about getting AIDS than those teenagers who are not sexually active (Brown, 1992). Those students with higher knowledge levels about AIDS have been found to have more positive attitudes toward persons with AIDS. Conversely, a fear of AIDS and antigay attitudes have been found to be correlated with a lack of knowledge about the disease (Temoshok et al., 1987). Compared with females, males have been found to have more negative attitudes toward persons with AIDS (Lester, 1989).

Public attitudes about AIDS may be a mixture of the fear of casual transmission and homophobia (see Chapter 7). AIDS is strongly associated with behaviors that have traditionally been considered deviant, such as homosexual behavior and drug abuse. Brandt (1988) suggests that this disease may have generated new fears as well as heightened old hostilities about homosexuality. There are three aspects of AIDS that make it different from other diseases. First is the fear of transmission; even though one may know that it is not casually transmitted, the fear of catching AIDS is constantly reinforced by the media (Friedland, 1988). Second, there is an issue of the social worth of the individuals who have been diagnosed with the disease. Because AIDS has been strongly associated with behaviors that have traditionally been considered deviant, an illusion is created that membership in a group other than those most at risk conveys protection (Friedland, 1988). Finally, there is the inability of society to comprehend the magnitude of this illness, which has left many people feeling isolated and frightened. Research has also shown that when confronted with danger, some deny the danger, while others overreact (Tanay, 1988).

In the early 1990s, when both Magic Johnson and Arthur Ashe announced that they were HIV positive, attitudes about AIDS changed slightly. Many people began to look at their own behaviors and evaluate whether or not they might be at risk. Suddenly, AIDS was something anyone could catch, and AIDS testing centers were overburdened with new patients requesting tests. It is interesting to note that this phenomenon did not occur when homosexual men were dying of AIDS, but only when heterosexual athletic heroes were infected.

Symptoms

Infection with HIV results in a gradual deterioration of the immune system through the destruction of T-helper lymphocytes (Friedman-Kien and Farthing, 1990). This decline in T-helper lymphocytes has been found to take an average of three years in those who are emotionally depressed and more than five years in those who are nondepressed (Bower, 1992).

Antibodies to HIV usually appear six weeks to six months after infection, but **seroconversion** may not occur for a year or longer (Friedman-Kien and Farthing, 1990). One study indicated that heavy alcohol consumption, moderate to heavy drug use, and younger age increased the likelihood of seroconversion in high risk individuals (Penkower et al., 1991). The average HIV-positive person will develop AIDS within eight to ten years (see Sexuality Today 13.1). Flulike symptoms such as fever, sore throat, chronic swollen lymph nodes in the neck or armpits, headaches, and fatigue may appear. After this period, an infected person will seem to recover, and all symptoms will disappear. Later symptoms may include **wasting syndrome**, which causes significant weight loss, and severe diarrhea, which persists for over one month; night sweats; **oral candidiasis**; gingivitis; oral ulcers; and persistent fever (Friedman-Kien and Farthing, 1990). In addition, a person might experience persistent dizziness, confusion, and blurring of vision or hearing. Be aware, however, that constant worry or fear about having AIDS can also cause many of these symptoms, as can many other diseases or problems. If you are concerned, it is a good idea to visit your local health department for a free, anonymous HIV test.

The deterioration of the immune system makes it easier for **opportunistic diseases** to develop. One of these is **pneumocystis carinii pneumonia (PCP)**, a type of pneumonia that was uncommon prior to 1980. As of 1987, it was the most common opportunistic disease of persons with AIDS; approximately 60% to 80% of people with AIDS develop PCP (Selik et al., 1987). Other opportunistic diseases include **toxoplasmosis**, **cryptococcosis**, **cytomegalovirus**, and **Kaposi's sarcoma**. Kaposi's sarcoma is a rare type of blood vessel cancer that occurs in homosexual men but is rarely seen in other populations. Lesions from Kaposi's sarcoma frequently occur around the ankle or foot, or they may be on the tip of nose, face, penis, eyelids, ears, chest, or back. Other STDs may appear or reappear, such as genital warts or syphilis, which may be resistant to treatment. Many people with AIDS also gray prematurely and lose some of their hair.

seroconversion: The immunological conversion from HIV negative to HIV positive.

wasting syndrome: Significant weight loss, often characteristic of AIDS.

oral candidasis: An infection in the mouth caused by the excess growth of a fungus that naturally occurs in the body.

opportunistic diseases: Diseases that occur when the immune system is depressed; often fatal.

pneumocystis carinii pneumonia (PCP): A rare type of pneumonia, which is an opportunistic disease that often occurs in people with AIDS.

toxoplasmosis: An often fatal disease caused by an infection with a microorganism; an opportunistic disease.

cryptococcosis: An opportunistic disease that may occur in persons with AIDS.

cytomegalovirus: An opportunistic disease that may occur in persons with AIDS.

Kaposi's sarcoma: A rare form of cancer that often occurs in people with AIDS.

In the later stages of AIDS, a person usually experiences a significant weight loss called wasting syndrome.

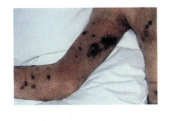

Kaposi's Sarcoma is a rare type of blood vessel cancer that occurs in homosexual men with AIDS but is rarely seen in other populations.

At first it was assumed that men and women developed similar symptoms after being infected with the AIDS virus. It was not until 1991 that it was discovered that many women develop different reactions to infection with the HIV virus. At that time, a revised definition of AIDS was proposed, which went into effect in January 1993. The definition of AIDS is important because the government uses this definition to calculate disability benefits and whether or not someone can participate in low-cost AIDS drug trials. Many AIDS activists felt that the old definition did not apply to women and many IV drug users who had been infected with the virus. In 1993, newer definitions almost doubled the number of Americans who, by definition, had AIDS.

SEX TALK

QUESTION **13.8** **When someone is diagnosed as having the HIV virus, is there a chance they will not ever develop AIDS? If not, about how long until they get AIDS?**

There is a median incubation period from the time of HIV infection to onset of AIDS symptoms of approximately eight to ten years (Moore et al., 1991). Some people do get sick immediately after infection, and those who are taking medication seem to live longer without developing symptoms. Although it is not clearly understood, 5% to 8% of people infected with HIV remain asymptomatic and completely healthy years after the initial infection (*Contemporary Sexuality*, 1994). However, at this point research indicates that almost all people who have the HIV virus will develop AIDS at some point in their lives.

After being infected with HIV, women's life expectancies have been found to be significantly shorter than men's (Williams, 1991). HIV-positive women also have an eight to eleven times higher rate of cervical dysplasia (which may lead to cervical cancer) on Pap smears compared with non-HIV-infected women. Other symptoms of HIV infection for women include PID, unexplained vaginal bleeding, bleeding after sexual intercourse, abnormal Pap smear results, persistent yeast infections, and the presence of other STDs including syphilis, herpes, and genital warts.

Diagnosis

Tests for HIV do not determine directly whether or not a person has HIV in his or her body, but whether the person's body has developed antibodies to fight HIV. The most widely used test is the **ELISA (enzyme-immunoabsorbent assay)**. To check for accuracy, if an ELISA test result is positive, a second test, known as the **Western Blot**, is used. These tests can determine the presence or absence of HIV antibodies. If there are none, the test results are negative, indicating that the person is probably not infected with HIV. It takes some time for the body to develop antibodies, and so there is a period where a person is infected with HIV but the test will not reveal it. If the test is positive, antibodies are present in the body and the person has HIV. It should be noted that **false negative** and **false positive** test results are also possible.

In 1985, approximately 79,000 tests for HIV were performed in public clinics in the United States; by 1990, this number had jumped to 1,350,000 (Higgens et al., 1991). Many college students ask whether or not they should be tested for HIV. This is an individual decision that depends on many factors (see Sexuality Today 13.2).

There has also been research on saliva-based AIDS tests. One company in Oregon has developed an oral saliva test that measures for the presence of HIV antibodies; they applied for FDA approval in 1991. Approval was granted in late 1994. The FDA imple-

ELISA (enzyme-immunoabsorbent assay): The screening test used to detect HIV antibodies in blood samples. Positive ELISA tests should be confirmed with a Western Blot test.

Western Blot: A test used to confirm a positive ELISA test; more accurate than ELISA tests, but too expensive to be used as the primary screening device for infection.

false negative: A negative AIDS test result that occurs in a person who is positive for the virus.

false positive: A positive AIDS test result that occurs in a person who is negative for the virus.

SEXUALITY *Today*   13.1

1993 Revised Classification System for HIV Infection

In 1993, the Centers for Disease Control (CDC) revised the classification system for HIV infection that was published by the CDC in 1986. Primarily this was done to emphasize the clinical importance of the T-lymphocyte count in the categorization of HIV-related clinical conditions. Prior to this new definition, a person had to develop an opportunistic disease before he or she was determined to have AIDS. However, as of 1993, an opportunistic disease or a T-lymphocyte count of less than 200 would classify a person as infected with AIDS. (A person without AIDS has a T-lymphocyte count of anywhere between 1000 and 1500.)

Measures of T-lymphocytes also help guide clinical and therapeutic management of those infected with HIV. In addition to adding the T-lymphocyte criterion to the definition of AIDS, three opportunistic infections were added to the case definition. These include pulmonary tuberculosis (which is the most common type of tuberculosis in persons infected with HIV throughout the world), recurrent pneumonia (the leading cause of HIV-related death), and invasive cervical cancer.

The addition of these diseases and T-lymphocyte counts to the AIDS definition had a tremendous impact on the number of reported cases of AIDS. It is anticipated that this definition change will help those with lower T-cell counts and those infected with these opportunistic diseases get the medical assistance they need as quickly as possible.

Morbidity and Mortality Weekly **(1992)**

SEXUALITY *Today*   *13.2*

Should I Get Tested for AIDS?

Many college students wonder whether or not they should be tested for AIDS. Professionals believe that AIDS testing may actually reduce the frequency of high risk sexual behaviors. At public clinics, tests are usually by appointment only, and they are either free or provided for a reduced fee. Blood is drawn and you must return for your results in one to two weeks. When you return for the results, a counselor provides you with your results, education, and information. If you are thinking about being tested for AIDS, you might want to consider the following questions.

1. Have you had unprotected sexual intercourse with a partner?
2. Have you engaged in unprotected anal intercourse?
3. Have you ever had a sexually transmitted disease?
4. Have you ever used IV drugs?
5. If you are a man, have you ever had anal sex with a man?
6. If you are a woman, have you ever had had sexual intercourse with a man who had sex with another man?
7. Have you ever had sex with a partner who used IV drugs?

If any of your answers to these questions was yes, you should seriously consider having an AIDS test.

mented strict restrictions on the use of these saliva-based tests. They can only be purchased through physicians and be used for diagnostic purposes (as opposed to screening blood donors) and cannot be used at home. Since effectiveness rates for saliva-based tests are lower than for blood tests, those who test positive are encouraged to follow up with an AIDS blood test. Eventually, a saliva-based AIDS test may be approved for in-home use.

Treatment

There is no cure for HIV. There are several medications that can help alleviate some of the symptoms of AIDS and prolong the time between outbreaks of symptoms. **Zidovudine (AZT)**, **zalcitabine (DDC)**, and **didanosine (ddI)** have been used to treat AIDS. A combination of these drugs may increase T-helper cell counts and improve neurological symptoms. In 1994, the FDA approved **stavudine (d4T)** as the fourth drug for the treatment of AIDS. All of these drugs work by blocking the ability of the virus to replicate, thus slowing the spread of the disease.

zidovudine (AZT): A medication that has been shown to prolong life in HIV-infected persons and to slow the progression to AIDS.

zalcitabine (DDC): A medication that has been shown to slow the progression to AIDS.

didanosine (ddI): A medication that has been shown to slow the progression to AIDS.

stavudine (d4T): A medication that has been shown to slow the progression to AIDS.

SEX TALK

QUESTION **13.9 What are the chances of actually finding a cure for AIDS?**

We believe that it will be a long time before there is a cure for AIDS. Many research studies are being done all over the world, and scientists are searching for vaccines, treatments, and cures. Because the virus is so complex and because it constantly reproduces and changes itself, finding a cure is very difficult. There is a much greater chance of finding a vaccine to immunize people against AIDS than of finding a cure for people who are already infected.

Other drugs are used to treat the individual opportunistic diseases. For example, in early 1993, the FDA approved the use of *Marinol* for severe weight loss and debilitation, which is often found in people with AIDS. *Marinol* contains an ingredient that is an active component of marijuana, which has long been known to increase appetite. Other effects of *Marinol* include drowsiness, dizziness, and impaired coordination, which are similar to effects of marijuana.

Several drug trials are being conducted that may produce other possible treatments for AIDS. Because the AIDS virus has the ability to change itself and elude the action of many medications, some researchers have attempted to strengthen the body's own immune system with drug therapy to help fight against the AIDS virus (Cotton, 1991). Strengthening the immune system would consist of increasing the T-helper cells. Unfortunately, this has not yet been successful. There have also been attempts to design an AIDS vaccine that would immunize the body against AIDS infected blood cells. Researchers at the Universities of Illinois and Pennsylvania are also attempting to develop a synthetic decoy that would interfere with the growth of the virus in the body (*Kansas City Star,* 1992f). This decoy would be made of amino acids shaped like the immune cells to which HIV attaches itself, and they would inhibit viral reproduction.

Many psychologists believe that after a patient has been diagnosed with HIV, it is important that he or she receives psychological counseling to provide information on the virus, promote a healthier lifestyle, reduce the risk of transmission to others, help him or her learn coping strategies, and abstain from high risk behaviors (Youngstrom, 1992). Without this intervention, it is possible that people who are diagnosed with HIV will become depressed and may even attempt suicide. The risk of suicide is higher in patients who are HIV positive than in non-HIV groups (Marzuk et al., 1988). Research has found that depressed men in the early stages of AIDS infection suffer a more rapid decline in their physical health and die earlier than do nondepressed men (Bower, 1992). Learning to combat the virus through the use of **psychoneuroimmunology** may also be helpful. One person with AIDS reported that he used visualization every night to help increase his T-helper cells. He would visualize the T-helper cells as an army that was fighting off the bad HIV cells in his body (Author's files).

psychoneuroimmunology: The field that studies the relationships between psychological factors (such as stress and attitudes) and the functioning of the immune system.

Prevention

In order to prevent the further spread of AIDS, people's behavior must change. Many programs have been started to achieve this goal, including educational programs, advertising, and mailings. Research has consistently found that people who are knowledgeable about AIDS are more likely to protect themselves, while those with less knowledge may not.

SEX TALK
QUESTION **13.10**   **If two people are free of the AIDS virus and have anal sex, could they then get AIDS from each other?**

If neither partner is infected with HIV, there is no way they can transmit the virus to each other—or to anyone else—regardless of their sexual behaviors.

A variety of educational programs have been developed, each designed for specific groups. Some are specifically targeted at those who are at increased risk for infection with HIV. For example, though IV drug using populations are difficult to reach, one program that provided education to IV drug users decreased drug use from 92% to 70% and decreased needle sharing from 67% to 24% (Stephens et al., 1991).

Sharing needles causes infected blood from one person to be injected into the bloodstream of another. In San Francisco, an exchange program provides clean needles in exchange for used needles for IV drug users. Clinic workers also roam the drug areas to hand out clean needles. Approximately 50% of needles were returned to collection sites within two weeks after distribution, which is encouraging (Guydish et al., 1991).

Gay men have made big strides in changing their behavior since the beginning of the AIDS crisis. When the AIDS crisis first began to spread in the homosexual community, gay men took action through education. This resulted in dramatic decreases in high risk behaviors such as unprotected anal and oral sex. In early 1980, approximately 40% of gay men reported engaging in risky sex, but by 1987 this number fell to 10% (Staver, 1992). These changes in behavior also resulted in lower rates of other STDs in homosexual men (Higgens et al., 1991). In addition, those gay men who tested HIV positive engaged in more safer sex behaviors than those who were either negative or untested. However, newer research reveals that some gay men have been relapsing into risky sexual behaviors (Lemp et al., 1994; Offir et al., 1993).

Many schools are beginning to include AIDS education in their classes. These programs provide students with information about risky sexual behaviors, facts about AIDS, and prevention strategies. Different educational programs emphasize different messages. One may discourage sexual activity, while a second encourages condom use, and a third stresses monogamy. All are similar in that the goal is to change behavior and increase self-responsibility. However, these programs have not progressed without controversy. People disagree about when these programs should start, how explicit they should be, and whether or not such education will increase sexual promiscuity. At UCLA, a class on AIDS And Other STDs is the most popular class in the history of the school (*Los Angeles Times,* 1994).

Educating people about condom use is necessary to slow the spread of AIDS. Using a condom has been found to be 10,000 times safer than not using one (McCase, 1992). In one study of persons who claimed to have engaged in high risk sex, 71% reported they had not used a condom (Catania et al., 1992). Between 15% and 31% of sexually active heterosexuals reported that they had engaged in a high risk behavior, and only 17% of those with multiple partners reported using condoms.

Once a diagnosis of HIV has been made, it is important to inform all past sexual contacts to prevent the spread of the disease. Because the virus can remain in the body for several years before the onset of symptoms, some people may not know that they have the virus and are capable of infecting others.

There are many social and political issues that surround AIDS, which have led to the formation of radical groups such as the "AIDS Coalition to Unleash Power" (ACT UP). This group uses aggressive and expressive social action to contest issues. ACT UP, which has chapters across the United States, falls under the umbrella of the "AIDS Coalition to Network, Organize, and Win" (ACT NOW). There are some who believe that ACT UP has gone too far and has gone beyond the bounds of "good taste." The group has staged events in which condoms are thrown about, couples passionately neck in public places, and people camp out in front of television cameras (Gamson, 1989).

Some believe that the only way to reach various high risk populations is through the broadcast and print media (Population Reports, 1989). Advertisements and public service announcements have aired that attempt to educate people about AIDS. However, there has been a strong reluctance in the media to use words such as *condoms* and *safer*

Today, the media is trying to educate people about AIDS.

sex. Even so, research is continually being done to determine the effectiveness of these methods of education.

AIDS panic has led to many types of new fears about infection. For example, despite more than a decade of AIDS and millions of physician–patient contacts, there has only been one *verified* case of a patient contracting AIDS from a health-care provider. This was the case of Kim Bergalis, who claimed that she acquired the AIDS virus from her HIV-positive dentist. Although the risk of such a route of infection is slim, it remains a possibility.

The AIDS quilt in Washington, D.C. Survivors of those who have died of AIDS often make pieces of the quilt to remember their loved ones.

It seems reasonable that before we can determine what will reduce high risk behaviors that contribute to increases in AIDS, we need to know the behaviors in which people are engaging. Yet data on sexual practices are lacking in the United States. Our assumptions about current sexual behaviors are based on the Kinsey studies from the 1940s and 1950s. We know very little about current rates of high risk behaviors, such as anal intercourse, extramarital or teenage sexuality, and homosexuality. The National Health and Social Life Study helped shine some light on these behaviors (see Chapter 2).

Families and AIDS

Families and friends of people with AIDS often do not receive the same social support as do families and friends of someone with other devastating diseases such as cancer or Alzheimer's disease. There is a great social stigma attached to AIDS, and many caregivers find that they have to deal with this pain on their own. Children whose parents become infected with the AIDS virus often have difficulties sorting through their own personal feelings about this (see Personal Voices 13.1).

Elizabeth Kubler-Ross (1969) believes that people progress through five stages when they receive news of their impending death. The five stages are denial, anger, depression, bargaining, and acceptance. Many families and friends of people with AIDS progress through a similar set of stages. Probably the hardest part of dealing with death from AIDS is that, in the majority of cases, the person dying of AIDS is young. We usually do not think of losing someone who is so young. Many people who are survivors of AIDS report that it is helpful to become involved in AIDS-related activities such as a support group. We have provided the names of several organizations at the end of this chapter.

*P*ersonal

V O I C E S

13.1

A Parent with AIDS

In January of 1991, I found out my father was gay. After a while of sorting out my feelings and realizing nothing had really changed, I came to accept it and deal with it. In December of 1991, I found out he was HIV positive from a blood transfusion he had because of a motorcycle accident. Needless to say, 1991 was not a good year at all. I cried a little, and I yelled a lot, but nothing changed, so I accepted it and I dealt with it all, or so I thought. I got information on AIDS and HIV so I could know what to expect, and in the information I found a phone number for support groups for families of those who are HIV positive. I never really thought about going. I figured I could work it all out on my own, but I had a lot of friends who would be there to offer a shoulder to cry on or an ear for listening (for the longest time I thought that crying in public was a sign of weakness and if I could help it, I wouldn't cry, and if I couldn't help it, I would cry only to a close friend). I just never thought about going to a group of people I did not know and pouring out my soul to them. Until the day I went to give blood.

It was like any other day, classes, and then lunch, and then work, only this day was the day for the blood drive. I went to the church (where the American Red Cross was taking blood) and I filled out the information. My temperature was taken and my pulse read, and then I went to the nurses station so they could make sure I hadn't had sex with a man who has had sex with another man and all that garbage they ask you ("just a formality" they say).

The nurse got to the question "Have you been exposed to anyone who is HIV positive or has the AIDS virus?" I asked, "What do you mean by exposed?" The nurse said, "Have you had sex with anyone who is HIV positive or has the AIDS virus?" I said, "No." She asked, "Have you shared a needle with anyone who is HIV positive or has the AIDS virus?" I said, "No." Then she asked, "Do you know of anyone who is HIV positive or has the AIDS virus?" I said, "Yes." She asked who and I told her. She asked me questions like "Does he cook for you and do you use the bathroom after him?" I said, "Well yes, he's my father." Then she went to talk to the head nurse in charge. After a few minutes, she came back to tell me they could not accept my blood because I had been exposed to the AIDS virus. I did not understand. Everything I had read said that a person cannot get AIDS from everyday contact. And yet here were "educated" people telling me differently. I understood they were just trying to be safe, but I had just given blood in November and here it was April. I figured if I had it, I would have been notified by now. But these people insisted that I not give blood, and the head nurse even called the main Red Cross to make sure she was doing the right thing. When she got off the phone, she wrote me a deferral letter stating I was no longer to give blood anywhere, under any circumstances. If I was asked to give blood, I was to say "no." I felt like I was already tried and convicted of having this disease before anyone really knew what was happening. I got really upset. I started crying in public and I did not know what to do. I asked if I could ever give blood again and she said "As long as you stay in contact with your father, no." To me, that was like saying—it's either us or him, and I knew I would pick him. After I left there I went to see a counselor friend of mine and she told me that the nurse did not know what she was talking about and that she agreed they had acted poorly. But I was still confused and this was just the beginning.

No one really knows how long a person can live with this disease, and if "educated" people were going to behave that poorly, who's to say that uneducated people wouldn't treat me worse when I don't even have it? The thought that the nurses could be right scared me so bad that I went up the next day to get my blood tested. The person there, who had heard about the incident from my counselor friend and the nurses at my school, told me there was really no reason to have the test, but she would give me one if it would make me feel better. I went ahead and did it. I also informed my boyfriend what was going on because if the nurses were right, then he could be at risk also.

I just could not understand why people would say such a thing. I was told that they were probably scared because they never came into contact with someone like me before. Also, they had new revisions for who could and could not give blood (she misunderstood the revisions, I was told later). But that is no excuse. It was very hard for me to imagine having such a terrible disease. I don't know how my father lives with it because I really don't think I could. I was angry at those nurses for suggesting and treating me as if I had it. I was and still am scared of what type of ignorance will be thrown my way next and if that ignorance will keep me from getting a good job or continuing my life the way I want to live it. I felt like I was found guilty before I even had a chance to go trial. I felt humiliated, having to walk out of the church with everyone watching and wondering why I couldn't give, and so very much alone; no one else at this school could possibly understand. I felt ashamed of my father. I felt embarrassed. I felt like giving up and wishing my father dead. Can you imagine wishing your own father dead? I have always been the strong one in my family until this, and it kills me to think about what my father will go through if a cure is not found. But it goes beyond that. I do not want to deal with him suffering and making my sisters and me suffer with him. I hated society for being so ignorant and treating me like I did something wrong. But overall, I felt scared that what they were saying was true, and I do have AIDS. I cannot bear to think about it now without wanting to cry. I guess the saying is that life goes on. I have decided to write a letter to the lady in charge of the support groups for people with family members with AIDS and ask her to send me some information. I figured if this was only the beginning, the future was going to get harder and I just may need some help.

Addendum: In late 1994, this student's father died of AIDS complications. She has since begun speaking publicly about the impact of AIDS on families.

Author's files

CROSS-CULTURAL ASPECTS OF AIDS

HIV and AIDS are also problems outside of the United States. As of 1990, intravenous drug use was the predominant route of infection for HIV in most countries, while in Australia and New Zealand homosexual sexual contact was the primary route of infection (Thirumoorthy, 1990). In Africa, HIV infection occurs equally in men and women and is primarily due to intravenous drug use and sexual contact with heterosexual drug users (Latif, 1990). Additional risk factors for AIDS in Africa include heterosexual promiscuity, polygamy, prostitution, and previous STDs. Because open sores facilitate the transmission of HIV, it is believed that the high frequency of STDs, including chancroids and gonorrhea, contributes to the heterosexual transmission of HIV in Africa (Latif, 1990). In Kenya, "widow inheritance laws" are still followed, in which a widow is "inherited" by her husband's brother, who must marry her (Ecker, 1994). Many of these women have lost their husbands to AIDS and carry the virus themselves. It is passed along to their new husbands via sexual intercourse. This is helping to spread the HIV infection.

In European countries, Switzerland has the highest proportion of AIDS cases, but France and Italy are quickly catching up. In Romania, AIDS has infected more than 1000 children, mostly through contaminated medical equipment (*The New York Times,* 1991k). A recent study in France revealed that 80% of sexually active teenagers reported they do not use condoms regularly because they are too expensive. In late 1992, the National AIDS Research Agency launched a new study to explore the sexual practices of 20,000 people in France.

Thailand has twice the number of people with AIDS as the United States, even though the United States has five times as many people (*Detroit News,* 1992). HIV first appeared among heroin users in Thailand, but it became established in the population within two years, mostly through legal prostitution (Rutherford, 1991). In Bangkok, there are approximately 200,000 prostitutes, and 30% of these have been found to be infected with the AIDS virus.

Asian culture often forbids the discussion of sexuality or condoms, which contributes to increasing AIDS rates. In poorer countries, such as Vietnam, a lack of funds limits anti-AIDS efforts. In the city of Ruili in China, it is policy for physicians and health-care workers *not* to inform patients of their positive HIV status. This is because of an ancient Chinese practice which does not allow advising patients of terminal illness (*Detroit News,* 1992). In late 1994, three blood donors in Beijing, China, were found to be infected with HIV. This was a startling finding because China had no policy of testing blood donors for HIV.

In mid-1994, a twenty-five-year-old man became only the fourth person in Japan to publicly admit that he had AIDS. Although there are fewer reported cases of AIDS in Japan than in the United States, the Japanese are fearful of disclosing their HIV status for fear of ostracism and loss of their jobs. In addition, people in Japan generally do not discuss personal issues in public.

Countries deal with their AIDS epidemics in different ways. In Buenos Aires, Argentine prison authorities often chain prisoners with AIDS to their beds so that they will not transmit the virus to other inmates, and these prisoners are labeled "extremely dangerous" (*Contemporary Sexuality,* 1991). Cuba has a compulsory testing program for HIV, where almost all members of the population are tested. Those found to be positive for HIV are quarantined (Perez-Stable, 1991). Between 1986 and 1989, more than five million Cubans were tested for HIV, and 434 persons were found to be HIV positive (315 men and 119 women). The Cuban government has established residential parks for people who are quarantined, and they provide housing, meals, exercise areas, and medical care. In addition, if an AIDS patient was previously employed, they are paid their full salary, while those who were unemployed are given a stipend. As of 1991, there were a total of six such facilities in Cuba. However, it has been estimated that between twenty-one to fifty-three of the persons who were quarantined may have been incorrectly diagnosed as HIV positive.

In Chile, AIDS informational flyers are being distributed in many neighborhoods. In addition, theatrical skits are being used to reach the younger children. Puppet shows, role-playing, plays, video drama, and songs have also been used in the United Kingdom, Zambia, and Chile (AIDS Health Promotion Exchange, 1990, 1991). Many educators claim that these methods help people discuss the issues because they can talk about the characters and not themselves. In Zimbabwe, flashcards are being used to promote storytelling about AIDS for different age levels.

In countries where prostitution is prevalent, there have been several attempts to reduce high risk behaviors. In the Netherlands, a group has been formed called the *Men and Prostitution Foundation.* This groups consists of men who have sex with prostitutes, and they distribute information to prostitutes and their clients in the red light district. This material provides information on reducing the AIDS risk. In Germany, posters were put up in high prostitution areas to promote condoms, and each poster uses the motto "*put it on man*" (AIDS Health Promotion Exchange, 1990). In addition, from 10 P.M. until midnight, approximately sixty people walk through this area and serve as "*human billboards*" with information attached to their clothing. Taxi drivers also handed out condoms to their passengers and played taped messages about AIDS.

In Brazil, male street-sex workers provide information on AIDS and safe sex. After six months of this program, condom use was found to increase from 15% to 65%, while safer sex practices increased from 9% to 70% (AIDS Health Promotion Exchange, 1990). Japan has been slow to respond to the AIDS crisis. However, in 1994, Japan hosted the Tenth Annual Conference on AIDS.

Treatment for AIDS in other countries is similar to treatment in the United States. AZT has been found to be effective, although in some countries there are limited accessibility and prohibitive costs. Many countries also have difficulty recognizing and treating opportunistic infections that occur with AIDS. It appears that opportunistic infections vary depending on what pathogens are in the local environment (Schopper and Walley, 1992). For example, *Pneumocystis carinii pneumonia* is one of the most common opportunistic diseases in the United States, while tuberculosis is very common in other countries. This makes it very difficult to train professionals in others countries to treat opportunistic diseases.

Recent research suggests that, in developing countries, counseling is being increasingly recognized as an important part of care for people with AIDS and their families. Providing education and information has also gained in popularity. In some countries, home-based health care is also being established to remove some of the burden from the hospitals, increase quality health care, and reduce costs.

PREVENTING STDS AND AIDS

There are many ways to reduce your chances of acquiring a STD. For example, using a barrier method of contraception, especially condoms, can help protect against transmission. Although some people believe that there are ways of practicing safe sex, others say there is no such thing as safe sex. The only effective preventive strategies, according to one physician, are "abstinence and sexual intercourse with one mutually faithful uninfected partner" (Noble, 1991).

SEX TALK

QUESTION **13.11** **If you have been diagnosed with a STD, do you need to use condoms for the rest of your life?**

It would be a good idea to talk to your health-care provider about this. Often, if you have been diagnosed with herpes, genital warts, or HIV, health-care providers will advise wearing condoms during sexual activity to decrease the risk of transmission to your sexual partner(s).

Early detection of a STD can help ensure that there are fewer long-term consequences, such as PID or infertility. In addition, notifying sexual partners as soon as a positive diagnosis is made helps to reduce the further transmission of a STD. It is also important to provide education about STDs and AIDS. This information must be presented in a nonjudgmental way. Shock and fear tactics have been found to be unsuccessful; in fact, these programs succeed in raising anxiety and decreasing effective precautions (Sherr, 1990). Educational campaigns, which work to increase knowledge and change attitudes, have been found to be most effective (Ross et al., 1990).

Summary

- There are many different types of STDs, including gonorrhea, syphilis, chlamydia, pubic lice, herpes, genital warts, chancroid, hepatitis, some vaginal infections, and human immunodeficiency virus.
- Certain contraceptive methods, such as condoms and nonoxynol-9 spermicide, offer some protection from STDs and HIV.
- Risk factors for STDs include multiple sexual partners, a partner who has had multiple sexual partners, early sexual activity, and the lack of consistent use of barrier contraceptives.
- STDs can be caused by bacteria, parasites, or viruses. Bacterial STDs are usually treated with antibiotics, while viral STDs are incurable.
- Gonorrhea is a bacterial STD. The majority of women are asymptomatic but are still capable of infecting their partners. Left untreated, gonorrhea may lead to PID in women. The majority of men are symptomatic and may experience urethral discharge, painful urination, and an increase in the frequency and urgency of urination. Gonorrhea is treated with antibiotics.
- Syphilis is a bacterial STD that is divided into three stages: primary, secondary, and tertiary. If left untreated, syphilis may lead to PID in women, and it may be fatal. Syphilis is treated with antibiotics.
- Chlamydia is a bacterial STD. In men, chlamydia can cause nongonococcal urethritis. Some researchers today claim that chlamydia is the most common bacterially induced STD. In women, chlamydia is often asymptomatic. If left untreated, chlamydia may cause PID. Chlamydia is treated with antibiotics.
- Pubic lice are parasites that attach themselves to pubic hair. Although they are often sexually transmitted, it is possible to become infected if a person shares towels or linens with a person who has pubic lice.
- Herpes is a viral STD. Once infected with herpes, a person will have the virus the rest of his or her life. HSV-1 usually causes cold sores in the mouth, while HSV-2 causes genital sores. Recurrent episodes depend upon the amount of the infectious agent, severity of infection, the type of herpes infection, and the timing of treatment.
- Genital warts are viral STDs. Once a person becomes infected with the papilloma virus, he or she will have the virus the rest of his or her life. There are several types of treatment available, depending upon the site of infection.
- Vaginal infections may be related to sexual intercourse. Several may cause vaginal discharge, while others are asymptomatic. These include trichomoniasis, hemophilus, nonspecific vaginitis, and yeast infections.
- Hepatitis is a viral disease that is often sexually transmitted. Symptoms may include nausea, vomiting, fever, liver enlargement, and fatigue. Long-term risks include cirrhosis, hepatic failure, and possibly death.
- Chancroid is a bacterial STD. The lesion that appears is similar to the syphilis sore, but the edges are soft instead of hard. Antibiotics are often used as treatment.
- Pelvic inflammatory disease is often caused by STDs. Long-term complications for women include infertility, chronic pelvic pain, and possibly death. Often PID results from undiagnosed or untreated STDs that move up into the pelvic area. Treatment usually involves antibiotics.
- AIDS, caused by the HIV, can be a sexually transmitted disease. The virus can be transmitted through blood, semen, or vaginal fluid. Symptoms of HIV infection can include weight loss, fatigue, night sweats, abnormal Pap smears, unexplained vaginal bleeding, persistent fevers, swollen lymph nodes, dry cough, white patches on the tongue, throat, or mouth, confusion, or blurring of vision. The symptoms may not occur for three to ten years after infection, although a person is able to infect others.
- Diagnosis of HIV is done through blood tests that look for antibodies the body has manufactured rather than the virus itself.
- Trials for new drugs are always being performed to look for new ways to treat the symptoms of HIV. These trials can be very expensive, which is why the drugs are also expensive.
- Education is the best weapon against AIDS. Programs have been developed for both high risk populations and schools.
- AIDS is also a problem outside of the United States, although it may occur in different ways. For instance, in Africa it is primarily a heterosexual disease. The high rates of prostitution also increase the AIDS risk in developing countries. Many interventions have been developed, including educational programs, plays, quarantine, and advertising campaigns.

R eflections on Sexuality

1. Why are women more at risk for STDs than men?
2. How does the punishment concept of disease explain some peoples attitudes about STDs?
3. How might the concept of latency contribute to the high incidence of certain STDs?
4. It is not the HIV virus that is fatal but rather the existence of opportunistic diseases. Explain why this is so.
5. Explain why the incidence of AIDS testing may have increased after Magic Johnson and Arthur Ashe announced their HIV status rather than after thousands of gay men were dying.
6. Why might the incidence of STDs vary from state to state in the United States? Why might it be different in other countries?
7. What symptoms might indicate the existence of a STD? Upon detecting such symptoms, what should a person do first?
8. What factors might cause college students to feel that they are invincible and not candidates for acquiring a STD?
9. What can you do to reduce your chances of acquiring a STD?
10. What are some ways that we might reduce the stereotypes that go along with having a STD? Outline an educational program that would present the information you learned in this chapter in a way that would help people understand exactly what STDs are and what implications there are when a person has one.
11. What are some behaviors that men and women can engage in that would reduce the risk of acquiring a STD? List behaviors that are specific to each gender and that reflect the underlying differences in men and women and their respective susceptibilities to different STDs.

R esources

AIDS Hotline, (800)342-2437.

Centers for Disease Control Public Inquiries Office, 1600 Clifton Rd, NE, Bldg. 1, Rm B63, Atlanta, GA 30333.

Gay Men's Health Crisis, PO Box 274, 132 W. 24th St., New York, NY 10011; (212)807-6655.

National Association of People with AIDS, PO Box 65472, Washington, DC 20035; (202)483-7979.

National Sexually Transmitted Diseases Hotline, American Social Health Association, (800)227-8922.

People with AIDS Hotline, (800) 828-3280.

S uggested Readings

BRANDT, A. M. (1985) *No Magic Bullet: A Social History of Venereal Disease in the United States.* New York: Oxford University Press.

FROMAN, P. K. (1992) *After You Say Goodbye: When Someone You Know Dies of AIDS.* New York: Chronicle Books.

GLASER, E., and L. PALMER. (1991) *In the Absence of Angels.* New York: G.P. Putnam.

HANDSFIELD, H. H. (1992) *Color Atlas and Synopsis of Sexually Transmitted Diseases.* New York: McGraw-Hill.

SHILTS, R. (1987) *And The Band Played On: Politics, People, and the AIDS Epidemic.* New York: St. Martin's Press, Inc.

14

Varieties of Sexual Expression

Joel is a forty-year-old man who likes to masturbate while attending adult movie theaters or watching sexually explicit movies at home. Recently, he has begun to go out for walks late at night, gazing into neighbors' windows in the hope of catching someone undressing. Joel has sexual relations with his wife about once every two weeks, but he masturbates almost daily while watching explicit movies or fantasizing about looking in people's windows and catching them undressing or having sex.

Laudan is a young woman with a high-powered job, long hours, and much responsibility. Laudan's sex life consists of picking up strangers at bars, supermarkets, museums, or wherever and bringing them home for one-night stands. She does this about three times a week, sometimes as often as five times a week. Laudan is very uncomfortable with her own behavior, and she is very frightened of getting AIDS. Yet she continues her behavior and says she is unable to stop herself.

Bernardo lives with his partner, Andy. In their basement, they have hooks in the ceiling, a bed with shackles, and various leather restraints and whips that they use in their sex play. They take turns being dominant and submissive, including whipping and "forcing" each other into sex acts but have never injured one another in any serious fashion.

Peter and his wife, Marta, had a fairly conventional sex life, although Peter often liked to make love while Marta wore a tight rubber skin-diving suit she owned. Peter began buying Marta more and more rubber clothing, insisting she wear it during sex, and finally admitted to her that he could not achieve erection without her wearing, or him fantasizing about, rubber. Marta insisted that Peter seek therapy.

WHAT IS "NORMAL" SEXUAL EXPRESSION?

Human sexuality can be expressed in many different ways. We tend to celebrate individual and cultural differences in most aspects of human life—in what people eat, how they dress, or how they dance, for example. Yet, we have been less tolerant of sexual diversity, and we have historically considered such behavior "deviant" or "perverted." More modern views of sexuality, however, do not categorize people as "deviant" versus "normal" but see sexual behavior as a continuum. For example, the sexual world is not really split into those who become sexually excited from looking at others naked or having sex (**voyeurs**) and those who do not; most people get aroused to some degree from visual sexual stimuli. Some people get more aroused than others, and at the upper limits are those who can *only* get aroused when watching sexual scenes; such people have taken a normal behavior to an extreme.

voyeur: One who observes people undressing or engaging in sex acts without their consent as a preferred or exclusive means of sexual arousal and orgasm.

Some medical and sexuality texts still categorize these kinds of behavior as *sexual deviance.* Many undergraduate texts discuss these behaviors in chapters titled *Abnormal, Unusual,* or *Atypical Sexual Behavior.* Yet how exactly do we decide whether a behavior is "normal"? What is "typical" sexual activity? Where do we draw the line? Do we call it "atypical" if 5% of sexually active people do it? Ten percent? Twenty-five percent? Sexual behaviors increase and decrease in popularity; oral sex, for example, was once considered a perversion, but now the majority of couples report that they

Men often look at women or sexual displays; a voyeur, however, takes such looking to an extreme, peeking into windows, for example, and finds such compulsive looking necessary for sexual arousal.

engage in it at least occasionally. Perhaps, then, we should consider as "deviant" only behaviors that may be harmful in some way. Yet masturbation was once believed to lead to mental illness, acne, and stunted growth, and now it is considered a normal, healthy part of sexual expression. If many of these desires exist to some degree in all of us, then the desire *itself* is not atypical, just the degree of the desire.

Social value judgments, not science, primarily determine which sexual behaviors are considered "normal" by a society. For example, in 1906, Krafft-Ebing defined sexual deviance as "every expression of (the sexual instinct) that does not correspond with the purpose of nature—i.e., propagation" (Brown, 1983:227). Certainly, most people would not go so far today. Freud himself stated that the criterion of normalcy was love and that defenses against "perversion" were the bedrock of civilization because perversion trivializes or degrades love (Cooper, 1991). Note that Freud's objections to perversion are not medical, as they were to most other mental disturbances, but moral. Even "modern" definitions can contain hidden value judgments: "The sexually variant individual typically exhibits sexual arousal or responses to inappropriate people (e.g., minors), objects (e.g., leather, rubber, garments), or activities (e.g., exposure in public, coercion, violence)" (Gudjonsson, 1986:192). "Appropriate" or "inappropriate" objects of sexual attention differ in different times, in different cultures, and for different people.

Despite these objections, certain groups of behaviors are considered the most common deviations from conventional heterosexual or homosexual behavior. The people who engage in these activities may see them as unproblematic, exciting aspects of their sexuality, or they may be very troubled by their behavior. Society may see the behavior as either solely the business of the individual in the privacy of their bedroom (e.g., sexual excitement from shoes or boots) or as a sign that the person is mentally ill (e.g., having sex with animals) or as dangerous and illegal (e.g., sex with underage children). In this chapter, we explore rarer sexual behaviors, theories of why people are attracted to unusual sexual objects, and how therapists have tried to help those who are troubled by their sexual desires.

PARAPHILIAS

paraphilia: Clinical term used to describe types of sexual expressions that are seen as unusual and potentially problematic.

The word **paraphilia** is made up of the Latin *philia* (love of) and *para* (beyond the usual). In other words, paraphilias are sexual behaviors that involve a craving for an erotic object that is "unusual." The DSM-IV (1994:522–523) defines paraphilias as "recurrent, intense sexually arousing fantasies, sexual urges, or behaviors, generally involving: (1) nonhuman objects, (2) the suffering or humiliation of oneself or one's partner, or (3) children or other nonconsenting persons, that occur over a period of at least 6 months." For some paraphiliacs, the fantasy or presence of the object of their desire is necessary for arousal and orgasm, while in others, the desire occurs periodically, or exists separately from their other sexual relationships.

SEX TALK

QUESTION **14.1** **If I fantasize about watching other people having sex or if I get turned on by being spanked, does that mean I have a paraphilia?**

A strong and varied fantasy life is the sign of healthy sexuality, and acting out fantasies in a safe sexual situation can add excitement to one's sex life. Problems may arise if (1) the fantasy or desire becomes so prominent or preoccupying that a person is unable to function sexually in its absence; (2) sexual play is taken to the point of physical or psychological injury; (3) the person feels extreme levels of guilt about the desire; or (4) the compulsion to perform a certain type of sexual behavior interferes with everyday life, disrupts personal relationships, or risks getting a person in trouble with the law. Under any of these circumstances, seeing a qualified sex therapist or counselor is advisable.

Levine et al. (1990:91) have offered three criteria that help identify a paraphilia.

1. *A long-standing unusual erotic preoccupation that is highly arousing.* This is always present, and it is one definition of a paraphilia.
2. *A pressure to act upon the erotic fantasy.* The desire, sometimes compulsion, to act on the fantasy is usually present and leads many to claim that "I just couldn't help myself"; others masturbate to relieve the sexual pressure, sometimes many times a day, to the point where normal daily activities may be disrupted.
3. *Sexual dysfunction of desire, arousal, or orgasm during conventional sexual behavior with a partner.* Many (but not all) paraphiliacs find it difficult to function sexually without the object (or fantasy of the object) of their erotic interest.

Many people find lingerie exciting, or enjoy watching sexual scenes, or enjoy being lightly bitten or scratched during sex. For the paraphiliac, however, the lingerie *itself* becomes the object of sexual attention, not a means of enhancing the sexuality of the partner. For this reason, some have suggested that the defining characteristic of paraphilia is that it replaces a whole with a part, that it allows the person to distance himself or herself from complex human sexual contact, and replace it with the undemanding sexuality of an inanimate object, a scene, or a single action (Kaplan, 1991).

Little is known about the prevalence of paraphilias in the general public, other than that they are more common in men than in women. Research on paraphilias has been drawn mostly from clinical and incarcerated samples, which are almost certainly not representative of the population as a whole. The number of people who live comfortably with uncommon sexual habits is hard to determine because people tend to be reluctant to admit to their sexual inclinations, especially if they seem unusual, even in confidential questionnaires. What is known is that people who do have paraphilias usually have more than one; in one report, the average number of paraphilias in the individuals studied was 4.8 (Abel et al., 1988). Paraphilias are also often found in people with substance abuse problems. One physician estimates that about one-half of the paraphiliacs referred to his practice had an alcohol problem (Langevin, 1992).

<u>SEX TALK</u>

QUESTION **14.2** **Don't women also engage in these behaviors? Why are paraphilias more common in men?**

No one really knows, although theories abound. Perhaps, some researchers suggest, paraphilias are developed visually, and the male tends, for some biological reason, to be more sexually aroused by visual stimuli than the female. Maybe cultural variables give men more sexual latitude in expressing what excites them. Or, perhaps, it has to do with the way we look at it; women may express their paraphilias in different, less obvious ways than men.

Paraphiliacs are often portrayed as sick, perverted, or potential sex offenders. There is thus an attempt to draw a clear line between paraphiliacs and "normal" people; yet the line is rarely that clear. One study took sexual histories and studied the arousal patterns of sixty college men who might typically be chosen as nonoffender or nonparaphilic controls in sex research (Templeman and Stinnett, 1991). Nearly two-thirds of the sample had engaged in some form of sexual misconduct or paraphilic behavior, from sexual contacts with children to coercive sex to voyeurism. Even more expressed a desire for such activities. These findings suggest that the difference between "paraphilic" and "normal" people may not be as great as researchers often suggest.

Certainly, there are paraphilic behaviors that can be dangerous or can threaten others. Men who expose themselves to young girls, people who violate corpses, strangers who rub against women on buses, or adults who seduce underage children must not be allowed to continue their behavior. There can even be legal problems with the paraphilias that are not in themselves dangerous; some **fetishists** resort to stealing the object of interest to them, and occasionally a voyeur will break into people's homes. Also, paraphiliacs are often compulsive masturbators, even up to ten times a day or more, which can make it difficult to hold certain jobs, for example. A number of therapies have been developed to help these people, but as you will see, it is very difficult to change a person's arousal patterns.

Other people live comfortably with their paraphilias. A man who has a fetish for lingerie, for example, may find a partner who very much enjoys wearing it for him. As you will see from Thomas Sargent's description of his rubber fetish in Personal Voices 14.1 on page 541, the behavior brings him comfort, excitement, and a sense of well-being, and he has no desire to see his fetish go away. Why should he want to put it to an end just because some other people find it distasteful, perverted, or abnormal? In what sense is such a person sick?

For this reason, paraphilias have become very controversial. Some theorists suggest that the term describes a society's value judgments about sexuality and not a psychiatric or clinical category (Silverstein, 1984). In fact, some theorists deny that terms like *paraphilia* really describe anything at all. Stoller (1991:39) objects to the idea of trying to create psychological explanations that group people by their sexual habits. He writes of a group of sadomasochists:

fetishist: One who focuses intensely on an inanimate object or body part (the *fetish*) for the arousal of sexual desire.

No one of them is very much like another except in their powerful commitment to getting erotic pleasure from giving or receiving pain. In their professions, hobbies, personality structures, empathy towards others, preferences in eating, television viewing, interest in sports, reading, clothes, optimism or pessimism, susceptibility to cigarette ads, insight into human behavior, use of recreational drugs, and psychiatric symptomatology,—in short, in any behavior and desire that reflects underlying character structure—they differ. . . . Given such immense differences, [it is wrong to] allege, via our "diagnosis," that these people are really much the same, that they are governed by the same dynamics coming out of the same early childhood experiences, conditioning experiences, synaptic chemistry, genes, or evolutionary ancestry.

Theories of the Origins of Paraphilia

Many researchers have theorized as to why and how paraphilias develop, but very little consensus has been reached. Paraphilias are undoubtedly complex behavior patterns, which, in different cases, may have biological, psychological or social origins—or aspects of all three.

Biological Theories

Biological researchers have found that a number of conditions can initiate paraphilic behavior. Men without previous paraphilia have begun to display paraphilic behavior when they developed temporal lobe epilepsy, brain tumors, and disturbances of certain areas of the brain (Langevin, 1992). This does not mean that everyone with a paraphilia has one of these diseases. Researchers have found that some paraphiliacs have differences in brain structure and brain chemistry and demonstrate lower intelligence scores, neuropsychological impairment, and other problems (Langevin, 1992). However, at most these are factors that may lead *some* people to be more likely to develop a paraphilia, and they do not explain the majority of paraphilic behaviors.

Psychoanalytic Theory

Psychoanalytic thought suggests that paraphilias can be traced back to the difficult time the infant has in negotiating his way through the Oedipal crisis and castration anxiety. Psychoanalytic theory thus can explain why paraphilias are more common among men in that both boys and girls identify strongly with the mothers, but girls can continue that identification while boys must, painfully, separate from their mothers to establish a male identity:

Little boys must perform an act of separation from their mothers not required of little girls; they must establish within themselves a barrier against the earliest stage of wanting to stay as one with their mothers, of not being individuals separate from their mothers, and therefore of not being sure they are fully male: fear of being female. Much of masculinity in all cultures is made up of manifestations of this conflict: emphasis on the phallus, fear of intimacy with women, fear of being humiliated by women, need to humiliate women (such as insulting, locker room vocabulary), fetishizing women

Stoller (1991:47)

Stoller goes on to suggest that the kernel of paraphilia may be in some kind of childhood trauma that, "like the pearl surrounding the grain of sand," grows into a paraphilia.

Louise Kaplan (1991:249), a psychoanalyst, suggests that *every* paraphilia involves issues of masculinity or femininity; as she writes, "every male perversion entails a masquerade or impersonation of masculinity and every female perversion entails a masquerade or impersonation of femininity." For example, men who expose themselves in public may be coping with castration anxiety by evoking a reaction to his penis from women. The exhibitionist in this view is "masquerading" as a man to cover up feelings of nonmasculinity; he is saying, in effect, "let me prove that I am a man by showing that I possess the instrument of masculinity." He even needs to demonstrate that his penis can inspire fear, which may be why exhibitionists disproportionately choose young girls, who are more likely to display a fear reaction (Kline, 1987). This confirms to the exhibitionist the power of his masculinity.

On the other hand, voyeurs, who are excited by looking at others nude or having sex, may be fixated on the experience that aroused their castration anxieties as children—the sight of genitals and sexuality (Kline, 1987). Looking while safely hiding allows the man to gain power over the fearful and hidden world of sexuality while safe from the possibility of contact. The visual component of castration anxiety is when the boy sees the power and size of the father's genitals and the lack of a penis on his mother or sisters. By the act of looking, castration anxiety begins, and in the voyeur, the looking has never ceased. Yet looking itself cannot really relieve the anxiety permanently, and so the voyeur is compelled to peep again and again. It is interesting, psychoanalytically speaking, that in the myth of Oedipus, the punishment he inflicts upon himself for his incestuous crimes is to put out his own eyes (Rosen, 1979).

Developmental Theories

Freud suggested that children are polymorphous perverse; that is, at birth we have a general erotic potential that can be attached to almost anything. We learn from an early age what sexual objects society deems appropriate for us to desire, but society's messages can get off track. For example, advertising tries to "sexualize" its products, and we have all seen shoe commercials, for example, that emphasize the long, sexy legs of the model while focusing on the shoes she wears. Some boys may end up focusing on those shoes as objects of sexual fantasy, which can develop into a fetish.

A theory that builds on similar ideas is John Money's (1984, 1986, 1990) **lovemaps**. Money suggests that the auditory, tactile, and (especially) the visual stimuli we experienced during childhood sexplay forms a template in our brain that defines our ideal lover and ideal sexual situation. If our childhood sexplay remains undisturbed, development goes on toward heterosexual desires. If, however, the child is punished for normal sexual curiosity or if there are traumas during this stage such as sexual abuse, the development of the lovemap can be disrupted in one of three ways:

1. In **hypophilia**, negative stimuli prevent the development of certain aspects of sexuality, and the genitals may be impaired from full functioning. Females are more likely to have their lovemaps disrupted in this way, resulting in an inability to orgasm, vaginal pain, or lubrication problems later in life.
2. In **hyperphilia**, the child defies the negative sexual stimulus and becomes overly sexually active, even becoming compulsively sexual (see hypersexuality, below).
3. In paraphilias, there is *substitution* of new elements into the lovemap. Since normal sexual curiosity has been discouraged or made painful, the child redirects erotic energy toward other objects that are not forbidden, such as shoes or

lovemaps: Term coined by John Money to refer to the picture of an ideal lover and sexual situation we develop as we grow up.

hypophilia: Lack of full functioning of the sexual organs due to missing stages of childhood development.

hyperphilia: Compulsive sexuality due to overcompensating for negative reactions to childhood sexuality.

rubber, or just looking; in other cases, the child turns his or her erotic energy inward and becomes excited by pain or humiliation. Once this lovemap is set, it becomes very stable, which explains why changing it is so difficult.

For example, Money (1984) suggests that sexual arousal to objects may arise when a parent makes a child feel shame about interest in an object. For example, a boy may be caught with his mother's panties, in the normal course of curiosity about the woman's body, but when he is severely chastised, the panties become forbidden, dirty, promising of sexual secrets, and he may begin to seek them out.

Another theory that tries to explain how these fixations occur is the idea of **courtship disorders** (Freund and Scher, 1983, Freund et al., 1984; Freund and Blanchard, 1986). Organizing paraphilias into "courtship" stages suggests that the paraphiliac's behavior becomes fixed at a preliminary stage of mating that would normally lead to sexual intercourse. Sexuality Today 14.1 explains the relationship between different courtship stages and behavior.

courtship disorders: A theory of paraphilias that links them to being stuck in different stages of the normal progression of courtship.

Boys and girls show natural curiosity about the clothing of the opposite sex. If made to feel shame for this curiosity, they may develop an intense interest, and eventually a compulsive interest, in the object.

SEXUALITY *Today*   <u>14.1</u>

Courtship Disorders

Freund and his colleagues (Freund and Scher, 1983, 1984) suggest that human sexual behavior goes through a series of stages before intercourse—seeing a potential partner, engaging them, tactile interaction (touching), and finally copulating. These courtship behaviors, Freund suggests, may be distorted by the paraphiliac; he or she may be "stuck" at one stage of courtship, unwilling or unable to progress to the next step. The list below gives some examples of paraphilias that may result from being stuck at different stages of courtship, or in the last case (which is not technically a paraphilia), if the person completely skips appropriate courtship behavior.

Courtship Stage	Paraphilia
Locating or viewing a potential partner	Voyeurism (compulsive looking)
Pretactile interaction	Exhibitionism (exposing oneself)
	Obscene telephone calling
Tactile interaction	Toucheurism (touching strangers)
	Frotteurism (rubbing up against strangers)
Almost entire omission of courtship behavior	Rape patterns

Behavioral Theories

Behaviorists suggest that paraphilias develop because some behavior becomes associated with sexual pleasure through conditioning (Wilson, 1987). For example, imagine that a boy receives an enema. While receiving it, the boy has an erection, either by coincidence or because he finds the stimulus of the enema pleasurable. Later, remembering the enema, he becomes excited and masturbates. As he repeats his masturbatory fantasy, a process called **conditioning** occurs, whereby sexual excitement becomes so associated with the idea of the enema that he has trouble becoming excited in its absence. You can imagine how similar situations could lead to other types of fetishes: a boy lies naked on a fur coat or rides "horsey" on aunty's high buttoned shoes or puts on his sister's panties or spies on a female house guest through the bathroom keyhole.

Sociological Theories

Another way of looking at the causes of paraphilias is to look at the ways society encourages certain behaviors. Feminists, for example, argue that in societies that treat women as sexual objects anyway, it is a natural development to replace the woman with another, inanimate sexual object. When men and their sexual organs are glorified, some men may need to reinforce their masculinity by exposing themselves and evoking fear. American society is ruled by images, saturated with television, movies, commercials, advertisements, and magazines, and most have highly charged sexual imagery. The result, some argue, is a world where the image takes the place of the reality, where it becomes common to substitute fantasies for reality. Surrounded by media, the society experiences things vicariously, through reading about it or seeing it rather than actually doing it. In such a climate, representations of eroticism may be easily substituted for sex itself, and so paraphilias become common.

conditioning: In behaviorism, the process whereby an organism associates a particular stimulus with a response; for example, if food repeatedly is served to a dog right after the sound of a bell, the dog will salivate at the sound of the bell even if no food is served.

Specific Paraphilias

Paraphilias have been grouped into a number of major categories by researchers and clinicians. Below we review some of the more common types of paraphilias.

Fetishism

A fetish is an inanimate object or a body part not usually associated with the sex act that becomes the primary or exclusive focus of sexual arousal and orgasm in an individual. The fetishist can develop a sexual response to an object, such as shoes, boots, panties, or bras; to a fabric, such as leather, silk, fur, or rubber; or to a body part, such as feet, buttocks, or hair. As with most paraphilias, the majority of fetishists are male.

There are different degress of attraction to an object. Many people enjoy using lingerie or even rubber or other fabrics as part of their lovemaking without becoming dependent upon them for arousal. The fetishist, on the other hand, *needs* the presence or the fantasy of the object in order to achieve arousal and sometimes cannot achieve orgasm in its absence. Some fetishists replace the human partner with the object, and they may cease having sexual intercourse altogether.

Some fetishists integrate the object of their desire into their sexual life with a partner; for others it remains a secret fetish, with hidden collections of shoes, or panties, or photographs of a body part, over which they masturbate in secret, ever fearful of discovery. Many fetishists see their sexual habits as a major part of their life, a source of their sense of identity; yet because fetishism is often regarded by society as shameful, they may be embarrassed to admit to their sexual desires. It is therefore rare to find a person who is open about their fetish and even has a sense of humor about it, as Sargent does in his description of his rubber fetish in Personal Voices 14.1.

People can become sexually fixated on almost any object, and they may have more than one fetish. For example, in one sample of forty-eight hospitalized fetishists studied by Chalkley and Powell (1983), individuals were fixated on such things as stockings, suspenders, slips, nylon knickers and panties, boots, rubber tubes and enemas, and handkerchiefs. Many had multiple fetishes; only seventeen of the forty-eight subjects were limited to a single object, while nine had two fetishes, twelve had three, six had four, and one each had five, six, seven, and nine fetishes. (There was one female among Chalkley and Powell's sample; she had a breast fetish.)

The fetishist is frequently content with his or her behavior, finding it arousing and harmless. Fetishists rarely volunteer for treatment, for, as Sargent tells us in Personal Voices 14.1, it provides a source of instant arousal, an ever-ready aphrodisiac. For some, though, the practice can be disruptive or even lead to criminal behavior; of the forty-eight fetishists studied by Chalkley and Powell (1983), thirteen had been referred to treatment because they were in some kind of legal trouble, most commonly stealing the object of their fetish. A publicist for Marla Maples, wife of Donald Trump, was arrested and tried for stealing dozens of her shoes; he admitted he had an "inappropriate and inordinate preoccupation with women's shoes," especially the imprint left in them after they had been worn (*Philadephia Daily News,* 1994). However, the problem most troubling to fetishists is the guilt and shame they feel about their behavior.

Different cultures hold up different body parts, objects, colors, or smells ("sign selection") as symbols of attraction and sexuality for mating. Fetishism is sign selection gone awry, where the person becomes sexually attracted to the sign itself, instead of what it represents. Put another way, for the fetishist, the object, unlike the living, breathing person, can stand for pure eroticism without the complication of having to deal with

The Story of a Rubber Fetishist

I am a rubber fetishist and professional therapist, in that order. This combination has given me a special view of unusual sexual practices both through my own personal experience and as a result of the large number of other individuals whom I have encountered professionally and personally.

I have four clear vignettes of memory associated with my early delight with rubber which I present either because they stimulate me in the telling or because they may be important to a therapist or client. One is of a woman with long dark hair playing with my penis by stroking it with soft rubber panties and moving her long hair gently and playfully over it. The whole image is intense and all involving. It is loving, fun, sexually exciting (I have no image of the state of my penis), secure, and safe. For me, rubber most often provides all of these experiences in one simultaneous concert of sensations. A second image is that of a moment of pleasant security when I pull back the bed covers far enough to place my hand gently on the rubber sheet of my bed in order to exchange the upset of a forgotten and unpleasant encounter with an adult for the quiet tranquility of the soft rubber and its loving associations. A third image is sliding under the cotton sheet to enjoy the rubber after I have been "tucked in" at night and then engaging in what my mother called "bounding up and down," still my favorite form of stimulation with my face and whole body gently moving over the rubber, skillfully massaging my penis between the rubber and my stomach. The fourth image is of a birthday. The rubber was in the form of solid rubber animals, smooth and rubber smelling but rather hard and of little sexual use. By the time I was three I was a full blown rubber fetishist. No raincoat, bathing cap, or pair of baby panties was (or is) safe from me. My pediatrician was warm and kind about it, and I appreciate the impact of his support on my life. I had no inkling of being weird, no guilt, in contrast with many of my fellow fetishists at the hands of their professionals. I hoped that I wouldn't outgrow it, and I didn't. By age nine, my grandfather's raincoat came into the house and I made love to it without ever being discovered. I still have a sheet of the rubber from it after fifty years. Simply stated, my life involved rubber as a central element from my earliest years and still does as I enter my sixties. Neither my mother nor professionals stimulated any guilt.

I had one encounter with a psychiatrist regarding my fetish. He told me that if I felt guilty (discovering that I was unusual seemed like guilt) I could either lay the guilt to rest or the rubber. Keeping both could be emotionally disruptive. I like this model of offering to eliminate guilt in place of eliminating sexual practice and have used it ever since as a therapist. For me, of course, I chose to keep the rubber.

In my own presentations of my rubber fetish I do not fail to enjoy some good laughs at myself. This is because I take myself seriously, seriously enough to laugh at things that are absurd. For example, I have received disapproving looks from women wearing rubber raincoats who thought I was looking at them, and from men who mistook my absorbed gaze as sexual attraction to them. I go nuts over rubber coats and will take the time to follow or cross a street just to prolong the delight of sound or vision. Then I will hurry to a place where I can love my rubber while fantasizing about the one I saw. Or I will lay one on top of another and be very promiscuous by loving the red while fantasizing about the blue and maybe go to get the blue and become distracted by the black. It's a delight. One day in a store I watched for a long time as a lady tried on a yellow poncho. She stood and posed in front of a mirror, smoothing the soft rubber over her breasts. I was standing at the rack, touching the same soft rubber. She came over, returning it with a smile. Dark hair and brown eyes—the coat was still warm as I scooped it up and bought it. It is still a favorite fantasy. Or the small department store that always had a supply of various kinds of rubber coats (if I don't have a particular size or color, I *must*). The salesman took me to a private loft upstairs where there were hundreds of rubber coats. I do not know if someone there shared my fetish, but it was my idea of heaven. I took lots of time, so the salesman asked if it was all right if he left me alone. All right? I went around my heaven with a delightful erection and sampled the softness of the rubber against my penis. Every coat in the collection. Then I took a few and laid them on a flat surface and made love to them. It was incredible. It's all silly, and fun.

Laughter, particularly at the self, dislodges the judgments and fears that are associated with most sexual behaviors because it provides a new perspective. The fetishes offer the therapist the opportunity to dislodge the seriousness which entrenches a distressed perspective, and discover the effectiveness of these approaches even to serious sexual difficulty and offenses. It is also effective. At best, a six foot man looks ridiculous in ten inch heels and knows it. If the therapist can't laugh, the message is clear to the client that it is as weird as he thought.

Sargent (1988)

another person's feelings, wants, and needs. It can be a refuge from the complexity of interpersonal sexual relations. In that sense, all the paraphilias we discuss below can be seen as a type of fetishism; pain and humiliation or women's clothes or looking at people having sex can each be a substitute for interpersonal sexuality.

Sadism and Masochism

sadism: Focus on administering pain and humiliation as the preferred or exclusive method of sexual arousal and orgasm.

Sadism refers to the intentional infliction of physical or psychological pain on another person in order to achieve sexual excitement. The term is named after Donatien Alphonse Françios de Sade (1740–1814), known as the Marquis de Sade. De Sade was sent to prison for kidnapping and terrorizing a beggar girl and then later for tricking some prostitutes into eating "Spanish Fly" (see Chapter 12), supposedly an aphrodisiac, but which caused such burning and blistering that one threw herself out a window. While in prison, de Sade wrote the novels *Justine* and *Juliette,* which described such tortures as being bound hand and foot, suspended between trees, set upon by dogs, almost being eviscerated (cut open), and so on. The highest form of sexual activity for women was pain, not pleasure, de Sade believed, because pleasure could be too easily faked. De Sade spent much of his life in prison and ended his life in a lunatic asylum (Bullough, 1976).

masochism: Focus on receiving pain and humiliation as the preferred or exclusive method of sexual arousal and orgasm.

Masochism, the achievement of sexual pleasure through one's own physical pain or psychological humiliation, was named after another novelist, Leopold Baron Von Sacher-Masoch (1836–1895). Sacher-Masoch believed that women were created to subdue men's "animal passions," and the whippings he describes in such novels as *Venus in Furs* (1888) he himself experienced at the hands of his mistresses (Bullough, 1976).

sadomasochism: The sexual activities of partners where one takes a dominant, "master," position, and the other takes a submissive, "slave," position.

Sadism and masochism both associate sexuality and pain, and most people who practice one are also involved with the other. Therefore, the phenomenon as a whole is often referred to as **sadomasochism**, or S&M. Since sadomasochism encompasses a wide variety of behaviors, how many people engage in it depends on how one defines it. In their survey, Janus and Janus (1993) found that 14% of men and 11% of women report some personal experience with S&M.

Some theorists have suggested that sadomasochism underlies many of the most interesting questions about sexuality and love. For example, Havelock Ellis, the pioneering sexuality researcher, wrote in 1903:

> *The relation of love to pain is one of the most difficult problems, and yet one of the most fundamental, in the whole range of sexual psychology. Why is it that love inflicts, and seeks to inflict, pain? Why is it that love suffers pain, and even seeks to suffer it?. . . [If] we succeed in answering it we shall come very near one of the great mysteries of love. At the same time we shall have made clear the normal basis on which rest the extreme aberrations of love.*
>
> ### Quoted in Moser (1988:43)

Sadomasochists often use props, like leather clothes, studs, collars, etc., to symbolize their dominance or submission.

Freud and his followers made sadomasochism central to their theorizing about adult sexuality. Freud believed that we all feel ambivalent to some degree about the ones we love and even, at times, feel the desire to hurt them. But we also feel guilty about it, especially in early childhood, and the guilt we feel is satisfied by turning that hurt upon ourselves. Later psychoanalytic theorists believed that the goal of masochism was not pain or punishment itself, but rather relinquishing the self to someone else in order to avoid responsibility or anxiety for sexual desires. To these theorists, we all engage in some sadistic and some masochistic behaviors in our love relationships.

Sexual responses to pain exist, to some degree, in many sexual relationships. Kinsey et al. (1953), for example, found that about half the men and women had some erotic response to being bitten and 24% of men and 12% of women had some erotic response to sadomasochistic stories. Surveys seem to indicate that between 5% and 10% of people have S&M fantasies or engage in S&M behavior at least occasionally (Moser and Levitt, 1987). Some couples use bondage, for example, as a variation on their love-making without any other strong sadomasochistic elements (Comfort, 1987).

The paraphilic sadomasochist takes these natural sadomasochistic tendencies to an extreme. S&M involves the use of physical pain, psychological humiliation, or both as part of sexuality. In most S&M encounters, one partner plays the **dominant** role ("master") and the other the **submissive** ("slave"). A variety of techniques are commonly used to physically dominate the submissive partner. Tying the submissive partner up or using restraints to render him or her helpless is often referred to as "bondage and discipline" (B&D). B&D is often accompanied by **flagellation**, **caning** or **birching**, or other painful or shocking stimuli on the skin such as the use of hot wax, ice, biting, etc. Psychological techniques can include sensory deprivation (through the use of face masks, blindfolds, ear plugs), humiliation (being subject to verbal abuse or being made to engage in embarrassing behaviors such as boot-licking, **scatophagic** behavior, **urolangia**, or acting like a dog), forced cross-dressing, or **infantilism** (DSM-IV, 1994; Gosselin, 1987; Moser, 1988). This is accompanied by verbal descriptions of what is to come and why the person deserves it, increasing in intensity over time to eventual sexual climax. Note that the pain is used as part of a technique to enhance sexuality—the pain *itself* is not exciting. If the submissive partner were beat up on his or her way home from a sexual encounter, he or she would not find the resultant pain in any way exciting.

S&M does not generally result in any lasting physical damage, as the encounter is usually a carefully scripted sexual ritual, with both sides knowing how far they can go and what roles to play. Still, sometimes S&M can go too far and result in accidental injury, or even death. Though a small number of people are nonconsensual, criminal sadists who derive joy in hurting or killing others, they bear little relation to the subculture of sadomasochists who use S&M as a mutual sexual activity.

People can participate in S&M to different degrees. For some couples, S&M is an occasional diversion in their lovemaking. Others pursue it in private; for example, most big cities have newspapers with advertisements for sadomasochistic services, where a **dominatrix** will offer her services to submissive males. Many report that executives and politicians and other men with power are among their biggest clients. For these men, the opportunity to absolve themselves of decision making and put their sexual lives completely in the hands of a dominant woman is very exciting.

A sadomasochistic subculture exists for those who have adopted S&M as a lifestyle. Partners meet in S&M clubs (often called "leather bars"), have S&M newsletters and magazines, and join organizations (such as the *Eulenspiegel Society,* or the *Society of Janus; SAMOIS* is a lesbian S&M group). Specialty shops cater to S&M advocates, selling restraints, whips, and other leather clothing. The sadomasochistic encounter, which is really a kind of drama or performance, is enhanced by both sides knowing their roles and dressing the part.

Much of S&M is about playing roles, usually with appropriate attitude, costuming, and scripted talk. These roles can change; contrary to popular belief, research has found that a large percentage of people into S&M switch between the dominant and submissive roles (Breslow et al., 1985, 1986). The S&M encounter is carefully planned, and the dominant partner is usually very careful not to actually hurt the submissive partner while "torturing" him or her. A "safe word" is usually agreed upon whereby the submissive partner can signal if he or she is in real distress. *The Masters' and Mistress' Handbook,* a

dominant: Taking the active role in sadomasochistic sexuality.

submissive: Taking the passive role in sadomasochistic activity.

flagellation: Striking a partner, usually by whipping.

caning: Beating someone with a rigid cane.

birching: Whipping someone using the stripped branch of a tree.

scatophagia *and* **urolangia:** The ingestion of feces and urine, respectively, often as a sign of submission.

infantilism: Treating the submissive partner as a baby, including dressing the person in diapers in which he or she is forced to relieve himself or herself.

dominatrix: A woman, often a prostitute, who humiliates and dominates submissive men.

guide to S&M encounters, offers a set of rules on how to torture one's partner without really causing harm:

> *Remember that a slave may suddenly start to cough or feel faint. If masked and gagged, choking or lack of oxygen may result in serious consequences within seconds. . . . Never leave a bound and gagged slave alone in a room. . . . It is essential that gags, nostril tubes, enema pipes, rods and other insertions should be scrupulously clean and dipped into mild antiseptic before use. . . . Never use cheap or coarse rope. This has no "give" and can quickly cause skin-sores.*
>
> *Quoted in Gosselin (1987:238–239)*

Sadomasochistic subcultures exist among gays, lesbians, and heterosexuals. In heterosexual S&M, power relations between the sexes are often overturned, with the female being the dominant partner and the male submissive. In both gay and lesbian S&M, the sadomasochistic drama is used to explore the nature of social relations by using sex as a means to explore power (Truscott, 1991). Both heterosexual and homosexual S&M practitioners derive sexual excitement from playing with power relations, from either being able to dominate another completely or to give in completely to another's will.

The S&M subculture uses symbols of authority and dominance taken from the general culture, such as whips, uniforms, and handcuffs, and uses them in a safe erotic drama where scripted roles take the place of "real self." It even mocks these symbols of authority by using them for erotic pleasure. This is expressed well by a porn writer and porn star (who is also a "world-class S&M whipmaster") interviewed by Stoller (1991:51):

> *See, I think S&M is savagely repressed in every society because it is inherently subversive to make fun of the symbols of authority. That's what people literally do in S&M—make fun of the symbols of authority and the symbolic behavior of domination, not necessarily consciously burlesquing them but using them for recreational purposes . . . this kind of perversion—perversion that has to do with mocking social rituals—is definitely subversion. That's why church and state conspire to crush it.*

Baumeister (1988) goes so far as to suggest that sadomasochism is a reaction to modern society itself. Noting that sexual masochism proliferated when Western culture became highly individualistic, Baumeister suggests that it relieves the submissive partner of a sense of responsibility for the self by placing one's behavior completely under someone else's control (which may be why many businessmen pay a dominatrix to humiliate them). For the sadistic partner, it relieves the sense of interaction and sensitivity usual to some degree in sexual intercourse; the personhood of the submissive partner is ignored and he or she can become a vehicle for the pleasure of the dominant partner.

Exhibitionism and Voyeurism

Visual stimuli are basic aspects of sexuality; most sexually active people enjoy looking at the nude bodies of their partners, and such things as lingerie and the act of undressing one's partner can enhance the sexual nature of the human form. The enormous industry of adult magazines and books, the almost obligatory nude scene in modern movies, the embarrassment most people feel when seen naked inappropriately, and even the common nighttime dream of being caught naked in public all show the fundamental psychological power of visual sexual stimuli.

Most advertisements for S&M services cater to the submissive male. Many such services also have submissives available for the dominant male.

For some people, looking at nudity or sexual acts or being seen naked or engaging in sex become the paramount activities of sexuality. The person who becomes sexually aroused primarily from displaying his (or, more rarely, her) genitals, nudity, or sexuality to strangers is an **exhibitionist**; the person whose primary mode of sexual stimulation is to watch others naked or engaging in sex is called a voyeur. Langevin and Lang (1987) review a number of studies that show that there is a close connection between exhibitionism and voyeurism; most exhibitionists engaged in voyeuristic habits before beginning to expose themselves.

exhibitionist: One who exposes his or her genitals to strangers as a preferred or exclusive means of sexual arousal and orgasm.

Exhibitionism. The exhibitionist (or "flasher"), who is usually male, achieves sexual gratification from exposing his genitals in public or to unsuspecting females. What excites the exhibitionist is not usually the nudity itself but the lack of consent of the victim as expressed in her shocked or fearful reaction. True exhibitionists would not get the same sexual charge being naked on a nude beach, for example, where everyone is naked. Exhibitionists usually have erections while exposing themselves, and they masturbate either then and there or later, while thinking about the reactions of the female victims.

Exhibitionism is the most common of all reported sexual offenses (Snaith, 1983). Legally classified as "indecent exposure," exhibitionism accounts for up to one-third of all sex convictions in the United States, Canada, and Europe (Langevin and Lang, 1987). While rates of exhibitionism are difficult to determine, between 33% and 35% of women in a United States college sample (Cox, 1988) and in a similar Hong Kong sample (Cox et al., 1982) reported being subjected to a male exhibitionist, most commonly in their early adolescence. Interestingly, 36% of the American sample reported knowing the man who exposed himself, which contradicts the DSM-IV criterion for exhibitionism, which states that the victim must be a stranger to the exhibitionist.

The exhibitionist usually exposes himself first while in his twenties (Blair and Lanyon, 1981). Many do not desire actual sexual union with the victim. Only 50% of the exhibitionists in one study claimed that they would have had sex with the woman if she had desired it (Langevin and Lang, 1987). Research has failed to confirm any personality characteristics that might be common to exhibitionists except that the behavior is compulsive and very difficult to stop (Snaith, 1983). Many exhibitionists have normal dating and sexual histories, are married and have normal sexual relations with their spouses, and do not seem to engage in their behavior *instead* of heterosexual intercourse (Langevin and Lang, 1987). Others tend to be shy, withdrawn, and marry their first girlfriend.

Exhibitionism in women is rare, although cases of it are reported in the literature (Grob, 1985; Rhoads and Boekelheide, 1985). Rhoads and Boekelheide suggest that the female exhibitionist may desire to feel feminine and appreciated, and seeing men admire her naked body reinforces the women's sense of sexual value and femininity. Perhaps, then, exhibitionism in women just takes a different form than in men. Another factor may be that women have much more opportunity to expose their bodies in social settings without being arrested. Even sophisticated evening wear often exposes the woman's cleavage, and short skirts and women's bathing suits (such as thong-style suits) cover very little. Women, therefore, have more legitimate ways to expose their bodies than men do. This type of exposure may be enough for female exhibitionists.

Obscene Telephone Callers. The exhibitionist must have the courage to confront his victims in person; the telephone allows a more anonymous kind of contact for the timid paraphiliac. **Scatolophilia**, the technical name for obscene telephone calling, is a form of exhibitionism where a person, almost always male, calls women and becomes excited as the victims react to his obscene suggestions. Most masturbate either during the call or afterward. Like the exhibitionist, the scatolophiliac is excited by the victim's reactions of fear, disgust, or outrage. Most scatolophiliacs have problems in their relationships and suffer from feelings of isolation and inadequacy. For many, scatolophilia is the only way they can express themselves sexually (Holmes, 1991).

scatolophilia: Sexual arousal from making obscene telephone calls.

SEX TALK

Q U E S T I O N   **14.3** **What should I do if I receive an obscene telephone call?**

The recipient of an obscene call should react calmly and not exhibit the reactions of shock, fright, or disgust that the caller finds exciting. Do not slam the phone down; simply replace it gently in the cradle. An immediate ring again is probably a callback; ignore it, or pick up the phone and hang up quickly without listening. Sometimes a gentle suggestion that the person needs psychological help disrupts the caller's fantasy. Persistent callers can be discouraged by suggesting that you have contacted the police. (Do not blow a police whistle into the phone, as some suggest; the caller can do the same to you later.) If you do get more than one call, notify the telephone company. Calls can be traced very quickly these days. Many phone companies now offer a two-digit code that sends the phone number of the last person to call your house directly to the phone company, who can then give it to the police. Check with your local telephone company to see if the service is available in your area.

The obscene telephone caller may boast of sexual acts he will perform on the victim, may describe his masturbation in detail, may threaten the victim, or may try to entice the victim to reveal aspects of her sexual life or even perform sexual acts such as masturbating while he listens on the phone. Some callers are very persuasive; many have great success in talking women into performing sexual acts while posing as product representatives recalling tampons or douches, as the police, or even as people conducting a sexual survey. (Please note: *no* reputable sexuality researchers conduct surveys over the phone. If you receive such a call, do not answer any sexually explicit questions.) Others threaten harm to the victim or her family if she does not do what he asks (obscene callers often know the victim's address, if only from the phone book). Some will get a woman's phone number while observing her writing a check at a place like the supermarket and then will frighten her more because he knows her address, appearance, and even some of her food preferences (Matek, 1988).

Currently, thousands of sexually explicit phone lines have been established where a person can pay to speak to a member of the opposite sex. Perhaps these lines may lessen the need of obscene callers to contact unsuspecting victims. However, new and potentially more intrusive types of obscene calls may be just around the corner. Computer online services provide an opportunity for people to type obscene messages to other users while online. Recently, also, the first picture-phones have been put into general use; these phones have a screen that transmits the picture of the person calling. The picture-phone may initiate a whole new type of obscene telephone call.

Voyeurism. Voyeurs, or **scopophiliacs**, are people whose main means of sexual gratification is through watching others naked or engaged in sex. Some would argue that we are a voyeuristic society; our major media—newspapers, television, movies, advertisements—are full of sexual images that are intended to interest and arouse us. Magazines and movies featuring nude women or couples are very popular. Even television shows display far more nudity and sexuality than would have been allowed in movies just a few years ago. In modern society, it seems, we have all become casual voyeurs to some degree.

Clinical voyeurs, however, are those for whom watching others naked or viewing erotica is a *compulsion*. Voyeurs are often called *Peeping Toms,* a revealing term because implicit in it are two important aspects of voyeurism. First, a "peeper" is one who looks without the knowledge or consent of the viewed, and the true voyeur is excited by the illicit aspect of their peeping. Second, the voyeur is usually male. Though it is becoming more acceptable for women in society to read magazines such as *Playgirl,* which show nude men, or to spend an evening watching male strippers such as the Chippendales, clinically speaking there are very few "Peeping Janes."

The typical voyeur is a heterosexual man in his twenties. **Primary voyeurism** is apparently rare. More often, voyeurism is mixed in with a host of other paraphilic behaviors (Langevin and Lang, 1987). In one study, less than 2% of voyeurs said that voyeurism was their only paraphilia (Abel et al., 1988). Still, voyeurs are generally harmless and are satisfied just with peeping, although they certainly can scare an unsuspecting person who sees a strange man peering in the window. In a few cases, however, voyeurism can lead to more and more intrusive sexual activity, including rape (Holmes, 1991). Voyeurs, when caught, are usually not charged with a sex crime but with trespassing or sometimes breaking and entering. Therefore, how many actually get in trouble with the law is difficult to determine.

Many voyeurs satisfy some of their urges by renting X-rated videos or going to live sex shows. For most voyeurs, however, these are ultimately unsatisfying, for part of the excitement is the knowledge that the victim does not know or approve of the fact that the voyeur sees them. Like exhibitionists, voyeurs tend to be immature, sexually frustrated, poor at developing relationships, and are chronic masturbators (Holmes, 1991).

scopophilia: The psychoanalytic term for voyeurism, literally "the love of looking."

primary voyeurist: A person for whom voyeurism is the main and exclusive paraphilia.

Personal

V O I C E S

14.2

Reactions to an Obscene Telephone Caller

The following personal account is from a twenty-eight-year-old woman, who was sharing a house with two roommates.

In May of 1990, after returning from a friend's wedding, I noticed that our phone machine had several messages on it. Many of these were very explicit and perverted. The guy who left them knew my name and said he was watching me, following all my moves, and had seen me taking a shower before. The whole time he kept breathing heavily. I was very scared because I didn't know who this person was, whether he was hiding in the bushes, or how he could know who I was.

From there his calls became more frequent and persisted throughout the summer. Each time he called he was very disgusting—saying things about pussy, vaginas, breasts, nipples, wanting to "fuck" me. He described what he thought it would be like to have sex with me—in fact, he also threatened to rape me. It was really disgusting. I was so scared and would cry all the time. I felt like he was everywhere because I didn't know who he was. The police told me to be careful about where I went and who I talked to.

Sometimes he would call in the afternoon, and sometimes at 3:00 in the morning. He told me what I had worn on particular days and knew what I looked like. I felt his closeness. . . . I felt like I was a threat to the safety of my roommates, who were frightened as well. My Dad brought over a shotgun and slept in the house one night. Actually that was the night that this guy told me he was going to come over and rape me.

Finally the phone company was able to trace the incoming calls to a specific phone number. It turned out it was a family number, and one of the kids living at home was making the calls. He was about nineteen to twenty years old. As it turns out, I found out he was the grocery clerk at the store that I shopped at. Every time I went there and checked out, he saw what I was wearing and also took all of the information off of my checks. Ironically, every time I went to the grocery store, I always made a point to go to this guy's checkout line. I thought that he was this young, little, innocent guy. He didn't sound anything like himself when he called me; I guess he changed his voice.

The arrest was made. He admitted to harassing about six other women over the phone. The charges that were filed against him were called harassment by communication. We began the trial, and I was lucky enough to get a female judge, which I think helped me. I really felt like all of the people that I interacted with respected and believed in me, which made me feel stronger. In court it was hard to go over everything that happened again. It was especially bad because the majority of people in the courtroom were men.

The guy was found guilty, sentenced to community service, and had to pay a fine of $500. He had to go to therapy 2–3 times a week. The judge told him that if she ever found him doing this again, he would go to jail and get a much stiffer sentence. I was mad, but at least it was over.

One month later, he started calling again. I couldn't believe it! I called the police and he was picked up and thrown in jail again.

In thinking about this now, I just wish that I wouldn't have waited so long to call the police the first time. I endured a whole month of his calls before I called the police. First, I believed that it would stop by itself. I was also really embarrassed about it and didn't think people would believe me. I also regret how paranoid I felt during all of those months. I blamed one guy, who was innocent. I just felt so distrustful of everyone. People who do things like this just don't understand how much it disrupted my life. This guy's phone calls totally took away the trust and compassion I had for other people.

Author's files

---

troilism: The act of a couple engaging in sex together while willingly being observed by a third party.

Troilism. Although it technically refers to a single couple copulating in front of others, **troilism** has come to mean any sex sessions involving multiple partners. Troilism is not new; in 1631, Mervyn Touchet, the Second Earl of Castlehaven, was executed in England for ordering his servants to have sex with his wife while he watched. The fact that they were servants and thus beneath his station was as damaging to him as the actual act (Bullough, 1976). Janus and Janus (1993) found that 14% of men and 8% of women in their survey had engaged in group sex.

Troilism may involve aspects of voyeurism, exhibitionism, and, sometimes, latent homosexual desires; an observer who gets excited, for example, by watching his wife fellate another man may be subconsciously putting himself in his wife's place. Some troilists install ceiling mirrors, video cameras, and other means to capture the sexual act for viewing later on. Others engage in sharing a sexual partner with a third party while they look on, or they engage in swinging (see Chapter 8). Many couples experiment with group sex, but to the troilist, engaging in or fantasizing about such sexual activity is their primary means of sexual arousal.

Transvestism

The **transvestite**, or **transgendered** person, obtains sexual pleasure from dressing up in the clothing of the opposite sex. True transvestites are almost always heterosexual males, although cross-dressing is common in a variety of contexts. Women in our culture, for example, often wear traditionally male clothing such as pants, suits, or ties. Male homosexual "drag queens" dress as females, and "butch" lesbians dress as males as part of the role-playing activities of the gay subculture. Cross-dressing is also frequently depicted in movies, such as Jack Lemmon and Tony Curtis in the classic Marilyn Monroe movie *Some Like It Hot,* or more recently Robin Williams in *Mrs. Doubtfire;* and it is a frequent comic diversion on television, such as the classic cross-dressing of Milton Berle in the 1950s, or the attempts of Corporal Klinger to get a psychiatric discharge for cross-dressing on *M*A*S*H.* Cross-dressing also has a long history; the Hebrew Bible, for example, expressly forbids wearing the clothing of the opposite sex. Agathon, a Greek tragic poet, would greet his friends dressed in a long female robe, saffron-colored tunic, and cape, with a bust-bodice, a hair net, and tight-fitting buskins (Tannahill, 1980). Joan of Arc was found guilty, among other things, of preferring male hairstyles and dress. Dekker and van de Pol (1989) document more than 100 cases of women who cross-dressed and lived as men in the seventeenth and eighteenth centuries. And Edward Hyde, the governor of colonial New York and New Jersey in the early eighteenth century, actually appears in flowing gown and lace hairpiece in his official state portrait!

Yet most of these are not cases of true transvestism, because the element of sexual excitement is missing. That is why true transvestism is often referred to as **fetishistic transvestism**, to emphasize the fact that the cross-dresser has an erotic attraction to the clothing he wears.

Transvestites are different from transsexuals. Male transsexuals feel that they are really women "trapped" in the body of a man, and many eventually pursue sex reassignment surgery (see Chapter 5). The male transvestite, however, does not desire to change his biological gender. The difference between transvestites and transsexuals seems to begin early in life; one study found that transsexuals, but not transvestites, lacked interest in playing with other boys while young, and transvestites, but not transsexuals, cross-dressed very early in life (Bullough et al., 1983). A small number of transvestites will go to great lengths to feminize their appearance, employing electrolysis (hair removal), taking hormones, or even getting surgical implants to simulate female breasts. But even most of these transvestites would stop at sex reassignment surgery because they enjoy heterosexual intercourse and being men.

Clothes are, in all cultures, symbols of sexual identity and gender roles. Many transvestites are not comfortable with the gender roles that society forces on them

transvestite: A person whose preferred or exclusive method of sexual arousal or orgasm is through wearing the clothing of the other sex.

transgendered: A recently coined term for transvestites and transsexuals, meant to indicate that they transcend simple categories of gender. "Intersexed" is also used.

fetishistic transvestism: A person whose preferred or exclusive method of sexual arousal or orgasm is through wearing the clothing of the other sex.

because of their biological gender, and they feel that cross-dressing liberates them from the expectation society puts on being male. As one cross-dresser put it:

> *Crossdressers of whatever persuasion, straight or gay, transvestites, transgen-*
> *derists, or transsexuals, are in the vanguard of men's liberation because we*
> *have faced that which frightens so many men: our inner femininity. We've met*
> *this erstwhile enemy and have made a degree of peace with her. . . . For most*
> *crossdressers, the feminine clothing simply gets them out of jail, so they can, for*
> *a limited time, be the kind of person they cannot be the rest of the time.*
>
> *Allen (1989)*

The degree to which transvestites assume a feminine identity differs in different men, but many adopt a name for their female side, and their spouses often say that when dressed as a woman, these men assume a very different personality (Allen, 1989). Cross-dressing may allow these men to relax, freed from the societal pressures of being male.

Some transvestites are very secretive about their habits, fearing that others will censure or ridicule them. Many have private collections of female clothes, and married transvestites may even hide their habit from their wives, although the majority do tell. This secrecy makes it difficult to determine how common transvestism actually is. Janus and Janus (1993) report that 6% of the men and 3% of the women in their survey reported some personal experience with cross-dressing.

SEX TALK

QUESTION **14.4 Aren't transvestites, deep down, really homosexual?**

No. Some male homosexuals enjoy dressing up as females, and some may derive a certain sexual satisfaction from it. But as Wayne expresses in Personal Voices 14.3, most heterosexual transvestites are not at all interested in sex with men. They seem all absorbed by women; they want to look, act, and behave like women and get a strong sexual attraction from women's clothes. Some like it when men approach them when they are cross-dressed but only because it affirms their abilities to pass as women.

Clinically speaking, we no more understand why people become transvestites than we understand any other fetishistic behavior. Most transvestites began cross-dressing at a very young age and began masturbating while wearing women's clothing during adolescence (Bullough et al., 1983). Male transvestites displayed more preadult feminine behaviors, such as preferring the company of girls, being called a sissy, or having female hobbies than a nontransvestite control group (Buhrich and McConaghy, 1985). Often, the intense sexual arousal of being dressed as female diminishes with age, but the behavior itself does not stop (Peo, 1988).

Many transvestites marry and raise families, which can cause problems if their spouses do not know of their habit. Bullough and Weinberg (1988) studied seventy wives of transvestites. Most had learned of their husbands' habit early in the relationship and tolerated or even supported it to some degree, although many also expressed resentment and fear of public exposure. However, most also characterized their marriage as happy and described their husbands as loving and good fathers. Some women married to transvestites fully support their husband's feminine identity, seeing "her" as a separate partner and friend from "him." In some families, the male's transvestism is completely open, and the children know about it and even help Daddy pick out clothes or do his nails (Allen, 1989).

A Transvestite and His (Her?) Wife

Elayne (alter ego of Wayne):

Last night I sat in a car with two crossdressers and held hands. Although we talked only about petty things, we touched. I can express my inner self as Wayne, but when I'm being Elayne, a few more bricks disappear. When I looked into Diane's eyes [another crossdresser], she looked right back into mine, but earlier, when I talked to [her as] Ed, he couldn't look at me. We spoke to the side of each other. But Diane and I didn't speak *to* each other, we spoke *within* each other.

I knew there was something different about me from the time I was six years old and I put on my sister's silk pajamas. They felt so good, but I was scolded and scoffed at. I grew up in a very conservative, redneck area of Iowa where "women were women and men were men." All through my childhood I wore black and white or muted plaid. When I was given crayons, I dared use only the black and white ones. I was so afraid of using color and being perceived as different.

I looked all over for information on crossdressing. I finally found something in Ann Landers—she told a wife that it was okay for her husband to wear her clothes. When I read that, I knew that there were others like me. I still have that column—it has turned yellow!

Elayne and his/her daughter.

When I dressed as Elayne, my son Ryan and I sometimes go for a ride through the woods and farms on our bicycles, and I'm sure most of the people who see us assume I'm his mother. I've always dressed around the kids. When they get older, maybe they'll tell their friends. I won't hide my crossdressing. I won't flaunt it either.

I don't feel particularly masculine. I tend to see men as hairy and fuzzy and bulky and aggressive. Men are dirty, and they don't know how to take care of themselves. I wouldn't want to have sex with a man.

Girls are usually encouraged to do the softer things, but if a boy starts into that softer area, he's held back. *Why should women have all the experiences in life?* I fantasized about having a baby and being pregnant, especially when Kaye was. If it were possible, I'd like to have a child. I'd be first in line to be the prototype mother-father!

I'd like to have breasts and have a baby suckle at my nipple. Kaye has beautiful, wonderful breasts. It's fun for her to lie on her back on top of me, and I can put my arms around her and feel the fantasy. She becomes part of me.

Kaye (Elayne/Wayne's wife):

Sometimes I find Elayne too pretty and overpowering. Sometimes I feel I'm married to two people. I like them both. They have different auras. Elayne is a different kind of outgoing. If I'm feeling good about myself, I find Elayne easier to take.

When I first heard about this crossdressing, I thought it was no big deal. What's so strange about that? I even assisted him in making a dress. At first I just thought he likes to wear women's clothes because they're prettier. Now I see it's also because it enables him to get into a different space where he is more conscious of the feminine side of himself and can make it more accessible. I don't think crossdressers should be seen any differently from artists or people who set fads.

I think Wayne's crossdressing has been, for the most part, a good learning experience for the children. It could make them more accepting of other people. Ryan climbs trees, but he also works with needlepoint. Sometimes I wonder if there'll be a backlash from the community if Elayne becomes more and more open.

Sometimes I get a little annoyed with Wayne when he decides to put on a dress just when we need to get someplace. I've got three kids to get ready and he's busy making himself pretty! Then, if I complain, instead of assisting he becomes a boss instead of a partner. I also get disgusted that he won't accept his male self—that he doesn't see its beauty or handsomeness.

Wayne, not Elayne, is my bed partner most of the time. He is gentle, though Elayne is even gentler. We both like to play the passive role. He prefers when I initiate and when I'm on top. He'll often wear a nightgown to bed. It's no big deal. I like the feeling of pantyhose in bed. It doesn't matter who wears them!

Allen (1989)

Transvestism is usually harmless, and most transvestites are not anxious to seek out therapy to stop their behavior. In any case, transvestism is usually so firmly fixed in a man's personality that eradication is neither possible nor desirable. The goal of therapy is to cope with the anxieties and guilt of the transvestite and the way he relates interpersonally and sexually with his partner and family (Peo, 1988). In the past few years, transvestite support groups have been organized in cities all over the country.

Pedophilia

pedophilia: Sex with children as a preferred or exclusive mode of sexual interaction in an adult; child molestation.

Pedophilia, which means "love of children," has been called many things throughout history: *child-love, cross-generational sex, man/child (or adult/child) interaction, boy-love, pederasty, Greek love, Knabenliebe, child abuse,* and *child sexual abuse* (Bullough, 1990). The variety of terms show how differently adult–child sexual interactions have been viewed in different periods of history. Although many people now consider sexual contact between adults and children to be one of the most objectionable of crimes, in many periods of history and in different cultures today, various types of child/adult sexual contact have been seen as acceptable. (See, for example, the discussion of Greek pederasty in Chapter 1, or the Sambian culture in Chapter 7.) Also, what exactly constitutes such contact in a society may be unclear. For example, as recently as the 1980s, a girl in the state of New Mexico could get married at age thirteen. If a thirty-year-old man marries a thirteen-year-old girl and has legal, consensual marital intercourse with her, is it pedophilia? What if they have consensual sex but are not married? Why should a piece of paper—a marriage certificate—make a difference in our definition?

Throughout most of history, a girl was considered ready for marriage and an adult sexual relationship as soon as she "came of age," that is, at menarche. It was common for much older men to be betrothed to very young women, and such marriages were seen as proper. For example, Saint Augustine decided to get married in order to try and curb his sexual promiscuity, and so he was betrothed to a prepubertal girl. Although intercourse was not permitted until she reached puberty, such early marriages were apparently common (Bullough, 1990). In England in the eighteenth to nineteenth centuries, twelve was considered the age of consent. In the eighteenth century as well, adult–child sex (especially same-sex pairings) were accepted in China, Japan, parts of Africa, Turkey, Arabia, Egypt, and the Islamic areas of India (Ames and Houston, 1990).

To some degree or another, then, what *legally* constitutes pedophilia is a matter of the laws in different societies. Yet, *clinically* speaking, pedophilia refers to "recurrent, intense sexually arousing fantasies, sexual urges, or behaviors involving sexual activity with a prepubescent child or children" (DSM-IV, 1994). Note that the child must be prepubertal, not just "young." Attraction to postpubertal boys and girls is called

ebhebephilia (sometimes just **hebephilia**): Attraction to children who have just passed puberty.

ebhebephilia, but it is not usually considered pathological. In fact, it has been shown that heterosexual males in almost all cultures are attracted to younger females, and homosexual males are attracted to younger or younger-appearing males (Ames and Houston, 1990; Feierman, 1990).

According to the DSM-IV, pedophiles often report an attraction to children of a particular age range, most often eight- to ten-year-olds in those attracted to girls and slightly older in those attracted to boys (attraction to prepubescent girls is more common). Some pedophiles are unable to function sexually with an adult, while others also maintain adult sexual relationships.

In the United States, an adult who has sexual contact with a boy or girl under the age of consent (usually eighteen, though it varies from state to state) to whom he or she is not married is guilty of child sexual abuse. A child sexual abuser may or may not be a pedophile; a person may sexually abuse a child because an adult is not available because children are easier to seduce than adults, out of anger, or because of other sexual, psychological, or familial problems. Some pedophiles are satisfied with undressing the child and masturbating, while others perform oral sex on the child or have the child do so to them, while still others engage in sexual intercourse with children.

No one knows exactly how common child–adult sexual contact is. Kinsey and his colleagues (Kinsey et al., 1948, 1953; Gebhard et al., 1965) found that about one-fourth of female respondents reported prepubertal sexual contact, although only 3% reported actual intercourse and 2% reported oral–genital contact. David Finkelhor (1980a, 1984), who has done extensive research into child abuse rates, found that 19% of female and 9% of male college students report some childhood sexual contact with an adult, although (as Kinsey found) actual intercourse was infrequent. In Tables 14.1a–d are some of Finkelhor's other findings. More recently, Janus and Janus (1993) found that 11% of the men in their sample, and 23% of women, reported being sexually abused as children.

Different types of pedophiles have been identified. Some engage in incest, forcing sex upon their own children, stepchildren, or other young relatives (see also Chapter 15). Though incest can occur with any adult relative, the most common situation involves a female child and her father or, more often, her *step*father. In fact, just *having* a stepfather is one of the most powerful predictors of sexual abuse. Finkelhor (1984) reports that fully half of females with stepfathers were victimized (though not necessarily *by* the stepfather, which may show that these families are generally less stable). Although girls are more likely to be abused by relatives, boys are more likely to be abused by casual acquaintances or strangers (Ames and Houston, 1990). Incest tends to be repetitive and progressive until the victim has come to expect the abuse and is frightened into a position of passive acceptance.

There is a difference between pedophiles who are attracted to girls and those attracted to boys. Boys are less likely to reject sexual advances and to report their sexual adventures to authorities than girls, and they will take the initiative in sexual encounters with adults more often than girls will (Brongersma, 1990). This may be the reason that violence is less common in sexual contact between men and boys than between men and girls.

Unfortunately, some pedophiles, realizing the chance of the child reporting the act, kill their victims. After one such murder of a young girl named Megan in New Jersey in 1994, her parents spearheaded a drive to pass "Megan's Law," which would make it mandatory for authorities to tell parents in a community when a convicted child molester moved into the neighborhood and would increase penalties for child molesters. The law was passed in New Jersey in 1994, and many other states are considering similar laws.

Female pedophiles also exist, although they often abuse children in concert with another person, usually their male partner. One expert suggests that many act to please their adult sexual partners rather than to satisfy their own pedophilic desires (*Contemporary Sexuality,* 1992). Others suggest that female sexual abuse, especially mother–child incest, is significantly underreported and may be much more prevalent than some believe (Holmes, 1991). Technically, an older women seducing an underage male is rape; yet movies such as *The Graduate* often glorify such sexual contact. Despite the fact that a boy can be traumatized if he is not ready for sex or is forced, some see seduction by an older woman as unproblematic. For example, one female high school teacher was acquitted of the charge of having sex with three of her young male students; one of the boys' fathers remarked that his son should consider himself lucky to have had a sexual experience with an older woman (Holmes, 1991)!

T a b l e **14.1a, b**

CHILD ABUSE AMONG A SAMPLE OF BOSTON FAMILIES

David Finkelhor surveyed 521 parents of children in the Boston area. He asked them whether their children had ever been sexually abused, and whether they themselves had been sexually abused when they were children. Twelve percent of parents (15% of the women and 6% of the men) had been sexually abused as children, and 9% said a child of theirs had been the victim of abuse or attempted abuse.`

PEOPLE RESPONDENT KNEW WHO HAD BEEN SEXUALLY ABUSED

IDENTITY OF VICTIMS	% OF RESPONDENTS WHO KNEW SUCH A VICTIM (N=521)
Self	12
Own Child	9
Relative	9
Friend	21
Child of friend or neighbor	20

AGE OF CHILD AND AGE OF PARENT (SELF-REPORT) AT TIME OF ABUSE/ATTEMPTED ABUSE

Age in Years	% CHILDREN (N=52)	% PARENTS SELF-REPORTS (N=78)
0–6	37	15
7–12	44	65
13–16	19	19

$x^2 = 8.3, p < .05$

A number of small organizations in Western countries, usually made up of pedophiles and ephebephiles, argue that man–boy love should be legalized, usually under the pretense of guarding "the sexual rights of children and adolescents" (Okami, 1990). In America, the North American Man–Boy Love Association (NAMBLA) argues for the abolition of age-of-consent laws. NAMBLA argues that there is a difference between those who simply want to use children for sexual release and those who develop long-lasting, often exclusive, and even loving relationships with a single boy. Suppe (1984) agrees that pederasty among postpubescent boys need not necessarily be harmful (which is not to deny that it often may be). On the other hand, those who work with sexually abused children vehemently deny the claim, pointing to children whose lives were ruined by sex with adults. Personal Voices 14.4 tells the story of one pedophiliac, a physician, who established emotional and intimate relationships with young boys before being caught and sentenced to a prison term.

Several factors may go into pedophilic behavior (Finkelhor, 1984, 1986). Pedophiles have been described as having had arrested psychological development, which makes them childlike with childish emotional needs. They may also have low self-esteem and poor social relations with adults, may be trying to overcome their own humiliations and pains from their childhood, or may exaggerate the social male role of dominance and

Table **14.1c, d**

SEXUAL ACTIVITIES IN CHILD REPORTS AND PARENT SELF-REPORTS

ACTIVITIES	% CHILD REPORTS (N=52)	% PARENT SELF-REPORTS (N=78)
Intercourse	2	9
Attempted Intercourse	8	10
Oral-genital	6	8
Touching sex organs	10	26
Fondle through clothes	20	27
Exhibit sex organs	26	11
Sexual Request	28	9

$x^2 = 16.79, p < .05$

IDENTITY OF PERPETRATORS IN CHILD REPORTS AND PARENT SELF-REPORTS

IDENTITY	% CHILD REPORTS (N=49)	% PARENT SELF-REPORTS (N=78)
Parent	2	8
Relative	8	24
Acquaintance	45	35
Stranger	45	33

$x^2 = 7.99, p < .05$

Reprinted with permission from Finkelhor (1984)

power over a weaker sexual partner. Because it has been found that many pedophiles were the victims of sexual abuse themselves when they were young, it has also been hypothesized that sexual victimization may make a person vulnerable to later desires to repeat or repair the experience. Conditions such as alcoholism or psychosis may also lessen the barriers to having sex with children.

Many media images sexualize childhood and associate sexuality with extreme youth. This may encourage pedophilic fantasies.

Pedophilia: An Autobiography

Dr. Silva (not his real name) is a physician who is incarcerated for having sex with a minor.

I believe that I was born a pedophile because I have had feelings of sexual attraction toward children and love for them as long as I can remember. I was not traumatized into this age orientation nor, certainly, did I ever make a conscious decision to be attracted in this way. Just as homosexuals and heterosexuals discover their sexual orientation, I discovered my age orientation as I grew, and I have been aware of it from a young age.

I remember being fascinated by children even during my own childhood. I can clearly remember, from before the age of 10, being at a popular gathering spot on my street and enjoying watching the younger children as they played and had a good time. . . . These feelings were confusing initially, and I tried to deny them. After all, in my peer group, "homosexual" was just about the worst epithet that could be hurled.

My developing experience with sex was occurring when I was 14 and 15 years old, and it was during this time that we in my peer group were befriended by a neighborhood man, about 25, who was known to "like boys." He drove us around and treated us to snacks and movies. At times, we went to his apartment, in pairs or as a group, where he took us individually into his bedroom to fellate us. I once spent the night with him. His mother and sister, with whom he lived, barely reacted to my presence there in the morning, as if it were not unusual for him to appear in the morning with a boy. While I enjoyed the oral sex he performed on me, the overall experience was unfulfilling. I was disappointed that he did not feel the emotional bond for me that I expected after such an intimate encounter. I felt satisfied physically but used. Subsequent experiences with him became acceptable once I adjusted my expectations and sought only sexual gratification.

In my second semester in medical school, I befriended Peter, a fellow medical student whose family lived in a nearby town. He invited me to meet his family and see the town. I will never forget the first time I met his brother Allen, who was 11 or 12 at the time. I loved the whole family, but what I felt for Allen was stronger than anything I had ever known before. During one of the earliest [visits to Peter's family], I had the opportunity to share a single bed with Allen. The closeness of our bodies as we lay there excited me so much that I was unable to sleep. Indeed, I experienced an intense orgasm as I held him close to me thinking he was asleep. He left the bed in order to sleep on the floor because, he told me later, he thought I had urinated in the bed. In future encounters he was wide awake and actively participated in our sexual relationship, which went on during the next two years and even later when I returned to visit. My relationship with him was the first true pedophilic/pedosexual relationship. After our sexual activity ceased, we maintained a close friendship that endures to this day.

In my fourth semester at medical school, I moved into a boarding house. Other students lived there with the host family, which consisted of a mother and three sons, ages 11, 12, and 13; the boys certainly were a factor in my choice. Thirteen-year-old John showed much interest in me. His curiosity was piqued by the issues of *Playboy* he came across, and we began to look at them. We became excited and it was not long before we had our clothes off and began fondling each other. Similar scenes were repeated over the next several nights, and we had an active, frequent sexual relationship during the ensuing three or four months. Our sexual activity consisted of my fellating or masturbating him or of mutual genital juxtaposition and friction. With a single exception to be described in a moment, never did I penetrate with my penis any of the boys with whom I was involved. On the single occasions that I attempted this behavior with John, once orally and once anally, he declined, and so I immediately desisted.

By now it was clear to me that I loved children, especially boys, and was happiest when I was in their company. When I took pleasure in most was seeing them happy and developing healthy in mind and body. So, I encouraged their interests if I felt these interests were healthy, or I exposed them to experiences that I thought would contribute to their educational or cultural edification.

It was in this period that I became friends with Eric, just about to turn 9, whose family recently had moved onto our street. . . . I had been dating Cathy [at the time], a foreign-born peer female who lived in my city and worked near our house. I enjoyed a good relationship, sexual and otherwise, with Cathy for about six month. Before we broke up, my relationship with Eric had become sexual and more pleasing than that with Cathy, and also she and I had been growing apart emotionally. I began to feel that I was maintaining our relationship for the sake of appearances and that young males were my true love—especially Eric.

Eric and I had become increasingly close. What made our relationship so beautiful and precious was the way in which it developed so gradually and so naturally....Most of the time, he just came over to my house and lay down with me for a few moments. One special time was a morning that he was on his way to school. He climbed into my room through my window, as he frequently did, removed his bookbag, and lay down next to me. We embraced for a few moments until we were satisfied and it was time for him to get to school. Not a word was spoken; all of our communication was physical on that occasion. Clearly, it was not sex that attracted me to him but, rather, our great emotional bond, which made sex so gratifying. Sex was a small but incredibly beautiful part of our relationship. The vast majority of the time we engaged in many other recreational and constructive activities.

The demise of our relationship began when his mother suspected some friends of mine were using marijuana in his presence. Eric was told we could no longer be friends. The next time I came over, she told me he did not want to see me anymore. Nevertheless, I often drove to his neighborhood, hoping to catch a glimpse of him near his home or school. Not long afterwards, he moved out of the country with his family.

I had been crushed when Eric's mother told me I could no longer see Eric. I cried every day for weeks and whenever I thought about him afterwards. Then, when he left the country, it was like a piece inside of me died. It still hurts me to think about him, and I do not think I will every fully recover.

**Reprinted with permission
from Silva (1990)**

Other Paraphilias

People can be sexually attracted to almost anything. A recent article in the *Journal of Forensic Sciences* tells of a man who was erotically attracted to his tractor; he wrote poetry to it, he had a pet name for it, and his body was found after he was asphyxiated by suspending himself by the ankles from the tractor's shovel in order to masturbate (O'Halloran, 1993). However, there are a number of other paraphilias which are relatively more common, although all are rare, and we will review a sample of them below.

Frotteurism or Frottage.

Frotteurism (or frottage) refers to the compulsive need to rub one's genitals against people, usually strangers, for sexual gratification. This is similar to **toucheurism**, where the compulsive desire is to rub strangers with one's hands. This desire, usually in men, finds expression on buses, trains, in shopping malls, while waiting in line, at crowded concerts, anywhere where bodies are pressed together. There have also been cases of frotteurism or toucheurism among doctors or dentists who rub against or touch their patients. Frotteurism, however, does not usually appear in isolation but as one of a number of paraphilias in an individual (Langevin and Lang, 1987).

frotteurism *or* **frottage:** The act of compulsively rubbing against strangers for sexual arousal.

toucheurism: The act of compulsively touching strangers with the hands to achieve sexual arousal.

Zoophilia.

Zoophilia is rare, although Kinsey and his colleagues (1948, 1953) found that up to 35% of boys raised on farms reported some sexual contact with animals; more recent studies put the number of farm contacts at about 17% (Holmes, 1991). In general, though, only 3.6% of the women and 8% of the men in Kinsey's sample reported animal contacts. Among the women, the contact was usually with a pet dog. Evidence indicates that zoophilia has been decreasing in recent years (Holmes, 1991).

zoophilia: The sexual attraction to animals in fantasy or through sexual contact as a preferred or exclusive means of sexual arousal and orgasm.

Contact between people and animals has been both practiced and condemned since earliest times. Greek mythology was populated by tales of interspecies sex, including Zeus raping Leda while in the guise of a swan. You have probably heard of the centaur, half-man and half-horse, the minotaur, half-man and half-bull, or the satyr, half-man and half-goat, who were the results of these sexual unions. (We have our own such myths; think about the sexual implications of *Beauty and the Beast* or *King Kong.*) The Hittite code (one of the earliest codes of law ever found), the Hebrew Bible, and the Jewish Talmud all impose the death penalty on people who engage in bestiality. The animal was often put to death also, especially if it was found guilty of complicity! In 1750, for example, Jacques Ferron was hung for copulating with a she-ass in France. The animal, however, was acquitted by the court on grounds that she was an unwilling victim of

SEXUALITY *Today* 14.2

Other Paraphilias

Each term below refers to an object or practice that the person finds extremely arousing and can become the preferred, or even exclusive, means for that person to achieve sexual arousal and orgasm.

Acrotomophilia and **Apotemnophilia:** The first term refers to finding sex with an amputee extremely arousing, and the second to the fantasy or reality of *being* an amputee. Some people with the latter desire will try to coerce or trick physicians into performing unnecessary amputations on them.

Asphyxiophilia or **hypoxyphilia:** Also known as autoerotic asphyxiation, these terms refer to the act of partly strangulating oneself to enhance orgasm. Often the person performs the act in front of a mirror and may use rope, a plastic bag, or a toxic inhalant to induce cerebral anoxia (the cutoff of oxygen to the brain), which is said to enhance orgasmic pleasure. This is very dangerous, and one estimate is that 31% of adolescent suicides is in a ten-year period were actually due to autoerotic asphyxiation that accidentally (or intentionally) went too far (Seehan and Garfinkel, 1988).

Autonepiophilia: Being diapered and treated as a baby.

Coprophilia and **Urophilia:** Contact with feces or urine. A man was convicted of lewd public behavior in California in 1992 after he was discovered under a women's outhouse at a state park. The man stood in the toilet pit vault and allowed urine and feces from women and girls to fall on his face and body (*Philadelphia City Paper*, 1992).

Formicophilia: The sensation of small creatures like snails, frogs, or cockroaches crawling on the body or genitals.

Gerontophilia: Sex with elderly persons.

Hyphephilia: The feel of a certain type of texture, such as skin, hair, fur, leather, etc.

Klismaphilia: Receiving an enema.

Mysophilia: Smelling, tasting, or coming into contact with filth and dirt, such as dirty underwear, used tampons, or smelly socks.

Narratophilia: Erotic or obscene talk, such as the pay-sex phone lines.

Olfactophilia: Smells of certain body parts, especially sexual and hairy areas.

Pictophilia: Erotic pictures (exclusively).

Pyrophilia (also known as pyromania): Lighting fires or watching things burn.

Stigmatophilia: Being pierced or tattooed.

**Adapted from Holmes (1991)
and Money (1984)**

---

violence. Character witnesses signed an affidavit that they knew the she-ass for four years and that she had always "shown herself to be of good character and had never given occasion of scandal to anyone" (Ford and Beach, 1951). Cotton Mather told of a man in Colonial New Haven, condemned to death for copulating with animals, who was forced before his death to witness the execution of his sexual partners—a cow, two heifers, three sheep, and two sows (Ford & Beach, 1951)!

necrophilia: The sexual attraction to dead bodies in fantasy or through sexual contact as a preferred or exclusive means of sexual arousal and orgasm.

Necrophilia. Tales of **necrophilia**, or having sex with corpses, have been found even in ancient civilizations. The Egyptians prohibited the corpses of the wives of important men from being delivered immediately to the embalmers for fear that the embalmers would violate them, and King Herod was rumored to have had sex with his wife for seven years after her death (Rosman and Resnick, 1989). More recently, the legends of the vampires imply necrophilia in the highly sexual approaches of the "undead." *Sleeping Beauty, Snow White,* and *Romeo and Juliet* all convey a sense of the restorative powers of loving the dead and thereby bringing the corpse back to life.

Rosman and Resnick (1989) suggest that necrophiliacs desire a partner who is unresisting and unrejecting, and to find one, many seek out professions that put them in contact with corpses. They identify three types of genuine necrophilia: *necrophilic fantasy,* where a person has persistent fantasies about sex with dead bodies without actually engaging in such behavior; *"regular" necrophilia,* which involves the use of already dead bodies for sexual pleasure; and *necrophilic homicide,* where the person commits murder to obtain a corpse for sexual pleasure. However, necrophilia is extremely rare and accounts for only a tiny fraction of murders.

A recent case of necrophilic homicide was the 1992 trial of serial killer Jeffrey Dahmer. Dahmer admitted to killing seventeen men, and he had sex with their corpses. He also mutilated their bodies, tried to create a "shrine" out of their organs that he thought would give him "special powers," and ate their flesh. In keeping with Rosman and Resnick's claim that necrophiliacs desire a partner who is unresisting and unrejecting, Dahmer bored holes into his victims' skulls while they were alive and poured in acid or boiling water, trying to create "zombies" who would fulfill his every desire (*Philadelphia Inquirer,* 1992). On the other hand, Dahmer also had sex with his victims while they were alive; perhaps he was an **erotophonophiliac**, which is someone who gets sexual excitement from the act of murder itself. Dahmer admitted his deeds but claimed he was insane. The jury found him sane and guilty, and he was sentenced to life in prison with no chance of parole; he was killed by another inmate in December 1994.

erotophonophiliac: Someone who gets sexual excitement from murdering others.

Other Philias: A number of other behaviors fall under the rubric of paraphilias, most of which are even rarer than the ones discussed above. Sexuality Today 14.2 lists a number of terms and their descriptions.

The Treatment of Paraphilias

For many people, paraphilias are unwanted disruptions to their lives. Their desires may get in the way of forming relationships, may get them into legal trouble, or may become such a preoccupation that they dominate their lives. For these people, a number of therapeutic solutions have been tried, with varying success. We review the assessment and treatment of paraphilias below.

Assessment

The first step in treating a person with a paraphilia of some sort is to assess the nature and scope of the problem. This can be done through self-report, through behavioral observation, or by physiological tests (Gudjonsson, 1986). Self-reports may not be reliable; someone under court order to receive treatment for pedophilia may be highly motivated to report that the behavior has ceased. Also, a person is not necessarily the best judge of their own desires and behavior; a man may truly believe he has overcome his sexual desires when in fact he has not. The second technique, behavioral observation, is limited by the fact that it cannot assess fantasies and desires; also, most people can suppress these behaviors for periods of time.

Physiological tests may be a bit more reliable. The most reliable technique for men is probably **penile plethysmography**, which is often used with male sex offenders. For example, a child molester can be shown films of nude children and the plethysmograph can record his penile blood volume. If he becomes excited at the pictures, then he is probably still having pedophilic desires and fantasies. A similar test is also available to test the sexual response of female offenders.

penile plethysmography: A test performed by measuring the amount of blood that enters the penis in response to a stimulus, which can indicate how arousing the stimulus is for the male.

Treatment Options

Therapies for paraphilias can be directed toward changing a patient's overt behaviors, subjective cognitions and emotions, and/or physiological responses (Gudjonsson, 1986). This can be done by trying to reinforce desirable sexual behaviors or by trying to decrease the undesirable behaviors. Whatever the technique, the most important goal of therapy must be to change a person's behavior. If behavior can be changed, even if fantasies and inner emotional life are not altered, then at least the person will not be harming others or himself or herself. That is why behavioral techniques have been the most commonly used and most successful of the treatments for paraphilias.

Positive behaviors can be encouraged by teaching paraphiliacs how to improve their social skills, allowing them to meet more men or women as potential sexual partners. To change emotions and thoughts, counseling, modeling (taking after a positive role model), or feedback can be used to change a person's attitudes toward the sexual object. In empathy training, which is useful when there is a victim, the person is taught to increase their compassion by putting themselves in the same situation as the victim. Incarcerated sex offenders may be exposed to relapse prevention therapies, which focus on controlling the cycle of troubling emotions, distorted thinking, and fanatasies that accompany their activities (Goleman, 1992). These techniques can be used in either group psychotherapy or individual counseling sessions.

Yet most find their desires difficult to suppress, and for them aversion therapy is one of the most common treatment strategies (Hawton, 1983). In aversion therapy, the undesirable behavior is linked with a noxious (unpleasant) stimulus. For example, the person might be shown pictures of nude boys or asked to fantasize about exposing himself to a girl, while an unpleasant odor, a drug that causes nausea, or an electric shock is administered. This technique has had some success (Hawton, 1983; Little and Curran, 1978), although its effectiveness decreases over time. In **shame aversion**, the noxious stimulus is shame; for example, an exhibitionist may be asked to expose himself in front of an audience.

Although removing the behavior itself may protect any victims, the person who still fantasizes about the behavior or has the same underlying attitude that led to it (such as fear of women) may not really be that much better off. The psychological underpinnings of the paraphilia also must be changed. In **systematic desensitization** (Wolpe, 1958), the person is taken through more and more anxiety-provoking or arousing situations and is taught to deeply relax at each step until the person learns to relax during even the most extreme situations (Hawton, 1983).

A number of therapies incorporate masturbation to try and reprogram a person's fantasies. In **orgasmic reconditioning**, the paraphiliac masturbates, and just as he feels orgasm is inevitable, he switches his fantasy to a more desired one, hoping thereby to

shame aversion: A type of aversion therapy where the behavior that one wishes to extinguish is linked with strong feelings of shame.

systematic desensitization: A technique by which a person learns to relax while experiencing arousal or anxiety-provoking stimuli.

orgasmic reconditioning: A sex therapy technique where a person switches fantasies just at the moment of masturbatory orgasm in order to try and *condition* himself or herself to become excited by more conventional fantasies.

The 1977 film *Looking for Mr. Goodbar* featured Diane Keaton, whose character compulsively sought sex from strange men at bars. In the end, Keaton's character is murdered by one of her pickups.

increasingly associate orgasm and, later, erection with the desirable stimulus. Similarly, in **satiation therapy** the person masturbates to a conventional fantasy and then right away masturbates again to the undesirable fantasy. The decreased sex drive and low responsiveness of the second attempt makes the experience less exciting than usual, and eventually the behavior may lose its desirability.

In addition to these behavioral therapies, a number of pharmacological and surgical means have also been tried. Chemotherapy of various kinds have been used to either decrease sexual drive or to treat psychological pathologies that are believed to underlie the undesirable behavior. There is evidence, for example, that progestogens are effective in decreasing the sex drive of hypersexual sex offenders (Cooper, 1986). Recently, both surgical and chemical castration have also been suggested. In early 1992, for example, a man convicted of molesting children agreed to be castrated rather than serve time in prison for his offense. The court rescinded the offer when no doctor could be found willing to perform the procedure. Castration may not be the answer to the violent or pedophilic offender; some use foreign objects on their victims, and so the inability to achieve erection is not necessarily an impediment to their activity. To the degree that such crimes are crimes of aggression, rather than of sex, castration may not address the underlying cause.

Ultimately, there is no certain way of changing a person's sexual desires. For many paraphiliacs whose desires are socially or legally unacceptable, life is a struggle to keep their sexuality tightly controlled.

satiation therapy: A therapy to lessen excitement to an undesired stimulus by masturbating to a desired stimulus and then immediately masturbating again when desire is lessened, to an undesired stimulus.

VARIATIONS IN SEXUAL FREQUENCY

Another form of variation in sexuality is variation in sexual frequency. Although there is a great range in frequency of sexual contact in the general population (see Chapter 9), some argue that certain people cross over the line from a vigorous sex life to an obsessed sex life. On the other side are those who, for various reasons, seem to have little or no sex drive at all.

Hypersexuality

Sexuality, like drugs, alcohol, gambling, and all other behaviors that bring a sense of excitement and pleasure, should involve some degree of moderation. Yet for some people, the need for repeated sexual encounters, which often end up being fleeting and unfulfilling, becomes almost a compulsion. In the past, there were unflattering terms for these people; women were usually called **nymphomaniacs**, while men were said to have **satyriasis** or **Don Juanism** or, in other cases, simply were referred to as "studs." Note that the female term is significantly more unflattering than the male term. Perhaps nowhere else is the double standard between the sexes so blatant as in the fact that women who enjoy frequent sexual encounters are considered "whores" or "nymphos" while men who enjoy similar levels of sexual activity are often admired.

Recently, however, "sexual addiction," also called compulsive sexual behavior, sexual compulsivity, sexual dependency, sexual impulsivity, and hypersexuality, has become popular and controversial in part due to the book *The Sexual Addiction* by Patrick Carnes (1983) (see also Chapter 12). Carnes's argument is that people who engage in many of the paraphilias we have discussed, not just hypersexuality, are really sexual addicts whose need for constant sexual encounters is similar to any addictive behavior. Sex and orgasm are mood-altering just as drugs are, and the addict will often sacrifice family, friends, work, health, and values in order to maintain the sexual behavior. Carnes suggests that the addict goes through four cycles repeatedly:

nymphomaniac: A term used to describe women who engage in frequent or promiscuous sex; usually used pejoratively.

satyriasis or **Don Juanism:** Terms used to describe men who engage in frequent or promiscuous sex; both are usually seen as flattering terms.

1. *Preoccupation* with thoughts of sex;
2. *Ritualization* of preparation for sex, such as primping oneself and going to bars;
3. *Compulsive sexual behavior* over which the addict feels he or she has no control; and
4. *Despair* afterward as the realization hits that he or she has again repeated the destructive sequence of events.

Sexual addiction can even be dangerous, as it may result in suicide, injury, and/or STDs.

SEX TALK

QUESTION **14.5** **I think about sex a lot—it seems like it is almost all the time. I also like to have sex as often as I can. Do I have sex addiction?**

Probably not. Thinking about sex is a universal human pastime, especially when a person is younger and just beginning to mature as a sexual being. Of course, older people frequently think about sex too. Sexual addiction becomes a problem when people find their sexual behavior becoming dangerous or uncomfortable. People who find that they cannot stop themselves from engaging in behaviors that put them at physical risk, that they find immoral, that make them feel extremely guilty, or that intrude on their ability to do other things in their life should probably seek counseling—but that is true whether or not the behavior is sexual.

Many have criticized the idea of sexual addiction, however. They argue that terms such as "sexual addiction" are really disguised social judgments. Sexual addiction may be nothing more than an attempt to "repathologize" sexual behaviors that became acceptable in the 1960s and 1970s (Levine and Troiden, 1988). Before the sexual freedom of the 1960s, those who engaged in promiscuous sex were often considered physically, mentally, or "morally" sick. Now that the moral climate is becoming more conservative, some scholars suggest that there is an attempt to return to a pathological model of sexuality, this time using the concept of addiction. In "sex-positive" cultures, where sex is seen as healthy and acceptable, having sex frequently, even several times every night, is seen as normal.

Although little systematic research has been done on sexual addiction, a number of psychologists have argued that sexual addiction is a real phenomenon that describes the behavior of a certain subgroup of people in both the heterosexual and homosexual communities (Pincu, 1989). Clinicians have found that sexual addicts tend to have a low opinion of themselves, distorted beliefs, a desire to escape from unpleasant emotions, difficulty coping with stress, a memory of an intense "high" that they experienced at least once before in their life (and that they are looking for again), and an uncanny ability to deny that they have a problem, even when it severely disrupts their lives (Earle and Crow, 1990). In response, a number of self-help groups have been organized, such as *Sexaholics Anonymous, Sex Addicts Anonymous, Sex and Love Addicts Anonymous,* and *Co-Dependents of Sexual Addicts.*

Hyposexuality

On the other side of the spectrum are those who have lost their sexual desire, or never had it in the first place. People with hyposexuality have no sexual fantasies or desire for sexual activity. In a related problem, called sexual aversion disorder, the person may desire but cannot actually engage in sex, feeling disgust, aversion, or fear when confronted by a sexual partner (DSM-IV, 1994). People with such conditions are different from those who choose celibacy as a sexual lifestyle, which we discussed in Chapter 8; these people either lack sexual desire altogether or desire a sexual life but are unable to have one. Their problems may be due to substance abuse, hormonal disturbances, or psychological causes, and various therapies may be recommended, depending on the cause. In Chapter 12 we discussed disorders of sexual desire in greater depth.

VARIATIONS OR DEVIATIONS?

What criteria should we use to decide whether or not a sexual behavior is "normal"? The number of people who engage in it? What a particular religion says about it? Popular opinion? Should we leave it up to the courts and the psychiatrists? Stoller (1991) suggests that we are all perverse to some degree. Why should some people be singled out as being too perverse, especially if they do no harm to anyone else?

Perhaps the need we feel to brand some sexual behaviors as perverse is summed up by Levine et al. (1990:92), who write, "Paraphilic images often involve arousal without the pretense of caring or human attachment." We tend to be uncomfortable with sex for its own sake, separate from ideas of love, intimacy, or human attachment, which is one reason that masturbation was seen as evil or sick for so many years.

Paraphilias are still labeled "perversions" by law and often carry legal penalties. Since even consensual adult sexual behavior, such as anal intercourse, is illegal in some states, it is not surprising that paraphilias are as well. Yet these laws also contain contradictions; for example, why is it illegal for men to expose themselves, yet women are not arrested for wearing see-through blouses? We must be careful while deciding that some sexual behaviors are natural and others are unnatural or some normal and others abnormal. Those which we call paraphilias may simply be part of human sexual diversity, unproblematic unless they cause distress or injury.

Summary

- Sexual behavior comes in many forms. For many people, sexuality is centered around objects (fetishes), particular behaviors (exhibitionism, voyeurism), or sexual partners who society views as unacceptable (pedophilia, necrophilia). These are all grouped under the term paraphilia, which refers to a set of sexual behaviors that are unusual or socially unacceptable.
- Paraphilic behavior is compulsive and can lead to troubles with law, personal distress, and secretiveness. Some paraphiliacs, on the other hand, are open about their desires, marry and have children, and may try and get their partners involved in their activities. Paraphilias are much more common in males.
- A number of theories have been offered about why people develop these types of sexual behaviors. Biologists look for origins in hormonal imbalances or neurological functioning. Psychoanalysts see it as a response to childhood castration anxiety and the Oedipal complex, where the child's attention turns to nonthreatening objects instead of the parent. Behaviorists and learning theorists see it as behavior that began early in life when sexual excitement and the object or activity happened at the same time, and then the person reinforced the connection by fantasizing about the behavior and masturbating. John Money suggests that we develop "lovemaps" as we grow, which define our ideal lover and ideal love situation, which can become disrupted, leading to these behaviors. Sociologists show how society encourages paraphilias by eroticizing objects in advertising, for example.
- People who direct their sexual attention exclusively to objects such as panties, fabrics such as rubber, or specific body parts such as feet are known as fetishists. They seem to substitute a part of sexuality for the whole and may find the object of their desires so stimulating that they may masturbate multiple times a day over the object.

- Inflicting and/or receiving pain as a necessary part of sexuality is called sadomasochism, or S&M. Sadomasochists may belong to elaborate subcultures and use props such as whips or leather restraints.
- Exhibitionism, the most common of the paraphilias, involves exposing one's genitals to unsuspecting and unwilling victims. The victim's shock, fear, or disgust is sexually stimulating to the exhibitionist, who often masturbates while remembering the incident.
- The voyeur is compelled to watch other people undressing or engaging in sexual acts. Voyeurs are often shy and withdrawn.
- Males whose preferred source of sexual stimulation is dressing up in women's clothes are transvestites. Transvestites are usually heterosexual and often are married with families.

- Pedophiliacs are sexually attracted primarily to children, often prepubescent. Pedophiliacs may seek out large numbers of children or may develop longer-lasting relationships with a single child. There may be differences between those attracted to young boys and those attracted to young girls.
- Another type of sexual variation is variation in frequency. Those with hypersexuality, or sexual addiction, feel compelled to engage in sex with great frequency, to the point where they may put themselves in danger or may neglect their jobs. Hyposexuality is the lack of sexual desire.
- There are a number of other, rarer forms of paraphilia, such as an obsessive desire to touch others, being attracted to corpses, or desiring sex with animals.
- Many treatments have been tried to rid people of unwanted paraphilic desires. Behavioral therapies have had the greatest success.

R e f l e c t i o n s   o n   S e x u a l i t y

1. What is "sexual deviance"? Why do you think the definitions of which behaviors are deviant change over time?
2. Is the definition of paraphilia based on science or values? Can you think of a definition that is not based on values?
3. Should a person who lives comfortably with a paraphilia be considered sick? Would you encourage such a person to seek treatment?
4. Why do you think paraphilias are more common among men?
5. How does society encourage fetishism?
6. Why do psychoanalytic theorists suggest that sadomasochism underlies both love and sexuality?
7. Paraphiliacs seem to replace interpersonal relationships with objects or activities that do not require interaction. Why do you think they might do that?
8. Pedophiles are sexually attracted to young boys and girls. Do you think the eroticization of childhood by advertising and television has encouraged pedophilia?
9. Do you think sexual addiction is a real syndrome or is a reaction against sexual freedom?

S u g g e s t e d   R e a d i n g s

ALLEN, M. P. (1989) *Transformations.* New York: E. P. Dutton.

BULLOUGH, V. L., and B. BULLOUGH. (1993) *Cross Dressing, Sex, and Gender.* Philadelphia: University of Pennsylvania Press.

CARNES, P. (1983) *The Sexual Addiction.* Minneapolis, MN: CompCare Publications.

FEIERMAN, J. (ed.). (1990) *Pedophilia: Biosocial Dimensions.* New York: Springer-Verlag.

FINKELHOR, D. (1984) *Child Sexual Abuse: New Theory and Research.* New York: Free Press.

HOLMES, R. (1991) *Sex Crimes.* Newbury Park, CA: Sage Publications.

WILSON, G. (ed.). (1987) *Variant Sexuality: Research and Theory.* Baltimore: Johns Hopkins University Press.

Power and Coercion

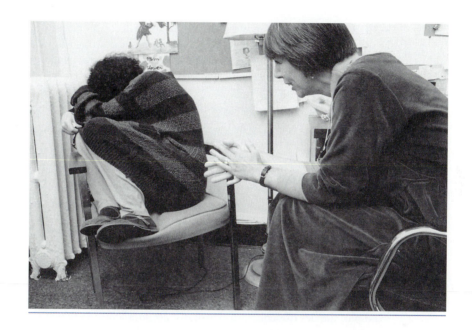

Jill is a nineteen-year-old college sophomore. After drinking too much at a party, she ends up kissing John on the dance floor. They eventually go up to John's room, and John begins to try to convince Jill to have intercourse. Jill says she does not want to but eventually has sex because she feels too drunk to put up a fight.

Jan has loved Sid, the lead singer of the "EgoManiacs," for two years. She has been to every one of his concerts and would do anything for him. He invites her back to his hotel room and she goes, understanding that sex is expected. As soon as they are finished, he asks her to leave.

Bill is a forty-two-year-old father of three. His youngest daughter is eight months old. Each time he changes her diaper he rubs her vulva. Although he feels a small amount of guilt, she seems to enjoy the sensation, and so he continues fondling her.

Dr. Thomas is a fifty-one-year-old professor of business at Pinnacle University. It is well known that one's grade can be increased if one is a good-looking male who shows the professor sexual attention. The more attention, the higher the grade.

Brenda, a twenty-six-year-old professional woman, goes out with Karl, a twenty-four-year-old professional man. She likes sex every night, which Karl agrees to even though he does not want to. He is afraid that if he does not, she will leave him.

Power is an aspect of all sexual relationships. Sexual relationships are healthy when power is shared and when the relationship empowers the partners. In sexuality, however, as everywhere in human life, power can also be used to degrade and oppress. For example, the act of seduction is usually an interaction between each partner's power, which is partly what makes dating and sexual anticipation so exciting. On the other hand, coercive sexuality involves the clash of personal power, with one partner overpowering the other.

rape: Forced sexual behavior with an individual without that person's consent.

Physically or psychologically forcing sexual relations on another person is usually referred to as **rape.** Sexual contact with a minor by an adult is called child sexual abuse and, in some societies, is also considered rape. There are also instances in which a person with more power entices, pressures, or encourages another person with less power into sexual activities, ranging from an unwanted glance or word to actual sexual contact. This is sexual harassment. This chapter will begin with the most extreme form of sexual coercion, rape, and will go on to explore other ways that power can be misused in sexual relationships.

PART ONE—RAPE

DEFINING RAPE AND SEXUAL ASSAULT

For most mammals, penile penetration of a female by a male is done only when the female is in estrus, or "heat" as it is commonly called. In some species, penetration takes place with a considerable amount of aggression and force; for instance, the male mink actually bites through the female's neck fur to stabilize their bodies during penetration (Abel et al., 1980). Humans can have sexual intercourse at any point in the menstrual cycle, which means other motivations determine when intercourse might take place. However, in humans, male and female desire for sexual contact may not coincide.

SEX TALK

QUESTION **15.1** **Why do people rape?**

There are several theories as to why rape exists in our society. Feminists argue that the nature of the relationships between the sexes fosters rape. Others argue that it exists because of the rapist's psychopathology. Still others claim it is because of how women dress, act, or behave. Today, most theorists agree that rape is a crime of power where sex is used as a weapon.

The line that separates rape from other categories of sexual activity can be blurry because of the fine distinctions between forced and consensual sex, as well as societal patterns of female passivity and male aggression (LaFree, 1982). For instance, we often expect that women will not initiate sexual activity, which is the primary responsibility of the man. These beliefs about how sex is *supposed* to be can make defining rape a difficult task.

There is not any single definition of rape (e.g., see Sexuality Today 15.1). For instance, in Georgia, rape is defined as "forcible penetration of the female sex organ by the male sex organ" (Rochman, 1991). In Pennsylvania, rape is defined as sexual intercourse with another person (who is not a man's spouse), by force, threat of force, [or] who is either unconscious or incapable of consent. Elements that are generally included are lack of consent, force or threat of force, and vaginal penetration. But penetration is also a hard concept to define. According to standard law, one inch of penetration is required. Ejaculation is not a necessary part of the definition; however, it does make for a stronger case if it eventually goes to court.

If there is no penis involved in the assault, many women do not consider it rape (Bart and O'Brien, 1985). This is because some women view rape as something that is done *by* a penis (intercourse, fellatio, sodomy) rather than something done *to* a vagina (digital penetration, cunnilingus, touching). However, research has shown us that these women still experience a trauma quite similar to that of a woman who is forced to endure penile penetration. A nonpenile sexual attack has also been referred to as **sexual battery** and is defined as the unwanted touching of an intimate part of another person, including the genitals, buttocks, and/or breasts, for sexual arousal.

While some states use the traditional definition of rape that only includes vaginal–penile intercourse, others broaden the definition by using the term **sexual assault,** which includes sexual penetration (vaginal, oral, anal) as well as unwanted sexual touching (Searles and Berger, 1987). This would include rape that occurs to both females and males.

Recently there has been a debate about the appropriate term for a person who has experienced a rape. Although the word *victim* emphasizes the person's lack of responsibility for the incident, it may also imply that the person was a passive recipient of the attack. The term *victim* can also become a permanent label. Some prefer the term *survivor,* which implies that the person had within themselves the strength to overcome and to survive the rape. It also confirms that the person made important decisions—for example, not to fight and possibly be killed—during the assault and thus was not completely passive. However, for clarity, we will use the term *victim* in this chapter to refer

In February 1992, boxer Mike Tyson was convicted of one count of rape and two counts of criminal sexual conduct for the 1991 date rape of Desiree Washington, an eighteen-year-old contestant in the Miss Black America beauty contest. Tyson was sentenced to six years in jail but was released in the summer of 1995.

sexual battery: Nonpenile sexual attack.

sexual assault: Coercion of a nonconsenting victim to have sexual contact.

SEXUALITY *Today* 15.1

Different Forms of Rape

Acquaintance rape (or date rape): involves forced sexual behavior by a date, boyfriend, girlfriend, casual acquaintance, or a friend of a friend. Because acquaintance rape in fraternities, dormitories, and college apartment complexes has received so much attention, it is sometimes referred to as campus rape.

Attempted rape: a rape may have been planned, but the assault is aborted for some reason.

Felony rape: occurs when an offender is engaging in some other felony such as burglary or robbery and also commits a rape because it appeals to the offender at the moment.

Gang rape: a rape in which several males take turns raping the victim. Also referred to as "pulling train" (in reference to the sequence of boxcars on a train).

Marital rape: occurs when a woman is legally the wife of her assailant. Marital rape is a relatively recent legal category. Until 1979, most rape laws protected husbands from prosecution for rape.

Prison rape: refers to the rape of an inmate by another inmate in prison (male or female).

Statutory rape: occurs when the victim is under the "legal age of consent," which varies by state regulations. Usually the age of consent is between thirteen and eighteen years old, and all states prohibit sexual activity with anyone under that age even if they fully consent to or initiate the act. A person under the legal age of consent is simply considered too young to make the decision to have sexual intercourse. The laws that regulate the age of consent were originally instituted for two reasons: to protect female virginity and to regulate youthful sexual conduct (Searles and Berger, 1987).

Stranger rape: is when an unknown assailant rapes a man or woman.

to a person who has survived a rape. In addition, we will primarily refer to females as the victims of rape, even though males can also be raped.

INCIDENCE OF RAPE

From 1985 to 1989, there was a dramatic increase in the number of rapes that were reported to the police in the United States. In 1990, the trend continued, with an increase of 6% over the number of rapes reported in 1989. On the average, a rape occurs every three minutes in the United States. One in four college women have experienced either rape or attempted rape since the age of fourteen (Koss et al., 1987), while one out of every fifteen male college students report that they have committed a rape in the previous twelve months (Yegidis, 1986). Although the definitions of *rape* and *sexual assault* may be different to various individuals in these studies, research on violence in dating relationships has found that 25% of women and 7% of men indicated that they had experienced violence in dating relationships (Aizenman and Kelley, 1988). On college campuses, 98% of sexual assaults are committed by someone the victim knows, often a fellow student (College Security Report, 1989).

Verbal sexual coercion is also prevalent on college campuses. Sanday (1990) refers to verbal sexual coercion as "working a yes out." Koss et al. (1987) found that 44% of female college students had engaged in unwanted sexual intercourse because of verbal pressure from their partners. Common coercive strategies include threatening to end the relationship or making the woman or man feel guilty (Muehlenhard and Schrag, 1991).

It is difficult, however, to assess the *actual* incidence of rape because forcible rape is one of the most underreported crimes in the United States (Federal Bureau of Investigation, 1988). The majority of rape victims never report the crime; one study found that only 21% of stranger rapes and 2% of acquaintance rapes were reported (Koss et al., 1987). Forty-four percent of one sample of adult women had been victims of either an attempted or completed rape, yet only 8% reported it to the police (Russell, 1984).

Why are women so unlikely to report being raped? Some women do not report it because they do not think that they were really raped, because they think that it was their fault because they did something to put themselves at risk, or because they feel shame and humiliation over the rape. Others fear no one will believe them or that nothing will be done legally. Many have heard stories about how difficult it is going to court and how women have been treated by the legal system when they report being raped.

The general sexual climate in society also affects the official rape rate (Jaffee and Straus, 1987). If a society does not tolerate violence against women and encourages reporting, the report rates will be higher. For example, rape rates appear to be higher in certain states such as California and Nevada (Baron and Straus, 1987). This could be because California and Nevada actually have higher incidences of rape or because people in these states feel more comfortable reporting rapes to the authorities.

THEORIES AND ATTITUDES ABOUT RAPE

What drives someone to rape another person? We discuss the most prominent theories of why rape occurs. These include the rapist psychopathology, victim precipitation, feminist and sociological theories.

Rapist Psychopathology

Modern ideas about why rape occurs evolved first from psychiatric theories, which suggested that men rape because of mental illness, uncontrollable sexual urges, or alcohol intoxication. This theory of **rapist psychopathology** suggests that it is either disease or intoxication that forces men to rape and that if they did not have these problems, they would not rape.

rapist psychopathology: A theory of rape that identifies psychological issues in a rapist that contribute to rape behavior.

According to this theory, the rape rate can be reduced by finding these sick individuals and rehabilitating them. The theory makes people feel safer because it suggests that only sick individuals rape, not "normal" people. However, research consistently fails to identify any significant distinguishing characteristics of rapists. Having psychological or alcohol problems does not predispose a person to be a rapist. In fact, men who rape are often found to be "normal" in every other way. Perhaps it is easier to see rapists as somehow sick than realize that the *potential* to rape exists in many of us.

Theories of rapist psychopathology were very common until the 1950s when feminist researchers began to refocus attention on rape's effect on the victim rather than on the offender. However, there are still those who accept psychopathological theories today.

Victim Precipitation Theory

Victim precipitation theory explores the ways victims make themselves vulnerable to rape, such as how they dress, act, or where they walk. By focusing on the victim and ignoring the motivations of the attacker, many have labeled this a "blame the victim" theory.

victim precipitation theory: A theory of rape that identifies victim characteristics or behaviors that contribute to rape.

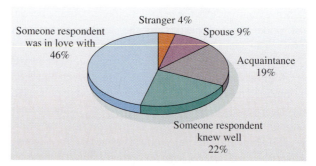

Note: Sample size = 204. Includes female respondents who reported that they had ever been "forced to do something sexual that they did not want to do by a man." Eighty-six women (or about 30% of all women who reported ever being forced) reported that they had been forced sexually by more that one person; they are not represented in the figure but the distribution of relationships to persons forcing is similar.

F i g u r e **15.1**

Relationship of women respondents to men who forced them to do something sexual.
Reprinted with permission from Michael et al (1994).

Victim precipitation theories claim that it is the victim's actions that cause a rape. In this scene from *The Accused,* Jodie Foster's character is dancing seductively.

The 1988 movie *The Accused* was based on an actual rape case that took place in New Bedford, Massachusetts, in the late 1980s. Jodie Foster played a character named Sarah Tobias, who is raped after dancing provocatively at a bar. Dressed in tight, sexy clothes and slightly intoxicated, Sarah begins to dance in a very sensuous way. The men in the bar watch her with interest, and soon one begins to dance with her. She kisses him as they continue to dance in a sexual way. As the excitement of the moment increases, he begins to initiate sex. Sarah tells him to stop and that she is not interested, but he ignores her wishes and forces her to have intercourse on a pinball machine as the other patrons watch and cheer him on. Other men in the bar follow and force themselves on her. Throughout the scene Sarah is screaming "No! Please, stop!"

Do you think Jodie Foster's character was "asking for it" just a little bit? After showing this film in class, students often report that they feel Jodie Foster's character was acting "sleazy" and "would sleep with anybody." Imagine you were on the jury that heard the case against the men accused of raping her: she was dressed in sexy clothes, had been drinking, was kissing one man, and was dancing in a provocative way. Do you think she was more to blame than a woman who was raped in the street by an unknown assailant? Do you think she was raped?

The victim precipitation theory of rape shifts the responsibility from the person who knowingly attacked to the innocent victim: "She was walking home too late at night," "She was drunk," "She was wearing too much makeup," or "She was flirting." The theory also serves to distance people from the reality of rape and lulls them into the false assumption that it could not happen to them or someone close to them because they would not act like "those other women." If we believe bad things happen to people who take risks, then we are safe if we do not take those risks. In the majority of rapes, however, women are not engaging in risky behavior. Brownmiller (1975) argues that rape forces a woman to stay in at night, to monitor her behavior, and to look to men for protection. This attitude also contributes to a rape victim's guilt because she then wonders: "If I hadn't worn what I did, walked where I walked, or acted as I did, maybe I wouldn't have been raped."

Feminist Theory

Feminist theorists view rape differently. They contend that rape and the threat of rape are tools used in our society to keep women in their place. This fear keeps women in traditional sex roles, which are subordinate to men's. Feminist theorists believe that the social, economic, and political separation of the genders has encouraged rape, which is viewed as an act of domination of men over women. Sex-role stereotyping—which reinforces the idea that men are supposed to be strong, aggressive, and assertive while women are expected to be slim, weak, and passive—encourages rape in our culture. Women are fearful and look to men to protect them. One study found that two-thirds of women reported being "very fearful" of rape (Warr, 1985). Even the clothing that men and women wear contributes to rape in our culture. In order to be fashionably dressed in society, women are encouraged to wear high heels, dresses, and pantyhose, which make it very difficult to run, fight, or move quickly. Men wear pants and flat soled shoes, which allow for free movement and easier fighting capabilities.

feminist theory: Theory of rape that contends that rape is a tool used in society to keep a woman in her place.

Sociological Theory

Sociological theory and feminist theory have much in common; in fact, feminist theorists are often sociological. Sociologists believe that rape is an expression of power differentials in society. When men feel disempowered by society, by changing sex roles or by their jobs, overpowering women with the symbol of their masculinity (a penis) reinforces, for a moment, the men's control over the world. In a sociologist's view, it is not coincidental that as male–female equality in society has increased, so has the rape rate.

sociological theory: A theory of rape that identifies power differentials in society as causing rape.

Sociologists explore the ways people guard their interests in society. For example, the wealthy class in a society may fear the poorer classes, who are larger in number and envy the possessions of the upper class. Since women have been viewed as "possessions" of men throughout most of Western history, fear of the lower classes often manifested itself in a belief that lower class males were "after our wives and daughters." During the slavery period in the United States, for example, it was widely believed that, if given the chance, black males would rape white women, while white males did not find black women attractive. Yet the truth was just the opposite; rape of white women by black males was relatively rare, while many white slave masters routinely raped their black slaves. Once again, this supports the idea that rape is a reflection of power issues rather than just sexual issues.

Measuring Attitudes About Rape

Researchers have used many techniques to measure attitudes about rape and rape victims, such as written vignettes, mock trials, videotaped scenarios, still photography, and newspaper reports. Where Do I Stand? 15.1 contains a questionnaire that will help you explore your own attitudes about rape victims. Take a few moments to take this test before you continue reading.

Gender Differences in Attitudes About Rape

How did you score on the test? Your scores may predict your general orientation to social issues. For example, it has been found that people who believe in the victim-precipitation

WHERE DO I *Stand?*   *15.1*

Attitudes Toward Rape Victims Scale

Below are a number of statements that have been made about sexual relations between men and women. Using the following scale, please indicate the degree to which you agree or disagree with each.

  1 = strongly disagree
  2 = somewhat disagree
  3 = undecided or no opinion
  4 = somewhat agree
  5 = strongly agree

1. _____ A raped woman is a less desirable woman.

2. _____ It is difficult for a man to tell when a woman really means "no."

3. _____ Most men would commit rape if they felt that they could get away with it.

4. _____ Women provoke rape by their appearance or behavior.

5. _____ Most women secretly desire to be raped.

6. _____ Women who go out alone at night put themselves in a position to be raped.

7. _____ It is impossible for a prostitute to say that she has been raped.

8. _____ If a woman doesn't fight a rapist, then she really wanted it.

9. _____ Women who wear short skirts or tight blouses are asking for it.

10. _____ If a woman dates a man several times, it is only natural that she should expect to have sex with him.

11. _____ Most women enjoy being sexually dominated by a strong partner.

12. _____ A little bit of force often makes sex more exciting.

Add up your total points. Scores will range from 12–60. A low score indicates more sensitivity toward a rape victim, while a higher score (above 50) indicates more conservative attitudes about rape victims.

Ward (1988)

model tend to have more conservative attitudes in general (Fischer, 1986). There are also strong gender differences in attitudes toward rape. Men have been found to be less empathetic and sensitive toward rape than women (Borden et al., 1988; Larsen and Long, 1987; Krulewitz, 1982; Malamuth and Check, 1981), especially those men who often watch pornography (Bales, 1993). Men and women have different feelings about rape; for example, some men believe that if a woman behaves as if she is sexually available, they have a right to force her to have sex (Bart and O'Brien, 1985). Men may also believe that a woman is signaling that she is sexually available when the woman thinks her behavior is simply friendly or even neutral (Saal et al., 1989). Females rate a rape as more justified and see the victim as more responsible for the rape when the woman was seen as "leading a man on" (Muehlenhard and MacNaughton, 1988). Some women believe that if they "led a man on," they gave up their right to refuse sex (Muehlenhard and Schrag, 1991).

RAPE IN DIFFERENT CULTURES

The United States has the highest number and rate of reported rapes in the world. In 1990, women in the United States were eight times more likely to be raped than were

European women, twenty-six times more likely than Japanese, and forty-six times more likely than Greek women (Mann, 1991). However, the incidence of rape varies depending on how each culture defines rape; one culture might accept sexual behavior that is considered rape in another culture.

In some cultures, rape was accepted as a punishment for women. Among the Cheyenne Indians, a husband who suspected his wife of infidelity could put her "out to field," where other men were encouraged to rape her (Hoebel, 1954). In the Marshall Islands of the Pacific Ocean, women were seen as the property of the males, and any male could force sexual intercourse upon them (Sanday, 1981). In Kenya, the Gusii people view intercourse as an act in which males overpower their female partners and cause her considerable pain. In fact, if she has difficulties walking the next morning, the man is seen as a "real man" and will boast of his ability to make his partner cry (Bart and O'Brien, 1985).

Rape has also been used for initiation purposes. In East Africa, the Kikuyu used to have an initiation ritual in which a young boy was expected to rape to prove his manhood (Broude and Greene, 1976). Until he did this, he could not engage in sexual intercourse or marry a woman. In Australia, among the Arunta, rape serves as an initiation rite for girls. After the ceremonial rape, she is given to her husband, and no one else has access to her.

During times of war, rape is also used as a weapon. During the Persian Gulf War in early 1991, many Kuwaiti women were raped by Iraqi soldiers, and they had very difficult recoveries. One woman even burned herself to death (Mann, 1991). In 1994, the war in Bosnia also witnessed the horror of rape, as young girls were raped in front of their parents. Support systems such as **Rape Crisis Centers** do not exist for these women; many of these women feel intensely isolated, rejected, and suicidal.

Research by Sanday (1981) indicates that the primary cultural factors that affect the incidence of rape in a society include relations between the sexes, the status of women, and male attitudes in the society. Societies that promote male violence have higher incidences of rape because men are socialized to be aggressive, dominating, and to use force to get what they want.

Rape Crisis Center: A center that provides treatment for rape victims, support, counseling, and education.

RAPE ON CAMPUS

Rape and Alcohol

On college campuses, alcohol use is one of the strongest predictors of acquaintance rape (Koss, 1988). For men, alcohol seems to "sexualize" the environment around them. Cues that might be taken as neutral if the men were not drunk (such as a certain woman talking to them or dancing with them) may be seen as an indication of sexual interest. In addition, alcohol increases the likelihood and intensity of male aggression toward women (Barnard, 1989). For women, alcohol may lead to increased teasing and flirting, which sends ambiguous messages. Muehlenhard and Cook (1988) found that 43% of college women reported regretting sexual intercourse they engaged in while intoxicated. Seventy-five percent of college men reported giving women alcohol or drugs in an attempt to obtain sex (Mosher and Anderson, 1986).

Even more, alcohol use on college campuses, as it relates to rape, is viewed very differently for men and women. A man who is drunk and is accused of rape is seen as *less* responsible because he was drinking ("Lighten up; he was so smashed he didn't even know what he was doing"); a woman who has been drinking is seen as *more* responsible for her behavior ("Can you believe her? She's had so much to drink that she's flirting with everyone—what a slut!") (Richardson and Campbell, 1982: Scully and Marolla, 1983). In court, women who have been drinking or were drunk are more likely to be discredited. Sexuality Today 15.2 describes a sexual offence policy used to safeguard against sexual abuse that occurs when the victim is incoherent because of alcohol or for other reasons.

SEX TALK
QUESTION **15.2** **What if you are drunk and she is too, and when you wake up in the morning she says you raped her?**

> **Claims of rape must be taken seriously. This is why men and women should be very careful in using alcohol and engaging in sexual activity. The best approach would be to delay engaging in sexual activity if you have been drinking. This way, you will not find yourself in the above situation.**

Fraternities and Rape

Initially, Greek organizations were established to help students join together to participate in social issues that they felt were largely ignored by their respective universities (Bryan, 1987). Today, however, many fraternities and sororities operate primarily for socializing. Unfortunately, fraternities tend to tolerate and may actually encourage the sexual coercion of women (Copenhaver and Grauerholz, 1991).

While rape does occur in residence halls and off-campus apartments, there are several ways in which fraternities create a riper environment for rape. Fraternities host large campus parties in which there is often excessive alcohol use and little university supervision. Some fraternity members may actually try to get the females drunk to have more access to sex. One fraternity was noted for serving what they referred to as "hunch punch," which was grain alcohol mixed only with Kool-Aid® powder. The fraternity was planning on giving this punch to women in a "prim and proper" sorority because having sex with these types of sorority girls was the goal (Martin and Hummer, 1989).

Many fraternities also revolve around an ethic of masculinity. Values that the members see as important include competition, dominance, willingness to drink alcohol, and "sexual prowess vis-à-vis women." There is considerable pressure to be sexually successful, and the members gain respect from other members through sex. This emphasis on masculinity and the protection of the group often provides a fertile environment for coercive sexuality (Martin and Hummer, 1989; Rapaport and Burkhart, 1984). Other factors that contribute to rape in fraternities are the inherent secrecy and protection of the group.

pulling train: A term that refers to the gang rape of a woman; refers to the succession of box cars on a train.

In her book *Fraternity Gang Rape: Sex, Brotherhood, and Privilege on Campus,* Sanday (1990) discusses the incidence of **pulling train** in fraternities. During an incidence of pulling train, or gang rape, fraternity brothers are encouraged to join in and those that do not are seen as either unmasculine or homosexual. Sanday argues that it is the homosexual desire of the members of the fraternity (for each other) that perpetuates this practice. Since the woman is usually either unconscious or too intoxicated to know what is going on, it is actually the men who are symbolically having sex with each other.

SEXUALITY *Today* 15.2

Dealing with Rape on Campus

Many colleges are grappling with how to deal with acquaintance rape on college campuses. A variety of different organizations have been formed, and many new policies against date rape have been proposed. Probably the most controversial of these policies was at Antioch College in Ohio. In 1992, the college adopted the *Sexual Offense Policy,* which requires students to obtain verbal consent at each stage of sexual intimacy. This means permission must be given by both partners before holding hands, kissing, and again before engaging in sexual intercourse. This policy was drafted and defended by a group of students and was approved by the school's Board of Trustees. It has the support of a majority of students, both female and male. Below are some excerpts from the *Sexual Offense Policy.*

All sexual contact and conduct on the Antioch College campus and/or occurring with an Antioch community member must be consensual.

Consent

1. For the purposes of this policy, "consent" shall be defined as follows: the act of willingly and verbally agreeing to engage in specific sexual contact or conduct.
2. If sexual contact and/or conduct is not mutually and simultaneously initiated, then the person who initiates sexual contact/conduct is responsible for getting the verbal consent of the other individual(s) involved.
3. Obtaining consent is an ongoing process in any sexual interaction. Verbal consent should be obtained with each new level of physical and/or sexual contact/conduct in any given interaction, regardless of who initiates it. Asking "Do you want to have sex with me?" is not enough. The request for consent must be specific to each act.
4. The person with whom sexual contact/conduct is initiated is responsible to express verbally and/or physically her/his willingness or lack of willingness when reasonably possible.
5. If someone has initially consented but then stops consenting during a sexual interaction, she/he should communicate withdrawal verbally and/or through physical resistance. The other individual(s) must stop immediately.
6. To take knowingly advantage of someone who is under the influence of alcohol, drugs and/or prescribed medication is not acceptable behavior in the Antioch community.

Adapted from the Antioch College *Sexual Offense Policy* (1992)

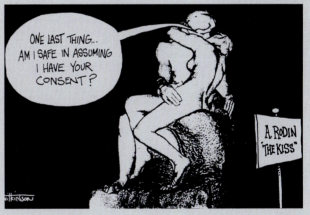

Some fraternities have begun to institute educational programs for their members. Others invite guest speakers from Rape Crisis Centers to discuss the problem of date rape. Until members of fraternities learn to use peer pressure against those who violate the rights of women, rape will certainly continue to be a problem.

SEX TALK

QUESTION **15.3 I am in a fraternity, and last semester there was a rape by one of my brothers. All of the members**

> **supported him when he said he did not do it, even though everyone knew he did. Why did they support him and not the woman?**
>
> This is a very difficult question to answer because it involves a group process in which these men agree to support each other "no matter what." There is a considerable amount of fear in telling the truth because the members of the fraternity will be angry and may even kick out the guy who tells or supports the woman. However, it appears that more and more fraternities are beginning to turn this peer pressure around. Some have even sponsored workshops for the fraternity members to teach them the laws and definitions of rape. Unfortunately, when a fraternity stands behind a rapist, they are silently encouraging his behavior.

EFFECTS OF RAPE

Rape is an emotionally, physically, and psychologically shattering experience for the victim. Immediately after a rape, many victims report feeling numb and disorganized. Some deny that the rape occurred at all, to avoid the pain of dealing with it. Others express disbelief, anger, vulnerability, and increased feelings of dependency. As time goes by, the healing process begins and feelings may shift to self-pity, sadness, and guilt. Anxiety attacks, nightmares, and fear slowly begin to decrease, although the incident is never forgotten. Some women never return to prior functioning levels and must create an entirely new view of the self to go on with life after a rape.

Rape Trauma Syndrome

Rape Trauma Syndrome (RTS): A two-stage stress response pattern that occurs after a rape.

Acute Phase: First stage of the rape trauma syndrome, in which a victim often feels shock, fear, anger, or other related feelings.

Researchers Burgess and Holmstrom (1974) coined the term **Rape Trauma Syndrome (RTS)**, which describes the effects of rape. RTS is a two-stage stress response pattern characterized by physical, psychological, behavioral, and/or sexual problems, and it occurs after forced, nonconsenting sexual activity. While not all victims respond to rape in the same manner, what follows is a description of what typically occurs.

The **Acute Phase** is the first stage of RTS. Most victims feel a fear of being alone, fear of strangers, or even fear of their bedroom or their car if that is where the rape took place. Other emotional reactions to rape include anger (at the assailant, the rape, healthcare workers, family, one's self, court), anxiety, depression, confusion, shock, disbelief, incoherence, guilt, humiliation, shame, and self-blame. The woman may also experience wide mood fluctuations. Difficulties with sleeping, including recurrent nightmares, are common. This phase begins immediately following the assault, may last from days to weeks and involves several stress-related symptoms.

Research indicates that approximately 60% of women eventually talk to someone about the experience (Golding et al., 1989). Most of the time they talk to friends or family members rather than to the police. Younger victims are more likely to tell someone than older victims, perhaps because older victims blame themselves more for the rape and may fear that others, too, will blame them. Women who are raped by a stranger are more likely to tell someone than someone who is raped by an acquaintance (Golding et al., 1989).

Depression often follows a rape, and some women report still feeling depressed eight to twelve months postrape. Family support is important in reducing depressive symptoms (Atkeson et al., 1982). Sometimes depressive feelings are so severe that victims' thoughts turn to suicide. Poverty, prior depression, and prior sexual assaults also increase feelings of depression, anxiety, and overall problems associated with the rape (Cohen and Roth, 1987).

Emotional reactions also vary depending on whether or not the victim knew her assailant. Women who report being raped by strangers experience more anxiety, fear, and startle responses, while those raped by acquaintances usually report more depression, guilt, and a decrease in self-confidence (Sorenson and Brown, 1990). A woman who knew her assailant may have initially trusted him and agreed to be with him, and so after the rape she may wonder how she could have had such bad judgment, why she did not see it coming, and feel a sense of betrayal (see Personal Voices 15.1).

Long-Term Reorganization is stage two of RTS and involves restoring order in the victim's lifestyle and reestablishing control. Many victims report that changing some aspect of their lifestyle, such as changing their address or phone number, helped them to gain control. Symptoms from both stages can persist for one to two years after the rape (Nadelson et al., 1982), although Burgess and Holmstrom (1979) found that 74% of rape victims recovered within five years. Recovery is affected by the amount and quality of care that the victim received after the rape. Positive crisis intervention and the support of others decrease the symptoms of the trauma.

Long-Term Reorganization: The second stage of the rape trauma syndrome, which involves a restoration of order in the victim's lifestyle and reestablishment of control.

Personal
V O I C E S
15.1

Acquaintance Rape

Below is a letter written by an eighteen-year-old college student who had been raped by an acquaintance. It is written to her assailant. Notice the lack of trust and vulnerability she expresses.

Once I called you a friend. Not anymore. Once I trusted you. You broke that trust by using it to get what you wanted. You are a thief. You stole something of mine. Something that had been very special to me. So special, that it was something I had reserved only for someone I loved. I will never forget that night. I will never forget how I said "NO" and you didn't listen, didn't care, and didn't stop. I will never forget the fact that you raped me. Although you didn't put a gun to my head, you didn't put a knife to my throat, and you didn't tie me up, the fact still remains the same. It was rape. I can never forget because of what it has done to me. When you took my body, you took every ounce of trust I had in me too. Because of what you did, I'm distrustful and suspicious of every male's intentions. Imagine being so frightened that when you catch someone simply looking at you, the hair on the back of your neck stands up and you wonder, what does he want?

Imagine freaking out if a guy accidentally touches you. Imagine being afraid to let a guy hold your hand or put his arm around you for fear he'll want more. Imagine always thinking that if he wants it, he'll TAKE it.

I wish I could show you what you have done to me. I wish I could make you feel every ounce of pain I have felt since you raped me. I wish you could see how much hurt is inside me. I wish you could hear my voice shaky and untrustworthy when I talk to men. I wish I could make you feel the tears that come to my eyes or the way my hands get ice cold when the word rape is mentioned. I wish you could see me when I hurt so much and am so incredibly scared of everyone and everything. I curl up into a ball and clutch a pillow. I wish you could hear how hysterically I sob at night.

You've made me feel so violated, isolated, sad, and angry. More scared than anything though. Of men, of sex. Every man I meet will pay for what you did. I pay for what you did. I have been through so much pain, you can't imagine. Sometimes I wonder "why me?" It doesn't seem fair. Fifteen minutes of self-gratification for you, but God only knows how many months of pain, suffering and fear I have already had to, and will have to, endure.

Author's files

During the first stage of Rape Trauma Syndrome, victims may feel depressed, confused, angry, guilty, or humiliated. Talking to a counselor can be very helpful in working through these feelings.

There are also many physical symptoms experienced by women who have been raped. Some of these include general body soreness, bruises, difficulties with swallowing and throat soreness if there was forced oral sex, vaginal itching or burning, rectal bleeding and/or pain, STD symptoms, and eating disorders. The emotional stress of the rape may also cause menstrual irregularities. However, some of these symptoms (nausea and menstrual irregularities) are also signs of pregnancy, which is why a pregnancy test is of utmost importance after a victim has been raped.

Recent research reveals that there is a higher incidence of pregnancy in women who have been raped than in women who engage in consensual sexual intercourse. One theory suggests that the fear response releases a hormone that can trigger ovulation (Krueger, 1988). Many rape victims are also concerned about the risk of acquiring HIV from their assailants (Salholz et al., 1990). Some rape victims are asking that their rapists be tested for AIDS. However, AIDS experts agree that one is unlikely to contract AIDS from a single exposure. It is also important to be checked for other STDs after a rape.

In the past, many researchers have argued that rape is a violent crime, not a sexual one. "Desexualizing" rape, or taking the sexual aspect out of it, has deemphasized postrape sexual concerns. Rape is indeed both a violent and a sexual crime, and the majority of victims report experiencing sexual problems postrape (Holmstrom and Burgess, 1978; Becker et al., 1986).

SEX TALK

QUESTION **15.4** Do women who are raped eventually have a normal sex life?

Although it may take anywhere from a few days to months, most rape victims report that their sex lives get back to what is normal for them. However, research indicates that lesbian women may have more difficulties with sexual problems postrape. Counseling, a supportive partner, and emotional support are extremely helpful.

Sexual difficulties can persist for a considerable period after the rape. Difficulties include fear of sex, desire and arousal disorders, and difficulties with sexual behaviors such as sexual intercourse, genital fondling, and oral sex. However, there do not appear to be any problems with masturbation and behaviors like hugging and cuddling. This may be because rapists rarely force their victims to engage in these behaviors (Feldman-Summers et al., 1979).

Counseling can be helpful for women suffering from postrape sexual difficulties. It is not uncommon for a woman to seek help for a sexual problem, such as anorgasmia (lack of orgasm), and during the course of therapy, reveal an experience with rape that she had never discussed.

Silent Rape Reaction

Silent Rape Reaction: A type of rape trauma syndrome that occurs in a victim who does not talk to anyone after the rape.

Some victims never discuss their rape with anyone and carry the burden of the assault alone within themselves. Burgess and Holmstrom (1974) call this the **Silent Rape Reaction**, and in many ways, it is similar to RTS. Feelings of fear, anger, and depression and physiological symptoms still exist; however, they remain locked inside. In fact, those who take longer to confide in someone usually suffer a longer recovery period (Cohen and Roth, 1987).

The Silent Rape Reaction occurs because some victims deny and repress the incident until a time when they feel stronger emotionally. This may be months or even years later. One woman who sought counseling had waited three years to deal with the memory. She was taking a course in psychology and noticed with frustration that as she read each chapter of the textbook, she would become extremely anxious if she saw the word *therapist*. When she explored why this was anxiety-producing, she replied that she could only read the word as "the rapist" and it frightened her. Perhaps her subconscious was letting her know that she was finally ready to work through the repressed experience. Slowly the memories of the rape came back, as did all of the pain and sorrow from the attack. After two months in counseling, she had worked through the memories sufficiently to feel that she was on her way to resolving her feelings about the rape (Author's files).

Effects of Rape in Special Populations

Marital Rape

It has been estimated that 10% to 14% of all married women are raped by their husbands, although this number is much higher in battered women (Russell and Howell, 1983; Yllo and Finkelhor, 1985). Although symptoms are similar to nonmarital rape, many of these women report feeling extremely betrayed and may lose the ability to trust others, especially men. In addition, there is often little social support for wives who are raped, and those who stay with their husbands often endure repeated attacks (Personal Voices 15.2 offers some explanations of why such women stay). The more often a woman experiences marital rape, the more emotional and physical symptoms she experiences (Yllo and Finkelhor, 1985). Unfortunately, marital rape may be one of the least discussed types of rape.

Lesbians

After a rape, lesbians also experience RTS. However, for many lesbians, it is very difficult to assimilate the experience of rape into their own self-image (Orzek, 1988). Many lesbians may also be "woman-identified" in most areas of their lives, and the rape may force them to reexamine the patriarchal society and their feelings about men. Some lesbians may have never experienced sexual intercourse with a man and may be unaccustomed to dealing with the fear of pregnancy, let alone the extreme feelings of being violated and abused.

Older Women

Many students believe that rape only happens to younger women. It is difficult to think about our mothers or grandmothers being raped. The stereotype that only young, attractive women are raped prevents our thinking about the risk of rape for older women. Although it is true that younger women are more at risk for rape, older women are also raped. Studies have estimated that between 3% and 12% of rape victims are over the age of fifty (Gebhard et al., 1965; Groth and Birnbaum, 1979). Older women are likely to be even more traumatized by rape than younger women because many have very conservative attitudes about sexuality, have undergone physical changes in the genitals (lack of lubrication and/or thinning of the walls of the vagina) that can increase the severity of physical injury, and they have less social support after a rape, which reinforces and intensifies their sense of vulnerability.

Nicole Brown Simpson experienced years of battering and abuse from her husband O. J. Simpson. In June 1994, she was found brutally murdered with her friend Ronald Goldman. In October of 1995, O.J. Simpson was found not guilty of two counts of murder.

Women with Disabilities

Unfortunately, handicapped people may be the most vulnerable to rape because of their diminished ability to fight back. In addition, mentally handicapped persons may have a more difficult time reading the preliminary cues that would alert them to danger. The impact of a rape may be very intense for these people because of a lack of knowledge about sexuality, loss of a sense of trust in others, and the lack of knowledgeable staff who can effectively work with these victims. In many cases, severely mentally handicapped persons who have been sexually assaulted may not realize that their rights have been violated and, therefore, may not report the crime. Because of these factors, the intensity and length of time of RTS is usually prolonged.

Prostitutes

Because a prostitute's job is to provide sex in exchange for payment, the question of consent is often difficult to judge. Also, because of the general disapproval of prostitution, a prostitute who reports rape is often treated with disdain. People tend not to

Personal
V O I C E S

Why Women Stay

Below is an essay written by a woman who lived with an abusive spouse. Notice the degree of manipulation and power he used to make her stay.

One of the most difficult emotional decisions to understand is why, at the first sign of aggression or mistreatment, a woman does not or cannot leave a man who abuses her. It sounds straightforward and easy, but is it?

Let me begin by saying that abusive relationships do not start with violence. Women do not enter into a relationship saying, "It's okay to hurt me." Even abusive relationships usually start romantically, sharing love and trust, building dreams together, and often having children —just as in a normal relationship.

Often, the spouse's controlling behavior is not seen immediately but develops slowly over time. When a woman realizes how damaging her relationships is, she often has really made an emotional commitment and developed a sense of loyalty to her partner. The bonds between the couple have been built over time and do not suddenly cease to exist. Once abuse enters the relationship, her emotional ties are a great source of turmoil. I know when I took my marriage vows, I meant "for better or for worse." But when "until death do us part" suddenly became a frightening reality, I was faced with some terrifying decisions.

There are myriad and complex reasons for staying in an abusive relationship. The simplest for society to grasp is the fact that many women have no other source of financial support or housing. We ask them to leave their homes behind, cloaked only by the temporary safety of darkness, to hide in community shelters (when there is room) or to live in the streets. Now add the responsibility of caring for several small children onto her shoulders. How many people would choose to take their children from their home, with no guarantee of food or shelter? How realistic are the options that we insist are the "obvious solutions" to this problem?

The fear of retaliation and further victimization by the abuser is another serious concern. The abused woman realizes that if the abuser catches her preparing to leave or finds her once she has gone, his threats to harm her or her family may soon become a reality. Once, when I tried to leave, my ex-husband took my dachshund puppy and beat him against the wall. He told me to remember those cries because if I ever left him or tried to get help, those cries would haunt me because they would be cries of my young niece. At that moment, I knew he was capable of every horrible threat he had ever made and my life was in grave danger.

Abuse by an intimate partner, either emotional or physical, is a commonly unrecognized cause of illnesses and injury among women. Recent estimates reveal that from 2 million to 4 million women are battered by their "significant other" each year. How long can we continue to ignore this horrifying crime? We must realize that your actions, or lack of action, can have a huge impact on a woman's life. Be aware that by not asking a woman about it, you could be closing your eyes to the fact that this woman will most likely return home, only to be beaten again and again.

Reprinted with permission from Bundow (1992)

---

believe that she was raped or may think that she is angry because she was not paid. Many prostitutes who are raped begin to question their involvement in prostitution. Believing and trusting her experience and performing a comprehensive medical checkup are imperative.

SEX TALK

QUESTION **15.5** **Why do prostitutes care if they are raped? Don't they just give it away anyway? I thought it was just like another customer who refused to pay.**

Prostitutes agree on a price in exchange for sexual activity. When a man has an agreement with a prostitute and then rapes her—which would be forceful and against her will—this simply reinforces the idea that every man has the right to a woman's body. Rape does not have anything to do with the availability of sex. These men are taking what they believe is theirs using force and doing it without the woman's consent. Prostitutes also take an enormous risk in their profession because rapists know that there is little chance that any retribution will follow.

Partners of Women Who Have Been Raped

When a man or woman's sexual partner is raped, the partner often feels anger, frustration, and intense feelings of revenge (Holmstrom and Burgess, 1979). Many men express a strong desire to "kill him" (the rapist), "make him pay," etc. In addition, some men experience a sense of loss, guilt, self-blame, and jealousy. If men believe that the rape was sexually motivated, they might either force sex on their partners to defend their own masculinity or they may reject the partner sexually (Foley, 1985). In cases of acquaintance rape, men may lose their trust in their partner, feeling that because their partner knew the assailant she may have expressed sexual interest in him. Often, these reactions further isolate the victims and reinforce their feelings of guilt.

All in all, rape places a great deal of stress upon a relationship. Couples often avoid dealing with rape entirely, believing that talking about it would be too stressful. Many men feel uncomfortable sharing their feelings about a rape because they worry about burdening their partners. However, open communication is extremely beneficial and should be encouraged. Even though dealing with a rape in a relationship can be traumatic, it has been found that women who have a stable and supportive partner recover from a rape more quickly than those without partners.

RAPE OF MEN

Can a man be raped? Each year in the United States, more than 9000 men are victims of rape or attempted rape (U.S. Department of Justice Statistics, 1990). However, male rape is even more underreported than female rape (Russell, 1984).

Rape of Men by Women

Students often laugh at the idea that a man could be raped by a woman because they believe the myth that men are always willing to have sex, and so a woman would never *need* to rape a man. However, the myth actually serves to make male rape more humiliating and painful for many men (see Personal Voices 15.3).

SEX TALK

QUESTION **15.6 Technically, can a man really be raped?**

Some people think that it is impossible for a woman to rape a man because he just would not get an erection. Even though men are anxious, embarrassed, or terrorized during a rape, they are able to have erections. Having an erection while being raped may be confusing and humiliating, just as an orgasm is for females. In fact, for some it may be the most distressing aspect of the assault (Sarrel and

Masters, 1982). Women who rape men can also use dildos, hands, or other objects to penetrate the anus. In addition, men can be orally or anally raped by men and forced to perform various sexual behaviors.

Men also report verbal sexual coercion. In a study of male college students, 34% reported coercive sexual contact: 24% from women, 4% from men, and 6% from both sexes (Struckman-Johnson and Struckman-Johnson, 1994). The majority of male rapes by women use psychological or pressured contact, such as verbal persuasion or emotional manipulation, rather than physical force. Although the majority of college men had no or very mild negative reactions to the unwanted female contact, 20% of the men experienced strong negative reactions.

Rape of Men by Men

Research estimates that between 2.5% and 5.0% of men are sexually victimized before the age of thirteen, and 84% of sexually assaulted boys reported that they had a male assailant (Finkelhor and Browne 1985). However, once again, this is probably an underrepresentation of the true incidence. The sexual assault of men is most commonly performed by older men who are outside of the family structure (e.g., a baby-sitter, teacher, or mother's boyfriend) (Finkelhor and Browne, 1985). We will discuss the rape of men by strangers here, and later in this chapter we will discuss the sexual abuse of male children.

It has been said that the incidence of male rape in the gay community is low because of the greater access to consensual sex in gay bars, bookstores, etc., and that it is more difficult to overpower another male than a female (Russell, 1984). Some feminists would argue that rape is a **misogynist's** act of hatred toward women, and that this is why the incidence in the gay community is lower.

Misogynist: A person who has a hatred toward women.

Mezey and King (1989) interviewed twenty-two men who had been raped by other men. Eleven of the assailants were gay men, three were bisexual, and three were hetero-

*P*_ers_*o*_n_*a*_l_

V O I C E S

15.3

The Rape of Men

This twenty-seven-year-old male, a 178-pound truck driver, was held captive for more than twenty-four hours, and when he was released, he did not tell anyone of his experience for fear of ridicule. He experienced severe erectile difficulties postrape (Sarrel and Masters, 1982).

[Sam] had been drinking and left a bar with a woman companion he had not known previously. They went to a motel where he was given another drink and shortly thereafter fell asleep. He awoke to find himself naked, tied hand and foot to a bedstead, gagged, and blindfolded. As he listened to voices in the room, it was evident that several women were present. When the women realized that he was awake, he was told he had to "have sex with all of them." He thinks that during his period of captivity four different women used him sexually, some of them a number of times. Initially he was manipulated to erection and mounted. After a very brief period of coitus, he ejaculated. He was immediately restimulated to erection and the performance was repeated . . . it became increasingly difficult for him to maintain an erection. When he couldn't function well, he was threatened with castration and felt a knife held to his scrotum. He was terrified that he would be cut and did have some brief improvement in erectile quality.

sexual (the others were unknown). Only two of these men reported their attacks to the police. Forced anal and oral sex, masturbation to ejaculation, and being urinated on were reported by the victims. The most common type of activity in the sexual assault of men by men is anal penetration followed by oral penetration (Groth and Burgess, 1980). Getting the victim to ejaculate is important in male rape by men. Many male assailants either masturbate or perform fellatio on the victim to the point of orgasm. The assailant may believe that if the victim has an orgasm, he will be less likely to report the attack or that it proves that the victim really "wanted it."

As in the case of female victims, male rape is an expression of power, a show of strength and masculinity, that uses sex as a weapon. One rapist commented:

> *I had the guy so frightened I could have made him do anything I wanted. I didn't have an erection. I wasn't really interested in sex. I felt powerful and hurting him excited me. Making him suck me was more to degrade him than for my physical satisfaction.*

Groth and Burgess (1980:808)

Many victims of male rape question their sexual orientation and feel that the rape makes them less of a "real man." The risk of suicide in men who have been raped has been found to be higher than in women (Mezey and King, 1989). Also, unlike women, male rape victims may increase their subsequent sexual activity to reaffirm their manhood.

Prison Rape

Rape in prison is usually violent and occurs in many different ways (see Personal Voices 15.4). Men who are in prison learn the same kind of avoidance techniques that women do in society—physical modesty, no eye contact, no accepting of gifts, and tempering of friendliness (Bart and O'Brien, 1985). Prison rape has been found to be an act of asserting one's own masculinity in an environment that rewards dominance and power (Peeples and Scacco, 1982). Sex, violence, and conquest are the only avenues open to men in the restrictive confines of prison. To rape another man is seen as the "ultimate humiliation" because it forces the victim to assume the role of a woman. The victim becomes the "property" of his assailant, who will, in turn, provide protection in return for anal or oral sex. However, the assailant often will "sell" favors to other inmates in exchange for cigarettes or money.

A man who rapes another man increases his sense of masculinity, while the victim often loses his and is referred to as a "whore," "bitch," "old lady," or even "pussy" (Rideau and Sinclair, 1982). In desperation, some victims turn to raping other men, and the cycle continues. Although prison rape occurs in the male population most frequently, it also occurs between female inmates using a variety of different objects to penetrate the vagina or anus.

Inmates who have been raped also experience RTS. The Acute Phase is characterized by feelings of fear, anxiety, anger, and guilt, as well as numerous physical problems. Because these men and women must continue to interact with their assailants, Long Term Reorganization may take longer to work through. In addition, there are no rape crisis services for those who have been raped in prison, nor is there any sympathy from the prison employees over the attack.

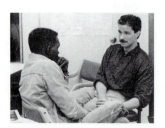

Men who have been raped also experienced Rape Trauma Syndrome and can benefit from counseling.

15.4

Prison Rape

Below is one account of a prison rape. Notice the degree of power used in this rape.

A rough, calloused hand encircled his throat, cutting off the scream rushing to his lips, the fingers digging painfully into his neck. "Holler, whore, and you die," a hoarse voice warned, the threat emphasized by the knife point at his throat. He nodded weakly as a rag was stuffed in his mouth. The hand left his neck. Thoughts of death moved sluggishly through his terror-stricken mind as his legs, weak with fear, threatened to give out from under him. An anguished prayer formed in his heart and his facial muscles twitched uncontrollably. He was thrown on the floor, his pants pulled off him. As a hand profanely squeezed his buttocks, he felt a flush of embarrassment and anger, more because of his basic weakness which prevented his doing anything to stop what was happening than what was actually going on. His throat grunted painful noises, an awful pleading whine that went ignored as he felt his buttocks spread roughly apart. A searing pain raced through his body as the hardness of one of his attackers tore roughly into his rectum. "Shake back, Bitch!" a voice urged. "Give him a wiggle!" His rapist expressed delight as his body flinched and quivered from the burning cigarette being applied to his side by other inmates gleefully watching.

Adapted from Peeples and Scacco (1982:3)

THE RAPIST

Rape is a man's right. If a woman doesn't want to give it, the man should take it. Women have no right to say no. Women are made to have sex. It's all they are good for. Some women would rather take a beating, but they always give in; it's what they are for.

—Incarcerated rapist (Scully and Marolla, 1985:261)

Who is it that rapes? What is your image of a "rapist"? A man in an alley? Someone who cannot control himself sexually? A drunk fraternity brother? A psychopath? As mentioned, psychologists used to believe that men rape because of uncontrollable sexual impulses, alcohol intoxication, or mental illness. Even today, however, the question of why men rape is still largely unanswered.

Research has shown that rapists are primarily from younger age groups, between the ages of fifteen and thirty, single (Amir, 1971; Russell, 1984), and tend to reduce their rape behavior as they get older (Kantrowitz and Gonzalez, 1990). The majority of rapists who are in prison deny their crime and justify their behavior by claiming the women wanted it or enjoyed it (Scully and Marolla, 1984). Some rapists try to excite their victims sexually and actually see themselves as lovers and not rapists (Russell, 1975). The challenge of convincing the woman that she really wanted the rape appears to be a primary motive. Other motives include revenge or punishment, hostility or a desire for domination, and power (Black, 1983; Scully and Marolla, 1985). One rapist commented:

Seeing them laying there helpless gave me the confidence that I could do it . . . with rape, I felt totally in charge. I'm bashful, timid. When a woman wanted to give in to normal sex, I was intimidated. In the rapes I was totally in command, she totally submissive.

Scully and Marolla (1985:259)

It is not only convicted rapists who are attracted to the idea of forcing a woman to engage in sex. In a study about the potential to rape, 356 college-age males were asked, "If you could be assured that no one would know and that you could in no way be punished for forcing a woman to do something she really didn't want to do (rape), how likely, if at all, would you be to commit such acts?" Sixty percent indicated that under the right circumstances, there was some likelihood that they would use force, or rape, or both (Ceniti and Malamuth, 1984).

Other research indicates that men who rape generally have sexist views about women, accept myths about rape (i.e., women enjoy rape), have low self-esteem, and are politically conservative (Peterson and Franzese, 1987). Correlations have also been found between being the victim of past sexual abuse and raping behavior (Stevenson and Gajarsky, 1992) and between the use of violent and degrading pornography and raping behavior (Koss and Dinero, 1989). However, despite the assumption that rapists are psychologically disturbed individuals, research does not support the assumption that they are any different from "normal" men (Cornett and Shuntich, 1991).

Treatment of Rapists

Can men who rape be treated so that they lose their desire to rape? Many different therapies have been tried, including shock treatment, psychotherapy, behavioral treatment, support groups, and the use of Depo Provera, a drug that can diminish a man's sex drive (see Chapter 11). The idea behind Depo Provera is that if the sex drive is reduced, so too will the likelihood of rape. So far these treatments have yielded inconclusive results. Many feminists argue that because violence, not sexual desire, causes rape, taking away sexual desire will not decrease the incidence of rape. For many men in treatment, the most important first step is to accept responsibility for their actions.

REPORTING RAPE

Telling the Police

As we learned earlier in the chapter, the majority of rape victims do not report the rape to the police. The likelihood of reporting such incidences is increased if the assailant was a stranger, if there was violence, or if a weapon was involved (Williams, 1984; LaFree, 1982). Women who report their rapes to the police tend to have a better adjustment and less emotional symptoms than those who do not report (Cohen and Roth, 1987). On college campuses, campus police are often notified before the local police. Campus police may be able to take disciplinary action, such as fines or dismissal if the assailant is a student, but they are not able to press formal charges. Pressing charges with the local police may be important for two reasons. First, it alerts the police to a crime and thus may prevent other women from being victimized. Second, if legal action is decided upon, a woman will need to have a formal report from the police (not the campus police).

Although police officers have become more sensitive to the plight of rape victims in the past few years, negative experiences are still reported. Society's victim-precipitated view of rape also affects the attitudes of the police. To make sure that a crime did indeed occur, police must interrogate each case completely, which can be very difficult for a vic-

SEXUALITY *Today*   15.3

What to Do If You Are Raped

1. **Know that it was not your fault.** When a woman is raped, she often spends a long time trying to figure out exactly what she did to put herself at risk for a rape. This is probably due to the fact that women have always been told to "be careful," "don't dress seductively," or "don't stay out late." In reality, a rape might happen anywhere and at any time. No one asks to be raped.

2. **Talk to a rape crisis counselor.** Some women like to talk to a rape crisis counselor before going to the hospital or police. This is very helpful because they can often give you advice. Besides this, they are knowledgeable about rape and the common symptoms. The help of a counselor can be priceless, and many hospitals have on-site counselors, usually volunteers from *Women Organized Against Rape*. Talking to a counselor also helps give the victim back her sense of control (see the Resources at the end of this chapter).

3. **Go to a hospital for a medical examination.** An immediate medical evaluation is imperative. If there is a nurse or health care provider on campus, you can see them, but it is better to go to a local emergency room in order to have a thorough physical examination. Medical evaluations are important for two reasons. One is to check for STDs that may have been transmitted during the rape. Since some of the STDs take time to show up positive on a culture, it is impor-

tant to be retested in the following weeks. Recently, some women have requested AIDS tests postrape, although infection with HIV also takes time to show up. If a woman was not using birth control or has reason to suspect that she may have become pregnant, the hospital can administer DES (the morning after pill), which will not allow a fertilized egg to implant.

4. **Do not shower or throw away any evidence of the rape.** Do not shower before you go to the hospital. If you decide to change your clothes, do not wash or destroy what you were wearing. If anything was damaged in the assault, such as glasses, jewelry, or bookbags, keep these too. Put all of this in a plastic bag and store it in a safe place. All this is necessary to preserve the evidence of the rape, which will be very important if you decide to press charges against the rapist.

5. **Decide if you want to file a police report.** You have a choice of filing either a formal or informal report. This is something that you will need to sort through and decide. A rape crisis counselor can be very helpful in this decision process.

6. **Decide whether you want to press charges.** Although you do not need to decide this right away, you will need to think about it as soon as possible. It is important to review this decision with a lawyer experienced in rape cases.

tim who has just been through a traumatic experience. In fact, some victims have reported that the process of contacting the police, going to the hospital, and appearing in court is as emotionally stressful as the actual rape. Still, many report that taking such legal action makes them feel back in control, that they are *doing* something about their situation.

It is also important for a victim to sit down and write out exactly what happened in as much detail as possible. When did the rape occur? Where was the victim? What time was it? Who was with the victim? What did the rapist look like? What was he or she wearing? Exactly what happened? Was alcohol involved? Was anyone else present? The victim should keep this for his or her own records for, if he or she decides to press charges, it will come in very handy. Over time memories fade and you can lose the important small details.

Pressing Charges

The decision to press official charges is a very difficult one that takes much consideration. It has often been said that a rape victim goes through a second rape because he or she seems to be put on trial more than the accused rapist. Constant delays in the process, and the fact that the ordeal is public, contribute to further feelings of victimization (Burgess and Holmstrom, 1974). Court proceedings take up a great deal of time, create considerable anxiety, and are often lengthy.

Victims of rape report that they pressed charges because they were angry, to protect others, or they wanted justice to be served. Reasons for refusing to press charges included being afraid of revenge, wanting to just forget, feeling sorry for the rapist, or feeling like it would not matter anyway because nothing will be done. Victims of rape can also file a civil lawsuit and sue the assailant for monetary damages. Civil lawsuits are generally easier to prove than criminal lawsuits (Wagner, 1991).

In 1994, President Clinton signed a crime bill into law. Two provisions directly affect rape trials. First, prosecutors are allowed to introduce evidence of an assailant's past sexual offenses. Prior to this time, this information was not allowed in court. Second, all rapists must undergo testing for HIV infection.

In the court proceedings, the victim's character is seen as very important. Victims who had engaged in sex outside of marriage, who used alcohol or drugs, and who knew the accused prior to the alleged rape are less likely to be believed (LaFree, 1989). In fact, the victim's moral character can be viewed as more important than both victim injury and medical evidence. In one case, a juror reported, "She was on birth control pills. She was experienced" (LaFree, 1989:217).

Going to Court

If a victim is undecided about whether or not to press charges, it may be helpful to sit in on a rape trial. Rape trials can be extremely difficult for all involved. However, the purpose of sitting in is not to scare a person but to prepare oneself. It is not easy to proceed with legal action, but many women report that going through this process made them feel more in control and assured them that they had done nothing wrong. It also helps to gather support from friends and family.

During court proceedings, the line of questioning of rape victims is often different from that in other crimes (see Sexuality Today 15.4). Should a victim decide to proceed with legal action, he or she must also be prepared for the possibility that the rapist may be found not guilty. Victims must consider how this would affect them and their recovery. One victim reported that she was so unprepared for a verdict of not guilty that, when it happened, she completely fell apart (Author's files).

AVOIDING RAPE

Avoidance Strategies

Rape is the only violent crime in which we expect a person to fight back. If someone is robbed, we understand that they willingly gave their money to the robbers rather than be harmed. However, it is different with rape because if a woman does not struggle, we question whether or not she wanted to have sex. Only with visible proof of a struggle (bruises and cuts) does society seem to have sympathy.

Some victims of rape have said that, at the time of the rape, they felt frozen with fear, that it was impossible to move because they just could not believe what was happening to them. One victim said:

SEXUALITY*Today*   15.4

Questioning the Victim—
Was He Asking for it?

Imagine a man who has been mugged going through the same type of cross-examination as a woman who has been raped:

"Mr. Henke, you were held up at gunpoint on the corner of Locust and 12th?"

"Yes."

"Did you struggle with the mugger?"

"No, I did not."

"Why not?"

"I saw he had a gun!"

"You decided to comply rather than to fight him?"

"Yes."

"Did you scream for help?"

"No. I was scared of the guy!"

"Mr. Henke, have you ever given away money?"

"Yes."

"And you did so willingly?"

"What are you getting at?"

"Well, the way I see it, Mr. Henke, you've given money away in the past. Maybe you just wanted someone to take your money forcibly."

"Yeah . . . sure."

"OK, what time did this mugging occur?"

"About 11:30 P.M. last evening."

"What were you doing out on the street that late?"

"Walking home."

"From where?"

"I had been out at a bar having cocktails with clients."

"So you were drinking?"

"Yes."

"What were you wearing?"

"A suit. I was still in my work clothes."

"An expensive suit?"

"Yeah, actually it is, I am a successful businessman you know. I have to wear nice clothes."

"In other words, Mr. Henke, you were walking around the city streets late at night, under the influence of alcohol, in an expensive suit that advertised your wealth, right? If we didn't know better, Mr. Henke, we might even think that you were asking for this to happen, mightn't we?"

Did you ever see a rabbit stuck in the glare of your headlights when you were going down a road at night? Transfixed—like it knew it was going to get it— that's what happened.

Brownmiller (1975:358)

Brownmiller (1975) discusses something known as "quid pro quo"—when a victim decides to let the rapist do what he or she is going to do in exchange for not killing. The decision to submit to the attack is a very difficult one. Postassault guilt or self-blame may increase as a result of submitting to the rapist. Giving in to the rapist ("I'll do what you want; don't hurt me") should only be used as a last resort, mainly because this may indicate submission to the rapist and a desire for the attack. In turn, this may intensify the attack (Prentky et al., 1986).

How does a person know when to fight back? What should his or her strategies be? If you are confronted with a potential or attempted rape, the first and best strategy is to try to escape. However, this may not be possible if you are in a deserted area, if there are multiple attackers, or if your attacker has a weapon. If you cannot escape, effective strategies include verbal strategies such as screaming, dissuasive techniques ("I have my period," or "I'm a virgin"), empathy (listening or trying to understand), negotiation ("Let's discuss this"), and stalling for time. However, if the rapist does not believe the victim, these techniques may cause more harm than good. Prentky et al. (1986) asserts that the safest strategy is to attempt to talk to the attacker

Self-defense training can help increase the physical and psychological skills necessary to fight a rapist.

and try to make yourself a real person to him ("I'm a stranger; why do you want to hurt me?").

Typology of Rapist and Avoidance Strategies

In Sex Facts 15.1 we discuss rapist typology. Since each of these rapists is looking for particular things in their victims, strategies for avoiding rape vary with each type of rapist. If it is not possible to escape, try to start talking to the assailant, saying calmly that you are a stranger and that there are other ways to express anger. Doing so will help refocus the rapist and may challenge the rapist's view of you as a person. If the rapist listens or starts talking, continue talking. Prentky et al. (1986) believes that this type of rapist would be a *compensatory* rapist. If, on the other hand, after you have tried to talk, the rapist ignores you and continues to force you to submit to sexual activity, this is probably an *exploitative* rapist. Try to continue talking and ask personal questions. If aggression continues to build, this could be either a *displaced anger* or *sadistic* rapist. If the rapist uses humiliation (for example, if he forces you to fellate him or uses highly abusive language), he is probably a displaced anger rapist. Try to continue talking and show some interest and concern. Most displaced anger rapists perceive women as being abusive. Finally, if he is a sadistic rapist, or one who uses eroticized and bizarre activities (such as the insertion of foreign objects into the anus or vagina), the best advice would be to do whatever it takes to escape or attract help (Prentky et al., 1986).

SEX *Facts* 15.1

Rapist Typology

Prentky et al. (1986:78–79) identify four types of rapists. These are:

1. *Compensatory Rapist:* This type of rapist derives his motivations to rape from his belief that he is so inadequate that no woman in her right mind would voluntarily have sex with him. Therefore, he must compensate for his acutely felt inadequacies as a male.

2. *Exploitative Rapist:* This type of rapist can be viewed as a "man on the prowl" for a woman to exploit sexually. Sexual behavior is impulsive and determined more by the situation than the person. They tend to be men with a distinctive macho style who cannot believe that a woman could say no. This type of rapist is the most commonly described in the rape literature.

3. *Displayed Anger Rapist:* The victim represents a hated individual. The rape may reflect a series of experienced or imagined insults from other people. Sex is used only to humiliate the victims. The most

distinctive feature of this offender is his persistent anger and negative attitudes toward women.

4. *Sadistic Rapist:* There is a fusion of sexual and aggressive feeling—arousal increases aggression and vice versa. Usually the sadist's violence is directed at certain body parts (such as the breast, buttocks, anus). The rapist usually views the victim as participating in the assault. This type of rapist is the rarest.

These types of rapists have also been found to differ in regard to whether or not they knew their victims. Compensatory rapists are more likely to rape strangers, whereas a sadistic rapist is more likely to rape an acquaintance. It is hypothesized that since a compensatory rapist cannot imagine anyone being attracted to him, he avoids confrontations with women who know him for fear of ridicule. A sadistic rapist, on the other hand, may rape someone he knows because he believes that person wants it like he does.

Of course, in the panic of the moment it is very difficult to keep a level head and to try to differentiate rapist type. However, if you can try various strategies and talk with the potential rapist, you may increase your chances of avoiding the rape.

PART TWO—SEXUAL ABUSE OF CHILDREN

Do you consider sexual play between a thirteen-year-old brother and his seven-year-old sister sexual abuse? How about an adult male who persuades a fourteen-year-old female to fondle his genitals? Or a mother who caresses her two-year-old son? Or a seventeen-year-old male who has sexual intercourse with his fourteen-year-old girlfriend? How about a fourteen-year-old-boy who willingly has sex with a twenty-five-year-old woman? How would you define the sexual abuse of children? Personal definitions of sexual abuse also affect how we perceive those who are participants in this behavior (Finkelhor, 1984).

Incest refers to sexual contact between a child, adolescent, or adult and a child they are closely related to (parent, stepparent, uncle, cousin, caretaker). There are several types of incest, including father–daughter, father–son, brother–sister, grandfather–grand-daughter, mother–daughter, and mother–son. Incest can also occur between stepparents and stepchildren or aunts and uncles and their nieces and nephews. Sexual activity between a child and someone who is responsible for the child's care (such as a baby-sitter) is also considered incest, though definitions for incest vary from state to state; for example, twenty-five states and the District of Columbia require vaginal penetration for incest to have occurred. In twelve states and the District of Columbia, a blood relationship between the victim and perpetrator is necessary to prosecute for incest.

Since most children look to their parents for nurturing and protection, incest with a parent, guardian, or someone else the child trusts can be extremely traumatic. The incestuous parent exploits this trust to fulfill sexual or power needs of his or her own. The particularly vulnerable position of children in relation to their parents has been recognized in every culture. The **incest taboo**—the absolute prohibition of sex between family members—is universal (Herman, 1981).

incest taboo: The absolute prohibition of sex between family members.

Although it is largely believed that father–daughter incest is the most common type of incest, there is evidence that brother–sister sexual relationships may be more common (Vanderbilt, 1992). There is some disagreement over whether sex play with siblings is traumatic, although most would agree it is not as bad as parent–child incest because it does not carry as much of a sense of betrayal. Some believe that it is not traumatic unless there is force or exploitation, while others believe that it leads to long-term difficulties with both interpersonal and sexual relationships (Daie et al., 1989).

INCIDENCE OF CHILD SEXUAL ABUSE

The overall reported incidence of **child sexual abuse** has been increasing over the past thirty years. In the Kinsey et al. (1953) study of 441 females, 9% reported sexual contact with an adult before the age of fourteen. By the late 1970s and early 1980s, reports of child sexual abuse were increasing dramatically; 1975 cases were reported in 1976, 22,918 in 1982 (Finkelhor, 1984), and 130,000 by 1986 (Jetter, 1991). In 1984 it was

child sexual abuse: Sexual contact with a minor by an adult.

conservatively estimated that a child was sexually abused or molested at least once every two minutes in the United States (Rogers and Thomas, 1984). Vanderbilt (1992) estimated that one in three children are sexually abused.

Sedney and Brooks (1984) found that 16% of college students reported a history of sexual abuse. In another study, 22% to 45% of adult women and 5% to 13% of adult males were found to have experienced some form of sexual victimization as children (Briere and Runtz, 1987).

Perhaps the increase in the incidence of child sexual abuse is a reflection of the changing sexual climate rather than an actual increase in the number of sexual assaults on children. The Women's Movement and the Child Protection Movement both have focused attention on child sexual abuse issues (Finkelhor, 1984). Women's groups often teach that child sexual abuse is due to the patriarchal social structure and must be treated through victim protection. The Child Protection Movement views the problem as one that develops out of a "dysfunctional family" and is treated through family therapy.

The reported incidence of child sexual abuse in other countries is much lower than in the United States (Finkelhor, 1984). However, note that the rate in the United States increased as the sexual climate changed. The incidence in other countries may be similar to the United States, but the United States may be more receptive to reports of abuse or may define child sexual abuse differently.

It is interesting to note that the frequency of fathers being accused of sexual abuse of their children in divorce cases has increased from 5% to 10% of cases in the late 1970s to 30% of cases by the late 1980s (Dullea, 1987). Usually the accusation arises in bitter custody battles; however, it is difficult to determine the truth of these reports. Are the accusations originating from a vengeful ex-spouse wanting custody, or is it easier to discuss the sexual abuse once the "bonds of secrecy" have been broken, as they typically are during divorce?

VICTIMS OF SEXUAL ABUSE

Although research is limited because of sampling and responding rates, it is estimated that between 2.5% and 8.7% of boys are sexually abused as children, usually by men (Finkelhor, 1984). Boys are more likely to be sexually abused by strangers (40% of boys, 21% of girls), while girls are more likely to have family members as assailants (29% of girls, 11% of boys) (Finkelhor et al., 1990). The median age for sexual abuse of both girls and boys is around eight or nine years old (Finkelhor et al., 1990; Feinauer, 1988).

Finkelhor (1984; 156–157) proposes three reasons that the reported rates of male sexual abuse may be lower than that for females: (1) boys grow up believing that they must be self-reliant and may feel that they should be able to handle the abuse; (2) male sexual abuse gets entwined with the stigma of homosexuality because the majority of offenders are male; and (3) because boys often have more freedom in our society than girls, they may have a great deal to lose by reporting a sexual assault.

Reactions to abuse vary. Many victims are scared to reveal the abuse, either because of shame, fear of retaliation, belief that they themselves are to blame, or fear that they will not be believed. Some victims only try to get help if they fear that a younger sibling is threatened. If they do get help, younger victims are more likely to go to a relative for help, while older victims may run away or enter into early marriages to escape the abuse (Herman, 1981). Victims of incest with a biological father delay reporting the longest, while those who have been victims of stepfather or live-in partners told more readily (Faller, 1989).

EFFECTS OF SEXUAL ABUSE

There have been conflicting findings regarding the traumatic effects of sexual abuse. There are some studies that indicate that children are not severely traumatized by sexual abuse (Fritz et al., 1981), while more recent studies indicate that it may have long-lasting effects, which may lead to other psychological problems, including antisocial behavior, drug abuse, and prostitution. Groth (1978) suggests that the greatest trauma of sexual abuse occurs when it exists over a long period of time, the offender is a person who is trusted, penetration occurs, and there is aggression.

Keep in mind that what follows is a discussion of what is typically experienced by a victim of childhood sexual abuse. As we have discussed before, it is impossible to predict what the experience of every child will be; the reaction of each child is different. There are a few factors that make the abuse more traumatic, including the intensity of the sexual contact and how the sexual abuse is handled in the family. If a family handles the sexual abuse in a caring and sensitive manner, the effects on the child are often reduced.

Many victims experience psychological symptoms such as depression, increased anxiety, nervousness, emotional problems, low self-esteem, and personality and intimacy disorders. Similar to reactions of rape victims, depression is the most prevalent emotional symptom, which may be higher in victims who are abused repeatedly (Feinauer, 1989). Guilt is usually severe, and many females develop a tendency to blame themselves for the sexual abuse. This is probably due to the fact that females have more internal **attributional styles**. People may also try to cut themselves off from a painful or unbearable memory, which can lead to what psychiatrists refer to as a **dissociative disorder**. In its extreme form, dissociative disorder may result in **multiple personality disorder (MPD)**, in which there are actually two or more distinct personalities in one body. Several studies indicate that there is a history of sexual abuse in the majority of MPD cases (American Psychiatric Association, 1994).

Perhaps the most frightening of all emotional symptoms in abuse victims is the inability to remember past events. It is not unusual for those who were abused as children to repress the entire experience. In a study of incest victims, 64% were found to partially repress their abuse and 28% of these severely repressed it (Herman and Schatzow, 1987).

The most devastating emotional effects occur when the sexual abuse is done by someone the victim trusts. In a study of the effects of sexual abuse by relatives, friends, or strangers, it was found that the stronger the emotional bond and trust between the victim and the assailant, the more distress the victim experienced (Feinauer, 1989).

It is not uncommon for children who are sexually abused to display what Finkelhor and Browne (1985) refer to as **traumatic sexualization**. Children may begin to exhibit compulsive sex play or masturbation and show an inappropriate amount of sexual knowledge. When they enter adolescence they may begin to show promiscuous and compulsive sexual behavior, which may lead to sexually abusing others in adulthood. These children have learned that it is through their sexuality that they get attention from adults. Women who have been sexually abused as children are also more vulnerable to revictimization later in life.

Recent research reveals a connection between eating disorders and sexual abuse (Jones and Emerson, 1994). In one study of 158 patients with eating disorders, 50% were found to have suffered sexual abuse (Hall et al., 1989). The obsessions about food become all-consuming and may temporarily replace the original trauma of the sexual abuse. When these patients discussed their past sexual abuse, they were often able to make significant changes in their eating patterns.

attributional styles: Pattern of internal or external styles of attributing meaning to various events.

dissociative disorder: Psychological disorder involving a disturbance of memory, identity, and consciousness, usually resulting from a traumatic experience.

multiple personality disorder (MPD): A dissociative disorder in which a person develops two or more distinct personalities.

traumatic sexualization: A common result of sexual abuse in which a child displays compulsive sex play or masturbation and shows an inappropriate amount of sexual knowledge.

Children who are sexually abused also commonly develop problems such as drug and alcohol addiction or prostitution. Finkelhor and Browne (1985) hypothesized that because of the stigma that surrounds the early sexual abuse, the children believe they were "bad," and the thought of "badness" is incorporated into their self-concept. As a result, they often gravitate toward behaviors that society sees as deviant.

It is not unusual for adults who had been abused as children to confront their offenders later in life, especially among those who have undergone some form of counseling or psychotherapy to work through their own feelings about the experience. They may feel a strong need to deal with the experience and often get help to work through it. Personal Voices 15.5 is a letter that was written by an eighteen-year-old incest victim to her father. She had been sexually assaulted by her father throughout her childhood, and this was the first time that she had confronted him.

THE ABUSER

Profiles of Sexual Abusers

Many of us would like to believe that sexual abusers are identifiable by how they look. They are not. Sexual abusers look like nice people. Yet there are things that distinguish the molester from those who do not abuse children. Research comparing child molesters to nonmolesters has shown us that molesters tend to have poorer social skills, lower IQs, unhappy family histories, lower self-esteem, and less happiness in their lives (Awad and Saunders, 1989; Langevin et al., 1988; Finkelhor et al., 1990; Milner and Robertson, 1990; Dwyer and Amberson, 1989). As surprising as it may seem, many abusers have strict religious codes, yet still violate sexual norms. In one study, for example, an incest offender who had been having sexual interactions with his daughter for seven years was asked why he had not had vaginal intercourse with her. He replied: "I only had anal sex with her because I wanted her to be a virgin" (Dwyer and Amberson, 1989:112).

Denying responsibility for the offense and claiming they were in a trancelike state is also common. The majority of offenders are also very good at manipulation, which they develop to prevent discovery by others. One man told his thirteen-year-old victim "I'm sorry this had to happen to you, but you're just too beautiful," demonstrating the typical abuser's trait of blaming the victim for the abuse (Vanderbilt, 1992:3). Ironically, those who abuse children also often report disdain for all sex offenders (Dwyer and Amberson, 1989).

Although males still account for the majority of sexual abusers, a growing number of juvenile females have been caught molesting boys and girls (Sleek, 1994). More research is needed in this area.

The Development of a Sexual Abuser

Three prominent theories that propose factors that make abuse more likely are learning, gender, and biological theories.

Learning theorists believe that what children learn from their environment or those around them contributes to their behavior later in life. Many child abusers were themselves sexually abused as children. Many reported an early "initiation ceremony,"

*P*ersonal

V O I C E S

Confronting the Incest Offender

The letter below was written by an eighteen-year-old female college student to her father. She had just begun to recall past sexual abuse by her father and was working on her memories in counseling. She decided to confront her father with this letter.

Dad: I can't hide it any longer! I know why I was treated differently than the other kids. I remember everything about when I was a little girl. For years I acted as if nothing ever happened; it was always there deep inside but I was somehow able to lock it away for many years. But Daddy, something has pried that lock open, and it will never be able to be locked away again. Yes Daddy, I remember everything! I remember being scared or sick and crawling into bed with my parents only to have my father's hands touch my chest and rear. I remember going on a Sunday afternoon to my father's office, innocently wanting to spend time with him, only to play with some machine that vibrated. Yes, I admit that it tickled, but why did he keep putting it near or on my private part? I remember sitting on my father's lap while he was on the phone. I had a halter top on at the time. I remember wondering what he was doing when he untied it then turned me around to face him so he could touch my stomach and chest. I remember many hugs, even as a teenager, in which my father's hand was on my rear. I remember those words, "I like what is underneath better," when I asked my father if he liked my new outfit. But Daddy, more than anything, I remember one night when mom wasn't home. I was scared so I crawled into bed with my father who I thought was there to protect me. I remember his hands caressing my still undeveloped breast. I remember his hand first rubbing the top of my underwear then the same hand working its way down my underwear. I remember thinking that it tickled, but yet it scared me. Others had never tickled me like this. I felt frozen until I felt something inside me. It hurt and I was scared. I said stop and started shaking. I remember jumping out of bed and running to my room where

I cried myself to sleep. I also remember those words I heard a few days later, "I was just trying to love you. I didn't mean to hurt you. No one needs to know about this. People would misunderstand what happened. No one needs to know about this." You don't have to deal with the memories of what this has done to my life, my relationships with men, my many sleepless nights, my days of depression, my feelings of filth being relieved through making myself throw-up and the times of using—abusing—alcohol in order to escape. You haven't even had to see the pain and confusion in my life because of this. You haven't even noticed that nothing tickles me anymore. I have two feelings, pain and numbness. You took my childhood away from me by making me lock my childhood away in the dark corners of my mind. Now that child is trying to escape and I don't know how to deal with her. She, this child, has caused me to sleep with many men because she wanted to feel loved, but she can only feel loved by a man when he expresses it the way her father did. She has caused me to be unable to say NO. Yes, Daddy, this girl you called your "pretty little princess" may as well be called your "pretty little slut." This little girl has even caused me to allow myself to be raped. Yes, it's true. RAPED! Does that word mean anything to you? Oh yes, I was raped. I didn't want it! I said NO, STOP, over and over. I was scared. I was shaking. I did not want it, but I can remember thinking, "Oh, well, it doesn't matter anyway, my body has been violated so many times already. The less I fight, the quicker it will be over with." Now because of this rape I am afraid of all men. How can I even begin to trust men? Oh what I'd give to have a man love me and not hurt me. This letter could go on forever because this is how long this is going to affect my life. I felt it was only fair that you know that it is no longer a secret. I have protected you long enough. Now it is time to protect myself from all of the memories. Daddy, I must tell you, even after all that has happened, for some reason I'm not sure of, I still feel love for you—that is, if I even know what love is.

Author's files

gender theories: Theories for sexual abuse that identify gender as an important aspect in the development of an abuser.

which taught them about sex at a young age. Many learned that such behavior was how adults show love and affection to children.

Gender theories recognize that sexual abusers are overwhelmingly male (Finkelhor et al., 1990). Males often are not taught how to express affection without sexuality, which leads to needing sex to confirm their masculinity, being more focused on the sexual aspect of relationships, and being socialized to be attracted to mates that are smaller (Finkelhor, 1984). Only about 4% of offenders are female (Russell, 1984). Keep in mind that the incidence of female offenders may be lower because of lower reporting rates for boys and/or because society accepts intimate female interaction with children as normal (Groth, 1978).

Biological theories suggest that physiology contributes to the development of sexual abusers (see Chapter 14). One study found that male offenders had normal levels of the male sex hormone testosterone but elevated levels of other hormones (Lang et al., 1990). Neurological differences have also been reported between incest offenders and nonsex criminal offenders, which are thought to contribute to violence (Langevin et al., 1988).

TREATMENT FOR SEXUAL ABUSE

The Victim

Currently, the most effective treatments for victims of sexual abuse include a combination of cognitive and behavioral psychotherapies, which teach victims how to understand and handle the trauma of their assaults more effectively. Many victims of sexual abuse also have difficulties developing and maintaining intimate relationships. Being involved in a relationship that is high in emotional intimacy and low in expectations for sex is beneficial (Maltz, 1990). Learning that they have the ability to say no to sex is very important and usually develops when they establish relationships based on friendship first, rather than sex. Many times the partners of victims of sexual abuse are confused; they do not fully understand the effects of abuse in the lives of their mates, and so they may also benefit from counseling (Cohen, 1988).

The Abuser

recidivism: A tendency to relapse into a former pattern of behavior.

In Chapter 14 we discussed treatment for pedophilia. Overall, the primary goal of treatment for sexual abusers is to decrease their level of sexual arousal to inappropriate sexual objects, such as children. This is attempted through behavioral treatment, psychotherapy, or drugs. Other goals of therapy include teaching them to interact and relate better with adults; assertiveness skills training; empathy and respect for others; increasing sexual education; and evaluating and reducing any sexual difficulties that they might be experiencing with their sexual partners (Abel et al., 1980). Since **recidivism** is high in these abusers, it is also important to find ways to reduce the incidence of engaging in these behaviors.

PREVENTION

How can we prevent child sexual abuse? One program that has been explored is the "just say no" campaign, which teaches young children how to say no to inappropriate sexual advances by adults. This program has received much attention. How effective is such a strategy? Even if we can teach children to say no to strangers, can we also teach them to say no to their fathers or sexually abusive relatives? Could there be any negative effects of educating children about sexual abuse? These are a few questions that future research will need to address.

Increasing the availability of sex education has also been cited as a way to decrease the incidence of child sexual abuse (Herman, 1981). Children from traditional, authoritarian families that have no sex education are at higher risk for sexual abuse. Educating children about sexual abuse—teaching that it does not happen to all children—may help victims to understand that it is wrong. Telling children where to go and whom to talk to is also important.

Another important factor in prevention is adequate funding and staffing of child welfare agencies. Social workers may be among the first to become aware of potentially dangerous situations. Physicians and educators must also be adequately trained in identifying the signs of abuse.

PART THREE—SEXUAL HARASSMENT

Sexual harassment may be the most widespread of all types of sexually coercive behavior (Siegel, 1992). Sexual harassment is a very broad term that includes anything from looks, jokes, unwanted sexual advances, a "friendly" pat, an "accidental" brush on a person's body, or an arm around a person (Cammaert, 1985). Because of the wide variety of actions that fall under this definition, many people are confused about what exactly constitutes sexual harassment.

MacKinnon (1987) defines sexual harassment as sexual pressure imposed on someone who is not in a position to refuse it. It may seem that sexual harassment is not as shocking as other forms of sexual coercion, but the effects of harassment on the victim can be traumatic and often cause long-term difficulties (see Personal Voices 15.6). Fitzgerald and Ormerod (1991:2) claim that "there are many similarities between sexual harassment and other forms of sexual victimization, not only in the secrecy that surrounds them but also in the mythology that support them."

sexual harassment:
Unwanted attention of a sexual nature from someone in school or the workplace; also includes the use of status and/or power to coerce or attempt to coerce a person into having sex, and unwelcome sexual jokes, glances, or comments.

INCIDENCE

It is estimated that 50% to 85% of American women will experience some form of sexual harassment during their professional life (Siegel, 1992). Sexual harassment has increased in the past few years, probably in relation to the increase in women in the workforce. By treating women as sexual objects, men may be reacting to the threat women pose to their jobs. Because of sexual harassment, women are nine times more likely than men to quit a job, five times more likely to transfer, and three times more likely to lose their jobs (Gutek and Konrad, 1986).

Although the majority of people that are sexually harassed are female, it can also happen to men. This is more common if they have a female boss. Women and men who are sexually harassed are typically young, unmarried, have a higher education, are in nontraditional jobs for their gender (i.e., female law enforcement, male secretaries), are supervised by someone of the other sex, work primarily with the other sex, and are in

P _ersona_ l
V O I C E S
<u>15.6</u>

Sexual Harassment

I was a first year graduate student working in the Psychiatry Department as a research assistant. One day I approached the 62-year-old psychiatrist that I was working with about a potential research project I was interested in. He was very busy and told me to come to his other office that evening. I had never known of his "other" office, but he gave me the directions. I was so excited about his interest in my project that I spent all day at the library collecting relevant articles for the paper. I arrived at his office at approximately 6 p.m. As soon as I stepped inside, I knew I had been foolish. It was an apartment, not an office, and he had a candlelight dinner set for two.

Although I probably should've known better, I still believed that he was interested in my research project. He said that we would eat a quick dinner and then get to work. All of the sudden in the middle of dinner he stood up, walked over to me and placed his hand on my breast. He asked how interested I was in publishing this paper. I was so frightened that I quickly grabbed my backpack and ran out of the building. At the encouragement of another psychiatrist in the Department, who had heard other reports about this psychiatrist's behavior, I reported the incident to the chairman of the Department. I was subsequently fired.

Author's files

trainee positions (Merit Systems Protection Board, 1981). The majority of the time harassers act alone. Same-sex harassment has also occurred.

Sexual harassment creates a hostile and intimidating environment. Most victims of sexual harassment never say anything about it (Siegel, 1992). This may be in part because women are socialized keep harmony in relationships. Others verbally confront the situation or leave their jobs in order to get away from it. Assertiveness is the most effective strategy, either by telling someone about it or confronting the offender. Many fear, however, that confronting a boss or teacher who is harassing them could jeopardize their jobs or their grades. Also, although these strategies increase the *chances* that the behavior will stop, they do not guarantee it. If you are being sexually harassed by someone in a university setting, the best advice is to talk to someone about it, such as a counselor or your advisor. If this is not possible, then you may want to go to a school official.

Women and men think differently about sexual harassment. If a male professor tells a female student how attractive she is every day, she might find it offensive or

In October 1991, during the Supreme Court nomination confirmation hearings, sexual harassment charges were brought up against Clarence Thomas by University of Oklahoma law professor Anita Hill. Hill was a former aide to Thomas. This case brought the issue of sexual harassment into the forefront of public thinking and helped women begin to talk about their experiences with sexual harassment.

uncomfortable; however, a male may find similar comments by a female professor to be flattering. In one study, approximately 75% of men who were asked how they would respond to sexual advances in the workplace said they would be flattered, while 75% of the women said they would be offended (Hayes, 1991). This is an extraordinary finding because it reveals that men and women interpret similar behaviors differently when it comes to sexual harassment. It is not surprising that women have a lower threshold for labeling certain behaviors as sexual harassment than do men (Johnson et al., 1991).

PREVENTION

The first step in reducing the incidence of sexual harassment is to acknowledge the problem. Too many people deny its existence. Since sexual harassers usually have more power, it is difficult for victims to come forward and disclose their victimization. University officials and administrators need to work together to provide educational opportunities and assistance for all students, staff, and employees. Establishing policies for dealing with these problems is also necessary. Workplaces also need to design and implement strong policies against sexual harassment.

Education, especially about the role of women, is imperative. As our society continues to change and as more and more women enter the workforce, we need to prepare men for this adjustment. Throughout history, when women have broken out of their traditional roles, there have always been difficulties. Today, as more and more women are working, we need research to explore the impact of women on the workforce.

Summary

- Sexually coercive behaviors, including rape, sexual abuse of children, incest, and sexual harassment, do exist. Research on rape has revealed that there has been an increase in the number of reported rapes in the last six years and that rape is still one of the most underreported crimes.
- Although many women are victims of rape and sexual assault, very few report it or take legal action. Men are less likely to report rape primarily because of the societal myth that says men cannot be raped.
- On college campuses, alcohol use is viewed very differently for men and women when it comes to rape. Fraternities may provide an environment that is conducive to rape due to alcohol and to the relationships of the members.
- Rape victims experience Rape Trauma Syndrome, which may take years to work through.
- Anyone can be raped, male or female, young or old, gay or straight, women with disabilities, or prostitutes.
- There are several types of rapists. Knowing the type of rapist may help to decide which avoidance strategies to employ.
- The majority of victims of sexual abuse are female, while the majority of offenders are male.
- Boys are more likely to be sexually abused by strangers, while girls are more likely to be abused by family members.

- The median age for sexual abuse is between eight and nine years old.
- Having an absent parent, a stepparent, or living in chemically dependent families may put a child at higher risk for sexual abuse.
- Many adults repress early sexual abuse and may remember it later in life.
- Eating disorders are common among victims of sexual abuse.
- Teaching a child to "just say no" may not be an effective method of prevention. Implementing sex education programs may help to decrease the frequency of child sexual abuse.
- Sexual harassment usually occurs in the context of an unequal power relationship.
- Establishing sexual harassment policies and providing education may help to decrease the incidence of sexual harassment. Only through increased reporting and sentencing will we be able to reduce the incidence of sexual assault.
- Throughout this chapter, we note the importance of prior sexual victimization in the offenders of these crimes. Rapists, child sexual molesters, and incest perpetrators all report a significant degree of past sexual victimization.

Reflections on Sexuality

1. What do you think should be done to encourage women (or men) to come forward to report a rape? What educational strategies could be employed?

2. How must society alter its views of rape (especially toward the rape of women) so that less blame is placed on the victim?

3. Name three different types of rapists and describe each.

4. Explain the theoretical views of rape. Which theory best encompasses how you feel about rape? Do you think that women are raped primarily because of risks that they take, such as getting drunk at a party or wearing tight clothing, or is it because of the nature of sex roles and the stereotypes about men and women in society? Is it because of the present disempowerment that men feel as a result of changing sex roles in society?

5. Who are the rapists of men? Why do you think a straight male would rape another male? Would this appear to you to be a sexually motivated crime?

6. What can be done to reduce the incidence of sexual harassment, specifically in the workplace? What can an individual do? What actions should the employer or business take to assure a harassment-free environment? What role, if any, should the government play?

7. Define incest, and give two examples of cases that would be considered incest cases.

8. What are the effects of childhood sexual abuse?

9. What can be done to help decrease the rates of child sexual abuse?

10. Explain some of the reasons that females are more likely to be the victims of sexual abuse and that men do not report abuse.

11. Why do you think males and females have different ideas about what constitutes sexual harassment?

12. Does your university have a policy for you to follow if you are a victim of sexual harassment? Who would you go to?

Resources

Rape

National Directory: Rape Prevention and Treatment U.S. Department of Health and Human Services, National Center for the Prevention and Control of Rape, (301) 443-3728.

Rape Crisis Centers can be located in your local telephone directory.

Sexual Assault

National Resource Center on Child Abuse and Neglect, 63 Inverness Drive East, Englewood, CO 80112-5117; (800)227-5242 (professional publications and public inquiries regarding child protective services and child abuse and neglect).

Planned Parenthood Federation of America, 810 Seventh Avenue, New York, NY 10019; (212)541-7800 (for informational materials).

Violence and Traumatic Stress Research, National Institute of Mental Health, 5600 Fishers Lane, Room 10C-24, Rockville, MD 20857; (301)443-3728 (for informational materials).

Sexual Abuse

Childhelp USA, 6463 Independence Avenue, Woodland Hills, CA 91367; (800)4-A-CHILD (to talk to a trained counselor about sexual abuse, information, and materials).

Incest Resources, Inc., Cambridge Women's Center, 46 Pleasant Street, Cambridge, MA 02139; (617)354-8807 (publishes literature on incest topics and provides patient referrals).

Incest Survivors Anonymous, PO Box 17245, Long Beach, CA 90807-7245; (310)428-5599 (a self-help peer support program with chapters nationwide for incest survivors).

National Committee for Prevention of Child Abuse, 332 South Michigan Avenue, Suite 1600, Chicago, IL 60604-4357 (provides information and statistics on child abuse and maintains an extensive publications list).

National Center for Missing And Exploited Children, 2101 Wilson Boulevard, Suite 550, Arlington, VA 22201; (800)843-5678 (for reporting missing children and child pornography. Provides free materials).

VOICES (Victims of Incest Can Emerge Survivors) in Action, Inc., PO Box 148309, Chicago, IL 60614; (312)327-1500 (a national network for incest survivors, partner,and other support people; newsletters and membership fees).

1

Morality, Religion, and Law

SEXUAL MORALITY

SEXUALITY AND RELIGION

SEXUALITY AND THE LAW

MAKING ETHICAL SEXUAL DECISIONS

SUMMARY

REFLECTIONS ON SEXUALITY

SUGGESTED READINGS

SEXUAL MORALITY

All sexually active human beings make decisions about when, where, and with whom they will engage in sexual activity. For most people, at least part of that decision is based on their views of what behaviors are morally acceptable, which may in large part be derived from their religious beliefs. For example, some people would not have sex with a partner they did not love, either because they feel it is immoral or against God's wishes; others find it acceptable if both partners are willing and go into the encounter openly and freely.

In addition to morality, people's sexual behaviors are also influenced by what is allowed in their particular society. For example, some men who would not use the services of a prostitute in Utah, where it is illegal, might be willing to do so next door in Nevada, where there are legal brothels (see Special Focus 3).

In this special-focus chapter, we discuss the ways morality, religion, and law shape our sexual behaviors. We present brief overviews of the major religious perspectives and discuss some of the ways laws in the United States try to structure the sexual behavior of citizens. We close the chapter by examining how people make ethical decisions about their sexuality.

Sexuality and Ethics

The sexual behavior of human beings differs from all other animals in part because it is so wrapped up in moral, religious, legal, and interpersonal values. How simple it seems for animals, who mate without caring about marriage, pregnancy, morals, or hurting their partners' feelings! Human beings are not (typically) so casual about mating; every culture has developed elaborate rituals, rules, laws, and moral principles that structure sexual relations between people. The very earliest legal and moral codes archaeologists have uncovered discuss sexual behavior at great length, and rules about sexual behavior make up a great part of the legal and ethical codes of the world's great civilizations and religions.

Yet, it is reasonable to ask why sexual desire and behavior, as opposed to other basic human needs such as hunger or sleep, should be subject to so many strong moral principles. What is it about sexuality that seems to demand such a close consideration of ethics?

There are many possible answers. For example, sexuality is one of the few basic drives that is *interpersonal*. Eating, for example, is basically a solitary act (even when we dine in groups, we eat individually). Sexual drive, on the other hand, usually involves the desire for a sexual partner. Conflict may arise, however, when that partner's feelings, needs, fears, and concerns are not the same as ours. People can be hurt, used, and taken advantage of sexually or be the victim of honest miscommunication, especially since sex is so difficult for many people to discuss.

Sexuality is also closely related to the formation of love bonds and to procreation. Every society has a stake in procreation; without adequate numbers of people a society can languish, and with too many people a society can be overwhelmed. Most societies create rules to prevent accidental births and births that do not fit conventional family structures (such as "illegitimate" births). Societies also formulate sexual rules to control the size of their population (such as the outlawing of contraception or abortion in cultures that want to encourage childbirth or the distribution of free contraception and free abortions, as they do in China, when the population gets too high).

Another reason sexuality and ethics are so closely linked is because the sexual drive emerges relatively late in life. Think about it—you have been eating, sleeping, loving, communicating, and otherwise exercising most of your basic drives since you were an infant. However, genital-based sexuality did not emerge in its present form until somewhere around puberty.* You must learn to cope with these new feelings at the very time that you are learning to cope with being an adult, establishing independence from parents, and forming your own identity.

SEX TALK

QUESTION **SF1.1**   **Aren't moral standards that used to surround sexuality out of date? I mean, even kids know about sex, and everyone does it, so why listen to old versions of morality anymore?**

Ours is not the most sexually free society in history; compared, for example, with ancient Greece, we are downright puritanical. Yet although sexual behaviors change, some things do not: sexuality involves the relationships between people who have their own fears, values, and expectations. Sexuality is a powerful drive that can easily tempt us into overlooking the needs of others. Wise men and women have been thinking and writing about these issues since ancient times, and drawing from their accumulated wisdom can help us develop our own sexual morality.

There are other reasons that morality and sexuality have been so closely intertwined throughout history in many countries. A more sociological explanation, for example, is based on the marriage contract signifying an economic as well as an interpersonal union. In some societies, marriage can include the transfer of enormous amounts of property, land, and prestige, often from the groom's side to the bride's side of the family. What the groom's side "pays" for in this contract is exclusive sexual access to the bride; strong laws are therefore in place to prevent the bride from losing her virginity before marriage and from thus losing her value to her father before he can exact his price from the groom. That is one explanation of why females have been allowed less sexual freedom than men. There are certainly other possible explanations for the moral and ethical standards that have developed around sexual behavior. Why do you think morality and sexuality are so closely bound?

---

* As we discuss in Chapter 4, even children have sexual needs and engage in sexual behavior. But the mature sexuality that begins to emerge in puberty has many features that make it distinct from childhood sexuality.

In many societies, the groom must still pay a price to the bride's family, sometimes through an elaborate ceremony such as this one in India. In that sense, the bride is considered "sold" by her father to the family of the groom.

SEXUALITY AND RELIGION

All great religious traditions have tried to set standards and rules about human sexuality, both to encourage moral behavior in individuals and to try to help maintain social cohesion. However, as times change and ideas change, religion changes, too; even the most fundamentalist believers worship differently than their ancestors did before them. Religions today must try to preserve their traditional sense of morality while dealing with the changing circumstances of the world around them, including modern attitudes toward sexuality and gender. For example, almost all the major religious groups in the United States have been debating issues of abortion, homosexuality, and admitting females to the clergy during the last decade, along with other sexual issues. Below we review some of the attitudes and rules that have been established by the major religions of the world.

*Judaism**

> *We who have the Torah and believe that God created all in his wisdom [do not believe that he] created anything inherently ugly or unseemly. If we were to say that intercourse is repulsive, then we blaspheme God who made the genitals. . . . Marital intercourse, under proper circumstances, is an exalted manner. . . . Now you can understand what our rabbis meant when they declared that when a husband unites with his wife in holiness, the divine presence abides with them.*
> *—from the* Iggeret ha-Kodesh *("Letter of Holiness"), early thirteenth century.*
>
> ***Quoted in Biale (1992:101)***

Judaism has long been regarded as having a positive attitude toward sexuality, in part because it is usually compared with historical Christianity, with its overwhelming

---

* See Chapter 1 for more on the Biblical background of Jewish belief.

suspicion of sex. However, although Judaism's official attitude toward sexuality has been *positive,* it has not been particularly *permissive.* As the quote above demonstrates, approval of sexuality was always within the marital bond, in keeping with Judaism's central focus on the maintenance and sanctity of the family. Premarital sex was never a particular concern of the rabbis (Jews historically got married early, and sexual contact was assumed to lead to marriage); but extramarital sex and homosexuality were strictly forbidden. Still, the rabbis of the **Talmud**, the Jewish code of laws and biblical interpretations, made it an obligation for men to please their wives sexually, even mandating the frequency of intercourse: men of leisure were to have sex with their wives every night, laborers who worked in the city twice a week, laborers who traveled outside the city once a week, scholars once a week (usually on Friday night, the Jewish Sabbath), camel drivers once a month, sailors once every five months, and so on.

Ancient Jewish history and tradition, including the Hebrew Bible and, later, the Talmud, include many sexual parables, rules, and laws. One of the most important moments in the Bible is the moment when God affirms his covenant with Abraham, telling him to circumcise all Hebrew males as "a token of the covenant betwixt you and me. . .and my covenant shall be in your flesh for an everlasting covenant" (Genesis 17:11,13). God wanted the covenant to last throughout the generations and so symbolically chose the cite of male procreation to carry its sign. The penis and its emission, semen, therefore became a powerful symbol of holiness in the Bible. Semen should not be wasted; for example, those having nocturnal emissions ("wet dreams") are considered ritually unclean, and masturbation is forbidden to males.

Procreation and, by extension, sexuality are sacred tasks, and so sexuality was taken seriously in Judaism. In the Talmud, a husband is instructed to have "pure" thoughts during intercourse and not engage in "levity" (joking around). He must also respect his wife's sexual needs and rights; he may not deprive her of sex and may not have sex with her if she does not want it or if she is asleep or intoxicated. The wife, likewise, has a sexual obligation to her husband and may not consistently withhold sex. These laws were innovative compared with the laws of other cultures of the time, and they were not adopted by Christianity until many centuries later (and some are still unique to Judaism). For example, Judaism celebrates marital sexuality, and celibacy is seen as sinful for it denies the very first commandment God gave humanity in the first chapter of Genesis: be fruitful and multiply.

Talmud: The rabbinical interpretations of the Torah, the Hebrew Bible, from which Jewish traditions and laws are derived.

Orthodox Jewish women wear modest clothes and cover their hair with scarves or wigs, believing that hair is a sexual part of the body and should be reserved for their husbands.

The attitudes of Jewish tradition toward nonprocreative sex are somewhat ambiguous. Within marriage, there are few sexual restrictions; there is no specific prohibition against oral or anal sex, for example. Sexual relations are encouraged even among the infertile and the elderly, who cannot procreate, indicating that Jewish tradition believes that sexuality has value outside of reproduction. On the other hand, the rabbis of the Talmud clearly condemned nonprocreative acts such as male masturbation (women's masturbation is never mentioned), to the point that some recommend that the man's hand be cut off or even that he be put to death! (Biale, 1992).

The rabbinical attitude toward women depends on which rabbi is speaking. At times the Talmud is clearly misogynistic ("Although a woman is a vessel filled with excrement and her mouth is filled with blood, everyone runs after her"), while at other times it views women with respect, and portrays them as important sexual partners, and emphasizes mutual sexual obligations (Biale, 1992).

Modern Judaism has inherited these ideas from its history, but it also has been profoundly influenced by modern life. Most Jews do not practice traditional sexual laws, and the major Jewish denominations, Orthodox, Conservative, and Reform (and, more recently, Reconstructionism), have different views of these rules.

Orthodox Jews are the most traditional in their interpretation of the Bible and the Talmud, and they closely follow rabbinical law. Orthodox men and women observe the Biblical **laws of Niddah**, which forbid sexual intercourse during, and for one week after, menstruation, during which the women is considered ritually unclean (much as a man is after a nocturnal emission). Whatever the original reasons for this prohibition, many have noted that the two-week intermission from intercourse brings the husband and wife back together sexually just as the woman is at the peak of her fertility cycle. Modern Orthodox Jews also emphasize the psychological benefits of having two weeks free of the pressures of sex and the special nature of the sexual rejoining afterward.

Conservative Jews are more liberal in their interpretation of traditional Jewish law than the Orthodox. For example, Conservative Judaism, after a long and sometimes bitter

laws of Niddah: Rules in the Jewish tradition concerning the behaviors of a menstruating woman, including sexual restrictions.

Conservative, Reform, and Reconstructionist branches of Judaism now permit female rabbis, although Orthodox Judaism still forbids it.

dispute, recently decided to ordain women as rabbis and is currently undergoing the same difficult struggle over the question of homosexual rabbis. Even more liberal are Reform Jews, who have long accepted female rabbis. Reconstructionist Judaism, the newest and smallest of the four major branches, is one of the few major religious groups in America that openly accepts homosexuality and homosexual clergy (Clark et al., 1990).

In general, Jews tend to be more liberal in their attitudes toward sex and gender roles than other American groups. Jews were found in one poll to be more accepting of premarital and extramarital sex and much more accepting of homosexuality than Catholics or Protestants (Cochran and Beeghley, 1991); in a poll of college students, Jews were more liberal than Protestants or Catholics on measure of such things as traditional attitudes toward women's sexuality, homosexuality, and male dominance (Lottes and Kuriloff, 1992).

On the other hand, Orthodox Judaism has been criticized for its male bias; for example, there is a prayer in the morning service where men thank God for not making them women; women are not counted as part of a prayer quorum, and there are no Orthodox female rabbis. Orthodox (male) rabbis often argue that clear gender role separation is part of traditional Jewish life and that it strengthens marriage. Yet there is also some unrest among Orthodox women, especially the well educated, who find their exclusion from full religious life disturbing, seeing it as ultimately harming Jewish life itself (Nelson, 1983). Non-Orthodox Jews have taken steps to improve the ritual equality of the sexes, by revising the prayers and rituals, creating new customs and practices, and ordaining female rabbis.

Christianity

In Chapter 1 we reviewed the history of Christian thought about sexuality. Traditional western Christianity has been a "sex negative" religion, bringing an overlay of sinfulness to almost every aspect of human sexuality (Bullough, 1992). Yet today, almost all Christian denominations are having serious debates about sexual behavior, homosexuality, and the role of women in religious life.

Sexuality issues have become, in Christianity, a primary way to discuss theology; in other words, questions about admitting homosexuals or women to the clergy or encouraging the use of condoms to prevent AIDS have become means to grapple with belief about the role of God's word and the Bible. Philip Turner (1993) has written that the great philosopher of modern sexuality, Michel Foucault, believed that

> *Sexuality now serves the same purpose as did the word "soul" in the Middle Ages. At that time, "soul" provided its users with a way to unite the various aspects of human identity and, in so doing, gave it significance. It is now the function of the word "sexuality" to do the same thing. Thus "sexuality," "self," and "identity" are closely linked by present usage—sometimes to the point that the notions meld one with another.*

In other words, debates over sexuality are now used to get at the most fundamental questions of faith. Let us review the sexual doctrines of a sample of religious denominations.

Catholicism

The Catholic Church's perspective on sexual behavior and ethics have shaped Western attitudes toward sex for centuries. The Catholic Church teaches that genital sexuality can be expressed only within a permanent and undissolvable marital union. The primary purpose of sexual intercourse is procreational, although it also serves a secondary, "unitive" purpose, that is, it also strengthens the love union (Nelson, 1983). Virginity and celibacy are seen as exalted states, and all artificial contraception (including condoms), artificial insemination (even with the husband's semen), divorce, masturbation, homosexual behavior, sexuality that cannot lead to procreation (anal and oral sex, for example), and all premarital and extramarital relations are forbidden (Curran, 1992). The Church considers these principles universal and eternal, applying to all people in all societies at all times in history.

The Roman Catholic Church has been consistent in its defense of these principles, and various popes have upheld the Church's traditional stand on sexual behavior. In 1976, a "Declaration on Certain Questions Concerning Sexual Ethics," approved by the pope, condemned the "unbridled exaltation of sex" and reinforced the Church's position that sex is only acceptable within the marital union, that all homosexual sexual activity is "intrinsically disordered," and that divorce is unacceptable. A 1983 Vatican pamphlet *Educational Guidance in Human Love* describes masturbation, extramarital sex, and homosexual acts as "grave moral disorders." The most recent statement, the 1992 **universal catechism** of the Roman Catholic Church reinforces many of these teachings. Abstinence or the rhythm method are the only acceptable forms of contraception, and "Any action which . . . envisages as a means or as an end to make procreation impossible, is intrinsically bad." While the catechism does say that homosexuals "do not choose their homosexual condition; for most of them it is an ordeal. They should be treated with respect, compassion, and sensitivity," it reiterates that homosexual acts are "intrinsically disordered" and so homosexuals are "urged to be chaste." The universal catechism also denies women the right to become priests and forbids abortion. In 1995, Pope John Paul II reiterated the Catholic Church's opposition to contraception in "Evangelism Vitae," the gospel of life (Bohlen, 1995). It is for these reasons that Catholicism in particular has been considered one of the most "sex negative" of religions. Its general attitude was summed up by Pope Gregory I, who wrote that "sexual pleasure can never be without sin."

Yet, just because Catholics answer to a central authority does not mean that Catholics think, believe, or behave alike. Andrew Greeley (1992a), a prolific Catholic priest and sociologist, argues that there are actually two Catholic traditions: the "High Tradition," which includes the thinking of the great theologians, and the "Popular Tradition," which includes the Catholicism that is practiced by the people, that is passed through families, and that is kept alive in the rituals, music, stories, and acts of individuals. Greeley argues that Catholic Popular Tradition is much more accepting of sexuality

universal catechism: An elementary book containing a summary of all the principles of a Christian religious tradition.

Priests in Catholicism are symbolically "married" to the Church.

than the High Tradition in that it better understands the role of sex in marriage. He supports his contention with statistics that show that Catholics have a high frequency of intercourse, stay sexually more active than other groups as they age, and are more sexually playful; in fact, he argues that Catholic Popular Tradition, combined with teachings of the High Tradition, lead Catholics to enjoy sex *more* than other groups!

Many Catholics in the United States have been seriously questioning some of the teachings of the High Tradition. Dissent in American Catholicism is strong, and it has been growing. For example, in 1963, 45% of American Catholics reported that they did not believe that birth control was wrong (Curran, 1992); by 1991, nine out of ten American Catholics accepted birth control, and six out of ten married Catholic women of childbearing age were actually using some form of artificial contraception (Greeley, 1992b). Also, many Catholics are arguing that the AIDS epidemic warrants a reconsideration of the use of condoms, because the value of saving a life supersedes the prohibition against contraception (Drane, 1992). American Catholics also seem to ignore the Church's teaching about premarital sex; according to polls, single Catholics are *more* likely than single Protestants to have had intercourse in the past year (Greeley, 1992b).*

Another area of disagreement between the Church and American Catholics is on attitudes toward homosexuality. In a Gallup poll, 48% of Catholics agreed that homosexuals should be eligible for the ministry (versus only 37% of Protestants) (*Religion Watch,* 1993). Forty-four percent of Catholics in the poll also agreed that homosexuality is an acceptable alternative lifestyle.

American Catholics are also questioning the Church's demand that the clergy be celibate. Celibacy was a late requirement of Catholic clergy (it was not mandatory until the sixteenth century), and many Americans believe that the requirement is a factor in the the sharp decline in the number of men entering the priesthood, especially in the United States. But the Church is remaining steadfast in demanding pledges of celibacy from Catholic priests.

Catholics throughout the world, including many in the United States, accept the Church's position on sexual behavior and believe that the Church's standards are God's will and lead to a moral life. On a recent trip to the United States, Pope John Paul II was greeted enthusiastically by a large, young audience, which brought into question the common belief that young Americans are disenchanted with Catholicism and the authority of the pope. Many made pledges of abstinence until marriage. On the other hand, many American Catholics argue that the world is changing and that Church doctrine must conform to the realities of modern life. The Vatican counters that Catholic morality is eternal and does not change just because peoples' lifestyles change. Only time will tell the results of these conflicts within the Roman Catholic Church. (See Sexuality Today SF1.1 for one example of a controversy over the teachings of the Catholic Church.)

Protestantism

Unlike Catholics, Protestants do not answer to a unified authority. Martin Luther fractured the unity of Christianity in the sixteenth century by rebelling against the need of the Church to mediate salvation—he believed salvation was available to the sinner directly from God. Martin Luther redirected Christian thought from the authority struc-

---

* American Catholics are more likely than other groups to use the pill as contraception. Since the pill is not a "barrier" method of contraception, and thus does not actively block the sperm and egg from joining, it may seem to Catholics less like a violation of the Church's dictates (Greeley, 1992b).

SEXUALITY *Today* SF1.1

American Bishops and Women's Role in the Church

The controversy in the United States over Catholic teaching is well illustrated in a proposed pastoral letter drafted in 1992 by some American bishops on women's place in Catholicism. For nine years the bishops wrote and rewrote the letter, trying to reach compromises between the Vatican, women's groups, and their own beliefs. As each draft was written, more radical aspects of the proposal were tempered.

The debate over acceptance of the letter was heated, with some bishops arguing that the letter went too far, others not far enough. The letter finally was defeated in a vote, the first time a proposed pastoral letter had failed to pass in the twenty-six-year history of the National Conference of Catholic Bishops.

Below are four excerpts of the same section of the letter, showing how the message of the letter changed over time. Note that the first draft urged a quick study of ordaining female deacons and strongly recommends studying the opening of other roles, while each subsequent version softens the message, until the final draft does not mention women and includes a statement about reflecting the official teaching of the Church.

First Draft, 1988:

In particular, we recommend that the question of admission of women to the diaconal office . . . be submitted to thorough investigation. . . . We urge that this study be undertaken and brought to completion soon. Women serving in pastoral ministry accomplish . . . many of the functions performed by ordained deacons and are capable of accomplishing all of them. The question of women being formally installed in the permanent diaconate arises quite naturally, and pastoral reasons prompt its evaluation.

Even more compelling is the question of women being installed in the lay ministries of lector and acolyte. The exclusion of women and girls from certain aspects of service at the altar likewise raises concern . . .

For this reason, we recommend that women participate in all liturgical ministries that do not require ordination.

Second Draft, 1990:

We recommend that the question of admission of women to the diaconal office . . . be submitted to thorough investigation. . . . We urge that this study be undertaken and brought to completion soon. We support further the study for admission of women to the lay ministries of lector and acolyte. The exclusion of women and girls from certain aspects of service at the altar likewise demands consideration. . . . For this reason, we encourage participation by women in all liturgical ministries that do not require ordination.

Third Draft, April 1992:

We also recognize the need for continuing dialogue and reflection on the meaning of ministry in the church, particularly in regard to the diaconate, to the office of lector and acolyte, and to servers at the altar.

Fourth Draft, September 1992:

We recognize the need also for continuing reflection on the meaning of ministry in the Church, particularly in regard to the diaconate, and the office of lector, acolyte, and to servers at the altar. Such study should proceed with an objectivity and serenity whose necessary context is respect for the authority of the magisterium of the Church.

The New York Times, 1992c

---

ture of the Church to the individual's private relationship with God. He therefore rejected the special role of priests, who were just men with the same need for salvation as other men, and so also rejected the celibacy of the clergy.

In most other ways, however, the attitudes of Protestant denominations toward sexual behavior did not significantly differ from that of Catholics, at least until recently. Like Catholicism, Protestantism has had a suspicion of sexuality, and Martin Luther (himself married to a former nun) called marriage a "hospital for the sick," believing that without marriage people would engage in sexual sinning. Protestant clergy, like the Catholic Church, have traditionally seen sexual behavior as legitimate only within marriage, and considered homosexuality and masturbation as sinful. On the other hand,

During the visit of Pope John Paul II in Denver in 1993, some American Catholics protested Vatican policy on sexuality. However, thousands also showed up to cheer the pope's message to return to basic sexual values.

Protestantism also shifted the focus of marriage and marital intercourse from procreation to the furthering of love and companionship (Nelson, 1983).

Different Protestant denominations have had different levels of openness to sexual controversies such as homosexuality and women in the clergy. Recently, many American Protestant denominations (especially the "**mainline**" denominations, which have been steadily losing membership) have been reassessing their definitions of acceptable sexual behavior. However, more traditional members of these denominations accuse the reformers of throwing away Biblical authority, which they interpret as forbidding these acts. The debates within Protestant denominations, some examples of which follow, have caused a great deal of internal turmoil and dissension.

mainline Protestant denominations: The older, more established Protestant denominations in the United States.

Presbyterians. In June 1991, an appointed Presbyterian committee presented a report on human sexuality, *Keeping Body and Soul Together: Sexuality, Spirituality and Social Justice,* which had taken three years to draft. The report called on the Church to replace prohibition of extra- and premarital relations with a "new ethic" that judged all relationships, married or unmarried, heterosexual or homosexual, on standards of responsibility, mutuality, and caring, rather than on whether the couple is married (*The New York Times,* 1991e). The report stated: "It may be said simply: Where there is justice-love, sexual expression has ethical integrity. That moral principle applies to single as well as to married persons, to gay, lesbian, and bisexual persons, as well as to heterosexual persons." Claiming that adoption of the report would violate the Bible, the Presbyterians rejected the document by a vote of 534 to 31 (*Time,* 1991).

On the other hand, the commissioners to the general assembly did vote to include in the Church's **canon** a statement affirming sexual equality. Presbyterians allow that abortion may be morally justified under certain conditions, including the socioeconomic status of the family, although they call on pregnant women to make "good moral choices" regarding abortion (Bullis and Harrigan, 1992; *Religion Watch,* 1992b). The Church also allows homosexuals to become members, although a pastoral letter calls on them to "transform their desires" or remain celibate. Practicing homosexuals may not become members of the clergy.

canon: A rule or law passed by a religious body.

Lutherans. The Lutheran Church has also been debating sexual issues, which has led to some bitterly fought campaigns over who was going to lead the Lutheran denomination (*Religion Watch,* 1992b). Part of the struggle has been between the Church's more liberal and more conservative wings and over issues such as the role of women in the Church and the Church's stand on sexual issues such as homosexuality and chastity. After four years of work, the Evangelical Lutheran Church developed a statement on human sexuality. The statement considered sinful and condemned adultery, promiscuity, prostitution, sexual abuse and manipulation, pornography, and the exploitation of sex in advertising and entertainment (Neff, 1992). Yet it also included the ideas that typical levels of masturbation were healthy, that condom distribution among teens was morally imperative, and that the Church should affirm homosexuals who live in lifelong committed relationships, all of which led to such a disapproving response from the clergy and laity that the statement is being rewritten (*The New York Times,* 1993a). An earlier proposed draft of a new stand on sexual issues, which would have loosened the Church's opposition to homosexuality, was defeated, and the Church continues the policy that homosexual practice contradicts God's intent.

Episcopalians. The Episcopalian Church has been shifting away from a more liberal theology toward a more conservative, traditional reading of scripture (*Religion Watch,* 1992c). Episcopalians ordain women, and at least two Episcopal congregations have ordained priests who are openly homosexual. Episcopal bishops affirmed in a pastoral document that marriage remains the foundation of the Church's sexual guidance, but they did express a greater sympathy for homosexuals. Although polls show a majority of Episcopalians to be fairly liberal on sexual issues, many experts see a move away from further liberalization on sexual issues and toward a growing conservative presence in the denomination.

Methodists. The United Methodist Church has perhaps the most accepting view of homosexuals, strongly rejecting homophobia and stating that there are no "easy moralisms" against homosexuality (Bullis and Harrigan, 1992). Yet the Protestant ambivalence toward homosexuality shows up even in this tolerant group. A special committee assigned to review the Church's prohibition against homosexual behavior ended up submitting two separate reports, one calling for repeal of the prohibition and one not (*Christian Century,* 1991).

Baptists. The Baptists are the largest Protestant denomination in the United States, and they tend to be conservative regarding sexual matters, relying on the Bible to guide them in sexual issues. At the American Baptist Churches' national meeting 1991, a number of issues of sexuality were discussed and voted on. A "statement of concern on human sexuality" was passed that asked the denomination to set up a committee to put together a guide to help local churches develop a Christian perspective on sexual issues. At the same meeting, a statement was adopted that accepts repentant homosexuals willing to "accept new relationships" but rejects the "homosexual lifestyle, homosexual marriage, ordination of homosexual clergy, or establishment of 'gay churches' or 'gay caucuses'" (*Christian Century,* 1991:713). A more moderate statement encouraging members to learn more about their own sexuality and "God's gift of sexuality in others" was defeated.

Southern Baptists, more than any other group of Baptists, have been struggling with issues of sexuality. After years of conflict, conservative, fundamentalist Baptist forces have wrested control of the Southern Baptist Convention from more moderate forces. The fundamentalists have tried to return Baptists to what they consider to be traditional Baptist values, including a prohibition of homosexuality, a rejection of women as pastors (even though many already exist), and a belief in the sinfulness of premarital sex, adultery, and abortion. This move to the right has led some of the more moderate members to resign from the denomination, while others have formed groups such as the Southern Baptist Alliance, which has tried to convince the denomination to take a more moderate line (Rebeck, 1988).

Other Protestant Groups. Many other Protestant groups have been struggling with these types of issues. The Christian Reformed Church, a conservative denomination, had a meeting to discuss the issue of women's ordination into the priesthood, and although there was greater support than in the past, women's ordination was again turned down (*Religion Watch,* 1992b). In the Disciples of Christ, another denomination, a dean of a seminary was nominated to the top position but was turned aside by the General Assembly largely because he favored ordaining homosexuals (*Christian Century,* 1991). On the other hand, the United Church of Christ took a stand in support of homosexual rights and ordination of homosexual clergy; it was then accused of **apostasy** by some other Christian groups.

apostasy: The rejection of one's birth religion.

The battles have also been raging in the Church of England, the mother church of the seventy-million-member Anglican Communion (of which the Episcopal Church in the United States is a part). In late 1992 the Church of England decided, in a very close vote, to admit women to its priesthood. The issue was so heated and divided the Church so strongly that some predicted that the Church might actually split into two churches over the issue. In March 1993, thirty-two women were ordained as priests in the Church of England, the first in its 460-year history. As a result of the decision, many priests are considering leaving the Anglican Church for the Roman Catholic Church or the Orthodox Churches.

Orthodox Churches, which include a number of national groups (such as the Greek or the Russian Orthodox Churches) tend to be very conservative and generally oppose the liberalizing movement of the Protestant Churches. In fact, there was strong opposition by Orthodox Churches to the Church of England's decision to admit women to the priesthood. The Greek Orthodox Church believes that "homosexuality should be treated by society as an immoral and dangerous perversion and by religion as a sinful failure," and the Eastern Orthodox Church forbids premarital intercourse and abortion other than when the mother's life is in danger (Bullis and Harrigan, 1992).

Protestant Sexual Morality. In addition to the particular sexual positions of Protestant denominations, there is also a growing fundamentalist Protestant movement in the United States. Fundamentalists believe that the Bible is the final source for making decisions about moral sexual behavior. Fundamentalists therefore tend to take firm stands against homosexuality, premarital sexuality, and variations from heterosexual intercourse within the marital union. Fundamentalism has a strong influence in the United States, especially in the southern states and areas of the Midwest.

Sexual morality is not determined only by which acts a religion forbids; Protestant sexual teaching also tries to guide believers toward developing loving and close sexual relations. Although each denomination within Protestantism has a somewhat different approach, all accept the Biblical emphasis on the importance of the family and so advocate healthy and loving sexual relations within the family unit.

Other Religions

There are thousands of religions in the world, and each creates its own unique set of standards about what sexual behaviors are encouraged or forbidden. In this section, we will briefly discuss three of the largest religions in the world: Islam, Hinduism, and Buddhism.

Islam

Islam is the third major Western religion, founded in the sixth century by the prophet Muhammed. Muhammed accepted Judaism and Christianity as God-inspired religions and accepted the divine origin of the Hebrew and Christian Bibles, but he felt that God had given, through him, a third testament, called the *Koran* (see Chapter 1). The Koran lays out the basis for Islamic faith, including laws about sexuality. A basic principle is *satr al-'awra,* or modesty, and in some traditional Islamic cultures women cover their bodies almost completely when in front of men other than their husbands. Islam is generally more tolerant of sexual activity than Christianity, and it has moderately accepting views of homosexuality, extramarital sex (though it is technically a sin), and other sexual acts. In this sense, Islam is a "sex positive" religion.

Islam is widely spread, and it is the dominant religion of many nations in the Middle East, Africa, parts of Asia, and even in Pacific island countries such as Indonesia. Practice differs greatly depending on the country and ranges from the extremely traditional behaviors of countries such as Iran to much more secular states such as Egypt or Turkey. In the more traditional states women lead restricted lives, while Turkey, for example, recently had a female prime minister.

According to fundamentalist Muslim interpretations of the Koran, Muslim males are forbidden to look at or touch women other than their wives or daughters. Fornication is punishable by whipping or stoning, as is adultery. So why is Islam characterized as a "sex positive" religion?

Daniel Easterman (1992), a scholar of Islam, argues that Islam does not separate the flesh from the spirit, as Christianity does. This can best be illustrated by the holy people who inspired these religions; while Mary was a virgin and Jesus, as far as we know, was celibate, Muhammed married numerous women and his sexuality was recorded in great detail. The result is that Islam celebrates foreplay, lovemaking, and sexual fantasy by appealing to Muhammed himself. In contrast to Christian history, celibacy was despised in Islam, and venerated religious scholars were noted for their enjoyment of lovemaking. Although promiscuous sexuality was forbidden, men could traditionally marry up to four wives and sleep with slave girls, divorce was easily obtained, contraception was permitted, and abortion was tolerated. In fact, there is even a form of temporary marriage in Islam known as *mut'a* ("pleasure"), which was used by men who had to travel

The Islamic principle of *satr al-'awra* as practiced in strict Muslim countries requires that a woman leave almost no part of her body explosed in public.

far from home. These men would temporarily "marry" a woman to have sexual companionship on their trip, and the *mut'a* was terminated on their return.

In addition, Easterman notes, Islam has a long history of erotic literature—almost entirely written by respected religious scholars! Books of religious law often contain detailed descriptions of lovemaking, and while Christianity conceives of heaven as a place of celibacy, in Islam it is likened to an ongoing orgasm. Islamic poetry can be very erotic as well, and it includes a large dose of homoerotic imagery.

On the other hand, sexuality in Islam is directed at and set up for men. Women are wholly subordinate to men, and their sexuality as well as their social interactions are strictly under men's control. As free as discussions of sex are in Islamic books, in practice Islamic societies can be extremely sexually repressed. There is, in Islam, a great tension between the image of powerful male sexuality and the strict laws of *satr al-'awra* that control women's lives. In those lands where fundamentalist Islam has been gaining power, women's roles have become more and more restricted.

Islam is now the third largest religion in the United States, after Christianity and Judaism, and American Muslims are becoming more vocal about moral and sexual issues in American culture. Like their brethren in other countries, American Muslims are generally traditional and take a conservative position on sexuality issues. Islam, like its closest relative, Judaism, is a family-oriented religion. It seems that American

Muslims will increasingly find themselves allied with conservative Christians on issues such as opposing pornography, abortion, safe-sex education, and condom distribution in schools (*Religion Watch,* 1992a).

Hinduism

Hinduism refers to a wide variety of religious forms that developed over thousands of years in India. In addition to pure Hindu groups, there are also associated groups (such as the Sikhs) and non-Hindu groups who have assimilated some Hinduism. Hinduism is thus not one religion with a unified philosophy; it comes in an almost infinite variety of forms (Renou, 1961).

This wide variety of forms is reflected in attitudes toward sexuality. In Chapter 1, we discussed India's sexual history, including temples adorned with explicit erotic art and the development of the *Kamasutra,* one of the world's greatest masterpieces of erotic literature. Sexuality also was a concern of those who taught yoga, a discipline of the mind and body, which joined with Buddhist elements to create Tantric yoga, a discipline concerned with sexual energies.

On the other hand, there have also been reactions against the eroticism of Indian history. First Muslim and later British rulers brought greater puritanism to India in recent centuries. Aristocratic Indians adopted Britain's puritanical attitude toward sex, and Mahatma Ghandi, who won India's independence from Britain, was quite **ascetic** in his lifestyle and preached a severe chastity.

ascetic: Living a lifestyle that rejects sensual pleasures such as drinking alcohol, eating rich foods, or engaging in sex.

Buddhism

Buddhism was founded by Gautama Siddhartha Sakya (560–480 B.C.) who found enlightenment sitting under the *Bodhi* ("Awakening") Tree and became known as the Buddha. Buddhism has since spread to many regions in many different forms and, like other religions, has had much disagreement about the role of sexuality and its place within the Buddhist view of the world.

Buddha believed that all suffering came from people having worldly attachments, and that full serenity and a state of perfect peace could only come if people renounced all attachments to worldly goods, people, and pleasures (including sexual). The most admired role in Buddhism, therefore, is the monk, who lives a life of renunciation and for whom sex is forbidden (monks are even forbidden to sleep under the same *roof* as a woman). As a religion of renunciation, Buddhism has had little to say about ideal family structure or sexual relations between spouses. Buddha urged chastity, although he accepted sexual relations within marriage. However, even though things such as extramarital sex were considered wrong, Buddhism never gave them much attention or a *uniquely* wicked role as did Christianity (Clasquin, 1992).

Various Buddhist traditions offer different views of sexuality. Both Theravada Buddhism, found mostly in South and Southeast Asia, and Mahayana Buddhism, found in East Asia and elsewhere, emphasize renunciation of activities that bring pleasure, and both have **ascetic monastic orders**. Both have an essentially sexless life as their ultimate goal. Zen Buddhism, on the other hand, a Japanese branch of Mahayana, is less legalistic and more open to sexuality. Focused on "compassion" as the chief value, sexuality is not "right" or "wrong" but must be assessed within the particulars of a correctly lived life (Clasquin, 1992). Tantric Buddhism, related to the Tantric yoga mentioned above and found particularly in Tibet, has developed elaborate techniques of sexual intercourse to increase a person's *Shakti* (natural energetic flow).

ascetic monastic orders: Groups of monks who live simple lives, rejecting sensual pleasures.

Tibetan monks are celibate and are so important to Tibetan Buddhism that at one point almost one-quarter of all men in Tibet were either monks or studying to become monks.

Religion's Role

What is the proper role of religion in determining how we should behave as sexual beings? Should religious leaders continue to promote traditional moral teachings, even if the majority of followers have changed their attitudes about behaviors such as premarital sex? Or should a religious tradition try to remold its teachings to be more relevant to the changing lifestyles of modern times?

These are the questions that modern religion grapples with in its attempts to provide guidelines to followers. Studies show, on the one hand, that religion does have a strong influence on people's sexual behaviors; for example, many studies have shown that more religious people have less frequent sex outside of marriage (and inside marriage as well) (Cochran and Beegley, 1991). Yet more than half of Americans claim that their religion has no influence on their opinions on issues such as sexuality and birth control (*U.S. News and World Report,* 1991).

Unlike the Middle Ages, when the Church had the power to imprison and execute people, the Church in the United States no longer has the power to coerce its followers into accepting particular beliefs. Instead, American religious systems offer their believers guidelines for behavior. In other words, religious or not, each individual must decide to what degree he or she will adopt the moral positions of a particular religious tradition. Such decisions cannot be made in a vacuum; they must be based on larger moral principles—it is up to each individual who engages in sexual contact with another to decide what values they bring to the encounter to ensure that each party is treated with respect and concern.

SEXUALITY AND THE LAW

Laws serve many purposes. They control aggression so that people can live together without harming each other. They regulate order so that large numbers of people can exist in one place without infringing on each other's rights. They protect property so that people can be secure knowing that what they own cannot be arbitrarily taken. And they define the government so people know who has legitimate power over their lives and property and who does not.

However, laws also serve another purpose. Since ancient times, societies have used laws to assure that people engage in acceptable *moral* behaviors, and sexuality has always been a large part of that moral code. Societies could regulate sexual behavior because there was no legal concept of privacy; **sexual propriety**, even behind closed doors, was everybody's business.

sexual propriety: A society or community's views of what is acceptable sexual behavior.

In the United States today, however, we claim to value the idea of privacy, a right that the Supreme Court has decided is implied in the Constitution (although the authors of the Constitution never mention the word *privacy* at all). The idea that what happens behind bedroom doors by consenting adults is nobody's business is a very modern idea, one that most Western cultures throughout most of history would find absurd. In fact, as we will see below, we ourselves do not adhere to it: a variety of laws in certain states allow the government to arrest us for private sexual behaviors such as homosexuality or oral sex.

There are many types of sexual behaviors that almost everyone would agree should be prohibited by law, such as coercive sex, sex with minors, or sexual behaviors (such as being a Peeping Tom) that infringe on others' privacy. However, many other sexual laws are there simply because people believe the behavior to be inherently immoral. In a pluralistic society such as that of the United States, where there are a great many ethnic and religious groups with different ideas of what is moral and immoral behavior, such laws are inevitably going to be challenged. Perhaps in a country with a more homogeneous population, such as Japan or Sweden, there may be some general agreement on moral issues. In a democracy with as diverse a population as the United States, however, consensus is far more difficult. Figure SF1.1 shows some of the types of laws related to sexuality in force in the fifty states, and Figure SF1.2 indicates the kinds of behaviors controlled in the countries of the world.

Take some time now to think of what kinds of laws should control our sexual lives. Should *all* private behaviors between consenting adults be allowed? Should the idea of immorality, sin, or perversion have a place in our legal codes? Should sexual behaviors be the business only of consenting adults' personal consciences and religious beliefs, and should the community have no right to comment on or control it? These questions are being argued in the United States right now, as the country continues to reassess its attitudes toward issues such as homosexuality, pornography, and abortion.

We might think of sexuality laws as falling into four broad categories—laws that regulate private sexual behavior, public sexual behavior, coercive sex, and commercial sex. Below, we examine some cases that illustrate each of these issues.

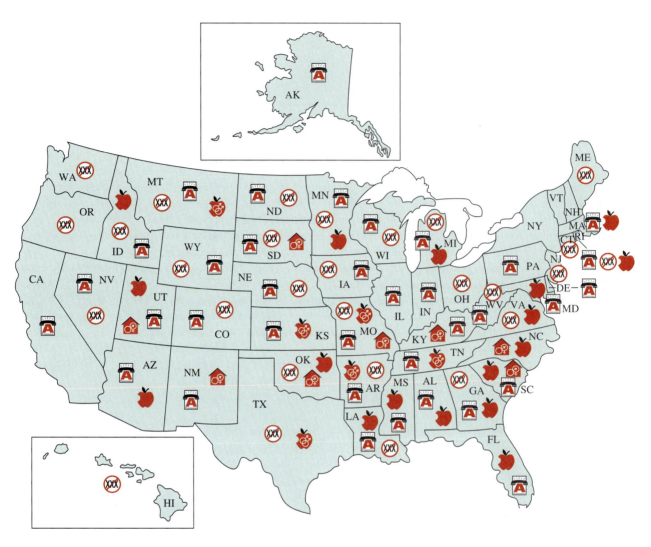

Key:

State where there is no law against marital rape

State where pornographic images are illegal if violent or offensive

State where minor must notify or get permission from parents in order to have an abortion

State that forbids sodomy altogether

State that forbids homosexual sodomy only

F i g u r e **SF1.1**
This map indicates where states stand legally on sexual issues such as adultery, sodomy, and pornography.

SEXUALITY *Today* SF1.2

Strange Sex Laws

Laws are sometimes passed that, when viewed later, can look quite strange. Laws stay on the books until they are specifically repealed, and so some laws are still technically in force although they have not been enforced since colonial days. In the early 1990s, a man brought his wife to court for adultery in Maine, and the old colonial law, still technically in force, called for a convicted women to stand for an hour with a noose around her neck, be given twenty lashes in public, or pay a fine of 100 English pounds! Below are some real laws on the books in various communities that show how sexuality can be the subject of strange legislative activity.

In Newcastle, Wyoming, an ordinance specifically bans couples from having sex while standing inside a store's walk-in meat freezer.

In Connorsville, Wisconsin, city fathers have banned lovers from shooting off a gun when the female partner reaches orgasm.

In Tremonton, Utah, no woman may have sex with a man while riding in an ambulance. A man, on the other hand, would not be charged.

In Alexandria, Minnesota, no man is allowed to make love to his wife with the smell of garlic, onions, or sardines on his breath.

In Clinton, Oklahoma, a man who masturbates while watching a couple make love in the back seat of a car at a drive-in theater can be charged with "molesting a vehicle."

Libido (**1993**)

Laws Regulating Private Sexual Behavior

Laws that regulate private sexual behavior implicitly accept the idea that two consenting adults do *not* always have the right to engage in whatever sexually related behaviors they want to, even in the privacy of their own home. (Sexuality Today SF1.2 lists a few of the more curious laws regulating sexual behavior.) In the United States, the Supreme Court has sometimes upheld the right to sexual privacy while in other cases it has upheld the right of states to regulate private sexual behaviors.

The first major case undermining the government's right to tell people what consensual sexual acts they could perform was *Griswold* v. *Connecticut* in 1965. In *Griswold,* the Supreme Court denied Connecticut the right to limit a couple's ability to acquire contraceptives and birth-control information from their physician. This was the case that firmly established the right to privacy by citing "zones of privacy," which are areas of life where the state does not have the right to venture. This right to privacy ultimately led to the 1973 *Roe* v. *Wade* decision, where the Supreme Court decided that a woman's decision to have an abortion fell into that "zone of privacy" (Samar, 1991). Yet the court has not consistently applied these privacy rights to people's sexual behaviors.

In 1986, a gay man in Georgia was arrested in his own bedroom while having oral sex with another man. A police officer, who was in the apartment for another reason, happened to glance through an open door and see the act. Georgia has a law prohibiting sodomy, defined as "any sex act involving the sex organs of one person and the mouth or anus of another." Although the charges against the man were dropped, he decided to pursue the case to prove that the prohibition was an unconstitutional invasion of his right to privacy.

At first glance, the case seemed similar in many ways to other right-to-privacy cases. On the basis of a right to privacy, the Supreme Court had overruled state laws

Figure **SF1.2**

Laws controlling sexuality are very different in different countries. **Adapted from Details (1994).**

Many disputes about which sexual behaviors are allowed in the United States are settled by the Supreme Court.

banning the use of contraception and abortion and had overturned a law prohibiting pornographic materials in the home (*Stanley* v. *Georgia,* 1969). In all these cases the court ruled that individuals have the right to regulate their own sexual conduct. Another interesting parallel can be drawn with the court's overruling of antimiscegenation laws (Nussbaum, 1992). These laws were passed originally because (like homosexuality) interracial marriage was highly unpopular and was said to offend the "moral sensibilities" of the people. The state clearly had some right to regulate marriage, such as demanding a marriage license or forbidding a person to marry two spouses. Yet the court ruled that the states could not forbid interracial marriage, for it infringed on people's rights.

The Georgia sodomy case, *Bowers* v. *Hardwick,* seemed to some to be just as clear. Though the Georgia law prohibited the act of sodomy between any two people, male or female, heterosexual or homosexual, it was used almost exclusively to arrest gay men and so was discriminatory. The U.S. Court of Appeals overturned the law as being an invasion of privacy.

Yet when the case finally reached the Supreme Court, the bitterly divided court decided five to four that the law *was* constitutional, for, as Justice White wrote, condemnation of homosexuality has "ancient roots" (the Georgia law itself went back to 1816). Interestingly, the discussion in the court and the decision of Justice White centered almost exclusively around issues of homosexuality, even though the law itself made both homosexual and heterosexual sodomy illegal. For that reason, Justice John Paul Stevens wrote a dissent in which he pointed out that the law itself was "concededly unconstitutional with respect to heterosexuals." In other words, had a heterosexual been arrested for doing exactly the same act, the court would undoubtedly have voted differently (*The New York Times,* 1986a,b).

SEX TALK
QUESTION **SF1.2**   **Why does the state have the right to tell me which sex acts I may or may not perform? Isn't it my own business what I do in the privacy of my bedroom?**

The idea that what one does in private does not effect the community at large is, believe it or not, a very recent one. Historically, many people believed that immoral behavior affected everyone and that sexual transgressions brought down the general moral level of the community; many people still believe that today. Many also believe that sexuality is such a powerful human force that if it is not monitored it can threaten the family, which the state has a stake in keeping together. Obviously, however, there is room for much disagreement on this, and attitudes about whether private sexual behaviors should be regulated—and if so, which ones—continue to be part of public debate (see Samar, 1991; Barnett, 1973).

Let us look at the justification used to uphold the Georgia sodomy laws. All fifty states had outlawed homosexual acts until 1961, and anal intercourse, known as buggery, had been illegal in the United States since colonial days and was punishable by death until the late eighteenth century. So, as Justice White had claimed, there is a long historical precedent. However, *any* law that is overturned for the first time has historical precedent. Slavery had been around for thousands of years, as had laws against abortion, miscegenation, womens' vote, and so on; yet each of these were overturned despite their "ancient roots." Why not sodomy?

There are a number of possible reasons that the court upheld the Georgia sodomy laws in *Bowers* v. *Hardwick*. First, if the court decided that homosexual acts were legal, some may have feared it would force the court to accept such things as homosexual marriages. Second, if the court overturned the Georgia law, it would be forced to overturn almost *all* laws that controlled sexual behavior between consenting adults, a move the court was not ready to make. Third, the court may have simply reflected society's discomfort with homosexuality.

Bowers v. *Hardwick* upheld the acceptability of laws regulating consenting adult behavior in the privacy of the bedroom. In response to the case, Minnesota, for example, started enforcing its antiadultery statute, reasoning that if the court was willing to uphold antisodomy laws, it would uphold antiadultery laws (Samar, 1991).

Twenty-four states and the District of Columbia still regard oral and/or anal sex between heterosexual or homosexual adults as illegal; seven states prohibit sodomy only between people of the same gender. In sixteen states, sodomy is a felony; in Michigan, sodomy is theoretically punishable by life in prison, and in Washington, D.C., sodomites are officially considered "sexual psychopaths." (According to Washington's law, the *majority* of Americans would be considered sexual psychopaths.)

Laws Regulating Public Sexual Behavior

Whatever rights to privacy we retain in our private lives do not extend to public sexual behavior. For example, even though obscene materials can be viewed in the privacy of one's home, the Supreme Court has allowed states to ban the mailing, importation, transportation, or public viewing (even in a movie theater for adults) of obscene materials (Samar, 1991). In public, laws can be passed against behaviors that offend a sense of public order, or what might be called "consensual morality," meaning that the public, in general, is offended by the behavior and thus should not be forced to observe or be the unwilling victim of the behavior (MacNamara and Sagarin, 1977).

Offensive behaviors usually include such things as exhibitionism and public nudity, voyeurism, transvestism, and the rarer examples of bestiality and necrophilia (see

Public laws about nudity differ from place to place. Some beaches allow more exposed flesh than others.

Chapter 14). Of course, "offending public morality" is a vague term; a man exposing his penis in public may be accused of offending public morality, while a woman wearing a see-through blouse may not. Some behaviors offend certain groups but not others, in certain places but not others. Some beaches allow women to wear thong-style bathing suits, showing their buttocks, while others do not, and there are special beaches set aside where nude bathing is legal. Sexual laws are not uniformly followed nor applied.

As one example, consider the current debates over "pornography," the term some people use for certain types of sexually explicit images (see Special Focus 4). As we mentioned, there are laws that restrict the mailing, transportation, and public display of sexual explicit materials. But in 1983, two nationally prominent feminists, Catherine MacKinnon and Andrea Dworkin, appeared before the City Council of Minneapolis to defend an antipornography ordinance they had authored (Downs, 1991). Their definition of *pornography,* fundamentally different from what had been accepted before, was "the sexually explicit subordination of women, graphically or in words." In other words, it was not the content of the pictures that defined what was pornography but its social and political effects. The existing law implied that pornography harmed the public sensibility and so was a criminal act; under MacKinnon and Dworkin's law it was considered part of a systematic oppression of women, which is a civil rights issue. Their law would therefore have switched enforcement of pornography violations from the city's Criminal Justice Division to its Civil Rights Commission. Also, under existing law, a work was not obscene if it contained "serious literary, artistic, political, or scientific value," while MacKinnon and Dworkin's law would follow the single criterion of whether or not there was female subordination. Their proposed law also contained a clause that allowed people to bring suit against pornographers if one was the victim of a crime and could prove that the attack had been motivated by the attacker's exposure to such materials (Downs, 1991).

Catherine MacKinnon and Andrea Dworkin, two feminists who have written and advocated new pornography laws.

The First Amendment of the Constitution protects speech from being prohibited because of its political or social implications; yet the Minneapolis amendment proposed by MacKinnon and Dworkin suggested that pornography be outlawed because of its political and social implications against women. The mayor of Minneapolis vetoed the measure as a violation of First Amendment rights, and a watered-down version, passed

SEXUALITY *Today* SF1.3

Sexual Fraud Suits

Imagine this: a person meets you at a bar and you begin flirting. In the course of conversation, the person tells you he or she is single and in good health, and you become interested. One thing leads to another, and you become sexual partners. Only afterward do you learn that the person lied and is actually married or, worse, has a sexually transmitted disease. What should you do now?

Some people think you should sue.

More and more, people are bringing law suits against sexual partners for false promises, lies, or misrepresentations. Though lawsuits alleging that a partner lied about a sexually transmitted disease are the most common, people also sue because partners lied about using birth controln or about being sterile or even because a partner sexually rejected them. In the case of people lying about STDs, juries in California have awarded plaintiffs amounts ranging from $15,000 to $450,000.

Jane Larson, a law professor at Northwestern University, has proposed that judges adopt a separate legal theory that would allow suits for "sexual fraud," defined as "an act of intentional, harmful misrepresentation made for the purpose of gaining another's consent to sexual relations." She insists that such misrepresentation is little different from economic fraud, except that the person is after sex instead of money.

Others, however, are hesitant to allow the courts to enter such previously private domains. Some judges and lawyers worry that every jilted lover or relationship gone sour would end up in the courts with each party suing the other for broken promises. They may have a point. In one recent case, a man sued his former wife for fraud because she had failed to tell him before they got married that she was not sexually attracted to him; the jury awarded him $242,000.

Derived from Pollock (1993)

by Indianapolis, was struck down for the same reason by a federal judge (Downs, 1991). But the influence of the movement begun by MacKinnon and Dworkin was felt in 1992 when a bill was introduced in Congress to allow people who were the victims of crimes to sue booksellers, publishers, and distributors of allegedly pornographic materials if it could be shown that such materials were used by the perpetrator and thus "caused" the attack. The bill was not passed by Congress. (See Sexuality Today SF1.3 for discussion of another proposed role for lawsuits in the realm of public sexual behavior.)

In Canada, on the other hand, the outcome was different. Canada does not have a strong history of free-speech protection as in the United States, and Canadian feminists, supported by MacKinnon and Dworkin, won a victory in 1992 when Canada's Supreme Court ruled that obscenity is to be defined by the harm it does to women's pursuit of equality. One supporter commented that the justices passed the law because "We showed them the porn—and among the seized videos were some horrifically violent and degrading gay movies. We made the point that the abused men in these films were being treated like women. . . . Porn makes women's subordination look sexy and appealing; it doesn't threaten men's jobs, safety, rights or credibility" (Landsberg, 1992:14). However, recently there has been strong criticism of the Canadian law, which has done little to control pronography and has been targeted at sexual minorities such as gays and lesbians (Toobin, 1994).

These types of cases have inspired greater debates about balancing freedom of speech with harm that might be caused by sexually explicit materials. Canada had previously ruled that the possible harm of pornography "must be borne" for the sake of free speech (Landsberg, 1992). In the United States, the strong free-speech tradition has limited how far legislators have been willing to go in restricting sexually explicit materials. But laws reflect the changing values of a culture and the pressures of special interest groups who lobby legislatures to change existing laws. Many, many groups become involved in these debates—feminist groups (some of which are antipornography; some of which feel that limiting any kind of speech is dangerous), civil liberties groups, religious groups, business lobbying groups, and so on. The courts and legislatures are, to one degree or another, strongly influenced by changing standards and public opinion.

Should there be laws restricting sexually explicit material? Must some kind of harm be demonstrated, or is it enough that it offends people? What about materials that are violent or show women being whipped or humiliated? Child pornography is illegal, but what about sexually explicit pictures of someone who is over eighteen but who looks much younger and is made up to resemble a child? Should technically legal material obviously designed to appeal to those who are sexually interested in children be allowed?

These are difficult issues. Laws that regulate public sexual behaviors must balance people's rights to behave sexually and other peoples' right not to be exposed to behaviors that they find offensive. However, this is itself problematic: where do we draw the line? If people in a certain area are offended by seeing two men kissing, should that be made illegal?

Some feminists, such as Andrea Dworkin, argue that the issue of pornography is not an issue of regulating public sexuality but a kind of coercive exploitation of women and therefore is more applicable to laws regulating sexual harassment and rape. Let us therefore turn to laws about coercive sexual behaviors.

Laws Regulating Coercive Sexual Behavior

Laws against coercive behavior refer to rape, sexual harassment, and sex with minors. In Chapter 15, we discuss the legal definitions of rape and harassment and some of the conceptual difficulties with those definitions. In this section, therefore, we will focus on recent political and legal controversies that illustrate the difficulties with our current legal structures.

Sexual Harassment

Feminists have long argued that rape and sexual harassment laws well illustrate women's plight in a sexist society. For example, when sexual harassment claims first started being litigated in the 1970s, judges tended to view harassing behavior either as isolated incidents, due to personality conflicts between employer and employee, or as a natural, universal, and therefore unremarkable part of the workplace interactions of men and women (Rhode, 1989). Sexual harassment in the workplace was not taken seriously until 1980, when the Equal Employment Opportunities Commission issued guidelines saying that harassment was a form of unlawful sex-based discrimination. In 1993, the Supreme Court made it easier to bring harassment suits by rejecting a lower court ruling that said that the harassment had to cause the workplace to be so hostile as to create "severe psychological injury." In the words of Justice Sandra Day O'Connor, the law should help the women before the "harassing conduct leads to a nervous breakdown." She suggested, instead, that harassment is actionable when "the environment would reasonably be perceived, and is perceived, as hostile or abusive" (*The New York Times,* 1993b).

Yet it is still difficult to bring such cases to court. First of all, bringing a harassment suit opens the person's attire, behavior, and sexual relationships to discussion in the courtroom setting. Also, courts have often mandated that the plaintiff (in most cases, a woman) show that she resisted the unwanted advances, even though such resistance might cost her job or a promotion; in fact, if the plaintiff is forced to submit, if a woman actually does sleep with the boss to keep her job, she is often assumed not to have suffered a legal injury at all (Rhode, 1989). There is still a great disparity between the ways many men and women view harassment and between the way women's experience and the law define sexual harassment.

Rape

Although rape laws have existed since ancient times, until recently the law considered rape an offense that a man does against *another man;* by "defiling" a man's wife or daughter, the rapist violates the man's property rights. Even as late as the 1950s, a *Yale Law Journal* article stated:

> *The consent standard in our society does more than protect a significant item of social currency for women; it fosters, and is in turn bolstered by, a masculine pride in the exclusive possession of a sexual object. The consent of a woman to sexual intercourse awards the man a privilege of bodily access, a personal "prize" whose value is enhanced by sole ownership. An additional reason for the man's condemnation of rape may be found in the threat of his status from a decrease in the value of his sexual possession which would result from forcible violation.*

> *Quoted in Tong (1984:90)*

English common law defined *rape* as the "illicit carnal knowledge of a female by force and against her will." Rape thus defined has four necessary conditions: (1) it is sex-specific (men rape women); (2) it must include penetration of a woman's vagina by a penis; (3) it must be outside of marriage; (4) it must be forcible (Tong, 1984). This discounts men raping men, women raping men, women raping women, men raping their wives, and men forcing women into sexual acts that do not include penile–vaginal penetration (usually called sexual assault). This formulation reflects the stereotypical view of rape: a stranger who coerces an otherwise chaste woman into intercourse (Rhode, 1989). Most rapes do not fit this pattern; yet only recently have laws begun to change to reflect the reality of coercive sexual relations.

Under the above formulation, a man who is separated from his wife can force her into having intercourse against her will and still not be charged with rape. Recent changes in the law have included spousal rape as a form of rape; in 1991, for example, a man in Florida was sentenced to fifteen years in jail for raping his wife after an argument. The prosecutor, reflecting current changes in thinking about rape, commented: "This case should send a message that a marriage license is not a license to rape. We're not in the Dark Ages, where men treat women as property" (*Philadelphia Daily News,* 1991).

Although progress has been made, rape is still a seriously underreported and misunderstood crime. Implicit in rape laws and attitudes are sexist assumptions about the relationship between women and men; that women desire, and thus subtly invite, forced sex; that women often fabricate charges of rape; that women "invite" rape by the way they dress or act; or that men cannot control their sexual urges. Rape laws also usually assume that rape refers to men raping women, and so ignore men who are raped. Rape laws and statistics also reveal racial and class biases. Black women are far more likely to be raped than white women, and rape usually remains within racial groups; yet the image of black men raping white women has had a long history in the American consciousness (Rhode, 1989).

SEXUALITY*Today*   *SF1.4*

Sexual Abuse by the Clergy

After years of quietly sweeping it under the rug, religious groups have recently begun to deal more seriously with the problem of the sexual abuse of parishioners by the clergy. In the early 1990s, a number of people who had been abused by clergy sued their churches, and these news stories empowered other victims to come forward. The bad publicity and the threat of monetary damages forced many religious groups to look more seriously at how they were going to respond to allegations of abuse.

To take just one example, cases against the Catholic Church have already cost more than $400 million, and some estimates suggest that the figure could go as high as $1 billion by the turn of the century (Berry, 1992). The National Conference of Catholic Bishops called upon the Church to "break this cycle of abuse," and the Church has finally begun to address explicitly how it plans to handle offending priests. Too often in the past, the Church had simply ignored abuse, or transferred the offending priest to another parish.

Clergy who abuse children (and adults) can leave long trails of injured people behind them. Clergy abuse is usually directed either at young boys or at women, and the trauma of sexual abuse is coupled with the sense of betrayal by a person who was supposed to represent trust and religious truth. The stories of those molested as children can be truly horrifying, such as the twelve-year-old boy who was molested by a religious brother at Boy Scout camp, and hung himself. Others were fed cake soaked in rum, used in pornographic movies, or even molested in the confessional.

It is difficult to determine how extensive the problem is. In his book on sexual abuse in the Catholic Church, Jason Berry (1992) estimates the actual number of clerics who are child molesters at 3,000, with each molester abusing up to 300 children; court records reveal that more than 200 pedophile priests have sought treatment at just one monastic center in New Mexico. Jeffrey Anderson, a lawyer in St. Paul, Minnesota, has himself brought more than 100 cases against Catholic priests and 40 more against clergy of other denominations. Until recently, there was little attempt to identify and punish those who violate their religious vows in this way. However, that seems to be changing. In December 1993, James Porter, a priest who was accused of sexual abuse by twenty-two former parishioners, was sentenced to eighteen to twenty years in prison.

Child Sexual Abuse

Almost every society has rules against sexual contact between adults and children. Children are, by their nature, considered too young to understand the implications of sexual contact. Children have little experience with the powerful feelings sexuality elicits, usually understand little about its mechanics or its long-term effects, and are susceptible to both adult threats and promises of rewards. Children occupy such a dependent position in relation to adults that even their willing consent can be seen as a product of implied desires to please or fears of rejection or punishment rather than true informed consent (see Sexuality Today SF1.4).

Statutory rape, which we discuss in Chapter 15, is the term used to refer to sex between a legal adult and a minor. *Child sexual abuse* or **impairing (or corrupting) the morals of a minor** are terms that imply lesser degrees of sexual contact. Most states clearly indicate at what age a person is considered an adult capable of making sexual decisions (usually between sixteen and eighteen), and under what age a person is not ever considered capable of making such decisions (ranging between twelve and eighteen) (MacNamara and Sagarin, 1977). Surprisingly, in many states children under the age of general consent can get married to a much older person, in which case intercourse is legal, but if they have consensual sex without a marriage certificate, it is rape. In current law, the degree of difference in age between the couple is usually considered, as is whether or not the adult knew the child was under age (MacNamara & Sagarin, 1977).

impairing (or corrupting) the morals of a minor: The legal term for an adult who engages a minor in sexually related acts (such as showing a minor sexually explicit movies); a lesser offense than child sexual abuse.

In our culture we use images of children as erotic objects, which may be a factor in our rates of child sexual abuse. This is a prepubescent Brooke Shields from the movie *Pretty Baby*.

In our society, we have made the issue of statutory rape more problematic by eroticizing childhood. In advertising and in other media, we often see children dressed in revealing ways, striking erotic poses, or actually having sexual contact. Children today are exposed to enormous amounts of sexual information at an early age and begin sexual experimentation earlier than their parents did (see Chapter 4). Society's natural protection of children has been complicated by its message that childhood sexuality is natural and that children can be "sexy."

Laws Regulating Commercial Sex*

Prostitution is often half-jokingly referred to as the "world's oldest profession." A certain level of prostitution has been tolerated in most societies throughout history, even where it was against the law. In the United States, it is easy to find prostitutes in most major cities, and there are legal brothels in Nevada.

A government has three choices of how to handle prostitution: it can make prostitution illegal, make it legal and regulate it, or decriminalize it—that is, remove it from the

---

* We discuss this aspect of law more fully in Special Focus 3.

criminal code while keeping it subject to health, tax, or business code standards (Rio, 1991). The arguments to keep prostitution illegal are either moral (it offends public sensibilities), medical (to prevent the spread of sexually transmitted diseases), or criminological (prostitution leads to other crimes, like drug abuse). Others argue that prostitution should be made illegal because it is harmful to the women themselves (Rio, 1991). On the other hand, proponents argue that a large percentage of people are in favor of decriminalizing prostitution, that legalizing prostitution would allow prostitutes to get medical attention without fear of arrest and thus decrease the spread of disease, and that the associated crime is due less to prostitution per se than prostitutes being forced to operate in a criminal underworld.

Making Ethical Sexual Decisions

In today's society, traditional codes of ethics and law must compete against the pressures of a sexual revolution that opened up previously forbidden behaviors, a media that constantly exposes sexuality to the public, and a rapidly changing family structure. Many people attack traditional Judeo-Christian values as old-fashioned, prudish, and unrealistic in today's world; defenders argue that a return to some basic traditional values would help alleviate soaring divorce rates, teenage pregnancy rates, and the apparent growing antagonism between the sexes.

Of course, somewhere between the arguments on both sides is the way most of us make decisions: we use our moral backgrounds as guidelines for behavior to be applied to the particular circumstances we are facing. It is foolish to simply discard systems of morality that have stood the test of thousands of years of human history; it is equally foolish not to recognize that the world is changing more rapidly than at any time in human history and that old codes of behavior must adapt to new circumstances.

So how does a person make ethical decisions about sexuality today? There are at least three different levels of decision making that are involved:

1. *Religious or moral background.* How involved are you in a religion or other system of moral guidance? Does that system offer guidelines for sexual behavior? Are there respected interpreters of that system who can offer you some guidance in your decisions? People have been thinking seriously about sexuality for thousands of years, and many theologians, philosophers, and other thinkers have written books about sexuality with ideas and values that you may have not considered. Your clergyperson can also be a source of guidance.

2. *Your personal needs and concerns.* Many people look back with regret at sexual encounters they have had where they were not true to their feelings. The key to avoiding regrets later is communication and honesty; neither is particularly easy where sexual matters are concerned. A popular book that was distributed on many college campuses in the 1970s was entitled *Sex Is Never an Emergency* (Pierson, 1973). The title reveals an important truth about sexuality: no matter how strong one's physical desires, viewing sex as an "emergency" is a recipe for disaster. There are questions to ask yourself: Is this the right time and the right person? After the sex act is finished, what will our relationship be, and will that be all right with me and with my partner? Am I doing this for the right reasons? Am I being honest with myself and with my partner?

3. *Your partner's needs and concerns.* Finally, sex (usually) involves the feelings, fears, and moral values of a partner. Overriding a partner's expressions of concern

is insensitive, if not immoral. Not exploring a partner's feelings in the first place often leads to awkward moments (and, not incidentally, awkward lovemaking).

When sexual desire beckons, it is easy to overlook doubts and concerns; later, we may wonder why we were in such a hurry. General principles of ethical behavior apply equally to sexuality: concern for others, respect for another's feelings, and openness and honesty.

S u m m a r y

- Because sexual relationships involve the feelings, wants, and needs of two vulnerable people, moral issues are an important part of all sexual relationships.
- Religions provide guidance about sexual morality. Judaism is a generally "sex positive" religion; it teaches that marriage is the correct relationship from which to express sexual pleasure.
- The Catholic Church has always taken a firm stand on sexual morality, restricting sexual relations to marriage and firmly forbidding birth control, homosexual relations, and female clergy. Many American Catholics have been vocal in their opposition to the Church's position recently.
- There are many Protestant denominations, and each has a somewhat different attitude toward sexuality. However, recently almost every group has begun to engage in public debates about sexuality, struggling with questions such as female and homosexual clergy, and attitudes toward premarital sex and abortion.
- Islam is a "sex positive" religion, and Islamic scholars have always been open about sexuality and even wrote erotic books. On the other hand, in many Islamic countries women are segregated out of society, must wear head-to-toe covering, and are considered the property of men.
- Hinduism, primarily in India, has thousands of gods and very different attitudes toward sexuality. Great temples have been built adorned with sexually explicit sculptures; yet there is also a strain of conservatism, brought in by the influence of Islam and British colonial power.
- Buddhism believes in renouncing earthly pleasures, including the sexual. The ascetic life of the monk is the highest value, although there are also strains of Buddhism that focus much more on sexuality and on sexual energies.
- Laws control people's actions, but they have also traditionally been used to establish a sense of morality in society.
- Sexual laws fall under four categories: (1) laws that regulate private sexual behavior, such as that upheld in *Bowers v. Hardwick,* the 1986 Supreme Court decision that Georgia could outlaw sodomy; (2) laws that regulate public sexual behavior such as public nudity; (3) laws regulating coercive sexual behavior such as rape, sexual harassment, and child sexual abuse; and (4) laws regulating commercial sex such as prostitution.
- We all must try to make ethical sexual decisions. To do so, we must consider (1) our religious and moral beliefs and the guidance of religious leaders; (2) our personal needs and concerns, as each of us are individuals with different sexual personalities; and (3) the needs and concerns of our partners.

R e f l e c t i o n s   o n   S e x u a l i t y

1. Why is sexuality so bound up with moral issues? What makes sexuality different, in that respect, from other basic drives?
2. Which of the major religions are "sex positive"? Which are "sex negative"? What is the difference in how these religions view sexuality?
3. How does being "family oriented" seem to influence a religion's attitude toward sexuality?
4. What are the major issues that religions are struggling with today? Why do you think these issues are so prominent today instead of, say, fifty years ago?

5. "United States law supports the idea that what goes on in private between two consenting adults is nobody else's business." Do you agree with this statement? Why or why not?
6. What are the arguments for and against further regulating pornography? What is your opinion?
7. What are your ethical standards for sexual relationships? If you had to write down a "code for sexual behavior," what would you include? Are there any sexual acts (homosexual, anal sex, adultery) that would be forbidden in your code?

Suggested Readings

ARMSTRONG, K. (1987) *The Gospel According to Women: Christianity's Creation of the Sex War in the West.* Garden City, NJ: Anchor Press.

BIALE, D. (1992) *Eros and the Jews.* New York: Basic Books.

DOMINIAN, J. (1989) *God, Sex, and Love: An Exercise in Ecumenical Ethics.* London: SCM Press.

GREEN, R. M. (1992) *Religion and Sexual Health.* Boston: Kluwer Academic Publishers.

RHODE, D. L. (1989) *Justice and Gender: Sex Discrimination and the Law.* Cambridge, MA: Harvard University Press.

TONG, R. (1984) *Women, Sex, and the Law.* Totowa, NJ: Rowman and Allanheld.

2

Sexuality Education

Sexuality education inspires powerful emotions and a considerable amount of controversy. In fact, sexuality education may be one of the most heated topics in the field of sexuality, as different sides debate whether and how sexuality education programs should be implemented in the schools. In this Special Focus, we present an overview of sexuality education from a variety of viewpoints, while exploring the history of sexuality education, its goals and effects, rationales for and against sexuality education, qualifications for teachers, sexuality education for older adults, heterosexism in sexuality education, and how other cultures outside of the United States handle sexuality education.

THE HISTORY OF SEXUALITY EDUCATION

People have always been curious about sex. However, it was only in the twentieth century that the movement to develop formal and effective sexuality education programs began. Public discussion of sexuality was due, in part, to the moral purity movement of the late nineteenth century and the medicalization of the sex movement in the early twentieth century. During the Victorian period, overt curiosity and discussion of sex had been suppressed, and a fearful, repressive atmosphere surrounded any public discussions of sexuality. Although this was happening in England, Victorianism influenced many parts of the world, including the United States. When Queen Victoria died in the early 1900s, sexual repression slowly began to dissolve, and formal sexuality education became possible.

Early Influences on Sexuality Education

Queen Victoria of England established very strict standards of personal morality in the nineteenth and early twentieth centuries, which eventually came to be known as "Victorianism."

Another early influence on sexuality education was Anthony Comstock (1844–1915) (see Chapter 1). Comstock was determined to eliminate the circulation of all materials he considered pornographic, including sexuality education materials. Comstock organized the New York Society for the Suppression of Vice and, in 1873, was successful in pressuring Congress to pass the Comstock Law, which made it illegal to send obscene or pornographic literature and/or advertisements through the mail. Comstock himself was appointed inspector for the U.S. Post Office, and he inspected all incoming mail with the power to arrest anyone who possessed or disseminated pornographic materials (including contraceptive information, obscene photographs, or sex information).

At about the same time, Margaret Sanger was working toward establishing the first birth control center in the United States (see Chapter 11). She had been sending out informational pamphlets about contraception to those who requested them. Since Comstock viewed these materials as pornographic, Sanger was arrested and put in jail. In fact, she was arrested and jailed several times, and her arrests eventually helped reverse the Comstock Law.

In 1937, the American Medical Association came out against the Comstock Law and in favor of access to sexual information. However, it was not until 1965 that the U.S. Supreme Court declared the unconstitutionality of such laws as the Comstock Law that prevented the dissemination of birth control information.

Several other developments in the United States also set the stage for sexuality education. Concern over skyrocketing rates of sexually transmitted diseases in the early 1900s resulted in the formation of a group called the American Society of Sanitary and Moral Prophylaxis and the American Federation for Sex Hygiene. Although these groups helped to further the cause of sexuality education, they concentrated their attention on venereal disease. Their approach was to use sexuality education to explain biology and anatomy and to reduce adolescents' natural sexual curiosity. School sexuality education was very scientific and avoided all discussions of interpersonal sexuality.

The Development of Sexuality Education Programs

Starting in the early 1900s, sexuality education was implemented by various national youth-serving groups including the YMCA, YWCA, Girl Scouts, Boy Scouts, and 4-H Clubs. These programs were developed mainly to demonstrate to young people the responsibilities required in parenting and to discourage early childbearing.

A society's attitudes toward sexuality education are the product of both the society's attitudes toward sexuality and its position on the role of schools. In the United States, for example, the opposition to sexuality education has often been due to two complementary attitudes: first, that sexuality is private, should be discouraged in children, and is best discussed in the context of a person's moral and religious beliefs; and second, that public schools are by their nature public, cannot discuss sex without giving children implicit permission to be sexual, and should not promote the moral or religious beliefs of any particular group. The result of these conflicting attitudes was the belief that sexuality education was best performed by parents in the home.

Attitudes toward sexuality, however, began to change and people began having sex earlier and more frequently. Sexuality education was seen as more important, due not only to the high teenage pregnancy rate (which shatters the illusion that kids are not actually having sex), but also to AIDS. Television and other media contributed by being so sex-saturated that sexuality was no longer a private topic. Yet, even with all these changes many still believe that public educational institutions will present a view of sexuality that they object to, and so they still oppose sexuality education in the United States.

Early sexuality education programs faced many problems. For example, who would be qualified to teach such programs? Very often an outside authority was brought in, such as a physician or a nurse. As a result, the lectures were often overly technical, which inhibited students from asking questions. Another problem that faced early sexuality education programs was which department should be responsible for implementing the programs, biology, psychology, health, or physical education. Should the courses be co-educational or separated by gender? Early programs separated the genders (which is still popular in some school districts today).

In the 1950s, sexuality education courses began appearing in colleges and universities in the United States. One of the first sexuality education and counseling programs in the United States was initiated at Yale University. It was very popular, and as a result, similar programs were implemented at other institutions. Do you know how long the sexuality course you are taking has been taught at your institution? It might be interesting to find out the background and history of the course.

Promoting Sexuality Education

In the 1960s, scientific journals began to focus on human sexuality. In 1964, the Sex Information and Education Council of the United States (SIECUS) was formed by Mary Calderone to help implement sexuality programs and promote sexual health. SIECUS proposed a list of principles for sexuality education, some of which are

1. Sexuality is a vital and basic human function.
2. It is learned as the result of a process that should not be left to chance or ignorance. The sexual learning process actually begins with the intimate relationships between the infant and the parents or parent-figures.
3. The developing child's sexuality is continually and inevitably influenced by daily contacts with persons of all ages, and especially by contacts with peers, the family, religion, school, and the media.
4. In many cultures, for both boys and girls, reproductive maturity precedes by some years emotional and social readiness for parenting.
5. The aim of sexuality education should be to facilitate a child's capacity and right to explore, enjoy, and integrate sexuality into his or her developing self-concept.
6. Television and other mass media have an important and widespread impact on the community. Their vast potential for informal and formal sexuality education should be put to productive use.
7. Sensitive sexuality education can be a positive force in promoting physical, mental, and social health. It should be geared to the three levels of learning—affective, cognitive, and operative—and should begin as early as possible.
8. All health, social science, religious, teaching, and counseling professionals should receive education in human sexuality.

In 1968, another sexuality organization was developed: the American Association of Sex Educators, Counselors, and Therapists (AASECT), which today provides

William Stayton, a theologian and sex therapist, believes that the natural curiosity each of us has about sexuality has become repressed in American culture today. We fear being *too* interested in sexuality, so we do not ask questions. Stayton believes that sexual ignorance is valued more than sexual knowledge.

Health Promotion Model: A model that emphasizes educating for sexual health rather than educating to avoid sexually transmitted diseases.

Disease Model: A model that emphasizes educating to reduce sexually transmitted diseases (such as herpes or AIDS) rather than educating for sexual health.

training and education for sexuality professionals. These organizations have helped build a foundation in support of sexuality education.

In 1990, SIECUS formed the National Coalition to Support Sexuality Education, which is comprised of fifty national nonprofit organizations. This group is dedicated to promoting sexuality education and is committed to assuring that comprehensive sexuality education is provided for all children and youth in the United States by the year 2000.

In 1991, under the auspices of SIECUS, a task force of twenty professionals who were working in the fields of sexuality, education, medicine, and youth services, developed the *Guidelines for Comprehensive Sexuality Education.* This comprehensive model was designed to promote and facilitate the development of sexuality education programs nationwide. Many schools use these guidelines in the development of their own curricula, textbooks, and programs. SIECUS has found that from kindergarten through twelfth grade, less than 10% of American teens receive comprehensive sexuality education (SIECUS, 1994).

GOALS OF SEXUALITY EDUCATION

Mary Calderone, a pioneer in the field of sexuality education, once said that before we can begin sexuality education we must be clear on whether we are educating *for* something or *against* something (Calderone, 1978). Are we using sexuality education to help students become healthier and have better relationships, or are we trying to help them avoid AIDS, STDs, and sexual dysfunctions? Educating for a healthy lifestyle is referred to as the **Health Promotion Model** of sexuality education, while educating to reduce problems is the **Disease Model** (see Sexuality Today SF2.1).

Sexuality education can have different goals. Knowledge acquisition, improving personal psychological adjustment, and improving relationships between partners are popular goals. Early sexuality education programs focused primarily on increasing knowledge levels and educating students about the risks of pregnancy (Kirby, 1992), believing that if knowledge levels were increased, then students would understand why it was important for them to avoid unprotected sexual intercourse. Soon sexuality education programs added values clarification and skills, including communication and decision-making skills. These second-generation sexuality education programs were based on the idea that if knowledge levels were increased *and* if students became more aware of their own values and had better decision-making skills, they would have an easier time talking to their partners and evaluating their own behavior.

Today, comprehensive sexuality education tries to help students develop a positive view of sexuality. *The Guidelines for Comprehensive Sexuality Education* (SIECUS, 1993) cite four main goals of sexuality education:

1. To provide accurate information about human sexuality
2. To provide an opportunity for young people to question, explore, and assess their sexual attitudes
3. To help young people develop interpersonal skills, including communication, decision-making, peer refusal, and assertiveness skills that will allow them to create satisfying relationships
4. To help young people develop the ability to exercise responsibility regarding sexual relationships

SEXUALITY *Today* SF2.1

The Disease Model of Sexuality Education Versus The Health Promotion Model

The Disease Model of sexuality education targets the increasing rates of disease in this country. Sexuality education should focus on teaching children and adults how to avoid STDs and teenage pregnancy. Recently, this model has been overshadowed by the Health Promotion Model of sexuality education. In this model, sexuality education is viewed as necessary for the health and well being of students. It teaches them how to improve their own self-concept, self-esteem, and communication and interpersonal skills. In addition, Scales (1986) adds that the Health Promotion Model should also promote:

- An awareness of what things in life are important to us; what makes us feel good and bad
- Knowledge of our cultural, religious, and family heritage
- Accepting our parents as fallible human beings
- Self-respect based on doing our best but not always being the best
- The ability to identify options and alternatives for behavior
- The ability to set priorities and to tell others what those priorities are
- Knowledge of how we treat our bodies well and how we mistreat them
- Awareness of different ways of dealing with uncomfortable feelings, especially anger

- The ability to see things from someone else's point of view
- Understanding that the range of "normal" in development and in behavior is very broad
- An ability to teach people younger than ourselves some of the things we have learned
- An interest in having and expressing our opinions
- Knowledge of how to seek help in our family if possible and outside if necessary or desired for birth control, chemical abuse, and feelings of suicide or depression
- The ability to describe the impact we have on other people
- The ability to set and work toward both realistic and impossible goals
- The ability to maintain relationships that are satisfying and to end or accept the ending of those that are not
- The ability to laugh at ourselves
- A tolerance for people who have different values and beliefs
- Knowledge of and respect for the principles of democracy

Scales (1986)

Unfortunately, many sexuality education programs today are based on the *crisis intervention theory*. In this approach, general biology is taught until there is a societal crisis and more information is necessary (Biehr, 1989). If the rate of teenage pregnancy in a community suddenly starts to skyrocket, education focuses on this problem; or if the incidence of AIDS increases, AIDS education is quickly added into the curriculum. Crisis intervention sexuality education is often unsuccessful because the students either do not have a foundation of information on which to build this new knowledge or because the information is simply presented too late.

Overall, what we have learned as sexuality educators is that it is impossible to design one sexuality education program that meets everyone's needs. Before implementing a sexuality education program, the needs, attitudes, values, and characteristics of a group must be taken into consideration. All programs must be tailored to the specific groups they are addressing.

Mary Calderone was the cofounder of the Sex Information and Education Council of the United States (SIECUS) and a pioneer in the area of sex education.

EFFECTS OF SEXUALITY EDUCATION

During the 1970s and 1980s, research showed that while sexuality education may have had some positive effects, overall, the incidence of unprotected sexual intercourse did not decrease (Kirby, 1992). However, in the mid-1980s, the U.S. Department of Health, Education and Welfare awarded a grant to a group called Mathtech for a comprehensive research study on the effects of sexuality education (Kirby, 1984). They found that, overall, sexuality education programs can increase knowledge levels, affect the attitudes, and/or change the behaviors of the students who take them. The most successful programs were those in which schools and parents worked together in developing the program.

Other studies have also found that sexuality education programs are successful in increasing the knowledge levels of the students who take them (Kilmann et al., 1981), particularly in sexual anatomy and physiology, sexual development, sexual behavior, and conception and contraception. Part of the task of increasing knowledge levels is to help teenagers understand their risk for pregnancy. Teenagers who understand the risks and are knowledgeable about sexuality are more likely to know about various methods of contraception (Eisen and Zellman, 1987), while myths about pregnancy ("you can't get pregnant the first time" or "jumping up after sex helps you avoid pregnancy") can interfere with their use of contraception. Attitudes also change in sexuality education; for example, attitudes toward sexual behaviors such as homosexuality or masturbation are likely to become more permissive after a sexuality education course, while attitudes toward abortion are the least likely to change (Weis et al., 1992).

College-level sexuality courses have also yielded favorable results. Students who take sexuality education courses become more accepting of the behaviors of others. In addition, they often feel less sexual guilt after taking a sexuality course (Wanlass et al., 1983). However, keep in mind that students who enroll in human sexuality courses already tend to have more sexual knowledge, to hold more permissive sexual attitudes, and to be more sexually experienced than college students in general (Weis et al., 1992).

Do sexuality education courses change people's actual sexual behavior? It is difficult to measure and evaluate behavioral changes after a sexuality education program, but it appears that there are some limited behavioral changes. Zelnik and Kim (1982) found that teenagers who had sexuality education were more likely to use contraception and had lower pregnancy rates. Although many opponents of sexuality education believe that sexuality education causes an increase in sexual behavior, virginity status has been found to be unrelated to whether or not a person took a sexuality education course (Eisen and Zellman, 1987). Increases are usually seen in *responsible* sexual behaviors, rather than just sexual behavior. However, overall, young people who have had sexuality education are not more likely to engage in sexual intercourse than those who have never taken a course (Marsigliano and Mott, 1986).

Specific programs have also yielded positive results. In South Carolina, a school-based sexuality education program with strong community support was found to reduce teenage pregnancy rates (Vincent et al., 1987). A school-based education program combined with a clinic program in Baltimore resulted in an increased use of contraception in males and females, a delay in first sexual intercourse, and an increased use of family planning clinics (Marsigliano and Mott, 1986). Another program in Atlanta for middle school students resulted in a decrease in the number of teenagers initiating sexual intercourse and fewer pregnancies than among those students who were not involved in the program (Howard and McCabe, 1990).

However, many effects of sexuality education programs may not be quantifiable. Programs may help students to feel more confident, be more responsible, improve their mental health, and increase their communication skills. We rarely measure for these changes.

FOR OR AGAINST SEXUALITY EDUCATION?

The controversy over whether or not to provide sexuality education has become heated and bitter. Sexuality education can foster strong emotional reactions in people because feelings, opinions, and beliefs are firmly held and not easily changed. Evaluating the sexuality education argument involves distinguishing opinions that may be based on emotion or bias from those based on a rational consideration of facts (Leone and O'Neill, 1983). In Where Do I Stand? SF2.1, we provide a list of various statements about sexuality education. Take a few minutes to complete this questionnaire before reading any further.

Rationale for Sexuality Education

Sexuality education is most effective when it promotes knowledge, attitudes, and skills that are also important in all aspects of life. Sexuality education ideally is education for living in a complex world. For instance, in teaching about different sexual values and the importance of tolerating and respecting these differences, students may also be helped to understand and respect cultural, racial, and religious differences. In learning how to talk about sexuality, youths also may learn transferable skills that help them talk about other emotionally laden subjects.

Scales (1987:117)

There are many reasons that proponents view sexuality education as necessary. One of the main arguments in support of sexuality education is that, even though there has been an increase in sexual behavior, most people still lack factual knowledge about sex. The widespread ignorance about sexuality helps promote myths. This, in turn, may lead to risky behaviors, the transmission of STDs, or unplanned pregnancies.

Increases in the spread of STDs and teenage pregnancy are also reasons that proponents of sexuality education cite for sexuality education. Many people simply do not know how to protect themselves. Finally, many mental health specialists are realizing that negative feelings about sexuality and sexual dysfunctions may lead to lower self-esteem or an increase in sexual guilt.

Children who receive sexuality education from their parents tend to engage in *less* premarital sexual activity than children who have no sexuality education from their parents. Adolescents are also more likely to incorporate the sexual values of their parents into their own value systems if there has been some communication between the parent and child about sexuality (Fisher, 1988). In fact, when parents talk with their children about sexuality, they strengthen family communication, leading to a stronger family unit. When young people can discuss sex with their parents, they tend to delay engaging in sexual intercourse, and when they do engage in sexual intercourse, they are more likely to use contraception (Gilgun and Gordon, 1983).

The artist formerly known as Prince has had a strong influence on the recording industry with his androgynous appearance and performances. In addition, many of his songs contain strong sexual messages. What effect do these lyrics have on young people today?

WHERE DO I $Stand$?   *SF2.2*

Distinguishing Bias from Reason

The topic of sexuality education creates powerful feelings in many people. As a result, many people let their feelings dominate their powers of reason. It is important to distinguish which opinions are based on emotion or bias and which are based on fact.

Consider each of the statements below. Put an "R" next to a statement if you believe it is based on reason or fact, a "B" if you believe it is based on bias, prejudice, or emotion, and an "I" if you believe it is impossible to tell. You might compare your answers with other students or ask your professor to discuss these in class.

1. The major goal of nearly all sexuality education curricula being taught in the schools is to teach teenagers (and sometimes children) how to enjoy sexual intercourse without having a baby and without feeling guilty.
2. One of the quickest ways to see how sexuality education classes change values and attitudes is to read the questionnaires given to the pupils (pre versus post).
3. Sexuality education is selective propaganda that artificially encourages children to participate in adult sex, while it censors out the facts of life about the unhappy consequences.
4. Sexuality education is robbing children of their childhood.
5. Since pregnancy is the major cause of female teenagers dropping out of school, sexuality education should be a part of their education.
6. Those teenagers who are most active sexually are usually those who know the least.
7. The central concept of sexuality education should deal not with acts and actions but with relationships.
8. The key to an effective sexuality education program is the extent to which students are helped to understand the basis for their decisions, why they do what they do—and the consequences.
9. There is no more reason to devote a special course to sex than one to digestion; digestion actually is more important for health, comfort, and happiness.
10. Sexual desire, when paired with strong feelings of love and respect, helps us develop important and exciting intimate relationships.
11. If you teach them about the sex perversions, they'll want to try them.
12. A proper understanding of the place of sex in our lives is necessary to our happiness and well being and is, accordingly, good for society.
13. Parents should not discuss sex with their youngsters of any age.
14. The need for sexuality education is made more urgent by the glorification of sex everywhere we look—in print, at the movies, on TV.
15. Parents, not schools or governments, are fundamentally responsible for the education of their children and those parents who do want to teach their own children about sex, on their own terms, should have the right to do so.

Reprinted with permission: Leone and O'Neill (eds.) (1983). *Sexual Values: Opposing Viewpoints*, **Greenhaven Press, Inc., p. 68. Copyright ©.**

SEX TALK

QUESTION **SF2.1**   **Why doesn't the government mandate some type of national sexuality education curriculum?**

The beginning of the AIDS epidemic was the first time the government became active in the promotion of sexuality and AIDS education in the schools. In 1986, the then Surgeon General, C. Everett Koop recommended that AIDS education begin in early elementary school. Besides this, however, Congress has steered clear of sexuality education, in part because curriculum development is typically considered to be a matter of state and local jurisdiction rather than a congressional issue. States are free to decide for themselves whether or not they will mandate sexuality education for their students. There are also structural problems in the government—for instance, the House of Representatives'

Committee on Education and Labor is responsible for education issues, while health issues are the responsibility of another committee. This leads to a diffusion of responsibility, which results in neither committee taking the lead on sexuality education. Congressional inaction on the topic of national sexuality education may also be due to it being controversial. Dr. Joycelyn Elders, Clinton's first Surgeon General, said that her goals were to introduce comprehensive school-based health education starting in the early grades and eventually leading up to sexuality education. Unfortunately, Dr. Elders resigned her position before these goals were realized. No matter what the government attempts to regulate as far as sexuality education is concerned, in the end, success will depend on the efforts of parents and the school systems to make sexuality education successful. As of 1995, there is no national law or policy on sexuality education in the United States.

Although many people claim that knowledge about sexuality may be harmful, studies have found that it is the *lack* of sexuality education, ignorance about sexual issues, or unresolved curiosity that is harmful (Gordon, 1986). Comprehensive sexuality education programs make students less permissive about premarital sex than students who do not take these courses. Accurate knowledge about sex may also lead to a more positive self-image and self-acceptance. Sexuality affects almost all aspects of human behavior and relationships with other persons. Therefore, if we understand and accept our own sexuality and the sexuality of others, we will have more satisfying relationships. Calderone (1983) believes that not talking to children about sex prior to adolescence is a primary cause of sexual problems later in life.

Another reason often given in support of sexuality education is that children receive a lot of information about sex through the media (see Special Focus 4). The media and peers are often primary sources of information about sexuality. Sex is present in the songs children listen to, the magazines they read, and the shows they watch on television. Many of these are poor sources of information, and many of the myths about sex are perpetuated, such as: "everyone's doing it," "only gays need condoms," "have fun while you're young," and "if you are still a virgin in high school, something is wrong with you." Teenagers learn very little (if anything) about intimacy, communication, and the need for contraception.

Many parents believe that they can be the sole sex educators of their children. As Sol Gordon (1986:22) points out:

> How can that be? You'll have to wrap your children in cotton and not allow them to leave their bedrooms, watch TV or read newspapers or current magazines. You certainly can't allow them to have any friends or go to any public school bathroom.

Proponents of sexuality education believe that sexual learning occurs even when there are no formalized sexuality education programs. When teachers or parents avoid children's questions or appear embarrassed or evasive, they reinforce children's ideas that sex is secret, mysterious, and bad (Brick, 1985).

As adolescents approach puberty, they may feel anxious about the changes in their bodies or in relationships with other people. Many teenagers feel uncomfortable asking questions and may be pressured by their peers to engage in sexual activity when they do not feel ready. Giving teenagers information about sex can help them to deal with these changes (see Personal Voices SF2.1).

Finally, at the college level, sexuality courses have also been found to have beneficial results. Students who take sexuality courses in college are more likely to discuss sexuality with their own children (King et al., 1993).

Phyllis Schlafly believes that sexuality education programs rob children of their innocence, and therefore, sex education should not be allowed in the schools.

Rationale Against Sexuality Education

What masquerades as sexuality education is not education at all. It is selective propaganda which encourages children to participate in adult sex, while it censors out the facts of life about the unhappy consequences. It is robbing children of their childhood.

Schlafly (1983)

While many people and groups support sexuality education in the United States, there has also been much criticism. Opponents of sexuality education range from very conservative groups or religious fundamentalists to nonreligious groups or parents who believe that sexuality education may increase sexual curiosity and lead to increases in sexual behavior. These people often believe that if sexuality education is given at all, it should be provided within the home, by the parents.

The primary arguments of many who oppose sexuality education are that school programs foster irresponsible and promiscuous behavior, that sexuality education programs reflect an obsession that our culture has with sex, and that sexuality education is the final straw in the moral decay of society (Weis et al., 1992). Some fear that sexuality education will ignore their own particular religious or moral perspective on sexuality. In addition, discussions about sex are thought to take away the purity and innocence of childhood.

Opponents of sexuality education programs believe that sexuality education contributes to high teenage pregnancy rates and the skyrocketing numbers of those infected with STDs. Ironically, these are the same issues that proponents of sexuality education believe can be decreased through sexuality education! Each year, there are more than one million unintended teenage pregnancies in the United States. Opponents of sexuality education argue that these increases are a direct result of the implementation of sexuality education programs. However, supporters argue that these increases are due to the declining age of puberty, the general increase in teenage sexual activity, changes in norms that regulate sexual activity, and a decrease in the number of teens who marry early.

Some school districts avoid the teaching of sexuality education to avoid controversy. In fact, resistance from the community, teachers, or parent groups is one of the most significant factors in the dearth of sexuality education in public schools today.

Recently, some districts have begun sexuality education programs for parents to enable them to educate their own children (Bundy and Poppen, 1990). In these programs, parents' confidence and comfort with sexuality is enhanced through learning about human sexual development, and then they are taught how to communicate with their children effectively. In addition, since many parents oppose sexuality education simply because they do not know what is being taught, increased communication between parents and schools could also help.

Sexuality education programs have also been tried in the workplace to reach parents (Caron et al., 1993). Parents who attended these programs felt more comfortable in discussing sexuality with their children. In addition, since the programs were done in the workplace, participants could interact and discuss the ideas with colleagues at work long after the programs were over. So far, preliminary studies have yielded promising results.

WHERE, WHEN, WHAT, AND HOW?

While many of the issues relating to sexuality education have been resolved, some issues still remain controversial. The four key questions: Where should it be taught? When should it be taught? What should be taught? How should it be taught?

*P*ersonal
V O I C E S
SF2.1

Teenagers and Sexuality Education

Below, teenagers from all over the United States comment on their own sexuality education.

Kathleen Sacco, 18, Pittsburgh, PA: *They showed us a film strip in ninth grade—it was hysterical. They had these little cartoon characters for everything. One of the characters was Captain Condom. You see this guy and this girl, and they're about to have sex, and all of a sudden, this character comes out—and it's CAPTAIN CONDOM! And they make up cute little names for the characters, who are supposed to represent venereal diseases. Like, one, her first name is Gona, and her last name is Ria. People do pay attention.*

Jessica DeVader, 17, Rossville, KS: *One problem is teachers who just don't take sexuality education seriously. They just don't understand that, to us, this is something important—even if some people are uneasy and kid around. They think, "Well, you just shouldn't be doing it, and that's it."*

Jason Perine, 17, Rossville, KS: *My dad had a talk with me, and I didn't really think it got anything out of it. It was basic stuff I already knew. This was about six years ago. But he at least tried. He at least knew what was going on—diseases and stuff. I'll always remember that he talked to me. At least he cares about what I do with my life. And, since then, he's brought it up in conversations when we're alone, when we're fishing, when we're driving together. He'll ask, "So what's going on?" and I can usually tell him, and he'll understand. And I feel I can ask him something if I want to.*

Robert Rachel, 19, North Miami, FL: *I was having sex when I was 8. The girl was 10. And my mom had no idea what was going on. I didn't know about contraceptives or fetuses or pregnancy. Or diseases. But, when I was 15, some teachers who saw me flirt a lot sat me down and talked to me. And then there started to be all this publicity about condoms. Did I listen? Yes.*

Jodi Rothman, 17, North Miami, FL: *Adults need to stop being scared to talk to us. Sexuality education in school needs to be taken a lot slower, and it needs to be practical. I read an article where a kid thought he had to puncture a hole in a condom so it didn't explode or something. A girl thought that for contraceptive jelly you could use, like, grape jelly. In TV and movies, whenever someone gets into a car, they put on their seat belt. And this promotes the wearing of seat belts. But whenever you see a couple going to bed together, they never stop and go, "Wait, let me get a condom." So people feel, "Well, Jean-Claude Van Damme doesn't have to use a condom. Why should my boyfriend?"*

Reprinted with permission from *Parade* (Copyright © 1993 by Lynn Minton)

Where Should It Be Taught?

One of the biggest debates in sexuality education is whether it should take place in the home, schools, or someplace else, such as the church or synagogue. We know children learn about sex from a variety of sources including parents, schools, siblings, friends, and the media. In 1993, most young people reported that their parents were their primary source of sexuality education. Friends were the second most popular source of information, school courses third, and television fourth (SIECUS, 1994).

Most people believe that parents should be the ones who teach their children about sex. In fact, parents *are* the primary sexuality educators of their children even if they say *nothing* at all about sexuality. Saying nothing gives very powerful messages about sexuality. Unfortunately, many parents today do not feel knowledgeable enough to provide sexuality education to their children, even though they may not feel comfortable saying so. While less than one in five parents in one study admitted that it is difficult to talk to their children about sex (Nolin and Petersen, 1992), when the children were asked, more than half of males and one-third of females said it was difficult to discuss sex with their parents. Another study found that 85% of parents want outside help in talking with their children about sex (Lapore, 1987). Many feel uncomfortable or embarrassed talking about sex, and they may not say anything for fear of saying the wrong thing (see Sexuality Today SF2.2). Even so, the majority of parents believe that children should be given accurate and understandable information about sex, whenever they desire it (Abramson et al., 1983).

There are some cultural differences in who talks about sexuality in the home. In a study to evaluate these differences, American parents of Mexican, Japanese, African, and European descent were surveyed about how comfortable they felt discussing sexuality with their children (Abramson et al., 1983). Overall, Mexican Americans expressed the most discomfort when discussing sexual issues. When parents were asked when a child should have sexuality education, Mexican Americans suggested that both

SEXUALITY *Today*　　　　　*SF2.2*

Sexuality Education:
Parent and Anxiety, Where Does it Come from?

When parents discuss the concept of sexuality education for their children, many report feeling very anxious and insecure about their own abilities. Wilson (1994:1–2) suggests that anxiety comes from many places:

1. **FEAR:** Many parents worry that something bad will happen to their children if they start talking to them about sex. They might be impregnated or impregnate their partner, be raped, or rape someone, or even become infected with a STD like AIDS. Parents also worry that they will wait too long, start too early, say the wrong thing, or give misinformation. The biggest fear is that providing sexuality education will rob their children of their innocence.
2. **LACK OF COMFORT:** Since most parents did not receive sexuality education from their parents, many feel

uncomfortable in presenting it themselves. Those who did receive it usually got it from their mothers. This causes many fathers to feel especially uncomfortable facing the prospect of educating their sons and daughters.

3. **LACK OF SKILLS:** Parents often do not know *how* to say what they want to say. Some resort to a lecture about the "birds and bees," while others simply ask their children, "Do you have any questions?"
4. **MISINFORMATION:** Many parents do not have the necessary facts about sexuality education. Having received little sexuality education themselves, many believe in the myths about sexuality.

Adapted from Wilson, (1994)

boys and girls should have some form of sexuality education between five and eight years old at the earliest, while the other groups (Japanese American, African American, and European American) said between nine and twelve years old. This age difference may be due to the fact that when early innocent sex play begins (usually around five to eight years old), Mexican Americans are more likely to begin trying to change these patterns of behavior. Although many parents may feel uncomfortable discussing sex with their children, European Americans were more likely to continue talking about sex even if it made them uncomfortable. This may be because as a group, European Americans tend to have higher levels of education, which has been found to be correlated with providing sexuality education to their children (Abramson et al., 1983).

In European American and African American cultures, mothers are generally the ones responsible for sexuality education at home (Nolin and Petersen, 1992). In one study, 60% of the time the mother was responsible for sexuality education, in 39% of the cases it was shared between the father and mother, and in only 1% of cases sexuality education was provided by the father (Abramson et al., 1983). Children often feel more comfortable discussing sex with their mothers because she has traditionally been more available, is often perceived as being more emotional, affectionate, and knowledgeable about reproduction, and is often not the disciplinarian. Mothers tend to go into more depth with their daughters than with sons; they give daughters more information on morals and values. This may be due to the double standard in which girls have more responsibility for avoiding sexual behavior.

In Japanese American families, it is often the father or both parents who discuss sex with male children. While overall, girls are more likely to talk to their mothers about sex questions, some cultural differences have been found among boys' preferences. In Mexican American and Japanese American homes, boys are more likely to approach their fathers with sex questions; but in African American or European American homes they are more likely to ask their mothers. Regardless of ethnic background, fathers who are better educated are more likely to talk to their children about sex.

At school, sexuality education typically begins some time during fifth or sixth grade in the United States, often with the boys and girls separated into groups. Girls are taught about menstruation, while boys learn about nocturnal emissions, and both learn the basic facts of conception. For some, this is the only formal sexuality education they have until entering college. Others receive more information around ninth grade (such as reproduction, anatomy, and the risks of sexual activity).

In the United States today, 70% of public school children take some type of sexuality education course. As of 1993, seventeen states require sexuality education, while thirty others recommend it; before 1986, only Maryland, Kansas, New Jersey, and the District of Columbia required sexuality education (see Table SF2.1). Still, only an estimated 15% of public school districts provide comprehensive sexuality education before tenth grade (Lapore, 1987).

When Should It Be Taught?

There is a joke about a mother whose nine-year-old son comes home from school one day and asks her *"Where did I come from?"* Believing that her son is ready for sexuality education, she sits him down and proceeds to tell him everything he needs to know about sex. After her hour-long speech is over, her son says "Wow, that's really something. Johnny said he was from St. Louis!" The important question here is, how does a parent know *when* to begin sexuality education?

Table **SF2.1**

STATE MANDATES ON SEXUALITY EDUCATION AND HIV/AIDS EDUCATION*

	MANDATES		RECOMMENDATIONS			MANDATES		RECOMMENDATIONS	
	SEXUALITY EDUC.	HIV/AIDS EDUC.	SEXUALITY EDUC.	HIV/AIDS EDUC.		SEXUALITY EDUC.	HIV/AIDS EDUC.	SEXUALITY EDUC.	HIV/AIDS EDUC.
Alabama		•	•		Montana			•	•
Alaska			•	•	Nebraska			•	•
Arizona		•	•		Nevada	•	•		
Arkansas	•	•			New Hampshire		•	•	
California		•	•		New Jersey	•	•		
Colorado			•	•	New Mexico	•	•		
Connecticut		•	•		New York		•	•	
Delaware	•	•			North Carolina		•	•	
Dist. of Col.	•	•			North Dakota			•	•
Florida	•	•			Ohio			•	
Georgia	•	•			Oklahoma		•	•	
Hawaii			•	•	Oregon		•	•	
Idaho		•	•		Pennsylvania		•	•	
Illinois		•	•		Rhode Island	•	•		
Indiana		•	•		South Carolina	•	•		
Iowa	•	•			South Dakota		•		
Kansas	•	•			Tennessee			•	
Kentucky			•	•	Texas			•	•
Louisiana			•	•	Utah	•	•		
Maine			•	•	Vermont	•	•		
Maryland	•	•			Virginia	•	•		
Massachusetts				•	Washington		•	•	
Michigan		•	•		West Virginia	•	•		
Minnesota		•	•		Wisconsin			•	•
Mississippi				•	Wyoming				
Missouri			•	•	**TOTAL**	**17**	**34**	**30**	**14**

*A state mandate is a requirement that all school districts provide sexuality education and/or HIV/AIDS education to their students, usually in the form of family life education programs or comprehensive health education. Mandates are usually accompanied by suggested curricula to be implemented at the local level.

Recommendations refer to any provisions by state legislatures or state departments of education, which support sexuality education and/or HIV/AIDS education but do not require it. While curricula may be suggested, it is left up to the local districts to design and implement such programs.

Source: *Guidelines for Comprehensive Sexuality Education: Kindergarten Through Twelfth Grade.* **National Guidelines Task Force, SIECUS, April 1993, page 51. Copyright Sex Information and Education Council of the U.S., Inc., 130 West 42nd Street, Suite 2500, New York, NY 10036. (212) 819-9770, fax (212) 819-9776**

Children begin to learn about sexuality from a very young age. From birth to age two, children are very curious about their bodies (including their genitals), and they begin to develop a positive or negative attitude toward their bodies. They are also encouraged to develop appropriate gender-typed behavior (see Chapter 4).

Between the ages of three and four, children begin to explore their own bodies and learn to masturbate (Wilson, 1991). They may begin to play "sex games" such as "doctor" or "mailman." They may also begin asking where they came from. All of these changes are great springboards for a discussion of sexuality.

Between the ages of five and eight, curiosity about sex continues to increase. Children often become interested in pregnancy and birth, sex roles, gender, and relationships. Sexuality education can include information on these topics.

As young children enter puberty (between the ages of nine and twelve), adolescents usually become more modest and experience a wide range of emotions. They may develop crushes on older people, including teachers, and sexual fantasies may begin. They also begin experimenting with adult sexuality, in some cases even with sexual intercourse (see Personal Voices SF2.1).

In developing sexuality education programs, we need to keep these developmental stages in mind. Education needs to be given to help students work through the issues they might be dealing with. Education must be comprehensive and **sequential**.

sequential: Characterized by sequence; sex education programs that are sequential involve building on information that has been learned in earlier units.

What Should Be Taught?

There is a continuing debate over what should be included in sexuality education. Some believe that only anatomy and physiology should be taught, while others believe we must include discussions of values, attitudes, and morals. Yet since people have different moral perspectives on sexuality, there is controversy about which values and morals to teach.

In the past, if sexuality education was provided in the schools, it was often merely a course in "plumbing," teaching the basics of anatomy and physiology. Today, courses may also include information on reproduction (e.g., learning about the development of a fetus), moral teaching (e.g., premarital sex is wrong), or the problems caused by sexual activity (e.g., unwanted pregnancy, infection with AIDS, infertility). Interpersonal aspects of sexuality, such as how it feels to be in love or why communication is important, are often ignored. In addition to teaching reproductive anatomy, physiology, and contraception, sexuality education needs to include more information about intimacy, communication, assertiveness, gender role expectations, values clarification, problem solving, and life planning.

Over the last few years, there have been many changes in the sexuality education curriculum, one of the most notable changes being the shift to what is called "**family life education**," mainly as a compromise with those who oppose sexuality education. This curriculum tends to focus on aspects of life such as getting along with parents, understanding emotions, what to do about sexual abuse, and information about AIDS. Outside of college-level courses, many states avoid teaching certain subjects in sexuality, such as sexual identity, sexual orientation, and abortion. They also tend to lack adequate balance between information about abstinence and safer sex (SIECUS, 1994). Less than one-third of states discuss sexual behaviors in their sexuality courses, and when they are discussed, the focus is often on the negative consequences of sexual activity rather than a promotion of sexual health and responsible decision making.

family life education: Forming in reaction to criticism of sex education from conservatives, this type of curriculum is expanding its focus to include information on relationships with parents, self-concepts, and STDs.

Young people's questions about sex help us determine what to include in sexuality education programs. Sexuality education programs that are based on students' questions are more congruent with the different developmental levels of students. Young children's questions about sexuality often involve reproduction ("How are babies made?"), differences between parents and child ("How come you have breasts and I don't?"), and gender differences ("Why do boys have a penis?"). Teenagers often want to know about penis size, masturbation, homosexuality, orgasm, love and intimacy, contraception, pregnancy, and various sexual behaviors. For more age-specific questions about sexuality, see Sexuality Today SF2.3.

How Should It Be Taught?

There are a variety of sexuality education programs today, concentrating on topics including abstinence, relationships, anatomy, contraception, and other issues. The main differences among these programs is whether they are abstinence-based or comprehensive. We will discuss a few of these programs below.

Abstinence-Based Programs

In the early 1990s, there was a proliferation of sexuality education programs that used fear to discourage students from engaging in sexual behavior. These programs were called "abstinence" or "fear-based" curricula and included mottos such as "Control your urgin'—be a virgin," "Don't be a louse—wait for your spouse," "Do the right thing—wait for the ring," or "Pet your dog—not your date." Typically, critical information was omitted from these programs, and there was an overreliance on avoiding sexual behavior, religion, and negative consequences of sexual behavior. These negative consequences are often exaggerated, and sexual behavior is portrayed as dangerous and harmful (Kantor, 1992). As of 1995, many of these programs have found their way into mainstream educational systems and have been the basis for sexuality education programs.

Overall, abstinence-based sexuality education programs have many similarities. They often use scare tactics to encourage abstinence; they omit information about contraception, abortion, and homosexuality; avoid any mention of the positive aspects of human sexuality; contain medical misinformation about abortion, STDs, HIV/AIDS, and sexual response; contain sexist, racist, and disabled biases; and view nontraditional families as "troubled" (Kantor, 1992).

One program (for junior high students) entitled Family Accountability Communicating Teen Sexuality (FACTS), cites the consequences of sexual behavior as

> [P]regnancy, financial aspect of fatherhood, abortion, guilt associated with abortion, AIDS, STDs, guilt, rejection, loss of reputation, inability to bond in the future, challenge not to compare sexual partners, alienation from friends and family, poverty, and inability to complete school.
>
> *Kantor (1992:3–4)*

Teen-Aid, a program for senior high school students developed by a group entitled Sexuality, Commitment and Family, claims the following to be consequences of premarital sexual behavior:

> [L]oss of reputation; limitations in dating/marriage choices; negative effects on sexual adjustment; negative effects on happiness (premarital sex, especially with more than one person, has been linked to the development of emotional illness [and the] loss of self-esteem); family conflict and possible premature separation from the family; confusion regarding personal value (e.g., "Am I loved because I am me, because of my personality and looks, or because I am a sex object?"); and loss of goals.
>
> *Kantor (1992:4)*

What Do They Want to Know and What Can We Teach Them at Different Ages?

In order to develop programs that can meet the needs of different age levels, educators often evaluate what types of questions students ask. Here we present questions typically asked at various ages and suggestions for what to include in sexuality education programs at these levels.

Ages Three to Five

During these years, children have short attention spans. Questions they have about sex may include:

What is that? (referring to specific body parts)

What do mommies do?

What do daddies do?

Where do babies come from?

At this level, sexuality education could focus on the roles of family members, the development of a positive self-image, an understanding that living things grow, reproduce, and die.

Ages Five to Eight

Children at these stages often become very curious about how the body works. Questions they have about sex may include:

Where was I before I was born?

How does mommy get a baby?

Did I come from an egg?

Sexuality education could include information on plant and animal reproduction, gender similarities and differences, growth and development, and self-esteem.

Ages Nine to Twelve

Curiosity about their bodies continues, and children are often interested in the other sex and reproduction. Questions they have about sex may include:

How does the reproductive system work?

Why do some girls have larger breasts than others?

Do boys menstruate?

Why don't some women have babies?

Sexuality education could focus on biological topics such as the endocrine system, menstruation and wet dreams, masturbation, sexual intercourse, birth control, abortion, self-esteem, and interpersonal relationships.

Ages Twelve to Fourteen

The onset of puberty causes many other physical changes such as changes in body shape, body control, reproductive ability, menstruation, breast and penis development, and voice changes, which can be very confusing. Questions they have about sex may include:

How can you keep yourself looking attractive?

Should your parents know if you're going steady?

Why are some people homosexual?

Does a girl ever have a wet dream?

Does sexual intercourse hurt?

Why do people get married?

Sexuality education could focus on increasing knowledge of contraception, intimate sexual behavior (why people do what they do), dating, and variations in sexual behaviors (homosexuality, transvestism, transsexualism).

Ages Fifteen to Seventeen

Adolescents tend to be interested in sexual topics, and they are curious about relationships with others, families, reproduction, and various sexual activity patterns. Many teenagers begin dating at this time. Questions they have about sex may include:

What is prostitution?

What do girls really want in a good date?

How far should you go on a date?

Is it good to have sexual intercourse before marriage?

Why is sex regarded as a dirty word?

Sexuality education could include more information on birth control, abortion, dating, premarital sexual behavior, communication, marriage patterns, sexual myths, moral decisions, parenthood, research in sexuality, sexual dysfunction, and the history of sexuality.

Adult Learners

Today, educators of adults, including college students, are trying to make up for lost time in sexuality education programs. They spend a considerable amount of time teaching biology, anatomy, and physiology, all of which should have been taught long before college. If students were receiving adequate sexuality education all along, as a regular part of their education, college-level sexuality education courses would be less crucial. As it is, college-level sexuality education courses for many people are the first time they are exposed to open, honest information about sexuality where they are encouraged to ask questions and find answers. It is also important to implement sexuality education programs for the elderly to help them have satisfying sexual relationships. Older men and women often have many questions about sexuality and dysfunctions in their changing bodies that can interfere with sexual satisfaction.

Although we have presented these general guidelines for sexuality education programs, keep in mind that any particular program must be designed according to the needs of the specific group to which it will be presented.

Adapted from Breuss and Greenberg (1981:223–231)

A happy and healthy future is also promoted as a reason for not engaging in sexual behavior. Facing Reality, a program for senior high school students, claims that there are rewards for those who avoid premarital sexual behavior. These include

> [C]ontinuing education, being able to serve others, mastering emotions and impulses, sharing family values for a lifetime, making more friends, becoming a leader, concentrating on important tasks, remaining physically healthy, raising a healthy family, making a clear-headed marriage choice, pursuing spiritual goals, making permanent commitments, excelling in athletics, giving example to others, creating positive peer pressure, enjoying a beautiful time of life, taking on greater responsibilities, [and] having piece of mind.

> *Kantor (1992:4)*

Sex Respect, one of the most popular abstinence-based programs used in junior high schools, was designed in 1983 by Coleen Mast, a former Catholic school teacher and an antiabortion activist. As of 1993, the program was being used in 1,600 school districts in all fifty states and also several foreign countries. Mast and her husband have also designed several products that promote abstinence including "Stop at the lips" T-shirts and "I'm worth waiting for" buttons. Overall, the message of this program is "DON'T DO IT," and this message is strongly enforced. Teachers who use these materials are not supposed to discuss controversial issues, such as masturbation, homosexuality, birth control, or abortion.

Do abstinence-based programs work? This is the important question, and the responses will differ, depending on who you ask. Supporters of abstinence-based programs often have very strong feelings about traditional sexuality education programs. Pat Robertson, the founder of the Christian Coalition and host of the *700 Club* television show, said that:

> [T]heir leaders are teaching them [schoolchildren] how to be homosexuals, teaching them how to be lesbians, teaching them how to have premarital sex in every way you can imagine without any benefit of marriage and without any concept of morality or the dignity or the beauty of sex.

> *SIECUS (1992:17)*

Supporters of abstinence-based programs claim that talking only about abstinence lets children and young adults know that this is the *only* choice. Those who believe in these programs would say that they are effective. On the other hand, many sexuality education experts believe that strictly abstinence-based programs may do more harm than good. They often fail to provide necessary factual information, and they support many myths and stereotypes about various topics in human sexuality (such as sexual assault, gender differences, sexual orientation, pregnancy options, and STDs).

Teenagers often claim that abstinence-based programs do not work. One nineteen-year-old said:

> Adults can't say children our age are not having sex. That's plain dumb. They can still promote abstinence, but tell us how to practice safe sex, or a lot of people in our generation are going to have AIDS. Sexuality education in eighth grade is way too late.

> *Minton(1993)*

However, it is important to keep in mind that there is a difference between "fear-based" abstinence programs and those that are "skill-based." Some abstinence-based

In abstinence-based sex education programs students are taught to abstain from sexual intercourse until marriage.

programs do not rely on scare or fear tactics. Often these programs incorporate skill-building into their programs. Will Power/Won't Power, a program for twelve- to fourteen-year-old girls, is one of these. Students are taught communication skills in addition to hearing about abstinence. Those who participated were found to be half as likely to have intercourse as those who did not participate (Girls, Inc., 1991). Postponing Sexual Involvement is a program for eighth graders, which provides students with skill-building exercises to deal with peer pressure. Compared with students who participated in this program, students who did not participate were four times more likely to have engaged in sexual intercourse by the end of eighth grade (Howard, 1982). It appears that when the abstinence message is combined with information about sexuality, these programs may be more successful at changing behavior.

Comprehensive Sexuality Education Programs

In 1991, the National Guidelines Task Force, which was comprised of fifteen national organizations and schools, established the *Guidelines for Comprehensive Sexuality Education.* Comprehensive Sexuality Education is based on the idea that sexuality education is:

> *...a lifelong process of acquiring information and forming attitudes, beliefs, and values about identity, relationships, and intimacy. It encompasses sexual development, reproductive health, interpersonal relationships, affection, intimacy, body image, and gender roles. Sexuality education addresses the biological, sociocultural, psychological, and spiritual dimensions of sexuality from (1) the cognitive domain, (2) the affective domain, and (3) the behavioral domain, including the skills to communicate effectively and make responsible decisions.*

> *SIECUS (1993)*

Comprehensive programs are developmentally appropriate and include information on self-esteem and feeling good about oneself. The primary goal of these types of programs is to promote sexual health.

The *Guidelines for Comprehensive Sexuality Education* identified six concepts that should be part of every sexuality education program: human development, relationships, personal skills, sexual behavior, sexual health, and society and culture (SIECUS, 1993). In addition, there are four levels of education that reflect different stages of development. Only developmentally appropriate information is presented at each level.

At the college level, sexuality courses use a variety of teaching methods. Your instructor might use a lecture or discussion format and may also incorporate films, guest speakers, slides, group discussions, and/or panel presentations by "experts" (Wanlass et al., 1983). These techniques have been found to be helpful in increasing knowledge levels and evaluating one's own attitudes. Discussion groups are also valuable in sexuality courses. Listening to a lecture and memorizing facts will probably help students pass a sexuality course, but developing an ability to think critically about one's own sexual values and experiences and to make good decisions will become much more important down the road, long after the course is over. For this reason, many sexuality courses rely on both discussion and lecture equally.

QUALIFICATIONS FOR SEXUALITY EDUCATORS

Teachers of sexuality education courses may be psychology professors, health or nursing instructors, physicians, doctoral students, or an interdisciplinary team of instructors, each with different areas of expertise (Kilmann et al., 1981). In kindergarten to twelfth-grade programs, teachers are usually drawn from health education, home economics, the home classroom, or physical education. In addition, experts from public health and local agencies may be invited to speak.

Sexuality education programs in high school have been criticized, for often the instructor is a gym or health teacher. Although they may (or may not) be qualified to teach physiology, anatomy, or health, they are rarely qualified to teach value systems or sexuality as a whole. Outside of college professors, many teachers have no background or specific training in sexuality education. In addition, the majority of states have no training programs or requirements for those responsible for teaching sexuality education. In fact, only nine states require training as a prerequisite to teaching human sexuality (SIECUS, 1993).

In 1958, a sex educator named Patricia Schiller, who founded AASECT, developed the first training program for sex educators in the United States. In 1972, the board of directors of AASECT approved a plan of standards by which sex educators could be certified. Today, many sex educators are certified each year through AASECT.

Overall, the most important criteria for a teacher of sexuality education is an accepting, nonjudgmental attitude and a level of comfort when discussing sexual issues. Discomfort with sexuality may lead to an overreliance on specific facts and less focus on feelings and thoughts related to sexuality issues. Students are quick to perceive that an instructor is uncomfortable with the topic, and they will be reluctant to ask questions.

HETEROSEXISM IN SEXUALITY EDUCATION

A recent criticism of sexuality education programs is that there is a strong heterosexist bias. There is an underlying assumption that *human* sexuality is *heterosexual* sexuality.

If homosexuals or bisexuals are left out of the sexuality education curriculum, in essence this is saying that they are "not fully sexual human beings" (Ellis, 1984). In many sexuality education courses today, homosexuality is discussed during one class period and the rest of the semester is spent exploring various aspects of heterosexuality (such as premarital, marital, and extramarital sex, contraception, and abortion). Textbooks on human sexuality typically offer one chapter on homosexuality, discussing primarily what *causes* it. Conversely, very little, if any, attention is paid to what *causes* heterosexuality. Perhaps the best way to reduce the heterosexism in sexuality education is to ask what causes sexual orientation in general (Ellis, 1984). Heterosexism is a problem in almost all topics in academia today, but it creates particular problems in the field of sexuality education.

SEXUALITY EDUCATION FOR OLDER ADULTS

Funny, you wouldn't think we would include a section on sexuality education for older adults, would you? When most people think about sexuality education, they think about teenagers and college students. But what about the older generation? Could they also benefit from sexuality education? The fact that we do not offer sexuality education for older adults reinforces the idea that older persons are either asexual and do not need any information about sex or that they already know everything there is to know. As sex educators, we believe that everyone is sexual from the day he or she is born until the day he or she dies. Only recently have we begun to expand sexuality to understand what happens during the entire life cycle rather than just during the reproductive years.

Most older people grew up during a period of relative sexual repression. Few had any type of sexuality education in their lifetime, and talking explicitly about sexuality was taboo. But it is never too late to learn about sexuality. Older persons need to learn age-specific information to deal with the physiological changes they may be experiencing and to increase their own personal comfort with sexuality. This, in turn, will help

The elderly also need sex education. These programs can help them understand physiological changes they may be experiencing and also can increase comfort levels with sexuality.

them understand sexuality and perhaps will help them discuss it with their own adult children or grandchildren.

In Chapter 12, we discussed some of the sexual dysfunctions that older persons may experience. Sexual difficulties may arise later in life because older persons are often not educated about the normal physiological changes of aging. When these problems begin to appear, they fear their sex life is over, which leads to worse sexual problems, even to a complete inability to function sexually. This, in turn, may lead to more negative self-images and depression. We can improve feelings of confidence and self-esteem by helping older generations understand their own sexuality.

SEXUALITY EDUCATION IN OTHER CULTURES

In a study done by the Alan Guttmacher Institute, the United States led nearly all other developed countries in the world in the rate of teenage pregnancy, abortion, and teenage childbearing. In fact, while teenage pregnancy rates have been decreasing in other developed countries, teenage pregnancy in the United States has been increasing. Overall, countries that have liberal attitudes toward sexuality, easily accessible birth control services for teenagers, and formal and informal sexuality education programs have the lowest rates of teenage pregnancy, abortion, and childbearing. Below, we review sexuality education in a variety of places.

Europe

The Netherlands has the lowest rates of teenage pregnancy, abortion, and childbearing in the world. The Alan Guttmacher Institute suggests that this may be due to compulsory (mandatory) sexuality education programs and easily accessible birth control services for adolescents. Sweden also liberalized contraceptive laws in 1975; this resulted in a decrease in the teenage abortion rates.

Over the years, Sweden has come to be known as the world leader in the area of sexuality education. Since 1956, Sweden has had compulsory sexuality education for all students beginning at the age of seven. There are national requirements for all sexuality education courses, a national curriculum, and a national handbook to guide in the training of teachers for these courses.

Outside the United States, sexuality education is also important, although it may be approached in many different ways. Here, a sexuality educator in India teaches a group of women about IUDs.

Brazil

In Brazil there is an annual *Carnival,* which is a time of liberation from the sexually repressive ways of Brazilian society. During the *Carnival,* television stations become much less conservative and air naked men and women, many engaging in public sexual activities. Yet, even with the open attitudes about sexuality during the *Carnival,* it has been difficult to establish sexuality education in Brazilian schools. The culture is highly patriarchal and has rigid gender roles. Only 32% of Brazilian parents discuss sex with their children (Suplicy, 1994).

As the rates of HIV and teenage pregnancies began increasing in Brazil, a group was set up to structure sexuality education. Paulo Freire, the Educational Secretary for the Municipality and leader of the program, said:

I want these children to learn to experience pleasure without feeling guilty. School has to sweep away taboos and sexual prejudices because sex is one of the most important sources of pleasure known to human beings.

Suplicy (1994:3)

In a study done in ten of the state capitals in Brazil in 1993, 86% of people interviewed favored including sexuality education in the school curriculum. These programs that have been implemented in the schools are very discussion oriented and interactive, and no grades are given. However, even with these gains, establishing comprehensive sexuality programs in Brazil has been difficult.

Asia

In Japan, there is opposition to sexuality education. One government employee said:

I believe that sexual matters should be secretive and should not be discussed in public. Everyone learns about sex through pornographic magazines or peer discussions when he or she becomes a teenager. Look at me! I'm very successful and doing fine as a city councilman, and nobody taught me about sex. The instruction of proper condom use will only encourage teenage sexual activity.

Kitazawa (1994:7)

In 1974, the Japanese Association for Sexuality Education (JASE) was founded to help establish comprehensive sexuality education in the schools, although abstinence education was very popular in Japan. As in the United States, popular sources of sex information in Japan include friends and older same-sex peers, magazines, and television.

In 1986, a new sexuality education curriculum was distributed to all middle and high schools in Japan (Kitazawa, 1994). In 1992, the Japanese Ministry of Education revised the sexuality curriculum and approved the discussion of secondary sex characteristics in coeducational fifth-grade classes. In fact, 1992 was called the "First Year of Sexuality Education," and sexuality education was required in schools. Prior to this time, there was no discussion of sexuality in elementary schools at all (Shimazaki, 1994).

Many teachers in the elementary schools have felt very uncomfortable with these changes. Talking about sexuality is very anxiety producing, both for teachers and many Japanese citizens. In addition, there is no formal sexuality training for these teachers. Today, however, the number of educators interested in teaching sexuality education is increasing. Workshops and educational programs add to the increasing comfort levels with sexuality. Overall, however, these open attitudes toward sexuality education have not been without opposition. In fact, sexuality education has been blamed for the changing norms in sexuality that resulted in an increase in divorce and a destruction of the family.

In Hong Kong, formal sexuality education programs began to appear on television in 1983 (Ng, 1993). Focusing at first on women and then on adolescent sexuality, they were conducted in a question-and-answer format with a specialist. After the television broadcast, a radio station opened its phone lines to continue the dialogue. Although these programs were considered controversial by some Hong Kong residents, others approved, and time will tell if these programs will continue after Hong Kong transfers to Chinese rule in 1997.

SEXUALITY EDUCATION IN THE FUTURE

In the future, it is likely that more sources of sexual information will be developed in the United States. For example, radio and television shows about sexuality have become mainstream. Magazines, books, cassettes, cable television, and videotapes also contribute to sexuality education, as do computer programs and bulletin boards (see Special Focus 4).

The content of sexuality education will surely change. For many years there has been pressure not to discuss the pleasurable aspects of sexuality; however, in the future, it is possible that sexuality will be discussed as pleasurable and enjoyable. Many specific sexual behaviors that are not related to reproduction (such as oral or anal sex) have often been described as deviations or perversions. Kirkendall and Libby (1984:67) point out that

> As the rigid atmosphere was relaxed, a perversion became an abnormality; then an abnormality became a deviancy; a deviancy became a variation; a variation became an option; an option became a choice; and now a choice has become a life-enhancing activity.

Ideally, in the future, kindergarten through grade-twelve sexuality education programs will discuss parenting, surrogate parenting, and divorce. Programs also need to be designed specifically for the needs of the disabled, another group that often has been viewed as asexual (see Chapter 12).

Finally, many groups are beginning to adopt policies that support sexuality education. In addition, in the United States, a group of more than sixty organizations called the National Coalition to Support Sexuality Education has formed and is committed to assuring that there will be comprehensive sexuality education for all students by the year 2000.

The Clinton Administration is planning to revise the long-standing "Just-Say-No" message to premarital sex by placing a stronger emphasis on contraception and the prevention of STDs. However, far-right groups are also mobilizing against comprehensive sexuality education. Since Congress won a Republican majority in 1994 and as more and more religious fundamentalists run for and are elected to state and local offices, the pressure against sexuality education will increase. As these groups work toward eliminating comprehensive sexuality education, it will become more important for proponents to voice their support.

Summary

- Overall, the most common goals for sexuality education programs include increasing knowledge; understanding one's own attitudes and values; reducing unhealthy sexual behavior; and respecting the attitudes and values of others. There has been a continuing debate about what topics are included in sexuality education programs. However, the majority of lower-level sexuality education programs in schools are primarily courses in anatomy and physiology.

- Sexuality education programs are effective in increasing knowledge levels, changing attitudes toward certain behaviors, developing more accepting attitudes toward the behavior of others, and decreasing levels of sexual guilt. They do not affect rates of sexual activity. However, some effects of sexuality education may not be quantifiable.

- Proponents of sexuality education claim that most people lack factual knowledge about sex, which can lead to irresponsible sexual behavior. They claim that these programs may decrease sexual activity, improve self-esteem, and help prevent sexual dysfunctions later in life.
- Opponents of sexuality education claim that sexuality education is responsible for the increasing rates of premarital sexual activity, STDs, and teenage pregnancy. They believe that formal programs in sexuality education increase students' curiosity, which may cause promiscuity. Other opponents of sexuality education feel that these programs take away from the parents' role as the primary sex educators of their children.
- The debate over sexuality education often focuses on where, when, what, and how to teach about sexuality. Where sexuality education should be taught, at what age, and by whom are all important questions.
- The mother is more likely to be the parent who talks to her children about sex because she is often viewed as more available, emotional, affectionate, and knowledgeable about reproduction. Even so, many parents feel uncomfortable discussing sexuality with their children and would like helping in doing so.
- Many different programs have appeared. Abstinence-only and comprehensive sexuality programs are two of the most popular types of sexuality education programs.

- Teachers of sexuality education programs are drawn from different disciplines. In the United States, most states have no training programs or requirements for teachers of sexuality education programs.
- Sexuality education programs have been criticized for having a heterosexist bias because homosexuality and bisexuality are often discussed in a very limited way. It is important to discuss the range of sexual orientation.
- Although we often think of sexuality education programs being directed toward younger persons, there have been many programs designed for older persons as well. Older persons can benefit from learning the age-specific physiological changes that may affect sexual functioning. In addition, programs can help to increase their comfort levels with sexuality.
- The United States, which has high teenage pregnancy, abortion, and childbearing rates, is one of the most conservative as far as sexuality education is concerned. Countries with liberal attitudes toward sexuality, easily accessible birth control services for teenagers, and formal and informal sexuality education programs have lower rates of teenage pregnancy, abortion, and childbearing.
- In the future, many more sources of information on sexuality will be available, such as magazines, cassettes, videotapes, and even computer software. Comprehensive sexuality education programs may also be developed and required in school systems.

*R**eflections on Sexuality*

1. Can you think of any reasons that parents might not want their children to be involved in sexuality education programs? Do you think parents have legitimate concerns?
2. What is the rationale for having sexuality education programs today? For not having them?
3. Do you think that teachers should be required to go through any specific training? Why or why not?

4. Explain how sexuality education differs outside the United States. Do you think that any of the programs developed for use in other countries would be appropriate for use in the United States?

*S**uggested Readings*

CALDERONE, M., and E. JOHNSON. (1989) *The Family Book About Sexuality.* New York: Harper and Row.

SIECUS (1993) *Guidelines for Comprehensive Sexuality Education: Kindergarten Through Twelfth Grade.* Third Printing New York. Developed by the National Guidelines Task Force, this is the first national consensus about what should be taught in sexuality education programs. Available from SIECUS for $5.75, 130 West 42nd St., Suite 2500, New York, NY 10036.

3

Prostitution

Karen, a twenty-five-year-old woman, goes out to dinner with a forty-five-year-old man. After dinner, they go back to her apartment and have sexual intercourse. The next day flowers arrive at her office and he gives her a pearl bracelet at lunch. She does not really care for him emotionally, but she appreciates his generosity.

Sue has been having a sexual relationship with a disabled male. He pays her $50 each time they have sexual intercourse. One night while lying in bed together after having sex, she realizes that she is falling in love with him, even though he is paying her.

Will is an attractive, heterosexual male who often dates older women. These women treat him very well by paying for everything he needs and wants. In return, he has sex with them on occasion. Although he often feels disgusted to be in bed with some of these older women, he does it because of what they can provide for him.

Tim, a heterosexual male bodybuilder, has sex with homosexual males once a month to make some extra cash. He does not enjoy these encounters at all. In fact, most of his friends would say that he is very homophobic and hates homosexuals.

Kimberly is hired for a position that she is not qualified for because she is sleeping with the boss. She quickly moves up the corporate ladder even though many others are more qualified to do so.

Sally, a fifteen-year-old female, works at a carnival one summer. To earn money she sells kisses to any man who will pay $5.00 per kiss. In one day, she earns $100.

Robin works at a sex therapy clinic as a sexual surrogate. A gentleman who does not have a sexual partner comes to the clinic for treatment for his erectile dysfunction. He hires Robin to engage in sexual intercourse to help him improve his sexual functioning.

Read through the scenarios listed on the preceding page. Which of these you would classify as exchanging sex for money? Which would you classify as prostitution? Is exchanging sex for material goods always prostitution? Defining prostitution is not easy. In fact, what is defined as prostitution in one culture might not be so defined in another. The U.S. legal code is also ambiguous about what constitutes prostitution; for instance, some state penal codes define prostitution as the act of hiring out one's body for sexual intercourse, while other states define prostitution as sexual intercourse in exchange for money or as any sexual behavior that is sold for profit. Dictionaries also have different definitions for prostitution. For example, the *Oxford English Dictionary* defines prostitution as "offering of the body to indicate lewdness for hire," while the *American Heritage Dictionary* defines a prostitute as "a person who solicits and accepts payment for sexual intercourse." Based on the first definition, Sue, Will, Tim, and Robin from the above scenarios are prostitutes, but by the second definition, only Sue and possibly Robin could be considered prostitutes. For our purposes in this chapter, we define prostitution as the act of a male or female engaging in sexual activity in exchange for money or other material goods.

Over the course of time, prostitutes have been called many slang terms, such as "whores," "hookers," "sluts," or "hustlers" (see Sexuality Today SF3.1). Some other terms often used when discussing prostitution include a **pimp,** who may act as a protector and business manager for many prostitutes; a **madam,** who is in charge of managing a home, **brothel,** or group of prostitutes. A **john** is a person who hires a prostitute, and a **trick** is the service that the prostitute performs (although recently a trick has come to mean the same as a john). Historically, most prostitutes worked in brothels, although with the exception of certain areas of Nevada, few brothels remain in the United States. However, brothels are still widespread in the Eastern and Oriental parts of the world.

SOCIOLOGIXCAL ASPECTS OF PROSTITUTION

Society has created social institutions such as marriage and the family in part to regulate sexual behavior. However, it is also true that, throughout history, people have had sexual relations outside these institutions. Prostitution has existed, in one form or another, as long as marriage has, which has led some to argue that it provides a needed sexual release. Whether a society should recognize this by allowing legal, regulated prostitution, however, raises a number of controversial social, political, economic, and religious questions.

Some sociologists suggest that prostitution developed out of the **patriarchal** nature of most societies. In a society where men are valued over women and where men hold the reins of economic and political power, some women exploit the only assets that cannot be taken away from them—their sexuality. The degree to which men govern a society has an influence over the type and degree of prostitution that exists in that society; however, prostitution is also linked to other economic, sociological, psychological, and religious factors (Bullough and Bullough, 1987).

Some sociologists used to claim that women actually benefited from prostitution because, from a purely economic point of view, they get paid for giving something away that is free to them. Kingsley Davis wrote:

> *The woman may suffer no loss at all, yet receive a generous reward, resembling the artist who, paid for his work, loves it so well that he would paint anyway. Purely from the angle of economic return, the hard question is not why so many women become prostitutes, but why so few of them do.*
>
> **As quoted in Benjamin (1961:876)**

pimp: A slang term that refers to the male in charge of organizing clients for a female prostitute.

madam: A slang term that refers to the woman who is responsible for overseeing a brothel.

brothel: A house of prostitution.

john: A slang term that refers to a prostitute's client.

trick: A slang term that refers to the sexual services of a prostitute; also may refer to a john.

patriarchal: Of or pertaining to a society or system that is dominated by male power.

The Language of Prostitution

Prostitutes often have their own language for prostitution activities. Below is a glossary of some of the terms used by prostitutes.

bitch: Word used affectionately by prostitutes to describe their coworkers.

bottom woman or *hoe:* One who has been with a particular pimp the longest and in whom he has the most confidence.

break luck: The first date a prostitute turns on a night-long tour.

bumper: A girl who steals while turning tricks.

car trick: Customers who choose to receive sexual services in their automobiles.

catching a date: Successfully interesting a man in paying for sex.

flatbacking: Engaging in conventional intercourse.

front money: Money that a pimp gives to his girl to start the evening; money for food and condoms.

greek sex: Anal sex.

half and half: A prostitute performing oral sex on a man and before ejaculation finishing with intercourse. Also known as a "suck and fuck."

ho: Street slang for whore or prostitute.

hoe game: The act of trying to interest and persuade a man to pay for sex.

hoe stroll: The street on which prostitutes work; also known as the track.

hot sheet hotel: Small, usually rundown hostelry which caters almost exclusively to street prostitutes and their customers.

outlaw: A prostitute living and working without a pimp.

pulling a girl: A pimp will talk to a girl on many occasions for many hours until he finally pulls her, which means he has convinced her to work for him.

put down: When a pimp drives a girl to work and drops her off, he has put her down to work.

rabbit: A girl who goes from pimp to pimp.

regulars: Tricks who come to a particular prostitute periodically.

renegading: The act of working the streets without a pimp.

rolling a trick: Stealing (usually money or credit cards) from a customer.

rubber man: Person who sells prophylactics to women on the street.

simp: A man pretending to be a pimp to pull girls in the hopes of actually becoming a pimp, who because of appearance and method of operation, does not command enough respect on the streets to succeed.

square: Anyone outside the life of prostitution.

trap: Money a woman has made on a given shift.

turn out: Someone who recently became a prostitute.

wife-in-law: Relationship of several women with the same pimp.

**Selected terms from Carmen (1985) and
Zausner (1986)**

THE PROSTITUTE

It is estimated that there are as many as two million prostitutes working in the United States today, some full-time and some part-time. Gay prostitution is also common (Perkins and Bennett, 1985), as is male prostitution for females, although there are more female prostitutes with male clients than all other forms combined (Goode, 1994). In recent years, however, female prostitution has been declining; male prostitution has been increasing (Earls and David, 1989).

What motivates a man or woman to sell sex for money? Is it just the money? Is it love? Is it fear? The majority of prostitutes say that their primary and maybe even sole motivation for prostituting is for the money (Rio, 1991). Prostitutes can make more money, on average, than their peers who work conventional jobs.

Many prostitutes say that the major drawback to their job is having to engage in sex with their clients. It is a myth that women become prostitutes because they love sex or because they are "nymphomaniacs." Those involved in the prostitution subculture say that if a prostitute enjoys sexual intercourse with clients, it "gets in her way" (Goode, 1994). If a prostitute enjoys the sexual interactions, she may lose sight of the importance of client pleasure, or she might want to spend more time with a particular client, which could reduce her income. One prostitute said:

I would say that nothing could prompt me to have an orgasm or even become excited with a john. . . . I doubt that I would be able to manage it. . . . I will always pretend to be excited, and to come at the moment he comes, but if I really got excited I would be all involved with myself, and the timing would be thrown off, and actually he wouldn't have a good time as if I were faking it. It's funny to think of, but he gets more for his money if it's a fake than if he were to get the real thing.

Wells (1970:139)

Prostitutes who are preoccupied with their own pleasure and orgasms are often referred to as "come freaks" (Goode, 1994).

The majority of prostitutes do not enjoy their work. Only 24% of prostitutes report that they like prostitution, mostly for the freedom it offers (both financially and personally) (Perkins and Bennett, 1985). Most prostitutes work full-time, with 49% of their clients being repeat customers, including some long-term customers (Freund et al., 1989). A "regular" customer visits the prostitute at least once a week, and some have sexual encounters two or three times each week with the prostitute or spend several hours at a hotel (or one of their homes) together.

SEX TALK
QUESTION **SF3.1**   **Do prostitutes enjoy having sex?**

Having sex with whom? Eighty percent of prostitutes have sexual lives outside of their professional lives (Savitz and Rosen, 1988). As for sex with clients, some prostitutes report that they enjoy both sexual intercourse and oral sex, although the majority do not. Some do experience orgasms in their interactions with clients, but again, the majority do not. In fact, in Masters and Johnson's early research on sexual functioning, they included prostitutes (see Chapter 2) but found that the pelvic congestion in prostitutes, which resulted from having sex without orgasms, made them poor subjects for their studies.

Female Prostitutes

In the United States, most female prostitutes are young. One study found that 75% of prostitutes were less than twenty-five years old (Potterat et al., 1990). The majority of female prostitutes enter the life of prostitution during adolescence. Most are either currently or previously married, and almost half have children (Freund et al., 1991). Those who become prostitutes have more sexual experience, on average, than nonprostitutes and receive less sex education from their parents (James and Meyerding, 1978).

Typically, female prostitutes live in an apartment or home with several other prostitutes and one pimp. This is known as a **pseudofamily** (Romenesko and Miller, 1989). The pseudofamily operates much like a family does; there are rules and responsibilities for all family members. The pimp is responsible for protecting the prostitutes, while the prostitutes are responsible for bringing home the money. Other household responsibilities are also agreed on. When the female ages and/or the male tires of her, she may be traded like a slave or simply disowned. The services of older prostitutes are less valuable; and by "older," we mean those over the age of twenty-two! (Visano, 1990).

Psychological problems are more common in prostitutes than nonprostitutes and more common in older prostitutes (de-Schampheleire, 1990). There are dangers associated with a life of prostitution, stressful family situations, and mistreatment by clients or pimps. To deal with these pressures, many prostitutes turn to drugs or alcohol, although many women enter prostitution to enable them to make enough money to support their preexisting addictions.

Entry into prostitution is often a gradual process (Goode, 1994). At first, the activity may bother them, but as time goes by, they become accustomed to the life and begin to see themselves and the profession differently. In Personal Voices SF3.1, one female prostitute shares her feelings about her work.

pseudofamily: A type of family that develops when prostitutes and pimps live together; rules, household responsibilities, and work activities are agreed on by all members of the family.

Predisposing Factors

Some common threads run through the lives of many prostitutes. The most common factor, according to researchers, is an economically deprived upbringing (Goode, 1994). However, since high-class prostitutes, who often come from wealthy backgrounds, are less likely to be caught and arrested, research studies may concentrate too much on poorer women.

Early sexual contact with many partners in superficial relationships has also been found to be related to prostitution. Davis (1971) speculated that after these early sexual experiences, the young woman experiences decreased self-esteem and begins to reevaluate herself in terms of her role in society. Prostitutes are also more often victims of sexual abuse, initiate sexual activity at a younger age, and experience a higher frequency of rape. Intrafamilial violence and past physical and sexual abuse are also common (Simons and Whitbeck, 1991; Earls and David, 1990). One study found that 73% of female prostitutes had been sexually abused in childhood (Bagley and Young, 1987), and the severity of the sexual abuse was correlated with poor mental health and diminished self-esteem. In addition, sexually abused children who ran away from home were more likely to become prostitutes than those who did not run away (Seng, 1989). Perhaps these experiences also affect a woman's decreasing sense of self-esteem.

Parents of prostitutes often report experiencing stress due to a history of failed intimate relationships, economic problems, and unstable relationships. In addition, many

VOICES

Female Prostitution

Lee is a thirty-seven-year-old prostitute in Sydney, Australia. She also raises a family at home.

I began prostituting when I was nineteen and met some working ladies. I was intrigued by what they were doing and saw the money they had and what they could do with it. . . .

I've made $2,000 in one week, which is very good money. I charge $20 minimum, short time, just for straight sex. That's ten minutes, which will not sound very long to most people, but when you consider that the average male only needs two or three minutes in sex—I had some guys finishing even before they get on the bed. I make all my clients wear a condom and I've put the condom on them and by the time I've turned around to get on the bed they've already blown it. In most of these cases it's the guys who are most apologetic and feel they have fallen down on the job.

I always check my clients both for any disease or body lice. If I am at all wary of a client I always get another girl to double-check. I go to the doctor once a week and get a report within ten minutes. There are some girls who will take anybody and don't use any protection, and they don't know how to check a client properly anyway. Girls on drugs are less careful than they should be, and in the parlors condoms are generally not insisted on.

Clients ask for a range of different sexual activities. It can range from good old fashioned straight-out sex to swinging from the chandeliers. Apart from bondage and discipline there are some weird requests such as golden showers, spankings and whippings, and the guy who wants a girl to shit on a glass-top table with him underneath the table. There's money to be made in these things but I won't do them because it's my own individual choice.

One guy wanted to be jumped on with stiletto heels, which to me is a complete turn-off, but others who have been with him have told me he has the ugliest scars from the days years ago when women used to wear very thin stilettos and these have punctured his stomach. I have one regular who wants to be ridden like a horse and I have to explain to him how he's going to be gelded. There's another guy who sits under an umbrella wearing nothing but a bowler hat and for every cigarette the woman here who sees him butts out on his penis he gives her $10 until he climaxes. There's another guy who wants his balls tied up so tightly that they turn purple. One guy carries his own dildo and wants the girl to strap it on and screw him.

As for a typical day for me, I get up between seven and seven-thirty and have the usual argument with getting kids off to school. I do my housework like any other housewife. I have pets, and I have a normal home. I eat, sleep and breathe like any normal human being. I enjoy cooking a lot. I keep my business quite separate from my home life, and the kids don't know what I do, my husband doesn't want to know about it and I don't want to discuss it with him. I try and spend as much time as I can with the kids. There are one or two guys among our friends who know about me but they haven't told their wives and we never discuss it. Work is work. I go to work to work and when I go home and close the doors on the house that's it. My occupation is not all that different from any nine-to-five worker except the hours are better, I'm my own boss, and the pay's better.

Perkins and Bennett (1985:71–85)

---

prostitutes grow up in poor neighborhoods, which provides easy access to prostitution careers, because active prostitution circles are common.

Keep in mind that though these factors contribute to a predisposition to prostitution, they do not *cause* a woman to become a prostitute. For example, we know that many prostitutes have had no early sex education; however, this does not mean that the lack of sex education *caused* them to become prostitutes. Different roads lead to a life of prostitution.

Types of Female Prostitution

Female prostitutes can solicit their services either in the street, bars, hotels, brothels, massage parlors, as **call girls** or **courtesans,** or out of an **escort agency** (Perkins and Bennett, 1985). These types of prostitutes differ with respect to the work setting, prices charged, and safety from violence and arrest. Streetwalkers make up about 20% of all prostitutes; bar girls are 15%; massage-parlor prostitutes are 25%; hotel prostitutes are 10%; brothel prostitutes are 15%; and call girls are 15% (Simon and Witt, 1982).

Streetwalkers. Also called street prostitutes, they are the most common type of prostitute and generally charge between $10 and $50. To attract customers, these prostitutes dress in tight clothes and high heels and may work on certain street corners. They are often victims of violence, rape, and robbery.

Streetwalkers generally approach customers and ask them questions such as "Looking for some action?" or "Do you need a date?" If the client is interested, the prostitute will suggest a price, and they will go to a place where the service can be provided (an alley, car, or cheap hotel room).

Typically, streetwalkers are looking to make as much money as possible, and they will try to "hustle" to make more (by suggesting more expensive types of sexual activity). Violence against prostitutes is highest in streetwalkers, which is why they usually have a pimp (we discuss pimps more later in this chapter).

Bar Prostitutes. Also called bar girls, they work in bars and hustle patrons for drinks and sexual activity. Since they usually work for the bar owner, they try to build up a client's bar bill. Unlike streetwalkers, bar girls have more protection from violence and police arrests. Bar prostitutes charge $20 to $100 or more, and the manager of the bar usually keeps 40–50% of the bar girls' nightly earnings.

Hotel Prostitutes. These prostitutes may be referred to hotel patrons by a bellboy or hotel manager. They keep 40–50% of the money they charge clients, while the hotel manager keeps the rest.

Brothel Prostitutes. Brothel prostitutes work out of a home or apartment that is shared by a group of prostitutes. A madam or pimp generally runs the house. Brothels offer more protection for prostitutes than the street. Services range from $20 to $100 or more.

In the United States, Nevada is the only state with counties in which brothels are legal. Prostitutes carry identification cards and are routinely examined for STDs. When a customer walks into a brothel in Nevada, he chooses a woman from a **line-up,** either when he first enters or after having a cocktail and spending some time talking to the girls. However, if a man takes too long to make his choice, the madam will usually choose a prostitute for him.

Once the choice is made, the prostitute and her client go to a room where he requests the services he wishes and she informs him of time limits and house prices for these services. The typical rate is $2 per minute, with more exotic services being more expensive. In Nevada brothels, conventional sexual intercourse has a time limit of 15 minutes and costs $30, while oral sex has a time limit of 20 minutes and costs $40 (Reynolds, 1986). After services are agreed on, the prostitute inspects the client's genitals for signs of sexually transmitted diseases and collects payment. A timer is set for the specified time period, and when time is up, the madam will knock on the door. Overtime can be negotiated during this time if desired. An average client spends $40 and stays for 20 minutes. The brothel prostitute keeps between 50 and 60% of her earnings, and the rest goes to the brothel owner.

call girl: A higher-class female prostitute who is often contacted by telephone and may either work by the hour or the evening.

courtesan: A prostitute who often interacts with men of rank or wealth.

escort agency: An agency set up to arrange escorts for unaccompanied males; sexual services are often involved.

In 1990, Julia Roberts played a prostitute in *Pretty Woman.* Unfortunately, prostitution in the movies is much more glamorous than it is in real life. In this movie, Richard Gere (a millionaire) hired her as a prostitute and later fell in love with her.

line-up: The lining up of prostitutes in a brothel so that when a client enters a brothel, clients can choose those prostitutes in which they are interested.

Brothels (such as the Mustang Ranch pictured here) are legal in certain counties in Nevada. Typically, several prostitutes live in a brothel with one madam.

bondage and discipline (B & D) prostitute: A prostitute who engages in sadomasochistic sexual services.

Massage Parlor Prostitutes. These prostitutes are masseuses who also provide sexual services. The owners of the massage parlor act as though they are unaware of this sexual activity. The most common service offered in massage parlors is fellatio or fellatio accompanied by sexual intercourse (Perkins and Bennett, 1985). Prices in massage parlors range from $20 to $50, and there is more protection through the use of security guards. However, the trade-off is that a parlor keeps more of the profit earned for working in their establishment.

Escort services, agencies that provide prostitutes who service as escorts, operate in ways similar to massage parlors, except that escort services do not have to take the responsibility for sexual activity since it does not occur on their premises.

Call Girls and Courtesans. Higher-class prostitution involves both call girls and courtesans. In 1993, Heidi Fleiss, the "Hollywood Madam," was arrested for her madam and prostitution activities with Hollywood actors and executives. Call girls are often contacted by telephone, and they may work by the hour or the evening. Some call girls charge $1,000 or more a night (Perkins and Bennett, 1985). Courtesans are also elite prostitutes, and many would argue that they are not prostitutes at all, even though they exchange sex for very expensive gifts.

Other Types of Prostitutes. Other, less common types of prostitutes include **bondage and discipline (B & D) prostitutes** who engage in sadomasochistic services, using such things as leather, whips, and/or chains. Women who specialize in B & D will advertise with pseudonyms like Madam Pain or Mistress Domination (Perkins and Bennett, 1985). B & D prostitutes may have dungeons, complete with whips, racks, and leg irons, and wear black leather, studded belts, and masks. Many do not have sexual intercourse with their clients at all but simply inflict pain or humiliation, which the client finds pleasurable. B & D prostitutes can make good money because few prostitutes choose to specialize in this area.

Lesbian prostitutes also exist, but we know little about them. Lesbian prostitutes tend to be older, and many take a younger woman on as a paid sexual partner (Perkins and Bennett, 1985). Lesbian prostitutes often have only one client at any given time.

Male Prostitutes

Some massage parlors are actually fronts for prostitution. On the outside they look like typical massage parlors. Often the owners claim they were unaware that any sexual activity was taking place on their property.

Male prostitutes who service women are referred to as "gigolos." Traditionally, gigolos are young men who are hired by older women. Male prostitutes who service other men are referred to as "hustlers" or "boys." Some male prostitutes service both men and women. In Personal Voices SF 3.2, one male prostitute discusses his work.

Male prostitutes who have sex with men may be otherwise heterosexual. For example, some bodybuilders hustle gay men for extra money (Klein, 1989). Ironically, many of these heterosexual, masculine bodybuilders are homophobic, which causes many conflicts between their attitudes and behaviors.

Approximately 50% of male prostitutes are homosexual, and 25% each are bisexual or heterosexual (Pleak and Meyer-Bahlburg, 1990). Like women, men tend to enter into the life of prostitution early, usually by the age of sixteen (with a range of anywhere from twelve to nineteen) (Cates and Markley, 1992). The majority of male prostitutes are between the ages of sixteen and twenty-nine and white (Earls and David, 1989).

Like female prostitutes, male street prostitutes have more psychopathology than nonprostitute peers (Simon et al., 1992), which may have to do with their dangerous and chaotic environments. They are more suspicious, mistrustful, hopeless, lonely, and iso-

Personal
V O I C E S

Male Prostitution

Stephen is an eighteen-year-old male prostitute who has been working on the streets since he was sixteen or seventeen years old. He identifies himself as gay and has sex primarily with male clients.

I only prostitute occasionally—about once or twice a week—but I used to do it nearly every day. I usually work for about two hours at a time until someone picks me up. I charge $40—sometimes $30—and make at the most $200 or $400 a week. Most of my money comes either directly or indirectly from prostituting. I also get an allowance from a past sugar daddy.

I got involved in prostitution because I knew I could make the money. It's taken as quite a common thing to do with the people I hang around with. None of us like it but it's easy money. I don't do it that much anymore but it's there if I need it. I'd like to stop but who's going to pay for the food? There's nothing else I can do to get an income.

The usual procedure is quite simple. First, I never really plan particular nights that I go out on, basically just whenever I need some money—which could even be in the middle of the day. So I just go to the park, take a seat and wait. Normally I don't have to wait too long—up to an hour at most. When a customer comes along we work out what's going to happen. We normally go to his place —sometimes mine. We do it, I get paid, he leaves his card or phone number and goes. Normally the whole thing usually takes about an hour and I usually see the guy again—in the next few weeks. But overall there is little preparation involved.

I don't mind doing this. It can be fun at times. You get to make a lot of money, working very small hours— normally everything goes well. If I thought there were better alternatives around (and there aren't), I'd take them, but at the present moment in time I don't mind.

Perkins and Bennett (1985:196–199)

---

lated than nonprostitutes. These feelings may develop out of the distrust that many have for their clients; clients may refuse to pay for services, hurt them, and/or force them to do things that they do not want to do. In fact, more than half of male prostitutes report that they are afraid of violence while they are hustling. The majority live alone, with no girlfriend, lover, or wife. This may be due to the type of lifestyle they lead or to the sense of hopelessness they carry with them. Although many would like to stop prostituting, they feel that they would not be able to find other employment (Simon et al., 1992).

Like the pimp for female prostitutes, many male prostitutes also have mentors, or "sugardaddies." One male prostitute said that his sugardaddy:

> *. . . showed me everything. He said that if you see something different you want, or you want to do this or you want to do that, you want to learn about the hustles, I'll show you. And he showed me bookstores, showed me the streets, the corners, the hustlers, the johns. He just showed me everything.*
>
> *Luckenbill (1986:288)*

When male prostitutes are asked what types of sexual behavior they engage in with their clients, 99% say that they perform fellatio, either alone or in combination with other activities; 80% say that they engage in anal sex, and 63% participate in **rimming** (Morse et al., 1992). In addition, many reported other activities including **water sports** and/or sadomasochistic behavior.

rimming: Oral stimulation of the anus.

water sports: Sexual services that involve urinating on or inside one's sexual partner.

In 1980, Richard Gere starred in *American Gigolo* as a male prostitute who was hired by older, wealthy women.

Predisposing Factors

Like females, males become prostitutes mainly for the money. However, many factors predispose a man to become a prostitute. Early childhood sexual experience (such as coerced sexual behavior) combined with a homosexual orientation increase the chances of choosing prostitution (Earls and David, 1989). Male prostitutes often experience their first sexual experience at a young age (approximately twelve years old) and have older partners. Some theorists believe that male homosexual prostitution is encouraged by accepting stereotypes that gay men have extraordinarily high sex drives and many casual sexual partners (Boyer, 1989). Sixty-four percent of male prostitutes had a male as their first sexual partner.

Male prostitutes have fewer career aspirations than nonprostitutes, abuse drugs and alcohol more often, and have greater alcohol use in their families. They also are likelier to view themselves as addicted to either drugs or alcohol than nonprostitutes (Cates and Markley, 1992). More than 50% of male prostitutes report using alcohol and a variety of drugs with their clients, and about half commonly accept drugs or alcohol as a trade for sex (Morse et al., 1992). Unlike female prostitutes, who tend to engage in drug use prior to prostitution, in males prostitution more often precedes drug use (Earls and David, 1989).

Like female prostitutes, male prostitutes have a history of troubled family backgrounds, as well as poor relationships with adult family members and friends (Price et al., 1984). They often perceive themselves as isolated, victimized, and unsuccessful in school and with peers. Still, one study found that family background was less important than was financial gain, early sexual experience, and homosexuality (Earls and David, 1989). Coleman (1989) found that faulty psychosexual and psychosocial development makes adolescent males more vulnerable to situational variables that may influence their decision to prostitute. Like female prostitutes, many roads lead men to prostitution.

Types of Prostitutes

Male prostitutes, like females, may engage in street hustling, bar hustling, and escort prostitution (Luckenbill, 1984). The differences between these types of prostitution are in income potential and personal safety.

Street and Bar Hustlers. These prostitutes solicit clients on the street or in parks that are known for the availability of the sexual trade. The majority of male prostitutes begin with street hustling, especially if they are too young to get into bars. Male prostitutes, like female prostitutes, ask their clients if they are "looking for some action." The average charge for male street prostitutes can be anywhere from $10 to $25 per trick.

Due to increasing fear and danger on the streets, many street hustlers eventually move into bars. One male prostitute said:

> *You got a lot of different kinds of assholes out there. When someone pulls up and says "get in," you get in. And you can look at their eyes, and they can be throwing fire out of their eyes, and have a knife under the seat. You're just in a bad situation. I avoid it by not hustling in the street. I hustle in the bars now.*
>
> *Luckenbill (1984:288)*

In the movie *My Own Private Idaho,* River Phoenix starred as a male prostitute who serviced older women and men.

Male prostitutes also report that bar hustling enables them to make more money than street hustling because they get to set their own prices. The average price for a bar trick ranges from $50 to $75.

Escort Prostitution. This is a natural progression after bar hustling. Escort prostitution involves finding someone who arranges clients but also takes a share of the profits. Each date that is arranged for an escort can bring from $150 to $200, and the prostitute usually keeps 60% for himself. However, escort services are not always well run or honest operations, and problems with escort operators may force a male prostitute to return to bar hustling. Compared with other types of male prostitutes, however, escort prostitutes are least likely to be arrested.

Call Boys. Like call girls, **call boys** keep a small group of clients with whom they have sex occasionally to earn money. Many of these prostitutes have had experience working both on the street and in bars, but they leave to go into business for themselves.

call boy: A higher-class male prostitute who is often contacted by telephone and may either work by the hour or the evening.

Transsexual and Transvestite Prostitutes. This type of prostitute is more common among male-to-female transsexuals than female-to-male (Perkins and Bennett, 1985). Some male transvestite prostitutes adopt an exaggerated female appearance and work beside female prostitutes (Elifson et al., 1993a), luring unsuspecting clients who do not always realize the prostitute is male. Most are homosexual males, but some are **she-males.** After being on hormonal therapy prior to sex reassignment surgery, they develop breasts but also still have their penis. In some places, these prostitutes are very popular.

she-male: A slang term that refers to a male who has been on hormones for sex reassignment but has not undergone surgery; she-males often have both a penis and breasts.

Adolescent Prostitutes

What we know about adolescent prostitution is disheartening. For adolescents who run away from home, prostitution offers a way to earn money and to establish their autonomy. Many of these adolescents have been sexually abused and have psychological problems, and many females among them have developed negative attitudes toward men (Gibson-Ainyette et al., 1988). Adolescent prostitution can have long-term psychological and sociological effects on the adolescents and their families (Landau, 1987).

It is estimated that between 750,000 and 1,000,000 minors run away from home each year in the United States and that more than 85% of these minors eventually become involved in prostitution (Landau, 1987). Others prostitute while living at home. See Personal Voices SF 3.3 for one adolescent's account of prostitution.

Pimps look for scared adolescent runaways at train and bus stations and lure them with promises of friendship and potential love relationships. A pimp will approach a runaway in a very caring and friendly way, offering to buy her a meal or give her a place to stay. At first, he makes no sexual demands whatsoever. He buys her clothes and meals and does whatever it takes to make her feel indebted to him. To him, all of his purchases are a debt she will one day repay. As soon as the relationship becomes sexual and the girl has professed her love for the pimp, he begins asking her to "prove" her love by selling her body. The girl may agree to do so only once, not realizing the destructive cycle she is beginning. This cycle is based on breaking down her self-esteem and increasing her feelings of helplessness. Male adolescents may enter into the life of prostitution in similar ways. Some may choose a life of prostitution to meet their survival needs or to support a drug habit.

Proponents of legalized prostitution in the United States believe that there should be minimum age requirements, similar to the age-of-consent restrictions (see Chapter 15). Outside the United States, adolescent prostitution is prevalent in many countries, such as Brazil and Thailand. Female adolescents in Brazil are drawn to prostitution primarily for financial and economic reasons (Penna-Firme et al., 1991). In Thailand,

Personal

VOICES

Adolescent Prostitution

Lynn—A thirteen-year-old adolescent prostitute

It was freezing cold that Friday afternoon as I stood on the street corner looking for buyers. The harsh wind made the temperature feel as though it were below zero, and I had been outdoors for almost two and a half hours already. I was wearing a short fake fur jacket, a brown suede miniskirt and spike heels. Only a pair of very sheer hose covered my legs, and I shook as I smiled and tried to flag down passing cars with male drivers. The cold bit at my skin, but if I had come out dressed in jeans and leg warmers, I'd have never gotten anywhere. After all, I was selling myself, and the merchandise had to be displayed.

Finally, a middle-aged man in an expensive red sports car pulled up to the curb. He lowered the car window and beckoned me over to him with his finger. I braced myself to start my act. Trying as hard as I could to grin and liven up my walk, I went over to his car, rested my chest on the open window ledge and said, "Hi ya, Handsome." It didn't matter what they looked like. That's what I always said. I had learned early on what they wanted to hear. And it usually worked.

He answered, "Hello, Little Miss Moffet. How'd you like Handsome to warm you up on a cold day like this?" I wished that I could have told him that I wouldn't like it at all. That even the thought of it made me sick to my stomach. He had called me Little Miss Moffet—they always made some remark about my age because I'm so young. Being thirteen has been a strong selling point for me. In any case, I hid my feelings and tried to look enthusiastic. They all want a happy girl who they think wants them.

So with the broadest smile I could manage, I answered, "there's nothing I'd like better than to be with you, Sir." I started to get into his car, but he stopped me, saying, "Not so fast, Honey, how much is this going to cost me?" I hesitated for a moment. I really wanted twenty dollars, but it had been a slow day and I had a strong feeling that this guy wasn't going to spring for it, so I replied, "Fifteen dollars, and the price of the hotel room."

We had sex in the same run-down dirty hotel that I always take my tricks to. It doesn't cost much, and usually that's all that really matters to them. Being with that guy was horrible, just like it always turns out to be. That old overweight man sweated all over me and made me call him Daddy the whole time. He really smelled bad too, once he got started. He may have thought that he was kissing me, but actually he just slobbered on my body. He kept calling me Marcy, and later he explained that Marcy was his youngest daughter.

Once he finished with me, the guy seemed in a big hurry to leave. He dressed quickly, and just as he was about to rush out the door, I yelled out, "But what about my money?" He pulled a ten-dollar bill out of his back pocket and laid it on the dresser, saying only, "Sorry, kid, this is all I've got on me right now."

At that moment I wished that I could have killed him, but I knew that there was nothing I could do. I was certainly in no position to take him on. Ten dollars wouldn't pay for a place for me to sleep in that night. If things got really bad, I thought that I could stay with a girl I knew for a night or two. But that didn't change the fact that I needed money to survive. The middle-class man in the expensive red sports car had cheated his thirteen-year-old hooker. That meant that I had to go back out on the street and brave the cold again in order to find another taker.

Landau (1987)

some parents sell their daughter's virginity for money or act as their managers and arrange jobs for them. One Thai prostitute said:

I started to work when I was fourteen years old. I worked at a "steakhouse," an entertainment place which was half a nightclub and half a restaurant. During this time, I went out with customers only when I wanted to. I had worked there for about one year before I met one man who took me to a brothel. This man was a friend of my friend. He said he would like to show me the beach. He took us four girls. He did not take us to the beach but to a brothel and he sold us to the owner. I had to stay in that house, in the brothel. Every day I had to receive fifteen men. If I did not obey the owner or did not get many men, I got beaten. I could finally escape from that brothel because one man helped me.

Pheterson (1989:64)

THE PIMP

Pimps play an important role in prostitution. In exchange for money, they offer the prostitute protection from both clients and the police. Pimps take all of the prostitute's earnings and manage the money, providing her with clothes, jewels, food, and sometimes, a place to live. Pimps recruit prostitutes and will often manage a group of prostitutes known as his "stable." His women are known by each other as "wives-in-law" (Ward et al., 1994).

A successful pimp can make a lot of money; in fact, one made $200,000 in a seven-month period (Reynolds, 1986). However, there are other motivating factors that attract men to pimping, including feelings of power and prestige within their peer group and the fact that the job is not particularly stressful for them. One pimp said:

I'm a professional gentleman of leisure. I have absolutely nothing to do. I stay in bed and take showers. I'm just a connoisseur of resting and a television freak. I do make more money than the President of the United States.

Quoted in Reynolds (1986:27)

THE CLIENT

As we mentioned earlier, clients of prostitutes are often referred to as "johns" or "tricks." The term *trick* has also been used to describe the behavior requested by the client. This term originated from the idea that the client was being "tricked" out of something, mainly his money (Goode, 1994).

What motivates people to go to prostitutes? An abnormally high sex drive? Variety in their sexual lives? Sigmund Freud believed that some men preferred sex with prostitutes because they were incapable of sexual arousal without feeling that their partner was inferior or a "bad" woman. Carl Jung went a step further and claimed that prostitution was tied to various unconscious **archetypes,** such as the "Great Mother." This archetype includes feelings of hatred and sexuality, which are connected to mother figures. This in turn leads men to have impersonal sex with partners whom they do not love or to whom they have no attraction.

archetypes: Ancient images that Carl Jung believed we are born with and influenced by.

We know more about the clients who visit female prostitutes, and so we will refer primarily to male clients below. These males visit prostitutes for a variety of reasons: for guaranteed sex, to eliminate the risk of rejection, for companionship, to have the undivided attention of the prostitute, because they have no other sexual outlets, because their sexual partners refuse to engage in certain behaviors, because of physical or mental handicaps, for adventure, curiosity, or to relieve loneliness (Rio, 1991). Married men sometimes seek out prostitutes when their wives will not perform certain behaviors, when they feel guilty about asking their wives to engage an activity, or when they feel the behaviors are too deviant to discuss with their wives.

Sadomasochistic behavior, with the woman as dominant and the man submissive, is the most common form of "kinky" sexual behavior requested from prostitutes (Goode, 1994). Other commonly requested behaviors from prostitutes include clients dressing as women, masturbating in front of nude clients, and rubber fetishes. One prostitute said:

> *These men couldn't have their wives do these things [that prostitutes do] because their wives would think that there was something wrong with them, and they would want a divorce. Some guys just can't get turned on by normal sex. This is the only way that they can get off.*
>
> *Zausner (1986:61) (quoted in Goode 1994:200)*

Clients may also seek out prostitutes because they are afraid of emotional commitments and want to keep things uninvolved; to build up their egos (many prostitutes fake orgasm and act very sexually satisfied); because they are starved for affection and intimacy; or because they travel a great deal or work in heavily male-populated areas (such as in the armed services) and desire sexual activity. Handicapped or disabled men may also use prostitutes for sex and companionship.

Kinsey found that clients of prostitutes are predominantly white, middle-class, married men who are between the ages of thirty and sixty (Kinsey et al., 1948). More recent research supports Kinsey's findings—the majority of men who visit prostitutes are middle-aged and most often married (Goode, 1994). They also tend to be regular or repeat clients; almost 100% go monthly or more frequently, and half of these go weekly or more frequently (Freund et al., 1991).

Male clients are most often solicited in their car on street corners in areas where female prostitution is common, but solicitation can also happen in hotels or transportation stops (Riccio, 1992). Of the clients who do seek male prostitutes, almost 75% of them also go to female prostitutes for sex (Morse et al., 1992). Overall, sexual intercourse and oral sex are the two most popular sexual behaviors requested from male prostitutes (Freund et al., 1991).

The majority of clients are not concerned with the police because enforcement of the law is usually directed at prostitutes rather the clients. At most, a client may be asked to testify in court against the prostitute, and if he does so, the charges against the client will be dropped (Rio, 1991). In fact, even though prostituting and engaging in sex with prostitutes are both illegal activities, arrests of the prostitute are 100 times greater than arrests of the client (James and Withers, 1975).

PROSTITUTION AND THE LAW

Prostitution is illegal in every state in the United States, except for certain counties in Nevada. However, even though it is illegal, it still exists in almost every U.S. city. In general, the government could address the issue of prostitution in two ways. Prostitution could remain a criminal offense, or it could be legalized and regulated. If prostitution were legalized, it would be subject to government regulation over such things as licensing, location, health standards, and advertising.

The biggest roadblock to legalized prostitution in the United States is that prostitution is viewed as an immoral behavior by the majority of people (Rio, 1991). Laws that favor legal prostitution would, in effect, be condoning this immoral behavior. Overall, however, the strongest objections to legalized prostitution are reactions to streetwalking. Today, the majority of Americans believe that the potential benefits of legalized prostitution should be evaluated.

Those who feel that prostitution should be legalized believe that this would result in lower levels of sexually transmitted diseases (because prostitutes could be routinely checked for STDs) and less disorderly conduct. Another argument in favor of legalization is that if prostitution were legal, the government would be able to collect taxes on the money earned by both prostitutes and their pimps. Assuming a 25% tax rate, this gross income would produce $20 billion *each year* in previously uncollected taxes.

Illegal prostitution is expensive in another way as well. For example, in 1971 the city of Seattle spent approximately one million dollars in an attempt to prohibit prostitution (James and Burstin, 1971). In California, it cost more than $1,000 to arrest and convict a single prostitute in the 1970s (Megino, 1977). Today, these numbers are probably much higher.

When college students were asked how they felt about the legalization of prostitution, those who scored high on scales of feminist orientation were more likely to view prostitution as an exploitation and subordination of women; they were also less likely to believe that women engage in prostitution for economic needs; and they believed that prostitution should not be legalized (Basow and Campanile, 1990). Overall, women are more likely than men to believe that prostitution should not be legalized and to see prostitution as exploitation and subordination of women.

In Nevada, where prostitution is legal (only in registered brothels, however, not streetwalking), the overwhelming majority of people report that they favor legalized prostitution. Ordinances for prostitution in Nevada vary by county, with each county responsible for deciding whether prostitution is legal throughout the county, only in certain districts, or not at all. For instance, there are no legal brothels in Reno or Las Vegas, perhaps because these cities enjoy large conventions and because many men attend these conventions without their wives. City officials felt that if a convention was held in a town with legalized prostitution, many wives might not want their husbands to attend; thus, there would be a decrease in the number of convention participants. Even so, there are several brothels near Reno and Las Vegas and also several that are close to state borders (such as near San Francisco). Usually, these are the largest of all the Nevada brothels. Brothels are locally owned small businesses that cater to both local and tourist customers.

Although prostitution in Nevada is not a criminal offense, there are laws against enticing people into prostitution, such as pimping or advertising for prostitutes (Reynolds, 1986). When a woman becomes a prostitute in Nevada, she is given a list of rules that she must follow.

Crackdowns on prostitution in other areas of the United States (where prostitution is not legal) often result in driving it further underground. This is exactly what happened in New York City in the 1980s. After law officials cracked down on prostitution in Manhattan, many brothels moved to Queens. Some of the prostitutes began operating out of "massage parlors" or private homes, which were supported through drug money.

There are many groups in the United States and abroad that are working for the legalization of prostitution. In San Francisco in 1973, an organization called COYOTE ("Call Off Your Old Tired Ethics") was formed by an ex-prostitute named Margo St. James to change the public's views of prostitution. Today, COYOTE is regarded as the best-known prostitutes' rights groups in the United States. To raise money, COYOTE throws extravagant Hookers' Masquerade Balls, which often raise more than $200,000.

COYOTE's mission is to repeal all laws against prostitution, to reshape prostitution into a credible occupation, and to protect the rights of prostitutes. They argue that contrary to popular belief, not all prostitution is forced—some women voluntarily choose to prostitute, and as a result, prostitution should be respected as a career choice.

Delores French, a prostitute, author, president of the Florida COYOTE group, and president of HIRE ("Hooking Is Real Employment") argues that:

> *A woman has the right to sell sexual services just as much as she has the right to sell her brains to a law firm when she works as a lawyer, or to sell her creative work to a museum when she works as an artist, or to sell her image to a photographer when she works as a model, or to sell her body when she works as a ballerina. Since most people can have sex without going to jail, there is no reason except old fashioned prudery to make sex for money illegal.*
>
> *Quoted in Jenness (1990:405)*

Organizations that support prostitution also appeared in the early 1970s in other parts of the world. In England, Helen Buckingham founded PLAN ("Prostitution Laws Are Nonsense") in 1975, and in West Germany similar groups were organized. CORP ("Canadian Organization for the Rights of Prostitutes") was founded in 1983 by Peggy Miller in Toronto, Canada. Many of these attempts at organization were met with resistance and, in some cases, even violence.

PROSTITUTION AND SEXUALLY TRANSMITTED DISEASES

Most prostitutes are knowledgeable about STDs and AIDS. They try to minimize their risks by using condoms, rejecting clients with STDs, and routinely taking antibiotics. However, while female prostitutes often do feel they are at risk of infection with STDs or AIDS with clients, they usually do not feel this way with their husbands or boyfriends (Dorfman et al., 1992). Condoms are used less frequently with their own sexual partners than with clients. Among homosexual male prostitutes, receptive anal intercourse without a condom is the most common mode of HIV transmission (Elifson et al., 1993a). Among female prostitutes, intravenous drug use is the most common mode of HIV transmission.

Eighty percent of prostitutes report using condoms with their clients (Pickering et al., 1992), 33% during oral sex (Freund et al., 1989; Freund et al., 1991). While 85% of prostitutes in Nairobi, Kenya, are infected with the AIDS virus, in the United States, only 13% of non-intravenous-drug-using prostitutes and 21% of intravenous-drug-using prostitutes are infected with AIDS (Lambert, 1988). These lower rates in the United States are presumably due to the higher use of condoms.

Less than half of the clients ask male prostitutes to wear a condom during sexual activity (Morse et al., 1992). When the client is the insertive partner, almost 50% wear condoms; if the prostitute is the insertive partner, 67% of clients do not ask them to wear a condom. In fact, many male prostitutes believe that clients may come to them primarily to engage in high-risk sexual behaviors. If the prostitute demanded his or her client wear a condom, the majority of clients say they would not engage in sex with them and would look for another prostitute.

Many opponents of legalized prostitution claim that legalization would lead to increases in the transmission of various STDs. However, STD transmission and prostitution have been found to have less of a relationship than you might think. Rates of STDs in Europe were found to *decrease* when prostitution was legalized and to increase when it was illegal (Rio, 1991). This is probably because when prostitution is legal, restrictions can be placed on the actual practice and medical evaluations are often required.

Many prostitutes take antibiotics sporadically to reduce the risk of STD infection; however, this practice has led some strains of STDs to become resistant to many antibiotics. Long-term use of antibiotics diminishes their effectiveness in an individual. Also, viral STDs, like AIDS and herpes, are not cured by antibiotics.

Male prostitutes have sex with multiple partners, are exposed to blood and semen, frequently practice high-risk sexual behaviors, and may continue prostituting even after they find out they are HIV positive. In addition, many have been infected with other STDs, which may make HIV transmission easier (Morse et al., 1991). Twenty-eight percent of male prostitutes who use IV drugs share needles with their clients. Clients of male prostitutes may serve to transmit HIV into the heterosexual community.

Outside the United States, increasing prostitutes' condom use and knowledge about AIDS has been an important task. There has been a lot of attention to AIDS transmission among prostitutes in Africa, for example. In Nigeria, AIDS prevention programs, which include health education, condom promotion and distribution, and a sexually transmitted disease treatment clinic, resulted in two-thirds of prostitutes using condoms (Williams et al., 1992). In Somalia, the prevalence of HIV in nonprostitute populations is 16 per 1,000, and in prostitutes, 30 per 1,000 (Corwin et al., 1991). Men and nonprostitute women knew more about AIDS and preventive information than female prostitutes. In Zaire, 99% of prostitutes reported hearing of AIDS, but only 77% knew that sex was the predominant mode of transmission (Nzila et al., 1991). Seventy-five percent of prostitutes had at least one sexually transmitted disease and 35% were HIV positive.

LIFE AFTER PROSTITUTION

Potterat et al. (1990) found that female prostitutes stay in the life for a relatively short time, usually four or five years. Some feel ready to leave, while others are forced out because of a deteriorating physical appearance or because of addiction to drugs or alcohol. Life after prostitution is often grim because most prostitutes have little money and few skills (which is why they turned to prostitution in the first place). In addition, there is usually little to show for the years they spent prostituting. Some seek psychotherapy as a way to handle leaving prostitution, and others spend a great deal of time in and out of prison for shoplifting or robbery. Tragically, some resort to suicide as a way out. An estimated 15% of suicides handled by large public hospitals are prostitutes (Reynolds, 1986).

Even so, there is a lot of disagreement about whether or not mandatory treatment programs should exist for prostitutes. If a person voluntarily chooses to engage in prostitution and he or she does not feel it is a problem, should the government require that he or she undergo treatment?

Even if it were possible to make prostitutes stop prostituting, few resources are available for them to establish a similarly salaried occupation (Rio, 1991). We need to evaluate how to best help a prostitute if he or she decides to stop prostituting. Also, since we have learned that the backgrounds of many prostitutes include a history of sexual abuse, familial violence, and alcohol abuse, perhaps we can offer intervention early on to help these people find alternative ways to make a living.

PROSTITUTION IN OTHER CULTURES

Prostitution exists all over the globe. Below we will explore how different countries handle prostitution and the different problems they encounter. In Focus on Diversity SF3.1, we present three women's stories about their lives of prostitution.

During World War II it is estimated that between 70,000 and 200,000 women from Japan, Korea, China, the Philippines, Indonesia, Taiwan, and the Netherlands were forcibly taken by the Imperial Japanese Army from their hometowns and put in brothels for Japanese soldiers. In 1993, Japan finally admitted to having forced women to prostitute themselves as **comfort girls,** and now these women are demanding to be compensated for the suffering they were forced to endure.

comfort *or* **hospitality girl:**
A prostitute in Japan or the Philippines who was forced into prostitution by the government to provide sex for soldiers.

In the Philippines, many prostitutes were similarly forced into prostitution and were called **hospitality girls.** Others freely chose to prostitute and may informally work when they need extra money or have lost their jobs. These women do not see themselves as prostitutes, and may have other jobs in addition to sporadic prostitution. The majority of police in the Philippines believe that prostitution is shameful for women (Guinto-Adviento, 1988).

Recently, a group named GABRIELA ("General Assembly Binding Women for Reforms, Integrity, Equality, Leadership, and Action") has formed in the Philippines in an attempt to fight prostitution, sexual harassment, rape, and battering of women. There are more than 100 women's organizations that belong to GABRIELA, which supports the economic, health, and working conditions of women. GABRIELA operates free clinics for prostitutes and also provides seminars and activities to educate the community about prostitution (West, 1989).

Thailand is often referred to as the prostitution capital of the world. In fact, organized "sex tours" to Thailand are run from many countries including the United States, Japan, Taiwan, South Korea, Australia, and Europe. In Bangkok, Thailand, there are at least 500,000 prostitutes. For many of these prostitutes, prostitution provides money to send to families and villages. Muecke (1992) claims that the culture views this as just another way for women to make money. Many Thai women have a *farang* (foreign tourist) boyfriend, with whom they have sex in exchange for money or material goods. These women are very good at manipulating these foreign boyfriends and may actually dominate the relationship, getting what they want in exchange for sex (Cohen, 1986). Sometimes teenage girls in Burma, just across the Thai border, are abducted and taken to Bangkok where their virginity is sold for about $40 each.

The World Health Organization estimates that by the year 2000, between two and four million Thais will be HIV positive; half of these will be women, and prostitution will be the key factor in HIV transmission. In the cheapest brothels in the Thai city of Chiang Mai (where most clients go), up to 80% of the prostitutes carry the AIDS virus (*The New York Times,* 1991). These numbers are high because Thai men do not generally wear condoms. Some maintain that they are immune from AIDS, and prostitutes are too afraid to ask their clients to wear condoms. Prostitution is so prevalent in Thailand that Thai men view a trip to a prostitute almost in the same regard as going to the store for

In Their Own Words

Prostitutes the world over have different opinions, attitudes, and concerns about prostitution. Below are several comments from prostitutes from different countries.

Frau Eva, Vienna, Austria

I have been in the business for eleven years and I founded the Austrian Association of Prostitutes. We organized in order to have a voice with public authorities.

Austria, like West Germany, is a federation of states. Prostitution politics differ from one state to another. In Vienna there are toleration zones and toleration times for prostitution. Prostitution is allowed only when it is dark outside and only in the police-controlled neighborhoods. Also, prostitution is allowed only in houses where no one lives, not even the prostitutes themselves, and only in areas where no kindergartens or schools or churches are nearby and where it is not too settled. Registration with the police is required, including registration of your work place. If you decide to deregister, it takes five years to get a letter of good conduct, something required for various jobs such as nursing or driving a taxi. The registration includes a photo, just like with criminals.

Prostitutes have to carry a little book when they're working that records weekly required medical checks. If you are shown to be sick, then your book is confiscated and you are not allowed to work. The police can demand to see your book anytime. At present prostitutes throughout Austria are also required to get a monthly AIDS test. If they fail to comply, they are fined up to the equivalent of $7,000 or given a prison sentence. There is no real choice of doctor because the AIDS test is free only when done by a state-designated agency.

Taxes are a major problem for us. Not only are we taxed, but we are taxed more heavily than other people since our income is overestimated. We don't have receipts and we are allowed few deductions. Despite the high taxes we are made to pay, they deny us representation and deny us social benefits. So, many women work illegally and avoid registration.

Mae, Bangkok, Thailand

Talking about the situation of prostitutes we might distinguish three main types: one is forced prostitutes, the second is so-called free prostitutes, and the third is migrant prostitutes abroad. Most of the first type who are forced are from the countryside and mostly they are deceived by agents or sold by their parents. The agents usually deceive them and say that they will be working in a restaurant or somewhere else other than prostitution. Often they are kept in a house of prostitution and not allowed to go out; they are given no freedom and many times little or no earnings. They will be beaten if they don't receive guests or if they don't obey the owner. And they have to work very hard; they have to receive at least ten to fifteen guests a day. The living condition is awfully bad. Many women have to sleep in one small room without enough air circulation; they get only two meals a day and not enough medical care. You can get away from the forced condition only by running away or when your body is not fit to work anymore. There was one very sad case of forced prostitution: In January, 1984, there was a big fire in Phuket Island in the South, in a tourist area. The fire broke out during the day and burnt down many houses in the area where there are a lot of brothels. Most of these brothels held forced prostitutes. Five women were burnt alive because they were sleeping after working the whole night and after taking sleeping pills. They were locked in behind iron gates and some of their bodies were chained.

Yolanda, Zurich, Switzerland

I'm a mother of four children. I have three children at school and one at home, plus I have my mother at home. I have been divorced for fourteen years, I raised the children all by myself, and I had to move very often because people discovered that I was a prostitute. So I'm not even entitled to my own private home. I have to pay three thousand francs rent in order to be left alone—yes, as soon as they know that you are a prostitute, they charge more; you are discriminated against. This is true for all women who are prostitutes. But we are the oldest profession of the world and everybody knows that. So it is time for all of us to stand up for our rights. We are people just like all other people. We have our profession, we make a living. A normal woman can buy what she wants, but we prostitutes cannot act as we want. We should be able to act as the others do! I also have a friend. We have a very good relationship. He comes and sees the children. I give my children love. They have parents. I didn't have that love when I was child but believe me, I am giving my children plenty of love.

Pheterson (1989:62–83)

A bargirl encourages a
client in Bangkok,
Thailand.

milk. It has also been suggested that since many Thais are Buddhists, they believe in
reincarnation and hope that they will not be a prostitute in their next life. This belief in
reincarnation often reduces the fear of death.

The survival of prostitution in Thailand has to do with the lack respect for women in
Thai culture. Women are viewed as pleasure providers. Interestingly, even with the
acceptability of prostitution, premarital sex is strictly prohibited. This double standard
may be most responsible for the success of prostitution.

In Amsterdam, Holland, there is a strip known as the Red Light District. The Red
Light District is crowded with sex shops, adult movie and live theater shows, and street
and window prostitutes. These prostitutes are named "window" prostitutes because they
sit behind a window and sell their bodies (see photo). There are approximately 200 such
windows in the Red Light District, which is one of the biggest tourist attractions in
Amsterdam. Travel services run tours through the Red Light District, although these
tourists do not generally use the prostitutes' services.

Window prostitutes in Amsterdam, Holland, solicit customers from their windows in the Red Light District.

In a beach resort bar in Thailand, a customer tries to examine a possible purchase.

Prostitution in Amsterdam is loosely regulated by authorities. Prostitutes pay taxes, get regular checkups, and participate in government-sponsored health and insurance plans (McDowell, 1986).

In Cuba, male prostitutes who solicit tourists are known as *jineteros. Jineteros* exchange sex for clothing or other luxuries brought over from other countries. In Havana, teenagers offer sex to older tourists in exchange for a six-pack of cola or a discotheque's cover charges. Female prostitutes in Cuba also ply the tourist trade. The government, in an attempt to encourage prostitution for the economy, requires that foreigners have a date to get into the discotheque, and they hire out women for this purpose.

Drugs and alcohol are also firmly tied to prostitution in several countries. In Scotland, the majority of prostitutes use both alcohol and illicit drugs, and many of the clients are also under the influence of drugs or alcohol at the time of contact (Plant et al., 1990). In Australia, 87% of female and 65% of male prostitutes use drugs other than alcohol or tobacco (Marshall and Hendtlass, 1986).

In New Zealand, prostitution is not illegal, but several laws exist to restrict solicitation to certain places. One prostitute in Dunedin, New Zealand, explained why it was difficult to get out of prostitution:

Lynne, a 24 year old, strolled into the sex industry from a normal childhood in a rural town in Southland. She has worked as an escort and in massage parlours for the last five years and would like nothing more than to "retire" and buy her own home in her old town. The trouble is the money is very, very good and it is hard for her to turn her back on such a highly-paid job. Besides, once you have worked in the business it is not easy to find a job elsewhere. How do you tell a prospective employer where you have worked for the last five years when you have no reference? How do you explain your range of skills in relating to people?

Otago Daily Times (1992:21)

Although prostitution exists all over the world, it is dealt with differently in each culture. We have much to learn from the way that other cultures deal with prostitution.

Summary

- According to sociologists, prostitution may have developed out of a patriarchal society.
- The primary motive for engaging in prostitution is for the money. Most prostitutes have been married at some point and have been prostituting for between three and ten years.
- There are several different types of female prostitutes, including streetwalkers; bar, hotel, and brothel prostitutes; call girls, and courtesans. Bondage-and-discipline and lesbian prostitutes also exist.
- Females may leave the life of prostitution for a variety of reasons, including deteriorating physical appearance or health, drug or alcohol addiction, or a desire to find other employment. Unfortunately, life after prostitution is often difficult because of a lack of money and skills.
- There are different types of male prostitutes. They may engage in street or bar hustling, escort prostitution, or as call boys. Transvestite and transsexual prostitutes also exist. The majority of males begin in street prostitution and may eventually move into bar and escort prostitution.
- Male prostitutes are often referred to as hustlers, gigolos, or boys. They can be heterosexual, homosexual, or bisexual.
- Adolescents may enter the life of prostitution after they run away from home, in order to make money. Many of them have been sexually abused and have psychological problems. Outside of the United States, adolescent prostitution is prevalent.
- Pimps play an important role in prostitution. They offer protection, recruit other prostitutes, may manage a group of prostitutes, and try to keep prostitutes hustling to make money. Successful pimps can make a great deal of money and often feel powerful in their role as a pimp.
- Clients go to prostitutes for a variety of reasons including guaranteed sex, to eliminate the risk of rejection, for companionship, to have the undivided attention of the prostitute, because there are no other sexual outlets, for adventure or curiosity, or to relieve loneliness.
- Many people believe that prostitution should be legalized so that it can be subjected to government regulation and taxation. However, others think that it would be immoral to legalize prostitution.
- Prostitutes are at high risk for acquiring STDs and AIDS. Overall, they are knowledgeable about these risks and use condoms some of the time. STDs have been found to decrease when prostitution is legal and to increase when it is illegal.
- Different groups, such as COYOTE, have organized to change the public's views of prostitution and to change the laws against it. These groups are also common outside the United States.
- Prostitution exists all over the world. Comfort girls existed in Japan during World War II. Hospitality girls were used for the same purposes in the Philippines.
- Although prostitution is illegal in Thailand, it is still referred to as the prostitution capital of the world. There are at least 500,000 male and female prostitutes in Bangkok, Thailand.

R eflections on Sexuality

1. How do sociologists view prostitution?
2. What factors have been found to be correlated with a life of prostitution?
3. What do we know about female prostitutes? Male prostitutes? Adolescent prostitutes?
4. Differentiate between the various types of male and female prostitutes.
5. What role do pimps play in prostitution?
6. What are your feelings about treatment aimed at societal interventions to improve conditions for men and women who prostitute by improving their education and training skills?
7. Describe the arguments for and against legalized prostitution.

S uggested Readings

LANDAU, E. (1987) *On The Streets: The Lives of Adolescent Prostitutes.* New York: Julian Messner Publishers.

SEIGLE, C. S. (1993) *Yoshiwara: The Glittering World of the Japanese Courtesan.* Honolulu: University of Hawaii Press.

WEST, D. (1993) *Male Prostitution.* New York: Naworth Press.

ZAUSNER, M. (1986) *The Streets: A Factual Portrait of Six Prostitutes as Told in Their Own Words.* New York: St. Martin's Press.

4

Sexual Images

EROTIC REPRESENTATIONS IN HISTORY

SEXUALITY, MEDIA, AND THE ARTS

GRAPHIC IMAGES: PORNOGRAPHY AND THE PUBLIC'S RESPONSE

SUMMARY

REFLECTIONS ON SEXUALITY

SUGGESTED READINGS

Without an element of the obscene there can be no true and deep aesthetic or moral conception of life. . . . It is only the great men who are truly obscene. If they had not dared to be obscene they could never have dared to be great.

—*Havelock Ellis*

Modern life is full of visual media. Magazines, newspapers, book covers, compact disc and videocassette packaging, cereal boxes and food products, even medicines are adorned with pictures of people, scenes, or products. Advertisements peer at us from magazines, billboards, buses, matchbook covers, and anywhere else that advertisers can buy space. Television, movies, computers, and other moving visual images surround us almost everywhere we go, and we will only depend upon them more as information technology continues to develop. We live in a visual culture whose images we simply cannot escape.

Many of these images are explicitly or subtly sexual. Barely clothed females and shirtless, athletic males are so common in our advertising media that we scarcely notice them anymore. The majority of movies today, even those directed at children, have sexual scenes that would not even have been permitted in movie theaters fifty years ago. The humor in television situation comedies has become more and more sexual, and nudity has begun to appear on prime-time network television shows. In addition, graphic depictions of sexuality, which until recently could only be found in adult bookstores and theaters, are now available at neighborhood video stores.

What is the effect of living in a society that is so saturated with sexual images? That is the question we will address in this chapter. Recently, there has been controversy over the effects of pornographic images on society, and scholars, presidential commissions, and the Supreme Court have all struggled to determine which types of sexual images should be acceptable and which might be harmful to society. Yet there is a tendency to overemphasize explicit sexual images and to neglect the sexualized images that appear almost everywhere in modern society.

We begin this chapter with a brief history of erotic representations. Next we take a look at how erotic representations are presented to us every day in books, television, advertising, and other media. Only then do we turn to the graphic sexual images of pornography. All along we will try to ask ourselves the question: What influence do these representations have on us? What are they trying to show us about ourselves? How do they subtly affect the way we think about men, women, and sexuality?

EROTIC REPRESENTATIONS IN HISTORY

Human beings have been making representations of themselves and the world around them since ancient times. Many of the earliest cave drawings and animal bone sculptures that were found have been representations of the human form, usually scantily dressed or naked. Often the poses or implications of the art seem explicitly erotic. Yet it is hard to know to what degree these images were considered erotic by preliterate people, for early erotic art was also sacred art whose purpose was to represent those things most important to early people—the search for food and the need to reproduce (Lucie-Smith, 1991). However, by the dawn of the great ancient civilizations such as Egypt, people were drawing erotic images on walls or pieces of papyrus just for the sake of eroticism (Manniche, 1987). Since that time, human beings have been fascinated with representations of the human form when naked or engaged in sexually explicit behavior; in turn, many governments have been equally intent on limiting or eradicating them.

Erotic representations have appeared in most societies throughout history, and they have been greeted with different degrees of tolerance. Ancient cultures often created public erotic tributes to the gods, including temples dedicated to phallic worship. India's sacred writings are full of sexual accounts, and some of the most explicit public sculptures in the world adorn its temples. Greece is famous for the erotic art that adorned

Early erotic art was often public art. The city of Pompeii included large, erect phalluses on street corners, and erotic frescoes adorned many people's homes.

objects like bowls and urns. When archaeologists in the eighteenth and nineteenth centuries uncovered the Roman city of Pompeii, buried in a volcanic blast in A.D. 79, they were startled and troubled to find that this jewel of the Roman Empire, which they had so admired, was full of brothels, had carved phalluses protruding at every street corner, and had private homes full of erotic **frescoes** (Kendrick, 1987). Authorities hid these findings for years by keeping the erotic objects in locked museum rooms and publishing pictures of the city where the phalluses were made to taper off like candles.

Not all sexual representations are explicit, and many of our greatest artists and writers included sexual components in their creations. The plays of Shakespeare, though hardly shocking by today's standards, do contain references to sexuality and the sexual act. The art of Michelangelo and Leonardo da Vinci also included graphic nudity without being titillating. Still, in their day, these pictures caused controversy; in the sixteenth century, for example, priests went around painting loincloths over nude pictures of Jesus and the angels. What one society or one period in history sees as obscene, another or later society can view as great art.

fresco: A type of painting done on wet plaster so that the plaster dries with the colors incorporated into it.

The Invention of Pornography

Most sexual representations created throughout history had a specific purpose, whether it was to worship the gods, to adorn pottery, or later, to criticize the government or religion. Very little erotic art seems to have been created simply for the purpose of arousing the viewer, as much of modern erotic art is. So most of history's erotic art cannot be considered "pornographic" in the modern sense (Hunt, 1993).

Pornography, which tends to portray sexuality for its own sake, did not emerge as a distinct, separate category until the middle of the eighteenth century. The word *pornography* did not even appear in the *Oxford English Dictionary* until 1857, and then it meant any offensive material, sexual or not. For most of history, sexuality itself was so imbedded in religious, moral, and legal contexts that it was not thought of as a separate sphere of life (Kendrick, 1987). Explicit words and pictures (along with other forms of writing, such as political writings) were controlled in the name of religion or in the name of politics, not in the name of public decency (Hunt, 1993). For example, **obscenity** was illegal among the Puritans (punishable originally by death and later by boring through the tongue with a hot iron) because it was an offense against God. That is why, before the nineteenth century, **hard-core** sexual representations were extremely rare. Such representations are only possible when sexuality is seen as a thing in and of itself.[1]

pornography: Any sexually oriented material that is not acceptable to the viewer; any sexual depictions that are in violation of the law.

obscenity: A legal term for materials that are considered offensive to standards of sexual decency in a society.

Another strong influence on the development of pornography was the development of the printing press and the mass availability of the printed word (sexually explicit books were printed within fifty years of the invention of movable type). For most of history, written or printed work was available only to a small elite because only they could afford it and, more important, only they could read.

Historians of pornography trace the modern pornographic novel back to the Renaissance Italian writer Pietro Aretino (1492–1556). The dialogue he created in his novel, *Ragionamenti,* became the model for almost all pornographic literature for the next century (Findlen, 1993). (Interestingly, Aretino was also one of the first authors in history to make his living entirely from writing.) Accompanying Aretino's prose was a

hard-core: A reference to explicit, genitally oriented sexual depictions; the opposite of soft-core, which displays sexual activity without explicit portrayal of genital penetration.

---

[1] Kendrick (1987) suggests that whereas in the past sex was integrated into other parts of life such as religious behavior or marital relationships, now we have stripped it of any meaning other than a pleasurable physical activity creating, as he puts it, "a notion of sex something like advanced calisthenics."

series of now famous pictures of various sexual positions (drawn by Marcantonio Raimondi), which have become known as "Aretino's positions" and which enjoyed widespread (if secretive) distribution during the Renaissance.

The most famous pornographic work of the eighteenth century was John Cleland's *Memoirs of a Woman of Pleasure* (better known as *Fanny Hill*), first published in 1748. Cleland made no pretenses of being political or philosophical, and his book contains neither humor nor satire; his work was aimed at sexually arousing the reader. Before Cleland, most sexually explicit books were about prostitutes because these women did "unspeakable" things (that could be described in graphic detail) and because they could end up arrested, diseased, and alone, thereby reinforcing society's condemnation of their actions. In fact, the word *pornography* literally means "writing about harlots."

Cleland's book was also about a prostitute, but it was radical in that the prostitute ends up married and happy, on a trip to an imagined pagan paradise (not even a Christian one)! *Fanny Hill* has a long history of being suppressed and censored; even when it *was* printed, a scene describing two men engaged in anal intercourse was usually left out (Trumbach, 1993). Although the book was first published in 1748, it was a court case over *Fanny Hill* in Massachusetts in 1966 that established the modern definition of pornography in the United States, as we will see below.

Cases like *Fanny Hill* teach us that to really understand the meaning of "pornography" we must understand the desire of the government and other groups to control it and suppress it. In other words, the story of pornography is not just about publishing erotic material, but also about the struggle between those who try to create it and those who try to stop them. Walter Kendrick (1987), who wrote a history of pornography, tried to capture that idea when he wrote that "'pornography' names an argument, not a thing." Both sides must be included in any discussion of pornography; without those who try to suppress it, pornography just becomes erotic art. In fact, the term **erotica**, often used to refer to sexual representations that are not pornographic, really just means pornography that a particular person finds acceptable. One person's pornography can be another person's erotica. As we shall see in this chapter, the modern arguments about pornography are some of the most divisive in the country, pitting feminists against feminists, allying some of the most radical feminist scholars with fundamentalist preachers of the religious right, and pitting liberals against liberals and conservatives against conservatives in arguments over the limits of free speech.

It is not only sexually explicit representations, as we noted, that are of interest to us. Sexuality is present in almost all our **media**, from the sultry model sensuously sipping a bottle of beer to the offhand sexual innuendos that are a constant part of television situation comedies. In fact, the entertainment media seems to be almost obsessed by sexual imagery; Michel Foucault, the French philosopher and historian of sexuality, has called it a modern compulsion to speak incessantly about sex. Before we discuss the sexually explicit representations of "pornography" with the heated arguments they often inspire, let us turn to the erotic images that present themselves to us in the popular media every day.

erotica: Sexually oriented media that are considered by a viewer or a society as within the acceptable bounds of decency.

media: All recorded forms of communication.

SEXUALITY, MEDIA, AND THE ARTS

mass media: Media intended for a large, public audience.

Over the last twenty-five years, representations in the **mass media** have become more explicitly erotic. We like to believe that we are so used to the media that we are immune to its influences. Does sex (or violence) on television, for example, really influence how

"Sex sells," and so advertisers use it.

promiscuous and violent our society becomes? Do the constant sexual stereotypes paraded before us in commercials and advertisements really help shape our attitudes toward gender relations? Does constant exposure to sexual images erode family life, encourage promiscuity, and lead to violence against women, as some conservative and feminist groups claim? Also, if we find out that sex and violence in the media does have an effect on how we behave, what should we do about it?

In this section, we will look at the history of how each medium has tested the boundaries of erotic representation and how the government and concerned citizens have tried to censure or control that medium.

Erotic Literature

Although the portrayal of sexuality is as old as art itself, *pornography* and *censorship* are more modern concepts, products of the mass production of erotic art in society. Throughout Western history, reactionary forces (usually the clergy) often censored nudity in public art, especially when it featured religious figures. The genitals of the nudes on Michelangelo's Sistine Chapel, for example, were painted over with loincloths and wisps of fabric by clerics. Still, since there was no way to mass produce these kinds of art, the reactions of the Church were on a case-by-case basis.

Pornography in the modern sense began to appear when printing became sophisticated enough to allow fairly large runs of popular books, beginning in sixteenth century. Intellectuals and clergy were often against this mass production of books. They worried that if everybody had books and could learn about things for themselves, why would anyone need teachers, scholars, or theologians? Religious and secular intellectuals quickly issued dire warnings about the corrupting effects of allowing people direct access to knowledge, especially provocative religious, political, or sexual materials, and set up mechanisms of control—censorship—to keep control over them (Findlen, 1993). By the seventeenth century, the Church was pressuring civic governments to allow them to inspect bookstores, and soon forbidden books, including erotica, were being removed; such books then became rarer and more valuable, and a clandestine business arose in selling them. It was this struggle between the illicit market in sexual art and literature and the forces of censorship that started what might be called a pornographic subculture, one that still thrives today.

Today, erotic literature of almost any kind is readily available. The sexual scenes described in the average romance novel today would have branded it as pornographic only a few decades ago, and the most prolific publishing house in the entire country is one that publishes exclusively sexually explicit books. One would think that such books would be the main targets of people trying to censor sexually explicit materials. Yet, most censorship battles over the written word are not fought over explicitly sexual material.

According to the Office for Intellectual Freedom of the American Library Association, the most censored books in the United States are *The Diary of Anne Frank, To Kill a Mockingbird, Of Mice and Men, 1984, Slaughterhouse Five, Catcher in the Rye, The Adventures of Huckleberry Finn, The Color Purple,* all the works of Stephen King and Judy Blume, and dictionaries such as *Webster's Seventh, Random House, Doubleday,* and *American Heritage* for defining "dirty" words (Pally, 1994). A number of groups, such as the National Coalition on Television Violence and the American Family Association, have been vocal in trying to censor literature and other media that offends their sense of decency; for example, they have been very active in trying to stop the distribution of books and literature that teach children about AIDS or sexuality. We discuss these groups in more detail later.

Although the early court cases that established the American legal attitudes toward pornography in the United States were often about books (especially about sending them through the mail), modern debates about pornography tend to focus more on explicit pictures and movies. Still, it was the erotic novel that first established pornographic production as a business in the Western world and provoked a response from religious and governmental authorities.

Television and the Movies

America has had a long love affair with the movies, going back to silent pictures. The advent of television has only increased our dependence on visual media, and it is probably no exaggeration to say that television is the single strongest influence on the modern American outlook toward life.

Television allows us to sit in the comfort of our home and have the world delivered to us. But the world we see on TV is only a small slice of the real world; television, like the movies, edits and sanitizes the world it displays. For example, although literally hundreds of acts of sexual intercourse are portrayed or suggested on television shows and in the movies every day, we rarely see a couple discuss or use contraception, discuss the morality of their action, contract a venereal disease, worry about AIDS, accidentally get pregnant, become impotent, or regret the act afterward. Most couples fall into bed shortly after initial physical attraction and take no time to build an emotional relationship before becoming sexually active. On soap operas, for example, extramarital sex is portrayed eight times more often than sex between spouses (Dietz and Strasburger, 1991). Homosexual contact, fetishes, transvestism, or variations of heterosexual intercourse are virtually absent on television, and only recently has homosexuality begun to appear in any serious way in Hollywood films. Although these trends are beginning to change somewhat, the sex we see on in the visual media still has only superficial resemblance to the sexuality of most people.

Yet television and movie producers believe that "sex sells," and so they fill their programming with it. What is seen every day on television soap operas would not have even been allowed in movie theaters fifty years ago. According to a study by Louis Harris and Associates (1988), Americans view approximately 27 instances of sexual behavior per hour on television, and networks broadcast about 65,000 sexual references per year. Though nudity is still rare on network television and though certain words are taboo, virtually any type of sex act can be hinted at or discussed, and many Americans can see more graphic sex on cable stations. Still, the networks have been trying to push as much nudity and sexual innuendo into their programming as possible. The 1992 season saw an episode of *Seinfeld* where the four main members of the cast had a contest to see who could go the longest without masturbating; the 1993 season introduced *NYPD Blue,* which featured nude lovemaking scenes showing female and male buttocks (and many stations refused to air the show at first); and at the last minute, the producers of the *Sisters* cut the 1992 season's opening dialogue, which showed a group of women in a steambath discussing their orgasms.

In an attempt to capture viewers back from cable stations, the major networks have been *increasing* the sexual content of their programming. The sexual content of soap operas has increased 103% since 1980 (Dietz and Strasburger, 1991). Television talk shows have also become decidedly more graphic in their content. As the number of talk show hosts has increased, so has competition for provocative guests, and a good sexual confession—men who cross-dress, mothers who sleep with their teenage sons' best friends, women who leave their spouses for other women, teenage prostitutes—are guaranteed at least to catch some attention.

Television magazine shows that imitate news reports but concentrate on two or three stories (e.g., *Hard Copy, A Current Affair*) often search for stories with lurid

Over time, television has used more and more explicitly sexual images. Soap operas, for example, have used sexual suggestion for years.

content, and if there is a sexual scandal or a rape accusation in the news, they are sure to feature it. Even the "hard" news shows, such as the networks' evening news reports, have turned a corner in their willingness to use graphic descriptions of sexual events. News shows, after all, also need ratings to survive, and one way to interest audiences is to report legitimate news stories that have a sexual content in a graphic and provocative way. These news reports deliver the sexually explicit information with the implicit message that they disapprove of it; but they still deliver it. As Walter Goodman (1991) wrote in *The New York Times:* "Television is like a brothel with rooms set aside for lectures on why visitors should stay out of brothels."

The AIDS epidemic was a key factor in opening up the way news organizations began to speak about sexuality (for example, the word *condom* would never have appeared on a major news network before AIDS). Another type of landmark came in the early 1990s. The rape trial of William Kennedy Smith (a member of the Kennedy family) and the accusations of sexual harassment against Supreme Court nominee Clarence Thomas, two of the biggest stories of the year, were covered by most evening news shows in explicit detail (Goodman, 1991). These incidents broke precedent and allowed the networks to use language and sexual references that would have been unthinkable just a few years before. The new frankness on television can, of course, be used to transmit important sexual information (such as safe-sex information), and it can help demystify sexuality through educational programming (see Sexuality Today SF4.1).

SEXUALITY *Today*

Sex Talk on the Radio *Janell L. Carroll, Ph.D.*

I've always believed that sex education was important. I've been doing it for over ten years. In 1990, I moved from Philadelphia to Lawrence, Kansas, which was quite an adjustment for me. Teaching sexuality became more of a challenge, you might say. Opponents to sexuality education were much more vocal and determined to do whatever it took to limit access to sex education. In September of 1992, I was hired by a very popular AM radio station in Kansas City to do a nightly call-in talk show called *Let's Talk About Sex* (featuring the song by Salt 'n' Pepa, of course). The show aired weeknights from 9 to 11 P.M. At first, it was slow going. I think people were shocked more than anything else to hear "sex" on the radio. But after only two months on the air, the show quickly became the most popular of all the shows on the station. Ratings were better than I ever could have imagined. People were calling in, asking questions, and really listening to the answers! It quickly became apparent to both myself and the station managers that Kansas City was really ready for this type of show.

What surprised me the most was how many fairly basic questions people had about human sexuality: What's the best way to avoid pregnancy? How does a woman reach orgasm? How can I talk to my partner about sex? Is my penis long enough? But also, there was a great deal of relief heard on the show. People who had been carrying around fears about their own sexuality were finally able to breathe a sigh of relief to know that they were "normal." One woman who called in had always thought of herself as inadequate because of her inability to orgasm during sexual intercourse. Imagine her relief when she learned that most women needed additional clitoral stimulation to reach orgasm during sexual intercourse. She had never heard this before!

In May of 1993, the first problems began. Some people felt the show was too racy, deferential, or just plain immoral. I was called just about every name in the book and received many negative letters. One woman blamed me for everything from the floods of 1993 to war, starvation, and homicide. "See what happens when you talk about sex?" Yet, there were also many positive and supportive letters and calls. Unfortunately, the voices in support are often not as vocal as those in opposition.

One man decided to make it his mission to force the station to cancel the show. He did this by contacting all of the advertisers and telling them false information about the show (saying that I promoted teenagers having sex, for instance). Suddenly, *Let's Talk About Sex* was being compared to other controversial programs such as the *Howard Stern Show* and the *Rush Limbaugh Show*. Advertisers were warned not to advertise on any of these controversial programs.

Unfortunately, in August of 1993, the pressure was too great for the station and they decided to pull the plug. There were many reasons they decided to cancel, but most important was the controversial nature of the show. I was really disappointed. It felt like the show was such a great service to the Kansas City area—so many people called in and even more were listening every night.

Today, I'm still working on putting together a national radio show on sexuality, but in this social climate it will take patience. Opposition to sex education is strong, and more importantly, vocal. I think the most important thing I've learned is that it's very important to stand up and fight for what you believe in—it can very easily be taken away from you.

However, the vast majority of sexual references are made to titillate, not inform, and sex is portrayed on television in an artificial and unrealistic light. When a news reporter announces, "Tonight at five-thirty: Sex in the Media," you can bet that the report will include either scantily clad women or a hint of sexual scandal; the news, like other forms of entertainment, uses sexual images as a way to attract viewers, even in the guise of educating the public about sex (see Sexuality Today SF4.2).

Television, Film, and Minority Sexuality

As sexually explicit as the visual media have become, they have a very poor track record in their portrayals of certain sexual behaviors, such as homosexuality, and certain minorities, such as the elderly, the disabled, and racial and ethnic minorities. In the case of homosexuality, television and the movies have (until very recently) been reluctant to treat gays and lesbians as other than perverts and criminals. Right before the 1991 Academy Award presentations, the Gay and Lesbian Alliance Against Defamation (GLAAD) issued a statement accusing the film industry as a whole of homophobia and of misinforming the public about homosexuality (*Philadelphia Daily News,* 1991). They were particularly upset by two very popular movies: *Silence of the Lambs,* in which a male cross-dresser is shown as a murdering psychopath, and *Basic Instinct,* where a lesbian was the killer. These movies implicitly link homosexuality to murder and mental illness, precisely the kind of stereotypes the gay rights movement has been trying to overcome.

When homosexuals are not being portrayed as murderers in movies and television, they have often been used for comic relief or portrayed as doomed, twisted, or sick. More often, homosexuality has just been ignored, as in the 1940s and 1950s when films eliminated the gay angle of many books and plays that were made into movies (such as Tennessee Williams's *Cat on a Hot Tin Roof*). What GLAAD wanted in its protest at the Oscars was to see homosexuals portrayed as ordinary people in ordinary roles, where their homosexuality is not made an issue but is simply another part of the character's life, like being tall, a father, or an African American. This is beginning to happen; more mainstream movies such as *Philadelphia,* which portrayed the struggles of a gay lawyer unfairly fired because he had AIDS, or *The Crying Game,* which shows a homosexual cross-dresser, are beginning to present explicit, if not typical, accounts of modern gay life.

The sexual lives of ethnic and racial minorities have also been neglected by the major media. African Americans have complained for many years that television and movies tend to portray them as criminals, drug pushers, or pimps; only recently have black actors begun appearing in stable roles and on situation comedies, although organizations like the NAACP still complain that these programs do not portray a realistic account of African-American life (*Jet,* 1991). However, even with the gains made in those areas, black sexuality still seems to be a taboo subject. African Americans are rarely given romantic leads and are not usually portrayed as romantic objects; even though there are a number of African-American situation comedies, at this writing there is not a single major dramatic show on television that is predominantly about African Americans. Insofar as the sexual lives of African Americans seem to be shown at all, it is through portrayals of single mothers and African-American prostitutes. On the other hand, at least African Americans are shown on television. Other minorities, such as Asian Americans, Latinos, and Native Americans, are rarely portrayed at all, and certainly not as romantic leads or as having sexual lives. Sex on television is written by, performed by, and tells the story of white Americans.

Things are a little better for minorities in the movies. African-American filmmakers such as Spike Lee have begun to release movies showing African-American sexual life

There has been some progress in portrayals of sexual minorities on TV and in the movies. In the sitcom *The Golden Girls,* elderly women were shown with sexual desires and making sexual jokes. Tom Hanks won an Academy Award for his sensitive portrayal of a gay man with AIDS in *Philadelphia.*

from the African-American perspective, and the popularity of black film stars such as Wesley Snipes and Denzel Washington have broken the barrier and encouraged movies with African-American romantic leads. Such portrayals are still rare, however, and with few exceptions mainstream movies rarely show minorities as romantic leads in movies where whites appear. Can you think of a movie (outside of Kung Fu movies) where an Asian man is a romantic lead?

Some progress has been made, and there are some advantages to being able to talk frankly about sex on television today. For example, television shows have broken sexual stereotypes, such as *The Golden Girls,* a sitcom that showed that older women also have sexual desires, make sexual jokes, and engage in sexual behaviors. The situation comedy *Roseanne* includes an openly lesbian character, and controversy was stirred when Roseanne was filmed in a deep, lingering kiss with Mariel Hemingway, who was playing a lesbian trying to pick her up in a bar; despite the worries of network executives, few viewers complained. So television is changing and trying to offer more realistic portrayals of minority sexuality.

Television, Film, and Gender

Television offers its viewers sexual information both explicitly (through such things as news, documentaries, and public service announcements) and implicitly (through the

SEXUALITY *Today*   *SF4.2*

Scandal!

Television news magazines, supermarket tabloids, and now even the more mainstream newspapers and magazines have become preoccupied with scandals. In fact, the term *tabloid journalism* is used to refer to sensational treatments of scandals or people's private lives in the guise of journalism. Scandal sells, and sex sells; so sexual scandals are every tabloid journalist's dream.

Scandals are not new. Shelly Ross (1988) has written a book about scandals in American political history, covering more than twenty-five major scandals, most of which involved sex. She tells of Lord Cornbury, Governor of Colonial New York in 1702, who presided over the state assembly wearing a dress; George Washington's love letter to his neighbor's wife; Alexander Hamilton's account of being sexually blackmailed; Andrew Jackson dissolving his entire cabinet over a sex scandal involving the wife of Secretary of War John Eaton; the illegitimate children of Benjamin Franklin, Grover Cleveland, and Warren Harding; and innumerable other presidential extramarital affairs (such as President Kennedy's with the girlfriend of top organized crime boss Sam Giancana). Sexual scandals have become a regular part of American popular culture, whether they involve politicians, entertainment figures, or other prominent citizens. Below are quick profiles of a few select sexual scandals of the last few years.

In July 1991, champion heavyweight boxer Mike Tyson persuaded Desiree Washington, an eighteen-year-old college freshman and Miss Black America contestant, to accompany him to his room. She later testified that Tyson raped

Mike Tyson

her despite her pleas to stop. Tyson was found guilty of one count of rape and two counts of criminal deviate conduct; he was sentenced to two six-year sentences to be served concurrently and a $30,000 fine. He was released from prison in April 1995.

Amy Fisher, a sixteen-year-old high school student, was having an affair with Joseph Buttafuoco, an automobile repairman from Long Island, New York. In May 1992, Fisher stalked Buttafuoco's wife, Mary Jo, eventually shooting her in the face. Fisher claimed that her lover, Joseph Buttafuoco, had encouraged her to shoot his wife, while Buttafuoco

Joey Buttafuoco

himself denied having the affair at all. Fisher, by then known as the "Long Island Lolita," eventually pled guilty to reduced charges that sent her to prison for at least five years. Buttafuoco was then brought to trial, pled guilty to one count of statutory rape, and received the maximum sentence of six months in prison, five years probation, and a $5,000 fine. The story received so much notoriety that the case became the subject of three television films, a musical play, and even a comic book.

Michael Jackson, arguably the most recognizable and popular entertainer in the world, was accused of child-molestation charges by a thirteen-year-old boy he had befriended. Jackson ended up paying the child and his family a large, undisclosed fee, and criminal prosecution was dropped when the boy refused to testify. Meanwhile, five of the singer's former bodyguards also filed

ways it portrays sexuality or gender relations in its programming) (Gunter and McAleer, 1990). One implicit message of television programming, almost since its inception, has been that men are in positions of leadership (whether they are the sheriff of a town or the head of the family), while women are either sexual temptations for men or are domestic servants who are subordinate to their husbands.[2] While the types of portrayals of

---

[2] The stereotyping of women is even more extreme in television commercials, which we consider in the section *Advertising*.

Michael Jackson

suit, saying that their services were terminated because they had come to know too much about Jackson's fondness for young boys.

Sex scandals are not unique to the United States. Queen Elizabeth II of England called 1992 a horrible year for her family, which has undergone a number of crises and scandals. It started in 1992, when Andrew and Sarah (known as "Fergie"), the Duke and Duchess of York, separated, after which the media published pictures of Fergie, topless, at a resort with her American boyfriend. Shortly afterward, Princess Anne divorced Captain Mark Phillips after eighteen years of

Prince Charles and Princess Diana

marriage. Most damaging of all was the scandal surrounding Prince Charles, heir to the throne, and Princess Diana. Andrew Morton published the book *Diana: Her True Story*, which chronicled the breakdown of the royal marriage, after which Charles and Diana announced their separation. In late 1989 and early 1990, a journalist bugged the royal phones, and the three recordings made showed that both Prince Charles and Princess Diana had lovers.

In Japan, Prime Minister Sosuke Uno was forced to resign due to *josei mondai*, or "women problems." Only two days after he assumed office, a geisha girl, Mitsuko Nakanishi, published a claim that Uno paid her $21,000 for a five-month affair in 1985 and 1986; later reports alleged that Uno had also had affairs with a sixteen-year-old apprentice geisha and a bar girl.

Prime Minister Sosuke Uno of Japan

In the ensuing elections, Uno's ruling Liberal-Democratic Party (LDP), which had ruled for almost forty years, lost control of the upper house of the Diet (the name for the Japanese congress). The upper house selected Socialist Party leader Takako Doi to be prime minister instead of Uno, making Doi the first woman to be named prime minister in Japanese history. Female voters, who outnumber male voters by 2.7 million, helped orchestrate the loss in their anger at Uno's sexual behavior.

Condensed from news sources

women's roles are changing and improving on television today, men still outnumber women in major roles, and the traditional role of woman as sex object (and, to a lesser extent, housewife) still predominates on television (Comstock and Paik, 1991).

The film industry has not been much different than the television industry in its treatment of sexual relations and gender stereotyping. Although it has a better history of portraying strong and independent women in the past (e.g., Katharine Hepburn, Bette Davis, and Mae West) and although there have always been maverick filmmakers who

Contrary to stereotype, many strong, independent women, such as Mae West, were portrayed in early movies.

challenged people's stereotypes, the typical Hollywood product has usually reflected society's expectations about the places of men and women. In movies, as in television, men's place has traditionally been on a horse with a gun, while the women's place has been either in the home, in bed, or out looking for a man.

In the last thirty years, sexual stereotyping has been one of the most researched areas of media studies. The conclusions of the research on television from the 1950s through the early 1980s has been almost unanimous: it mattered little whether the program was a crime drama or a soap opera, whether it was children's programming or adult programming, or whether it was a comedy or a tragedy; men initiated most of the action on television, initiated most of the conversation, and were portrayed as dominant and action oriented, while females were subordinate and helpless (Kalisch and Kalisch, 1984). When there was a male–female interaction in prime-time programming, it was the men who were ordering or advising the women 70% of the time. Women on television tended to be portrayed as emotional, passive, and dependent, usually waiting for a man to protect them.

Many of these stereotypes persist. Soap operas, because they are aimed at women, do portray women as more competent, especially in the personal sphere of life, than other programming (Geraghty, 1992). Yet even soap operas send subtle messages about keeping women in their place; women who "stand by their men" and are sexually more reserved tend to be portrayed sympathetically, while those who are more sexually active and independent of men tend to be portrayed as evil or unsympathetic. Another example of sexual stereotyping is medical shows. Kalisch and Kalisch's (1984) study of prime-time portrayals of nurses and physicians from 1950 to 1980 found that most nurses were female, most physicians were male, and the nurses, who were totally dependent on and subservient to male physicians, rarely were shown contributing to the patient's welfare. Even more recent medical shows, such as *ER* and *Chicago Hope,* show men in most of the positions of power. The same is true in news shows, where television executives have long resisted allowing women to become anchors. It was not until 1993 that Connie Chung became the first woman to anchor a major evening network newscast (with a male coanchor, Dan Rather), and Chung was fired from the job in 1995. Newswomen have also accused executives of choosing them for their appearance instead of their credentials, and some female reporters, such as Christine Craft, have sued networks claiming that they were fired when they began to show wrinkles around their eyes.

Fortunately, some gender stereotypes on television are changing. Men are now being shown as single or stay-at-home dads, and there is a tendency to mock the old "macho man" stereotypes on programs such as *Home Improvement. Roseanne* and *Murphy Brown* represent the new television woman: forceful, working outside the home, and dealing with the real-life problems of balancing family, social life, and occupation. The women on these shows do not wear tight-fitting clothes, and their primary concern is not how to attract men; they have more important things to worry about. Newer police, lawyer, and medical shows, which traditionally starred males, now regularly show women in leading roles. In situation comedies, also, the stay-at-home housewife is a thing of the past. Still, there are areas where the old patterns persist. Women are still often used as window-dressing, to appear as sexy backdrops to whatever action is happening on the screen, while shows like *Baywatch* still focus on the tightness of its stars' bathing suits. Also, while female news commentators have made great strides, serious news shows still rely disproportionately on male experts. But perhaps the place where female roles are the most absent is in children's television.

Television and Children

By the time today's youth are seventy years old, they will have spent about *seven years* of their lives watching television! Television viewing begins early; two- to five-year-olds spend almost twenty-eight hours a week watching television, and teenagers about twenty-two. By the time they graduate from high school, teenagers will have watched 15,000 hours of TV, compared with only 11,000 hours of formal classroom instruction (Strasburger, 1989). Children spend more time watching television than on any activity other than sleep (Signorielli and Lears, 1992).

SEX TALK

QUESTION **SF4.1**   **Most kids today know all about sex at an early age. Then why are people so uptight about showing nudity on television? What do they think it will do to their kids?**

Even in a society like ours, which has begun to discuss sex more openly, it is still a difficult subject for children to understand. Many parents believe that it

Sesame Street, and Saturday morning cartoons such as *The Teenage Mutant Ninja Turtles,* and most other children's programs are dominated by male characters, although recently a few more shows with strong female leads are appearing.

is their job to introduce the topic to their children, to explain it to them, and to teach their children whatever values the parents believe are appropriate around sexuality. This may be undermined when children see fairly uncensored sexuality on television, which is usually shown without any discussion of values and without any way to address the children's questions about what they are seeing.

Researchers have begun to ask serious questions about the impact of all this television watching, especially since television is so inundated with sexuality and sexual stereotypes.[3] For example, children are very concerned with sexual roles, and they often see the world in terms of "boy's" behavior and "girl's" behavior (see Chapter 5). Children are taught from a young age to behave in ways appropriate to their gender, and they quickly begin to tease other children who do not follow these stereotypes (such as effeminate boys). Still, research shows that when children are exposed to books or films that portray nonstereotyped gender behaviors, their gender stereotypes are reduced (Comstock and Paik, 1991).

Children's television lacks female role models and offers stereotyped portrayals of men and women. For example, an analysis of more than 200 television programs directed at children, adolescents, and teens found that not a single one was devoted to any female character's academic activities or career plans as a major part of the plot (Steenland, 1992). Instead, it was found that young women on television programs are preoccupied with grooming, fashion, and dating. The problem is even worse for younger viewers; "educational" television shows and Saturday morning cartoons have been tra-

---

[3] The other important issue is the impact on children of the enormous amount of violence on television, which even has the American Medical Association concerned (see Centerwall, 1992).

ditionally characterized by a virtual absence of female lead characters. For example, although *Sesame Street* has a human cast of mixed ethnicities and genders and even a number of female muppets, its most notable muppet figures (from Kermit to Bert and Ernie to Big Bird to the Count) have all been male. It was only with the introduction of Zoe in 1993 that a female muppet managed to gain a high profile. Television executives argue that boys will not watch cartoons with a female lead, but girls will watch cartoons with a male lead, and so it makes more economic sense to produce cartoons featuring males. The result is that it is hard for young girls to find good gender role models on television.[4] It is understandable why researchers have found that more television viewing is correlated with greater sexual stereotyping in certain groups of children (Gunter and McAleer, 1990).

Television is a powerful teacher of children, and programming directed at teens, such as MTV, is full of graphic sexuality and gender stereotypes (Lewis, 1990). Perhaps television's attitudes toward sexuality explains why studies find that adolescents who watch more television with sexual content are more likely to have had sexual intercourse (Brown and Newcomer, 1991).

The Movement Against the Sexualization of the Visual Media

The irony is that networks have turned to sex to increase their ratings, yet the constant presence of sexual themes on television is beginning to turn viewers away. A Gallup poll in the late 1980s, for example, found that six out of ten parents reported feeling uncomfortable watching television with their kids because of its sexual content, and surveys show that the majority of Americans want stronger regulation of sexual content and profanity. Nearly three out of four people say they would support boycotting the sponsors of objectionable shows (Alster, 1991).

Portrayal of sexuality in movies has also long been a source of controversy. There was no control over motion picture content until the 1930s, when the industry began policing itself with The Motion Picture Code. A rating system was eventually developed, starting with ratings of G (general audience), M (mature audiences), R (restricted to those over 17 unless accompanied by an adult), and X (adults only). Later, PG (Parental Guidance) and PG-13 (Parental Guidance, under thirteen not recommended) replaced M, and NC-17 was substituted for X if the movie was intended for general release (as opposed to movies made explicitly for the adult, X-rated market). These categories and, for that matter, the whole rating system are controversial. First of all, they change over time; what is allowed in many PG-13 movies today probably would have earned an R rating not too long ago, and many R movies would have been rated X. Also, rating standards seem preoccupied with sexuality and ignore excessive violence; there is little problem showing a body being blown to bits, but a body cannot be shown making love.

---

4 It is not just gender that is stereotyped on children's television and not only girls who have trouble finding role models. Children's programming presents a severely restricted portrait of humanity. A comprehensive study of 38 hours of children's television found, as we suggested, that more than 75% of the 1145 characters who appeared were men. But that is not all; less than 1% of the men (and 3% of the women) were elderly, and almost none were overweight. Close to 90% of the characters were white, with only 6% African Americans and 6% other ethnicities. (Another problem is that the "bad guy" in cartoons usually has a foreign accent and nonwhite features.) Characters also tended to be from the upper classes, and 70% were in technical or professional occupations (Dietz and Strasburger, 1991).

The rating system has not stopped the movies from trying to be as sexually explicit as they can within their rating categories. Hollywood seems to try to push the limits of the R rating as far as possible, and a number of directors have had to cut sexually explicit scenes out of their movies. In fact, some movies are made in two or three versions; the least sexually explicit version is for release in the United States, a more explicit copy is released in Europe (where standards are looser), and a third, even more explicit version, is released on videocassette.

A backlash does seem to be developing, and Hollywood has been reducing the sexual explicitness of its general release movies. Michael Medved (1992), a noted movie critic, argued in his book *Hollywood vs. America* that the movie and television industries are out of touch, too dedicated to violence, profanity, and sex, and do not really understand what consumers want to see on television and in the movies. He showed that sex does not necesarily sell by showing that G- and PG-rated movies actually make more money than R-rated movies. Combined with the fact that the baby boom generation is looking for movies for their young children, the 1990s have seen a return of the family movie.

Several small but well-organized groups (such as the National Coalition for Better TV) have tried to use advertiser boycotts to convince network programmers to change their portrayals of sexuality. One group, the American Family Association of Tupelo, Mississippi, and its president, Donald Wildmon, have organized letter-writing campaigns and boycotts against shows such as *Roseanne, Married With Children, Murphy Brown,* and *L.A. Law* (Dwyer, 1992). Wildmon's organization protests portrayals of homosexuality, extramarital sex, and abortion on television. These groups argue that television has gotten to the point where it offends most people, and so violates standards of **decency**. However, polls show that while many people feel that there is too much gratuitous sex and violence on television, most do not support the opinions or tactics of groups like the American Family Association.

Standards of decency can be very different in different countries; the same shows that result in public protests and sponsors pulling their advertising in the United States are shown in Canada with little or no protest and no sponsorship loss. England, which used to be extremely conservative in its television programming, recently ran a prime-time feature showing a close-up of female genitalia at the moment of orgasm (*The New York Times,* 1992d). In fact, the countries of Europe, even those who have tried to join together in a single economic community, have very different standards of decency. Sweden, for example, forbids some British TV shows because of their violence but allows hard-core pornography that Britain has traditionally prohibited.

Some of the shows that groups such as the American Family Association are boycotting get high ratings for the very reasons that they are boycotted: because they are willing to deal with complex issues such as abortion and homosexuality in a frank and honest (if sometimes sensationalistic) manner. It will be interesting to see whether advertisers are scared away by these groups or continue to sponsor provocative and controversial programs.

decency: Conformity to recognized standards of propriety, good taste, and modesty—as defined by a particular group (standards of decency differ among groups).

Advertising

Advertising is a modern medium, and its influence pervades modern life. There is practically no area that is free from its effects, from the media to consumer products and even to nature itself—billboards obscure our views from highways, and planes drag advertising banners at our beaches. People proudly wear advertisement for soft drinks or fashion designers on their shirts, sneakers, or hats, not realizing that they often spend more for such clothing, paying money to help the company advertise!

The almost universal presence of advertising means that it becomes part of the way that we look at the world (Comstock and Paik, 1991). According to estimates, children see up to 40,000 advertisements on television every year! Studies have shown that advertising has a profound effect on the way children think about the world (as consisting of "products I want to have," for example), and it influences the way they begin to form their ideas of sexuality and gender roles (Durkin, 1985; Gunter and McAleer, 1990).

Advertising and Gender Role Portrayals

In his groundbreaking book *Gender Advertisements,* Erving Goffman (1976) used hundreds of pictures from print advertising to show how men and women are positioned or displayed to evoke sexual tension, power relations, or seduction. Advertisements, Goffman suggested, do not show actual portrayals of men and women but present clear-cut snapshots of the way we *think* they behave. Advertisements try and capture ideals of each sex: men are shown as taller than women or are standing while the woman is sitting, to suggest their dominant position in the encounter. Men are shown as more confident and authoritative, while women are more childlike and deferential (Belknap and Leonard, 1991). Since Goffman's book was published, advertisements have become more blatantly sexual, and analyzing the gender role and sexual content of advertisements has become a favorite pastime of those who study the media.

The studies that have been published since Goffman seem to suggest that plenty of commercials still draw on sexual stereotyping (Bretl and Cantor, 1988). Studies of television commercials, for example, still show differences between the way men and women are portrayed. A study of more than 300 television commercials aired during prime time showed that 90% of the voice-overs were done by men, and when women were used, they were often speaking to subordinates (pets, children) and not directly to the audience (Lovdal, 1989). Men were pictured in three times the number of occupational categories as women, and women were more likely than men to be in commercials that featured the home.

These kinds of findings are not only true in television. A study of recent advertising for fitness and health products in magazine ads found that women were placed in subordinate positions to men, were posed in unnatural positions, were portrayed as body parts, and were displayed with a focus on sexuality rather than wellness (Rudman and Hagiwara, 1992). Even medical advertisements in major medical journals show these kinds of biases. A study of thirty-two major medical journal ads found that almost 96% of the physicians portrayed in the advertisements were male, while almost all the nurses were female (in fact, close to 20% of physicians in the United States are female, and the number is rapidly increasing; while only about 4% of nurses are male, that number is also rising quickly) (Hawkins and Aber, 1993). In keeping with the common advertising theme that women should be portrayed as subordinate to men, women were more than twice as likely as men to be pictured as patients or medical consumers (68.1% of medical ads that pictured patients featured women versus 31.9% featuring men), women's body parts were shown more often, and women appeared naked four times more often than men. So even in advertisements directed at physicians, who are presumably less swayed by the sight of the naked (female) body, the same stereotypical images are used.

There are signs that advertising companies are trying to put more women into ads in positions of authority and dominance (*Business Week,* 1991). Men are also being shown in traditionally female roles, such as cuddling babies or cooking. However, the naked body is still a primary means of selling products, and even if gender roles are becoming more egalitarian, portrayals of sexuality are still blatant.

Advertising and Portrayals of Sexuality

One glance at television or magazine advertisements shows how deeply advertisers believe that (heterosexual) sex sells. The purpose of advertising is to (1) get your attention; (2) get you excited; and (3) associate that excitement with the product being advertised. The excitement can be intellectual, emotional, physical (sports, for example), or visual (fast-moving action, wild colors); but when you think of "getting excited," what immediately comes to mind? Well, that is what comes to the mind of advertising executives also, and so ads often use sexual images or suggestions to provoke, to entice—in short, to *seduce.*

Sexuality (especially female sexuality) has been used to sell products since the turn of the century. In an analysis comparing magazine advertisements in 1964 with advertisements in 1984, Soley and Kurzbard (1986) found that while the percentage of

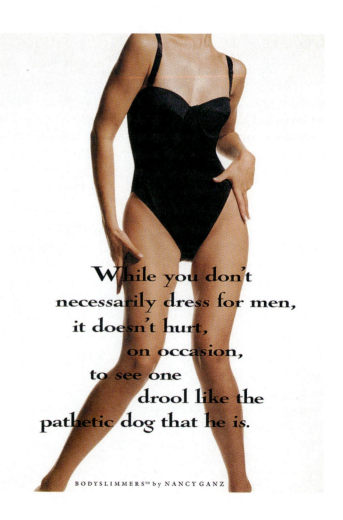

Advertisers play on sexuality and gender relations to gain attention for the products.

advertisements portraying sexuality did not change, sexual illustrations had become more overt and visually explicit in 1984. By the 1990s, a variety of advertisers were challenging the limits with advertising campaigns that featured graphic nudity or strong sexual implications. A pair of pictures for Nordica Ski Equipment featuring a male and a female nude on skis were banned in 1991 from the major ski magazines, even though the models were posed so that no sexual areas were exposed. Brooke Shield's fabulously successful 1980 Calvin Klein ads ("Nothing comes between me and my Calvins. Nothing.") convinced Calvin Klein that, as he put it, "Jeans are about sex." This led to a series of more and more graphic Calvin Klein ads, culminating a 116-page advertising insert in *Vanity Fair* in 1991 that featured more naked torsos than actual pictures of his clothing line (Prud'homme, 1991). Other clothing manufacturers and perfume companies (Calvin Klein also produced some erotic and provocative ads for his perfume *Obsession*) soon followed in what seemed to be a race to see who could out-eroticize who in the advertising industry.

Not all portrayals of sexuality are this blatant, however. Some are suggestive, such as sprays of soda foam near the face of an ecstatic looking women, models posing with food or appliances placed in obviously phallic positions, models posed in sexual positions even if clothed (in one case, the words "We're having a BIG sale" were written between a model's spread thighs), or ads that show women and, less often, men whose faces are contorted in sexual excitement. Some authors even claim that advertisements have tried to use **subliminal** sexuality—pictures of phalluses or breasts or the word *sex* worked into advertisements so they cannot be seen without extreme scrutiny (Levine, 1991). Whether these strategies work is a matter of much debate, but Calvin Klein's ads were so provocative that news reports about them appeared in newspapers and on television news shows—and that is just what advertisers want most for their ads and the products they represent: for people to talk and think about them.[5]

subliminal: The use of images or words, often sexual, that are not immediately apparent to the viewer of an advertisement, intended to excite the subconscious mind and improve the viewer's reaction to the ad.

Sexuality and Gender in New Media

There are other forms of media that we have not discussed. For example, we could easily explore sexuality and gender issues in live theater, in men's and women's magazines, in newspaper reports, in rock videos and public musical performances, in graffiti and other public art, in posters, calendars, and pinup art; or we could discuss studies that show how sexual stereotyping is common in such things as the Sunday comics (see Brabant and Mooney, 1986). Because sexuality pervades our lives, it also pervades our art and our media.

There are other types of media that deal with sexuality also. Sex-advice columns are common now, and they run in many newspapers and magazines across the country. There are also thousands of "900 number" telephone lines offering sexual services of various kinds across the country. People call the number and pay a certain amount per minute (or use their credit cards for a flat fee) and can talk either to other people who have called in on a party line or to professionals who will discuss sex or play the part of the caller's sexual fantasy. These phone lines cater to men and women (though more commonly to men) and to heterosexuals and homosexuals.

As new forms of media are developed, sexual and gender issues are arising there, too. For example, computers have generated whole new forms of communications. Computer networks such as *Internet,* which links up thousands of academically based

---

[5] Calvin Klein, though, was finally forced to withdraw ads in 1995 that some claimed mimicked child pornography.

computer users all over the country, allow almost completely unregulated interaction. Literally thousands of sexually explicit conversations, art works, and computer games go zipping over public telephone lines between the users of computer networks every day. Anyone with a modem on his or her computer, from ten-year-olds to college professors, can have virtually unlimited access to explicit sexual materials.

Computer technology has been taken even one step further: virtual reality (VR). In VR, pictures generated by computer are projected into goggles put over the eyes, and as the head and eyes move, the picture moves accordingly. The user is given the illusion of actually being in the scene before him or her. Recently, enterprising VR producers have been making sexually explicit VR movies, which are coordinated with "stimulators" (vibrators) attached to sensors at the groin; one can actually feel like one is acting in the pornographic scene while the computer responds to the user's own physical states of excitement and stimulates the user to orgasm. Certainly, new forms of media will present challenges to those who want to regulate or control the public's access to sexually explicit materials.

GRAPHIC IMAGES: PORNOGRAPHY AND THE PUBLIC'S RESPONSE

I am convinced that this traffic in hard-core pornography is . . . pollution as surely as sewage, and it ought to be equally subject to Federal control through the commerce clause.

Report of the Commission on Obscenity and Pornography

[Radio talk show hosts who use "smutty" language] *may just find themselves in the gutter. . . . This new breed of air pollution, the prurient trash that is the stock-in-trade of the sex-oriented radio talk show, complete with the suggestive, coaxing, pear shaped tones of the smut-hustling host. . . . This is garbage pure and simple.*

Dean Burch, Chairman of the Federal Communications Commission

We will drive the vermin away.

Alexander Cohen, Broadway producer, on a local gay movie house; Quotes from Davis (1983:89–90)

Pollution . . . sewage . . . gutter . . . air pollution . . . smut . . . garbage . . . vermin . . . why do sexually explicit images evoke such passionate responses? Why are people, even thoughtful and sober people, so quick to reach for words like *sewage* and *vermin* to describe sexually explicit images and the people who make and sell them?

Pornography has always aroused passions, but the debate over pornography is particularly active today because never before in history has pornography been so widely available. The pornography industry produces thousands of books and movies every year, and the availability of home VCRs, cable, satellite dishes, and even computer networks allows people almost unlimited access to these materials. Throw in arguments from free-speech advocates, antiporn (and anti-antiporn) feminists, religious groups, presidential commissions, the American Civil Liberties Union, and a powerful pornography industry, and you can begin to see the extent of the fights that have developed over this issue.

We begin this section by reviewing the disputes over the legal and governmental definitions of pornography as they have been argued in presidential commissions and in the highest courts in the country. Then we look at how those same debates are discussed among the scholars and activists who are trying to influence the country's policies toward pornography. We also examine the basic claim of modern opponents of pornography: that pornography is harmful in its effects on individuals and society as a whole. Finally, we examine the public's attitudes toward pornography.

Legal and Governmental Definitions of Obscenity

Court Decisions

The First Amendment to the Constitution of the United States, enacted in 1791, includes the words: "Congress shall make no law . . . abridging the freedom of speech, or of the press." Ever since, the court system has struggled with the meaning of those words, for it is obvious that they cannot be taken literally; we do not have the right to make false claims about other people, lie in court under oath, or, in the famous phrase, "yell 'fire' (falsely) in a crowded theater," even though that limits our freedom of speech.

The legal definition of obscenity dates back to the 1868 case of *Regina* v. *Hicklin* in England, where the court defined obscenity as material that tended "to deprave and corrupt those whose minds are open to such immoral influences" (quoted in Berger et al., 1991:113). The *Hicklin* decision permitted the confiscation of obscene materials due only to their sexual content, which remained the American standard until the 1930s. Since then, American courts have reinterpreted and liberalized obscenity laws significantly. Sexuality Today SF4.3 lists some important court decisions that have helped shape the American legal attitudes toward obscene representations.

Court cases in the United States have established the three-part definition of obscenity, quoted in Sexuality Today SF4.3, that has determined how courts define pornography. For something to be obscene it must (1) appeal to the **prurient** interest; (2) offend contemporary community standards; and (3) lack serious literary, artistic, political, or scientific value.

But these criteria are not without critics. What are "community standards"? Which people in a community get to decide what that community's standards are? What about minority groups in a community with different standards? What is "prurient interest"? How do we decide if a work, as a whole, appeals to those interests? The only way to make these decisions, it seems, is by impression; as Supreme Court Justice Potter once said in trying to come to grips with these problems, "I can't define [pornography], but I know it when I see it."

Some argue that the criteria of prurience, offensiveness, and community standards turn moral fears into legal "harms," which are more imaginary than real, and so we end up with arbitrary discussions of what is "prurient" and which speech has "value" (Hunter et al., 1993). On the other hand, antiporn feminists argue that pornography laws were made to reflect a male preoccupation with "purity" of thought and insult to moral sensibilities and to ignore the true harms of pornography: the exploitation of women (see below) (Berger et al., 1991).

Obscenity laws have been used in the twentieth century to control almost anything of a sexual nature. Books now considered classic—James Joyce's *Ulysses,* Henry Miller's *Tropic of Cancer,* the *Kama Sutra,* Havelock Ellis' pioneering *Studies in the Psychology of Sex,* and hundreds of others—were banned at one time or another. It is in part because of past abuses that there is so much resistance to laws that have recently been proposed to further restrict pornography.

prurient: Characterized by lascivious thoughts; used as criteria for deciding what is pornographic.

Some Major American
Supreme Court Decisions on Obscenity

Year	Case	Finding
1934	*United States* v. *One Book by James Joyce Entitled Ulysses*	*Ulysses* was constitutionally protected in spite of "pornographic" passages. Rejecting the English precedent of *Regina* v. *Hicklin*, Judge Woolsey of the district court commented that the legal standard required that the author have "pornographic intent" or that the work as a whole served to "stir the sex impulses" or led to "sexually impure or lustful thoughts" in the reader. The effect of isolated passages on particular readers was no longer the issue.
1942	*Chaplinsky* v. *New Hampshire*	The First Amendment does not protect certain categories of expression, such as "the lewd and obscene, the profane, the libelous, and the insulting or 'fighting' words—those which by their very utterance inflict injury or tend to incite immediate breach of the peace" because they serve "no essential part of any exposition of ideas, and are of such slight social value as a step to truth that any benefit that may be derived from them is clearly outweighed by the social interest in order and morality."
1957	*Roth* v. *United States*	Obscenity is not protected by First Amendment because it is "utterly without redeeming social importance"; obscenity is redefined in terms of "whether to the average person, applying contemporary community standards, the dominant theme of the material as a whole appeals to the prurient interest."
1966	*A Book Called "John Cleland's Memoirs of a Woman of Pleasure" ("Fanny Hill")* v. *Attorney General of Massachusetts*	In order to be deemed obscene, material must (1) be patently offensive to contemporary community standards, going substantially beyond the customary limits of candor; (2) appeal to the prurient interest of the average person; and (3) be utterly without redeeming social value.
1969	*Stanley* v. *Georgia*	Individuals have the right to possess even obscene materials in their own homes. "The right to receive information and ideas, regardless of their social worth, is fundamental to our free society." This decision virtually legalized pornography.
1973	*Miller* v. *California*	The standard three-part test of obscenity, first described in *Memoirs* (above), is put in its current form by Chief Justice Warren Burger. Obscenity is defined by a) whether the average person, applying contemporary community standards, would find that the work, taken as a whole, appeals to the prurient interest; and b) whether the work depicts or describes, in a patently offensive way, sexual conduct specifically defined by the applicable state law; and c) whether the work, taken as a whole, lacks serious literary, artistic, political, or scientific value.
1982	*New York* v. *Ferber*	People may not distribute child pornography, even if it can be shown to have "value," because such materials "bear so heavily and pervasively on the welfare of children engaged in its production" that they do not enjoy the benefit of the First Amendment.
1984	*American Booksellers Association, Inc.* v. *Hudnut*	Striking down an ordinance sponsored by antiporn feminists that made it possible to remove pornography that could be shown to subordinate women, the court decided that it restricted an enormous amount of speech—even more than *Miller* (above)—without showing direct harm. This was a blow to those who were trying to create antipornography ordinances that are acceptable under the court's interpretation of the First Amendment.

Derived from Berger et al. (1991), Downs (1989), and Hunter et al. (1993)

Presidential Commissions

1970 Commission on Obscenity and Pornography. In 1967, President Lyndon Johnson set up a commission to study "a matter of national concern": the impact of pornography on American society. The commission was headed by a behavioral scientist who brought on other social scientists, and although the commission also included experts in law, religion, broadcasting, and publishing, its findings were based on empirical research and much of its $2 million budget was used to fund more scientific studies (Einsiedel, 1989). The commission (which used the terms *erotica* or *explicit sexual material* rather than *pornography*), studied four areas: pornography's effects, traffic and distribution of pornography, legal issues, and positive approaches to cope with pornography (Berger et al., 1991).

The 1970 Commission operated without the benefit of the enormous research on pornography that has appeared in the last twenty-five years, and so it has been criticized for such things as not distinguishing between different kinds of erotica (for example, violent versus nonviolent), for including homosexuals, exhibitionists, and rapists all under the same category of "sex offenders," and for relying on poor empirical studies. Still, while calling for more research and better designed and funded studies in the future, the Commission did perform most comprehensive study of the evidence up until that time and concluded that:

1. "empirical research . . . has found no reliable evidence to date that exposure to elicit sexual materials plays a significant role in the causation of delinquent or criminal sexual behavior among youth or adults," so
2. "greater latitude can safely be given to adults in deciding for themselves what they will or will not read." (quoted in Einsiedel, 1989:89)

In other words, the Commission recommended that the state stop worrying so much about pornography, which it saw as a relatively insignificant threat to society. The U.S. Senate was not happy with the Commission's conclusions and condemned them. President Nixon, who was by then in office, tried to suppress the report, warning that "an attitude of permissiveness . . . regarding pornography . . . would contribute to an atmosphere condoning anarchy . . . [and threaten] our social order [and] moral principles" (quoted in Berger et al., 1991:24).

The 1986 Attorney General's Commission on Pornography (The "Meese Commission"). In 1985, President Ronald Reagan appointed Attorney General Edwin Meese to head a new commission that he expected to overturn the 1970 Commission's findings. In fact, the official charter of the Meese Commission was to find "more effective ways in which the spread of pornography could be contained" (Berger et al., 1991:25) and so already assumed that pornography is dangerous or undesirable and needs containment. Since the Commission was a creation of the Attorney General's office, it took a law-enforcement approach, was made up predominantly of lawyers (there was only one social scientist on the Meese Commission), and was chaired by an antipornography prosecutor who was praised by Reagan for "closing down every adult bookstore in his district" (Berger et al., 1991). It also included representatives of antipornography groups, religious fundamentalists, and a Franciscan priest. While the 1970 Commission focused on social science, the Meese Commission listened to experts and laypeople through public hearings around the country, most of whom supported restricting or eliminating sexually graphic materials. Virtually every claim made by antipornography activists was cited in the report as fact with little or no supporting evidence, while those who did not support the Commission's positions were treated rudely or with hostility (Berger et al., 1991). The Meese Commission issued a 1,960-page report summarizing its findings.

The 1986 Meese Commission came to the opposite conclusions of the 1970 Commission. The Meese Commission divided pornography into four categories: (1) violent pornography, (2) "degrading" pornography (e.g., anal sex, group sex, homosexual depictions), (3) nonviolent/nondegrading pornography, and (4) nudity. The Commission used a selection of scientific studies to claim that the first two categories are damaging and may be considered a type of social violence and that they hurt women most of all:

> *Pornography is degrading to women. . . . It is provided primarily for the lustful pleasure of men and boys who use it to generate excitation. And it is my belief, though evidence is not easily obtained, that a small but dangerous minority will then choose to act aggressively against the nearest available females. Pornography is the theory; rape is the practice.*
>
> **Quoted in Williams (1989:16)**

The Meese Commission made a number of recommendations:

- Antipornography laws were sufficient as they were written, but law enforcement efforts should be increased at all levels.

This picture of Edwin Meese, reading the Attorney General's Report on Pornography with the exposed breast of the statue of justice over his shoulder, got wide distribution.

- Convicted pornographers should forfeit their profits and be liable to have property used in production or distribution of pornography confiscated, and repeat offenses against the obscenity laws should be considered felonies.
- Religious and civic groups should picket and protest institutions that peddle offensive materials.
- Congress should ban obscene cable television, telephone sex lines, and child pornography in any form.

Reaction to the Meese Commission was immediate and strong. Many of the leading sexuality researchers that the Commission cited in support of its conclusions condemned the report and accused the Commission of intentional misinterpretation of their scientific evidence. The Moral Majority, the religious right, and conservative supporters hailed the findings as long overdue. Women's groups were split on how to react to the report. On the one hand, the report used feminist language and adopted the position that pornography damages women. Antiporn feminists saw in Meese a possible ally to get pornography banned or at least restricted and so supported the Meese Commission's conclusions, if not its spirit. Other women's groups, however, were very wary of the Commission's antigay postures and conservative bent, and they worried that the report would be used to justify wholesale censorship.

SEX TALK

QUESTION **SF4.2** **Why are men so turned on by seeing naked women, while I find that looking at pictures of naked men doesn't do much for me sexually?**

Some theorists have suggested that men are more visual than women, that visual stimuli are more important to men's sex lives than to women's. In higher primates, for example, the female's vulva swells and turns various shades of pink and purple, which is a sign to males to mate with her. Perhaps human males are more visual as a holdover from our primate days. Others, however, suggest that male's greater use of pornography is socially determined. Males are socialized more into seeing females as sexual objects to be ogled, and women are socialized into using makeup and bright clothes to make themselves more visually attractive to men. No one knows exactly to what extent each of these factors contributes to men's greater use of pornography.

The Pornography Debates

The argument over pornography has created some unlikely allies. Lesbian feminist scholars such as Andrea Dworkin find themselves allied with Christian evangelical leaders such as Jerry Falwell, and law professors specializing in First Amendment issues find themselves defending the rights of publishers of the most graphically explicit magazines and movies.

The religious-conservative opposition to pornography is based on a belief that people have an inherent human desire to sin and that pornography reinforces that tendency and so undermines the family, traditional authority, and the moral fabric of society (Berger et al., 1991). Unless strong social standards are kept, people will indulge themselves in individual fulfillment and pleasure, promoting material rather than spiritual or moral values (Downs, 1989). Users of pornography become desensitized to shocking sexual behaviors, and pornography teaches them to see sex as simple physical pleasure rather than a part of a loving, committed relationship. This leads to increased teen pregnancy rates, degradation of females, and rape; in this, at least, the religious-conservative antipornography school agrees with the antiporn feminists.

Nowhere has the issue of pornography been as divisive as it has been among feminist scholars, splitting them into two general schools. The antipornography feminists, led by Catherine MacKinnon and Andrea Dworkin, see pornography as an assault on women that silences them, renders them powerless, reinforces male dominance, and indirectly encourages sexual and physical abuse against women. The other side,[6] which includes groups such as the Feminist Anticensorship Taskforce (FACT), argue that censorship of sexual materials will eventually (if not immediately) be used to censor such things as feminist writing and gay erotica and would therefore endanger women's rights and freedoms of expression (Cowan, 1992). Let us use these two schools to explore the arguments of each side in the pornography debates.

Antipornography Arguments

One of the scholars who has written most forcefully and articulately against pornography is Catherine MacKinnon (1985; 1987; 1993; Dworkin and MacKinnon, 1988). MacKinnon argues that pornography cannot be understood separate from the long history of male domination of women and that it is in fact an integral part and a reinforcing element of women's second-class status. Pornography is less about sex than power; MacKinnon defines pornography as "the sexually explicit subordination of women, graphically depicted, whether in pictures or words," which is "central in creating and maintaining the civil inequalities of the sexes." MacKinnon does not see pornography as a result of sexual exploitation or even as a cause of exploitation but as a form of sexual exploitation itself. She argues that pornography is a discriminatory social practice that institutionalizes the inferiority and subordination of one group by another, the way segregation institutionalized the subordination of blacks by whites. That is why MacKinnon sees pornography not as a free speech issue but as a civil rights issue; the existence of pornography denies women equality with men and so is a violation of women's civil rights.

MacKinnon suggests that defending pornography on First Amendment terms as protected free speech is to misunderstand the influence of pornography on the everyday life of women in society. Rather than thinking of censoring pornography as a violation of the First Amendment right to free speech, she suggests thinking of pornography itself as a violation of a woman's right not to be discriminated against, guaranteed by the Fourteenth Amendment. Imagine, she suggests, if the thousands of movies and books produced each year by the $8 billion pornographic industry were not showing women, but rather Jews, African Americans, the handicapped, or some other minority splayed naked, often chained or tied up, urinated and defecated upon, with foreign objects inserted into their orifices, while at the same time physical assaults and sexual assaults against that group were epidemic in society (as they are against women). Would people still appeal to the First Amendment to prevent some kind of action? In fact, MacKinnon argues, in the case of pornography it is a mistake to distinguish speech from action; pornography is itself *an act,* linked to the general disempowerment of women.

---

6 Some who argue against the antipornography feminists call themselves the "anti-antiporn" contingent, but for simplicity's sake we will refer to them simply as the "anticensorship" group.

Feminists opposed to pornography argue that images like these demean women and ultimately create a climate of discrimination against them.

Some other feminists take this argument a step further and claim that male sexuality is by its nature subordinating; Andrea Dworkin (1981; 1987), for example, a close ally of MacKinnon, is uncompromising about men and their sexuality. Dworkin, like MacKinnon, sees pornography as a central aspect of male power, which she sees as a long-term strategy to elevate men to a superior position in society by forcing even strong women to feign weakness and dependency. She believes that laws and customs protect male power and that history and myth glorify it; pornography is just the most raw depiction of male power over women. Even sexuality reflects male power: Dworkin sees every act of intercourse as an assault, because men are the penetrators and women are penetrated.

Although MacKinnon does not seem to go as far as Dworkin, she does argue that men do not see the parallel between subordination of women and that of other minorities because pornography exploits men's sexual excitation:

The message of [pornography] *is . . . "get her.". . . This message is addressed directly to the penis, delivered through an erection and taken out on women in the real world.*

Quoted in Posner (1993:31–32)

Because pornography is harmful in and of itself, such authors claim, it should be controlled or banned. To that end, MacKinnon and Dworkin have sponsored or consulted on antipornography legislation in cities such as Minneapolis and Indianapolis, as well as in Canada (see Special Focus 1). Although they have not had much success passing laws in the United States, their strong arguments have set the agenda for the public debate over pornography.

Anticensorship Arguments

A number of critics have responded to the arguments put forth by people like MacKinnon and Dworkin (Dworkin, 1993; Kaminer, 1992; Posner, 1993; Romano, 1993; Wolf, 1991, 1993). First of all, many argue that a restriction against pornography cannot be separated from a restriction against writing or pictures that show other oppressed minorities in subordinate positions. Once we start restricting all portrayals of minorities being subordinated, we are close to a society ruled by censorship. Also, they ask, how far should we go in removing offensive pornography from society? Many Hollywood movies, television shows, and even women's romance novels portray women as subordinate or secondary to men; are all of those to be censored, too? MacKinnon seems to make little distinction between *Playboy* and movies showing violent rape; are *any* sexual portrayals of the female body or of intercourse not harmful to women?

In response to MacKinnon and Dworkin's attempt to pass a pornography-harms bill in Indianapolis, anticensorship feminists Nan Hunter and Sylvia Law wrote to the court hearing the case:

> *Society's attempts to protect women's chastity through criminal and civil laws have resulted in restrictions on women's freedom to engage in sexual activity, to discuss it publicly and to protect themselves from the risks of pregnancy. These disabling restrictions reinforced gender roles which have oppressed women for centuries. The Indianapolis ordinance resonates with the traditional concept that sex itself degrades women, and its enforcement would reinvigorate those discriminatory moral standards which have limited women's equality in the past.*
>
> **Quoted in Peterson (1992:37)**

MacKinnon's portrayal of women as subject to wholesale domination by men has also been questioned because society is made up of a large number of different subcommunities (for example, gay communities, different ethnic communities, youth subcultures) where interpretations of women's roles vary. Also, what of lesbian pornography, where the models and the intended audience are female, with men almost wholly excluded? Many of these portrayals are explicitly geared toward resisting society's established sexual hierarchies; should they also be censored (Henderson, 1991)? Once sexually explicit portrayals are suppressed, anticensorship advocates argue, so are the portrayals that try to challenge sexual stereotypes.

A more complicated issue is the claim of the antiporn group that pornography harms women in some fashion. One response is to suggest that such an argument once again casts men in a more powerful position than women and by denying women's power, supports the very hierarchy it seeks to dismantle. But the question of whether it can be demonstrated that pornography actually harms women is a difficult one.

Pornography and Harm

Both sides of the pornography debate produce reams of studies that support their side; the Meese Report and antiporn feminists such as MacKinnon and Dworkin produce papers showing that pornography is tied to rape, assault, and negative attitudes toward women, while others produce studies showing that pornography has no effects or is secondary to more powerful forces (Fisher and Barak, 1991). Who is right?

Societywide Studies

In 1969, J. Edgar Hoover, Director of the F.B.I., submitted evidence to the Presidential Commission on Obscenity and Pornography claiming that police observation had led him to believe that

A disproportionate number of sex offenders were found to have large quantities of pornographic materials in their residences . . . more, in the opinion of witnesses, than one would expect to find in the residences of a random sample of non-offenders of the same sex, age, and socioeconomic status, or in the residences of a random sample of offenders whose offenses were not sex offenses.

Quoted in Hunter et al. (1993:226)

Correlations like these have been used since the early nineteenth century to justify attitudes toward pornography (Hunter et al., 1993). Such claims are easily criticized on scientific grounds because a "witnesses' opinion" cannot be relied upon (and there has never been a study that has reliably determined the amount of pornography in the "average" nonoffender or non–sex offender's home). Better evidence is suggested in the state-by-state studies of Baron and Straus (1987; 1989), and Scott and Schwalm (1988). Both groups of researchers found a direct nationwide correlation between rape and sexually explicit magazines: rape rates are highest in those places with the highest circulation of sex magazines.

SEX TALK

QUESTION **SF4.3**   **I agree that in many cases pornography is degrading to women, but I still find it turns me on. How can I find something to be disgusting intellectually and yet still find it sexually arousing?**

Sexuality, as we have emphasized, is a complicated, often confusing part of life. Sexual arousal has physiological, psychological, and social aspects to it, which combine in different ways in different people, which is what makes studying sexuality so interesting. Pornography often tries to bypass the brain and shoot right for the groin, in the sense that it shows sexuality in its most obvious, raw, and uncreative forms. There is no reason to feel guilty that pictures of sexual situations are arousing to you. However, if you want to avoid looking at pictures that are demeaning to women, you may want to search out erotic materials that treat the sexes with greater equality. Erotic videos, pictures, and magazines that treat both sexes with respect, often produced by women, are now widely available, and you may find them just as stimulating.

On the other hand, Denmark, which has no laws against pornography at all, and Japan, in which pornography is sold freely and tends to be dominated by rape and bondage scenes, have low rates of reported rape, relative to the United States (Posner, 1993). In a study of four countries over twenty years, Kutchinsky (1991) could find no increase in rape relative to other crimes in any of the countries even as the availability of pornography increased dramatically. Baron (1990), the same researcher who found that rape rates correlated with explicit magazines, did a further study, which showed that gender equality was higher in states with higher circulation rates of sexually explicit magazines. This may be because those states are generally more liberal. Women in societies that forbid or repress pornography (such as Islamic societies) tend to be more oppressed than those in societies where it is freely available. All in all, the effects of pornography on a society's violence toward women are far from clear.

Individual Studies

Several laboratory studies have sought to determine the reaction of men exposed to different types of pornography. In most cases, men are shown pornography and then a test is done to determine if their attitudes toward women, sex crimes, etc., are altered. While little evidence indicates that nonviolent, sexually explicit films provoke antifemale reactions in men (Padgett et al., 1989), many studies have shown that violent or degrading pornography does influence attitudes. Viewing sexual violence and degradation increases fantasies of rape, the belief that some women secretly desire to be raped, acceptance of violence against women, insensitivity to rape victims, desire for sex without emotional involvement, the treatment of women as sex objects, and desire to see more violent pornography (Fisher and Barak, 1991; Linz, 1989; Berger et al., 1991). On the other hand, these studies are under artificial conditions (would these men have chosen to see such movies if not in a study?), and feelings of sexual aggression in a laboratory may not mirror a person's activities in the real world. It is also unclear how long such feelings last and whether they really influence behavior (Kutchinsky, 1991). Other studies show that men's aggression tends to increase after seeing any violent movie, even if it is not sexual, and so the explicit sexuality of the movies may not be the important factor (Linz and Donnerstein, 1992).

What Is Harm?

Lahey (1991) argues that the attempt to determine the effects of viewing pornography misses the point because once again the focus is on men and their reactions; is it not enough that women feel belittled, humiliated, and degraded? Is it not "harm" that pornography reinforces the loathsome idea that women exist solely to service men sexually? The voice of women is silent in pornography studies. For example, a variety of studies show that women tend to have negative reactions to viewing pornography, but women's reactions are not generally considered relevant to the discussion. The questions focus on whether pornography induces sexual violence in men.

Pornography, Lahey (after MacKinnon and Dworkin) argues, is the form that female victimization takes in American culture. Pornography harms women by teaching falsehoods about women (that they enjoy painful sexuality, are not as worthy as men, secretly desire sex even when they refuse it, and do not know what they really like); it harms women's self-esteem; and it harms women by reproducing itself in men's behavior toward women.

Certainly, there is an argument to be made that certain kinds of sexually explicit materials contribute little to society and cause much pain directly and indirectly to women. Many who defend sexually explicit materials that show consensual sex abhor the violent and degrading pornography that is the particular target of feminist ire. Whether the way to respond to such materials is through new laws (which may do little to stop its production; child pornography, which is illegal, flourishes in the United States) or through listening to the voices of women, who are its victims, is an open question.

Public Attitudes Toward Pornography

It is not only scholars and activists who disagree about pornography; the general public seems profoundly ambivalent about it as well. A *Newsweek* (1985) poll found that most people did not want stricter controls on pornography; for example, 60% were against banning X-rated movie theaters. Still, a majority wanted to ban violent pornography and felt that pornography can lead to a loss of respect for women, acts of violence, and rape.

This may be due to the general anticensorship feeling in America. In fact, one study of a county in Wisconsin (Thompson et al., 1990) showed that even people who felt that pornography had negative effects on others were opposed to regulating it. Interestingly, the most important factor in people's attitudes toward pornography was their beliefs about how pornography affected others who saw it; most people believed that pornography had a greater influence over other people than over themselves. Even though people believed that pornography had negative effects, such as violating women's rights, they opposed censorship.

Pornography is a difficult, controversial problem in American society. By arguing that sex is the only part of human life that should not be portrayed in our art and media, the core conflict over sexuality is revealed: people seem to believe that although sexuality is a central part of human life, it should still be treated differently than other human actions, as a category unto itself.

S u m m a r y

- Erotic representations have existed in almost all societies at almost all times; they have also been the subject of censorship by the religious or governmental powers.
- The term *pornography* refers not just to the production of erotic representations (which is better termed *erotica*) but to the struggle between some who want to create erotic representations and others who want to stop them.
- The erotic novel first established pornographic production as a business in the Western world, and it provoked a response of censorship from Church and governmental authorities.
- Television and, to a lesser extent, movies have become the primary media in the United States, and they contain enormous amounts of sexually suggestive material. Children are particularly subjected to this barrage of sexual images. In addition, TV offers little in the way of positive sexual role models for children. Certain groups have begun to organize

to change the content of television programming.
- Advertising has commercialized sexuality and uses an enormous amount of sexual imagery to sell products. Ads are becoming more explicit in the general media in the United States.
- Pornography is one of the most difficult issues in public life in America. Feminists, conservatives, and the religious right argue that pornography is destructive, violates the rights of women, corrupts children, and should be banned or severely restricted. Liberals and critics of banning pornography argue that creating a definition of pornography that protects art and literature is impossible, that people have the right to read whatever materials they want in their own homes, and that censorship is a slippery slope that leads to further censorship. The public is split between these positions.

R e f l e c t i o n s   o n   S e x u a l i t y

1. Has pornography as we know it today always existed in history?
2. How is television's portrayal of sexuality different than the way sexuality is experienced by most people in the real world? What does television tend to focus on, and what does it ignore?
3. Why do advertisers rely so much on sexually suggestive ads to sell their products? Does such advertising work?

4. What is the legal definition of obscenity today? How has it changed over time?
5. What are the major arguments of antipornography feminists such as Catherine MacKinnon? How do anticensorship scholars respond to their views?
6. What does the research show on the question of whether pornography actually inspires men to sexual violence?

Suggested Readings

BARTHEL, D. (1988) *Putting on Appearances: Gender and Advertising.* Philadelphia: Temple University Press.

BERGER, R. J., P. SEARLES, and C. E. COTTLE. (1991) *Feminism and Pornography.* New York: Praeger.

GOFFMAN, E. (1976) *Gender Advertisements.* New York: Harper Colophon Books.

HUNTER, I., D. SAUNDERS, and D. WILLIAMSON. (1993) *On Pornography: Literature, Sexuality and Obscenity Law.* New York: St. Martin's Press.

LEWIS, L. A. (1990) *Gender Politics and MTV.* Philadelphia: Temple University Press.

5

Sexual Humor

THEORIES OF SEXUAL HUMOR

Introduction

Sexual humor is found in every society and throughout recorded history. Sexual jokes and cartoons were scribbled on the walls of pyramids and tombs by ancient Egyptian workmen (Manniche, 1987), were common in ancient Rome (Richlin, 1992), and are found in ancient Chinese texts (Levy, 1973) (see Focus on Diversity SF5.1) It is not surprising that sexuality is the subject of so much humor, since humor tries to expose our hidden selves, and society often tries to hide the sexual sides of our nature. That is why there is no more absurd image than a well-dressed man with his pants down: when the genitals are exposed, so is the basic truth that "civilized" people are also animals, try as they might to hide that fact.

What is sexual humor? The answer is not as easy as you might think. Clearly, a joke that concerns genitals or intercourse is considered sexual humor; but what about a joke like this:

"What reading material would you choose if you were marooned on a desert island?" the young lady was asked. She replied, "A tattooed sailor!"

Here, sex is vaguely implied. Is that a sexual joke? Or what about jokes about marriage, or relationships, that are about male–female relationships but not about sex?

What's a man's idea of helping with housework? Lifting his legs so you can vacuum.

It is difficult to know where sexual joking ends, and jokes about life begin.

Humor and sex may go together well because they are so similar in how they are experienced. Like lovemaking, a good joke or story involves slowly increasing tension until the tension suddenly breaks in convulsive bodily jerking; a good laugh is, in many ways, similar to a good orgasm. But laughter releases this tension more quickly than orgasm, and, while not everyone can experience multiple orgasms, almost everyone can experience multiple bouts of laughter.

Sexuality is an anxiety-producing part of human life, and good sexual humor exposes the contradictions and problems of being sexual animals. So much tension and anxiety is built up around sexuality that it is easy to provoke

Focus
on Diversity
SF5.1

Erotic Humor in Ancient Civilizations

There is nothing new about sexual jokes. Ancient civilizations used sexual humor; in fact, some of the earliest examples of humor that we have found are sexual. Different cultures find different things funny; for example, in Japan, flatulence (farting) is considered a symbol of good fortune, while in China, it is a cause for embarrassment or shame (Levy, 1973). So, as you might imagine, they are portrayed differently in the humor the two cultures.

The sexual jokes of ancient Egyptians are illustrated in the cartoons and graffiti that have survived on flakes of pottery and on papyrus. Although many of the cartoons look humorous to us today, it is difficult to tell if they were intentionally drawn as comedy. Do you think the cartoon pictured here was meant to be funny?

In her book about sexuality and aggression in Roman humor, Amy Richlin (1992) shows that Roman writings and poems were full of sexual satires, insults and mockery, and aggressive sexual humor. The following graffiti, taken from the walls of the Italian city of Pompeii, buried by a volcano more than 1,900 years ago (A.D. 79), seem like they could be found on walls today: *"Sabina, you give blojobs, you don' do good"* (it is misspelled in the original Latin). *"Equitas' slave Cosmus is a big queer and a cocksucker with his legs wide open."*

China also has a history of sex jokes, dating back at least hundreds of years (Levy, 1973). Interestingly, while the West has a long history of humor directed at women, in East Asian humor women are rarely portrayed as foolish, while men are often so portrayed. Also, Chinese jokes, even sexual ones, often also have a political theme and imply some criticism of Chinese officials. Since virginity was valued in women, many Chinese sexual jokes focus on a woman who accidentally reveals that she is not a virgin on her wedding night, or who is sensuous, aggressive, or sexually active. *A girl was intimate with a man, and her parents found out and scolded her. She bowed submissively and explained: "It's all because I was raped that day, it wasn't my idea!" "Then why didn't you cry out?" her parents asked. "Mama, I felt like crying out but just think—how could I cry out when my tongue was pressed deeply into his mouth?"*

Sometimes sexual humor can crop up where you least expect it. The Talmud, the basic explanation of Jewish law, is a serious discussion by the rabbis of their interpretation of the Bible and its laws. But it also relates stories and anecdotes, such as this seemingly irrelevant account (a "kav" is a liquid measure, like an ounce): *Rabbi Jonathan said: "Rabbi Ishmael's penis was like a wineskin of nine kav's capacity." Rev Pappa said: "Rabbi Jonathan's penis was like a wineskin of five kav's capacity." Some report him as giving the measurement as three kav's capacity. And what about Rav Pappa himself? His penis was like a Harpanian jug* (Bava Metsia 84a).

blue humor: A term referring to sexually oriented jokes.

burlesque: A theatrical form that uses coarse, vulgar, or sexual humor and was commonly performed in houses of burlesque throughout the first half of the twentieth century.

laughter simply by a sexual suggestion or innuendo (which explains why many comedians rely so much on **blue humor**). However, since so many taboos also center on sexuality, comedians must be careful about timing and audience when using sexual humor; what is funny to one group of people may be offensive to another. It is this tension between the allowed and the forbidden, the obvious (that humans have sex) and the hidden (we are not allowed to show it), that makes sexual humor so effective.

The tension between humor and eroticism was used by houses of **burlesque**, where comedians would come out after strippers and "puncture" the erotic tension by causing the patrons to laugh (Davis, 1983). This cycle of erotic tension followed by humorous release is also used in films and television, which only go so far in showing eroticism, and then relieve the erotic tension through humor. Often, if the film itself fails to do that, an audience member's well-placed wisecrack can serve the same purpose.

Houses of burlesque often featured strippers, chorus girls, and vaudeville acts with a Master of Ceremonies, usually a comedian, who tied the acts together with lewd, humorous remarks.

Humor is taken seriously by psychologists and other researchers trying to understand the human mind. Freud himself wrote a whole treatise on humor and why we find things funny. Let us review some of the general theories about humor and then try to see where sexual humor fits in.

Theoretical Perspectives

Humor is a fundamental part of human communication. Watch two people talking, and take note of how often they laugh and smile, and you will begin to appreciate how common and important a part of normal conversation joking, humor, and laughter are. Yet laughter is one of the most curious of human behaviors. Crying, in comparison, is easy to understand; it is an expression of grief or loss or pain, and it seems to help lessen the tensions associated with those emotions. But why laugh? Why are things funny? Theorists have come up with a variety of explanations about why we laugh, and what humor is.

Biological Theories

One set of theories suggests that humor and laughter are physiologically built into us; they are part of our nervous system and serve some adaptive evolutionary function. Many researchers have speculated over the years about how exactly humor is beneficial physiologically; laughter has been said to help circulation, massage the vital organs, facilitate digestion, or oxygenate the blood. Others believe that humor is an instinct, developed to help people cope with the minor irritations of living without becoming depressed about them. Still others have suggested that laughter is a leftover trace of other ancient behaviors, in the same way that our appendix is a leftover organ whose function we no longer need. For example, perhaps laughter developed before language and was used to indicate good news or that the group was safe and could relax. One theorist suggests that laughter is the remnant of a successful attack against a foe (Keith-Spiegel, 1972). Laughter involves many of the same actions as attacking—exposing teeth, sudden screaming, contorting the face, sprawling the limbs—and may have eventually become a substitute, as people began to live together in civilization, for actual assaults.

Some biological theorists have suggested that laughter is an evolutionary leftover from acts of aggression. Note the similarities in the aggressive expression of the ape and the laughing face of the human being.

The problem with these types of theories is similar to looking at sexuality only through a biological lens: it does not explain the subtleties and complexity of human behavior. A purely biological view cannot explain why we laugh at different things in different cultures, or why some things make us laugh and others do not. It cannot account for complex verbal humor such as irony or satire. Surely there is a biological component to laughter, but it is too complex to leave it at that.

Superiority Theories

Aristotle suggested that our sense of humor (or our sense of the "ludicrous," as he put it) comes from noting some defect, deformity, or ugliness in others that gives us a sense of superiority. Other theorists have also suggested that humor, to some degree, arises from comparing ourselves with others, or with other situations, and feeling a sense of mastery or control (Wyer and Collins, 1992). Even if we feel sympathy for another's misfortune, laughter arises because, just for a moment, we get a feeling that (compared with the other guy) we are O.K. That may be why we laugh more at people who are considered socially undesirable than those who are above us in social rank.

For example, in the early 1990s a whole series of "blond" jokes appeared: jokes that made fun of blond women:

> *Why did the blond stare for an hour at the frozen orange juice container? Because the box said "concentrate."*

> *Parked together in a romantic spot, the boy said to his blond girlfriend, "Honey, why don't you go get comfortable in the back seat?" She replied, "Gee, I'd rather stay up here with you."*

Why are these jokes (supposed to be) funny? Because they instill in the listener a sense of superiority: "I could not be that stupid!" Pretty soon, some male jokes appeared to offset the blond jokes:

Why are dumb blond jokes so short? So men can understand them.

Some men did not find those jokes as funny as blond jokes (which made them feel superior to women), while many women thought they were a scream (in part because they made them feel superior to men). All jokes, to some degree or another, instill that sense, say superiority theories.

Release and Relief Theories

We laugh to release tension and anxiety, say release theorists, and the laughter response itself—the spasms of the diaphragm, the release of air, the momentary sense of relaxation and even exhaustion we feel after a good laugh—all point to its function in relieving tension. Theorists have taken different positions on exactly what tensions and anxieties jokes are supposed to release, such as aggressive impulses or, in the case of Freud, our sexual impulses (see "Psychoanalytic Theories" below).

Incongruity, Configurational, and Surprise Theories

This commonly held group of theories suggest that we laugh when a situation disrupts our normal ways of thinking, or our normal routines. However, each of these three theories suggest that humor is disruptive in different ways. **Incongruity theory** suggests that we find it funny when two things are put together that seem to emphasize a contradiction or contrariness in the other. A joke sets up a line of reasoning that we think we follow, and then disrupts our expectations with an unexpected punch line (Wyer and Collins, 1992).

> *A young Catholic priest is walking through town when he is approached by a prostitute. "How about a quickie for twenty dollars?" she asks. The priest, puzzled, shakes her off, and continues on his way, only to be stopped by another prostitute. "Twenty bucks for a quickie," she offers. He rushes on. Finally, he approaches his home in the country, and as he walks up to the door he sees a nun. "Pardon me, sister," he says, "But what's a quickie?" "Twenty dollars, same as in town," she replies.*

Here, the expected sanctity of the nun is turned around by the punch line, after the joke has already reinforced the expectation that religious people are sexually naive by the priest's behavior. Many incongruity theorists suggest that the foundation of humor is putting two (or more) things together that are basically conflicting, like the religiosity of the nun and her sexual response.

Configurational theories are like incongruity theories but suggest that it is not the tension between two opposing things itself that leads to the humor response, but the coming together, the "falling into place" or insight that makes us laugh.

> *A woman says to her physician, "Doctor, every time my husband and I make love, I feel either very hot or very cold." The doctor examines the woman and finds nothing wrong. Finally, he calls her husband and asks for his explanation, and the husband replies: "Very simple—once in the summer, once in the winter."*

incongruity theory: A theory that humor involves bringing two things together that seem to highlight a contradiction in each other.

configurational theory: The theory that laughter happens when a situation of seeming contradiction falls into place all at once.

Figure **SF5.1**

We expect construction workers to whistle or come on to a female, not to make comments on her shoes; incongruity theory would explain that the contradiction is what makes this cartoon funny.

punch line: The final line of a joke, which resolves the joke; the line that people are supposed to respond to with laughter.

Our puzzlement at the woman's complaint is resolved, and laughter begins, at the **punch line**; the story becomes funny when it is resolved through a single thought that "punches" us, or strikes us as it resolves incongruity. Humor is almost a type of problem solving, and laughter comes when all becomes clear to us, when the contradictions are resolved.

A related idea to these two theories is **surprise theory**, in which surprise, suddenness, or shock is cited as a necessary (although not always sufficient) aspect of humor. Like incongruity, suddenness breaks through routine courses of thought or action, and many theorists blend surprise and incongruity theories.

surprise theory: A theory that says that humor or laughter comes from the act of being surprised or shocked during the course of a joke or situation.

> *The female student wiggled up to her professor after class and murmured suggestively, "I didn't do very well on the test today, but I'll do anything to pass this course—and I mean anything!" "Really?" asked the professor. "Absolutely!" she purred. "Try studying," snapped the professor.*

Surprise theorists can also explain why hearing a joke over again is not as funny as the first time; the shock or surprise is gone.

Ambivalence Theories

ambivalence theory: A theory of humor that suggests humor comes from a conflict of emotions in the listener.

Ambivalence theorists suggest that laughter does not come from a conflict of perception, as incongruity theorists suggest, but a conflict of *emotions*. Socrates said that laughter arises from the simultaneous pleasure and pain one gets from envy and malice. Ambivalence theorists have suggested that laughter comes from a mixture of joy and sorrow, love and hate, mania and depression, superiority and limitation, sympathy and animosity, or other conflicting emotions.

> *A woman was complaining to her friend about her husband's lack of sexual attentiveness. "Why, if anything ever happened to me," she said, "he wouldn't even be able to identify the body!"*

This joke works, say ambivalence theorists, because it elicits in us feelings of both sympathy (for her) and superiority (this would never happen to me).

Psychoanalytic Theories

Sigmund Freud was, in one sense, a release theorist. Release theorists, we noted above, suggest that laughter occurs when a strain is alleviated or anxiety is broken. Freud (1960 [1905]) suggested that there is a similarity between jokes and dreams: both are our attempts to get around our internal censor to express those things that we cannot usually express in society because of our inhibitions. Dreams disguise our forbidden thoughts, while jokes hide our inhibitions behind innuendo and suggestion. To Freud, the tension that is broken in humor is the "psychic energy" that is stored up as our superegos censor our infantile desires and wishes, which are often sexual. In his book, *Jokes and Their Relation to the Unconscious,* Freud (1960 [1905]:96–97) wrote:

> *The purpose of jokes can easily be reviewed. Where a joke is not an aim in itself—that is, where it is not an innocent one—there are only two purposes that it may serve, and these two can themselves be subsumed under a single heading. It is either a hostile joke, (serving the purpose of aggressiveness, satire, or defense) or an obscene joke (serving the purpose of exposure).*

Aggression and sexuality are the two things that society forces us to repress; hostile and erotic jokes are ways to release the stress caused by trying to stop these desires.

The problem with all the theories above is that they seem to be able to explain some types of jokes, but not others. A joke that builds a situation and resolves it with a punch line is one thing; but how is a quick, throwaway one-liner in a social context able to build up tensions and release them? How is the laughter that greets someone who spills coffee on his or her pants explained by ambivalence theory? Why do we laugh at a funny walk or expression? That no one has managed to explain a simple act like human laughter in satisfactory manner shows how complex and difficult it is to understand any human behavior.

TYPES OF SEXUAL HUMOR

Even though the most common jokes worldwide are those that focus on some aspect of male–female relationships, they are not usually explicitly sexual. American humor is more sexually explicit than that of other countries. Europeans tend to think of American humor as "smutty," and sexually explicit humor is so foreign to Africans and Asians that they often do not understand it at all, even in translation (Janus et al., 1986).

American humor expresses our unique national ambivalence about sex. We come from a Puritan background that demanded suppression of sexuality, and we still retain a general disapproval of sexuality; yet we allow an enormous amount of sexual material and erotic suggestion in our movies, television, advertising, and other media. The humor of other countries, like American humor, tends to focus on male–female relationships; it is just that the sexual aspects are suggested more than spoken, hinted at more than revealed.

Forms of Humor

Sexual humor comes in many forms, including visual jokes, verbal jokes, written jokes, funny poetry, cartoons, etc. Below, we review some of the more prominent ways sexual humor is communicated.

"Dirty" Jokes

Why are jokes about sexuality considered "dirty"? Why is the idea of being soiled part of our attitude toward sex in general and sexual humor in particular? Perhaps it can be traced back to the Bible's use of the term "unclean" to refer to various sinful states. But it remains a part of the undercurrent of American thought that sexual language makes one somehow unclean; that is why children who used profanity used to get their mouths washed out with soap. On the other hand, as we mentioned, its forbidden nature may be part of what makes sexual humor so funny.

In his classic two-volume book about sexual humor, *The Rationale of the Dirty Joke*[1] (one of the first scholarly treatments of sexual humor, and still one of the best), Gershon Legman (1968) divided sexual jokes into fifteen categories, including children, animals, sadism, adultery, homosexuality, prostitution, castration, and "disease and disgust," among others. Each category was subdivided into sections; for example, below is the Table of Contents entry under "Women":

With all these categories in just one chapter, you can imagine the kinds of jokes he recounts in the chapter on "scatology" (excrement). There are no taboo subjects in sexual humor; in those things that are most forbidden, anxiety is the greatest, and humor is therefore at its most effective.

---

[1]The book was later reprinted as *No Laughing Matter.*

Legman believed that dirty jokes were told and appreciated mostly by men, and served to define and clarify their relationship to women. He took primarily a Freudian view of humor, which he saw as a way to relieve tensions built up over our anxiety about sexual issues. Legman also believed that the kind of sexual humor a person particularly enjoys holds a key to that person's character, and by asking a person "What is your favorite joke?" we can reveal something about their deepest problems, concerns, or pre-occupations. For example:

> *Adam To Eve, right after being created, as he looks down at himself: "Stand back! I don't know how big this thing gets!"*

Here, many things combine to make this joke funny. We need to have a knowledge of Adam and Eve, we must understand that the joke refers to his erection, we have to realize that Adam and Eve would be sexually naive, and we must not find the joke religiously or otherwise offensive. If any of these elements are missing, the joke will not seem funny.

SEX TALK

QUESTION **SF5.1**   **What does it reveal about a person who uses sexual humor all the time?**

People may use sexual humor for a variety of reasons. Sexual humor is usually intended to shock, which brings attention. Some people may have a hard time getting the attention they want, and may find that sexual humor at least gets a reaction out of people. Sexual humor, like all other kinds of humor, works best in moderation.

Today, the humor section of any good bookstore is filled with collections of dirty jokes. Jokes with sexual implications are routinely used by comedians on television, and some of our most famous stand-up comedians have night club acts that would have had longshoremen blushing and women fainting in an earlier day. But things have changed, not in small part due to the career and humor of Lenny Bruce, recounted in Personal Voices SF5.1. Bruce, more than any other entertainer, showed how sexually oriented humor could reveal truths about our society and its attitudes toward sex.

Poetry

Poetry has its own sexual form: the limerick. The definitive book on the limerick was written by Gershon Legman (1969), the same person who wrote the definitive work on the dirty joke. Legman points out that the limerick has always been primarily an indecent verse form, and "clean" limericks have never really been of interest to anyone. Though limericks had been used in nursery rhymes as far back as the fourteenth century, dirty limericks became a fad in both England and the United States in the 1860s, when literally thousands were written and circulated.

The real appeal of limericks is that they are a *folk* art form. Limericks were passed around through word of mouth, and because of their explicitly sexual content, publishers were always reluctant to print them. Legman's exhaustive book (in two volumes; Volume I has seventeen hundred limericks—all dirty) has chapters with titles like "Strange Intercourse," "Abuses of the Clergy," "Zoophily" (sex with animals), and "Buggery" (anal sex). Most limericks are just five-line stanzas:

*P*ersonal
V O I C E S

SF5.1

Stand-Up Comedy:
An American Art Form

Throughout history, the professional humorist has served as a critic of society, pointing out its flaws. The court jester, for example, was the only person who was allowed to make fun of the king, and his humor was usually directed toward pointing out the king's foibles and failings. Other great humorists expressed their critiques of society through books and plays.

Stand-up comedy is a relatively new form of professional humor, and a particularly American one. Will Rogers traveled across the country with his uniquely American brand of stand-up humor and was one of the most beloved men of the twentieth century. Milton Berle ushered in the age of television by appearing in a dress (which elicited gales of laughter), and comics like George Burns and Gracie Allen got most of their material through playing on male–female and marital relations. The history of stand-up comedy in America goes hand-in-hand with the modern history of sexual humor in America. But the man who really broke all taboos about sexual humor in the United States was Lenny Bruce.

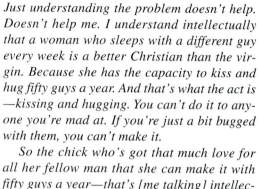

Lenny Bruce

Lenny Bruce was more than a comedian, for his satire was directed at the sexual and racial injustices he saw in society. Bruce's successful career deteriorated as he was banned in many cities, arrested for obscenity and possession of drugs, and finally declared a bankrupt pauper shortly before he died in 1966. But he opened the way for the modern stand-up comics today who can talk about sex and use profanity without fear of being hauled off the stage by the police. When we read his routines today, they seem tame, yet his routines were radical and shocking in the 1950s. Here is a sample of a Bruce routine where he considers the hypocrisy of a man valuing virginity while ogling sexy women:

Just understanding the problem doesn't help. Doesn't help me. I understand intellectually that a woman who sleeps with a different guy every week is a better Christian than the virgin. Because she has the capacity to kiss and hug fifty guys a year. And that's what the act is —kissing and hugging. You can't do it to anyone you're mad at. If you're just a bit bugged with them, you can't make it.

So the chick who's got that much love for all her fellow man that she can make it with fifty guys a year—that's [me talking] intellectually; but emotionally, I don't want to be that fifty-first guy. Cause I learned my lesson early, man. The people told me, "This is the way it is, Virgin is Good, Virgin is Good." Yeah that's really weird.

This conflict, you know, like you talk to the average guy:

"Isn't that a pretty chick?"

"Yeah, she's beautiful."

"What's her beauty—to you?"

"Well, ah, she's got a pretty face, nutty jugs. . . ."

"Well, ah, would you marry a woman like that?"

"Of course."

"You'd like her for your wife?"

"Sure!"

"Would you let your wife dress that way?"

"No no no!"

"Why not?"

"Cause she got her jugs stickin out, man."

"What'd you dig her for in the first place?"

"Cause her jugs stickin out."

"But you don't want her to dress that way."

"No, no!"

So that's where the conflict is—we want for a wife a combination kindergarten teacher and a hooker.

Derived from Cohen (1967)

In the Garden of Eden sat Adam,
Happily stroking his Madam.
   Great was his mirth,
   For on all the earth,
There were only two balls—and he had 'em.

Limericks can be linked into themes, such as the famous story of "The Farter from Sparta" (found in the chapter of Legman's book entitled "Excrement"), which is made up of twelve limericks (See Personal Voices SF5.2.)

Of course, erotic poems come in other forms as well. Walt Whitman, the great American poet, has many erotic passages in his book-length poem "Leaves of Grass"; and a best-selling book of the late 1980s, *The White Hotel,* began with a long poem that was extremely erotic in content. But in terms of having an erotic poetic form, the limerick wins, hands down.

Cartoons

From the artisans who made the pyramids to modern magazines, sexual cartoons have been a favorite form of sexual humor. In the United States, *Playboy* magazine has been the premier magazine for sexual cartoons for many years. Started by Hugh Hefner in 1953, *Playboy* was an overnight success, due to its air of urban sophistication, its articles and fiction from the nation's top-ranked authors, its tasteful pictures of nudity, and its humor pieces, especially cartoons. In fact, according to Dines-Levy and Smith (1988), who did a study of *Playboy* cartoons, *Playboy* had more cartoons in the 1970s (erotic or otherwise) than any other mass circulation magazine in the United States, and it was dubbed by some "America's chief humor magazine" for that reason. Since then, many other magazines (men's, women's, and general) also include cartoons with sexual humor. Even the *New Yorker,* America's most sophisticated cartoon humor magazine, includes cartoons that focus on marriage, gender, and even (implied) sexuality.

The single-frame cartoons featured in *Playboy* are very popular; in fact, cartoons are the most highly rated part of *Playboy* and *Playgirl* magazines (even more than the

"Why won't you cuddle?"

Figure SF5.2
The *New Yorker* often has cartoons that play on gender relations in the United States.

Personal
VOICES

The Farter from Sparta
(written between 1938 and 1948)

There was a young fellow from Sparta
A really magnificent farter,
 On the strength of one bean
 He'd fart "God Save the Queen"
And Beethoven's Moonlight Sonata.

He could vary, with proper persuasion,
His fart to suit any occasion.
 He could fart like a flute,
 Like a lark, like a lute,
This highly fartistic Caucasian.

This sparkling young farter from Sparta,
His fart for no money would barter.
 He could roar from his rear
 Any scene from Shakespeare
Or Gilbert and Sullivan's Mikado.

He'd fart a gavotte for a starter,
And fizzle a fine serenata.
 He could play from his anus
 The Coriolanus:
Oof, boom, er-tum, tootle, um tah-dah!

He was great in the Christmas Cantata,
He could double-stop fart the Toccata
 He'd boom from his ass,
 Bach's B-Minor Mass,
And in counterpoint, La Traviata.

Spurred on by a very high wager
With an envious German named Bager
 He'd proceeded to fart
 The complete oboe part
Of a Hadyn Octet in B-major.

His repertoire ranged from classics to jazz,
He achieved new effects with bubbles of gas
 With a good dose of salts
 He could whistle a waltz
Or swing it in razzamatazz.

His basso profundo with timbre so rare
He rendered quite often with power to spare.
 But his great work of art,
 His fortissimo fart,
He saved for the Marche Militare.

One day he was dared to perform
The William Tell Overture Storm,
 But naught could dishearten
 Our spirited Spartan
For his fart was in wonderful form.

It went off in capital style,
And he farted it through with a smile,
 Then feeling quite jolly
 He tried the finale,
Blowing double-stopped farts all the while.

The selection was tough, I admit,
But it did not dismay him one bit,
 Then, with ass thrown aloft
 He suddenly coughed . . .
And collapsed in a shower of shit.

His bunghole was blown back to Sparta
Where they buried the rest of our farter,
 With a gravestone of turds
 Inscribed with the words:
"To the Fine Art of Farting, A Martyr."

Quoted in Legman (1969:152–154)

nude pictures) (Dines-Levy and Smith, 1988). Cartoons are simple, quick, visually appealing, make few demands on the reader, and can reveal a truism about life in a very compact space (which is why political cartoons are so popular). On the other hand, the content of the cartoons in *Playboy* have been strongly criticized for reinforcing stereotypes of women as sexual objects and men as lecherous and promiscuous (Dines-Levy and Smith, 1988).

Cycles of Humor

Most of us learn jokes from our friends, not by reading them in magazines or seeing them on TV. Jokes and limericks are part of the popular culture, part of our collective folklore. For example, periodically a group of jokes on the same topic circulates around the country, and within a short time everyone seems to have heard them. That is what we mean by a **cycle of humor**.

Some of these joke cycles become very familiar to most Americans in a short time. Alan Dundes (1987), in *Cracking Jokes: Studies of Humor Cycles and Stereotypes*, describes the rise and fall of America's fascination with dead baby jokes, quadriplegic jokes, elephant jokes, Jewish-American Princess jokes, ethnic humor, lightbulb jokes, and even describes the joke cycles that circulate in other countries. These jokes come and go; elephant jokes were the rage in the 1960s, and are now all but forgotten:

> *What's big and gray and comes in quarts? An elephant.*

> *What do you get when you cross an elephant with a prostitute? A three-quarter-ton pickup.*

Why do we have these cycles of sexual jokes? Dundes suggests that "jokelore," as he calls it, serves an important purpose in folk society by allowing people to comment on those things that cause them the most anxiety and are uppermost in their thoughts. For example, we do not have a lot of underground political jokes in the United States because we have a free press, and so we can read political criticism every day; more oppressed countries are usually filled with them. However, sexuality, racism, disease, national disasters, and gruesomeness are less open to discussion, are more repressed, and find an outlet in popular humor. That is why cycles of jokes often come after particularly painful disasters; jokes followed the Challenger Shuttle disaster, the Chernobyl nuclear accident in Russia, the Gulf War, the burning of the Davidian compound of David Koresh in Waco, Texas, the AIDS epidemic, and almost all other national disasters; they also followed stories like the Bobbit case, the Rodney King beating in Los Angeles, and the O. J. Simpson trial. These "**gallows humor**" jokes also appear in operating rooms, morgues, and any other place where the touch of death and disaster threaten to overwhelm people. Laughter in those places, no matter how gruesome the joke, breaks the tension and helps people to function in the face of tragedy or discomfort.

cycle of humor: Groups of jokes with common themes that circulate widely among people, often in response to national circumstances.

gallows humor: Jokes that are made in situations of stress or fear to help break the tension; originated from the jokes often made by people about to be hanged on the gallows.

SEXUAL HUMOR AND GENDER

Sigmund Freud had a very specific view of the purpose of a sexual joke in a social context. He wrote:

> *We know what is meant by "smut": The intentional bringing into prominence of sexual facts and relations by speech. . . . It is a further relevant fact that smut is directed to a particular person, by whom one is sexually excited and who, on hearing it, is expected to become aware of the speaker's excitement and as a result to become sexually excited in turn. Instead of this excitement the other person may be led to feel shame or embarrassment, which is only a reaction against the excitement and, in a roundabout way, is an admission of it. Smut is thus originally directed towards women and may be equated with attempts at seduction. If a man in the company of men enjoys telling or listening to smut, the original situation, which owing to social situations*

> *cannot be realized, is at the same time imagined. A person who laughs at smut that he hears is laughing as though he were the spectator of an act of sexual aggression.*
>
> *Freud (1960 [1905]:97)*

This is an astonishing statement, for in it Freud, who has often been accused of neglecting women or even of being a misogynist, presages the arguments of many feminist critics more than half a century later: that sexually explicit language by men, including sexual jokes, are in essence an attack on women, and in that sense are a type of sexual assault.

What is the relationship of sexual joking to the relation between the sexes? Are sexual jokes necessarily hostile to women? Aren't there "gender neutral" sexual jokes? And how about jokes that are hostile to men?

Jokes That Are Disparaging to Women

One of the striking things about a historical look at humor in general (not just sexual humor) is how much of it is directed at women and marriage. Even in 1923, in his seminal book *The Psychology of Laughter and Comedy,* Greig noted this trend. Aristophanes, Greig noted, never tired of making fun of Athenian women, and throughout the Middle Ages, women were the most frequent objects of humor (with clergy coming in a close second). He also noted that many of the jokes of the early twentieth century were simply the jokes of centuries past, rewritten slightly to fit the times, but with the same ideas and similar punch lines. Greig (1923:5) seems to quickly get to the heart of the matter with his musings on why men enjoy joking about women so much:

> *How are we to explain this immortal laughter of men? It would seem that the general attitude of man towards woman is what the psycho-analysts would call ambivalent. Woman is for man the natural object of both love and hate, and his attitude towards her is now predominantly the one, now predominantly the other, and generally both together in some measure. The ambivalence of emotion may be, and constantly is, disguised.*

When we think of the classic gender jokes, and the classic categories of gender jokes, most are jibes at women: jokes about wives, mothers-in-law, "women's logic," women drivers, promiscuous women. Even a male category such as the "henpecked husband" is really about the wife who dominates him (Dundes, 1987).

Greig claimed that most jokes are created by men, and that men do more joking than women. It is difficult to determine whether or not most jokes throughout history are the creations of men; it may just be that, since men did more writing than women throughout history, more men's jokes survive. For a long time, even among psychologists and others who study humor, it was assumed that men were blessed with a sense of humor while women were basically humorless. In 1885, in response to these types of claims, Kate Sanborn wrote a book called *The Wit of Women* to demonstrate women's unique brand of humor (Sheppard, 1986). Yet the stereotype persisted for years. For example, it is only recently that women have begun to appear with any regularity as stand-up comics; even though there were many examples of funny women in the 1960s and 1970s (Phyllis Diller, Carol Burnett, Lucille Ball, Joan Rivers, etc.), most people in the entertainment industry believed that women simply were not as funny as men (Janus et al., 1986).

Of course, both men and women tell jokes, create jokes, laugh at jokes, and appreciate jokes. In a study of gender and humor, Crawford and Gressley (1991) could detect no differences in how men and women describe their sense of humor or in what they consider important components of humor. There were differences in the types of humor each enjoyed (men preferred hostile humor, jokes, and cartoons, while women preferred anecdotes and stories). Yet even in their study, both men and women were more likely to choose a male model as embodying a good sense of humor. In that sense, people still buy society's stereotype of humor as a masculine trait.

Another reason women may have seemed humorless to some is that such a large percentage of men's jokes insult women, and women may not find those jokes funny. Carolyn Miller, one of the creators of the "Antioch Sense of Humor Inventory," which measures preferences for different types of humor, writes:

> *We* [the inventors of the inventory] *found it necessary to distinguish sexual jokes that express hostility toward men or women from those that are "purely" sexual—ie, that simply celebrate or laugh at sexuality without a backhand slam at the opposite sex. Much of what has traditionally been considered sexual humor actually involves hostility to women, and research with our test indicates that when one separates the two, women enjoy sexual humor as much as men do. (It's only fair, however, to point out that women take as much delight in humor that degrades men as men do in humor that degrades women.)*
>
> *Miller (1985:173)*

Changes in Gender and Humor

As gender roles have changed over the last thirty years, so has the nature of humor. Feminism has made it less socially acceptable to tell jokes that disparage women, although those jokes still exist. Similarly, women seem to be more willing to publicly tell jokes that paint men in a less than flattering light. Let us examine some of these trends.

Women's Humor

The relationship between gender and humor is changing in two different ways. First, more and more jokes are appearing that make men their target; and second, more and more women's humor is being published and performed by professional female comedians. These new outlets for female humor allow women to joke about what it is like to be a woman—especially having to deal with men. Men are not used to being the butt of women's jokes, while women have put up with it for years; it is interesting to watch men listening to some of the modern female comedians who insult them, for they seem much more uncomfortable when they are the target of women comedians than women do when being made fun of by men. Even in popular jokes the battle of the sexes is in full swing. In Sexuality Today SF5.1, for example, we recount a cycle of humor, created by average people, which was passed between friends until it included hundreds of jokes. The humor itself is quite telling about the way the two sexes regarded each other in the 1980s.

The amount of comedy by and for women has been rapidly increasing. Despite the fact that feminists have often been stereotyped as lacking a sense of humor (*How many feminists does it take to screw in a lightbulb? That's not funny!*), many of the first collections of women's humor were published by feminist comedians, such as *Titters: The*

SEXUALITY *Today*

Men and Women Confront Each Other—With Jokes

For a while, the photocopy machine became a new tool in the distribution of jokes and humor (it has now probably been taken over by the fax and computer networks). During the 1980s, photocopies began appearing in offices entitled: "Ninety-Seven Reasons Why Cucumbers Are Better than Men." Ninety-seven reasons eventually multiplied into hundreds of reasons, and the collections were even published in two books. Men soon got into the act, and responded with "The Reasons Sheep are Better than Women." Below are a few of the reasons from each list. Note that the humor (and the sting) of these jokes is in their truth; these jibes reveal things that really bother each sex about the other. Try to read these as an anthropologist from another culture might read them, as a study in American attitudes between the sexes as much as in the study of sexual humor. What can you tell about the dissatisfaction between the sexes from these jokes?

Why Cucumbers Are Better than Men

The average cucumber is at least six inches long.

Cucumbers stay hard for a week.

A cucumber will always respect you in the morning.

You can go to a movie with a cucumber and see the movie.

A cucumber won't ask: "Am I the first?"

Cucumbers won't tell other cucumbers you're not a virgin anymore.

Cucumbers will never make a scene because there are other cucumbers in the refrigerator.

A cucumber won't care what time of the month it is.

Cucumbers don't leave whisker burns, fall asleep on your chest, or drool on your pillow.

Cucumbers won't make you sleep on the wet spot.

A cucumber doesn't use your toothbrush, roll-on, or hairspray.

A cucumber never forgets to flush the toilet, and the seat is always the way you left it.

A cucumber will never leave you for:
—another woman
—another man
—another cucumber

A cucumber never snaps your bra or pinches your butt.

A cucumber never has to call its wife.

Cucumbers don't play the guitar and try to find themselves.

You don't have to wait until half-time to talk to your cucumber.

The Reasons Sheep are Better than Women

The Woolgrower's Association isn't nearly as nasty as the National Organization of Women.

There is a livestock auction once a week.

Sheep don't have a gag reflex, or upper teeth.

You can get a better grip on sheep's ears.

Cottonmouth is easier to get rid of than a social disease.

A sheep won't compare your technique to former boyfriends or her first husband.

Sheep won't drink your liquor, smoke your weed, snort your coke, and then tell you they have to be home early.

Sheep never ask about your former lovers and then get pissed off when you tell them.

Sheep don't get moody once a month.

A sheep doesn't expect you to support her for the rest of her life after one roll in the hay.

A sheep never wears curlers and a mud pack to bed.

A sheep doesn't stop screwing after the honeymoon.

A sheep won't lead you on and then tell her parents she was raped.

A sheep won't expect you to pay for the baby-sitter, to pay her way through school, to pay $100 an hour for her therapist, to pay . . . and pay . . . and pay.

A sheep will never sue you for palimony.

A sheep won't care if your secretary is better looking than she is.

Sheep won't cheat on you with your best friend.

Sheep never have a headache.

Derived from Dundes (1987)

Figure SF5.3
Female cartoonists are beginning to produce cartoons that show their views of men and the relations between the sexes.

First Collection of Humor by Women (Stillman and Beatts, 1976). Other collections of women's humor have been appearing recently, such as *In Stitches: A Patchwork of Feminist Humor and Satire* (Kaufman, 1991); *Pulling Our Own Strings* (Kaufman and Blakely, 1980); and *Women's Glib* and *Women's Glibber* (Warren, 1991; 1992). Much of this humor is directed at men, as a corrective, perhaps, to centuries of mother-in-law and wife jokes.

Gay and Lesbian Humor

Another trend worthy of noting is the increase in comedians and comedy devoted to gay and lesbian issues. Gay nightclubs are now full of gay comedians, commenting on the particular humor of gay life, and at the annual lesbian festival in Mount Holyoke,

Massachusetts, lesbian comics perform every year. Gay magazines like the *Advocate* and lesbian magazines like *Off Our Backs* routinely run gay and lesbian cartoons. Although these comedians often find it hard to break into mainstream comedy clubs, lesbian humor often makes it into general women's anthologies (Kaufman, 1991; Warren, 1991, 1992).

Gay humor has been more successfully mainstreamed in the theater. It began with the groundbreaking *La Cage Aux Folles,* a play and movie about a gay couple in France, and since then there has been great success with Broadway shows such as *Angels in America.* In fact, plays with gay themes are extremely popular, and New York theater now routinely has four or five plays running that have some gay content.

HUMOR AND SEXUALITY

One more category of humor and sex should be mentioned: the connection between a sense of humor and sexuality. One mistake that adolescents often make is to take sexuality with complete seriousness; although the decision to be sexually active and the precautions needed to be sexually safe certainly deserve the most serious attention, sexuality itself can be playful, joyous, and funny. Ruch and Hehl (1988) found a correlation between appreciation of sex humor and scales of sexual libido, satisfaction, experience, and pleasure; those who had a good sense of sexual humor also had good sex lives. In other words, do not be afraid to laugh at yourself, and at the human condition—we all have sex hang-ups to one degree or another, and the best thing to do is to laugh at them and not take things *too* seriously!

Summary

- Sexual humor is universal, and encompasses humor about sexuality, sexual relationships, and gender.
- Sexuality and humor go together naturally, in part because orgasm and laughter are physiologically similar, and because sexuality is a scary and tension-filled part of life.
- There are many theories about why we laugh. Biological theories suggest that laughter is an evolutionary or physiological adaptation. Superiority theories suggest we laugh when we feel superior to something, in order to gain mastery and control. Release and relief theories say we laugh to release built-up tensions. Incongruity-type theories suggest that we laugh when surprised by the sudden resolution of a situation that is internally inconsistent or contradictory. Ambivalence theory views laughter as a result of conflicting emotions. And psychoanalytic theory follows Freud's idea that we accumulate psychic energy by repressing our sexual and aggressive thoughts, and this energy is released through laughter.
- Humor, including sexual humor, comes in many forms. Most common are "dirty" jokes where verbal humor is spread through riddles and jokes. Erotic poetry also exists, most notably the limerick, which originated and persists as an erotic poetic form. Erotic cartoons, especially as begun by *Playboy* magazine, also are a popular form of erotic humor.
- Cycles of humor refer to types of jokes—lightbulb jokes, dead baby jokes—that make their way through the culture. These folk forms of humor are common and popular, and they often follow national tragedies.
- Throughout history, men's humor has been predominant, and women have been accused of being humorless. This may be in part because men's humor has been directed at women and disparages them, and women may well not find this kind of humor funny. More recently, however, women have become more visible as comics and collections of women's humor have been published.
- Humor and sexuality also go together in the sense that studies show that people who have a sense of sexual humor have fuller and more satisfying sex lives.

R eflections on Sexuality

1. Why is sexual humor found in almost every society? What makes sexual humor such a potent form of humor?
2. To what extent is laughter biological? What are the weaknesses of purely biological explanations of humor?
3. What are the major theories of humor? What are their strengths and weaknesses?
4. What are cycles of humor? How are they generated, and how do they spread?
5. Why are their so many jokes that seem to demean women? How is the relation between humor and gender changing?
6. Does humor have a place in sexual relationships? Should the bedroom be a place of serious lovemaking only, or is there room for humor in sexuality?
7. What kinds of sexual jokes do you think are funny, and what kind are not funny to you? What is the difference between them?

S uggested Readings

CHAPMAN, A. J., and H. C. FOOT. (eds.) (1976) *Humour and Laughter: Theory, Research and Applications.* London: John Wiley and Sons.

LEGMAN, G. (1968) *No Laughing Matter: An Analysis of Sexual Humor.* Bloomington: Indiana University Press.

MACHOVEC, F. J. (1988) *Humor: Theory, History, Applications.* Springfield, IL: Charles C. Thomas.

POWELL, C., and G. E. C. PATON. (eds.) (1988) *Humour in Society: Resistance and Control.* New York: St. Martin's Press.

ZIV, A. (1988) *National Styles of Humor.* New York: Greenwood Press.

6

Enriching Personal Sexuality

SELF-ESTEEM

COMMUNICATION

MASTURBATION

WHAT DO WE LOOK FOR IN A PARTNER?

WHAT MAKES A GOOD LOVER?

SEXUAL FANTASY

SEXUAL PROBLEMS

SUMMARY

REFLECTIONS ON SEXUALITY

SUGGESTED READINGS

If you are like many college students, this was probably one of the first chapters you turned to the first time you looked through this book. It is perfectly okay to do so, but you must understand that it is difficult to learn to be a good lover and to really appreciate your own sexuality if you have not learned all that precedes this chapter. It is like trying to build a house without first building a foundation. This chapter includes information on decorating, while the rest of this book has been the floors, walls, and ceilings of the house. Decorating involves making the best out of what we have available to us.

Before we can really understand sexuality, we need to understand our anatomy, physiology, hormones, our capacity to love, gender issues and differences, as well as the possibilities of contracting STDs, and many other social issues. All of these help give meaning to what sexuality is all about. In this Special Focus, we discuss how to enrich your own sexuality; not only does this chapter discuss how to be a good lover, but it also discusses how to feel good about yourself and your relationships with others. No one is born a good lover; it takes learning and patience. The information in this chapter may be valuable to you throughout your life, as your relationships change and mature.

SELF-ESTEEM

Healthy sexuality depends upon feeling good about yourself. If you have a poor self-image, or do not like certain aspects of your body or personality, how can you demonstrate to a lover why you are attractive? Imagine a man or woman who is overly concerned about his or her body while in bed with a partner. Maybe a woman is worried that her partner will not be attracted to her body—her flat (or large) chest, thighs, stomach, or her inverted nipples. Perhaps a man is consumed with anxiety over the size of his penis, worrying that his partner won't find it appealing. All of these fears interfere with our ability to let go, relax, and enjoy the sexual experience. Before anyone else can accept us, we need to accept ourselves.

In American society, learning to like our bodies is often difficult. Magazines, television, and advertisers all play to our insecurities with their portrayals of the ideal body. The beauty images that the media present to us are often impossible to live up to, and leave many of us feeling unattractive by comparison. We are encouraged to buy products that will make us look more attractive or sexy (also see Special Focus 4). To sell products, advertisers must first convince us that we are not okay the way we are, that we need to change our looks, our smells, our habits. The endless diet products currently on the market also increase our dissatisfaction with our bodies. This, in turn, has led to a preoccupation with weight and eating disorders such as **anorexia** and **bulimia**. Many young women who are convinced that they are overweight consciously starve themselves (sometimes to death) in an attempt to be thin.

In the United States in particular, we put a high value on physical attractiveness throughout the life cycle, and our body image greatly affects how attractive we feel. Many American women go on diet after diet, have breast augmentation or, less often, reduction surgery, endure **liposuction**, or other types of cosmetic surgery to correct what they see as "figure flaws" (thighs, eyelids, chests, necks, cheekbones). Many women also repeatedly cut and color their hair, worry constantly about their makeup, or lay in tanning beds to look and feel better about themselves. Many American men (and women) spend hours in gyms lifting weights, and perhaps even take steroids, to achieve the "perfect" body.

Everyone has parts of his or her body they wish they could change. In fact, most of us are much more critical of our bodies than our partners would ever be. Not all of us are blessed with the looks of Kathy Ireland or Mel Gibson!

Self-esteem is related to our emotional and mental health. Mental health professionals agree that improving mental health includes improving one's self-acceptance, autonomy, and self-efficacy (being able to function in the world), resilience (not to get overburdened by anger, depression, or guilt), interest in one's own careers and lives, and close relationships with others (Wolfe, 1992). All of these are important in establishing good mental health and, therefore, good sexual relationships.

anorexia: An eating disorder characterized by self-induced weight loss, distorted body-image, and other perceptual disturbances and the physiological changes that result from nutritional depletion.

bulimia: An eating disorder characterized by overeating (at least twice a week) followed by purging through self-induced vomiting, strict dieting or fasting, vigorous exercise, and/or use of laxatives.

liposuction: The suction of fat cells from various parts of the body.

SEX TALK

QUESTION **SF6.1**   **Is there a difference between "having sex" and "making love"?**

Most people would agree that there is a difference. "Having sex" implies little emotional attachment, with the emphasis put on orgasm and physical pleasure. "Making love," on the other hand, implies that the emotional component is very important, and the intimacy created in the act of sexual intercourse derives from the feelings the partners have for one another.

COMMUNICATION

Although we have already discussed communication in Chapter 6, we mention it again here because part of being a good lover is knowing how to communicate your desires to your partner, and also knowing how to listen to what your partner is communicating to you. Good communication is one of the most important factors in a satisfying sexual relationship (Sarrel and Sarrel, 1980). Further, the Sarrels noted that:

the ability to share thoughts and feelings about sex with your partner is the one single factor most highly correlated with a good sexual relationship . . . the good communicators had intercourse [more often] and were likelier to be satisfied with its frequency.

Quoted in Barbach (1982:104)

Eating disorders reflect unhappiness with one's body. In some cases, anorexics will starve themselves to death.

Sex symbols, such as Kathy Ireland and Mel Gibson, are often seen as standards that we have to live up to in order to be happy with ourselves and our bodies.

Too often, we assume that being a good lover also means being a mind-reader. Somehow, we are just supposed to know what turns our partner on. In reality, nothing could be further from the truth; good lovers are not mind-readers—they are able and willing to listen and communicate with their partners. Where Do I Stand? SF6.1 includes a questionnaire to help you determine whether or not you rely on mind-reading more than communicating with your partner. Take a moment to complete this questionnaire before moving on.

Even though communication is important, it is not always easy. Telling your partner what you really want and need during sexual activity can be very difficult. Why is this? Perhaps you are worried that he or she will not like your openness, or will think differently about you if he or she knows you like a certain behavior. Also, men and women worry that if they tell their partner that they do not like how a certain touch feels, their partner will become insulted and feel that their lovemaking is being criticized. As a result, they say nothing even though what their partner is doing is not pleasurable to them. Ultimately, this is self-defeating, since they may end up feeling resentful of their partner.

Telling a partner what we want sexually makes us feel vulnerable. We have put ourselves on the line, without knowing what kind of reaction we will get. Women often have more difficulty telling their partners what they desire sexually and what feels good. This may be due to the strong double standard in American society that says that women are not supposed to enjoy sex. If a woman knows what type of sexual stimulation turns her on, she may be viewed as promiscuous or easy. Men, on the other hand, often believe that they are supposed to know everything about sex. However, both men and women should know that good lovers are not born that way—they *learn* to be good lovers.

Overall, it is interesting that many people find it easier to be physically sexual with someone than it is to be open, honest, and communicate with their partner. Some couples have an easier time having sex than they do sitting down and talking to each other about their needs and desires. Then they complain that their sexual partner is not what they wish they would be! Yet most of the time, their partners are not uncaring or selfish; they simply do not know what they are expected to do. They *could* be better lovers if their partners would just talk to them about what they desire in bed. After all, couples who have the most exciting sex lives are those who actively show or tell their partners what they want.

WHERE DO I *Stand?*   SF6.1

Is Your Partner A Mind-Reader?

Many people believe that if they are in love, they will be able to read their partner's mind. Somehow, they will just "know" what turns their partner on. Below is a list of some of the ways in which people might be expecting their partners to read their minds.

Give yourself points for how frequently a statement applies to you. (If you are not sexually active right now, try to *imagine* how you would act in the given situations.)

Often	*3 points*
Sometimes	*2 points*
Never	*1 point*

1. *You* know what really turns you on, but you don't tell your partner.
2. You don't come out and tell your partner you are in the mood to make love, but let him/her know you're interested by how you behave, what you wear to bed, or by "hinting around."
3. When you like something your partner is doing to you sexually, you don't show him/her how excited you are or let him know what she/he's doing right.
4. You are on the quiet side when you make love, and don't make much noise.
5. When you don't like something your partner is doing to you sexually, you move your body away or lie there not responding, rather than tell your partner you'd rather have him/her do something else.
6. You get impatient because your partner doesn't know the "right" thing to do or the "right " way to touch you.

7. You don't say "romantic" things during your love-making.
8. When you feel like stopping your lovemaking, you don't tell your partner directly, but respond less, hoping she/he'll get the message.
9. You think talking during sexual play "ruins" the mood.

Now add up your score:

9–11 points: You are good at asking for what you want in bed. Have fun!

12–21 points: You are relying too much on mind-reading in bed. Practice talking about what you want and how you feel.

22–27 points: Either your partner is a good mind reader or you aren't getting what you want in bed. Admit that you have a problem communicating and start working to change it.

Relying too much on mind reading can lead to resentment, frustration, and a decrease of passion in your relationship. Communicate with your partner about what you like and don't like, what you are afraid of, and what makes lovemaking good for you.

Reprinted with permission from DeAngelis (1987)

SEX TALK
QUESTION **SF6.2** **I really enjoy having sexual intercourse with my partner, but I wish we could spend more time with foreplay. How can I ask him without making him feel defensive?**

The best way to handle it is to be honest and communicate your desires to your partner. After all, he will not know unless you tell him. When you bring it up, here are a few suggestions: do not begin discussing it while you are in the middle of sexual activity—wait until you are in a neutral place and then bring it up (while taking a walk together or going for a drive). How you tell your partner about this is also very important. Saying "Why didn't you continue to caress my clitoris?" will probably cause more defensiveness on his part than anything else (see Sexuality Today SF6.1). Try to own the feelings you are having ("I really love it when you touch me there"), rather than blaming him ("Why don't you touch me more there?"). Remember to use "I" language as much as possible (i.e., I feel, I think, I want), rather than "you" language (you always, you never). "You" language will usually succeed only in getting a defensive reaction from your partner.

Although verbal communication is far better than nonverbal communication, nonverbal communication can express your sexual desires, and it can be much less threatening than verbal communication. For example, if you would like your partner to stimulate your nipples more during foreplay, show him or her this by moving your body more when he or she is doing what you like, or moving his or her hands to your breasts. Moan, or even move more, to communicate your pleasure to him or her.

You might also try performing the behavior on your partner that you wish she or he would do to you. However, there are problems with some types of nonverbal communication. As this couple demonstrates, it can often be misunderstood:

> *One woman attempted to communicate her preference for being kissed on the ears by kissing her partner's ears. However, [she] found that the more she kissed her partner's ears, the less he seemed to kiss hers. Over a period of time her kissing of his ears continued to increase while his kissing of her ears stopped altogether. Finally she asked him why he never kissed her ears anymore, only to discover that he hated having his ears kissed and was trying to communicate this by not kissing hers. After their discussion, he began to kiss her ears, she stopped kissing his, and both were happier for the exchange.*
>
> *Barbach (1982:105)*

In this case, nonverbal communication needed to be clarified through verbal information.

In new relationships, it can take time to feel comfortable enough with your partner to share your own sexual preferences and desires. However, even though it might not feel comfortable right away, sharing personal information can lead to a stronger and more satisfying relationship, regardless of how long the relationship lasts. Barbach (1982:106) believes that:

> *Letting your partner know early in a relationship what you like and don't like sexually helps to prevent negative patterns from developing. What frequently occurs in a new relationship is that people make love to a new partner by doing what turns* them *on, or by doing what pleased a previous partner, or what they have read women or men like. During the honeymoon stages of a relationship everything tends to feel good, but people become more discriminating after a while. At that point, if you don't let your partner know what turns you on or off, you will only reinforce the belief that what is being done is fine, thus leading to more of the same behavior.*

Remember, communication is a way for both partners to become more sexually satisfied. In turn, this leads to a better and more fulfilling relationship. However, if you are having problems communicating with your sexual partner and telling him or her what you need, do not worry; it does not get easier overnight. As long as you keep attempting to communicate, it will gradually get easier. Realize that the discomfort may make you feel self-conscious, but do not let this get in your way. Try talking with your partner about *why* it is so difficult to talk about sex; this can help initiate the

SEXUALITY *Today*   *SF6.1*

Non-constructive Communication Patterns

Below are some common mistakes couples make in their communication patterns. These can often lead to arguments, misunderstandings, and conflicts. How many of the following occur in your own relationships? You might want to discuss this with your partner and see if you agree.

1. **Overgeneralization:** Do you make "you always..." or "you never..." statements?

2. **Name-calling or stereotyping words:** Do you ever call your partner a "selfish bastard," "male chauvinist pig," "nag," "hysterical female" or other derogatory term?

3. **Dig at the past:** Do you continue to dwell on a past event, even though there is nothing that can be done to change it now?

4. **Collect resentments:** Instead of dealing with issues as they present themselves, do you collect them until one day when you finally explode?

5. **Use overkill:** Do you threaten the worst if your needs are not met?

6. **Fail to see the world from his or her viewpoint:** Can you get into your partner's shoes and see the issues as he or she sees them?

7. **Repeat old arguments and accusations:** Do you continue to argue old issues?

8. **Fail to mention positives:** Do you neglect to say anything nice about what your partner has recently done?

9. **Use "guilt trips":** Do you try to make your partner feel guilty by playing the "poor me" routine?

10. **Use "kitchen sink":** Do you throw too many issues into the conversation at once, large and small, which results in no issues being solved?

11. **Overwhelmed by anger, hate, or despair:** Do you yell, scream, interrupt, talk louder, leave the room, or become totally silent?

12. **Use the "accusatory you":** Do you use the "you always do this," "you don't love me," or "you never listen"?

Clinging to any of these communication patterns can interfere with the resolution of problems and concerns. See if you can talk about these communication styles and catch yourself when you are engaging in them.

Reprinted with permission from Wolfe (1992)

conversation. Like anything else, learning to communicate takes practice. In Where Do I Stand? SF6.2, we have included a questionnaire to assess your sexual functioning. Take a few moments to fill out this survey. You might consider discussing your results with your sexual partner.

MASTURBATION

Throughout this book we have discussed the practice, frequency, and specifics of masturbation. However, we discuss it again here because masturbation can actually help a person become a better lover. Masturbation helps us learn what turns *us* on, and where we like to be touched. It may help you to learn what kind of pressure and manipulation gives you the greatest pleasure and orgasmic response (see Chapter 9, Sexuality Today 9.2 and Personal Voices SF6.1).

After you learn to masturbate, it may be helpful to share this information with your partner so he or she can also learn how to best stimulate you. Masturbation can also be exciting for couples to use during sexual activity. They may masturbate themselves or each other, either simultaneously or one at a time.

Whether or not you choose to masturbate is an entirely personal decision. You do not need to masturbate to be a good lover; in fact, some people who never masturbate are terrific lovers. For some people, masturbation may be unacceptable for personal or religious reasons.

What Do We Look For in a Partner?

We look for many things in a sexual partner: someone who is honest, fun, sensitive, good looking, someone that we can talk to and with whom we can have a good sex life.

In the United States, attractiveness in women is often viewed in terms of physical attributes such as height, weight, eye and hair color, complexion, and smile. Julia Roberts is considered a very attractive woman.

SEX TALK

QUESTION **SF6.3** **Are looks more important to men or women?**

Men often report that physical attractiveness is important to them when looking for a partner. Women are less likely to identify looks as one of the most important characteristics. However, women are more likely than men to report that what a person does (career) is very important. In essence, it seems that men value looks more, while women place more value on success. We must keep in mind, however, that these differences may be due to the fact that men and women feel more comfortable saying that these characteristics are important. In the past, women have not been socialized to value attractiveness in men, while men have not been socialized to value success in women (see Chapter 6).

When college students were asked who the ideal man and ideal woman were, their answers were very interesting (see Personal Voices SF6.2).

What Makes a Good Lover?

It would be impossible to list all the qualities that make people good lovers. People look for many different things in a partner, and what makes someone a good lover to you might not make them a good lover to someone else. Overall, good lovers are sensitive to their partner's needs and desires, can communicate their own desires, and are patient, caring, and confident. Being nervous or feeling silly can interfere with lovemaking abilities. It is hard to concentrate when you are worried about performing.

Where Do I Stand? SF6.3 offers a quiz for men that will help you evaluate your sexual abilities with women.

Men and women sometimes have different views of the same sexual behaviors. In the movie *Annie Hall,* the lead characters, Annie and Albey, each go to see their respective therapists, and are each asked how often they have sex. Annie replies, "Oh, all the time, at least three times a week," while Albey says, "Hardly ever, maybe three times a week." Do you think this reflects a gender difference?

In the United States, attractiveness in men is often viewed in terms of physical attributes such as height, weight, build, eye and hair color, and smile. Arnold Schwarzenegger is considered a very attractive man.

W H E R E   D O   I *S t a n d ?*   *SF6.2*

Test Your Sexual Performance

This questionnaire is designed to help you to assess your sexual performance and judge for yourself which special areas of your sex life need to be improved. Answer as honestly as you can, because the more truthful you are, the more accurate your assessment will be. From an accurate assessment, you will be able to improve your sexual capabilities much more quickly and effectively.

1. Most of the time, I am easily sexually stimulated. Yes/No
2. I am often too tired for lovemaking. Yes/No
3. I always enjoy sex. Yes/No
4. I do not think I make love often enough. Yes/No
5. I enjoy exposing myself sexually to my partner. Yes/No
6. I do not like making love with the lights on. Yes/No
7. I am prepared to try any sexual act. Yes/No
8. I do not know very much about sex. Yes/No
9. I would like to find out more about different sexual acts. Yes/No
10. I would never consider masturbating in front of my partner. Yes/No
11. I have frequently indulged in oral sex. Yes/No
12. I think that sex should be confined to the bedroom. Yes/No
13. I have told my partner my most secret erotic thoughts. Yes/No
14. I would never use vibrators or other sex toys. Yes/No
15. I have told my partner what stimulates me the most. Yes/No
16. I have faked a climax more than once. Yes/No
17. I frequently try to have sex more than once a night. Yes/No
18. I find it hard to keep my concentration during sex. Yes/No
19. I enjoy casual sexual touching during the day. Yes/No
20. I think sex magazines and videos are repulsive. Yes/No
21. I get completely involved in lovemaking. Yes/No
22. I think that the importance of sex is overrated. Yes/No
23. I would dress up in erotic clothing to stimulate my partner. Yes/No
24. I think some sexual acts are dirty. Yes/No
25. I think that better sex is one important reason to keep fit. Yes/No
26. I do not think that I am a particularly outstanding lover. Yes/No
27. I always try to find out what my partner's sexual needs are. Yes/No
28. I think my partner is completely satisfied sexually. Yes/No
29. I always try to make sure that my partner climaxes. Yes/No
30. I do not like my partner touching me anally. Yes/No
31. I enjoy kissing and caressing my partner whether we make love or not. Yes/No
32. I expect my interest in sex to decline as I get older. Yes/No
33. It still excites me to see my partner naked. Yes/No
34. My partner's sexual demands sometimes seem too extreme. Yes/No
35. I would be interested in improving my sexual performance. Yes/No
36. I would never let my partner make sex videos of me. Yes/No
37. I would like to achieve a more intensive climax. Yes/No

Even sexual techniques can be viewed differently. In a discussion about a couple's early sexual experiences, a man said:

I'll never forget the first time. She was lying on her parent's bed with the lamp-light shining on her, naked and suntanned all over. . . . I climbed on that bed and I lifted her up onto my thighs—she was so light I could always pick her right up—and I opened up her [vagina] with one hand and I rammed my cock

Score three points for every *even-numbered* question to which you answered no and deduct three points for every *even-numbered* question to which you answered yes. Deduct three points for every *odd-numbered* question to which you answered no and score three points for every *odd-numbered* question to which you answered yes.

93–108: You are a highly sexually motivated individual who recognizes not only the importance of your own sexual needs but also the sexual needs of your partner. You are generous and giving when it comes to sex, because you know that by giving pleasure, you will receive pleasure in return. You do not flinch from sexual experimentation, and you have a healthy respect for your own body. You are open-minded about new sexual experiences, although you have a tendency to think that your sex life is so good that it does not require any major improvement.

72–93: You are an unusually caring and daring lover, and you enjoy sex wholeheartedly. You do not always concentrate fully on your lovemaking, however, because you allow domestic or professional anxieties to interfere instead of thinking only of sexual pleasure—both for you and for your partner. You have a positive attitude about the role of sexual satisfaction in your life, but you are not as adventurous as you might be. You would be prepared to listen to advice about improving your sexual pleasure, but you would be likely to select only those activities and exercises that did not embarrass you or go against your preconceived ideas about what is and is not sexually acceptable.

54–72: You understand that sex is a critical part of your life, but you are lacking in sexual knowledge and sexual self-confidence—not necessarily through any fault of your own. You are inhibited by the feeling that sex is an activity that should be performed only in bed and only at bedtime and not freely discussed at any other time. You have strong sexual fantasies but your are often afraid to express them to your partner, fearing that s/he may consider them offensive or upsetting. Although you derive a good deal of satisfaction from your lovemaking, you tend not to criticize your partner or to show him or her how to stimulate you more intensely. There have been many occasions when you have gone without a climax or simulated one.

33–54: You have strong inhibitions about sex that you should consider as carefully and as self-analytically as possible. Did your parents have a very restrictive attitude about sex? Was your first introduction to lovemaking painful or awkward or embarrassing? Did you have an unhappy sexual relationship? Do personal or family problems make it hard for you to concentrate on your sexual satisfaction and well-being? Do you have sexual difficulties, such as climaxing too soon (if you are a man) or failing to reach orgasm (if you're a woman)? Whatever it is, don't despair. Sexual problems, because of the physical and emotional tensions involved, almost always seem worse to the sufferer than they really are.

If you scored lower than 33, you may need to talk to a professional counselor about your sexual reserve. You will need to take a metaphorical deep breath, relax, and then work calmly and systematically on adjusting your feelings about love and sex. Sex is a pleasure. Sex is a joy. Sex is a source of satisfaction and excitement. There is nothing that you can do with your partner that is wrong or degrading if both of you enjoy it.

Reprinted with permission from Masterton (1992)

---

up there like it was a Polaris missile. Do you know, she screamed out loud, and she dug her nails in my back, and without being too crude about it I [screwed] her until she didn't know what the hell was happening. . . . She loved it. She screamed out loud every single time. I mean I was an active, aggressive lover.

Masterton (1987:70)

Yet at the same time, his partner was evaluating the sexual activity very differently.

What did I think about it? . . . I don't know. I think the only word you could use would be "flabbergasted." He threw me on the bed as if he were Tarzan, and tugged off all of my clothes, and then he took off his own clothes so fast it was almost like he was trying to beat the world record. . . . He took hold of me and virtually lifted me right up in the air as if I were a child, and then he pushed himself right up me, with hardly any loveplay or any preliminaries or anything.

Masterton (1987:73)

This is another reason that communication is so important. Here is a man thinking he is doing exactly what she wants, and a woman wondering *why* he is doing it. Eventually, this couple's marriage ended, mainly due to a lack of communication, which left both feeling confused and frustrated.

Pleasing Women

What do women want in a sexual relationship? What do they feel is the biggest turn-on for them? When female college students were asked what qualities they think an "ideal lover" would have, their answers were varied:

An ideal lover wouldn't pressure me about sex. It would just happen naturally. I would love to cuddle and sleep together without having sexual intercourse. My partner would be very gentle, sensitive, and romantic.
—twenty-year-old female

My ideal lover wouldn't push it or make it harsh or rushed in any way. It is supposed to be enjoyable for both of us. He would personally please me—slow, comfortable, soft, loving. I don't want to be used just to make someone else feel good. Foreplay is necessary, and so is a slow down afterwards, talking, cuddling, and cooling off. —nineteen-year-old female

Author's files

Many women desire a partner who will be patient and take it slowly. Being pressured into sexual activity can be a tremendous turn-off. Other women report that they like the emotionality of sex and want their lovers to be more sensitive to their emotional needs.

I don't personally regard sex as a strictly physical experience and I feel downgraded when it gets treated as such. The best thing my partner can do in and out of bed is make me feel very loved. Sex for the sake of sex means nothing— making love, on the other hand, is wonderful. That involves us being very kind and gentle and taking our time. I like for him to tell me he loves me and then to show me through sex. —twenty-one-year-old female

Author's files

Overall, when women are given the choice between foreplay, sexual intercourse, and afterplay, they rate foreplay as their favorite part of sexual activity. This is not all that surprising, since women are more likely to orgasm during foreplay than during any of these other activities (see Chapter 9).

People often believe that the purpose of foreplay, kissing, and fondling are to prepare for sexual intercourse. They believe that sexual intercourse is the goal of sexual activity and that the exclusive focus is on penile–vaginal sexual intercourse, rather than

Personal

VOICES

Sex For One

Around the age of ten, I wanted to see what I looked like "down there." One afternoon when the house was empty, I got mother's hand mirror and went into my bedroom. Sitting by the window with sunlight pouring in, I looked at my sweet little child's genitals and was instantly horrified. There hanging down were the same funny-looking things that dangled from a chicken's neck. Right on the spot, I swore off masturbation and made a deal with God. If He got rid of those things that hung down, I promised to stop playing with myself, keep my room clean, and love my little brothers. After a couples of weeks of abstinence, which wasn't easy, I examined my genital deformity again. Upon more careful observation, I saw that my left inner lip was shorter than the right one. I cleverly decided to switch sides and continue playing with myself until they evened up, and then stop forever. Throughout the rest of my childhood, into adulthood, I masturbated with my finger on the left side of my genitals. My inner lips never evened up or dropped off. I simply kept the knowledge of my genital deformity to myself. It was just another one of the many things wrong with me, and I quietly settled into confirmed body loathing.

[Today I believe that] masturbation is a way for all of us to learn about sexual response. It's an opportunity for us to explore our bodies and minds for all those sexually secrets we've been taught to hide, even from ourselves. What better way to learn about pleasure and being sexual creative? We don't have to perform or meet anyone else's standards, to satisfy the needs of a partner, or to fear criticism or rejection for failure. Sexual skills are like any other skills; they're not magically inherited, they have to be learned.

Masturbation is our first natural sexual activity. It's the way we discover our erotic feelings, the way we learn to like our genitals and to build sexual self-esteem. It's the best way to gain sexual self-knowledge and to let go of old sexual fears and inhibitions. For women especially, it's a way to build confidence so we can communicate clearly with our lovers. When we're asked what feels good, we will have the courage to let go of our little white lie, "Oh, everything you do feels good."

Aside from its importance as a form of sexual self-help, the benefits of masturbation are many. Masturbation provides sexual satisfaction for people unable to find partners. It's a way for teenagers with irrepressible sex drives to have orgasms without the possibility of pregnancy. Masturbation also provides a sexual outlet for couples when they are separated, when one partner is ill, when one partner is not interested in sex, or when either partner cannot get enough stimulation to reach orgasm through sexual intercourse.

My futuristic fantasy for sexual liberation goes like this—it's New Year's Eve, 1999. All the television networks have agreed to let me produce "Orgasms Across America." Every TV screen will be showing high-tech, fine-art porn created by the best talent this country has to offer. At the stroke of midnight, the entire population will be masturbating to orgasm for World Peace.

Reprinted with permission from Dodson (1987)

---

on focusing on what feels good for the moment. This belief can lead to problems. Consider this: when someone asks you if you had "sex" last night, what do they mean? Are they asking if you had sexual intercourse? Probably. We have been taught to believe that sex equals intercourse, and without it, we often do not think that "sex" occurred. The problem is that the overemphasis on sexual intercourse neglects the pleasure of activities such as cuddling, kissing, hugging, or body massage.

SEX TALK

QUESTION **SF6.4** **I've read that in order for a man to be a good lover, he needs to have a larger-than-average penis. Is this true?**

Actually, the truth is that penis size has nothing at all to do with how good a lover a man is. Maybe you have heard the saying "it's not the size of the ship that matters, it's the motion of the ocean." The majority of nerve endings in a woman's vagina are located in the outer third, which means that a woman's greatest sensitivity is near the opening of her vagina. A large penis can actually cause discomfort for some women. One woman said: "I make love to the whole man, not his penis. My partner has a smaller penis than my first lover, but I enjoy sex with him more. Why? Because nothing is more satisfying than making love with someone you love" (*Glamour,* 1993). Overall, being a good lover has less to do with penis size than the man himself and the partners' relationship.

Some women want to wait until they are married to experience sexual intercourse. For them, the "ideal lover" will be their husband. One woman said:

I've never been in a relationship, but I think that the ideal lover must be a Christian, attractive, intelligent, willing to listen to me, understands there will be no intercourse until after marriage, willing to pray with and for me, has a good smile, and is willing to communicate.   —nineteen-year-old female

Author's files

Throughout this book, we have encouraged you to explore your own attitudes and values. If you feel premarital sexuality is wrong, or not for you, do not be pressured into it. Listen to yourself.

What Do Women Like?

Every woman has particular erogenous zones, which are especially sensitive to touch during sexual activity, and there are as many different combinations of erogenous zones as there are women. In Sexuality Today SF6.2, we show the results of one study on what women value in a sexual encounter.

Although we discuss primarily heterosexual women, lesbians enjoy many of the same activities, with the exception of sexual intercourse. Many women like to have their backs stroked, their necks kissed, words whispered in their ears, or their hair played with. Some may like to have their nipples and breasts stroked, while others feel their breasts are too sensitive to touch during foreplay. Some women enjoy a finger being inserted into their vaginas prior to sexual intercourse, while others do not enjoy it. Some women like to kiss and hug during sexual activity; others do not.

Try asking your partner where she likes to be touched, and/or try different areas to see where she is most responsive. It is possible that she may not know where these areas are; explore and find them together.

Some women find "dirty" talk during sexual activity to be very arousing and exciting. Although you might think that a woman who screams "Oh, please give it to me!! Harder!! Faster!!" may have some kind of problem, in actuality, she may just feel more comfortable telling her partner what it is she wants. Some women may talk dirty about the sexual act, their partner, or they may pretend they are someone else, using fantasy to increase sexual arousal.

Prior to sexual activity, sometimes even before going out for the night, some women (and men) like to whisper into their partner's ear, telling them what they would like to do with them in bed later on, which can be very erotic. However, if this makes you uncomfortable, share this with your partner and try to come up with different ways to increase your arousal together.

Personal

V O I C E S

The Ideal Man and Woman

College students offered a wide array of answers to the question, "Who is the Ideal Man or Woman?" They also provided information on why they thought this person was ideal. Before reading this list, who do you think is the Ideal Man or Woman? What qualities do they have that makes them ideal?

My dad is my ideal man. He has the *best* sense of humor. My ideal man *must* be able to make me laugh and know how to take a joke. He has to be very caring and sincere. I'd also like for him to be sports-minded, smart, and know what's going on in the world. Not a dork or a know-it-all.

Mel Gibson, because he is funny, handsome, smart, has blue eyes, is well-built, and has a nice butt!

Denzel Washington has a really nice body and is also very sexy.

Robin Williams, because he has a sense of humor, is attractive, has an intense love for his children and family, is sincere, caring, and intelligent.

Prince, because he can dance, he dresses very sexy, and is just *plain* sexy!

My mom is my Ideal Woman. She is compassionate, down to earth, fun-loving, jokes around, is trustworthy, and doesn't expect or ask for too much.

Cindy Crawford, because she is beautiful, rich, successful in her career, athletic, and sexy.

Janet Jackson is my ideal person because she has a great body and is very sexy. It is perfect, and her face is fine.

Lorenzo Lamas is my ideal man because he is muscular and his hair is so nice.

Kathy Ireland, because she is gorgeous, rich, has good taste for things, has *great* eyes, and I just love her style.

To me, the ideal woman would have the looks and body of Cindy Crawford, but would be the type of person who would think of others before thinking of herself. She would also stand for what she believes in. She must be athletic, and not afraid to argue. Finally, she has to have a good sense of humor.

Traci Lords, because she is completely all-around, beautiful, "more" than outgoing, dumb as a rock, has all kinds of experience, and has that look in her eye.

Rosanne Arnold, because she is voluptuous, sensual, intelligent, funny, and physically fit.

Author's files

During sexual activity, women report that clitoral stimulation is important. As we discussed in Chapter 3, the clitoris contains erectile tissue just as the penis does. During arousal, the clitoris erects and is very sensitive to touch. However, do not get overly eager and immediately go for the clitoris. Prior to this, lightly stroke her legs, hips, breasts, and inner thighs. Then *slowly* move to the clitoris. Some women like to have their clitoris stroked hard and vigorously, while others like to have it lightly stroked. This can be done with one or two fingers, used in a circular motion around the clitoris and labia. It is also important to make sure that the clitoris is sufficiently lubricated so that stimulation is not irritating. Women also like to have their vulva fondled. It can be helpful to stroke her clitoris and intermittently move down and spread her labia, perhaps even inserting a finger into her vagina (please remember to have washed your hands *prior* to engaging in these behaviors).

Again, remember that all women differ in what arouses them. The best advice is to take it *slowly.* Being patient and moving slowly are the keys to helping a woman become fully aroused. Women often take longer to become fully aroused than do men. In fact, this is one difference between heterosexual and lesbian sexual activity. Lesbian couples

W H E R E   D O   I $Stand$?   *SF6.3*

FOR MEN: How Good a Lover Are You?

Heterosexual women between the ages of eighteen and thirty-eight were asked what they considered to be the ideal qualities in a great lover. These factors are listed below. In order to find out how a woman would rate your sexual prowess, try taking this questionnaire. Be as honest as you can; only in this way can you learn to be a better lover. Answer yes or no to the following statements.

1. I always try to ensure that she is satisfied after sex.
2. I always talk to her during the sexual act, complimenting, flattering, and stimulating her.
3. When necessary, I delay my own climax so that she can get closer to hers.
4. I always caress her breasts during lovemaking.
5. I always undress her before we make love.
6. I am always trying to think of new ways of stimulating her.
7. I often arouse her orally (that is, by licking her sexual organs).
8. I always make sure that there is no possibility of her becoming pregnant.
9. I know what her most vivid sexual fantasy is.
10. I would do anything in bed that she asked me to do.
11. I have told her what sexual variations arouse me the most.
12. I caress and stimulate her even when I don't feel like sex.
13. I have made love to her in many different locations (out of doors, for instance, or in front of the fire).
14. When she does something that really turns me on, I always let her know.
15. During sex, I always make a point of telling her how much I love her.
16. I always make sure that I am well-groomed before making love to her.
17. I often kiss her and openly show her affection.
18. I know how to stimulate her in order to bring her quickly to a climax.
19. She is one of my best friends.
20. I am happy to let her take a dominant role when she feels like it.

Although this is not a comprehensive and exhaustive list of all the qualities that make a man a good lover, it does reflect some of the qualities which many woman find important in their partners. Give yourself one point for every question you answered yes to.

SCORES	WHAT IT MEANS
18–20	Congratulations! You are a considerate and creative lover. Don't forget, however, that there is always room for improvement.
15–18	You are an A-rated lover, but some of your sexual attitudes may be a little selfish. Try worrying less about your own pleasure, and think more of hers.
10–15	You might be sympathetic and trying hard, but not remembering often enough that a woman likes a lot of care and attention during the course of a sexual relationship. You are in danger of letting her feel as if you're using her for your own enjoyment and not much else.
Below 10	You may need to reevaluate your lovemaking strategies. Try talking to your partner, to find out what it is she wants and likes in a lover.

Reprinted with permission from Masterton (1987)

spend more time with body massage, caressing, and generalized sensuality than do heterosexual couples. In addition, lesbians have also been found to be more orgasmic than heterosexual women. Perhaps this is because they have more sexual knowledge about each other's bodies.

As we stated earlier, lesbians use many of the same techniques as heterosexual couples. Orgasms through body rubbing, mutual masturbation, and receiving and performing cunnilingus are very popular. Overall, cunnilingus is the preferred technique, with mutual masturbation and body rubbing taking a close second and third. Even though cunnilingus is the preferred sexual activity, masturbation is more frequently engaged in. In lesbians, activities are often focused more on providing orgasms and pleasure for their partners than for themselves.

For some women, a soft rubbing of the anus and shallow penetration is very erotic. However, prior to trying this, be sure to talk to your partner about it.

SEX TALK

QUESTION **SF6.5** **Do women like the sensation of penetration? What does it feel like?**

> **Many women do enjoy the vaginal sensations of penetration, whether it is with a penis, finger, or a vibrator. Many women report the feeling of "penile containment," when the penis is fully inside the vagina. However, the nerve endings in the vagina are located primarily in the outer third, so this is where the sensations of penetration are felt most strongly. In addition, it is important to keep in mind that penetration feels pleasurable to women only when they have had the time to produce vaginal lubrication. Without adequate stimulation and lubrication, penetration can be very uncomfortable or even painful.**

Usually, memories about the best sexual experience we have had can give some information about what arouses us the most. For example, when one woman was asked to remember her best sexual experience, she said:

> *He undressed me real slow. I don't think I'd ever been undressed like that before. He ran his fingers down my back, inside my blouse, and that really made me shiver. He laid me down on the rug and loosened my belt and took off my jeans. I wasn't wearing any panties underneath but then I never do. It was then that he quickly stripped off his own clothes so that he was naked. He ran his fingers all over my bare body; the first time he did that it was like electricity, and I kind of opened my legs up expecting him to climb onto me right away. But he held me close, and caressed my breasts, and ran his hand through my hair, and kissed my face, and we rolled over and over on the floor just feeling the warmth and the nakedness of each other. At last he touched me between the legs, and the way he did it was so gentle, but strong too, as if he wanted me real bad. He let his finger slip up inside me, and his thumb rub slowly round and round on my clitoris, but very lightly so that I could scarcely feel it to begin with, but then the feeling gradually built up and it was incredible. I grabbed hold of his shoulders, and said, "I want you," and he smiled and kissed me, and said, "I want you, too," and do you know something? He was driving me crazy, I didn't want him to stop what he was doing, but at the same time I had a very urgent need to have his cock inside of me.*
>
> *Masterton (1987:29–30)*

If you are sexually experienced, try to think back to your best sexual encounter. What made it the best? What characteristics about this experience do you feel are important in sexual relationships? If you have not had a sexual experience yet, think about what will be important to you when that time comes. Where would you like to be? Who would you like to be with? How would you like for it to happen?

What Do Women Want?

Women were asked "What do you expect from a man when you go to bed with him?" Below is a compilation of these answers. Not all factors are important for all sexual experiences; during one sexual activity, talking and caressing may be most important, while during another, orgasm is most important. Also, this list may not represent what all women expect during a sexual encounter. Why not ask your partner, and see what her top ten list looks like?

1. **Kissing:** This is one of the things many women enjoy the most about intimacy whether it is on the lips, head, eyes, breasts, or anywhere else for that matter. In long-term relationships, kissing seems to decrease in frequency, even though men and women still enjoy it.

2. **Talking while making love:** Many people are afraid to talk when they are making love. Let your partner know how you feel. Talking during sex can be very arousing, exciting, romantic, and encouraging. Some couples find dirty talk during sex very exciting.

3. **Caressing:** Many people immediately think of caressing their partner's genitals during sex, but full body caressing is also important, including the head, neck, shoulders, and backs.

4. **Playing:** Women often rate foreplay as their favorite part of sexual activity. Many women are more likely to reach orgasm during foreplay than during intercourse.

5. **Climax:** Men and women both report that they expect to reach an orgasm when they have sex with their partners.

6. **Oral sex:** The majority of women like to have cunnilingus performed on them. One of the biggest hurdles, however, is the fear that their vagina is dirty, bad, or it tastes and/or smells bad. Taking a bath together prior to oral sex can be helpful.

7. **Sexual intercourse:** Many women enjoy the vaginal penetration and thrusting of sexual intercourse. Certain positions, such as female-on-top, are more likely to help a woman to reach orgasm (see Chapter 9).

8. **Body language:** During sex, it is important to pay attention to your lover's body language. Is she breathing heavily? Is she close to orgasm? Is she enjoying what you are doing? Ignoring her body language can result in hurt feelings, rejection, and an overall negative sexual experience.

9. **Afterplay:** What can disappoint a woman more than anything else is having her partner roll over and fall asleep directly after sexual intercourse. Most women like a little cuddling, kissing, hugging, or quiet conversation.

10. **Sex in the morning:** All women might not agree, but many women express a desire for sex in the morning after a long night together, or maybe it is just a good way to start the day!

Adapted from Masterton (1987:79–86)

Pleasing Men

What do men want in a sexual relationship? What do they feel is the biggest turn-on for them? When college men were asked what qualities they think an "ideal lover" would have, many cited the importance of the ability to communicate and tell them what is wanted. In addition, a partner who can relax and experiment is often important to men.

> *Someone who's open and honest about what he or she likes or doesn't like. And also open to the extent that sex is not a completely serious act and isn't afraid to make sex fun and experimental.   —twenty-year-old male*

> *During intercourse I wish my partner would be more confident and get into it more; be more active during intercourse. I also wish she would be more open about discussing the act. Tell me what she liked and disliked.   —twenty-one-year-old male*

I think the ideal lover would be able to just get wild during sex and let herself go. In fact, the best sexual experience I ever had was when my girlfriend went wild one night but we were both drunk at the time, so it wasn't very memorable. I want her to let herself go and do anything and everything.   —twenty-year-old male

Author's files

Men consistently report that they wish their partners could tell them what it is they want and do not want during sexual activity. After all, for many years now, there has been a tremendous amount of pressure put on men. Generally, men have been expected to control the initiation, timing, and rhythm of lovemaking, and also to be an expert in sexual technique. Society simply expects men to be knowledgeable about sex.

Freud once said that one question he could not answer was, "What do women want?" Most men do not know what it is a woman wants. What kind of man does not know how to please a woman? An honest one. Even though women may expect men to know all there is to know about sex and pleasing women, many men would say that they have no idea what turns a woman on.

To be a good lover, a heterosexual man needs to be knowledgeable about both female *and* male anatomy. After taking this course, you should know not only how your own genitals function, but also how the sexual response cycle affects the male and female genitals and anatomy and physiology. Knowledge is a very powerful tool in becoming a better lover.

SEX TALK
QUESTION **SF6.6**   What do men think about during sex?

Like women, men think about a variety of things during sex. If he is trying to prolong an erection, he may think about sports, classes, the weather, or a dull meeting he has to go to. In India, in fact, men who want to be good lovers are taught to perform mathematical calculations in their heads while they are having sexual intercourse (Davis, 1984). To increase arousal, some men may think about their partner and the behaviors that they are engaging in. It's possible that using fantasy may also be used to increase sexual arousal (we discuss this more below). It is impossible to identify all the things that may go through a man's mind during sexual activity.

What Do Men Like?

In Where Do I Stand? SF6.4 we have presented a questionnaire for women to measure how much they know about men and sexuality. Take a moment to complete this questionnaire before continuing.

Most men like partners who feel comfortable with themselves, can communicate their sexual needs, and who will explore their sexuality with them. One man said:

The nicest thing a woman can do for me is to treat me the way she likes to be treated. What men "really want" is just the same thing women really want. They want to be respected. They want to be treated well. They want to be recognized as individuals.

Davis (1984:20)

Gay men also enjoy many of the same activities as heterosexual men, with the exception of penile–vaginal intercourse. Many men enjoy it when their partner initiates sexual activity. In addition, like women, men have different erogenous zones that they like to have stimulated. Some men like to have their necks, eyelids, ears, backs, or shoulders kissed, while others prefer having their backs rubbed. Men also like to be caressed and massaged. The inside of the thighs are another area on a man's body that are highly sensitive to touch.

Like women, men like to have their genitals lightly stroked. A light brushing of the penis and testicles is often very pleasurable. Men do not necessarily like their partner to immediately grab the penis and begin stimulating it. They prefer to be aroused slowly and teased as stimulation gets closer to the penis.

Some men also like to have their nipples licked or pinched. Although men's nipples have fewer nerve endings than women's, they are very responsive to touch. In addition, some men like to have their anus stroked or penetrated, but you should talk to your partner about this. There are many psychological reasons that couples may not see the anus as a source of sexual pleasure, and some may find stimulation of the anus distasteful. After you talk to your partner about it, try taking a bath together beforehand so that you are both clean and relaxed. For some men, a slow, soft rubbing of the anus and the skin between the anus and scrotum can be immensely pleasurable. Your partner can let you know what feels best.

Be sure to pay attention to the physical signs of arousal. In men, this includes faster breathing, an increase in heart rate, increased muscular tension in the legs and stomach, erect nipples, sex flush, a thickening of the skin covering the testicles, movement of the testicles up toward the penis, a reddening in the head of the penis, and more vigorous thrusting (also see the sexual response cycle in Chapter 9). In addition, there are many individual signs that men show (such as certain movements, phrases, or eye contact).

Men also enjoy variety in their locations in which they engage in sexual behavior. One man said:

> [My girlfriend] *is just great. In the three years we've been together, she's never once said, "Oh, no, not here." And believe me, we've made love in some pretty weird places. We tried it in a hammock under some palm trees on a Caribbean island—and did I look ridiculous when I fell out! Once it was on a fishing boat, once it was in the backseat of a friend's car while it was parked in his garage. It doesn't always work out . . . but we have a lot of fun experimenting.*
>
> *Davis (1984:54)*

Engaging in sex in a variety of locations may be so exciting because it implies that your passion just cannot wait.

Despite common stereotypes, men's best sexual experiences often do not involve powerful thrusting and endless erections. Many times the emotional aspects are very important.

> *My best sexual experience involved a long-term non-sexual relationship. For two years, we shared everything with each other. We knew each other so well, that we reached a point where sex was the last way we could open and give of ourselves to each other. The actual sexual experience was neither intense nor passionate. It was more of an awakening. It was tender and nurturing, almost spiritual.*
>
> *Author's files*

There are also some things that many men do not enjoy when it comes to sex. In Sexuality Today SF6.3 are a list of the top twenty sexual turn-offs for men.

Like heterosexual men, homosexual men engage in a variety of sexual techniques including hugging, kissing, mutual masturbation, performing and receiving anal and oral sex, and orgasm through body rubbing. In gay men, fellatio is the most common sexual behavior. White homosexual men engage in hand–genital contact next most frequently, while African-American men are more likely to engage in anal intercourse. Overall, like heterosexuals, younger homosexual men experiment more with sexual behaviors, while older homosexuals tend to settle on one or two techniques over time.

SEXUAL FANTASY

Most people use sexual fantasy at some point during their sexual activity. In fact, what we understand today is that people who fantasize the most usually have higher levels of sexual activity (see Chapter 9). Sexual fantasies can help increase arousal during foreplay, sexual intercourse, or masturbation. In addition, they can help relieve boredom during sexual activity. Sexual fantasies range in content and explicitness. Some fantasies are romantic in nature, while others are forceful or violent. Overall, female sexual fantasies tend to be more romantic than male fantasies. As we discuss in Chapter 9, sexual fantasies are a normal part of sexual activity. They can help increase sexual arousal and desire. Would you be comfortable sharing your sexual fantasies with your partner? Why or why not?

SEXUAL PROBLEMS

In Where Do I Stand? SF6.5 there is a questionnaire that can help you explore your own thoughts and feelings about your own sexuality at this point in your life. It will help you locate any problems or issues that might cause problems later on down the road. Take a few moments to complete this questionnaire. You might have your sexual partner fill it out as well. How do your answers compare?

Physical and psychological dysfunctions can interfere with a healthy and satisfying sexual relationship (see Chapter 12). It is important to communicate about sexual problems and dysfunctions in a relationship. If this is not done, partners may blame themselves for the problem. For example, if a man begins to develop a problem obtaining or maintaining an erection, and he does not discuss this with his partner, she may feel that he does not love her anymore or that she is sexually undesirable. Refusing to talk about it, or ignoring the problem, will make the situation much worse in the long run.

Some people believe that talking about sexual problems only makes them worse. In reality, what usually happens is that a man has a problem getting an erection one night, or a woman does not reach orgasm, and they begin to worry: "What if this happens again tomorrow?" Soon their worry becomes a self-fulfilling prophecy, and their initial secrecy has led to further problems down the road.

If you notice that your partner is having difficulties with some aspect of his or her sexual functioning, talk about it. Do not ignore it. Also, do not take it personally and think that it is your fault. As we discussed in Chapter 12, there are several causes for

WHERE DO I *Stand*?   *SF6.4*

FOR WOMEN: A Sex Quiz

How much do you really know about men and sex? Take this quiz to find out. Ask yourself if you think the following statements are True or False.

1. Men love women who are mysterious in bed.
2. Men are turned off by women who show that they like sex too much.
3. When a woman laughs and acts playful in bed, it makes men feel judged and uncomfortable.
4. Women care much more about men's grooming and hygienic habits than men care about these same habits in women.
5. If you tell a man what you want in bed, he will feel like you are trying to take control, and will secretly resent it.
6. It doesn't really matter to a man whether or not you like him to perform oral sex on you, as long as you perform it on him.
7. The main reason that men talk less than women do during sex is that men are afraid to open up and be vulnerable.
8. When a man has an erection, it means he's turned on and ready to have sex.
9. Men secretly feel that a woman who frequently initiates sex is too aggressive and doesn't give her partner a chance to feel like a man.
10. The best time to talk with your partner about your sex life is in bed.

If you think that *even one* of these statements is true, you don't know everything you should about men and sex. If you answered that *most or all* of these statements were true, there are many important things to learn. The fact is, most men are turned off by all of these.

Reprinted with permission from DeAngelis (1990:165–166)

Our sexual fantasies are often as unique as we are. Some people might fantasize about an intimate encounter in the woods, while others have very different fantasies. Your fantasies may be very different from your partner's. What do you fantasize about?

SEXUALITY*T o d a y*   *SF6.3*

The Top Twenty Sexual Turn-offs For Men

Barbara DeAngelis, a relationship expert in California, compiled a list of the top twenty sexual turn-offs men want women to know about. Although this may not be representative of all men at all times, it might be interesting to talk to your partner about each of these. See which he agrees or disagrees with, and talk about others that he feels should be on the list. What are your top twenty sexual turn-offs?

1. Women who act as if they do not like sex, make derogatory comments, or have a "let's get it over with" attitude.
2. Women who never initiate sex.
3. Women who act unfamiliar with a man's body and are uncomfortable touching him, or who immediately stimulate his penis, ignoring other parts of his body.
4. Women who make men responsible for their orgasms.
5. Women who have to be in control all the time during sex, who give lots of instructions, and constantly correct their partners' techniques.

6. Women who are unresponsive in bed, both verbally and physically.
7. Women who talk too much in bed.
8. Women who do not take care of themselves.
9. Women who do not like their own bodies and put themselves down.
10. Women who are too concerned with their appearance.
11. Women who do not like receiving oral sex.
12. Women who are sloppy kissers.
13. Women who are too serious.
14. Women who are excessively needy and clingy.
15. Women who are selfish, self-absorbed, or superficial.
16. Women who care only about a man's financial status.
17. Women who use their sexuality to manipulate men.
18. Women who talk about former lovers.
19. Women who are not sexually spontaneous.
20. Women who wear ugly underwear.

Adapted from DeAngelis (1990:213–280)

---

sexual problems. Try to stay level-headed about it, and do not jump to any conclusions ("This just proves she's having an affair; I knew it all along!"). The sexual organs are part of the body, and can malfunction just as your stomach or lungs can. No one says when his or her spouse gets a stomach ache, "He or she doesn't love me anymore!"

Finally, do not assume that once you have read this book, you will be a great lover. Being a good lover takes practice, patience, and work. It is not uncommon for lovers in long-term relationships to let go of some of the responsibility for maintaining their sex lives. Good lovers do not let themselves fall into predictable sexual patterns. Try something new, experiment, and play. Think of new and different ways to surprise and excite your partner, and continue to communicate your own sexual desires and needs.

S u m m a r y

- To become a better lover, a person must first understand the basics of human sexuality, such as anatomy and physiology, hormones, love, and many other areas.
- Healthy sexuality depends upon feeling good about oneself. A positive self-concept helps us to feel good about ourselves, which our partners pick up on.
- Masturbation can also help us to learn to be better lovers.

People who masturbate tend to be more aware of what type of stimulation feels best to them.
- We look for many qualities in our sexual partners. Often these qualities include attractiveness, personality, tenderness, and sexual ability. A good lover is sensitive to his or her partner's needs and desires, can communicate his or her own desires, and is patient, caring, and confident.

WHERE DO I *Stand?* SF6.5

Sharing Sexual Thoughts and Feelings

Learning what turns ourselves and our partners on can be very helpful. Below we have listed several questions that you and your partner should answer separately. Take your time and really think about these questions. After you are done, share your list with your partner. You might find you learn some new things about your sexual partner.

1. My favorite sexual or sensual experience with you was when (describe in as much detail as possible):

_____
_____
_____
_____

2. Three wonderful things you could do that could turn me on or improve sex for me are (kinds of touching, talking, positions, etc.):

_____
_____
_____
_____

3. The best way for me to orgasm is (describe in as much detail as possible):

_____
_____
_____
_____

4. Two things that I find sexually frustrating in our relationship are:

_____
_____
_____
_____

5. A fantasy I might like to act out with you is (write out a detailed scenario, including what each of you is doing, feeling, hearing, tasting).

6. Two things I am afraid might happen if I have sex more regularly with you are:

_____
_____
_____
_____
_____

7. The thing I'm most embarrassed to tell you about is (things like, I haven't been having orgasms, I'd like you to stimulate me anally, or I feel inadequate about certain behaviors):

_____
_____
_____
_____

8. One of the most erotic or sensuous experiences I ever had was:

_____
_____
_____

What made it good was:

_____
_____
_____

9. One of the worst sexual experiences I ever had was:

_____
_____
_____

What made it bad was:

_____
_____
_____

Reprinted with permission from Wolfe (1992:249)

S u m m a r y

- Most women believe that an ideal lover is slow, patient, and will respect the emotionality of sex, while most men believe that an ideal lover is open-minded, can talk about what she likes or dislikes, and will experiment and explore her sexuality.
- The majority of people use sexual fantasy to increase their sexual arousal at some point during their lives. Overall, female fantasies tend to be more romantic, while male fantasies tend to be more overtly sexual.
- Many sexual dysfunctions can interfere with a healthy and satisfying sexual relationship. It is important to talk about these concerns and issues as they occur, rather than ignoring them, which can cause bigger problems later on.
- Overall, being a good lover takes practice, patience, and work.

R e f l e c t i o n s   o n   S e x u a l i t y

1. Why are self-esteem and communication important to a relationship?
2. What are nonconstructive communication patterns? Give an example. How might these patterns cause problems in relationships?
3. What can you do to improve your own sex life or to assure you will find it enjoyable later on?
4. What makes a good lover? Explain.
5. What do women want in a sexual relationship? What do men want?

S u g g e s t e d   R e a d i n g s

COMFORT, A. (1991) *The New Joy of Sex: A Gourmet Guide for Lovemaking for the Nineties.* New York: Crown publishers.

DEANGELIS, B. (1987) *How to Make Love All the Time.* New York: Rawson Associates, a division of MacMillan Publishers.

DEANGELIS, B. (1990) *Secrets About Men Every Woman Should Know.* New York, Dell Publishing.

FARRELL, W. (1992) *The Liberated Man: Freeing Men and Their Relationships with Women.* New York: Berkley Books.

HEIMAN, J. and J. LOPICCOLO. (1988) *Becoming Orgasmic: A Sexual and Personal Growth Program for Women.* New York: Prentice Hall.

Masterton, G. (1987) *How to Drive Your Woman Wild in Bed.* New York: Penguin Books.

Masterton, G. (1993) *Drive Him Wild: A Hands-on Guide to Pleasuring Your Man in Bed.* New York: Penguin Books.

WOLFE, J. (1992) *What to Do when He Has a Headache.* New York: Penguin Books.

Glossary

abortifacients: Any substance or device that causes an abortion.

abortion: Induced termination of a pregnancy before fetal viability.

abstinence: In sexuality, the refraining from intercourse and often other forms of sexual contact.

acquired immune deficiency syndrome (AIDS): A condition of increased susceptibility to opportunistic diseases; results from an infection with the HIV, which destroys the body's immune system.

acrosin: The chemical in the head of the spermatozoon that breaks down the outer membrane of the ovum to allow penetration.

acrosome: The head of a spermatozoon that contains enzymes that facilitate the penetration of a spermatozoon into a secondary oocyte.

Acute Phase: First stage of the rape trauma syndrome, in which a victim often feels shock, fear, anger, or other related feelings.

acyclovir: A topical ointment used to reduce the pain and swelling of the herpes blisters.

adrenal glands: Two glands, one above each kidney. The adrenal glands produce small amounts of both female and male sex hormones.

adrenogenital syndrome (AGS): An inherited disorder involving an overproduction of androgen in the adrenal glands. Females born with this condition frequently have masculinized genitals because of excess prenatal androgen exposure. In males, genital appearance is usually unaffected.

affective disorders: A class of mental disorders that affect mood.

age-grading: The tendency of cultures to determine people's social positions and allowable behaviors in terms of their chronological age.

alveoli: The milk-secreting portion of mammary glands.

ambivalence theory: A theory of humor that suggests humor comes from a conflict of emotions in the listener.

amenhorrea: The absence of menstruation.

amniocentesis: A diagnostic procedure in which amniotic fluid is extracted from a pregnant woman's uterus to examine fetal cells for chromosomal defects that can cause genetic disorders or other abnormalities in the unborn child.

amnion: The innermost fetal membrane that holds the fetus suspended in amniotic fluid.

amniotic fluid: The fluid in the amniotic cavity; initially produced by the mother's blood and later from fetal urine.

ampulla: A sac-like widening of a canal.

anal fixation: If the conflict of the anal stage is not successfully resolved, anal character traits such as stubbornness, orderliness, or cleanliness might result.

anal sphincter: a ring-like muscle that surrounds the anus; it usually relaxes during normal physiological functioning.

anal stage: The psychosexual stage of development in which the anal region is the primary erogenous zone.

analingus: oral stimulation of the anus.

androgen: The general name for male hormones such as testosterone and androsterone.

androgen-insensitivity syndrome (AIS): A condition where a genetic males cells are insensitive to androgens, resulting in the development of female external genitalia (but no internal reproductive organs). People with AIS are raised as females.

androgyny: The strong presence of both masculine and feminine gender role characteristics in a single individual.

andropause: The hormonal changes accompanying old age in men that correspond to menopause in women.

anencephaly: The absence of all or part of the brain.

angina: Though the term technically refers to any spasmodic or choking pain, it is usually used by the lay public to refer to the chest pains that accompany heart disease.

anorexia: An eating disorder characterized by self-induced weight loss, distorted body-image, and other perceptual disturbances and the physiological changes that result from nutritional depletion.

anorgasmia: An inability to reach orgasm.

anti-miscegenation laws: Laws forbidding sexuality, marriage, or breeding between members of different races.

Apgar: A numerical expression of the condition of a newborn infant based on the combined assessment of heart rate, respiratory effort, muscle tone, reflex irritability, and color evaluated one minute after birth.

aphasia: Defects in the ability to express and/or understand speech, signs, or written communication, due to damage to the speech centers of the brain.

aphrodisiac: A substance that increases, or is believed to increase, a person's sexual desire.

apostasy: The rejection of one's birth religion.

archetypes: Ancient images that Carl Jung believed we are born with and influenced by.

areola: The pigmented ring around the nipple of the breast.

arousal disorders: Sexual dysfunctions that occur during the excitement stage of sexual response.

artificial insemination: Inserting semen into a woman's vagina or uterus for the purpose of inducing pregnancy by means other than sexual intercourse.

ascetic: Living a lifestyle that rejects sensual pleasures such as drinking alcohol, eating rich foods, or engaging in sex.

ascetic monastic orders: Groups of monks who live simple lives, rejecting sensual pleasures.

asexual: Relationships that do not involve sexual behavior.

asymptomatic: Describes diseases that occur without recognizable symptoms.

atheoretical: Research that is not structured by a particular theory.

attributional styles: Pattern of internal or external styles of attributing meaning to various events.

autoerotic: Characterized by sexual desire for or sexual behavior with oneself.

autoinoculate: To cause a secondary infection in the body from an already existing infection.

autosomes: Any chromosome that is not a sex chromosome. There are 22 autosomes in the normal human cell, which appear in homologous pairs.

aversion therapy: (In behavior therapy) a technique that reduces the frequency of maladaptive behavior by associating it with real or imagined a aversive stimuli during a conditioning procedure.

back-alley abortions: Illegal abortions, which were all that were available prior to the legalization of abortion.

barren: Unable to have children. Being childless was often considered to be the woman's fault in ancient civilizations.

Bartholin's glands: A pair of glands on either side of the vaginal orifice that open by a duct into the space between the hymen and the labia minora; also called greater vestibular glands.

basal body temperature (BBT): The body's resting temperature, which is taken first thing in the morning prior to arising and used to calculate ovulation in the sympto-thermal method of contraception.

behavior modification: Therapy based on operant conditioning and classical conditioning principles, used to change behaviors.

behaviorists: Theorists who believe that behavior is learned through rewards and punishments and can be altered using the same technique.

benign: Not malignant; favorable for recovery; a mild disease.

benign prostatic hypertrophy: The common enlargement of the prostate that occurs in most men after about age fifty.

berdache: A social role among some Native American tribes in which people of one biological gender lived their lives as members of the other biological gender.

bestiality: The act of having intercourse with an animal.

bibliotherapy: Using books and educational materials for the treatment of sexual dysfunction.

biphobia: A suspicion, antipathy, or dislike of bisexuals whether coming from heterosexuals or homosexuals.

birching: Whipping someone using the stripped branch of a tree.

birth control: Another term for contraception.

bisexual: A person who is sexually attracted to both sexes.

blastocyst: The hollow ball of embryonic cells that enters the uterus from the Fallopian tube and eventually implants. Once implantation has been achieved, pregnancy has begun.

bloody show: The combination of the mucus plug and blood that are expelled from the vagina before labor begins.

blue humor: A term referring to sexually oriented jokes.

body image: A person's feelings and mental picture of his or her own body's beauty.

bondage and discipline (B & D) prostitute: A prostitute who engages in sadomasochistic sexual services.

Braxton–Hicks contractions: Intermittent contractions of the uterus after the third month of pregnancy that do no indicate that labor has begun.

break-through bleeding: Slight blood loss which occurs from the uterus when a woman is taking oral contraceptives.

breast buds: The first swelling of the area around the nipple that indicates the beginning of breast development.

breech birth: An abnormal and often dangerous birth during which the baby's feet, knees, or buttocks emerge before the head.

brothel: A house of prostitution.

buggery: A term used in some legal documents and in popular circles for anal sex.

bulbourethral gland: One of a pair of glands located under the prostate gland on either side of the urethra that secretes a fluid into the urethra; also called a **Cowper's gland.**

bulemia: An eating disorder characterized by overeating (at least twice a week) followed by purging through self-induced vomiting, strict dieting or fasting, vigorous exercise, and/or use of laxatives.

bundling: An American practice of putting a wooden board or hanging sheets in the middle of the bed, or wrapping the body in tight clothes, in order to allow an unmarried couple to spend the night together without sex.

burlesque: A theatrical form that uses coarse, vulgar, or sexual humor and was commonly performed in houses of burlesque throughout the first half of the twentieth century.

butch: Lesbian role-playing of a masculine-type female.

call boys: A higher-class male prostitute who is often contacted by telephone and may either work by the hour or the evening.

call girl: A higher-class female prostitute who is often contacted by telephone and may either work by the hour or the evening.

Candida albicans: Fungus that causes yeast infections (candidiasis) in women.

caning: Beating someone with a rigid cane.

cannula: A tube, used in an abortion procedure, through which the uterine contents are emptied.

canon: A rule or law passed by a religious body.

case study: A research methodology that involves an in-depth examination of one subject or a small number of subjects.

castration anxiety: The fear a boy experiences during the phallic stage of psychosexual development that his father will cut off his genitals.

cauterization: A sterilization procedure that involves burning or searing the Fallopian tubes or vas deferens for permanent sterilization.

celibacy: The state of remaining unmarried; often used today to refer to abstaining from sex.

cervical cap: A plastic or rubber cover for the cervix that provides a contraceptive barrier to sperm.

cervical effacement: The stretching of the cervix in preparation for birth.

cervical intraepithelial neoplasia (CIN): The lesion that signals the possible beginning of cervical cancer.

cervical laceration: Cuts or tears on the cervix of the uterus.

cervix: The donut-shaped bottom part of the uterus that protrudes into the top of the vagina and contains an opening (os) through which sperm enter and menstrual fluid and babies exit the uterus.

cesarean section: A surgical procedure in which the woman's abdomen and uterus are cut open and a child is removed; used when vaginal birth may endanger a mother and/or child.

chancre: A small, red-brown sore that results from syphilis infection; the sore is actually the site in which the bacteria entered the body.

chancroid: A bacterial STD that is characterized by small bumps that eventually rupture and form painful ulcers.

chastity: The quality of being sexually pure, either through abstaining from intercourse or by adhering to strict rules of sexuality.

child sexual abuse: Sexual contact with a minor by an adult.

chlamydia: A STD that is caused by an infection with *Chlamydia trachomatis;* although often asymptomatic, it is also one of the most damaging of all the STDs.

Chlamydia trachomatis: Bacteria that causes chlamydia.

chorionic villus sampling (CVS): The sampling and testing of the chorion for fetal abnormalities.

chromosome: A threadlike structure in the nucleus (central body) of a cell that carries the genetic information of the cell.

chronic obstructive pulmonary diseases (COPD): Diseases of the lung and breathing.

chronic pelvic congestion: A vasocongestive buildup in the uterus that can occur when arousal does not lead to orgasm.

circumcision: Surgical removal of the foreskin (prepuce), the fold of skin over the glans penis, or, in some societies, the removal of the clitoris in women.

climacteric: The combination of physiological and psychological changes that develop at the end of a female's reproductive life; usually includes menopause.

clitoris: An erectile organ of the female located under the prepuce; it is an organ of sexual pleasure and is homologous to the male penis.

cognitive theory: A theory that proposes that our thoughts are responsible for our behaviors.

cohabitation: Living together in a sexual relationship when not legally married.

coitus interruptus: A contraceptive method involving a withdrawal of the penis from the vagina prior to ejaculation.

coitus reservatus: A contraceptive method that involves stopping sexual intercourse prior to ejaculation and allowing the penis to detumesce.

colostrum: A thin, yellowish fluid, high in proteins and antibodies, that is secreted from the nipples at the end of pregnancy and during the first few days after delivery.

colposcopy: Magnified examination used by physicians to identify changes in the cervical cells.

combination birth control pills: An oral contraceptive containing synthetic estrogen and progesterone.

comfort *or* **hospitality girl:** A prostitute in Japan or the Philippines respectively, who was forced into prostitution by the government to provide sex for the soldiers.

coming out: The process of a person recognizing his or her own homosexuality, coming to personal terms with it, and then informing his or her family and the public.

common-law marriage: A marriage existing by mutual agreement over a period of years, rather than through legal means, between a man and a woman.

communicable diseases: Diseases that can be transmitted from one person to another.

companionate or **conjugal love:** A love that develops over time in committed couples, involving a sense of intimacy, trust, mutual respect, comfort and ease, and deep affection. Companionate love can also be quite sexual and sensual but usually without the sense of urgency found in romantic love.

concubine: Primarily in older societies, a woman who served as a secondary wife, whose social and legal status was inferior to that of the primary wife, but whose children were considered legitimate.

conditional love: Accepting others conditionally, making restrictions on their behaviors or thoughts.

conditioning: In behaviorism, the process whereby an organism associates a particular stimulus with a response; for example, if food repeatedly is served to a dog right after the sound of a bell, the dog will salivate at the sound of the bell even if no food is served.

condom: A latex or animal membrane sheath that fits over the penis and is used for protection against pregnancy and sexually transmitted diseases; latex female condoms, that protect the vaginal walls, are also available.

confession: A Catholic practice of revealing one's sins to a priest.

confidentiality: Keeping all materials collected in a research study private and confidential.

configurational theory: The theory that laughter happens when a situation of seeming contradiction falls into place all at once.

Confucianism: More a Chinese philosophy than a religion, Confucianism, based on the sayings of Confucius, was directed toward principles of justice and righteousness in human interaction.

congenital syphilis: Syphilis that is transmitted from an infected mother to her developing child.

consanguineous marriage: A marriage that takes place between persons who are related by blood or family lineage.

conscious: In Freud's theory, the part of the personality that contains the material of which we are currently aware.

constructionism: The scientific theory that sexual orientation is a product of social forces rather than an innate part of a person's biological makeup.

contagion: Disease transmission by direct or indirect contact.

contemporaneous bisexuality: When bisexuals have sex with members of both sexes in the same time period.

contraception: Prevention of pregnancy by abstinence or the use of certain devices or surgical procedures to prevent ovulation, fertilization, or implantation.

contraceptive sponges: Polyurethane sponges impregnated with spermicide, inserted into the vagina for contraception.

corona: The ridge of the glans penis.

corpora cavernosa: Plural of corpus cavernosum (cavernous body), areas in the penis and clitoris that fill with blood during erection.

corpus luteum: Meaning "yellow body," a yellowish endocrine gland in the ovary formed when a follicle has discharged its secondary oocyte; it secretes estrogen and progesterone to help prepare the uterus for implantation.

corpus spongiosum: Meaning "spongy body," the erectile tissue in the penis that contains the urethra.

correlational: Research that examines the relationship between two or more variables.

correlations: Numbers that indicate a degree of a relationship between two variables.

courtesan: A prostitute who often interacts with men of rank or wealth.

courtship disorders: A theory of paraphilias that links them to being stuck in different stages of the normal progression of courtship.

couvade: The experiencing of the symptoms of pregnancy and/or childbirth.

Cowper's glands: See **bulbourethral gland.**

cremaster muscle: The "suspender" muscle that raises and lowers the scrotum to control scrotal temperature.

crowning: The emergence of a baby's head at the opening of the vagina at birth.

crus and **crura** (plural): Tapered, internal portion of the penis or clitoris that is part of the root and is attached to muscles anchoring the organ.

cryosurgery: Surgery suing freezing techniques to destroy part of an organ.

cryptococcosis: An opportunistic disease that may occur in persons with AIDS.

cunnilingus: The act of sexually stimulating the female genitals with the mouth.

curette: A surgical instrument, which is shaped like a spoon or scoop, used to empty the uterus during an abortion procedure.

cycle of humor: Groups of jokes with common themes that circulate widely among people, often in response to national circumstances.

cystectomy: The surgical removal of the bladder.

cytomegalovirus: An opportunistic disease that may occur in persons with AIDS.

dartos muscles: Muscles in the scrotum that are responsible for raising and lowering the testes.

decency: Conformity to recognized standards of propriety, good taste, and modesty—as defined by a particular group (standards of decency differ among groups).

deoxyribonucleic acid (DNA): A nucleic acid in the shape of a double helix, in which is encoded all genetic information in the organism.

dependent variable: A variable in which changes are contingent upon changes in the independent variable.

Depo Provera: Medroxyprogesterone, an injectable contraception available in the United States and in many other countries.

DES: Diethstilbestrol, a potent synthetic estrogen.

detumescence: The return of an erect penis to the flaccid state.

diaphragm: A birth-control device consisting of a latex dome on a flexible spring rim; used with spermicidal cream or jelly.

didanosine (ddI): A medication that has been shown to slow the progression to AIDS.

differentiation: The process in development when simple cells begin to take on complex shapes and functions.

Dihydrotestosterone (DHT): A derivative of testosterone, an androgen that stimulates the growth of certain male cells in fetal development and at puberty.

dilation: The expansion of the opening of the cervix in preparation for birth.

dilation and curettage: The surgical scraping of the uterine wall with a curette (spoon-shaped instrument).

dilation and evacuation (D&E): A second-trimester abortion procedure that involves cervical dilation and vacuum aspiration of the uterus.

dilation rods: A series of graduated metal rods that are used to dilate the cervical opening during an abortion procedure.

dilators: A graduated series of metal rods used in the treatment of vaginismus.

diploid: Having two complete sets of chromosomes, characteristically found in the somatic cells of an organism.

discrepancy in desire: Differences in levels of sexual desire in a couple.

Disease Model: A model that emphasizes educating to reduce sexually transmitted diseases (such as herpes or AIDS) rather than educating for sexual health.

disinhibition: The loss of normal control over behaviors, such as expressing sexuality or taking one's clothes off in public.

dissociative disorder: Psychological disorder involving a disturbance of memory, identity, and consciousness, usually resulting from a traumatic experience.

dizygotic: Pertaining to or derived from two separate zygotes.

dominant: Taking the active role in sadomasochistic sexuality.

dominatrix: A woman, often a prostitute, who humiliates and dominates submissive men.

Down's syndrome: A problem that occurs on the twenty-first chromosome of the developing fetus that can cause mental retardation.

dry sex: Sexual activity that does not involve the transfer of any bodily fluids.

ductus epididymis: A tightly coiled tube inside the epididymis in which spermatozoa undergo maturation.

due date: The projected birth date of a baby; it gives a general idea of the day of birth but is not meant to be exact.

dysmenorrhea: Painful menstruation.

dyspareunia: Painful intercourse.

ebhebephilia (sometimes just hebephilia): Attraction to children who have just passed puberty.

eclampsia: A progression of toxemia with similar, but worsening, conditions.

ectopic pregnancy: The implantation of the fertilized egg outside the uterus, for example, in the Fallopian tubes or the abdomen.

edema: An excessive accumulation of fluid in a part of the body causing swelling.

effectiveness rates: Estimated rates of the number of women who do not become pregnant each year using each method of contraception.

ego: According to Freud, the part of the personality that mediates between environmental demands (reality), conscience (superego), and instinctual needs (id).

ejaculation: The reflex ejection or expulsion of semen from the penis.

ejaculatory duct: A tube that transports spermatozoa from the vas deferens to the urethra.

ejaculatory inevitability: A feeling, just prior to orgasm, that ejaculation can no longer be controlled; the vas deferens, seminal vesicles, and prostate have already started to contract.

Electra complex: The incestuous desire of the daughter for sexual relations with the father.

ELISA (enzyme-immunoabsorbent assay): The screening test used to detect HIV antibodies in blood samples. Positive ELISA tests should be confirmed with a Western Blot test.

embryo: The unborn organism during the first eight weeks after fertilization.

endocrine glands: Glands that secrete hormones into the blood.

endometriosis: The growth of endometrial tissue outside the uterus.

endometrium: The mucous membrane lining the uterus.

endorphins: Neurotransmitters, concentrated in pituitary gland and parts of the brain, that inhibit physical pain.

engagement: When the fetus moves down toward the birth canal prior to delivery.

entremetteuse: A woman who procures sexual partners for men; in older days, one who also taught men about lovemaking.

epididymitis: An inflammation of the epididymis in men, usually resulting from STDs.

epidural block: A nerve block used during delivery that is administered through a needle in the back into the space between the spinal cord and the outer membrane.

episiotomy: A cut made with surgical scissors to avoid tearing of the perineum at the end of the second stage of labor.

erectile dysfunction: The inability to obtain or maintain an erection firm enough for penetration.

erection: The hardening of the penis (or clitoris) caused by blood engorging the erectile tissue.

erogenous zones: According to Freud (in psychoanalytic theory), the mouth, anus, and genital regions are particularly sensitive to touch, and the various pleasures associated with these regions are sexual.

erotica: Sexually oriented media that are considered by a viewer or a society as within the acceptable bounds of decency.

erotophonophiliac: Someone who gets sexual excitement from murdering others.

escort agency: An agency set up to arrange escorts for unaccompanied males; sexual services are often involved.

essentialism: The scientific theory that sexual orientation is innate, part of a person's biological makeup.

estrogen: A general term for female sex hormones produced by the ovaries (and elsewhere) and concerned with development and maintenance of female reproductive structures and secondary sex characteristics, such as estradiol and estriol.

estrus: The (usually monthly) state of female mammals in sexual excitement; in higher primates it is accompanied by a swelling and coloration of the hindquarters. (In males, the corresponding word is *rut*.)

eunuchs: From the Greek word for "bed-watcher," castrated males (or less often males with their penis removed) who guarded harems. At times, children were make eunuchs in childhood in order to sing soprano in church choirs. In the Bible Jesus mentions eunuchs who castrated themselves for religious reasons.

excitement: The first stage of the sexual response cycle, in which an erection occurs in males and vaginal lubrication occurs in females.

exhibitionist: One who exposes his or her genitals to strangers as a preferred or exclusive means of sexual arousal and orgasm.

extended families: Family members in addition to the nuclear family, such as grandparents or uncles and aunts, living together as a family unit.

failure rates: Measurable rates of the number of women who become pregnant each year using each method of contraception.

Fallopian tubes: The ducts that transport ova from the ovary to the uterus; also called oviducts.

false negative: A negative AIDS test result that occurs in a person who is positive for the virus.

false negative: Incorrect result of a medical test or procedure that wrongly shows the lack of a finding, condition, or disease.

false positive: A positive AIDS test result that occurs in a person who is negative for the virus.

false postitive: An incorrect result of a medical test or procedure that wrongly shows the presence of a finding, condition, or disease.

family life education: Forming in reaction to criticism of sex education from conservatives, this type of curriculum is expanding its focus to include information on relationships with parents, self-concepts, and STDs.

fellatio: The act of sexually stimulating the penis with the mouth.

female infanticide: The killing of female infants; practiced in some countries that value males more than females.

femininity: The set of behavioral expectations of women in a particular culture.

feminist theory: Theory of rape that contends that rape is a tool used in society to keep a woman in her place.

femme: Lesbian role-playing of a feminine-type female.

fertility awareness: Basal body temperature charting used in conjunction with another method of contraception.

fertilization: Penetration of the ovum by a spermatozoon and the subsequent union of the nuclei of the two cells.

fetal alcohol syndrome (FAS): A disorder involving growth deficiencies, nervous system damage, and facial abnormalities found in the offspring of mothers who consumed large quantities of alcohol during pregnancy.

fetal distress: When a fetus has an abnormal heart rate or rhythm.

fetish: An inanimate object, or a body part, that serves as the focus of sexual desire.

fetishist: One who focuses intensely on an inanimate object or body part (the fetish) for the arousal of sexual desire.

fetishistic transvestite: A person whose preferred or exclusive method of sexual arousal or orgasm is through wearing the clothing of the other sex.

fimbria: The branched, fingerlike border at the end of each Fallopian tube.

first-trimester abortion: Termination of pregnancy within the first twelve weeks of pregnancy.

fisting: Sexual technique that involves inserting the fist and even part of the forearm into the anus.

fixation: The tying up of psychic energy at one psychosexual stage, which results in adult behaviors characteristic of the stage.

flagellation: Striking a partner, usually by whipping.

flagellum: The taillike end of a spermatozoon that propels it forward.

Food and Drug Administration: An agency in the U.S. federal government which has the power to approve and disapprove new drugs.

foreskin: The fold of skin that covers the glans penis, often removed by circumcision; also called the prepuce.

fornication: Engaging in sexual intercourse while unmarried.

fraternal twins: Two offspring developed from two separate ova fertilized by different spermatozoon.

free association: A technique used in psychoanalytic therapy in which a client flows with any feelings or thoughts by reporting them immediately without censorship.

Free Love Movement: A movement of the early nineteenth century that preached that love should be the factor that determines whether one should have sex (not to be confused with the free love movement of the 1960s). The movement was against promiscuity, which does not include true love of the partner.

frenulum: Any small fold of mucous membrane that connects two parts of an organ and limits movement.

fresco: A type of painting done on wet plaster so that the plaster dries with the colors incorporated into it.

frotteurism or **frottage:** The act of compulsively rubbing against strangers for sexual arousal.

fundus: The part of a hollow organ farthest from the opening; in the uterus, the topmost portion.

gallows humor: Jokes made in situations of stress or fear to help break the tension; originated from the jokes often made by people about to be hanged on the gallows.

gamete intra-Fallopian tube transfer: A reproductive technique in which the sperm and ova are collected and injected into the Fallopian tube prior to fertilization.

gamete or germ cell: A male or female reproductive cell; the spermatozoon or ovum.

gay bar: A bar that serves a predominantly homosexual clientele.

gay baths: Public baths that served a predominantly homosexual clientele and were often used for sexual pick-ups; many were closed, voluntarily or involuntarily, as the AIDS epidemic became known.

gender constancy: The realization in the young child that one's gender does not normally change over the life span.

gender dysphoria: The state of feeling and believing that one is not really a member of one's anatomical gender (see **transsexualism**).

gender hierarchy: The ranking of the genders, with one gender (usually male) being dominant and considered superior.

gender identity: The inner sense of one's maleness or femaleness.

gender reassignment surgery: Surgery for transsexuals, designed to re-form male genitals into female genitals or female genitals into male.

gender role behavior: The learned set of behaviors that are expected of a person of one's gender.

gender-role nonconformity: The act of not behaving as society expects of one's gender.

gender roles: A set of culturally prescribed behaviors that determines how members of each gender are expected to behave in a particular society.

gender schema: The network of ideas and associations that guides the way we think about gender and gender roles.

gender theories: Theory for sexual abuse that identifies gender as an important aspect in the development of an abuser.

gender traits: Biologically determined characteristics that differentiate men from women.

genderlects: Deborah Tannen's word for the fundamentally different strategies males and females use to communicate.

gene: A basic unit of genetic material that is carried in a particular site on a chromosome. A gene is made up of DNA.

generalizability: Pertaining to objects, symbols, principles, etc. formulated in such a manner that they have wide applicability.

generalizable: Able to be applied to the general population.

genital stage: The final psychosexual stage in which the ability to engage in adult sexual behavior is developed.

genital warts: Wartlike growths on the genitals; also called venereal warts, condylomata, or papilloma.

gestation: The period of intrauterine fetal development.

gestational carrier: A woman who carries another couple's zygote to term for them.

glans clitoris or penis: The flaring tip of the penis or clitoris, from the word *glandes* meaning "acorn" (because of its shape).

glans penis: The flaring, enlarged region at the end of the penis.

global sexual dysfunction: A sexual dysfunction that occurs in every sexual situation.

gonads: The glands that produce gametes and hormones; the ovary in the female and the testis in the male.

gonococcus bacterium: The bacterium that causes gonorrhea (*Neisseria gonorrhoeae*).

gonorrhea: A STD that is caused by an infection with *Neisseria gonorrhoeae;* symptoms in men include a puslike discharge and frequent urination; many women are asymptomatic; if left untreated, gonorrhea can lead to serious complications.

gossypol injections: An ingredient in cottonseed oil that, when injected or implanted, may inhibit sperm production.

Grafenberg Spot (G-spot): A controversial structure that is said to lie on the anterior (front) wall of the vagina and that is reputed to be a seat of sexual pleasure when stimulated.

gynecologist: A physician who specializes in gynecology, the branch of medicine dealing with the study and treatment of disorders of the female reproductive system.

gynecomastia: Abnormal breast development in the male.

haploid: Having one set of chromosomes, half the number characteristically found in the somatic cells of an organism.

hard-core: A reference to explicit, genitally oriented sexual depictions; the opposite of soft-core, which displays sexual activity without explicit portrayal of genital penetration.

harem: Abbreviation of the Turkish word *harêmlik* (*harâm* in Arabic) meaning "women's quarters" or "sanctuary."

Health Promotion Model: A model that emphasizes educating for sexual health rather than educating to avoid sexually transmitted diseases.

hemiplegia: Paralysis of one side of the body.

hemophilus: A vaginal infection caused by the organism *Hemophilus vaginalis;* often this infection is asymptomatic.

Hemophilus ducreyi: Bacteria that causes chancroid infection.

Hemophilus vaginalis: Organism that causes hemophilus, a vaginal infection.

hemorrhoids: Dilated or varicosed blood vessels in the anal region.

hepatitis B virus (HBV): Virus that causes one form of hepatitis.

hermaphrodite: A rare condition where both male and female sex organs exist in one person.

herpes: A highly contagious viral infection that causes eruptions of the skin of mucous membranes.

herpes simples I (HSV-1): A viral infection that causes cold sores on the face and lips.

herpes simplex II (HSV-2): A viral infection that is sexually transmitted and causes genital ulcerations.

herpes simplex virus (HSV): The virus that causes herpes.

heterophobia: The antipathy or dislike that homosexuals feel toward heterosexuals.

heterosexism: An attitude where heterosexuality is assumed to be the norm, and where social power is used to promote the validity of one heterosexual model of loving over other forms.

heterosexual: A person who is predominantly sexually attracted to the opposite sex.

Homo sapiens: The technical name for the species that all human beings belong to.

homoerotic: Artistic or literary works that focus on the sexual or love relations between members of the same sex.

homologous: Organs or other organic structures are said to be homologous when they correspond in structure, position, or origin but not necessarily in function. The female's labia minora and the male scrotum are homologous, for example, because they both originate from the same fetal tissue.

homophobia: A deep antipathy, disgust, or dislike of homosexuals.

homosexual: A person who is predominantly sexually attracted to the same sex.

homosocial play: The tendency for children to play with others of their own gender.

hormone: A secretion of endocrine glands that alters the physiological activity of target cells of the body.

hot flashes: A symptom of menopause consisting of the feeling of sudden heat often accompanied by a flush.

human chorionic gonadotropin (hCG): The hormone that stimulates production of estrogen and progesterone to maintain pregnancy.

human immunodeficiency virus (HIV): The retrovirus responsible for the development of AIDS; can be sexually transmitted.

human papilloma virus (HPV): A viral infection that can cause wartlike growths and/or increase the risk of cervical cancer.

hymen: A thin fold of vascularized mucous membrane at the vaginal orifice.

hyperestrogenemia: Having an excessive amount of estrogens in the blood.

hyperphilia: Compulsive sexuality due to overcompensating for negative reactions to childhood sexuality.

hyperprolactinemia: A condition in which there is an overproduction of prolactin which may interfere with sexual functioning.

hypersexuality: Abnormally expressive or aggressive sexual behavior, often in public; the term usually refers to behavior.

hypertension: Abnormally high blood pressure.

hypogonadism: A condition in which there is an underproduction of gonadal hormones which may interfere with sexual functioning.

hypophilia: Lack of full functioning of the sexual organs due to missing stages of childhood development.

hyposexuality: Abnormal suppression of sexual desire and behavior, the term usually refers to behavior due to some disturbance of the brain.

hypothalamus: A portion of the forebrain that controls important functions such as hunger and thirst, body temperature, and sexual function.

hysterectomy: The surgical removal of the uterus.

hysteria: A psychological disorder characterized by excessive or uncontrollable fear or other strong emotion.

hysterotomy: A second-trimester abortion procedure that involves a surgical removal of the fetus through the abdomen.

id: In Freud's theory, the collection of unconscious urges and desires that continually seek expression.

identical twins: Two offspring developed from one single ovum fertilized by one spermatozoon.

impairing (or corrupting) the morals of a minor: The legal term for an adult who engages a minor in sexually related acts (such as showing a minor sexually explicit movies); a lesser offense than child sexual abuse.

imperforate hymen: An abnormally closed hymen that usually does not allow exit to menstrual fluid.

impulse control: The ability to delay gratification of one's immediate desires.

in vitro fertilization: A procedure in which a woman's ova are removed from her body, fertilized with sperm in a laboratory, and then surgically implanted into her uterus.

incest taboo: The absolute prohibition of sex between family members.

incompetent cervix: A condition in which the cervix begins to open prematurely without labor or contractions and may result in premature delivery or miscarriage.

incongruity theory: A theory that humor involves bringing two things together that seem to highlight a contradiction in each other.

incontinence: The inability to withhold defecation or urination.

indentured servants: People who became servants to pay off a debt and were often treated as little more than slaves.

independent variable: The variable controlled by the experimenter and applied to the subject in order to determine its effect on the subject's reaction.

indwelling catheter: A permanent catheter, inserted in the bladder, to allow the removal of urine in those who are unable to urinate or are incontinent.

infantilism: Treating the submissive partner as a baby, including dressing the person in diapers in which the partner is forced to relieve himself or herself.

infertility: The inability to conceive (or impregnate) after one year of regular sexual intercourse without the use of birth control.

infibulation: The ritual removal of the clitoris, prepuce, and labia and the sewing together of the vestibule. Practiced in many African societies, there are now movements to try to eliminate the practice.

informed consent: Informing subjects about what will be expected of them before they participate in a research study.

infundibulum: The funnel or trumpet-shaped, open end of the Fallopian tube.

inguinal canal: The tubular passage through the lower layers of the belly wall.

inguinal hernia: A condition where the intestines bulge through a hole in the abdominal muscles of the groin.

inhibin: A hormone that, when injected or implanted, inhibits sperm production.

inhibited sexual desire (ISD): A sexual dysfunction in which a person experiences very low sexual desire.

Institutional Review Board: A committee at universities that works to approve research proposals.

intimacy repertoire: The set of attitudes and behaviors we learn in adolescence about how to form close friendships and love relations. For example, we might learn that a different set of behaviors is appropriate for a love interest than for a person with whom we plan to have a casual sexual relationship.

intracavernous injections: A treatment method for erectile dysfunction in which vasodilating drugs are injected into the penis for the purpose of creating an erection.

intrauterine device: A small, plastic device that is inserted into the uterus for contraception.

introitus: Any entrance to a body cavity, such as the vagina.

intromission: Insertion of the penis into the vagina or anus.

john: A slang term that refers to a prostitute's client.

judicial bypass option: Abortion legislation that allows for a judge to bypass parental consent or notification for a minor to acquire an abortion.

Kaposi's sarcoma: A rare form of cancer that often occurs in people with AIDS.

karma: The idea that there is a cycle of birth, death, and rebirth and that deeds in one's life affect one's status in a future life.

Klinefelter's syndrome: A genetic disorder in which there are three sex chromosomes, XXY, instead of two; characterized by small testes, low sperm production, breast enlargement, and absence of facial and body hair.

Koran: The holy book of Islam.

labia majora: Two longitudinal folds of skin extending downward and backward from the mons pubis of the female.

labia minora: Two small folds of mucous membrane lying within the labia majora of the female.

lactation: The collective name for milk creation, secretion, and ejection from the nipple by the mammary glands.

lactiferous ducts: The openings in the nipple through which milk is secreted.

lactiferous sinuses: The area of the breast where milk is stored for eventual secretion from the nipple.

Lactobacillus: Bacteria in the vagina that help maintain appropriate pH levels.

Lamaze method: A prepared childbirth method in which couples are provided information about the birth process and are taught breathing and relaxation exercises to use during labor.

laminaria: Seaweed that grows in cold ocean waters and can swell three to five times its original diameter; when dried laminaria may be used in second-trimester abortion procedures to dilate the cervix.

lanugo: The downy covering of hair over the fetus.

laparoscope: Instrument inserted through a small abdominal incision to view organs, remove fluids and tissues, drain ovarian cysts, stop bleeding, or perform other procedures.

laparoscopy: A procedure that allows a physician to have a direct view of all the pelvic organs, including the uterus, Fallopian tubes, and ovaries; also allows a physician to perform a number of important surgical procedures.

latency: A period in which a person is infected with a STD but does not test positive for it; the length of latency varies for different diseases.

latency stage: The psychosexual stage of development that follows resolution of the Oedipus complex and in which sexual desires are weak.

laws of Niddah: Rules in the Jewish tradition concerning the behaviors of a menstruating woman, including sexual restrictions.

lechery: Excessive indulgence in sexual desire.

lesbian: A woman who is attracted to and/or has sex with other women; comes from the Greek island of Lesbos, where Sappho, who wrote love poetry to women, lived.

leydig cells: The cells in the testes that produce hormones.

libido: According to Freud, the energy generated by the sexual instinct, also known as the "life" instinct.

ligation: A sterilization procedure that involves the tying or binding of the Fallopian tubes or vas deferens.

limerence: A term coined by Dorothy Tennov, referring to a sense of passionate obsession with object of desire, a preoccupation with love feelings, and a sense of dependency on the other person, similar to infatuation.

line-up: The lining-up of prostitutes in a brothel so when a client enters a brothel, clients can choose those prostitutes in which they are interested.

liposuction: The suction of fat cells from various parts of the body.

Long Term Reorganization: The second stage of the rape trauma syndrome, which involves a restoration of order in the victim's lifestyle and re-establishment of control.

lovemaps: Term coined by John Money to refer to the picture of an ideal lover and sexual situation we develop as we grow up.

lumpectomy: A modern surgical procedure for breast cancer where the tumorous lump and a small amount of surrounding tissue are removed.

machismo: A Spanish term for standards of masculinity.

madam: A slang term that refers to the woman who is responsible for overseeing a brothel.

mainline Protestant denominations: The older, more established Protestant denominations in the United States.

major depression: A persistent, chronic state in which the person feels he or she has no worth, cannot function normally, and entertains thoughts of or attempts suicide.

malignant: Technically, a cancerous condition that will spread; often used to mean any life-threatening condition.

mammary ducts: The tube that deposits the milk into the lactiferous sinuses.

mammary glands: The milk-producing glands of the mature female; breasts.

mammography: A procedure for internal imaging of the breasts to evaluate for breast disease or screen for breast cancer.

mania: A symptom of mental disorder characterized by excessive activity, feelings of elation, overtalkativeness, and irritability.

masculinity: The set of behavioral expectations of men in a particular culture.

masochism: Focus on receiving pain and humiliation as the preferred or exclusive method of sexual arousal and orgasm.

mass media: Media intended for a large, public audience.

mastectomy: The surgical removal of a breast.

master status: A primary characteristic or role that determines the way one is regarded; for example, being African American, gay, a movie star, or female.

maternal-serum alpha-fetoprotein-screening (MSAFP): A blood test used during early pregnancy to determine neural tube defects such as spina bifida or anencephaly.

meatus: An opening in the body, such as the orifice of the urethra.

media: All recorded forms of communication.

menarche: The start of menstrual cycling, usually during early puberty.

menopause: The cessation of menstrual cycling in women.

menorrhagia: Excessive menstrual flow.

menses: The blood and tissues discharged from the uterus during menstruation.

menstrual extraction: Removal of the contents of the uterus prior to a positive pregnancy test.

methotrexate: An experimental drug being tested as a post-coital method of contraception or abortion; when taken, it causes a fertilized ovum to be expelled.

midwife: A person who assists women during childbirth.

minipill: A type of birth-control pill that contains only synthetic progesterone and no estrogen.

miscarriage: A spontaneous abortion or pregnancy that terminates on its own.

misogynist: A person who has a hatred toward women.

mitosis: The division of the nucleus of a cell into two new cells such that each new daughter cell has the same number and kind of chromosomes as the original parent.

mittelschmerz: German for "middle pain," a pain in the abdomen or pelvis that some women feel that indicates ovulation has occurred.

modeling behavior: The act of young children mimicking the behavior of adults, usually their parents, in an attempt to learn adult behaviors.

monogamous: Being married to one mate; often used to mean not having sexual relations outside the marital unit.

monophasic: Oral contraceptives containing stable levels of hormones during the entire month; the doses and types of hormones do not vary.

monozygotic: Pertaining to or derived from a single zygote.

mons veneris or **mons pubis:** Literally Latin for "mountain of Venus" (Venus was the Roman goddess of love and beauty), the mound of fatty tissue over the female pubic bone, also called mons pubis meaning "pubic mound."

"morning after" pill: A contraceptive method that involves taking a high dose of hormones to interrupt a pregnancy within forty-eight hours of conception.

morning sickness: One of the signs of pregnancy that most women experience; it can occur at any time of day.

motherhood mandate: The belief that there is something psychologically wrong with a woman if she is childless at a certain age.

mucus plug: A collection of thick mucus in the cervix that prevents bacteria from entering the uterus.

Müllerian duct: One of a pair of tubes in the embryo that will develop, in female embryos, into the Fallopian tubes, uterus, and part of the vagina.

Müllerian inhibition factor: A hormone secreted in male embryos that prevents the Müllerian duct from developing into female reproductive organs.

multimodal: Using a variety of techniques.

multiphasic: Oral contraceptives that contain varying levels of hormones during the month; each week the hormonal dosage is changed.

multiple orgasms: More than one orgasm experienced within a short period of time.

multiple personality disorder: A dissociative disorder in which a person develops two or more distinct personalities.

mutual masturbation: Simultaneous masturbation of both sexual partners by each other.

myocardial infarction: A cutoff of blood to the heart muscle, causing damage to the heart; also called a heart attack.

myometrium: The smooth muscle layer of the uterus.

myotonia: Involuntary contractions of the muscles.

Naegeles Rule: A means of figuring the due date by subtracting three months from the first day of the last menstrual period and adding seven days.

narcissism: Obsession with the self, conceit, and selfishness, named for the Greek mythical character Narcissus, who gazed at his own reflection in a pool and fell in love with himself. Unlike healthy self-love, narcissism involves total self-absorption.

natural family planning: A contraceptive method that involves calculating ovulation and avoiding sexual intercourse during ovulation and at unsafe times.

necrophilia: The sexual attraction to dead bodies in fantasy or through sexual contact as a preferred or exclusive means of sexual arousal and orgasm.

Neisseria gonorrhoeae: The bacteria that causes gonorrhea.

neuroleptics: A class of antipsychotic drugs.

neurosis: A category of psychological disorders in which an individual experiences emotionally distressing symptoms.

nipple: A pigmented, wrinkled protuberance on the surface of the breast that contains ducts for the release of milk.

nocturnal emissions: Male orgasm and ejaculation while sleeping, often during erotic dreams; also known as wet dreams.

nocturnal penile tumescence (NPT) test: A study that is done to evaluate erections during sleep; tumescence of the penis is noted during certain stages of sleep, and this helps clarify the erectile dysfunction etiology.

no-fault divorce: The legal dissolution of a marriage without having to establish one partner's guilt.

nondemand pleasuring: Non-goal-oriented sexual activity.

nongonococcal urethritis (NGU): Urethral infections in men that are usually caused by an infection with chlamydia.

Nonoxynol-9: A spermicide that has been found to be highly effective for the prevention of pregnancy and protection from sexually transmitted diseases.

nonspecific vaginitis: A vaginal infection caused by the bacteria hemophilus; symptoms may include an increase in vaginal discharge, soreness, and itching.

Norplant: A hormonal method of birth control using doses that are implanted in a woman's arm and that can remain in place for up to five years.

nuclear family: A family unit consisting of a mother, father, and their children, without extended members such as grandparents.

nymphomaniac: A term used to describe women who engage in frequent or promiscuous sex; usually used pejoratively.

obscenity: A legal term for materials that are considered offensive to standards of sexual decency in a society.

Oedipus complex: A male child's sexual attraction at about age five for his opposite sex parent and the consequent conflicts.

100% sampling: A research strategy in which all members of a particular group are included in the sample.

oocyte: A cell in the ovary that develops into the ovum.

oophorectomy: The surgical removal of the ovaries.

operant conditioning: Learning resulting from the reinforcing response a subject receives following a certain behavior.

opportunistic diseases: Diseases that occur when the immune system is depressed; often fatal.

oral candidasis: An infection in the mouth caused by the excess growth of a fungus that occurs naturally in the body.

oral contraceptives: The "pill"; a preparation of synthetic female sex hormones that blocks ovulation.

oral stage: The psychosexual stage of development in which the mouth, lips, and tongue together are the primary erogenous zone.

orgasm: The third stage of the sexual response cycle, which involves an intense sensation during the peak of sexual arousal and results in a release of sexual tension.

orgasmic platform: The thickening of the walls of the outer third of the vagina, which occurs during the plateau stage of the sexual response cycle.

orgasmic reconditioning: A sex therapy technique where a person switches fantasies just at the moment of masturbatory orgasm to try and *condition* himself or herself to become excited by more conventional fantasies.

os: The opening of the cervix that allows passage between the vagina and the uterus.

osteoporosis: An age-related disorder characterized by decreased bone mass and increased susceptibility to fractures as a result of decreased levels of estrogens.

ostomies: Operations to remove part of the small or large intestine or the bladder, resulting in the need to create an artificial opening in the body for the elimination of bodily wastes.

Ottoman Empire: An empire based in Turkey that lasted over 600 years and ruled over large parts of Asia, Europe, and Africa, until its collapse after World War I.

outpatient surgery: Surgery performed in the hospital or doctor's office, after which a patient is allowed to return home; inpatient surgery requires hospitalization.

ovarian cysts: Small, fluid-filled sacs that can form on the ovary, which do not pose a health threat under most conditions.

ovary: The female gonad, responsible for the production of ova and female sex hormones.

oviducts: See **Fallopian tubes.**

ovum or **ova:** The female egg; ova is plural.

oxytocin: A hormone secreted by the hypothalamus that stimulates contraction of both the uterus for delivery of the newborn and the ducts of mammary glands for the secretion of milk from the nipple.

palimony: Payments awarded by a court to a woman (usually), from a man with whom she has cohabited.

Papanicolaou ("Pap") smear or **test:** Named for its inventor, a test that scrapes some cells from the cervix to detect cervical cancer.

papaverine: A vasodilator that is injected directly into the penis to increase erectile response.

paradigm: A plan of research based on specific concepts.

paraphilia: Clinical term used to describe types of sexual expressions that are seen as unusual and potentially problematic.

paraplegia: Paralysis of the legs and lower part of the body, affecting both sensation and motor response.

parental consent: Abortion legislation that requires the consent of the parents of a minor prior to an abortion procedure.

parental notification: Abortion legislation that requires the notification of the parents of a minor prior to an abortion procedure.

participant-observation: A research methodology that involves actual participation in the event that is being researched.

passing women: Women, predominantly in the early twentieth century, who dressed, acted, and lived as men—even marrying other women—without revealing their true gender to the public.

patriarchal: Of or pertaining to a society or system that is dominated by male power.

pederasty: Sexual contact between adult men and (usually) postpubescent boys.

pedophilia: Sex with children as a preferred or exclusive mode of sexual interaction in an adult; child molestation.

peer-reviewed: A process of research study approval, prior to the study being carried out. Usually universities have a committee that approves proposals.

pelvic inflammatory disease (PID): Widespread infection of the female pelvic organs.

penectomy: The surgical removal of the penis.

penile plethysmography: A test performed by measuring the amount of blood that enters the penis in response to a stimulus, which can indicate how arousing the stimulus is for the male.

penile strain gauge: A device that was used by Masters and Johnson to measure penile engorgement during arousal.

penis: The male copulatory and urinary organ, used both to urinate and introduce spermatozoa into the female vagina; it is the major organ of male sexual pleasure and is homologous to the female clitoris.

penis envy: A girl's desire to have a penis and to be like a male.

penitents: Those who come to confess sins (from the word *penance,* meaning "to repent").

perfect use: Refers to the probability of contraceptive failure for a perfect user of each method.

performance fears: The fear of not being able to perform during sexual behavior.

perimetrium: The outer wall of the uterus.

Peyronie's disease: Abnormal calcifications in the penis, which may cause painful curvature, often making sexual intercourse impossible.

phallic stage: The psychosexual stage of development in which the genital region is the primary erogenous zone and in which the Oedipus complex develops.

phallus: The penis; often used to refer to the penis as a symbol of power and aggression.

photoplethysmograph: A device used to measure physiological sexual arousal in females.

pimp: A slang term that refers to the male in charge of organizing clients for a female prostitute.

pitocin: A drug used during delivery to induce uterine contractions.

pituitary gland: A small endocrine gland lying beneath the hypothalamus, nicknamed the "master gland" because of its importance in hormonal secretion.

placebo pills: Seven pills that are at the end of a 28-day cycle of oral contraception; these pills are sugar pills and do not contain any hormones; used to help a woman remember to take a pill every day.

placenta: The structure through which the exchange of materials between fetal and maternal circulations occurs.

placenta previa: A condition in which the placenta is abnormally positioned in the uterus so that it partially or completely covers the opening of the cervix.

placentophagia: The act of eating the placenta directly following birth.

plateau: The second stage of the sexual response cycle, occurring prior to orgasm, in which vasocongestion builds up.

platonic friendship: Named after Plato's description, a deep, loving friendship between men (and now also between men and women) that is devoid of sexual contact or desire.

pneumocystis carinii pneumonia (PCP): A rare type of pneumonia, which is an opportunistic disease that often occurs in people with AIDS.

podophyllin: Acidic solution used to burn off genital warts.

polygamy: The practice of men or women marrying more than one partner.

polygyny: The practice of having more than one wife at a time.

pornography: Any sexually oriented material that is not acceptable to the viewer; any sexual depictions that are in violation of the law.

postcoital methods: Methods of birth control that are used after a pregnancy is confirmed or suspected.

postcoital drip: A vaginal discharge (dripping) that occurs after sexual intercourse.

postpartum depression: The feelings of sadness found in some women after childbirth, usually mild, but that can, in rare cases, result in deep, clinical depression; also called baby blues.

postpartum psychosis: The rare occurrence of severe, debilitating depression or psychotic symptoms in the mother after childbirth.

preconscious: In Freud's theory, the part of the personality that contains thoughts that can be brought into awareness with little difficulty.

premature: A baby born early, weighing less than 5.5 pounds.

premature ejaculation: Unintentional ejaculation either during foreplay, during penetration, or soon after intercourse begins.

premenstrual syndrome (PMS): Symptoms of physical and emotional stress occurring late in the postovulation phase of the menstrual cycle.

prepubescence: The period just before puberty.

prepuce: The loose-fitting skin covering the glans of the penis and clitoris.

prevalence: The state of widely or commonly occurring or existing.

priapism: A condition in which erections are longlasting and often painful.

primary (early) syphilis: The first stage of the syphilis infection, in which a sore called a chancre develops.

primary follicle: The site in the ovary of the immature ovum.

primary sexual dysfunction: A sexual dysfunction that has always existed.

primary voyeurist: A person for whom voyeurism is the main and exclusive paraphilia.

primitive gonads: The gonads early in development that have not yet assumed the shape or functions of the male or the female.

probability sampling: A research strategy that involves acquiring a random sample for inclusion in a study.

pro-choice supporters: People who believe that the abortion decision should be left up to the woman, and not regulated by the government.

prodromal phase: The tingling or burning feeling in the genitals that precedes the development of herpes blisters.

progesterone: A female sex hormone produced by the ovaries that helps prepare the endometrium for implantation of a fertilized ovum and the mammary glands for milk secretion.

prolactin: A hormone secreted by the pituitary gland that initiates and maintains milk secretion by the mammary glands.

pro-life supporters: People who believe that abortion should be illegal or strictly regulated by the government.

prostaglandin procedure: A second-trimester abortion procedure that involves injecting the uterus with prostaglandins, which cause uterine contractions and fetal expulsion.

prostate gland: A doughnut-shaped gland that wraps around the urethra as it comes out of the bladder which contributes fluid to the semen.

prostatectomy: The surgical removal of the prostate gland.

prosthesis implantation: A treatment method for erectile dysfunction in which a prosthesis is surgically implanted into the penis.

prurient: Characterized by lascivious thoughts; used as criteria for deciding what is pornographic.

pseudocyesis: A condition in which a woman believes she is pregnant and experiences signs of pregnancy, even though she is not.

pseudofamily: A type of family that develops when prostitutes and pimps live together; rules, household responsibilities, and work activities are agreed on by all members of the family.

pseudohermaphrodite: A person who has the gonads of one sex and the genitalia of the other or is born with ambiguous genitalia.

psychoanalysis: The system of psychotherapy developed by Freud that focuses on uncovering the unconscious material responsible for a patient's disorder.

psychogenic: Relating to psychological causes.

psychoneuroimmunology (PNI): The field that studies the relationships between psychological factors (such as stress and attitudes) and the functioning of the immune system.

psychosexual development: The childhood stages of development (oral, anal, phallic, latency, genital) during which, according to Freud, the id's pleasure-seeking energies focus on distinct erogenous zones.

puberty: The period of life at which both males and females develop the capacity to reproduce.

pubococcygeus muscle: A muscle that surrounds and supports the vagina.

pubic lice: Parasites that primarily infest the pubic hair and can be transmitted through sexual contact; also called crabs.

pudendum: Derived from a Latin word meaning "that about which one should have modesty," a name for the female genitalia.

pulling train: A term originated by Sanday (1990) that refers to the gang rape of a woman; refers to the succession of box cars on a train.

punch line: The final line of a joke which resolves the joke; the line that people are supposed to respond to with laughter.

punishment concept: The idea that people who had become infected with certain diseases, especially STDs, had done something wrong and were being punished.

punishment: In therapy, a process to decrease the frequency of an undesired behavior by following the occurrence of the behavior with an aversive stimulus.

Puritan: A sixteenth and seventeenth century religious movement from England that wanted to purge the church of elaborate ceremonies and simplify worship: has come to mean any person or group who is excessively strict in regard to sexual matters.

quadriplegia: Paralysis of all four limbs.

quadruped: Any animal that walks on four legs.

quadruplets: Four offspring having coextensive gestation periods and delivered at the same birth.

radical mastectomy: A surgical procedure where the breast, its surrounding tissue, the muscles supporting the breast, and axillary (underarm) lymph nodes are removed.

radical prostatectomy: The surgical removal of the prostate.

radioimmunoassay (RIA): A procedure in which a radioactive substance known to react with a certain protein is injected into the bloodstream to detect the amount of that protein in the body.

random sample: A number of cases taken from the entire population of persons, values, scores, etc. in such a way as to ensure that any one selection has as much chance of being picked as any other and that the sample will be a valid representation of the entire population.

randomly assign: Assigning subjects to groups in an experiment such that each subject has an equal chance of being assigned to each group.

rape: Forced sexual behavior with an individual without that person's consent.

Rape Crisis Center: A center for rape victims that provides treatment, support, counseling, and education.

Rape Trauma Syndrome: Two-stage stress response pattern that occurs after a rape.

rapist psychopathology: A theory of rape that identifies psychological issues in a rapist that contribute to rape behavior.

recanalization: The rejoining of the vas deferens or Fallopian tubes after a sterilization procedure.

recidivism: A tendency to relapse into a former pattern of behavior.

refractory stage: The period of time after an ejaculation in which men cannot be stimulated to further orgasm.

reinforcement: An event that when made contingent on a response, increases its probability; a reward or punishment.

reliability: The dependability of a test as reflected in the consistency of its scores upon repeated measurements of the same group.

replacement partner: A partner, other than the spouse, brought in by the subject; used in Masters and Johnson's physiological studies of sexual behavior.

representative sample: A sample that resembles the breakdown of the general population. Certain factors (such as ethnicity, gender, or age) are appropriately proportioned.

repression: A coping strategy by which unwanted thoughts or prohibited desires are forced out of consciousness and into the unconscious mind.

resolution: The fourth stage of the sexual response cycle, in which the body returns to the pre-aroused state.

retarded ejaculation: Condition in which ejaculation is impossible or occurs only after strenuous efforts.

revascularization: A procedure used in the treatment of vascular erectile dysfunction in which the vascular system is rerouted to ensure better blood flow to the penis.

reverse transcriptase: A chemical that is contained in the RNA of HIV; it helps to change the virus to DNA.

Rhogam: A drug given to mothers whose Rh is incompatible with the fetus's; it prevents the formation of antibodies that can imperil future pregnancies.

rhythm method: A contraceptive method that involves calculating the date of ovulation and avoiding sexual intercourse around this time.

rimming: Oral stimulation of the anus.

role repertoire: A set of roles we learn in adolescence (for example, our role as "friend," "lover," "student," "car driver," etc.), each of which has certain behaviors and attitudes associated with it. We carry these roles throughout life.

romantic love: The type of love that is focused on physical attraction, feelings of ecstasy, and passion, romance, and exclusivity. Only recently in history has romantic love become the preferred love leading to long-term relationships.

rooting reflex: When a hungry infant keeps its head in contact with an object that touches its mouth or cheek.

RU-486: A drug that when taken early in pregnancy with prostaglandin, causes a nonsurgical termination of the pregnancy.

sadism: Focus on administering pain and humiliation as the preferred or exclusive method of sexual arousal and orgasm.

sadomasochism: The sexual activities of partners where one takes a dominant, "master," position, and the other takes a submissive, "slave," position.

safe sex: Sexual behaviors that do not pose a risk for the transmission of sexually transmitted diseases.

safer sex: Sexual behaviors that reduce the risk of transmission of a sexually transmitted disease.

saline abortion: A second-trimester abortion procedure in which amniotic fluid is removed and replaced with a saline solution, which causes premature delivery of the fetus.

samples of convenience: A research methodology that involves using samples that are easy to collect and acquire.

satiation therapy: A therapy to lessen excitement to an undesired stimulus by masturbating to a desired stimulus and then immediately masturbating again when desire is lessened, to an undesired stimulus.

satyriasis or **Don Juanism:** Terms used to describe men who engage in frequent or promiscuous sex; both are usually seen as flattering terms.

scatophagia *and* **urolangia:** The ingestion of feces and urine, respectively, often as a sign of submission.

scatolophilia: Sexual arousal from making obscene telephone calls.

schema: A network of associations that organizes and guides an individual's perceptions.

schizophrenia: Any of a group of mental disorders that affects the individual's ability to think, behave, or perceive things normally.

scopophilia: The psychoanalytic term for voyeurism, literally "the love of looking."

secondary follicle: The name of the site in the ovary where the matured ovum sits before being released.

secondary oocyte: A mature ovum ready to be released from the ovary.

secondary sexual characteristics: The physical characteristics other than the genitalia, that distinguish male from female; for example, breasts, sex-based distribution of body hair, voice pitch, body shape, and muscle development.

secondary sexual dysfunction: A sexual dysfunction in a person who has functioned well in the past.

secondary syphilis: The second stage of syphilis, in which the bacteria invade the central nervous system causing a rash on the body. The lymph glands may also become swollen and enlarged.

secondary tubules: The tubes that transport milk from the alveoli of the breast to the mammary ducts.

second-trimester abortion: Termination of pregnancy between twelve and twenty-four weeks of pregnancy.

self-actualized: Fulfillment of an individual's potentialities; the actualization of aptitudes, talents, etc.

self-disclosure: The act of telling or showing another person intimate aspects of one's cognitive or emotional life. One can self-disclose facts, opinions, vulnerabilities, fears, hopes, insecurities, etc.

seminal vesicles: The pairs of pouchlike structures lying next to the urinary bladder that secrete a component of semen into the ejaculatory ducts.

seminiferous tubules: The tightly coiled ducts located in the testes where spermatozoa are produced.

semirigid rods: Flexible rods that are implanted into the penis during prosthetic surgery.

sensate focus: A series of touching experiences (nonsexual and sexual) that are assigned to couples in sex therapy to teach nonverbal communication and reduce anxiety.

sequential: Characterized by sequence; sex education programs that are sequential involve building on information that has been learned in earlier units.

sequential bisexuality: When bisexuals have sex exclusively with one sex in any given period; the opposite of **contemporaneous bisexuality.**

sequential homosexuality: In some cultures, homosexuality is structured into a particular part of a person's life, to be followed by periods of heterosexuality; age-structured homosexuality is one example (see Focus on Diversity 7.1).

seroconversion: The immunological conversion from HIV negative to HIV positive.

Sertoli cells: Cells in the wall of the seminiferous tubules that provide nutrients for the developing sperm and serve in hormone regulation. These cells have been referred to as "nurse cells" since they nourish spermatocytes, spermatids and spermatozoa.

sex chromosomes: The twenty-third pair of chromosomes, designated X and Y, that determines the genetic sex of an individual; in males the pair is XY and in females it is XX.

sex flush: A temporary reddish or rashlike color change that sometimes develops during sexual excitement; mostly occurs on the chest and abdomen but can spread to other parts of the body.

sex guilt: A generalized expectancy for self-mediated punishment for violating or anticipating violating internalized standards of proper sexual conduct.

sex reassignment surgery: Surgery for transsexuals, designed to reform male genitals into female genitals, or female genitals into male.

sex typing: The development of stereotypical ideas about men and women that are then applied to particular individuals and provide expectations of how that individual will behave.

sexologist: A professional who studies sexuality.

sexology: The scientific study of sexuality.

sexual assault: Coercion of a nonconsenting victim to have sexual contact.

sexual aversion disorder: A phobia or irrational fear of sexual activity or the thought of sexual activity which leads to an avoidance of sexual situations.

sexual battery: Nonpenile sexual attack.

sexual dimorphism: The process of splitting groups of people conceptually into two genders, male and female.

sexual harassment: Unwanted attention of a sexual nature from someone in school or the workplace; also includes the use of status and/or power to coerce or attempt to coerce a person into having sex, and unwelcome sexual jokes, glances, or comments.

sexual orientation: A term used to denote the gender(s) one is sexually attracted to.

sexual pathology: Sexual disorders.

sexual propriety: A society or community's views of what is acceptable sexual behavior.

sexual reproduction: The creation of offspring through the combination of the genes of two parents.

sexual script: The sum total of a person's internalized knowledge about sexuality.

sexual surrogate: A professional who may work with a sex therapy team and serves as a sexual partner for the client while the client is in therapy.

sexuality: A general term for the feelings and behaviors of human beings concerning sex.

shaft: The main body of the penis or clitoris.

shame aversion: A type of aversion therapy where the behavior that one wishes to extinguish is linked with strong feelings of shame.

she-males: A slang term that refers to a male who has been on hormones for sex reassignment but has not undergone surgery; she-males often have both a penis and breasts.

siamese twins: Twins who are born physically joined together in any manner.

Silent Rape Reaction: The rape trauma syndrome that occurs in a victim who does not talk to anyone after the rape.

simple mastectomy: The surgical removal of the breast tissue.

situational homosexuality: When people have sex with members of the same sex because of a situation that does not allow them access to the opposite sex; same-sex activity in prison and on naval vessels are examples.

situational sexual dysfunction: A sexual dysfunction that occurs only in specific situations.

sixty-nine position: Oral sex that is performed simultaneously.

skenes glands: Small glands on either side of the female urethra.

smegma: The collected products of sweat and oil glands that can accumulate under the clitoral hood or penile foreskin in cases of insufficient cleanliness.

social learning theory: A theory that grew out of behaviorism and focused on both internal and external events as causing our behaviors.

socialization: The process whereby social values and knowledge are taught to and assimilated by individuals throughout the life cycle.

sociobiology: A theory that incorporates both evolution and sociology and looks for trends in behaviors.

sociological theory: A theory of rape that identifies power differentials in society as causing rape.

sodomy: A vague legal category for "unnatural" sex acts that can include oral sex, anal sex, and/or sex with animals.

somatic cells: The cells that make up the body other than germ cells, such as skin cells, brain cells, blood cells, etc.

sonography: Another name for ultrasound; a way of seeing the developing fetus by bouncing sound waves off it.

spectatoring: Acting as an observer or judge of one's own sexual performance.

speculum: An instrument for dilating the vagina to examine the cervix and other internal structures.

sperm: The male germ cell, produced in the testes.

sperm bank: A place that stores frozen sperm for later use.

spermatids: The cells that make up the final intermediate stage in the production of sperm.

spermatocyte: The intermediate stage in the growth of a spermatozoon.

spermatogenesis: The production of sperm in the testes.

spermatogonium: The immature sperm cells that will develop into spermocytes.

spermatozoon: A mature sperm cell.

spina bifida: A congenital defect of the vertebral column in which the halves of the neural arch of a vertebra fail to fuse in the midline.

spirochetes: Microorganisms that cause syphilis.

spontaneous abortion: A natural process whereby the body expels a developing embryo.

squeeze technique: A technique used for the treatment of premature ejaculation in which the ejaculatory reflex is reconditioned using a firm grasp on the penis.

stalking: Obsessively following and spying on another person, usually to see if they are involved romantically with someone else. Stalking is now against the law in most states.

start day: The actual day that the first pill is taken in a pack of oral contraceptives.

stavudine (d4T): A medication that has been shown to slow the progression to AIDS.

sterilization techniques: Surgical contraceptive methods that cause permanent sterility.

stillbirth: An infant who is born dead.

stoma: Surgical opening made in the abdomen to allow waste products to exit the body.

stop–start technique: A technique used for the treatment of premature ejaculation in which the ejaculatory reflex is reconditioned using intermittent pressure on the glans of the penis.

straight: A commonly used word for heterosexual.

strokes: Occur when blood is cut off from part of the brain, usually because a small blood vessel bursts.

subliminal: The use of images or words, often sexual, that are not immediately apparent to the viewer of an advertisement, intended to excite the subconscious mind and improve the viewer's reaction to the ad.

submissive: Taking the passive role in sadomasochistic activity.

superego: According to Freud, the social and parental standards the individual has internalized; the conscience.

surprise theory: A theory that says that humor or laughter comes from the act of being surprised or shocked during the course of a joke or situation.

surrogate mother: A woman who donates her ovum (which is fertilized by the father's sperm) and then carries the zygote to term.

surrogate parenting: Use of a woman who, through artificial insemination or invitro fertilization, gestates a fetus for another woman or man.

surrogate partner: A partner supplied by Masters and Johnson for subjects who did not have an available partner.

sympto-thermal method: A contraceptive method that involves monitoring both cervical mucous (sympto) and basal body temperature (thermal) to determine ovulation.

syphilis: A STD that is caused by an infection with *Treponema pallidum;* syphilis is divided into primary, secondary, and tertiary stages.

systematic desensitization: A treatment method for sexual dysfunction that involves neutralizing the anxiety-producing aspects of sexual situations and behavior by a process of gradual exposure.

Talmud: The rabbinical interpretations of the Torah, the Hebrew Bible, from which Jewish traditions and laws are derived.

temple prostitutes: Women in many ancient cultures who would have sex with worshippers at pagan temples to provide money for the temple or as a form of worshipping the gods.

tenting effect: During sexual arousal in females, the cervix and uterus pull up, making a larger opening in the cervix—presumably for the sperm to pass through. In addition, the upper third of the vagina balloons open.

testicles or **testes:** The male gonads, or sex glands, that rest in the scrotum and are responsible for the production of sperm and certain male sex hormones. The word "testes" comes from the Latin word "to testify," for Roman soldiers would put their hand over their genitals (presumably their most valued possessions) when they took an oath.

testosterone: A male sex hormone (androgen) secreted by the Leydig cells of mature testes; controls the growth and development of male sex organs, secondary sex characteristics, spermatozoa, and body growth.

testosterone therapy: The use of testosterone to replace missing hormones in males with hormone disorders.

test-tube baby: A slang term for any zygote created by mixing sperm and egg outside a woman's body.

thanatos: According to Freud, the self-destructive instinct, often turned outward in the form of aggression; (also known as the "death" instinct).

theory: A formal statement about the relationship between constructs or events.

T-lymphocytes (T-helper cells): Type of white blood cell that helps to destroy harmful bacteria in the body.

toucheurism: The act of compulsively touching strangers with the hands to achieve sexual arousal.

toxemia: A condition of a mother involving high blood pressure, edema, protein in the urine, and convulsions during the latter half of pregnancy; may result in coma or death of a mother.

toxic shock syndrome: An infection of Staphylococci bacteria usually caused by tampons that includes high fever, vomiting and diarrhea, and sore throat, and that if left untreated, may lead to shock, loss of limbs, or death.

toxoplasmosis: An often fatal disease caused by an infection with a microorganism; an opportunistic disease.

transgendered: A recently coined term for transvestites and transsexuals, meant to indicate that they transcend simple categories of gender.

transgression: Sin.

transition: The last period in labor, in which contractions are strongest and the periods in between contractions are the shortest.

transudation: The passing of a fluid through a membrane, especially the lubrication in the vagina during sexual arousal.

transsexualism: Extreme gender dysphoria that has persisted without fluctuation for at least one or two years.

transvestite: A person whose preferred or exclusive method of sexual arousal or orgasm is through wearing the clothing of the other sex.

traumatic sexualization: A common result of sexual abuse in which a child displays compulsive sex play or masturbation and shows an inappropriate amount of sexual knowledge.

Treponema pallidum: The bacterium that causes syphilis.

triangulation: The psychological dynamic of three family members where two ally themselves against the third.

tribadism: Body rubbing.

Trichomonas vaginalis: Organism that causes trichomonas, a vaginal infection.

trichomoniasis: A vaginal infection caused by the protozoan *Trichomonas vaginalis,* which may result in discomfort, discharge, and inflammation.

trick: A slang term that refers to the sexual services of a prostitute; also may refer to a john.

trimester: A period of three months; pregnancies usually consist of three trimesters.

triphasic model: A model of sexual response proposed by Kaplan in which there are three phases—sexual desire, vasocongestion, and muscular contractions.

triphasil pills: A type of multiphasic oral contraceptive that contains three different types of pills, each of which contains a different hormonal dosage.

triplets: Three offspring having coextensive gestation periods and delivered at the same birth.

Triple-X syndrome: A genetic abnormality where a female has an extra X sex chromosome; characterized by decreased fertility, some genital abnormality, and slight mental retardation.

triolism: The act of a couple engaging in sex together while willingly being observed by a third party.

tubal sterilization: A surgical procedure in which the Fallopian tubes are cut, tied, or cauterized, for permanent contraception.

tubercle: A small rounded protuberance.

tumescence: The swelling of the penis due to vasocongestion, causing an erection.

Turner's syndrome: A genetic disorder in females when there is only one X sex chromosome instead of two; characterized by lack of internal female sex organs, infertility, short stature, and mental retardation.

typical use: Refers to the probability of contraceptive failure for a typical user of each method.

umbilical cord: The long, ropelike structure containing the umbilical arteries and vein that connect the fetus to the placenta.

unconditional positive regard: Accepting others unconditionally, without restrictions on their behaviors or thoughts.

unconscious: In Freud's theory, all the ideas, thoughts, and feelings of which we are not and cannot normally become aware.

universal catechism: An elementary book containing a summary of all the principles of a Christian religious tradition.

unrequited love: Love for another that is not returned by the person loved.

urethra: The tube from the urinary bladder to the exterior of the body that conveys urine in females and urine and semen in males.

uterine perforation: Tearing a hole in the uterus.

uterus: The hollow muscular organ in females that is the site of menstruation, implantation of the fertilized ovum, and labor; also called the womb.

vacuum aspiration (suction): The termination of a pregnancy by using suction to empty the contents of the uterus.

vacuum aspirator: A vacuum pump that is used during abortion procedures.

vacuum constriction devices: Treatment devices for erectile dysfunction used to pull blood into the penis.

vagina: A muscular tubular organ, situated between the urinary bladder and the rectum in the female, that leads from the uterus to the vestibule and is used for sexual intercourse and the passage of the newborn from the uterus.

vaginal contraceptive film (VCF): Spermicidal contraceptive film that is placed in the vagina.

vaginismus: Involuntary spasms of the muscles around the vagina in response to attempts at penetration.

validity: The property that a measuring device measures, what it is intended to measure.

varicocele: An unnatural swelling of the veins in the scrotum that may lead to sterility in males.

varicose veins: Unnaturally swollen veins.

vas deferens: One of two long tubes that convey the sperm from the testes and in which other fluids are mixed to create semen.

vasectomy: A surgical procedure in which the vas deferens are cut, tied, or cauterized for permanent contraception.

vasocongestion: An increase in the blood concentrated in the male and female genitals, as well as in the female breasts, during sexual activity.

vernix caseosa: Cheesy substance that coats the fetus in the uterus.

vestibule: The area between the labia minora, which contains the opening to the urethra and vagina, among other things.

viability: When a fetus is capable of living and reaching a stage of development that will permit survival under normal conditions.

victim precipitation theory: A theory of rape that identifies victim characteristics or behaviors that contribute to rape.

voyeur: One who observes people undressing or engaging in sex acts without their consent as a preferred or exclusive means of sexual arousal and orgasm.

vulva: Literally meaning "covering," the collective designation for the external genitalia of the female; also called the pudendum.

wasting syndrome: Significant weight loss, often characteristic of AIDS.

water sports: Sexual services that involve urinating on or inside one's sexual partner.

Western Blot: A test used to confirm a positive ELISA test; more accurate than ELISA tests, but too expensive to be used as the primary screening device for infection.

wet-nurse: A woman brought in to breast feed an infant for another woman.

widow/widower syndrome: A range of symptoms, including sexual dysfunction, that many widows and widowers experience after losing their sexual partners.

Wolffian duct: One of a pair of structures in the embryo that when exposed to testosterone, will develop into the male reproductive system.

women's suffrage: The movement to get women the right to vote.

XYY syndrome: A genetic abnormality where a male has an extra X sex chromosome; characterized by decreased fertility, some genital abnormality, and slight mental retardation.

yeast infections: Vaginal infections caused by the fungus *Candida albicans,* which is often sexually transmitted.

yin and **yang:** The Chinese belief that the universe is run by the interaction of two fundamental principles, one (yin) negative, passive, weak, yielding, and female, and the other (yang) positive, assertive, active, strong, and male.

yohimbine: This substance is derived from the bark of a tree and has been used as an aphrodisiac.

zalcitabine (DDC): A medication that has been shown to slow the progression to AIDS.

zidovudine (AZT): A medication that has been shown to prolong life in HIV-infected persons and to slow the progression to AIDS.

zona reaction: The reaction of the ovum to the penetration by a spermatozoon that makes the egg impenetrable by any other sperm.

zoophilia: The sexual attraction to animals in fantasy or through sexual contact as a preferred or exclusive means of sexual arousal and orgasm.

zygote: The single cell resulting from the union of a male and female gamete; the fertilized ovum.

zygote intra-Fallopian transfer: A reproductive technique in which the sperm and ova are collected and fertilized outside the body, and the fertilized zygote is then placed into the Fallopian tube.

Bibliography

AAUW (American Association of University Women). (1994). *Shortchanging girls, shortchanging America.* AAUW, Washington, DC: Author.

Abel, E. L. (1985). *Psychoactive drugs and sex.* New York: Plenum Publishing.

Abel, G., et al. (1988). Multiple paraphiliac diagnoses among sex offenders. *Bulletin of the American Academy of Psychiatry & Law, 2,* 153–168.

Abel, G., Becker, J., & Skinner, L. (1980). Aggressive behavior and sex. *Psychiatric Clinics of North America, 3,* 133–135.

Abramson, P. R., Moriuchi, K. D., Waite, M. S., & Perry, L. B. (1983). Parental attitudes about sexual education. *Archives of Sexual Behavior, 12,* 381–397.

Adam, B. D. (1987). *The rise of a gay and lesbian movement.* Boston: Twayne Publishers.

Adams, G., Addams-Taylor, S., & Pittman, K. (1989). Adolescent pregnancy and parenthood: A review of the problem, solutions, and resources. *Family Relations, 38,* 223–229.

Adler, M. W. (1990). The epidemiology of sexually transmitted diseases in the West. *Seminars in Dermatology, 9,* 96–101.

Adler, N. E., David, H. P., Major, B. N., et al. (1992). Psychological factors in abortion. *American Psychologist, 47,* 1194–1204.

Adler, N. E., David, H. P., Major, B. N., Roth, S. H., Russo, N. F., & Wyatt, G. E. (1990). Psychological responses after abortion. *Science, 248,* 41–44.

Afek, D. (1990). Sarah and the women's movement: The experience of infertility. *Women and Therapy, 10,* 195–203.

Ahmed, J. (1986). Polygyny and fertility differentials among the Yoruba of western Nigeria. *Journal of Biosocial Sciences, 18,* 63–73.

AIDS Health Promotion Exchange. (1990). Country watch. *AIDS Health Promotion Exchange, 2,* 6–10.

AIDS Health Promotion Exchange. (1991). Country watch. *AIDS Health Promotion Exchange, 4,* 7–10.

AIDS Update. (1991). Health and fitness of body and mind. AIDS Update, December, 13.

Ainsworth, M. D. S., Blehar, M. C., Waters, E., & Wall, S. (1978). *Patterns of attachment: A psychological study of the strange situation.* Hillsdale, NJ: Erlbaum.

Aizenman, M., & Kelley, G. (1988). The incidence of violence and acquaintance rape in dating relationships among college men and women. *Journal of College Student Development, 29,* 305–311.

Albert, A., & Porter, J. R. (1988). Children's gender-role stereotypes: A sociological investigation of psychological models. *Sociological Forum, 3,* 184–210.

Alan Guttmacher Institute. (1981). *Teenage pregnancy: The problem that hasn't gone away.* New York: Alan Guttmacher Institute.

Alan Guttmacher Institute. (1991). *State Reproductive Health Monitor 2(1).*

Allen, M. P. (1989). *Transformations.* New York: E. P. Dutton.

Alster, N. (1991). Crude doesn't sell. *Forbes* January 21, 60–61.

Alter, M. J., Hadler, S. C., Margolis, H. S., et al. (1990). The changing epidemiology of hepatitis B in the United States. *Journal of the American Medical Association, 263,* 1218–1222.

Altman, D. (1982). *The homosexualization of America, the Americanization of the homosexual.* New York: St. Martin's Press.

Altman, D. (1986). *AIDS in the mind of America.* New York: Anchor Press, Doubleday.

Alzate, H. (1985). Vaginal eroticism: A replication study. *Archives of Sexual Behavior, 14,* 529–537.

Alzate, H., & Hoch, Z. (1986). The "G spot" and "female ejaculation": A current appraisal. *Journal of Sex and Marital Therapy, 12,* 211–220.

Amato, R., & Booth, S. (1991). The consequences of divorce for attitudes toward divorce and gender roles. *Journal of Family Issues 12(3),* 306–322.

American Psychiatric Association. (1994). *Diagnostic and statistical manual of mental disorders* (4th ed). Washington, DC: American Psychiatric Association Publishers.

Ames, M. A., & Houston, D. A. (1990). Legal, social, and biological definitions of pedophilia. *Archives of Sexual Behavior, 19,* 333–342.

Amir, M. (1971). *Patterns in forcible rape.* Chicago: University of Chicago Press.

Andersen, B. L. (1981). A comparison of systematic desensitization and directed masturbation in the treatment of primary orgasmic dysfunction in females. *Journal of Consulting and Clinical Psychology, 49,* 568–570.

Anderton, D., & Emigh, R. (1989). Polygynous fertility: Sexual competition vs. progeny. *American Journal of Sociology 94(4),* 832–855.

Andrews, F. M., Abbey, A., & Halman, L. J. (1991). Stress from infertility, marriage factors, and subjective well-being of wives and husbands. *Journal of Health and Social Behavior, 32,* 238–253.

Annas, G. J. (1988). Death without dignity for commercial surrogacy: The case of Baby M. *Hastings Center Report,* April–May, 21–24.

Apfel, R. J., & Handel, M. H. (1993). *Madness and loss of motherhood.* Washington, DC: American Psychiatric Press.

Aral, S., Vanderplate, C., & Madger, L. (1988). Recurrent genital herpes: What helps adjustment? *Sexually Transmitted Diseases, 15,* 164–166.

Aral, S. O., Mosher, W. D., & Cates, W. (1991). Self-reported pelvic inflammatory disease in the U.S., 1988. *Journal of the American Medical Association, 266,* 2570–2573.

Archer, J., & Lloyd, B. (1985). *Sex and gender.* Cambridge, UK: Cambridge University Press.

Aries, P. (1962). *Centuries of childhood: A social history of family life.* New York: Vintage Books.

Arowolo, O.(1981). Plural marriage, fertility, and the problem of multiple causation.

Atchley, R. (1985). *Social forces and aging.* Belmont, CA: Wadsworth Publishing.

Atkeson, B. M., Calhoun, K. S., Resick, P. A., & Ellis, E. M. (1982). Victims of rape: Repeated assessment of depressive symptoms. *Journal of Consulting and Clinical Psychology, 50,* 96–102.

Awad, G., & Saunders, E. (1989). Adolescent child molesters: Clinical observations. *Child Psychiatry and Human Development, 19,* 195–206.

Baber, K., & Monaghan, P. (1988). College women's career and motherhood expectations. *Sex Roles 19(3–4),* 189–203.

Bagley, C., & Young, L., (1987). Juvenile prostitution and child sexual abuse: A controlled study. *Canadian Journal of Community Mental Health, 6,* 5–26.

Bailey, J. M., & Bell, A. P. (1993). Familiarity of female and male homosexuality. *Behavior Genetics, 23,* 313–322.

Bailey, J. M., Benishay, D. S. (1993). Familial aggregation of female sexual orientation. *American Journal of Psychiatry, 150,* 272–277.

Bailey, J. M., & Pillard, R. C. (1993). A genetic study of male sexual orientation. *Archives of General Psychiatry 50(3),* 240–241.

Baker, S. A., Thalberg, S. P., & Morrison, D. M. (1988). Parents' behavioral norms as predictors of adolescent sexual activity and contraceptive use. *Adolescence, 23,* 265–282.

Baladerian, N. J. (1991). Sexual abuse of people with developmental disabilities. *Sexuality and Disability, 9,* 323–334.

Baldassare, J. S. (1991). Update on the management of sexually transmitted diseases. *Philadelphia Medicine, 87,* 230–233.

Baldwin, J. (1993). In nations where gays serve, many soldiers keep sexuality quiet. *The Philadelphia Inquirer,* January 28, A6.

Bales, J. (1993). Definition, effect of pornography studied. *American Psychological Association Monitor,* November, 8.

Bandura, A. (1969). *Principles of behavior modification.* Austin, TX: Holt, Rinehart & Winston.

Barbach, L. (1982). *For each other: Sharing sexual intimacy.* New York: Penguin Group.

Barker, W. J., & Perlman, D. (1975). Volunteer bias and personality traits in sexual standards research. *Archives of Sex Behavior, 4,* 161–171.

Barlow, D. H. (1986). Causes of sexual dysfunction: The role of anxiety and cognitive interference. *Journal of Consulting and Clinical Psychology, 54,* 140–148.

Barnard, C. P. (1989). Alcoholism and sex abuse in the family: Incest and marital rape. Special issue: Aggression, family violence and chemical dependency. *Journal of Chemical Dependency Treatment, 3,* 131–144.

Barnett, W. (1973). *Sexual freedom and the constitution.* Albuquerque, NM: University of New Mexico Press.

Baron, J. A., LaVecchia, C., & Levi, F. (1990). The antiestrogenic effect of cigarette smoking in women. *American Journal Obstetrics and Gynecology 162(2),* 502–14.

Baron, L. (1990). Pornography and gender equality: An empirical analysis. *The Journal of Sex Research, 27,* 363–380.

Baron, L., & Straus, M. A. (1987). Four theories of rape: A macrosociological analysis. *Social Problems, 34,* 467–489.

Barrientos, T. (1993). Like a virgin. *The Philadelphia Inquirer,* October 10, K1.

Bart, P. B., & O'Brien, P. H. (1985). *Stopping rape: Successful survival strategies.* New York: Pergamon Press.

Basow, S. A., & Campanile, F. (1990). Attitudes toward prostitution as a function of attitudes toward feminism in college students: An exploratory study. *Psychology of Women Quarterly, 14,* 135–141.

Bauer, H. M., Ting, Y., Greer, C. E., Chambers, J. C., et al. (1991). Genital human papillomavirus infection in female university students as determined by a PCR-based method. *Journal of the American Medical Association, 265,* 472–477.

Baumeister, R. F. (1988). Masochism as escape from self. *Journal of Sex Research, 25,* 28–59.

Bayer, R. (1981). *Homosexuality and American psychiatry: The politics of diagnosis.* New York: Basic Books.

Beach, S. R. H., & Tesser, A. (1988). Love in marriage: A cognitive account. In R. J. Sternberg & M. L. Barnes (Eds.), *The psychology of love* (pp. 330–358). New Haven and London, CT: Yale University Press.

Becker, G., Landes, E., & Michael, R. (1977). An economic analysis of marital stability. *Journal of Political Economy 85,* 1141–1187.

Becker, J. V., et al. (1986). Level of postassault sexual functioning in rape and incest victims. *Archives of Sexual Behavior, 15,* 37–50.

Belknap, P., & Leonard II, W. M. (1991). A conceptual replication and extension of Erving Goffman's study of gender advertisements. *Sex Roles, 25,* 103–118.

Bell, A. P., & Weinberg, M. S. (1978). *Homosexualities: A study of diversity among men and women.* New York: Simon and Schuster.

Bell, A. P., Weinberg, M. S., & Hammersmith, S. K. (1981). *Sexual preference: Its development in men and women.* Bloomington: Indiana University Press.

Bem, S. L. (1974). The measurement of psychological androgyny. *Journal of Consulting and Clinical Psychology, 42,* 155–162.

Bem, S. L. (1976). Probing the promise of androgeny. In A. G. Kaplan & J. P. Bead (Eds.), *Beyond sex-role stereotypes: Readings toward a psychology of androgeny.* Boston: Little Brown.

Bem, S. L. (1977). On the utility of alternative procedures for assessing psychological androgyny. *Journal of Consulting and Clinical Psychology, 45,* 196–205.

Bem, S. L. (1981). Gender schema theory: A cognitive account of sex-typing. *Psychological Review, 88,* 354–364.

Bem, S. L. (1984). Androgeny and gender schema theory: A conceptual and empirical integration. In T. B. Sonderegger (Ed.), *Psychology and gender* (pp. 179–226). Lincoln: University of Nebraska Press.

Bem, S. L. (1987). Masculinity and femininity exist only in the mind of the perceiver. In J. M. Reinisch, L. A. Rosenblum, & S. Stephanie (Eds.), *Masculinity/femininity: Basic perspectives* (pp. 304–311). New York: Oxford University Press.

Bem, S. L. (1989). Genital knowledge and gender constancy in preschool children. *Child Development, 60,* 649–662.

Benjamin, H. (1961). Prostitution. *Encyclopedia of sexual behavior.* New York: Hawthorn Books.

Bennett, N., Blanc, A., & Bloom, D. E. (1988). Commitment and the modern union: Assessing the link between premarital cohabitation and subsequent marital stability. *American Sociological Review, 53,* 127–138.

Benokraitis, N. V. (1993). *Marriages and families.* Englewood Cliffs, NJ: Prentice Hall.

Benowitz, N. (1991). Nicotine replacement therapy during pregnancy. *Journal of the American Medical Association 266(22),* 3174–3177.

Benson, R. C. (1983). *Handbook of obstetrics and gynecology.* Los Altos, CA: Lange Medical Publishers.

Benton, J., Mintzes, J., & Kendrich, A. (1993). Alternative conceptions in STD's: A cross-age study. *Journal of Sex Education and Therapy, 19,* 165–182.

Beral, V., Hannaford, P., & Kay, C. (1988). Oral contraceptive use and malignancies of the genital tract. *The Lancet 2(8624),* 1331–1335.

Berg, E. (1988). The AIDS experience. *Footnotes,* December, 3–10.

Berg, J. H., Archer, R. L. (1980). Disclosure or concern: A second look at liking for the norm-breaker. *Journal of Personality, 48,* 245–257.

Berger, G., Hank, L., Rauzi, T., & Simkins, L. (1987). Detection of sexual orientation by heterosexuals and homosexuals. *Journal of Homosexuality, 13,* 83–100.

Berger, R. J., Searles, P., & Cottle, C. E. (1991). *Feminism and pornography.* New York: Praeger.

Berger, R. M. (1990). Men together: Understanding the gay couple. *Journal of Homosexuality, 19,* 31–49.

Bergmann, M. S. (1987). *The anatomy of living.* New York: Fawcett Columbine.

Bergstrom, W., & Nielsen, H. (1990). Sexual expression among 60–80 year old men & women. *Journal of Sex Research, 27,* 289–295.

Berkey, B. R., Perelman-Hall, T., & Kurdek, L. A. (1990). The multidimensional scale of sexuality. *Journal of Homosexuality, 19,* 67–87.

Berkowitz, G. S., Skovron, M. L., Lapinski, R. H., & Berkowitz, R. L. (1990). Delayed childbearing and the outcome of pregnancy. *The New England Journal of Medicine, 322,* 659–664.

Bernard, M. L., & Bernard, J. L. (1983). Violent intimacy: The family as a model for love relationships. *Family Relations, 32,* 283–286.

Berne, L. (1988). Abortion attitude scale. In Davis, et al. (Eds.), *Sexuality related measures* (p. 1). Lake Mills, IA: Graphic Publishing.

Bernstein, G. (1989). Counseling the male diabetic patient with erectile dysfunction. *Medical Aspects of Human Sexuality, 23,* 20–23.

Berrill, K. T., & Herek, G. M. (1990). Primary and secondary victimization in anti-gay hate crimes. *Journal of Interpersonal Violence, 5,* 401–413.

Berry, J. (1992). *Lead us not into temptation: Catholic priests and the sexual abuse of children.* New York: Doubleday.

Biale, D. (1992). *Eros and the Jews.* New York: Basic Books.

Bidwell, R. J., & Deisher, R. W. (1991). Adolescent sexuality: Current issues. *Pediatric Annals, 20,* 293–302.

Bieber, I., et al. (1962). *Homosexuality: A psychoanalytic study.* New York: Basic Books.

Biehr, B. (1989). Problem sexual behavior in school-aged children and youth. *Theory Into Practice, 28,* 221–226.

Bigner, J. J., & Jacobsen, R. B. (1989a). The value of children of gay and heterosexual fathers. *Journal of Homosexuality, 18,* 163–172.

Bigner, J. J., & Jacobsen, R. B. (1989b). Parenting behaviors of homosexual and heterosexual fathers. *Journal of Homosexuality, 18,* 173–186.

Bittles, et al. (1991). Chap. 8.

Black, D. (1983). Crime as social control. *American Sociological Review, 48,* 34–45.

Blackwood, E. (1984). Sexuality and gender in certain Native American tribes: The case of the cross-gender females. *Signs: Journal of Women in Culture and Society, 10,* 27–42.

Blagojevic. (1989). Chap. 8.

Blanchard, R., Clemmens, L. H., & Steiner, B. W. (1987). Heterosexual and homosexual gender dysphoria. *Archives of Sexual Behavior, 16,* 139–152.

Block, J. (1983). Differential premises arising from differential socialization of the sexes: Some conjectures. *Child Development, 54,* 1335–1354.

Blumstein, P., & Schwartz, P. (1983). *American couples.* New York: William Morrow.

Blumstein, P. W., & Schwartz, P. (1976). Bisexuality in men. *Urban Life, 5,* 339–359.

Bly, R. (1990). *Iron J.: A book about men.* Reading, MA: Addison-Wesley.

Bohlen, C. (1995). In strongest terms, he assails abortion and capital punishment. *The New York Times,* March 31, A1, A13.

Bolton, F. G., MacEachron, A. E. (1988). Adolescent male sexuality: A developmental perspective. *Journal of Adolescent Research, 3,* 259–273.

Borden, L. A., Karr, S. K., & Caldwell-Colbert, A. T. (1988). Effects of a university rape prevention program on attitudes and empathy toward rape. *Journal of College Student Development, 29,* 132–136.

Bornstein, D. (Ed.). (1979). *The Feminist Controversy of the Renaissance.* Delmar, NY: Scholars' Facsimiles & Reprints.

Boston Women's Health Collective. (1992). *The new our bodies, our selves.* New York: Simon & Schuster.

Boswell, J. (1980). *Christianity, social tolerance, and homosexuality: Gay people in western Europe from the beginning of the Christian era to the fourteenth century.* Chicago: The University of Chicago Press.

Bower, B. (1992). Depression, early death noted in HIV cases. *Science News, 142,* 53.

Boyer, D. (1989). Male prostitution and homosexual identity. Special Issue: Gay and lesbian youth. *Journal of Homosexuality, 17,* 151–184.

Bozett, F. W. (1989). Gay fathers: A review of the literature. *Journal of Homosexuality, 18,* 137–162.

Brabant, S., & Mooney, L. (1986). Sex role stereotyping in the Sunday comics: Ten years later. *Sex Roles, 14,* 141–148.

Bracher, M., & Santow, G. (1992). Premature discontinuation of contraception in Australia. *Family Planning Perspectives, 24,* 58–65.

Brandt, A. M. (1985). *No magic bullet: A social history of venereal disease in the United States.* New York: Oxford University Press.

Brandt, A. M. (1988). The syphilis epidemic and its relation to AIDS. *Science, 239,* 375–380.

Brecher, E., & the Editors of Consumer Report Books. (1984). *Love, sex and aging.* Boston: Little, Brown.

Brecher, E. M., & Brecher, J. (1986). Extracting valuable sexological findings from severely flawed and biased population samples. *Journal of Sex Research, 22,* 6–20.

Breslow, N., Evans, L., & Langley, J. (1985). On the prevalence and roles of females in the sadomasochistic subculture: Report of an empirical study. *Archives of Sexual Behavior, 14,* 303–317.

Bretl, D. J., & Cantor, J. (1988). The portrayal of men and women in U.S. television commercials: A recent content analysis and trends over 15 years. *Sex Roles, 18,* 595–609.

Bretschneider, J. G., & McCoy, N. L. (1988). Sexual interest and behavior in healthy 80 to 102 year olds. *Archives of Sexual Behavior, 17,* 109–129.

Breuss, C. E., & Greenberg, S. (1981). *Sex education/theory and practice.* Belmont, CA: Wadsworth Publishing Co.

Brewer, T. F., & Derrickson, J. (1992). AIDS in prison: A review of epidemiology and preventive policy. *AIDS, 6,* 623–628.

Brick, P. (1985). Sexuality education in the elementary school. *SIECUS Report, 13,* 1–4.

Briere, J., & Runtz, M. (1987). Post sexual abuse trauma: Data and implications for clinical practice. *Journal of Interpersonal Violence, 2,* 367–379.

Briggs, D. (1994). Church draft offers mixed view on gays. *The Philadelphia Inquirer,* July 28, A10.

Bromwich, P., & Parsons, T. (1990). *Contraception: The facts* (2d ed.). Oxford, England: Oxford University Press.

Brongersma, E. (1990). Boy-lovers and their influence on boys: Distorted research and anecdotal observations. *Journal of Homosexuality, 20,* 145–173.

Brooks-Gunn, J., & Furstenberg, F. F. (1989). Adolescent sexual behavior. *American Psychologist, 44,* 249–257.

Brooks-Gunn, J., Furstenberg, F. F. (1990). Coming of age in the era of AIDS: Puberty, sexuality, and contraception. *Milbank-Quarterly, 68,* 59–84.

Broude, G. J., & Greene, S. J. (1976). Cross-cultural codes on twenty sexual attitudes and practices. *Ethnology, 15,* 409–428.

Brown, J. D., & Newcomer, S. F. (1991). Television viewing and adolescents' sexual behavior. In *Research on adolescent sexual socialization* (pp. 77–91). Chapel Hill, NC: Haworth Press.

Brown, J. R. W. C. (1983). Paraphilias: Sadomasochism, fetishism, transvestism and transsexuality. *British Journal of Psychiatry, 143,* 227–231.

Brown, L. K. (1992). Comparison of HIV related knowledge, attitudes, intentions, and behaviors among sexually active and abstinent young adolescents. *Journal of Adolescent Health, 13,* 140.

Brownmiller, S. (1975). *Against our will: Men, women, and rape.* New York: Simon & Schuster.

Brubaker, T. (1985). *Later life families.* Beverly Hills, CA: Sage Publications.

Bryan, W. A. (1987). Contemporary fraternity and sorority issues. *New Directions for Student Services, 40,* 37–56.

Bryson, Y. J., Pang, S., Wei, L. S., et al. (1995). Clearance of HIV infection in a perinally infected infant. *The New England Journal of Medicine 332(13),* 833–838.

Buchanan, M., & Robbins, C. (1990). Early adult psychological consequences for males of adolescent pregnancy and its resolution. *Journal of Youth and Adolescence, 19,* 413–424.

Buffum, J. (1982). Pharmacosexology: The effects of drugs on sexual function: A review. *Journal of Psychoactive Drugs 14(1–2),* 5–44.

Buffum, J., Smith, D. E., Moser, C., et al. (1981). Drugs and sexual function. In H. Lief (Ed.), *Sexual problems in medical practice* (pp. 211-242). Chicago: American Medical Association.

Buhrich, N., & McConaghy, N. (1985). Preadult feminine behaviors of male transvestites. *Archives of Sexual Behavior, 14,* 413–419.

Buhrmester, D., & Furman, W. (1987). The development of companionship and intimacy. *Child Development, 58,* 1101–1113.

Bulatao, R., Palmore, J. A., & Ward, S. E. (1990). *Choosing a contraceptive: Method choice in Asia and the U.S.* Boulder, CO: Westview Press.

Bulcroft, R., & Bulcroft, K. (1991). The nature and functioning of dating in later life. *Research on Aging 13(2),* 244–260.

Bullis, R. K., & Harrigan, M. P. (1992). Religious denominational policies on sexuality. *Families in Society,* May, 304–312.

Bullough, V. L. (1973). *The subordinate sex: A history of attitudes toward women.* Urbana, IL: University of Illinois Press.

Bullough, V. L. (1976). *Sexual variance in society and history.* New York: Wiley.

Bullough, V. L. (1979). *Homosexuality: A history.* New York: New American Library.

Bullough, V. L. (1990). History in adult human sexual behavior with children and adolescents in Western societies. In J. Feierman (Ed.), *Pedophilia biosocial dimensions* (pp. 69–90). New York: Springer-Verlag.

Bullough, V. L. (1992). Christianity and sexuality. In R. M. Green (Ed.), *Religion and sexual health* (pp. 3–16). Boston: Kluwer Academic Publishers.

Bullough, V., & Bullough, B. (1987). *Women and prostitution: A social history.* Buffalo, NY: Prometheus Books.

Bullough, V. L., Bullough, B., & Smith, R. (1983). A comparative study of male transvestites, male to female transsexuals, and male homosexuals. *Journal of Sex Research, 19,* 238–257.

Bullough, V. L., & Weinberg, J. S. (1988). Women married to transvestites: Problems and adjustments. *Journal of Psychology and Human Sexuality, 1,* 83–104.

Bundow, G. L. (1992). Why women stay. *Journal of the American Medical Association 267(23),* 3229.

Bundy, M. L., & Poppen, M. A. (1986). School counselor effectiveness as a consultant. *Elementary School Guidance and Counseling, 20,* 215–222.

Burbidge, M., & Walters, J. (1981). *Breaking the silence: Gay teenagers speak for themselves.* London: Joint Council for Gay Teenagers.

Bürgel, J. C. (1979). Love, lust and longing: Eroticism in early Islam as reflected in literary sources. In Al-Sayyid-Marsot & A. Lutfi (Eds.), *Society and the sexes in medieval Islam.* Malibu, CA: Undena Publications.

Burgess, A. W., & Holmstrom, L. L. (1974). Rape trauma syndrome. *American Journal of Psychiatry, 131,* 981–986.

Burgess, A. W., & Holmstrom, L. L. (1979). *Rape: Crisis and recovery.* Bowie, MD: Robert J. Brady Publishers.

Burgess, J. P. (1993). Can't stop talking about sex. *Christian Century,* July 28, 732–734.

Burnell, G. M., & Norfleet, M. A. (1987). Women's self-reported response to abortion. *Journal of Psychology, 121,* 71–76.

Burns, L. H. (1990). An exploratory study of perceptions of parenting after infertility. *Family Systems Medicine, 8,* 177–189.

Buss, D. (1989). Conflict between the sexes: strategic interference and the evocation of anger and upset. *Journal of Personality and Social Psychology 56(5),* 735–747.

Buss, D. (1989). Sex differences in human mate preferences: Evolutionary hypotheses tested in 37 cultures. *Behavioral and Brain Sciences, 12,* 1–49.

Butcher, A. H., Manning, D., & O'Neal, E. (1991). HIV-related sexual behaviors of college students. *Journal of American College Health, 40,* 115–118.

Buunk, B. (1987). Conditions that promote breakups as a condition of extradyadic involvements. *Journal of Social and Clinical Psychology 5(3), 271–284.*

Buunk, B., & Hupka, R. B. (1987). Cross-cultural differences in the elicitation of sexual jealousy. *Journal of Sex Research, 23,* 12–22.

Byers, E., & Heinlein, L. (1989). Predicting initiating and refusals of sexual activities in married and cohabiting couples. *Journal of Sex Research 26,* 210–231.

Byrne, D., & Murnen, S. K. (1988). Maintaining loving relationships. In R. J. Barnes & M. L. Sternberg (Eds.), *The psychology of love* (pp. 293–310). New Haven & London: Yale University Press.

Cabaj, R. P. (1988). Gay and lesbian couples: Lessons on human intimacy. *Psychiatric Annals, 18,* 21–25.

Cado, S., & Leitenberg, H. (1990). Guilt reactions to sexual fantasies during intercourse. *Archives of Sexual Behavior 19(1),* 49–63.

Cain, R. (1991). Stigma management and gay identity development. *Social Work, 36,* 67–73.

Calderone, M. (1978). The challenge ahead: In search of healthy sexuality. In H. A. Otto (Ed.), *New sex education* (pp. 346–358). Chicago: Follett Publishing Co.

Calderone, M. (1983). On the possible prevention of sexual problems in adolescence. *Hospital and Community Psychiatry, 34,* 528–530.

Callan, V. (1986). Single women, voluntary childlessness and perceptions about life and marriage. *Journal of Biosocial Science, 18,* 479–487.

Cammaert, L. (1985). How widespread is sexual harassment on campus? Special issue, Women in groups and aggression against women. *International Journal of Women's Studies, 8,* 388–397.

Carnes, P. (1983). *The sexual addiction.* Minneapolis: CompCare.

Caron, S., Knox, C., & Rhodes, C. (1993). Sexuality education in the workplace: Seminars for parents. *Journal of Sex Education and Therapy, 19,* 200–211.

Caron, S. L., Davis, C. M., Wynn, R. L., & Roberts, L. W. (1992). America responds to AIDS, but did college students? Differences between March, 1987, and September 1988. *AIDS Education and Prevention, 4,* 18–28.

Carrier, J. M. (1989). Gay liberation and coming out in Mexico. *Journal of Homosexuality, 17,* 225–252.

Carroll, J. L., Volk, K. D., & Hyde, J. S. (1985). Differences between males and females in motives for engaging in sexual intercourse. *Archives of Sexual Behavior, 14,* 131–139.

Carroll, L. (1991). Gender, knowledge about AIDS, reported behavioral change, and the sexual behavior of college students. *Journal of American College Health, 40,* 5–12.

Cass, V. C. (1979). Homosexual identity formation: A theoretical model. *Journal of Homosexuality, 4,* 219–235.

Cass, V. C. (1984). Homosexual identity formation: Testing a theoretical model. *The Journal of Sex Research, 20,* 143–167.

Castadot, R. G. (1986). Pregnancy termination: Techniques, risks, and complications and their management. *Fertility and Sterility, 45,* 5–17.

Catania, J. A., et al. (1989). Older Americans and AIDS: Transmission risks and primary prevention research needs. *Gerontologist, 29,* 373–381.

Catania, J. A., Coates, T. J., Kegeles, S. M., et al. (1989). Implications of the AIDS risk-reduction model for the gay community: The importance of perceived sexual enjoyment and help-seeking behaviors. In V. M. Mays, G. W. Albee, & S. F. Schneider (Eds.), *Primary prevention of AIDS: Psychological approaches* (pp. 242–261). Newbury Park, CA: Sage Publications.

Catania, J. A., Coates, T. J., Stall, R., Turner, H., et al. (1992). Prevalence of AIDS related risk factors and condom use in the United States. *Science, 258,* 1101–1106.

Catania, J. A., McDermott, L. J., & Pollack, L. M. (1986). Questionnaire response bias and face-to-face interview sample bias in sexuality research. *Journal of Sex Research, 22,* 52–72.

Catania, J. A., & White, C. B. (1982). Sexuality in an aged sample: Cognitive determinates of masturbation. *Archives of Sexual Behavior, 11,* 237–245.

Cates, J. A., & Markley, J. (1992). Demographic, clinical, and personality variables associated with a male prostitution by choice. *Adolescence, 27,* 695–706.

Cates, W. (1990). The epidemiology and control of STDs in adolescents. In M. Schydlower & M. A. Shafer (Eds.), *AIDS and other STDs* (pp. 409). Adolescent Medicine: State of the Art Reviews.

Cates, W., & Hinman, A. R. (1991). STDs in the 1990's. *New England Journal of Medicine, 325,* 1368–1369.

Cates, W., Rolfs, R. T., & Aral, S. O. (1990). STDs, PID, and infertility: An epidemiologic update. *Epidemiology Review, 12,* 199–220.

Cates, W., & Stone, K. (1992). Family planning, STDs, and contraceptive choice: A literature update Part I. *Family Planning Perspectives, 24,* 75–84.

Ceniti, J., & Malamuth, N. (1984). Effects of repeated exposure to sexually violent or nonviolent stimuli on sexual arousal to rape or nonrape depictions. *Behavior Research and Therapy, 22,* 535–548.

Centers for Disease Control. (1991). Advance report on final divorce statistics, 1988. *National Center for Health Statistics 39(12).*

Centers for Disease Control. (1994). Personal communication.

Centerwall, B. S. (1992). Television and violence. *Journal of the American Medical Association, 267,* 3059–3063.

Chalkley, A. J., & Powell, G. E. (1983). The clinical description of forty-eight cases of sexual fetishism. *British Journal of Psychiatry, 142,* 292–295.

Chan, C. S. (1989). Issues of identity development among Asian-American lesbians and gay men. *Journal of Counseling and Development, 68,* 16–20.

Chia, R. C., Chong, C. J., Cheng, B. S., et al. (1985). Attitude toward marriage roles among Chinese and American college students. *Journal of Social Psychology 126(1),* 31–35.

Chick, D., & Gold, S. R. (1987–88). A review of influences on sexual fantasy: Attitudes, experience, guilt, and gender. *Imagination, Cognition, and Personality, 7,* 61–76.

Chilman, C. S. (1983). *Adolescent sexuality in a changing American society.* New York: Wiley.

Chilman, C. S. (1986). Some psychosocial aspects of adolescent sexual and contraceptive behaviors in a changing American society. In J. B. Lancaster & B. A. Hamburg (Eds.), *School-age pregnancy and parenthood: Biosocial dimensions* (pp. 191–217). New York: Aldine DeGruyter.

Chodorow, N. (1978). *The reproduction of mothering: Psychoanalysis and the sociology of gender.* Berkeley: University of California Press.

Christensen, A., & Shenk, J. L. (1991). Communication, conflict, and psychological distance in nondistressed, clinic, and divorcing couples. *Journal of Consulting and Clinical Psychology 59(3),* 458–463.

Christian Century. (1991). War, sex, dissension: Religion stories of 1991. *Christian Century, 108,* 1187–1190.

Chu, J., & White, E. (1987). Decreasing incidence of invasive cervical cancer in young women. *American Journal Obstetrics and Gynecology, 157,* 1105.

Church, C. A., & Geller, J. (1990). Voluntary female sterilization: Number one and growing. *Population Reports—Series J, (39),* 2–31.

Clark, D. A. (1994). Does immunological intercourse prevent pre-eclampsia? *The Lancet, 344,* 969–970.

Clark, J. M., Brown, J. C., & Hochstein, L. M. (1989). Institutional religion and gay/lesbian oppression. *Marriage and Family Review 14(3–4),* 265–284.

Clark, M. S., & Reis, H. T. (1988). Interpersonal processes in close relationships. *Annual Reviews in Psychology, 39,* 609–672.

Clasquin, M. (1992). Contemporary Theravada and Zen Buddhist attitudes to human sexuality: An exercise in comparative ethics. *Religion, 22,* 63–83.

Class of 78. (1983–84). An investigation of remarriages in Hongkou district, Shanghai. *Chinese Sociology and Anthropology 16(1–2),* 117–127.

Cobb, N. J., Stevens-Long, J., & Goldstein, S. (1982). The influence of televised models on toy preference in children. *Sex Roles, 8,* 1075–1080.

Cochran, J. K., & Beeghley, L. (1991). The influence of religion on attitudes toward nonmarital sexuality: A preliminary assessment of reference group theory. *Journal for the Scientific Study of Religion, 30(1),* 45–62.

Cohen, E. (1986). Lovelorn farangs: The correspondence between foreign men and Thai girls. *Anthropological Quarterly, 59,* 115–127.

Cohen, J. (1967). *The essential Lenny Bruce.* New York: Ballantine Books.

Cohen, J. (1991). The efficiency and efficacy of IVF and GIFT. *Human Reproduction, 6,* 613–618.

Cohen, L. (1988). Providing treatment and support for partners of sexual-assault survivors. *Psychotherapy, 25,* 94–98.

Cohen, L., & Roth, S. (1987). The psychological aftermath of rape: Long-term effects and individual differences in recovery. *Journal of Social and Clinical Psychology, 5,* 525–534.

Cole, T., & Cole, S. (1981). Sexual health and physical disease. In H. Lief (Ed.), *Sexual problems in medical practice* (pp. 191–198). Chicago: American Medical Association.

Coleman, E. (1982). Developmental stages of the coming-out process. *American Behavioral Scientist, 25,* 469–482.

Coleman, E. (1989). The development of male prostitution activity among gay and bisexual adolescents. Special Issue: Gay and lesbian youth. *Journal of Homosexuality, 17,* 131–149.

Coleman, M., & Ganong, L. H. (1985). Love and sex role stereotypes: Do macho men and feminine women make better lovers? *Journal of Personality and Social Psychology, 49,* 170–176.

Coleman, S. (1983). *Family planning in Japanese society.* Princeton, NJ: Princeton University Press.

Coles, R., & Stokes, G. (1985). *Sex and the American teenager.* New York: Harper & Row.

College Security Report. (1989). Stanford survey reveals high rate of forced sex. *College Security Report, 1,* 1–3.

Collier, J. F., Rosaldo, M. Z. (1981). Politics and gender in simple societies. In S. Ortner & H. Whitehead (Eds.), *Sexual meanings* (pp. 275–329). Cambridge, UK: Cambridge University Press.

Collins, R. (1988). *Sociology of marriage and the family.* Chicago: Nelson-Hall.

Comfort, A. (1987). Deviation and variation. In G. D. Wilson (Ed.), *Variant sexuality: Research and theory* (pp. 1–20). Baltimore: Johns Hopkins University Press.

Comfort, A. (1991). *The new joy of sex: A gourmet guide to lovemaking for the nineties.* New York: Crown Publishers.

Comstock, G., & Paik, H. (1991). *Television and the American child.* San Diego, CA: Academic Press.

Constantine, L. L., & Martinson, F. M. (1981). Child sexuality: Here there be dragons. In L. L. Constantine & F. M. Martinson (Eds.), *Children and sex: New findings, new perspectives* (pp. 3–8). Boston: Little, Brown.

Contemporary Sexuality. (1991). AIDS patients chained to bed in Argentina. 25: 7.

Contemporary Sexuality. (1994). HIV without AIDS. 28:1.

Contemporary Sexuality. (1992). Sex Addict or Sexual Narcissist? 26: 1–2.

Cooper, A. J. (1986). Progestogens in the treatment of male sex offenders: A review. *Canadian Journal of Psychiatry, 31,* 73–79.

Cooper, A. M. (1991). The unconscious core of perversion. In G. I. Fogel & W. A. Myers (Eds.), *Perversions and near-perversions in clinical practice: New psychoanalytic perspectives* (pp. 17–35). New Haven: Yale University Press.

Copenhaver, S., & Grauerholz, E. (1991). Sexual victimization among sorority women: Exploring the link between sexual violence and institutional practices. *Sex Roles, 24,* 31–41.

Corey, L., Adams, H. G., Brown, Z. A., et al. (1983). Genital herpes simplex virus infections. *Annals of Internal Medicine, 98,* 958–972.

Corne, S., Briere, J., & Esses, L. (1992). Women's attitudes and fantasies about rape as a function of early exposure to pornography. *Journal of Interpersonal Violence, 7,* 454–461.

Cornett, M., & Shuntich, R. (1991). Sexual aggression: Perceptions of its likelihood of occurring and some correlates of self-admitted perpetration. *Perceptual & Motor Skills, 73,* 499–507.

Corwin, A. L., Olson, J. G., Omar, M. A., Razaki, A., et al. (1991). HIV-1 in Somalia: Prevalence and knowledge among prostitutes. *AIDS, 5,* 902–904.

Cotton, P. (1991). Immune boosters disappoint AIDs researchers. *Journal of the American Medical Association, 266,* 1613–1614.

Coulson, N. J. (1979). Regulation of sexual behavior under traditional Islamic law. In Al-Sayyid-Marsot & A. Lutfi (Eds.), *Society and the sexes in medieval Islam* (pp. 63–68). Malibu, CA: Undena Publications.

Covey, H. C. (1989). Perceptions and attitudes toward sexuality of the elderly during the Middle Ages. *The Gerontologist, 29,* 93–100.

Cowan, G. (1992). Feminist attitudes toward pornography control. *Psychology of Women Quarterly,* 165–177.

Cowley, G. (1993). Family matters. *Newsweek,* December 6, 46–52

Cox, D. J. (1988). Incidence and nature of male genital exposure behavior as reported by college women. *Journal of Sex Research, 24,* 227–234.

Cox, D. J., Tsang, K., & Lee, A. (1982). A cross cultural comparison of the incidence and nature of male exhibitionism among female college students. *Victimology: An International Journal, 7,* 231–234.

Cramer, P., & Skidd, J. E. (1992). Correlates of self-worth in preschoolers: The role of gender-stereotyped styles of behavior. *Sex Roles, 26,* 369.

Crawford, M., & Gressley, D. (1991). Creativity, caring, and context. *Psychology of Women Quarterly, 15,* 217–231.

Creinen, M. D., & Darney, P. D. (1993). Methotrexate and Misoprostol for early abortion. *Contraception, 48,* 339–348.

Crime Codes of Pennsylvania. (1991). *Crime codes of Pennsylvania.* New York: Gould Publications.

Critelli, J., Myers, E., & Loos, V. (1986). The components of love: Romantic attraction and sex role orientation. *Journal of Personality, 54,* 355–370.

Curran, C. E. (1992). Sexual ethics in the Roman Catholic tradition. In R. M. Green (Ed.), *Religion and sexual health* (pp. 17–35). Boston: Kluwer Academic Publishers.

Currier, R. L. (1981). Juvenile sexuality in global perspective. In L. L. Constantine & F. M. Martinson (Eds.), *Children and sex: New findings, new perspectives* (pp. 9–19). Boston: Little, Brown.

Dagg, P. K. B. (1991). The psychological sequelae of therapeutic abortion—denied and completed. *American Journal of Psychiatry, 148,* 578–585.

Daie, N., Wilztum, E., & Eleff, M. (1989). Long-term effects of sibling incest. *Journal of Clinical Psychiatry, 50,* 428–431.

Dancey, C. P. (1990). Sexual orientation in women: An investigation of hormonal and personality variables. *Biological Psychology, 30,* 251–264.

Darling, C. A., Davidson, J. K., & Passarello, L. C. (1992). The mystique of first intercourse among college youth: The role of partners, contraceptive practices, and psychological reactions. *Journal of Youth and Adolescence 21(1),* 97–117.

Darnton, J. (1994). After 460 years, the Anglicans ordain women. *The New York Times,* March 13, A1, A11.

D'Augelli, A. R. (1989). Lesbians' and gay men's experiences of discrimination and harassment in a university community. *American Journal of Community Psychology, 17,* 317–321.

D'Augelli, A. R., & Rose, M. L. (1990). Homophobia in a university community: Attitudes and experiences of heterosexual freshman. *Journal of College Student Development, 31,* 484–491.

David, H. P. (1994). Reproductive rights and reproductive behavior. *American Psychologist, 49,* 343–349.

Davidson, J. K., & Darling, C. A. (1986). The impact of college level sex education on sexual knowledge, attitudes, and practices: The knowledge/sexual experimentation myth revisited. *Deviant Behavior, 7,* 13–30.

Davidson, J. K., & Darling, C. A. (1993). Masturbatory guilt and sexual responsiveness among post-college-age women: Sexual satisfaction revisited. *Journal of Sex and Marital Therapy, 19,* 289–300.

Davidson, J. K., & Moore, N. B. (1994). Masturbation and premarital sexual intercourse among college women: Making choices for sexual fulfillment. *Journal of Sex and Marital Therapy, 20,* 178–199.

Davis, J. (1984). *Making love: A woman's guide.* New York: Signet Books.

Davis, K. (1971). Prostitution. In R. K. Merton & R. Nisbet (Eds.), *Contemporary social problems* (pp. 341–351). New York: Harcourt Brace Jovanovich.

Davis, K. E., & Latty-Mann, H. (1987). Love styles and relationship quality: A contribution to validation. *Journal of Social and Personal Relationships, 4,* 409–428.

Davis, K. E., & Todd, M. (1982). Friendship and love relationships. In K. E. Davis & T.O. Mitchell (Eds.), *Advances in descriptive psychology* (pp. 79–122). Greenwich, CT: JAI Press.

Davis, M. S. (1983). *Smut: Erotic reality/obscene ideology.* Chicago: The University of Chicago Press.

DeAmicis, L. A., Goldberg, D. C., LoPiccolo, J., Friedman, J., & Davies, L. (1985). Clinical follow-up of couples treated for sexual dysfunction. *Archives of Sexual Behavior, 14,* 467–489

DeAngelis, B. (1987). *How to make love all the time.* New York: Rawson Associates.

DeAngelis, B. (1990). *Secrets about men every woman should know.* New York: Dell Publishing.

DeBuono, B. A., Zinner, S. H., & Daamen, M. (1990). Sexual behavior of college women in 1975, 1986, and 1989. *New England Journal of Medicine, 322,* 821–825.

Deevey, S. (1990). Older lesbian women: An invisible minority. *Journal of Gerontological Nursing, 16,* 35–39.

DeLamater, J. (1987). A sociological approach. In J. H. Geer & W. T. O'Donohue (Eds.), *Theories of human sexuality* (pp. 237–253). New York: Plenum Press.

D'Emilio, J., & Freedman, E. (1988). *Intimate matters: A history of sexuality in America.* New York: Harper & Row.

Derogatis, L. R., Meyer, J. K., & Dupkin, C. N. (1976). Discrimination of organic versus psychogenic impotence with the DSFI. *Journal of Sex and Marital Therapy, 2,* 229–240.

de-Schampheleire, D. (1990). MMPI characteristics of professional prostitutes: A cross-cultural replication. *Journal of Personality Assessment, 54,* 343–350.

Details. (1994). Geography of desire 2: Illegal sex around the world. *Details* May, 26–27

Detroit News. (1992). Taboos hinder AIDS prevention in Asian cultures. 10A.

Diamond, M., & Diamond, G. H. (1986). Adolescent sexuality: Biosocial aspects and intervention. In P. Allen-Meares & D. A. Shore (Eds.), *Adolescent sexualities: Overviews and principles of intervention* (pp. 3–13). New York: The Haworth Press.

Dietz, P. E., Evans, B. (1982). Pornographic imagery and prevalence of paraphilia. *American Journal of Psychiatry, 139,* 1493–1495.

Dietz, W. H., & Strasburger, V. C. (1991). Children, adolescents, and television. *Current Problems in Pediatrics,* January, 8–32.

Dimeff, R., & Malone, D. (1988). Psychiatric disorders in weight lifters using anabolic steroids. *Medicine and Science in Sports and Exercise, 1991,* 23.

Dines-Levy, G., & Smith, G. W. H. (1988). Representations of women and men in Playboy magazine. In C. Powell & G. E. C. Paton (Eds.), *Humour in society: Resistance and control* (pp. 234–259). New York: St. Martin's Press.

Dion, K. L., & Dion, K. K. (1988). Romantic love: Individual and cultural perspectives. In R. J. Sternberg & M. L. Barnes (Eds.), *The Psychology of Love* (pp. 264–292). New Haven & London: Yale University Press.

DiVasto, P. V., Pathak, D., & Fishburn, W. R. (1981). The interrelationship of sex guilt, sex behavior, and age in an adult sample. *Archives of Sexual Behavior, 10,* 119–122.

Dodge-Tripet, L. J., Glasgow, R. E., & O'Neill, H. K. (1982). Bibliotherapy in the treatment of female orgasmic dysfunction. *Journal of Consulting and Clinical Psychology, 50,* 442–443.

Dodson, B. (1987). *Sex for one: The joy of self-loving.* New York: Crown Trade Publishers.

Donnan, H. (1988). Marriage among Muslims; preference and choice in northern Pakistan. New York: E. J. Brill.

Dorfman, L. E., Derish, P. A. & Cohen, J. B. (1992). Hey girlfriend: An evaluation of AIDS prevention among women in the sex industry. *Health Education Quarterly, 19,* 25–40.

Dormen, L. (1992). Does penis size matter? *Glamour, 90,* 90.

Dormont, P. (1989). Life events that predispose to erectile dysfunction. *Medical Aspects of Human Sexuality,* 17–19.

Dorner, G. (1976). *Hormones and brain differentiation.* Amsterdam: Elsevier.

Dorner, G. (1988). Neuroendocrine response to estrogen and brain differentiation in heterosexuals, homosexuals, and transsexuals. *Archives of Sexual Behavior, 17,* 57–75.

Douhitt, R. A. (1989). The division of labor within the home: Have gender roles changed? *Sex Roles, 20,* 693–704.

Downs, D. A. (1989). *The new politics of pornography.* Chicago: The University of Chicago Press.

Doyle, J. (1985). *Sex and gender.* Dubuque, IA: Brown.

Dressler, J. (1978). Gay teachers: A disesteemed minority in an overly esteemed profession. *Rutgers Camden Law Journal, 9,* 399–445.

Dressler, J. (1979). Study of law student attitudes regarding the rights of gay people to be teachers. *Journal of Homosexuality, 4,* 315–329.

DSM-IV (Diagnostic and Statistical Manual of Mental Disorders). (1994). Washington: American Psychiatric Association.

Dundes, A. (1987). *Cracking jokes: Studies of sick humor cycles and stereotypes.* Berkeley, CA: Ten Speed Press.

Dunham, C., Myers, F., McDougall, A., & Barnden, N. (1992). *Mamatoto: A celebration of birth.* New York: Penguin Group.

Dunlap, D. W. (1995). Some states trying to stop gay marriages before they start. *The New York Times,* March 13, A18.

Dunn, M. E., & Trost, J. E. (1989). Male multiple orgasms: A descriptive study. *Archives of Sexual Behavior, 18,* 377–399.

Durkin, K. (1985). *Television, sex roles, and children.* Milton Keynes, UK: Open University Press.

Dutton, D. G., & Aron, A. P. (1974). Some evidence for heightened sexual attraction under conditions of high anxiety. *Journal of Personality and Social Psychology, 30,* 510–517.

Dworkin, A. (1981). *Pornography: Men possessing women.* New York: Putnam.

Dworkin, A. (1987). *Intercourse.* New York: The Free Press.

Dwyer, S. M., & Amberson, J. I. (1989). Behavioral patterns and personality characteristics of 56 sex offenders: A preliminary study. *Journal of Psychology and Human Sexuality, 2,* 105–118.

Dwyer, V. (1992). Prime-time sparks: Pressure groups try to sanitize TV shows. *MacLean's, 7,* 52–53.

Earle, R. H., & Crow, G. M. (1990). Sexual addiction: Understanding and treating the phenomenon. *Contemporary Family Therapy, 12,* 89–104.

Earls, C. M., & David, H. (1989). A psychosocial study of male prostitution. *Archives of Sexual Behavior, 18,* 401–419.

Earls, C. M., & David, H. (1990). Early family and sexual experience of male and female prostitutes. *Canada's Mental Health, 38,* 7–11.

Easterman, D. (1993). The erection is eternal. *New Statesman & Society, 6,* 26–27.

Ecker, N. (1994). Culture and sexual scripts out of Africa. *SIECUS Report, 21,* 18.

Edgar, T. F., & Hammond, S. L. (1992). Strategic sexual communication: Condom use resistance and response. *Health Communication, 4,* 83–104.

Edgren, G. (1991). The transformation of Tula. *Playboy, 38,* 102–105.

Einsiedel, E. (1989). Social science and public policy: Looking at the 1986 commission on pornography. In S. Gubar & J. Hoff (Eds.), *For adult users only* (pp. 87–107). Bloomington: Indiana University Press.

Einstein, Z. R. (1988). *The female body and the law.* Berkeley: University of California Press.

Eisen, M., & Zellman, G. (1987). Changes in incidence of sexual intercourse of unmarried teenagers following a community-based sex education program. *Journal of Sex Research, 23,* 527–533.

Eisenberg, A., Murkoff, H. E., & Hathaway, S. E. (1991). *What to expect when you're expecting.* New York: Workman Publishing.

Eisenhart, M. A., & Holland, D. C. (1992). Gender constructs and career commitment: The influence of peer culture on women in college. In T. L. Whitehead & B. V. Reid (Eds.), *Gender constructs and social issues* (pp. 142–180). Chicago: University of Illinois Press.

Elifson, K. W., Boles, J., Posey, E., Sweat, M., et al. (1993). Male transvestite prostitutes and HIV risk. *American Journal of Public Health, 83,* 260–261.

Elifson, K. W., Boles, J., & Sweat, M. (1993). Risk factors associated with HIV infection among male prostitutes. *American Journal of Public Health, 83,* 79–83.

Ellerbrock, T. V., Bush, T. J., Chamberland, M. E., et al. (1991). Epidemiology of women with AIDs in the US, 1981 through 1990. *Journal of the American Medical Association, 265,* 2971–2975.

Ellis, B., & Symons, D. (1990). Sex differences in sexual fantasy: An evolutionary psychology approach. *Journal of Sex Research, 27,* 527–555.

Ellis, L., Ames, M., Ashley, P. W., & Burke, D. (1988). Sexual orientation of human offspring may be altered by severe maternal stress during pregnancy. *The Journal of Sex Research, 25,* 152–157.

Ellis, L., Burke, D., & Ames, M. (1987). Sexual orientation as a continuous variable: A comparison between the sexes. *Archives of Sexual Behavior, 16,* 523–529.

Ellis, M. (1984). Eliminating our heterosexist approach to sex education. *Journal of Sex Education and Therapy, 10,* 61–63.

Engel, J. W., & Saracino, M. (1986). Love preferences and ideals: A comparison of homosexual, bisexual, and heterosexual groups. *Contemporary Family Therapy, 8,* 241–250.

Epstein, C. F. (1986). Symbolic segregation: Similarities and differences in the language and non-verbal communication of women and men. *Sociological Forum, 1,* 27–49.

Epstein, C. F. (1988). *Deceptive distinctions sex, gender, and the social order.* New Haven: Yale University Press.

Erikson, K. (1986). *Wayward Puritans.* New York: Macmillan Publishing Company.

Erlanger, S. (1991). A plague awaits. *The New York Times,* July 14, 24.

Estrin, H. M., & Do, S. H. (1988). Chlamydia trachomatis, monoclonal antibody testing, wet mount screening, and the university health service. *Journal of the American College Health, 37,* 61–64.

Etaugh, C., & Liss, M. (1992). Home, school, and playroom: Training grounds for adult gender roles. *Sex Roles, 26,* 129–147.

Falk, P. J. (1989). Lesbian mothers: Psychosocial assumptions in family law. *American Psychologist, 44,* 941–947.

Faller, K. C. (1989). The role relationship between victim and perpetrator as a predictor of characteristics of intrafamilial sexual abuse. *Child and Adolescent Social Work Journal, 6,* 217–229.

Faludi, S. (1991). Backlash: *The undeclared war against American women.* New York: Crown Publishers.

Family Planning Perspectives (1991). Accessibility of abortion services in the U.S. *Family Planning Perspectives 23.*

Farah, M. (1984). *Marriage and sexuality in Islam.* Salt Lake City: University of Utah Press.

Farnsworth. (1992). Argentine homosexual gets refugee status in Canada. *The New York Times,* February 14, A10.

Fay, R. E., Turner, C. F., Klassen, A. D., & Gagnon, J. H. (1989). Prevalence and patterns of same-gender sexual contact among men. *Science, 243,* 338–348.

Federal Bureau of Investigation. (1988). *Crime in the United States: Uniform crime reports.* Washington: U.S. Department of Justice.

Feeney, J., & Noller, P. (1990). Attachment style as a predictor of adult romantic relationships. *Journal of Personality and Social Psychology, 58,* 281–291.

Feierman, J. R. (1990). A biosocial overview of adult human sexual behavior with children and adolescents. In J. Feierman (Ed.), *Pedophilia: Biosocial dimensions* (pp. 8–68). New York: Springer-Verlag.

Feinauer, L. (1988). Relationship of long term effects of childhood sexual abuse to identity of the offender: Family, friend, or stranger. *Women and Therapy, 7,* 89–107.

Feinauer, L. (1989). Comparison of long-term effects of child abuse by type of abuse and by relationship of the offender to the victim. *American Journal of Family Therapy, 17,* 46–48.

Feldman-Summers, S., Gordon, P. E., & Meagher, J. R. (1979). The impact of rape on sexual satisfaction. *Journal of Abnormal Psychology, 88,* 101–105.

Ferree, M. M., & Hess, B. B. (1985). *Controversy and coalition: The new feminist movement.* Boston: Twayne.

Fine, M. (1988). Sexuality, schooling, and adolescent females: The missing discourse of desire. *Harvard-Educational Review, 58,* 29–53.

Fine, M., & Asch, A. (1988). Disability beyond stigma: Social interaction, discrimination, and activism. *Journal of Social Issues, 44,* 3–21.

Finkelhor, D. (1980a). Risk factors in the sexual victimization of children. *Child Abuse and Neglect, 4,* 265–273.

Finkelhor, D. (1980b). Sex among siblings: A survey on prevalence, variety, and effects. *Archives of Sexual Behavior, 9,* 171–194.

Finkelhor, D. (1984). *Child sexual abuse: New theory and research.* New York: The Free Press.

Finkelhor, D. (1985). Sexual abuse of boys. In A. W. Burgess (Ed.), *Rape and sexual assault* (pp. 97–109). New York: Garland Publishing.

Finkelhor, D., & Browne, A. (1985). The traumatic impact of child sexual abuse. *American Journal of Ortho-Psychiatry, 55,* 530–541.

Finkelhor, D., Hotaling, G., Lewis, I. A., & Smith, C. (1990). Sexual abuse in a national survey of adult men and women: Prevalence, characteristics, and risk factors. *Child Abuse and Neglect, 14,* 19–28.

Fischer, G. J. (1986). College student attitudes toward forcible date rape. *Archives of Sexual Behavior 15(6),* 457–466.

Fisher, T. (1988). The relationship between parent–child communication about sexuality and college students' sexual behavior and attitudes as a function of parental proximity. *Journal of Sex Research, 24,* 305–311.

Fisher, W. A., & Barak, A. (1991). Pornography, erotica, and behavior: More questions than answers. *International Journal of Law and Psychiatry, 14,* 65–83.

Fitzgerald, L. F., & Ormerod, A. J. (1991). Perceptions of sexual harassment: The influence of gender and academic context. *Psychology of Women Quarterly, 15,* 281–294.

Flaceliére, R. (1962). *Love in ancient Greece.* New York: Crown Publishers.

Fletcher, J. L. (1991). Perinatal transmission of human papillomavirus. *American Family Physician, 43,* 143.

Foley, T. S. (1985). Family response to rape and sexual assault. In A. W. Burgess (Ed.), *Rape and sexual assault* (pp. 159–188). New York: Garland Publishing.

Ford, C. S., & Beach, F. A. (1951). *Patterns of sexual behavior.* New York: Harper & Brothers.

Forrest, J. D. (1993). Timing of reproductive life stages. *Obstetrics and Gynecology, 82,* 105–110.

Forrest, J. D., & Fordyce, R. R. (1993). Women's contraceptive attitudes and use in 1992. *Family Planning Perspectives 25(4),* 175–179.

Forsé, M., Jaslin, J. P., Yannick, M., et al. (1993). *Recent social trends in France 1960–1990.* Frankfurt-am-Main: Campus Verlag.

Forstein, M. (1988). Homophobia: An overview. *Psychiatric Annals, 18,* 33–36.

Foucault, M. (1978). *The history of sexuality: An introduction.* New York: Vintage Books.

Foucault, M. (1986). On the genealogy of ethics: An overview of a work in progress. In P. Rabinow (Ed.), *The Foucault reader.* Harmondsworth, UK: Penguin Books.

Foucault, M. (1987). *The history of sexuality: Volume 2, The use of pleasure.* London: Penguin Books.

Foucault, M. (1988). *The history of sexuality: Volume 3, The care of the self.* New York: Random House.

Frank, E., & Anderson, C. (1989). The sexual stages of marriage. In M. Henslin (Ed.), *Marriage and family in a changing society* (pp. 190–195). New York: The Free Press.

Frank, E., Anderson, C., & Rubinstein, D. N. (1978). Frequency of sexual dysfunction in normal couples. *New England Journal of Medicine, 299,* 111–115.

Frank, P. L. (1991). The effect of induced abortion on subsequent pregnancy outcome. *British Journal of Obstetrics and Gynecology, 98,* 1015.

Freud, S. (1960). *The ego and the id.* New York: W. W. Norton.

Freud, S. (1963). *A general introduction to psychoanalysis.* New York: Pocket Books.

Freud, S. (1963). *General psychological theory.* New York: Colliers.

Freund, K., & Blanchard, R. (1986). The concept of courtship disorder. *Journal of Sex and Marital Therapy, 12,* 79–92.

Freund, K., Scher, H., & Hucker, S. (1983). The courtship disorders. *Archives of Sexual Behavior, 12,* 369–379.

Freund, K., Scher, H., & Hucker, S. (1984). The courtship disorders: A further investigation. *Archives of Sexual Behavior, 13,* 133–139.

Freund, K. M. (1992). Chlamydial disease in women. *Hospital Practice,* 175–186.

Freund, M., Lee, N., & Leonard, T. (1991). Sexual behavior of clients with street prostitutes in Camden, New Jersey. *Journal of Sex Research, 28,* 579–591.

Freund, M., Leonard, T. L., & Lee, N. (1989). Sexual behavior of resident street prostitutes with their clients in Camden, New Jersey. *Journal of Sex Research, 26,* 460–478.

Friedan, B. (1963). *The feminine mystique.* New York: Dell.

Friedl, K. (1993). Effects of anabolic steroids on physical health. In C. Yesalis (Ed.), *Anabolic steroids in sport and exercise* (pp. 107–150). Champaign, IL: Human Kinetics Publishers.

Friedland, G. (1988). AIDS and compassion. *Journal of the American Medical Association, 259,* 2898–2899.

Friedman, R. M. (1986). The psychoanalytic model of male homosexuality: A historical and theoretical critique. *The Psychoanalytic Review, 73,* 484–519.

Friedman-Kien, A. E., & Farthing, C. (1990). Human immunodeficiency virus infection: A survey with special emphasis on mucocutaneous manifestations. *Seminars in Dermatology, 9,* 167–177.

Friedrich, W. N., Grambsch, P., Broughton, D., Kuiper, J., & Beilke, R. L. (1991). Normative sexual behavior in children. *Pediatrics, 88,* 456–464.

Fyfe, B. (1983). 'Homophobia' or homosexual bias reconsidered. *Archives of Sexual Behavior, 12,* 549–554.

Gagnon, J. H. (1977). *Human sexualities.* Glenview, IL: Scott, Foresman.

Gagnon, J. H. (1985). Attitudes and responses of parents to preadolescent masturbation. *Archives of Sexual Behavior, 14,* 451–466.

Gallagher, D. (1992). Young, female, and gay. *The Philadelphia Inquirer,* April 29, D1, D20.

Gamba, R. (1990). Attitudes and expected behaviors towards persons with AIDS: The importance of information among University students. *Interamerican Journal of Psychology, 24,* 57–68.

Gamson, J. (1989). Silence, death, and the invisible enemy: AIDS activism and social movement "newness." *Social Problems, 36,* 351–367.

Gamson, J. (1990). Rubber wars: Struggles over the condom in the United States. *Journal of the History of Sexuality, 1,* 262–282.

Gaskell, J. S. (1992). *Gender matters from school to work.* Philadelphia: Open University Press.

Gass, G. Z., & Nichols, W. C. (1988). Gaslighting: A marital syndrome. *Contemporary Family Therapy 10(1),* 3–16.

Gayle, H. D., Keeling, R. P., Garcia-Tunon, M., et al. (1991). Prevalence of HIV among university students. *New England Journal of Medicine, 323,* 1538–1541.

Gebhard, P., et al. (1965). *Sex offenders: An analysis of types.* New York: Harper & Row.

Gebhard, P., & Johnson, A. (1979). *The Kinsey data: Marginal tabulations of the 1938–1963 interviews conducted by the Institute for Sex Research.* Philadelphia: W. B. Saunders.

Gebhard, P. H., Gagnon, J. H., Pomeroy, W. B., & Christenson, C. V. (1965). *Sex offenders: An analysis of types.* New York: Harper & Row.

Geer, J. H., & O'Donohue, W. T. (1987). A sociological approach. In *Theories of human sexuality* (pp. 237–253). New York: Plenum Press.

Geer, J. H., & O'Donohue, W. T. (1987). *Theories of human sexuality.* New York: Plenum Press.

Gelbard, M. (1988). Dystrophic penile classification in Peyronie's disease. *Journal of Urology, 139,* 738–740.

George, W. H., Gournic, S. J., & McAfee, M. P. (1988). Perceptions of postdrinking female sexuality: Effects of gender, beverage choice, and drink payment. *Journal of Applied Social Psychology, 19,* 1295–1317.

Geraghty, C., et al. (1992). A woman's space: Women and soap opera. In *Imagining women* (pp. 221–236). United Kingdom: Polity Press.

Gergen, K. J. (1991). *The saturated self.* New York: Basic Books.

Geringer, W. M., Marks, S., Allen, W. J., & Armstrong, K. A. (1993). Knowledge, attitudes, and behavior related to condom use and STDs in a high risk population. *Journal of Sex Research, 30,* 75–83.

Gibbs, J. T. (1986). Psychosocial correlates of sexual attitudes and behaviors in urban early adolescent females: Implications for intervention. In P. Allen-Meares & D. A. Shore (Eds.), *Adolescent sexualities: Overviews and principles of intervention* (pp. 81–97). New York: The Haworth Press.

Gibson-Ainyette, I., Templer, D. I., Brown, R., & Veaco, L. (1988). Adolescent female prostitutes. *Archives of Sexual Behavior, 17,* 431–438.

Gilgun, J., & Gordon, S. (1983). The role of values in sex education programs. *Journal of Research and Development in Education, 16,* 27–33.

Gilmore, D. D. (1990). *Manhood in the making: Cultural concepts of masculinity.* New Haven: Yale University Press.

Girls, Inc. (1991). *Truth, trust and technology.* New York: Girls, Inc.

Gladue, B. (1990). Adolescents' sexual practices: Have they changed? *Medical Aspects of Human Sexuality,* November, 53–54.

Glamour Magazine. (1993). Verdict in: Penis size matters. October, 84.

Glatzer, W., Hondich, K. O., Noll, H., et al. (1993). *Recent social trends in West Germany, 1960–1990.* Frankfurt-am-Main: Campus Verlag.

Glick, P. S., & Spanier, G. B. (1981). Cohabitation in the U.S. In P. J. Stern (Ed.), *Single life: Unmarried adults in social context* (pp. 194–209). New York: St. Martin's Press.

Goeman, J., & Piot, P. (1990). The epidemiology of STDs in Africa and Latin America. *Seminars in Dermatology, 9,* 105–108.

Goffman, E. (1976). *Gender advertisements.* New York: Harper Colophon Books.

Goitein, S. D. (1979). The sexual mores of the common people. In Al-Sayyid-Marsot & A. Lutfi (Eds.), *Society and the sexes in medieval Islam* (pp. 43–62). Malibu, CA: Undena Publications.

Gold, R. (1990). *Abortion and women's health, a turning point for Americans.* New York: Alan Guttmacher Institute.

Gold, S., & Clegg, C. (1990). Sexual fantasies of college students with coercive experiences and coercive attitudes. *Journal of Interpersonal Violence, 5,* 464–473.

Gold, S., & Gold, R. (1991). Gender differences in first sexual fantasies. *Journal of Sex Education & Therapy, 17,* 207–216.

Gold, S. R., & Chick, D. A. (1988). Sexual fantasy patterns as related to sexual attitude, experience, guilt, and sex. *Journal of Sex Education and Therapy, 14,* 18–23.

Golding, J., Siegel, J., Sorenson, S. B., et al. (1989). Social support sources following sexual assault. *Journal of Community Psychology, 17,* 92–107.

Goldman, R., & Goldman, J. (1982). Children's sexual thinking: Report of a cross-national study. *SIECUS Report, 10,* 3–7.

Goleman, D. (1992). Therapies offer hope for sexual offenders. *The New York Times,* April 14, C1, C11.

Golombok, S., Spencer, A., & Rutter, M. (1983). Children in lesbian and single-parent households: Psychosexual and psychiatric appraisal. *Journal of Child Psychology and Psychiatry, 24,* 551–572.

Goode, E. (1994). *Deviant behavior.* Englewood Cliffs, NJ: Prentice Hall.

Goodman, W. (1991). Sex? Viewers are shocked. Shocked! *The New York Times,* December 22, Section 2: 1, 32.

Gordon, B. N., Schroeder, C. S., & Abrams, J. M. (1990). Age and social-class differences in children's knowledge of sexuality. *Journal of Clinical Child Psychology, 19,* 33–43.

Gordon, S. (1986). What kids need to know. *Psychology Today, 20,* 22–26.

Gore, W. (1972). The relationship between sex roles, mental illness and marital status. *Social Forces, 51,* 34–44.

Gore, W., Hughes, M., & Styles, L. (1983). Does marriage have positive effects on the psychological well-being of the individual? *Journal of Health and Social Behavior, 24,* June, 122–131.

Gorman, M. (1982). *Abortion and the early church.* New York: Paulist Press.

Gosselin, C. C. (1987). The sadomasochistic contract. In G. D. Wilson (Ed.), *Variant sexuality: Research and theory* (pp. 229–257). Baltimore: Johns Hopkins University Press.

Gould, S. J. (1981). *The mismeasure of man.* New York: W. W. Norton.

Grady, W. R., Tanfer, K. (1994). Condom breakage and slippage among men in the U.S. *Family Planning Perspectives, 26,* 107–112.

Greeley, A. (1992). Sex and the married Catholic: The shadow of St. Augustine. *America,* October 31, 318–323.

Greeley, A. (1992). Sex and the single Catholic: The decline of an ethic. *America,* November 7, 342–359.

Greeley, A. M. (1991). *Faithful attraction.* New York: Tom Doherty Associates, Inc.

Green, J. (1991). This school is out. *The New York Times Magazine,* October 13, 32–36, 59–60, 68.

Green, R. (1987). *The "Sissy Boy Syndrome" and the development of homosexuality.* New Haven: Yale University Press.

Green, R. (1988). The immutability of (homo)sexual orientation: Behavioral science implications for a constitutional (legal) analysis. *The Journal of Psychiatry and the Law, 16,* 537–575.

Green, R., Mandel, J. B., Hotvedt, M. E., Gray, J., & Smith, L. (1986). Lesbian mothers and their children: A comparison with solo parent heterosexual mothers and their children. *Archives of Sexual Behavior, 15,* 167–184.

Greenblat, C. S. (1989). Sexuality in the early years of marriage. In J. M. Henslin (Ed.), *Marriage and family in a changing society* (pp. 180–189). New York: The Free Press.

Greenhouse, L. (1995). Supreme court to rule on anti-gay rights law in Colorado. *The New York Times,* February 22, A17.

Greenhouse, P. (1987). Female to female transmission of HIV. *The Lancet, 2,* 401–402.

Greenwald, E., & Leitenberg, H. (1989). Long-term effects of sexual experiences with siblings and nonsiblings during childhood. *Archives of Sexual Behavior, 18,* 289–400.

Gregory, N., Sanchez, M., & Buchness, M. R. (1990). The spectrum of syphilis in patients with HIV infection. *Journal of the American Academy of Dermatology, 22,* 1061.

Greig, J. Y. T. (1923). *The psychology of laughter and comedy.* New York: Dodd, Mead.

Greil, A. L., Leitko, T. A., & Porter, K. T. (1988). Infertility: His and hers. *Gender and Society, 2,* 172–199.

Griffin, J.L. (1992). The gay baby boom. *The Chicago Tribune,* September 3, C1, C2.

Griffitt, W., & Veitch, R. (1971). Hot and crowded: Influence of population density and temperature on interpersonal affective behavior. *Journal of Personality and Social Psychology, 17,* 92–98.

Grob, C. S. (1985). Single case study: Female exhibitionism. *Journal of Nervous and Mental Disease, 173,* 253–256.

Grosskurth, P. (1980). *Havelock, Ellis, A biography.* New York: Alfred A. Knopf.

Groth, A. N. (1978). Patterns of sexual assault against children and adolescents. In A. W. Burgess, A. N. Groth, L. L. Holmstrom, & S. M. Sgroi (Eds.), *Sexual assault of children and adolescents.* Toronto: Lexington Books.

Groth, A. N., & Birnbaum, H. J. (1979). *Men who rape: The psychology of the offender.* New York: Plenum Press.

Groth, N., Burgess, A. (1980). Male rape: Offenders and victims. *American Journal of Psychiatry, 137,* 806–810.

Grunebaum, A., et al. (1983). Association of human papillomavirus infection with cervical intraepithelial neoplasia. *Obstetrics and Gynecology, 62,* 448.

Gudjonsson, G. H. (1986). Sexual variations: Assessment and treatment in clinical practice. *Sexual and Marital Therapy, 1,* 191–214.

Guinto-Adviento, M. L. (1988). The human factor in law enforcement: An exploratory study of the attitudes of policemen toward prostitution. *Philippine Journal of Psychology, 21,* 12–33.

Gundersen, B. H., Melas, P. S., & Skar, J. E. (1981). Sexual behavior of preschool children: Teachers' observations. In L. L. Constantine & F. M. Martinson (Eds.), *Children and sex: New findings, new perspectives* (pp. 45–61). Boston: Little, Brown.

Gunter, B., & McAleer, J. L. (1990). *Children and television: The one eyed monster?* London: Routledge, Chapman, Hall.

Gutek, B., & Konrad, A. M. (1986). Impact of work experiences on attitudes toward sexual harassment. *Administrative Science Quarterly 31.*

Guydish, J., Clark, G., Garcia, D., Downing, M., et al. (1991). Evaluating needle exchange: Do distributed needles come vaccinated? *American Journal of Public Health, 81,* 617–619.

Haas, A. (1979). Male and female spoken language differences: Stereotypes and evidence. *Psychological Bulletin, 86,* 616–626.

Haas, A. (1979). *Teenage sexuality—A survey of teenage sexual behavior.* New York: Macmillan.

Hall, J. A. (1978). Gender effects in decoding nonverbal cues. *Psychological Bulletin, 85,* 845–857.

Hall, R. C., Tice, L., Beresford, T. P., & Wooley, B. (1989). Sexual abuse in patients with anorexia nervosa and bulimia. *Psychosomatics, 30,* 73–79.

Halperin, D. M. (1990). *One hundred years of homosexuality: And other essays on Greek love.* New York: Routledge.

Hamabata, M. M. (1990). *Crested kimono: Power and love in the Japanese business family.* Ithaca, NY: Cornell University Press.

Hamburg, B. A. (1986). Subsets of adolescent mothers: Developmental, biomedical, and psychosocial issues. In J. B. Lancaster & B. A. Hamburg (Eds.), *School-age pregnancy and parenthood: Biosocial dimensions* (pp. 115–145). New York: Aldine DeGruyter.

Hamer, D. H., et al. (1993). A linkage between DNA markers on the X chromosome and male sexual orientation. *Science, 261,* 321–327.

Hamilton, W. S. (1991). *Nutrition: Concepts and controversies.* New York: West Publishing Co.

Handler, A., Davis, F., Ferre, C., & Yeko, T. (1989). The relationship of smoking and ectopic pregnancy. *American Journal of Public Health, 79,* 1239–1242.

Handsfield, H. (1992). Recent development in STDs: Viral and other syndromes. *Hospital Practice,* 175–200.

Handsfield, H. H., Rice, R. J., Roberts, M. C., et al. (1989). Localized outbreak of penicillinase-producing neisseria gonorrhoeae paradism for introduction and spread of gonorrhea in a community. *Journal of the American Medical Association, 261,* 2357.

Hankinson, S. E., Hunter, D. J., Colditz, G. A., et al. (1993). Tubal ligation, hysterectomy, and risk of ovarian cancer: A prospective study. *Journal of the American Medical Association 270(23),* 2813–2818.

Hansen, B. (1989). American physicians' earliest writings about homosexuals, 1880–1900. *The Milbank Quarterly, 67,* 92–108.

Hansen, C. H., & Hansen, R. D. (1988). How rock music videos can change what is seen when boy meets girl: Priming stereotypic appraisal of social interactions. *Sex Roles, 19,* 287–316.

Hardy, J. B. (1988). Premature sexual activity, pregnancy, and sexually transmitted diseases: The pediatrician's role as a counselor. *Pediatrics in Review, 10,* 69–76.

Hariton, E. B. (1973). The sexual fantasies of women. *Psychology Today,* 39–44.

Harkness, C. (1992). *The infertility book.* Berkeley, CA: Celestial Arts.

Harlow, H. F. (1959). Love in infant monkeys. *Scientific American, 200,* 68–70.

Harris, J. R., Lippman, M. E., Veronesi, U., & Willett, W. (1992). Breast Cancer (1). *New England Journal of Medicine, 327(5),* 319–328.

Harris, L., et al. (1988). *Sexual material on American network television during the 1987–88 season.* New York: Planned Parenthood Federation of America.

Harrison, J. (1978). Warning: The male sex role may be dangerous to your health. *Journal of Social Issues, 34,* 65–86.

Harry, J. (1990). A probability sample of gay males. *Journal of Homosexuality, 19,* 89–104.

Harry, P. (1977). *Les enfants, le sexe et nous.* Toulouse: Privot, 167.

Hart, C. W. M., & Pilling, A. R. (1960). *The Tiwi of North Australia.* New York: Holt, Rinehart & Winston.

Harvard Law Review. (1990). *Sexual orientation and the law.* Cambridge, MA: Harvard University Press.

Hatcher, R. A., et al. (1990). *Contraceptive technology 1990–1991.* New York: Irvington Publishers.

Hatcher, R. A., Guest, F., Stewart, F., Stewart, G., et al. (1988). *Contraceptive technology 1988–1989.* New York: Irvington Publishers.

Hatcher, R. A., Trussell, J., Stewart, F., Stewart, G., et al. (1994). *Contraceptive technology.* New York: Irvington Publishers.

Hatfield, E. (1988). Passionate and companionate love. In R. J. Sternberg & M. L. Barnes (Eds.), *The psychology of love* (pp. 191–217). New Haven and London: Yale University Press.

Hatfield, E., Rapson, R. (1987). Gender differences in love and intimacy: The fantasy vs. the reality. *Journal of Social Work and Human Sexuality* (Special Issue: Intimate Relationships), *5,* 15–22.

Hatfield, E., & Sprecher, S. (1986). Measuring passionate love in intimate relationships. *Journal of Adolescence, 9,* 383–410.

Hawkins, J. W., & Aber, C. S. (1993). Women in advertisements in medical journals. *Sex Roles, 28,* 233–242.

Hawkins, R. O. (1990). The relationship between culture, personality, and sexual jealousy in men in heterosexual and homosexual relationships. *Journal of Homosexuality, 19,* 67–84.

Hawton, K. (1983). Behavioural approaches to the management of sexual deviations. *British Journal of Psychiatry, 143,* 248–255.

Hayes, A. S. (1991). Courts concede the sexes think in unlike ways. *The Wall Street Journal,* B1–B5.

Hays, D., Samuels, A. (1989). Heterosexual women's perceptions of their marriages to bisexual or homosexual men. *Journal of Homosexuality, 18,* 81–100.

Hazan, C., & Shaver, P. (1987). Romantic love conceptualized as an attachment process. *Journal of Personality and Social Psychology, 52,* 511–524.

Health (1992). Missing persons: 60 million women. *Health, 14,* 16.

Health Magazine. (1992a). Herpes simplex is sneaky and sexist. *Health Magazine,* 15–16.

Health Magazine. (1992b). Cervical cancer and vitamin B. *Health Magazine,* 12–14.

Heath, D. (1984). An investigation into the origin of copious vaginal discharge during intercourse: "Enough to wet the bed"—That "is not urine." *The Journal of Sex Research, 20,* 194–210.

Hedges, C. (1994). With Mullahs' sleuths eluded, hijinks in the hills. *The New York Times,* August 8, A3.

Heiman, J., & LoPiccolo, J. (1992). *Becoming orgasmic: A sexual and personal growth program for women.* New York: Simon & Schuster.

Hemmer, J. D., & Kleiber, D. A. (1981). Tomboys and sissies: Androgynous children? *Sex Roles, 7,* 1205–1212.

Hemphill, E. (1991). *Brother to brother.* Boston: Alyson Publications.

Henderson, L. (1991). Lesbian pornography: Cultural transgression and sexual demystification. *Women and Language, 14,* 3–12.

Hendrick, C., & Hendrick, S. S. (1989). Research of love: Does it measure up? *Journal of Personality and Social Psychology, 56,* 784–794.

Hendricks, S. E., Graber, B., & Rodriguez-Sierra, J. F. (1989). Neuroendocrine responses to exogenous estrogen: No differences between heterosexual and homosexual men. *Psychoneuroendocrinology, 14,* 177–185.

Henshaw, S. (1990). Induced abortion: A world review, 1990. *Family Planning Perspectives, 22,* 76–89.

Henshaw, S. K., Forrest, J. D., & Van Vort, J. (1987). Abortion services in the United States, 1984 and 1985. *Family Planning Perspectives, 19,* 63–70.

Henshaw, S. K., Koonin, L. M., & Smith, J. C. (1991). Characteristics of U.S. women having abortions, 1987. *Family Planning Perspectives, 23,* 75–81.

Henshaw, S. K., & Kost, K. (1992). Parental involvement in minors' abortion decisions. *Family Planning Perspectives, 24,* 200.

Henshaw, S. K., & Silverman, J. (1988). The characteristics and prior contraceptive use of U.S. abortion patients. *Family Planning Perspectives, 20,* 158–168.

Henshaw, S. K., & Van Vort, J. (1994). Abortion services in the U.S., 1991 and 1992. *Family Planning Perspectives, 26,* 100–106, 112.

Hentoff, N. (1991). A case of loathing. *Playboy,* 94–98, 164–166.

Herdt, G. (1981). *Guardians of the flutes: Idioms of masculinity.* New York: McGraw-Hill.

Herdt, G. (1988). Cross-cultural forms of homosexuality and the concept 'gay.' *Psychiatric Annals, 18,* 37–39.

Herdt, G. (1989). Introduction: Gay and lesbian youth, emergent identities, and cultural scenes at home and abroad. In G. Herdt (Ed.), *Gay and Lesbian Youth* (pp. 1–42). New York: Harrington Park Press.

Herek, G. M. (1984). Beyond 'homophobia': A social psychological perspective on attitudes toward lesbians and gay men. In J. P. DeCecco (ed.), *Homophobia: An overview* (pp. 1–21). New York: The Haworth Press.

Herek, G. M. (1986). The social psychology of homophobia: Toward a practical theory. *New York University Review of Law & Social Changes, 14,* 923–935.

Herman, J., & Schatzow, E. (1987). Recovery and verification of memories of childhood sexual trauma. *Psychoanalytic Psychology, 4,* 1–14.

Herman, J. L. (1981). *Father-daughter incest.* Cambridge, MA: Harvard University Press.

Herold, E. S., & Mewhinney, D. M. (1993). Gender differences in casual sex and IDS prevention: A survey of dating bars. *Journal of Sex Research 30(1),* 6–42.

Herrero, R., Brinton, L. A., Reeves, W. C., et al. (1990). Sexual behavior, venereal diseases, hygiene practices, and invasive cervical cancer in high-risk population. *Cancer, 65,* 380.

Hersch, P. (1991). Sexually transmitted diseases are ravaging our children: Teen epidemic. *American Health, 10,* 42–45.

Higgens, D. L., Galavotti, C., O'Reilly, K. R., et al. (1991). Evidence for the effects of HIV antibody counseling and testing on risk behaviors. *Journal of the American Medical Association, 266,* 2419–2429.

Hinsch, B. (1990). *Passions of the cut sleeve: The male homosexual tradition in China.* Berkeley: University of California Press.

Hirayama, H., & Hirayama, K. (1986). The sexuality of Japanese Americans. Special issue: Human sexuality, ethnoculture, and social work. *Journal of Social Work and Human Sexuality, 4(3),* 81–98.

Hite, S. (1976). *The Hite report.* New York: Macmillan.

Hite, S. (1981). *The Hite report on male sexuality.* New York: Alfred Knopf.

Hite, S. (1987). *Women and love: A cultural revolution in progress.* New York: Alfred Knopf.

Hoebel, E. A. (1954). *The law of primitive man.* Boston: Harvard University Press.

Hoeffer, B. (1981). Children's acquisition of sex-role behavior in lesbian-mother families. *American Journal of Orthopsychiatry, 51,* 536–544.

Holbrook, S. M. (1990). Adoption, infertility, and the new reproductive technologies: Problems and prospects for social work and welfare policy. *Social Work, 35,* 333–337.

Holden, C. (1991). Is "gender gap" narrowing? *Science, 253,* 959–960.

Holmes, R. (1991). *Sex crimes.* Newbury Park, CA: Sage Publications.

Holmstrom, L. L., & Burgess, A. W. (1978). *The victim of rape: Institutional reactions.* New York: Wiley.

Holmstrom, L. L., & Burgess, A. W. (1979). Rape: The husband's and boyfriend's initial reactions. *The Family Coordinator, 28,* 321–330.

Hook, E. W., & Marra, C. M. (1992). Acquired syphilis in adults. *New England Journal of Medicine, 326,* 1060–1068.

Hooker, E. (1957). The adjustment of the male overt homosexual. *Journal of Projective Techniques, 21,* 18–31.

Hooper, R. R. (1978). Cohort study of venereal disease. *American Journal of Epidemiology, 108,* 136.

Hopkins E. (1992). Tales from the baby factory. *The New York Times Magazine,* March 15, 40.

Hort, B. E., Fagot, B. I., & Leinbach, M. D. (1990). Are people's notions of maleness more stereotypically framed than their notions of femaleness? *Sex Roles, 23,* 197–211.

Hotchner, T. (1984). *Pregnancy and childbirth.* New York: Avon Books.

Howard, M. (1982). Delaying the start of intercourse among adolescents. *Adolescent Medicine, 3,* 181–193.

Howard, M., & McCabe, J. (1990). Helping teenagers postpone sexual involvement. *Family Planning Perspectives, 27(1),* 21–26.

Hudson, F., & Ineichen, B. (1991). *Taking it lying down: Sexuality and teenage motherhood.* Hampshire: MacMillan.

Huerta-Franco, M. R., & Malacara, J. M. (1993). Association of physical and emotional symptoms with the menstrual cycle and life-style. *Journal of Reproductive Medicine, 38(6),* 448–54.

Hunt, L. (1993). Introduction: Obscenity and the origins of modernity, 1500–1800. In L. Hunt (Ed.), *The invention of pornography* (pp. 9–45). New York: Zone Books.

Hunt, M. (1974). *Sexual behavior in the 1970's.* New York: Dell Publishing.

Hunter, I., Saunders, D., & Williamson, D. (1993). *On pornography: Literature, sexuality and obscenity law.* New York: St. Martin's Press.

Hurlbert, D. F.(1992). Factors influencing a woman's decision to end an extramarital sexual relationship. *Journal of Sex and Marital Therapy, 18(2),* 104–113.

Hutchins, L., & Kaahumanu, L. (1990). *Bi any other name: Bisexual people speak out.* Boston: Alyson Publications.

Hutter, M. (1981). *The changing family: Comparative perspective.* New York: Wiley.

Iammarino, N. K., & Scardino, P. T. (1991). Testicular cancer: The role of the primary care physician in prevention and early detection. *Texas Medicine, 87(5),* 66–71.

Imperato-McGinley, J., Peterson, R. E., Gaultier, T., & Sturla, E. (1979). Androgens and the evolution of male gender identity among male pseudohermaphrodites with 5 alpha reductase deficiency. *New England Journal of Medicine, 300,* 1233.

Ingham, R., Woodcock, A., & Stenner, K. (1991). Getting to know you. . .Young people's knowledge of their partners at first intercourse. Special Issue: Social dimensions of AIDS. *Journal of Community and Applied Social Psychology, 1(2),* 117–132.

Ingrassia, M. (1994). Virgin cool. *Newsweek,* October 17, 59–69.

Irvine, J. (1990). *Disorders of desire, sex, and gender in modern American sexology.* Philadelphia: Temple University Press.

Isay, R. A. (1989). *Being homosexual.* New York: Farrar, Straus, & Giroux.

Iverson, J. S. (1991). A debate on the American home: The antipolygamy controversy, 1880–1890. *Journal of the History of Sexuality, 1,* 585–602.

Jackson, M. (1984). Sex research and the construction of sexuality: A tool of male supremacy? *Women's Studies International Forum, 7,* 43–51.

Jaffee, D., & Straus, M. A. (1987). Sexual climate and reported rape: A state-level analysis. *Archives of Sexual Behavior, 16,* 107–125.

Jake. (1993). Secrets of female sexuality. *Glamour Magazine,* 283–286.

JAMA. (1992). Induced termination of pregnancy before and after Roe vs. Wade. *Journal of the American Medical Association, 268,* 3231–3238.

James, J., & Burstin, N. (1971). Prostitution in Seattle. *Washington State Bulletin News 25.*

James, J., & Meyerding, J. (1978). Early sexual experience as a factor in prostitution. *Archives of Sexual Behavior, 7,* 31–42.

James, J., & Withers, J. (1975). *The politics of prostitution.* New York: Social Research Associates Press.

James, W. (1971). The reliability of reporting coital frequency. *Journal of Sex Research, 7,* 312–314.

Janczewski, Z., Bablok, L., Fracki, S., & Smith, A. (1992). Histological structure of the testes in andropause. *Polski Tygodnik Lekarski, 47,* 530–2.

Janeway, E. (1971). *Man's world, woman's place: A study in social mythology.* New York: W. Morrow & Company.

Janus, S. S., & Bess, B. E. (1981). Latency: Fact or fiction? In L. L. Constantine & F. M. Martinson (Eds.), *Children and sex: New findings, new perspectives* (pp. 75–82). Boston: Little, Brown.

Janus, S. S., Janus, C., & Vincent J. (1986). The psycho-sexuality of stand-up comedy. *Journal of Psychohistory, 14,* 133–140.

Janus, S. S., & Janus, C. L. (1993). *The Janus report on sexual behavior.* New York: Wiley.

Jayne, C. (1981). A two-dimensional model of female sexual response. *Journal of Sex and Marital Therapy, 7,* 3–30.

Jedlicka, D., & Robinson, I. E. (1987). Fear of venereal disease and other perceived restraints of premarital coitus. *Journal of Sex Research, 23,* 391–396.

Jenness, V. (1990). From sex as sin to sex as work: Coyote and the reorganization of prostitution as a social problem. *Social Problems, 37,* 403–420.

Jet (1991). NAACP cites shortage of blacks in film and TV. *Jet, 80* (October 14), 52.

Jetter, A. (1991). Faye's crusade. *Vogue,* 147–151: 202–204.

Johnson, C. B., Stockdale, M. S., & Saal, F. E. (1991). Persistence of men's misperceptions of friendly cues across a variety of interpersonal encounters. *Psychology of Women Quarterly, 15,* 463–475.

Johnson, J., & Alford, R. (1987). The adolescent quest for intimacy: Implications for the therapeutic alliance. *Journal of Social Work and Human Sexuality* (Special issue: Intimate Relationships) *5,* 55–66.

Johnson, J. H. (1989). Weighing the evidence on the pill and breast cancer. *Family Planning Perspectives, 21,* 89–92.

Jones, R. (1984). *Human reproduction and sexual behavior.* Englewood Cliffs, NJ: Prentice Hall.

Jones, W. P., & Emerson, S. (1994). Sexual abuse and binge eating in a nonclinical population. *Journal of Sex Education and Therapy, 20,* 47–55.

Jorgenson, C. (1967). *Christine Jorgenson: Personal biography.* New York: Erickson.

Kaats, G. R., & Davis, K. E. (1971). Effects of volunteer biases in studies of sexual behavior and attitudes. *Journal of Sex Research, 7,* 26–34.

Kaeser, F. (1992). Can people with severe mental retardation consent to mutual sex? *Sexuality and Disability, 10,* 33–42.

Kahn, Y. (1989–90). Judaism and homosexuality: The traditionalist/progressive debate. *Journal of Homosexuality, 18,* 47–82.

Kain, E. (1987). A note on the integration of AIDS into the sociology of human sexuality. *Teaching Sociology, 15,* 320–323.

Kalisch, P. A., & Kalisch, B. J. (1984). Sex-role stereotyping of nurses and physicians on prime-time television: A dichotomy of occupational portrayals. *Sex Roles, 10,* 533–553.

Kaltreider, N. B., Goldsmith, S., & Margolis, A. (1979). The impact of midtrimester abortion techniques on patients and staff. *American Journal of Obstetrics and Gynecology, 135,* 235–238.

Kaminer, W. (1992). Feminists against the first amendment. *Atlantic Monthly,* November, 111–117.

The Kansas City Star. (1992a). Barbie storms Russia in her pink, blond glory. July 20, A1, A4.

The Kansas City Star. (1992b). Scientists in India create vaccine for women to prevent pregnancy. October 10, A5.

The Kansas City Star. (1992c). Woman gives birth to her sister's triplets. May 10, A6.

The Kansas City Star. (1992d). In age of AIDS, women can die of gender proprieties. July 24, C5.

The Kansas City Star. (1992e). Estimate on AIDS higher. June 4, A3.

The Kansas City Star. (1992f). Decoy helps protect cells from AIDS, scientists say. July 5, A14.

The Kansas City Star. (1993a). Detectives relish Valentines day. February 14, A5.

The Kansas City Star. (1993b). Survey: Most spouses faithful. October 19, A5.

Kantor, L. (1992). Scared chaste? Fear based educational curricula. *SIECUS Reports, 21,* 1–15.

Kantrowitz, B., & Gonzalez, D. (1990). Examining the mind of the rapist. *Newsweek,* July 23, 46–53.

Kaplan, D. A. (1993). Is it torture or tradition? *Newsweek,* December 20, 124.

Kaplan, H. S. (1974). Fiction and fantasy: No-nonsense therapy for six sexual dysfunctions. *Psychology Today, 8,* 77–86.

Kaplan, H. S. (1974). *The new sex therapy.* New York: Bruner/Mazel.

Kaplan, L. J. (1991). Women masquerading as women. In G. I. Fogel & W. A. Meyers (Eds.), *Perversions and near-perversions in clinical practice: New psychoanalytic perspectives* (p. 127–152). New Haven: Yale University Press.

Kassler, W. J., & Cates, W. (1992). The epidemiology and prevention of sexually transmitted diseases. *Urologic Clinics of North America, 19,* 1–12.

Kaufman, G. (Ed.). (1991). *In stitches: A patchwork of feminist humor and satire.* Bloomington, IN: Indiana University Press.

Kaufman, G., & Blakely, M. K. (Eds.). (1980). *Pulling our own strings*. Bloomington: Indiana University Press.

Kayongo-Male, D., Onyango, P. (1984). *The sociology of the African family*. London: Longman.

Keating, J., & Over, R. (1990). Sexual fantasies of heterosexual and homosexual men. *Archives of Sexual Behavior, 19,* 461–475.

Kedia, K. (1983). Ejaculation and emission: Normal physiology, dysfunction, and therapy. In R. J. Krane, M. B. Siroky, & I. Goldstein (Eds.), *Male sexual dysfunction* (pp. 37–54). Boston: Little, Brown.

Keen, S. (1991). *Fire in the belly: On being a man*. New York: Bantam.

Kegel, A. M. (1952). Sexual functions of the pubococcygeus muscle. *Western Journal of Surgery, Obstetrics, and Gynecology, 60,* 521–524.

Keith-Spiegel, P. (1972). Early conceptions of humor: Varieties and issues. In J. Goldstein & P. E. McGhee (Eds.), *The psychology of humor* (pp. 4–39). New York: Academic Press.

Kelly, J. A., O'Brien, G. G., & Hosford, R. (1981). Sex roles and social skills: Considerations for interpersonal adjustment. *Psychology and Women Quarterly, 5,* 758–766.

Kelly, J. B. (1989). Mediated and adversarial divorce: Respondents' perceptions of their processes and outcomes. *Mediation Quarterly, 24,* 71–88.

Kelly, M. P., Strassberg, D. S., & Kircher, J. R. (1990). Attitudinal and experiential correlates of anorgasmia. *Archives of Sexual Behavior, 19,* 165–177.

Kendrick, W. M. (1987). *The secret museum: Pornography in modern culture*. New York: Viking.

Kerfoot, W. W., & Carson, C. C. (1991). Pharmacologically induced erections among geriatric men. *Journal of Urology, 146,* 1022–1024.

Kettl, P., et al. (1991). Female sexuality after spinal cord injury. *Sexuality and Disability, 9,* 287–295.

Kilmann, P. R., Wanlass, R. L., Sabalis, R. F., & Sullivan, B. (1981). Sex education: A review of its effects. *Archives of Sexual Behavior, 10,* 177–203.

King, B. M., Parisi, L. S., & O'Dwyer, K. R. (1993). College sexuality education promotes future discussions about sexuality between former students and their children. *Journal of Sex Education and Therapy, 19,* 285–293.

Kinnaird, K. L., & Gerrard, M. (1986). Premarital sexual behavior and attitudes toward marriage and divorce among young women as a function of their mothers' marital status. *Journal of Marriage and the Family, 38(4),* 757–765.

Kinsey, A., Pomeroy, W. B., & Martin, C. E. (1948). *Sexual behavior in the human male*. Philadelphia: Saunders.

Kinsey, A. C., Pomeroy, W., Martin, C. E, & Gebhard, P. (1953). *Sexual behavior in the human female*. Philadelphia: Saunders.

Kirby, D. (1984). *Sexuality education: An evaluation of programs and their effects, an executive summary*. Bethesda, MD: Mathtech, Inc.

Kirby, D. (1992). Sexuality education: It can reduce unprotected intercourse. *SIECUS Report, 21,* 19–25.

Kirkendall, L., & Libby, R. (1984). Sex education in the future. *Journal of Sex Education and Therapy, 10,* 64–67.

Kirkpatrick, M., & Smith, C. R. R. (1981). Lesbian mothers and their children: A comparative study. *American Journal of Orthopsychiatry, 51,* 545–551.

Kitazawa, K. (1994). Sexuality issues in Japan. *SIECUS Report,* 7–11.

Kleerekoper, M. (1991). Oral contraceptive use may protect against low bone mass. *Archives of Internal Medicine, 151,* 1971–1976.

Klein, A. M. (1989). Managing deviance: Hustling, homophobia, and the bodybuilding subculture. *Deviant Behavior, 10,* 11–27.

Klein, F. (1978). *The bisexual option: A concept of one-hundred percent intimacy*. New York: Arbor House.

Klein, F. (1990). The need to view sexual orientation as a multi-variable dynamic process: A theoretical perspective. In D. P. McWhirter, S. A. Sanders, & J. M. Reinisch (Eds.), *Homosexuality/Heterosexuality: Concepts of Sexual Orientation* (pp. 277–282). New York: Oxford University Press.

Klein, F., et al. (1985). Sexual orientation: A multi-variable dynamic process. *Journal of Homosexuality, 11,* 35–49.

Klein, M. (1988). *Your sexual secrets: When to keep them, when and how to tell*. New York: E. P. Dutton.

Kline, P. (1987). Sexual deviation: Psychoanalytic research and theory. In G. D. Wilson (Ed.), *Variant sexuality: Research and theory* (pp. 150–175). Baltimore: Johns Hopkins University Press.

Klitsch, M. (1988). FDA approval ends cervical cap marathon. *Family Planning Perspectives, 20,* 137–138.

Knopp, L. M. (1990). Social consequences of homosexuality. *Geographical Magazine,* May, 20–25.

Knowlden, H. A. (1990). The pill and cancer: A review of the literature. *Journal of Advanced Nursing, 15,* 1016–1020.

Kohler, K., Schweikert-Stary, M. T., & Lubkin, I. (1990). Altered mobility. In I. M. Lubkin (Ed.), *Chronic illness impact and interventions* (pp. 86–110). Boston: Mones & Barlett Publishers.

Kolata, G. (1995a). Man's world, woman's world? Brain studies point to differences. *The New York Times,* February 28, C1, C7.

Kolata, G. (1995b). Men and women use brain differently, study discovers. *The New York Times,* February 16, A1, A22.

Kolk, C. J. V., Chubon, R. A., & Kolk, J. K. V. (1992). The relationship among back injury, pain, and sexual functioning. *Sexuality and Disability, 10(3),* 153–161.

Kolodny, R. C. (1980). Adolescent sexuality. Presented at the Michigan Personnel and Guidance Association Annual Convention (Detroit), November, 1980.

Kopelman, L. (1988). The punishment concept of disease. In C. Pierce & D. Vandeveer (Eds.), *AIDS, ethics, and public policy.* Belmont, CA: Wadsworth Publishing Co.

Koss, M. (1988). Hidden rape: Sexual aggression and victimization in a national sample in higher education. In A. Burgess (Ed.), *Rape and sexual assault* (pp. 3–25). New York: Garland.

Koss, M., Dinero, T. (1989). Predictors of sexual aggression among a national sample of male college students. *Annals of the New York Academy of Sciences, 528,* 133–147.

Koss, M. P., Gidycz, C. A., & Wisniewski, N. (1987). The scope of rape: Incidence and prevalence of sexual aggression and victimization in a national sample of higher education students. *Journal of Consulting and Clinical Psychology, 55,* 162–170.

Koutsky, L. A., Galloway, D. A., & Holmes, K. K. (1988). Epidemiology of genital human papillomavirus infection. *Epidemiological Review, 10,* 122–163.

Krilov, L. (1991). What do you know about genital warts? *Medical Aspects of Human Sexuality, 25,* 39–41.

Krogh, G. V. (1990). STDs in five continents. *Seminars in Dermatology, 9,* 91–95.

Kroon, S. (1990). Genital herpes—when and how to treat. *Seminars in Dermatology, 9,* 133–140.

Krueger, M. M. (1988). Pregnancy as a result of rape. *Journal of Sex Education and Therapy, 14,* 23–27.

Krulewitz, J. E. (1982). Sex differences in evaluations for females and male victims' responses to assault. *Journal of Applied Social Psychology, 11,* 460–474.

Kubler-Ross, E. (1969). *On death and dying.* New York: MacMillan.

Kuhn, T. (1962). *The structure of scientific revolutions.* Chicago: University of Chicago Press.

Kutchinsky, B. (1991). Pornography and rape: Theory and practice? *International Journal of Law and Psychiatry, 14,* 47–64.

LaFree, G. (1982). Male power and female victimization. *American Journal of Sociology, 88,* 311–328.

Lahey, K. A. (1991). Pornography and harm—learning to listen to women. *International Journal of Law and Psychiatry, 14,* 117–131.

Lambert, B. (1988). AIDS among prostitutes not as prevalent as believed, studies show. *The New York Times,* September 20, B1.

Lancaster, J. B. (1986). Human adolescence and reproduction: An evolutionary perspective. In J. B. Lancaster & B. A. Hamburg (Eds.), *School-age pregnancy and parenthood: Biosocial dimensions* (pp. 17–37). New York: Aldine DeGruyter.

Lancaster, R. N. (1988). Subject honor and object shame: The construction of male homosexuality and stigma in Nicaragua. *Ethnology, 27,* 111–125.

Lancet (1990). Contraceptive efficacy of testosterone-induced azoospermy in normal men. *Lancet, 2,* 955.

Landau, E. (1987). *On the streets: The lives of adolescent prostitutes.* New York: Julian Messner.

Landers, A. (1992). A 'Simple Truth' about an Aspect of Sexuality. June 1, C2.

Landsberg, M. (1992). Canada: Antipornography breakthrough in the law. *Ms.,* May/June, 14–15.

Lane, H. C., Holmberg, S. D., & Jaffee, H. W. (1991). HIV seroconversion and oral intercourse. *American Journal of Public Health, 81,* 658.

Laner, M. R., & Laner, R. H. (1979). Personal style or sexual preference: Why gay men are disliked. *International Review of Modern Sociology, 9,* 215–228.

Lang, R., Flor-Henry, P., & Frenzel, R. (1990). Sex hormone profiles in pedophilic and incestuous men. *Annals of Sex Research, 3,* 59–74.

Langevin, R. (1992). Biological factors contributing to paraphiliac behavior. *Psychiatric Annals, 22,* 307–314.

Langevin, R., & Lang, R. A. (1987). The courtship disorders. In G. D. Wilson (Ed.), *Variant sexuality: Research and theory* (pp. 202–228). Baltimore: Johns Hopkins University Press.

Langevin, R., Wortzman, G., Dickey, R., Wright, P., et al. (1988). Neuropsychological impairment in incest offenders. *Annals of Sex Research, 1,* 401–415.

Langfeldt, T. (1981a). Processes in sexual development. In L. L. Constantine & F. M. Martinson (Eds.), *Children and sex: New findings, new perspectives* (pp. 37–44). Boston: Little, Brown.

Langfeldt, T. (1981b). Childhood masturbation: Individual and social organization. In L. L. Constantine & F. M. Martinson (Eds.), *Children and sex: New findings, new perspectives* (pp. 63–72). Boston: Little, Brown.

Lapore, J. (1987). National call to action. Planned Parenthood Federation of America 4.

Larkin, M. (1992). Reacting to patients with sexual problems. *Headlines, 3,* 2, 3, 6, 8.

Larsen, K. S., & Long, E. (1987). *Attitudes towards rape.* Paper presented at the annual meeting of the Western Psychological Association, Long Beach, CA.

Larson, A. (1981). *Patterns of contraceptive use around the world.* Washington: Population Reference Bureau.

Latif, A. (1990). STDs in Africa. *Genitourinary Medicine, 66,* 235–237.

Lauer, R. H., Lauer, J. C., Kerr, S. T. (1985). The long-term marriage: Perceptions of stability and satisfaction. *International Journal of Aging and Human Development, 31(3),* 189–195.

Lauersen, N. H., & Bouchez, C. (1991). *Getting pregnant: What couples need to know right now.* New York: Fawcett Columbine.

Laumann, E. C., Gagnon, J. H., Michael, R. T., et al. (1994). *Social organization of sexuality.* Chicago: University of Chicago Press.

Lavee, Y. (1991). Western and non-Western human sexuality: Implications for clinical practice. *Journal of Sex and Marital Therapy, 17,* 203–213.

Lawlis, G., & Lewis, J. (1987). Relationship problems in adolescence. *Medical Aspects of Human Sexuality,* September, 62–67.

Lee, J. A. (1974). The method for measuring love. *Psychology Today, 8,* 43–51.

Lee, J. A. (1977). A typology of styles of loving. *Personality and Social Psychology Bulletin, 3,* 173–182.

Lee, J. A. (1989). Invisible men: Canada's aging homosexuals: Can they be assimilated into Canada's 'liberated' gay communities? *Canadian Journal on Aging, 8,* 79–97.

Legman, G. (1968). *No laughing matter: An analysis of sexual humor.* Bloomington: Indiana University Press.

Legman, G. (1969). *The limerick.* New York: Bell Publishing.

Leitenberg, H., Detzer, M. J., & Srebnik, D. (1993). Gender differences in masturbation and the relation of masturbation experience in preadolescence and/or early adolescence to sexual behavior and sexual adjustment in young adulthood. *Archives of Sexual Behavior, 22,* 87–98.

Lemp, G. F., Hirozawa, A. M., & Givertz, D. (1994). Seroprevalence of HIV and risk behaviors among young homosexual and bisexual men. *Journal of the American Medical Association, 272,* 449–454.

Leone, B., & O'Neill, M. T. (1983). *Sexual values: Opposing viewpoints.* St. Paul, MN: Greenhaven Press.

Leslie, G. R., & Korman, S. K. (1989). *The family in social context.* New York: Oxford University Press.

Lester, D. (1989). Attitudes toward AIDS. *Personality and Individual Differences, 10,* 693–694.

Levay, A. N., Sharpe, L., & Kugel, A. (1981). The effects of physical illness on sexual functioning. In H. Lief (Ed.), *Sexual problems in medical practice* (pp. 169-190). Chicago: American Medical Association.

LeVay, S. (1991). A difference in hypothalamic structure between heterosexual and homosexual men. *Science, 253,* 1034–1037.

Levine, J. (1991). Search and find. *Forbes, 148,* 134–135.

Levine, M. P., & Troiden, R. R. (1988). The myth of sexual compulsivity. *Journal of Sex Research, 25,* 347–363.

Levine, R. J., et al. (1990). Differences in the quality of semen in outdoor workers during summer and winter. *New England Journal of Medicine, 323(1),* 12–16.

Levine, S. B., Risen, C. B., & Althof, S. E. (1990). Essay on the diagnosis and nature of paraphilia. *Journal of Sex & Marital Therapy, 16,* 89–102.

Levy, H. S. (1973). *Chinese sex jokes in traditional times.* Washington: The Warm-Soft Village Press.

Lewes, K. (1988). *The psychoanalytic theory of male homosexuality.* New York: Meridian.

Lewis, L. A. (1990). *Gender politics and MTV.* Philadelphia: Temple University Press.

Lewis, M. (1987). Early sex role behavior and school age adjustment. In J. M. Reinish, L. A. Rosenblum, & S. A. Sanders (Eds.), *Masculinity/femininity: Basic perspectives* (pp. 202–226). New York: Oxford University Press.

Lewis, R. J., & Janda, L. H. (1988). The relationship between adult sexual adjustment and childhood experiences regarding exposure to nudity, sleeping in the parental bed, and parental attitudes toward sexuality. *Archives of Sexual Behavior, 17,* 349–362.

Li, V. C., Wong, G. C., Qiu, S., Cao, F., et al. (1990). Characteristics of women having abortion in China. *Social Science and Medicine, 31,* 445–453.

Libido. (1993). Looney sex laws. *Libido, 5,* 21–22.

Lieberman, B. (1988). Extrapremarital intercourse: Attitudes toward a neglected sexual behavior. *The Journal of Sex Research, 24,* 291–298.

Liebowitz, M. R. (1983). *The chemistry of love.* Boston: Little, Brown.

Lightfoot-Klein, H. (1989). The sexual experience and marital adjustment of genitally circumcised and infibulated females in the Sudan. *Journal of Sex Research, 26,* 375–392.

Lilley, L. L., & Schaffer, S. (1990). Human papillomavirus: A sexually transmitted disease with carcinogenic potential. *Cancer Nursing, 13,* 366–372.

Linz, D. (1989). Exposure to sexually explicit materials and attitudes toward rape: A comparison of study results. *The Journal of Sex Research, 26,* 50–84.

Linz, D., Donnerstein, E. (1992). Research can help us explain violence and pornography. *The Chronicle of Higher Education,* September 30, B3–B4.

Lipman, A. (1986). Homosexual relationships. *Generations 10(4),* 51–54.

Little, L. M., & Curran, J. P. (1978). Covert sensitization: A clinical procedure in need of some explanations. *Psychological Bulletin, 3,* 513–531.

Llewelyn-Davies, M. (1981). Women, Warriors, and patriarchs. In S. Ortner & H. Whitehead (Eds.), *Sexual meanings* (pp. 330–358). Cambridge, UK: Cambridge University Press.

Longo, D. J., Clum, G. A., & Yaeger, N. J. (1988). Psychosocial treatment for recurrent genital herpes. *Journal of Consulting and Clinical Psychology, 56,* 61–66.

LoPiccolo, J., & Lobitz, W. C. (1972). The role of masturbation in the treatment of orgasmic dysfunction. *Archives of Sexual Behavior, 2,* 163–171.

LoPiccolo, J., & Stock, W. E. (1986). Treatment of sexual dysfunction. *Journal of Consulting and Clinical Psychology, 54,* 158–167.

Lopresto, C. T., Sherman, M. F., & Sherman, N. C. (1985). The affects of a masturbation seminar on high school males' attitudes, false beliefs, and behavior. *Journal of Sex Research, 21,* 142–156.

The Los Angeles Times. (1994). AIDS 101. April 28, B1.

Lott, A. J., & Lott, B. E. (1961). Group cohesiveness, communication level, and conformity. *Journal of Abnormal and Social Psychology, 62,* 408–412.

Lottes, I. L., & Kuriloff, P. J. (1992). The effects of gender, race, religion, and political orientation on the sex role attitudes of college freshmen. *Adolescence, 27,* 675–688.

Lovdal, L. T. (1989). Sex role messages in television commercials: An update. *Sex Roles, 21,* 715–724.

Lovejoy, F. H., & Estridge, D. (Eds.). (1987). *The new child health encyclopedia.* New York: Delacorte Press.

Lowhagen, G. B. (1990). Syphilis: Test procedures and therapeutic strategies. *Seminars in Dermatology, 9,* 152–159.

Lowry, T., & Williams, G. (1983). Brachioroctic eroticism. *Journal of Sex Education and Therapy, 9(1),* 50–52.

Lucie-Smith, E. (1991). *Sexuality in Western art.* London: Thames & Hudson.

Luckenbill, D. F. (1984). Dynamics of the deviant scale. *Deviant Behavior, 5,* 337–353.

Lunde, I., Larsen, G., Fog, E., & Garde, K. (1991). Sexual desire, orgasm, and sexual fantasies: A study of 625 Danish women born in 1910, 1936, and 1958. *Journal of Sex Education and Therapy, 17,* 111–115.

Lurie, A. (1990). The cabinet of Dr. Seuss. *The New York Review of Books, 37,* 50–52.

Maccoby, E. E. (1987). The varied meanings of "masculine" and "feminine." In J. M. Reinisch, L. A. Rosenblum, & S. Stephanie (Eds.), *Masculinity/femininity: Basic perspectives* (pp. 227–239). New York: Oxford University Press.

MacKinnon, C. A. (1985). Pornography: Reality, not fantasy. *The Village Voice,* March 26.

MacKinnon, C. A. (1986). Pornography: Not a moral issue. (Special Issue: Women and the law.) *Women's Studies International Forum, 9,* 63–78.

MacKinnon, C. A. (1987). *Feminism unmodified: Discourses on life and law.* Cambridge, MA: Harvard University Press.

MacKinnon, C. A. (1993). *Only words.* Cambridge, MA: Harvard University Press.

Macklin, E. D. (1980). Nontraditional family forms: A decade of research. *Journal of Marriage and the Family, 42(4),* 905–922.

MacNamara, D. E. J., & Sagarin, E. (1977). *Sex, crime, and the law.* New York: The Free Press.

Magai, C. (1992). Fact sheet: RU486. *Psychology of Women Newsletter, 19,* 10–11.

Mahlstedt, P. (1987). The crisis of infertility. In G. Weeks & L. Hof (Eds.), *Integrating sex and marital therapy: A clinical guide* (pp. 121–148). New York: Bruner/Mazel Publishers.

Major, B., Cozzarelli, C., Sciacchitano, A. M., & Cooper, M. (1990). Perceived social support, self-efficacy, and adjustment to abortion. *Journal of Personality and Social Psychology, 59,* 452–463.

Major, B., Mueller, P., & Hildebrandt, K. (1985). Attributions, expectations, and coping with abortion. *Journal of Personality and Social Psychology, 48,* 585–599.

Malamuth, N. M., & Check, J. V. P. (1981). The effects of mass media exposure on acceptance of violence against women: A field experiment. *Journal of Research in Personality, 15,* 436–446.

Maltz, W. (1990). Adult survivors of incest: How to help them overcome the trauma. *Medical Aspects of Human Sexuality,* December, 38–43.

Mann, J. (1991). Kuwaiti rape a doubly savage crime. *Washington Post* March 29, C3.

Manniche, L. (1987). *Sexual life in ancient Egypt.* London: KPI Ltd.

Margulis, L., & Sagan, D. (1991). *Mystery dance: On the evolution of human sexuality.* New York: Summit Books.

Markman, H. J. (1979). Application of a behavioral model of marriage in predicting relationship satisfaction of couples planning marriage. *Journal of Consulting and Clinical Psychology, 47,* 743–749.

Markman, H. J. (1981). Prediction of marital distress: A 5-year follow-up. *Journal of Consulting and Clinical Psychology, 49,* 760–762.

Marshal, D., & Suggs, R. (1971). *Human sexual behavior: Variations in the ethnographic spectrum.* Englewood Cliffs, NJ: Prentice Hall.

Marshall, N., & Hendtlass, J. (1986). Drugs and prostitution. *Journal of Drug Issues, 16,* 237–248.

Marsigliano, E., & Mott, F. (1986). The impact of sex education on sexual activity, contraceptive use, and premarital pregnancy among American teenagers. *Family Planning Perspectives.*

Martin, C. L., & Halverson, C. F. (1983). The effects of sex-typing schemas on young children's memory. *Child Development, 54,* 563–574.

Martin, H. P. (1991). The coming-out process for homosexuals. *Hospital and Community Psychiatry, 42,* 158–162.

Martin, P. Y., & Hummer, R. A. (1989). Fraternities and rape on campus. (Special issue: Violence against Women.) *Gender and Society, 3,* 457–473.

Martinson, F. M. (1981a). Eroticism in infancy and childhood. In L. L. Constantine & F. M. Martinson (Eds.), *Children and sex: New findings, new perspectives* (pp. 23–35). Boston: Little, Brown.

Martinson, F. M. (1981b). Preadolescent sexuality: Latent or manifest? In L. L. Constantine & F. M. Martinson (Eds.), *Children and sex: New findings, new perspectives* (pp. 83–93). Boston: Little, Brown.

Marzuk, P. M., Tierney, H., Tardiff, K., et al. (1988). Increased risk of suicide in persons with AIDS. *Journal of the American Medical Association, 259,* 1333–1337.

Masters, W. H., & Johnson, V. E. (1966). *Human sexual response.* Boston: Little, Brown.

Masters, W. H., & Johnson, V. E. (1970). *Human sexual inadequacy.* Boston: Little, Brown.

Masters, W. H., & Johnson, V. E. (1979). *Homosexuality in perspective.* Boston: Little, Brown.

Masters, W. H., Johnson, V. E., & Kolodny, R. (1994). *Heterosexuality.* New York: HarperCollins.

Masters, W. H., Johnson, V. E., & Kolodny, R. C. (1982). *Human sexuality.* Boston: Little, Brown.

Masterton, G. (1987). *How to drive your woman wild in bed.* New York: Penguin Books.

Masterton, G. (1992). *Wild in bed together.* New York: Penguin Group.

Matek, O. (1988). Obscene phone callers. (Special issue: The sexually unusual: Guide to understanding and helping.) *Journal of Social Work and Human Sexuality, 7,* 113–130.

Mayer, K., & DeGruttola, V. (1987). HIV and oral intercourse. *Annals of Internal Medicine, 107,* 428–429.

Mayhook, J. J. (1990). Crimes from the heart. *Human Rights, 17,* 46–51.

McBrien, R. P. (1993). Teaching the truth. *Christian Century,* October 20, 1004–1005.

McCarthy, J., & McMillan, S. (1990). Patient/partner satisfaction with penile implant surgery. *Journal of Sex Education and Therapy, 16,* 25–37.

McCase E. (1992). Letter to members of the NYC Board of Education from the co-chair of the HIV/AIDS Advisory Council of NYC concerning Ronald Carey et al., The effectiveness of latex condoms. *Sexually Transmitted Diseases,* July–August.

McCormick N., & Jones, A. (1989). Gender differences in nonverbal flirtation. *Journal of Sex Education and Therapy, 15,* 271–282.

McDowell, B. (1986). The Dutch touch. *National Geographic, 170,* 501–525.

McGregor, J. A. (1989). Chlamydial infection in women. *Sexually Transmitted Diseases, 16,* 565–592.

McKirnan, D. J., & Peterson, P. L. (1989). Alcohol and drug use among homosexual men and women: Epidemiology and population characteristics. *Addictive Behaviors, 14,* 545–553.

McLaren, A. (1990). *A history of contraception.* Cambridge, MA: Basil Blackwell.

McNamara, R., & Grossman, K. (1991). Initiation of dates and anxiety among college men and women. *Psychological Reports, 69(1),* 252–254.

McWhirter, D. P., & Mattison, A. M. (1984). *The male couple: How relationships develop.* Englewood Cliffs, NJ: Prentice Hall.

Medved, M. (1992). *Hollywood vs. America: Popular culture and the war on traditional values.* New York: HarperCollins.

Megino, G. R. (1977). *Prostitution and California law.* California Legislative Senate Committee on Judiciary.

Melchert, T., & Burnett, K. (1990). Attitudes, knowledge, and sexual behavior of high-risk adolescents: Implications for counseling and sexuality education. *Journal of Counseling & Development, 68,* 293–298.

Merit Systems Protection Board. (1981). *Sexual harassment in the federal workplace: Is it a problem?* Office of Merit Systems Review and Studies. Washington, DC: U.S. Government Printing Office.

Mertus, J. A. (1990). Fake abortion clinics: The threat to reproductive self-determination. *Women and Health, 16,* 95–113.

Meyer-Bahlburg, H. F. L. (1977). Sex hormones and male homosexuality in comparative perspective. *Archives of Sexual Behavior, 6,* 297–325.

Mezey, G., & King, M. (1989). The effects of sexual assault on men: A survey of 22 victims. *Psychological Medicine, 19,* 205–209.

Mhloyi, M. M. (1990). Perceptions on communication and sexuality in marriage in Zimbabwe. *Women and Therapy, 10(3),* 61–73.

Michael, R. T., Gagnon, J. H., Laumann, E. O., et al. (1994). *Sex in America.* Boston: Little, Brown.

Mihalik, G. (1988). Sexuality and gender: An evolutionary perspective. *Psychiatric Annals, 18,* 40–42.

Miller, B. C., McCoy, J. K., & Olson, T. D. (1986). Parental discipline and control attempts in relation to adolescent sexual attitudes and behavior. *Journal of Marriage and the Family, 48,* 503–512.

Miller, W. B. (1986). Why some women fail to use their contraceptive method: A psychological investigation. *Family Planning Perspectives, 18,* 27.

Milner, J., & Robertson, K. (1990). Comparison of physical child abusers, intrafamilial sexual child abusers, and child neglecters. *Journal of Interpersonal Violence, 5,* 37–48.

Minton, L. (1993). What kids say. *Parade Magazine,* August 1: 4–6.

Moatti, J. P., Bajos, N., Durbec, J. P., Menard, C., & Serrand, C. (1991). Determinants of condom use among French heterosexuals with multiple partners. *American Journal of Public Health, 81,* 106–109.

Moller, L. C., Hymel, S., & Rubin, K. H. (1992). Sex typing in play and popularity in middle childhood. *Sex Roles, 26,* 331–353.

Monat-Haller, R. K. (1992). *Understanding and experiencing sexuality.* Baltimore: Paul H. Brookes Publishing.

Money, J. (1984). Paraphilias: Phenomenology and classification. *American Journal of Psychotherapy, 38,* 164–179.

Money, J. (1985). *The destroying angel.* Buffalo, NY: Prometheus Books.

Money, J. (1986). *Venuses penises: Sexology, sexophy, and exigency theory.* Buffalo, NY: Prometheus Books.

Money, J. (1987). Sin, sickness, or status? Homosexual gender identity and psychoneuroendocrinology. *American Psychologist, 42,* 384–399.

Money, J. (1990). Pedophilia: A specific instance of new phylism theory as applied to paraphiliac lovemaps. In J. Feierman (Ed.), *Pedophilia biosocial dimensions* (pp. 445–463). New York: Springer-Verlag.

Money J., & Norman, B. F. (1987). Gender identity and gender transposition: Longitudinal outcome study of 24 male hermaphrodites assigned as boys. *Journal of Sex and Marital Therapy, 13,* 75.

Moore, J. R., Daily, L., Collins, J., et al. (1991). Progress in efforts to prevent the spread of HIV infection among youth. *Public Health Reports, 106,* 678–686.

Morales, A. (1993). Nonsurgical management options in impotence. *Hospital Practice, 28(3a),* 15–24.

Morbidity and Mortality Weekly. (1992). 1993 Revised Classification System for HIV Infection and Expanded Surveillance Case Definition for AIDS Among Adolescents and Adults. Issue 41, Atlanta, GA: U.S. Department of Health and Human Services.

Moreau, R. (1992). Sex and death in Thailand. *Newsweek, 120,* 50–51.

Morgan, S. P., & Rindfuss, R. (1985). Marital disruption: Structural and temporal dimensions. *American Journal of Sociology, 90(5),* 1055–1077.

Morokoff, P. J. (1986). Volunteer bias in the psychophysiological study of female sexuality. *Journal of Sex Research, 22,* 35–51.

Morris, R. J. (1990). Aikane: Accounts of Hawaiian same-sex relationships in the journals of Captain Cook's third voyage (1776–1780). *Journal of Homosexuality, 19,* 21–54.

Morrison, D. (1989). Predicting contraception efficacy: A discriminant analysis of three groups of adolescent women. *Journal of Applied Social Psychology, 19,* 1431–1452.

Morse, E. V., Simon, P. M., Balson, P. M., & Osofsky, H. J. (1992). Sexual behavior patterns of customers of male street prostitutes. *Archives of Sexual Behavior, 21,* 347–357.

Morse, E. V., Simon, P. M., Osotsky, H. J., Balson, P. M., & Gaumer, R. (1991). The male street prostitute. *Social Science Medicine, 32,* 535–539.

Moseley, D. T., Follingstad, D. R., & Harley, H. (1981). Psychological factors that predict reaction to abortion. *Journal of Clinical Psychology, 37,* 276–279.

Moser, C. (1988). Sadomasochism. Special issue: The sexually unusual: Guide to understanding and helping. *Journal of Social Work and Human Sexuality, 7,* 43–56.

Moser, C., & Levitt, E. E. (1987). An exploratory-descriptive study of a sadomasochistically oriented sample. *Journal of Sex Research, 23,* 322–337.

Mosher, D. L., & Anderson, R. D. (1986). Macho personality, sexual aggression, and reactions to guided imagery of realistic rape. *Journal of Research in Personality, 20,* 77–94.

Mosher, D. L., & Tomkins, S. S. (1988). Scripting the macho man: Hypermasculine, socialization, and enculturation. *Journal of Sex Research, 25,* 60–84.

Mosher, W. D., & Bachrach, C. A. (1987). First premarital contraceptive use: United States, 1960–62. *Study of Family Planning, 18,* 83–95.

Mosher, W. D., & Pratt, W. F. (1990). Contraceptive use in the United States, 1973–1988. *Patient Education and Counseling, 16(2),* 163–72.

Muecke, M. A. (1992). Mother sold food, daughter sells her body: The cultural continuity of prostitution. *Social Science and Medicine, 35,* 891–901.

Muehlenhard, C. L., & Cook, S. W. (1988). Men's self-reports of unwanted sexual activity. *Journal of Sex Research, 24,* 58–72.

Muehlenhard, C. L., & MacNaughton, J. S. (1988). Women's beliefs about women who "lead men on." *Journal of Social and Clinical Psychology, 7,* 65–79.

Muehlenhard, C. L., & Schrag, J. (1991). Nonviolent sexual coercion. In A. Parrot & L. Beckhofer (Eds.), *Acquaintance rape—The hidden crime* (pp. 115–128). New York: Wiley.

Mueller, P., & Major, B. (1989). Self-blame, self-efficacy, & adjustment of abortion. *Journal of Personality & Social Psychology, 57,* 1059–1068.

Muir, J. G. (1993). Homosexuals and the 10% fallacy. *The Wall Street Journal,* March 31, A14.

Munson, M. (1987). How do you do it? *On Our Backs 4(1).*

Murphy, L. R. (1990). Defining the crime against nature: Sodomy in the United States appeals courts, 1810–1940. *Journal of Homosexuality, 19,* 49–66.

Nacci, P. L., & Kane, T. R. (1983). The incidence of sex and sexual aggression in federal prisons. *Federal Probation, 47,* 31–36.

Nadelson, C. C., Notman, M. T., Zackson, H., & Gornick, J. (1982). A follow-up study of rape victims. *American Journal of Psychiatry, 139,* 1266–1270.

NARAL (National Abortion Rights Action League). (1992). *Who decides? A state by state review of abortion rights.* Author.

National Abortion Federation (1988). *Teenage women, abortion, and the law.* Washington, DC: National Abortion Federation.

National Abortion Rights Action League (1989). *The voices of women. Abortion in their own words.* Washington DC.

NCHS (1991). Advance report of final natality statistics. Monthly Vital Statistics Report, 1989: 40. Hyattsville, MD: Public Health Service.

Neff, D. (1993). How Lutherans justify sex. *Christianity Today, 37,* 16–17.

Neisen, J. H. (1990). Heterosexism: Redefining homophobia for the 1990s. *Journal of Gay and Lesbian Psychotherapy, 1,* 21–35.

Nelson, J. B. (1982). Sexuality issues in American religious groups: An update. *Marriage & Family Review, 6,* 35–46.

New, J. F. H. (1969). *The Renaissance and Reformation, A short history.* New York: Wiley.

The New Republic. (1992). Kondomski. *The New Republic, 207,* 28–29.

The New York Times. (1991a). Coming out in India, with a nod from the Gods. August 15, A4.

The New York Times. (1991b). Anti-homosexual t-shirts prompt suspension of Syracuse fraternity. June 26, B4.

The New York Times. (1991c). Houston police set trap to quell the tide of violence against homosexuals. August 9, A–12.

The New York Times. (1991d). Gay images, TV's mixed signals. May 19, 1, 32.

The New York Times. (1991e). Presbyterians reject report on sex. June 11, A18.

The New York Times. (1991f). Lesbian ordained Episcopal Priest. June 6, A1, A20.

The New York Times. (1991g). Greek Church suspends ties to National Council. July 24, 11.

The New York Times. (1991h). Militants back 'queer', shoving 'gay' the way of 'negro.' April 26, 23–24.

The New York Times. (1991i). When grandmother is the mother, until birth. August 5, A1–A11.

The New York Times. (1991j). W.H.O. says 40 million will be infected with AIDs virus by 2000. June 18, C3.

The New York Times. (1992a). Sexual behavior levels compared in studies in Britain and France. C3.

The New York Times. (1992b). No cookie-cutter answers in 'mommy wars.' September 2, B1, B5.

The New York Times. (1994a). With church preaching in vain, Brazilians embrace birth control. September 2, A1, 3.

The New York Times. (1994b). Company wants to sell genital herpes drug over the counter. May 22, Sect. 1, p. 19, col. 1.

Newcomer, S. F., & Udry, J. R. (1985). Oral sex in an adolescent population. *Archives of Sexual Behavior, 14,* 41.

Newsweek. (1983). Newsweek poll on homosexuality. August 8, 33.

Newsweek (1995). Bisexuality. July 17, 44–50.

Ng, M. (1993). Public responses to the sex education series of radio- television: Hong Kong. *Journal of Sex Education and Therapy, 19,* 64–72.

NGLTF (National Gay & Lesbian Task Force). (1991a). Anti-gay/lesbian violence, victimization & defamation in 1990. Washington, DC: National Gay and Lesbian Task Force Policy Institute.

NGLTF (National Gay and Lesbian Task Force). (1991b). Where do the states stand on hate crime? Washington, DC: National Gay and Lesbian Task Force Policy Institute, February.

NGLTF (National Gay and Lesbian Task Force). (1994a). The right response: A survey of voter's attitudes about gay-related issues. Washington, DC: National Gay and Lesbian Task Force Policy Institute.

NGLTF (National Gay and Lesbian Task Force). (1994b). General overview of anti-gay/lesbian/bisexual violence. Anti-Gay/Lesbian/Bisexual Violence Fact Sheet, April.

Nichols, M. (1990). Lesbian relationships: Implications for the study of sexuality and gender. In D. McWhiter, S. A. Sanders, & J. Reinish (Eds.), *Homosexuality/heterosexuality: Concepts of sexual orientation* (pp. 350–364). The Kinsey Institute Series. New York: Oxford University Press.

Nilsson, L. (1990). *A child is born.* New York: Delacorte Press, Bantam Books.

Niruthisard, S., Roddy, R. E., & Chutivongse, S. (1991). The effects of frequent nonoxynol-9 use on the vaginal and cervical mucosa. *Sexually Transmitted Diseases, 18,* 176–179.

Noble, R. (1991). There is no safe sex. *Newsweek 8.*

Noh, S., et al. (1990). AIDS epidemic, emotional strain, coping and psychological distress in homosexual men. *AIDS Education and Prevention, 2(4),* 272–283.

Nolin, M. J., & Petersen, K. K. (1992). Gender differences in parent-child communication about sexuality: An exploratory study. *Journal of Adolescent Research, 7,* 59–79.

Nussbaum, M. (1992). Venus in robes. *The New Republic,* April 20, 36–41.

Nutter, D. E., & Condron, M. K. (1985). Sexual fantasy and activity patterns of males with inhibited sexual desire and males with erectile dysfunction versus normal controls. *Journal of Sex and Marital Therapy, 11,* 91–98.

Nzila, N., Laga, M., Thiam, M., Mayimona, K., et al. (1991). HIV and other sexually transmitted diseases among female prostitutes in Kinshasa. *AIDS, 5,* 715–721.

Offir, J. T., Fisher, J. D., Williams, S. S., & Fisher, W. A. (1993). Reasons for inconsistent AIDS-preventative behaviors among gay men. *Journal of Sexual Relationships, 30,* 62–69.

Ogunbanjo, B. (1989). Sexually transmitted diseases in Nigeria. A review of the present situation. *West African Journal of Medicine, 8,* 42–49.

Ohalloran, R. L., & Dietz, P. E. (1993). Autoerotic fatalities with power hydraulics. *Journal of Forensic Sciences, 38,* 359–364.

Okami, P. (1990). Sociopolitical biases in the contemporary scientific literature of adult human sexual behavior with children and adolescents. In J. Feierman (Ed.), *Pedophilia biosocial dimensions* (pp. 91–121). New York: Springer-Verlag.

Oliver, M. B., & Hyde, J. S. (1993). Gender differences in sexuality: A meta-analysis. *Psychological Bulletin, 114,* 29–51.

O'Neill, N., & O'Neill, G. (1972). Open marriage: A new life style for couples.

Ortner, S., & Whitehead, H. (1981). Introduction: Accounting for sexual meanings. In S. Ortner & H. Whitehead (Eds.), *Sexual meanings* (pp. 1–27). Cambridge, UK: Cambridge University Press.

Ortner, S. B. (1974). Is female to male as nature is to culture? In M. Z. Rosaldo & L. Lamphere (Eds.), *Woman, culture, and society.* Stanford, CA: Stanford University Press.

Orzek, A. M. (1988). The lesbian victim of sexual assault: Special considerations for the mental health professional. (Special issue: Lesbianism: Affirming nontraditional roles.) *Women and Therapy, 8,* 107–117.

Ostrov, E., Offer, D., Howard, K., Kaufman, B., & Meyer, H. (1985). Adolescent sexual behavior. *Medical Aspects of Human Sexuality, 19,* 28–36.

Otago Daily Times (New Zealand). (1992). Working girls: Sex industry on legal tightrope. March 21, 21.

O'Toole, C. J., & Bregante, J. L. (1992). Lesbians with disabilities. *Sexuality and Disability, 10,* 163–172.

Padgett, V. R., Brislin-Slutz, J. A., & Neal, J. A. (1989). Pornography, erotica, and attitudes toward women: The effects of repeated exposure. *The Journal of Sex Research, 26,* 479–491.

Padian, N. S., Shiboski, S. C., & Jewell, N. P. (1991). Female to male transmission of HIV. *Journal of the American Medical Association, 266,* 1664.

Painton, P. (1993). The shrinking ten percent. *Time,* April 26, 27–29.

Palca, J. (1991). Fetal brain signals time for birth. *Science, 253,* 1360.

Pally, M. (1994). *Sex and sensibility: Reflections on forbidden mirrors and the will to censor.* Hopewell, NJ: Ecco Press.

Parelman, A. (1983). *Emotional intimacy in marriage: A sex roles perspective.* Ann Arbor: University of Michigan Press.

Parker, R. (1989). Youth, identity, and homosexuality: The changing shape of sexual life in contemporary Brazil. *Journal of Homosexuality, 17,* 269–289.

Parsons, N. K., Richards, H. C., & Kanter, G. D. (1990). Validation of a scale to measure reasoning about abortion. *Journal of Counseling Psychology, 37,* 107–112.

Patterson, J, & Kim, P. (1991). *The day America told the truth.* New York: Plume/Penguin

Paul, J. P. (1984). The bisexual identity: An idea without social recognition. *Journal of Homosexuality, 9,* 45–63.

Payer, P. J. (1991). Sex and confession in the thirteenth century. In J. E. Salisbury (Ed.), *Sex in the Middle Ages.* New York: Garland.

Pearson, V., & Klook, A. (1989). Sexual behaviour following paraplegia. *Disability, Handicap & Society, 4,* 285–295.

Peck, M. S. (1978). *The road less traveled: A new psychology of love, traditional values, and spiritual growth.* New York: Simon & Schuster.

Peele, S. (1988). Fools for love: The romantic ideal, psychological theory, and addictive love. In R. J. Sternberg & M. L. Barnes (Eds.), *The psychology of love.* New Haven and London: Yale University Press.

Peele, S., & Brodsky, A. (1976). *Love and addiction.* New York: New American Library.

Peeples, E. H., & Scacco, A. M. (1982). The stress impact study technique: A method for evaluating the consequences of male-on-male sexual assault in jails, prisons, and other selected single-sex institutions. In A. M. Scacco (Ed.) *Male rape: A casebook of sexual aggressions* (pp. 241–278). New York: AMS Press.

Pelletier, L. A., & Herold, E. S. (1988). The relationship of age, sex guilt, & sexual experience with female sexual fantasies. *Journal of Sex Research, 24,* 250–256.

Penkower, L., Dew, M. A., Kingsley, L., et al. (1991). Behavioral health and psychosocial factors and risk for HIV infection among sexually active homosexual men. *American Journal of Public Health, 81,* 194–196.

Penna-Firme, T., Grinder, R. E., & Linhares-Barreto, M. S. (1991). Adolescent female prostitutes on the streets of Brazil: An exploratory investigation of ontological issues. *Journal of Adolescent Research, 6,* 493–504.

Peo, R. (1988). Transvestism. *Journal of Social Work and Human Sexuality, 7,* 57–75.

Pepe, M. V., Sanders, D. W., & Symons, C. W. (1993). Sexual behaviors of university freshmen and the implications for sexuality educators. *Journal of Sex Education and Therapy, 19,* 20–30.

Peplau, L. A., & Conrad, E. (1989). Beyond nonsexist research: The perils of feminist methods in psychology. *Psychology of Women Quarterly, 13,* 381–402.

Peplau, L. A., & Gordon, S. L. (1985). Women and men in love: Sex differences in close heterosexual relationships. In V. O'Leary et al., *Women, gender and social psychology.* Hillsdale, NJ: Erlbaum

Peplau, L. A., Rubin, W., & Hill, C. T. (1977). Sexual intimacy in dating relationship. *Journal of Social Issues, 33(2),* 86–109.

Perelman, D., Gerson, A. C., & Spinner, B. (1978). Loneliness among senior citizens. *Essence, 2(4),* 239–248.

Perez-Stable, E. (1991). Cuba's response to the HIV epidemic. *American Journal of Public Health, 81,* 563–567.

Perkins, R., & Bennett, G. (1985). *Being a prostitute: Prostitute women and prostitute men.* Boston: Allen & Unwin.

Perper, T. (1985). *Sex signals: The biology of love.* Philadelphia: ISI Press.

Perrow, C., & Guillén, M. F. (1990). *The AIDS disaster.* New Haven, CT: Yale University Press.

Person, E. S., Terestman, N., Myers, W. A., Goldberg, E., et al. (1992). Associations between sexual experiences and fantasies in a nonpatient population. *Journal of American Academy of Psychological Analysis, 20,* 75–90.

Petersen, A. C., & Crockett, L. (1986). Pubertal development and its relation to cognitive and psychosocial development in adolescent girls: Implications for parenting. In J. B. Lancaster & B. A. Hamburg (Eds.), *School-age pregnancy and parenthood: Biosocial dimensions* (pp. 147–175). New York: Aldine DeGruyter.

Peterson, L. (1988). The issues—and controversy—surrounding adolescent sexuality and abstinence. *SIECUS Report, 17,* 1–8.

Peterson, S., & Franzese, B. (1987). Correlates of college men's sexual abuse of women. *Journal of College Student Personnel, 28,* 223–228.

Pfeiffer, E., Verwoerdt, A., & Davis, G. (1972). Sexual behavior in middle life. *American Journal of Psychiatry, 128,* 1262–1267.

Pheterson, G. (1989). *A vindication of the rights of whores.* Seattle: Seal Press.

Philadelphia City Paper. (1992). News quirks. November 8, 9.

Philadelphia Daily News. (1991). 15 years for raping wife. October 30, 14.

Philadelphia Daily News. (1994). Jones admits to a 'sexual' thing. February 15, 6.

Philadelphia Inquirer. (1991). Health plans exclude gay families. June 12, 17–A.

Philadelphia Inquirer. (1992). Psychologist: Dahmer driven to necrophilia. February 6, A4.

Philadelphia Inquirer. (1994). Couples who stay together can collect pay together. October 2, A3.

Piaget, J. (1951). *Play, dreams, and imitation in children.* New York: Norton.

Picard, J., Guerrier, D., Kahn, A., & Josso, N. (1989). Molecular biology of anti-Mullerian hormone. In S. S. Wachtel (Ed.), *Evolutionary mechanisms in sex determination* (pp. 209–217). Boca Raton, FL: CRC.

Pickering, H., Todd, J., Dunn, D., & Pepin, J. (1992). Prostitutes and their clients: A Gambian survey. *Social Science and Medicine, 34,* 75–88.

Pierson, E. C. (1973). *Sex is never an emergency: A candid guide for young adults.* Philadelphia: Lippincott.

Pillard, R. C. (1988). Sexual orientation and mental disorder. *Psychiatric Annals, 18,* 52–56.

Pincu, L. (1989). Sexual compulsivity in gay men: Controversy and treatment. *Journal of Counseling and Development, 68,* 63–66.

Plant, M. L., Plant, M. A., & Thomas, R. M. (1990). Alcohol, AIDS risks, and commercial sex: Some preliminary results from a Scottish study. *Drug and Alcohol Dependence, 25,* 51–55.

Platt, R., Rice, P., & McCormack, W. (1983). Risk of acquiring gonorrhea and prevalence of abnormal adnexal findings. *Journal of the American Medical Association, 250,* 3205.

Pleak, R. R., & Meyer-Bahlburg, H. F. (1990). Sexual behavior and AIDS knowledge of young male prostitutes in Manhattan. *Journal of Sex Research, 27,* 557–587.

Plummer, K. (1989). Lesbian and gay youth in England. *Journal of Homosexuality, 17,* 195–223.

Plummer, K. (1991). Understanding childhood sexualities. *Journal of Homosexuality, 20,* 231–249.

Podell, J. (1990). *The reference shelf: Abortion.* New York: HW Wilson.

Pollitt, K. (1991). The smurfette principle. *The New York Times Magazine,* April 7, 22–24.

Pollock, E. J. (1993). As remedy for certain broken promises, professor proposes 'sexual fraud' suits. *The Wall Street Journal,* June 11, B1–B2.

Pomerleau, A., Bolduc, D., Malcuit, G., & Cossette, L. (1990). Pink or blue: Environmental gender stereotypes in the first two years of life. *Sex Roles, 22,* 359–367.

Pomeroy, W. B. (1982). Dr. Kinsey and the Institute for Sex Research. New Haven, CT: Yale University Press.

Ponse, B. (1980). Lesbians and the worlds. In J. Marmor (Ed.) *Homosexual behavior: A modern reappraisal.* New York: Basic Books.

Population Reports. (1989). Mass media programs for the general public. *AIDS education: A beginning.* Series L, 7–14.

Porter, R. (1982). Mixed feelings: The Enlightenment and sexuality in eighteenth-century Britain. In P.-G. Goucé (Ed.), *Sexuality in eighteenth-century Britain* (pp. 1–27). Manchester, England: Manchester University Press.

Posner, R. A. (1993). Obsession. *The New Republic, 209,* 31–36.

Pothen, S. (1989). Divorce in Hindu society. *Journal of Comparative Family Studies, 20(3),* 377–392.

Potterat, J. J., Woodhouse, D. E., Muth, J. B., & Muth, S. Q. (1990). Estimating the prevalence and career longevity of prostitute women. *Journal of Sex Research, 27,* 233–243.

Prentky, R., Burgess, A., & Carter, D. (1986). Victim response by rapist type: An empirical and clinical analysis. *Journal of Interpersonal Violence, 1,* 73–98.

Price, V., Scanlon, B., & Janus, M. (1984). Social characteristics of adolescent male prostitution. *Victimology, 9,* 211–221.

Prud'homme, A. (1991). What's it all about, Calvin? *Time, 138,* 44.

Quimby, E., & Friedman, S. R. (1989). Dynamics of black mobilization against AIDS in New York City. *Social Problems, 36,* 403–415.

Radlove, S. (1983). Sexual response and gender roles. In E. R. Allgeier & N. B. McCormick (Eds.), *Changing boundaries: Gender roles and sexual behavior.* Palo Alto, CA: Mayfield.

Rado, S. (1949, rev. 1955). An adaptional view of sexual behavior. *Psychoanalysis of behavior: Collected papers.* New York: Grune & Stratton.

Ragab, M. J. (1993). Walker, NOW give new visibility to mutilation. *National NOW Times,* November, 1–2.

Raghavan, D. (1990). Towards the earlier diagnosis of testicular cancer. *Australian Family Physician, 19(6),* 865–75.

Rancour-Laferriere, D. (1985). *Signs of the flesh.* New York: Mouton de Gruyter.

Rapaport, K., & Burkhart, B. R. (1984). Personality and attitudinal characteristics of sexually coercive college males. *Journal of Abnormal Psychology, 93,* 216–221.

Rebek, V. A. (1988). The Southern Baptist alliance: The loyal opposition organizes. *The Christian Century,* June 1, 542–544.

Reevy, W. R. (1967). In A. Ellis & A. Abarbanel (Eds.), *The encyclopedia of sexual behavior.* New York: Hawthorn.

Register, C. (1987). *Living with chronic illness.* New York: Macmillan.

Reingold, A. L. (1991). Toxic shock syndrome: An update. *American Journal of Obstetrics and Gynecology, 165(4, pt. 2),* 1236.

Reinisch, J. (1990). *The Kinsey Institute new report on sex.* New York: St. Martins Press.

Reis, J., & Herz, E. (1989). An examination of young adolescents' knowledge of and attitude toward sexuality according to preconceived contraceptive responsibility. *Journal of Applied Social Psychology, 19,* 231–250.

Reiss, I. L. (1982). Trouble in paradise: The current status of sexual science. *Journal of Sex Research, 18,* 97–113.

Reiss, I. L. (1986). *Journey into sexuality: An exploratory voyage.* Englewood Cliffs, NJ: Prentice Hall.

Reiter, E. O. (1986). The neuroendocrine regulation of pubertal onset. In J. B. Lancaster & B. A. Hamburg (Eds.), *School-age pregnancy and parenthood: Biosocial dimensions* (pp. 53–76). New York: Aldine DeGruyter.

Religion Watch. (1992a). American Muslim activism on moral issues taking shape. *Religion Watch, 7,* 1–2.

Religion Watch. (1992b). Church convention focuses on gender, sexuality, authority. *Religion Watch, 7,* 1–2.

Religion Watch. (1992c). Future church trends viewed through an Episcopal lens. *Religion Watch, 8,* 1–2.

Religion Watch. (1992d). Catholicism and abusive priests. *Religion Watch, 8(2),* 5–6.

Religion Watch. (1993). 1992 brings changes and continuities to religious scene. *Religion Watch, 8,* 1–2.

Renou, L. (1961). *Hinduism.* New York: Braziller.

Resnick, S. K. (1992). Weep for health. *Natural Health,* May/June, 56, 58.

Reynolds, H. (1986). *The economics of prostitution.* Springfield, IL: Charles C. Thomas.

Rhoads, J. M., & Boekelheide, P. D. (1985). Female genital exhibitionism. *The Psychiatric Forum,* Winter, 1–6.

Rhode, D. L. (1989). *Justice and gender.* Cambridge, MA: Harvard University Press.

Riccio, R. (1992). Street crime strategies: The changing schemata of streetwalkers. *Environment and Behavior, 24,* 555–570.

Rich, A. (1983). Compulsory heterosexuality and lesbian existence. In A. Snitow, C. Stinsell, & S. Thompson (Eds.) *Powers of desire: The politics of sexuality* (pp. 177–205). New York: Monthly Review Press.

Richardson, D., & Campbell, J. L. (1982). The effect of alcohol on attributions of blame for rape. *Personality and Social Psychology Bulletin, 8,* 468–476.

Richer, S. (1990). *Boys and girls apart: Children's play in Canada and Poland.* Ottawa, Canada: Carleton University Press.

Richie, J. P. (1993). Detection and treatment of testicular cancer. *CA: A Cancer Journal for Clinicians, 43(3),* 151–175.

Richlin, A. (1992). *The Garden of Priapus: Sexuality and aggression in Roman humor.* New York: Oxford University Press.

Richter, A. (1993). *The dictionary of sexual slang.* New York: Wiley.

Rideau, W., & Sinclair, B. (1982). Prison: The sexual jungle. In A. M. Scacco (Ed.). *Male rape: A casebook of sexual aggressions* (pp. 4–29). New York: AMS Press.

Riessman, C. K., Whalen, M. H., Frost, R. O., & Morgenthaw, J. E. (1987). Romance and health seeking among college women. *Women and Health, 17(4),* 21–47.

Rio, L. M. (1991). Psychological and sociological research and the decriminalization or legalization of prostitution. *Archives of Sexual Behavior, 20,* 205–218.

Rischer, C. E., & Easton, T. A. (1992). *Focus on human biology.* New York: HarperCollins.

Risman, B., & Schwartz, P. (1988). Sociological research on male and female homosexuality. *Annual Review of Sociology, 14,* 125–147.

Rittenhouse, C. A. (1991). The emergence of premenstrual syndrome as a social problem. *Social Problems, 38(3),* 412–425.

Rochman, S. (1991). Silent victims: Bringing male rape out of the closet. *The Advocate, 582,* 38–43.

Rogers, C., & Thomas, J. (1984). Sexual victimization of children in the USA. *Clinical Proceedings, Children's Hospital National Medical Center, 40,* 211–221.

Rogers, S. C. (1978). Woman's place: A critical review of anthropological theory. *Comparative Studies in Society and History, 20,* 123–162.

Rokach, A. (1990). Content analysis of sexual fantasies of males and females. *Journal of Psychology, 124,* 427–436.

Romenesko, K., & Miller, E. M. (1989). The second step in double jeopardy: Appropriating the labor of female street hustlers. (Special issue: Women and crime.) *Crime and Delinquency, 35,* 109–135.

Roscoe, B., Diana, M. S., & Brooks, R. H. (1987). Early, middle, and late adolescents' views on dating and factors influencing partner selection. *Adolescence, 22,* 59–68.

Rosen, I. (1979). Exhibitionism, scopophilia, and voyeurism. In I. Rosen (Ed.), *Sexual deviation* (pp. 139–194). New York: Oxford University Press.

Rosen, R. (1994). Sexual dysfunction in the 1990's: Current research and theory. Paper delivered at the SSSS Midwest Meeting, May 26–29, 1994, Austin, Texas.

Rosen, R. C., & Leiblum, S. R. (1987). Current approaches to the evaluation of sexual desire disorders. *Journal of Sex Research, 23,* 141–162.

Rosenberg, K. P. (1994). Notes and comments: Biology and homosexuality. *Journal of Sex & Marital Therapy, 20(2),* 147–151.

Rosenthal, R., & Rosnow, R. L. (1975). *The volunteer subject.* New York: Wiley.

Rosman, J. P., & Resnick, P. J. (1989). Sexual attraction to corpses: A psychiatric review of necrophilia. *Bulletin of the American Academy of Psychiatry and the Law, 17,* 153–163.

Ross, M. W., Rigby, K., Rosser, B. R., et al. (1990). The effect of a national campaign on attitudes toward AIDS. *AIDS Care, 2,* 339–346.

Ross, S. (1988). *Fall from grace: Sex, scandal, and corruption in American politics from 1702 to the present.* New York: Balantine Books.

Rossi, A. (1977). The biosocial basis of parenting. *Daedalus, 106,* 1–31.

Rossi, A. S. (1978). The biosocial side of parenthood. *Human Nature, 1,* 72–79.

Roth, N. (1991). "Fawn of my delights": Boy-love in Hebrew and Arabic verse. In J. E. Salisbury (Ed.), *Sex in the Middle Ages* (pp. 157–172). New York: Garland.

Rotheram-Borus, M. J., Koopman, C., Haignere, C., & Davies, M. (1991). Reducing HIV sexual risk behaviors among runaway adolescents. *Journal of the American Medical Association, 266,* 1237–1241.

Rothman, S. M. (1978). *Woman's proper place.* New York: Basic Books.

Ruan, F. F., & Bullough, V. L. (1992). Lesbianism in China. *Archives of Sexual Behavior, 21,* 217–226.

Ruan, F. F., & Tsai, Y. M. (1988). Male homosexuality in contemporary mainland China. *Archives of Sexual Behavior, 17,* 189–199.

Rubin, L. B. (1991). *Erotic wars: What happened to the sexual revolution?* New York: Harper Perennial.

Rubin, Z. (1970). Measurement of romantic love. *Journal of Personality and Social Psychology, 16,* 265–273.

Rubin, Z. (1973). *Liking and loving: An invitation to social psychology.* New York: Holt, Rinehart & Winston.

Rubinson, L., & deRubertis, L. (1991). Trends in sexual attitudes and behaviors of a college population over a 15 year period. *Journal of Sex Education and Therapy, 17(1),* 32–41.

Ruch, W., & Hehl, F. J. (1988). Attitudes to sex, sexual behavior, and enjoyment of humour. *Personality and Individual Differences, 9,* 983–994.

Rudman, W. J., & Hagiwara, A. F. (1992). Sexual exploitation in advertising health and wellness products. *Women & Health, 18,* 77–89.

Rugh, A. B. (1984). *Family in contemporary Egypt.* Syracuse, NY: Syracuse University Press.

Russell, D. E. H. (1974). *The politics of rape: The victim's perspective.* New York: Stein & Day.

Russell, D. E. H. (1984). *Sexual exploitation: Rape, child sexual abuse, and workplace harassment.* Beverly Hills, CA: Sage Publications.

Russell, D. E. H., & Howell, N. (1983). The prevalence of rape in the United States revisited. *Signs: Journal of Women in Culture and Society,* 688–695.

Russo, V. (1987). *The celluloid closet: Homosexuality in the movies.* New York: Harper & Row.

Rutherford, G. W. (1991). Heterosexually transmitted human immunodeficiency virus infection in Asia. *Archives of AIDS Research, 5,* 31–43.

Saal, F. E., Johnson, C. B., & Weber, N. (1989). Friendly or sex? It may depend on who you ask. *Psychology of Women Quarterly, 13,* 263–276.

Sabo, D. (1990). The myth of the sexual athlete. In F. Abbott (Ed.), *Men and intimacy* (pp. 16–20). Freedom, CA: The Crossing Press.

Sack, A. R., Keller, J. F., & Hinkle, D. E. (1984). Premarital sexual intercourse: A test of the effects of peer group, religiosity, and sexual guilt. *Journal of Sex Research, 20(2),* 168–185.

Sadava, S. W., & Matejcic, C. (1987). Generalized and specific loneliness in early marriage. *Canadian Journal Behavioral Science, 19,* 57–66.

Sadker, M., & Sadker, D. (1985). Sexism in the schoolroom of the 80's. *Psychology Today, 19,* 54, 57.

Salholz, E., Springen, K., DeLaPena, N., & Witherspoon, D. (1990). A frightening aftermath. *Newsweek 116,* 53.

Salovey, P., & Rodin, J. (1985). The heart of jealousy. *Psychology Today,* September, 22–29.

Samar, V. (1991). *The right to privacy: Gays, lesbians, and the Constitution.* Philadelphia: Temple University Press.

Samet, N., & Kelly, E. W. (1987). The relationship of steady dating to self-esteem and sex role identity among adolescents. *Adolescence, 22(85),* 231–245.

Sanday, P. R. (1981). The socio-cultural context of rape: A cross-cultural study. *Journal of Social Issues, 37,* 5–27.

Sanday, P. R. (1990). *Fraternity gang rape: Sex, brotherhood, and privilege on campus.* New York: New York University Press.

Sandowski, C. L. (1989). *Sexual concerns when illness or disability strikes.* Springfield, IL: Charles C. Thomas.

Santee, B., & Henshaw, S. K. (1992). The abortion debate: Measuring gestational age. *Family Planning Perspectives, 24,* 172–173.

Sargent, T. (1988). Fetishism. *Journal of Social Work and Human Sexuality, 7,* 27–42.

Sarrel, P., & Masters, W. (1982). Sexual molestation of men by women. *Archives of Sexual Behavior, 11,* 117–131.

Sarrel, P., & Sarrell, L. (1980). The Redbook report on sexual relationships. *Redbook 77.*

Sarrel, P. M. (1990). Sexuality and menopause. *Obstetrics & Gynecology, 75(4 Supp.),* 26S–30S.

Satullo, C. (1994). A call for a truce in the housework wars. *The Philadelphia Inquirer,* October 11, A11.

Savitz, L., & Rosen, L. (1988). The sexuality of prostitutes: Sexual enjoyment reported by "streetwalkers." *Journal of Sex Research, 24,* 200–208.

Sawyer, R. G., & Moss, D. J. (1993). STD's in college men: A preliminary clinical investigation. *Journal of American College Health, 42,* 111–114.

Scales, P. (1986). The changing context of sexuality education: Paradigms and challenges for alternative futures. *Family Relations, 35,* 265–274.

Scales, P. (1987). Today's sexuality education represents the essence of democratic society. In R. T. Francoeur (Ed.), *Taking sides: Clashing views on controversial issues in human sexuality* (pp. 113–122). Guildford, CT: Dushkin.

Schachter, S., & Singer, J. E. (1962). Cognitive, social, and physiological determinants of emotional state. *Psychological Review, 69,* 379–399.

Schiavi, R. C., & White, D. (1976). Androgens and male sexual function: A review of human studies. *Journal of Sex and Marital Therapy, 2,* 214–228.

Schiller, Z. (1991). Sex still sells—but so does sensitivity. *Business Week,* March 18, 100.

Schlafly, P. (1983). Sex education promotes sexual activity. In B. Leone & M. T. O'Neill (Eds.), *Sexual values: Opposing viewpoints.* St. Paul, MN: Greenhaven Press.

Schnarch, D. (1993). *The sexual crucible.* New York: Norton.

Schneider, A., et al. (1987). Human papillomaviruses in women with a history of abnormal Papanicolaou smears and in their male partners. *Obstetrics and Gynecology, 69,* 554.

Schneider, M. (1989). Sappho was a right-on adolescent: Growing up lesbian. *Journal of Homosexuality, 17,* 111–130.

Schogol, M. (1994). The skinny on Barbie. *The Philadelphia Inquirer,* January 24.

Schopper, D., & Walley, J. (1992). Care for AIDS patients in developing countries: A review. *AIDS Care, 4,* 89–102.

Schover, L., & Jensen, S. B. (1988). *Sexuality and chronic illness.* New York: The Guilford Press.

Schuchat, A., & Broome, C. V. (1991). Toxic shock syndrome and tampons. *Epidemiologic Reviews, 13,* 99–112.

Schwartz, B., Gaventa, S., Broome, C. V., et al. (1989). Nonmenstrual toxic shock syndrome associated with barrier contraceptives. *Reviews of Infectious Diseases, 2,* 543–549.

Schwebke, J. R. (1991). Syphilis in the 90's. *Medical Aspects of Human Sexuality,* April, 44–49.

Scott, J. E., & Schwalm, L. A. (1988). Rape rates and the circulation rates of adult magazines. *Journal of Sex Research, 24,* 241–250.

Scully, D., & Marolla, J. (1983). *Incarcerated rapists: Exploring a sociological model.* Final Report for Department of Health and Human Services, NIMH.

Scully, D., & Marolla, J. (1984). Convicted rapists vocabulary of motive: Excuses and justifications. *Social Problems, 31,* 530–544.

Scully, D., & Marolla, J. (1985). Riding the bull at Gilley's: Convicted rapists describe the rewards of rape. *Social Problems, 32,* 251–263.

Searles, P., & Berger, R. J. (1987). The current status of rape reform legislation. *Women's Rights Law Reporter, 10,* 25–44.

Seavey, C. A., Katz, P. A., & Zalk, S. R. (1975). Baby X: The effect of gender labels on adult responses to infants. *Sex Roles, 1,* 103–109.

Sedney, M. A., & Brooks, B. (1984). Factors associated with a history of childhood sexual experience in a nonclinical female population. *Journal of the American Academy of Child Psychiatry, 23,* 215–218.

Selik, R. M., Starcher, E. T., & Curran, J. W. (1987). Opportunistic diseases reported in AIDS patients. *AIDS, 1,* 175–182.

Seminars in Dermatology. Sexually transmitted diseases and abortions: The present situation for medical care of sexually transmitted diseases in Sweden. *Seminars in Dermatology, 9,* 190–193.

Seng, M. J. (1989). Child sexual abuse and adolescent prostitution: A comparative analysis. *Adolescence, 24,* 665–675.

Sevely, J. L., & Bennett, J. W. (1978). Concerning female ejaculation and the female prostate. *The Journal of Sex Research, 14,* 1–20.

Shafik, A. (1991). Testicular suspension: Effect on testicular function. *Andrologia, 23(4),* 297–301.

Shain, R. N. (1991). Impact of tubal sterilization and vasectomy on female marital sexuality. *American Journal of Obstetrics and Gynecology, 164,* 763.

Shaklee, H. (1983). Sex differences in children's behavior. *Advances in Developmental and Behavioral Pediatrics, 4,* 235–285.

Shanin, R. N., Miller, W. B., Holden, A. E. C., & Rosenthal, M. (1991). Impact of tubal sterilization and vasectomy on female marital sexuality: Results of a controlled longitudinal study. *American Journal of Obstetrics and Gynecology, 164,* 763–771.

Shapiro, S., & Nass, J. (1986). Postpartum psychosis in the male. *Psychopathology, 19,* 138–142.

Shaver, P., Hazan, C., & Bradshaw, D. (1988). Love as attachment: The integration of three behavioral systems. In R. J. Sternberg & M. L. Barnes (Eds.), *The psychology of love* (pp. 68–99). New Haven and London: Yale University Press.

Shaver, P., Schwartz, J., Kirson, D., & O'Connor, C. (1987). Emotion knowledge: Further exploration of a prototype approach. *Journal of Personality and Social Psychology, 52,* 1061–1086.

Sheehan, W., & Garfinkel, B. D. (1988). Case study: Adolescent autoerotic deaths. *Journal of the American Academy of Child and Adolescent Psychiatry, 27,* 367–370.

Sheppard, A. (1986). From Kate Sanborn to feminist psychology: The social context of women's humor, 1885–1985. *Psychology of Women Quarterly, 10,* 155–170.

Sherfey, J. (1972). *The nature and evolution of female sexuality.* New York: Random House.

Sherr, L. (1990). Fear arousal and AIDS: Do shock tactics work? *AIDS, 4,* 361–364.

Shettles, L, & Rorvik, D. (1970). *Your baby's sex: Now you can choose.* New York: Dood, Mead.

Shimazaki, T. (1994). A closer look at sexuality education and Japanese youth. *SIECUS Report,* 12–15.

Shitz, R. (1987). *And the band played on: Politics, people, and the AIDS epidemic.* New York: St. Martin's Press.

SIECUS. (1993). *Guidelines for comprehensive sexuality education: Kindergarten through twelfth grade.* New York: SIECUS National Guidelines Task Force.

SIECUS. (1994). *SIECUS fact sheet #3 on comprehensive sexuality education: Sexuality education and the schools: Issues and answers.* New York: SIECUS.

Siegel, D. L. (1992). *Sexual harassment: Research and resources.* The National Council for Research on Women.

Siegel, K., Mesagno, F. P., Chen, J., & Christ, G. (1989). Factors distinguishing homosexual males practicing risky and safer sex. *Social Science and Medicine, 29,* 561–569.

Signorielli, N., & Lears, M. (1992). Children, television, and conceptions about chores: Attitudes and behaviors. *Sex Roles, 27,* 157–170.

Silva, D. C. (1990). Pedophilia: An autobiography. In J. Feierman (Ed.), *Pedophilia biosocial dimensions* (pp. 464–487). New York: Springer-Verlag.

Silverstein, C. (1984). The ethical and moral implications of sexual classification: A commentary. *Journal of Homosexuality, 9,* 29–38.

Silvestre, L., Dubois, C., Renault, M., et al. (1990). Voluntary interruption of pregnancy with Mifepristone (RU 486). and a prostaglandin analogue: A large-scale French experience. *The New England Journal of Medicine, 322,* 645–648.

Simkins, L., & Rinck, C. (1982). Male and female sexual vocabulary in different interpersonal contexts. *The Journal of Sex Research, 18,* 160–172.

Simon, C. P., & Witt, A., (1982). *Beating the system: The underground economy.* Boston: Auburn House.

Simon, P. M., Morse, E. V., Osofsky, H. J., & Balson, P. M. (1992). Psychological characteristics of a sample of male street prostitutes. *Archives of Sexual Behavior, 21,* 33–44.

Simon, W., & Gagnon, J. (1986). Sexual scripts: Permanence and change. *Archives of Sexual Behavior, 15,* 97–120.

Simons, R. L., & Whitbeck, L. B. (1991). Sexual abuse as a precursor to prostitution and victimization among adolescent and adult homeless women. *Journal of Family Issues, 12,* 361–379.

Sivan, I. (1988). International experience with Norplant-2 contraceptives study. *Family Planning Perspectives, 19,* 81–94.

Skinner, B. F. (1953). *Science and human behavior.* New York: Macmillan.

Skolnick, A. (1992). *The intimate environment: Exploring marriage and the family.* New York: HarperCollins.

Sleek, S. (1994). Girls who've been molested can later become molesters. *American Psychological Monitor, January,* 34.

Smith, K. T. (1971). Homophobia: A tentative personality profile. *Psychological Reports, 29,* 1091–1094.

Smith, T. (1991). Adult sexual behavior in 1989: Number of partners, frequency of intercourse, and risk of AIDS. *Family Planning Perspectives, 23,* 102–107.

Snaith, R. P. (1983). Exhibitionism: A clinical conundrum. *British Journal of Psychiatry, 143,* 231–235.

Sneddon, I., & Kremer, J. (1992). Sexual behavior and attitudes of university students in Northern Ireland. *Archives of Sexual Behavior, 21,* 295–312.

Socarides, C. W. (1981). Psychoanalytic psychotherapeutic perspectives on female homosexuality: A discussion of the lesbian as a 'single' woman. *American Journal of Psychotherapy, 35,* 510–515.

Society for Adolescent Medicine. (1991). Society for adolescent medicine position paper on reproductive health care for adolescents. *Journal of Adolescent Health, 12,* 649–661.

Soley, L., & Kurzbard, G. (1986). Sex in advertising: A comparison of 1964 and 1984 magazine advertisements. *Journal of Advertising, 15,* 46–54.

Sorenson, R. C. (1973). *Adolescent sexuality in contemporary America.* New York: World.

Sorenson, S., & Brown, V. (1990). Interpersonal violence and crisis intervention on the college campus. *New Directions for Student Services, 49,* 57–66.

Spector, T. D., Roman, E., & Silman, A. J. (1990). The pill, parity, and rheumatoid arthritis. *Arthritis and Rheumatology, 33,* 782.

Spence, J. T. (1984). Gender identity and its implications for the concepts of masculinity and femininity. In T. B. Sonderegger (Ed.), *Psychology and gender* (pp. 59–95). Lincoln: University of Nebraska Press.

Spencer, S. L., & Zeiss, A. M., (1987). Sex roles and sexual dysfunction in college students. *Journal of Sex and Marital Therapy, 23,* 338–347.

Spolan, S. (1991). Oh, by the way. *Philadelphia City Paper,* March 22, 7.

Stack, S., & Gundlach, J. H. (1992). Divorce and sex. *Archives of Sexual Behavior, 21(4),* 359–367.

Starr, B., & Weiner, M. B. (1981). *Sex and sexuality in the mature years.* New York: Stein & Day.

Staver, S. (1992). Gay men may be relapsing into risky sex. *American Medical Association News,* November 9, 10.

Steenland, S. (1989). Prime-time girls just want to have fun. *Media & Values, 49,* 34.

Stehle, B. F. (1985). *Incurably romantic.* Philadelphia: Temple University Press.

Steinberg, L. (1983). *The sexuality of Christ in Renaissance art and in modern oblivion.* New York: Pantheon.

Stephens, R. (1963). *The Muria of Africa.* New York: Random House.

Stephens, R. C., Feucht, T. E., & Roman, S. W. (1991). Effects of an intervention program on AIDs-related drug and needle behavior among IV drug users. *American Journal of Public Health, 81,* 568–571.

Sternberg, R. J. (1986). A triangle theory of love. *Psychological Review, 93,* 119–135.

Sternberg, R. J. (1987). Liking versus loving: A comparative evaluation of theories. *Psychological Bulletin, 102,* 331–345.

Sternberg, R. J. (1988). *The triangle of love: Intimacy, passion, commitment.* New York: Basic Books.

Stevenson, M., & Gajarsky, W. (1992). Unwanted childhood sexual experiences relate to later revictimization and male perpetration. *Journal of Psychology and Human Sexuality, 4,* 57–70.

Stillman, D., & Beatts, A. (Eds.) (1976). *Titters: The first collection of humor by women.* New York: Collier.

Stoller, R. J. (1991). The term perversion. In G. I. Fogel & W. A. Myers (Eds.), *Perversions and near-perversions in clinical practice: New psychoanalytic perspectives.* (pp. 36–58). New Haven, CT: Yale University Press.

Stoller, R. J., & Herdt, G. H. (1985). Theories of origins of male homosexuality. *Archives of General Psychiatry, 42,* 399–404.

Storms, M. D. (1980). Theories of sexual orientation. *Journal of Personality and Social Psychology, 38,* 783–792.

Storms, M. D. (1981). A theory of erotic orientation development. *Psychological Review, 88,* 340–353.

Strasburger, V. C. (1989). Adolescent sexuality and the media. *Pediatric Clinics of North America, 36,* 747–773.

Strathern, M. (1981). Self-interest and the social good: Some implications of Hagen gender imagery. In S. Ortner & H. Whitehead (Eds.), *Sexual meanings* (pp. 166–191). Cambridge, UK: Cambridge University Press.

Strauss, R., Wright, J., Finerman, G., & Catlin, D. (1983). Side effects of anabolic steroids in weight-trained men. *Physical Sports Medicine, 11,* 87–96.

Strommen, E. F. (1989). 'You're a what?': Family member reactions to the disclosure of homosexuality. *Journal of Homosexuality, 18,* 37–58.

Struckman-Johnson, C., & Struckman-Johnson, D. (1994). Men pressured and forced into sexual experience. *Archives of Sexual Behavior, 23,* 93–115.

Suplicy, M. (1994). Sexuality education in Brazil. *SIECUS Report,* 1–6.

Suppe, F. (1984). Classifying sexual disorders: The diagnostic and statistical manual of the American Psychiatric Association. *Journal of Homosexuality, 9,* 9–28.

Sutherland, P. (1987). I want sex, just like you. *The Village Voice, 32(14),* 25.

Swaab, D. F., & Hofman, M. A. (1990). An enlarged suprachiasmatic nucleus in homosexual men. *Brain Research, 537,* 141–148.

Tanay, E. (1988). Psychiatric reflections on AIDs education. *Psychiatric Annals, 18,* 594–597.

Tannahill, R. (1980). *Sex in history.* New York: Stein & Day.

Tannen, D. (1990). *You just don't understand: Women and men in conversation.* New York: Ballantine Books.

Taylor, C. (1986). Extramarital sex: Good for the goose? *Women and Therapy, 5(2–3),* 289–295.

Temoshok, L., et al. (1987). A three city comparison of the public's knowledge and attitudes about AIDS. *Psychology and Health, 1,* 43–60.

Templeman, T. L., & Stinnett, R. D. (1991). Patterns of sexual arousal and history in a "normal" sample of young men. *Archives of Sexual Behavior, 20,* 137–150.

Tepper, M. S. (1992). Sexual education in spinal cord injury rehabilitation: Current trends and recommendations. *Sexuality and Disability, 10,* 15–31.

Terry, J. (1990). Lesbians under the medical gaze: Scientists search for remarkable differences. *The Journal of Sex Research, 27,* 317–339.

Thirumoorthy, T. (1990). The epidemiology of sexually transmitted diseases in Southeast Asia and the western Pacific. *Seminars in Dermatology, 9,* 102–104.

Thomasset, C. (1992). The nature of woman. In C. Klapisch-Zuber (Ed.), *A history of women in the West, Volume II: Silences of the Middle Ages* (pp. 43–70). Cambridge, UK: Belknap Press.

Thompson, A. P. (1984). Emotional and sexual components of extramarital relations. *Journal of Marriage and the Family, 46,* 35–42.

Thomson, E., & Colella, U. (1992). Cohabitation and marital stability: quality or commitment? *Journal of Marriage and the Family, 54,* 259–267.

Tietze, C., & Henshaw, S. K. (1986). *Induced abortion: A world review, 1986.* New York: Alan Guttmacher Institute.

Tietze, C. (1983). *Induced abortion: A world review, 1983.* New York: The Population Council.

Time. (1991). What does God really think about sex? *Time,* June 24, 48–50.

Timmreck, T. C. (1990). Overcoming the loss of a love: Preventing love addiction and promoting positive emotional health. *Psychological Reports, 66,* 515–528.

Ting-Toomey, S. (1991). Intimacy, expressions in three cultures: France, Japan, and the United States. *International Journal of Intercultural Relations, 15,* 29–46.

Tong, R. (1984). *Women, sex, and the law.* Totowa, NJ: Rowman & Allanheld.

Toobin, J. (1994). X-rated. *Atlantic Monthly,* October 3, 70–78.

Torres, A., & Forrest, J. (1988). Why do women have abortions? *Family Planning Perspectives, 20,* 169–176.

Tortora, G. J., & Grabowski, S. R. (1993). *Principles of anatomy and physiology.* New York: HarperCollins.

Treffke, H., Tiggemann, M., & Ross, M. (1992). The relationship between attitude, assertiveness, and condom use. *Psychology and Health, 6,* 45–52.

Tremble, B., Schneider, M., & Appathurai, C. (1989). Growing up gay or lesbian in a multicultural context. In G. Herdt (Ed.), *Gay and lesbian youth* (pp. 253–267). New York: Harrington Park Press.

Trocki, K. F. (1992). Patterns of sexuality and risky sexuality in the general population of a California county. *Journal of Sex Research, 29,* 85–94.

Troiden, R. R. (1989). The formation of homosexual identities. In G. Herdt (Ed.), *Gay and lesbian youth* (pp. 43–73). New York: Harrington Park Press.

Trudel, G., & Desjardins, G. (1992). Staff reactions toward the sexual behaviors of people living in institutional settings. *Sexuality and Disability, 10,* 173–188.

Trumbach, R. (1990). Is there a modern sexual culture in the West, or, did England never change between 1500 and 1900? *Journal of the History of Sexuality, 1,* 206–309.

Trumbach, R. (1990). Sodomy transformed: Aristocratic libertinage, public reputation, and the gender revolution of the 18th century. *Journal of Homosexuality, 19,* 105–124.

Trumbach, R. (1993). Erotic fantasy and male libertinism in enlightenment England. In L. Hunt (Ed.), *The invention of pornography* (pp. 253–282). New York: Zone Books.

Truscott, P. (1991). S/M: Some questions and a few answers. In M. Thompson (Ed.), *Leatherfolk: Radical sex, people, politics, and practice* (pp. 15–36). Boston: Alyson Publications.

Turell, S. C., Armsworth, M. W., & Gaa, J. P. (1990). Emotional response to abortion: A critical review of the literature. *Women and Therapy, 9,* 49–68.

Turner, B. F., & Adams, C. G. (1988). Reported change in preferred sexual activity over the adult years. *Journal of Sex Research, 25,* 289–303.

Tyler, C. W. (1981). Epidemiology of abortion. *Journal of Reproductive Medicine, 26,* 459.

U.S. Bureau of Census. (1991). *Fertility of American women.* Current Population Reports. Series P–20, #454.

U.S. Department of Justice Statistics. (1990). *Sourcebook of Criminal Justice Statistics—1989.* Washington, DC: U.S. Government Printing Office.

U.S. News and World Report. (1991). The gospel on sex. *U.S. News and World Report,* June 10, 59–64.

Ulbrich, P. M., Coyle, A. T., & Llabre, M. M. (1990). Involuntary childlessness and marital adjustments: His and hers. *Journal of Sexual and Marital Therapy, 16,* 147–158.

Vanderbilt, H. (1992). Incest: A chilling report. *Harper's Bazaar Magazine,* February.

Vincent, M., Clearie, A., & Schluchter, M. (1987). Reducing adolescent pregnancy through school and community-based education. *Journal of the American Medical Association, 257(24),* 3382–3386.

Vinovskis, M. A. (1986). Adolescent sexuality, pregnancy, and childbearing in early America: Some preliminary speculations. In J. B. Lancaster & B. A. Hamburg (Eds.), *School-age pregnancy and parenthood: Biosocial dimensions* (pp. 303–322). New York: Aldine DeGruyter.

Visano, L. A. (1990). The impact of age on paid sexual encounters. *Journal of Homosexuality, 20,* 207–226.

Voigt, H. (1991). Enriching the sexual experience of couples: The Asian traditions and sexual counseling. *Journal of Sex and Marital Therapy, 17,* 214–219.

Voydanoff P., & Donnelly, B. W. (1990). *Adolescent sexuality and pregnancy.* Newbury Park, CA: Sage Publications.

Vukovic, L. (1992). Cold sores and fever blisters. *Natural Health,* November–December, 119–120.

Wagner, E. (1991). Campus victims of date rape should consider civil lawsuits as alternatives to criminal charges or colleges' procedures. *The Chronicle of Higher Education,* August 7, B2.

Walen, S. R., & Roth, D. (1987). A cognitive approach. In J. H. Geer & W. T. O'Donahue (Eds.), *Theories of human sexuality* (pp. 335–360). New York: Plenum Press.

Walfish, S., & Myerson, M. (1980). Sex role identity and attitudes toward sexuality. *Archives of Sexual Behavior, 9,* 199–203.

The Wall Street Journal. (1993). Vasectomies might increase cancer risk. *The Wall Street Journal,* B9.

Walsh, M. W. (1993). Canada takes lead on gay rights. *The Philadelphia Inquirer,* January 3, A2.

Walster, E., Berscheid, E. (1974). A little bit about love: A minor essay on a major topic. In T. L. Huston (Ed.), *Foundations of interpersonal attraction* (pp. 355–381). New York: Academic Press.

Wanlass, R. L., Killmann, P., Bella, B. S., & Tarnowski, K. J. (1983). Effects of sex education on sexual guilt anxiety and attitudes: A comparison of instruction formats. *Archives of Sexual Behavior, 12,* 487–502.

Ward, C. (1988). The attitudes toward rape victims scale: Construction, validation, and cross-cultural applicability. *Psychology of Women Quarterly, 12,* 127–146.

Ward, D., Carter, T., & `Perrin, D. (1994). *Social deviance: Being, behaving, and branding.* Needham Heights, MA: Allyn & Bacon.

Warr, M. (1985). Fear of rape among urban women. *Social Problems, 32,* 238–250.

Warren, R. (1991). *Women's glib: A collection of women's humor.* Freedom, CA: The Crossing Press.

Warren, R. (1992). *Women's glibber: State-of-the-art women's humor.* Freedom, CA: The Crossing Press.

The Washington Post. (1993). AIDS scientist Gallo, rival meet to discuss cooperation. *The Washington Post,* January 9, A2, col. 4.

Wasserheit, J. N. (1992). Interrelationships between HIV infection and other STDs. *Sexually Transmitted Diseases, 19,* 61–77.

Weinberg, M. S., & Williams, C. J. (1988). Black sexuality: A test of two theories. *Journal of Sex Research, 25(2),* 197–218.

Weis, D. L., Rabinowitz, B., & Ruckstruhl, M. F. (1992). Individual changes in sexual attitudes and behavior within college level human sex courses. *Journal of Sex Research, 29,* 43–59.

Weitzman, L. J. (1986). *The divorce revolution.* New York: The Free Press.

Welch, L. (1992). *Complete book of sexual trivia.* New York: Carol Publishing Group.

Wells, J. W. (1970). *Tricks of the trade.* New York: New American Library.

Wells, J. W., & Kline, W. B. (1987). Self-disclosure of homosexual orientation. *Journal of Social Psychology, 127,* 191–197.

Wendel, G. D. (1989). Early and congenital syphilis. *Obstetrics and Gynecology Clinics of North America, 16,* 479–494.

West, L. (1989). Philippine feminist efforts to organize against sexual victimization. *Response to the Victimization of Women and Children, 12,* 11–14.

Westermarck, E. (1972). *Marriage ceremonies in Morocco.* London, UK: Curzon Press.

Weston, K. (1991). *Families we choose: Lesbians, gays, kinship.* New York: Columbia University Press.

Whalen, R. E., Geary, D. C., & Johnson, F. (1990). Models of sexuality. In D. P. McWhirter, S. A. Sanders, & J. M. Reinisch (Eds.) *Homosexuality/heterosexuality: Concepts of sexual orientation* (pp. 61–70). New York: Oxford University Press.

Whelan, C. I., & Stewart, D. E. (1990). Pseudocyesis: A review and report of six cases. *International Journal of Psychiatry in Medicine, 20,* 97–108.

White, C. B. (1982). Sexual interest, attitudes, knowledge, and sexual history in relation to sexual behavior in the institutionalized aged. *Archives of Sexual Behavior, 11,* 11–21.

White, S. D., & DeBlassie, R. R. (1992). Adolescent sexual behavior. *Adolescence, 27,* 183–191.

Whitehead, H. (1981). The bow and the burden strap: A new look at institutionalized homosexuality in native North America. In S. Ortner & H. Whitehead (Eds.), *Sexual meanings* (pp. 80–115). Cambridge, UK: Cambridge University Press.

Whiting, B., & Edwards, C. P. (1988). A cross-cultural analysis of sex differences in the behavior of children aged 3 through 11. In G. Handel (Ed.), *Childhood socialization* (pp. 281–297). New York: Aldine De Gruyter.

Whiting, B. B., & Whiting, J. W. (1975). *Children of six cultures: A psycho-cultural analysis.* Cambridge, MA: Harvard University Press.

Wight, D. (1992). Impediments to safer heterosexual sex: A review of research with young people. *AIDS Care, 4,* 11–23.

Wikan, U. (1977). Man becomes woman: Transsexualism in Oman as a key to gender roles. *Man, 12,* 304–391.

Williams, C. W. (1991). *Black teenage mothers: Pregnancy and child rearing from their perspective.* Lexington, MA: Lexington Books.

Williams, E., Lamson, N., Efem, S., Weir, S., et al. (1992). Implementation of an AIDS prevention program among prostitutes in the Cross River State of Nigeria. *AIDS, 6,* 229–230.

Williams, J. E., & Best, D. L. (1982). *Measuring sex stereotypes: A thirty-nation study.* Beverly Hills, CA: Sage Publications.

Williams, L. (1984). The classic rape: When do victims report. *Social Problems, 31,* 459–467.

Williams, L. (1989). *Hard core: Power, pleasure, and the "frenzy of the visible."* Berkeley, CA: University of California Press.

Williams, P. (1991). A new focus on AIDs in women. *ASM News, 57,* 130–134.

Williams, W. L. (1986). *The spirit and the flesh: Sexual diversity in American Indian culture.* Boston: Beacon Press.

Williams, W. L. (1990). Book review: P. A. Jackson, Male homosexuality in Thailand: An interpretation of contemporary Thai sources. *Journal of Homosexuality, 19,* 126–138.

Wilson G. (1981). *The Coolidge effect: An evolutionary account of human sexuality.* New York: William Morrow.

Wilson, G. D. (1987). An ethological approach to sexual deviation. In G. D. Wilson (Ed.), *Variant sexuality: Research and theory* (pp. 84–115). Baltimore: Johns Hopkins University Press.

Wilson, J. (1988). Androgen abuse of athletes. *Endocrinology Review, 9,* 181–199.

Wilson, P. (1991). *When sex is the subject: Attitudes and answers for young children.* Santa Cruz, CA: Network Publications.

Wilson, P. (1994). Forming a partnership between parents and sexuality educators. *SIECUS Report, 22,* 1–5.

Wilson S., & Medora, N. (1990). Gender comparisons of college students' attitudes toward sexual behavior. *Adolescence, 25,* 615–627.

Winkler, J. J. (1990). *The constraints of desire: The anthropology of sex and gender in ancient Greece.* New York: Routledge.

Woestendiek, J. (1992). Oregon's Measure 9 brings the gay lifestyle to a vote. *The Philadelphia Inquirer,* October 27, A1, A6.

Wolchik, S. A., Braver, S. L., & Jensen, K. (1985). Volunteer bias in erotica research: Effects of intrusiveness of measure and sexual background. *Archives of Sexual Behavior, 14,* 93–107.

Wolf, N. (1991). *The beauty myth: How images of beauty are used against women.* New York: W. Morris.

Wolfe, J. (1992). *What to do when he has a headache.* New York: Penguin Press.

Wolff, C. (1971). *Love between women.* New York: Harper & Row.

Wolpe, J. (1958). *Psychotherapy by reciprocal inhibition.* Stanford, CA: Stanford Univ. Press

Working Woman. (1991). Success and the newly single girl. April, 100.

Wurtele, S. K., Melzer, A. M., & Kast, L. C. (1992). Preschoolers' knowledge of, and ability to learn genital terminology. *Journal of Sex Education and Therapy, 18,* 115–122.

Wyer, R. S., & Collins II, J. E. (1992). A theory of humor elicitation. *Psychological Review, 99,* 663–688.

Xian, F. (1983–1984). Marriage and birth aspirations of young rural women in a Jiangsu Province village. *Chinese Sociology and Anthropology 16, (1–2),* 138–144.

Yegidis, B. L. (1986). Date rape and other forced sexual encounters among college students. *Journal of Sex Education and Therapy, 12,* 51–54.

Yesalis, C., Wright, J., & Bahrke, M. (1989). Epidemiological and policy issues in the measurement of the long term effects of anabolic-androgenic steroids. *Sports Medicine, 8,* 129–138.

Yesalis, C. E. (1993). Incidence of anabolic steroid use: A discussion of methodological issues. In C. Yesalis (Ed.) *Anabolic steroids in sport and exercise* (pp. 49–69). Champaign, IL: Human Kinetics Publishers.

Yesalis, C. E., Kennedy, N. J., Kopstein, A. N, & Bahrike, M. S. (1993). Anabolic-Androgenic Steroid Use in the United States. *Journal of the American Medical Association, 270,* 1217–1221.

Yllo, K., & Finkelhor, D. (1985). Marital rape. In A. W. Burgess (Ed.), *Rape and sexual assault* (pp. 146–158). New York: Garland.

Youngstrom, N. (1991). Sex behavior studies are derailed. *The American Psychological Association Monitor, 22,* 1.

Youngstrom, N. (1992). Counseling buoys people with HIV. *American Psychological Association Monitor, 23,* 24.

Zausner, M. (1986). *The streets: A factual portrait of six prostitutes as told in their own words.* New York: St. Martin's Press.

Zelnik, K., & Kim, Y. (1982). Sex Education and its association with teenage sexual activity, pregnancy, and contraceptive use. *Family Planning Perspectives, 14,* 117–126.

Zelnik, M., Kantner, J., & Ford, K. (1981). *Sex and pregnancy in adolescence.* Beverly Hills, CA: Sage Publications.

Zelnik, M., & Kantner, J. F. (1980). Sexual activity, contraceptive use, and pregnancy among metropolitan-area teenagers: 1971–1979. *Family Planning Perspectives, 12,* 230–237.

Zilbergeld, B. (1978). *Male sexuality.* New York: Bantam Books.

Zinn, M. B., & Eitzen, S. D. (1993). *Diversity in families.* New York: HarperCollins.

Zolese, G., & Blacker, C. V. R. (1992). The psychological complications of therapeutic abortion. *British Journal of Psychiatry, 160,* 742–749.

Zucker, K. J. (1990). Psychosocial and erotic development in cross-gender identified children. *Canadian Journal of Psychiatry, 35,* 487–495.

Zuger, B. (1989). Homosexuality in families of boys with early effeminate behavior: An epidemiological study. *Archives of Sexual Behavior, 18,* 155–166.

Credits

Photos

Chapter 1

Page 1: © Ashmolean Museum, Oxford; **4L:** © Gerard Lacz/Animals, Animals; **4R:** © Adam woolfitt/Robert Harding Picture Library; **5T:** © Erich Lessing/Naturhistorisches Museum, Vienna, Austria/Art Resource; **5B:** © Fitsroy Barrett/Retna, Ltd.; **6L:** © The British Museum; **6R:** © The British Museum; **10:** © Ashmolean Museum, Oxford; **15R:** © The Bettmann Archive; **15L:** © Giraudon/Art Resource; **18B:** © Museo del Prado, Madrid, Spain/Erich Lessing/Art Resource; **18T:** © Scala/Art Resource; **22:** © 1994, The Art Institute of Chicago; **21:** © Scala/Art Resource; **24:** © Wellcome Institute Library, London; **27:** © Massachusetts Historical Society; **30:** © American Social Health Assoc. Records, Social Welfare History Archives; Univ. of Minnesota Libraries

Chapter 2

Page 35: © Photo by Dellenback, Courtesy of the Kinsey Institute, Indiana University; **36:** © The Bettmann Archive; **41:** © Ken Heyman/Black Star; **47:** © Janell Carroll; **49:** © The Bettmann Archive; **50T:** © The Bettmann Archive; **50B:** © Photo by Dellenback, Courtesy of the Kinsey Institute, Indiana University; **53:** © UPI/Bettmann; **57:** © UPI/Bettmann Newsphotos

Chapter 3

Page 67: © Biophoto Associates/Science Source/Photo Researchers; **70:** © Biophoto Associates/Science Source/Photo Researchers; **77:** © Bergman & Associates; **79L:** © Dr. John Money, PhD.; **79R:** © Dr. John Money, PhD.; **83L:** © Tee A. Corrine; **8M:** © Tee A. Corrine; **83R:** © Tee A. Corrine; **90TL:** © Joel Gordon; **90TR:** © Bergman & Associates; **90BL:** © Bergman & Associates; **90BR:** © Robert Holland/The Image Bank; **97:** © Joel Gordon; **107TL:** © Bergman & Associates; **107TR:** © Joel Gordon; **107B:** © Bob Durham

Chapter 4

Page 121: © Hella Hammid/Photo Researchers; **123:** © Ann Purcell/Photo Researchers; : © Thomas Heinser Studio; **126T:** © Erika Stone/Photo Researchers; **126B:** © Monkmeyer Press Photo Service; **128:** © Hella Hammid/Photo Researchers; **139T:** © Stephen Trimble; **139B:** © Courtesy Paul Wolpe; **144:** © Richard Hutchings/Photo Researchers; **145:** © Richard Hutchings/Photo Researchers; **157:** © Greig Cranna/Stock Boston

Chapter 5

Page 161: © Ronnie Kaufman/The Stock Market; **166T:** © Popperfoto/Archive Photos; **166B:** © The Kobal Collection; **167:** © Archive Photos; **168:** © Doug Menuez/Stock Boston; **177T:** © Roger Stevens/Custom Medical Stock; **177B:** © Dr. William Stayton; **185:** © Alan D. Carey/Photo Researchers; **187:** © Ronnie Kaufman/The Stock Market; **189:** © Mary Kate Denny/Photo Edit; **192:** © Gary Hershorn/Reuters/Bettmann; **194:** © Rhoda Sidney/Stock Boston

Chapter 6

Page 199: © Dan Coffey/The Image Bank; **200:** © Emil Muench/Photo Researchers; **203:** © Dan Coffey/The Image Bank; **204:** © Springer/Bettmann Film Archive; **214:** © Jeff/Greenberg/dMRp/Photo Edit; **215L:** © Dashow/Anthro-Photo File; **215R:** © Rowe/Anthro-Photo File; **227L:** © Lionel Delevingne/Stock Boston; **227R:** © Charles Gupton/Stock Boston; **228:** © Rich Meyer/The Stock Market

Chapter 7

Page 233: © Chloe Atkins; **235:** © Vanessa Vick/Photo Researchers; **242:** © Mitch Reardon/Photo Researchers; **247:** © Giraudon/Art Resource; **260:** © Joel Gordon; **266:** © Chloe Atkins; **268:** © Robert Brenner/Photo Edit; **269:** © Donna Binder/Impact Visuals; **272:** © Reuters/Bettmann

Chapter 8

Page 275: © David Barritt/Gamma Liaison; **283:** © Steve Dipaola/Allsport USA; **300:** © Chris Helgren/Reuters/Bettmann; **303:** © Joel

Gordon; **307:** © Robert Frerck/Odyssey Productions; **309:** © David Barritt/Gamma Liaison

Chapter 9

Page 313: © Joel Gordon; **326–327:** from "The World According to He and She" by Julie Logan and Arthur Howard, Copyright © 1992 by Julie Logan & Arthur Howard. Used by permission of Dell Books, a division of Bantam Doubleday Dell Publishing Group; **353:** Courtesy Paul Wolpe

Chapter 10

Page 363: © Mariette Pathy Allen; **367T:** © Prof. P. Motta/Dept. of Anatomy/University "La Sapienza", Rome/Science Photo Library/Photo Researchers; **367B:** © David Phillips/Science Source/Photo Researchers; **381:** © Lowell J. Gerogia/Photo Researchers; **383:** © Custom Medical Stock; **384TL:** © Petit Format/Nestle/Photo Researchers; **384TM:** © Petit Format/Nestle/Science Source/Photo Researchers; **384TR:** © John Watney/Photo Researchers; **384BL:** © James Stevenson/Science Photo Library/Photo Researches; **384BM:** © Petit Format/Nestle/Science Source/Photo Researchers; **386:** © Kermani/Gamma Liaison; **393:** © Andy Levin/Photo Researchrs; **396:** © Mariette Pathy Allen; **399:** © Courtesy of Janell Caroll; **405:** © Custom Medical Stock Photo

Chapter 11

Page 407: © Joel Gordon; **413T:** © Joel Gordon; **413B:** © Joel Gordon; **414:** © Tony Freeman/Photo Edit; **417:** © Joel Gordon; **418:** © Joel Gordon; **419:** © Benn Mitchell/The Image Bank; **423T:** © Joel Gordon; **423B:** © Joel Gordon; **425:** © Tony Freeman/Photo Edit; **426:** © Joel Gordon; **442:** © Alan McLaughlin/Impact Visuals

Chapter 12

Page 455: ©1980 Hella Hammid; **258:** © Courtesy of Helen S. Kaplan; **467:** © Voja Miladinovic/Sipa Press; **472:** © Courtesy of American Medical Systems, Inc.; **479:** © Biophoto Associates/Photo Researchers

Chapter 13

Page 493: © Mike Theiler/Reuters/Bettmann; **499:** © Lester Bergman & Assoc.; **501T:** © Biophoto Associates/Photo Researchers; **501B:** © Center For Disease COntrol, Atlanata, GA.; **502:** © Lester Bergman & Assoc.; **503:** © Western Ophthalmic Hospital/Science Photo Library/Photo Researchers; **504T:** © Lester Bergman & Assoc.; **504B:** © Lester Bergman & Assoc.; **505T:** © Custom Medical Stock Photo; **505B:** © Lester Bergman & Assoc.; **507T:** © Marc S. Berger/Medichrome; **507B:** © Centers For Disease Control, Atlanta, GA.; **518T:** © Thierry Falise/Gamma Liaison; **518B:** © Dept. of Medical Photography, St. Stephen's Hospital, London/Science Photo Library/Photo Researchers; **523:** © Michael J. Okoniewski/The Image Works; **524:** © Mike Theiler/Reuters/Bettmann

Chapter 14

Page 531: © Mariette Pathy Allen; **533:** © Gatewood/The Image Works; **538:** © Courtesy of Paul Wolpe; **542:** © Joel Gordon; **545:** © New Esoteric Press, PO Box 300689, JFK Station, Jamaica, NY 11430; **551:** © Mariette Pathy Allen; **555:** © Tom McCarthy/Photo Edit; **560:** © The Kobal Collection

Chapter 15

Page 565: © Joel Gordon; **567:** © Brent Smith/Reuters/Bettmann; **570:** © The Kobal Collection; **575:** © Signe Wilkinson/Cartoonists & Writers Syndicate; **578:** © Joel Gordon ; **580:** © Fred Prouser/Reuters/Bettmann;

584: © Joel Gordon; **590:** © Robert Ullmann/Design Conceptions; **598:** © L. Mark/UPI/Bettmann

Special Focus 1

Page 603: © C. Rancinan/Sygma; **604:** © Feinblatt-Media/Sipa Press; **605:** © Irene Perlman/Stock Boston; **607:** © Luciano Mellace/Reuters/Bettmann; **610:** © UPI/Bettmann; **615:** © David Austen/Stock Boston; **616:** © Joel Gordon; **622:** © Collection, The Supreme Court Historical Society; **624T:** © Reuters/Bettmann; **624M:** © Hazel Hankin/Impact Visuals; **624B:** © Donna Binder/Impact Visuals; **629:** © The Kobal Collection

Special Focus 2

Page 634: © UPI/Bettmann; **636:** © Courtesy Dr. William R. Stayton; **637:** © SIECUS; **639:** © Cliff Ginsburg/UPI/Bettmann; Newsphotos; **642:** © Art Phillips/UPI/Bettmann; **651:** © Steven Rubin/JB Pictures; **653:** © The Stein Center; **654:** © Philip Jones Griffiths

Special Focus 3

Page 665: © Archive Photos/Fotos International; **666T:** © T. Campion/Sygma; **666B:** © Joel Gordon; **668T:** © The Kobal Collection; **668B:** © The Kobal Collection; **678:** © Patric Zachmann/Magnum Photos; **679T:** © Reuters/Bettmann; **679B:** © Patric Zachmann/Magnum Photos

Special Focus 4

Page 684: © Museo Archeologico Nazionale, Naples, Italy/Erich Lessing/Art Resource; **687:** © Joel Gordon; **690:** © National Broadcasting Company; **691:** © Courtesy Janell Carroll; **693L:** © Fotos International/Archive Photos; **693R:** © National Broadcasting Company; **696:** © The Kobal Collection; **698L:** © Richard Termine/Children's Television Workshop; **698R:** © Fred Wolf Films; **694T:** © Jeff Christensen/Reuters/Bettmann; **694B:** © Robin Jerstad/Reuters/Betmann; **695T:** © Garcia Stills/Retna, Ltd.; **695M:** © Masaharu Hatano/Reuters/Bettmann; **695B:** © Pat Benic/Rueters/Bettmann Newsphotos; **702:** © BODYSLIMMERS by Nancy Ganz; **708:** © UPI/Bettmann; **711:** © Gabriel Pico/Sipa Press

Special Focus 5

Page 718: © The British Museum; **719:** © Archive Photos; **720L:** © G.C. Kelley/Photo Researchers; **720R:** © Stephen Marks/Stockphotos, Inc./The Image Bank; **726:** © The Bettmann Archive; **733:** © Roberta Gregory

Special Focus 6

Page 738: © Brian Plonka/Impact Visuals; **739L:** © Steve Granitz/Retna, Ltd.; **739R:** © Navarro/Leparisten/Retna; **743T:** © B/S-Camera Press/Retna Ltd.; **743B:** © Steve Granitz/Retna Ltd.; **756:** © P.Turner/The Image Bank

Text

Chapter 2

Page 48: Figure on Chronology of Sex Research from HUMAN SEXUALITIES by John Gagnon. Copyright © 1977 by John Gagnon. Reprinted by permission of the author.

Chapter 4

Page 130: Guilford Publications, Inc., Table, "Preschoolers' Knowledge of and Ability to Learn Genital Terminology" from Journal of Sex Education and Therapy, 18, 1992. Reprinted by permission of Guilford Publications, Inc. **132:** L. Constantine, Excerpt from CHILDREN AND SEX: NEW FINDINGS by L. Constantine, pages 75–82. Copyright © 1981 by L. Constantine. Reprinted by permission of Little, Brown and Company. **134:** Richard Currier, "Juvenile Sexuality in Global Perspective" by Richard L. Currier. Copyright 1981 by Richard L. Currier. Reprinted by permission of Little, Brown & Company. **136:** John Gagnon, "Attitudes and Responses of Parents to Preadolescent Masturbation" by John Gagnon from ARCHIVES OF SOCIAL BEHAVIOR (14), 1985, pages 455 and 463. Copyright © 1985 by John Gagnon. Reprinted by permission of Plenum Publishing and the author. **140:** Jane B. Lancaster, Figure 2.2 from SCHOOL AGE PREGNANCY AND PARENTHOOD by Jane B. Lancaster. Reprinted by permission of Aldine de Gruyter, a division of Walter de Gruyter, Inc. and the author. **153:** Sex Information and Education Council of the U.S., SR Vol. 17 (1) 1988, The Issue and Controversy Surrounding Adolescent Sexuality and Abstinence.

Chapter 5

Page 188: Katha Pollitt, "The Smurfette Principle" by Katha Pollitt, The New York Times, April 7, 1991 Magazine. Copyright © 1991 by The New York Times. Reprinted by permission. **190:** Jane S. Gaskell, Gender Matters from School to Work by Jane S. Gaskell. Copyright © 1992 by Jane S. Gaskell. Reprinted by permission.

Chapter 6

Page 204: Copyright © 1964, Renewed 1992 by Mayerling Productions Ltd. and Jerry Brock. Copyright © 1964, Renewed 1992 by Joseph Stein, Mayerling Productions, Ltd. and Jerry Brock. Used by permission. **205:** John Alan Lee, "The Styles of Loving" by John Alan Lee from PSYCHOLOGY TODAY, 8 (5): 43–51, 1974. Copyright © 1974 by Sussex Publishers, Inc. Reprinted with permission from PSYCHOLOGY TODAY Magazine. **207:** Robert J. Sternberg, "A Triangle Theory of Love" by Robert J. Sternberg from PSYCHOLOGICAL REVIEW, 93 (2): 119–135. Copyright © 1986 by the American Psychological Association. Reprinted by permission. **209:** Elaine Hatfield and Susan Sprecher, Excerpt from "Measuring Passionate Love in Intimate Relationships" by Elaine Hatfield and Susan Sprecher from the Journal of Adolescence, 9:383–410. Copyright © 1986 by Academic Press, Inc. London. Reprinted by permission. **216:** David Buss, "Sex Differences in Human Mate Preferences: Evolutionary Hypotheses Tested in 37 Cultures" from BEHAVIORAL AND BRAIN SCIENCES, 12: 1–49, 1989. Reprinted with the permission of Cambridge University Press. **218:** Don Sabo, Excerpt from "The Myth of the Sexual Athlete" by Don Sabo from CHANGING ME: ISSUES IN GENDER, SEX AND POLITICS. Copyright © 1990 by Don Sabo. Reprinted by permission of the author. **220:** Bernard F. Stehle, Excerpt and picture from "Murray and Francis, A Tale of Committed Love" from INCURABLY ROMANTIC by Bernard F. Stehle. Copyright © 1985 by Bernard F. Stehle. Reprinted by permission.

Chapter 7

Page 237: H. Kinsey, From SEXUAL BEHAVIOR IN THE HUMAN MALE by H. Kinsey, 1948. Reprinted by permission of the Kinsey Institute for Research in Sex, Gender and Reproduction; Bloomington, IN. **238:** Fritz Klein, "The Need to View Sexual Orientation as a Multi-Variable Dynamic Process: A Theoretical Perspective" by Fritz Klein

from HOMOSEXUALITY/HETEROSEXUALITY, pages 277–282. Copyright © 1990 by The Oxford University Press. Reprinted by permission. **256:** Vivienne C. Cass, "Homosexual Identity Formation" by Vivienne C. Cass from Journal of Homosexuality, Volume 4, 1979, pages 219–235. Reprinted by permission of The Haworth Press, Inc.

Chapter 8

Page 280: Robert Michael, John Gagnon, Edward Laumann, and Gina Kolata, Figure 1 from SEX IN AMERICA by Robert Michael, John Gagnon, Edward Laumann, and Gina Kolata. Copyright © 1994 by CSG Enterprises, Inc. Reprinted by permission of Little, Brown & Company. **281:** Personal Ads, THE NEW TIMES, Kansas City, MO. **283:** Focus on the Family, Excerpt from story on "Fatherhood: Not Yet" from FOCUS ON THE FAMILY, June 1993, p. 2–4. Reprinted by permission of Focus on the Family. **285:** Philip Blumstein and Pepper Schwartz, Chart on p. 207, "Sexual Initiation" from AMERICAN COUPLES by Philip Blumstein and Pepper Schwartz. Copyright © 1983 by Philip Blumstein and Pepper Schwartz. Reprinted by permission of William Morrow & Company, Inc. **290:** Jeffry Larson, "The Marriage Quiz: College Students' Beliefs in Selected Myths About Marriage" by Jeffry H. Larson, 37:1, pp 3–11. Reprinted by permission of The National Council on Family Relations. **293:** Chart on p. 196, "Sexual Frequency"; **296:** Chart on p. 274, "Instances of Non-monogamy" from AMERICAN COUPLES by Philip Blumstein and Pepper Schwartz. Copyright © 1983 by Philip Blumstein and Pepper Schwartz. Reprinted by permission of William Morrow & Company, Inc. **298:** James Patterson and Peter Kim, Table, "Adultery: How It Happens" from THE DAY AMERICA TOLD THE TRUTH by James Patterson and Peter Kim. Copyright 1991 by James Patterson and Peter Kim. Used by permission of Prentice Hall Press, A Division of Simon & Schuster. **301:** Mazine Zinn and Stanley Eitzen, Figure 11.1 "Annual Divorce Rates in the US: 1860–1990 from DIVERSITY IN FAMILIES by Maxine B. Zinn and Stanley D. Eitzen. Copyright © 1993 by Maxine B. Zinn and Stanley D. Eitzen. Reprinted by permission of HarperCollins College Publishers.

Chapter 9

Pages 317–319, 322: W. Masters, V. Johnson and R. Kolodny, Drawings from page 51–52, 58, 59, and 60 from HETEROSEXUALITY by W. Masters, V. Johnson, and R. Kolodny. Copyright © 1994 by W. Masters, V. Johnson and R. Kolodny. Reprinted by permission of HarperCollins College Publishers. **326–327:** Julie Logan and Arthur Howard, Excerpt from THE WORLD ACCORDING TO HE AND SHE by Julie Logan and Arthur Howard. Copyright © 1992 by Julie Logan and Arthur Howard. Used by permission of Dell Books, a division of Bantam Doubleday Dell Publishing Group, Inc. **337:** Chart on p. 236, "Oral Sex" from AMERICAN COUPLES by Philip Blumstein and Pepper Schwartz. Copyright © 1983 by Philip Blumstein and Pepper Schwartz. Reprinted by permission of William Morrow & Company, Inc. **332:** Betty Dodson, From SEX FOR ONE: THE JOY OF SELF-LOVING by Betty Dodson. Copyright © 1974, 1983, 1987 by Betty Dodson. Reprinted by permission of Harmony Books, a division of Crown Publishers, Inc. **356:** Figure 5; **360:** Figure 18 from SEX IN AMERICA by Robert Michael, John Gagnon, Edward Laumann, and Gina Kolata. Copyright © 1994 by CSG Enterprises, Inc. Reprinted by permission of Little, Brown & Company.

Chapter 11

Page 410: Robert Hatcher, Contraceptive Comfort and Confidence Scale by Robert Hatcher from CONTRACEPTIVE TECHNOLOGY,

16th Edition. Copyright © 1994 by Robert Hatcher. Reprinted by permission of Irvington Publishers. **435:** Linda Berne, Abortion Attitude Scale by Linda Berne. Reprinted by permission of the author. **448:** Sally Tisdale, Excerpt from "We Do Abortions Here" by Sally Tisdale. Reprinted by permission of the author. **452:** Stanley K. Henshaw, "Induced Abortion: A World Review, 1990" from FAMILY PLANNING PERSPECTIVES, Volume 22, Number 2, March/April 1990. Reproduced with the permission of The Alan Guttmacher Institute.

Chapter 12
Page 497: William Yarber, STD Attitude Scale by William Yarber. Copyright © 1988 by William Yarber. Reprinted by permission of William Yarber.

Chapter 13
Page 513: Ian Worpole, Illustration on page 94 from HIV: INFECTIONS THE CLINICAL PICTURE by Robert R. Redfield and Donald S. Burke. Scientific American, October, 1988. Reprinted by permission of Scientific American.

Chapter 14
Page 541: Thomas Sargent, "Fetishism" in Journal of Social Work and Human Sexuality, 1988. Copyright © 1988 by Thomas Sargent. Reprinted by permission of The Haworth Press, Inc. **551:** Patti Allen, From TRANSFORMATIONS by Mariette Patty Allen. Copyright © 1989 by Mariette Pathy Allen. Used by permission of the publisher, Dutton, an imprint of New American Library, a division of Penguin Books USA Inc. **554–555:** David Finkelhor, Tables 6.1, 6.3, 6.4, 6.5 from CHILD SEXUAL ABUSE: New Theory and Research by David Finkelhor. Copyright © 1984 by David Finkelhor. Reprinted with the permission of The Free Press, a division of Macmillan, Inc. **Pages 556–557:** Donald C. Silva, "Excerpt from Pedophilia: An Autobiography" from PEDOPHILIA: BIOSOCIAL DIMENSIONS, by Donald C. Silva. Copyright © 1990 by Donald C. Silva. Reprinted by permission of Springer-Verlag Publishers and the author.

Chapter 15
Page 570: Figure 21 from SEX IN AMERICA by Robert Michael, John Gagnon, Edward Laumann, and Gina Kolata. Copyright © 1994 by CSG Enterprises, Inc. Reprinted by permission of Little, Brown & Company. **572:** Calleen Ward, Attitudes About Rape Victim Scale by Calleen Ward. Reprinted by permission of the author. **581:** G. Bundow, Excerpt from "Resident Forum: Why Women Stay" from Journal of the American Medical Association, Vol. 267, 23. Reprinted by permission of The American Medical Association.

Special Focus 2
Page 640: O'Neil and Leone, Box from Sexual Values: Opposing Viewpoints by O'Neill and Leone. Copyright 1985 by Greenhave Press, Inc. Reprinted by permission. **637:** Photograph of Mary Calderone which appeared in Winter issue of SIECUS Developments, page 4, Vol. 2, Issue 2. Copyright 1988 by Sex Information and Education Council of the U.S., Inc. Reprinted by permission. **643:** Lynn Minton, "Fresh Voices" by Lynn Minton, Parade Publications, August 1, 1993. Copyright © 1993 by Lynn Minton. Reprinted by permission of Parade Publications, Inc. **646:** "Guidelines for Comprehensive Sexuality Education: K–12th," National Guidelines Task Force.

Special Focus 3
Page 661: Arlene Carmen, SELECTED TERMS from WORKING WOMEN: THE SUBTERRANEAN WORLD OF STREET PROSTITUTION by Arlene Carmen. Copyright © 1985 by Judon Memorial Church. Michael Zausner, Excerpt from THE STREETS by Michael Zausner. Copyright © 1986 by Michael Zausner. Reprinted by permission of St. Martin's Press. Reprinted by permission of HarperCollins Publishers, Inc. **670:** Elaine Landau, Excerpt from ON THE STREETS by Elaine Landau. Copyright © 1987 by Elaine Landau. Reprinted by permission of Silver Burdett Press, an imprint of Julian Messner.

Special Focus 5
Page 726: John Cohen, Excerpt form THE ESSENTIAL LENNY BRUCE by John Cohen. Copyright © 1967 by John Cohen. Reprinted by permission of Ballantine Books.

Special Focus 6
Page 740: Barbara DeAngelis, Ph.D., Excerpt from HOW TO MAKE LOVE ALL THE TIME by Barbara De Angelis, Ph.D. Copyright © 1987 by Barbara De Angelis, Ph.D. Reprinted with the permission of Rawson Associates, an imprint of Simon & Schuster, Inc. Pages **742:** Janet Wolfe, "Nonconstructive Communication Patterns" from WHAT TO DO WHEN HE HAS A HEADACHE by Janet Wolfe. Copyright © 1992 by Janet Wolfe. Reprinted by permission of Hyperion Books. **745:** From WILD IN BED TOGETHER by Graham Masterton. Copyright © 1992 by Graham Masterton. Used by permission of Dutton Signet, a division of Penguin Books USA Inc. **747:** Betty Dodson, From SEX FOR ONE: THE JOY OF SELFLOVING by Betty Dodson. Copyright © 1974, 1983, 1987 by Betty Dodson. Reprinted by permission of Harmony Books, a division of Crown Publishers, Inc. **750, 752:** Graham Masterton, from HOW TO DRIVE YOUR WOMAN WILD IN BED by Graham Masterton. Copyright © 1987 by Graham Masterton; **758:** Janet Wolfe, "Nonconstructive Communication Patterns" from WHAT TO DO WHEN HE HAS A HEADACHE by Janet Wolfe. Copyright © 1992 by Janet Wolfe. Reprinted by permission of Hyperion Books. **756, 757:** From SECRETS ABOUT MEN EVERY WOMAN SHOULD KNOW by Barbara DeAngelis, PhD. Copyright © 1990 by Barbara DeAngelis, PhD. Used by permission of Del Books, a division of Bantam Doubleday Dell Publishing Group, Inc.

Index